KODANSHA ENCYCLOPEDIA OF JAPAN

Distributors
JAPAN: KODANSHA LTD., Tokyo.
OVERSEAS: KODANSHA INTERNATIONAL LTD., Tokyo.
U.S.A., Mexico, Central America, and South America: KODANSHA INTERNATIONAL/USA LTD. through HARPER & ROW, PUBLISHERS, INC., New York.
Canada: FITZHENRY & WHITESIDE LTD., Ontario.
U.K., Europe, the Middle East, and Africa: INTERNATIONAL BOOK DISTRIBUTORS LTD., Hemel Hempstead, Herts., England.
Australia and New Zealand: HARPER & ROW (AUSTRALASIA) PTY. LTD., Artarmon, N.S.W.
Asia: TOPPAN COMPANY (S) PTE. LTD., Singapore.

Published by Kodansha Ltd., 12-21, Otowa 2-chome, Bunkyo-ku, Tokyo 112 and Kodansha International/USA Ltd., 10 East 53rd Street, New York, New York 10022.

Printed in Japan.
First edition, 1983.

LCC 83-80778
ISBN 0-87011-629-0 (Volume 9)
ISBN 0-87011-620-7 (Set)
ISBN 4-06-144539-1 (0) (in Japan)

Library of Congress Cataloging in Publication Data
Main entry under title:

Kodansha encyclopedia of Japan.

Includes index.
1. Japan—Dictionaries and encyclopedias. I. Title: Encyclopedia of Japan.
DS805.K633 1983 952'.003'21 83-80778
ISBN 0-87011-620-7 (U.S.)

KODANSHA ENCYCLOPEDIA OF JAPAN

9

KODANSHA

ACADEMIC ADVISERS

ARUGA Yūshō	marine biology	Associate Professor Department of Fisheries Tōkyō University of Fisheries Tōkyō
ASAI Kiyoshi	Japanese literature	Professor Department of Letters and Education Ochanomizu Women's University Tōkyō
FUKUSHIMA Yasuto	military affairs	Professor National Defense College National Defense Agency Tōkyō
HARADA Katsumasa	Japanese history	Lecturer Wakō University Machida, Tōkyō Prefecture
HOSHIKAWA Kiyochika	agriculture	Professor Faculty of Agriculture Tōhoku University Sendai, Miyagi Prefecture
HOSHINO Yoshirō	natural science	Science commentator Kyōto
HOSOYA Chihiro	international relations	Professor Department of Law Hitotsubashi University Kunitachi, Tōkyō Prefecture
IMAIZUMI Yoshiharu	zoology	Professor Department of Literature Tsuru University Tsuru, Yamanashi Prefecture
ISHII Shirō	law	Professor Faculty of Law Tōkyō University Tōkyō
ISHIYAMA Akira	clothing	Professor Department of Home Economics Bunka Women's College Tōkyō
ITŌ Mikiharu	ethnology	Professor National Museum of Ethnology Suita, Ōsaka Prefecture
IWAI Hiroaki	social problems	Professor Department of Sociology Tōyō University Tōkyō
KAGESATO Tetsurō	Japanese art	Director Mie Prefectural Art Museum Tsu, Mie Prefecture
KANAI Madoka	Japanese history	Professor Historiographical Institute Tōkyō University Tōkyō
KAWASAKI Shinjō	Buddhist philosophy	Assistant Professor Institute of Philosophy Tsukuba University Tsukuba Academic New Town, Ibaraki Prefecture
KURITA Ken	labor relations	Professor Department of Commerce Meiji University Tōkyō
MASHIMO Keimei	medicine	Director Tōkyō Welfare Pension Hospital Tōkyō
MATSUDA Osamu	plant folklore	President Japan Association of the Friends of Plants Tōkyō

MIYAZAWA Ken'ichi	economics	Professor, Department of Economics President, Hitotsubashi University Kunitachi, Tōkyō Prefecture
NAGAZUMI Akira	international relations	Professor Faculty of Letters Tōkyō University Tōkyō
NARA Hakujun	Buddhist philosophy	Assistant Professor Institute of Philosophy Tsukuba University Tsukuba Academic New Town, Ibaraki Prefecture
NISHIKAWA Osamu	geography	Professor College of Arts and Sciences Tōkyō University Tōkyō
NISHIMURA Masae	anthropology	Professor Department of Education Waseda University Tōkyō
NODA Kazuo	management	Professor Department of Sociology Rikkyō University Tōkyō
NOMACHI Akira	Western philosophy	Professor Institute of Philosophy Tsukuba University Tsukuba Academic New Town, Ibaraki Prefecture
OKAMURA Tadao	political science	Professor Faculty of General Education Hōsei University Tōkyō
ŌMORI Wataru	government administration	Assistant Professor College of Arts and Sciences Tōkyō University Tōkyō
ŌSHIMA Yasumasa	Western philosophy	Professor World Problems Research Institute Kyōto Sangyō University Kyōto
SAITŌ Shōji	animal and plant folklore	Professor Department of Science and Engineering Tōkyō Denki University Tōkyō
SEIKE Kiyosi	architecture	Professor and Dean School of Fine Arts Tōkyō University of Fine Arts and Music Tōkyō
SHIKI Masahide	geography	Professor Department of Letters and Education Ochanomizu Women's University Tōkyō
SUZUKI Zenji	biology	Professor Faculty of Liberal Arts Yamaguchi University Yamaguchi, Yamaguchi Prefecture
TADA Michitarō	cultural anthropology	Professor Research Institute for Humanistic Studies Kyōto University Kyōto
TAKAGI Keijirō	medicine	President Japan Society of Pharmacists Tōkyō
TAKAKUWA Yasuo	education	Professor Faculty of Education Nagoya University Nagoya, Aichi Prefecture

TAKUMI Hideo	Japanese art	Director Kanagawa Prefectural Museum of Modern Art Kamakura, Kanagawa Prefecture
TANAKA Akira	Japanese history	Professor Faculty of Letters Hokkaidō University Sapporo, Hokkaidō
TANAKA Hideo	law	Professor and Chairman Faculty of Law Tōkyō University Tōkyō
TSUJI Shizuo	Japanese cooking	President Tsuji Professional Culinary Institute Ōsaka
TSUKUBA Hisaharu	agriculture	Assistant Professor Department of Economics Waseda University Tōkyō
UMETANI Noboru	international relations	Professor Faculty of Letters Ōsaka University Ōsaka
UWANO Zendō	linguistics	Assistant Professor Faculty of Letters Tōkyō University Tōkyō
WAKASUGI Akira	accounting	Professor and Dean Department of Economics Yokohama National University Yokohama, Kanagawa Prefecture
WATANABE Tōru	sports	Professor College of Arts and Sciences Tōkyō University Tōkyō
YAMADA Terutane	traditional medicine	Standing Director Japan Institute of Traditional Medicine Tōkyō
YUI Tsunehiko	management	Professor Department of Business Management Meiji University Tōkyō

EDITORIAL CONSULTANTS

CAMBRIDGE

Tadatoshi AKIBA
Takashi EGUCHI
Robert FELDMAN
Glen S. FUKUSHIMA
Andrew GORDON
Hiroshi WATANABE

TŌKYŌ

AMAKI Shihomi
ARATA Yōji
ARITA Seiko
Theodore F. COOK
Louise CORT
ENOMOTO Tōru
FUJINAGA Tamotsu
HAMADA Kōsaku
HATANO Sumio
HIROI Yūichi
Dangshi HUANG
INUTA Mitsuru
IWATA Rei
Japan Academy
Japan Foundation
KANNO Hiroomi
KATŌ Yasutake
KAWAI Masakazu
KOBAYASHI Michihiko
KUBOTA Takeshi
Joseph LOVE
MACHIDA Kōichi
MAYUZUMI Hiromichi
MOMOSE Kesao
MUKAE Ryūji
MURATA Harumi
NAITŌ Masao
NAKAGAWA Fumio
NAKAI Jun
NAKAZATO Toshikatsu
NASU Kunio
NISHIMURA Hiroko
OKADA Shigehiro
OKUMURA Hideo
ŌTSUJI Kiyoshi
Lawrence REPETA
SAITŌ Masao
SATŌ Tadao
SEKI Nobuko
SUEMATSU Yasukazu
SUZUKI Tomonari
TAKEHANA Rintarō
TANAKA Masaaki
TOMOI Masatoshi
TONOOKA Shin'ichiro
TSUCHIANA Fumito
TSUJI Keigo
URANO Ayako
WASHI Haruo
YAUCHI Kenji

CONTRIBUTORS

ABE Gihei	Assistant Professor, National Museum of Japanese History, Chiba Prefecture, Japan
ABE Hiromu	Chief, Preservation Section, Shōsōin Office, Nara, Japan
ABE Mikio	Executive Vice-President, Nomura Research Institute, Kanagawa Prefecture, Japan
ABE Takeshi	President, Tōkyō Gakugei University, Tōkyō, Japan
ABE Tokiharu	Secretary, Itō Foundation for the Advancement of Ichthyology, Tōkyō, Japan
ABE Yasushi	Music commentator
James C. ABEGGLEN	Vice-President, Boston Consulting Group, Inc, Boston, Massachusetts, US
ACHIWA Gorō	Physician
Barbara C. ADACHI	Author of *The Living Treasures of Japan* (1973) and *The Voices and Hands of Bunraku* (1978)
ADACHI Tetsuo	Deputy Manager, London branch, Long-Term Credit Bank of Japan, Ltd, London, England
Stephen ADDISS	Associate Professor, Department of Art History, University of Kansas, Lawrence, Kansas, US
AIDA Kō	Professor, Department of Home Economics, Ochanomizu Women's University, Tōkyō, Japan
AKASHI Yōji	Professor, Department of Foreign Languages, Nanzan University, Aichi Prefecture, Japan
Tadatoshi AKIBA	Associate Professor, Tufts University, Medford, Massachusetts, US
AKIYAMA Terukazu	Professor, Department of Literature, Gakushūin University, Tōkyō, Japan
AMAGI Isao	Advisor to the Minister, Ministry of Education, Tōkyō, Japan
AMANO Ikuo	Associate Professor, Faculty of Education, Tōkyō University, Tōkyō, Japan
AMANO Takashi	Commentator on fishing topics
Walter AMES	Author of *Police and Community in Japan* (1981)
J. L. ANDERSON	Manager for operations at WGBH in Boston; President of Mass Comm/Masu Komi media consultants; coauthor of *The Japanese Film* (rev ed, 1982)
Nancy ANDREW	Translator of *Almost Transparent Blue* by Ryū Murakami (1976)
Allan A. ANDREWS	Associate Professor, Department of Religion, University of Vermont, Burlington, Vermont, US
ANZAI Shin	Professor, Department of Literature, Sophia University, Tōkyō, Japan
Haruo AOKI	Professor and Chairman, Department of Oriental Languages, University of California, Berkeley, Berkeley, California, US
Michiko Y. AOKI	Roger Williams College, Bristol, Rhode Island, US
AOKI Tamotsu	Associate Professor, Department of Anthropology and Sociology, Ōsaka University, Ōsaka, Japan
AOMI Jun'ichi	Professor, Faculty of Law, Tōkyō University, Tōkyō, Japan
ARA Hide	Dean, Institute of Social Sciences, Tsukuba University, Ibaraki Prefecture, Japan
ARAI Eiji (d 1981)	Professor, College of Humanities and Sciences, Nihon University, Tōkyō, Japan
ARAI Naoyuki	Professor, Department of Literature, Sōka University, Tōkyō Prefecture, Japan
James T. ARAKI	Professor, Department of East Asian Literature, University of Hawaii at Manoa, Honolulu, Hawaii, US
ARAMAKI Shigeo	Professor, Earthquake Research Institute, Tōkyō University, Tōkyō, Japan
ARASE Yutaka	Professor, Institute of Journalism and Communication, Tōkyō University, Tōkyō, Japan
Diane Wright ARIMOTO	
ARIMOTO Takafumi	Lecturer, Department of Fisheries, Tōkyō University of Fisheries, Tōkyō, Japan
ARIYAMA Teruo	Associate Professor, Department of Sociology, Momoyama Gakuin University, Ōsaka Prefecture, Japan
Barbara L. ARNN	Department of Modern Languages and Literatures, University of Oklahoma, Norman, Oklahoma, US
Paul H. ARON	Executive Vice-President, Daiwa Securities America Inc, New York, New York, US
ARUGA Yūshō	Associate Professor, Department of Fisheries, Tōkyō University of Fisheries, Tōkyō, Japan
ASAI Kiyoshi	Professor, Department of Letters and Education, Ochanomizu Women's University, Tōkyō, Japan
ASAJIMA Shōichi	Professor, Department of Business Management, Senshū University, Tōkyō, Japan
Janet ASHBY	Staff Writer, *Encyclopedia of Japan*
AWAJI Takehisa	Professor, Department of Law, Rikkyō University, Tōkyō, Japan
AWAYA Kentarō	Associate Professor, Department of Literature, Rikkyō University, Tōkyō, Japan
AZUMA Hiroshi	Professor, Faculty of Education, Tōkyō University, Tōkyō, Japan
Jane BACHNIK	Assistant Professor, Department of Anthropology, University of North Carolina, Chapel Hill, North Carolina, US
Robert L. BACKUS	Associate Professor, Department of Eastern Languages, University of California, Santa Barbara, Santa Barbara, California, US
Frederick BAEKELAND	Associate Professor, Department of Psychiatry, State University of New York Downstate Medical Center, Brooklyn, New York, US
Hans H. BAERWALD	Professor, Department of Political Science, University of California, Los Angeles, Los Angeles, California, US
BAI Kōichi	Professor, Faculty of Law, Tōkyō Metropolitan University, Tōkyō, Japan
Robert J. BALLON	Chairman, Socio-Economic Institute, Sophia University, Tōkyō, Japan
BAMBA Nobuya	Professor, Faculty of Law, Ōsaka University, Ōsaka, Japan

BANNO Junji	Associate Professor, Institute of Social Science, Tōkyō University, Tōkyō, Japan
Susan BARBERI	
Gina Lee BARNES	Assistant Lecturer, Department of Archaeology, University of Cambridge, Cambridge, United Kingdom
Mary W. BASKETT	
James C. BAXTER	Acting Assistant Professor, Department of History, University of Virginia, Charlottesville, Virginia, US
Edward R. BEAUCHAMP	Associate Professor, College of Education, University of Hawaii at Manoa, Honolulu, Hawaii, US
Johanna BECKER	Professor, Department of Art, College of St. Benedict, St. Joseph, Minnesota, US
George BEDELL	Associate Professor, Department of Linguistics, University of California, Los Angeles, Los Angeles, California, US
Lawrence W. BEER	Kirby Professor of Civil Rights, Department of Government and Law, Lafayette College, Easton, Pennsylvania, US
Burton F. BEERS	Professor, Department of History, North Carolina State University at Raleigh, Raleigh, North Carolina, US
Harumi BEFU	Professor, Department of Anthropology, Stanford University, Stanford, California, US
BEKKI Atsuhiko	Professor Emeritus, Rikkyō University, Tōkyō, Japan
John W. BENNETT	Professor, Department of Anthropology, Washington University, St. Louis, Missouri, US
Gordon M. BERGER	Director, East Asian Studies Center and Associate Professor, Department of History, University of Southern California, Los Angeles, California, US
Gail Lee BERNSTEIN	Associate Professor, Department of Oriental Studies, University of Arizona, Tucson, Arizona, US
Paul BERRY	
Jonathan W. BEST	Assistant Professor, Art Department, Wesleyan University, Middletown, Connecticut, US
John BESTER	Lecturer, College of Arts and Sciences, Tōkyō University, Tōkyō, Japan
Theodore C. BESTOR	Social Science Research Council, New York, New York, US
Monica BETHE	Coauthor of *Nō as Performance: An Analysis of the Kuse Scene of Yamaba* (1978).
BITŌ Masahide	Professor, Faculty of Letters, Tōkyō University, Tōkyō, Japan
Carmen BLACKER	Lecturer, Faculty of Oriental Studies, University of Cambridge, Cambridge, United Kingdom
Dorothy BLAIR	Retired Consultant, The Corning Museum of Glass, Corning, New York, US
Peter BLEED	Associate Professor and Chairman, Department of Anthropology, University of Nebraska at Lincoln, Lincoln, Nebraska, US

Alfred BLOOM	Professor, Department of Religion, University of Hawaii at Manoa, Honolulu, Hawaii, US
Tuvia BLUMENTHAL	Associate Professor, Department of Economics, Ben Gurion University, Israel
Audie BOCK	Pacific Film Archives, University Art Museum, Berkeley, California, US
Felicia G. BOCK	Translator of *Engi-shiki: Procedures of the Engi Era,* Books I-V (1970), Books VI-X (1972)
Harold BOLITHO	Associate Professor, Department of Japanese, Monash University, Clayton, Victoria, Australia
Andrea BOLTHO	Magdalen College, University of Oxford, Oxford, United Kingdom
Robert BORGEN	Assistant Professor, Department of East Asian Languages, University of Hawaii at Manoa, Honolulu, Hawaii, US
Adriana BOSCARO	Director, Seminario di Lingua e Letteratura Giapponese, Università degli Studi di Venezia, Venice, Italy
Roger W. BOWEN	Assistant Professor, Department of Government, Colby College, Waterville, Maine, US
Gordon T. BOWLES	Professor Emeritus, Department of Anthropology, Syracuse University, Syracuse, New York, US
C. R. BOXER	Professor Emeritus, University of London, London, United Kingdom
John H. BOYLE	Professor, Department of History, California State University, Chico, Chico, California, US
Karen BRAZELL	Professor, Department of Asian Studies, Cornell University, Ithaca, New York, US
Martin BRONFENBRENNER	Professor, Department of Economics, Duke University, Durham, North Carolina, US
Robert H. BROWER	Professor, Department of Far Eastern Languages and Literatures, University of Michigan, Ann Arbor, Michigan, US
Delmer M. BROWN	Director, Inter-University Center for Japanese Language Studies in Tōkyō; Professor Emeritus, Department of History, University of California, Berkeley, Berkeley, California, US
Philip BROWN	Assistant Professor, University of North Carolina, North Carolina, US
Sidney DeVere BROWN	Professor, Department of History, University of Oklahoma, Norman, Oklahoma, US
Michael Lee BROWNE	Professor, Department of Art and History, Wayne State University, Detroit, Michigan, US
James CAHILL	Professor, Department of History of Art, University of California, Berkeley, Berkeley, California, US
Carlo CALDAROLA	Professor, Department of Sociology, University of Alberta, Edmonton, Alberta, Canada
Kent E. CALDER	Lecturer, Japan Institute and Member, Program on US–Japan Relations, Center for International Affairs, Harvard University, Cambridge, Massachusetts, US
Alan CAMPBELL	Executive Editor, *Encyclopedia of Japan*

John Creighton CAMPBELL	Associate Professor, Department of Political Science and Director, Center for Japanese Studies, University of Michigan, Ann Arbor, Michigan, US
Jeanne CARREAU	Potter
William R. CARTER	Historian; translator of *Guide to the Asuka Historical Museum* issued by the Nara National Research Institute of Cultural Properties (1978)
Ann B. CARY	Staff Writer, *Encyclopedia of Japan*
Ellen F. CARY	
Otis CARY	Professor, Department of Literature, Dōshisha University, Kyōto, Japan
Richard T. CHANG	Professor, Department of History, University of Florida, Gainesville, Florida, US
Edward I-te CHEN	Associate Professor, Department of History, Bowling Green State University, Bowling Green, Ohio, US
John J. CHEW	Professor, Department of Anthropology, University of Toronto, Toronto, Ontario, Canada
Madeleine CHI	Professor, Fu-jen University, Taipei, Taiwan
Soon Sung CHO	Professor, Department of Political Science, University of Missouri, Columbia, Missouri, US
Kee Il CHOI	Former Professor, College of Wooster, Wooster, Ohio, US
Thomas W. CLEAVER	Assistant Professor, Department of Economics, Villanova University, Villanova, Pennsylvania, US
Diane Shaver CLEMENS	Associate Professor, Department of History, University of California, Berkeley, Berkeley, California, US
Richard S. CLEVELAND	Curator of Oriental Art, St. Louis Art Museum, St. Louis, Missouri, US
Maida S. COALDRAKE	Senior Lecturer, Department of History, University of Tasmania, Hobart, Tasmania, Australia
William H. COALDRAKE	Department of Fine Arts, Harvard University, Cambridge, Massachusetts, US
Bruce A. COATS	
Joel COHN	Staff Writer, *Encyclopedia of Japan*
Robert E. COLE	Professor, Department of Sociology, University of Michigan, Ann Arbor, Michigan, US
Rex COLEMAN	Senior Partner, Coleman & Gresser, Attorneys at Law, Los Angeles, California, US
Samuel J. COLEMAN	Carolina Population Center, University of North Carolina, Chapel Hill, North Carolina, US
Martin C. COLLCUTT	Associate Professor, Department of East Asian Studies, Princeton University, Princeton, New Jersey, US
Walter Ames COMPTON	Author of *Nippon-tō: Art Swords of Japan* (1976)
Ellen P. CONANT	Lecturer and writer
Hilary CONROY	Professor, Department of History, University of Pennsylvania, Philadelphia, Pennsylvania, US
Michael COOPER	Editor, *Monumenta Nipponica*, Sophia University, Tōkyō, Japan
Louise Allison CORT	Freer Gallery of Art, Smithsonian Institution, Washington, DC, US
Teruko CRAIG	Staff Writer, *Encyclopedia of Japan*
Lloyd CRAIGHILL	Professor of East Asian Studies, Kansai University of Foreign Studies, Ōsaka Prefecture, Japan
Edwin A. CRANSTON	Professor and Chairman, Department of East Asian Languages and Civilizations, Harvard University, Cambridge, Massachusetts, US
Sydney CRAWCOUR	Professorial Fellow and Head, Department of Far Eastern History, Research School of Pacific Studies, Australian National University, Canberra, Australia
Liza CRIHFIELD	Author of *Ko Uta: Little Songs of the Geisha World* (1979).
Doris CROISSANT	Privatdozent, Kunsthistorisches Institut, Universität Heidelberg, Heidelberg, West Germany
William K. CUMMINGS	Department of Sociology, National University of Singapore, Singapore
Louisa CUNNINGHAM	Curatorial Assistant, Oriental Art Department, Yale University Art Gallery, New Haven, Connecticut, US
Michael CUNNINGHAM	Oriental Department, Cleveland Museum of Art, Cleveland, Ohio, US
Michael A. CUSUMANO	Staff Writer, *Encyclopedia of Japan*
Frederick F. CZUPRYNA	Staff Writer, *Encyclopedia of Japan*
Kenneth J. DALE	Professor, Japan Lutheran College and Theological Seminary, Tōkyō, Japan
Donald J. DALY	Professor, Faculty of Administrative Studies, York University, Downsview, Ontario, Canada
Eugene A. DANAHER	Milgrim Thomajan Jacobs & Lee, New York, New York, US
Roger DANIELS	Professor, Department of History, University of Cincinnati, Cincinnati, Ohio, US
Brett de BARY	Assistant Professor, Asian Studies Department, Cornell University, Ithaca, New York, US
Jane DEVITT	Research Fellow, Japanese Economic and Management Studies Center, University of New South Wales, Kensington, New South Wales, Australia
George DEVOS	Professor, Department of Anthropology, University of California, Berkeley, Berkeley, California, US
Roger DINGMAN	Associate Professor, Department of History, University of Southern California, Los Angeles, California, US
Donna L. DOANE	
Miyoko DOCHERTY	Lecturer, Department of the Far East, School of Oriental and African Studies, University of London, London, United Kingdom
Paula DOE	Author of *A Warbler's Song in the Dusk: The Life and Work of Ōtomo Yakamochi* (1982)

DOI Teruo	Professor, Department of Law, Waseda University, Tōkyō, Japan
Michael W. DONNELLY	Associate Professor, Department of Political Science, University of Toronto, Toronto, Ontario, Canada
Ronald P. DORE	Assistant Director, Technical Change Center, London, United Kingdom
Grisha DOTZENKO	Kodansha Famous Schools, Inc, Tōkyō, Japan
John W. DOWER	Professor, Department of History, University of Wisconsin–Madison, Madison, Wisconsin, US
Peter DRYSDALE	Professorial Fellow, Research School of Pacific Studies, Australia–Japan Research Center, Australian National University, Canberra, Australia
Heinrich DUMOULIN	Professor Emeritus, Sophia University, Tōkyō, Japan
Charles DUNN	Professor, Department of the Far East, School of Oriental and African Studies, University of London, London, United Kingdom
Jerry DUSENBURY	
Mary DUSENBURY	
David DUTCHER	Lecturer, Ōsaka University, Ōsaka, Japan
Masayo Umezawa DUUS	Author of *Tokyo Rose* (1979)
Peter DUUS	Professor, Department of History, Stanford University, Stanford, California, US
Richard E. DYCK	Specialty Materials Department, General Electric Company, Worthington, Ohio, US
Yoshiko Kurata DYKSTRA	Professor, Kansai University of Foreign Studies, Ōsaka Prefecture, Japan
H. Byron EARHART	Professor, Department of Religion, Western Michigan University, Kalamazoo, Michigan, US
David M. EARL	Department of History and Philosophy, Eastern Michigan University, Ypsilanti, Michigan, US
Lane R. EARNS	
David G. EGLER	Assistant Professor, Department of History, Western Illinois University, Macomb, Illinois, US
EJIMA Yasunori	Assistant Professor, Faculty of Letters, Tōkyō University, Tōkyō, Japan
EJIRI Kōichi	Suwada Farm, Chiba Prefecture, Japan
George ELISON	Professor, Department of East Asian Languages and Cultures, Indiana University, Bloomington, Indiana, US
ENDŌ Hiroshi	Professor, Department of Law, Gakushūin University, Tōkyō, Japan
ENDŌ Takeshi	Head Professor and Curator, Dressmaking Museum, Bunka Women's University, Tōkyō, Japan
Gerhild ENDRESS	Dozent, Abteilung Für Ostasienwissenschaften, Universität Bochum, Bochum, West Germany
ENOKI Kazuo	Deputy Director, Oriental Library, Tōkyō, Japan
Robert ENTENMANN	
Frances ERGEN	
Mark D. ERICSON	American Consulate, Ottawa, Ontario, Canada
Steven J. ERICSON	Staff Writer, *Encyclopedia of Japan*
Earle ERNST	Senior Professor of Drama and Theatre (Emeritus), University of Hawaii at Manoa, Honolulu, Hawaii, US
ETŌ Fumio	Professor, Department of Literature, Seikei University, Tōkyō, Japan
ETŌ Kyōji	Professor, School of Education, Nagoya University, Aichi Prefecture, Japan
Robert EVANS, JR	Professor, Department of Economics, Brandeis University, Waltham, Massachusetts, US
Lee W. FARNSWORTH	Professor, Department of Political Science, Brigham Young University, Provo, Utah, US
Wayne FARRIS	
Dallas FINN	
Richard B. FINN	Administrative Director, Program on US–Japan Relations, Center for International Affairs, Harvard University, Cambridge, Massachusetts, US
Jerry K. FISHER	Associate Professor, Department of History, Macalester College, St. Paul, Minnesota, US
Pat FISTER	
Scott C. FLANAGAN	Professor, Department of Government, Florida State University, Tallahassee, Florida, US
Wm. Miles FLETCHER III	Assistant Professor, Department of History, University of North Carolina at Chapel Hill, Chapel Hill, North Carolina, US
James H. FOARD	Assistant Professor, Department of Religious Studies, Arizona State University, Tempe, Arizona, US
Grace FOX	Author of *Britain and Japan 1858–1883* (1969)
Andrew FRASER	Senior Fellow, Department of Far Eastern History, Research School of Pacific Studies, Australian National University, Canberra, Australia
Cal FRENCH	Professor, Department of the History of Art, University of Michigan, Ann Arbor, Michigan, US
Peter FROST	Professor, Department of History, Williams College, Williamstown, Massachusetts, US
FUJII Toshiko	Chief, Women Workers Section, Women and Minors Bureau, Ministry of Labor, Tōkyō, Japan
FUJIKAWA Kinji	Curator, Japanese Sword Museum, Tōkyō; President, Society for the Preservation of Japanese Swords, Tōkyō, Japan
FUJIKURA Kōichirō	Professor, Faculty of Law, Tōkyō University, Tōkyō, Japan
FUJIMURA Michio	Professor, Department of Literature, Sophia University, Tōkyō, Japan

FUJINO Ichirō	Chief, Ōsaka branch of Nishikawa Industries, Ōsaka, Japan
FUJITA Tomio	Professor, Department of General Education, Rikkyō University, Tōkyō, Japan
FUKAGAWA Tsuneyoshi	Professor, Shōbi College of Music, Saitama Prefecture, Japan
FUKUDA Hideichi	Professor, National Institute of Japanese Literature, Tōkyō, Japan
FUKUDA Kizō (d 1982)	Professor, Department of Literature, Seikei University, Tōkyō, Japan
Haruhiro FUKUI	Professor, Department of Political Science, University of California, Santa Barbara, Santa Barbara, California, US
Glen S. FUKUSHIMA	Consultant, *Encyclopedia of Japan*
FUKUSHIMA Shingo	Professor, Department of Law and Head, Graduate School of Law Studies, Senshū University, Tōkyō, Japan
FUNAKOSHI Tōru	Professor, Department of Engineering, Tōkyō Denki University, Tōkyō, Japan
Jean FUNATSU	
FURUTA Hikaru	Professor, Faculty of Education, Yokohama National University, Kanagawa Prefecture, Japan
FURUYA Kōzō	Former Chief, Tea Research Station, Ministry of Agriculture, Forestry, and Fisheries, Tōkyō, Japan
Toyomasa FUSÉ	Professor, Department of Sociology, Faculty of Arts, York University, Downsview, Ontario, Canada
GANBE Eiichi	Former Director, Electric Communication Research Institute, Nippon Telegraph and Telephone Public Corporation, Tōkyō, Japan
C. Harvey GARDINER	Research Professor of History (Emeritus), Southern Illinois University, Carbondale, Illinois, US
Kenneth GARDNER	Deputy Keeper, Department of Oriental Manuscripts and Printed Books, The British Library, London, United Kingdom
Robert GARFIAS	Professor, Department of Music, University of Washington, Seattle, Washington, US
B. J. GEORGE, JR	Professor, New York Law School, New York, New York, US
Van C. GESSEL	Assistant Professor, Department of Modern and Classical Languages, University of Notre Dame, Notre Dame, Indiana, US
Kalyan Kumar GHOSH	Reader, Center for Southeast Asia, Jadavpur University, Calcutta, India
GŌDA Yoshimasa	Assistant, Department of Literature, Aoyama Gakuin University, Tōkyō, Japan
David I. GOLDBERG	Professor, Leningrad State University, Leningrad, USSR
Grant K. GOODMAN	Professor, Department of History, University of Kansas, Lawrence, Kansas, US
Theodore W. GOOSSEN	

Andrew GORDON	Instructor, Department of History, Harvard University, Cambridge, Massachusetts, US
GOTŌ Kazuhiko	NHK Theoretical Research Center, Tōkyō, Japan
Patricia J. GRAHAM	
Allan G. GRAPARD	Assistant Professor, Department of Asian Studies, Cornell University, Ithaca, New York, US
Maribeth GRAYBILL	Acting Assistant Professor, Department of the History of Art, University of California, Berkeley, Berkeley, California, US
Edward G. GRIFFIN	
Jane T. GRIFFIN	
Peter M. GRILLI	Director, Education and Communications and Japan Film Center, Japan Society, Inc, New York, New York, US
Willem A. GROOTAERS	Formerly Lecturer, Graduate School of Linguistics, Sophia University, Tōkyō, Japan
HABE Tadashige	Professor, Faculty of Marine Science and Technology, Tōkai University, Shizuoka Prefecture, Japan
Roger F. HACKETT	Professor, Department of History, University of Michigan, Ann Arbor, Michigan, US
Eleanor M. HADLEY	Adjunct Professor, Department of Economics, George Washington University, Washington, DC, US
HAGA Namio	Adviser, Mining and Metallurgical Institute of Japan, Tōkyō, Japan
HAGA Noboru	Head Professor, Institute of History and Anthropology, Tsukuba University, Ibaraki Prefecture, Japan
HAGA Tōru	Professor, College of Arts and Sciences, Tōkyō University, Tōkyō, Japan
Kanji HAITANI	Professor, Department of Economics and Business Administration, State University of New York College at Fredonia, Fredonia, New York, US
Yoshito S. HAKEDA	Professor, Department of Religion, Columbia University, New York, New York, US
David HALE	
John O. HALEY	Associate Professor, School of Law, University of Washington, Seattle, Washington, US
Ivan P. HALL	Associate Executive Director, Japan–US Friendship Commission, Tōkyō, Japan
John W. HALL	Professor, Department of History, Yale University, New Haven, Connecticut, US
Robert B. HALL	Professor, Department of History and Director, Center for Asian Studies, University of Rochester, Rochester, New York, US
Robert King HALL (d 1981)	Editor of *Kokutai no hongi: Cardinal Principles of the National Entity of Japan* (1949) and author of *Education for a New Japan* (1949, reprint 1971)

HAMAKAWA Yoshihiro	Professor, Department of Electrical Engineering, Faculty of Engineering Science, Ōsaka University, Ōsaka, Japan
HAMANO Takuya	Writer of children's books; Lecturer, Tōkyō Gakugei University and Nihon University, Tōkyō, Japan
HANAMI Tadashi	Dean, Department of Law, Sophia University, Tōkyō, Japan
HANAMURA Masaru	Lecturer and trustee, Kunitachi College of Music, Tōkyō Prefecture, Japan
Mikiso HANE	Professor, Department of History, Knox College, Galesburg, Illinois, US
Susan B. HANLEY	Associate Professor, School of International Studies, University of Washington, Seattle, Washington, US
HARADA Katsumasa	Lecturer, Wakō University, Tōkyō Prefecture, Japan
HARADA Yukihiro	Senior Economist, Economics Division, Long-Term Credit Bank of Japan, Ltd, Tōkyō, Japan
Helen HARDACRE	Assistant Professor, Department of Religion, Princeton University, Princeton, New Jersey, US
Eileen HARGADINE	
Phillip T. HARRIES	Lecturer, School of Oriental and African Studies, University of London, London, United Kingdom
HARUHARA Akihiko	Professor and Chairman, School of Journalism, Department of Literature, Sophia University, Tōkyō, Japan
HASHIKAWA Bunzō	Professor, Department of Politics and Economics, Meiji University, Tōkyō, Japan
HASHIMOTO Nobuyuki	Associate Professor, Department of Law, Kansai Gakuin University, Ōsaka Prefecture, Japan
HASHIMOTO Sumiko	Senior Researcher, Tōkyō National Museum, Tōkyō, Japan
HASUMI Otohiko	Professor, Department of Education, Tōkyō Gakugei University, Tōkyō, Japan
HATA Ikuhiko	Professor, Department of Politics and Economics, Takushoku University, Tōkyō, Japan
HATORI Tetsuya	Professor, Department of Literature, Seikei University, Tōkyō, Japan
Milan HAUNER	Department of History, University of Wisconsin–Madison, Madison, Wisconsin, US
William B. HAUSER	Associate Professor and Chairman, Department of History, University of Rochester, Rochester, New York, US
T. R. H. HAVENS	Professor, Department of History, Connecticut College, New London, Connecticut, US
HAYAKAWA Kunihiko	Director, Hayakawa and Associates, Architects, Tōkyō, Japan
HAYAKAWA Zenjirō	Professor, Department of Sociology, Rikkyō University, Tōkyō, Japan
HAYASHI Kunio	Fashion commentator
HAYASHI Kyōhei	Tsubouchi Memorial Theater Museum, Waseda University, Tōkyō, Japan
HAYASHI Shigeju	Professor, Department of Literature, Seikei University, Tōkyō, Japan
HAYASHI Takeji	Former President, Miyagi University of Education, Miyagi Prefecture, Japan
HAYASHI Yasaka	Former Professor, Department of Agriculture, Tōkyō University of Agriculture, Tōkyō, Japan
HAYASHI Yutaka	*Go* commentator
HAYASHI Yūzō	Standing Director, Japan Physical Education Facilities Management Company, Tōkyō, Japan
Benjamin H. HAZARD	Professor, Department of History, San Jose State University, San Jose, California, US
Graham HEALEY	Acting Director, Center for Japanese Studies, University of Sheffield, Sheffield, United Kingdom
Waldo HEINRICHS	Professor, Department of History, Temple University, Philadelphia, Pennsylvania, US
HEMMI Takemitsu	Professor, School of Mental Health, Faculty of Medicine, Tōkyō University, Tōkyō, Japan
Dan Fenno HENDERSON	Professor, School of Law, University of Washington, Seattle, Washington, US
Paul HENRIQUES	Instructor, Asian Division, University of Maryland, Tōkyō Prefecture, Japan
Howard S. HIBBETT	Professor, Department of East Asian Languages and Civilizations, Harvard University, Cambridge, Massachusetts, US
HIBI Yutaka	Professor, Faculty of Education, Nagoya University, Aichi Prefecture, Japan
Brian HICKMAN	Assistant Librarian for Japanese and Korean Collections, School of Oriental and African Studies, University of London, London, United Kingdom
Money HICKMAN	Department of Asiatic Art, Museum of Fine Arts, Boston, Massachusetts, US
HIDANO Tadashi	Professor and Director, Research Division, National Center for University Entrance Examinations, Tōkyō, Japan
HIGASHI Jutarō	Professor, Department of Art and Science, Tsuda College, Tōkyō, Japan
HIJIKATA Kazuo	Professor, Faculty of General Education, Nagoya University, Aichi Prefecture, Japan
HINOTANI Akihiko	Professor, Department of Literature, Keiō University, Tōkyō, Japan
Noburu HIRAGA	Lecturer, Department of Asian Languages and Literatures, University of Washington, Seattle, Washington, US
Atsuko HIRAI	Department of History, Michigan State University, East Lansing, Michigan, US
HIRANO Kunio	Professor, Department of Arts and Science, Tōkyō Women's Christian University, Tōkyō, Japan
HIRANO Ryūichi	President and Professor, Faculty of Law, Tōkyō University, Tōkyō, Japan
HIRASAWA Yutaka	Professor, Department of Fisheries, Tōkyō University of Fisheries, Tōkyō, Japan
HIRATA Masami	Chief Editorial Writer, Kyōdō News Service, Tōkyō, Japan
HIRATSUKA Masunori (d 1981)	Director, National Institute for Educational Research, Tōkyō, and Professor Emeritus, Faculty of Education, Kyūshū University, Fukuoka Prefecture, Japan
HIROI Nobuko	Lecturer, Department of Fine Arts, Kyōto City University of Arts, Kyōto, Japan

HIRONAKA Wakako	Writer and translator
HIROSAKI Yoshitsugu	Director, Enoshima Aquarium, Kanagawa Prefecture, Japan
HIROSE Hideo (d 1981)	Professor, Senshū University, Tōkyō, Japan
Johannes HIRSCHMEIER (d 1983)	President, Nanzan University, Aichi Prefecture, Japan
HITOTSUMATSU Shin	Professor, Research Institute for Mathematical Sciences, Kyōto University, Kyōto, Japan
Frank HOFF	Associate Professor, Department of East Asian Studies, University of Toronto, Toronto, Ontario, Canada
HŌJŌ Yoshio	Chief of Research, Department of Physiology and Heredity, Agricultural Technology Research Institute, Ibaraki Prefecture, Japan
HOKAMA Hiroshi	Professor, Department of Law, Chūō University, Tōkyō, Japan
Wendy HOLDEN	Department of the History of Art, University of Michigan, Ann Arbor, Michigan, US
Leon HOLLERMAN	Professor Emeritus, Department of Economics, Claremont McKenna College, Claremont, California, US
Inger-Johanne HOLMBOE	Lund Law School, Malmo, Sweden
HOMMA Yasuhei	Professor, Department of Sociology, Rikkyō University, Tōkyō, Japan
William D. HOOVER	Associate Professor and Chairman, Department of History, University of Toledo, Toledo, Ohio, US
Kyotsu HORI	Tōkyō Risshō Junior College for Women, Tōkyō, Japan
HORIUCHI Mamoru	Professor, Department of Education, Nagoya University, Aichi Prefecture, Japan
H. Mack HORTON	Translator of *Architecture in the Shoin Style* by Fumio Hashimoto (1981)
HOSHIKAWA Kiyochika	Professor, Faculty of Agriculture, Tōhoku University, Miyagi Prefecture, Japan
HOSHINO Akira	Professor and Chairman, Division of Education, College of Liberal Arts, International Christian University, Tōkyō Prefecture, Japan
HOSHINO Eiki	Lecturer, Department of Literature, Taishō University, Tōkyō, Japan
HOSODA Kazuo	Professor, Department of Home Economics, Shōwa Women's University, Tōkyō, Japan
HOSOYA Chihiro	Professor, Department of Law, Hitotsubashi University, Tōkyō Prefecture, Japan
HOSOYA Toshio	Professor Emeritus, Tōkyō University, Tōkyō, Japan
John F. HOWES	Associate Professor, Department of Asian Studies, University of British Columbia, Vancouver, British Columbia, Canada
HOYANAGI Mutsumi	Vice-President, Tōkyō Geographical Society, Tōkyō, Japan
Francis L. K. HSU	Professor and Director, Center for the Study of Culture in Education, School of Education, University of San Francisco, San Francisco, California, US
Thomas M. HUBER	Assistant Professor, Department of History, Duke University, Durham, North Carolina, US
David W. HUGHES	
G. Cameron HURST III	Professor and Chairman, Department of East Asian Languages and Cultures, University of Kansas, Lawrence, Kansas, US
Julia HUTT	Research Assistant, Far Eastern Section, Victoria and Albert Museum, London, United Kingdom
ICHIKAWA Kenjirō	Professor, Department of Fisheries, Tōkyō University of Fisheries, Tōkyō, Japan
ICHIKI Toshio	National Defense College, Tōkyō, Japan
Fumiko IKAWA-SMITH	Associate Professor and Chairman, Department of Anthropology, McGill University, Montreal, Quebec, Canada
Hiroko IKEDA	Professor Emeritus, Department of East Asian Literature, University of Hawaii at Manoa, Honolulu, Hawaii, US
IMAI Jun	Professor, Department of Humanities, Musashi University, Tōkyō, Japan
IMAI Shigeru	Associate Professor, Kyūshū Institute of Design, Fukuoka Prefecture, Japan
IMAIZUMI Yoshiharu	Professor, Department of Literature, Tsuru University, Yamanashi Prefecture, Japan
IMAIZUMI Yoshinori	Visiting Professor, Tōkyō University of Agriculture, Tōkyō, Japan
IMAMICHI Tomonobu	Former Professor and Dean, Faculty of Letters, Tōkyō University, Tōkyō, Japan
IMAMURA Yoshio	
IMAZEKI Rokuya	Former President, Mycological Society of Japan, Tōkyō, Japan
INABA Eiko	Formerly on staff of the Long-Term Credit Bank of Japan, Ltd, Tōkyō, Japan
INAGAKI Shisei	Social historian
INŌ Tentarō	Professor, Department of Literature, Chūō University, Tōkyō, Japan
INOKUCHI Shōji	Director, Folklore Society of Japan, Tōkyō, Japan
INOUE Hiroshi	Deputy Chief, Department of Botany, National Science Museum, Tōkyō, Japan
INOUE Kaoru	Professor Emeritus, Ōsaka University, Ōsaka, Japan
INOUE Keizō	Inoue Ski School, Niigata Prefecture, Japan
INOUE Munemichi	Manager, Economic Research Section, Marubeni Corporation, Tōkyō, Japan
INOUE Shōbi	Professor, Department of Education, Tōkyō Gakugei University, Tōkyō, Japan
INOUE Shun	Professor, Faculty of General Education, Ōsaka University, Ōsaka, Japan
INOUE Teruko	Associate Professor, Department of the Humanities, Wakō University, Tōkyō Prefecture, Japan
Daniel K. INOUYE	United States Senator from Hawaii

Akira IRIYE	Professor and Chairman, Department of History, University of Chicago, Chicago, Illinois, US
Mitsuko IRIYE	
Chiyoko ISHIBASHI	
Hoyu ISHIDA	Staff Writer, *Encyclopedia of Japan*
ISHIDA Ichirō	Professor, Department of Literature, Tōkai University, Kanagawa Prefecture, Japan
ISHIGE Naomichi	Associate Professor, National Museum of Ethnology, Ōsaka Prefecture, Japan
ISHII Ryōsuke	Professor, Department of Law, Sōka University, Tōkyō Prefecture, Japan
ISHII Susumu	Professor, Faculty of Letters, Tōkyō University, Tōkyō, Japan
ISHIKAWA Minoru	Professor, Department of Law, Sophia University, Tōkyō, Japan
ISHIMINE Keitetsu	Professor, Department of Law and Letters, Ryūkū University, Naha, Okinawa Prefecture, Japan
ISHIMURA Zensuke	Professor, Department of Law, Tōkyō Metropolitan University, Tōkyō, Japan
ISHIYAMA Akira	Professor, Department of Home Economics, Bunka Women's College, Tōkyō, Japan
ISHIZAKA Etsuo	Professor, Department of Sociology, Hōsei University, Tōkyō, Japan
ISHIZAKI Jūrō	Advisor to Daikyō Oil Co, Ltd, and to Abu-Dhabi Oil Co, Ltd
ISOBE Kiichi	Professor Emeritus, Tōkyō Institute of Technology, Tōkyō, Japan
ITASAKA Tsuyoshi	Film commentator
ITŌ Hajime (d 1980)	Commentator on economic affairs
ITŌ Masami	Judge, Supreme Court, Tōkyō, Japan
ITŌ Mikiharu	Professor, National Museum of Ethnology, Ōsaka Prefecture, Japan
ITŌ Nobuo	Director, National Cultural Properties Research Institute, Tōkyō, Japan
ITŌ Shigeo	Instructor, Legal Training and Research Institute, Supreme Court, Tōkyō, Japan
ITŌ Zen'ichi	Professor, Department of Arts and Science, Tōkyō Women's Christian University, Tōkyō, Japan
Hiroshi ITOH	Professor, Department of Political Science, State University of New York College at Plattsburgh, Plattsburgh, New York, US
IWADARE Hiroshi	Editorial staff, *Asahi shimbun*, Tōkyō, Japan
IWAI Hiroaki	Professor, Department of Sociology, Tōyō University, Tōkyō, Japan
IWAMOTO Tokuichi	Professor, Department of Literature, Kokugakuin University, Tōkyō, Japan
Yoshio IWAMOTO	Professor, Department of East Asian Languages and Cultures, Indiana University, Bloomington, Indiana, US
IWANAGA Shinkichi	Managing Director, Shimbun Tsūshin Chōsakai; author of *The Story of Japanese News Agencies* (1980)
IWASHIMA Hisao	Professor and Director, First Research Office of War History, National Defense College, Tōkyō, Japan
Masakazu IWATA	Professor, Department of History, Biola College, La Mirada, California, US
Tōru IWATAKE	Postdoctoral Research Fellow, Department of Music, University of Queensland, Brisbane, Australia
IYANAGA Teizō	Professor, Department of Literature, Sophia University, Tōkyō, Japan
Marius B. JANSEN	Professor, Department of East Asian Studies, Princeton University, Princeton, New Jersey, US
Donald JENKINS	Director, Portland Art Association, Portland, Oregon, US
JIMBO Genji	Professor, Department of Chemical Engineering, Nagoya University, Aichi Prefecture, Japan
Chalmers JOHNSON	Professor and Chairman, Department of Political Science, University of California, Berkeley, Berkeley, California, US
Gine JOHNSON	
Eleanor H. JORDEN	Professor, Department of Modern Languages and Linguistics, Cornell University, Ithaca, New York, US
John JUNKERMAN	Staff Writer, *Encyclopedia of Japan*
KAGESATO Tetsurō	Director, Mie Prefectural Art Museum, Mie Prefecture, Japan
KAI Michitarō	Professor, Department of Law, Ōsaka City University, Ōsaka, Japan
KAKEGAWA Tomiko	Professor, Department of Sociology, Kansai University, Ōsaka Prefecture, Japan
Yoshiko KAKUDŌ	Curator of Japanese Art, Asian Art Museum of San Francisco, San Francisco, California, US
KAMACHI Noriko	Professor, Department of History, University of Michigan-Dearborn, Dearborn, Michigan, US
KANAI Madoka	Professor, Historiographical Institute, Tōkyō University, Tōkyō, Japan
KANASEKI Hiroshi	Professor and Dean, Department of Arts and Sciences, Tenri University, Nara Prefecture, Japan
KANAZAWA Yoshio	Attorney, Kanazawa Law Office, Tōkyō, Japan
Christine Guth KANDA	Assistant Professor, Department of Art and Archaeology, Princeton University, Princeton, New Jersey, US
James KANDA	
KANEKO Hiroshi	Professor, Faculty of Law, Tōkyō University, Tōkyō, Japan
KANEKO Yoshimasa	President, Seika Jikken Sha, Tōkyō, Japan
KANNO Kōki	Professor, Department of General Education, Iwate University of Medicine, Iwate Prefecture, Japan
KANŌ Hisashi	Nara National Cultural Properties Research Institute, Nara Prefecture, Japan
Eugene J. KAPLAN	Japan Economic Institute of America, Washington, DC, US
Catherine KAPUTA	Cotranslator of *Kanō Eitoku* by Tsuneo Takeda (1977)
KARASAWA Tomitarō	Professor, Department of Education, Sōka University, Tōkyō Prefecture, Japan

KARATSU Hajime	Managing Director, Matsushita Communication Industrial Co, Ltd, Kanagawa Prefecture, Japan
KARITA Yoshio	Chief, First Section, North American Bureau, Ministry of Foreign Affairs, Tōkyō, Japan
KATA Kōji	Commentator; formerly Editor, *Shisō no Kagaku*
KATAGIRI Kazuo	Professor, Department of Literature, Aoyama Gakuin University, Tōkyō, Japan
KATŌ Hiroaki	
KATŌ Hiromi	Economic Research Institute, Economic Planning Agency, Tōkyō, Japan
KATŌ Hiroshi	Professor, Department of Economics, Keiō University, Tōkyō, Japan
KATŌ Ichirō	Professor Emeritus, Faculty of Law, Tōkyō University and Chancellor, Seijō Gakuen, Tōkyō, Japan
KATŌ Jōji	Vice-Director, Productivity Research Institute, Japan Productivity Center, Tōkyō, Japan
KATŌ Kōji	Senior Researcher, National Institute for Educational Research, Tōkyō, Japan
KATŌ Kōzaburō	Professor, Department of Economics, Senshū University, Tōkyō, Japan
KATŌ Masashi	Senior Planning Officer, Planning Bureau, Economic Planning Agency, Tōkyō, Japan
KATŌ Shunjirō	Lecturer, Tottori University, Tottori Prefecture, Japan
KATŌ Shunpei	Professor, Department of Engineering, Tōkyō Institute of Science and Technology, Tōkyō, Japan
KATORI Tadahiko	Tōkyō National Museum, Tōkyō, Japan
KATSURA Yoshio	Professor, Department of Education, Kōbe University, Hyōgo Prefecture, Japan
KAWAHARA Sumiyuki	Senior Specialist for Cultural Properties, Monuments and Sites Division, Agency for Cultural Affairs, Tōkyō, Japan
KAWAI Takeshi	Professor, Department of Law, Hitotsubashi University, Tōkyō Prefecture, Japan
KAWAKAMI Hiroshi	Professor, Department of Literature and Arts, Seijō University, Tōkyō, Japan
KAWAMOTO Akira	Professor and Dean, Department of Sociology, Meiji Gakuin University, Tōkyō, Japan
KAWAMOTO Ichirō	Professor, Faculty of Economics, Kōbe University, Hyōgo Prefecture, Japan
KAWAMOTO Takashi	Senior Vice-President, The Bank of Tōkyō Trust Company, New York, New York, US
Fujiya KAWASHIMA	Associate Professor, Department of History, Bowling Green State University, Bowling Green, Ohio, US
KAWAUCHI Hachirō	Professor, Department of Humanities, Ibaraki University, Ibaraki Prefecture, Japan
KAWAZOE Noboru	Director, Communication Design Institute, Kyōto, Japan
KAZAKI Hideo	Professor, Department of Science, Tōhō University, Tōkyō and Professor Emeritus, Tōkyō Metropolitan University, Tōkyō, Japan

Donald KEENE	Professor, Department of East Asian Languages and Cultures, Columbia University, New York, New York, US
James T. KENNEY	Staff Writer, *Encyclopedia of Japan*
Roger KEYES	Coauthor of *The Theatrical World of Osaka Prints* (1973)
KIDA Hiroshi	Director, National Institute for Educational Research, Tōkyō, Japan
KIDA Jun'ichirō	Commentator on publishing
J. Edward KIDDER, JR	Vice-President, and Professor, Division of Humanities, International Christian University, Tōkyō Prefecture, Japan
KIKKAWA Shūhei	Lecturer, Department of Literature, Kagoshima Women's University, Kagoshima Prefecture, Japan
Cornelius J. KILEY	Associate Professor, Department of History, Villanova University, Villanova, Pennsylvania, US
Hee-Jin KIM	Associate Professor, Department of Religious Studies, University of Oregon, Eugene, Oregon, US
Yongdeok KIM	Department of Asian History, College of Humanities, Seoul National University, Seoul, Korea
KIMURA Eiichi	Professor, Department of Commerce, Hitotsubashi University, Tōkyō Prefecture, Japan
KIMURA Hidemasa	Chairman, Japan Committee for Civil Aviation Studies, Tōkyō, Japan
KIMURA Hiroshi	Senior Researcher, National Institute for Education Research, Tōkyō, Japan
KIMURA Kiyotaka	Lecturer, Shitennōji International Buddhist University, Ōsaka Prefecture, Japan
KIMURA Masanori	Professor, Department of Literature, Gakushūin University, Tōkyō, Japan
KIMURA Shigemitsu	Associate Professor, Department of Education, Tōkyō Gakugei University, Tōkyō, Japan
KIMURA Tsuyoshi	Minister's Secretariat, Ministry of Posts and Telecommunications, Tōkyō, Japan
Masako KINOSHITA	
KINOUCHI Kiyoko	Professor, Department of Home Economics, Ōtsuma Women's University, Tōkyō, Japan
Maurine A. KIRKPATRICK	
KISAKA Jun'ichirō	Professor, Department of Law, Ryūkoku University, Kyōto, Japan
KISHINO Hisashi	Lecturer, Department of Education, Rikkyō University, Tōkyō, Japan
Sandy KITA	Elvejhem Museum of Art, University of Wisconsin–Madison, Madison, Wisconsin, US
Joseph M. KITAGAWA	Professor, Department of Far Eastern Languages and Civilizations, University of Chicago, Chicago, Illinois, US
KITAHARA Yasusada	Executive Vice-President, Nippon Telegraph and Telephone Public Corporation, Tōkyō, Japan
John KITAHARA-FRISCH	Professor, Life Science Institute, Sophia University, Tōkyō, Japan
KITAMURA Bunji	Professor, Department of Literature, Kokushikan University, Tōkyō, Japan

KITAZAWA Masahiro — Professor, Faculty of Law, Nagoya University, Aichi Prefecture, Japan

Gisaburō N. KIYOSE — Assistant Professor, Department of East Asian Languages, University of Hawaii at Manoa, Honolulu, Hawaii, US

Jill KLEINBERG — Staff Writer, *Encyclopedia of Japan*

Lothar G. KNAUTH — Professor, Universidad Nacional Autonoma de Mexico, Villa Obregon, Mexico

KOBAYAKAWA Yōichi

KOBAYASHI Kazuhiro — Publications specialist

KOBAYASHI Manabu — Professor, Department of Education, Tsukuba University, Ibaraki Prefecture, Japan

KOBAYASHI Saburō — Professor, Archaeological Institute, Meiji University, Tōkyō, Japan

T. James KODERA — Associate Professor, Department of Religion, Wellesley College, Wellesley, Massachusetts, US

KOGIKU Kiichirō — Professor, Department of Economics, University of California, US

Byung Chul KOH — Professor, Department of Political Science, University of Illinois at Chicago, Chicago, Illinois, US

KOIKE Chie — Professor, Department of Home Economics, Bunka Women's University, Tōkyō, Japan

KOIZUMI Iwao — Professor, Department of Technology, Kanazawa University, Ishikawa Prefecture, Japan

KOJIMA Kazuto — Associate Professor, Department of Liberal Arts, Saitama University, Saitama Prefecture, Japan

KOJIMA Takeshi — Professor, Department of Law, Chūō University, Tōkyō, Japan

KOJIMA Tomiko — Lecturer, Department of Music, Tōkyō University of Fine Arts and Music, Tōkyō, Japan

KOKUBO Takeshi — Executive Editor, *Encyclopedia of Japan*

Akira KOMAI — Professor, Department of Far Eastern Languages and Civilizations, University of Chicago, Chicago, Illinois, US

KOMATA Yūsuke — Lecturer, Tankang University, Taipei, Taiwan

KOMATSU Sakyō — Science fiction writer

KOMINE Takao — Domestic Research Section, Economic Planning Agency, Tōkyō, Japan

KONDŌ Shinji — National Defense College, Tōkyō, Japan

KONISHI Jin'ichi — Professor Emeritus, Tsukuba University, Ibaraki Prefecture, Japan

KŌNO Motomichi — Lecturer, Komazawa University, Tōkyō and at Hokkaidō Education University, Hokkaidō, Japan

KŌNO Tomomi — Professor, Ōsaka Kun'ei Women's College, Ōsaka and Director, Kōno Food Research Institute, Ōsaka, Japan

KOSHIBA Harumi — Associate Professor, Department of Humanities and Arts, Tōkai University, Tōkyō, Japan

KOTANI Kōzō — Deputy Director-General, Government Pension Bureau, Prime Minister's Office, Tōkyō, Japan

KŌUCHI Saburō — Professor, Institute of Journalism, Tōkyō University, Tōkyō, Japan

KOYANAGI Shun'ichirō — Lecturer, Faculty of Education, Yamanashi University, Yamanashi Prefecture, Japan

KOYASU Nobukuni — Professor, Faculty of Literature, Ōsaka University, Ōsaka, Japan

KOZAWA Tadahiro — Staff Writer, *Encyclopedia of Japan*

Klaus KRACHT — Lecturer, Abteilung für Ostasienwissenschaften, Ruhr-Universität Bochum, Bochum, West Germany

Ellis S. KRAUSS — Associate Professor, Department of Political Science, Western Washington University, Bellingham, Washington, US

Hyman KUBLIN — Professor, Department of History, Brooklyn College, Brooklyn, New York, US

KUBO Fuminae — Director-General, Japan Pharmaceutical Information Center, Tōkyō, Japan

KUBOTA Kinuko — Professor, Department of Law, Tōhoku Gakuin University, Miyagi Prefecture, Japan

KUBOTA Takeshi — Teacher, Tōkyō Metropolitan Nishi Senior High School, Tōkyō, Japan

KUDŌ Masanobu — Director, Japan Ikebana Art Society, Tōkyō, Japan

KUMA Rakuya — Executive Director and General Manager, Research Laboratory, Kobayashi Kōsē Co, Ltd, Tōkyō, Japan

Fumie KUMAGAI — Professor, Department of Sociology, University of New Hampshire, Durham, New Hampshire, US

KUMAGAI Hiroshi — President, Japanese Association of Medical Sciences, Tōkyō, Japan

KUMAKURA Isao — Associate Professor, Institute of History and Ethnology, Tsukuba University, Ibaraki Prefecture, Japan

KUMATORI Toshiyuki — Director-General, National Institute of Radiological Sciences, Chiba Prefecture, Japan

KURANISHI Shigeru — Professor, Department of Engineering, Tōhoku University, Miyagi Prefecture, Japan

KURATA Bunsaku (d 1983) — Director, Nara National Museum, Nara, Japan

KURAUCHI Shirō — Professor, Department of Literature, Tōyō University, Tōkyō, Japan

KURITA Ken — Professor, Department of Commerce, Meiji University, Tōkyō, Japan

KURIYAMA Shigehisa — Staff Writer, *Encyclopedia of Japan*

KURODA Nobuyuki — Professor, School of Law, Kansei Gakuin University, Hyōgo Prefecture, Japan

Michio KUSHI — Kushi Institute, Boston, Massachusetts, US

KUWATA Tadachika — Professor Emeritus, Department of Literature, Kokugakuin University, Tōkyō, Japan

George KUWAYAMA — Senior Curator, Far Eastern Art, Los Angeles County Museum of Art, Los Angeles, California, US

Patricia Hagan KUWAYAMA	Manager, Foreign Exchange Department, Federal Reserve Bank of New York, New York, New York, US
William R. LAFLEUR	Associate Professor, Department of Oriental Languages, University of California, Los Angeles, Los Angeles, California, US
Whalen LAI	Associate Professor, Department of Religious Studies, University of California, Davis, Davis, California, US
Harry J. LAMLEY	Professor, Department of History, University of Hawaii at Manoa, Honolulu, Hawaii, US
H. G. LAMONT	Department of Oriental Languages, University of California, Los Angeles, Los Angeles, California, US
Richard LANE	Author of *Masters of the Japanese Print* (1962), *Shunga Books of the Ukiyo-e School, Series I-VI* (1973–82), and *Images from the Floating World* (1978).
Betty B. LANHAM	Professor, Department of Sociology and Anthropology, Indiana University of Pennsylvania, Indiana, Pennsylvania, US
T. C. LARKIN	New Zealand Ambassador to Japan 1972–76; Consultant, International Trade Development, Asia Pacific Research Unit Limited, Wellington, New Zealand
Joyce C. LEBRA	Professor, Department of History, University of Colorado, Boulder, Colorado, US
Takie Sugiyama LEBRA	Professor, Department of Anthropology, University of Hawaii at Manoa, Honolulu, Hawaii, US
Gari LEDYARD	Professor and Chairman, Department of East Asian Languages and Cultures, Columbia University, New York, New York, US
Changsoo LEE	Assistant Professor, School of Public Administration, University of Southern California, Los Angeles, California, US
George Alexander LENSEN (d 1980)	Professor, Department of History, Florida State University, Tallahassee, Florida, US
Robert W. LEUTNER	Assistant Professor, Department of Asian Languages and Literature, University of Iowa, Iowa City, Iowa, US
Solomon B. LEVINE	Professor, School of Business, University of Wisconsin–Madison, Madison, Wisconsin, US
Young Ick LEW	Associate Professor, Department of History, University of Houston, Houston, Texas, US
Bruno H. LEWIN	Professor, Abteilung für Ostasienwissenschaften, Ruhr-Universität Bochum, Bochum, West Germany
Olof LIDIN	Professor, East Asian Institute, University of Copenhagen, Copenhagen, Denmark
Thomas B. LIFSON	Assistant Professor, Graduate School of Business Administration, Harvard University, Cambridge, Massachusetts, US
Anthony V. LIMAN	Associate Professor, Department of East Asian Studies, University of Toronto, Ontario, Canada
Edward J. LINCOLN	Vice-President, Japan Economic Institute of America, Washington, DC, US
Howard A. LINK	Curator of Asian Art, Honolulu Academy of Arts, Honolulu, Hawaii, US
Noriko Mizuta LIPPIT	Associate Professor, Department of East Asian Languages and Cultures, University of Southern California, Los Angeles, California, US
Victor D. LIPPIT	Associate Professor, Department of Economics, University of California, Riverside, Riverside, California, US
David J. LU	Professor, Department of History and Director, Center for Japanese Studies, Bucknell University, Lewisburg, Pennsylvania, US
Jack A. LUCKEN	Associate Professor, Graduate School of Management, Rutgers–The State University of New Jersey, Newark, New Jersey, US
Leonard LYNN	Associate Professor, Department of Social Sciences, Carnegie-Mellon University, Pittsburgh, Pennsylvania, US
Kathleen MCCARTHY	
Paul MCCARTHY	Associate Professor, Faculty of General Education, Rikkyō University, Tōkyō, Japan
James D. MCCAWLEY	Professor, Department of Linguistics, University of Chicago, Chicago, Illinois, US
Harold A. MCCLEERY	Vice-President, Tōkyō office, Chemical Bank, Tōkyō, Japan
Edwin MCCLELLAN	Professor, Department of East Asian Languages and Literatures, Yale University, New Haven, Connecticut, US
Aya Louisa MCDONALD	Acting Assistant Professor, Department of Art, Wellesley College, Wellesley, Massachusetts, US
Terry Edward MACDOUGALL	Associate Professor, Department of Government, Harvard University, Cambridge, Massachusetts, US
Miles K. MCELRATH	Associate Professor, Department of East Asian Languages and Literatures, Ohio State University, Columbus, Ohio, US
MACHIDA Yōji	Manager, Industrial Research Division, Long-Term Credit Bank of Japan, Ltd, Tōkyō, Japan
James MCMULLEN	Lecturer, Oriental Institute, University of Oxford, Oxford, United Kingdom
Theodore MCNELLY	Professor, Department of Government and Politics, University of Maryland, College Park, Maryland, US
Wayne C. MCWILLIAMS	Associate Professor, Department of History, Towson State University, Towson, Maryland, US
MAEDA Kazutoshi	Professor, Department of Management, Komazawa University, Tōkyō, Japan
MAEDA Wakaki	Sports Section, Tōkyō Office, *Chūnichi shimbun,* Tōkyō, Japan
MAKABE Tetsuo	Deputy Manager, International Project Finance Division, Long-Term Credit Bank of Japan, Ltd, Tōkyō, Japan
John M. MAKI	Professor Emeritus, Department of Political Science, University of Massachusetts, Amherst, Massachusetts, US
MAKI Masami	Head, Section IV, Institute for National Educational Research, Tōkyō, Japan

MAKINO Noboru — Vice-President, Mitsubishi Research Institute, Inc, Tōkyō, Japan

William P. MALM — Professor, School of Music, University of Michigan, Ann Arbor, Michigan, US

Alfred H. MARKS — Professor, Department of English, State University of New York at New Paltz, New Paltz, New York, US

Susan H. MARSH — Associate Professor, Department of Political Science, Providence College, Providence, Rhode Island, US

Byron K. MARSHALL — Professor, Department of History, University of Minnesota at Minneapolis St. Paul, Minneapolis, Minnesota, US

Samuel E. MARTIN — Professor, Department of Linguistics, Yale University, New Haven, Connecticut, US

MARUOKA Hideko — Writer on Japanese women's problems

Penelope E. MASON — Associate Professor, Department of Art, Florida State University, Tallahassee, Florida, US

Jeffrey MASS — Professor, Department of History, Stanford University, Stanford, California, US

MASUDA Yoshio — Professor, College of Arts and Sciences, Tōkyō University, Tōkyō, Japan

MASUDA Yūji — Senior Researcher, Economic Research Institute, Japan Society for the Promotion of Machine Industry, Tōkyō, Japan

MASUI Ken'ichi — Professor, Department of Commerce, Keiō University, Tōkyō, Japan

MASUNAGA Shizuto — Executive, Iōkai Shiatsu Center, Tōkyō, Japan

Francis MATHY — Professor, Department of Literature, Sophia University, Tōkyō, Japan

Susan MATISOFF — Associate Professor, Department of Asian Languages, Stanford University, Stanford, California, US

MATSUBARA Mitsunori — Prior, Yakushiin, Okayama Prefecture, Japan

Naoko MATSUBARA — Artist, printmaker

MATSUDA Osamu — President, Japan Association of the Friends of Plants, Tōkyō, Japan

MATSUI Hideji — Director, Research Center of Health, Physical Fitness and Sports, University of Nagoya, Aichi Prefecture, Japan

Amy T. MATSUMOTO — Associate Professor, Department of East Asian Languages, University of Minnesota at Minneapolis St. Paul, Minneapolis, Minnesota, US

MATSUMOTO Saburō — Professor, Department of Law, Keiō University, Tōkyō, Japan

Tomone MATSUMOTO — Lecturer, School of Modern Asian Studies, Griffith University, Nathan, Queensland, Australia

MATSUNAGA Seiji — Deputy Manager, Operations Administration Division, Long-Term Credit Bank of Japan, Ltd, Tōkyō, Japan

MATSUNAMI Yoshihiro — Associate Professor, Department of Buddhism, Taishō University, Tōkyō, Japan

MATSUO Takayoshi — Professor, Faculty of Letters, Kyōto University, Kyōto, Japan

MATSUSHITA Mitsuo — Professor, Department of Law, Sophia University, Tōkyō, Japan

MATSUURA Kaoru — Professor, Faculty of Law, Nagoya University, Aichi Prefecture, Japan

Marlene J. MAYO — Associate Professor, Department of History, University of Maryland, College Park, Maryland, US

MAYUZUMI Hiromichi — Professor, Department of Literature, Gakushūin University, Tōkyō, Japan

Meron MEDZINI — Visiting Senior Lecturer, School for Overseas Students, Hebrew University, Jerusalem, Israel

Julia MEECH-PEKARIK — Associate Curator, Far Eastern Art, The Metropolitan Museum of Art, New York, New York, US

Joan MELLEN — Professor, Department of English, Temple University, Philadelphia, Pennsylvania, US

Richard L. MELLOTT

MERA Kōichi — Professor, Institute of Socioeconomic Planning, Tsukuba University, Ibaraki Prefecture, Japan

Charles M. MERGENTIME

Daniel A. METRAUX — Department of History, Philosophy, and Government, Anderson College, Anderson, Indiana, US

MIHARA Takeshi — Staff, General Research and Planning Department, Fukutoku Mutual Bank, Ōsaka, Japan

MIKAMI Terumi — Professor, Department of Literature, Chūō University, Tōkyō, Japan

MIKI Seiichirō — Assistant Professor, Faculty of Literature, Nagoya University, Aichi Prefecture, Japan

Frank O. MILLER — Chairman, Department of Political Science, College of Wooster, Wooster, Ohio, US

Roy Andrew MILLER — Professor, Department of Asian Languages and Literature, University of Washington, Seattle, Washington, US

Douglas E. MILLS — Lecturer, Faculty of Oriental Studies, University of Cambridge, Cambridge, United Kingdom

MINAMIZUKA Shingo — Assistant Professor, Faculty of Literature, Chiba University, Chiba Prefecture, Japan

Richard H. MINEAR — Professor, Department of History, University of Massachusetts, Amherst, Massachusetts, US

MINEGISHI Kentarō — Assistant Professor, Department of Humanities, Tōkyō Metropolitan University, Tōkyō, Japan

MINEGISHI Sumio — Assistant Professor, Department of Humanities, Tōkyō Metropolitan University, Tōkyō, Japan

Earl MINER — Professor, Department of East Asian Studies, Princeton University, Princeton, New Jersey, US

Sharon A. MINICHIELLO — Associate Professor, Department of History, Loyola Marymount University, Los Angeles, California, US

MISUMI Haruo — Tōkyō National Cultural Properties Research Institute, Tōkyō, Japan

Arthur M. MITCHELL	Attorney, Tanaka & Takahashi, Tōkyō, Japan
C. H. MITCHELL	Author of *The Illustrated Books of the Nanga, Maruyama, Shijō and Other Related Schools of Japan: A Biobibliography* (1972)
Richard H. MITCHELL	Professor, Department of History, University of Missouri at St. Louis, St. Louis, Missouri, US
MIYACHI Seiya	Professor, Department of Economics, Kokugakuin University, Tōkyō, Japan
Hiroshi MIYAJI	Professor, Department of Oriental Studies, University of Pennsylvania, Philadelphia, Pennsylvania, US
MIYAKE Hitoshi	Professor, Department of Literature, Keiō University, Tōkyō, Japan
MIYAKE Masahiko	Professor, Department of Education, Aichi University of Education, Aichi Prefecture, Japan
MIYAMOTO Mataji	Professor Emeritus, Ōsaka University, Ōsaka, Japan
MIYAMOTO Mizuo	Lecturer, Department of Literature, Waseda University, Tōkyō, Japan
MIYANO Nobuyuki	Director, Indirect Tax Division, Takamatsu National Tax Bureau, Kagawa Prefecture, Japan
MIYAO Shigeo (d 1982)	Cartoonist and folklore researcher
MIYATA Setsuko	Lecturer, Department of Literature, Waseda University, Tōkyō, Japan
Dixon Y. MIYAUCHI	Professor, Department of History, State University of New York at Plattsburgh, Plattsburgh, New York, US
MIYAWAKI Osamu	Professor, Faculty of Education, Yokohama National University, Yokohama, Japan
MIYAZAWA Ken'ichi	President, Hitotsubashi University, Tōkyō Prefecture, Japan
Masao MIYOSHI	Professor, Department of English, University of California, Berkeley, Berkeley, California, US
MIZOGUCHI Toshiyuki	Professor, Institute of Economic Research, Hitotsubashi University, Tōkyō Prefecture, Japan
MIZUBAYASHI Takeshi	Associate Professor, Faculty of Law, Tōkyō Metropolitan University, Tōkyō, Japan
MOCHIDA Minoru	Deputy Manager, Business Department, Meiji Mutual Life Insurance Company, Tōkyō, Japan
Brian MOERAN	Department of Anthropology and Sociology, School of Oriental and African Studies, University of London, London, United Kingdom
Robert MOES	Curator, Department of Oriental Art, The Brooklyn Museum, Brooklyn, New York, US
Kathleen MOLONY	
MOMOSE Hiroto	Deputy Manager, Business Development Division, Long-Term Credit Bank of Japan, Ltd, Tōkyō, Japan
MOMOSE Kesao	Professor, Office for the Compilation of Historical Materials, Tōkyō University, Tōkyō, Japan
Tazuko MONANE	Professor, Department of Foreign Languages, University of Hawaii at Hilo, Hilo, Hawaii, US
Betty Iverson MONROE	Associate Professor, Department of Art History, Northwestern University, Evanston, Illinois, US
Wilbur F. MONROE	Author of *Japanese Financial Markets and the World Economy* (1973) and *Japanese Exports to the United States* (1978)
MORI Masumi	Researcher, Japanese Business History Institute, Tōkyō, Japan
MORIMOTO Minoru	Section Chief, Ministry of Agriculture, Forestry, and Fisheries, Tōkyō, Japan
MORINAGA Hiroshi	Professor and Director, Misasa Branch, Okayama University Hospital, Okayama Prefecture, Japan
James R. MORITA	Associate Professor, Department of East Asian Languages and Literatures, Ohio State University, Columbus, Ohio, US
MORIYAMA Tsuneo	Professor, Faculty of Education, Kumamoto University, Kumamoto Prefecture, Japan
Carol MORLAND	
Robert E. MORRELL	Associate Professor, Department of Japanese and Chinese, Washington University, St. Louis, Missouri, US
Mark MORRIS	Lecturer, Centre for Asian Studies, University of Adelaide, Adelaide, South Australia, Australia
Helmut MORSBACH	Senior Lecturer, Department of Psychology, University of Glasgow, Glasgow, Scotland
Anne Nishimura MORSE	
Ronald A. MORSE	Director, East Asia Center for Scholars, Washington, DC, US
William F. MORTON	Associate Professor and Chairman, Department of History, York College of the City University of New York, Jamaica, New York, US
William G. MORTON	
Karl MOSKOWITZ	Assistant Professor, Department of East Asian Languages and Civilizations, Harvard University, Cambridge, Massachusetts, US
MOTEGI Kiyoko	Lecturer, Takasaki College of Music, Gumma Prefecture, Japan
Frank T. MOTOFUJI	Professor, Department of Oriental Languages, University of California, Berkeley, Berkeley, California, US
Ross MOUER	Lecturer, School of Modern Asian Studies, Griffith University, Nathan, Queensland, Australia
MOZAI Torao	Professor, Department of Oceanography, Tōkai University, Kanagawa Prefecture, Japan
Chieko MULHERN	Associate Professor, Center for East Asian Studies, University of Illinois, Urbana, Illinois, US

Hugo MÜNSTERBERG	Professor Emeritus, Department of Art History, State University of New York College at New Paltz, New Paltz, New York, US
MURAKAMI Shigeyoshi	Lecturer, Department of Social Sciences, Hitotsubashi University, Tōkyō Prefecture, Japan
MURAKAMI Yumi	Security Analyst, Paine, Webber, Mitchell Co, New York, New York, US
MURAKOSHI Sueo	Professor, Department of General Education, Ōsaka City University, Ōsaka, Japan
MURAMATSU Teijirō	Professor, Institute of Industrial Science, Tōkyō University, Tōkyō, Japan
MURATA Hiroshi	President, Japan Institute of Life Insurance, Tōkyō, Japan
MURATA Yoshio	Professor, Tōkyō University of Agriculture, Tōkyō, Japan
Patricia MURRAY	Executive Editor, *The Japan Interpreter*, Tōkyō, Japan
MUTŌ Shunkō	Judge, Tōkyō Higher Court, Tōkyō, Japan
MUTSU Gorō	Director, International Relations Office, National Defense College, National Defense Agency, Tōkyō, Japan
William E. NAFF	Professor, Department of Asian Languages and Literatures, University of Massachusetts, Amherst, Massachusetts, US
NAGAHAMA Yōichi	Professor, Department of Law, Waseda University, Tōkyō, Japan
NAGAHARA Keiji	Professor, Department of Economics, Hitotsubashi University, Tōkyō Prefecture, Japan
NAGAI Hiroo	Professor, Department of Science and Literature, Nihon University, Tōkyō, Japan
NAGANO Gorō	Lecturer, Seian Women's College, Kyōto, Japan
NAGAO Masakazu	Tokio Marine and Fire Insurance Co, Ltd, Vancouver, British Columbia, Canada
NAGAO Ryūichi	Professor, College of Arts and Sciences, Tōkyō University, Tōkyō, Japan
Susumu NAGARA	Professor, Department of Far Eastern Languages and Literatures, University of Michigan, Ann Arbor, Michigan, US
NAGASAWA Katsuo	Professor Emeritus, Chiba University, Chiba Prefecture, Japan
NAGASE Akira	Japan Equipment Inspection Institute, Tōkyō, Japan
NAGASHIMA Atsushi	Professor, Department of Law, Tōyō University, Tōkyō, Japan
NAGATOYA Yōji	Lecturer, School of Medicine, Ōsaka University, Ōsaka, Japan
NAGAZUMI Akira	Professor, Faculty of Letters, Tōkyō University, Tōkyō, Japan
NAITŌ Kinju	Research and Study Department, Japan Travel Bureau, Tōkyō, Japan
NAITŌ Motoo	Professor Emeritus, Tōkyō University, Tōkyō, Japan; Professor, Nippon College of Veterinary and Zootechnical Science, Tōkyō, Japan
Tetsuo NAJITA	Professor, Center for Far Eastern Studies, University of Chicago, Chicago, Illinois, US
NAKAGAWA Kōji	Deputy Executive Secretary, Economic and Social Commission for Asia and the Pacific, Bangkok, Thailand
NAKAGAWA Masayuki	Deputy Manager, Operations Administration Division, Long-Term Credit Bank of Japan, Ltd, Tōkyō, Japan
Kate NAKAI	Assistant Professor, Department of History, University of Oregon, Eugene, Oregon, US
Yoshiyuki NAKAI	Assistant Professor, Department of Chinese and Japanese, University of Oregon, Eugene, Oregon, US
NAKAJIMA Kawatarō	Professor, Department of Literature and Home Economics, Wayō Women's University, Chiba Prefecture, Japan
NAKAJIMA Kenzō	Professor, Department of Education, Tōkyō Gakugei University, Tōkyō, Japan
NAKAJIMA Naotada	Professor, Research Division, National Center for University Entrance Examination, Tōkyō, Japan
NAKAMURA Hajime	Director, The Eastern Institute, Inc, Tōkyō, Japan
Kyōko Motomochi NAKAMURA	Assistant Professor, Liberal Arts Division, Kawamura Junior College, Tōkyō, Japan
NAKAMURA Masanori	Professor, Department of Economics, Hitotsubashi University, Tōkyō Prefecture, Japan
NAKANE Chie	Professor, Institute of Oriental Culture, Tōkyō University, Tōkyō, Japan
NAKANE Takehiko	Professor, Department of Science, Kagoshima University, Kagoshima Prefecture, Japan
Don T. NAKANISHI	Assistant Professor, Asian American Studies Center, University of California, Los Angeles, Los Angeles, California, US
NAKASA Hideo	Chief, Programming Division, National Association of Commercial Broadcasters in Japan, Tōkyō, Japan
NAKASATO Toshikatsu	Head, First Section, Department of Restoration Techniques, Tōkyō National Research Institute of Cultural Properties, Tōkyō, Japan
NAKAUCHI Tsuneo	Professor, Department of Arts and Sciences, International Christian University, Tōkyō Prefecture, Japan
Shigeru NAKAYAMA	Lecturer, College of Arts and Sciences, Tōkyō University, Tōkyō, Japan
Dick K. NANTO	Assistant Professor, Department of Economics, Brigham Young University, Provo, Utah, US
NAOI Atsushi	Assistant Professor, Faculty of Letters, Tōkyō University, Tōkyō, Japan
NARAMOTO Tatsuya	Historian
NARITA Katsuya	Professor, Tōkyō University, Tōkyō, Japan
NARITA Yoriaki	Professor, Faculty of Economics, Yokohama National University, Kanagawa Prefecture, Japan
NASU Hiroshi (d 1979)	Professor, Department of Economics, Gifu University of Economics, Gifu Prefecture, Japan
Karin C. NELSON	

Margret NEUSS	Professor, Abteilung Japanologie, Philipps-Universität, Marburg, West Germany
J. V. NEUSTUPNÝ	Chairman, Department of Japanese, Monash University, Clayton, Victoria, Australia
NIKI Isao	Japan Raw Silk and Sugar Price Stabilization Agency, Tōkyō, Japan
NINOMIYA Masato	Attorney
Ian NISH	Reader, London School of Economics, University of London, London, United Kingdom
NISHIDA Makoto	Professor, Faculty of Science, Chiba University, Chiba Prefecture, Japan
NISHIDA Shunji	Assistant Manager, Personnel Division, Long-Term Credit Bank of Japan, Ltd, Tōkyō, Japan
NISHIJIMA Sadao	Professor Emeritus, Tōkyō University; Professor, Department of Humanities, Niigata University, Niigata Prefecture, Japan
NISHIKAWA Osamu	Professor, College of Arts and Sciences, Tōkyō University, Tōkyō, Japan
NISHIMIZU Mieko	Assistant Professor, Department of Economics, Princeton University, Princeton, New Jersey, US
NISHIMOTO Yōichi	Professor, Department of Politics and Economics, Tōkai University, Tōkyō, Japan
NISHIMURA Makoto	Professor, Department of Literature, Tōyō University, Tōkyō, Japan
Harry K. NISHIO	Professor, Department of Sociology, University of Toronto, Toronto, Ontario, Canada
Tamako NIWA	Associate Professor, Department of Asian Languages and Literature, University of Washington, Seattle, Washington, US
NIWATA Noriaki	Professor, Department of Commerce, Keiō University, Tōkyō, Japan
Agnes M. NIYEKAWA	Professor, Department of East Asian Languages, University of Hawaii at Manoa, Honolulu, Hawaii, US
NODA Kazuo	Professor, Department of Sociology, Rikkyō University, Tōkyō, Japan
NOGUCHI Takehiko	Assistant Professor, Department of Literature, Kōbe University, Hyōgo Prefecture, Japan
NOGUCHI Takenori	Professor, Department of Literature and Arts, Seijō University, Tōkyō Prefecture, Japan
NOGUCHI Yukio	Professor, Department of Economics, Hitotsubashi University, Tōkyō Prefecture, Japan
NOHARA Hiroshi	Nohara Office for Technicians, Kanagawa Prefecture, Japan
Sharon NOLTE	Assistant Professor, Department of History, Southern Methodist University, Dallas, Texas, US
NOMURA Tadao	Managing Director, Hōsō Bunka Foundation, Tōkyō, Japan
NOMURA Yoshihiro	Professor, Faculty of Law, Tōkyō Metropolitan University, Tōkyō, Japan
Edward NORBECK	Professor, Department of Anthropology, Rice University, Houston, Texas, US
NOSE Takayuki	Professor, Department of Public Health, School of Medicine, Tottori University, Tottori Prefecture, Japan
F. G. NOTEHELFER	Associate Professor, Department of History, University of California, Los Angeles, Los Angeles, California, US
NOZAKI Shigeru	Director, Broadcasting Research Institute, National Association of Commercial Broadcasters in Japan, Tōkyō, Japan
NUMATA Satoshi	Assistant Professor, Department of Literature, Aoyama Gakuin University, Tōkyō, Japan
James A. O'BRIEN	Professor, Department of East Asian Languages and Literature, University of Wisconsin, Madison, Wisconsin, US
OCHIAI Shigenobu	Kōbe Municipal Central Library, Hyōgo Prefecture, Japan
ODA Takeo	Professor Emeritus, Kyōto University, Kyōto, Japan
ODA Yukio	Assistant Manager, General Planning and Administration Division, Long-Term Credit Bank of Japan, Ltd, Tōkyō, Japan
ODAKA Kōnosuke	Professor, Institute of Economic Research, Hitotsubashi University, Tōkyō Prefecture, Japan
OGASAWARA Nobuo	Senior Researcher, Industrial Arts Section, Art and Science Division, Tōkyō National Museum, Tōkyō, Japan
OGATA Shijūrō	Executive Director, Bank of Japan, Tōkyō, Japan
OGAWA Yoshio	Professor Emeritus, Tōkyō University of Foreign Studies, Tōkyō, Japan
ŌGUCHI Yūjirō	Professor, Department of Letters and Education, Ochanomizu Women's University, Tōkyō, Japan
OGURA Michio	Professor, Department of Fisheries, Tōkyō University of Fisheries, Tōkyō, Japan
OGURI Junko	Lecturer, Gakujutsu Kenkyūjo, Tōkyō, Japan
OHARA Satoru	Professor, Department of Literature, Sophia University, Tōkyō, Japan
ŌHARA Satoshi	Professor, Department of Economics, Tōkyō Keizai University, Tōkyō, Japan
OKA Takashi	Associate Professor, Department of Law, Hōsei University, Tōkyō, Japan
OKADA Yasushi	Manager, Industrial Research Divsion, Long-Term Credit Bank of Japan, Ltd, Tōkyō, Japan
Shumpei OKAMOTO	Professor, Department of History, Temple University, Philadelphia, Pennsylvania, US
Frank Masao OKAMURA	Brooklyn Botanic Garden, Brooklyn, New York, US
ŌKI Yasue	Director, Kanagawa Prefectural Hot Spring Institute, Kanagawa Prefecture, Japan
Daniel I. OKIMOTO	Assistant Professor, Department of Political Science, Stanford University, Stanford, California, US
OKONOGI Masao	Associate Professor, Department of Law, Keiō University, Tōkyō, Japan
OKUDA Shinjō	Professor, Faculty of Education, Yokohama National University, Kanagawa Prefecture, Japan

OKUDAIRA Yasuhiro	Professor, Institute of Social Science, Tōkyō University, Tōkyō, Japan
ŌMORI Kazuko	Professor, Department of Home Economics, Tōkyō Kasei University, Tōkyō, Japan
ŌNAMI Yūji	Priest, Russian Orthodox Church, Tōkyō, Japan
P. G. O'NEILL	Professor, School of Oriental and African Studies, University of London, London, United Kingdom
ŌNISHI Harutaka	Professor, Department of Literature, Nara University, Nara Prefecture, Japan
ONO Kōji	Dean, Department of Law, Daitō Bunka University, Tōkyō, Japan
ŌNO Tōru	Professor, Department of Foreign Languages, Ōsaka University of Foreign Studies, Ōsaka, Japan
ŌNO Tsutomu	Writer on Social Thought and Contemporary Social Problems
ONODA Yōichi	Director, Shin Nampeidai Clinic, Tōkyō, Japan
Herman OOMS	Associate Professor, Department of History, University of Illinois at Chicago Circle, Chicago, Illinois, US
Alfred C. OPPLER (d 1982)	Jurist; Author of *Contemporary Japan* (1952) and *Legal Reform in Occupied Japan: A Participant Looks Back* (1976)
ORITA Kōji	Chief, Production Room, Theatrical Division, National Theater of Japan, Tōkyō, Japan
Masako M. ŌSAKO	Assistant Professor, Department of Sociology, University of Illinois, Chicago, Illinois, US
OSHIMA Mitsuo	Professor Emeritus, Tōkyō Gakugei University, Tōkyō, Japan
ŌSUMI Seiji	Far Seas Fishery Research Laboratory, Fisheries Agency, Shizuoka Prefecture, Japan
ŌTA Rin'ichirō	Librarian, Keiō University Library, Tōkyō, Japan
ŌTA Yoshimaro	Professor, Department of Literature, Sophia University, Tōkyō, Japan
Yūzō ŌTA	Associate Professor, Department of History, McGill University, Montreal, Quebec, Canada
ŌTŌ Tokihiko	Professor Emeritus, Seijō University, Tōkyō, Japan
ŌTSUKA Shigeru	Councillor, Foreign Affairs Division, Japanese National Railways, Tōkyō, Japan
ŌTSUKA Shigeru	Professor, Department of Literature, Mukogawa Women's University, Hyōgo Prefecture, Japan
ŌTSUKA Sueko	President, Ōtsuka Gakuin, Tōkyō, Japan
ŌTSUKA Yasuo	Vice-President, Oriental Medicine Research Center, Kitasato Institute, Tōkyō, Japan
ŌUCHI Eishin	Abbot, Shōenji, Nagasaki Prefecture, Japan
ŌUCHI Minoru	Center for International Studies, Cornell University, Ithaca, New York, US
OWADA Hisashi	Minister, Japanese Embassy, Moscow, USSR
David OWENS	Japan Society, Inc, New York, New York, US
Robert S. OZAKI	Professor, Department of Economics, School of Business and Economics, California State College at Hayward, Hayward, California, US
OZAWA Terutomo	Professor, Department of Economics, Colorado State University, Fort Collins, Colorado, US
George R. PACKARD	Dean, School of Advanced International Studies, John Hopkins University, Washington, DC, US
Allan PALMER	Tea ceremony teacher, Urasenke Foundation, Kyōto, Japan
Hugh PATRICK	Professor, Department of Economics, Yale University, New Haven, Connecticut, US
Erich PAUER	Lecturer, Japanologisches Seminar, Universität Bonn, Bonn, West Germany
Diana PAUL	Assistant Professor, Department of Religious Studies, Stanford University, Stanford, California, US
Mark R. PEATTIE	Visiting Professor, Department of History, University of California, Los Angeles, Los Angeles, California, US
Joseph A. PECHMAN	Director, Economic Studies Program, The Brookings Institution, Washington, DC, US
T. J. PEMPEL	Director, China–Japan Program, Cornell University, Ithaca, New York, US
Susan J. PHARR	Professor, Department of Political Science, University of Wisconsin–Madison, Madison, Wisconsin, US
Rulan Chao PIAN	Professor, Department of East Asian Languages and Civilizations, Harvard University, Cambridge, Massachusetts, US
Stuart D. B. PICKEN	Professor, Division of Humanities, International Christian University, Tōkyō Prefecture, Japan
John D. PIERSON	Manager, Planning and Development, Signode Nippon, Ltd, Kōbe, Japan
Ernest D. PIRYNS	Lecturer, International Department, Sophia University, Tōkyō, Japan
Joseph PITTAU	Former President, Sophia University, Tōkyō, Japan
David W. PLATH	Professor, Department of Anthropology, University of Illinois, Urbana, Illinois, US
Herbert E. PLUTSCHOW	Associate Professor, Department of Oriental Languages, University of California, Los Angeles, Los Angeles, California, US
Christian POLAK	Research Scholar, Maison Franco-Japonaise, Tōkyō, Japan
David POLLACK	Assistant Professor, Department of Foreign Languages, Literatures, and Linguistics, University of Rochester, Rochester, New York, US
Junco Sato POLLACK	
Edythe POLSTER	
Barbara PORTER	
Brian POWELL	Lecturer, Oriental Institute, University of Oxford, Oxford, United Kingdom
Irena POWELL	Oriental Institute, University of Oxford, Oxford, United Kingdom

Cyril H. POWLES	Professor, Faculty of Divinity, Trinity College, Toronto, Ontario, Canada
C. Kenneth QUINONES	Assistant Professor, Department of History, Trinity College, Hartford, Connecticut, US
Judith N. RABINOVITCH	Assistant Professor, Department of East Asian Languages and Literatures, Yale University, New Haven, Connecticut, US
Robert B. RADIN	Former Director of Japanese Studies, Department of History, University of Miami, Coral Gables, Florida, US
Esperanza RAMIREZ-CHRISTENSEN	Staff Writer, *Encyclopedia of Japan*
Daniel B. RAMSDELL	Professor, Department of History, Central Washington State College, Ellensberg, Washington, US
William V. RAPP	Vice-President, Morgan Guaranty Trust Company, New York, New York, US
C. Tait RATCLIFFE	President, International Business Information, Inc, Tōkyō, Japan
Kirsten REFSING	Former Lecturer, Asahikawa College, Asahikawa, Hokkaidō, Japan
Michael R. REICH	Coauthor of *Six Lives, Six Deaths: Portraits from Modern Japan* (1979)
Haru REISCHAUER	Writer
David K. REYNOLDS	Director, ToDo Institute, Los Angeles, California, US
Robert RHODES	Lecturer, Department of Literature, Ōtani University, Kyōto, Japan
Richard RICE	Assistant Professor, Department of History, University of Tennessee, Knoxville, Tennessee, US
Kenneth L. RICHARD	Assistant Professor, Department of East Asian Studies, University of Toronto, Toronto, Ontario, Canada
Bradley RICHARDSON	Professor, Department of Political Science, Ohio State University, Columbus, Ohio, US
Donald RICHIE	Author of *The Films of Akira Kurosawa* (1965), *Ozu* (1971), and *The Japanese Movie* (rev ed, 1982) and coauthor of *The Japanese Film* (rev ed, 1982).
J. T. RIMER	Professor and Chairman, Department of Chinese and Japanese, Washington University, St. Louis, Missouri, US
Alan RIX	Australia-Japan Economics Research Project, Department of Economics, Australian National University, Canberra, Australia
Laurance ROBERTS	Author of *A Dictionary of Japanese Artists* (1976) and *Roberts' Guide to Museums* (1978)
Gary E. ROBERTSON	
B. W. ROBINSON	Keeper Emeritus, Far Eastern Section, Victoria and Albert Museum, London; Adviser, Sotheby's, London, United Kingdom
Lawrence W. ROGERS	Associate Professor, Department of East Asian Languages, University of Hawaii at Hilo, Hilo, Hawaii, US
Thomas P. ROHLEN	Research Associate, Stanford University, Stanford, California, US
Thomas ROHLICH	Assistant Professor, Department of Asian Languages and Literature, University of Iowa, Iowa City, Iowa, US
Robert ROLF	Foreign Instructor, Department of Education, Fukuoka University of Education, Fukuoka Prefecture, Japan
John M. ROSENFIELD	Professor, Department of Oriental Arts, Harvard University, Cambridge, Massachusetts, US
Eugene ROTWEIN	Professor, Department of Economics, Queens College of the City University of New York, Flushing, New York, US
Gilbert ROZMAN	Professor, Department of Sociology, Princeton University, Princeton, New Jersey, US
Barbara RUCH	Associate Professor, Department of Oriental Studies, and Director, Institute for Medieval Japanese Studies, University of Pennsylvania, Philadelphia, Pennsylvania, US
Marleigh Grayer RYAN	Dean, Department of Liberal Arts and Sciences, State University of New York College at New Paltz, New Paltz, New York, US
Carole A. RYAVEC	
SAEKI Arikiyo	Professor, Department of Literature, Seijō University, Tōkyō, Japan
SAEKI Shōichi	Professor, College of Arts and Sciences, Tōkyō University, Tōkyō, Japan
SAGARA Iichi	President, University of the Sacred Heart, Tōkyō, Japan
SAGARA Tōru	Professor, Department of Literature and Arts, Kyōritsu Women's University, Tōkyō, Japan
SAIKI Kazuma	Professor, Department of Literature, Taishō University, Tōkyō, Japan
SAITŌ Hiroshi	Professor, Centro de Estudos Japonêses, Universidade de São Paulo, São Paulo, Brazil
SAITŌ Kenjirō	Professor, Department of Education, Utsunomiya University, Tochigi Prefecture, Japan
SAITŌ Masako	Professor, Department of Literature, University of the Sacred Heart, Tōkyō, Japan
SAITŌ Ryōsuke	Editor, *Asahi shimbun*, Tōkyō, Japan
SAITŌ Shizuo	Professor, Faculty of International Politics and Economics, Aoyama Gakuin University, Tōkyō, Japan; Council Member, United Nations University, Tōkyō, Japan
SAITŌ Shōji	Professor, Department of Science and Engineering, Tōkyō Denki University, Tōkyō, Japan
SAITŌ Tadashi	Professor Emeritus, Taishō University, Tōkyō, Japan
SAKAGUCHI Nobuhiko	Nihon Shōgi Remmei, Tōkyō, Japan
Akira SAKAI	Tōkyō Regional Immigration Bureau, Tōkyō, Japan

Robert K. SAKAI	Professor, Department of History, University of Hawaii at Manoa, Honolulu, Hawaii, US
SAKAI Tadayasu	Curator, The Museum of Modern Art, Kanagawa Prefecture, Japan
Hiroshi SAKAMOTO	Senior Lecturer, Department of Asian Languages, Stanford University, Stanford, California, US
SAKANOUE Masanobu	Professor, Department of Sciences, Kanazawa University, Ishikawa Prefecture, Japan
Mitsugu SAKIHARA	Associate Professor, Department of History, University of Hawaii at Manoa, Honolulu, Hawaii, US
SAKURABAYASHI Makoto	Professor, Department of Economics, Teikyō University, Tōkyō, Japan
SAKURADA Katsunori (d 1977)	Professor, Shiraume Gakuen Junior College, Tōkyō Prefecture, Japan
Ralph SAMUELSON	
SANEYOSHI Tatsuo	Freelance nonfiction writer
James H. SANFORD	Associate Professor, Department of Religion, University of North Carolina at Chapel Hill, Chapel Hill, North Carolina, US
SAOTOME Masahiro	Researcher, Tōkyō National Museum, Tōkyō, Japan
SASABUCHI Tomoichi	Adviser, Modern Culture Research Institute, Shōwa Women's University, Tōkyō, Japan
SASAKI Kinzō	Professor, Department of Law, Senshū University, Tōkyō, Japan
SASAKI Tadayoshi	Former President, Tōkyō University of Fisheries, Tōkyō, Japan
SASAYAMA Haruo	Assistant Professor, Faculty of Letters, Tōkyō University, Tōkyō, Japan
Elizabeth S. SATŌ	Professor, Department of History, University of Cincinnati, Cincinnati, Ohio, US
SATŌ Hideo	Chief, Research Room for Educational Materials, National Institute for Educational Research, Tōkyō, Japan
Hiroaki SATŌ	Translator of Japanese poetry
Kazuo SATŌ	Professor, Department of Economics, State University of New York at Buffalo, Buffalo, New York, US
SATŌ Kōji	Professor, Faculty of Law, Kyōto University, Kyōto, Japan
Ryūzō SATŌ	Professor, Department of Economics, Brown University, Providence, Rhode Island, US
SATŌ Seizaburō	Professor, College of Arts and Sciences, Tōkyō University, Tōkyō, Japan
SATŌ Tadashi	Professor, Institute of Geoscience, Tsukuba University, Ibaraki Prefecture, Japan
SATŌ Tamotsu	Professor, Department of Letters and Education, Ochanomizu Women's University, Tōkyō, Japan
Toshihiko SATŌ	Professor, Department of English, Virginia State College, Petersburgh, Virginia, US
E. Dale SAUNDERS	Professor, Department of Oriental Studies, University of Pennsylvania, Philadelphia, Pennsylvania, US
SAWADA Keisuke	Professor, Department of Education, Sōka University, Tōkyō Prefecture, Japan
SAWAKI Takao	Chairman, Department of Law, Rikkyō University, Tōkyō, Japan
SAWANOBORI Toshio	Professor, Department of Law, Kokugakuin University, Tōkyō, Japan
SAWAYAMA Hiroshi	Assistant Manager, Economics Division, Long-Term Credit Bank of Japan, Ltd, Tōkyō, Japan
Gary R. SAXONHOUSE	Professor, Center for Research on Economic Development, University of Michigan, Ann Arbor, Michigan, US
C. Franklin SAYRE	Assistant Professor, Department of Art and Art History, Oakland University, Rochester, Michigan, US
Paul SCHALOW	
Wolfgang SCHAMONI	Privatdozent, Institut für Ostasienkunde (Japanologie), Universität Munchen, Munich, West Germany
Irwin SCHEINER	Professor, Department of History, University of California, Berkeley, Berkeley, California, US
Kim SCHUEFFTAN	Editor, Kodansha International, Ltd, Tōkyō, Japan
A. C. SCOTT	Professor Emeritus, Department of Theater and Drama, University of Wisconsin, Madison, Wisconsin, US
Christopher SEELEY	Lecturer, Department of Asian Languages, University of Canterbury, Christchurch, New Zealand
Edward G. SEIDENSTICKER	Professor, Department of East Asian Languages and Cultures, Columbia University, New York, New York, US
SEIKE Kiyosi	Professor and Dean, School of Fine Arts, Tōkyō University of Fine Arts and Music, Tōkyō, Japan
Kyōko Iriye SELDEN	
SENGEN Ryūichirō	Professor, Department of Law, Dōshisha University, Kyōto, Japan
SENSHŪ Shin'ichi	Director, Civil Engineering Technology Research Laboratory, Electric Power Central Research Institute, Tōkyō, Japan
Carl SESAR	Translator of *Takuboku: Poems to Eat* (1966)
Joseph SEUBERT	
Jack SEWARD	Author of *Hara-kiri* (1968), *Japanese in Action* (1969), and *The Japanese* (1972)
Nancy SHATZMAN-STEINHARDT	Department of the History of Art, Bryn Mawr College, Bryn Mawr, Pennsylvania, US
Charles D. SHELDON	Lecturer, Faculty of Oriental Studies, University of Cambridge, Cambridge, United Kingdom
Paul SHEPHERD	
James E. SHERIDAN	Professor, Department of History, Northwestern University, Evanston, Illinois, US
SHIBANUMA Susumu	Director, The National Chuō Youth Center, Tōkyō, Japan

SHIGEMATSU Itsuzō	Chairman, Radiation Effects Research Foundation, Hiroshima Prefecture, Japan
SHIKI Masahide	Professor, Department of Letters and Education, Ochanomizu Women's University, Tōkyō, Japan
Ben-Ami SHILLONY	Chairman, Department of East Asian Studies, Hebrew University, Jerusalem, Israel
SHIMADA Jirō	Professor, Department of Economics, Chūō University, Tōkyō, Japan
SHIMADA Masahiko	Professor, Department of Literature, Kanazawa University, Ishikawa Prefecture, Japan
SHIMBORI Michiya	Professor, School of Education, Hiroshima University, Hiroshima Prefecture, Japan
SHIMIZU Hideo	Professor, Department of Law, Aoyama Gakuin University, Tōkyō, Japan
SHIMIZU Tetsuo	Poet
Yoshiaki SHIMIZU	Curator of Japanese Art, Freer Gallery of Art, Smithsonian Institution, Washington, DC, US
SHIMMI Hiroshi (d 1979)	General Secretary, Japan Bible Society, Tōkyō, Japan
SHIMOKAWA Kōichi	Professor, Department of Business Management, Hōsei University, Tōkyō, Japan
SHINADA Yutaka	Inspector of Cultural Properties, Agency for Cultural Affairs, Ministry of Education, Tōkyō, Japan
SHINAGAWA Fujirō	Professor, Department of Music, Senzoku Gakuen University, Kanagawa Prefecture, Japan
SHINJI Isoya	Associate Professor, Department of Landscape Architecture, Tōkyō University of Agriculture, Tōkyō, Japan
Minoru SHINODA	Professor, Department of History, University of Hawaii at Manoa, Honolulu, Hawaii, US
SHINOMIYA Toshiyuki	Assistant Professor, Faculty of Humanities, Hirosaki University, Aomori Prefecture, Japan
SHINRA Ichirō	Professor Emeritus, Meiji University, Tōkyō, Japan
Hiroki SHIOJI	Staff Writer, *Encyclopedia of Japan*
SHIONO Hiroshi	Professor, Faculty of Law, Tōkyō University, Tōkyō, Japan
SHIRAI Kunihiko	Chief, Birds and Animals Research Section, Forestry Experimental Station, Ministry of Agriculture, Forestry, and Fisheries, Tōkyō, Japan
SHIRAI Yoshio	Director, Japanese Film Critics' Pen Club, Tōkyō, Japan
SHIRAISHI Masaya	Assistant Professor, Thai-Vietnamese Department, Ōsaka University of Foreign Studies, Ōsaka, Japan
SHIRAISHI Teizō	Professor, Department of Humanities, Fukuoka University, Fukuoka Prefecture, Japan
Zenryū SHIRAKAWA	Assistant Professor, Department of Modern Foreign Languages, Boston University, Boston, Massachusetts, US
Ichirō SHIRATO	Senior Lecturer, Department of East Asian Languages and Cultures, Columbia University, New York, New York, US
SHIROTA Fumihiko	Chief, Internal Medicine Department, Nissan Kōseikai Tamagawa Hospital, Tōkyō, Japan
SHISHIDO Toshio	Vice-President, International University of Japan, Niigata Prefecture, Japan
Donald H. SHIVELY	Professor, Department of Japanese History and Literature, Harvard University, Cambridge, Massachusetts, US
William F. SIBLEY	Associate Professor, Department of Far Eastern Languages and Civilizations, University of Chicago, Chicago, Illinois, US
Jeanne SIGÉE	Translator and Editor of *Les Spectres de Yotsuya* by Tsuruya Namboku (1979)
George A. R. SILVER	Professor, Department of History, Earlham College, Richmond, Indiana, US
Bradford L. SIMCOCK	Assistant Professor, Department of Sociology and Anthropology, Miami University, Oxford, Ohio, US
Robert T. SINGER	Art historian and writer
Patricia SIPPEL	
Joseph W. SLADE	Professor, Department of English, Long Island University, Brooklyn Center, Brooklyn, New York, US
Richard SMETHURST	Associate Professor, Department of History, University of Pittsburgh, Pittsburgh, Pennsylvania, US
Barbara F. SMITH	
Henry D. SMITH II	Associate Professor, Department of History, University of California, Santa Barbara, Santa Barbara, California, US
Lawrence SMITH	Keeper of Oriental Arts, The British Museum, London, United Kingdom
Malcolm D. SMITH	Visiting Professor, Department of Law, University of British Columbia, Vancouver, British Columbia, Canada
Robert J. SMITH	Professor, Department of Anthropology, Cornell University, Ithaca, New York, US
SŌDA Hajime	Managing Director, Japan Society of Medical History, Tōkyō, Japan
SOEDA Yoshiya	Professor, Institute of Sociology, Tsukuba University, Ibaraki Prefecture, Japan
Michael SOLOMON	Assistant Professor, Department of History, Oakland University, Rochester, Michigan, US
SOMEYA Shirō	Councillor and Professor Emeritus, Institute of Public Health, Tōkyō, Japan
SONE Ken'ya	Professor, Junior College of Mechanical Engineering, Nihon University, Tōkyō, Japan
SONODA Minoru	Professor, Department of Literature and Executive Secretary, Institute for Japanese Culture and Classics, Kokugakuin University, Tōkyō, Japan
Isao SORANAKA	Assistant Professor, Department of History, University of Western Ontario, London, Ontario, Canada
Eugene SOVIAK	Associate Professor, Department of History, Washington University, St. Louis, Missouri, US
Dennis M. SPACKMAN	Staff Writer, *Encyclopedia of Japan*
Douglas E. SPARKS	Gnostic Concepts, Inc, Menlo Park, California, US

Norman SPARNON	Author of *Japanese Flower Arrangement, Classical and Modern* (1960)
Robert M. SPAULDING	Associate Professor, Department of History, Oklahoma State University, Stillwater, Oklahoma, US
Thomas A. STANLEY	Department of Oriental Studies, University of Arizona, Tucson, Arizona, US
Richard STANLEY-BAKER	Department of History in Art, University of Victoria, Victoria, British Columbia, Canada
Oliver STATLER	Author of *Japanese Inn* (1961), *The Pilgrimage* (1983), and others
M. William STEELE	Associate Professor, Division of Humanities, International Christian University, Tōkyō Prefecture, Japan
Kurt STEINER	Professor Emeritus, Department of Political Science, Stanford University, Stanford, California, US
Patricia G. STEINHOFF	Professor, Department of Sociology, University of Hawaii at Manoa, Honolulu, Hawaii, US
John J. STEPHAN	Professor, Department of History, University of Hawaii at Manoa, Honolulu, Hawaii, US
William E. STESLICKE	Visiting Scholar, Department of Medical Care Organization, School of Public Health, University of Michigan, Ann Arbor, Michigan, US
Margo STIPE	
J. A. A. STOCKWIN	Director, Nissan Institute of Japanese Studies, Oxford, United Kingdom
Richard STORRY (d 1982)	Director, Far Eastern Centre, St. Antony's College, University of Oxford, Oxford, United Kingdom
Giuliana STRAMIGIOLI	Professor, Instituto di Studi dell'India e dell'Asia Orientale, Università degli Studi di Roma, Rome, Italy
Tal STREETER	Sculptor; author of *The Art of the Japanese Kite* (1974)
Kenneth STRONG	Former Lecturer, Department of the Far East, School of Oriental and African Studies, University of London, London, United Kingdom
Nathan O. STRONG	Assistant Professor, Curriculum and Instruction Program, University of San Francisco, San Francisco, California, US
SUCHI Tokuhei	Writer
SUDA Ken	Former Professor, Tōkyō University of Navigation, Tōkyō, Japan
SUDŌ Haruo	Assistant Professor, Department of Sociology, Hōsei University, Tōkyō, Japan
SUENAKA Tetsuo	Professor, Department of School Education, Hyōgo University of Education, Hyōgo Prefecture, Japan
SUGENO Kazuo	Professor, Faculty of Law, Tōkyō University, Tōkyō, Japan
SUGIHARA Shirō	President, Kōnan University, Hyōgo Prefecture, Japan
SUGIYAMA Akio	Professor, Department of Education, Kōbe University, Hyōgo Prefecture, Japan
SUGIYAMA Tadayoshi	Professor, Department of Agriculture, Tōkyō University of Agriculture, Tōkyō, Japan
SUGIYAMA Yasushi	Professor, School of International Affairs, Aoyama Gakuin University, Tōkyō, Japan
SUYAMA Kazuyuki	Deputy Manager, Yokohama Branch, Long-Term Credit Bank of Japan, Ltd, Kanagawa Prefecture, Japan
SUZUKI Eichi	Assistant Professor, Department of Education, Ibaraki University, Tochigi Prefecture, Japan
SUZUKI Hiroaki	Joint General Manager, Division II, Credit Analysis, Long-Term Credit Bank of Japan, Ltd, Tōkyō, Japan
SUZUKI Kōichi	Director, Bank of Japan Centennial History Project, Bank of Japan, Tōkyō, Japan
SUZUKI Masao	Chief Researcher, Chiyoda Ward Library, Tōkyō, Japan
SUZUKI Mitsuru	Professor, Faculty of Engineering, Hiroshima University, Hiroshima Prefecture, Japan
SUZUKI Norihisa	Professor, Department of Education, Rikkyō University, Tōkyō, Japan
SUZUKI Ryōichi	Historian
SUZUKI Yoshio	Director General, Correction Bureau, Ministry of Justice, Tōkyō, Japan
SUZUKI Yukihisa	Professor, Department of Foreign Languages, Kyōto University of Foreign Studies, Kyōto, Japan
SUZUKI Zenji	Professor, Faculty of Liberal Arts, Yamaguchi University, Yamaguchi Prefecture, Japan
David L. SWAIN	Editor, *Japan Christian Quarterly*, Tōkyō, Japan
Barbara Bowles SWANN	
Thomas E. SWANN	Visiting Assistant Professor, University of Minnesota, Minneapolis, Minnesota, US
Thomas D. SWIFT	Professor, Department of History, California State University, Sacramento, California, US
Elizabeth de Sabato SWINTON	Research Curator in Oriental Art, Worcester Art Museum, Worcester, Massachusetts, US
Kenneth M. TAGAWA	
Mildred TAHARA	Associate Professor, Department of East Asian Literature, University of Hawaii at Manoa, Honolulu, Hawaii, US
Kōji TAIRA	Professor, Department of Economics, University of Illinois, Urbana-Champaign, Urbana, Illinois, US
TAKABATAKE Michitoshi	Professor, Department of Law and Politics, Rikkyō University, Tōkyō, Japan
TAKAGI Noritsune	Professor, Institute of Journalism and Communication Studies, Tōkyō University, Tōkyō, Japan
TAKAGI Shōsaku	Professor, Historiographical Institute, Tōkyō University, Tōkyō, Japan
TAKAHASHI Ken'ichi	Professor, Department of Literature, Sophia University, Tōkyō, Japan
TAKAHASHI Masao	
TAKAHASHI Naoki	Senior Lecturer, Department of Law, Senshū University, Tōkyō, Japan

TAKAKURA Shō	Professor, Institute of Education, Tsukuba University, Ibaraki Prefecture, Japan
TAKAKUWA Yasuo	Professor, Faculty of Education, Nagoya University, Aichi Prefecture, Japan
TAKAMURA Hisao	Social Education Supervisor, Social Education Bureau, Ministry of Education, Tōkyō, Japan
TAKANO Keiichi	Professor, Faculty of Education, Kyūshū University, Fukuoka Prefecture, Japan
TAKANO Shinji	Director, Wild Bird Society of Japan, Tōkyō, Japan
Ted T. TAKAYA	Assistant Professor, Department of Modern Languages and Literature, University of the Pacific, Stockton, California, US
TAKEBE Yoshiaki	Professor, Institute of Language Teaching, Waseda University, Tōkyō, Japan
TAKEDA Fumio	Sports Writer, *Asahi shimbun*, Tōkyō, Japan
TAKEDA Katsuhiko	Professor, Department of Politics and Economics, Waseda University, Tōkyō, Japan
TAKEDA Yukimatsu	Adviser, Nippon Electric Company, Tōkyō, Japan
TAKEHISA Yoshihiko	Professor, Department of Literature, Nara Women's University, Nara Prefecture, Japan
TAKENAKA Kazurō	Professor, Department of Sociology, Tsukuba University, Ibaraki Prefecture, Japan
TAKEUCHI Akio	Professor, Faculty of Law, Tōkyō University, Tōkyō, Japan
TAKEUCHI Hitoshi	Professor Emeritus, Tōkyō University, Tōkyō, Japan
Melinda TAKEUCHI	Assistant Professor, School of Art, Stanford University, Stanford, California, US
TAKEUCHI Rizō	Former Professor, Faculty of History, Tōkyō University, Tōkyō, Japan
TAKUMA Shinpei	Director, Department of Educational Technology, National Institute of Special Education, Kanagawa Prefecture, Japan
TAKUMI Hideo	Director, Kanagawa Museum of Modern Art, Kanagawa Prefecture, Japan
TAMAI Kensuke	Director, Centro de Estudos Japonêses, Universidade de São Paulo, São Paulo, Brazil
TAMIYA Hiroshi	Professor, Department of Law, Rikkyō University, Tōkyō, Japan
George J. TANABE, JR	Professor, Department of Religion, University of Hawaii at Manoa, Honolulu, Hawaii, US
Atsuko TANABE DE BABA	Universidad Nacional Autónoma de México, Mexico City, Mexico
TANAKA Akira	Professor, Faculty of Letters, Hokkaidō University, Hokkaidō, Japan
TANAKA Jirō	National Research Institute of Aquaculture, Fisheries Agency, Mie Prefecture, Japan
TANAKA Masaaki	Professor, Department of Arts, The Women's College of Fine Arts, Tōkyō, Japan
TANAKA Minoru	Professor, Department of Law, Keiō University, Tōkyō, Japan
TANAKA Shigeaki	Professor, Faculty of Law, Kyōto University, Kyōto, Japan
TANAKA Takeo	Professor, Historiographical Institute, Tōkyō University, Tōkyō, Japan
TANAKA Yōnosuke	Chairman, Council for the Study of Industrial Information, Tōkyō, Japan
TANAKA Yutaka	Assistant Judge, Civil Affairs Bureau, The Supreme Court of Japan, Tōkyō, Japan
TANIGUCHI Yasuhei	Professor, Faculty of Law, Kyōto University, Kyōto, Japan
TANIKAWA Atsushi	Lecturer, Department of Literature, Kokugakuin University, Tōkyō, Japan
TANIKAWA Hisashi	Professor, Department of Law, Seikei University, Tōkyō, Japan
TANJI Kenzō	Chief, Yono City History Compilation Office, Yono City Municipal Office, Saitama Prefecture, Japan
TANSŌ Akinobu	Professor, Department of Law, Ritsumeikan University, Kyōto, Japan
TASHIMO Masaaki	Manager, Industrial Research Division, Long-Term Credit Bank of Japan, Ltd, Tōkyō, Japan
TASHIRO Hikaru	
TATSUKI Mariko	Senior Lecturer, Department of Economics, Teikyō University, Tōkyō, Japan
TATSUTA Misao	Professor, Faculty of Law, Kyōto University, Kyōto, Japan
TAURA Takeo	Professor, Faculty of Education, Nagoya University, Aichi Prefecture, Japan
TERAI Minako	Kimono specialist
TERASAKI Masao	Professor, Faculty of Education, Tōkyō University, Tōkyō, Japan
John E. THAYER III	Director, The Peabody Museum of Salem, Salem, Massachusetts, US
Sarah THOMPSON	Department of Prints, Philadelphia Museum of Art, Philadelphia, Pennsylvania, US
Arthur H. THORNHILL III	
Donald R. THURSTON	Associate Professor, Department of Political Science, Union College, Schenectady, New York, US
David A. TITUS	Professor, Department of Government, Wesleyan University, Middletown, Connecticut, US
Ronald P. TOBY	Assistant Professor, Department of History, University of Illinois, Urbana-Champaign, Urbana, Illinois, US
TODA Yoshio	Former Lecturer, Department of Literature, Kokugakuin University, Tōkyō, Japan
TOGAI Yoshio	Professor, Department of Business Management, Matsuyama University of Commerce, Ehime Prefecture, Japan
TOGANOO Shōzui	Asiatic Department, Boston Museum of Fine Arts, Boston, Massachusetts, US
TOKUZEN Yoshikazu	Professor, Japan Lutheran Theological College-Seminary, Tōkyō, Japan
TOMATSU Hidenori	Assistant Professor, Department of Law, Seijō University, Tōkyō, Japan
TOMIKI Kenji (d 1979)	Former President, Japan Aikidō Society, Tōkyō, Japan; Professor, Kokushikan University, Tōkyō, Japan

TOMISAWA Konomi	Industrial Research Division, Long-Term Credit Bank of Japan, Ltd, Tōkyō, Japan
TOMITA Torao	Professor, Department of Literature, Rikkyō University, Tōkyō, Japan
TONOKI Keiichi	Professor, School of Information and Communication, Bunkyō University, Saitama Prefecture, Japan
Conrad TOTMAN	Professor, Department of History, Northwestern University, Evanston, Illinois, US
George Oakley TOTTEN III	Professor, Department of Political Science, University of Southern California, Los Angeles, Los Angeles, California, US
TOYODA Takeshi	Former Professor, Department of Literature, Chūō University, Tōkyō, Japan
TSUCHIDA Mitsufumi	Professor, Bunkyō University's Women's College, Tōkyō, Japan
TSUCHIDA Naoshige	Curator, National Museum of Japanese History, Chiba Prefecture, Japan
TSUCHIDA Tomoaki	Staff Writer, *Encyclopedia of Japan*
TSUCHIYA Rokurō	Professor, Department of Economics, Chūō University, Tōkyō, Japan
TSUCHIYA Shin'ichi	Councillor, Secretariat, Ministry of Justice, Tōkyō, Japan
TSUDA Hideo	Professor, Department of Literature, Kansai University, Ōsaka Prefecture, Japan
TSUJI Shizuo	President, Tsuji Professional Culinary Institute, Ōsaka, Japan
Matsuo TSUKADA	Professor, Department of Botany, University of Washington, Seattle, Washington, US
Toshio G. TSUKAHIRA	Foreign Service Institute, US Department of State, Washington, DC, US
Reiko TSUKIMURA	Professor, Department of East Asian Studies, University of Toronto, Toronto, Ontario, Canada
TSUKUBA Hisaharu	Assistant Professor, Department of Economics, Waseda University, Tōkyō, Japan
TSUMORI Makoto	Professor, Department of Home Economics, Ochanomizu Women's University, Tōkyō, Japan
TSUMURA Akinobu	Executive Director, Japan National Oil Corporation, Tōkyō, Japan
E. Patricia TSURUMI	Associate Professor, Department of History, University of Victoria, Victoria, British Columbia, Canada
Yoshihiro TSURUMI	Professor, Department of Marketing, Baruch College, City University of New York, New York, New York, US
Kinya TSURUTA	Professor, Department of Asian Studies, University of British Columbia, Vancouver, British Columbia, Canada
TSUTSUI Michio	Professor, Faculty of Agriculture, Tōkyō University, Tōkyō, Japan
Royall TYLER	Assistant Professor, Department of East Asian Languages and Literatures, University of Wisconsin, Madison, Wisconsin, US
William J. TYLER	Assistant Professor, Department of Oriental Studies, University of Pennsylvania, Philadelphia, Pennsylvania, US
UCHIDA Michio	Professor, Department of Education, Tōkyō Gakugei University, Tōkyō, Japan
UCHIKAWA Yoshimi	Professor, Institute of Journalism and Communication Studies, Tōkyō University, Tōkyō, Japan
UDAGAWA Akihito	Professor, Faculty of Economics, Yokohama National University, Kanagawa Prefecture, Japan
UDAGAWA Masaru	Assistant Professor, Department of Business Management, Hōsei University, Tōkyō, Japan
UEDA Kenji	Professor, Department of Literature, Kokugakuin University, Tōkyō, Japan
UEDA Kiichi (d 1980)	Former Professor, Shōwa University, Tōkyō, Japan
Makoto UEDA	Professor, Department of Asian Languages, Stanford University, Stanford, California, US
UEDA Masaaki	Professor, Faculty of Liberal Arts, Kyōto University, Kyōto, Japan
UEDA Nobuhiro	Assistant, Faculty of Law, Tōkyō University, Tōkyō, Japan
Toyoaki UEHARA	Associate Professor, Department of East Asian Languages and Cultures, Indiana University, Bloomington, Indiana, US
UENO Yoshiya	Assistant Professor, Faculty of Letters, Tōkyō University, Tōkyō, Japan
UKAI Nobushige	Professor, Faculty of Law, Tōkyō University, Tōkyō, Japan
UMETANI Noboru	Professor, Faculty of Letters, Ōsaka University, Ōsaka, Japan
J. Marshall UNGER	Assistant Professor, Department of East Asian Languages, University of Hawaii at Manoa, Honolulu, Hawaii, US
UNNO Fukuju	Professor, Department of Literature, Meiji University, Tōkyō, Japan
Taitetsu UNNO	Professor, Department of Religion, Smith College, Northampton, Massachusetts, US
UNNO Yoshirō	Professor, Department of Law, Niigata University, Niigata Prefecture, Japan
Frank K. UPHAM	Visiting Professor of Law, Harvard Law School, Cambridge, Massachusetts, US
URANO Tatsuo	Assistant Professor, Department of Law, Nihon University, Tōkyō, Japan
Marian URY	Associate Professor, Comparative Literature Program, University of California, Davis, Davis, California, US
Sharlie Conroy USHIODA	Instructor, Saddleback Community College, Mission Viejo, California, US
USHIOGI Morikazu	Professor, Department of Education, Nagoya University, Aichi Prefecture, Japan
USHIRO Masatake	Management Consultant, McKinsey & Co, Ltd, Tōkyō, Japan
USUI Katsumi	Professor, Institute of Sociology, Tsukuba University, Ibaraki Prefecture, Japan
UWANO Zendō	Assistant Professor, Faculty of Letters, Tōkyō University, Tōkyō, Japan
Allie Marie UYEHARA	Author of *Ten Keys to Modern Japanese Flower Arrangement* (1975)
Cecil H. UYEHARA	Author of *Leftwing Social Movements in Japan: An Annotated Bibliography* (1959)

H. Paul VARLEY	Professor, Department of East Asian Languages and Cultures, Columbia University, New York, New York, US
Susan Downing VIDEEN	
Valdo H. VIGLIELMO	Professor, Department of East Asian Literature, University of Hawaii at Manoa, Honolulu, Hawaii, US
Savitri VISHWANATHAN	Reader, Department of Chinese and Japanese Studies, University of Delhi, Delhi, India
Ezra F. VOGEL	Professor and Director, US–Japan Program, Harvard University, Cambridge, Massachusetts, US
Suzanne H. VOGEL	Supervisor, Clinical Social Work, University Health Services, Harvard University, Cambridge, Massachusetts, US
Frits VOS	Professor and Director, Center for Japanese and Korean Studies, Leiden State University, Leiden, Holland
Meredith WADDELL	Formerly at Dentsū Inc, New York, New York, US
Hiroshi WAGATSUMA	Professor, Department of Anthropology, University of California, Los Angeles, Los Angeles, California, US
WAGATSUMA Takashi	Chief, Department of Obstetrics and Gynecology, National Medical Center Hospital, Tōkyō, Japan
WAKASUGI Akira	Professor and Dean, Department of Economics, Yokohama National University, Kanagawa Prefecture, Japan
WAKITA Osamu	Assistant Professor, Faculty of Letters, Ōsaka University, Ōsaka, Japan
WATANABE Akira	Assistant Professor, Department of Education, Tōkyō Gakugei University, Tōkyō, Japan
WATANABE Hiroshi	Architectural critic; Principal Associate, Wathos Planning, Tōkyō, Japan
WATANABE Hiroshi	Assistant Professor, Faculty of Law, Tōkyō University, Tōkyō, Japan
WATANABE Ichirō	Professor, Institute of Physical Education, Tsukuba University, Ibaraki Prefecture, Japan
WATANABE Tadashi	Former Deputy Secretary General, Science Council of Japan, Tōkyō, Japan
WATANABE Takeshi	Director and Chief, Construction Headquarters, Teito Rapid Transit Authority, Tōkyō, Japan
WATANABE Tōru	Professor, College of Arts and Sciences, Tōkyō University, Tōkyō, Japan
Tsugumichi WATANABE	Milbank Tweed Hadley & McCloy, New York, New York, US
WATANABE Yoshirō	Professor, Institute of Socioeconomic Planning, Tsukuba University, Ibaraki Prefecture, Japan
David B. WATERHOUSE	Professor, Department of East Asian Studies, University of Toronto, Toronto, Ontario, Canada
Glenn T. WEBB	Associate Professor, Department of Art History, University of Washington, Seattle, Washington, US
Herschel WEBB	Professor, Department of East Asian Languages and Cultures, Columbia University, New York, New York, US
Peter WEBER-SCHÄFER	Professor, Politische Wissenschaft Sektion, Abteilung fur Ostasienwissenschaften, Ruhr-Universität Bochum, Bochum, West Germany
C. G. WEERAMANTRY	Professor, Faculty of Law, Monash University, Clayton, Victoria, Australia
Gail Capitol WEIGL	Assistant Professor, Department of Art, University of Maryland, College Park, Maryland, US
Lucie R. WEINSTEIN	Associate Professor, Department of Art, Southern Connecticut State College, New Haven, Connecticut, US
Stanley WEINSTEIN	Professor, Department of East Asian Languages and Literatures, Yale University, New Haven, Connecticut, US
Theodore F. WELCH	Assistant University Librarian and Lecturer, Oriental and African Languages Program, Northwestern University, Evanston, Illinois, US
D. Eleanor WESTNEY	Department of Sociology, Yale University, New Haven, Connecticut, US
William WETHERALL	
Carolyn WHEELWRIGHT	Assistant Professor, Department of the History of Art, Yale University, New Haven, Connecticut, US
John A. WHITE	Professor, Department of History, University of Hawaii at Manoa, Honolulu, Hawaii, US
Merry I. WHITE	Associate in Research, Fairbank Center for East Asian Studies and Director, Project on Human Potential, Harvard Graduate School of Education, Cambridge, Massachusetts, US
George M. WILSON	Professor, Department of History, Indiana University, Bloomington, Indiana, US
William R. WILSON	Translator of *Hōgen monogatari: Tale of the Disorder in Hōgen* (1971)
Manfred WIMMER	Japan Go Association, Tōkyō, Japan
Clark WORSWICK	Editor of *Japan: Photographs 1854–1905* (1979) and *Imperial China: Photographs, 1850–1912* (1978)
Yasuko YABE	
YAGI Atsuru	Professor, Department of Humanities, Yamaguchi University, Yamaguchi Prefecture, Japan
YAMADA Katsumi	Professor, Department of Foreign Languages, Tōkyō University of Foreign Studies, Tōkyō, Japan
YAMADA Makiko	Associate Professor, Graduate School, International University of Japan, Niigata Prefecture, Japan
YAMADA Terutane	Physician and Standing Director, Japan Institute of Traditional Medicine, Tōkyō, Japan
YAMADA Tokubei	Specialist in Japanese dolls; Yoshitoku Co, Tōkyō, Japan
YAMADA Toshio	Professor, Department of Art and Literature, Seijō University, Tōkyō, Japan
YAMAGUCHI Kazuo	Professor, Department of Business Management, Sōka University, Tōkyō Prefecture, Japan

YAMAGUCHI Makoto	Professor, Department of Elementary Education, Kantō Junior College, Gumma Prefecture, Japan
YAMAGUCHI Osamu	Professor, Department of Literature, University of the Sacred Heart, Tōkyō, Japan
George K. YAMAMOTO	Professor, Department of Sociology, University of Hawaii at Manoa, Honolulu, Hawaii, US
YAMAMOTO Tadashi (d 1981)	Former Chief, Tōkyō Clinical Medicine Comprehensive Research Institute, Tōkyō, Japan
YAMAMOTO Takeo	Professor, Historiographical Institute, Tōkyō University, Tōkyō, Japan
Kozo YAMAMURA	Professor, Department of East Asian Studies, University of Washington, Seattle, Washington, US
YAMANAKA Seigō	Professor, Department of Arts and Literature, Seijō University, Tōkyō, Japan
YAMANO Aiko	Principal, Yamano Beauty School, Tōkyō, Japan
YAMANOBE Tomoyuki	Director, Tōyama Memorial Hall Art Museum, Saitama Prefecture, Japan
YAMARYŌ Kenji	Teacher, Azabugakuen High School, Tōkyō, Japan
YAMASHITA Kikuko	Staff Writer, *Encyclopedia of Japan*
YAMASHITA Ryūji	Professor, Faculty of Letters, Nagoya University, Aichi Prefecture, Japan
YAMAZAKI Isao	Essayist; former member of the Editorial Board, *Yomiuri shimbun,* Tōkyō, Japan
YAMAZAKI Yukio	Assistant Professor, Department of Humanities, Niigata University, Niigata Prefecture, Japan
Philip YAMPOLSKY	Adjunct Professor, Department of East Asian Languages and Cultures, Columbia University, New York, New York, US
Minoru YANAGIHASHI	Assistant Professor, Department of Oriental Studies, University of Arizona, Tucson, Arizona, US
YANAI Kenji	Professor, Department of Literature, Komazawa University, Tōkyō, Japan
Minja YANG	Information Officer, Office of the United Nations High Commissioner for Refugees, Tōkyō, Japan
YANO Tōru	Professor and Chairman, Social Sciences Section, Center for Southeast Asian Studies, Kyōto University, Kyōto, Japan
Richard YASKO	Associate Professor, Department of History, University of Wisconsin–Whitewater, Whitewater, Wisconsin, US
Kenneth YASUDA	Professor, Department of East Asian Languages and Cultures, Indiana University, Bloomington, Indiana, US
YASUDA Motohisa	Professor, Department of Literature, Gakushūin University, Tōkyō, Japan
YAZAWA Taiji	Professor Emeritus, Tōkyō Metropolitan University, Tōkyō, Japan
M. YOCHUM	
Karl G. YONEDA	
YONEKURA Mamoru	Art writer, *Asahi shimbun,* Tōkyō, Japan
YONEMOTO Kanji	Executive Director, Japan Industrial Robot Association, Tōkyō, Japan
Ann YONEMURA	Assistant Curator of Japanese Art, Freer Gallery of Art, Smithsonian Institution, Washington, DC, US
YOSHIDA Hiroo	Professor, Department of Literature, Chiba University, Chiba Prefecture, Japan
YOSHIDA Hiroshi	Assistant Manager, Economic Welfare Policy Section, Economic Welfare Bureau, Economic Planning Agency, Tōkyō, Japan
YOSHIDA Yoshio	Professor, National Institute for Research on Polar Regions, Ibaraki Prefecture, Japan
Takehiko YOSHIHASHI (d 1978)	Formerly of the School of International Service, American University, Washington, DC, US
YOSHIKAWA Yōko	Assistant Professor, Department of Foreign Languages, Kyōto Sangyō University, Kyōto, Japan
YOSHIKOSHI Tatsuo	Photographer
I. Roger YOSHINO	Professor, Department of Sociology, University of Arizona, Tucson, Arizona, US
Masatoshi M. YOSHINO	Professor, Institute of Geoscience and Director, Environmental Research Center, Tsukuba University, Ibaraki Prefecture, Japan
Michael Y. YOSHINO	Professor, Department of Business Administration, Harvard Business School, Cambridge, Massachusetts, US
YOSHITAKE Yoshinori	Professor Emeritus, Musashino Women's College, Tōkyō Prefecture, Japan
YOSHITOSHI Yawara	President, School of Medicine, Hamamatsu University, Shizuoka Prefecture, Japan
YOSHIZAWA Akira	President, International Origami Society, Tōkyō, Japan
Ernest P. YOUNG	Professor, Department of History, University of Michigan, Ann Arbor, Michigan, US
John YOUNG	Professor and Director, Institute of Far Eastern Studies, Seton Hall University, South Orange, New Jersey, US
YUASA Michio	Professor, Department of Law, Aichi Gakuin University, Aichi Prefecture, Japan
Nobuyuki YUASA	Translator and editor of *The Zen Poems of Ryōkan* (1981)
YUI Tsunehiko	Professor, Department of Business Management, Meiji University, Tōkyō, Japan
YUKAWA Osamu	Professor Emeritus, Nihon University, Tōkyō, Japan
Leon M. ZOLBROD	Professor, Department of Asian Studies, University of British Columbia, Vancouver, British Columbia, Canada

TRANSLATORS

The *Encyclopedia* is particularly grateful to Professor Michael K. YOUNG of Columbia University for his translations and advice concerning Japanese law.

ARAI Yasuko
Janet ASHBY
Carol BABA
BABA Shin'ya
Jerome E. BARNETT
Monica BETHE
James R. BRECKENRIDGE
James H. BRODERICK Jr
Theodore COOK
Kenneth DALE
Barry DUELL
Richard J. EMMERT
ENDŌ Akira
Mark ERICSON
FURUTA Minako
Paul GRONER
William D. JOHNSON
KANEKO Yoshihisa
KUSAKA Sae
Edward J. LAMPERT
John C. MARALDO
Lewis MARKS
MARUMO Teruyoshi
Julia M. MATISOO
Roland MONSON
ŌE Hidefusa
Roderick H. SEEMAN
Paul SHEPHERD
TAMURA Keiichi
TSURUOKA Atsuo
UETSUHARA Tokio
Marian URY
Michiko Nakanishi VIGDEN
Erika D. WHITE

TRANSLATION SERVICES

ISS International, Inc
National Translation Institute of Science and Technology
Translation Center for Industry and Technology, Inc

ART AND DESIGN

Art director: SUGIURA Kōhei

Assistant art director: KAIHO Tōru

Illustration design: Six, Co
ITŌ Katsuko
MIYASHITA Katsuyuki
SHIBA Masami
TAKEŻAWA Shigeru

Cartography: Tanshi Co
KOZAKI Kenzō
SUGAI Minoru
Nihon Kōbō Co
Morishita Co
Chizuseihan Cartographic Co
SHIRAMASA Akiyoshi

PRODUCTION

Dai Nippon Printing Co, Ltd
DNP America Inc
Kimura Zugei Co
Komiyama Printing Co
Lehigh/ROCAPPI
Ellen VANOOK

INDEX

Richardson Associates:
Dr. William J. RICHARDSON (director)
J. Edmund DE STEFANO (chief indexer)

ACKNOWLEDGMENTS

Photographs

ABE Michiaki
ADACHI Michio
Agricultural Land Development Public Corporation
ASANO Kiichi
Benridō
Bon Color Photo Agency Co, Ltd
Bridgestone Museum of Art, Ishibashi Foundation, Kurume
Bridgestone Museum of Art, Ishibashi Foundation, Tōkyō
Bunraku Society
Byōdōin
Camera Tōkyō Service Co, Ltd
CHINO Takayasu
Chion'in
Chishakuin
Chōgosonshiji
Chōkōji
Chūō Kōron Sha, Inc
Chūō Ward Office
Chūsonji
Daiichi Publication Center
Daikakuji
Daisen'in
Dandy Photo Co, Ltd
EBARA Takao
Education Commission, Higashi Ōsaka
Egawa Museum of Art
Eisei Bunko
ENDŌ Norikatsu
Engakuji
Enman'in, Onjōji
Enryakuji
Fine Photo Agency Co, Ltd
FUDEMOTO Hiromasa
FUJI Hiroko
FUJII Manabu
FUJIMORI Takeshi
FUJISHIMA Ayako
Fukuoka Art Museum
Fukuoka City Branch Office, Tōkyō
FUSE Masanao
Gakken Co, Ltd
Gakushūin Daigaku Shiryōkan
Gotō Art Museum
Government Buildings Department
  Minister's Secretariat, Ministry of Construction
HAGA Hideo
HAGIWARA Hidesaburō
HANAYAGI Shigeka
HATTORI Masatsugu
HAYASHI Shigeo
Henjōkōin
HIDAKA Katsuhiko
HIGUCHI Hatsuko
HIRATA Gōyō
Hōkyōji
Hōryūji
Hosokawaryū Bonseki Iemoto
HOSOMI Minoru
Idemitsu Art Gallery
Ii Art Museum
Ikenobō
Imperial Household Agency (Tōkyō)
  Katsura Detached Palace Office
  Kyōto Office of the Imperial Household
  Office of the Shōsōin Treasure House
Institute of Oriental Culture, Tōkyō University
IRIE Taikichi
ISHII Takanori
ISHIMOTO Yasuhiro
Ishiyamadera
Itsukushima Shrine
Itsuō Art Museum
Iwanami Shoten Publishers
Iwasaki Art Publications
IWASA Tamayo
IWATA Kikue
IZUMI Kōji
Izumo Shrine
Japanese National Railways
Japan Federation of Artists
Japan Film Library Council (Kawakita Memorial Film Institute)
Japan Magazine Publishers Association
Japan Press Photo Co, Ltd
Japan Travel Bureau Photo Library
Jingoji
Jingū Bunko
Jōbon Rendaiji
J. O. Co
Jōgon'in
Jōjuin, Kiyomizudera
Kagawa Prefectural Tourist Office, Tōkyō
Kakubei Jishi Hozonkai
KANAYA Fumio
KANEKO Keizō
Kangikōji
Kansai Electric Power Co, Inc
Kanshinji
Kantō Sha Co
KANZE Motomasa
Kararī Co, Ltd
Kawabata Yasunari Memorial Society
KAWAI Hajime
KAWAMURA Noriyuki
Keiō University
Kendō Nihon
Kenninji

Kinki Nippon Railway Co, Ltd
Kitano Temmangū Shrine
Kiyomizudera, Kyōto Prefecture
Kiyomizudera, Nagasaki Prefecture
Kiyoshikōjin Seichōji
K. Mikimoto & Co, Ltd
Kōbe City Branch Office, Tōkyō
Kōdaiji
Kōdansha International Ltd
Kōdansha Photography Department
Kōfukuji
Kojimadera
Kongōbuji
Kōryūji
Kōtokuin
Kōzanji
KUBO Katsutaka
Kyōdō News Service
Kyōto Furitsu Sōgō Shiryōkan
Kyōto National Museum
Kyūgetsu
Kyūkaen
Maeda Ikutokukai Foundation
MAEDA Setsu
MAEJIMA Hisao
Mainichi Shimbun
MATSUMOTO Norio
Matsuo Taisha Shrine
Meiji University Archaeological Collection
M. G. S. Photo Library
Mitsubishi Heavy Industries, Ltd
Mitsui Bunko
MITSUI Shinako
Miyagi Michio Memorial Museum
Miyagi Prefectural Office, Tōkyō
MIYAZAKI Kazuo
MIYAZAKI Manabu
MOA Museum of Art
MORI Atsuki
MŌRI Hōkōkai
MORITA Jūshirō
MORIYA Nobutaka
Motoori Norinaga Memorial Museum
Mōtsuji
Mt. Kōya Cultural Properties Preservation Society
MUNAKATA Chiya
Musashino Local Museum
Museum of Modern Japanese Literature
Myōchiin, Tenryūji
Myōhōin
Myōhokkeji
Myōshinji
Nagasaki Municipal Museum
Nagasaki Prefectural Museum of History and Folklore
Nagasaki Prefectural Tourist Office, Tōkyō
NAGATA Seiji
NAKAMATA Masayoshi
NAMBU Hideo
Nara National Research Institute of Cultural Properties
Nara Prefectural Trade Office, Tōkyō
NARIYAMA Tetsurō
National Theater
New Tōkyō International Airport Authority
Nezu Art Museum
NHK Service Center
Nijō Castle
Nikkō Tōshōgū
Nippon Express Co, Ltd
Nippon Gakki Co, Ltd
Nippon Steel Corporation
Nishi Honganji
Nishizawa Toy Collection
Ōbaiin, Daitokuji
Ōbunsha Publishing Co, Ltd
ODA Hideo
OGAWA Isshin
OGAWA Tomoji
Oguro Kikaku Co, Ltd
OKUMURA Akira
ONCHI Kunio
Ōsaka Castle Museum
ŌTA Eiichi
Ōtsuka Kōgei Sha Co, Ltd
ŌTSUKA Seigo
Pentax Gallery, Asahi Kōgaku Co, Ltd
Photo Pac Co
Riccar Art Museum
Rinnōji
Rokuharamitsuji
Rokuonji
Ryōanji
Ryūsen'an
Saidaiji
Saigō Family
Sainenji
SAKAI Tadamasa
Sakamoto Manshichi Photography Research Co, Ltd
SASAKI Fumitsuna
SATŌ Haruki
Sekai Bunka Photo
Sendai City Museum
Shibundō Publishing Co
Shitamachi Museum
Shitennōji
Shizuoka Prefectural Trade and Tourist Office, Tōkyō
Shōgakukan Publishing Co, Ltd
Shōjūji
Shōren'in

Silk Museum
Sōgetsu Shuppan, Inc
Sōgō Art Co
SUGANUMA Baku
Suntory Museum of Art
SUZUKI Jūzō
Taishūkan Publishing Co, Ltd
Taizōin
TAKAMURA Kimie
TAMURA Tadatsugu
Tekisui Art Museum
Tessai Art Museum
Tochigi Prefectural Tourist Office, Tōkyō
Tochigi Prefectural Trade Office, Tōkyō
Tōdaiji
Tōfukuji
Tōji
Tokugawa Reimeikai Foundation
Tōkyō Aerial Photo Research Institute
Tōkyō Gakuso
Tōkyō Metropolitan Central Library
Tōkyō Metropolitan Government Office
Tōkyō National Museum
Tōkyō National Museum of Modern Art
Tōkyō National Research Institute of Cultural Properties
Tōkyō University of Fine Arts and Music
Toppan Idea Center, Toppan Printing Co, Ltd
Tōshōdaiji
Tōyama Studio Co, Ltd
Tōyō Bunko
Toyokuni Shrine
Toyota Motor Corporation
Tsubouchi Memorial Theater Museum
Uesugi Shrine
UMEHARA Ryūzaburō
UMEWAKA Manzaburō
Umezawa Memorial Gallery
Uni Photos Co, Ltd
Urasenke Konnichian
USHIO Yoshimichi
Waseda University Library
WATANABE Manabu
Yaesu Art Gallery
Yagi Photo Library
Yakuōin
Yakushiji
YAMAHATA Yōsuke
YAMAZAKI Kane
Yamato Bunkakan
Yoita Kyōdo Shiryōkan
Yokkaichi City Branch Office, Tōkyō
Yokohama City Port Department
YOKOYAMA Takashi
YOSHIDA Chiaki
Yoshikawa Kōbunkan Publishing Co, Ltd
YOSHIKOSHI Tatsuo
Yoshitoku Collection
Yūzenshikai
Yuzu Henshū Kōbō Co
Zauhō Publications
Zenkōji
Zenrinji

Special Acknowledgment

KŌMA Yoshiko
OSAKU Taiko

AIZAWA Takeshi
Fuji Photo
IMAJIMA Minoru
Ina Kōgei
KANAI Hiroo
KATAKURA Nobuhiro
KAWAMATA Takashi
KENZO TANGE & URTEC
KIKUCHI Sadao
KOBAYASHI Tadashi
MIURA Tōseki
PEC Co, Ltd
TSUNODA Eriko
YANO Takehiko

THE ROMANIZATION RULES OF THE *ENCYCLOPEDIA OF JAPAN*

Spelling

Japanese words are spelled according to the Hepburn system of romanization with macrons being used to indicate long vowels. The *Encyclopedia* uses *m* instead of *n* before *p, b,* or *m,* and an apostrophe is used to distinguish syllable-final *n* from *n* at the beginning of a syllable. Foreign words in Japanese phrases are spelled as pronounced in Japanese.

Italicization

All Japanese words have been italicized except for proper nouns, which have been capitalized and set in roman letters. Certain Japanese words that were judged to be familiar to Western readers—such as *kabuki, haiku, kimono,* and *samurai*—were italicized on their first use in an article only and thereafter set in regular type.

Word division

The basic principle followed in word division was to divide Japanese words and phrases into units consisting of from one to three Chinese characters in the case of words of Chinese origin *(kango)* or from one to six syllables in the case of words of native origin (Yamato *kotoba*). Words or phrases of more than three Chinese characters or six syllables were divided into smaller units according to meaning or grammatical relationship. However, prefixes or suffixes that would be spelled solid according to this rule were spelled open if they were joined in sense to compounds of two or more words as a whole rather than to the first or last word (e.g., *nihonshi* "Japanese history" vs *gendai nihon shi* "history of modern Japan"). In another exception, compounds of four Chinese characters—spelled open by this rule—were hyphenated if a change in sound had accompanied compounding (e.g., *temmoku-jawan,* from *temmoku* and *chawan*).

An effort was also made to avoid repeating information in Japanese and English when English paraphrases or equivalents were needed to clarify the meaning of Japanese terms. Thus, as *ji* means "temple" in Japanese, Tōdaiji, for example, would be referred to as "Tōdaiji" or "the temple Tōdaiji" and *not* as "Tōdaiji Temple." Common geographical suffixes in this category include *kawa/gawa* "river" ("Sumidagawa" or "the river Sumidagawa," not "the Sumida River" or "the Sumidagawa River"), *shima/jima* "island," and *san/zan* "mountain."

HOW TO USE THE INDEX

Typography

Boldface type (e.g., **Anglo-Japanese Alliance**) indicates entries for which there are articles in the *Encyclopedia of Japan* while lightface type is used for topics discussed within articles (e.g., Marxism). Indented headings indicate aspects of the entry:

Scandinavia
  Japanese studies **4**:43b

The heading "Japanese studies" under the index entry "Scandinavia" indicates the location of information on Japanese studies in Scandinavia. The page references present the volume number in boldface followed by the page number and a letter indicating the left half (a) or the right half (b) of the page. Thus the reference for Japanese studies in Scandinavia, **4**:43b, indicates that this information will be found in volume 4 on page 43 in the righthand column. Numbers in italics direct the reader to photographs.

Headings in italics are the titles of books, newspapers, magazines, films, plays, or art works. Quotation marks indicate poems, short stories, sections of books, and slogans. Words in foreign languages, with the exception of the Latin names of plants, are not set in italics unless they fall into the categories listed above.

Alphabetization

The entries in the index are alphabetized letter by letter, not word by word, so that not all of the entries beginning with the same word will fall together:

New Liberal Club
New religions
News agencies
Newspapers
New Tōkyō International Airport

Mc is alphabetized as if it were spelled out as Mac and St. as Saint.

Chinese characters

Chinese characters are provided for all Japanese personal names, place names, and titles of books as well as for select words.

Cross references

Cross references direct the reader to the form used in the index (e.g., Japan External Trade Organization. *See* **JETRO**).

A

Aa gyokuhai ni hana ukete ······ ああ玉杯に花うけて ········ 7:166b
Aa mujō ··········· 噫無情 ········ 4:316b
Abacus ································ 1:1a
wasan ································ 8:231a
Abalones [(awabi) family Haliotidae] ···················· 1:1a-1b; 2:284a; 7:81b
Abashiri (city) ········ 網走 ······· 1:1b, *1b*
Abashiri, Lake ····· 網走湖 ······· 1:1b-2a
Abashiri Quasi-National Park ······· 網走国定公園 ·········· 1:1b
Abdomen ····················· 3:100a-100b
Abe Akira ·········· 阿部昭 ·········· 1:2a
Abe Collection
Ōsaka Municipal Museum of Fine Arts ································ 6:121b
Abe family 安倍氏, 阿部氏 ·········· 1:2a
samurai against ························ 7:7b
Abegawa. *See* **Abekawa**
Abe ichizoku ····· 阿部一族 ········· 4:85a
Abe Isoo ········· 安部磯雄 ······· 1:2a-2b; 7:281a
education ······························ 1:2a
labor involvements ·············· 1:2a-2b
pacifism ······························ 6:144a
political career ················· 1:2a-2b
Shakai Minshutō ················ 7:74a-74b
Shakai Taishūtō ······················ 7:74b
Abe Jirō ········· 阿部次郎 ·········· 1:2b
Abekawa ··········· 安倍川 ·········· 1:2b
Abe Kōbō ········ 安部公房 1:2b-3b; 7:38b
life ································ 1:2b-3a
shingeki ······························ 7:113b
works ····························· 1:3a-3b
literary devices ······················· 1:3a
prose themes ························· 1:3a
scientific ······························ 1:3a
Abe Masahiro ···· 阿部正弘 ············ 1:3b
kabunakama revival ················ 4:100a
Perry, Matthew Calbraith ··········· 3:189b
Abe Nobuyuki ··· 阿部信行 ······· 1:3b-4a
Abe no Hirafu · 阿倍比羅夫 ··· 1:4a; 7:263a
Abe no Munetō ·· 安倍宗任 ·········· 1:4a
Abe no Nakamaro ··············· 阿倍仲麻呂 ·········· 1:4a
Sui and Tang (T'ang) China, embassies to ································ 7:259b
Abe no Sadatō ··· 安倍貞任 ·········· 1:4a
Abe Nōsei. *See* **Abe Yoshishige**
Abe no Yoritoki · 安倍頼時 ······· 1:4a-4b
Abe Shigetaka ··· 阿部重孝 ·········· 1:4b
Abe Shinnosuke ·············· 阿部真之助 ·········· 1:4b
Abe Shōō ········ 阿部将翁 ·········· 1:4b
Abe Shōzō. *See* **Minakami Takitarō**
Abe Tadaaki ····· 阿部忠秋 ·········· 1:4b
Abe Tomoji ······ 阿部知二 ·········· 1:4b
Shinkō Geijutsu Ha ················ 7:119b
Abe Yoshishige ·· 安倍能成 ·········· 1:5a
Abe Yutaka ········ 阿部豊 ········ 2:268b
Abhidharmakośa ························ 4:320a
Abhinayadarpanam ···················· 8:21b
Abiko ··············· 安孫子 ·········· 1:5a
Aboku shingo ···· 亜墨新語 ········ 4:369b
A-bomb Medical Law ················· 1:110b
Abō Pass ·········· 安房峠 ·········· 1:5a
northern Japan ······················ 2:238b
Abortion (datai) ·· 1:5a; 2:234b, 246b-247b; 6:224a, 225a; 8:263a
criminality ··························· 2:48a
Abu Dhabi Oil Co, Ltd ·············· 2:61a
Abugawa ·········· 阿武川 ·········· 1:5a
Abugawa Dam · 阿武川ダム ·········· 1:5a
Abukumagawa ··· 阿武隈川 ·· 1:5a; 2:366b
Abukuma Mountains ··············· 阿武隈山地 ·· 1:5b; 2:366b
Abuna-e (risqué pictures) ········· 7:187b
Aburakasu ··········· 油糟 ········ 7:140a
Abura kōmori *(Pipistrellus abramus)* ································ 1:146b
Aburatsubo ·········· 油壺 ············ 1:5b
Abuse of right ························ 1:5b
ownership rights ···················· 6:137a
Abutsu Ni ·········· 阿仏尼 ······ 1:5b-6a; 2:356a
life ···································· 1:5b
works ·································· 1:6a
Academic Degree Order (1887) ····· 1:6a
Academic degrees ··················· 1:6a
Academic freedom 1:6a-6b; 6:220b; 8:171a
constitutional guarantee ············ 2:396b
Kyōto University Incident ···· 4:339a-339b
Morito Incident ······················ 5:254a
Academy Prize ··························· 4:9b
Accent in the Japanese language 1:6a-8a
dialects ················· 1:7a-7b; 2:91b
history ····························· 1:7b-8a
modern standard
intonation system ···················· 1:7a
long syllables ························ 1:6b
mora ·································· 1:6b
parts of speech ······················ 1:7a
short syllables ······················· 1:6b
Accounting and auditing ········ 1:8a-10a
auditing practices ····················· 1:9a
balance sheets ················· 1:9b-10a
certified public accountant (kōnin kaikeishi) ························ 1:266a
consolidated financial statement ····························· 1:360a-360b
early history ·························· 1:8a
income statements ·················· 1:10a
principles ····························· 1:8b
profession ··························· 1:8b-9a
professionalization ················ 1:8a-8b
tax accounting ········· 1:10a; 7:351b-352a
tax accountants ····················· 7:351b
Acheson statement ············ 1:10a-10b
Achievement tests ··················· 1:10b
Achilles Corporation ················ 1:10b
Acquisition by prescription ········· 7:68a
Actors' Analects, The ················· 8:21b
Acupressure ····························· 7:83b
Acupuncture ············· 1:10b; 5:146a
psychotherapy ······················ 6:261a
Adachi Buntarō ··············· 足立文太郎 ········· 1:11a
Adachi Kagemori 安達景盛 ········· 1:11a
Adachi Kenzō ··· 安達謙蔵 ········· 1:11a
Kokumin Dōmei ····················· 4:260a
Adachi Mineichirō ················· 安達峰一郎 ······· 4:373b
Adachi Tadashi ···· 足立正 ········· 1:11a
Adachi Ward ········ 足立区 ········· 1:11a
Adams, William ········· 1:11a-11b; 5:3b
Dutch trade ························ 2:135b
Saris, John ··························· 7:22a
Adatarasan ···· 安達太良山 ·········· 1:11b
Administered prices ················ 1:11b
Administrative acts ············· 1:13a, 14a
types ································· 1:14a
Administrative Board (Mandokoro) 5:101b
Administrative Case Litigation Law · 1:13a
Administrative Court ····· 1:11b-12a, 13a; 7:277b
abolishment ························· 4:378a
Okano Keijirō ························ 6:80b
public law ··························· 6:265b
tax laws ····················· 7:355a-358b
"Administrative disposition" ········ 1:13a
Administrative guidance ······· 1:12a-13a; 2:118a, 316a; 4:379b
description ·························· 1:12a
effectiveness ························ 1:12b
enforcement methods ················ 1:12b
exports ······························ 1:12a
foreign trade ························ 2:326a
industrial policy ···················· 3:297a
Industrial Structure Council ······· 3:302b
legal challenges ····················· 1:12b
Ministry of International Trade and Industry ····························· 4:190b
Securities Exchange Law ············· 1:8b
technological development ········· 7:370a
Administrative law ········ 1:13a-13b, 14a
Administrative litigation ········ 1:13b-14a
seizures ······························ 7:55b
types ································· 1:13b
Administrative Management Agency (AMA) ··············· 1:14a, 219a; 2:118a
Administrative Management and Inspection Commission ··········· 1:14a
Administrative procedure ·········· 1:14a
Administrative Reform, Provisional Council on ·························· 1:14a
Administrative scrivener ······· 1:14a-14b
Adogawa ············ 安曇川 ·········· 1:14b
Adoption ··· 1:14b-15b; 2:242a-242b; 6:163a
characteristics ················· 1:14b-15a
foundlings ··························· 1:15b
historical perspective ··············· 1:15a
in literature ························· 1:15a
marriage ···························· 5:116a
modern Japan ················· 1:15a-15b
principle of succession ······· 3:259b-260a
provisional or temporary ··········· 1:15a
purposes ····························· 1:14b
urban ································ 1:15b
Adoptive marriage ············ 2:242a-242b
ADR ····························· 1:51b-52a
Adult, legal definition of ············ 1:16a
Adultery ······················· 1:15b-16a
Adulthood ·················· 1:16a; 5:4b-5a
Adulthood Day ························ 3:17a
"Advance to the North" (hokushinron) group ································ 1:87b
"Advance to the South" (nanshinron) group ································ 1:87b
Advertising ···················· 1:16a-17b
cost ·································· 1:16a
financing ···························· 1:17b
future prospects ···················· 1:17b
history ···························· 1:16b-17a
industry structure ·············· 1:17a-17b
Japan Advertisers Association ········ 4:9b
Japan Advertising Review Organization ····························· 4:9b-10a
postwar history ······················ 1:17a
self-regulation ························ 4:9b
signboards ················· 7:193b-194a
Advertising agencies ·········· 1:17b-18a
Daikō Advertising Inc ·········· 2:60a-60b
Dentsū ································ 2:87a
first ··························· 1:16b, 17b
Hakuhōdō ···························· 3:88a
number ·················· 1:16a, 17b-18a
Advertising revenues ················· 1:16a
postwar growth ······················ 1:17a
Advisory Council on the Welfare of the Physically Handicapped ··········· 6:186a
Adzuki beans. *See* **Azuki**
Aeba Kōson ····· 饗庭篁村 ·········· 1:18a
Shinshōsetsu ························ 7:125a

Aeba Yosaburō. *See* **Aeba Kōson**
Ae no Koto ········· 2:*259a*
  ta no kami ········· 7:344a
Aerophones ········· 5:282b
Aesop's Fables ········· 3:183b, 347b
Aesthetics ········· 1:18a-19a
  concepts
    aware ········· 5:246b-247a
    fūryū ········· 2:374a-374b
    iki ········· 3:267b-268a
    ma ········· 5:77a
    mono no aware ········· 5:246b-247a
    okashi ········· 6:81a
    sabi ········· 6:361a-361b
    shibui ········· 7:85b-86a
    wabi ········· 8:197a
    yojō ········· 8:328b
    yūgen ········· 8:355a-355b
  historical trends ········· 1:18a-18b
    Edo period ········· 1:18b
    Heian period ········· 1:18a
    medieval ········· 1:18b
  modern ········· 1:19a
  premodern characteristics ········· 1:18b
    beauty ········· 1:18b
    elegance ········· 1:18b
    impermanence ········· 1:18b
    simplicity ········· 1:19a
    symbolic representation ········· 1:18b
  shibui ········· 7:85b-86a
Africa and Japan ········· 1:19a-19b
  aid ········· 1:19b
  diplomatic relations ········· 1:19a; 3:322a-323b
  trade ········· 1:19a; 3:322a-323b
Africa Committee ········· 4:188a
African Development Fund (AfDF) ········· 1:19b
Afro-Asian Conferences ········· 1:19b-20a
Afro-Asian Peoples' Solidarity Conferences ········· 1:19b
Afterlife ········· 1:20a
  avatar ········· 1:122b-123a
  Buddhist view ········· 1:20a
  Emma ········· 2:201b
  realms ········· 1:20a
  representations ········· 1:20a
  Shintō view ········· 1:20a
  this-worldliness ········· 8:24b
  traditional belief ········· 1:20a
After the Banquet case ········· 1:20a-20b, 85a, 255a; 6:249b
Afurisan ········· 雨降山 ········· 6:137b
Afuri Shrine 雨降神社
  Ōyama ········· 6:137b
Aganogawa ········· 阿賀野川 ········· 1:20b
Agano ware ········· 上野焼 ········· 1:20b; 2:295b
  Kobori Enshū ········· 4:238b
Agatai ········· 県居 ········· 4:129a
Agatameshi no Jimoku ········· 県召の除目 ········· 4:57b
Agata no Inukai no Tachibana no Michiyo ········· 県犬養橘三千代 ········· 1:20b-21a
Agatanushi ········· 県主 ········· 1:21a
Agatsumagawa ········· 吾妻川 ········· 1:21a
Agawa Hiroyuki ········· 阿川弘之 ········· 1:21a
Age, legal definition of ········· 1:21a-21b
Agechirei ········· 上地令 ········· 1:21a; 3:189b
Agedatami-bon ········· 上畳本 ········· 4:161b
Agency for Cultural Affairs (Bunkachō) ········· 1:75a; 5:186b
Agency for Spiritual Guidance ········· 7:245b
Agency of Industrial Science and Technology ········· 1:21b; 6:304a
Agency system ········· 2:66b-67a
Ageo ········· 上尾 ········· 1:21b
Age of Glass ········· 6:112a
Age of the Six Poetic Geniuses ········· 8:208b
Age reckoning ········· 5:3b-4a
Aging ········· 5:149a
Ago Bay ········· 英虞湾 ········· 1:21b
Agrarianism ········· 6:32a-32b
Agrarian nationalism (nōhon shugi) ········· 6:205a
  Gondō Seikyō ········· 3:45a
  Ishiguro Tadaatsu ········· 3:341a
  Tachibana Kōzaburō ········· 7:292a
  ultranationalism ········· 8:144b
Agrarian Reform Recording Committee ········· 8:289a
Agricultural Administration Council 1:32a
Agricultural Chemicals Control Law 1:30b
Agricultural cooperative associations (nōkyō) ········· 1:21b-22b, 139b; 6:238a; 7:214a
  land reform programs ········· 1:24b
  Nōrin Chūkin Bank ········· 6:37b
  postwar ········· 1:22a-22b
    membership ········· 1:22a
    problems ········· 1:22a
    structure ········· 1:22a
  prewar ········· 1:21b
    government support ········· 1:21b
    national networks ········· 1:22a
    prefectural federations ········· 1:21b
Agricultural rites ········· 1:22b-23a, *23a*, 160b, 194b; 2:258a
  corn raising ········· 1:22b
  folk religion ········· 2:298a-300b
  harvest ········· 1:22b
  New Year ········· 1:23a
  rice growing ········· 1:22b
Agriculture ········· 1:23b-32a; 2:284a
  in Asia, development of ········· 7:178a-178b
  brewing ········· 1:169b-170a
  climate ········· 1:327b-328a
  commercial ········· 2:148a, 150a-150b
  early modern economy ········· 2:153a-153b
  farming techniques ········· 1:28b-31a
    animal husbandry ········· 1:29b-30a
    chemicals ········· 1:30b
    dry field farming ········· 1:29a-29b
    fertilizers ········· 1:30b
    horticulture ········· 1:30a
    implements ········· 1:30a-30b
    insect pests ········· 1:30b
    irrigation ········· 1:29b
    land improvement ········· 1:29b
    new varieties (plant breeding) ········· 1:30a
    plant diseases ········· 1:30b
    rice planting ········· 1:28b-29a
  farmland ········· 1:26a
    climate ········· 1:26a
    cultivation areas ········· 1:26a
    farm households ········· 1:26a
    volcanoes ········· 1:26a
  financial depression of 1930s ········· 7:173b
  forestry ········· 2:326b-327a
  gōnō (rich farmers) ········· 3:45b-46a
  governmental policy ········· 1:31a-32a
    Basic Agriculture Law of 1961 ········· 1:31a
    income doubling plan ········· 1:31a
    present problems ········· 1:32a
    self-sufficiency ········· 1:31a-32a
    tenant-farming ········· 1:31a
  government policy
    bakuhan system ········· 1:131a-133a
  history ········· 1:23b
    Edo period ········· 1:24a
    modern era ········· 1:24a
    political power ········· 1:23b-24a
  horticulture ········· 3:231b
  industrial structure ········· 3:299b-302a
  labor movement ········· 4:353b
  landlordism ········· 4:362b
  land reclamation ········· 7:109b-110a
  livestock production ········· 1:27b-28b
    beef cattle ········· 1:28b
    chicken ········· 1:28b
    climate for ········· 1:27b-28a
    dairy cattle ········· 1:28b
    history ········· 1:27b-28a
    native breeds ········· 1:28b
    pork ········· 1:28b
  mechanization ········· 1:25a, 26a
  modernization ········· 1:24a-26a
    land reform and migration ········· 1:24b
    postwar changes ········· 1:24b-26a
  part-time basis ········· 2:308a
  plant crops ········· 1:26b-27b
    apples ········· 1:71a
    azuki bean ········· 1:27a, 127a
    chestnuts ········· 1:270a
    cucurbits ········· 2:52a-52b
    eggplants ········· 2:184b
    fruit trees ········· 1:27a
    grapes ········· 1:27a; 3:60b
    green tea ········· 1:27b
    industrial ········· 1:27b
    mikan ········· 1:27a; 5:170a-170b
    mushrooms ········· 1:27b; 5:282a-282b
    peaches ········· 1:27b; 6:169b
    pears ········· 6:170a
    persimmons ········· 6:178a
    potatoes and yams ········· 6:231b
    radishes ········· 1:27a; 6:276a-276b
    rice ········· 1:26b; 6:308a-310a
    soybeans ········· 1:27a; 7:239a
    vegetables, green ········· 8:189a
    vegetables, Western ········· 8:189a-189b
    Welsh onions ········· 8:241a
    wheat and barley ········· 1:26b; 8:251a
  premodern economy ········· 2:147a-148a
  primary industries ········· 6:240a
  religious aspects ········· 2:252b-254a
  sericulture ········· 7:68b-69a
  tea ········· 7:359b-360a
  terrace farming ········· 1:*25a*
Agriculture, White Paper on ········· 1:32a
"Agriculture-first" (nōhon shugi) ········· 1:26a
Agriculturists
  Andō Hirotarō ········· 1:55a
  Fesca, Max ········· 2:252a
  Fukuba Hayato ········· 2:361b
  Kellner, Oscar ········· 4:190b-191a
  Miyazaki Yasusada ········· 5:222b
  Ōkura Nagatsune ········· 6:98a
  Satō Nobuhiro ········· 7:28b
  Yokoi Tokiyoshi ········· 8:331b
Agronome français: Dictionaire économique ········· 4:294b
Aguinaldo, Emilio ········· 1:32a-32b
Agura ········· 7:248b
Agura nabe ········· 安愚楽鍋 ········· 4:135a
Ai ········· 3:290a
Aichi Canal ········· 愛知用水 ········· 1:32b, *32b*
Aichi Irrigation Project ········· 8:237a
Aichi Machine Industry Co, Ltd 1:32b-33a
Aichi Prefecture ········· 愛知県 ········· 1:33a
Aichi Steel Works, Ltd ········· 1:33a-33b
  Toyoda Automatic Loom Works, Ltd ········· 8:90a
Aida Gozan ········· 会田吾山 ········· 4:31b
Aida Masae ········· 会田昌江 ········· 3:102a
Aikawa ········· 相川 ········· 1:33b
Aikawa Yoshisuke ········· 鮎川義介 ········· 1:33b
Aikidō ········· 合気道 ········· 1:34a, *34b*
  jūjutsu ········· 1:34a
  jūjutsu techniques ········· 1:34a
  modern systematization ········· 1:34a
  practice forms ········· 1:34a
Aikoku Fujinkai (Patriot's Women's Association) ········· 愛国婦人会 ········· 1:34a; 7:105a
  Okumura Ioko ········· 6:96b; 8:261a

Aikokuhan (patriotic groups) 愛国班 **4**:284a
Aikoku Kinrōtō
  Shimpeitai Incident **7**:108a
Aikoku Kōtō (Public Party of Patriots) 愛国公党 **1**:34b; **6**:207a
  Freedom and People's Rights Movement **2**:334a
  Gotō Shōjirō **3**:54a
  Hayashi Yūzō **3**:118a
  Itagaki Taisuke **3**:349a
Aikokusha (Society of Patriots) 愛国社 **1**:34b; **2**:373b; **6**:207a
  Freedom and People's Rights Movement **2**:334b
  Itagaki Taisuke **3**:349a
  League for Establishing a National Assembly **4**:372b-373a
Aikyōgen 間狂言 **4**:324b, 326a
Aikyōjuku 愛郷塾 **1**:34b
  Tachibana Kōzaburō **7**:292a
Ainotake 間ノ岳
  Shirane Sanzan **7**:147a
Ai no kawaki (Thirst for Love) 愛の渇き **6**:231a
Ai no korīda (Realm of the Senses) 愛のコリーダ **2**:*275a*
Ainu **1**:34b-36a
  Batchelor, John **1**:145b
  dance **1**:36a
  dialects **2**:92a
  economy **1**:35b
  Ezo **2**:238b
  folk crafts **2**:294a
  folktales **1**:36a
  general description **1**:34b-35a
  Jōmon skulls **4**:34b
  Koganei Yoshikiyo's study of **4**:248a
  land rights **4**:113a
  language **1**:36a-37b
    affinities **1**:37a-37b
    general description **1**:36a-36b
    Japanese language **4**:23b
    Kindaichi Kyōsuke **4**:212a
    literature **1**:37a
    phonology **1**:36b
    studies **1**:36b
    syntax and grammar **1**:36b-37a
    vocabulary **1**:37a
  lifestyle **1**:35b
  minorities **5**:195a
  music **1**:36a, 37b
    affinities **1**:37a
    general description **1**:37b
  musical instruments **1**:37b
  origins **1**:35b
  physical characteristics **1**:35b; **4**:35a-38a
  population **1**:35a
  religion **1**:36a
  Russia **6**:340b
  Sakhalin **7**:1b
  social organization **1**:36a
Ainu-English-Japanese Dictionary **1**:145b
Ainu jojishi yūkara no kenkyū I-II **4**:212a
Aioi 相生 **1**:37b
Aircraft industry. *See* **Aviation**
Air pollution **2**:227b-228a
  coal **2**:216a
  control **2**:227a-229a
  diseases **2**:226b-227a
Airport Law of 1952 **1**:38a
Airports **1**:37b-38a
  classes **1**:37a
  maintenance **1**:38a
  New Tōkyō International (Narita) **1**:37b; **5**:370b-371b
  Ōsaka International **1**:37b
  Tōkyō International (Haneda) **1**:37b
Air Self Defense Force **7**:60a-60b
Air transportation **8**:102b-103a
Aisai monogatari
  Shindō Kaneto **7**:111a
Aisin Seiki Co, Ltd **1**:38a
  Toyota Motor Co, Ltd **8**:93b
Ai to ninshiki to no shuppatsu 愛と認識との出発 **4**:312a
Aizawa Seishisai 会沢正志斎 **1**:38a
  Fujita Tōko **2**:347a
  Fujita Yūkoku **2**:347a
  Mito school **5**:205a
  Shinron **7**:124a
Aizawa Tadahiro 相沢忠洋 **1**:38a
  Iwajuku site **3**:358a
Aizen katsura 愛染かつら **4**:177b
Aizu, Battle of. *See* **Boshin Civil War**
Aizu Basin 会津盆地 **1**:38a
Aizu Book of Agriculture **1**:38b
Aizu Hongō ware 会津本郷焼 **1**:38b
Aizukoma 会津駒 **4**:265a
Aizu Komagatake 会津駒ケ岳 **4**:265a
Aizu nōsho 会津農書 **1**:38b
Aizu Wakamatsu 会津若松 **1**:38b
Aizu Yaichi 会津八一 **1**:38b
Ajia Afurika Kaigi **1**:19b-20a
Ajikawa 安治川 **1**:38b
Ajinomoto Co, Inc **1**:38b-39a
Ajirogi 網代木 **4**:180a
Ajisai. *See* **Hydrangea, Japanese**
Akabane Kōsaku Bunkyoku 赤羽工作分局 **1**:39a
Akabane Manufacturing Branch **1**:39a
Akabira 赤平 **1**:39a
Akabori Shirō 赤堀四郎 **1**:39a
Akaezo fūsetsu kō 赤蝦夷風説考 **1**:39a; **4**:302a
Akagami **7**:168a
Akagisan 赤城山 **1**:39a
Akahata 赤旗 **1**:39b; **2**:339a; **4**:180b; **7**:91b
  circulation **4**:12a
  Japan Communist Party **4**:11a
Akahata Incident. *See* **Red Flag Incident of 1908**
Akahata Jiken. 赤旗事件 *See* **Red Flag Incident of 1908**
Akahito 赤人 **8**:287b
Akahon. 赤本 *See* **Kusazōshi**
Akai daiya 赤いダイヤ **4**:115a
Akai Electric Co, Ltd **1**:39b
Akaishidake 赤石岳 **1**:39b
Akaishi Mountains 赤石山脈 **1**:39b
Akai tori 赤い鳥 **1**:39b-40a
Akakurage **4**:50b
Akakura Hot Spring 赤倉温泉 **1**:40a
Akama Shrine 赤間神宮 **1**:40a
  Shimonoseki **7**:105b
Akamatsu family 赤松氏 **1**:40a; **7**:8b
Akamatsu Katsumaro 赤松克麿 **1**:40a-40b
  Kokumin Kyōkai founder **4**:260b-261a
Akamatsu Mitsusuke 赤松満祐 **1**:40b
Akamatsu Sōtan 赤松宗旦
  Tonegawa zushi **8**:74a
Akame, 48 Falls of 赤目四十八滝 **1**:40b
Akan, Lake 阿寒湖 **1**:40b
Akan National Park 阿寒国立公園 **1**:40b
Akasaka Detached Palace **1**:40b
Akashi (city) 明石 **1**:40b-41a
Akashi Strait 明石海峡 **1**:41a
Akashi Women's Normal School
  Shin Kyōiku Undō **7**:121b
Akashiya no Dairen アカシヤの大連 **4**:232b
Aka to kuro (Red and Black) 赤と黒 **3**:76a; **4**:183a
"Akatombo" (Red Dragonflies) 赤とんぼ **2**:133b
Akatsuchi no ie 赤土の家 **4**:139a
Akatsuki to yūbe no shi 暁と夕の詩 **7**:293a
Akazome Emon 赤染衛門 **1**:41a; **5**:37a
  Eiga monogatari **3**:153a
Akazukin-chan ki o tsukete 赤頭巾ちゃん気をつけて **7**:163a
Akebi (*Akebia quinata*) **1**:*41a*; **2**:305a
  baskets **4**:104b
Akebonokai あけぼの会 **5**:19b
Akechi Mitsuhide 明智光秀 **1**:41a-41b; **2**:280b, 361b; **7**:104a
  Honnōji Incident **3**:224a
  Kameoka **4**:125b
Akegarasu nochi no masayume 明烏後正夢 **7**:333b
Aki 安芸 **1**:41b
Akiba Shrine 秋葉神社 **1**:41b
Akibiyori 秋日和 **3**:102b
Akigawa 秋川 **1**:41b
Akihito, Crown Prince 明仁親王 **1**:41b-42a
  Imperial household **3**:277b
Akimoto Matsuyo 秋元松代 **1**:42a
Aki no hi 秋の日 **4**:169a
Aki no hitomi 秋の瞳 **8**:284a
Aki no koe (Voice of Autumn) 秋の声 **6**:139b
Aki no yo no naga monogatari (Long Tale for an Autumn Night)
  otogi-zōshi **6**:130a
Akirame あきらめ **1**:42a
Akishima 昭島 **1**:42a
Akishinodera 秋篠寺 **1**:42a
Akita 秋田 **1**:42b
Akita Castle 秋田城 **1**:42b
Akita Incident 秋田事件 **1**:42b
Akitajō 秋田城 **1**:42b
Akita Komagatake 秋田駒ケ岳 **4**:264b-265b
Akita Oil Fields 秋田油田 **1**:42b
Akita Plain 秋田平野 **1**:42b
Akita Prefecture 秋田県 **1**:42b-43a
Akita school 秋田派 **1**:43a-43b
  main principles **1**:43b
  major painters **1**:43a
  Odano Naotake **6**:65a
  Satake Shozan **7**:25b
Akitsu 安芸津 **1**:43b
Akiyama Saneyuki 秋山真之 **1**:43b-44a
Akiyama Teisuke 秋山定輔 **1**:44a
Akiyoshidai 秋吉台 **1**:44a, *44b*
Akiyoshidai Quasi-National Park 秋吉台国定公園 **1**:44b
Akiyoshidō 秋芳洞 **1**:44a-44b; **5**:352b
Akiyoshi Toshiko 秋吉敏子 **1**:44b
Akizuki Rebellion of 1876 秋月の乱 **1**:44b
  chitsuroku shobun **1**:297a
Akkadō 安家洞 **1**:44b
Akō 赤穂 **1**:44b-45a
Akogigaura. *See* **Akogiura**
Akogiura 阿漕浦 **1**:45a

Akō Incident of 887 阿衡事件 1:45a
Miyoshi Kiyoyuki 5:224a
Uda, Emperor 8:125b
Akō Incident of 1703. *See* **Forty-Seven Rōnin Incident**
Akubasho 4:95b
Akuma 悪魔 4:160b; 7:342b
Akuma ga kitarite fue o fuku 悪魔が来りて笛を吹く 8:333b
Akumyō 悪名 4:174b
Akune 阿久根 1:45a
Aku okeno 灰汁桶の 6:299b
Akutagawa Prize
Akutagawa Ryūnosuke (1935) 1:46a
Endō Shūsaku 2:214a
Gomi Yasusuke (1953) 3:44b
Hotta Yoshie (1951) 3:239b-240a
Inoue Yasushi 3:311b
Ishihara Shintarō 3:341
Ishikawa Tatsuzō 3:345a
Kaikō Ken 4:111a
Kikuchi Kan 4:206b
Kita Morio (1960) 4:227a
Kiyooka Takayuki (1969) 4:232b
Lee Hwe-song (1972) 4:374b
Matsumoto Seichō 5:138a
Nakayama Gishū (1938) 5:318b
Ōe Kenzaburō (1958) 6:66a
Ozaki Kazuo (1937) 6:139b
Shōji Kaoru (1969) 7:163a
Shōno Junzō (1954) 7:167a
Tanabe Seiko (1964) 7:335b
Yasuoka Shōtarō (1953) 8:319b
Akutagawa Ryūnosuke 芥川龍之介 1:45a-46a, 313b; 5:13a, 55a-55b; 7:26b, 72b, 81a, 103b; 8:173b
birth and education 1:45a
death 1:46b
earlier period 1:45a
final period 1:45b
Kokon chomonjū used 4:256b
Konjaku monogatari's influence on 4:271a
middle period 1:45b
Shinchō 7:109a
Shinshichō 7:125a
Shinshōsetsu 7:125b
works 1:45a-45b
Akutagawa Ryūnosuke Literary Prize. *See* Akutagawa Prize
Akutō 悪党 1:46a, 97b
Ālayavijñāna 1:177b
Album leaf (sōshi) 6:150a
Alcock, Rutherford 1:46a; 7:29a
Shimonoseki Bombardment 7:106a
Alcoholic beverages in Japanese society 1:46a-47a
earliest record 1:46a
premodern drinking habits 1:46a-46b
present day use
among women 1:47a
consumption 1:47a
social 1:47a
urban life 8:179a
varieties 1:47a
wedding ceremony 1:47a
sake 7:1a-1b
Aleutian Islands 4:223b
Alexander, Wallace McKinney 1:47a
Algae 7:46b
Alien Land Acts 1:47a-47b
ineffectiveness 1:47b
1913 1:47a; 8:155b
1920 1:47b
Alien registration 1:47b; 2:314a
Alien Registration Law of 1952 1:47b; 2:313a
Aliens. *See* **Foreigners, legal status of**
Allegory. *See* **Waka**
Allerlie aus Japan 6:312a
Allied Council for Japan 1:47b-48a, 117a-117b
Ball, William MacMahon 1:135a-135b
Far Eastern Commission 2:248a
land reforms of 1946 4:364a
Occupation 6:51b
Sebald, William Joseph 7:47a
Allied Occupation. *See* **Occupation**
All-Japan Bookbinding Association (Zen Nihon Seihon Kōgyō Kumiai Rengōkai) 6:246b
All Japan Federation of Electrical Machine Workers' Unions 2:87a
All Japan Federation of Proletarian Arts (Zen Nihon Musansha Geijutsu Remmei) 6:255b
All Japan Kendō Federation (Zen Nihon Kendō Remmei) 4:196a
All-Japan Printing Association 6:246b
All Men Are Brothers 8:336a
All Nippon Airways Co, Ltd (ANA) 1:48a; 8:102b
All Nippon News Network (ANN) 1:92a, 93a
Allowances
nonstatutory 8:200a
statutory 8:200a
All Quiet on the Western Front 6:255b
Almanac of Publishing 6:267b-268a
Almeida, Luis de 2:172b
Alphabet. *See* Language: Japanese language
Alps Electric Co, Ltd 1:48a
Altaic languages, Japanese and 4:18b-20a
Alternate attendance 7:14a-14b
Altiona peto 6:100a
Aluminum
manufacturers 6:10b-11a; 7:173a, 268b-269a
smelters 7:173a
Ama 1:48a-48b
female 1:48a-48b
male 1:48a-48b
"Amabune" 海人舟 4:269b
Amache Relocation Center 1:48b
Amae 1:48b-49a; 4:39b; 6:261a; 7:262b, 275b
Doi Takeo 1:49a
vs enryo 2:221a
general description 1:48b
usages 1:48b-49a
adult relationships 1:48b
child-parent 1:48b, 277b
Amae no kōzō 甘えの構造 1:49a
Amagasaki 尼ケ崎 1:49a
Amagatari 天語り 2:138a
Amagi 甘木 1:49a
Amagi Pass 天城峠 1:49b; 4:146b
Amagisan 天城山 1:49b; 2:342b
Amagi Yugashima 天城湯ケ島 8:355a
Amagoi. *See* **Rain, rituals for**
Amako family 尼子氏 1:49b
Amakudari 1:49b
Amakusa (town) 天草 1:49b-50a
Amakusa Islands 天草諸島 1:50a, *50b*
Amakusa Sea 天草海 1:50a
Amakusa Shirō. 天草四郎 *See* **Shimabara Uprising**
Amami Islands 奄美諸島 1:50a; 7:30b
agricultural rites 1:23a
Yoronjima 8:339a
Amami Ōshima 奄美大島 1:50a, *50b*; 4:105b, 205a
Amanohashidate 天橋立 1:50a, *51a*; 6:*152b*
Amanojakko 1:50a
Amanojaku 1:50a-50b
Amanokaguyama 天香久山 8:310b
Amanosagume 1:50a
Amano Tameyuki 天野為之 1:50b-51a
Amano Teiyū 天野貞祐 1:51a
Amano Tōkage 天野遠景 1:51a
Amaterasu Ōmikami 天照大神 1:51a-51b, 125a; 2:2b; 4:125b; 7:15b, 276a, 278b, 280a; 8:236b, 256b, 307b
account 1:51b
birth 5:293a
Daijōsai 2:59a-59b
disappearance 5:293b
feuding with Susanoo 5:293a-293b
Hirota Shrine 3:150b
imperial descent 4:191b
imperial regalia 3:278b-279a
Ise Shrine 3:338a
Izumo Shrine 3:367a
Jinnō shōtō ki 4:59b-60a
Kannamesai 4:144a
kokutai concept 4:263a
messengers 5:294a-294b
Ryōbu Shintō 6:351a
Shingon sect 7:115a
Shinsen shōjiroku 7:124b
Takachihonomine 7:310b
Takamagahara 7:314a
tama 7:332a
worship 1:51b
Amateru Kami 天照神 7:276b
Amatsukami 天津神 4:125b
Amatsu Kominato 天津小湊 1:51b
Amatsu tsumi 天津罪 3:101a
Ame no Futodama no Mikoto 天太玉命 1:125a
Amenomori Hōshū 雨森芳洲 1:51b
American Communist Party 7:229b
American Depositary Receipts (ADR) 1:51b-52a
American Pacific Mail Steamship Company 3:362b
Amerika Hikozō. *See* **Hamada Hikozō**
Amerika jigoku meguri (Touring the American Hell) アメリカ地獄巡り 8:13a
Amerika kanjō ryokō アメリカ感情旅行 8:319b
Amerika kyōiku shisetsudan 8:164b
Amerika Mura アメリカ村 1:52a
"Amerikan Sukūru" アメリカンスクール 4:252a
Amida 1:52a, 176a, 179a *201a*; 2:360a; 4:62a; 7:63a, 67b
Byōdōin temple 1:227a
East Asian Buddhism 1:52a
Jōdo Shin sect 4:68b
Jōruriji 4:77b
Kinkakuji 4:213a
Kiyozawa Manshi 4:233a
Kyōgyōshinshō and 4:330a
monasticism 5:238a
Namu Amida Butsu 5:327a-327b
Ōjōyōshū 6:77a
popularization of Buddhism 3:171a-172a
Primal Vow 1:52a
Tannishō 7:344a
Pure Land Buddhism 4:144b
raigōzu 6:276b
Sanzen'in 7:19b

Shinran ··· 7:123a
statues ··· 4:111a
thought and culture ··· 8:27a-28a
visual arts ··· 1:52a
worship ··· 1:52a
Amida no munewari ··· 阿弥陀の胸割 ··· 4:76b
Amida sculpture ··· 4:66b
Amida's Riven Breast ··· 4:76b
Amida triad ··· 6:*124b*
Amino Kiku ··· 網野菊 ··· 1:52a-52b
Ami school ··· 阿弥派 ··· 1:52b-53a
connoisseurship ··· 1:53a
Geiami ··· 1:52b; 3:14a
influence ··· 1:53a
ink painting ··· 3:306b
Nōami ··· 1:52b; 6:29b-30a
origin ··· 1:52b
painting ··· 6:151b
Sōami ··· 1:52b; 7:207b
Amitābha Buddha ··· 3:328b-329a
Amity, Commerce and Navigation, Treaty of (between Philippines and Japan) ··· 4:370a; 6:184b
Amma ··· 1:53a
Amnesty (taisha)
criminal law ··· 2:49a
ritsuryō system ··· 6:328a
Amō Eiji ··· 天羽英二 ··· 1:53a
Amoenitatum Exoticum ··· 4:102a
Amoghavajra
Shingon sect ··· 7:114a
Amō statement ··· 天羽声明 ··· 1:53a; 7:92a
Amphibians ··· 1:60a-60b, 62a
frogs ··· 2:339b-340a
imori ··· 3:275a
salamanders ··· 7:5a-5b
Ampo Riots of 1960
pacifism ··· 6:145a
Ampo tōsō. *See* **Peace movement**
Amur River Society ··· 1:53b
annexation of Korea ··· 4:282a
Gen'yōsha ··· 3:24b-25a
nationalism ··· 5:342b-343a
Russo-Japanese War ··· 6:346a
tairiku rōnin ··· 7:302b
Uchida Ryōhei ··· 8:124a
ultranationalism ··· 8:145b
World War II ··· 8:271b
Analects ··· 2:57a; 4:277a
Itō Jinsai's study ··· 4:247b
Anami Korechika 阿南惟幾 ··· 1:53b
Anan (city) ··· 阿南 ··· 1:53b
Anan Coast ··· 阿南海岸 ··· 1:53b
Anarchism ··· 1:53b-54a; 4:345a
Anarchist League of Japan ··· 3:344a
Anarcho-syndicalism ··· 5:231a-231b
Anatomische Tabellen ··· 7:258b
Anatomy of Dependence ··· 1:49a
Ancestor worship ··· 1:54a-55a; 6:295b
background ··· 1:54a-54b
butsudan ··· 1:225b
ceremonies and festivals ··· 1:54b
features ··· 1:54a-54b
in Hirata Atsutane's thought ··· 4:259a
memorial tablets ··· 1:54a
social control of household ··· 1:54b
state influence ··· 1:54a
An Chung-gŭn ··· 1:55a
Ancient Learning (Kogaku) ··· 古学 ··· 4:246b-248a; 8:290b
Ancient private records ··· 4:255a-255b
Ando ··· 安堵 ··· 1:55a
Andō Hiroshige ··· 安藤広重 ··· 3:148a-149b
Andō Hirotarō ··· 安藤広太郎 ··· 1:55a
Andon. *See* **Lanterns**
Andō Nobumasa 安藤信正 ··· 1:55a-55b
Andō Sanesue ··· 安東実季 ··· 3:179b
Andō Shōeki ··· 安藤昌益 ··· 1:55b-56a
egalitarian thought ··· 1:55b-56a
metaphysics ··· 1:55b-56a
theory of medicine ··· 1:56a
Anegawa, Battle of ··· 姉川の戦 ··· 1:56a, 94a, 95a; 5:300a
Asai Nagamasa ··· 1:94a
firearms usage ··· 2:279a
Oda Nobunaga ··· 6:63a
Anemone, Japanese [(shūmeigiku) *Anemone japonica*] ··· 1:56a
Anesaki Chōfū. 姉崎嘲風 *See* Anesaki Masaharu
Anesaki Masaharu ··· 姉崎正治 ··· 1:56b
Anglerfishes [(ankō) family Lopliidae] ··· 1:56b
Anglican-Episcopal Church ··· 7:51b
Angling ··· 2:287a
Anglo-Japanese Alliance ··· 1:56b-57b, 87b, 238b; 2:332b; 7:29b, 198b; 8:152a, 270b, 291b, 343b
abrogation ··· 1:237b
background ··· 1:56b
in Britain ··· 1:57a
Denison, Henry Willard ··· 2:86b
dissatisfaction ··· 1:57a
in Japan ··· 1:57a
from outside ··· 1:57a
Hayashi Tadasu ··· 3:118a
international relations ··· 3:321a
Japanese control in Korea ··· 4:282a
Japanese factions ··· 1:57a
Komura Jutarō ··· 4:268a
Korea's annexation ··· 4:287a
neutrality ··· 3:196b
original agreement and revisions ··· 1:56b-57a
Russo-Japanese agreements of 1907–1916 ··· 6:344b
Russo-Japanese War ··· 6:346a
termination ··· 1:57a-57b; 2:330a
Tripartite Pact ··· 8:107a
Twenty-One Demands ··· 8:120b
United States ··· 8:157a
Washington Conference ··· 8:234a
Anglo-Japanese Commercial Trade Treaty of 1894
Denison, Henry Willard ··· 2:86b
Anglo-Japanese Commercial Treaty of 1894 ··· 1:57b; 8:152a
international relations ··· 3:320b
Mutsu Munemitsu ··· 5:289a
Treaty of Shimonoseki ··· 7:106a
Unequal Treaties revision ··· 8:148a
Anglo-Japanese relations. *See* **United Kingdom and Japan**
Angoin. 安居院 *See* **Asukadera**
Animals ··· 1:57b-62a
agriculture ··· 1:27b-28b, 61b
amphibians ··· 1:60a-60b, 62a
arthropods ··· 1:62a
birds ··· 1:59b-60a, 61b
characteristics ··· 1:57b-59a
endemic species ··· 1:59a
living fossils ··· 1:59a
zoogeographic divisions ··· 1:59a
in contemporary Japan ··· 1:61b
fishes ··· 1:60b-61a, 61b-62a
husbandry ··· 1:29b-30a
insects ··· 1:61a
in Japanese culture ··· 1:61a-61b
mammals ··· 1:59a-59b, 61b
prevention of cruelty ··· 7:167a
protected ··· 5:352a
reptiles ··· 1:60a-60b, 62a
Animism ··· 1:62a
Anjō ··· 安城 ··· 1:62a
An Jūkon ··· 安重根 ··· 1:55a
Ankō ··· 1:56b
Ankokuji ··· 安国寺 ··· 3:269b
Ankokuji Ekei ··· 安国寺恵瓊 ··· 1:62a; 7:56b
Anna Incident ··· 安和の変 ··· 1:62a-62b
Annaka ··· 安中 ··· 1:62b
Annals of the Institute of Statistical Mathematics ··· 7:246a
Annual events. *See* **Festivals**
"Annual tribute" ··· 5:360a-361b
Anotsu ··· 安濃津 ··· 1:62b
Anrakuan Sakuden ··· 安楽庵策伝 ··· 1:62b-63a
comic monologue ··· 6:282a
early life and education ··· 1:62b
literary pursuits ··· 1:63a
prelate of Jōdo sect ··· 1:62b-63a
Anraku no mon ··· 安楽の門 ··· 6:81b
Ansei commercial treaties ··· 安政五か国条約 ··· 1:63a; 4:333a; 7:29a
gaikoku bugyō ··· 3:3a
Harris Treaty ··· 3:105a
import tariffs ··· 4:112b-113a
Iwakura mission ··· 3:359a
Kōbe ··· 4:238a
Kōmei, Emperor ··· 4:266a
Mutsu Munemitsu ··· 5:288b
Nagai Uta ··· 5:301b
Nagasaki trade ··· 5:306a
naichi zakkyo ··· 5:309b-310a
Netherlands ··· 5:362a
Opening of Japan ··· 6:114b
Sakuradamongai Incident ··· 7:4b
Sawa Nobuyoshi ··· 7:31a
Shimonoseki Bombardment ··· 7:106a
shogunate missions to the West ··· 7:161a
Takenouchi Yasunori ··· 7:325a
territory of Japan ··· 8:13b
Tokugawa Iemochi ··· 8:48a
Unequal Treaties revision ··· 8:148a
Yokoi Shōnan ··· 8:331a
Ansei gokakoku jōyaku ··· 安政五か国条約 ··· 1:63a
Ansei Purge ··· 安政の大獄 ··· 1:63a-64a
general description ··· 1:63a-63b
Harris Treaty ··· 1:63b
Hashimoto Sanai ··· 3:110a
Ii Naosuke ··· 3:263a
levels ··· 1:63b
Sakuradamongai Incident ··· 1:63b; 7:4b
shogunal succession ··· 1:63b
sonnō jōi ··· 5:156a-156b
Umeda Umpin ··· 8:146b
Yoshida Shōin ··· 8:346a
Antarctic research ··· 1:64a-64b
history ··· 1:64a
Japanese Antarctic Research Expedition (JARE) ··· 1:64a
present status ··· 1:64a
special features ··· 1:64a
Antenna ··· 2:192a
Anthologies
imperial. *See* **Imperial anthologies**
Man' yōshū. *See* **Man'yōshū**
"unofficial" or private (shisenshū) ··· 8:204a
Anthologies of the Thirty-six Poetic Geniuses ··· 1:234b, *234b*
Anthropological Association (Anthropological Society of Nippon), ··· 8:110a
Anthropological Association of Tōkyō ··· 1:77a
Anthropologists
Adachi Buntarō ··· 1:11a

Benedict, Ruth Fulton ········ **1**:149b
Embree, John Fee ········ **2**:200a
Hasebe Kotondo ········ **3**:106b
Imanishi Kinji ········ **3**:274a
Ishida Eiichirō ········ **3**:340a
Izumi Seiichi ········ **3**:366a
Kida Minoru ········ **4**:202a
Kiyono Kenji ········ **4**:232b
Koganei Yoshikiyo ········ **4**:248a
Nakane Chie ········ **7**:218a
Torii Ryūzō ········ **8**:79a
Tsuboi Shōgorō ········ **8**:110a
Anti-Christian edicts ···· **1**:64b-65a; **3**:185b
Azuchi-Momoyama
Oda Nobunaga ········ **1**:64b
Toyotomi Hideyoshi ········ **1**:64b
Edo period
Madre de Deus Incident ········ **1**:65a
Tokugawa Ieyasu ········ **1**:65a
Nagasaki trade ········ **5**:306a
National Seclusion ········ **5**:346b
Ōmura Sumitada ········ **6**:104b
Ōtomo Sōrin ········ **6**:132b
Takayama Ukon ········ **7**:321a
Anti-Comintern Pact ······ **1**:65a-65b, 88a; **2**:332b; **3**:202a; **8**:272a, 344a
international relations ········ **3**:321b
Ōshima Hiroshi ········ **6**:125b
Russia and Japan ········ **6**:343a
Russo-Japanese fisheries ········ **6**:345b
Tripartite Pact ········ **8**:107a
Anticommunism ········ **7**:201b-202a
Antimonopoly Law (1947) ····· **1**:65b-67b; **4**:378b; **8**:363a
administrative guidance ········ **1**:12b
cartels ········ **1**:66b, 245a
computer industry ········ **1**:345a
enforcement procedures ········ **1**:67b
holding companies ········ **3**:216a; **4**:189b
industrial organizations ········ **3**:293b
merger, corporate ········ **5**:164a
private monopolization ········ **1**:65b-66b
control ········ **1**:66a
definition ········ **1**:65b
exclusion ········ **1**:65b
mergers ········ **1**:66a-66b
particular field of trade ········ **1**:66a
public interest ········ **1**:66a
stock acquisitions ········ **1**:66a-66b
unfair business practices ········ **1**:67a-67b
abuse of economic power ········ **1**:67a-67b
coercion ········ **1**:67a
definition ········ **1**:67a
discriminatory acts ········ **1**:67a
inducement ········ **1**:67a
price setting ········ **1**:67a
restrictive agreements ········ **1**:67a
unreasonable restraint
cartel agreements ········ **1**:66b
definition ········ **1**:66b
exemptions ········ **1**:66b
trade associations ········ **1**:66b
unreasonable restraint of trade ·· **1**:66b-67a
Anti-Russia Fellow Activists' Society ········ **7**:303a
"Antislavery" law ········ **6**:257a
Antiwar movement. *See* **Peace movement**
Antoku, Emperor 安徳天皇 ···· **1**:40a, 67b; **4**:1a
Ants [(ari) family Formicidae] ·· **1**:67b-68a
An'ya kōro ······ 暗夜行路 ········ **4**:114a
Anzai Fuyue ····· 安西冬衛 ········ **1**:68a
Anzai Masaru. *See* **Anzai Fuyue**
ANZUS Pact ········ **1**:117a-117b
Aobeka monogatari ········ あおべか物語 ········ **8**:299b
Aōdō Denzen ·· 亜欧堂田善 ········ **1**:68a
Aohon ········ 青本 ·· **4**:201b, 319b
Aoi Bunko. *See* **Aoi Library**
Aoi Festival ········ 葵祭 · **1**:68a; **2**:*253a*, **4**:130a, 164a, 174a, 336b
Aoi getsuyōbi ·· 青い月曜日 ········ **4**:111b
Aoi Library ········ 葵文庫 ····· **1**:68a-68b
Aoi Matsuri. *See* **Aoi Festival**
Aoi sammyaku (Blue Mountains) ····· 青い山脈 ········ **6**:221b
Aoki [(Japanese laurel) *Aucuba japonica*] ········ **1**:68b
Aoki-Kimberley Treaty ········ **7**:198a
Aoki Kon'yō ····· 青木昆陽 ········ **1**:68b
Aoki Mokubei ···· 青木木米 ··· **1**:68b, 211a
Aoki Shigeru ······ 青木繁 ········ **1**:69a
education ········ **1**:69a; **6**:155b
romanticism ········ **1**:69a
seascapes ········ **1**:69a
Umi no Sachi (Gifts of the Sea) ···· **1**:*69a-69b*
Wadatsumi no iroko no miya ········ **1**:69a
Aoki Shūzō ······ 青木周蔵 **1**:57b, 69a-69b
shigi kempō ········ **7**:92b
Aomori ········ 青森 ········ **1**:69b
Aomori ken no semushi otoko (The Hunchback of Aomori) ········ 青森県のせむし男 ········ **8**:13a
Aomori Prefectural Museum ········ **1**:69b
Aomori Prefecture ·青森県 ····· **1**:69b-70a
economy ········ **1**:70a
festivals ········ **1**:70a
geographical description ········ **1**:69b
tourist attractions ········ **1**:70a
Aoneko ········ 青猫 ········ **3**:76a
Aonodōmon ····· 青ノ洞門 ········ **1**:70a
Aono Suekichi ··· 青野季吉 ···· **1**:70a-70b; **5**:13a
political involvements ········ **1**:70b
principal works ········ **1**:70b
Aoshima ········ 青島 ········ **1**:70b
Aoto Fujitsuna ··· 青砥藤綱 ····· **1**:70b-71a
Aoto-zōshi hana no nishiki-e ········ **4**:*95a*
Aoyagi Tanenobu 青柳種信 ········ **1**:76b
Aoyama Gakuin University ········ **1**:71a
Aoyama Tanemichi ········ 青山胤通 ········ **1**:71a
Apartment living ········ **5**:6a
Aporon no shima ········ アポロンの島 ········ **6**:69b
"Apostate's oath" ········ **7**:186b
Apparel. *See* Clothing
Appeals (Jōso) ········ **2**:51a
Appellate courts ········ **4**:81a
Apples [(ringo) *Malus pumila*] ······ **1**:71a
Appliance industries **1**:298a; **3**:207a; **4**:52b; **5**:141b; **7**:14a
Apprentice system ········ **1**:71a-71b
April 16th Incident ········ **1**:71b
Tanaka Giichi ········ **7**:336a-336b
Aquapolis ········ **4**:207b
Aquariums ········ **1**:71b
history ········ **1**:71b
number and location ········ **1**:71b
Arabian Oil Co, Ltd ····· **1**:71b-72a; **6**:182a
Aragoto ········ 荒事 ········ **3**:257a; **4**:91a-91b, 97b
Arahata Kanson ·荒畑寒村 ···· **1**:72a-72b, 155a
Japan Communist Party ······ **1**:72a; **4**:11a
Japan Socialist Party ········ **1**:72a
Kanno Suga ········ **4**:145b
labor movement ········ **1**:72a
Red Flag Incident ········ **6**:285a
socialism ········ **1**:72a
works ········ **1**:72a-72b
Arahitogami ········ 現人神 ········ **6**:204b
Arai (city) ········ 新井 ········ **1**:72b
Arai, Clarence ········ **4**:15b
Arai Hakuseki ··· 新井白石 ····· **1**:72b-73a
concept of periodization ········ **3**:155a
historiography ········ **3**:155a
political program ········ **1**:72b
Shōtoku no Chi ········ **7**:171a
training and samurai service ········ **1**:72b
works ········ **1**:72b-73a
Confucianism ········ **1**:73a
historical ········ **1**:73a
Arainegi ········ **2**:25a
Arai Ōsui ········ 新井奥邃 ········ **1**:73a
education ········ **1**:73a
evangelical activities ········ **1**:73a
Harris, Thomas Lake ········ **1**:73a; **3**:104a
visit to United States ········ **1**:73a
writings ········ **1**:73a
Arajotai (The New Household)
Tokuda Shūsei ········ **8**:45a
Arakawa ········ 荒川 ···· **1**:73a-73b, 272a
Arakawa Toyozō ·荒川豊蔵 ········ **1**:73b
Arakawa Ward ····· 荒川区 ········ **1**:73b
Arakida Moritake ········ 荒木田守武 ········ **1**:73b
Arakida Rei ······ 荒木田麗 ····· **1**:73b-74a
Arakida Reijo ·荒木田麗女 ····· **1**:73b-74a
novels ········ **1**:73b-74a
poetry ········ **1**:73b-74a
style ········ **1**:73b-74a
Araki Mataemon ········ 荒木又右衛門 ········ **3**:108a
Araki Moriaki ···· 荒木守晨 ········ **4**:194b
Araki Sadao ····· 荒木貞夫 ········ **1**:74a
February 26th Incident ········ **2**:250a
gumbatsu ········ **3**:66a-66b
Kōdōha leader ········ **4**:243a
Araki Sōtarō ··· 荒木宗太郎 ········ **1**:74a
Arakurekai ········ **5**:19a
Ara Masahito ······ 荒正人 ········ **1**:74a; **5**:316b-317a
Arao ········ 荒尾 ········ **1**:74b
Araragi ········ アララギ ·· **1**:74b; **7**:28b, 99b
Koizumi Chikashi ········ **4**:250b
Orikuchi Shinobu ········ **6**:118b
Saitō Mokichi ········ **6**:374a
Shimaki Akahito ········ **7**:99b
Araragi school ·アララギ派 ········ **5**:19b
Arashi Kanjūrō ··嵐寛寿郎 ········ **1**:74b
Arashi no nagori ········ あらしのなごり ········ **6**:332b
Arashiyama ········ 嵐山 ·· **1**:74b; **6**:*24b*
Aratama Michiyo 新珠三千代 ····· **2**:*273a*
Arbitration ······ **1**:74b-75a; **2**:118b; **4**:349b
Tripartite commissions ········ **4**:351b
Arc ········ **7**:324b
Archaeological museums ···· **5**:277b-278a
Archaeological sites and remains
Fukui Cave ········ **2**:363b
Heijō Palace site ········ **3**:124a
Hoshino ········ **3**:235a
Iba ········ **3**:253b
Iha shell mound ········ **3**:262a
Ishibutai tomb ········ **3**:339b
Iwajuku ········ **3**:358a
Kamegaoka ········ **4**:125a
Karako ········ **4**:157b
Kasori shell mounds ········ **4**:163b
Moyoro shell mound ········ **5**:261b
Mukōgaoka shell mound ········ **5**:262b
Nintoku Mausoleum ········ **6**:8a-8b
Nogawa ········ **6**:31a
Ojin Mausoleum ········ **6**:76b
Okinoshima site ········ **6**:92b
Ōmori shell mounds ········ **6**:103b
Ōyu Stone Circles ········ **6**:138b-139a
Suku ········ **7**:266a
Takamatsuzuka tomb ········ **7**:314b-315a

Togariishi ········ 8:35b-36a
Toro ········ 8:80b
Archaeological Society (Archaeological Society of Nippon) ········ 1:77a, 179b
Archaeologists
Aizawa Tadahiro ········ 1:38a
Gotō Shuichi ········ 3:54a-54b
Hamada Kōsaku ········ 3:89b
Harada Yoshito ········ 3:100b
Kobayashi Yukio ········ 8:306b
Miyake Yonekichi ········ 5:219a
Morimoto Rokuji ········ 5:250b
Takahashi Kenji ········ 7:312a; 8:306b
Torii Ryūzō ········ 8:79a
Tsuboi Shōgorō ········ 8:110a
Umehara Sueji ········ 8:147a, 306b
Yamanouchi Sugao ········ 8:302b
Archaeology ········ 1:75a-80b
haniwa ········ 3:97b-98a
inscriptions ········ 3:313b-314a
Jōmon culture ········ 4:72a-74a
kofun ········ 4:244a-246a
mokkan (wooden tablets) ········ 5:234a
Okhotsk culture ········ 6:83b-84a
Paleolithic culture ········ 6:159b-160a
Satsumon culture ········ 7:30b
shell mounds ········ 7:82b-83a
studies. *See* Archaeology, studies of
Yayoi culture ········ 8:321a-322a
Archaeology, studies of
general characteristics ········ 1:75a
excavations ········ 1:75a
popular and governmental support 1:75a
scholarly discipline ········ 1:75a
historical ········ 1:79a-80b
early period ········ 1:79a
formal establishment (1926-1945) · 1:79b
late 19th and early 20th century ········ 1:79a-79b
new trends in ········ 1:80a
postwar period ········ 1:79b
ideographs ········ 4:142b-143a
inscriptions ········ 3:313b-314a
prehistoric ········ 1:75a-76a
early period ········ 1:75a-75b
modern period ········ 1:75b
protohistoric ········ 1:76a-79a
early period ········ 1:76a-76b
early 20th century: typological and chronological studies ········ 1:77a-78a
immediate postwar period: academic excavations and research ········ 1:77a-78a
late 19th century: postrestoration innovations ········ 1:76b-77a
recent developments: salvage excavations and tomb preservations ········ 1:78b-79a
shell mounds ········ 7:82b-83a
Archery (kyūdō) ········ 4:340a
contests (tōshiya) ········ 7:13a-13b
civil ········ 4:340a-340b
military ········ 4:340a-340b
mounted (yabusame) ········ 8:283a-283b
Archipelago
administrative divisions ········ 4:2b
remodeling plan ········ 5:381b
territory ········ 4:2b
Architects
Bertin, Louis-Emile ········ 1:150a
Conder, Josiah ········ 1:349b
Horiguchi Sutemi ········ 3:227b
Isozaki Arata ········ 3:348a
Kikutake Kiyonori ········ 4:207b
Kobori Enshū ········ 4:238b
Kurokawa Kishō ········ 4:316b
Maekawa Kunio ········ 5:82a
Maki Fumihiko ········ 5:85b
Murano Tōgo ········ 5:267a
Raymond, Antonin ········ 6:284b
Satō Takeo ········ 7:28b
Shirai Seiichi ········ 7:145b
Tange Kenzō ········ 7:340b
Taniguchi Yoshirō ········ 7:341b
Tatsuno Kingo ········ 7:349b
Taut, Bruno ········ 7:351a-351b
Waters, Thomas James ········ 8:237a
Wright, Frank Lloyd ········ 8:279a
Yoshida Isoya ········ 8:341a
Yoshimura Junzō ········ 8:348a
Architectural Institute of Japan ········ 1:81b; 7:349b
Architectural Standards Law ········ 1:80b
ownership rights ········ 6:137a
Architecture ········ 1:80b-82b
bridges ········ 1:170a-170b
Buddhist ········ 1:182a-184b
Genshin ········ 1:189b
Pure Land ········ 1:189b
castles (shiro) ········ 1:245b-249a
domestic ········ 7:110a-111a
gates ········ 3:12a-13a
esoteric Buddhist ········ 1:188a
gasshō-zukuri
Shirakawa ········ 7:146b
gates ········ 3:12a, 13a
Karayō ········ 1:191b
Mahāyāna Buddhist ········ 1:185b
modern ········ 1:80b-81b, *81a*
post-World War II ········ 1:81a-81b
naval
Hiraga Yuzuru ········ 3:142b
Yamagata Masao ········ 8:293b
new style ········ 7:33a
Nippon ········ 7:351b
residential ········ 7:162a-163a
Rokumeikan ········ 6:335a
rural, Hida Folklore Village ········ 3:129b
schools ········ 7:33a-33b
Shinden-zukuri mode ········ 1:189b
Shintō art ········ 7:135b
Shoin-zukuri style ········ 1:227a
storehouses ········ 7:248a
Sukiya-zukuri techniques ········ 1:81a
temple gates ········ 3:12a
traditional domestic ········ 1:81b-82b
climate ········ 1:81b
construction ········ 1:81b-82a
elements ········ 3:244a
materials ········ 1:81b-82a
shoin-zukuri ········ 7:162a-163b
spatial concepts ········ 1:82a-82b
unit of measure ········ 1:82b
Western influence ········ 1:80b-81a
Bank of Japan Building ········ 1:140b
criticism ········ 1:80b
Meiji Restoration ········ 1:80b
Zen ········ 1:191b-192a
Archives ········ 5:336a-336b
Archives and Mausolea Department, Imperial Household Agency ········ 1:82b; 8:381b
Archives of Great Japan ········ 2:65a
Arechi ········ 荒地 ········ 1:82b-83a
founding ········ 1:125b-126a
Argot ········ 3:303b-304a
Ari ········ 1:67b-68a
Ariake Bay ········ 有明湾 ········ 1:83a, *83a*
Aribaba ········ アリババ ········ 4:157b
Arida ········ 有田 ········ 1:83a
Aridagawa ········ 有田川 ········ 1:83a
Arige Kemi ········ 有毛検見 ········ 4:191a
Arikata no kotoba ········ 有形の言葉 ········ 7:281a
Arima, Prince ········ 有間皇子 ········ 1:83b-84a
Arima Harunobu · 有馬晴信 ········ 1:83a-83b; 7:98b
alliances ········ 1:83b
Christian daimyō ········ 1:305b
conversion to Christianity ········ 1:83a-83b
exile and death ········ 1:83b
foreign involvements ········ 1:83b
Arima Hot Spring 有馬温泉 ········ 1:83b
Arima Ineko ········ 有馬稲子 ········ 1:83b
Arima Shinshichi 有馬新七 ········ 1:84a
Arima Yoriyasu ·· 有馬頼寧 ········ 1:84a
Arisaka Hideyo ·· 有坂秀世 ········ 1:84a
Arisawa Hiromi ·· 有沢広巳 ········ 1:84a-84b
Arishima Ikumitsu ········ 有島行光 ········ 5:250a
Arishima Takeo ·· 有島武郎 ········ 1:84b-85a; 7:27b, 103b, 109a
death ········ 1:84b-85a
humanism ········ 1:84b
Shirakaba school ········ 7:145b-146a
works ········ 1:84b
Aristocracy ········ 6:170a
Aristocratic age ········ 3:152a-153b
periodization ········ 6:176b
Arisugawa no Miya Taruhito 有栖川宮熾仁親王 ·· 1:85a, 165a; 7:16b
Arita ········ 有田 ········ 1:85a
Arita Hachirō ········ 有田八郎 ········ 1:20b, 85a; 7:92a
Arita ware ········ 有田焼 1:85a-85b, *85a, 260b*; 4:337a
museums ········ 5:279b
Wagener, Gottfried ········ 8:199a
Ariwara family ········ 在原氏 ········ 1:85b
Ariwara no Narihira ········ 在原業平 ········ 1:85b-86a; 7:13a; 8:208b
Ise monogatari ········ 3:337a
Kokinshū ········ 4:254b
Kokinshū criticism ········ 1:85b
Rokkasen ········ 6:334b
Ariyoshi Sawako ········ 有吉佐和子 · 1:86a; 7:103b
Armed forces, imperial Japanese ········ 1:86b-88b
China War (Sino-Japanese War of 1937-1945) ········ 1:88a-88b; 7:198a-202a
civilian control ········ 1:88a
disarmament era ········ 1:88a
foreign models ········ 1:85a
founding ········ 1:86a-86b
conscription ········ 1:86a-86b
Japanese independence ········ 1:86a-86b
sonnō jōi ········ 1:86a
imperial expansion ········ 1:87a
Korea ········ 1:87a; 4:287a-287b
Russian threat ········ 1:87a
size of military ········ 1:87a
militarism ········ 5:173a-175a
militarism era ········ 1:88a; 5:173a-175a
national defense policy, split ········ 1:87b
"Advance to the North" group ········ 1:87b
"Advance to the South" group ········ 1:87b; 7:236a-237a
Pacific War and dissolution of military
defeat ········ 1:88b
Potsdam Declaration ········ 1:88b
size of military ········ 1:88b
Russo-Japanese War ········ 1:87b
Sino-Japanese War ········ 1:87b
supreme command ········ 1:86b-87a; 8:85a
Army General Staff Office ········ 1:87a
Imperial Headquarters ········ 1:87a; 2:58b
independence of ········ 1:86a
Naval General Staff Office 1:87a; 5:358b
World War I ········ 1:87b-88a
World War II ········ 8:271b

Armor 1:89b
- dōmaru or haramaki type 1:89b
- dyes and dye colors 2:136a-136b
- Kofun period 1:89b
- ōyoroi 1:89b
- tōsei gusoku 1:90a

Arms and armor 1:88b-89b, *90a-90b*
- armor. *See* Armor
- bows 1:89b
- early weapons 1:89a
- firearms 1:89b; 2:279a-279b
- jitte 1:90a
- kusarigama 1:90a
- museums 5:280a
- naginata 1:89a-89b
- possession 1:88b-89a
- saddlery 1:90a
- sasumata 1:90a
- shields 1:89b
- sodegarami 1:90a
- spears 1:89b
- swords 1:89a; 7:285a-288a
- tetsubō 1:90a

Arms Export, Three Principles of 1:90a-90b
Army, Imperial. *See* **Armed forces, imperial Japanese**
Army Academy 1:90b
- National Defense Academy 5:338b

Army Academy Incident 6:41b-42a
Army camps 1:292a
Army Day 6:347a
Army General Staff Office 1:90b-91a
- independence 1:87a
- power 8:85a
- Sugiyama Hajime 7:258b

Army Ministry 1:91a
- Navy Ministry 5:358b

"Arranged marriage" (miai) 5:320b
Arrest (taiho) 2:49b
Arsenals 3:210a
Arsenic poisoning 6:219a
Art 1:91a-91b
- aesthetics 1:18a-19a
- architecture, traditional domestic 1:81b-82b
- bonsai 1:161b-163a
- Buddhist architecture 1:182a-184b
- Buddhist art 1:184b-194b
- Buddhist sculpture 1:197a-204a
- bunjinga 1:210a-211a
- calligraphy 1:232b-236b
- ceramics 1:256a-265b
- crests 2:42a-43b
- design 2:88a-90a
- emakimono 2:198a-200a
- flower arrangement 2:288a-292a
- folk crafts 2:293b-296a
- folk pictures
  - ōtsu-e 6:133b-134a
- gardens 3:8a-11b
- influence of China 1:91a
- ink painting 3:305b-307b
- inrō 3:313a-313b
- lacquer ware 4:360b-362a
- masks 1:93a, 197a; 5:125b-127b
- merging with religion 1:18b
- modern prints 5:232a-233b
- namban art 5:322a-323a
- netsuke 5:363a-365a
- painting 6:147b-159a
- photography 6:185a-186a
- religious symbolism 6:295b-296a
- screen and wall painting 7:41a-43b
- Shintō architecture 7:132a-134a
- Shinto art 7:134b-137b
- Shōsōin art repository 1:184b, 200b; 7:168a-170a
- shunga 7:187a-188a
- swords 7:285a-288a
- textiles 8:16b-20a
- tie-dyeing 8:29b
- tsuba 8:108a-109b
- ukiyo-e 8:138a-144a
- zenga 8:374b-375a

Arte Breve da Lingoa Iapoa 6:334a
Arte da Lingoa de Iapam 6:334a
Articles of incorporation
- limited liability company 5:10a
- limited partnership company 5:10b

Artisans 7:165a
Artistic names 5:325a-326a
Artists. *See* Painters
Artists' Alliance of Farmers and Workers 7:175a
Art Theatre Guild of Japan Co, Ltd 1:91b; 2:275b
Aruga Kizaemon 有賀喜左衛門 1:91b
Aru hareta hi ni ある晴れた日に 4:169b
Aru onna 或る女 1:84b
Aru otoko 或る男 4:114a
Asa 1:91b
Asabuki Eiji 朝吹英二 1:91b-92a
Asada Gōryū 麻田剛立 1:92a
Asada Sōhaku 浅田宗伯 1:92a
Asagao 5:255a
Asagaoichi 5:255a
Asa-gasuri 4:164b
Asagiri gunka (War Song of the Morning Mist) 朝霧軍歌 8:319b
Asahi 旭 1:92a
Asahi Breweries, Ltd 1:92a; 4:221a
Asahi Chemical Industry Co, Ltd 1:92a-92b; 7:57b
Asahi chōja 朝日長者 7:269b
Asahi Denka Kōgyō 1:92b
Asahigawa 旭川 1:92b
Asahi Glass Co, Ltd 1:92b
Asahikawa 旭川 1:92b
Asahi Mountains 朝日山地 1:92b-93a, 136b
Asahi National Broadcasting Co, Ltd 1:92a, 93a, 172b, 173b
Asahina Yasuhiko 朝比奈泰彦 1:93a, 268a
Asahi Optical Co, Ltd 1:93a
Asahi Pentax 1:93a
Asahi shimbun 朝日新聞 1:18a, 93a-93b; 2:371b; 4:139b; 5:128b, 369b-370a; 7:258a
- founding 1:93a
- Ikebe Sanzan 3:264b
- other publications 1:93b
- Rice Riots of 1918 1:93a
- self-censorship 1:253a

Asahi ware 朝日焼 1:93b
- Kobori Enshū 4:238b
- Wagener, Gottfried 8:199a

Asai Chū 浅井忠 1:93b
- Fontanesi, Antonio 2:304a

Asai family 浅井氏 1:93b-94a
Asai Nagamasa 浅井長政 1:94a; 7:84b
Asai Ryōi 浅井了意 1:94a; 5:46a
- *Ukiyo monogatari* 4:136b

Asaka (city) 朝霞 1:94a
Asaka Canal 安積疏水 1:94a; 4:293b
- Inawashiro, Lake 3:283b

Asakasha あさ香社 5:19b
Asaka Tampaku 安積澹泊 1:94b
Asakawa Kan'ichi 朝河貫一 1:94a
Asakura family 朝倉氏 1:94a; 7:84a
- fortress 2:363b
- mansion excavation 1:80a-80b

Asakura Fumio 朝倉文夫 1:94b
Asakura Takakage Jōjō 朝倉孝景条々 1:94b
Asakura Toshikage, 17-Article Code of 朝倉敏景十七箇条 1:94b-95a
- kabegaki 4:90a

Asakura Yoshikage 朝倉義景 1:95a; 7:84b
Asakusa Bunko 浅草文庫 1:95a-95b; 5:1a
Asakusa Kannon (Sensōji) 8:*63a*
Asakusa Kurenaidan 浅草紅団 4:176a; 7:175b
Asama Hot Spring 浅間温泉 1:95b
Asamayama 浅間山 1:*95a*, 95b
- Onioshidashi 6:107b

Asami Keisai 浅見絅斎 1:95b; 7:27b
- *Seiken igen* 7:51b

Asamushi Hot Spring 浅虫温泉 1:95b
Asan Mountains 阿讃山脈 7:18b
Asano Cement. *See* **Nihon Cement Co, Ltd**
Asano Nagamasa 浅野長政 1:95b
Asano Naganori 浅野長矩 2:327a
Asano Sōichirō 浅野総一郎 1:95b-96a; 7:52a
Asano Yoshinaga 浅野幸長 1:96a
Asano zaibatsu 浅野財閥 1:95b
Asanuma Gumi Co, Ltd 1:96a
Asanuma Inejirō 浅沼稲次郎 1:96a
"Asanuma statement" 1:96a
Asaoka Ruriko 浅丘ルリ子 2:*275a*
Asayama Bontō 朝山梵燈 1:96a-96b
Asayama Nichijō 朝山日乗 1:96b
Asceticism 1:96b
- organizing 7:182a
- kugyō 1:96b
- mountain 8:287b
- present day Japan 1:96b
- shamanism 7:76b
- shugyō 1:96b

ASEAN and Japan 1:96b-97a; 2:309a; 3:324b
Asebi [(Japanese andromeda) *Pieris japonica*] 1:97a
Ash-glazed wares 1:261b-262a
Ashibetsu 芦別 1:97a
Ashibetsudake 芦別岳 1:97a; 8:354b
Ashibi 馬酔木 1:74b; 4:169b; 5:307b
Ashida Enosuke 芦田恵之助 1:97a-97b
- Seikatsu Tsuzurikata Undō development 7:51a

Ashida Hitoshi 芦田均 1:97b
- Japan Socialist Party 4:48a

Ashide 葦手 1:97b
Ashigaru 足軽 1:97b-98a
- yoriki 8:338b

Ashihara Yoshishige 芦原義重 1:98a
Ashikaga (city) 足利 1:98b
- silk weaving 2:296a

Ashikaga family 足利氏 1:98b-99b; 7:25b
- Ashikaga Yoshimitsu 1:99a
- decline of shogunate 1:99b
- Muromachi history 1:99a; 3:172b
- origins 1:99a
- Patrons of the Arts 1:99b
- rivalry for leadership 3:173b
- Shiba family branch 7:83b

Ashikaga Gakkō · 足利学校 · · · 1:99b-100a, 151b; 4:136a
education · 2:172b
Ashikaga Gakkō Bunko
· · · · · · · · · · · · · 足利学校文庫 · · · · · · · · · · 5:1a
Ashikaga Gakkō Iseki Toshokan
· · · · · · 足利学校遺跡図書館 · · · · · · · · 1:100a
Ashikaga Masatomo. 足利政知
See **Horikoshi Kubō**
Ashikaga military government
decrees (tokusei) · · · · · · · · · · · · · · · · · · 8:58b
Ashikaga Mochiuji
· · · · · · · · · · · · · · · · 足利持氏 · · · · · · · · · 1:99b
Uesugi Norizane · · · · · · · · · · · · · · · · · · · 8:130a
Ashikaga shogunate. *See* **Muromachi shogunate**
Ashikaga Tadayoshi
· · · · · · · · · · · · · · · · 足利直義 · · · · · · · · 1:100a
Kannō Disturbance · · · · · · · · · · · · · · · 4:144b
Ashikaga Takauji 足利尊氏 · · · · · · · · · 1:40a, 100a-101a; 2:204b; 2:265a; 8:341b, 356a
betrayal · 4:192a
Genkō Incident · 3:21a
Kanenaga, Prince · · · · · · · · · · · · 4:139b-140a
Kannō Disturbance · · · · · · · · · · · · · · · · 4:144b
Kemmu Restoration · · · · · · · · · · · · · · · 4:191a
Muromachi shogunate · · · · · · · · · · · · · 5:271b
portrait · 1:*100b*
Sasaki Takauji · 7:23b
Shiba family · 7:84a
warrior government · · · · · · · · · · · · · · · 8:229b
Ashikaga Yoshiaki
· · · · · · · · · · · · · · · · 足利義昭 · · · · · · · 1:101b; 3:172b, 178b
Shinchō kō ki · 7:109b
Ashikaga Yoshimasa
· · · · · · · · · · · · · · · · 足利義政 1:101a; 3:173a; 7:67a; 8:301b
Higashiyama culture · · · · · · · · · · · · · · 3:132b
Hino Tomiko · 3:141a
posthumous portraits · · · · · · · · · · · · · · 4:147b
shinden-zukuri · · · · · · · · · · · · · · · · · · · 7:110b
Ashikaga Yoshimitsu
· · · · · · · · · · · · · · · · 足利義満 · · · · · · · · · 1:99a, 101a-101b; 2:204b, 265a
China · 1:283b
Kaei sandai ki · · · · · · · · · · · · · · · · · · · 4:101b
Kan'ami · 4:135b
Kitayama culture · · · · · · · · · · · · · · · · · · 4:229a
tally trade · 7:331b
Ashikaga Yoshimochi
· · · · · · · · · · · · · · · · 足利義持 · · 1:99a; 3:173a
Ashikaga Yoshinori
· · · · · · · · · · · · · · · · 足利義教 · · · 1:99a, 101b; 3:174a
assassination · · · · · · · · · · · · · · · · · · 4:196b-197a
Ashikari · · · · · · · · · · · · · 蘆刈 · · · · · · · · 7:342b
Ashinoko · · · · · · · · · · · 芦ノ湖 · · · · · · · 1:101b; 2:342b; 3:*86a*
Ashio · · · · · · · · · · · · · · · · · 足尾 · · · · · · · · 1:101b
Ashio Copper Mine
· · · · · · · · · · · · · · · 足尾銅山 · · · 2:372a-372b
Ashio Copper Mine Incident · · · · · ·
· · · · · · · 足尾銅山鉱毒事件 · · · 1:73a, 102b; 4:349b; 7:99a
Fukuda Hideko · · · · · · · · · · · · · 2:362a-362b
Tanaka Shōzō · · · · · · · · · · · · · · · · 7:338b-339b
Yokohama mainichi shimbun · · · · · · · · · 8:330a
Ashio Copper Mine labor dispute · 1:102a
Ashio Kōdoku Jiken. *See* **Ashio Copper Mine Incident**
Ashiya (Honshū) · · · · · 芦屋 · · · · · · · · 1:102a
Ashiya (Kyūshū) · · · · · · 芦屋 · · · · · · · · 1:102a
Ashizurimisaki · · · · · 足摺岬 1:102a; 7:334a
Ashizuri-Uwakai National Park 足摺宇和海国立公園 · · · · · · · · 1:102b
Ashura · 4:244*b*
Asia
culture · 7:177b-179a
Japanese immigration · · · · · · · · 2:362a-362b
Japanese studies · · · · · · · · · · · · · · · · · · · 4:44b
Asia Development Board · · · · · · · · · · 1:102b
Asia faction
Shigemitsu Mamoru · · · · · · · · · · · 7:91b-92b
Asian American concept · · · · · · · · · · · · 4:14b
Asian Americans · 4:14b
Asian Games · 1:102b
Asian Relations Conference · · · · · · · · · 1:19b
Asia Trade Development Association
· 3:319b
Aso · · · · · · · · · · · · · · · · · 阿蘇 · · · · · · · · 1:102b
Asobase-kotoba · 2:251a
Asō Hisashi · · · · · · · · 麻生久 · · · 1:102b-103a
Shakai Taishūtō · 7:74b
Shinjinkai · 7:115b
Ason · · · · · · · · · · · · · · · · · · 朝臣 · · · · · · · · 1:103a
Aso National Park
· · · · · · · · · · · · 阿蘇国立公園 · · · · · · · · 1:103a
Asosan · · · · · · · · · · · · · 阿蘇山 · · 1:103a, *103a*
Aso Shrine · · · · · · · 阿蘇神社 · · · · · · · · 1:103b
Aso Volcanic Zone · · · · · · · · · · · · · · · · 7:346a
Assembly and Political Association Law (Shūkai Oyobi Seisha Hō) · · · · · · · 6:266a
Assembly of Prefectural Governors
· 1:103b; 4:203a; 7:16b
Association for Mystery Writers of Japan · 2:170b
Association for the Study of Materialism (Yuibutsuron Kenkyūkai) · · · · · · · · · · 8:81b
Association of American Libraries · 6:269a
Association of Booksellers · · · · · · · · · · 6:268a
Association of Eastern European Studies · 2:142b
Association of Japanese Geographers
· 1:103b
Kiuchi Shinzō · 4:231b
tachimono · 7:293b
Association of Patriotic Japanese Literature · 7:176b
Association of Southeast Asian Nations. *See* **ASEAN and Japan**
Assumption of risk · · · · · · · · · · · · 1:103b-104a
Aston, William George · · · · · · · · · · · · 1:104a
Astrology
On'yōryō · 6:113b
Astronomical observatories · · · · · · · 1:104a
Kwasan (Kasan) Astronomical Observatory · 1:104a
Latitude Observatory of Mizusawa · 1:104a
Tōkyō Astronomical Observatory · · 1:104a
Astronomy · 1:104a-104b
history of studies · · · · · · · · · · · · 1:104a-104b
On'yōryō · 6:113b
Publications of The Astronomical Society of Japan · 1:104b
recent developments · · · · · · · · · · · · · · · 1:104b
celestial physics · · · · · · · · · · · · · · · · · 1:104b
radio astronomy · · · · · · · · · · · · · · · · · · 1:104b
universities training researchers · · 1:104b
Asuka (region) · · · · · · · 飛鳥 · · · 1:105a-105b
Asuka (village) · · · · 明日香 · · · 1:104b-105a
Asukabehime · · · · · · · · · 安宿媛 · · · · · · · · 4:268b
Asuka culture · · · · 飛鳥文化 · · · · · · · · 1:105b
Asuka Daibutsu · · 飛鳥大仏 · · · · · · · · · 2:55b
Asukadera · · · · · · · · · · · 飛鳥寺 · · 1:105b-106b, 182a; 7:85a
history · 1:106a
temple · 1:106a
excavation · 1:106a
Asukagawa · · · · · · · · 飛鳥川 · · · · · · · · 1:106b
Asuka Historical Museum · · · · · · · · · 5:333b
Asuka history. *See* **History of Japan**
Asukai Masaari 飛鳥井雅有 · · · · · · · · 1:106b
Asukai Masatsune
· · · · · · · · · · · · · · · · 飛鳥井雅経 · · 1:106b-107a; 5:41a
Shin kokinshū · 7:119b
Asuka Kiyomihara Code
· · · · · · · · · · 飛鳥浄御原律令 · · 1:107a, 151a
Dajōkan · 2:69b
ritsuryō system · · · · · · · · · · · · · · · · · · · 6:331a
Taika Reform · 7:295b
Asuka Kiyomihara no Miya · · · · · · · 飛鳥浄御原宮 1:107a; 2:350a
Asuka period · · · · 飛鳥時代 · · · · · · · · · 1:107a
Asukata Ichio · 飛鳥田一雄 · · · · · · · · 1:107b
Japan Socialist Party · · · · · · · · · · · · 4:48a-49a
Atae · 直 · · · 4:89a, 310a
Atagawa Hot Spring
· · · · · · · · · · · · · · · · · · 熱川温泉 1:107b; 2:342b
Atago Daigongen
· · · · · · · · · · · · · · · · · 愛宕大権現 · · · · · · · · 1:107b
Atago Jinja · · · · · · 愛宕神社 · · · · · · · · · 1:107b
Atago Shrine · · · · 愛宕神社 · · · · · · · · · 1:107b
Atagoyama · · · · · · · · · 愛宕山 · · · · · · · · 1:107b
Tamba Mountains · · · · · · · · · · · · · · · · · 7:333a
Ataka · · · · · · · · · · · · · · · · · · 安宅 · · · · · · · · · 4:98a
Atami · · · · · · · · · · · · · · · · · 熱海 · · · · · · · · · 1:107b
Atarashiki Mura · · 新しき村 · · · 5:281a-281b
Atarashiki tsuchi · 新しき土 · · · · · · · · · 3:102b
Athenée Français · · · · · · · · · · · · · · · · · 2:332b
Ātman · 1:176b
Atomic bomb · · · · · · · · · 1:107b-111b; 8:276a
aftereffects · · · · · · · · · · · · · · · · · · · 1:109a-110b
deaths · 1:109a-109b
family and livelihood · · · · · · · · · · · · 1:110a
material loss · 1:109b
medical effects · · · · · · · · · · · · · · · · · · 1:109b
non-Japanese hibakusha · · · · 1:110a-110b
psychological · 1:110a
American justification · · · · · · · · · · · · · 1:108a
destructive power · · · · · · · · · · · · 1:108a-109a
blast effects · 1:108b
fire storms · 1:109a
radiation effects · · · · · · · · · · · · · · · · · 1:109a
thermal radiation effects · · · · · · · · · 1:108a
hibakusha
message · 1:111a-111b
organizations · 1:111a
Hiroshima · · · · · · · · · · · 1:*108b*; 3:*149a*, 149b
historical background · · · · · · · · · · · · · · 1:108a
Nagasaki · · · · · · · · · · · · · 1:*109a*; 5:304a, *304b*
Occupation · 6:51a
postwar developments · · · · · · · 1:110b-111a
foreign assistance · · · · · · · · · · · · · · · · 1:111a
hibakusha organizations · · · · · · · · · · 1:111a
Japanese government · · · · · · · · · · · · 1:110b
local governments · · · · · · · · · · · 1:110b-111a
medical community · · · · · · · · · · · · · · · 1:111a
peace movement · · · · · · · · · · · · · · · · · · 1:111a
religious leaders · · · · · · · · · · · · · · · · · 1:111a
United States government · · · · · · · 1:110b
Truman, Harry S · · · · · · · · · · · · · · · · · · 8:107b
Atomic Bomb Casualty Commission (ABCC) · · · · · · · · · · · · · · · · 1:110b, 111b; 4:37b
Atomic bomb related disease 1:111b-114a
Bikini radiation injuries
clinical course · · · · · · · · · · · · · · · · 1:113b-114a
exposure mode · · · · · · · · · · · · · · · · · · · 1:113b
fallout exposure · · · · · · · · · · · · · · · · · 1:113b
periodic examinations · · · · · · · · · · · · 1:114a
burns · 1:112a
clinical course of sustained injuries 1:112a
Hiroshima and Nagasaki · · · · · 1:111b-112a
mechanical injuries · · · · · · · · · · · · · · · · 1:112a
radiation injuries
acute effects · 1:112b
exposure doses · · · · · · · · · · · · · · 1:112a-112b
late · 1:112b

Atomic Disasters Anniversary World Conference against Atomic and Hydrogen Bombs ······ 6:166a
Atomic energy, laws concerning ······ 1:114a-114b
Atomic Energy Commission ······ 7:167a
Atomic Energy Research Institute, Japan ······ 1:114b; 7:38a
Atomic weapons, movement to ban ······ 1:114b-115a; 6:144b
Atomi Gakuen Women's University 1:115a
Atomi Girls' School ······ 1:115a
Atomi Kakei ······ 跡見花蹊 ······ 1:115a
Ato ni tsuzuku o shinzu (They Will Follow) ······ 後に続くを信ず ······ 8:319b
Ato no Chitoko no nikki kokiroku ······ 4:255a
Atsuakira, Prince 敦明親王 ······ 4:249b-250a
Atsugi ······ 厚木 ······ 1:115a-115b
Atsugi Bonjin ······ 厚木凡人 ······ 2:76a
Atsugi Motor Parts Co, Ltd ······ 1:115b
Atsuita ······ 厚板 ······ 1:115b
  Nō theater ······ 1:115b
  origin and description ······ 1:115b
Atsumichi, Prince 敦道親王 ······ 3:366a
Atsumi Kiyoshi ······ 渥美清 1:115b; 2:*275a*, 275b
Atsumi Peninsula 渥美半島 ······ 1:115b
Atsumonozaki ······ 厚物咲 ······ 5:318b
Atsumorisō ······ 4:305a
Atsuta Shrine ······ 熱田神宮 ······ 1:115b-116a; 2:51a
  imperial regalia ······ 3:278b
  Owari Province ······ 6:136b
  site ······ 5:309a
Attaining Enlightenment in This Very Existence ······ 7:114b
Attendant ······ 4:296a
Attorneys. *See* **Lawyers**
Attorneys Law (Bengoshi Hō) ······ 4:371b
Attu ······ 1:116a
Audio equipment industry ······ 7:17b
Audio industries
  Nippon Columbia Co, Ltd ······ 6:8b
  Pioneer Electronic Corporation ······ 6:189a
  Sansui Electric Co. Ltd. (Sansui Denki) ······ 7:17b
  Trio-Kenwood Corporation ······ 8:92ba
Audiovisual education ······ 1:116a
Auditing. *See* **Accounting and auditing**
Auditing standards ······ 1:116a-116b
  field work ······ 1:116a-116b
  general ······ 1:116a-116b
  reporting ······ 1:116a-116b
Audit officers ······ 4:104b
Audit options ······ 1:9a
August First declaration ······ 1:116b, 289a; 7:47b-48a
Aung San ······ 1:116b
Australia and Japan ······ 1:116b-118b
  historical background ······ 1:116b-117a
    immigration issue ······ 1:116b-117a
    trade issue ······ 1:116b-117a
  Japanese studies ······ 4:44a-44b
  language studies ······ 4:21a
  postwar development
    ANZUS Pact ······ 1:117a
    Ball, William MacMahon ······ 1:117a-117b, 135a-135b
    British Commonwealth Occupation Force ······ 1:117a-117b, 170a
    Evatt, H.V. ······ 1:117a-117b
  relation in 1970s
    cultural ······ 1:117b-118b
    oil crisis of 1973-74 ······ 1:117b-118b
    trade ······ 1:117b-118b
  trade ······ 1:117b
    Agreement on Commerce ······ 1:117b
    Australia-Japan Business Cooperative Committee ······ 1:117b, 118b-119a
    beef ······ 1:117b
    General Agreement on Tariffs and Trade (GATT) ······ 1:117b
    mineral resources ······ 1:117b
    1970s ······ 1:117b
    pre-World War II ······ 1:117a
    sugar ······ 1:117b
    1970s ······ 1:117b
  World War II ······ 1:116b-117a
Australia, Japan, and Western Pacific Economic Relations Research Project (1972) ······ 1:117b-118b
Australia-Japan Business Cooperative Committee (AJBCC) ······ 1:118b-119a
  Pacific Basin Economic Council ······ 6:143b
Australia-Japan Foundation ······ 1:117b-118b
Australian immigration policy and Japan ······ 1:119a-119b
Austria and Japan ······ 1:119b-120b
  between wars ······ 1:120a
  early Austro-Hungarian relations ······ 1:119b
    Pfizmaier, August ······ 1:119b
    von Benyowsky, Moritz August ······ 1:119b
  Japanese studies ······ 4:43a
  Meiji Restoration to World War I
    constitutional law ······ 1:119b-120a
    diplomatic relations ······ 1:119b-120a
    Iwakura mission ······ 1:119b-120a
    scientific exchange with ······ 1:119b-120a
    sericulture ······ 1:119b-120a
    Siebold, Heinrich von ······ 1:119b-120a
    trade ······ 1:119b-120a
    Unequal Treaties ······ 1:119b-120a
    World Exhibition of 1873 ······ 1:119b-120a
  post-World War II ······ 1:120a
Austronesian ······ 4:20a-20b
Authors (modern). *See* Novelists
Authors (premodern)
  Anrakuan Sakuden ······ 1:62b-63a
  Arakida Reijo ······ 1:73b-74a
  Asai Ryōi ······ 1:94a
  Bakin ······ 1:130b-131a
  Chikamatsu Monzaemon ······ 1:275a-276a
  Ejima Kiseki ······ 2:188a
  Hanasanjin ······ 3:94b
  Hirata Atsutane ······ 3:145a-145b
  Hirose Tansō ······ 3:148a
  Hōseidō Kisanji ······ 3:234b
  Jippensha Ikku ······ 4:61a-61b
  Kada no Arimaro ······ 4:100b
  Kamochi Masazumi ······ 4:128a
  Kamo no Chōmei ······ 4:128b-129a
  Kamo no Mabuchi ······ 4:129a-129b
  Kan Sazan ······ 4:152a
  Katō Chikage ······ 4:167b
  Katori Nahiko ······ 4:169a
  Keichū ······ 4:187b-188a
  Koikawa Harumachi ······ 4:250a
  Miyako no Nishiki ······ 5:219b
  Miyako no Yoshika ······ 5:219b
  Motoori Norinaga ······ 5:257a-258b
  Motoori Ōhira ······ 5:259a
  Murasaki Shikibu ······ 5:267b
  Murata Harumi ······ 5:269b
  Nishizawa Ippū ······ 6:20a
  Ōmi no Mifune ······ 6:102a
  Ryūtei Rijō ······ 6:359a
  Ryūtei Tanehiko ······ 6:359a-359b
  Saikaku ······ 6:369b-371a
  Sakurada Jisuke ······ 7:4a-4b
  Santō Kyōden ······ 7:18a-18b
  Segawa Jōkō ······ 7:48b
  Sei Shōnagon ······ 7:52a-54a
  Shikitei Samba ······ 7:96b-97b
  Shimizu Hamaomi ······ 7:104a
  Sugawara no Takasue no Musume 7:257b
  Tamenaga Shunsui ······ 7:333b-334a
  Tayasu Munetake ······ 7:359a
  Tsuga Teishō ······ 8:113a
  Ueda Akinari ······ 8:126a-126b
  Yashiro Hirokata ······ 8:317a
  Yoshida Kenkō ······ 8:341a-342b
  Yoshishige no Yasutane ······ 8:349b
Autobiography of Yukichi Fukuzawa, The ······ 1:155a
Autoharp ······ 6:354b
Automatic Train Control ······ 7:118a
Automation ······ 7:202b
  quality control ······ 6:274a
Automobile Company (Ōtomōbiru Shōkai) ······ 1:120b
Automobile Damage Compensation Security Law, liability under ······ 4:384a
Automobile Liability Security Law 1:120b
  compensation guarantee ······ 1:120b
  compulsory liability ······ 1:120b
  heavy liability ······ 1:120b
Automobile Liability Security Law of 1955 ······ 1:120b
Automobile pollution ······ 6:218a
Automotive industry ······ 1:120b-122b; 8:102a
  companies
    Aichi Machine Industry Co, Ltd ······ 1:32b-33a
    Aisin Seiki, Co, Ltd ······ 1:38a
    Atsugi Motor Parts Co, Ltd ······ 1:115b
    Automobile Company ······ 1:120b
    Bridgestone Tire Co, Ltd ······ 1:170b
    Daihatsu Motor Co, Ltd ······ 2:58b
    Fuji Heavy Industries, Ltd ······ 2:343a
    Hino Motors, Ltd ······ 3:140b-141a
    Honda Motor Co, Ltd ······ 3:219a-219b
    Isuzu Motors, Ltd ······ 3:348b
    Kantō Auto Works, Ltd ······ 4:153a
    Mitsubishi Motors Corporation ······ 5:208b
    Nihon Radiator Co, Ltd ······ 5:381a
    Nippondensō Co, Ltd ······ 6:9a
    Nissan Diesel Motor Co, Ltd ······ 6:20b
    Nissan Motor Co, Ltd ······ 6:20b
    Nissan Shatai Co, Ltd ······ 6:20b
    Suzuki Motor Co, Ltd ······ 7:283a
    Tōyō Kōgyō Co, Ltd ······ 8:92a
    Toyota Auto Body Co, Ltd ······ 8:93a
    Toyota Motor Corporation ······ 8:93b
    Yamaha Motor Co, Ltd ······ 8:296a
    Yokohama Rubber Co. Ltd ······ 8:330b
  early history ······ 1:120b-122b
    foreign imports ······ 1:121a
    Military Vehicle Subsidy Law of 1918 ······ 1:121a
    problems ······ 1:121a
    trial productions ······ 1:121a
  in 1970s ······ 1:122a
  postwar developments ······ 1:121b-122b
    government protection ······ 1:121b-122a
    passenger car production ······ 1:122a
  between Wars ······ 1:121a-121b
    Automotive Manufacturing Industries Law of 1935 ······ 1:121b
    foreign vehicles restriction ······ 1:121b
    zaibatsu ······ 1:121b
  World War II ······ 1:121b
Automotive Manufacturing Industries Law of 1935 ······ 1:121b
Autumn and Winter Landscapes ······ 7:*17a*
"Autumn in the Forest" ······ 7:105b
Autumn Landscape ······ 1:68b
Avalokitésvara ······ 4:144b-145a
Avatar ······ 1:122b-123a
Avertimentos y avisos acerca dos costumes e catangues de Jappão ······ 8:189a
Aviation ······ 1:*123a*, 123b-124a

destruction and revival ············ 1:124a
early history ······················ 1:123a
foreign technology ················ 1:123a
gross sales ························ 1:124a
warplanes ·························· 1:123b
world records ······················ 1:123b
Aviation Cadets of the Imperial
Japanese Navy ···················· 8:329a
Awabi ······························ 1:1a-1b
Awa Dance ······ 阿波踊り ·· 1:124a, *124b*, 161b
Awajishima ········ 淡路島 ········ 1:124a
Awakening of Japan, The ··· 6:79b; 7:294b
Awa maru ·········· 阿波丸 ········ 1:124b
Awano Seiho ·· 阿波野青畝 ········ 1:124b
Awara ················ 芦原 ··· 1:124b-125a
Awards. *See* **Decorations**
Aware. *See* **Mono no aware**
Awase-jōyu ························ 2:25b
Awasezu ···························· 2:25b
Awashima ············ 粟島 ········ 1:125a
Awa Shrine ······ 安房神社 ········ 1:125a
Awataguchi Yoshimitsu
··············· 粟田口吉光 ········ 1:125a
Aya, Prince ·········· 礼宮 ········ 3:*277a*
Ayabe ················ 綾部 ········ 1:125a
Aya family ············ 漢氏 ········ 1:125b
Ayame. *See* **Irises**
Ayase ················ 綾瀬 ········ 1:125b
Ayatakedai ························ 4:308a
Ayatsuri jōruri ··· 操浄瑠璃 ··· 1:212a-215b
Ayrton, William Edward ············ 1:125b
Ayu [(sweetfish) *Plecoglossus altivelis*]
······ 1:14b, 115b, 125b; 2:26a, 283b, 287b
Ayukawa Gisuke. *See* **Aikawa Yoshisuke**
Ayukawa Nobuo · 鮎川信夫 ········ 1:82b, 125b-126a
Ayumu hito ········ 歩む人 ········ 4:179b
Azai family. *See* **Asai family**
Azai Nagamasa. *See* **Asai Nagamasa**
Azaleas [(tsutsuji) family Ericaceae]
···························· 1:126a-126b
Azami ······························ 8:24b
Azamukazaru no ki
············ 欺かざるの記 ········ 4:309a
Azuchi ················ 安土 1:126b; 4:340b
Azuchi Castle ······ 安土城 · 1:126b; 7:91a
description ························ 1:248a
Kanō Mitsunobu ···················· 4:147b
Oda Nobunaga ······················ 6:63b
paintings ·················· 3:181b; 4:146a
Azuchi-Momoyama history. *See* **History of Japan**
Azuchi-Momoyama period
············· 安土桃山時代 ········ 1:126b
Azuchi Shūron ··· 安土宗論 ··· 1:126b-127a
Azuki *(Phaseolus angularis)* ······· 1:127a
Azuma kagami ····· 吾妻鏡 ·· 1:127a-127b, 294b; 2:342b; 5:44b; 7:152b
arrangement ························ 1:127a
extant editions ···················· 1:127b
Kanazawa edition ·················· 1:127b
Kikkawa edition ··················· 1:127b
Shimazu edition ··················· 1:127b
general description ··········· 1:127a-127b
hentai kambun ················ 3:126b-127a
historiography ····················· 3:154a
Azuma Ryōtarō ·· 東龍太郎 ········ 1:127b
Azumasan ············ 吾妻山 ········ 1:127b
Azumazasa *(Sasaella ramosa)* ····· 1:136a
Azusagawa ·········· 梓川 ········ 1:127b

B

Baba Katsuya ···· 馬場勝弥 ········ 1:129a
Baba Keiji ······· 馬場敬治 ········ 1:129a
Baba Kochō ····· 馬場孤蝶 · 1:129a; 7:54b
Baba Tatsui ······ 馬場辰猪 ········ 1:129a
Kōjunsha formed ··················· 4:252b
naichi zakkyo ····················· 5:309b
Baba Tsunego ··· 馬場恒吾 ··· 1:129a-129b
Baby carriers ······················ 6:101a
Bachiru ···························· 7:169b
Bacon, Alice Mabel ················ 1:129b
Iwakura mission ··················· 1:129b
Tsuda Umeko ························ 1:129b
writings ··························· 1:129b
Bacteriologists
Hata Sahachirō ····················· 3:112b
Kitazato Shibasaburō ·············· 4:229a
Noguchi Hideyo ····················· 6:31b
Shiga Kiyoshi ······················ 7:89b
Badger. *See* **Tanuki**
Badminton ························ 1:129b
Baibunsha ········ 売文社 ········ 1:72a, 129b-130a
Baien ················ 煤煙 ········ 5:253b
Baika namako (sea cucumber) ····· 7:45a
Baiken (deed) ······················ 4:253b
Baikenjō (deed) ···················· 4:253b
Bail ······················ 1:130a; 2:49b-50a
Baishin ················ 陪臣 ········ 1:130a
Baishōron ·········· 梅松論 ··· 1:130a-130b
general description ················ 1:130a
historiography ····················· 3:154a
literary comparisons ·············· 1:130b
versions ·················· 1:130a-130b
Baiu ································· 4:8a
Bakan Sensō ···· 馬関戦争 ··· 7:105b-106a
Bakemono ························ 1:130b
hitotsume kozō ···················· 3:208b
kappa ······························ 4:156b
mononoke ·························· 5:247a
oni ································· 6:106a
tengu ································ 8:5b
yamamba ···························· 8:297a
Bakin ················ 馬琴 ·· 1:130b-131a, 211b, 295, 378a; 5:11b, 16b, 48b
gesaku ······························ 3:28b
kusazōshi ·························· 1:130b
life ································ 1:130b
Nansō Satomi Hakkenden ··········· 5:329a
nonfiction writings ········· 1:130b-131a
works of ···················· 1:130b-131a
yomihon ···························· 1:130b
Bakufu. 幕府 *See* **Shogunate**
Bakufu kengai shisetsu
············ 幕府遣外使節 ··· 7:161a-161b
Bakuhan system ············ 1:131a-133a, 211b; 2:1a, 108b; 3:186a; 4:377b
chōnin ····························· 1:301b
farmers and taxes ··········· 1:131b-132a
general description ················ 1:131a
governmental developments ······· 1:133a
hyakushō ··························· 3:249b
landlordism ························ 4:362b
provinces ·························· 6:260a
rural development ··········· 1:132a-132b
oyakata ···························· 1:132b
productivity ······················· 1:132b
profit ······························ 1:132b
taxation ··················· 1:132a-132b
Samurai and government ···· 1:131a-131b
mobilization ··············· 1:131a-131b
prebureaucratic lines ·············· 1:131b
salaries ···························· 1:131a
shogunate missions to the West ··· 7:161a
social structure and class policy
··························· 3:187b-188a
tenryō ································ 8:10a
Tokugawa shogunate ················· 8:55b
townsmen and commerce ············ 1:132a
craftsmen ·························· 1:132a
merchants ·························· 1:132a
urban development ·········· 1:132b-133a
toiya and kabunakama ·············· 1:132b
uchikowashi ························ 1:132b
Bakushū ·············· 麦秋 ········ 3:102b
Balance of payments ········· 1:133b-135a
definitions and data summary 1:133b-134a
current account balance ··········· 1:133b
merchandise trade balance ········ 1:133b
net long-term capital ·············· 1:133b
overall balance ···················· 1:134a
flow of funds ······················ 2:293a
foreign exchange control ·········· 2:314b
foreign trade ················ 2:324a-324b
IMF ································· 3:274b
Japan's performance ·········· 1:134a-135a
1950s and 1960s ············· 1:134a-135a
1966-71 ···························· 1:135a
1971- ······························ 1:135a
modern economy ·············· 2:163b-164a
monetary policy ···················· 5:241a
research and development ········· 6:305a
tariffs ······················ 7:346b-347a
Balance of trade ···················· 2:314b
Balkan states ······················ 2:142a
Ball, William MacMahon ···· 1:117a-117b, 135a-135b
Ballad-drama (kōwaka) ··············· 5:45a
Ballet. *See* Dance, Western-style
Balloonflower ······················ 4:207b
Balneotherapy ················ 3:239a-239b
history ····························· 3:239a
present conditions ··········· 3:239a-239b
Balneotherapy Institute ············ 3:239a
Bälz, Erwin von ············ 1:135b, 4:35a
Ba Maw ··························· 1:135b
Greater East Asia conference ······· 3:61b
Bambetsu 番別
Shinsen shōjiroku ················· 7:124b
Bamboo [(take; sasa) family Gramineae]
························· 1:135b-136a
baskets ····················· 4:104b-105a
traditional furniture material ····· 2:371b
Bamboo and White Crane ·········· 4:147b
Bamboo craftwork ·················· 2:295b
"Bamboo horse" ···················· 7:246a
Bamboo ware ················ 1:136a-136b
B-aminoisobutyric acid (BAIB) ······ 4:37a
Ban'ampō ·········· 万安方 ··· 4:114b-115a
Banchōkai
Teijin Incident ···················· 7:375b
Bancroft, Edgar Addison ·········· 1:136b
Bandai-Asahi National Park ··· 磐梯朝日国立公園 ·· 1:11b, 127b, 136b-137a; 2:366a-366b
Ban Dainagon ekotoba (Picture Story of the Courtier Ban Dainagon)
··········· 伴大納言絵詞 1:137a; 6:*152a*; 8:81b
Ōtemmon Conspiracy ················ 6:129b
Bandaisan ········· 磐梯山 ········· 1:37a
Bandō Tamasaburō ·················
············· 坂東玉三郎 ········ 4:91a

Bandō Tsumasaburō 阪東妻三郎 1:137a-137b; 2:268b
Bangkok Conference 7:197a
Banishment 1:137b
edo jūri shihō-barai 1:137b
tokoro-barai 1:137b
Banka (Dirge) 挽歌 8:319b
Banka poems
defined 5:105a-105b
Bankata 番方 1:137b
Bank Bookkeeping Guide (1872) 1:6a
Bankei Yōtaku 盤珪永琢 1:137b
Banking Bureau 5:188a
Banking system 1:137b-140a, 242a
corporate finance 2:28b-29b, 35a
corporate funds 4:189a
economic growth 2:161a
foreign exchange 1:140b
functions 1:140a
bonds 1:140a
debenture floatation 1:140a
financing 1:140a
securities 1:140a
small business 7:164a
trust transactions 1:140a
history 1:137b-139a
agriculture and industrial banks 1:139a
Bank of Japan 1:138b
Bank of Japan Law of 1942 1:139a
central bank 1:138b
consolidation 1:139a
early modern 2:151b-152a, 153a
Financial Crisis of 1927 1:139a
foreign exchange 1:138b-139a
Kawase kaisha 1:138a
long-term credit banks 1:139a
Mitsui 1:138a
National Bank Ordinance of 1872 1:138a
national banks 1:138a-138b
Ono houses 1:138a
post-World War II 1:139a; 2:155b-156a
Ryōgaeshō 1:137b
Savings Bank Ordinance of 1890 1:138b
savings banks 1:138b
monetary policy 5:240a
mutual financing 5:262b
overloan 2:158a-158b
present 1:139a-140a
Bank of Japan 1:139a
commercial banks 1:139a-139b
cooperative associations 1:139b-140a
credit association 1:139b
exports 1:139a-140a
foreign banks 1:139b
long-term credit banks 1:139b
mutual savings and loan banks (sōgo ginkō) 1:139a-140a
postal savings system 1:139b-140a
public corporation 1:139b
trust banks 1:139a-140a; 3:327b-328a
Shibusawa Eiichi 7:86a-86b
Taika Shakkandan 7:297a-297b
Bank of Japan (Nippon Ginkō or Nihon Ginkō) 1:140a-140b
business cycles 1:224b
domestic exchange 2:130b
establishment 1:140a
Financial Crisis of 1927 2:277a-277b
Financial System Research Committee 2:278b
flow of funds compilation 2:292a
foreign trade controls 2:320a
founding 2:30b
general description 1:140b
Inoue Junnosuke 3:309b
interest rate structure 3:317b-318a
Matsukata fiscal policy 5:133b-134a
monetary policy 5:239b-241b
national banks 5:336b
reorganization 1:140b
role 1:140b
technological development 7:369a-369b
Bank of Japan Building 1:140b
Tatsuno Kingo 7:349b
Bank of Japan Case 6:201b
Bank of Japan Law of 1942 1:139a
Bank of Korea 1:303b
Bank of Taiwan 7:307b, 309b
Bank of Tōkyō, Ltd (Tōkyō Ginkō) 1:140b-141a
Yokohama Specie Bank 8:330b
Bank of Yokohama, Ltd 1:141a
Banko ware 万古焼 1:141a, 264a
Bankruptcy 1:141a
alternatives 1:141a
Bankruptcy Law of 1922 1:141a
Okano Keijirō 6:81a
Banks
Bank of Japan 1:140a-140b
Bank of Korea 1:303b
Bank of Tōkyō, Ltd (Tōkyō Ginkō) 1:140b
Bank of Yokohama, Ltd 1:141a
Dai-Ichi Kangyō Bank, Ltd 2:58b
Daiwa Bank, Ltd 2:68b
Export-Import Bank of Japan 2:237b
Fuji Bank, Ltd 2:342a
Hokkaidō Takushoku Bank, Ltd 3:214a
Industrial Bank of Japan, Ltd 3:291a
Japan Development Bank 4:12b
Kyōwa Bank Ltd 4:339b-340a
Long-Term Credit Bank of Japan, Ltd 5:73a
Mitsubishi Bank, Ltd 5:206b-207a
Mitsubishi Trust & Banking Corporation 5:209a
Mitsui Bank, Ltd 5:211a
Mitsui Trust & Banking Co, Ltd 5:212b-213a
Nippon Credit Bank, Ltd 6:9a
Nōrin Chūkin Bank 6:37b
Saitama Bank, Ltd 6:372b
Sanwa Bank, Ltd 7:18b-19a
Shōkō Chūkin Bank 7:164a
Sumitomo Bank, Ltd 7:267b
Sumitomo Trust & Banking Co, Ltd 7:269b
Taiyō Kobe Bank, Ltd. 7:310a
Tōkai Bank, Ltd 8:40b
Tōyō Trust & Banking Co, Ltd 8:93b-94a
Yasuda Trust & Banking Co, Ltd 8:318a
Yokohama Specie Bank 8:330b
Bannermen (hatamoto) 3:111b-112a
Ban Nobutomo 伴信友 1:141b
Ban on Heterodox (Kansei Igaku no Kin) 2:174a; 4:152b; 5:132a
"Banreki aka-e" 万暦赤絵 7:176a
Bansha 蛮社 1:141b
Bansha no Goku 蛮社の獄 1:141b, 211b
Shinkiron 7:119a
Takano Chōei 7:316b
Torii Yōzō 8:80a
Banshi 番士 1:137b
Banshokō 蕃薯考 1:68b
Bansho Shirabesho 蕃書調所 1:141b-142a
French-Japanese relations 2:331a
Western learning 8:243a
Banshū 番衆 1:137b
Banshun 晩春 3:102b
Banshū-ori 播州織 4:160b
Banshū Plain 播州平野 3:139a
Bansugoroku 7:259a
Ban-the-bomb movement 1:114b
Ban Tsuma 阪妻 1:137a
Banzai 1:142a
Banzuke 7:272a
Baptist Church 1:142a
Bar Association. *See* **Japan Federation of Bar Associations**
"Bara tōnin" 薔薇盗人 7:176a
Barley. *See* **Wheat and barley**
Barrier of Nakoso 5:321b
Barriers, ancient fortified 5:321b
Barrier stations 7:57a
Basal metabolism 4:37a
Baseball 1:142a-143a
amateur 1:142b
nonstudent 1:142b
student 1:142b
Japan-United States games 1:142b-143a
professional 1:142b
Dai Nihon Baseball Club 1:142b
two-league system 1:142b
rubber ball 1:142b
Bashaku 馬借 1:143a-143b
Bashaku ikki 馬借一揆 1:143b-144a
Bashō 芭蕉 1:144a-145b, 181b-182a, 276a; 5:12a, 16a, 39a; 6:297a-297b, 298b, 299b; 7:5b, 24a, 259a
disciples
Hattori Ransetsu 3:114a
Kagami Shikō 4:102b
Kawai Sora 4:179a
Morikawa Kyoroku 5:250a
Mukai Kyorai 5:262a
Naitō Jōsō 5:311a
Ochi Etsujin 6:59b
Sugiyama Sampū 7:259a
Takarai Kikaku 7:318a
Fūryū concept 2:374b
haibun 3:77b
haiku 3:78b-79a
Issa 3:348a
life 1:144a-145a
Masaoka Shiki's criticisms 5:123b
northern journey 1:144b-145a
Shinkei 7:119a
Shin kokinshū 7:120b
studies
Hattori Tohō 3:114a
westward journies 1:144a-144b
1684 1:144a
1687 1:144b
works
Fuyu no hi 1:144a
"Genjūan no ki" 1:145a
Haikai shichibushū 3:78a
Kashima mōde 8:105b
Minashiguri 1:144a
Nozarashi kikō 1:144a
"Oi no kobumi" 1:144b
Oku no hosomichi 1:145a
"Saga nikki" 1:145a
"Sarashina kikō 1:144b
"Sarumino" 1:145a
Sumidawara 1:145a
Tōsei montei dokugin nijikkasen 1:144a
Bashō kukai 芭蕉句解 6:126a
Bashō school 5:18a
Basic Agriculture Law of 1961 1:32a
Basic Law concerning Atomic Energy of 1955 1:114a
Basic Law concerning the Execution of Duties by Police Officials 8:171a
Basic Law for Environmental Pollution Control 2:224b-225b, 228a-228b
Basic Relations between Japan and the Republic of Korea, Treaty on 4:287b
Basins
Chichibu 1:271b
Hita 3:206a
Hitoyoshi 3:208b
Ina 3:281b

Kamikawa ········· 4:126b
Kitakami ········· 4:226a
Kōfu ········· 4:243b; 8:301a
Kōriyama ········· 4:293b
Kyōto ········· 4:336b-337a
Matsumoto ········· 5:137b
Miyakonojō ········· 5:219b
Miyoshi ········· 5:223b
Nara ········· 5:332a-332b
Ōdate ········· 6:65a
Ōmi ········· 6:101a
Saku ········· 7:3a
Takayama ········· 7:320a
Tsuyama ········· 8:119b
Ueno ········· 8:128b
Yamaguchi ········· 8:294a
Bassui Tokushō · 抜隊得勝 ········· 1:145b
Bataan ········· 1:145b
Batchelor, John ········· 1:145b
Bateren ········· 1:145b-146a
Bath ········· 1:146a
customs ········· 1:146b
mixed ········· 1:146b
modern family ········· 1:146a-146b
public ········· 1:146a
sentō ········· 1:146a
temple ········· 1:146a
Batik ········· 7:21a
Bats [(kōmori) order Chiroptera] ·· 1:146b
Batsu ········· 1:146b-147b; 6:205b; 7:62b
general description ········· 1:147a
types ········· 1:146b-147a
gakubatsu ········· 1:147a; 3:3b
gumbatsu ········· 1:147a; 3:65b-67a
habatsu ········· 1:147a; 3:73a
hambatsu ········· 1:147b; 3:91b-92a
keibatsu ········· 1:147a
mombatsu ········· 1:147a
zaibatsu ········· 1:147a; 8:361b-363b
Batsuzoku ········· 3:92a
Battledore ········· 3:77a
Battle of the Carriages ········· 4:148b, 149b
Bays
Ago ········· 1:21b
Ariake ········· 1:83a
Dōkai ········· 2:127b
Hiroshima ········· 3:149b
Ise ········· 3:336b-337a
Kagoshima ········· 4:105a
Kojima ········· 4:251b
Matsushima ········· 5:140a
Mikawa ········· 5:170b
Mutsu ········· 5:288b
Nago ········· 5:308b
Ōsaka ········· 6:120a
Sagami ········· 6:363b
Sendai ········· 7:63b
Sukumo ········· 7:266a
Suruga ········· 7:278b
Tōkyō ········· 8:66a
Tosa ········· 8:81a
Toyama ········· 8:88a
Tsuruga ········· 8:116b
Uchiura ········· 8:125a
Be ········· 部 · 1:125b, 147b; 2:103b; 4:166b; 7:256a
classification ········· 1:147b
ownership ········· 1:147b
prototype ········· 1:147b
Shintō ········· 7:126a
uji-kabane system ········· 8:131b
Beads, ancient ········· 1:147b-148a
bead-making sites ········· 1:148a
glass ········· 3:35b
kofun deposits ········· 4:244b
Shintō art ········· 7:134b
types ········· 1:148a
Beanbag ········· 1:148a
Bean curd ········· 8:35a
Bean paste. *See* **Miso**
Bean-scattering ceremony ········· 7:71b
Beard, Charles Austin ········· 1:148a-148b
Bears [(kuma) family Ursidae] ········· 1:148b
"Beatles" ········· 6:112a
"Beatnik" movement ········· 7:207a
Beauties beneath Trees (juka bijin) ········· 6:*149a*
Bedding ········· 1:148b-149a; 2:371a
kakebuton ········· 1:149a
mosquito nets ········· 1:149a
pillows ········· 1:148b
shikibuton ········· 1:149a
Beef production ········· 1:28b
Bees and wasps [(hachi) order Hymenoptera] ········· 1:149a
Beetle, Japanese ········· 4:22b
Before the Dawn ········· 4:103b
Beheiren. *See* **Peace for Vietnam Committee**
Beigoma ········· 1:149b
Beijing (Peking) Customs Conference ········· 7:88b
Beijing (Peking) theater ········· 8:22b-23a
Beijing Treaty of 1905 ········· 6:228a
Beiō kairan jikki ········· 米欧回覧実記 3:359b; 4:307b
Bekkōbachi (spider wasps) ········· 1:149a
Bekkō-zaiku ········· 8:80b-81a
Belgium, Japanese studies ········· 4:43a-43b
Bells, wind ········· 8:254a
Benedict, Ruth Fulton ·· 1:149b; 4:38a, 39a
Ben'en ········· 1:*192b*
Benevolence (jin) ········· 4:141b
Bengaru no tora ········· ベンガルの虎 ········· 4:157b
Benikujaku ········· 紅孔雀 ········· 8:339a
Benizuri-e ("safflower printed pictures") 紅摺絵 ········· 8:141a
Benkei ········· 弁慶 ········· 1:149b
kabuki depiction ········· 4:97b
Gikeiki ········· 3:32b
Benshi ········· 2:267b-268a
Benten ········· 弁天 ········· 5:296a
Bentenjima ········· 弁天島 ·· 1:150a; 4:2b
Benzaiten. *See* **Tembu**
Benzoin umbellatum ········· 4:316b
Beppu ········· 別府 ········· 1:150a
Beppu Bay ········· 別府湾 ········· 1:150a
Bereaved Families Association ········· 8:319b
Beriberi Investigation Committee ·· 7:311a
Berrien, F.K. ········· 4:39b-40a
Berry, John Cutting ········· 1:150a; 2:51b
Bertin, Louis-Emile ········· 1:150a
Berurin hyōhaku ········· ベルリン漂泊 ········· 4:162b
Besshi Copper Mine ········· 別子銅山 ········· 4:182b
Besshi Copper Mine labor disputes ········· 1:150a-150b
Besshi Dōzan sōgi ········· 別子銅山争議 ········· 1:150a
Bessho ········· 3:137a
Betonamu ni Heiwa o Shimin Rengō ········· 6:145b, 166a
Betsugen Enshi ·· 別源円旨 ········· 1:150b
Betsuri ········· 別離 ········· 8:219a
Bettelheim, B.J. ········· 4:32a
Bibai ········· 美唄 ········· 1:150b
Bible, translations of ········· 1:150b-151a
colloquial ········· 1:151a
Japanese Common Bible Translation project ········· 1:151a
Meiji version ········· 1:150b
oldest extant ········· 1:150b
Protestant ········· 1:150b
Roman Catholic ········· 1:150b-151a
16th century ········· 1:150b
Bible studies. See *Seisho no kenkyū*
Bibliography ········· 1:151a-154b
characteristics of extant manuscripts and printed books ········· 1:153a-154a
external ········· 1:153a-153b
internal ········· 1:153b-154a
descriptive ········· 1:154a
form and characteristic of Japanese books ········· 1:151b-153a
manuscripts ········· 1:152a
printed books ········· 1:152a-153a
origin and transmission of books ········· 1:151a-151b
Bicycle theft ········· 4:86b
Biddle, Francis ········· 4:17b
Bigelow, William Sturgis ········· 1:154b
Big Four combines ········· 8:361b, 364a
Bigot, Georges ········· 1:154b-155a
Bijin ········· 4:109b, 201a
Bijinga ········· 6:158b
Itō Shinsui ········· 3:356a
Kaburagi Kiyokata ········· 4:100a
Bikini Island ········· 1:114b; 5:75b
Bikini radiation injuries ········· 1:113a-114a
Bills and Notes Law ········· 1:339a-339b
Bimbōgami ········· 1:155a
Bimbō monogatari (Story of the Poor) ···· 貧乏物語 4:180b; 8:264b
Bindweed ········· 3:151a
Bingata. *See* **Okinawan textiles**
Biochemistry ········· 1:156a
Biochemists
Akabori Shirō ········· 1:39a
Hayaishi Osamu ········· 3:114b
Shibata Keita ········· 7:84b
Biography and biographical fiction ········· 1:155a-155b
autobiographical ········· 1:155a-155b
biographical ········· 1:155a-155b
Biologists
Fujii Kenjirō ········· 2:343a
Imanishi Kinji ········· 3:274a
Kihara Hitoshi ········· 4:204b
Makino Tomitarō ········· 5:87a
Minakata Kumakusu ········· 5:176a
Morse, Edward Sylvester ········· 5:256a
Oka Asajirō ········· 6:77b
Ono Ranzan ········· 6:111b
Thunberg, Carl Peter ········· 8:29b
Toyama Kametarō ········· 8:88a
Whitman, Charles Otis ········· 8:252b
Yamamoto Senji ········· 8:299a
Yatabe Ryōkichi ········· 8:319b-320a
Biology ········· 1:155b-156a
biochemistry ········· 1:156a
genetics ········· 1:156a
Meiji period ········· 1:155b-156a
physiology ········· 1:156a
premodern ········· 1:155b
Bird-and-flower painting (kachōga) ········· 1:156a-156b; 6:158b-159a
Bird, Isabella Lucy ········· 1:156b
"Bird rattles" ········· 5:334b
Birds ········· 1:59b-60a, 61b
bush warbler ········· 1:223b-224a
chicken, Japanese ········· 1:272b-273b
cranes ········· 2:41b
crows ········· 2:51b-52a
cuckoos ········· 2:52a
geese ········· 3:13b
gulls ········· 3:65b
hawks and eagles ········· 3:114b
herons ········· 3:127b-128a
kite, black ········· 4:229b
komadori ········· 4:264b
larks ········· 4:368b
mandarin duck ········· 5:100b-101b

pheasants 6:182b
plovers 6:192b
ptarmigan 6:262b
rails 6:277b
reed warblers 6:285b
sparrows 7:241a
thrushes 8:29b
wagtails 8:200b-201a
wild ducks 8:253a-253b
woodpeckers 8:269b
Birds and Flowers 4:110b
Birds and Flowers of the Four Seasons 4:150b
Birds of Prey 4:148b
Birōjima 枇榔島 1:156b
Birth control 6:224b; 7:11a
family planning 2:246b-247b
Birthday celebrations 4:151a
Birthplace history 5:71b
Birth rate 2:246b-247a; 6:222a, 223b-224a, 225a
economic implications 6:232a
Bisai 尾西 1:156b
Bishamonten 毘沙門天 5:296a
"Bishō" (The Smile) 微笑 8:333b
Bishū 尾州 6:136b
Bitasen 鐚銭 1:156b-157a
copper 1:156a
iron and brass 1:156b-157a
Bitchūguwa 4:322a
Bitō Nishū 尾藤二洲 1:157a
Biwa, Lake 琵琶湖 1:*157a*, 157b-158a; 7:90b
Biwa (lute) 琵琶 1:157a-157b; 2:301a; 7:*168b*, 195a
Chikuzen 1:157a-157b
court music 1:157a
gagaku 3:2a
general description 1:157a
gunka 3:69a
national anthem 5:336a
Satsuma mōsō 1:157a
Biwa hōshi 琵琶法師 1:157b; 5:44a; 7:61b
Biwako Canal 琵琶湖疏水 1:157b; 4:336a
Bizen 備前 1:158a
Bizenkurage 4:50b
Bizen ware 備前焼 1:158a, 263a; 7:256a
early 1:158a
Edo-period 1:158a
general description 1:158a
jar 1:*259a*
Kaneshige Tōyō 4:140a
Momoyama period 1:158a
museums 5:279b
present 1:158a
Black Cat 6:*157a*
Black Dragon Society. *See* **Amur River Society**
Black, John Reddie 1:158b; 4:46a
Black Ocean Society (Gen'yōsha) 3:24b-25a
Black Rain 3:255a
Blacks, attitudes toward 2:312a-313a
Black-seal certificate 7:184a
Black Stream (kuroshio) 4:318b
Bloch, Bernard 1:158b
Blood chemistry 4:35b-36b
"Blood Debt" Incident 1:158b-159a; 5:88a; 7:196b
"Blood seal" 4:200a
"Blood tax" riots (Ketsuzei ikki) 4:200a-200b
Blue Cat 3:76a
"Bluestocking Society" 7:54a-54b
Board of Audit 1:159a; 2:276b; 3:56a; 6:264b
Board of Censors 4:185b
ritsuryō system 6:323a
Board of directors 1:159a-159b
Board of Inquiry (Monchūjo) 5:239a
Board of Retainers (Samurai-dokoro) 7:8b
Boats, traditional. *See* **Ships**
Bōchō kaiten shi 防長回天史 1:159b; 7:255b
Bodhicitta 4:67b
Bodhidharma 4:158a
Bodhisattva 1:159b; 4:66a, 144b; 7:169a
Jizō 4:66a
Bodhisena 3:288a
Bōeichō 防衛庁 2:82a
Bōei Daigakkō 5:338b
Bōei hakusho 2:82b
Bōei Kenshūsho 5:338b
Bōfū 3:127b
Bohai (Po-hai) 1:159b-160a; 2:347b; 7:257a, 261a
China invaded 4:277b
Boissonade de Fontarabie, Gustave Emile 1:160a, 166a; 4:378a
Civil Code 1:316b-317a
French-Japanese relations 2:332a
legal reform activities 2:316b, 319a
Sandai Jiken Kempaku Movement (Movement to Memorialize Three Important Items) 7:9b
Bojutsu yume monogatari 戊戌夢物語 1:141b; 7:316b
Bo Juyi 8:210a
Bokkai 渤海 1:159b-160a
Bōkokurei Jiken. *See* **Grain embargo controversy**
Boku Eikō 朴泳孝 6:159b
Boku Retsu 朴烈 6:159a-159b
Boku Seiki 朴正熙 6:159a
Bokuseki 1:192b
Sōhō Myōchō 1:*235a*
Bokuseki no utsushi 墨跡の写し 1:236a
Bokuseki soshi den 墨跡祖師伝 1:236a
Boller, Anton 4:18b
Bolshevik Revolution (1917) 6:342b-343a; 7:192a; 8:271a
Bolshevism 5:231b
"Bolshevist Group" 6:255a
Bolshoi Ballet 2:76a
Bombori lanterns 4:368a
Bommōkyō 梵網経 1:234a
Bon dance. *See* **Bon odori**
Bond market 1:242b
Bonds, public 1:160a
foreign exchange control 2:315a
public investment 6:265a
Bone articles 1:160a-160b
Jōman culture 4:72a-74a
Kamegaoka site 4:125a
Okhotsk culture 6:84a
paleolithic culture 6:159b-160a
Bon Festival 盆 1:20a, 124a, 160b; 2:258a; 5:4b; 7:246a, 249b
chūgen 1:312a
cooking 2:22a
Daimonji Okuribi 2:61a
dance 2:75a
funerals 2:370b
dances 2:374a
importance 2:299a
nembutsu odori 5:360a
religion 6:291b
Tanabata Festival 7:334b-335a
Bongaku Shinryō 梵学津梁 4:64a
Bonin Islands ボニン諸島 4:7a
Bonito [(katsuo) family Scombridae] 1:160b-161a
Bonkei and bonseki 1:161a
Bon odori 1:160a
Awa 1:124a
Bō no Tsu 坊津 1:161b
Bonsai 1:*162a*, 161b-163a
abroad 1:163a
aesthetics and philosophy 1:162a-163a
ferns 2:252a
general description 1:161b-162a
growing 1:162a
fertilizer 1:162a
instruments 1:162a
seasons 1:162a
soil 1:162a
temperature and moisture 1:162a
varieties 1:162a
major styles 1:161b-162a
cascading 1:161b
clumped 1:162a
forest 1:162a
rock planting 1:162a
slanting 1:161b
twin-trunk 1:162a
twisting-trunk 1:161b
upright 1:161b-162a
weeping-cascade 1:161b
Shin-zen-bi 1:163a
styles 1:162a
classic 1:162a-162b
dramatic 1:162a-162b
Bontō An 梵燈庵 1:96a-96b
Bonus 1:163a-163b; 2:18b, 243b; 4:348a
seasonal 8:200a
Book catalogs 3:219a
Book and magazine distributors 1:163b
Bookbinding
modern 6:245b
types 1:153a-153b
traditional types 1:153a-153b
Book illustration 1:163b-164a
emakimono 2:198a-200b
kusazōshi 4:319b-320a
Bookkeeping methods
accounting 1:8a-10a
auditing 1:8a-10a
Book of Changes
omikuji 6:101b
ommyōdō 6:103a
Book of Filial Piety 孝経 2:57a
Book of History
in Ogyū Sorai's thought 4:247b
Book of Odes
in Ogyū Sorai's thought 4:247b
Book of Tea, The 5:12a; 6:79b; 7:294b
Books
censorship 1:252a
external characteristics 1:153a-153b
bindings 1:153a-153b
paper 1:153b
scripts and writing styles 1:153b
form 1:151b-153a
manuscripts 1:152a
printed books 1:152a-153a
internal characteristics 1:153b-154a
"one-yen" (empon) 2:212b
origin and transmission 1:151a-151b
early 1:151a
Kana 1:151b
preservation 1:151b
8th century 1:151b
9th century 1:151b
publishing 6:267b
Books of the floating world 8:144a-144b
Booth, Eugene 1:164a
"Boroya no shunjū" ボロ屋の春秋 8:147b

Bosatsu ········ 1:159b; 7:*169a*
Bose, Rash Behari ········ 1:164a-164b
Bose, Subhas Chandra ········ 1:164b-165a
Indian National Army ········ 3:289b
Bōshibari ········ 棒縛 ·· 4:*326b*, 327a
Boshi jojō ········ 母子叙情 ········ 6:80a
Boshin Civil War 戊辰戦争 ·· 1:165a-165b
debate ········ 1:165a-165b
events ········ 1:165a
French-Japanese relations ········ 2:331b
Goryōkaku, Battle of ········ 3:47a
Itagaki Taisuke ········ 3:349a
Kabayama Sukenori ········ 4:89b
Kan'eiji destruction ········ 4:138a
Kawai Tsugunosuke ········ 4:179b
Kawakami Sōroku ········ 4:181b
Kido Takayoshi ········ 4:202b
Kiheitai ········ 4:204b
Kogosho Kaigi ········ 4:249b
Meiji Restoration ········ 5:159b
Ōuetsu Reppan Dōmei ········ 6:135b
Shinsengumi ········ 7:124b
Takenouchi Tsuna ········ 7:325a
Tōgō Heihachirō ········ 8:36a
Tokugawa Yoshinobu ········ 8:57b
United Kingdom ········ 8:151a
White Tiger Brigade ········ 1:226b
Willis, William ········ 8:253b
Boshin Shōsho ·· 戊申詔書 ········ 1:165b
Bōshū ········ 防州 ·· 7:276b-277a
Bōsō Peninsula ·· 房総半島 ········ 1:165b
Boston Symphony Orchestra
Ozawa Seiji ········ 6:140b
Botan. *See* **Peonies**
Botanical Garden (Leyden) ········ 7:193a
Botanical gardens ········ 1:165b-166a
nonuniversity ········ 1:165b
specialty ········ 1:165b-166a
university ········ 1:165b
Botanists
Hirase Sakugorō ········ 3:144b
Iinuma Yokusai ········ 3:263b
Ikeno Seiichirō ········ 3:266b
Itō Keisuke ········ 3:354b
Makino Tomitarō ········ 5:87a
Maksimovich, Kark Ivanovich ········ 5:87b
Matsumura Jinzō ········ 5:138a
Miyabe Kingo ········ 5:216b
Miyoshi Manabu ········ 5:224a
Nakao Sasuke ········ 7:177b
Noro Genjō ········ 6:39a
Siebold, Philipp Franz von ·· 7:192b-193a
Thunberg, Carl Peter ········ 8:29b
Yatabe Ryōkichi ········ 8:319b-320a
Botchan ········ 坊ちゃん ········ 5:350a
Botekishū ········ 暮笛集 ········ 7:279b
Bousquet, Georges Hilaire ········ 1:166a
Bowing ········ 6:76a
Bows and arrows. *See* **Arms and armor**
Boxer Protocol of 1901 ········ 7:199a
Boxer Rebellion 1:166a-166b, 287a; 3:196b; 5:9b; 7:29a, 198b
aftereffects ········ 1:166a-166b
cause ········ 1:166a
climax ········ 1:166a
Fukushima Yasumasa ········ 2:367a
Komura Jutarō ········ 4:268a
Russia and Japan ········ 6:342a
Russo-Japanese War ········ 6:346a
Tairo Dōshikai ········ 7:303a
Tōgō Heihachirō ········ 8:36a
"Boxers" ········ 1:166a
Boxes ········ 1:166b-167a
design ········ 1:166b-167a
haribako ········ 3:103b
Kōrin ········ 1:*166b*
materials ········ 1:166b
types ········ 1:166b
writing box (suzuribako) ········ 1:166b, *166b*
Box Man, The ········ 1:3a
Boycotts ········ 2:14b
Boy Scouts ········ 1:167a
Boy's Day. *See* **Children's Day**
Braccialini, Scipione ········ 3:350b
Bracelets, ancient ········ 1:148a, 167a
chokkomon ········ 1:299b
Jōmon ········ 1:167a
Kofun ········ 1:167a
Yayoi ········ 1:167a
Brandt, Max August Scipio von ·· 1:167a; 3:26b
Brass bands ········ 5:286a
Braun, Hans Wolfgang ········ 3:26a
Brazil and Japan ········ 1:167a-169a
early relations ········ 1:167b
immigration contracts ········ 1:167b
treaty of amity (1895) ········ 1:167b
Japanese immigrants ········ 1:169a-169b; 2:200b-201b
community leaders ········ 3:142b; 5:317b; 7:105a; 8:130b, 221b, 298b
large-scale economic cooperation ········ 1:168b-169a
postwar relations
investments ········ 1:168a-168b
trade ········ 1:168b
prewar commerce ········ 1:167b-168a
Brazilian-Japanese Cultural Association (Aliança Cultural Brasil-Japão) ········ 8:298b
Bretton Woods Agreement ········ 8:161a
IMF ········ 3:274b
Brewing ········ 1:169b-170a
method ········ 1:169b-170a
miso ········ 1:170a
sake ········ 1:170a
soy sauce ········ 1:170a
Bribery, political ········ 6:202a
Bridges ········ 1:170a-170b
European techniques ········ 1:170a
modern technology ········ 1:170b
premodern ········ 1:170a
Bridgestone Museum of Art ········ 3:339b
Bridgestone Tire Co, Ltd ········ 1:170b
Ishibashi Shōjirō ········ 3:339a
Brinkley, Frank ········ 1:170b-171a; 2:311a
British Commonwealth Occupation Force (BCOF) · 1:117a-117b, 171a; 7:32b; 8:152b
British Commonwealth Peace Conference ········ 1:117a
British Origami Society ········ 6:118b
Broadcast College ········ 1:171a-171b
Broadcasting ········ 1:171b-173b
commercial ········ 1:173a-173b
educational ········ 2:179a
history ········ 1:171b-172b
first ········ 1:171b
FM ········ 1:172b
government control ········ 1:171b
Nippon Hōsō Kyōkai (NHK) ········ 1:171b-173b; 5:374a
postwar ········ 1:172a-172b
television ········ 1:172a-172b
"Three Radio Laws" ········ 1:172a
late-night ········ 1:173b
present-day ········ 1:172b-173a
financing ········ 1:173a
general characteristics ········ 1:172b
networks ········ 1:172b-173a
programming ········ 1:172b
television viewing ········ 1:173a
public ········ 1:93a
radio ········ 4:382a
wire-relayed ········ 8:254b
Broadcasting companies
Asahi Broadcasting Corporation (ABC) ········ 1:92a
Asahi National Broadcasting Co, Ltd. ········ 1:93a
Chūbu Nippon Broadcasting Co, Ltd ········ 1:311a
Far East Network (FEN) ········ 2:248b-249a
Fuji Telecasting Co, Ltd ········ 2:347b
Kyokutō Hōsō ········ 4:332b
Mainichi Broadcasting System Inc (MBS) ········ 5:84b
Nippon Broadcasting System, Inc ········ 6:8b
Nippon Cultural Broadcasting, Inc ········ 6:9a
Nippon Television Network Corporation ········ 6:13a-13b
Television Tōkyō Channel 12, Ltd · 7:380a
Tōkyō Broadcasting System, Inc (TBS) ········ 8:66a
Yomiuri Telecasting Corporation ·· 8:337a
Broadcasting Law of 1950 ·· 1:171b-172b, 173b
freedom of speech regulation ········ 2:339a
freedom of the press ········ 2:339a
Brocade (nishiki) ········ 6:17b
Broken Thread ········ 6:188a
Bronze age ········ 1:173b-174a
Bronze bell ········ 1:78b
Bronze mirrors ········ 1:77a, 78a, 167a, 174a, *174b*; 7:266a, 280a-280b
chokkomon ········ 1:299b
history ········ 1:174a
Imperial Regalia ········ 1:174a; 3:278b
inscriptions ········ 1:174a; 3:314a
Kagami to ken to tama ········ 7:312a
kofun ········ 4:244a
Ōzuka tomb ········ 6:141a
treasures and ritual implements ········ 1:174a
Bronze weapons 1:167a, 174a-175a; 7:266a
Dōhoko dōken no kenkyū ········ 7:312a
fern frond design ········ 2:252a
halberd heads ········ 1:175a
history ········ 1:174a-175a
spearheads ········ 1:175a
swords ········ 1:175a
Brooke, John Mercer ········ 1:175a-175b
Hamada Hikozō ········ 3:89a
Kanrin maru ········ 4:151b
Brotherhood of the New Life ········ 3:104a
Brother Industries, Ltd ········ 1:175b
Brown algae ········ 7:46b
Brown, Nathan ········ 1:142a
Brown, Samuel Robbins ········ 1:175b
Brown, Winthrop Gilman ········ 4:285b
Bruno Taut ········ 3:10a
Brunton, Richard Henry ·· 1:175b; 2:311b
Brussels Conference ········ 1:175b-176a
Brussels Tariff Nomenclature
United States (1945-1973) ········ 8:161b
Bryan note ········ 1:176a
B-29 bomber ········ 1:176a
World War II ········ 8:276a
Bu ········ 4:193b
Buckwheat, cultivation of ········ 7:178b-179a
Buddha ········ 1:52a
Amida ········ 1:176a
Dainichi ("Great Sun") ········ 1:176a; 2:64b
epithet ········ 6:281a-281b
images ········ 1:201b-203a; 7:67b
power of ········ 7:347a
Shaka ········ 1:176a
Yakushi ········ 8:285b
"Buddha's-Footprint-Stone-Songs, The" ········ 2:137b
Buddha tiles ········ 1:176a-176b
Buddhism · 1:176b-180a; 7:122b-123b, 217a
Asian diffusion ········ 1:177b-178a
China ········ 1:178a

Southeast ····· 1:177b-178a
Azuchi Disputation ····· 1:126b-127a
bodhisattva ····· 1:159b
canon of texts ····· 1:187b
ceremonies
Gosaie ····· 8:286a
incense ····· 3:284b
Kōfukuji (place) ····· 8:286a
Saishōe ····· 8:286a
Yakushiji ····· 8:286a
Yuimae ····· 8:286a
China and Japan ····· 1:281b-282b
coexistence with Shintō ····· 7:126b
dharma ····· 2:91b
doctrines
emptiness ····· 2:212b-213a
hongaku (primordial enlightenment) ····· 3:221a
inga ····· 3:303b
interdependent origination (engi) ····· 2:217a-217b
mujō ····· 5:262a
satori (awakening; enlightenment) · 7:28b
this-worldliness ····· 8:24b
early ····· 1:176b-177a
Brahmanism ····· 1:176b
doctrine ····· 1:176b-177a
economic principles ····· 1:177a
literature ····· 1:177a
rules for religious life ····· 1:177a
sangha ····· 1:177a
state theory ····· 1:177a
education ····· 2:173a
esoteric (mikkyō) ····· 2:231a-231b
financial support ····· 6:293a
flower arrangement ····· 2:288a-290a
folk religion ····· 2:298a
fund-raising ····· 3:136b-137a
gankake ····· 3:7b
Good Law
Tale of Genji ····· 7:330b-331a
hijiri ····· 3:136b-137a
holy men ····· 3:136b-137a
iconography ····· 7:381a
India and Japan ····· 3:288a
influence on housing ····· 3:243a-243b
inzō ····· 3:328a
Japanese sects ····· 1:178a-180a
characteristics ····· 1:179b-180a
history ····· 1:178a-179b
introduction ····· 1:178a-179b
Jōdo ····· 4:67a-68a
Jōdo Shin ····· 4:68a-69a
Nara Buddhism ····· 5:332b
Nichiren sect ····· 1:179a; 5:376b-377a
present ····· 1:180a
Pure Land Buddhism ····· 1:179a; 6:270a-270b
Ritsu ····· 6:332a
Shingon sect ·· 1:178b-179a; 7:113b-115a
Tendai sect ····· 1:178b; 8:4a-5b
Yūzū Nembutsu ····· 8:359b
Zen Buddhism ····· 1:179a-179b; 6:318b-320a; 7:233a-234b; 8:370a-374b
Japanese literature ····· 1:180a-182a; 1:292a-296a; 6:194a
kikajin introduction ····· 4:205b
lay believers (danka) ····· 4:362b; 4:372a; 8:123a
lay devotional associations ····· 4:372a
literature ····· 1:292a-295b; 5:26a; 6:194a
monasticism ····· 5:236a-239a
money offerings ····· 5:242a
music ····· 5:283a-283b
nature ····· 5:357b
new religions ····· 5:366b; 7:224b
Okinawa ····· 6:85a
oshi ····· 6:124b
portrait painting ····· 6:226b
prayer ····· 6:233a
priesthood ····· 6:238b-239a
priests. *See individual sect*
religion ····· 6:290b-293b
rites. *See* **Buddhist rites**
ritual implements. *See* **Buddhist ritual elements**
rosaries ····· 1:197a
sculpture. *See* **Buddhist sculpture**
setsuwa bungaku ····· 7:72a
Shingaku ····· 7:112a
Shintoism ····· 1:179b-180a
shrines. *See* Shrines
spread ····· 1:177a-177b
Brahmanism ····· 1:177b
Mahāyāna ····· 1:177b
syncretism ····· 7:289a-290a
temples. *See* **Temples**
thought and culture ····· 8:24b
community-ism vs. universalism ·· 8:27b
functionalism and classicism ·· 8:28a-29a
life-centeredness vs. transcendence ····· 8:26b-27a
Tokugawa shogunate ····· 8:53a
tolerance in Japanese religion ····· 8:70b
warrior-monks ····· 8:230b-231a
weddings ····· 8:239a
women in ····· 8:256b, 258b
Buddhist architecture ····· 1:182a-184b
bell tower ····· 1:183a
buildings for monks ····· 1:183a
gates and corridor ····· 1:182b-183a
pagoda and principal temple halls ····· 1:182a-182b
storehouse ····· 1:183a
styles ····· 1:183a-183b
Asuka ····· 1:183a
daibutsuyō ····· 1:183b
eclectic ····· 1:183b
Karayō ····· 1:191b
Tang ····· 1:183a
wayō ····· 1:183a
Sutra repository ····· 1:183a
Buddhist art ····· 1:184b-194b
Daruma ····· 1:*193a*
emakimono ····· 1:*191a*
esoteric ····· 1:187b-189a
architecture ····· 1:188a
Goma ceremony ····· 1:188a
Kannon, Eleven-Headed ··· 1:187b, 189a
mandala ····· 1:188a
painting ····· 1:188b-189a
Ryōbu Shintō ····· 1:187b-188a
sculpture ····· 1:188b-189a
statues, wood ····· 1:189a
types of buildings ····· 1:188a
Hakuin ····· 1:*193a*
Heian-period ····· 1:189a
Hōryūji ····· 1:*185a*
Kichijōten ····· 1:*185a*
latter-day ····· 1:193a-194b
painting ····· 1:193b-194a
sculpture ····· 1:194a
Lotus Sutra ····· 1:186a, 187b
Mahāyāna ····· 1:184b-187b
architecture ····· 1:185b
calligraphy ····· 1:187a-187b
emakimono ····· 1:186b-187a
painting ····· 1:185b-187a
printing ····· 1:187a-187b
sculpture ····· 1:185b-187a
masks ····· 1:189b
Minchō ····· 1:*192b*
Pure Land ····· 1:189a-191a
architecture ····· 1:189b
painting ····· 1:189b-191a
sculpture ····· 1:189b-191a
Raigōzu ····· 1:190a, *190a-190b*
Relic hall (shariden) ····· 1:*191a*
Sanjūsangendō ····· 1:*189a*
Scroll of Hungry Ghosts ····· 1:*191a*
sculpture. *See* **Buddhist sculpture**
Takuma School ····· 1:190a
tapestry ····· 1:189b
Tosa school ····· 1:193b
Zen ····· 1:191a-193a
architecture ····· 1:191b-192a
painting ····· 1:192a-193a, *193a*
portraits ····· 1:192a
sculpture ····· 1:192a-193a
zenga ····· 1:*193a*
Buddhist castings ····· 6:125a
Buddhist family altar ····· 2:307a
Buddhist images ····· 7:94a
Buddhist rites ····· 1:194b-195a
agricultural rites ····· 1:194b
esoteric
Goma ceremony ····· 1:195a
musical instruments ····· 1:195b-196a
nembutsu ····· 1:194b
pilgrimages ····· 1:194b
Buddhist ritual implements ·· 1:195a-196b
esoteric Buddhism ····· 1:196a
keman ····· 1:*196b*
Pure Land Buddhism ····· 1:196a-196b
reliquary (sharitō) ····· 1:*195a*
vajra ····· 1:*196b*
Zen ····· 1:196b
Buddhist rosaries ····· 1:197a
Buddhist sculpture ··· 1:197a-204a; 2:327a
Amida ····· 1:*201a*
Ashura ····· 4:*244b*
daibutsu ····· 2:*55a*
Five Wisdom Kings ····· 1:*200b*
Fukūkenjaku Kannon ····· 1:*187a*
Gakkō, statue of ····· 1:*198a*
Ganjin, statue of ····· 3:*7a*
Hakuhō culture ····· 3:87b-88a
Heian period ····· 1:198a-199a
historical survey ····· 1:197a-199b
iconography and sizes ····· 1:202b-203a
image types ····· 1:201b
inscriptions inside ····· 1:203b
Jizō ····· 1:201a, *201a*
Jōchō ····· 1:*201a*
Kaikei ····· 1:*201a*
Kamakura period ····· 1:199a-199b
Kuratsukuri no Tori ····· 1:*197a*
materials and construction
trees ····· 1:201b
materials and techniques ····· 1:200a-202a
clay figures ····· 1:200a
dry-lacquer statues ····· 1:200a
gilt-bronze Buddhist images ····· 1:200a
Respoussé bronze placques ····· 1:201a
stone sculpture ····· 1:200a–201a
tiles ····· 1:200b
wood-core dry-lacquer images ····· 1:200a-200b
wood sculpture ····· 1:201a–201b
Miroku, statue of ····· 1:*197b*
Muchaku ····· 1:*186b*
Niō ····· 1:*186b*
Nyoirin Kannon ····· 1:*188b*
objects inside Buddhist images ····· 1:203b
pre-Buddhist clay figures ····· 1:197a-197b
preservation programs ····· 1:203b-204a
Renge Kokūzō ····· 1:*187a*
Rushana ····· 1:*199a*
sculptors ····· 1:199b-200a
See also **Sculptors**
Shaka Triad ····· 1:*197a*
Shikkongōshin, statue of ····· 1:*198b*
Tempyō culture ····· 8:3b
tools ····· 1:201b

Unkei 1:*186b*
Yakushi 1:*188b*
Yakushi Triad 1:*199a*
Budget, national 1:204b-206a
Diet 2:95a
education 1:205b
Foodstuff Control Special Account 1:205b
local allocation tax 1:205b-206a
public works 1:205a-205b
roads 6:332b
social security 1:204b-205a
Budget Bureau 5:187b
Budō 3:60b; 5:118b-120a
Budō shoshin shū (Introduction to the Way of the Warrior) 武道初心集 2:56b
Bugaku 舞楽 2:*73a*; 3:1a; 7:22a
costumes 8:23a-23b
dance 3:47b
masks 5:126a-126b
gosechi no mai 3:47b
Bugaku zusetsu (music) 舞楽図説 6:134b
Bugei jūhappan 武芸十八般 1:206a
Bugyō 奉行 1:206a
jisha 4:62b
Buildings Protection Law 4:374a
Bukan 武鑑 1:206a
Buke (age of military houses) 6:176b
Buke densō 武家伝奏 1:206a-206b
Buke giri monogatari 武家義理物語 8:144a
Bukehō 武家法 1:206b
Goseibai Shikimoku 3:47b-48a
Buke-mono (aspects of samurai life) 武家物 8:144a
Buke myōmoku shō 武家名目抄 8:358b
Buke nikki 武家日記 4:101b
Buke seiji 8:228b-230b
Buke Shohatto 武家諸法度 1:206b-207a; 3:187a; 4:85a
laws 1:206b
samurai declassment 4:108b
Tokugawa Ieyasu 8:50b
Tokugawa shogunate 8:53a
Buki Yushutsu Sangensoku 1:90a-90b
Bukka Tōsei Rei 物価統制令 6:238b
Bukkenron 物権論 7:255b
Bukkyō Daigaku 7:342a
Bukkyōgo daijiten 仏教語大辞典 5:314b-315a
Bukōsan 武甲山 1:207a
"Bullet Train" 7:116b-119a
Bullfighting 1:207a, 251b
Bumbuku chagama 分福茶釜 1:207a-207b
tanuki 7:345a
Bummei Ittōki 文明一統記 1:207b
Bummei Kaika 文明開化 3:359a; 5:154a
Bummeiron no gairyaku 文明論之概略 1:207b; 2:368a
historiography 3:156a
kokutai 4:263a
Bun 1:207b; 4:123b
Bunchi seigen rei 分地制限令 1:208a
Bunchō. *See* **Tani Bunchō**
Bunchō gadan 文晁画談 7:341a
Bundan 1:208a-208b
Bundy, William Putnam 4:285b
Bungaku jidai 文学時代 7:175b
Bungakukai 文学界 1:208b-209a; 4:69a, 180a; 6:66a
Kitamura Tōkoku 4:227b
Bungakukai group 5:52a
Bungaku no sanjūnen (Thirty Years of Literature) 文学の三十年 8:173b
Bungakuza
shingeki 7:113a
Tokugawa Musei 8:52a
Bungei 文芸 1:209a
Bungei jidai 文芸時代 1:209a-209b
founding 5:19a
Shinkankaku school 7:116a-116b
Bungei Kakushin Kai 5:19a
Bungei kurabu 文芸倶楽部 1:209b; 7:309b
Bungei Kyōkai 文芸協会 5:18b
shingeki 7:112b
Bungei seiki 文芸世紀 7:176a
Bungei sensen 文芸戦線 1:209b
leading theoretician 7:175a
proletarian literature movement 6:254b
Senki 7:66b
Tanemakuhito 7:340a-340b
Bungei shunjū 文芸春秋 1:209b-210a
Bungei Shunjū, Ltd 1:210a; 2:373a
Ikejima Shimpei 3:266b
Bungo Channel 豊後水道 1:210a
Bungo Takada 豊後高田 1:210a
Bun'ikō 文意考 4:129b
Bunjin artists 1:210a; 3:28b
Ike no Taiga 1:*210b*
Jūben jūgi (The Ten Conveniences and Ten Pleasures) 1:*210b*
Okada Beisanjin 6:77b
Okada Hankō 6:78a
Okamoto Toyohiko 6:80b
Tazaki Sōun 7:359a
Yosa Buson 1:*210b*
Bunjinga 文人画 1:210a-211a; 6:154a
screen and wall painting 7:43a
Bunji seiji 文治政治 3:189a
Bunka and Bunsei eras 文化文政時代 1:211a-211b
culture and learning 1:211b
foreign ships 1:211b
shogunate and economy 1:211b
Bunka Gakuin 4:184a
Bunka Hōsō. *See* **Nippon Cultural Broadcasting, Inc**
Bunkai hitsuroku (Reading Notes) 文会筆録 8:312a
Bunka shūreishū 文華秀麗集 1:211b-212a; 2:350b; 4:189a; 5:29b
Bunkazai Hogo Hō 2:52b-53a
Bunke 4:218a
Bunkengaku 文献学 1:154a
Bunko 文庫 4:199a
Bunkobon 6:162a
Bunkoku 分国 1:274a
Bunkokuhō 分国法 1:212a
bukehō 1:206b
Imagawa Kana Mokuroku 3:271b
kabegaki 4:90a
kakun 4:119a
Ōuchike Kabegaki 6:135b
Shingen Kahō 7:113b
Yūkike Hatto 8:357a
Bunkyō Ward 文京区 1:212a
Bunkyū Sannen Hachigatsu Jūhachinichi no Seihen 文久三年八月十八日の政変 2:39a-39b
Bunraku 文楽 1:212a-215b; 2:274a; 8:21b-22a
costumes 8:23b-24a
early history 1:213b-214a
final stage 1:215a-215b
Kanadehon chūshingura 1:*212b*
Kiritake Monjūrō II 4:222a
puppeteer 1:*213a*
puppet heads 1:*214b*
Sonezaki shinjū 1:*212b*
stage, chanter, and audience 1:*213a*
stages of development 1:214a-215a
Takemoto Gidayū I 7:324b
theater conventions 1:212b-213b
Toyotake Yamashiro no Shōjō 8:93b
See also **Jōruri**
Bunroku Keichō no Eki (Bunroku Campaign) 文禄・慶長の役 3:326b-327a
Bunshō sekai 文章世界 4:148b; 7:309b
Bunshoshō 聞書抄 7:342b
Bunten 文展 1:215b; 8:328a
Japan Art Academy 4:10b
modern painting 6:158a
Bun'ya no Yasuhide 文屋康秀 4:254b
Buraiha writers 6:230b
"Buraikan" 無頼漢 7:122b
Burakumin 1:216a-217a, 324a, 7:217a
minorities 5:195a
Bureaucracy 1:217a-221a; 6:214a; 7:214a
administrative guidance 1:220b
Administrative Management Agency 1:14a
Cabinet Orders 1:220b
competition 1:220a
Constitution of 1947 2:11b-12a
coordination 1:220a
court rank (ikai) 2:39b
executive branch (government) 3:55b-56a
gakubatsu 3:3b-4a
history and development 1:217a-220a
Imperial Ordinances 1:218a
Meiji Constitution 1:217b
ministries 1:218b-219a
national civil service system 1:219b-220a
politics 1:220a-220b
post-World War I return 3:199b-200a
premodern 1:217a-217b
present day 1:218b-219a
Privy Council 1:217b
public policy formation 1:220a-220b
public unionization 1:220b
reform 1:220b-221a
strikes 1:220b
Bureaucrats, ritsuryō system 7:150b-151a
court ranks 2:39b-41a
"Bureaucrats' parties" 6:321b
Bureau of Archivists 4:315b
Bureau of Books 8:381a-381b
Bureau of Poetry 4:1b
Bureau of Yin and Yang 6:113a-113b
Buri 8:323b
Burials, prehistoric 4:244a-246b; 6:235a-235b
dolmen (shisekibo) 6:235a-235b
flexed (kussō) 6:235a
hōkei shūkōbo ("square, ditched graves") 6:235b
jar (kamekan) 6:235a
shell mounds 7:83a
Burma and Japan 1:221a-221b
Aung San 1:116b
Ba Maw 1:135b
Burners, hibachi 3:128b-129a
Bushi ("military gentry") 武士 7:7a
Bushidan 武士団 1:221b
ienoko and rōtō 3:261a
Kammu Heishi 7:299a
kokufu 4:257a
myōshu 5:291b
samurai 7:7a
Seiwa Genji 5:177b
shōen 7:155a

- sōryō system 7:232a
- yorioya and yoriko 8:338b

Bushidō 1:20a, 221b-223b; 4:85a; 8:290a
- early warrior society 1:222a
- *Hagakure* 3:75a
- legacy 1:223a-223b
- samurai 7:8a
- tea ceremony 4:159a
- transition to Tokugawa 1:222a-223a

Bushū 武州 5:275a-275b

Bush warbler [(uguisu) *Cettia diphone*] 1:223b-224a

Business
- and government 5:92b
- code of ethics 1:302b-303a
- Commercial Code 1:337b-339a
- **concentration** 1:224a
- consumer movement 2:14a-15b
- contemporary economy 2:158b-159a
- cooperative associations (kyōdō kumiai) 2:25b
- corporate culture 2:26a-28b
- corporate history 2:29b-33b
- corporations 2:34b-37a
- **cycles** 1:224a-224b
- funding 2:161a
- practices. *See* Business practices
- post-World War II, one-set principle 6:106a
- stability laws 7:205b
- **wholesale and retail** 1:224b

Business Accounting Council (BAC) 1:8b

Business and Professional Women's Clubs, Federation of 8:263b

Business guidance laws 7:205b

Business leaders
- Adachi Tadashi 1:11a
- Aikawa Yoshisuke 1:33b
- Asabuki Eiji 1:91b-92a
- Asano Sōichirō 1:95b-96a
- Ashihara Yoshishige 1:98a
- Dan Takuma 2:77b
- Dokō Toshio 2:127b
- Fujii Heigo 2:343b
- Fujita Denzaburō 2:346a
- Fujiwara Ginjirō 2:348b
- Fujiyama Aiichirō 2:359a
- Fujiyama Raita 2:359a
- Furukawa Ichibei 2:372b-373a
- Gō Seinosuke 3:48a
- Gotō Keita 3:53a
- Hara Yasusaburō 3:103b
- Hattori Kintarō 3:113b
- Hibi Ōsuke 3:129a
- Hiratsuka Tsunejirō 3:146a
- Hirose Saihei 3:147b
- Honda Sōichirō 3:219b
- Horie Shigeo 3:227b
- Hori Kyūsaku 3:228a
- Hotta Shōzō 3:239b
- Ibuka Masaru 3:254a
- Ichimura Kiyoshi 3:258a
- Idemitsu Sazō 3:259a
- Ikeda Shigeaki 3:266a
- Inayama Yoshihiro 3:284a
- Ishibashi Shōjirō 3:339a
- Ishida Taizō 3:340b
- Ishikawa Ichirō 3:342a
- Ishizaka Taizō 3:347a; 8:304b
- Iwasaki Koyata 3:361b-362a; 8:289a
- Kagami Kenkichi 4:102b
- Kaneko Naokichi 4:139a
- Katō Takeo 4:170b
- Kawakami Gen'ichi 4:180b
- Kikawada Kazutaka 4:205b
- Kobayashi Ataru 8:304b
- Kobayashi Ichizō 4:236b
- Kuhara Fusanosuke 4:302b-303a
- Kurata Chikara 4:311b-312a
- Magoshi Kyōhei 5:83b
- Masuda Takashi 5:129b-130a
- Matsunaga Yasuzaemon 5:139a
- Matsushita Kōnosuke 5:141a
- Minomura Rizaemon 5:195a
- Miyajima Seijirō 5:218a
- Mizuno Shigeo 5:226b
- Mogi Keizaburō 5:233b
- Mori Nobuteru 5:251b
- Morita Akio 5:253a
- Motoyama Hikoichi 5:259a
- Mukai Tadaharu 5:262a
- Murata Shōzō 5:270a
- Mutō Sanji 5:288a
- Nagano Shigeo 5:303a
- Nakajima Chikuhei 5:313b
- Nakamigawa Hikojirō 5:314a-314b
- Nakano Tomonori 5:317a
- Nakayama Sohei 5:319a-319b
- Nezu Kaichirō 5:373b-374a
- Noguchi Shitagau 6:32a
- Odaira Namihei 6:61a
- Ogura Masatsune 6:71a
- Ōhara Magosaburō 6:73b
- Ōhara Sōichirō 6:73b
- Okauchi Hideo 6:81a-81b
- Ōkawa Heizaburō 6:81b
- Ōkura Kihachirō 6:98a
- Saji Keizō 6:375a
- Sakurada Takeshi 7:4b
- Seki Hironao 7:56b
- Shibusawa Eiichi 7:86a-86b
- Shibusawa Keizō 7:86b
- Shōda Heigorō 7:154b
- Shōda Hidesaburō 7:154b
- Shōriki Matsutarō 7:167a
- Sugi Michisuke 7:257b
- Suzuki Masaya 7:282b
- Takahata Seiichi 7:313b
- Tashiro Shigeki 7:347b
- Torii Shinjirō 8:79b
- Tsutsumi Yasujirō 8:119a
- Uemura Kōgorō 8:127b
- Watanabe Tetsuzō 8:236b
- Yamamoto Jōtarō 8:298a-298b
- Yamamoto Tamesaburō 8:299b
- Yamashita Tarō 8:304b
- Yano Tsuneta 8:316a
- Yasukawa Daigorō 8:319a
- Yoshida Tadao 8:346a

Business machines 5:359a

Businessmen's Association 4:64a

Business practices
- amakudari 1:49b
- bankruptcy 1:141a
- pricing 1:11b
- unfair 1:67a-67b
  - abuse of economic power 1:67a-67b
  - coercion and inducement 1:67a
  - definition 1:67a
  - discriminatory acts 1:67a
  - price settings 1:67a
  - restrictive agreements 1:67a

Business stability laws 7:205b

Buson 蕪村 1:*144b*, 211a, 224b-225a, 181b; 5:12a, 16a; 6:297b, 298b, 299b; 7:5b, 17b
- haibun 3:78a

Bussangaku 物産学 1:225a

Bussan kaisho 物産会所 4:262a

Bussho 仏所 1:225a-225b
- founder 1:303b

Bussokuseki 仏足石 1:225b

Bussokuseki no uta or "Buddha's Foot-Stone Poem" 8:202b

Butsuda 1:176a

Butsudan 1:160b, 225b

Butsugu 1:195a-196b

Butsumo dai kujaku myōō kyō 佛母題孔雀明王経 6:248a

Butsurui shōko 物類称呼 1:225b
- Japanese dialects 4:31b

Butterbur 2:360a

Butterflies [(chō) order Lepidoptera] 1:225b-226a

Buyaku 夫役 1:226a-226b

Buyō (dance) 8:63b

Buyō Inshi 武陽陰士 7:55b

Buzen 豊前 1:226b

Byakkotai 白虎隊 1:38b, 226b
- Iimoriyama 3:262b

"Byakuya" 白夜 7:176a

Byōbu 2:371a; 7:41a-43b

Byōbu-e (paintings on screens) 7:41b

Byōbugaura 屏風ケ浦 1:226b-227a

Byōdōin 平等院 1:227a-227b; 2:358a; 7:41b
- door panels 7:328a
- gardens 3:9a
- Phoenix Hall (Hōōdō) 1:*226b*; 7:328a
- raigōzu 6:277a

By the Lake 6:*156b*

C

Cabinet. *See* **Prime minister and cabinet**

Cabinet Information Bureau 2:339a; 7:176b

Cabinet Law 1:13a; 2:6b

Cabinet Library 1:229a
- National Archives 5:336a-336b

Cabinet order 1:229a

Cabinet Order concerning the Definition of Nuclear Raw Materials of 1957 1:114b

Cable television 1:229a

Cabral, Francisco 1:229a-229b

Cachon, Mermet de 1:229b

Cadastral register (Ōtabumi). *See* **Census**

Cai E (Ts'ai O) 1:229b

Cairo Conference 1:229b, 290a
- Taiwan 7:309a

Calendar, dates, and time 1:229b-232b; 2:258a, 259a-259b, 299a
- annual calendar 2:205a
- festivals 2:258a-262a
- Japanese, "National Era" 1:232a
- jikkan jūnishi 4:57a
- Jingūreki (Ise Shrine Calendar) 1:*231a*
- months 1:232a-232b
- nengō 1:231b-232a; 6:174b
- old civil 1:231a-231b
- old solar 1:230b
- periodization 6:175a
- reign years 1:232a
- sexagenary cycle 1:232a
- solar and lunar 1:230a-230b
- times of day 1:232b

Calico 7:21a

Calligraphers
- Fujiwara no Sukemasa 2:355a
- Fujiwara no Yukinari 2:358b
- Gion Nankai 3:34a
- Gyokuen Bompō 3:71a-71b

Hakuin 3:88a
Hon'ami Kōetsu 3:218b
Hosoi Kōtaku 3:236a
Ichikawa Beian 3:256b
Ike no Taiga 3:267a
Ikkyū 3:269b-270b
Jakugon 4:1a-1b
Kang Hŭi-an 8:325a
Kitao Shigemasa 4:228b
Konoe Iehiro 4:273b
Konoe Nobutada 4:273b
Kūkai 1:187b
Maki Ryōko 5:87a-87b
Matsumura Goshun 5:138a
Miyamoto Musashi 5:220a
Nakamura Fusetsu 5:314b
Onoe Saishū 6:110a
Ono no Tōfū 6:111b
Ōtagaki Rengetsu 6:128b
Ryōkan 6:352a
Saichō 1:187b
Sengai Gibon 7:63b
Shōkadō Shōjō 7:163a
Takuan Sōhō 7:237b
Tesshū Tokusai 8:16a
Calligraphy 1:232b-236b; 2:358b
Azuchi-Momoyama period 1:236a
bokuseki 1:192b, 235b-236a
Chinese 1:283a; 4:142b; 7:170a
diplomatics 2:97b
early history 1:233b-234a
Edo period 1:236a
education 2:172b
general description 1:232b-233b
aim 1:232b
Chinese-character scripts 1:233b
connoisseurship and collection activities 1:233b
history 1:232b-233b
implements 1:233b
Heian period 1:234a-235b
Hosshōji school 1:236a
Kokinshū poems 1:234b
Kōzei style 1:235b-236a
Kūkai 1:234a
Saga, Emperor 1:234a
Sampitsu 1:234a
Sanseki 1:234a-234b
Tachibana no Hayanari 1:234a
wayō trend 1:234b-235b
implements 1:*233a*
ink painting 3:305b
"ink traces" 1:192b
kaisho 7:170a
Kamakura and Muromachi periods 1:235b
Chinese Song calligraphy 1:235b
Fujiwara no Sadaie 1:235b
Fujiwara no Toshinari 1:235b
Sesonji school 1:235b
Sugawara no Michizane 1:235b
Kantei style 4:153a
kinki shoga 4:213b
Mahāyāna Buddhist 1:187a-187b
daizōkyō 1:187b
issaikyō 1:187b
minchōtai 7:170a
museums 5:280a
new Chinese influences 1:236a
script style, Chinese 7:170a
seichōtai 7:170a
sōchōtai 7:170a
style
Ashide 1:97b
Western-style painting 8:328a
Calligraphy Museum 5:314b
Calpico 1:236b
Calpis 7:220b
Calpis Food Industry Co, Ltd 1:236b
Cambodia and Japan 1:236b
refugees 6:286a
Camellias [(tsubaki) *Camellia* spp.] 1:236b-237a; 2:326b
Cameras 6:233b
Camphor tree [(kusunoki) *Cinnamomum camphora*] 1:237a; 2:326b
Canada and Japan 1:237b-238a
Japanese immigrants 1:238b-239b
post-1949 1:239b
1877-1941 1:238b
1941-1949 1:238b-239a
Japanese studies 4:42a
postwar relations 1:237b-238a
prewar relations 1:237b
relations today 1:238a
Canals
Aichi 1:32b
Asaka 1:94a-94b
Biwako 1:157b
Hakone 3:86a
Meiji 5:153a
Minumadai 5:198a
Takasegawa 7:318b
Teizambori 7:377a
Toyogawa 8:90b
Cancer, medical research 5:151b-152a
Candles 5:9a
Cannibalism 7:323b
Canon, Inc. 1:239b
Cant. *See* Ingo
Cao Rulin (Ts'ao Ju-lin) 1:239b
Capacity to act 1:239b-240a
Capacity to enjoy rights 1:240a
Capes
Ashizurimisaki 1:102a
Daiōzaki 2:66b
Echizemmisaki 2:144a
Erimomisaki 2:230b
Hinomisaki 3:140b
Inubōzaki 3:325b
Iragomisaki 3:329b
Irōzaki 3:336a
Murotozaki 5:274b
Nagasakibana 5:304a
Nosappumisaki 6:40b
Noshappumisaki 6:41a
Notsukezaki 6:41b
Omaezaki 6:100b
Ōmazaki 6:100b
Satamisaki 7:25b
Shionomisaki 7:141a
Sōyamisaki 7:239a
Tappizaki 7:346a
Toimisaki 8:38a
Capital
foreign 2:315b
industrial funds 3:291b-292a
Capital formation 1:240a-242a
developments in 1970s 1:242a
general description 1:240a-241a
historical and international comparisons 1:241a-241b
production and welfare 1:241b
saving 1:241a
Capitalism
debate 5:382-383b
"Lectures on the History of the Development of Japanese Capitalism" 5:382b
Capitalism, Japanese. *See* **Nihon shihon shugi ronsō**
Capital-liability ratio 1:243b
Capital markets 1:242a-243a; 2:35a, 276a-276b
banks and bond market 1:242b
equity market 1:242b
internationalization 1:243a
Japanese 1:242a
Capital of the Tycoon 1:46a
Capital Outflow Prevention Law 2:314b
Capital Provinces 4:211b-212a
Capital punishment 1:243a-243b; 6:172b
Capital Region Development Commission 8:180b
Capital Region Development Plan 8:180b
Capital stock 2:160a-160b
Capital structure 1:243b
Capron, Horace 1:243b; 2:311a
Caraway, Paul Wyatt 1:243b-244a
Card games 4:381b
Cardinal Principles of the National Entity of Japan 4:264a
Career-long employment 2:210b-211a; 8:6a
Caretaker 6:347a
Carp [(koi) *Cyprinus carpio*] 1:244a; 2:26a, 281b
Carpenters' tools 1:244a-245a
Carriage 6:301a
Carrying poles. *See* **Tembimbō**
Cartels 1:66b, 245a; 2:32a-32b, 324b
industrial organization 3:295b-296a
international 1:66b-67a
legal 3:295b-296a
administrative guidance 3:295b-296a
depression 3:296a
private government control over 4:370b
Cary, Otis 1:245a-245b
Casio Computer Co, Ltd 1:245b; 7:80a
Caste system 6:324b
Castellan 4:66b
"Castle culture" 3:178a
Castles 1:245b-249b
ancient fortifications 1:245b-246b
grid-pattern city 1:245b-246a
mountain fortress 1:246a
palisade 1:246b
Azuchi-Momoyama and Edo periods 1:247b-248a; 2:170a
decline of castle 1:248a
rise of castle 1:248a
building techniques and design 1:248a-249a; 2:279a
Fushimi 2:375a
gates 3:13a
Himeji 1:*247a*; 3:139a
Itojō 3:354b
Matsumoto 5:137b
medieval 1:246b-247b
mountain fort 1:246b-247b
plain castle 1:247b
museums 5:278b
Nagoya 5:309a-309b
Ōsaka 6:120a-120b
remains 1:248b
Tagajō 7:294a
warfare 2:266a
Castle towns (jōka machi) 1:131a, 249a-249b; 2:266b
chōnin 1:301a
development 1:248a
economy 2:149b
map 2:*62a-62b*
premodern economy 2:148b
samurai 4:194a
urbanization 8:176a
urban life 8:177b
urban planning 8:179b
warrior government 8:230a
"Catching a Catfish with a Gourd" 4:77b
Catfishes [(namazu) family Siluridae] 1:249b
Cathode-ray tube 2:192a

Catholic Church. *See* **Christianity**
Catholicism. *See* **Christianity**
Catholic missionaries, modern ··· 1:249b-251a; 4:52a
charitable and social welfare institutions ··· 1:250b
contemplatives ··· 1:250b-251a
current ··· 1:250b
educational institutions ··· 1:250a
Kōlbe, Maxmilian ··· 1:250b
origins ··· 1:249b-250a
scholars ··· 1:250a-250b
Cats [(neko) *Felis catus*] ··· 1:251a
mythology ··· 5:296b
Utagawa Kuniyoshi ··· 1:*251a*
Cattle (ushi) ··· 1:251a-251b
Cattle production ··· 1:28b
CATV (Community Antenna Television) ··· 1:229a
Caudill, William ··· 4:39b
Caves, paleolithic ··· 6:159b-160a
Cedar, Japanese. *See* **Sugi**
Celebrations. *See* Ceremonies; **Festivals**
Celestial beings, mythology ·· 5:295a-295b
Celestial physics ··· 1:104b
Cement industry ··· 1:251b
Censorship ··· 1:251b-255a
early Shōwa period
books ··· 1:253a-253b
newspapers ··· 1:253a
political and social movements ··· 1:253a
Edo period ··· 1:251b-252a
Christian writings ··· 1:251b
sexual materials ··· 1:252a
shogunal government and official ideology ··· 1:252a
Tokugawa Ieyasu and Tokugawa family ··· 1:251b-252a
films ··· 2:339a
freedom of speech ··· 2:338a
freedom of speech, regulation of ··· 2:338a-338b
Ienaga textbook review case ··· 3:261a
laws ··· 2:338b
literary societies ··· 1:208b
Meiji period ··· 1:252a-252b
freedom of speech ··· 1:252a-252b
Libel Law of 1875 ··· 1:252a-252b
newspapers ··· 1:252a
prepublication ··· 1:252b
Press Law of 1909 ··· 6:236a
Press Ordinance of 1875 (Shimbunshi Jōrei) ··· 1:252b
Publication Law of 1893 (Shuppan Hō) ··· 6:262b
Publication Ordinance of 1869 ··· 1:252a
Publication Ordinance Penalties (Shuppan Jōrei Bassoku) ··· 1:252b
socialism ··· 1:252b
Motion Picture Code Committee ·· 5:256b
newspapers and other publications ··· 2:338b-339a
Occupation period ··· 1:254a-254b
China and Soviet Union ··· 1:254b
elimination of censorships procedures ··· 1:254a
Occupation Press Code ··· 1:254a
writings censored ··· 1:254b
Ōsaka Asahi Hikka Incident ··· 6:120a
post-Occupation period ··· 1:254b-255a
citizen organizations ··· 1:255a
Constitution of 1947 ··· 1:254b
invasion of privacy ··· 1:255a
obscenity and Supreme Court ··· 1:254b-255a
political pressure ··· 1:255a
self-censorship codes ··· 1:254b-255a
Subversive Activities Prevention Law ··· 7:254a-254b
textbook authorization ··· 1:255a
radio broadcasting ··· 2:339a
Broadcasting Law of 1950 ··· 1:173b
Taishō period ··· 1:252b-253a
magazines ··· 1:252b
newspapers ··· 1:252b
Peace Preservation Law of 1925 ·· 1:253a
War period ··· 1:253b-254a
National Mobilization Law of 1941 ··· 1:253b
Nihon Shuppankai (Japan Publishers Association) ··· 1:253b
penalties ··· 1:253b
Publications Control Committee · 1:253b
social thought and history ·· 1:253b-254a
Census ··· 1:255a-255b; 2:107a; 6:223b
ritsuryō system ··· 6:330a
Census registration ··· 4:60b-61a
ritsuryō system ··· 6:324a
Center for Archaeological Operations ··· 5:333b
Center for Japanese-Brazilian Studies ··· 5:317b
Central America
diplomatic relations ··· 3:323a-323b
Japanese studies ··· 4:45a
trade ··· 3:323a-323b
Central Council for Education ··· 1:51a, 255b; 5:254b
Central Council on Youth Problems ··· 1:255a
Central East Atlantic Fisheries Commission ··· 2:283a
Central Eugenic Protection Council ··· 2:234b
Central Finance Corporation for Commercial and Industrial Cooperatives ··· 7:204b
Central Glass Co, Ltd ··· 1:255b-256a
Central Labor Relations Commission (Chūō Rōdō Iinkai) 1:218b, 256a; 4:358b; 7:189b, 255b
Ōta Kaoru ··· 6:129a
strike injunctions ··· 4:352a
Central West Atlantic Fisheries Commission ··· 2:283a
Centro Diffusione Origami ··· 6:118b
Ceramic bowl ··· 7:*168b*
Ceramic industries
NGK Insulators, Ltd ··· 5:374a
Noritake Co, Ltd ··· 6:37b-38a
Tōtō, Ltd ··· 8:85b
Ceramics ··· 1:256a-265b
Agano ware ··· 1:20b
Aizu Hongō ware ··· 1:38b
Arita ware ··· 1:85b, *260b*
ash-glazed (shirashi) ··· 1:261b-262a; 7:71a
Chinese influence ··· 1:262a
kilns ··· 1:262a
Sue ware ··· 1:261b
Banko ware ··· 1:141a
Bizan ware ··· 1:158a-259a
Bizen ware jar ··· 1:*259a*
design techniques ··· 7:266b
Echizen ware ··· 2:144a
Edo period ··· 1:263b-264a
decline and resurgence ··· 1:264a
decorated wares ··· 1:263b
general ··· 1:263b
Korean noborigama (climbing kiln) ··· 1:263b
Rimpa ··· 1:264a
utilitarian wares ··· 1:263b
folk craft ··· 2:295b-296a
furniture material, traditional ··· 2:371b
Hagi ware ··· 3:76b-77a
Haji ware ··· 3:84a
Hirashimizu ware ··· 3:145a
history ··· 1:256a-261b
Iga ware ··· 3:261b
Imari ware ··· 1:*260b*
iron-glazed ··· 7:71b
Kakiemon ware ··· 1:*261a*; 4:116b
Karatsu ware ··· 1:*260b*; 4:159a
Kutani ware ··· 1:*261a*; 4:321b
Kyōto ··· 1:*262b*; 4:337a-337b
lead-glazed ··· 1:262a-263a
Kyōto ··· 1:262b
origin ··· 1:262a-262b
Sanage ··· 1:263a
technique ··· 1:262a-262b
types ··· 1:262b
Mashiko ware ··· 2:*294b*; 5:125a
medieval ··· 1:263a
Kamakura period ··· 1:263a
Muromachi period ··· 1:263a
"Six Old Kilns" ··· 1:263a
types ··· 1:263a
Mino ware ··· 5:196a-196b
Nabeshima ware ··· 5:299a-299b
Ogidō shell mound ··· 6:70a
Onta ware ··· 6:113a
Oribe ware ··· 1:*258b*; 5:196a-196b
production techniques ··· 1:264a-265b
glazes ··· 1:265a-265b
kilns ··· 1:264b-265a
tools ··· 1:264b
Raku ware ··· 1:*258b*; 6:283a
Sanage ··· 7:9a-9b
Satsuma ware (satsuma-yaki) ··· 7:30a
Seto ware ··· 1:*257b*; 7:71a-71b
Shigaraki ware ··· 7:91a-91b
Shino ware ··· 1:*259a*; 5:196a-196b
Sōma ware ··· 7:226b-227a
Sue ware ··· 1:*257a*; 7:256a
Takatori ware ··· 7:319b-320a
Tamba ware ··· 7:333a
Tokoname ware ··· 8:43b-44a
Tsuboya ware ··· 8:111a
Tsutsumi ware ··· 8:119a
Yayoi pottery ··· 8:322a-322b
Ceramics museums ··· 5:279b
Ceramists
modern
Arakawa Toyozō ··· 1:73b
Hamada Shōji ··· 3:89b
Ishiguro Munemaro ··· 3:340a-341b
Itaya Hazan ··· 3:351b
Kaneshige Tōyō ··· 4:140a
Katō Hajime ··· 4:168a
Katō Tōkurō ··· 4:170b
Kawai Kanjirō ··· 4:178a-179b
Kitaōji Rosanjin ··· 4:228a
Miwa Kyūwa ··· 5:216a
Tomimoto Kenkichi ··· 8:71a-71b
premodern
Aoki Mokubei ··· 1:68b
Chōjirō ··· 1:298b
Eiraku Hozen ··· 2:186b
Hon'ami Kōetsu ··· 3:218b-219a
Kenzan ··· 4:199b-200a
Miura Ken'ya ··· 5:215b
Nin'ami Dōhachi ··· 6:4b
Nonomura Ninsei ··· 6:35a
Okuda Eisen ··· 6:95a
Ri Sampei ··· 6:320b
Sakaida Kakiemon ··· 4:116b
Cerebral apoplexy ··· 5:147b
Ceremonies
coming-of-age ··· 3:17a
gempuku ··· 3:17a
yūsoku kojitsu ··· 8:358a-358b
Cerqueira, Luis de ··· 1:265b-266a
Certain Woman, A ··· 1:84b; 4:309a

Certificate of Alien Registration ···· **1**:47b
Certified public accountant (CPA) ·· **1**:8b, 266a
Certified Public Accountants Law (1948) ···· **1**:8b
Cha. *See* **Tea**
Chabana (tea-ceremony flower arrangement) ···· **2**:*289a*
Chadō. *See* **Tea ceremony**
Chaguchagu Umakko ···· チャグチャグ馬子 ···· **1**:266a
Chairs ···· **2**:371a
Chaji ···· **7**:361b
Chakaiseki ryōri ···· 茶懐石料理 ··· **2**:*21a*, 305a, 306a
Chakaiseki ryōri cuisine ···· **2**:21b-22a
Chakushi ···· **6**:326a
Chambara ···· **1**:266a; **2**:271a, 274b
Chamberlain, Basil Hall ···· **1**:266a-266b; **2**:311a
  Hearn, Lafcadio ···· **3**:120b
Chamberlains' Office ···· **4**:315b
Chamber music ensembles ···· **4**:65a
Chamber of Elders ···· **3**:22a
Chambers of commerce
  establishment ···· **2**:32a
  regional ···· **4**:11a
Changed circumstances, principle of ···· **6**:245a-245b
Changgufeng (Ch'ang-ku-feng) Incident ···· **1**:266b
Chang Hsüeh-liang. *See* **Zhang Xueliang (Chang Hsüeh-liang)**
Chang Myōn ···· **4**:285a
Chang Po-go ···· **1**:266b
  Silla's trade controlled by ···· **4**:277b
Chang Tso-lin. *See* **Zhang Zuolin (Chang Tso-lin)**
Chang Tzu-p'ing. *See* **Zhang Ziping (Chang Tzu-p'ing)**
Chanoine, Charles Sulpice Jules ···· **1**:266b-267a; **2**:331b
Cha no yu. 茶の湯 *See* **Tea ceremony**
Chanson ···· **6**:354b
Chanter, puppet theater ···· **1**:213b
Chants, religious ···· **5**:283a-283b
Chao Fu ···· **4**:146b
Chapbooks ···· **4**:221b
Characters. *See* **Kanji**
Character sketches ···· **2**:188a; **5**:48b
"Charcoal-Maker Millionaire, The" ···· **7**:269b-270a
Charcoal making ···· **1**:267a
Chartered merchants ···· **3**:57a
Charter Oath · **1**:267a-267b; **2**:310b; **6**:204a; **7**:54a, 55a
  composition ···· **1**:267a-267b
  Fukuoka Takachika ···· **2**:365b
  Iwakura mission ···· **3**:193b
  Kido Takayoshi ···· **4**:203a
  kōgi seitai ron ···· **4**:248b
  Meiji Restoration ···· **5**:159b
  purpose ···· **1**:267a
  text ···· **1**:267a
  Yuri Kimimasa ···· **8**:358a
"Chart of the 50 sounds" ···· **3**:40b-41a
Chasen ···· **1**:136a
Chashaku ···· **1**:136a
Chashitsu ···· **7**:361b-362a
Chausudake. 茶臼岳 *See* **Nasudake**
Chawan ···· **7**:363b-364a
Chaya Shirojirō ···· 茶屋四郎次郎 ···· **1**:267b
Cheerleading ···· **6**:66b
Chemical industry ···· **1**:267b-268a
companies
  Asahi Chemical Industry Co, Ltd. ···· **1**:92a-92b
  Asahi Denka Kōgyō ···· **1**:92b
  Chisso Corporation ···· **1**:297b
  Daicel Chemical Industries, Ltd ···· **2**:56a
  Hitachi Chemical Co, Ltd ···· **3**:206b
  Kanegafuchi Chemical Industry Co, Ltd ···· **4**:137b
  Kaō Corporation ···· **4**:156a
  Kumiai Chemical Industry Co, Ltd ···· **4**:308a
  Kyōwa Hakkō Kōgyō Co, Ltd ···· **4**:340a
  Lion Corporation ···· **5**:10b
  Mitsubishi Chemical Industries, Ltd ···· **5**:207a
  Mitsubishi Gas Chemical Co, Inc ···· **5**:207b-208a
  Mitsubishi Petrochemical Industries, Ltd ···· **5**:212a
  Mitsui Petrochemical Industries, Ltd ···· **5**:212a
  Mitsui Tōatsu Chemicals, Inc ···· **5**:212b
  Nippon Kayaku Co, Ltd ···· **6**:10a
  Nippon Shokubai Kagaku Kōgyō ···· **6**:12a-12b
  Nippon Soda Co, Ltd ···· **6**:12b
  Nippon Zeon Co, Ltd ···· **6**:13b
  Nissan Chemical Industries, Ltd ···· **6**:20a
  Nittō Chemical Industry Co, Ltd ···· **6**:22b
  Sekisui Chemical Co, Ltd ···· **7**:57b
  Shin-Etsu Chemical Co, Ltd ···· **7**:11b
  Shōwa Denkō ···· **7**:173a
  Sumitomo Chemical Co, Ltd **7**:267b-268a
  Teijin, Ltd ···· **7**:375b
  Tōagōsei Chemical Industry Co, Ltd ···· **8**:30b
  Tokuyama Soda Co, Ltd ···· **8**:60b
  Tōray Industries, Inc ···· **8**:76b-77a
  Tōyō Soda Mfg Co, Ltd ···· **8**:93a
  Ube Industries, Ltd ···· **8**:123a
Chemical Society of Japan Award · **1**:268a
Chemistry ···· **1**:268a-268b
  Japanese achievements ···· **1**:268b
Chemists
  Akabori Shirō ···· **1**:39a
  Asahina Yasuhiko ···· **1**:93a
  Divers, Edward ···· **2**:120a
  Fukui Ken'ichi ···· **2**:363b
  Ikeda Kikunae ···· **3**:265b
  Kondō Heisaburō ···· **4**:269a
  Majima Toshiyuki ···· **5**:85a
  Mizushima San'ichirō ···· **5**:227b-228a
  Nagai Nagayoshi ···· **5**:301a
  Nitta Isamu ···· **6**:22a
  Nozoe Tetsuo ···· **6**:42a
  Ochiai Eiji ···· **6**:59a
  Sakurada Ichirō ···· **7**:4a
  Takamine Jōkichi ···· **7**:315b
  Yabuta Teijirō ···· **8**:283b
Chemulp'o, Treaty of **1**:268b; **4**:280a-280b; **7**:68b
Cheng Ch'eng-kung. *See* **Zheng Chenggong (Cheng Ch'eng-kung)**
Cheng Hsiao-hsü. *See* **Zheng Xiaoxu (Cheng Hsiao-hsü)**
Chen Mingshu (Ch'en Ming-shu) ·· **2**:342a
Chen Shou (Ch'en Shou) ···· **8**:305a
Chen Tianhua (Ch'en T'ien-hua) ·· **1**:269a
Ch'en T'ien-hua. *See* **Chen Tianhua (Ch'en T'ien-hua)**
Cherries and Maples (panels) ·· **7**:*41a-41b*
Cherry, flowering [(sakura) *Prunus* spp.] ···· **1**:269a-270a
  culture ···· **1**:269a-269b
  foreign ···· **1**:269b-270a
  varieties ···· **1**:269b
Cherry Blossom Society ···· **7**:5a
Cherry blossom viewing ···· **3**:94a-94b
Chestnut [(kuri) *Castanea crenata*] **1**:270a
Chests ···· **2**:371a
Chi ···· **4**:141b
Chiang Kai-shek ···· **1**:270a-270b, 288b; **6**:260a, 285b, 302a; **7**:228a; **8**:377b
  He-Umezu (Ho-Umezu) Agreement ···· **3**:128b
  Nanjing (Nanking) Incident ·· **5**:328b-329a
  Second United Front ···· **7**:47b-48a
  Shanghai Incident ···· **7**:77b
  World War II ···· **8**:275a
  Xi'an (Sian) Incident ···· **8**:281a
Chian Iji Hō ···· 治安維持法 ··· **6**:168a-169b
Chian Keisatsu Hō. 治安警察法 *See* **Public Order and Police Law of 1900**
Chiaochou concession. *See* **Jiaozhou (Kiaochow)**
Chiba ···· 千葉 ···· **1**:271a
Chiba Nikkō Company ···· **2**:304b
Chiba Prefecture ··· 千葉県 ···· **1**:271a
Chiba Shūsaku ·· 千葉周作 ···· **8**:303a
Chiba University ···· **1**:271a
Chibetto ryokōki ···· チベット旅行記 ···· **4**:177b
Chichi ariki (There was a Father) ···· 父ありき ···· **6**:141b
Chichibu, Prince ··· 秩父宮 ···· **1**:272a
  February 26th Incident ···· **2**:250a
Chichibu (city) ···· 秩父 ··· **1**:271a-271b
Chichibu Basin ·· 秩父盆地 ···· **1**:271b
Chichibu Cement Co, Ltd ···· **1**:271b
Chichibu geosyncline ···· 秩父地向斜 ···· **4**:9a
Chichibu Incident ···· 秩父事件 ··· **1**:271b-272a
  Farmers' Movement ···· **2**:249a
  Iida Incident ···· **3**:262b
  Jiyūtō ···· **4**:65b
Chichibu-Tama National Park ··· 秩父多摩国立公園 **1**:272a; **5**:318b
Chichijima ···· 父島 ··· **1**:272a-272b
Chichi no shanikusai (Father's Carnival) ···· 父の謝肉祭 ···· **8**:289b
Chicken, Japanese [(nipponkei) *Gallus gallus domesticus*] ···· **1**:272b-273b
  breeds and varieties ···· **1**:272b-273a
  history and folklore ···· **1**:273a-273b
    introduction ···· **1**:273a
Chicken production ···· **1**:30a
Chidori ···· **6**:192b
Chifuren ···· **1**:273b
Chigasaki ···· 茅ケ崎 ···· **1**:274a
Chigo ···· 稚児 ···· **1**:274a
Chigo monogatari 稚児物語 ···· **6**:130a
Chigyō ···· 知行 **1**:274a; **2**:265b
Chigyōkoku system ···· 知行国制 ···· **1**:274a
Chihōban ···· **1**:152b
Chihōkan Kaigi 地方官会議 ···· **1**:103b
Chihōshi ···· 地方史 ···· **5**:71a-71b
Chihōzei. *See* **Taxes, national and local**
Chiji ···· 知事 ···· **4**:197b
Chijimi ···· **1**:274b
Chijin no ai ···· 痴人の愛 ···· **7**:342b
Chijiwa Miguel ···· 千々石ミゲル ···· **1**:274b
Chikamatsu Hanji ···· 近松半二 · **1**:274b, 276a; **5**:49b
  Naniwa miyage ···· **5**:328b
Chikamatsu Monzaemon ···· 近松門左衛門 ···· **1**:*275a*, 275b-276a; **2**:274a; **3**:22b; **4**:77a; **5**:16a, 47a; **6**:269b; **7**:262a
  bunraku ···· **1**:214a
  Forty-Seven Rōnin Incident ···· **2**:328a

giri and ninjō ········ **3**:34b
kabuki works ········ **1**:276a; **4**:91b
Naniwa miyage ········ **5**:328a
puppet plays ········ **1**:275a-276a
Sakata Tōjūrō collaboration ···· **4**:91a-19b; **6**:379b
Semimaru ········ **7**:62a
works ········ **5**:47a
Chikamatsu Shūkō ········ 近松秋江 ········ **1**:276a
Chiken (title deed) ········ **4**:253b
Chikubashō ········ 竹馬抄 · **1**:276b; **7**:84a
Chikubujima Festival Mandala ····· **7**:136b
Chikubushima ····· 竹生島 ········ **1**:276b
Chikugo ········ 筑後 ········ **1**:276b
Chikugogawa ······ 筑後川 ··· **1**:83a, 276b
Chikugo shōshi gundan ········ 筑後将士軍談 ········ **1**:76b
Chikuhakukai ······ 竹柏会 ········ **5**:19b
Chikuhō Coalfield ········ 筑豊炭田 **1**:276b; **5**:314a
Tagawa ········ **7**:294a
Chikujō Daiten ·· 竺常大典 ········ **3**:353b
Chikumagawa ····· 千曲川 ········ **1**:276b
Shinanogawa ········ **7**:109a
Chikuma Shobō Publishing Co, Ltd ········ **1**:276b
Chikura ········ 千倉 ········ **1**:277a
Chikusai ········ 竹斎 ········ **4**:136b
Chikushino ········ 筑紫野 ········ **1**:277a
Childbirth ········ **2**:234b
Child Care Leave Bill of 1975 ······ **8**:262a
Childhood and child rearing **1**:277a-278b; **4**:38a-38b
age and sex differences ······ **1**:278a-278b
children in folk culture ········ **1**:277a
contemporary culture ········ **1**:277b
father and mother as disciplinarians ········ **1**:278a
games ········ **3**:6a
legal definition ········ **1**:277a
moral masochism and feelings of guilt ········ **1**:278a
physical and emotional closeness ··· **1**:48b, 277b
recent developments ········ **1**:278b
shitsuke ········ **1**:277b-278a
Children
abandonment ········ **7**:279b
entertainment for ········ **6**:275b
and **television** ········ **1**:278b-279a
"Children for Hire" ········ **8**:173b
Children's Day ········ **1**:146b, 277b, *279a*, 279a-279b; **2**:*261a*, 262a; **5**:4a
carp streamers ········ **1**:244a
dolls ········ **2**:129b
flags and banners ········ **2**:288a
kites ········ **4**:229b
Children's groups ········ **5**:4a
Children's literature ········ **1**:279b-280a
Akaitori ········ **1**:39b
Iwaya Sazanami ········ **3**:364a
Ogawa Mimei ········ **6**:70a
Suzuki Miekichi ········ **7**:282b
Children's songs ········ **1**:280a; **2**:301a
Child Welfare Law ··· **1**:280a-280b; **6**:235b; **7**:55b, 209b, 212a; **8**:265b
juvenile crime ········ **4**:86b
Chile ········ **4**:369b
Chimakizasa *(Sasa paniculata)* ···· **1**:136a
Chimmoku ········ 沈黙 ········ **2**:214a
Chin ········ **4**:40b-41a
China and Japan ········ **1**:280b-291b
Buddhism ········ **1**:178a; **2**:186a-186b
calligraphic styles of ········ **7**:170a
Chinese-Japanese character dictionary ········ **2**:93a-93b
cultural sphere ········ **2**:141b-142a
diplomatic envoys, ancient ··· **7**:259b-261a
ethics ········ **2**:232a
influence in medicine ········ **5**:145b-146b
kampō (Chinese medicine) · **5**:150b-151b
Neo-Confucianism ········ **7**:190a-191b
(to 1911) ········ **1**:280b-287b
ancient period ········ **1**:281a-283a
Edo period ········ **1**:284b-286a
medieval period ········ **1**:283a-284b
Meiji period ········ **1**:286a-287b
prehistory ········ **1**:281a
(after 1912) ········ **1**:287b-291b
anti-warlord and anti-imperialist movements ········ **1**:288a-288b
Chinese Revolution of 1911 and Twenty-One Demands ········ **1**:287b; **8**:120b-121a
diplomatic relations ········ **1**:291a-291b
Manchurian Incident ······ **1**:288b-289a; **5**:97b-98a
May Fourth Movement and Washington Conference ··· **1**:287b-288a; **5**:143a-143b
North China problem ······ **1**:289a-289b
outbreak of Pacific War and Japan's defeat ········ **1**:289b-290a
postwar relations ··· **1**:290a-290b; **3**:205b
Sino-Japanese War of 1894-1895 ········ **7**:197b-198b
Sino-Japanese War of 1937-1945 **1**:289b; **7**:199a-202a
trade with China and Nationalist government opposition ····· **1**:290b-291a
unification of China by Nationalist government ········ **1**:288b
wakō ········ **8**:220b
postwar relations ········ **3**:205b
religion ········ **6**:290a-293b
songs from ········ **5**:197a-197b
Taiwan ········ **7**:306a-309a
Chinaberry [(sendan) *Melia azedarach* var. *japonica*] ········ **1**:291b
China Critic ········ **7**:337b
China Enterprise Company ········ **5**:249b
China Incident of 1937. *See* **Sino-Japanese War of 1937-1945**
China-Japan Peace and Friendship Treaty ········ **1**:291a-292a; **7**:202a
antihegemony principle ········ **1**:292a
China War (1937-1945) ······ **3**:201a-202a; **7**:199a-202a
Ch'in-ch'i shu-hua ········ **4**:213b-214a
Chindai ········ 鎮台 ········ **1**:292a
Chinese
minorities ········ **5**:195a-195b
resident foreigners ········ **2**:313a-313b
Chinese bellflower ········ **4**:207b
Chinese characters. *See* **Kanji**
Chinese Communist Party
August First declaration ········ **1**:116b
Second United Front ········ **7**:47b-48a
Chinese Eastern Railway (CER) ········ **1**:292a-292b; **7**:237a
Hirota Kōki ········ **3**:150a
Ioffe (Joffe), Adolf Abramovich ···· **3**:328a
Russia and Japan ········ **6**:341b, 343a
World War I ········ **8**:270b
Chinese Exclusion Act (US) ········ **4**:14a
Chinese Guomindang (Kuomintang) Party. *See* Guomingdang
Chinese Lions (Karajishi zu) ······ **4**:146b, *146a-146b*
Chinese literature and Japanese literature ········ **1**:292b-296a; **5**:195a-196b
characteristics ········ **5**:25a-25b
Edo period ········ **1**:294b-295b
Heian period ········ **1**:293a-294a
Kamakura and Muromachi periods ········ **1**:294a-294b
modern period ········ **1**:295b-296a
Nara period ········ **1**:293a
poetry ········ **5**:29a-32a
prose ········ **5**:29b-30a
recording and transmission ····· **5**:26a-27a
Yamato period ·· **1**:292b-293a; **5**:193b-194a
Chinese-style painting ········ **4**:157a
Ching ········ **8**:119a-119b
Chinjufu ········ 鎮守府 ········ **1**:296a
Chinju no kami ········ **1**:296a-296b
Chinkasai (Soothing of the Flowers) ········ 鎮花祭 ········ **6**:191b
Chinkon ritual ········ **4**:107a
Chin Nampin ······· 沈南蘋 ········ **7**:83b
Chino ········ 茅野 ········ **1**:296b
Chinowa ········ **5**:308b
Chinsetsu yumiharizuki ········ 椿説弓張月 ········ **1**:130b
Chinsō ········ **1**:192a; **6**:227b
Chin Tenka ········ 陳天華 ········ **1**:269a
Chion'in ········ 知恩院 **1**:296b; **4**:336b
Chiossone, Edoardo ······ **1**:296b; **2**:311b
cultural exchange ········ **3**:350b-351a
Chiran ········ 知覧 ········ **1**:297a
Chirigaku hyōron ········ 地理学評論 ········ **1**:103b
Chiri Mashiho · 知里真志保 ········ **1**:36b
Chirimen ········ **1**:297a
Chiritsubaki ········ **1**:237a
"Chirizuka" ········ 塵塚 ········ **4**:179b
Chiryū ········ 知立 ········ **1**:297a
Chishakuin ········ 智積院 ········ **1**:297a
Shingon sect ········ **7**:115a
Shinshōji ········ **7**:125a
Chishima Islands. *See* **Kuril Islands**
Chishimakan Incident ········ 千島艦事件 ········ **1**:297a
Chishima Rettō ·· 千島列島 ········ **4**:313a
Chishima Volcanic Zone ········ 千島火山帯 ········ **1**:297a
Chishimazasa *(Sasa kurilensis)* ···· **1**:136a
Chishitsu Chōsajo ········ **3**:26a
Chiso Kaisei ····· 地租改正 · **4**:365b-366b
Chisso Chemical Company ········ **2**:304a
Chisso Corporation ········ **1**:297b
pollution ········ **2**:226a
Chisuji no kurokami ········ 千すじの黒髪 ········ **7**:335b
Chita ········ 知多 ········ **1**:297b
Chita Peninsula · 知多半島 ········ **1**:297b
Chiteiki ········ 池亭記 ········ **4**:129a
Chitose ········ 千歳 ········ **1**:297b
Chitose ware ······· 千歳焼 ········ **3**:145a
Chitsuroku shobun ········ 秩禄処分 ··· **1**:297b-298a
dissolution of samurai class ········ **7**:8b
Chi-tung Fang-kung Tzu-chih Cheng-fu ········ **2**:142b
Chiyari Fuji ······ 血槍富士 ········ **4**:166a
Chiyoda Chemical Engineering & Construction Co, Ltd ········ **1**:298a
Chiyoda Saiichi ········ 千代田才一 ········ **4**:189b
Chiyoda Ward ··· 千代田区 ········ **1**:298a
Chiyogami ········ **1**:298b
Chiyo Ni kushū 千代尼句集 ········ **4**:102b
Chlorella (*Chlorella* spp.) · **1**:298b; **7**:334a
Chō ········ **1**:225b-226a
Chōchin lanterns ········ **4**:368a
Chōchō satsujin jiken ········ 蝶々殺人事件 ········ **8**:333b
Chōdensu. *See* **Minchō**
Ch'oe Mu-sŏn ········ **4**:278a
Ch'oe Yŏng ········ **4**:278a
Chōfu (city) ········ 調布 ········ **1**:298b
Chōfu (district) ······· 長府 ········ **1**:298b

Chō Gakuryō 張学良 **8**:377b
Chōhei hantai ikki 徴兵反対一揆 **4**:200a
Chōheirei 徴兵令 **1**:359a
Cho Hōkō 張宝高 **1**:266b
Chōjirō 長次郎 **1**:298b; **2**:346a; **4**:337a
Chōjū giga 鳥獣戯画 **1**:298b-299a; **2**:*199a-199b*; **8**:32a
Chōka **1**:299a-299b
  decline **4**:115b
  Heian period **5**:30a
  Kakinomoto no Hitomaro **4**:117a
  waka **8**:202b
Chōkaisan 鳥海山 **1**:299b
Chokai shōsetsu tengu 嘲戒小説天狗 **8**:288b
Chōkai Volcanic Zone 鳥海火山帯 **1**:299b
Chōkata 帳方 **4**:119b
Chōkei, Emperor 長慶天皇 **1**:299b
Chokkomon 直弧文 **1**:160b, 167a, 299b
Chōkōdō ryō 長講堂領 **1**:299b-300a
Chōkohō Jiken 張鼓峰事件 **1**:266b
Chō kokka shugi 超国家主義 **8**:144b-146a
Chōkokuji. 長谷寺 *See* **Hasedera**
Chokurei **3**:278b
Chokusenshū 勅撰集 **3**:275b
Chokushimon **1**:183a
Chokusho 勅書 **7**:62a
Chōkyōsai Eiri 鳥橋斎栄里 **1**:300a
Chommage **4**:127b
Chōmonkyō 長門峡 **1**:5a, 300a
Chōna hajime 手斧始め **4**:195a
Chōnaikai **1**:300a; **5**:359b
Chongguo Renmin Jiukuo Hui **5**:346a
Chongqing (Chungking) government **1**:300b
Chōnin 町人 **1**:132a, 300a-302b; **3**:191a
  culture **1**:302b
  daily life **1**:302a-302b
  early history **1**:301a
  Edo **2**:168b-169b
  emergence **1**:301a-301b
  further development **1**:301b-302a
  Hiroshige **1**:*300b*
  Junkeichō yomise no zu (Night Stalls in Junkeichō) **1**:*300b*
  shi-nō-kō-shō **7**:122b
  strata **1**:302a
  urban life **8**:177b
Chōnindō 町人道 **1**:302a-303a
Chōnin kōken roku 町人考見録 **1**:303a
Chōnin-mono (economic life) 町人物 **8**:144a
Ch'ŏphaesinŏ **7**:163a
Chopping board (manaita) **2**:24b
Chopsticks **2**:305b
Chordophones **5**:282b
Chōri Co, Ltd **1**:303a
Chō Sakurin 張作霖 **8**:378a
Chōsan 逃散 **1**:303a-303b
Chōsei 長勢 **1**:199b, *303a*, 303b
Chōsen 庁宣 **1**:303b
Chōsen Ginkō **1**:303b
Chōsen Kaikyō. *See* **Korea Strait**
Chōsen Sensō 朝鮮戦争 **4**:292a-292b
Chōsen tsūshinshi 朝鮮通信使 **1**:303b-304a
  Chōsenjin shisetsu raihei daigyōretsu ryakuzu (Sketches of the Procession of the Korean Tributory Mission) **1**:*304a-304b*
  Korean-Japanese relations **4**:279a
Choshi
  bibliography **1**:153b
Chōshi 銚子 **1**:153b, 304a
Chō Shihei 張資平 **8**:377b-378a
Chōshū domain 長州藩
  Western naval expedition against **7**:105b
Chōshū Expeditions 長州征伐 **1**:86a, 304a-304b
  Meiji Restoration **5**:158a-158b
  Satsuma-Chōshū Alliance **7**:29b
    Tokugawa Iemochi **8**:48a
    Tokugawa Yoshinobu **8**:57b
  yonaoshi rebellions **8**:337b
Chōsokabe family 長宗我部氏 **1**:304b
Chōsokabe Motochika 長宗我部元親 **1**:304b; **8**:302a
Chōsokabe Motochika, 100-Article Code of 長宗我部元親百箇条 **1**:304b
Chōsokabe Okitegaki 長宗我部掟書 **1**:304b
Chosŏn. *See* **Taehan Empire**
Chōson gappei **8**:87b
Chōtei. *See* **Conciliation**
Chou En-lai. *See* **Zhou Enlai (Chou En-lai)**
Chou Hung-ch'ing Incident. *See* **Zhou Hongqing (Chou Hung-ch'ing) Incident**
Chou Tso-jen. *See* **Zhou Zuoren (Chou Tso-jen)**
Chōya gunsai 朝野群載 **1**:305a
Chōya shimbun 朝野新聞 **1**:129a
Chōzen naikaku 超然内閣 **8**:97b
Christian art, 16th and 17th centuries. *See* **Namban art**
Christian Churches, Japan Association of **1**:305a
Christian daimyō **1**:64b, 305a-306a
  Arima Harunobu **1**:83a
  Konishi Yukinaga **4**:270b
  Ōmura Sumitada **6**:104b
  Takayama Ukon **7**:321a
Christianity **1**:306a-310a; **6**:290a
  Anti-Christian edicts **1**:64b-65a
  Azuchi-Momoyama **3**:183a
  bateren **1**:145b-146a
  Catholic **1**:308a
  Deusu **2**:91a
  Edo period **4**:32a
  education **2**:172b; **6**:293a
  expansion **1**:306b-307a
  government censorship **1**:251b
  introduction to Japan **1**:306b
  Japanese literature **4**:32a
  Kakure Kirishitan **1**:308a; **4**:119a
  martyrdoms **1**:307a
  missionaries **1**:249b-250b; **6**:257a-258b
  mission to Europe of 1582 **5**:203a
  music **5**:283b
  Nagasaki **5**:304a
  nationalism **1**:309a-309b
  "national isolation directives" **7**:186a
  natural sciences **5**:355b
  nonchurch (mukyōkai) **5**:262b-263a
  Okinawa **6**:87a
  Orthodox **1**:308a-308b
  persecution and suppression **1**:307a-308a; **7**:185b
  Protestant **1**:308b
  publications **6**:248a
  reintroduction **1**:308a
  sects **7**:242b
  social activity **1**:309a
  social work **6**:293a
  statistics **1**:309b
  Tokugawa shogunate **8**:53a
  tolerance in Japanese religion **8**:70b
  Toyotomi Hideyoshi **8**:95a
  Urakami persecutions **6**:178a
  warrior government **8**:230b
  weddings **8**:239a
  women in **8**:256b
Christian Mansion **4**:221b-222a
Christian schools **6**:295b
  mission schools **5**:202b-203a
Christmas **1**:310a
Chronicle of Gods and Sovereigns, A **4**:59b-60a
Chronicle of Great Peace. *See Taiheiki*
Chronicle of Japan **1**:141b; **5**:383b-384a
Chronicle of the Kemmu Era **4**:191b
Chronicles, historiography **3**:152a-158a
Chronicles of Masakado **7**:165b
"Chronicles of the Three Kingdoms" **8**:240b
Chronological Records of the Money-Changing Houses **6**:351b
Chrysanthemum and the Sword **1**:149b
Chrysanthemum Festival **1**:310a; **2**:260b
Chrysanthemums [(kiku) *Chrysanthemum morifolium*] **1**:310a-311a
Chūbu Electric Power Co, Inc **1**:311a
Chūbu-Nippon Broadcasting Co, Ltd (CBC) **1**:311a
Chūbu region 中部地方 **1**:311a-311b
Chūbu Sangaku National Park 中部山岳国立公園 **1**:5a, 127b, 311b
Chūchō jijitsu 中朝事実 **1**:311b; **8**:290b
Chūgan Engetsu 中巌円月 **1**:311b; **3**:58b
Chūgen (retainer) 中間 **1**:311b-312a
Chūgen (gifts) 中元 **1**:312a; **7**:49a
  kaeshi **3**:30b; **4**:102a
  kokorozuke **4**:256b
Chūgoku Electric Power Co, Inc **1**:312a
Chūgoku Mountains 中国山脈 **1**:312a
Chūgoku region 中国地方 **1**:312a-312b; **4**:151b
Chūgū 中宮 **1**:312b
Chūgūji 中宮寺 **1**:312b
Chu Hsi school. *See* **Shushigaku**
Chu Hsi studies **7**:190a-191b
Chūji tabi nikki (Chūji's Travel Diary) 忠治旅日記 **2**:*268b*
Chūkai 中海 **5**:318b
Chūka Minkoku Ishin Seifu 中華民国維新政府 **6**:285b-286a
Chūka Minkoku Rinji Seifu 中華民国臨時政府 **6**:260a-260b
Chūkan shōsetsu **1**:312b-313a
  postwar literature **6**:231a
Chūken kigyō **7**:205a
Chūki 中気 **1**:231a
Chūkyō, Emperor 仲恭天皇 **4**:72a
Chūkyō Industrial Zone 中京工業地帯 **1**:313a
  Nagoya **5**:308b-309a
Chūkyōshin **1**:255b
Chūma 中馬 **1**:313a
Chūmon (inner gate) **1**:182b; **3**:*12b*; **7**:111a
Chung-hua Min-kuo Linshih Cheng-fu **6**:260a-260b
Chung-hua Min-kuo Wei-hsin Cheng-fu **6**:285b-286a
Chungking government. *See* **Chongqing (Chungking) government**
Chung Kuei **7**:163b
Chung-kuo Jen-min Chiu-kuo Hui **5**:346a
Chūnichi shimbun 中日新聞 **1**:313a

Chūō kōron ······ 中央公論 ·· **1**:313a-313b; **4**:114a; **6**:267b; **7**:100a, 309b, 338a; **8**:348b
banning ········ **1**:252b
Kajii Motojirō ········ **4**:114a
Takita Choin ········ **7**:327a
Yokohama Incident ········ **8**:330a
Chūō Kōron New Writer's Prize ··· **7**:163a
Chūō Kōron Sha, Inc ······ **1**:313b; **2**:343a
Shimanaka Yūsaku, president **7**:100a-100b
Chūō Kyōiku Shingikai ········ **1**:255b
Chūō Rōdō Iinkai ········ **1**:256a
Chūō University ········ **1**:313b
Chūō Ward ········ 中央区 ········ **1**:313b
Churchill, Winston
Yalta Conference ········ **8**:286b
Church of Perfect Liberty, The ···· **6**:192b
Chūritsu Rōren (Federation of Independent Labor Unions) ········ 中立労連 ·· **1**:313b-314a; **4**:347b, 360a; **6**:238a; **7**:189b
Chūseikai ········ **1**:314a
Kenseikai ········ **4**:198a
Chūshin ········ **4**:247b
Chūshingura ······· 忠臣蔵 · **4**:171b, 275a; **5**:49b; **8**:184a
Chūshingura okame hyōban ·· 忠臣蔵岡目評判 ········ **4**:61a
Chu Shun-shui ········ **7**:191b
Chūsonji ········ 中尊寺 ······· **1**:195b, 314a-314b
Chūuki. 中右記 *See* **Chūyūki**
Chūyūki ········ 中右記 ········ **1**:314b
Chūzan'ō ········ 中山王 ········ **1**:314b
Chūzenji, Lake ·· 中禅寺湖 ··· **1**:315a; **6**:*3a*
Cicadas [(semi) family Cicadidae] · **1**:315a
Cien Dashi ········ **8**:286a
Circle, Triangle, and Square ······ **8**:*374b*
Cities
Amami
Naze ········ **5**:359a
Awajishima
Sumoto ········ **7**:274b
China
Harbin ········ **3**:103b
Hokkaidō
Abashiri ········ **1**:1b
Akabira ········ **1**:39a
Asahikawa ········ **1**:92b
Ashibetsu ········ **1**:97a
Bibai ········ **1**:150b
Chitose ········ **1**:297b
Date ········ **2**:78a
Ebetsu ········ **2**:143a
Eniwa ········ **2**:218a
Fukagawa ········ **2**:359b
Furano ········ **2**:370b
Hakodate ········ **3**:85b
Iwamizawa ········ **3**:360b
Kitami ········ **4**:226b
Kushiro ········ **4**:320b
Mikasa ········ **5**:170b
Mombetsu ········ **5**:236a
Muroran ········ **5**:274b
Nayoro ········ **5**:358b
Nemuro ········ **5**:360a
Noboribetsu ········ **6**:30a
Obihiro ········ **6**:49a
Otaru ········ **6**:129a-129b
Rumoi ········ **6**:340b
Sapporo ········ **7**:20a
Shibetsu ········ **7**:85b
Sunagawa ········ **7**:274b
Takikawa ········ **7**:326b
Tomakomai ········ **8**:70b
Utashinai ········ **8**:187a
Wakkanai ········ **8**:220a
Yūbari ········ **8**:354b
Honshū
Abiko ········ **1**:5a
Ageo ········ **1**:21b
Aioi ········ **1**:37b
Aizu Wakamatsu ········ **1**:38b
Akashi ········ **1**:40b-41a
Akigawa ········ **1**:41b
Akishima ········ **1**:42a
Akita ········ **1**:42b
Akō ········ **1**:45a
Amagasaki ········ **1**:49a
Anjō ········ **1**:62a
Annaka ········ **1**:62b
Aomori ········ **1**:69b
Arai ········ **1**:72b
Arida ········ **1**:83a
Asahi ········ **1**:92a
Asaka ········ **1**:94a
Ashikaga ········ **1**:98b
Ashiya ········ **1**:102a
Atami ········ **1**:107b
Atsugi ········ **1**:115a
Ayabe ········ **1**:125a
Ayase ········ **1**:125b
Bisai ········ **1**:156b
Bizen ········ **1**:158a
Chiba ········ **1**:271a
Chichibu ········ **1**:271a-271b
Chigasaki ········ **1**:274a
Chino ········ **1**:296b
Chiryū ········ **1**:297a
Chita ········ **1**:297b
Chōfu ········ **1**:298b
Chōshi ········ **1**:304a
Daitō ········ **2**:67b
Ebina ········ **2**:143a
Ena ········ **2**:213a
Enzan ········ **2**:229b
Esashi ········ **2**:231a
Fuchū (Tōkyō Prefecture) ········ **2**:340a
Fuchū (Hiroshima Prefecture) ···· **2**:340a
Fuji ········ **2**:341b
Fujieda ········ **2**:342a
Fujiidera ········ **2**:343a
Fujimi ········ **2**:343b
Fujinomiya ········ **2**:344a
Fujioka ········ **2**:344a
Fujisawa ········ **2**:345b
Fuji Yoshida ········ **2**:359a
Fukaya ········ **2**:359b
Fukuchiyama ········ **2**:361b
Fukui ········ **2**:363a
Fukuroi ········ **2**:365b
Fukushima ········ **2**:366a
Fukuyama ········ **2**:367b
Funabashi ········ **2**:368a
Furukawa ········ **2**:372a
Fussa ········ **2**:375a
Futtsu ········ **2**:376b
Gamagōri ········ **3**:5a
Gifu ········ **3**:31a
Gobō ········ **3**:38b
Gojō ········ **3**:40b
Gose ········ **3**:47b
Gosen ········ **3**:48b
Goshogawara ········ **3**:50a
Gotemba ········ **3**:51a
Gōtsu ········ **3**:54b
Gyōda ········ **3**:71a
Habikino ········ **3**:73a
Hachinohe ········ **3**:74b
Hachiōji ········ **3**:74b
Hadano ········ **3**:75a
Hagi ········ **3**:75b
Hakui ········ **3**:88a
Hamada ········ **3**:89a
Hamakita ········ **3**:90b
Hamamatsu ········ **3**:90b
Hanamaki ········ **3**:94a
Handa ········ **3**:95a
Hannō ········ **3**:99b
Hanyū ········ **3**:100a
Haramachi ········ **3**:102a
Hashima ········ **3**:109b
Hashimoto ········ **3**:109b
Hasuda ········ **3**:111a
Hatogaya ········ **3**:112b
Hekinan ········ **3**:126a
Higashi Hiroshima ········ **3**:131b
Higashi Kurume ········ **3**:132a
Higashi Matsuyama ········ **3**:132a
Higashi Murayama ········ **3**:132a
Higashine ········ **3**:132a
Higashi Ōsaka ········ **3**:132a-132b
Higashi Yamato ········ **3**:132b
Hikari ········ **3**:137b
Hikone ········ **3**:138b
Himeji ········ **3**:139a
Himi ········ **3**:139b
Hino ········ **3**:140b
Hirakata ········ **3**:143a
Hirata ········ **3**:145a
Hiratsuka ········ **3**:146a
Hirosaki ········ **3**:147b
Hiroshima ········ **3**:149b
Hisai ········ **3**:151b
Hitachi ········ **3**:206b
Hitachi Ōta ········ **3**:207a
Hōfu ········ **3**:209a
Honjō (Akita Prefecture) ········ **3**:223a
Honjō (Saitama Prefecture) ······ **3**:223a
Hōya ········ **3**:246b
Ibara ········ **3**:253a
Ibaraki ········ **3**:253a
Ichihara ········ **3**:255b
Ichikawa ········ **3**:256b
Ichinomiya ········ **3**:258a
Ichinoseki ········ **3**:258b
Iida ········ **3**:262a
Iiyama ········ **3**:263b
Ikeda ········ **3**:264b-265a
Ikoma ········ **3**:270b
Imaichi ········ **3**:272b-273a
Ina ········ **3**:281b
Inagi ········ **3**:282b
Inazawa ········ **3**:284a
Innoshima ········ **3**:308b
Inuyama ········ **3**:326b
Iruma ········ **3**:336a
Ise ········ **3**:336b
Isehara ········ **3**:337a
Isesaki ········ **3**:338a
Ishinomaki ········ **3**:345a
Ishioka ········ **3**:345a
Itami ········ **3**:351b
Itō ········ **3**:351b
Itoigawa ········ **3**:353b
Iwai ········ **3**:357b
Iwaki ········ **3**:358a
Iwakuni ········ **3**:358a
Iwakura ········ **3**:358b
Iwanuma ········ **3**:361b
Iwata ········ **3**:363b
Iwatsuki ········ **3**:364a
Izumi (Miyagi Prefecture) ········ **3**:365a
Izumi (Ōsaka Prefecture) ········ **3**:365a
Izumi Ōtsu ········ **3**:366a
Izumi Sano ········ **3**:366a
Izumo ········ **3**:367a
Jōetsu ········ **4**:69a
Jōyō ········ **4**:78b
Kadoma ········ **4**:101a
Kaga ········ **4**:102a
Kainan ········ **4**:111b
Kaizuka ········ **4**:114a
Kakamigahara ········ **4**:115a

Kakegawa 4:115a
Kakogawa 4:117b
Kakuda 4:118a
Kamagaya 4:120b
Kamaishi 4:120b
Kamakura 4:120b
Kameoka 4:125b
Kameyama 4:125b
Kami Fukuoka 4:126a
Kaminoyama 4:127a
Kamo 4:128a
Kamogawa 4:128a
Kanazawa 4:136a
Kanuma 4:154a
Kariya 4:160a
Kasai 4:160b
Kasama 4:161a
Kasaoka 4:161a
Kashihara 4:162a
Kashiwa 4:162b
Kashiwara 4:162b-163a
Kashiwazaki 4:163a
Kasugai 4:163b
Kasukabe 4:164a
Katano 4:166a
Katsuta 4:174b
Katsuura 4:174b
Katsuyama 4:175a
Kawachi Nagano 4:177a
Kawagoe 4:177b
Kawaguchi 4:177b
Kawanishi 4:182a
Kawasaki 4:183a
Kazo 4:185b
Kazuno 4:185b
Kesennuma 4:200a
Kimitsu 4:208b
Kiryū 4:222a
Kisarazu 4:222b
Kishiwada 4:223b
Kita Ibaraki 4:225b
Kitakami 4:226a
Kitakata 4:226b
Kitamoto 4:227a
Kiyose 4:232b
Kōbe 4:238a
Kodaira 4:241a
Kōfu 4:243b
Koga 4:246a
Koganei 4:248a
Kokubunji 4:257a
Komae 4:264b
Komagane 4:264b
Komaki 4:265a
Komatsu 4:265b
Komoro 4:267b
Kōnan 4:268b
Kōnosu 4:275a
Kōriyama 4:293b
Kosai 4:294b
Koshigaya 4:295b
Kōshoku 4:296a
Kudamatsu 4:302a
Kuji 4:303a
Kuki 4:304a
Kumagaya 4:305b
Kumano 4:306b
Kunitachi 4:310a
Kurashiki 4:311b
Kurayoshi 4:312a
Kure 4:312b
Kurobe 4:313b
Kuroishi 4:316a
Kuroiso 4:316a
Kusatsu 4:319a-319b
Kuwana 4:322a
Kyōto 4:334a
Machida 5:78b
Maebashi 5:79b
Maizuru 5:85a
Masuda 5:129b
Matsubara 5:131a
Matsudo 5:132b
Matsue 5:132b
Matsumoto 5:137b
Matsusaka 5:140a
Mattō 5:142a
Mihara 5:168b-169a
Miki 5:171a
Minami Ashigara 5:176b
Mine 5:184a
Mino 5:194a
Mino Kamo 5:194b
Minoo 5:195a
Misato 5:198a
Misawa 5:198a
Mishima 5:199a
Mitaka 5:203b-204a
Mito 5:204b
Mitsukaidō 5:213a
Mitsuke 5:213a
Miura 5:214a-214b
Miyako 5:219a
Miyazu 5:223b
Miyoshi 5:223b
Mizunami 5:226a
Mizusawa 5:227b
Mobara 5:228a
Mōka 5:234a
Moriguchi 5:249b
Morioka 5:252b
Moriyama 5:254b
Mukō 5:262b
Murakami 5:266a
Murayama 5:270a
Musashi Murayama 5:275a
Musashino 5:275a
Mutsu 5:288a
Nabari 5:299a
Nagahama 5:300a
Nagai 5:300a
Nagano 5:302a
Nagaoka 5:303b
Nagaokakyō 5:303b
Nagareyama 5:303b
Nagato 5:307a
Nagoya 5:308b-309a
Nakaminato 5:314b
Nakano 5:315b-316a
Namerikawa 5:324a
Nanao 5:327b
Nan'yō 5:330a
Nara 5:331b-332a
Narashino 5:334a
Narita 5:334b
Natori 5:349b
Neyagawa 5:373a
Nihommatsu 5:378b
Niigata 5:385a
Niimi 5:386b
Niitsu 5:386b
Niiza 5:386b
Nikkō 6:2b-3a
Ninohe 6:7a
Nirasaki 6:13b-14a
Nishinomiya 6:19a
Nishio 6:19a
Nishiwaki 6:19b
Noda 6:30a-30b
Noshiro 6:41a
Numata 6:44b
Numazu 6:44b
Obama 6:47b
Obanazawa 6:48a
Ōbu 6:50b
Ōda 6:60b
Ōdate 6:65a
Odawara 6:65b
Ōfunato 6:67b
Oga 6:68a
Ōgaki 6:68a
Ojiya 6:77a
Okaya 6:82b
Okayama 6:82b
Okazaki 6:83a
Okegawa 6:83b
Ōmachi 6:100a-100b
Ōmagari 6:100b
Ōme 6:101a
Ōmi Hachiman 6:101b
Ōmiya 6:102b
Ono (Hyōgo Prefecture) 6:108b
Ōno (Fukui Prefecture) 6:108b
Onoda 6:109a
Onomichi 6:110b
Ōsaka 6:120a
Ōta 6:128a
Ōtake 6:129a
Ōtawara 6:129b
Ōtsu 6:133b
Ōtsuki 6:134a
Owari Asahi 6:136b
Owase 6:136b
Oyabe 6:137a
Oyama 6:137b
Rikuzen Takata 6:317b
Ryōtsu 6:353a
Ryūgasaki 6:353b
Sabae 6:361a
Sagae 6:363a
Sagamihara 6:363b
Sakado 6:375a
Sakai 6:375b
Sakaiminato 6:376b
Sakata 6:379b
Saku 7:3a
Sakura 7:4a
Sakurai 7:4b
Sanda 7:9b
Sanjō 7:12a
Sano 7:15b
Sawara 7:31b
Sayama 7:31b
Seki 7:56a
Sendai 7:63b
Sennan 7:66b
Seto 7:71a
Settsu 7:73a
Shibata 7:84b
Shibukawa 7:86a
Shijōnawate 7:94a
Shiki 7:95b
Shimada 7:99a
Shimizu 7:104a
Shimminato 7:104b
Shimoda 7:104b
Shimodate 7:104b
Shimonoseki 7:105b
Shimotsuma 7:107a
Shingū 7:115a
Shinjō 7:116a
Shin Nan'yō 7:121b
Shinshiro 7:125a
Shiogama 7:140a
Shiojiri 7:140b
Shirakawa 7:146b
Shiroishi 7:148a
Shirone 7:148a
Shizuoka 7:153a
Shōbara 7:154a
Sōja 7:224a
Sōka 7:224b
Sōma 7:226b
Suita 7:264b

Sukagawa 7:265a
Sumoto 7:274b
Susono 7:279a
Suwa 7:280a
Suzu 7:280b
Suzuka 7:280b
Tachikawa 7:293a
Tagajō 7:294a
Tajimi 7:310a
Takahagi 7:311a
Takahama 7:311a
Takahashi 7:311b
Takaishi 7:314a
Takaoka 7:317b
Takarazuka 7:318a
Takasago 7:318b
Takasaki 7:318b
Takatsuki 7:320a
Takayama 7:320a
Takefu 7:323b
Takehara 7:324a
Tama 7:332a
Tamano 7:332b
Tanabe 7:335a
Tanashi 7:339b
Tatebayashi 7:348b
Tateyama 7:349b
Tatsuno 7:349b
Tendō 8:5b
Tenri 8:8b
Tenryū 8:10a
Toba 8:31a
Tochigi 8:33a
Tochio 8:33a-33b
Toda 8:33b
Tōgane 8:35b
Tōkai 8:40b
Tōkamachi 8:42a-42b
Toki 8:42b
Tokoname 8:43b
Tokorozawa 8:44a
Tokuyama 8:60b
Tōkyō 8:60b-66a
Tomioka 8:71b-72a
Tonami 8:73a
Tondabayashi 8:74a
Tōno 8:75a
Toride 8:77a
Tottori 8:85b-86a
Towada 8:86b
Toyama 8:87b
Toyoake 8:89a
Toyohashi 8:90b
Toyokawa 8:91b
Toyonaka 8:92a-92b
Toyooka 8:92b
Toyosaka 8:92b
Toyota 8:93a
Tsu 8:108a
Tsubame 8:109b
Tsuchiura 8:112a
Tsuru 8:116b
Tsuruga 8:116b
Tsuruoka 8:117a
Tsushima 8:117b
Tsuyama 8:119b
Ube 8:123a
Ueda 8:125b
Ueno 8:128b
Uji 8:131a
Uozu 8:174b
Urawa 8:175b
Urayasu 8:176a
Utsunomiya 8:188a
Wajima 8:201a
Wakayama 8:219a
Wakō 8:220a
Warabi 8:223a
Yachiyo 8:283b
Yaita 8:284b
Yaizu 8:284b
Yamagata 8:290b
Yamaguchi 8:294a
Yamanashi 8:301a
Yamato 8:308a
Yamato Kōriyama 8:310a
Yamato Takada 8:310b
Yanai 8:315b
Yao 8:316a
Yashio 8:317a
Yasugi 8:318b
Yawata 8:320a-320b
Yōkaichi 8:329a
Yōkaichiba 8:329a
Yokkaichi 8:329b
Yokohama 8:329b
Yokosuka 8:334a
Yokote 8:334a
Yonago 8:337a
Yonezawa 8:338a
Yono 8:338a
Yūki 8:356b
Yuzawa 8:358b
Zama 8:367b
Zushi 8:381a
Kyūshū
Akune 1:45a
Amagi 1:49a
Arao 1:74b
Beppu 1:150a
Bungo Takada 1:210a
Buzen 1:226b
Chikugo 1:276b
Chikushino 1:277a
Dazaifu 2:79a
Ebino 2:143b
Fukue 2:362b
Fukuoka 2:364b
Hirado 3:141b
Hita 3:206a
Hitoyoshi 3:208b
Hondo 3:220a
Hyūga 3:252b
Ibusuki 3:255a
Iizuka 3:264a
Imari 3:274a
Isahaya 3:336b
Izumi 3:365a-365b
Kagoshima 4:105a
Kanoya 4:151a
Karatsu 4:159a
Kaseda 4:161a
Kashima 4:162a
Kasuga 4:163b
Kikuchi 4:206a
Kita Kyūshū 4:226b
Kitsuki 4:231b
Kobayashi 4:236a
Kokubu 4:256b
Kumagaya 4:305b
Kumamoto 4:305b
Kurume 4:318b
Kushikino 4:320a
Kushima 4:320a
Makurazaki 5:88a
Matsuura 5:141b
Minamata 5:176a
Miyakonojō 5:219b
Miyazaki 5:221a-221b
Nagasaki 5:303b
Nakama 5:314a
Nakatsu 5:318a
Naze 5:359a
Nichinan 5:375a
Nishinoomote 6:19a
Nobeoka 6:30a
Nōgata 6:31a
Ogōri 6:71a
Ōita 6:75b
Ōkawa 6:81b
Ōkuchi 6:95a
Ōmura 6:104a
Ōmuta 6:104b-105a
Ōnojō 6:110a
Saga 6:363a
Saiki 6:371a
Saito 6:373a
Sasebo 7:24a
Sendai 7:63b
Shimabara 7:98b
Tagawa 7:294a
Takeo 7:325a
Taketa 7:325b
Taku 7:327b
Tamana 7:332b
Tarumizu 7:347b
Tosu 8:85a
Tsukumi 8:115a
Usa 8:181a
Ushibuka 8:181b
Usuki 8:182a
Uto 8:187b
Yamada 8:288b
Yamaga 8:290a
Yame 8:313a
Yanagawa 8:313b
Yatsushiro 8:320a
Yukuhashi 8:357b
Okinawa
Ginowan 3:33b
Gushikawa 3:70b
Hirara 3:144b
Ishigaki 3:340b
Ishikawa 3:342a
Itoman 3:354b
Nago 5:308b
Naha 5:309b
Okinawa 6:84b
Urasoe 8:175b
Shikoku
Aki 1:41b
Anan 1:53b
Hōjō 3:210b
Imabari 3:271b
Iyo 3:364a
Iyo Mishima 3:364b
Kan'onji 4:148b
Kawanoe 4:182a
Kōchi 4:239b
Komatsushima 4:266a
Marugame 5:120b
Matsuyama 5:141b
Muroto 5:274b
Nakamura 5:314b
Nankoku 5:329a
Naruto 5:335b
Niihama 5:386a
Ōzu 6:141a
Saijō 6:369b
Sakaide 6:376a
Sukumo 7:266a
Susaki 7:278b
Takamatsu 7:314a-314b
Tokushima 8:58b
Tosa 8:81a
Tosa Shimizu 8:82a-82b
Tōyo 8:89a
Uwajima 8:188b
Yawatahama 8:320b
Zentsūji 8:377a
Cities, new industrial 5:365a
Citizenship, naturalization 5:351b
Citizens' movements 1:315a-316a; 6:206b, 215b, 237b

consumer movement 2:14b
early postwar 1:315a
environmental 1:315a
major pollution suits 1:315b
organization 1:315b
victims' movements 1:315a-315b
lawsuits 1:315
women in 8:263b
Citizen Watch Co, Ltd 1:316a
C. Itoh & Co, Ltd 1:316a; 2:344a
City commissioner 5:78b
City elders 2:184b-185a
City Planning Law 8:180b
Civic education 1:316a
Civil Code 1:160a, 166a, 316b; 2:6b; 3:240a-241a; 5:118a-118b; 6:162b-163a
abuse of rights 1:5b
administrative law 1:13a-13b
adulthood 1:16a
bankruptcy 1:141a
capacity to act 1:239b-240a
capacity to enjoy rights 1:240a
contracts 2:20a
assumption of risk 1:103b-104a
customary 2:53b
dairi 2:66b-67a
damages, compensation for 2:72a
divorce 2:121b
of 1898
marriage law 5:118a
women's suffrage 8:268b
environmental law 2:225a
environmental rights 2:229a-229b
foreign juristic persons 3:3a
foreign law influence 2:319a
government compensation 3:55a
guardians (kōkennin) 4:253b-254a
inheritance law 3:304a
inkyo 3:307b
juristic acts 4:86a
kōjo ryōzoku 4:252b
kōkennin 4:253b
liability for negligence 4:383b
liability without fault 4:383b
old age and retirement 6:99a
Oppler, Alfred C. 6:115a
ownership rights 6:136b
parental power 6:162b
partnership 6:164a
person without capacity 6:178a
prescriptive period 6:235b
privacy, right to 6:249b
problems 4:378b
product liability 6:253b
public law 6:265b
revision 2:332a
sex discrimination 2:362a
support provisions 7:277a
Tomii Masaaki 8:71a
torts 8:81a
trust 8:107b
Wagatsuma Sakae 8:198b
wills 8:254a
women in 8:261b
Civil Code controversy 1:316b-317b
Civil Engineering Society 2:372a
Civil Execution Law (Minji Shikkō Hō) 6:260a
Civilian control of the military 1:317b
Civil Information and Education Section of SCAP 1:254b, 317b
Civil liberties, protection of 1:317b-318a
1947 constitution 4:378a
Civil Liberties Bureau 2:118a
Oppler, Alfred C. 6:115a
Civil Procedure, Code of 1:318a-321a
appellate system 1:321a
comparisons between Japanese and American systems 1:320a-321a
compulsory execution 1:321a
court system 1:319a
definitions 1:318a
discovery procedures 1:320b
format 1:319b-320a
function 1:318a-318b
historical background 1:318b-319a
law of evidence 4:371a
private international law 6:251b
provisional disposition 6:260a
relation to other laws 1:319a-319b
remedies, legal 1:321a
seizure 7:55b
witnesses 8:255a
Civil rights, 1889 Constitution and 4:378a
Civil service 1:219b-220a; 6:264b
examination 8:326a
National Personnel Authority 5:344b
Civil Service Appointment Ordinance (Bunkan Nin'yō Rei) 1:217b
Civil War of 672 4:60a-60b
Clan 8:131a
Clan names 5:324b-325a
Clark, Edward Warren 1:321b; 2:311a
Clark, William Smith 1:321b; 2:311b; 7:20a
Class consciousness 7:216b
rise 7:218a
Classical Japanese 1:321b-322b; 7:34b
grammar 1:322b
kakari-musubi 4:115a
orthography 1:322a-322b
Classical Standard 3:16b
Classicism 8:27b
Classified Collection of Japanese Classics 3:69b
Classified National History 6:340a
Classroom plans 7:33b
Class structure 1:322b-325a; 2:107a-107b
continuities from past 1:324a-325a
elitism 1:324b
Meiji era 1:323b
modern classes 1:323b
modern debate over 1:323b-324a
villages 6:119b
Claudel, Paul Louis Charles 1:325a; 2:332b
Clause final expressions 7:231b
Clean Government Party 4:266b-267a
Clerks 4:308b
Climate 1:325a-328a
cyclones 1:328a-328b
early summer 1:325b
heating 1:327b
land utilization 1:327b-328a
crop damage due to weather 1:328a
drought 1:328a
floods 1:328a
foehn phenomenon 1:328a
highland areas 1:328a
rice cultivation 1:327b-328a
warm districts 1:328a
monsoons 1:327a-327b
rice cultivation 1:327b-328a
seasons 1:325b-326b; 4:7b-8a
baiu 1:325b-326a
fall 1:326b
midsummer 1:326a-326b
monsoon 1:325b
shūrin 1:326b
spring 1:325b
summer 1:325b-326b
winter 1:325b
snow country 1:327a
typhoons 1:326b
weather and Japanese life 1:326b-327b
heating and changes in lifestyle 1:327b
monsoons 1:327a
snow country 1:327a
summer lifestyle and air conditioning 1:327b
Clinics, health care 3:120b
Cliques. *See* **Batsu**
Cloisonné 1:328b-329a
Cloister government 3:314b-315a
Cloister Office 3:315a
Clothing 1:329a-333a
Azuchi-Momoyama period 1:332b
Edo period 1:332b-333a
footwear 3:30a
headgear 3:118b-119b
Heian period 1:329b-332a
men's 1:330a-330b
women's 1:331a-332a
Kamakura and Muromachi periods 1:332a
men's 1:332a
women's 1:332a
kimono 4:209a-210b
komon used for 4:267a
modern developments 1:333a
obi 6:48b-49a
prehistoric 1:329b; 8:321b-322a
raingear 6:280a
sashiko 7:24a-24b
tabi 7:291a
tasuki 7:348a
tekkō 7:377a
uchikake 1:332a-332b
uchiki 1:332a
uniforms 8:149b-150a
Western influence 1:333a
Yamato and Nara periods 1:329b
Clouds and Dragons 4:*110a-110b*
Coal 1:333a-333b; 5:352b
alternate energy source 2:215a
power 2:191a-191b
Coastal areas
Dannoura 2:76b
Fukiagehama 2:360a
Futamigaura 2:376a
Jōdogahama 4:67a
Katsurahama 4:173a
Kujūkurihama 4:303b
Maiko 5:84b
Sanriku Coast 7:16a
Shichirigahama 7:88a
Sosogi Coast 7:232b
Sotomo 7:233a
Tōjimbō 8:39a
Tottori Sand Dunes 8:86b
Coastal Fishing Ground Improvement Law 2:285a
Cochran, George 1:237b
Cockfighting 1:333b-334a
Cocks, Richard 1:334a; 7:22a
Coeducation 1:334a
Coffee houses 1:334a-334b
Cofradia 7:241a
Coins
eirakusen 2:186b
ginza (silver) 4:219b-220a
kinza (gold) 4:219b-220a
koban 4:234b
kōchō jūnisen 4:239b
minting 5:242b-243a
ōban 6:47b-48a
premodern 5:242a
selecting (erizeni) 2:230b; 3:176a
yen 8:323b
Wadō kaihō 8:198a
zeniza (lesser) 4:219b-222a
Cold War 3:324a
Cold-war diplomacy 7:10a

Collection for Ten Thousand Generations or Collection of Ten Thousand Leaves 5:26a; 8:287b
Collection of a Thousand Years 7:68a-68b
Collection of Chinese and Japanese Poems for Singing 8:218a
Collection of Gleanings 7:184b-185a
Collection of Golden Leaves 4:219a-219b
Collection of Jeweled Leaves 3:71b-72b
Collection of Sand and Pebbles 7:80b-81a
Collection of Verbal Flowers 7:95a-95b
Collective bargaining right 1:334b; 2:369a; 4:347b-348a, 360a; 7:188b-189a
Collective labor agreements 1:334b
  grievance procedure 3:62b
Colloquial Standard 3:16b
Colonialism 1:335a-336b; 4:7a
  goals and outcome 1:336b
  Guandong Peninsula 1:335b; 3:64b-65a
  institution 1:335b-336a
  Sakhalin (Karafuto) 1:335b; 7:2a
  Taiwan 7:307b
Colonization Office. *See* **Kaitakushi**
Colorado River Indian Reservation 6:229b
Color blindness 4:36b
Color of Stream and Hue of Mountains 7:181a
Color television industry, Japanese, in U.S 4:23a
Combined Fleet, Imperial Japanese Navy 1:336b
Combs 1:337a
  hairstyles 3:83a
Comedy 6:281b
Comic magazines 1:337a
Comic pictures 5:101b-102a
Coming Nation, The 4:138b
Coming-of-age ceremonies. *See* **Gempuku**
Coming-of-Age Day 2:254a; 5:4b
Comintern 7:229a
Comintern 1927 Thesis 1:337b
  Japan Communist Party 4:11b
Comintern 1932 Thesis 1:337b
Commentary on the Constitution 4:192b-193a
Commentary on the Lotus Sutra 1:234a
Commerce, Navigation, and Delimitation, Treaty of, (1855; between Russia and Japan) 8:13b
Commercial banks 1:139a-139b
  city (toshi ginkō) 1:139b
  establishment 1:139a
  function 1:139a-139b
  regional (chihō ginkō) 1:139a
Commercial Code 1:159a, 337b-339a; 5:10b, 164a; 7:48b, 247a-247b
  attitudes toward 1:339a
  Checks Law 1:339a
  commercial entities 1:338b
  Commercial Law in Japan's industrial economy 1:337b-338a
  commercial transactions 1:338b-339a
  contracts 1:338b
  development 1:338a-338b
  financial reporting requirements 2:277b-278a
  foreign law influence 2:319a
  joint-stock company 4:70a-71a
  limited liability company 1:337b
  Okano Keijirō 6:81a
  other commercial laws 1:338b
  partnership 6:164a
  private international law 6:251b
  public law 6:265b
  Roesler, Karl Friedrich Hermann 6:334a
  tax laws 7:357b
  Ume Kenjirō 8:147a
  unlimited partnership company 8:173a
Commercial districts 7:149b-150b
Commercialization
  before 1600 2:148a
  Edo-period 2:149b-150a
Commercial law
  codification 1:8a
  tax accounting 7:352a
Commercial paper 1:339a-339b
Commissariat rice 3:252a-252b
Commissioner of foreign affairs 3:3a
Commissioner of Hakodate 3:86a
Commissioner of Sado 6:363a
Commissioners, premodern Japan 1:206a
Commissioners of finance 4:143b-144a
Commissioners of temples and shrines 4:62b
Commission on the Constitution 1:339b-340a; 2:13b-14a
Commission to Investigate the National Language 4:31b
Committee for the Compilation of Documents 7:335b
Committee of Seven to Appeal for World Peace 1:340a
Committee to Promote Anti-Prostitution Laws 6:257b
Commonage rights 8:71a
Commoners 3:125b
Commoner's News 3:125b
Common-law marriage 1:340a-340b
  Factory Law of 1911 1:340a
  Workers' Compensation 1:340a
Communication, symbolic 2:233b
Communication gestures 3:29a-30a
Communications
  international 3:318b-319a
  telecommunications systems 7:377a-379b
  telephones 7:379b-380a
Communion. *See* **Naorai**
Communism 5:229b-232a
  April 16th Incident 1:71b
  censorship 1:252a, 254b
  labor federations 4:346b
  March 15th Incident 5:113a
  Matsukawa Incident 5:136a-136b
  Mitaka Incident 5:204a
  Proletarian literature movement 6:255b
  publications 2:339a
  Sino-Japanese War of 1937-1945 7:201b-202a
  Yokohama Incident 8:330a
Communist associations 2:337b
Communist League 6:284b
Communist Manifesto 4:297b
Communist movement
  Comintern 1927 Thesis 1:337b
  Comintern 1932 Thesis 1:337b
Communist Party. *See* **Japan Communist Party**
Communists, public trial of 1:340b-341a
Community centers 1:314b, 341a
Community Chest 1:341a-341b
Community education 1:341b-342a
  future issues 1:342a
  history 1:341b
  system and present conditions 1:341b-342a
Community education officers 1:342a
Commutation (genkei) 2:49a
Commuting 1:342a-342b
"Companions of Barbarian Studies" 7:167b
Companion stories
  otogishū 6:129b
  otogi-zōshi 6:129b-130a
Company welfare system 1:342b-343b; 4:344b
  Factory Law of 1911 1:342b
  future 1:343b
  growth 1:342b
  level 1:343a-343b
  paternalism 6:165a
  post-World War II development 1:342b-343a
Compendiums of Edo period (1600-1868) 4:233b
Compensation
  company welfare system 1:343a
  for damages 7:226a
  government 3:54b-55b
Compilation of Japanese History 4:262b
Complete Catalog of Japanese Books 1:154b
Comprehensive National Development Law (1950) 8:180a
Comprehensive National Land Development Plan 1:343b-344a; 8:180a
Compromise 2:118b-119a
Comptrollers 4:144a
Compulsory education 1:344a; 2:176b, 223b
  school system 2:177a
  elementary and secondary education 2:195a-195b
Computer industry 1:344a-346b; 2:167a-167b
  companies
    Fujitsū, Ltd 2:347b
    Hitachi, Ltd 3:206b-307a
    IBM Japan, Ltd 3:253b
    Japan Electronic Computer Company (JECC) 1:345a
    Nippon Electric Co, Ltd (NEC) 6:9a-9b
    Nippon Univac Kaisha, Ltd 6:13b
    Tōshiba Corporation 8:82b
  governmental role 1:345a-345b
    hardware and software incentives 1:345b
    Information Technology Promotion Agency (IPA) 1:345b
    Japan Electronic Computer Company (JECC) 1:345a-345b
    research and development projects 1:345b
  history 1:345b-346b
  incentives for development 1:345b
  Information Technology Promotion Agency (IPA) 1:345b
  Ministry of International Trade and Industry (MITI) 1:345b
  research and development projects 1:345b
  state 1:344a-344b
  structure 1:344b-345a
Computer technology 1:346b-349a
  communications 1:347b-349a
  development 2:194a
  mainframe makers 1:347b
  national projects 1:347a-347b
  relations with IBM 1:347a
  research and development 1:347a
  trends 1:347b
Comte de Monte Cristo, Le 4:316b
COMTRAC
  Shinkansen 7:118a-118b
Conciliation 1:349a; 2:117a, 118b; 4:81b
  contemporary law 4:379a-380b
  labor 4:349b
    Tripartite commissions 4:351b
  litigation vs 4:370a-370b
Concordia Society 1:349a-349b; 5:96b-97a
Conder, Josiah 1:80b, 349b; 2:292a; 6:335a-335b
Condolence gifts 1:349b-350a
  kaeshi 4:102a
Conduct codes 1:206b-207a
Confections 1:350a-350b

azuki 1:127a
Western influence 1:350a
Conference of Administrative Vice-Ministers 6:244a
Conference of Asian and Pacific Accountants (1951) 1:8b
Conference on Modern Japan 5:228b-229a
Confession 1:350b; 2:49b
law of evidence 4:371a
Confessions of Lady Nijō, The 8:87a
Confiscation (bosshū) 2:49a
Conflict resolution 1:350b-352b
conflict 1:350b-351b
factional 1:351a
group 1:351a
individual versus group 1:351a
vertical 1:350b-351a
consensus decision making 1:351b
institutionalized 1:351b-352a
mediation 1:351b
processes 1:351a-351b
ritualization 1:352a-352b
Confucianism 1:352b-358b; 6:290a; 7:213b
Ancient Learning (Kogaku) 4:246b-248a
Chinese
ancient 1:352b-353a
medieval 1:354b-355a
corporate culture 2:26a-27a
Edo period 1:355b-357b
patronage and education 1:355b-356b
thought 1:356b-357b
education 2:173a-173b
Five Classics 2:329b
Four Books 2:329b
Japanese
ancient 1:353a-354b
medieval 1:355a-355b
Kobunjigaku 4:239a
limitations to influence 1:356b
meritocracy 1:354a, 358a
modern 1:357b-358b
Ogyū Sorai 6:72b-73a
Okinawa 6:85a
rei 6:288b
religion and society 6:294a
religious dimension 1:354a
scholars 7:191b
Setchūgaku 7:71a
Shingaku 7:112a
Shushigaku 7:190a-191b
tolerance in Japanese religion 8:70b
virtues 5:87b
women in 8:258b
Congress of Industrial Labor Unions of Japan (Zen Nihon Sangyōbetsu Rōdō Kumai Kaigi) 6:212b; 7:6a
Connoisseurs 4:83a
"Conquer Korea" debate. *See* **Seikanron**
Conroy, Hilary 4:22a
Consanguineous marriages 4:38a
Consanguinity 1:358b-359a
Conscription
ancient Japan 7:2a-2b
modern 1:86a, 359a
ritsuryō system 6:330a
Conscription Ordinance of 1873 1:86a, 359a; 2:361a; 8:190a, 291a
Chitsuroku shobun 1:297b
ketsuzei ikki 4:200a
militarism 5:173a-173b
Nishi Amane 6:14a
shizoku 7:151a
Yamagata Aritomo 4:204b
Conservation 1:359a-360a
Association for the Preservation of Historic Sites, Places of Scenic Beauty, and Natural Monuments 1:359b
Comprehensive National Development Plan 1:359b
Comprehensive National Land Development Law 1:359b
energy 2:215b-216a
Environment Agency 1:359b
Japan Union of Nature Conservation 1:359b
Law for the Preservation of Historic Sites, Places of Scenic Beauty, and Natural Monuments 1:359b
Law for the Protection of Cultural Properties 1:359b
National Parks Association of Japan 1:359b
National Parks Law 1:359b
Natural Environment Preservation Law 1:359b
Natural Parks Law 1:359b
Nature Conservation Society of Japan 1:359b
Conservative Faction 7:259b
Consolidated financial statements 1:360a-360b
Consort 1:312b
Constitution. *See* Constitution of 1947; Constitution of the Empire of Japan (Meiji Constitution)
Constitution, dispute over revision of 2:13b-14a
Constitutional Association 4:198a
Constitutional Association of Friends 6:314b
Constitutional Democratic Party 6:315a
Constitutional Imperial Rule Party 6:315b
Constitutional litigation 2:13a-13b
Constitutional Nationalist Party 6:314b-315a
Constitutional Party 4:198a-198b
Constitutional Problems Study Group 2:13b; 5:223b
Constitutional Reform Party 6:314b
Constitution of 1868. *See* **Seitaisho**
Constitution of 1947 2:3b-7a
Bill of Rights 2:5a-5b
cabinet 2:5b-6a
civil liberties 1:317b
Commission 1:339b-340a
courts 2:6a
democracy 2:84b
enactment 2:3b-4b
executive branch of government 3:55b-56a
finance 2:6a
fundamental freedoms
assembly 2:337a
association 2:337a-337b
religious faith 2:337b-338a
speech 2:338a
press 2:339a
Habeas Corpus Law 3:73a
interpretation 2:6a-6b
labor rights 2:369a
liberties 2:369a; 5:62a-62b
local autonomy 2:6a
minority rights 5:195b-196a
national defense 5:336b-338b
national legislature 2:5b
no-war, no-arms provision 2:5a
pacificism 6:144b
political system 6:214b-215a
popular sovereignty 2:4b-5a
practice 2:6b-7a
text 2:9b-13a
Amendments 2:12b-13a
Cabinet 2:11b-12a
Diet 2:11a-11b
Emperor 2:9b-10a
finances 2:12b
Judiciary 2:12a-12b
local self-government 2:12b
preamble 2:9b
renunciation of war 2:10a
rights and duties of people 2:10a-11a
supplementary provisions 2:13a
supreme law 2:13a
women in 8:261b
Constitution of the Empire of Japan (Meiji Constitution) 2:1a-3b; 3:195b-196b
constitutional government 2:3a
debates 2:1a-2a
foreign models 2:2a
Fukuzawa Yukichi 2:2a
Genrōin draft 2:1b
Inoue Kaoru 2:1b
Inoue Kowashi 2:1b-2a
Itagaki Taisuke 2:1b
Itō Hirobumi 2:1b
Iwakura Tomomi 2:1b
Kido Takayoshi 2:1a
kokutai 2:2a
Motoda Nagazane 2:2a
newspaper 2:2a
Ōki Takatō 2:2a
Ōkubo Toshimichi 2:1a-1b
Ōkuma Shigenobu 2:1b
shigi kempō 7:92b
Ueki Emori 2:2a
Yamagata Aritomo 2:1b
democracy 2:84b
drafting 2:2b
drafters 2:2b
Emperors' authority 2:2b-3a
European influence 2:2b
Peerage Ordinance of July 1884 2:2b
promulgation 2:2b
general description 2:1a
Genrōin 3:22a
Great Court of Cassation 3:60b
Inoue Kowashi 3:311a
Itō Hirobumi 3:353a
Itō Miyoji 3:355a
Iwakura Tomomi 3:360a
Kaneko Kentarō 4:138b
political system 6:213b-214b
rights of people 2:3a
Roesler, Hermann 6:334a
text 2:7b-9b
Emperor 2:7b-8a
Finance 2:9a-9b
Imperial Diet 2:8a-8b
imperial oath 2:7a
Judicature 2:9a
Ministers of State and Privy Council 2:8b
preamble [or edict] (Jōyu) 2:7b
promulgation rescript 2:7b
rights and duties of subjects 2:8a
supplementary rules 2:9b
Construction industry 2:14a
Construction industry companies
Asanuma Gumi Co, Ltd 1:96a
Chichibu Cement Co, Ltd 1:271b
Chiyoda Chemical Engineering & Construction Co, Ltd 1:298a
Fujita Corporation 2:346a
Hazama-Gumi Ltd 3:118b
Hitachi Plant Engineering & Construction Co, Ltd 3:207a
Kajima Corporation 4:114b
Kumagai Gumi Co, Ltd 4:304b
Maeda Construction Co, Ltd 5:79b
Misawa Homes Co, Ltd 5:198b

Mitsubishi Mining & Cement Co, Ltd 5:208a-208b
Mitsui Construction Co, Ltd 5:211a-211b
Nihon Cement Co, Ltd 5:379a
Nishimatsu Construction Co, Ltd 6:17b
Ohbayashi-Gumi, Ltd 6:74a
Okumura Corporation 6:96b
Onoda Cement Co, Ltd 6:109a
Ōsaka Cement Co, Ltd 6:120b-121a
Penta-Ocean Construction Co, Ltd 6:173b
Satō Kōgyō Co, Ltd 7:27a-27b
Sekisui House, Ltd 7:57b
Shimizu Construction Co, Ltd 7:104a
Sumitomo Cement Co, Ltd 7:267b
Sumitomo Construction Co, Ltd 7:268a
Taisei Corporation 7:303a
Takenaka Kōmuten Co, Ltd 7:324b
Tobishima Corporation 8:32b
Toda Construction Co, Ltd 8:33b
Tōkyū Construction Co, Ltd 8:70a
Zenitaka Corporation 8:375b
Construction machinery industry 2:14a
Construction Standards Law 6:313a
Consumer credit 2:17b
Consumer expenditures 2:17a-17b
Consumer goods, durable 5:7a
Consumer movement 2:14a-15b, 304a-304b
international influence 2:14b
issues of 1:315b
Consumer organizations 7:181b
Consumer price index 3:303a
Consumer protection laws 2:15b-16b
characteristics of basic 2:15b-16a
local level 2:16b
private laws 2:16b
specific statutes 2:16a
Consumers 2:16b-17b, 243b
expenditure patterns 2:17a-17b
apparel 2:17a
credit 2:17b
discretionary 2:17a-17b
food 2:17a
housing 2:17a
market segments 2:17b
savings 2:17b
income 2:16b-17a
population 2:16b
role in economy 2:168a-168b
shopping patterns 2:119b
Consumers' cooperatives 2:14b, 17b-18a
Consumption and saving behavior 2:18a-20a; 5:7b
asset portfolio 2:18b-19a
economic growth 2:161a
expenditure patterns 2:19a-20a
saving out of income 2:18a-18b
Containers
hisago 3:151b
lacquer ware 3:313a
wooden utensils 6:83b
Contemporary Japan 4:44a
Contraception 6:224a
Contracts 2:20a-20b; 4:86a
assumption of risk 1:103b-104a
employment 2:209a-209b
formal legal principles 2:20a
freedom of 2:337b
jidan 4:53b
managerial ideology 5:92a
principle of changed circumstances 6:245a-245b
role and use 2:20b
standard-form 7:243b
technological assistance 2:315b-316a
Contract workers 2:212a
Control faction, Imperial Army. *See* Tōseiha
Cooking, Japanese 1:*314b*; 2:20b-25b; 3:127b
general description 2:20b-21b
history 2:304b-306b
implements 2:24b-25a
hōchō (knives) 2:24b
kama and kamado (rice pot and hearth) 2:25a
makisu (bamboo for rolling and shaping) 2:25a
manaita (chopping board) 2:24b
nabe (saucepans or pots) 2:24b
nagashikan (mold with dual bottoms) 2:25a
oroshigane (grater) 2:25a
shamoji (spatula) 2:25a
suribachi and surikogi (mortar and pestle) 2:24b-25a
zaru (basket) 2:25a
methods, general 2:22b-24b
agemono (deep-fried) 2:23a-23b
aemono 2:23b-24a
dashijiru (stock) and condiments 2:22b
gohan-mono (white rice with water) 2:24a
menrui (noodles) 2:24a-24b
mushimono (steamed) 2:23b
nabemono (at table) 2:24b
nerimono (mashed) 2:24a
nimono (stewed) 2:23a
shirumono (soups) 2:22b
sunomono (vinegared) 2:23a-24b
yakimono (grilled or broiled) 2:22b-23a
yosemono (molded) 2:24a
methods, specific
meshi 5:164a
miso 5:202a
nattō 5:351a
nori 6:37a-37b
pickles 6:187b
rāmen 6:283a
sashimi 7:24b
soy sauce 7:239a-239b
sukiyaki 7:265b
sushi 7:278b-279a
tempura 8:3a-3b
teriyaki 8:13a
tōfu 8:35a
umeboshi 8:146b
regional 2:22a-22b
tableware 2:25a, 307a
chawan (ceramic bowl) 2:25a
hachi (deep bowl) 2:25a
hashi (chopsticks) 2:25a
kyūsu and dobin (teapots) 2:25a
sara (ceramic plate or dish) 2:25a
tokkuri and sakazuki (bottle and cup) 2:25a
wan (soup bowl) 2:25a
zen (little table for one person) 2:25a
terms 2:25a-25b
arainegi (long green onion) 2:25a
awase-jōyu (soy sauce) 2:25b
awasezu (dressing) 2:25b
itamae (cook) 2:25b
kaishiki (leaves or paper) 2:25b
kakushiaji (hidden flavor) 2:25b
keshōjio (salt) 2:25b
momijioroshi (red pepper) 2:25b
nerimiso (paste) 2:25b
sakana (appetizer with sake) 2:25b
sammaioroshi (cut fish) 2:25b
shimofuri (fat or taint treatment) 2:25b
sujime (treatment to eliminate fishy smell) 2:25b
traditional 2:21b-22a
chakaiseki ryōri 2:21b-22a
gyōji ryōri 2:22a
honzen ryōri 2:21b
kaiseki ryōri 2:22a
shōjin ryōri 2:22a
Cooperative associations 2:25b
Cooperative communities 7:121b
Cooperative Democratic Party (Kyōdō Minshutō) 4:260b
Cooperatives
agricultural 1:21b
business 2:25b
consumers' 2:17b-18a
Cooperativism, theory of 7:174b
Copernican theory 5:355b-356a
Copper
mining 5:185a
mining companies 7:266b-267a
Copper coins
eirakusen 2:186b
kōchō jūnisen 4:239b
Wadō kaihō 8:198a
zeniza 4:220a
Copyright Law 2:25b-26a; 6:262b
Design Law 2:91a
translation rights 8:98a
Coral Island 7:324b
Cormorant fishing 2:26a, *26a*, 287b
in Nagaragawa 5:303b
Corporate culture 2:26a-28b
Confucian and Utilitarian influences 2:27a
emergence 2:26b-27a
general description 2:26a-26b
ideology and practice 2:27a-27b; 4:344b
informal reinforcement 2:28a
multinational enterprises 5:263b
socialization of new employees 2:27b-28a
Corporate diversification 3:318a
Corporate finance 2:28b-29b
capital structure 1:243b
creditworthiness 2:28b-29a
funds 4:189a
future trends 2:29a-29b
origins 2:29a
Corporate history 2:29b-33b
business development, Japanese-style 2:33a
business organizations 2:32a-32b
Edo-period merchants 2:29b
entrepreneurs and business leaders 2:30a-30b
forms of business 2:31b-32a
joint-stock company 2:31b
limited liability 2:31b
limited partnership 2:31b
unlimited partnership 2:31b
zaibatsu 2:31b-32a
management of labor 2:32b-33a
Meiji government as modernizer 2:29b-30a
modern business 2:30b-31b
banks 2:30b
cotton spinning 2:31a
foreign trade 2:30b-31a
internal commerce 2:30b
mining 2:31a-31b
periods 2:30b
railways 2:31a
shipbuilding 2:31a
shipping 2:31a
Corporate recruitment 2:33b
Corporate Reorganization Law 1:141a; 2:33b-34a; 4:378b
Corporate stock 2:34a
Corporate Tax Law 7:352a
Corporate training programs 2:34a-34b
Corporations 2:34b-38a
board of directors 1:159a

bureaucracies ················ 1:219a-219b
changing ························ 2:37a
corporate identity ················ 2:37a
corporate image ·················· 2:317b
employment practices ·········· 2:36a-36b
enterprise groups and subsidiaries
························· 2:35b-36a
establishment ················ 2:37b-38a
expense accounts ············ 2:237a-237b
financial characteristics ········ 2:34b-35a
governmental relations ············ 2:35b
labor union relations ·········· 2:36b-37a
overseer ························ 6:136a
publicly traded
exchanges for ·············· 7:246b-247a
stockholders' general meeting ···· 7:247a
purchase of equity ·············· 2:315b
Corrections Bureau ················ 6:249a
Correspondence forms ·············· 7:376a
Corvée labor ······················ 8:327a
Cosigner ·························· 6:301a
Cosmetics ···················· 2:38a-38b
beni (rouge) ······················ 2:38a
mayuzumi (eyebrow-paint) ······ 2:38a-38b
ohaguro (tooth blackening) ········ 2:38a
oshiroi (white powder) ············ 2:38a
Shiseidō Co, Ltd ·················· 7:148b
Cosmogony ·············· 2:38b; 6:290b
Cosmos ·························· 8:138a
Cost accounting standards ········ 2:38b
Cotia Cooperative Society ·········· 5:317b
Shimomoto Kenkichi ················ 7:105a
Cotton ·························· 8:16b, 19b
India and Japan ·················· 3:288b
sarasa (calico; batik) ·············· 7:21a
Councillor (sangi) ············ 7:11a-11b
Councillors, junior (wakadoshiyori) 8:217a -217b
Council of Business Accounting of the Ministry of Finance ·············· 2:38b
Council of Public Corporation and National Enterprise Workers' Unions
································ 4:294a
Council of State ·················· 3:252a
Council on the National Language (Kokugo Shingikai) ····· 2:38b-39a; 4:78b
Ueda Kazutoshi ···················· 8:127a
Counseling, educational ····· 2:179a-179b
"Counterculture" ·················· 6:206b
Counters ························ 2:39a
Coups d'État, periodization ········ 6:175a
Coup d'Etat of 30 September 1863
······ 2:39a-39b; 5:317b; 7:12b, 31b, 102a
Chōshū Expeditions ················ 1:304a
Hamaguri Gomon Incident ············ 3:90a
Hirano Kuniomi ···················· 3:143b
Kido Takayoshi ···················· 4:202b
Shichikyō Ochi ······················ 7:88a
Tenchūgumi Rebellion ················ 8:4a
Couriers ···················· 3:138b-139a
Court-appointed attorneys ·········· 2:39b
Courtesans
portrayal of, in sharebon ······ 7:79b-80a
women in ·························· 8:259b
Courtet, Guillaume ················ 2:330b
Court for the Impeachment of Judges
································ 3:275b
Court liaison officers ········ 1:206a-206b
Court Music Bureau ················ 2:74a
Court nobles. *See* **Kugyō**
Court Organization Law ··· 2:6a; 4:80b-81a
Oppler, Alfred C. ·················· 6:115a
Court ranks ················ 2:39b-41a
Courts. *See* Judiciary
Courtyards ························ 7:147a
shirasu ···························· 7:147a
Cowra Prisoner-of-War Outbreak ··· 2:41a
Coxinga. *See* **Zheng Chenggong (Cheng Ch'eng-kung)**
Crabs [(kani) tribe Brachyura] · 2:41a-41b, 285b
horseshoe ·························· 3:231a
Crafts. *See* **Folk crafts**
Craftsmen of Various Trades ······ 4:150a
Cram schools ············ 2:41b; 4:83b-84a
entrance examinations ············ 2:223a
universities and colleges ·········· 8:170b
Cranes [(tsuru) family Gruidae] ···· 2:41b
Crane Wife, The ···················· 8:117a
Crawford, Sir John Grenfell · 1:118a-118b; 2:41b
Creation Society ······ 3:70a; 8:355a, 378a
Creation story. *See* **Cosmogony**
Credit Guaranty Associations Law 7:205b
Credit unions, agricultural ·········· 1:22a
Crepe fabrics ······················ 1:274b
Crests ················ 2:42a-43b, 280b
categories ·························· 2:43b
clothing ···················· 2:43a-43b
general description ················ 2:42a
8th century ························ 2:42a
12th-13th centuries ·········· 2:42b-43a
14th-16th centuries ················ 2:43a
texts ······························ 2:43a
Crickets [(kōrogi) subfamily Gryllinae]
························ 2:43b-44b; 4:220b
Crime ······················ 2:44a-46a
areas of concern ············ 2:44b-45a
drug abuse ························ 2:45a
female ···························· 2:45a
juvenile delinquency ········ 2:44b-45a
organized ·························· 2:45a
political terrorism ················ 2:45a
white collar ······················ 2:45a
collective responsibility of family (enza)
································ 2:229b
Criminal Justice Administration 2:45b-46a
clearance rate ···················· 2:45b
imprisonment ······················ 2:46a
juvenile cases ·············· 2:45b-46a
penalties ·························· 2:45b
pretrial screening ················ 2:45b
Daibon Sankajō ···················· 2:55b
international ······················ 3:319a
shioki ······························ 7:140b
Shipbuilding Scandal of 1954 ······ 7:143a
Shōchū Conspiracy ················ 7:154b
social factors ······················ 2:46a
statistics ·················· 2:46a-46b
historical trends ·················· 2:46a
international comparison ····· 2:46a-46b
Teigin Incident ···················· 7:375b
Crime victims, compensation for ··· 2:46b
Criminal code ······················ 1:160a
abortion ···························· 1:5a
capital punishment (shikei) ··· 1:243a-243b
parenticide ························ 6:163a
privacy, right to ·················· 6:249b
Criminal Compensation Law of 1950
································ 2:47a
Criminal investigation ·········· 2:47a-47b
Criminal justice administration · 2:45b-46a
clearance rate ······················ 2:45b
imprisonment ······················ 2:45b
juvenile cases ·············· 2:45b-46a
penalties ·························· 2:45b
pretrial screening ·················· 2:45b
penalties ·························· 2:45b
Criminal law ················ 2:47b-49b
general doctrine
immaturity ························ 2:48a
general doctrines ············ 2:48a-48b
impaired mental condition ········ 2:48a
intoxication ························ 2:48a
mistake ···························· 2:48a
necessity ·················· 2:48a-48b
principle of legality ·············· 2:48a
self-denunciation ·················· 2:48b
history ···························· 2:47b
pardon ···························· 2:49a
penal code organization ········ 2:47b-48b
provisional release ················ 2:49a
punishment of attempts ········ 2:48b-49a
abettor ···························· 2:48b
accessories ························ 2:48b
conspirational coprincipals ········ 2:48b
coprincipals ························ 2:48b
death ······························ 2:48b
incarceration ················ 2:48b-49a
misui ······························ 2:48b
pecuniary sanctions ················ 2:49a
Criminal penalty ············ 2:45b; 6:339b
Criminal procedure (Keiji Soshō Kisoku)
························ 2:49b-51b
appeal (jōso) ······················ 2:51a
basic characteristics ················ 2:49b
decision ···················· 2:50b-51a
acquittal ·························· 2:51a
criminality and punishment ········ 2:51a
guilty ······························ 2:50b
defendant's constitutional rights 2:50a-50b
compulsory process ················ 2:50a
impartial tribunal ·················· 2:50a
presence of defendant ·············· 2:50a
privilege against self-incrimination 2:50a
protection against repeated prosecutions ························ 2:50b
public trial ························ 2:50a
punishment according to procedures established by law ················ 2:50b
right to counsel ···················· 2:50a
speedy trial ························ 2:50a
detention (kōryū) ············ 2:49b-50a
extraordinary remedial proceedings
························ 2:51a-51b
extraordinary appeal ················ 2:51b
reopening ·························· 2:51a
history ···························· 2:49b
institution of charges
accusations (kokuhatsu) ············ 2:50a
complaints (kokuso) ················ 2:50a
prosecution ························ 2:50a
investigation ······················ 2:49b
arrest ······························ 2:49b
interrogation ······················ 2:49b
search and seizure ········ 2:49b; 7:55b
law of evidence ···················· 4:371a
Minor Offenses Law ················ 5:196a
noncoercive ························ 2:49b
revision ···························· 4:378a
trial procedure ······················ 2:50b
Criminology ························ 2:51b
Hanzai ron josetsu ················ 7:327a
"Cross recognition", policy of ····· 4:287a
Crows [(karasu) *Corvus* spp.] · 2:51b-52a
Crows Rising in Spring Mist ········ 6:78a
Crucian carp [(funa) *Carassius* spp.]
························ 2:26a, 52a
Crustaceans ························ 7:179b
Crypto-Christians ············ 7:185b, 186b
Cuckoos [(hototogisu) family Cuculidae]
································ 2:52a
Cucurbits (family Cucurbitaceae)
························ 2:52a-52b
cucumber ·························· 2:52a
general ···························· 2:52a
melons ···························· 2:52b
squashes ·························· 2:52b
Cuisine, Japanese. *See* Cooking, Japanese
Culpability ························ 2:48a
Cultivators' rights ···················· 7:5a

Culturalism 5:230b-231a
Cultural Properties Law 1:75a; 2:52b-53a, 295b
administrative acts 2:52b-53a
cultural properties 2:52b
promulgation 2:52b
purpose 2:52b
Culture and personality 4:39a
Cumulative guidance record 2:53a
report cards 6:302b
Cuong De 2:53a
Currency
bitasen 1:156b-157a
coins. *See* Coins
Dajōkan satsu 2:70b
hansatsu 3:99b
Matsukata fiscal policy 5:133b
premodern 5:243a
ryō 6:347b
yen 8:323b-324a
Currency management 7:174a
Current Contents of Academic Journals 4:46a
Currents, ocean 5:114b
Curriculum 7:34a-36a
Japanese children abroad 7:37a-37b
Customary law 2:53b; 4:379b-380a
Cuttlefish. *See* **Squid and cuttlefish**
Cycling 2:53b
Cymbidium 7:188b
Cypresses [(hinoki) *Chamaecyparis obtusa*] 2:53b-54b
Cypress Trees 4:146b
Cypripedium japonicum 4:305a
"Cyrano de Bergerac" 7:121a
Czechoslovakia 2:142b; 7:192a
Japanese studies 4:43b

D

Dahl, Otto Christian 4:20a
Daianji 大安寺 1:182a; 2:55a-55b; 7:16b
Daibikan 7:107b
Daibon Sankajō 大犯三箇条 2:55b
Daibosatsu Mountains 大菩薩連嶺 2:55b
Daibosatsu Pass 大菩薩峠 2:55b
Daibosatsu Tōge 大菩薩峠 5:320a; 6:221a; 8:339a
Daibutsu 大仏 2:55b-56a; 4:120b; 7:168a
Daibutsuden (great Buddha hall) 8:*33a*
Daibutsuyō 大仏様 1:183b
Daicel Chemical Industries, Ltd 2:56a
Fuji Photo Film Co., Ltd 2:56a
Daichō 大帳 4:187b
Daidairi 大内裏 3:122a
Daidairi zu kōshō 大内裏図考証 1:79a
Daidairon 大々論 3:*59a*; 5:101b
Dai Dembōin 大伝法院 4:118a
Daidō Danketsu Movement 大同団結運動 2:56a, 336a
Daidōji Yūzan 大道寺友山 2:56a-56b
Daidō Steel Co, Ltd 2:56b
Daiei Co, Ltd 2:56b, 271b-272a
Daiei, Inc 2:56b
Daigakuin 3:59b
Daigaku Rei (University Order) 6:252b
Daigakuryō 大学寮 2:56b-57a; 7:256b
court ranks 2:40b
decline 2:172b
establishment 2:172b
Kangakuin 4:140a
Daigaku wakumon 大学或問 4:307b
Daigenkai 大言海 2:57a; 6:134a
Daigennin (advocates) 4:371b
Daigo 大子 2:57a
Daigo, Emperor 醍醐天皇 2:57a
Engi Tenryaku no chi 2:217b
Fujiwara family 2:348a-348b
Shin kokinshū 7:120a
Shinkokushi 7:121b
Sugawara no Michizane 7:257a
Daigo Fukuryū maru 第五福竜丸 1:113b; 5:75b-76a
Daigo Fukuryū maru Jiken 第五福竜丸事件 4:75b-76a
Daigoji 醍醐寺 1:183a; 2:57a-58a
Shingon sect 7:115a
Daigoji Treasure House 2:58a
Daigokuden 大極殿 1:79b; 2:58a
Heiankyō 3:122a-122b
Daihannyaharamitta kyō 大般若波羅蜜多経 4:322b
Daihatsu Motor Co, Ltd 2:58b
passenger car production 1:122a
Toyota Motor Co, Ltd. 8:93b
Daihon'ei 大本営 1:87a; 2:58b
Dai-Ichi Bank, Ltd 2:58b
Daiichi Chūō Kisen Kaisha 2:58b
Daiichi Electric Railway Co 4:188b
Dai-Ichi Kangyō Bank, Ltd 1:140a; 2:58b
Dai-Ichi Mutual Life Insurance Co 2:58b-59a
Daiinkun. 大院君 *See* **Taewon'gun**
"Dai isshō" 第一章 7:176a
Dai Jitao (Tai Chi-t'ao) 2:59a
Daijiten 大辞典 2:93b; 4:31b
Daijōe bemmō 大嘗会便蒙 4:100b
Daijōin jisha zōji ki 大乗院寺社雑事記 2:59a
Daijōkan. 太政官 *See* **Dajōkan**
Daijō kishin ron (The Awakening of Mahāyāna Faith) 大乗起信論 6:247b
Daijōsai 大嘗祭 2:59a-59b, 298b
kagura uta 4:108a
Shintō rites 7:139a
Daijō tennō (retired sovereign) 太上天皇 4:64a
Dai kagura 太神楽 4:107b; 7:250a
Daikakuji 大覚寺 2:59b, 289a
Daikan 代官 2:60a; 8:9b-10a
kanjō bugyō 4:143b-144a
Daikan Daiji 大官大寺 2:55a
Daikan Teikoku 大韓帝国 7:293b
Dai kanwa jiten 大漢和辞典 2:60a, 93b; 5:255a-255b
Daikeichō 大計帳 4:187b
Daiken Home Co 2:60a
Daiken Trade & Industry Co, Ltd 2:60a
Daiken Home Co 2:60a
Daikin Kōgyō Co, Ltd 2:60a
Daikō Advertising, Inc 1:17a; 2:60a-60b
Daikōgi 大公儀 4:248b
Daikoku 大黒 2:60b; 5:296a
Daikoku dancers 4:101b
Daikoku-mai 大黒舞 7:250a
Daikokuten 大黒天 2:60b; 7:73a
Shintō family altars 7:137b
Daikokuya Kōdayū 大黒屋光太夫 2:60b; 4:173a
Daikon 6:276a-276b
Daikuhara Gintarō 大工原銀太郎 2:60b
Daikyoku 太極 3:126a
Daikyō Oil Co, Ltd 2:60b-61a; 6:182a
Daily Japan Herald 4:46a
Daimaru, Inc 2:61a
Daimoku 題目 1:179a; 5:327b
Daimonji Okuribi 大文字送り火 1:160b; 2:61a
Daimonjiyama 大文字山 2:61a; 4:336b
Daimyō 大名 1:131b; 2:61a-64b; 4:7a, 55a; 7:256b
Abe Masahiro 1:3b
Abe Tadaaki 1:4b
accounting agents 4:116a
Amako family 1:49b
Andō Nobumasa 1:55a
Arima Harunobu 1:83a-83b
Asai Nagamasa 1:94a
Asakura Yoshikage 1:95a
bakuhan system 2:63a-64a
codes of conduct 1:206b-207a
declassment 4:108b
domains 1:221b
Edo period 2:63b, 171b
education 2:174a
feudalism 2:265a-267a
Fukushima Masanori 2:366b
Gamō Ujisato 3:6b
genealogies 4:138a
general description 2:61a
Gosanke 3:47b
hatamoto 3:111b
highway travel 4:108b
Hoshina Masayuki 3:235a
Hosokawa Tadaoki 3:236b
Hosokawa Yūsai 3:237a
Hotta Masayoshi 3:239b
Ii Naosuke 3:263a
Ikeda Mitsumasa 3:265b
Ikeda Terumasa 3:266a
Imagawa Yoshimoto 3:272b
inns 3:223a
Itakura Katsukiyo 3:350a
Kaisakuhō 4:112a
Kamakura shogunate 2:61a-61b
Kan'eiji 4:137b-138a
Katō Kiyomasa 4:168b
Kuroda Nagamasa 4:314b
Kuroda Yoshitaka 4:315a
Kutsuki Masatsuna 4:321b
Kuze Hirochika 4:322b-323a
land laws 1:208a
Maeda Toshiie 5:80b-81a
Maeda Tsunanori 5:81a-81b
Matsudaira Katamori 5:131a-131b
Matsudaira Sadanobu 5:131b-132a
Matsudaira Tadanao 5:132a
Matsudaira Tadayoshi 5:132b
Matsudaira Yoshinaga 5:132b
Matsukura Shigemasa 5:136b-137a
Meiji Restoration 2:64a; 5:156a-157a
military unification 2:61b, 63a
Mizuno Tadakuni 5:226b-227b
Mōri Motonari 5:250b
Muromachi shogunate 2:61b
Nabeshima Kansō 5:299a
Oda Nobunaga reforms 2:61b, 63a
Ōuchi Yoshitaka 6:135b
registers 1:206a
rice tax transport 4:112b
ryōshu 6:353a
sankin kōtai (alternate attendance) rule 7:14a

Satake Shozan · · · 7:25b
sengoku · · · 2:61b; 7:64a
Shimazu Nariakira · · · 7:102a-102b
Shimazu Yoshihiro · · · 7:102b
shōgun · · · 7:160b
shugo · · · 2:61b
Takeda Katsuyori · · · 7:322b
Takeda Shingen · · · 7:323a-323b
Tōdō Takatora · · · 8:34b-35a
Tokugawa Akitake · · · 8:45b
Tokugawa Mitsukuni · · · 8:51b-52a
Tokugawa Nariaki · · · 8:52a
Tokugawa shogunate · · · 8:55a
Toyotomi Hideyoshi reforms · · · 2:63a
Tsutsui Junkei · · · 8:118b
Uesugi Harunori · · · 8:129a
Uesugi Kagekatsu · · · 8:129b
Uesugi Kenshin · · · 8:129b-130a
Ukita Hideie · · · 8:137b-138a
Yamanouchi Toyoshige · · · 8:302b
Daimyō disturbances · · · 6:74a-74b
Daimyō loans · · · 大名貸 · · · 2:64b
Kajimaya · · · 4:114b
kakeya · · · 4:116a
Kōnoike family · · · 4:274a
Daimyō plays · · · 4:327a
Daimyō processions 大名行列 · · · 2:64b
sankin kōtai · · · 7:14a
Dainichi · · · 1:176a, 184b, 187b; 2:64b
dual aspects · · · 4:269b-270a; 7:310a
Pure Land worship · · · 4:118a
Shingon sect · · · 7:113b-115a
Dainichikyō · · · 大日経 · · · 7:310a
Dainichi-Nippon Cables, Ltd · · · 2:65a
Dainichi Nyorai · · · 大日如来 · · · 4:269b
Dai Nihon Butokukai (All Japan Martial Virtues Society) · · · 4:196a
Dai Nihon chimei jisho · · · 大日本地名辞書 · 2:65a; 6:288a; 8:127a
Dai Nihon chishi · · · 大日本地誌 · · · 6:288a
Dai Nihon Eiga Kyōkai · · · 4:202a
Dai Nihon enkai jissoku zenzu 大日本沿海実測全図 · 2:65a; 5:112b
Dai Nihon hennenshi · · · 大日本編年史 · · · 4:307b
Dai Nihon kahei shi · · · 大日本貨幣史 · · · 8:240a
Dai Nihon Kajin Kai · · · 大日本歌人会 · · · 5:19b
Dai Nihon Kajin Kyōkai · · · 大日本歌人協会 · · · 5:19b
Dai Nihon Kannon Kai · · · 6:78b
Dai Nihon kokugo jiten · · · 大日本国語辞典 · · · 2:57a, 65a, 377a
Dainihonkoku zokusannō Shōtoku taishi hōsan · · · 8:231a
Dai Nihon komonjo · · · 大日本古文書 · · · 2:65a, 105a
Dai Nihon Sangyō Kumiai Chūōkai · 1:21b
Dai Nihon shi (History of Great Japan) · · · 大日本史 · · 1:94b, 285b, 357b; 2:65a-65b
historiography · · · 3:154b
Kuriyama Sempō, compiler · · · 4:313b
Mito school · · · 5:205a
Miyake Kanran · · · 5:218b
Nagakubo Sekisui · · · 5:302a
Shōkōkan · · · 2:347a
Tokugawa Mitsukuni · · · 2:347a;8:51b
Dai Nihon shiryō · · · 大日本史料 · · · 2:65b
Dai Nihon Teikoku Kempō · · · 大日本帝国憲法 · · · 2:1a-3b
Dai Nippon Fujinkai (Great Japan Women's Society) · · · 大日本婦人会 · · 1:34a; 2:65b; 8:261a
Dai Nippon hennenshi · · · 大日本編年史 · · · 3:156a
Dainippon Ink & Chemicals, Inc · · · 2:66a
Takenaka Kōmuten Co, Ltd · · · 7:324b
Dai Nippon Kokubō Fujinkai (National Defense Women's Association) · · · 大日本国防婦人会 · · 2:66a; 8:261a
Dai Nippon Kokusuikai (Great Japan National Essence Society) · · · 大日本国粋会 · · · 2:66a
Tokonami Takejirō · · · 8:44a
Dai Nippon Pharmaceuticals · · · 8:21a
Dai Nippon Printing Co, Ltd · · · 2:66a-66b
Toppan Printing Co, Ltd · · · 8:76a
Dai Nippon Rengō Seinendan · · · 2:66b
Tanaka Giichi · · · 7:336a-336b
Dai Nippon Seisantō · · · 3:25a; 7:108a
Dai Nippon shōgyō shi: Fu Hirado bōeki shi · · · 7:256b
Dai-Nippon Sugar Manufacturing Co, Ltd · · · 2:66b, 359a
Dai Nippon Teikoku · · · 大日本帝国 · · · 2:66b
Dai Nippon Teikoku Kaigun · · 大日本帝国海軍 · · · 3:278a
Dai Nippon Teikoku Rikugun · · 大日本帝国陸軍 · · · 3:278a
Daini Seikōsha Co · · · 4:200b
Daiōzaki · · · 大王崎 · · · 2:66b
Dairi · · · 内裏 · · · 2:66b-67a
Dairi (inner palace grounds)
Heiankyō · · · 3:122a
Heijōkyō · · · 3:124a
Dairy cattle production · · · 1:28b
Daisen · · · 大山 · · · 2:67a; 7:66a
Daisen-Oki National Park · · · 大山隠岐国立公園 · · · 2:67a-67b; 6:83a; 7:101b
Daisetsuzan · · · 大雪山 · · · 2:67b
Daisetsuzan National Park · · · 大雪山国立公園 · · 1:92b; 2:67b, 370b
Daishin'in · · · 大審院 · · · 3:60b
Daishōwa Paper Mfg Co, Ltd · · · 2:67b
Daisūteki seisūron · · · 代数的整数論 · · · 7:311a
Daitō · · · 大東 · · · 2:67b
Dai Tōa Kyōeiken · · · 大東亜共栄圏 · · · 3:60b-62a
Daitō Islands · · · 大東諸島 · · · 4:224b
Daitōjuku · · · 大東塾 · · · 2:67b-68a
Daitokuji · · · 大徳寺 · · · 2:68a-68b; 4:336b; 7:67a
Ikkyū · · · 3:269b-270a
paintings · · · 4:148a
Daiwa Bank, Ltd · · · 2:68b
Daiwa House Industry Co, Ltd · · · 2:68b
Daiwa Securities Co, Ltd · · · 2:68b
Daiwa Spinning Co, Ltd · · · 2:68b-69a
Daizōkyō · · · 大蔵経 · · · 1:187b
Daizu · · · 7:239a
Dajōkampu · · · 太政官符 · · · 4:130a
Dajōkan (Grand Council of State) · · · 太政官 2:2b, 69a-70b, 104a; 6:246a; 7:16b
early Meiji · · · 2:70a-70b; 3:193a-194a
authority under Seitaisho · · · 7:54a
censorship · · · 1:252a
Navy Ministry · · · 5:358b
Sanshoku · · · 7:16b-17a
Taikyō Sempu · · · 7:297b
ritsuryō system · · · 2:69a-70a; 3:163b; 6:329b-330a
ryōge no kan · · · 6:351b
regency government · · · 6:286b-288a
Dajōkan satsu · · · 太政官札 · · · 2:70b
Dake Hot Spring · · · 岳温泉 · · · 2:70b-72a
Damages, compensation for · · · 2:72a
Damask · · · 2:131a
Dampatsurei · · · 断髪令 · · 2:72a; 4:127b
Dampatsushiki · · · 7:272b
Dams · · · 2:72a-73b
classification · · · 2:72b
construction history · · · 2:72b-73a
Futagawa · · · 1:83a
Kurobe · · · 4:313b
Mihoro · · · 5:169a
Ogōchi · · · 6:71a
Oku Tadami · · · 6:98b
postwar · · · 2:73a
Sakuma · · · 7:3a-3b
Tagokura · · · 7:294b
Dance
Ainu · · · 1:36a
Awa · · · 1:124a
Bon odori · · · 1:161a
dengaku · · · 2:86a-86b
dojōsukui · · · 2:127b
masks · · · 5:126a-126b
sculpture · · · 1:197a
shishi-mai · · · 7:148b-149a
shishi odori · · · 7:149a
traditional · · · 2:73b-75b
bugaku · · · 2:*73a*; 3:1b
Hanayagiryū · · · 2:*74b*
kabuki · · · 2:*74b*
since Meiji Restoration · · · 2:75b
Nō · · · 2:*73a*, 74b-75a
Western-style · · · 2:75b-76b
Danchi · · · 3:*244b*, 254a
Dancing religion. *See* Tenshō Kōtai Jingūkyō
Dangai. *See* **Impeachment**
Danger years (yakudoshi) · · · 8:285a-285b
Dangibon · · · 4:256a
Dangyokei · · · 断魚渓 · · · 2:76b
Dan Ikuma · · · 團伊玖磨 · · · 2:76b
Danjōdai · · · 弾正台 · · · 4:185b
Danjō Garan · · · 壇場伽藍 · · · 4:269b
Danka · · · 2:76b
Kakure Kirishitan · · · 4:119a-120a
Dan Kazuo · · · 檀一雄 · · · 2:76b
Dan Kizui · · · 段祺瑞 · · · 2:134b
Dannoura · · · 壇ノ浦 · · · 2:76b
Dannoura, Battle of · · · 壇ノ浦の戦 · · 1:67b; 2:77a; 7:263a
imperial regalia · · · 3:279a
Minamoto no Yoshitsune · · · 5:183a
Shimonoseki · · · 7:105b
Taira-Minamoto War · · · 7:300b
Taira no Munemori · · · 7:301b
Taira no Tomomori · · · 7:302b
Danrin, Empress 檀林皇后 · · · 2:77a
Danrin school · · · 談林派 · · · 2:77a-77b; 4:270a; 5:18a, 46b; 6:297a
yakazuhaikai · · · 3:79a
Danrin toppyakuin · · · 談林十百韻 · · 2:77b; 6:20a
Danshi (" 'creped" paper) · · · 檀紙 · · · 8:233a
Dan Takuma · · · 団琢磨 · · · 2:77b
assassination · · · 2:32a; 4:373a
Dantani Plywood Co, Ltd · · · 2:77b
Danzan Shrine tower · · · 6:147b
Daochuo · · · 4:67a
Daoxuan · · · 2:131b

"Darakuron" ······· 堕落論 ·· 6:230b, 375b
Dare da? Hanazono o arasu mono wa! ······· 7:119b
Darkness in Summer ······· 4:111b
Dart fishing ······· 2:287a
Daruma ······· 1:*193a*
Daruma dolls ······· 2:77b
Daruma fairs ······ 達磨市 2:*77a*, 77b-78a
Takasaki ······· 7:318b
Dashi ······· 山車 ······· 2:78a
Das Japanische Inselreich ······· 6:288a
Das Kapital ······· 7:310a
Date (city) ······· 伊達 ······· 2:78a
Date Chihiro ····· 伊達千広 ······· 3:155b
Date family ······· 伊達氏 ······· 2:78a
Date Masamune 伊達政宗 ···· 2:78a-78b; 3:179b; 7:63b
Date family ······· 2:78a
French and Japanese relations ······ 2:330a
Hasekura Tsunenaga ······· 3:109a
Sekigahara, Battle of ······· 7:56b
Vatican expedition ······· 4:369a
Date Sōdō ······· 伊達騒動 ······· 2:78b
Davydov, Gavrill Ivanovich ······· 6:341a
Day-care centers ······· 6:235b
Day laborers ······· 7:202b
Day lilies [(kisuge) *Hemerocallis thunbergii*] ······· 2:78b-79a
Dazaifu ······· 太宰府 ······· 2:79a
Dazaifu (Government Headquarters) ···· 大宰府 ······· 1:4a; 2:79a-79b, 104b, 364b-365a; 8:303a
Kōrokan ······· 4:293a-294b
Mongol invasions of Japan ··· 5:243b-244b
sakimori ······· 7:2a
Sugawara no Michizane ······· 7:257a
urbanization ······· 8:176a
Dazaifu Shrine ······· 太宰府天満宮 · 2:79b; 7:257a
temmangū ······· 7:381a
Dazai Osamu ······ 太宰治 ···· 2:79b-80a, 274a; 6:230b; 7:176a
Dazai Shundai ··· 太宰春台 ······· 2:80b
Death ······· 2:80b-81a
euthanasia ······· 2:235b-236a
Death day anniversary ······· 5:5a
Death penalty ······· 2:48b; 6:172b
Death rate ······· 6:223b-224a
Debayashi ······· 4:99a
Debenture ······· 2:81a
joint-stock company ······· 4:70a-71b
Debtors, seizure ······· 7:55b
December Ninth Movement ···· 2:81a-81b
Doihara-Qin (Doihara-Ch'in) Agreement ······· 2:126b
National Salvation Association ····· 5:346a
Decision making
leader's role ······· 5:90b
participants ······· 5:90b-91a
process ······· 5:90a-91a
Declining industries ······· 2:81b
Decorations (awards) ······· 2:41a, 81b
Decorative techniques
cloisonné ······· 1:328b
kirikane (gold- or silver-leaf) · 4:220b-221a
lacquer ······· 4:361a-361b
maki-e ······· 5:85a-85b
mother-of-pearl inlay (raden) ······ 5:256b
Rimpa ······· 6:317b-318a
string (mizuhiki) ······· 5:225b-226a
tortoiseshell work ······· 8:80b-81a
Decorum (rei) ······· 4:141b
Decoux, Jean ······· 2:333a
Decree of the Cancellation of Debts ······· 4:152b
Deer, Japanese [(shika) *Cervus nippon*] ······· 2:82a
Deer Cry Pavilion ······· 6:335a-335b
Deer dance ······· 7:149a
Defendant
acquittal ······· 2:51a
constitutional rights ······· 2:50a-50b
compulsory process (shōnin o motomeru kenri) ······· 2:50a
impartial tribunal (kōhei na saibansho) ······· 2:50a
presence (shuttō) ······· 2:55a
public trial (kōkai saiban no kenri) 2:50a
punishment, legally mandated ···· 2:50b
repeated prosecutions, protection against (ichiji fusairi) ······· 2:50b
right to counsel (bengonin o irai suru kenri) ······· 2:50a
self-incrimination, privilege against (mokuhiken) ······· 2:50a
speedy trial (jinsoku na saiban o ukeru kenri) ······· 2:50a
conviction ······· 2:51a
Defense, national ······· 5:336b-338b
Defense Agency (Bōeichō) ·· 1:218b; 2:5a, 82a; 6:242b, 264b; 7:59a
Defense Facilities Administration Agency ······· 2:82a; 7:59b
Defense industry ······· 2:82a-82b
Defense Secrets Protection Law ·· 2:339a
Defense White Paper ······· 2:82b
Defilement ······· 4:186a-186b
Deguchi Nao ···· 出口なを ···· 2:82b-83a; 7:76b
Deguchi Nobuyoshi ······· 出口延佳 ······· 4:59a
Deguchi Onisaburō ······· 出口王仁三郎 ······· 2:83a
Deification. *See* **Ikigami**
Deities
bimbōgami-type ······· 1:155a
Buddhist prototype ······· 3:222b-223a
creation of ······· 3:364b
Daikokuten (god of wealth) ······· 2:60b
feast days (ennichi) ······· 2:219a
festivals ······· 2:254a
Izanagi and Izanami ······· 3:364b-365a
Jizō ······· 5:4a
ubusunagami ······· 8:123a
water (suijin) ······· 7:263b
yakubyōgami ······· 1:155a
zashiki warashi ······· 8:368b
See also **Kami**
Dejima ······· 出島 2:*83a*, 83a-83b; 5:306a
Dutch trading enclave ······· 2:330b
Kaempfer, Engelbert ······· 4:101b-102a
National Seclusion ······· 5:347b
Takashima Shūhan ······· 7:319a
Dekasegi ······· 2:83b-84a; 4:343b, 356b
industrial structure ······· 3:301a
Delegation of power to legislate ···· 2:84a
De Long, Charles E. ······· 2:84a
Dembō kanjō ···· 伝法灌頂 ······· 4:117b
Demetaka ······· 出目高 ······· 2:84a
Democracy ······· 2:84a-85a; 7:215b
history ······· 2:84b
modernization ······· 5:229a
postwar development ······· 2:84b-85a
Democratic education ······· 2:223b
Democratic Liberal Party
Occupation ······· 6:54a
Democratic Party ······· 5:197b
Occupation ······· 6:54a
Democratic People's Republic of Korea, Japanese relations with. *See* **Korea and Japan**
Democratic Socialist Party [(DSP) Minshatō] ····· 2:85a-85b; 6:212b; 7:215b
ban-the-bomb movement ···· 1:114b-115a
Diet ······· 2:96b
Dōmei ······· 2:130a
Kasuga Ikkō ······· 4:163b
labor unions ······· 4:347a
national defense ······· 5:336b-338b
Nishio Suehiro ······· 6:19a
peace movement ······· 6:166b
pressure groups ······· 6:238a
Sasaki Ryōsaku ······· 7:23a
Demokurashī ····· デモクラシー · 7:115b
Demons
mononoke ······· 5:247a
oni ······· 6:106a
pacification ······· 8:285a
yamamba ······· 8:297a
Dempata Eitai Baibai Kinshi Rei. *See* **Tahata Eitai Baibai Kinshi Rei**
Dempwolff, Otto ······· 4:20a
Denden taiko ······· 2:85b-86a
Den'en ni shisu (To Die in the Country) ·田園に死す ······· 8:13a
Dengaku ······· 田楽 ···· 2:86a-86b, 297b, *298b*, 301a
dance, traditional ······· 2:73b-74b
furyū development ······· 2:374a
Nō ······· 6:23b
sarugaku ······· 7:22a
Dengaku nō ······· 田楽能 ······· 4:324b
Den Hideo ······· 田英夫 ······· 2:86b
Denison, Henry Willard ······· 2:86b, 311a
Denki bungaku ······· 1:155a-155b
Denki Kagaku Kōgyō ······· 2:86b-87a
Denki Rōren ······· 2:87a
Denkōroku ······· 伝光録 ······· 4:190b
Denmark
Japanese studies ······· 4:43b
Denryoku Chūō Kenkyūjo ······· 2:192a
"Densely inhabited district" (DID) · 8:176b
Denshi Gijutsu Sōgō Kenkyūjo ···· 2:195a
Dentists ······· 3:120a
Dentsū, Inc ······· 1:17a; 2:87a; 7:56b
Department stores ······· 2:30b, 87a-87b
Deposit money ······· 2:87b
Depression ······· 2:153b; 3:200a
Depression of the 1930s ······· 2:320a
De Rijke, Johannes ······· 2:87b
Dermatoglyphs ······· 4:35b
De Sade case ······· 2:87b-88a; 4:362a
obscenity ······· 6:50b
Descendants of Cain, The ······· 1:84b
Design ······· 2:88a-90a
modern ······· 2:89a-90a
commercial ······· 2:89b-90a
industrial ······· 2:89a-89b
premodern ······· 2:88a-88b
Design in textiles ······· 2:90a-91a
Design Law of 1959 ······· 2:91a; 6:164b
Desks ······· 2:371a
Detective Story Writers Club ······ 2:170b
Deusu (*Deus*) ······· 2:91a
Deutzias. *See* **Unohana**
Deva ······· 7:381a
Deva Seizing a Demon ······· 4:147a
Devils ······· 5:296a
DeVos, George ······· 4:39b
Dewa Mountains 出羽山脈 · 1:136b; 2:91a
Dewa Sanzan Shrines ······· 出羽三山神社 ····· 2:91a-91b
Dewey, John ······· 2:180b
De Witt, John L. ······· 4:17b-18a
Dharma ······· 1:192a; 2:91b
footprints of Buddha ······· 1:225b
Dharma Bums, The ······· 7:207a
Dharmakāya ······· 4:68b
Dhyāna ······· 1:179b
Dialectical materialism theory ····· 3:141a
Dialects ······· 2:91b-93a; 4:23b-24a
boundaries ······· 2:91b
centers ······· 2:91b

divisions ··· 2:91b
Honshū ··· 2:91b-92a
Kyūshū ··· 2:91b
East-West boundary ··· 2:92a-92b
social ··· 2:92b-93a
"Dialogue on Poverty" ("Hinkyū mondō") ··· 8:303a
Diamond realm ··· 4:269b-270a
Diamond realm mandala ··· 6:*150b*
Diana ··· 5:100a; 6:270b, 349a-351a; 7:141b
Diaries ··· 5:33b; 6:2a-2b
Chichi no shūen nikki ··· 3:348a
Chūyūki ··· 1:314b
description ··· 6:2a
Gaun nikkenroku ··· 3:13b
Hanazono Tennō shinki ··· 3:95a
Izayoi nikki ··· 1:6a
Izumi Shikibu nikki ··· 3:366b
Kagerō nikki ··· 4:104a-104b
Murasaki Shikibu nikki ··· 5:267b
Nakatsukasa Naishi no nikki ··· 5:318a-318b
Sanuki no Suke no nikki ··· 7:18b
Sarashina nikki ··· 7:21a-21b
Tosa nikki ··· 4:216b
Towazugatari ··· 8:87a-87b
travel ··· 8:104b-106a
Umezu Masakage nikki ··· 8:147b
Uwai Kakuken nikki ··· 8:188b
Diary of a Japanese Convert ··· 1:155a
Diary of Lady Sanuki, The ··· 7:18b
Diary of Nakatsukasa Naishi ··· 5:318a-318b
Dictionaries ··· 2:93a-94a
Butsurui shōko ··· 1:225b
Daigenkai ··· 2:56a
Dai kanwa jiten ··· 3:60a
Dai Nihon kokugo jiten ··· 2:65a
Gagen shūran ··· 3:3a
Gensen ··· 3:23a-23b
Iroha jirui shō ··· 3:332a
Nihon daijisho ··· 5:379a
Nippo jisho ··· 6:8b
Rigen shūran ··· 6:312a
Ruiju myōgi shō ··· 6:340a
Setsuyōshū ··· 7:72b-73a
shinsen jikyō ··· 7:124b
Wakun no shiori ··· 8:221b
Wamyō ruiju shō ··· 8:222a
Dictionnaire historique du Japon ··· 4:42b
Didactic writing ··· 5:50a
Diesel Kiki Co, Ltd ··· 2:94a
Diet ··· 2:*94a*, 94b-96b; 4:37a
cabinet orders ··· 1:229a
Constitution of 1947 ··· 2:11a-11b
delegation to power ··· 2:84a
democracy ··· 2:84b
elections ··· 2:189a-190a
executive branch of government 3:55b-56a
history ··· 2:94a-94b
Occupation ··· 6:52a
organization ··· 2:94b-95a
revision of tax system ··· 7:172b
workings ··· 2:95a-96b
See also **Imperial Diet**
Diet Law ··· 2:6b
Diet member legislation ··· 2:96b
Ding Ruchang (Ting Ju-ch'ang) ··· 2:96b-97a; 8:287a
Diplomatics ··· 2:97a-100b, 112b-115a
documents. *See* **Documents**
external characteristics of documents ··· 2:97a-98b
calligraphy styles ··· 2:97b
language styles ··· 2:97b
orthography ··· 2:97b
semantic problems ··· 2:97b-98a
writing materials ··· 2:97a-97b
hammotsu ··· 2:*100a-100b*
historical documents ··· 2:99a-100b
Azuchi-Momoyama and Edo periods ··· 2:100a-100b
Kamakura and Muromachi periods ··· 2:99b-100a
Nara and Heian periods ··· 2:99a-99b
internal characteristics
date ··· 2:99a
issuing agent ··· 2:98b
main text ··· 2:98b-99a
recipient ··· 2:98b
Diplomatic seals ··· 7:184a
Diplomats
Aoki Shūzō ··· 1:69a-69b
Arita Hachirō ··· 1:85a
Ashida Hitoshi ··· 1:97b
EnomotoTakeaki ··· 2:219b-220a
Gotō Shimpei ··· 3:53b-54a
Hayashi Tadasu ··· 3:118a
Inoue Kaoru ··· 3:310a-310b
Ishii Kikujirō ··· 3:341a
Iwakura Tomomi ··· 3:360a
Katō Takaaki ··· 4:169b-170b
Katsura Tarō ··· 4:173b-174a
Komura Jutarō ··· 4:268a-268b
Makino Nobuaki ··· 5:86b
Matsuoka Yōsuke ··· 5:139a-139b
Mutsu Munemitsu ··· 5:288b-289a
Nomura Kichisaburō ··· 6:34a
Ōkuma Shigenobu ··· 6:95b-96b
Saitō Hiroshi ··· 6:373b-374a
Satō Naotake ··· 7:28a
Shidehara Kijūrō ··· 7:88a-89a
Shigemitsu Mamoru ··· 7:91b-92b
Soejima Taneomi ··· 7:219b
Tanaka Giichi ··· 7:336a-336b
Tōgō Shigenori ··· 8:36b
Uchida Kōsai ··· 8:123b
Ugaki Kazushige ··· 8:130b-131a
Yoshida Shigeru ··· 8:343a-345a
Yoshizawa Kenkichi ··· 8:352a
Direct demand ··· 2:100b-101a
Disabled persons ··· 4:353a
Disarmament
post-World War I ··· 1:88a
post-World War II ··· 6:301a-301b; 8:276a-277a
Discipline of Japanese history: a guide to research ··· 2:101a-116b
See also Historical scholarship
Discrimination ··· 1:216a-216b; 2:314a; 5:195a-195b
Diseases ··· 5:147b-149a
allergic disorders ··· 5:148b
atomic bomb related ··· 1:111b-114a
blood ··· 5:148b
circulatory ··· 5:148a-148b
collagen ··· 5:148b
digestive ··· 5:148b
endocrine and metabolic ··· 5:148b
infectious ··· 5:147b-148a
prevention ··· 5:149b
intractable ··· 2:116b
neoplasm ··· 5:148a
nervous disorders ··· 5:148b
occupational ··· 6:55b
parasitic ··· 5:148a
poisoning ··· 5:148b-149a
pollution-related diseases ··· 6:217b-220a
quarantine ··· 6:274a
respiratory ··· 5:148a
venereal ··· 8:189b
Dismissal of an employee ··· 2:117a
Dispute resolution systems other than litigation ··· 2:117a-119a
in court ··· 2:118b-119a
arbitration ··· 1:74b-75a; 2:118b
compromise ··· 2:118b-119a
conciliation (chōtei) ··· 2:118b
historical background ··· 2:117a-117b
social methods ··· 2:117b-118a
Dispute settlement ··· 4:53b
Distilling industries
Nikka Whisky Distilling Co, Ltd ··· 6:1b
Suntory, Ltd ··· 7:276a
Takara Shuzō Co, Ltd ··· 7:318a
Distribution system ··· 2:119b-120b
business ··· 1:224b
1868-1937 ··· 2:30b
fragmented
implications ··· 2:120a
sources ··· 2:119b-120a
trends of change ··· 2:120b
District courts ··· 4:80b-81b
Divers, Edward ··· 2:121a
Divers ··· 2:286b; 4:37a
Dividends (kabushiki haitō) ··· 2:121a
Divination ··· 2:121a-121b
futomani ··· 2:121a
incubation ··· 2:121b
kiboku ··· 2:121a
kites ··· 4:230a
shamanistic medium ··· 2:121b
Yi jing ··· 2:121b
"Divine Soldiers" Incident ··· 7:108a-108b
Divine Wind League ··· 4:58a
Divorce (rikon) ··· 2:121b-122b, 244b; 7:214b
adultery ··· 1:15b-16a
settlements ··· 2:122a
custody of children ··· 2:122a
disposition of property ··· 2:122a
general terms ··· 2:122a
trends ··· 2:122a-122b
types ··· 2:121b-122a
agreement ··· 2:121b
arbitration ··· 2:121b
family court ··· 2:121b
judicial decision ··· 2:121b-122a
Divorce temple. *See* **Kakekomidera**
Doboku Kenkyūjo ··· 6:267a
Dōbōshū ··· 同朋衆 ··· 4:62a
Dobu ··· どぶ ··· 7:111a
Dochirina kirishitan ··· どちりな・きりしたん ··· 4:119b
Dōchū hizakurige ··· 道中膝栗毛 ··· 4:61a
Doctrina Christan ··· 4:*52b*, 119b
Documents
bugyōnin hōsho ··· 2:99b
diplomatics. *See* **Diplomatics**
gejijō ··· 3:15b
imperial edict ··· 3:277a
inzen ··· 2:99b
kampu ··· 4:130a
kaō ··· 4:155a-156a
kudashibumi ··· 4:302a
migyōsho ··· 2:98a-99a
mokkan ··· 2:99a; 5:234a
seals ··· 7:45a
semmyō ··· 7:62a
shotai ··· 7:170a
shuinjō ··· 7:184a
tasshi ··· 2:100a
Dodge, Joseph M. ··· 2:122b-123a, 157b
Dodge line ··· 2:122b-123a; 4:347a
business cycles ··· 1:224a
economy ··· 2:157b-158a
Ministry of International Trade and Industry ··· 5:190b
Price Control Order of 1946 ··· 6:238b
Shimoyama Incident ··· 7:107a
Doeff, Hendrik ··· 2:123a
French-Japanese relations ··· 2:330b
Dog, Japanese [(nihonken) *Canis familiaris* var. *japonicus*] ··· 2:124b-126a
folklore ··· 2:125b-126a
history ··· 2:125a-125b

types ········ 2:124b-125a
large (ōgata) ········ 2:124b-125a
medium (chūgata) ········ 2:125a
small (kogata) ········ 2:125a
Dōgashima ········ 堂ケ島 ········ 2:123a
Dōgen ········ 道元 1:179b; 2:*123a*, 123b-124a; 7:154a
calligraphic works ········ 1:235b
education ········ 2:172b
Eiheiji temple ········ 2:186a-186b
Rinzai sect ········ 6:319a
Sōtō sect ········ 7:233b-234a
Watsuji Tetsurō ········ 8:237b
Dogfighting (tōken) ········ 2:124a-124b
Tosa dog ········ 8:81b
Dōgo Hot Spring 道後温泉 2:126a; 5:*141a*
Dōgoyama ········ 道後山 ········ 2:126a
Dog shooting (inuoumono) ········ 2:125b
Dogtooth violet ········ 4:165b
Dogū ········ 土偶 ········ 4:74a-74b
Dogū mokugū ········ 土偶木偶 ········ 4:242b
Dohi Keizō ········ 土肥慶蔵 ········ 2:126a
Dōhō ········ 同胞 ········ 7:115b
Dōhoko ········ 1:175a
Dohyō ········ 7:271a
Dohyō's shōmen ········ 7:272b
Doi Bansui ········ 土井晩翠 ········ 2:126a-126b; 5:12a
Doigahama ········ 土井ケ浜 ········ 6:235a
excavation of ········ 1:78a
Doihara-Chi'n Agreement. *See* **Doihara-Qin (Doihara-Ch'in) Agreement**
Doihara Kenji 土肥原賢二 ········ 2:126b
Doihara-Qin (Doihara-Ch'in) Agreement ········ 2:126b
Doihara Kenji ········ 2:126b
Doi Kiyoyoshi ········ 土居清良 ········ 7:52a
Do ikki. 土一揆 *See* **Tsuchi ikki**
Doi Takeo ········ 土居健郎 ········ 1:49a
Doi Tatsuo ········ 土井辰雄 ········ 2:126b
Doi Toshikatsu ········ 土井利勝 ········ 2:126b-127a
Dōji ········ 道慈 ········ 2:55a
Dōjima Rice Market ········ 堂島米市場 ········ 2:127a
chōnin ········ 1:301b
Kajimaya ········ 4:114b
Dōjinsha school ········ 同人社 ········ 5:315a
Dojōgaku kenkyū ········ 土壌学研究 ········ 7:140b
Dōjōji ········ 道成寺 ········ 4:154b, 326a
Dojōsukui ········ 2:127b
Dōka ········ 1:175a
Dōkai Bay ········ 洞海湾 ········ 2:127b
Dōken ········ 1:175a
Dokkoishi ········ 7:248a
Dokō Toshio ········ 土光敏夫 ········ 2:127b
Dokuganryū Masamune ········ 独眼竜政宗 ········ 2:78a; 4:166a
Dokugen aika ········ 独絃哀歌 ········ 4:123a
Dokugin hyakuin 独吟百韻 ········ 1:73b
Dokuritsu Bijutsu Kyōkai (Independent Art Association) ········ 6:157b
Dokuritsu hyōron (Independent Review) ········ 独立評論 ········ 8:296a
Dokuro hai ········ どくろ杯 ········ 4:139a
Dokusen Kinshi Hō ········ 1:65b-67b
Dōkyō ········ 道鏡 ········ 2:127b
Fujiwara no Nakamaro ········ 2:353b
Doll Festival ········ 1:277b, 279b; 2:*127a*, 127b-128a; 5:4a
festivals ········ 2:260b
katashiro ········ 4:166b
origami ········ 6:116b
religious symbolism ········ 6:296a
sekku ········ 7:58a
shiohigari ········ 7:140b
Dolls ········ 2:128a-130a
dogū ········ 2:128a
Doll Festival. *See* **Doll Festival**
Edo period ········ 2:129a-130a
gosho ningyō ········ 2:*128b*, 129b
haniwa ········ 2:128a
Heian through Azuchi-Momoyama periods ········ 2:128a-128b
Hirata Gōyō ········ 2:129b, *130b*
inu hariko ········ 3:325b
ishō ningyō ········ 2:*129a*, 129b
kokeshi ········ 4:254a
Meiji period to present ········ 2:130a
Saga ningyō ········ 2:*129a*, 129b
Sakuma Kōho ········ 2:*129a*, 129b
tsuchiningyō (earthen or clay) ········ 2:129b
Doll's House, A ········ 7:112b
Dolmen burials. *See* **Prehistoric burials**
Dolphins. *See* **Whales**
Domain ········ 3:92b
monopolies ········ 3:96a
Domainal code. *See* **Bunkokuhō**
Domainal paper money ········ 3:99b
Domain clique ········ 3:91b-92a
Domain currency ········ 3:99b
Domain economies ········ 2:149a
Domain schools ········ 2:174a-174b
Dōmei (Japanese Confederation of Labor) ········ 同盟 ········ 2:85b, 130a; 4:347a-347b, 360a; 6:238a; 7:189a
labor unions ········ 1:313b-314a
Shinsambetsu ········ 7:124a
Takita Minoru ········ 7:327a
Dōmei Tsūshinsha (Domei News Agency) ········ 2:130a; 4:54b; 5:369a
censorship ········ 1:254a
presidents ········ 2:373a
Domestic Affairs Adjustment Law · 2:118b, 246a
Domestic colonization doctrine ········ 7:236b
Domestic Competitive Painting Exhibitions (Naikoku Kaiga Kyōshinkai) ········ 8:327b
Domestic exchange ········ 2:130a-130b
Domestic Painting Competitive Exhibitions ········ 7:359a
Dominicans ········ 2:130b
Dōmino ········ 7:249a
Dōmoto Inshō ········ 堂本印象 ········ 2:57b, 130b
Donchō ········ 2:130b
Don Francisco de Velasco. *See* **Tanaka Shōsuke**
Dong Du Movement ········ 6:182a
Dongya Heqin Hui ········ 8:31a
Dōni ō dōwa ········ 道二翁道話 ········ 5:320a
Donjon ········ 1:248a
Donker Curtius, Jan Hendrik 2:130b-131a
Donsu (damask) ········ 2:131a
Door-to-Door Sales Law ········ 2:131a
Doppo gin ········ 独歩吟 ········ 4:309a
Dore, Ronald ········ 4:42a
Dōri no kankaku ········ 道理の感覚 ········ 1:51a
Dormouse, Japanese ········ 2:131a-131b
Doro-e ········ 泥絵 ········ 2:131b
Dorokyō ········ 瀞峡 ········ 2:131b
Shingū ········ 7:115a
Dōsen ········ 道璿 ········ 2:131b
Dōshikai. *See* **Rikken Dōshikai**
Dōshin ········ 同心 ········ 8:338b
Dōshisha University · 2:131b-132a; 5:386a; 6:258a
Dōshō ········ 道昭 1:106a; 2:132a
Dōshū ········ 堂衆 ········ 2:132a
Dosō ········ 土倉 ········ 2:132a-132b; 4:161b; 7:266b
Shinran ········ 7:122b
Dōsojin ········ 道祖神 ········ 2:132b
konsei, variation ········ 4:275b
Dōsōkai (alumni group) ········ 6:205b
Dōtaku ········ 銅鐸 1:257b; 2:132b
Karako site ········ 4:157b
Shintō ········ 7:126a
Dōtoku ········ 2:232b; 5:248a
Dōtombori ········ 道頓堀 ········ 6:*119a*
Double Fantasy ········ 6:112a
"Doughnut phenomenon" ········ 8:176b
Douglas, Archibald ········ 7:242b
Douglas Reef ········ 6:93a
Dōwa Mining Co, Ltd ········ 2:132b-133a
Dōyaku (or *Zūfu*) *Haruma* (Halma Translated by Doeff) ········ 道訳法児馬 2:123a; 8:242b
Doyō fujin ········ 土曜夫人 ········ 6:65a
Dozō ········ 7:248b
Dōzoku ········ 4:218a; 7:214b
Draft Law to Control Radical Social Movements ········ 2:133a-133b
Draft notification slips ········ 7:167b-168a
Dragon and Tiger ········ 3:109b
Dragonflies ········ 2:133b
Dragon Palace ········ 5:295b
Drama
modern ········ 5:57b-60a
post-World War II ········ 5:59a-60a
pre-World War II ········ 5:58a-59a
radio ········ 6:275a
Shingeki ········ 7:112a-113b
Shingeki ········ 7:112a
Western
criticism ········ 7:124b-125a
Draper, William ········ 4:69b
Dress. *See* **Clothing**
Drivers' licenses ········ 2:133b-134a
Road Traffic Law ········ 6:333a
Drug abuse ········ 2:45a, 134a-134b
deaths ········ 4:86b
Narcotics Control Law ········ 5:334b
Drugs ········ 5:150a-150b
kampō ········ 5:151a
medicine ········ 5:150a-150b
psychotherapy ········ 6:261a
Drums ········ 5:282b
taiko ········ 7:297b
tsuzumi ········ 8:119b-120a
Drunken drivers ········ 6:333a
Dry field farming ········ 1:29a-29b
Drying Fishnets ········ 4:111a
DSP ········ 2:85a-85b
Dual Shintō (Ryōbu Shintō) ········ 4:188a; 6:351a-351b
Dual sovereignty ········ 6:86a
Dual structure ········ 2:324a
Duan Qirui (Tuan-Ch'i-jui) ········ 2:134b
Duan Qirui cabinet ········ 4:384b
Du Bousquet, Albert Charles ········ 1:166a; 2:134b-135a
Du Fu ········ 6:297b
Dulles, John Foster ·· 2:135a-135b; 6:302b; 7:10b-11a
Dutch East India Company
Dutch Factory ········ 2:135b
Dutch trade ········ 2:135b
Dutch Factory ········ 2:135b
Doeff, Hendrik ········ 2:123a
Dutch interpreters. *See* **Oranda tsūji**
Dutch-Japanese Treaty of Amity ········ 2:130b-131a
Dutch-language interpreters ········ 6:116a
Dutch Learning. *See* **Western Learning**
Dutch New Year ········ 6:116a
Dutch reports ········ 6:115b
Dutch trade ········ 2:135b-136a
Dyeing ········ 7:13b; 8:16b-21a, 29b-30a, 237b-238a, 359a
Dyen, Isidore ········ 4:20a

Dyes and dye colors · · · 2:136a-136b; 8:18a
design · · · 2:90a
indigo · · · 3:290a
murasaki root · · · 5:267b

E

Eagles · · · 3:114b
Earlier Nine Years' War · · · 1:4a-4b; 2:137a
samurai in · · · 7:7b
Early Japanese History · · · 6:288b
Early Japanese song. *See* Music, song, early
Early literature. *See* **Literature**
Ear ornaments, ancient · · · 2:138b
Kofun period · · · 2:138b; 4:245a
Earthenware · · · 1:256b-258a
Haji ware · · · 3:84a-84b
Jōmon pottery · · · 4:75a-75b
Earthquake Disaster Prevention, Committee for · · · 2:140b
Earthquake Research Institute · · · 2:141a; 6:305b
Earthquakes · · · 2:138b-140a; 4:7b
causes and distribution · · · 2:139a-139b
crustal distortion and faulting · · · 2:139a
mantle convection and horizontal displacement · · · 2:139b
crustal movement · · · 4:8b-9a
prediction · · · 2:139b
damage prevention · · · 2:139b-140a
research · · · 2:139b
Tōkyō Earthquake of 1923. *See* **Tōkyō Earthquake of 1923**
Earthquake scale · · · 2:140a
Earth sciences · · · 2:140a-141a
geology · · · 2:141a
Meiji period · · · 2:140a-141a
seismology · · · 2:140b-141a
Earthworms [(mimizu) class Oligochaeta] · · · 2:141a-141b
East Asia Common Culture Society 8:30a
East Asia cultural sphere · · · 2:141a-142a
East Asia Friendship Society · · · 8:31a
East Asian League · · · 8:30b
East Asia Research Institute · · · 8:289a
East Asia: The Great Tradition · · · 6:289a
East Asia: The Modern Transformation · · · 6:289a
East China Sea · · · 2:142a
Eastern European nations and Japan · · · 2:142a-142b
diplomatic relations · · · 3:323a-323b
Japanese studies · · · 4:43b-44a
trade · · · 3:323a-323b
Eastern Japan · · · 2:142b
Eastern Sea Road · · · 8:40b-41b
East Germany · · · 3:27b; 4:43b-44a
East Hebei (Hopeh) Anticommunist Autonomous Government · · · 2:142b
December Ninth Movement · · · 2:81a
Yin Rugeng · · · 8:325b
East India Company (Dutch). *See* Dutch East India Company
East India Company (English) · · · 1:334a
E-awase · · · 絵合せ · · · 7:167a
Ebara Corporation · · · 2:142b-143a
Ebashi Setsurō · · 江橋節郎 · · · 2:143a
Ebetsu · · · 江別 · · · 2:143a
Ebi · · · 7:179b
Ebina · · · 海老名 · · · 2:143a
Ebina Danjō · · 海老名弾正 · · · 2:143a
Ebine *(Calanthe discolor)* · · · 2:143a-143b
Ebino · · · えびの · · · 2:143b
Ebino Kōgen · · えびの高原 2:143b; 4:221b
Ebisu · · · 恵比須 2:143b; 5:296a
Shintō family altars · · · 7:137b
Ebisukaki · · · 恵比須舁き · · · 6:269b
Ebune · · · 1:324a
Eburimanshi no yūga na seikatsu · 江分利満氏の優雅な生活 · · · 8:294b
Ebusshi · · · 絵仏師 · · · 2:143b
Jigoku-zōshi · · · 4:54b
Kose school · · · 4:295a
Takuma school · · · 7:328a
Echigo-jishi · · · 越後獅子 · · · 4:118a
Echigo Mountains · · · 越後山脈 · · 2:143b, 336b
Echizemmisaki · · · 越前岬 · · · 2:144a
Echizen ware · · · 越前焼 · · · 2:144a
museums · · · 5:279b
Echizen'ya Chōjirō. 越前屋長次郎 *See* **Tamenaga Shunsui**
Eckert, Franz · · · 5:286a
Econometric models · · · 2:144a-145a
economic planning · · · 2:144a
Japanese planning · · · 2:144a
macroeconomic · · · 2:144a-144b
microeconomic · · · 2:144b
recent developments and future prospects · · · 2:144b-145a
regional industry · · · 2:144b
static · · · 2:144b
turnpike · · · 2:144b
Economic Aspects of Japan, The · 7:324a
Economic cooperation · · · 1:205b
Economic Council · · · 2:167a-167b
Economic efficiency · · · 2:145a-146b
Economic growth, contemporary · · · 2:163a-165a
first phase · · · 2:163b
government's role · · · 2:163a-163b
major continuities · · · 2:163a
turning points · · · 2:163b-165a
Economic history. *See* Economy, contemporary; Economy, early modern; Economy, Occupation-period; Economy, premodern
Economic independence · · · 2:165b
Economic planning · · · 2:165b-167b
foreign investment control · · · 2:317a
Income-Doubling Plan · · · 3:287a
industry choice · · · 2:167a-167b
managerial ideology · · · 5:92b
models · · · 2:144a
modern · · · 2:163a
Economic Planning Agency (EPA) · · · 2:167b-168a; 4:190b
function · · · 2:165b-167a
Income-Doubling Plan · · · 3:287a
national wealth · · · 5:349a-349b
White Paper on the Economy · · · 8:251b
White Paper on the National Standard of Living · · · 8:251b
Economic Reconstruction Round Table · · · 4:385b
Economic stabilization · · · 6:4b-5b
Economic Stabilization Board (ESB) · · · 1:8b; 2:168a
Economic Planning Agency · · 2:167b-168a
economic reform · · · 2:155b-156a, 157a
Nagano Shigeo · · · 5:303b
Economic Welfare Council · · 2:168a-168b
Economists
Amano Tameyuki · · · 1:50b-51a
Arisawa Hiromi · · · 1:84a-84b
Crawford, Sir John Grenfell · · · 2:41b
Fukuda Tokuzō · · · 2:362b
Hirano Yoshitarō · · · 3:143b
Inomata Tsunao · · · 3:309a
Ishibashi Tanzan · · · 3:339b
Kaiho Seiryō · · · 4:110a
Kanai Noburu · · · 4:135b
Kawakami Hajime · · · 4:180b
Koizumi Shinzō · · · 4:250b
Kushida Tamizō · · · 4:320a
Masuchi Yōjirō · · · 5:129b
Mayet, Paul · · · 5:142b
Minobe Ryōkichi · · · 5:194a
Morishima Michio · · · 5:253a
Morito Tatsuo · · · 5:254b
Nakayama Ichirō · · · 5:318b
Noro Eitarō · · · 6:38b
Ōshima Sadamasu · · · 6:126a
Ōtsuka Hisao · · · 6:134a
Ōuchi Hyōe · · · 6:135a-135b
Sakisaka Itsurō · · · 7:2b-3a
Shiozawa Masasada · · · 7:141b
Sōda Kiichirō · · · 7:219a
Sugimoto Eiichi · · · 7:258a
Sugimura Kōzō · · · 7:258a
Taguchi Ukichi · · · 7:294b
Takata Yasuma · · · 7:319b
Uno Kōzō · · · 8:173b-174a
Yamada Moritarō · · · 8:289a
Yanaihara Tadao · · · 8:315b
Yasui Takuma · · · 8:318b-319a
Economy
balance of payments · · · 1:133b-135a
business concentration · · · 1:224a
business cycles · · · 1:224a-224b
hunting and gathering · · · 4:72a
income distribution · · · 3:285b-287a
industrial organization · · · 3:292a-296b
industrial revolution in Japan · · · 3:298a
industrial structure · · · 3:299b-302a
Industrial Structure Council · · · 3:302a
inflation and price stability · · · 3:303a
input-output analysis · · · 3:312b-313a
Matsukata era · · · 3:194b
Matsukata fiscal policy · · · 5:134b
maturing process · · · 5:241a-241b
Meiji period · · · 2:29b-30a
occupational structure · · · 6:55b-57b
postwar growth · · · 3:203a-203b
occupation · · · 3:240a
pre-World War II recovery · · · 3:201a
price guidelines
incomes policy · · · 3:287b
recovery of during Shōwa depression · · · 7:174a
White Paper on the Economy · · · 8:251b
White Paper on the National Standard of Living · · · 8:251b
wholesale and retail · · · 1:224b
World War I · · · 3:199b-200a
Economy, premodern (to 1867) · · · 2:146b-151a
before 1600 · · · 2:147a-149a
autonomous domains · · · 2:148b
commercialization and monetary expansion · · · 2:148a-148b
domain economics · · · 2:149a
foreign trade · · · 2:148a
protohistorical period · · · 2:147a
ritsuryō system · · · 2:147a-147b
shōen · · · 2:147b-148a
unification · · · 2:149a
urbanization · · · 2:148b-149a
Edo period · · · 1:149a-151a
commercial expansion · · · 2:149b-150a
diffusion of trade and handicraft industry · · · 2:150a
employment options · · · 2:150b

fiscal deficits and impoverished samurai ········ **2**:150b
foreign trade ········ **2**:150a
regional variation ········ **2**:150a-150b
shipping ········ **2**:149b
urbanization ········ **2**:149a-149b
Economy, early modern (1868-1945) ········ **2**:151a-154a
foreign capital and commerce **2**:151a-151b
growth industries ········ **2**:152b-153a
growth problems ········ **2**:153a-154a
industrialization and modernization ········ **2**:151a-152a
private sector ········ **2**:152a
production ········ **2**:152a-152b
Economy, Occupation-period (1945-52) ········ **2**:154a-158b
conclusions ········ **2**:158b
Dodge line ········ **2**:157b-158a
end of war ········ **2**:154a-155a
policy makers ········ **2**:154b
SCAP ········ **2**:154b-155a
Korean War ········ **2**:158a-158b
reform ········ **2**:155a-156b
economic aid ········ **2**:155a
economic purgation ········ **2**:155a
inflation and inflation control ········ **2**:155a-156b
reparation payments ········ **2**:155a
reverse course ········ **2**:156b-157b
Economy, contemporary (from 1952) ········ **2**:158b-165b
economic heritage ········ **2**:158b-159a
economic performance overview ········ **2**:159a-161b
growth ········ **2**:159b-160b
investment and saving ········ **2**:160b-161a
labor force ········ **2**:161a-161b
technology ········ **2**:161b
growth benefits and costs ········ **2**:165a
growth environment ········ **2**:163a-165b
first phase ········ **2**:163b
government's role ········ **2**:163a-163b
major continuities ········ **2**:163a
turning points ········ **2**:163b-165a
structural changes ········ **2**:161b-162a
industrial organization ········ **2**:162b-163a
production and workers distribution ········ **2**:162a-162b
Edachi ········ 役立ち ········ **8**:327a
E-dai ········ **4**:164b
Eda Saburō ········ 江田三郎 ········ **2**:168b
Japan Socialist Party ········ **4**:49a
Eda Satsuki ········ 江田五月 ········ **2**:168b
Edict of Expulsion ········ **8**:95a
"Edicts on Compassion for Living Things" (Shōrui awaremi no rei) ········ **8**:56a-56b
Edo ········ 江戸 ·· **2**:168b-169b
castle town ········ **1**:249a
chōnin class ········ **1**:301b
development ········ **2**:168b-169a
influence ········ **2**:169b
journeys to ········ **2**:171b
land reclamation ········ **4**:364a
land use ········ **2**:169a-169b
population ········ **8**:178a
rice riot ········ **8**:124a
urbanization ········ **8**:176a, 177b
Edo Castle ········ 江戸城 ··· **2**:169b-170a
chōnin ········ **1**:301b
Kaempfer, Engelbert ········ **4**:101b
Nakaoku ········ **2**:170a
Ōhiroma ········ **6**:74a
Ōoku ········ **6**:113b
Ōta Dōkan ········ **6**:128b
Tokugawa Ieyasu ········ **8**:50a
paintings ········ **4**:151a
Edo city commissioners ········ **2**:171a
Edogawa ········ 江戸川 ········ **2**:170b
Edogawa Rampo ········ 江戸川乱歩 ·· **2**:170b-171a; **5**:291b
Edogawa Rampo Prize ········ **2**:171a
Edogawa Ward ·· 江戸川区 ········ **2**:171a
Edo hakkei (Eight Views of Edo) ·· 江戸八景 ········ **8**:184b
Edo hanjō ki ··· 江戸繁昌記 ········ **8**:11b
Edo history. *See* **History of Japan**
Edokko ········ 江戸子 ········ **4**:61b
Edokoro ········ 絵所 ········ **2**:171a
Edo kouta ········ 江戸小唄 ········ **4**:298a
Edokyahan ········ **4**:323b
Edo literature. *See* **Literature**
Edo machi bugyō ········ 江戸町奉行 · **2**:171a; **5**:78b; **7**:6a
Itakura Katsushige ········ **3**:350a
Ōoka Tadasuke ········ **6**:113b
Tōyama Kinshirō ········ **8**:88a
Edo Murasaki ······ 江戸紫 ········ **4**:199a
Edo period ······ 江戸時代 ··· **2**:171a-171b
Edo-period education. *See* **Education**
Edo-period wares. *See* **Ceramics**
Edo sampu ······ 江戸参府 ········ **2**:171b
Dejima ········ **2**:83a
Dutch Factory ········ **2**:135b
Kaempfer, Engelbert ········ **4**:101b
EDR ········ **2**:235b
Education ········ **2**:171b-179a
academic degrees ········ **1**:6a
academic freedom ········ **1**:6a-6b
academic pressures ········ **5**:6b
administration ········ **2**:177a-178b, 181a
local ········ **2**:177b-178a
national ········ **2**:177b
adult ········ **1**:341b-342a
audiovisual ········ **1**:116a; **2**:181b
authorization system ········ **7**:37b
before 1600 ········ **2**:172a-172b
ancient Japan ········ **2**:172a-172b
medieval education ········ **2**:172b
boards ········ **2**:178a
Central Council for Education ········ **1**:255b
children of returnees ········ **2**:182a
Chinese characters required ········ **4**:331b
civic ········ **1**:316a
civil service ········ **1**:218a, 219b-220a
coeducation ········ **1**:334a
commoners school ··· **4**:113b, 340a; **7**:182a
community ········ **1**:341a, 342a; **2**:182a
compulsory ········ **1**:344a; **2**:183a-183b, 195a-195b, 223b; **7**:35b
corporate management ········ **2**:32b
corporate training and ········ **2**:28a
correspondence ········ **2**:181b-182a
cram schools ········ **2**:41b
cumulative guidance record (shidō yōroku) ········ **2**:53a
curriculum ········ **7**:34a-36a
elementary and secondary ········ **7**:34a-35b
extracurricular activities ········ **7**:35b
foreign language training ·· **2**:318b; **7**:35b
health and physical education ········ **7**:35b
history ········ **7**:35b-36a
home economics ········ **7**:35b
language ········ **7**:34b
mathematics ········ **7**:35a
music and art ········ **7**:35b
physics ········ **4**:10a; **6**:186b
school course guidelines ········ **7**:34a
science ········ **7**:35a
social studies ········ **7**:34b-35a
structure ········ **7**:34b-35b
democratization ········ **2**:180a-180b
Edo period ········ **2**:172b-175a
Confucian scholarship and school formation ········ **2**:173a-173b
domain schools ········ **2**:174a-174b
heterodoxy and new orthodoxy ·· **2**:173b
other schools ········ **2**:174b-175a
elementary ········ **2**:195b-196a
entrance examinations ·· **2**:181a, 222a-223a
environmental ········ **2**:224a
expenses ········ **2**:179b-180a
finance ········ **2**:178a-178b
local ········ **2**:178a
national ········ **2**:178a
financial aid ········ **2**:277a
foreign students in Japan ········ **2**:319a
schools ········ **3**:3a
gakubatsu ········ **1**:147a; **3**:3b-4a
government policy ········ **2**:178b
decentralization ········ **2**:178b
equal opportunity ········ **2**:178b, 230b
finance ········ **2**:178b-179a
private schools ········ **2**:179a
single-track school system ········ **2**:178b
teacher status, quality, and renumeration ········ **2**:178b
graduate schools ········ **3**:59b
higher. *See* Higher education
home ········ **2**:181b
humanization ········ **2**:180b
Iwakura mission and ········ **3**:359b
Japanese children abroad ······ **7**:36a-37b, 48b-49a
judges
Legal Training and Research Institute ········ **1**:320b
levels
elementary (shotō kyōiku) ·· **2**:194a-195b
high schools (kōtō gakkō) ········ **2**:195b
junior colleges ········ **4**:84a-84b
preschool ········ **6**:235b
secondary (chūtō kyōiku) ·· **2**:194a; **7**:52a
university. *See* **Universities and colleges**
lifelong learning ········ **5**:5b
lifestyles ········ **5**:6b, 8b
literacy ········ **2**:172b-173a; **5**:10b-11a
management ········ **5**:89b
mass communications ········ **5**:129a-129b
medical ········ **3**:120a-120b
Meiji period ········ **2**:152b
militaristic ····· **2**:176a-176b, 183b; **5**:175a; **7**:52a
miscellaneous schools ········ **5**:198b
mission schools ········ **5**:202b-203a
modern ········ **2**:175a-176b
characteristics ········ **2**:175a-175b
consolidation ········ **2**:176a
establishment ········ **2**:175b-176a
expansion ········ **2**:176a
post-World War II reforms ······ **2**:176b
wartime ········ **2**:176a-176b
moral ········ **5**:248a-248b; **7**:191b
music ········ **5**:285a
national budget ········ **1**:204b
nationalism ········ **2**:176a, 183b
private schools ········ **7**:94a-94b
professional schools ········ **7**:62a
progressive ········ **7**:31b
provision, by parent or guardian ···· **1**:21b
PTAs ········ **6**:262b
reform ········ **2**:176a-176b; **2**:183a-184a
early 20th century ········ **2**:183b
interwar period ········ **2**:183b
Meiji period ········ **2**:183a-183b
of 1947 ········ **2**:180a-180b
post-World War II ········ **2**:183b-184a
religious ······ **6**:290b, 295a-295b; **7**:191a
report cards ········ **6**:302b
research ········ **2**:180b-181a
Shin Kyōiku Undō ········ **7**:121b

scholastic ability measurement 2:180b-181a
school administration 7:33a
school orders (gakkōrei) 7:36b
school system 2:176b-177a
secondary 2:195b
sex 7:73b
single-track system 2:178b
special 7:241b
teachers 7:365a-367a
teacher-training systems 6:38a; 7:365b
teaching methods 7:367a-367b
testing 1:10b
textbooks 7:37b
tutoring schools (juku) 2:223a
United States education missions to Japan 8:164b
universities and colleges 3:133a-135a; 8:170a-171a
village schools (gōgaku) 3:40a
vocational 8:192b-193a
Vocational Training Law 8:193a-193b
Western Learning 4:306a; 8:241a-243a
Western influence 2:175b-176a
women 8:260a; 267a-268a
contemporary 8:262b-263a
youth schools 7:52a
Education, Fundamental Law of 2:182a-182b
aims 2:180a
content 2:178b
Education Act of 1872 ..... 7:191b
Educational broadcasting 2:179a
Educational counseling 2:179a-179b
cases 2:179b
Educational expenses 2:179b-180a
Educational Personnel Certification Law 7:366a
Educational Public Employees Special Law 8:171a
Educational Reforms of 1947 2:180a-180b
coeducation 1:334a
Educational research 2:180b-181a
administration 2:181a
entrance examination system 2:181a
humanization and curriculum revision 2:180b
moral education 2:181a
National Institute for 2:181a
scholastic ability measurement 2:180b-181a
school role and function 2:181a
Educational Research, National Institute for 2:181a
Educational technology 2:181b
Education law 2:182b
"Education mother" 2:181b
Education Order of 1872 ..... 2:175b, 182b-183a, 230b, 361a; 3:193b; 5:11a; 7:241b
coeducation 1:334a
compulsory education 1:344a
Murray, David 5:275a
normal schools 6:38a
Ōseidasaresho 6:124a
private schools 6:252a
Tanaka Fujimaro 7:336a
teachers 7:365a-365b
Verbeck, Guido Herman Fridolin 8:190a
women's education 8:267b
Education Order of 1879 ..... 2:183a
Education Reform Council 1:51a, 255b; 2:183a
Fundamental Law of Education 2:182a
Occupation 6:53a
United States education missions to Japan 8:164b

Educators
American
Bacon, Alice Mabel 1:129b
Berry, John Cutting 1:150a
Brown, Samuel Robbins 1:175b
Clark, Edward Warren 1:321b
Clark, William Smith 1:321b
Fenollosa, Ernest Francisco 2:251b-252a
Griffis, William Elliot 3:62b
Janes, Leroy Lansing 4:2a
Kauffman, James Lee 4:175a
Mason, Luther Whiting 5:127b-128a
Murray, David 5:275a
Scott, Marion McCarrell 7:41a
Shaw, Glenn William 7:81a
Vining, Elizabeth Gray 8:192a
Vories, William Merrel 8:195b
Warner, Langdon 8:228a
British
Conder, Josiah 1:349b
Murdoch, James 5:270b
German
Fröbel, Friedrich Wilhelm August 2:339b
Hausknecht, Emile 3:114a-114b
Hearn, Lafcadio 3:120b-121a
Japanese
Abe Isoo 1:2a
Abe Jirō 1:2b
Abe Shigetaka 1:4b
Abe Yoshishige 1:5a
Amano Tameyuki 1:50b-51a
Amano Teiyū 1:51a
Ashida Enosuke 1:97a-97b
Atomi Kakei 1:115a
Azuma Ryōtarō 1:127b
Daikuhara Gintarō 2:60b
Fukuzawa Yukichi 2:367b-368a
Hamao Arata 3:91a
Hasegawa Tai 3:108a
Hatano Kanji 3:112a
Hatoyama Haruko 3:112b
Hirose Tansō 3:148a
Inoue Enryō 3:309b
Inoue Tetsujirō 3:311a
Itō Jinsai 3:354a
Iwamoto Yoshiharu 3:360b
Izawa Shūji 3:365a
Kaigo Tokiomi 4:109b
Kanō Jigorō 4:147a
Kawai Michi 4:179a
Kawasaki Natsu 4:184a
Kikuchi Dairoku 4:206a
Kozaki Hiromichi 4:300a
Maeda Tamon 5:80b
Makiguchi Tsunesaburō 5:85b
Miura Baien 5:214b-215a
Miwata Masako 5:216a-216b
Miyake Yonekichi 5:219a
Mori Arinori 5:248b-249a
Morito Tatsuo 5:254b
Motoda Nagazane 5:257a
Nakai Chikuzan 8:292a
Nakai Riken 8:292a
Nambara Shigeru 5:323b
Naruse Jinzō 5:335a
Nishi Amane 6:14a-14b
Nishimura Shigeki 6:17b-18b
Nitobe Inazō 6:21b-22a
Obara Kuniyoshi 6:48a
Ogura Kinnosuke 6:71a
Ōhara Yūgaku 6:73b
Oikawa Heiji 6:74b-75a
Okamoto Kansuke 6:80a
Ōse Jintarō 6:124a-124b
Ototake Iwazō 6:133b
Sawayanagi Masatarō 7:31b
Shimoda Utako 7:105a
Sugiura Shigetake 7:258b
Tachibana Kōzaburō 7:292a-292b
Takada Sanae 7:310b
Takagi Kenkan 7:311a
Takamine Hideo 7:315a-315b
Tanaka Fujimaro 7:336a
Tanimoto Tomeri 7:342a
Tejima Seiichi 7:377a
Tosaka Jun 8:81b
Toyama Masakazu 8:88a
Tsuda Umeko 8:112b-113a
Tsunoda Ryūsaku 8:116a
Yajima Kajiko 8:284b
Yanaihara Tadao 8:315b
Yasui Tetsu 8:319a
Yoshida Shōin 8:345b-346a
Yuasa Hachirō 8:354b
Eejanaika · ええじゃないか 2:184a
Eel, Japanese [(unagi) *Anguilla japonica*] 2:184a, 287b
Efu ..... 衛府 2:184a
Efumi ..... 絵踏 4:119a
Egami Namio ..... 江上波夫 1:78b
horse-rider theory 3:230a
E-gasuri 4:*164b*
Egawa Hidetatsu · 江川英龍 2:184b
Egawa Tan'an. 江川坦庵 *See* **Egawa Tarōzaemon**
Egawa Tarōzaemon ..... 江川太郎左衛門 2:184b
Eggplant [(nasu) *Solanum melongena*] 2:184b
Ego 2:184b
Egonoki [(Japanese snowbell) *Styrax japonica*] 2:184b
Egōshū ..... 会合衆 2:184b-185a
Eguchi ..... 江口 4:135b
Ehime Prefecture ..... 愛媛県 2:185a-185b
Ehon butai ōgi 絵本舞台扇 8:141a
Ehon mushi erami 画本虫撰 · 8:142a, 185b
Eibutsuka poems 5:106a
Eichelberger, Robert Lawrence 2:185b; 7:33a
Eidaka ..... 永高 2:185b-186a; 4:137a
Eifuku Mon'in ..... 永福門院 2:186a
Eiga monogatari · 栄華物語 · 2:186a; 5:37a, 246a
Akazome Emon 1:41a
Fujiwara no Michinaga 2:186a
historiography 3:153a
Eigen Jakushitsu wajō goroku 永源寂室和上語録 4:2a
Eighteen Kabuki numbers 4:97b-99a
Eight Eight Fleet 3:73b
Eight Outrages 3:73b
Eight Provinces of Kantō 4:141b
Eight Views of Ōmi 6:101b
Eight Views of the Xiao (Hsiao) and Xiang (Hsiang) Rivers 7:167b; 8:13a
Eiheiji ..... 永平寺 2:186a-186b, 364a
training 2:172b
Eihei shingi ..... 永平清規 2:172b
Eikoku sangyō kakumei shi ron 英国産業革命史論 8:127a
Eikosaku ..... 永小作 2:186b
Eikyō Disturbance 7:322a
E inga kyō ..... 絵因果経 2:199a; 6:148a, 149a
Eiraku Hozen ..... 永楽保全 2:186b
Eirakusen ..... 永楽銭 1:156b; 2:186b; 5:242b
erizeni 2:230b
kandaka 4:137a
Eirin 5:256b
Eisai ..... 栄西 · 1:179b, 294a; 2:187a-187b; 3:171b
calligraphic works 1:235b

Rinzai sect ······ 6:319a
Eisai Co, Ltd ······ 2:187b
Eisei Bunko Foundation ······ 5:276b
Eison ······ 叡尊 ··· 2:187b-188a
Eiten ······ 2:187b
Eitoku. 永徳 *See* **Kanō Eitoku**
Eiyokei ······ 栄誉刑 ······ 7:140b
Eiyū taibōron (Awaiting Heroes) ······ 英雄待望論 ······ 8:117a
Eizon ······ 叡尊 ··· 2:187b-188a
monasticism ······ 5:238b
Eji ······ 衛士 ······ 2:184a
Ejima Incident ··· 絵島事件 ······ 2:188a
Kaigetsudō Ando ······ 4:109b
Ejima Kiseki ···· 江島其磧 · 2:188a; 5:48b
fūzoku shōsetsu ······ 2:278a
Ejō ······ 懐奘 ······ 2:186b
Ekayāna (One Vehicle) doctrine ···· 4:67b
Ekiben ······ 2:188a-188b
Ekisei ······ 駅制 ······ 2:188b
Elderly ······ 5:5a
institutions ······ 7:211b-212a
lifestyles ······ 5:7a
otona ······ 6:132b
respect for ······ 5:5a
social security ······ 4:353a
suicides among ······ 7:209a
welfare ······ 7:211b-212a
Elder statesmen ······ 3:21b-22a
Election Law of 1945 ······ 8:263a
Elections ······ 2:188b-190a
democracy ······ 2:84b-85a
Diet ······ 2:94a
Imperial Diet ······ 3:276a
registration ······ 2:190a
voter participation ······ 2:190a
Electoral system ······ 2:190a
Electrical products manufacturers ······ 7:174a
Electric power ······ 2:190a-191b
companies
Chūbu Electric Power Co, Inc ···· 1:311a
Chūgoku Electric Power Co, Inc ·· 1:312a
Hokkaidō Electric Power Co, Inc · 3:214a
Hokuriku Electric Power Co, Inc · 3:215a
Kansai Electric Power Co, Inc ······ 4:151b-152a
Kyūshū Electric Power Co, Inc ··· 4:340b
Shikoku Electric Power Co, Ltd ··· 7:97b
Tōhoku Electric Power Co, Inc ···· 8:37a
Tōkyō Electric Power Co, Inc ···· 8:37a
dams ······ 2:72a-73b
development ······ 2:191b
distribution ······ 2:191a-191b
industrialization ······ 2:191a
periods
first ······ 2:190b
second ······ 2:190b
third ······ 2:190b-191a
suppliers ······ 4:10b
system ······ 2:191a
transmission ······ 2:191a-191b
Electric Power Development Co, Ltd ······ 2:191b-192a
Electric Power Industry, Central Research Institute of ······ 2:192a
Electric Power Management Law · 2:191b
Electric power system ······ 2:191a
Electronics ······ 2:192a-195a
companies
Akai Electric Co, Ltd ······ 1:39b
Alps Electric Co, Ltd ······ 1:48a
Casio Computer Co, Ltd (Kashio Keisanki) ······ 1:245b
Fujitsū, Ltd ······ 2:347b
Hitachi, Ltd ······ 3:206b-207a
Matsushita Electric Industrial Co, Ltd ······ 5:140b
Matsushita-Kotobuki Electronics Industries, Ltd ······ 5:141a-141b
Mitsubishi Electric Corporation ······ 5:207a-207b
Nippon Electric Co, Ltd ······ 6:9a-9b
Oki Electric Industry Co, Ltd ······ 6:84a
Omron Tateisi Electronics Co, Ltd ······ 6:104a
Pioneer Electronic Corporation ··· 6:189a
San'yō Electric Co, Ltd ······ 7:19a
Sharp Corporation ······ 7:80a-80b
Sony Corporation ······ 7:228b-229a
Tōshiba Corporation ······ 8:82b
Trio–Kenwood Corporation ······ 8:106b
Victor Co. of Japan, Ltd ······ 8:191b
consumer grade ······ 2:194a-194b
computer industry ······ 1:344a
development ······ 2:192a
after 1955 ······ 2:193b-194a
postwar (1945-54) ······ 2:193b
industry structure ······ 2:194a-195a
manufacturers ······ 2:194a
Shinagawa Ward ······ 7:108b
to 1945 ······ 2:192a
Electrotechnical Laboratory ······ 2:195a; 6:305b
Elementary and secondary education ······ 2:195b-196a
Elementary Japanese for College Students ······ 2:196b
El Filibusterismo ······ 6:332b
Eliot, Charles Norton Edgcumbe · 1:149b; 2:196a
Elisséeff, Serge ······ 2:196a-196b; 4:42b
Elite, political and social ······ 8:325a
Elizabeth Saunders Home ·· 2:196b; 7:30b
konketsuji in ······ 4:271b
Ema ······ 絵馬 · 2:196b, *197a*, 197b-198a; 7:*144b*, 256b
Kanō school ······ 4:149b
Emaki. *See* **Emakimono**
Emakimono ······ 絵巻物 ·· 2:198a-200a; 6:150a
Ban Dainagon ekotoba ······ 1:137a; 6:*152a*
Buddhist art ······ 1:186b-187a
Chōjū giga (Scrolls of Frolicking Animals and Humans) ······ 1:298b; 2:*199a-199b*
format ······ 2:198a-199b
Gaki-zōshi ······ 1:190b, 191a
Genji monogatari emaki · 1:163b; 2:*198a-198b*
Heiji monogatari emaki ······ 3:123b; 6:*152a*
history ······ 2:199a-200a
Jigoku-zōshi ······ 1:190b
Kanō school ······ 4:149b
Scrolls of Hungry Ghosts ······ 1:190b
Shigisan engi emaki ······ 7:92b-93a, *93a*
Sumiyoshi school ······ 7:270a
Toba Sōjō ······ 2:*199a-199b*; 8:31b-32a
Tosa school ······ 8:82a
Embree, John Fee ··· 2:200a; 4:38b; 7:73b, 255a
Embroidery ······ 2:200a
Embushū ······ 閻浮集 ······ 8:16a
Emigrant Protection Art ······ 2:200b
Emigration ······ 2:200a-201b
early ······ 2:200b
effects ······ 2:201b
exclusionism ······ 2:200b
growth of empire ······ 2:200b
to Latin America ······ 4:369a
Okinawa ······ 6:87b
postwar ······ 2:201a-201b
prewar ······ 2:200b-201a
See also **Immigration**
Emigration and immigration control ······ 2:201b
Emigration Bureau ······ 2:200b
Emi no Oshikatsu ······ 恵美押勝 ······ 2:353b
Emishi. 蝦夷 *See* **Ezo**
Emi Suiin ······ 江見水蔭 ······ 4:199a
Emma ······ 2:201b
hell ······ 3:126a
Emmeiji ······ 延命寺 ······ 4:177a
Emperor ······ 2:202a-209a
early ······ 2:203a-204b
Edo period ······ 2:204b-205b
"Emperor System" (Tennōsei) ····· 2:207b
Heian period ······ 2:204a
hōō (priestly retired sovereign) ···· 3:227a
Kamakura period ······ 2:204a-204b
legal status ······ 2:208b-209a
list of ······ 2:*202a-203a*
meaning ······ 2:208a-208b
Meiji Constitution ······ 2:2b-3a; 3:195b
Meiji period ······ 2:206b; 5:153a-154a
Meiji Restoration ······ 2:205b-206b
Muromachi and Azuchi-Momoyama periods ······ 2:204b
1947 Constitution ······ 2:207b-208a
organ-of-state theory ······ 8:8a
present ······ 2:207a-207b
religion ······ 6:291a
renunciation of divinity ······ 2:209a
"Symbol Emperor System" (Shōchō Tennō Sei) ······ 2:208a
Taishō period ······ 2:206b-207a
theocracy ······ 8:24a
veneration of ······ 6:290b
"Emperor art" ······ 7:351a-351b
Emperor-as-organ theory. *See* **Tennō kikan setsu**
Emperors ······ 2:202a-203a
Antoku ······ 1:40a, 67b
Chōkei ······ 1:299b
Daigo ······ 2:57a
En'yū ······ 1:62b
Fushimi ······ 2:375a
Go-Daigo ······ 1:99a, 100a-100b; 3:39a
Go-Fukakusa ······ 3:39b
Go-Hanazono ······ 3:40a
Go-Ichijō ······ 3:40a-40b
Go-Kameyama ······ 3:41b-42a
Go-Komatsu ······ 3:43b
Go-Mizunoo ······ 1:193b; 3:44b
Go-Saga ······ 3:47a
Go-Sanjō ······ 3:47a
Go-Shirakawa ······ 1:189b; 3:49b
Go-Toba ······ 1:40a
Go-Uda ······ 3:54b
Hirohito ······ 1:41b; 3:147a
Ichijō ······ 3:255b-256a
Jimmu ······ 4:57a-57b
Juntoku ······ 4:85a
Kameyama ······ 4:125b
Kammu ······ 4:128a
Kazan ······ 4:185a
Keikō ······ 4:189a
Keitai ······ 4:190a-190b
Kimmei ······ 4:208b
Kōbun ······ 4:238b
Kōgon ······ 4:249a
Kōkō ······ 1:45a
Kōmei ······ 4:266a-266b
Kōtoku ······ 4:297b
Meiji ······ 5:153a-154a
Mommu ······ 5:236a
Nintoku ······ 6:8a
Ōjin ······ 6:76a-76b
Reizei ······ 1:62a
Saga ······ 6:363b
Sanjō ······ 7:12a
Shirakawa ······ 7:146b
Shōmu ······ 1:184b, 198a
Sujin ······ 7:264b

Sutoku ·········· 7:279b-280a
Taishō ·········· 7:305a-305b
Temmu ·········· 7:381b-382b
Tenji ·········· 8:5b-6a
Toba ·········· 8:31b
Tsuchimikado ·········· 8:112a
Uda ·········· 1:45a; 8:125b
Empire of Great Japan ·········· 2:66b
growth ·········· 2:200b
Employee benefits
company welfare system ······ 1:342b-343b
Employees' Pension Insurance ··· 6:173a; 7:211b
Employees' Pension Law ·········· 6:173a
Employers' liability ·········· 2:209a
Employment
compensation ·········· 5:90a
recruitment (saiyō) ·········· 2:33a
training programs (shanai kenshū) ·········· 2:34a-34b
corporate culture ·········· 2:26b-27a
dismissal ·········· 2:117b; 4:349b
Edo period ·········· 2:211b-212a, 2:150b
fudai ·········· 2:211b-212a
hiyō ·········· 2:211b-212a
hōkōnin ·········· 2:211b-212a
nenki hōkōnin ·········· 2:211b-212a
forms ·········· 2:209b
group hiring ·········· 3:62b-63a
high level ·········· 2:159a-159b, 160b
ie concept ·········· 3:260b
industrial robots ·········· 3:298b-299b
investigations ·········· 1:217a
medical and health insurance 5:144b-145a
modern ·········· 2:210a-211a
career-long ·········· 2:210b-211a
"closed" ·········· 4:344b
enterprise unionism ·········· 2:211a
seniority system ·········· 2:211a
trends ·········· 2:210a-210b
variations ·········· 2:211a
motivation
internal organization of Japanese companies ·········· 3:318a
permanent ·········· 2:33a
personnel reassignment ·········· 7:185a
practices ·········· 2:36a-36b
premodern ·········· 2:211b-212b
contract workers ·········· 2:212a-212b
Edo period ·········· 2:211b-212a
rights of employees ·········· 2:212b
before 17th century ·········· 2:211b
promotion ·········· 2:211a
resignations ·········· 2:211a
reward system ·········· 5:90a
self ·········· 7:60b
seniority system ·········· 5:90a; 7:65a
socialization ·········· 2:27b
trends ·········· 2:210a, 210b
wage differentials ·········· 8:198b
wage system ·········· 8:199b-200b
women ·········· 5:7a
work-related accidents
industrial injuries ·········· 3:292a
Employment contracts ·········· 2:209a-209b
work regulations ·········· 8:270b
Employment Measures Law ·········· 2:210a
Employment Promotion Corporation
Vocational Training Law ·········· 8:193b
Employment Referral Law of 1921 (Shokugyō Shōkai Hō) ·········· 6:265a
Employment security ·········· 4:347b
labor disputes ·········· 4:350a
Employment Security Law of 1947 (Shokugyō Antei Hō) ···· 2:210a; 4:352b, 358a; 6:265a
Employment system ·········· 2:210a-212b
teinensei ·········· 7:376b
Empon ······ 円本 ······ 2:212b
Empress, nonreigning. *See* **Chūgū; Kōgō**
Empresses ·········· 1:312b
Gemmei ·········· 3:124a
Jitō ·········· 4:63b-64a
Kōgyoku ·········· 7:371a
Kōken ·········· 4:253b
Saimei ·········· 7:371a
Shōtoku ·········· 4:253a
Suiko ·········· 1:197b; 7:264a
Emptiness ·········· 2:212b-213a; 7:16a
En ······ 縁 ······ 7:359a; 8:323b-324a
Ena ······ 恵那 ······ 2:213a
Enakyō ······ 恵那峡 ······ 2:213a
Enameling ·········· 1:328b-329a
Enami Kiemon ······ 榎並喜右衛門 ······ 4:214a
Enasan ······ 恵那山 ······ 2:213a
Enchi Fumiko ···· 円地文子 ······ 2:213b
Enchin ······ 円珍 ······ 2:213b
Encouragement of Learning, An · 3:4a-4b
Enden ·········· 2:213b
Endogamy ·········· 5:116b-117a
Endō Shūsaku ··· 遠藤周作 2:214a; 7:103b
Christianity ·········· 4:32a
education ·········· 2:214a
fiction ·········· 2:214a
Endowment insurance ·········· 5:5b
Endō Yukio ······ 遠藤幸雄 ······ 2:214a
Enduring Art of Japan, The ······ 8:228a
En el Pais del Sol ·········· 7:291a
Energy
balance ·········· 2:217a
conservation ·········· 2:215b-216a
nuclear power ·········· 2:214b
Energy industries ·········· 2:214a-214b
Energy revolution ·········· 2:214b
Energy sources ·········· 2:214b-217a
alternatives ·········· 2:215b-217a
coal ·········· 1:333a-333b; 2:216a
dams ·········· 2:72b
electric power ·········· 2:190a-191b
natural gas ·········· 2:216a
nuclear ·········· 2:216b-217a
oil crisis ·········· 2:215a-215b
solar energy ·········· 2:216a-215b
vulnerability ·········· 2:214b-215a
Energy vulnerability ·········· 2:214b-215a
Engagement ·········· 5:4b
Engakuji ······ 円覚寺 1:*191a*; 2:217a; 4:120b; 7:76a
Engakukyō ······ 円覚経 ······ 6:247b
Engawa ·········· 1:82a
Engi ······ 縁起 ······ 1:177a; 2:217a-217b
Engi Kyaku ······ 延喜格 ······ 6:332a
Engi Kyakushiki. *See* **Engi Shiki**
Engi Reform (902) ······ 延喜の改革 ··· 2:57a, 104b
Engi Shiki ······ 延喜式 · 2:217b; 7:96a
background ·········· 2:217b
Daigo, Emperor ·········· 2:57a
daijōsai ·········· 2:59a-59b
harae ·········· 3:101a
ritsuryō system ·········· 6:332a
Shintō ·········· 7:126b, 138b
Engi Tenryaku no chi ······ 延喜・天暦の治 ·· 2:217b-218a
Shin kokinshū ·········· 7:120a
England and Japan. *See* **United Kingdom and Japan**
English ivy ·········· 8:320a
English Peninsular and Oriental Navigation Company (P & O) ···· 3:362b
Engo ·········· 8:203b
Eniwa ······ 恵庭 ······ 2:218a
Eniwa case ·········· 2:218a
judicial review ·········· 4:79b
Enkai ·········· 2:218a
Enkiridera ······ 縁切寺 ······ 4:115b
Enkō sugi ·········· 7:257b
Enkū ······ 円空 · 1:194a, 199b; 2:218a-218b
Enkyoku ······ 宴曲 ······ 2:218b
Enlightenment ·········· 7:28b
Enlightenment Faction ·········· 4:101b
Ennen ······ 延年 ······ 2:74a, 218b-219a, 259a, 297b
furyū ·········· 2:218b-219a, 373b
kaiko ·········· 2:218b
renji ·········· 2:219a
Enni ······ 円爾 · 2:219a; 7:80b
Enni Ben'en. 円爾弁円 *See* **Enni**
Ennichi ·········· 2:219a; 7:250a
Ennin ······ 円仁 ······ 2:219a
raigōzu ·········· 6:277a
Risshakuji ·········· 6:320b-321a
wasan ·········· 8:231a
Ennin's Diary: The Record of a Pilgrimage to China in Search of the Law ··· 6:289a
Ennin's Travels in T'ang China ···· 6:289a
En no Gyōja ······ 役行者 ·· 2:219a-219b; 7:67a
En no Ozunu ······ 役小角 ······ 5:295b
Ennō Zenji ······ 円応禅師 ······ 4:1b-2a
Enoken ······ エノケン ······ 2:219b
Enola Gay ·········· 1:176a
Enomoto Ken'ichi ······ 榎本健一 ······ 2:219b
Furukawa Roppa ·········· 2:373a
Enomoto Kikaku. *See* **Takarai Kikaku**
Enomoto Takeaki 榎本武揚 · 1:165a, 167b; 2:219b-220a
French-Japanese relations ·········· 2:331b
Goryōkaku, Battle of ·········· 3:47a
Kaigun Denshūjo ·········· 4:110a
Enoshima ······ 江ノ島 · 2:220a, 345b; 7:88a
"Enrai no kyakutachi" ······ 遠来の客達 ······ 7:228b
"Enrich the Country and Strengthen the Military" ······ 1:86a; 2:360b-361a
Enryakuji ······ 延暦寺 · 1:178b, 182b; 2:220a-221a, *220b*, 221a; 4:138a, 163a; 6:149b; 7:91a
monasticism ·········· 5:237b-238a
Tendai sect ·········· 8:4a
Enryakuji, burning of ······ 延暦寺焼き打ち ······ 2:221a
Enryakuji community ·········· 2:187a
Enryo ·········· 2:221a
En school ······ 円派 ······ 2:221a
founder ·········· 1:303b
En Seigai ······ 袁世凱 ··· 8:354a-354b
Ensuikō Sugar Refining Co, Ltd ·········· 2:221a-221b
Entairyaku ······ 園太暦 ······ 2:221b
Enterprise ·········· 7:252b
Enterprise groups ·········· 1:139a; 2:221b
one-set principle ·········· 6:106a
Enterprise Incident ·········· 2:221b-222a
Enterprise unions. *See* **Labor unions**
Entō ······ 遠島 ······ 2:222a
Entrance examinations · 2:41b, 222a-224a; 4:83b-84a; 7:215a
children of returnees ·········· 2:182a
research ·········· 2:181a
universities and colleges ·········· 8:170b
Entrepreneurs
Fujita Denzaburō ·········· 2:346a
Fujiyama Raita ·········· 2:359a
Furukawa Ichibei ·········· 2:372b-373a
Godai Tomoatsu ·········· 3:39a-39b

Gotō Keita 3:53a
Gunji Shigetada 3:68b
Hattori Kintarō 3:113b
Ibuka Masaru 3:254a
Idemitsu Sazō 3:259a
Iwasaki Yatarō 3:362a
Kaneko Naokichi 4:139a
Mitsunaga Hoshio 5:214a
Mori Kaku 5:249b
Ōhara Magosaburō 6:73b
Ōkura Kihachirō 6:98a
Shibusawa Eiichi 7:86a-86b
Takenouchi Tsuna 7:325a
Environment Agency 1:219a; 2:224a
standards 2:226a
Environmental conservation 1:359a-360a
Environmental education 2:224a
Environmental law 2:224a-225b
courts 2:225b
statutory framework 2:224b-225b
Environmental movements 1:315a
Environmental Pollution Countermeasures Council 6:217a
Environmental quality 2:225b-229a
antipollution measures
expenditures and personnel 2:228b-229a
research, technology, and planning 2:229a
assessment 2:229a
natural 2:228a
pollution 2:226a-228a
air 2:227b-228a
exhaust gas regulation 2:236a-236b
forms 2:228a
public health 2:226a-227b
protection legislation and administration 2:228a-228b
women in 8:263b
Environmental right 2:229a-229b
civil liberties 1:318a
En'ya Hangan Takasada 塩谷判官高貞 4:275a
Enza 縁坐 2:229b; 7:249b
Enzan 塩山 2:229b
Epictetus' *Discourses* 4:233a
Epidemiologists
Futaki Kenzō 2:376a
Episōdo エピソード 4:169a
Epistolary style 7:230a-231b
Equality of the sexes under the law 2:229b-230a
marriage law 5:118a
Equality under the law 2:230a-230b
Equal opportunity in education 2:230b
Equestrianism. *See* **Horsemanship**
Equity market 1:243a
Era 4:203b-204a
Era names 5:360a
"Eriko to tomo ni" ("Together with Eriko") えり子とともに 8:125a
Erimomisaki 襟裳岬 2:230b
Erisen. 撰銭 *See* **Erizeni**
Erithacus akahige 4:264b
Erizeni 撰銭 2:230b
EROA 2:155a, 158a-158b
Ero guro nansensu bungaku
Shinkō Geijutsu Ha 7:119b
Eroshenko, Vasilii Iakovlevich 2:230b-231a
Erosion control 2:72b
Erotic art. *See* **Shunga**
Eruption Smoke (Fun'en) 6:*156b*
Esaki Reona 江崎玲於奈 2:231a
Esashi 江差 2:231a
"Escalator schools" 2:222b
Eschatology 2:101b, 231a
Rinzai sect 6:319a
Shinran 7:123a
Eshi no sōshi 絵師草紙 2:199b
Esoteric Buddhism 1:185a, 187b-189a; 2:231a-231b; 7:15b
architecture 1:188a
art 1:187b-189a
Dainichi ("Great Sun") 2:64b
Goma ceremony 1:188a, 195b
inzō 3:328a
Kannon, Eleven-Headed 1:187b, 189a
Kongōkai 4:269b
Kūkai 4:304a
prayer 6:233a
ritual implements 1:196a
Ryōbu Shintō 1:187b-188a
Saichō 6:365a-366b
Shingon sect 7:113b-115a
Shintō 7:127a
statues, wood 1:189a
symbols 5:99b-100b
Esperanto 2:231b
Essayists
Baba Kochō 1:129a
Hirata Tokuboku 3:145b
Kamo no Chōmei 4:128b-129a
Sei Shōnagon 7:52a-54a
Terada Torahiko 8:11a
Yoshida Kenkō 8:341a-342b
Essays 3:77a-78a; 8:106a
Essentials of Civil Law 8:147a
Esso Standard Oil Co, Ltd 2:231b
Tōa Nenryō Kōgyō 8:30b
Estate stewards 4:62b-63b; 7:183a
Esugoroku 7:259a
Eta Funayama Tomb 江田船山古墳 2:231b
Tamana 7:332b
Etajima 江田島 2:231b
Eta (outcasts) 8:178b
shi-nō-kō-shō 7:122b
Etchan 悦ちゃん 7:148b
Etching, modern 5:233b
Ethics, East and West 2:232a-232b
Confucianism 1:352b-358b
corporate culture 2:26b-27a
vs etiquette 2:232b
evil 2:236a
religious codes 6:290a
townsmen 1:302b-303a
utilitarian 2:27a
Ethnographical museums 5:278a-278b
Ethnologists
Iha Fuyū 3:262a
Minakata Kumakusu 5:176a
Etiquette 2:232b-234a
behavior 2:233a
vs ethics 2:232b
military 6:69a
ojigi 6:76a
rei 6:288b
social organization 2:233b
symbolic communication 2:233b-234a
tatemae-honne, giri-ninjō, and omote-ura 2:233a-233b
Eto. 干支 *See* **Jikkan jūnishi**
Etō Jun 江藤淳 2:234a
Etorofu 択捉 2:234a
Russia 6:340b
Etō Shimpei 江藤新平 1:34b; 2:234a-234b
Civil Code 2:319a
Freedom and People's Rights Movement 2:334a
Itagaki Taisuke 3:349b
Saga Rebellion 6:364b-365a
Eugenic Protection Council 2:234b
Eugenic Protection Law 1:5a; 2:48a, 234b, 247b; 6:224a
Eugenics movement 2:234b
Eulalia 7:279a
Eulenberg, Ambassador Graf Fritz zu 3:26b
Eulenburg, Friedrich Albert 1:167a; 2:234b-235a
European Atomic Energy Community (EURATOM) 2:235a
European Coal and Steel Community (ECSC) 2:235a
European Community and Japan 2:235a-235b
European Depositary Receipts 2:235b
European Economic Community (EEC) 2:235a; 8:164a
Euthanasia 2:235b-236a
dying with dignity 2:235b-236b
legislation 2:236a
Evil 2:236a
Evolution 4:33b-34a
Ewing, James Alfred
earth sciences 2:140b
Excavations 1:78a-78b
Exceptional Provisions to the Copyright Law 8:98a
Excessive Economic Power Decentralization Law 5:303a
Exchange of Sakhalin for the Kuril Islands, Treaty of 6:371a; 8:13b
Exclusionism 2:200b
Execution of judgment 4:333a
Executive branch of government 3:55b-56a
Exhaust gas regulation 2:236a-236b
Exile 6:339b
Existentialism 2:236b
Exorcism 2:236b-237a; 6:295b; 7:71b
Exoteric Buddhism 1:195b-196a
Expansionism 3:320b-321a
Ex parte Endo (323 US 283) 4:18a
Expense accounts 2:237a-237b
taxes 7:353a
Explorers
Kawaguchi Ekai 4:177b
Kondō Jūzō 4:269a-269b
Mamiya Rinzō 5:88b-89a
Matsuura Takeshirō 5:141b
Mogami Tokunai 5:233b
Okamoto Kansuke 6:80a
Shirase Nobu 7:147a
Uemura Naomi 8:128a
Export-Import Bank of Japan 1:139b; 2:237b; 6:190a
China 1:290b
fiscal system 2:281b
foreign aid policy 2:310a
import financing 2:326a
reorganization 2:321a
Export Insurance Law 6:190a
Exports
arms 1:90a-90b
computers 1:344b
oil 1:71b-72a
steel 3:335b-336a
Exposition of the Administrative Laws 6:352b
Expo '70 2:237b-238a; 7:264b
Expressways 2:238a
roads 6:332b
urban life 8:178b
"Expulsion Ordinance"
Peace Preservation Law of 1887 6:167b
Extended family 7:213a
honke and bunke 3:223a
Extracurricular activities 7:35b
Extradition 2:238a
Extraordinary Council on Education 6:318b

Extraterritoriality, principle of ······· 7:78a
Eyebrow paint (mayuzumi) ····· 2:38a-38b
Ezaki Glico Co, Ltd ·········· 2:238a-238b
Ezo ···················· 蝦夷 ······· 1:211b; 2:238b; 7:263a
  aborigines ························· 2:238b
  development ························ 4:113a
  military campaigns against ········ 2:370b
  northern regions ··················· 2:238b
    Russo-Japanese frontier ·········· 2:238b
    settlement ······················· 2:238b
  saku (stockades; palisades) ············ 7:3a
  samurai ······························ 7:7b
  shōgun ····························· 7:160a
  suppression ························ 4:189a
  war against ························ 7:294a
Ezo Mountains ··蝦夷山系··· 2:239a-239b
  Ishikari Mountains ················ 3:342a

F

Fabian ····························· 2:241a
  Hayashi Razan ······················ 3:117b
"Face" ································ 4:155a
Face of Another, The ··················· 1:3a
Facial powder (oshiroi) ················ 2:38a
Facing Two Ways ······················ 4:169b
Factionalism ··························· 3:315a
Factions. *See* **Batsu**
Factories
  government-operated, Meiji period ··············· 3:56a-56b
  industrial zones ··················· 3:303a
Factory Law of 1911 · 2:241a-241b; 4:351a, 357b-358a; 7:209a
  conditions of factory workers ······ 7:164a
  industrial injuries ················· 3:292a
  job safety regulations ·············· 2:241b
  Katsura Tarō ······················· 2:241b
  minimum working age ················ 2:241b
  women ······························ 8:264b
  worker's compensation ·············· 8:270a
  work hours ························· 8:270a
Factory workers, labor conditions · 7:164a
Fa-hsiang Tsung ·············· 3:237a-237b
Fairies and celestial beings ·· 5:295a-295b
Fair Trade Commission (Kōsei Torihiki Iinkai) ···· 3:296a; 4:378b
  antimonopoly law ···················· 1:65b
  antimonopoly proceedings ············ 1:67b
  industrial organization ······· 3:293b, 296a
  public employees ···················· 6:264b
"Falcon" (fighter plane) ················ 3:114b
Falconry ···························· 2:241b
Familism ······························· 7:213b
Family ························ 2:241b-245b
  average, living conditions of ·· 7:243b-244a
  child rearing and education ·· 1:277a-278b; 2:244b-245a
    entrance examinations ············ 2:245a
    father's role ···················· 2:244b
    mother's role ············· 2:244b-245a
  contemporary ················ 2:243a-245b
  cyclic variations ············ 2:242a-242b
    adoption ························· 2:242a
    primogeniture ···················· 2:242a
  dating and marriage planning 2:243b-244a
    marriage age ····················· 2:244a
  divorce ····················· 2:121b-122b
  education at home ·················· 2:181b
  filial piety ················ 2:245a, 267a
  functions ·················· 2:242b-243a
    oyabun-kobun ···················· 2:243a
  genealogy ····················· 3:17b-18a
  grandparents ················ 2:245a-245b
    retirement ······················ 2:245b
  housewives ················· 3:241a-242a
  husband ·························· 3:242a
  husband-wife relationships ··· 2:244a-244b
    division of labor ················ 2:244a
    divorce ·························· 2:244b
    emotional intimacy ··············· 2:244b
  marriage ··················· 7:214b-215a
    age ······························ 2:44a
    planning ················· 2:243b-244a
  parental relationships ······· 1:277b-278a
  religion ·························· 6:291a
  ritsuryō system ·············· 6:324b-325a
  "ritual parents" ··················· 1:277a
  roles ····························· 2:242b
  terminology ················ 2:241b-242a
    ie ······························· 2:242a
    kazoku ··························· 2:242a
    setai ···························· 2:242a
  traditional ················· 2:241b-243a
  training and discipline ······ 1:277b-278a
  typical life ······················· 2:243b
    leisure-time activities ··········· 2:243b
    standard of living ················ 2:243b
  women working ····················· 2:245a
  yorioya and yoriko ················ 8:338b
Family court ········· 2:245b-246b; 7:277a
  domestic cases ···················· 2:246a
    conciliation procedure ··········· 2:246a
    determination procedures ········· 2:246a
  history and concept ·········· 2:245b-246a
    probation officers ················ 2:246a
    structure ················· 2:245b-246a
  juvenile cases ·············· 2:246a-246b
    hearings ························· 2:246b
  juvenile crime ····················· 4:87a
  juvenile law ······················· 4:87b
  juvenile reformatories ············· 4:87b
  penal system ······················ 6:172a
  present and future ················ 2:246b
  probation officers ················ 2:246a
Family courts ············ 2:45b; 4:80b, 81b
Family law. *See* Shinzoku Hō
Family names ·················· 5:324b-325a
Family planning ······ 2:246b-247b; 8:261a
  abortion ················· 1:5a; 2:247a-247b
    Eugenic Protection Law ··········· 2:247b
  birth rate ·················· 2:246b-247a
  contraception ················ 2:247a-247b
    Ogino Kyūsaku ···················· 2:247a
  movement ··················· 2:246b-247a
    Katō Shizue ················ 4:169a-169b
    Margaret Sanger ·················· 2:246b
    zero population growth ··········· 2:247a
  role of government and other organizations ······················ 2:247b
Family Planning Research Institute ····························· 2:247b
Family Registers. *See* **Household Registers**
Family Registration Law (Koseki Hō) ············ 4:33a, 60b; 8:91b
Family Registration Law Enforcement Regulations (Koseki Hō Sekō Kisoku) ································· 8:91b
Family-state ························ 4:185b
Family succession system ············ 6:324a
Famines ···························· 7:381b
Fans ······················ 2:247b-248a
  construction ················ 2:247b-248a
  symbols of office ················· 2:248a
  types ····························· 2:248a
Far East Command ················· 2:248a
  MacArthur, General Douglas ······ 2:248a; 5:77a-78a
  Ridgway, Matthew ········ 2:248a; 6:311b
Far Eastern Commission (FEC) ·· 1:237b; 2:248a
  Allied Council for Japan ···· 1:48a; 2:248a
  Australia ·················· 1:117a-117b
  Canada ···························· 1:237b
  Occupation ························ 6:51b
  Potsdam Declaration ················ 2:248a
  reparations for Southeast Asia ····· 6:302b
  Russia and Japan ··················· 6:343b
  San Francisco Peace Treaty · 2:248a; 7:10b
  Sansom, George Bailey ··············· 7:17a
  SCAP ······························· 7:32b
  strike report ······················ 7:250b
  United Kingdom ····················· 8:153a
Far Eastern Conference ················ 8:37a
Far Eastern Republic ······ 2:248b; 3:328a
  Ioffe, Adolf Abramovich ············ 2:248b
  Russia and Japan ··················· 6:343a
Far East Network (FEN) ····· 2:248b-249a
  Radio Law ························· 2:249a
Far East Society ······················ 8:37a
Farewell gifts ······················ 2:249a
Farmers
  bakuhan system ············· 1:131b-132a
  hyakushō ·················· 3:249a-249b
  landholding ······················· 4:194b
  rōnō ······························ 6:337b
  as social class ···················· 1:323a
  See also **Agriculture**
Farmers' Movement ················· 2:249a
Farm households ······················· 1:26a
Farmhouses ··················· 5:192-193b
Farming
  equipment
    sembakoki ························· 7:61a
    threshers ························· 7:61a
  mechanization ······················ 1:25a
  postwar changes ·············· 1:24b-26a
  riots ······························ 8:124a
  storage facilities ················· 7:248a
Farming techniques ····· 1:28a-32a; 7:178a
  agricultural chemicals ·············· 1:30b
  agricultural implements ······· 1:30a-30b
  animal husbandry ·············· 1:29b-30a
  dry field farming ·············· 1:29a-29b
  fertilizers ························ 1:30b
  horticulture ······················· 1:30a
  insect pests ······················· 1:30b
  irrigation ························· 1:29b
  land improvements ·················· 1:29b
  new varieties ······················ 1:30a
  plant diseases ····················· 1:30b
  rice planting ·················· 1:28b-29a
Farmland. *See* **Agriculture**
FAS Association ······················ 3:151b
Fascism ···················· 2:111b; 6:204a
Faulds, Henry ················ 2:249a-249b
  Morse, Edward S. ··················· 2:249b
Faxiang Zong ················· 3:237a-237b
February First Strike. *See* **General Strike of 1947**
February 26th Incident 二・二六事件 ························ 2:249b-250b; 8:344a
  Araki Sadao ························ 2:250a
  Chichibu, Prince ··················· 2:250a
  Hayashi Senjūrō ···················· 3:117b
  Hirohito, Emperor ·········· 2:249b; 3:147a
  Hirota Kōki ························ 2:250a
  Ishiwara Kanji ····················· 3:345b
  Kawai Eijirō ······················· 4:178b
  Kita Ikki ··················· 2:250a; 4:226a
  Kōno Hisashi ······················· 2:250a
  Makino Nobuaki ····················· 2:249b
  Mazaki Jinzaburō ··················· 2:250a

Mishima Yukio ········ 2:250b
Nagata Tetsuzan ········ 2:250a
Nishida Mitsugi ········ 2:250a
Nonaka Shirō ········ 2:250a
Okada Keisuke ········ 2:249b
Saitō Makoto ········ 2:249b
Shōwa Depression ········ 7:174a
Shōwa Restoration ········ 7:176b-177a
Suzuki Kantarō ········ 2:249b
Takahashi Korekiyo ········ 2:249b; 7:312a
Takami Jun ········ 2:250b
Takeda Taijun ········ 2:250b
Tatekawa Yoshitsugu ········ 7:349a
Terauchi Hisaichi ········ 8:12a
Watanabe Jōtarō ········ 2:249b; 8:235b
World War II ········ 8:271b
Young Officers Movement ········ 2:250a

FEC. *See* **Far East Command; Far Eastern Commission**

Federation of Economic Organizations (Keidanren) ········ 4:188a-188b; 6:237b

Federation of Independent Unions of Japan (Chūritsu Rōren) ········ 1:313b-314a; 4:188b; 7:189b

Federation of Youth Groups of Japan ········ 2:66b

Feminine language ········ 2:250b-251b
asobase-kotoba ········ 2:251a
femininity expression ········ 2:250b
nyōbō kotoba ········ 2:250b; 6:45a-45b
patterns ········ 2:251a-251b
Sei Shōnagon ········ 2:250b
women's social status ········ 2:250b-251b

Feminism ········ 8:260b
organizations representing Seitōsha ········ 7:54a-54b

Feminists
Fukuda Hideko ········ 2:362a-362b
Hiratsuka Raichō ········ 3:146a
Ichikawa Fusae ········ 3:257a
Itō Noe ········ 3:355a
Kaneko, Josephine Conger ········ 4:138a
Kanno Suga ········ 4:145a-145b
Katō Shizue ········ 4:169a
Kawasaki Natsu ········ 4:184a
Kishida Toshiko ········ 5:313b-314a
Kozai Shikin ········ 4:300a
Kubushiro Ochimi ········ 4:301b
Oku Mumeo ········ 6:96b
Sakai Magara ········ 7:57a
Sasaki Toyoju ········ 7:23b
Takamure Itsue ········ 7:316b
Tanno Setsu ········ 7:344a
Tatewaki Sadayo ········ 7:349b
Yamada Waka ········ 8:289b
Yamakawa Kikue ········ 8:297a
Yamataka Shigeri ········ 8:307b

FEN. *See* **Far East Network**

Fencing ········ 3:253a; 4:195b

Fenimore Cooper ········ 1:175a

Fenollosa, Ernest Francisco 2:251b-252a, 311a
art preservation ········ 2:252a
Bigelow, William Sturgis ········ 1:54b
career ········ 2:251b-252a
Kanō Hōgai ········ 4:147a
Kiyozawa Manshi ········ 4:233a
works ········ 2:252a

Fenton, John William ········ 5:286a

Ferdinand, Crown Prince Franz ········ 1:120a

Fern frond design ········ 1:174a; 2:252a
Kamegaoka site ········ 4:125a
Ōzuka tomb ········ 6:141a

Ferns [(shida) order Filicales] ········ 2:252a

Fertility rites ········ 2:86a; 6:290b

Fertilizers ········ 1:30b
rice ········ 6:309a

Fesca, Max ········ 2:252a

Festival of Hōkoku Shrine ········ 4:150a

Festivals ········ 2:252b-262a; 7:71b; 8:183a
Ae no Koto ········ 2:*259a*
Aoi ········ 1:68a; 2:*253a*
Atami ········ 1:107b
Bon Festival ········ 1:160b
Boys' Day ········ 1:279a
Children's Day ········ 1:279a-279b; 2:*261a*
Chrysanthemum Festival ········ 1:310a
dashi ········ 2:78a
Dazaifu Shrine ········ 2:79b
dealing with sex ········ 7:74a
doll ········ 1:277b, 279b; 2:127b-128a
ennichi ········ 8:322b
folk performing arts ········ 2:296b-298a
Gion ········ 3:33b-34a
Hakata Dontaku ········ 3:85a
hanagasa ········ 8:290b
hana matsuri ········ 3:94a
hari kuyō observance ········ 2:*260b*
hatsumōde ········ 2:*259b*
hatsuuma ········ 3:113b
Hi Matsuri ········ 2:*259a*
Hiratsuka ········ 7:335a
horse (Chaguchagu Umakko) ········ 1:266a
iris ········ 1:279a
Japanese cooking ········ 2:22a
Jidai Matsuri ········ 2:258b; 4:53a
kagura ········ 4:106a-107b
kakizome ········ 2:*259b*
kamakura ········ 2:*252b*
Kamakura Matsuri ········ 2:*252b*
Kanda ········ 4:137a
Kantō ········ 2:*255a*
kawabiraki ········ 4:177a
kites ········ 4:229b-231b
list of ········ 2:*256a-257b*
masks ········ 5:126b-127a
matsuri ········ 2:252b-258a
communion ········ 2:254b-255b
deity ········ 2:254a
essentials ········ 2:254a-255b
Gion Festival ········ 2:255b
group ········ 2:255b
hare and ke ········ 2:253b-254a
modern society ········ 2:258a
offerings ········ 2:254b
purificatory asceticism ········ 2:254a-254b
seasons ········ 2:254a
village and city festivals ········ 2:255b
Mitaue Matsuri ········ 1:103b
Momo no Sekku (Peach Festival) ········ 7:58a
mura matsuri ········ 6:205a
Nanakusa Sekku (Seven Herb Festival) ········ 7:58a
National Sports Festival ········ 5:348a
nebuta ········ 1:69b; 2:*255a*
Nenchū gyōji ········ 2:252b-253a, 258a-262a
annual events ········ 2:*262b*
Bon Festival ········ 1:160b
Boys' Day ········ 1:279a
Children's Day ········ 1:279a-279b
Chrysanthemum Festival ········ 1:310a; 2:260b
hana matsuri ········ 2:260a; 3:94a
hari kuyō ········ 2:*260b*
hatsumōde ········ 2:259b
hatsuuma ········ 2:260a
higan ········ 2:260a
kakizome ········ 2:*259b*
Momo no Sekku (Peach Festival) ········ 7:58a
Nanakusa Sekku (Seven Herb Festival) ········ 7:58a
National Sports Festival ········ 5:348a
New Year ········ 5:371b-372a
post-Heian period ········ 2:260b-262a
pre-Heian antecedents ········ 2:258b-259b
sekku ········ 2:260a
setsubun ········ 2:259a-259b, *260b*
shichigosan ········ 2:*261b*, 262a
Shōbu no Sekku ········ 7:58b
sources ········ 2:258a-258b
tanabata ········ 2:260b
tōrō nagashi ········ 2:*261a*
toshi no ichi (year-end fair) ········ 2:*262a*
tsukimi (moon viewing) ········ 2:*261b*
New Year ········ 5:371b-372a
Nomaoi Matsuri ········ 2:*254b*
Okunchi ········ 2:*258b*
Peiron ········ 1:37b
religion ········ 6:290a
rice ········ 1:103b; 6:309b
Rice-Transplanting Festival ········ 2:*254b*
Sanja Festival (Sanja Matsuri) ········ 2:*253a*; 7:11b
Sannō Festival (Sannō Matsuri) ········ 7:15a
Sendai ········ 7:335a
setsubun ········ 2:*260b*
shichigosan ········ 2:*261b*
Shintō rites ········ 7:139a
Shōbu no Sekku ········ 7:58b
Snow Festival (Yuki Matsuri) ········ 2:*252b*
Sōma Nomaoi ········ 7:226b
Takayama ········ 7:320a
Tango ········ 1:279a
tōrō nagashi ········ 2:*261a*
toshi no ichi (year-end fair) ········ 2:*262a*
tsukimi (moon viewing) ········ 2:*261b*
Yamaguchi Gion ········ 8:294a

Fēton gō Jiken ········ フェートン号事件 ········ 6:182a

Feudal age
historiography ········ 3:153b-154b
periodization ········ 6:176b

Feudalism ········ 2:263a-267a; 7:218a
abolition ········ 3:192a-194b
bushidō ("the Way of the warrior") ········ 1:221b-223b
decline: Edo period ········ 2:266a-267a
bakuhan system ········ 1:131a
bureaucracy ········ 2:266b
daimyō vassalage ········ 2:266a-266b
economic growth ········ 2:266b-267a
Sankin Kōtai system ········ 2:266b
urbanization ········ 2:266b
gains ········ 4:63a
mature: late Muromachi and Azuchi-Momoyama periods ········ 2:265a-266a
daimyō ········ 2:265a-266a
fief holders ········ 2:265b
instability ········ 2:266a
oath of allegiance ········ 2:265b
Sengoku period ········ 2:265a
vassalage ········ 2:265b-266a
problems of definition ········ 2:263a-263b
characteristics ········ 2:263b
Japanese ········ 2:263a-263b
Marxist ········ 2:263a
Western ········ 2:263a
protofeudalism: Kamakura period ········ 2:264a-264b
Carolingian ········ 2:264b
go-on ("favor") ········ 2:264a
government centralization ········ 2:264a
hōkō ("service") ········ 2:264a
limited character ········ 2:264b
rise of warrior class ········ 2:263b-264a
alliances ········ 2:264a
hereditary aspect ········ 2:263b-264a
origins ········ 2:263b
warfare ········ 2:264a
transition to: early Muromachi period ········ 2:264b-265a
gokenin system ········ 2:264b
kokujin ········ 2:265a
shugo rebellion ········ 2:265a

warrior government ········ 8:228b
Fiction
Edo period ········ 3:28a-29a; 5:48b-49b
modern ········ 5:50b-56a; 6:220b-221b
pre-modern ········ 5:14a, 245b-246b
Fiction literary groups ········ 5:18b-19b
Fidelity and good faith, principle of ········ 6:245b
Fidelity (shin) ········ 4:141b
Fields Prize ········ 3:147b; 7:311a
Figure painting ········ 6:158b
Figurines, clay ········ 4:74a-74b
Filial piety ········ 2:245a-245b, 267a; 6:163a
religion ········ 6:291a
censorship ········ 2:338b
Film, Japanese ········ 2:267a-276a
actors and actresses
Aratama Michiyo ········ 2:*273a*
Asaoka Ruriko ········ 2:*275a*
Atsumi Kiyoshi ········ 1:115b; 2:*275a*
Fuji Tatsuya ········ 2:*275a*
Funakoshi Eiji ········ 2:*273a*
Hanayagi Shōtarō ········ 3:95a
Hara Setsuko ········ 2:*271a*; 3:102a-102b
Hasegawa Kazuo ········ 3:107a
Hayakawa Sesshū ········ 3:115a
Hidari Sachiko ········ 2:*274b*; 3:130a-130b
Ichikawa Utaemon ········ 3:258a
Inoue Masao ········ 2:*268b*
Iwashita Shima ········ 2:*274b*
Katsu Shintarō ········ 4:174b
Kazami Akiko ········ 2:*269a*, 270b
Matsuda Eiko ········ 2:*275a*
Mifune Toshirō ········ 2:*270b-271a*; 5:168a-168b
Mikuni Rentarō ········ 5:172b-173a
Mochizuki Yūko ········ 5:228b
Mori Masayuki ········ 2:*272b*
Nakadai Tatsuya ········ 2:*273a*
Nakamura Kichiemon ········ 2:*274b*
Okada Eiji ········ 6:78a
Ōkōchi Denjirō ········ 2:*268b*; 6:93a
Otowa Nobuko ········ 6:133b
Ryū Chishū ········ 2:*271a*; 6:353b
Saitō Tatsuo ········ 2:269a
Shimura Takashi ········ 7:108b
Takakura Ken ········ 7:314a
Takamine Hideko ········ 2:*272b*; 7:315a
Tanaka Kinuyo ········ 2:*270b*; 7:337a
Wakao Ayako ········ 8:218b
Yamaguchi Yoshiko ········ 8:295b
Yamamoto Fujiko ········ 8:297b
Yorozuya Kinnosuke ········ 8:339a
Ai no korīda (Realm of the Senses) · 2:*275a*
benshi and storytelling cinema ········ 2:267b-268a
editing techniques ········ 2:268a
live performances ········ 2:267b
vocal styles ········ 2:267b
censorship ········ 2:271b, 338b
compliance ········ 2:271b
military themes ········ 2:271b
Chūji tabi nikki (Chūji's Travel Diary) ········ 2:*268b*
companies
Daiei Co, Ltd ········ 2:56b, 271b-272a
Nikkatsu Corporation 2:267b-268a, 270b; 6:1a-1b
Shin Tōhō Co, Ltd ········ 2:271b, 273b
Shōchiku Co, Ltd ········ 2:268a, 269b
Tōei Co, Ltd ··· 2:272a, 273a-273b, 274b; 8:35a
Tōhō Co, Ltd ········ 2:270b; 8:36b
directors
Fukasaku Kinji ········ 2:359b
Gosho Heinosuke ········ 3:50a
Hani Susumu ········ 3:97a-97b
Ichikawa Kon ········ 3:257b-258a
Imai Tadashi ········ 3:273a
Imamura Shōhei ········ 3:273b-274a
Inagaki Hiroshi ········ 3:282a
Itami Mansaku ········ 3:351b
Itō Daisuke ········ 3:351b-352a
Kinoshita Keisuke ········ 4:215b
Kinugasa Teinosuke ········ 4:218b-219a
Kobayashi Masaki ········ 4:237a; 8:300b
Kumai Kei ········ 4:305b
Kumashiro Tatsumi ········ 4:307a
Makino Masahiro ········ 5:86b
Makino Shōzō ········ 5:87a
Matsuyama Zenzō ········ 5:141b-142a
Mizoguchi Kenji ········ 5:225a-225b
Murata Minoru ········ 5:269b
Naruse Mikio ········ 5:335a-335b
Ōshima Nagisa ········ 6:125b-126a
Ozu Yasujirō ········ 6:141a-142b
Shimazu Yasujirō ········ 7:102b
Shinoda Masahiro ········ 7:122a-122b
Tasaka Tomotaka ········ 7:347b
Teshigahara Hiroshi ········ 8:15a
Toyoda Shirō ········ 8:90a-90b
Uchida Tomu ········ 8:124a
Yamada Yōji ········ 8:289b-290a
Yamamoto Kajirō ········ 8:298b
Yamamoto Satsuo ········ 8:299a
Yamanaka Sadao ········ 8:300b
Yoshimura Kōzaburō ········ 8:348a
documentary ········ 2:275b-276a
early history ········ 2:267a-267b
importance ········ 2:267a
early postwar era ········ 2:271b-272a
communist purge ········ 2:271b
labor unions ········ 2:271b
Occupation film policy ········ 2:271b
theaters ········ 2:272a
first gendaigeki ········ 2:268b-269a
comedies ········ 2:269a
influences ········ 2:268b
genres
chambara ········ 2:271a, 274b
geidō-mono ········ 2:271a
gendaigeki ········ 2:267b, 269b, 271b
haha-mono ········ 2:269b
hōmu dorama ········ 2:269b
jidaigeki · 2:267b-268a, 269b, 271b, 274a
kaidan jidaigeki ········ 2:273a
Meiji-mono ········ 2:269b
merodorama ········ 2:269b
pinku ········ 2:275a
rensageki ········ 2:267b
roman poruno ········ 2:275a
shimpa ········ 2:267b, 268b
shōshimin geki ········ 2:270a
taiyōzoku ········ 2:273b
torimonochō ········ 2:271b
tsuma-mono ········ 2:269b
yakuza ········ 2:343a
Hadaka no shima ········ 3:75a
Kurutta ippeiji (A Page Out of Place) 2:*268b*
late 1920s and early 1930s ··· 2:269b-270a
mainstream ········ 2:269b
characteristics ········ 2:269b
genres ········ 2:269b
motif ········ 2:269b
rival productions ········ 2:269b
series and remakes ········ 2:269b
new wave ········ 2:273b-274a
literary sources ········ 2:274a
television ········ 2:273b
thematic changes ········ 2:273b-274a
Nijūshi no hitomi (Twenty-Four Eyes) ········ 2:*272b*
1970s ········ 2:275b
independent film making ········ 2:275b
largest grossing film ········ 2:275b
Ningen no jōken (The Human Condition) ········ 2:*273a*
Nippon konchūki (The Insect Woman) ········ 2:*274b*
Nobi (Fires on the Plain) ········ 2:*273a*
obscenity cases ········ 1:255a
Otoko wa tsurai yo; Torajirō wasurenagusa (*Hard to Be a Man*; Tora's Forget-me-not) ········ 2:*275a*
producers
Kido Shirō ········ 4:202a
Makino Shōzō ········ 5:87a
Nagata Masaichi ········ 5:306b-307a
radio drama ········ 6:275b
reformation of early 1920s ··· 2:268a-268b
female impersonators ········ 2:268a
film criticism ········ 2:268a
manzai ········ 2:268a
popular cultural influence ········ 2:268a
retrenchment and 1960s ········ 2:274a-274b
anti-heroes ········ 2:274a
minorities as theme ········ 2:274a
Saikaku ichidai onna (The Life of Oharu) ········ 2:*270b*
screenwriters
Hashimoto Shinobu ········ 3:110b
Hisaita Eijirō ········ 3:151b
Itami Mansaku ········ 3:351b
Matsuyama Zenzō ········ 5:141b-142a
Mizuki Yōko ········ 5:226a
Noda Kōgo ········ 6:30b
Tanaka Sumie ········ 7:339b
Terayama Shūji ········ 8:12b-13a
Yasumi Toshio ········ 8:319b
Yoda Yoshikata ········ 8:326b
Shichinin no samurai (Seven Samurai) ········ 2:*271a*
Shinjū Ten no Amijima (Love Suicide at Amijima; Double Suicide) ········ 2:*274b*
talkie ········ 2:270a-271b
fantasy films ········ 2:270b-271a
literary influences ········ 2:270b
output ········ 2:271a-271b
realism ········ 2:270a-270b
television age ········ 2:274b-275a
movie attendance ········ 2:275b
sexual themes ········ 2:275a
Third Golden Age ········ 2:272a-273b
comedy ········ 2:272b-273a
creativity ········ 2:272a
monster movies ········ 2:273b
Motion Picture Code Committee · 2:280b
Rashōmon ········ 2:272a
sexual themes ········ 2:273b
violence as theme ········ 2:273a-273b
war as theme ········ 2:272a-272b
Tōkyō monogatari (Tōkyō Story) ········ 2:*271a*
Tsuchi (Earth) ········ 2:*269a*
Tsuchi to heitai (Mud and Soldiers) · 2:*270b*
Ukigumo (Floating Clouds) ········ 2:*272b*
Umarete wa mita keredo (I Was Born, But . . .) ········ 2:*269a*
Film libraries ········ 2:276a
Finance ········ 2:276a-276b
capital markets ········ 2:276a-276b
corporate ········ 2:28b-29b
cost accounting standards ········ 2:38b
dividends ········ 2:120b-121a
financial intermediaries ········ 2:276a-276b
government bonds ········ 3:54b
household ········ 2:18b-20a
insurance, miscellaneous ········ 3:316a
insurance system ········ 3:316b-317a
interest rate structure ········ 3:317b-318a
iron and steel industry ········ 3:335b
loans ········ 3:56b-57a; 6:16a
museums ········ 5:280a-280b
national budget ········ 1:204b-206a

reserve funds 7:87a-87b
Finance, local government 2:276b-277a
budgets 2:276b
equalization grants 2:276b-277a
revenues 2:276b
taxes 7:353b
Finance law 1:160a; 2:6b, 276b
Public Accounts law 2:276b
Tax Allocation to Local Governments law 2:276b
Tax law 2:276b
Financial Accounting Standard on Consolidated Financial Statements 2:278a
Financial aid for students 2:179b-180a, 277a
scholarship loans 2:277a
Financial circles 8:366b-367a
Financial Crisis of 1927 2:277a-277b
French-Japanese relations 2:332b
Inoue Junnosuke 3:309b-310a
Itō Miyoji 3:355a
Suzuki Shōten 4:139a
Taiwan Ginkō 7:309b
Takahashi Korekiyo 7:312b
Tanaka Giichi 7:336a-336b
Financial depression of 1930 7:173b-174a
Financial reporting 2:277b-278a
cultural influences 2:277b
directors' function 2:277b
stockholders 2:277b
legal influences 2:277b-278a
Commercial Code 2:277b-278a
Securities Exchange Law 2:277b-278a
western influences and consolidated statements 2:278a
Financial statements 2:278b
interim 2:278b
limited liability company 5:10a
periodic 2:278b
Financial System Research Committee 2:278b
Fine arts exhibitions 1:215b
Fines, nonpenal 2:49a; 6:35a-35b
Finger pressure treatment. *See* **Shiatsu**
Fingerprints 2:249b
Firearms 1:89b
hinawajū 3:140a
introduction of 2:279a-279b
Firearms and Sword Possession Control Law 2:278b-279a
licensing criteria 2:279a
Fire Defense Agency 2:280a
Fire Defense College 2:280a
Fire Defense Research Institute 2:280a
Fire defense system 2:279b-280a
history 2:279b
operations 2:279b
fire prevention 2:279b
preservation of order 2:279b
rescue and ambulance operations 2:279b
organization and system 2:279b
Fire fighters 3:137b-138a
Fireflies [(hotaru) family Lampyridae] 2:280a-280b
Firefly viewing 2:280b
Firemen's uniforms, traditional 2:280b-281a
Fire Services Law 2:280a
Fireworks 2:281a
Firipin Oki Kaisen フィリピン沖海戦 4:383b
Fiscal investment and loan program 8:367b
Fiscal system 2:281a-281b
government-affiliated agencies 2:281b
national government accounts 2:281a-281b
Fish. *See* **Animals**
Fish and shellfish farming 2:281b-282b
farming 2:281b-282b
techniques 2:282b
freshwater fish culture 2:281b-282a
carp 2:281b
production 2:281b-282a
tilapia 2:282a
method of culture 2:282a-282b
disease 2:282a-282b
feeding 2:282a-282b
oxygen requirements 2:282a
rare species 1:60b-61a
saltwater fish culture 2:282a
nori 2:282a
production 2:282a
seaweed 2:282a
Fisheries Preservation and Control Act 2:283a
Fishery agreements 2:282b-283a, 285b
bilateral 2:282b-283a
Korean 4:284b-285a
multilateral 2:282b
Russo-Japanese 6:344a, 345b
200-mile fishing zone 2:283a
Fishery Convention 7:238a
Russo-Japanese fisheries 6:345a-345b
Fishery zones 2:283a-283b
Russo-Japanese fisheries 6:345b
Fishes 1:60b-61a
abalones 1:1a-1b
anglerfishes 1:56b
ayu 1:125b
bonito 1:160b-161a
carp 1:244a
catfishes 1:249b
crucian carp 2:52a
eel, Japanese 2:184a
globefishes 3:36b-37a
gobies 3:38b
goldfish 3:43b
herring 3:128a
mackerel 5:79a
octopuses 6:60a-60b
salmons 7:5b
samma 7:6b-7a
sardines 7:21b
sea bream 7:45a
tuna 8:120a
whitebait 8:251a
yellowtail 8:323b
Fish farming. *See* **Fish and shellfish farming**
Fish finders 2:286a
Fishing 2:283b-284a
Fishing industry 2:284a-287b
ama 1:48a
companies
Hōkō Fishing Co, Ltd 3:214b
Kyokuyō Co, Ltd 4:332b
Nichiro Gyogyō Kaisha, Ltd 5:378a
Nippon Suisan Kaisha, Ltd 6:13a
Taiyō Fishing Co, Ltd 7:309b-310a
conclusion 2:287b
future prospects 2:285a-285b
modernization 2:286a-286b
equipment 2:286a-286b
fish finders 2:286a
other devices 2:286a
offshore fishing grounds 2:284a
principal fisheries 2:285b-286a
northern sea operations 2:285b
Pacific saury net 2:285b
purse seining 2:285b
set net 2:286a
skipjack pole-and-line 2:286a
squid 2:286a
trawlnet 2:285b
tuna longline 2:285b-286a
production 2:284a
state of industry 2:284a
aquiculture 2:284a
companies 2:284a
employees 2:284a
traditional Japanese fisheries 2:286b-287b
angling 2:287a
ayu 2:287b
cormorant fishing 2:26a, 287b
eels 2:287b
octopuses 2:287a
pearls 2:287a
sea cucumbers 2:287a
types 2:284a-285a
drift netting 2:284b
longline angling 2:284b
mackerel 2:284b
offshore 2:284a
pelagic 2:284b
pollack 2:285a
purse seining 2:284b
sardines 2:284b
squid and cuttlefish 2:284b
whaling 2:284b
Fishing tackle 7:105b
Fish weir 2:287b
Five Amakusa Bridges 8:174a
Five Commissioners (Gobugyō) 1:95b
"Five government enterprises" 6:264b
Five Great Elders (Gotairō) 8:95b-96a
Five Highways, The 3:41a-41b
Five Kings of Wa 倭の五王 2:161a, 287a-288b
lineage 2:287b-288a
tomb mounds 1:79a
"Five-man groups" 3:45a-45b
Five Men of the Pear Chamber (Nashitsubo no Gonin) 5:179a
Five Peaks of Aso 1:103a
Five-Power Treaty
Washington Naval Treaty of 1922 8:235b
Five Regents' Houses 3:48a-48b
Five Temples. *See* **Gozan**
Five Wisdom Kings 1:*200b*
Flag, national 5:339a
Flags and banners 2:288a
Flexed Burials. *See* **Prehistoric burials**
Floats 7:15a
Flood control 2:72a-72b
Floor mat 7:348a
Flora Japonica 4:316b
Florenz, Karl 3:27b; 4:42b
Flower arrangement 2:288a-292a
Adachi Chōka 2:291a
chabana (tea-ceremony) 2:*289a*
design 2:88a
fūryū 2:374b
iemoto 3:260b
Ikenobō Sengyō 2:288b
leisure-time activity 4:382a
modern ikebana
abroad 2:292a
avant-garde 2:291b, 292b
free-style 2:291a-291b
moribana 2:290b-291a
schools 2:291b
today 2:291b-292a
modern (free style) nageire 2:*291a*
moribana-style 2:*291a*
Ohara Hōun 2:291a
religion 6:292a
rikka-style 2:*288b*
contemporary 2:*293a*
shōka-style 2:*290b*
contemporary 2:*293a*
Teshigahara Hiroshi 2:*292b*
Teshigahara Sōfū 2:290a

traditional ikebana · · · 2:288a-290a
historical development · · · 2:288a-288b
modern · · · 2:290a-290b
nageire · · · 2:289b-290a
rikka · · · 2:288b-289b
schools · · · 2:288b
shōka · · · 2:290a
"Flower divination" · · · 6:191b
Flower Festivals · · · 3:94a-94b
Flowering hazel · · · 8:81b
Flowers
chrysanthemums [(kiku) *Chrysanthemum morifolium*] · · · 1:310a-311a
day lilies [(kisuge) *Hemerocallis thunbergii*] · · · 2:78b-79a
gardenia [(kuchinashi) *Gardenia jasminoides*] · · · 3:8a
gentians [(rindō) *Gentiana scabra* var. *buergeri*] · · · 3:24a
hirugao [(bindweed) *Calystegia japanica*] · · · 3:151a
irises · · · 3:331b-332a
kikyō [(balloonflower) *Platycodon grandiflorum*] · · · 4:207b
morning glories [(asagao) *Pharbitis*] · 5:255a
peonies [(botan; shakuyaku) *Ranunculaceae*] · · · 6:173b
roses · · · 6:339a
shimotsuke (*Spiraea japonica*) · · 7:106b-107a
violets [(sumire) *Violaceae*] · · · 8:192a-192b. *See also* **Plants**
Flower viewing · · · 3:94a, *94b*
Flower-viewing party · · · 6:191b
Flow of funds · · · 2:292b-293b
corporate deficits · · · 2:292b
development · · · 2:292b
double-entry bookkeeping · · · 2:292b
personal sector · · · 2:292b
Flute Player on a Buffalo · · · 6:77b
Flying Granary, The · · · 7:*93a*
Flying squirrels · · · 2:293b
Folding-screen panel · · · 7:*169b*
Folk crafts · · · 2:293b-296a
classification · · · 2:295b-296a
ceramics · · · 2:*294b*, 295b
metalwork · · · 2:295b
paper · · · 2:296a
textiles · · · 2:*295a, 295b-296a*; 8:19b
typography · · · 2:296a
wood and bamboo · · · 2:294b, 295b
Hamada Shōji · · · 3:89b
history of tradition · · · 2:295a-295b
decline · · · 2:295a-295b
Japan Folk-Craft Museum · · · 4:46a
Kawai Kanjirō · · · 4:178b
Leach, Bernard Howell · · · 4:372b
mingu · · · 5:184a
Munakata Shikō · · · 5:532b, *233a*, 264b
museums · · · 5:278a
traditional
makers · · · 7:165a
Yanagi Muneyoshi · · · 2:293b-295a; 8:314a
Folk culture. *See* Folklore
Folk dances. *See* **Dance, traditional**
Folklore
ghosts · · · 3:30a
Kintarō (Golden Boy) · · · 4:218b
New Year
Ōtoshi no kyaku · · · 6:133b
Folklore studies · · · 2:296a-296b, 302a
contemporary status · · · 2:296b
historical development · · · 2:296a-296b
literary-philosophical approach · · · 2:296b
local history · · · 5:71a-71b
Orikuchi Shinobu · · · 2:296b
scholars · · · 7:256b
Shibusawa Keizō · · · 7:86b
Yanagi Muneyoshi · · · 2:296b
Folk performing arts · · · 2:296b-298a
dengaku · · · 2:*298b*
festival context · · · 2:297b-298a
furyū · · · 2:*299a*
general characteristics · · · 2:297a-297b
agricultural nature · · · 2:297a
processions · · · 2:297a-297b
purification · · · 2:297a
seasonal nature · · · 2:297b
Honda classification · · · 2:297b
kadozuke · · · 4:101a
kagura · · · 2:*297a*
Kuromaru odori (dance) · · · 2:*299a*
nembutsu odori · · · 5:360a
rain dances · · · 6:280b
range and diversity · · · 2:296b-297a
rice · · · 6:309b
Folk religion · · · 2:298a-300b; 6:291a; 7:76a
characteristics · · · 2:298a-298b
historical development · · · 2:298b
modern · · · 2:299b-300b
nationalism · · · 2:299b
new religions · · · 2:300a
revival · · · 2:300a
patterns · · · 2:298b-299b
rites of passage · · · 2:299b
seasonal · · · 2:299a
Folk Shintō · · · 民間神道 · · · 2:300b
dimensions · · · 2:300b
matsuri · · · 2:253a
Folk song · · · 2:300b-301a
instrumental accompaniment · · · 2:301a
musical structure · · · 2:301a
Ryōjin hishō · · · 6:351b
ryūkōka · · · 6:354a
study and collection · · · 2:301b-302a
types · · · 2:301a-301b
historical · · · 2:301b
regional · · · 2:301a-301b
Folktales · · · 2:302a-304a
"Ash Scatterer" · · · 2:303a
Bumbuku chagama · · · 1:207a-207b
diffusion routes to Japan · · · 2:303b-304a
foxes · · · 2:330a
Hamamatsu Chūnagon monogatari · 3:90b-91a
Hanasaka jijii · · · 3:94b
history of study · · · 2:302a-302b
interrelationship between oral and written literature · · · 2:302b-304a
Issumbōshi · · · 3:348b
Itō Einosuke · · · 3:352a
"Kachikachi mountain" · · · 2:303a-303b
monkeys · · · 5:245a-245b
oni · · · 6:106a
"Peach Boy" · · · 2:302b
publication · · · 2:302a-302b
"Sarukani kassen" ("The Battle between the Monkey and the Crab") · · · 7:22b
Shitakiri suzume ("Tongue-cut Sparrow") · · · 2:303a; 7:149b
type and motif · · · 2:302b
Uji shūi monogatari · · · 8:137b
Urashima Tarō · · · 8:175b
"Urikohime" ("The Melon Princess") · · · 8:181a
"Wen Removed" · · · 2:302b-303a
writing style · · · 4:132a-132b
Yoru no nezame ("Nights of Fitful Waking") · · · 8:339a
Yuriwaka legend · · · 8:358a
Fontanesi, Antonio · · · 2:304a
Asai Chū · · · 1:93b; 2:304a
Yamamoto Hōsui · · · 2:304a; 8:298a
Food additives and contamination · · · 2:304a-304b
consumer reaction · · · 2:304b
fish contamination · · · 2:304b
Kanemi Oil Poisoning Incident · · · 2:304b
Minamata disease · · · 2:304a
Morinaga Powdered Milk Incident · 2:304a
political issue · · · 2:304b
Food and eating · · · 2:304b-307a
consumer expenditure · 2:17a; 7:244a-245a
household · · · 2:19a
contemporary · · · 2:306b-307a
changes in eating habits · · · 2:307a
eating customs · · · 2:306a-307a
seasoning and cooking · · · 2:306a
staple foods and side dishes · · · 2:306b
cooking · · · 2:20b-25b
history of Japanese · · · 2:304b-306b
Azuchi-Momoyama period · · · 2:306a
Chinese influence · · · 2:304b-305a
Edo period · · · 2:306a-306b
Heian period · · · 2:305b
Jōmon period · · · 2:305a
Kamakura period · · · 2:305b
Kofun and Nara periods · · · 2:305b
Korean influences · · · 2:305a
modern period · · · 2:306a-306b
Muromachi period · · · 2:305b-306a
Western influences · · · 2:305a
Yayoi period · · · 2:305a
instant · · · 3:315b
Food May Day · · · 4:358a; 7:165a
Food processing industry · · · 2:307a
Food products industries
Ajinomoto Co, Inc · · · 1:38b-39a
Calpis Food Industry Co, Ltd (Karupisu Shokuhin Kōgyō) · · · 1:236b
House Food Industrial Co, Ltd · · · 3:240a
Itō Ham Provisions Co, Ltd · · · 3:352a
Marudai Food Co, Ltd · · · 5:120b
Nippon Flour Mills Co, Ltd · · · 6:9b
Nippon Reizō · · · 6:11b-12a
Nisshin Flour Milling Co, Ltd · · 6:20b-21a
Nissin Food Products Co, Ltd · · · 6:21b
Q. P. Corporation · · · 6:273a
Snow Brand Food Co, Ltd · · · 7:206b
Tōyō Seikan Kaisha, Ltd · · · 8:92b
Tōyō Suisan Kaisha, Ltd · · · 8:93a
Food Sanitation Law · · · 2:307a-307b
Foodstuff Control Law · · · 6:310a
Foodstuff Control Special Account · · · 2:307b
rice surplus · · · 2:307b
transfers to · · · 1:205b
Food supply · · · 2:308a
improvement measures · · · 2:308a
rice · · · 2:308a
self-sufficiency · · · 2:308a
wheat · · · 2:308a
Fool's Dance · · · 1:124a
Footgear, traditional · · · 2:308a
rain · · · 6:280b
Footprints in the Snow · · · 8:59b
Forbidden Room, The · · · 5:198a
Forceful appeals · · · 3:50a
Ford, Gerald · · · 4:18a
Foreign aid policy · · · 2:308a-310a
administration · · · 2:309b
changes · · · 2:308b-309b
developing nations · · · 2:309a-309b
economic interests · · · 2:309a
emphases · · · 2:309b
geographic distribution · · · 2:309b
political aspects · · · 2:309b
international comparisons · · · 2:308a-308b
Overseas Economic Cooperation Fund · · · 6:136a
Foreign concessions, 19th century. *See* **Kyoryūchi**
Foreign currency reserves · · · 2:310a
Foreign employees of the Meiji period · · · 2:310b-311b
Bälz, Erwin von · · · 1:135b

Boissonade de Fontarabie, Gustave Emile ··· **1**:160a; **2**:311a
Bousquet, Georges Hilaire ··· **2**:166a
Brinkley, Frank ··· **1**:170b; **2**:311a
Brunton, Richard Henry · **1**:1:175b; **2**:311b
Capron, Horace ··· **1**:243b; **2**:311a
Chamberlain, Basil Hall ··· **1**:266a-266b; **2**:311a-311b
Chiossone, Edoardo ··· **1**:296b; **2**:311b
Clark, Edward Warren ··· **1**:1:321b; **2**:311a
Clark, William Smith ··· **1**:321b; **2**:311b
Denison, Henry Willard ··· **2**:86b; **2**:311a
Du Bousquet, Albert Charles · **2**:134a-134b
Fenollosa, Ernest Francisco ··· **2**:251b-252a
Griffis, William Elliot ··· **2**:311a; **3**:62b
Mayet, Paul ··· **5**:142b
Morse, Edward Sylvester ··· **2**:311a; **5**:256a
Mosse, Albert ··· **5**:256a-256b
Murray, David ··· **2**:311a; **5**:275a
Roesler, Karl Friedrich Hermann ·· **2**:311a; **6**:334a
Verbeck, Guido Herman Fridolin ·· **2**:311a; **8**:189b-190a

Foreigners, attitudes toward · **2**:311b-313a
Dejima ··· **2**:83a-83b
East and West in Japanese culture · **2**:312a
Japan's modern History and the West
nationalistic factors ··· **2**:312a
political factors ··· **2**:311b
Japan's modern history and West ··· **2**:311b-312a
konketsuji ··· **4**:271a-271b
Whites and Blacks ··· **2**:312a-313a
discontinuity with Japanese ··· **2**:312a
negative feeling toward ··· **2**:312b-313a
positive feelings toward ··· **2**:313a

Foreigners in Japan ··· **2**:313a-314a
adjustment problems ··· **2**:313b-314a
Alien Registration Law ··· **2**:313a
ethnic discrimination ··· **2**:314a
historical roles ··· **2**:313b
konketsuji ··· **4**:271a-271b
legal status ··· **2**:314a
sex discrimination ··· **2**:313b
national differences ··· **2**:313a-313b
demographic factors ··· **2**:313b
sex ratio ··· **2**:313a-313b
percentage of population ··· **2**:313a

Foreign Exchange and Foreign Trade Control Law ··· **1**:13b; **2**:314a-314b, 320b
prewar ··· **2**:314a
trade controls ··· **2**:314b

Foreign exchange control ··· **2**:314b-316b
background ··· **2**:314b
postwar ··· **2**:314b
prewar ··· **2**:314b
budget ··· **2**:315b
capital control ··· **2**:315b
direct and portfolio investments · **2**:315b
yen base system ··· **2**:315b
evolution of system ··· **2**:316a-316b
liberalization ··· **2**:316a
Foreign Trade Control Law ··· **2**:314b
enforcement ··· **2**:315a
objective ··· **2**:315a
Investment Law ··· **2**:315a
coverage ··· **2**:315a
modern economy ··· **2**:163b
standard settlement ··· **2**:315b
tariffs ··· **7**:346b-347a
technology imports ··· **2**:315b-316a
contract categories ··· **2**:316a

Foreign Exchange Control Law of 1980 ··· **2**:315b-316a, 320a
monetary policy ··· **5**:240b

Foreign exchange quotas ··· **2**:325a

Foreign Investment Council ··· **2**:316b
foreign exchange control ··· **2**:316b
foreign investment in Japan ··· **2**:316b
Organization for Economic Cooperation and Development (OECD) ··· **2**:316b
technology transfer ··· **7**:374b

Foreign investment in Japan
guidelines for foreign firms ·· **2**:316b-319a
foreign executives ··· **2**:318a-318b
image ··· **2**:317b
Japanese interdependency ·· **2**:317b-318a
Japanese personnel ··· **2**:318a
perceptions of the Japanese ··· **2**:317b
history ··· **2**:316b-317a
after World War II ··· **2**:317a
relaxation of restrictions ··· **2**:317a

Foreign Investment Law. *See* **Foreign exchange control**

Foreign Investment Law ··· **2**:314a-314b, 320b; **6**:180a
technology transfer ··· **7**:374b

Foreign language training in the schools ··· **2**:318b; **7**:35b

Foreign law, study of ··· **2**:318a-319a
Civil Code ··· **2**:319a
foreign scholars ··· **2**:319a
modernization ··· **2**:318a-319a

Foreign Mission Society of Paris (MEP) ··· **1**:249a

Foreign museums ··· **5**:280b

Foreign relations. *See* **International relations;** *specific country*

Foreign ships, decree concerning **7**:125b

Foreign students in Japan ··· **2**:319a-319b

Foreign trade ··· **2**:319b-324b; **8**:161a-164b
Ansei commercial treaties ··· **1**:63a
Azuchi-Momoyama history ··· **3**:184b
balance-of-payments ··· **2**:324a-324b
deficits ··· **2**:324a
before 1600 ··· **2**:148a
Brazil ··· **1**:167a-169a
postwar ··· **1**:168a-168b
prewar ··· **1**:167b-169a
commodity composition of exports ··· **2**:321b-322a
developing countries ··· **2**:322a
home market expansion ··· **2**:321b-322a
definition ··· **2**:319b
Dutch ··· **2**:135b-136a
early modern ··· **2**:151a-151b
economic rehabilitation ··· **2**:320a-320b
Greater East Asia Coprosperity Sphere ··· **2**:320a
Edo period ··· **2**:150a
export performance ··· **2**:321b
annual rate ··· **2**:321b
percentage of world total ··· **2**:321b
export promotion ··· **2**:320b-321a
Export-Import Bank of Japan ··· **2**:321a
import licenses ··· **2**:320b-321a
Ministry of International Trade and Industry ··· **2**:320b
geographical distribution ··· **2**:322a-322b
horizontal trade relations ··· **2**:322b
Harris Treaty ··· **2**:319b
import dependence ··· **2**:322b-323a
raw materials ··· **2**:322b
import liberalization ··· **2**:323a-324a
industrial structure ··· **2**:323b
International Monetary Fund ··· **2**:323b
interwar period ··· **2**:320a
Depression effects ··· **2**:320a
protective policies ··· **2**:320a
role of colonies ··· **2**:320a
iron and steel industry ··· **3**:335b-336a
Italy ··· **3**:351a
Iwakura mission ··· **3**:359b
modern era, advent of (1868 to World War I) ··· **2**:319b-320a
dualistic pattern ··· **2**:319b
Taiping Rebellion ··· **2**:319b
tariff autonomy ··· **2**:320a
Unequal Treaties ··· **2**:320a
multinational enterprises ··· **5**:263a-264a
postwar protectionism ··· **2**:320b
Foreign Exchange and Foreign Trade Control Law ··· **2**:320b
tariff levels ··· **2**:320b
trading partners ··· **2**:320b
post-World War II ··· **2**:157a
regulations limiting ··· **7**:171a
Thailand ··· **8**:20b
trading companies ··· **2**:324a

Foreign trade, government policy on ··· **2**:324b-326b
administrative guidance ··· **2**:326a
balance-of-payments ··· **2**:324b
cartels ··· **2**:325a
export quality checks ··· **2**:325a
foreign exchange quotas ··· **2**:325a
Greater East Asia Coprosperity Sphere ··· **2**:325a
history ··· **2**:324b
importance ··· **2**:324b
industrialization ··· **2**:325b
liberalization ··· **2**:325b-326b
linkage system ··· **2**:325b
Ministry of International Trade and Industry (MITI) ··· **2**:325a
national seclusion ··· **2**:324b
protectionist ··· **2**:325a
research and development ··· **2**:325a
tariffs ··· **2**:325a

Forestry ··· **2**:326b-327a
forest conditions ··· **2**:326b
species ··· **2**:326b
total forest area ··· **2**:326b
history of wood utilization ··· **2**:327a
construction ··· **2**:327a
fuel ··· **2**:327a
Tōkyō Earthquake of 1923 ··· **2**:327a
operations ··· **2**:326b-327a
national forests ··· **2**:326b-327a
private ··· **2**:327a
profit-sharing ··· **2**:326b-327a
supply and demand of wood ··· **2**:326b

Formosa. *See* **Taiwan**

Formulary of Adjudications ··· **3**:47b-48a

Fortune-telling ··· **6**:101b
ommyōdō ··· **6**:103a

Forty-Seven Rōnin Incident 赤穂事件 **2**:327a-328a; **7**:28a; **8**:293a
Akō ··· **1**:44b
background ··· **2**:327a-327b
Confucian scholars' opinions ··· **2**:327b
Muro Kyūsō ··· **2**:327b
Ogyū Sorai ··· **2**:327b
Satō Naotaka ··· **7**:28a
Yamagata Daini ··· **8**:293a
dramatic portrayal ··· **2**:269b
katakiuchi ··· **4**:165a
Kanadehon chūshingura ··· **4**:96a
public reaction ··· **2**:327b-328a
dramatic portrayals ··· **2**:328a
Tokugawa Tsunayoshi ··· **2**:328a
shogunate's dilemma ··· **2**:327b
vendetta ··· **2**:327b
Kira Yoshinaka ··· **4**:220a
Ōishi Yoshio ··· **2**:327b

Fossa Magna ··· **2**:328a, 345a; **4**:8b
earthquakes ··· **2**:139a-139b, 141a
Naumann, Edmund ··· **5**:358a

Fossils ··· **2**:328a-329b
characteristics ··· **2**:328b-329b
cenozoic ··· **2**:329a
cretaceous ··· **2**:329a
jurassic ··· **2**:328b
mesozoic ··· **2**:328b-329a

neogene 2:329a
paleogene 2:329a
paleozoic 2:328b
pleistocene 2:329a
triassic 2:328b
Foster child 8:338b
Foster family program 7:26b
Foster parent 8:338b
Foujita, Léonard 2:347a
Foundlings 1:15b
Fountains, legends 5:295a
Four Books and Five Classics 2:329b
Four Elegant Pastimes, The 4:146a
442nd Regimental Combat Team 2:329b-330a; 4:15a
Four Great Kings 7:298a
"Four Great Surnames" 7:292a
Four Guardian Kings of Classical Poetry (Waka Shitennō) 8:73b
Four Monk-Writers 4:1b
Four Pleasures 4:110b
Four-Power Treaty of 1921 2:330a
Anglo-Japanese Alliance 1:57a; 8:152a
United States 8:157a
Washington Conference 8:234b
" 'Four S's" 7:316a-316b
Fowl. *See* **Chicken, Japanese**
Foxes [(kitsune) *Vulpes vulpes*] 2:330a
hondokitsune 2:330a
Inari, symbol of 3:283a
Kitakitsune 2:330a
legends 2:330a
mythology 5:296b
Foxtrot 6:354b
"Framework Agreement for Economic Cooperation between Japan and Canada" 1:238a
France and Japan 2:330a-333b
closed Japan 2:330b-331a
Dutch influence 2:330b-331a
Kanagawa Treaty 2:331a
Edo period (latter part) 2:331a-331b
first French consul-general 2:331a
foreign trade agreements 2:331b
Japanese delegations to France 2:331a-331b
first contact 2:330a
Japanese expansion 2:332a-333a
cultural agreements 2:333a
diplomatic agreements 2:332a-332b
economic agreements 2:332b
Financial Crisis of 1927 2:332b
Indochina 2:333a; 3:290b
Sino-Japanese War 2:332b
Japanese studies 4:42a-42b
Meiji period 2:331b-332a
Boshin Civil War 2:331b
Constitution 2:332a
educational system 2:332a
Freedom and People's Rights Movement 2:332a
French political thought 2:331b-332a, 2:335b
military cooperation 2:331b-332a
post-World War II 2:333a
France Bed Co, Ltd 2:333b
Franciscans 2:333b
Franco-Japanese Agreement of 1907 2:332b, 333b
Franco-Japanese Treaty on Trade and Navigation 2:332a
Franz Xaveri Sein Leben und Seiner Zeit (Francis Xavier: His Life and Times) 8:281a
Fraternal associations (kō) 4:234a
Free Artists Association 8:294b
Freedom and People's Rights Movement 2:1b, 333b-337a; 7:92b, 99a, 251a; 8:291b
Akita Incident 1:42b
Baba Tatsui 1:129a
background 2:333b-334a
Korean debate 2:334a
leadership 2:334a
Chichibu Incident 1:271b
Daidō Danketsu Movement 2:56a
Dajōkan (Grand Council of State) 2:70b
early organization 2:334a-334b
Aikoku Kōtō 1:34b
Aikokusha 2:334b
elitist nature 2:334a
Ōsaka Conference of 1875 2:334b
Risshisha 2:334a
eclipse 2:336a
Constitution 2:336a
Daidō Danketsu Movement 2:336a
Ōsaka Incident 2:336a
Peace Preservation Law of 1887 2:336a
France and Japan 2:332a
freedom of speech 2:338b
Fukuda Hideko's involvement 2:362a
Fukushima Incident 2:335a, 366a
Furusawa Shigeru 2:373a
fundamental liberties 2:369a
Gakumon no susume 3:4b
Gumma Incident 3:67b
ideology 2:335b-336a
European influence 2:335b-336a
natural rights 2:335b-336a
Iida Incident 3:262b
Inoue Kaoru 3:310b
interpretations 2:336a-337a
authoritarianism 2:336a
individualism 2:336b
regionalism 2:336a-336b
Itagaki Taisuke and 3:349a
Kabasan Incident 4:89a
Kawakami Otojirō 4:181a
Kishida Toshiko 4:223a
Kitamura Tōkoku 4:227b
kōgi seitai ron used by 4:249a
Kokumin no tomo reflected 4:261a
local societies 2:334b-335a
League for Establishing a National Assembly 2:335a
non-elitist nature 2:334b-335a
military expansion criticism 2:361a
modern philosophy 5:229b
naichi zakkyo 5:309b-310a
Nakae Chōmin 5:311b-312a
Nakajima Nobuyuki 5:313b-314a
nationalism 5:342b
news agencies 5:396a
Ōi Kentarō 6:75a
opposition 2:361b
Ōsaka Incident 6:121a
Peace Preservation Law of 1887 6:167b
Political Crisis of 1881 6:202b
Press Ordinance of 1875 6:236a
Proletarian literature movement 6:254b
Publication Ordinance of 1869 6:262b
rise of parties 2:335a-335b
Jiyūtō 2:335a
Minto 2:335a
organization 2:335a
Rikken Kaishintō 2:335a
socioeconomic composition 2:335b
Risshisha 6:321a
Sandai Jiken Kempaku Movement (Movement to Memorialize Three Important Items) 7:9b
Sanshimpō ("Three New Laws") 7:16b
seiji shōsetsu 7:50a
shimpa 7:107b
shizoku 7:152a
Tanaka Shōzō 7:338b-339b
Taoka Reiun 7:346a
Tarui Tōkichi 7:347a
Tōyama Mitsuru 8:88a
Ueki Emori 8:127a
Unequal Treaties revision 8:149a
women in 8:260b
women's suffrage 8:268b
Yokohama mainichi shimbun 8:330a
Freedom injuristic acts, principle of 4:86a
Freedom of assembly 2:337a
constitutional guarantee 2:369b
Public Order and Police Law of 1900 2:337a
Tōkyō ordinance decision (20 July 1960) 8:68b
Freedom of association 2:337a-337b
constitutional guarantee 2:369b
Peace Preservation Law of 1925 2:337b
Public Order and Police Law of 1900 2:337b
Subversive Activities Prevention Law 2:337b
Freedom of contract 2:337b; 4:86a
Freedom of religious faith 2:337a-338a; 4:372a
constitutional guarantee 2:369b
legal interpretations 2:337b-338a
separation of state and religion 2:337b-338a
Freedom of speech 1:254b; 2:338a
constitutional guarantee 2:369b
freedom of the press 2:338a
obscenity 2:338a; 6:49b-50a
Peace Preservation Law of 1925 2:338a
Press Law of 1909 2:338a
Publication Law of 1893 2:338a
Freedom of speech, regulation of 1:251b-255a; 2:338a-338b
Edo period 2:338b
Meiji and Taishō periods 2:338b-339a
censorship system 2:338b
films 2:338b-339a
newspapers 2:338b-339a; 6:236a
publication 6:262b
radio broadcasting 2:339a
Shōwa period 2:339a
censorship repeal 2:339a
Freedom of the press 2:338a, 339a-339b; 6:236a, 267b
constitutional guarantee 2:369b
privacy, right to 6:249b
restrictions 2:339a-339b
Free markets 6:282b
Free Thai Movement (FTM) 2:339b; 6:238b; 7:65b; 8:20b
Fregat Pallada (Frigate *Pallas*) 3:45a; 6:270b
Friends 1:3b
Friendship and Commerce, Treaty of (between Russia and Japan) 6:341b
Friendship Association 8:354a
Friends of Constitutional Government Party 6:315a-315b
Fringed pink [(kawara nadeshiko) *Dianthus superbus*] 2:339b
Fröbel, Friedrich Wilhelm August 2:339b
Frogs [(kaeru) order Anura] 2:339b-340a
Frois, Luis 1:96b; 2:340a
Fruit. *See specific fruit*
Fruit trees production 1:27a-27b
Fūbaika 風媒花 7:323b
Fucan Fabian. *See* **Fabian**
Fuchi 扶持 2:340a
Fuchimai 扶持米 2:340a
Fuchū (central Honshū) 府中 2:340a
Fuchū (western Honshū) 府中 2:340a

Fudai 譜代 1:131b; 2:340b; 3:186b; 5:308b; 8:56b-57a
daimyō 2:340b
peasants 2:340b
rōjū 6:334a
Fudasashi 札差 2:340b-341a
chōnin 1:302a
functions 2:340b
Kansei Reforms 4:152b
monopoly associations 2:340b
origins 2:340b
Fude (brush) 1:232b
Fude no susabi 筆のすさび 4:152a
Fudō 不動 4:98b
Fudōchō 不同調 4:130b
Fudoki 風土記 1:151b; 2:296a, 341a-341b; 7:76a; 8:175b
Bungo 2:341b
geography 6:288a
Harima 2:341b
Hitachi 2:341a
Hizen 2:341b
Izumo 2:341a
mythology 5:292a
religious symbolism 6:295b
thought and culture 8:25b
uses 2:341a
Fudoki texts 4:20b
Fudō Myōō 不動明王 4:147a; 6:*151a*
Fuefuki dōji 笛吹童子 8:339a
Fuefukigawa 笛吹川 2:341b, 343b; 4:122b
Fuel Research Institute 6:305b
Fuels. *See* **Energy, sources**
Fūgai Ekun 風外慧薫 2:341b
Fugaku sanjūrokkei (Thirty-six Views of Mt Fuji) 富嶽三十六景 3:*215a*
Fūgashū (Collection of Elegance) 風雅集 2:186a; 8:213b, 214b
Fugitive Criminal Extradition Law 2:238a
Fugu 3:36b-37a
Fuhito 史 4:89a
Fuji 富士 2:341b; 7:48a
Fuji. *See* **Wisteria, Japanese**
Fuji, Mount. 富士山 *See* **Fujisan**
Fujian (Fukien) People's Government 福建人民政府 2:341b-342a
Fuji Bank, Ltd 1:168a; 2:342a
Fujieda 藤枝 2:342a
Fujieda Shizuo 藤枝静男 2:342a
Fuji Electric Co, Ltd 2:342a-342b, 347a, 372b
Fuji Five Lakes 富士五湖 2:342b, 345a, 359b; 4:177b
Fujigawa, Battle of 富士川の戦 2:342b
Azuma kagami 2:342b
Minamoto no Yoritomo 5:181b
Taira-Minamoto War 7:300a
Fuji-Hakone-Izu National Park 富士箱根伊豆国立公園 1:49b, 107b; 2:342b-343a; 4:135a
Fuji Heavy Industries, Ltd 2:343a; 5:313b
Nissan Motor Co, Ltd Affiliation 2:343a
passenger car production 1:122a
Fujiidera 藤井寺 2:343a
Fujii Heigo 藤井丙午 2:343a
Fujii Kenjirō 藤井健次郎 2:343a
Fuji Junko 藤純子 2:343a-343b
Fujikawa 富士川 2:341b, 343b; 4:122b
Fujikawa Yū 富士川游 2:343b
Fuji Kōsan Co, Ltd 2:343b
Fujikoshi 5:299b
Fujikura, Ltd 2:343b
Fujimi 富士見 2:343b
Fujimori Seikichi 藤森成吉 2:343b
Shin Nihon bungaku 7:122a
Fujimoto Kizan 藤本箕山 7:95b-96a
Fujin bungei 婦人文芸 4:126a
Fujin kōron 婦人公論 2:344a; 7:100a
Fujin Kyōfūkai 婦人矯風会 4:324b
Fujin no tomo 婦人之友 2:344a
Fujinomiya 富士宮 2:344a
Fujin Sanseiken Undō 婦人参政権運動 8:169a
Fuji Oil Co, Ltd 2:344a
Fujioka 藤岡 2:344a
Fujioka Sakutarō 藤岡作太郎 2:344a-344b
Fuji Photo Film Co, Ltd 2:344b, 359a
Fujisan 富士山 2:*344b*, 344b-345b, 347b; 4:177b
height 2:344b
plants, animals, and man 2:345a
religious faith and climbing 2:345a-345b
religious symbolism 6:295b
scale and location 2:344a-345a
Fujisan Hongū Sengen Jinja 富士山本宮浅間神社 7:64a
Fujisawa 藤沢 2:345b; 4:135a
Fujisawa Pharmaceutical Co, Ltd 2:345b
Fujisawa Takeo 藤沢桓夫 2:345b
Fujishima Takeji 藤島武二 2:345b-346a
Kokusen (Black Fan) 2:*346b*
Fuji Spinning Co, Ltd 2:346a
Fujita Art Museum 2:346a; 5:277a
Fujita Corporation 2:346a
Fujita Denzaburō 藤田伝三郎 2:346a-346b
museums 5:277a
Fujita Gorō 藤田五郎 3:46b
Fujitani Mitsue 富士谷御杖 2:346b; 5:17b
Fujitani Nariakira 富士谷成章 2:346b-347a; 5:17a; 7:281a
Fujita Tōko 藤田東湖 2:347a
Fujita Yūkoku 2:347a
Fujita Tsuguharu 藤田嗣治 2:347a
Fujita Tsuguji 藤田嗣治 2:347a
Fuji Tatsuya 藤竜也 2:*275a*
Fujita Yūkoku 藤田幽谷 2:347a-347b
Fujita Tōko 2:347a
Fuji Telecasting Co, Ltd 1:173a; 2:347b; 7:14a
Fuji Tradition 7:303b
Fujitsū, Ltd 2:342b, 347b
Fuji Volcanic Zone 富士火山帯 2:345a, 347b
Fujiwara culture 藤原文化 2:347b-348a
Fujiwara family 藤原氏 1:190b; 2:166a, 348a-348b; 7:7b, 19b, 45b, 74a, 166a, 256b
alliances 2:264a
Asukai Masatsune 1:106b
branch families 2:348a, 350b-351a
Buddhist sculptors 1:199b
decline 2:348b
insei 3:314b
founder 2:351a
founding 2:348a
Fujiwara culture 2:347b
Fujiwara no Fuhito 2:350b
Fujiwara no Michinaga 2:352a
Fujiwara no Yoshifusa 2:358a
Gosekke (Five Regents' Houses) 3:48a-48b
Ichijō, Emperor 3:255b-256a
Jien 4:53b
Konoe family 4:272b
libraries 5:1a
Murasaki Shikibu 5:267b
narrative histories 3:153a
power 2:352b
regency government 6:286a
regents 2:348a
rule 2:204a-204b
Tōshi kaden 8:83a
women in 8:258b
Fujiwara Foundation of Science 2:348b
Fujiwara Ginijrō 藤原銀次郎 2:348b
Fujiwara Iwaichi 藤原岩市 2:348b; 3:289b
Fujiwara Kei 藤原啓 1:260b
Fujiwara Kikan 藤原機関 2:348b, 350a
Fujiwarakyō 藤原京 1:182a; 2:350a
excavations 1:79b
mokkan 5:234a, *234b*
Fujiwara no Akihira 藤原明衡 2:350a; 5:37b
literature 1:293a
Meigō ōrai 5:152b-153a
Fujiwara no Akisuke 藤原顕輔 2:350a; 5:38a
Fujiwara no Kiyosuke 2:352b
Kenshō 4:198b
Shika wakashū 7:95a-95b
Fujiwara no Fuhito 藤原不比等 2:348a, 350b
Kaifūsō 4:109a
Taihō Code 7:295b
Yōrō Code 8:339a
Fujiwara no Fujifusa 藤原藤房 2:350b
Fujiwara no Fuyutsugu 藤原冬嗣 2:350b
Fujiwara no Hidehira 藤原秀衡 2:350b
Fujiwara no Hidesato 藤原秀郷 2:350b
Fujiwara no Hirotsugu, Rebellion of 藤原広嗣の乱 2:351a; 7:91a
Fujiwara no Ietaka 藤原家隆 2:351a; 5:41a
Shin kokinshū 7:119b
Fujiwara no Kamatari 藤原鎌足 2:348a, 351a-351b
naidaijin 5:310a-310b
Taika Reform 7:295b
Tōshi kaden 8:83a
Yamashinadera established 4:243b
Fujiwara no Kaneie 藤原兼家 2:351b
regency 2:352b
Fujiwara no Kanemichi 藤原兼通 2:351b; 7:26a
Fujiwara no Kanesuke 藤原兼輔 2:351b; 7:13a
Fujiwara no Kanezane 藤原兼実 4:303b
Fujiwara no Kintō 藤原公任 1:18a; 2:258a, 352a-353b; 5:14a; 8:210a
critical influence 2:352a
Sanjūrokkasen (The Thirty-Six Poetic Geniuses) 7:12b
Shūi wakashū 7:184b
Wakan rōeishū 8:218a
Fujiwara no Kiyohira. 藤原清衡 *See* **Ōshū Fujiwara family**
Fujiwara no Kiyokawa 藤原清河 2:352a-352b
Fujiwara no Kiyosuke 藤原清輔 2:352b
Fujiwara no Korechika 藤原伊周 2:352b; 7:53a
Fujiwara no Michinaga 2:352b-353a
Fujiwara no Kōzei 藤原行成 1:234a-234b; 2:358b
Fujiwara no Ietaka 藤原家隆 3:51a-52b
Fujiwara no Masatsune 藤原雅経 1:137a

Fujiwara no Michinaga 藤原道長 2:348b, 352b-353a; 5:34a-34b; 7:53b
Byōdōin temple 1:227a
Fujiwara no Kintō 2:352a
Fujiwara no Korechika 2:352b
Fujiwara no Yorimichi 2:357b-358a
Kagerō nikki 4:104a
Midō Kampaku ki 5:167b
regency 2:351b, 352b, 6:286b
Sanjō, Emperor 7:12a
Fujiwara no Michinori 藤原通憲 2:353a
Fujiwara no Michitoshi 藤原通俊 2:353a-353b; 5:38a
Fujiwara no Michitsuna no Haha. 藤原道綱母 *See* **Kagerō nikki**
Fujiwara no Mitsuyoshi 藤原光能 6:227a
Fujiwara no Motohira. 藤原基衡 *See* **Ōshū Fujiwara family**
Fujiwara no Mototoshi 藤原基俊 2:353b; 5:15a, 38b; 7:68a; 8:211a
Fujiwara no Mototsune. 藤原基経 *See* **Akō Incident of 887**
Fujiwara no Toshinari 2:357a
Fujiwara no Nakamaro 藤原仲麻呂 2:353b
Fujiwara no Nobuzane 藤原信実 2:353b-354a
Fujiwara no Takanobu 2:355b
Fujiwara no Norinaga 藤原教長 1:137a
Fujiwara no Sadaie 藤原定家 1:5b; 2:348b, 351b, 354a-355a; 4:*133b*; 5:14b, 42a; 7:61b, 96b
Fujiwara no Takanobu 2:355b
Fujiwara no Tameie 2:355b
Fujiwara no Toshinari 2:356b
Fujiwara no Toshinari no Musume 2:357b
Go-Toba, Emperor 3:51b-52a
heirs 4:254a
Jakuren 4:1b
Lady Daibu 4:197b
life 2:354a-354b
orthographic studies 4:133b
poetry and poetic ideals 2:354b-355a
Shinkei 7:119a
Shin kokinshū 7:119b
Teika kanazukai 4:133b
treatises and criticism 2:354b-355a
Fujiwara no Sadanaga 藤原定長 4:1b
Fujiwara no Sanekata 藤原実方 7:53b
Fujiwara no Sari. 藤原佐理 *See* **Fujiwara no Sukemasa**
Fujiwara no Shōshi. *See* **Jōtō Mon'in**
Fujiwara no Shunzei 藤原俊成 2:355a, 356b; 5:39a; 8:211b, 355b *See* **Fujiwara no Toshinari**
Fujiwara no Sukemasa 藤原佐理 1:234a; 2:355a
Fujiwara no Sumitomo 藤原純友 2:355a-355b
Fujiwara no Tadamichi. 藤原忠通 *See* **Hōgen Disturbance**
Fujiwara no Takanobu 藤原隆信 2:355b; 5:*181a*; 6:227a
Fujiwara no Nobuzane 2:353b
Jingoji 4:58b
Sei Shōnagon 7:53a-53b
Fujiwara no Tameie 藤原為家 1:5b; 2:348b, 354a, 355b-356b; 8:213b
Fujiwara no Teika 藤原定家 2:354a; 8:211b, *See* **Fujiwara no Sadaie**
Fujiwara no Teishi 藤原定子 2:356b
Fujiwara no Korechika 2:352b
Fujiwara no Toshinari 藤原俊成 1:181a; 2:348b, 354a, 356b-357b; 4:128b; 5:39a, 42a; 7:96b; 8:211b, 355b
Fujiwara no Ietaka 2:351a
Fujiwara no Mototoshi 2:353b
Fujiwara no Tameie 2:355b
Go-Toba, Emperor 3:51a-52b
Jakuren 4:1b
Kamo no Chōmei 4:128b
life 2:356b
poetic career 2:356b-357a
poetic ideals 5:14b
poetic ideals and principles 2:357a-357b
poetry 2:357a
Senzai wakashū 7:68a-68b
Shinkei 7:119a
Fujiwara no Toshinari no Musume 2:357b
Shin kokinshū 7:120a
Fujiwara no Tsugikage 藤原継蔭 3:336b
Fujiwara no Yasuhira. 藤原泰衡 *See* **Ōshū Fujiwara family**
Fujiwara no Yorimichi 藤原頼通 2:357b-358a
Byōdōin temple 1:227a
regency 2:353a, 6:286b
Fujiwara no Yorinaga. 藤原頼長 *See* **Hōgen Disturbance**
Fujiwara no Yoshifusa 藤原良房 2:348a, 358a
kampaku 4:130a
Jōwa conspiracy 4:78a
sesshō 7:69b
Fujiwara no Yoshitsune 藤原良経 2:358a-358b; 5:40b
posthumous portraits 4:147b
Shin kokinshū 7:119b
Fujiwara no Yukinari 藤原行成 1:234a; 2:358b
Fujiwara no Sukemasa 2:355a
Gonki 3:45b
Sei Shōnagon 7:53a-53b
Fujiwara Regency Government 2:69b
Fujiwara Seika 藤原惺窩 2:358b-359a
education 2:173a
Hayashi Razan 3:117a
Fujiwara Technological University 2:348b
Fuji Xerox Co, Ltd 2:344b, 359a; 6:311b
Fujiya Confectionery Co Ltd 2:359a
Fujiyama Aiichirō 藤山愛一郎 2:359a
Fujiyama Raita 藤山雷太 2:66b, 359a
Fujiyama Aiichirō 2:359a
Fuji Yoshida 富士吉田 2:359a-359b
Fuju Fuse sect 不受不施派 2:359b; 5:375a-377b; 8:12b
Fukagawa 深川 2:359b
Fukai Shidōken den 深井志道軒伝 4:256a
Fukan zazengi 普勧坐禅儀 2:123b
Fukasaku Kinji 深作欣二 2:275b, 359b
Fukaya 深谷 2:359b
Fukazawa Shichirō 深沢七郎 2:360a; 7:100a
Fukeizai. *See* **Lese majesty**
Fuke sect 普化宗 7:75b
Fuki [(butterbur) *Petasites japonicus*] 2:360a
Fukiagehama 吹上浜 2:360a
Fukidera 富貴寺 2:360a
Fukien People's Government, *See* **Fujian (Fukien) People's Government**
Fukin and fugin 夫金, 夫銀 2:360a-360b
Fukinuki yatai 2:360b
Genji monogatari emaki 3:20b
Fukken Jimmin Seifu 福建人民政府 2:341b-342a
Fukkisō *(Pachysandra terminalis)* 2:360b
Fukko Shintō 復古神道 6:306a-306b
Fukko Yamato-e school 復古大和絵派 2:360b
Fuko 封戸 2:360b
Fukoku kyōhei 富国強兵 1:86a; 2:360b-361a
Fuku 4:163b, 321b
Fukuba Bisei 福羽美静 2:361a-361b
Fukuba Hayato 福羽逸人 2:361b
Fukuba Yoshishizu. *See* **Fukuba Bisei**
Fukubiki 2:361b
Fukuchi Gen'ichirō 福地源一郎 2:361b
Rikken Teiseitō 6:315b
Fukuchiyama 福知山 2:361b
Fukuda Doctrine of 1977 7:196b, 236a; 8:192a
Fukuda Eisuke 福田英助 5:219b
Fukuda Gyōkai 福田行誡 2:361b-362a
Fukuda Heihachirō 福田平八郎 2:362a
Fukuda Hideko 福田英子 2:362a-362b; 7:54a, 56a
Fukuda Shōji. *See* **Shōji Kaoru**
Fukuda Takeo 福田赳夫 2:362b
foreign aid policy 2:309b
Fukuda Tokuzō 福田徳三 2:362b
Reimeikai 6:288b
Fukuda Tsuneari 福田恆存 2:362b; 5:13b
Shingeki 7:112a
Fukue 福江 2:362b
Fukuejima 福江島 2:363a
Fukugen Movement (Restoration of the Original Teachings)
Tenrikyō 8:9a
Fukuharakyō 福原京 2:363a
Fukui 福井 2:363a-363b
Fukui Cave 福井洞穴 2:363b; 4:75a
Fukui Ken'ichi 福井謙一 2:363b
Fukuin shūhō 福音週報 8:127b
Fukui Plain 福井平野 2:363b
Fukui Prefecture 福井県 2:364a
Fukūkenjaku Kannon 不空羂索観音 1:*187a*; 4:253a
Fukumoto Kazuo 福本和夫 2:364a
Japan Communist Party 4:11b
Fukunaga Takehiko 福永武彦 2:364a-364b
Fuku no kami 福ノ神 4:*325a*, 327a
Fukuoka 福岡 2:364b, 365a
Fukuoka nichinichi shimbun 福岡日日新聞 4:207b
Fukuoka Plain 福岡平野 2:364b
Fukuoka Prefecture 福岡県 2:364b-365b
Fukuoka Takachika 福岡孝弟 2:365b; 7:54a, 55a
Fukuroda Falls 袋田滝 2:365b
Fukuroi 袋井 2:365b
Fukurokuju 福禄寿 5:296a
Fukurotoji 1:153b
Fukushi Kōjirō 福士幸次郎 2:365b-366a
Fukushima 福島 2:366a
Fukushima Basin 福島盆地 2:366a
Fukushima Incident 福島事件 2:335b, 366a
cause 2:366a

effects. 2:366a
Kabasan Incident 4:89a
Kōno Hironaka 4:274a
Fukushima Kazuo 福島和夫 2:366b
Fukushima Masanori 福島正則 2:366b
Fukushima Prefecture 福島県 2:366b-367a
Fukushima Yasumasa 福島安正 2:367a
Fukutoshin 8:181a
Fuku warai 2:367a-367b
Fukuyama 福山 2:367b
Fukuzawa Yukichi 福沢諭吉 1:8a, 16b, 155a; 2:*367a*, 367b-368a; 4:384b; 7:338b
Bummeiron no gairyaku 1:207b
Freedom and People's Rights Movement 2:335b
French-Japanese relations 2:331a
Gakumon no susume 3:4a
historiography 3:156a
Kaehwap'a 4:101b
Keiō University 4:189a
Koizumi Shinzō, specialist 4:251a
Kōjunsha 4:252b
Korean enlightenment 4:280b
Meirokusha 5:161a
nephew 5:314a-314b
Seiyō jijō 7:54b
westernization 2:311b; 4:387a
works 2:367b-368a
Fulbright, William 4:50a
Fulbright Commission 4:50a-50b
Fulbright scholars 4:50a
Fumai. 夫米 *See* **Fukin and fugin**
Fumie 踏絵 2:*368a*
Funa. *See* **Crucian carp**
Funabashi 船橋 2:368a-368b
Funa Benkei 船弁慶 4:154b, 326a
Funadama 2:368b
Funahashi Seiichi 舟橋聖一 2:368b; 7:103b
fūzoku shōsetsu 2:378b
Shinkō Geijutsu Ha 7:119b
Funakoshi Eiji 船越英二 2:*273a*
Fundamental labor rights 2:369a; 6:312a-312b
collective bargaining 1:334b
Fundamental Law of Education
Occupation 6:53a
Fundamental liberties 2:369a-369b
absolute guarantee 2:369a
Western concepts 2:369a
Fundoshi 2:369b
Funeral goods. *See* **Funerary sculptures**
Funerals 2:369b-370b
commemorative rites and services 2:370a-370b
hōyō 2:370b
kōdengaeshi 2:370b
customs 2:105a
post-funerary rites 2:307a
kichū 2:370a
mochū 2:370a
rites and services 2:370a
ihai 2:369a, 370a
incense money 2:370a
mikoto 2:370a
mourning period 2:370a
oharai 2:370a
sakaki 2:370a
senreisai 2:370a
shimenawa 2:370a
shinobite 2:370a
tamagushi 2:370a
wake 2:370a
Funerary sculptures 1:75b, 77a
Fun'ya no Watamaro 文室綿麻呂 2:370b
Furandoru no fuyu フランドルの冬 4:102b
Furano 富良野 2:370b
Furano Basin 富良野盆地 2:370b
Fūren, Lake 風蓮湖 2:370b
Fūren Shōnyūdō 風連鍾乳洞 2:370b
Fūrin. *See* **Wind-bells**
Furisode Fire. *See* **Meireki Fire**
Furniture, traditional 2:370b-371b
cabinets 2:371a
chabudai 2:*371a*
chairs 2:371a
charcoal braziers 2:371b
chests 2:371a
continuing use 2:371a
decoration 2:371b
desks 2:371a
earliest examples 2:370b
lamps 2:371b
materials 2:371b
screens 2:371a
tables 2:371b
tansu 2:*371a*
towel racks 2:371b
Furoshiki 1:146b; 2:295b, 371b
Furugaki Tetsurō 古垣鉄郎 2:371b
Furuhashi Hironoshin 古橋広之進 2:371b
Furuhata Tanemoto 古畑種基 2:371b-372a
Furuichi Kimitake 古市公威 2:372a
Furui Yoshikichi 古井由吉 2:372a
Furukawa (city) 古川 2:372a
Furukawa (industrial combine) 古河 2:372a
government enterprise sales 4:138a
mining 2:31b
Furukawa Co, Ltd. 1:92b; 2:372b
Furukawa Electric Co, Ltd 1:92b; 2:342a-342b, 372b
Yokohama Rubber Co, Ltd 8:330b
Furukawa Ichibei 古河市兵衛 2:372b
Furukawa Roppa 古川緑波 2:373a
Furuno Inosuke 古野伊之助 2:373a
Furuoka Hideto 古岡秀人 3:3b
Furusawa Shigeru 古沢滋 2:373a-373b
Furusawa Uruo 古沢滋 2:373a
Furuta Oribe 古田織部 2:373b; 7:361a
Furuta Shigenari 古田重然 2:373b
Furuyama Komao 古山高麗雄 2:373b
Furuyama Moromasa 古山師政 2:373b
Furyoki (Prisoner of War) 俘虜記 6:113b
Furyū (dance) 風流 2:74a, 255b, 373b-374a; 3:183a-184b; 4:326a; 6:23b
creative spirit 2:373b
folk performing arts 2:297b
folk song 2:301a
subtypes 2:373b-374a
Fūryū (refinement of taste) 風流 2:374a-374b
Fūryū Fukagawa uta 風流深川唄 7:108a
Fūryū mijinzō 風流微塵蔵 4:242b
Furyū monji 2:374b
Fūryū mutan Incident. 風流夢譚事件 *See* **Shimanaka Incident**
Fūryū Shidōken den 風流志道軒伝 3:142a; 4:256a
Fūryū yomo byōbu 風流四方屛風 8:78b
Fusain Society (Fyūzankai) 6:156a
Fusang youji (Fu-sang yu-chi; A Record of Travels in Japan) 8:222b
Fusen Jōyaku 不戦条約 4:191a
Fusen Kakutoku Dōmei (Women's Suffrage League) 婦選獲得同盟 2:374b; 8:260b, 268b
Ichikawa Fusae 3:257b
Fuseya Soteki 伏屋素狄 2:374b-375a
Fushi 4:77a
Fushimi, Emperor 伏見天皇 2:375a
calligraphy 1:235a
Go-Uda, Emperor 4:125b
Gyokuyō wakashū 3:71b
Fushimi Castle 伏見城 1:126b; 2:375a; 3:178a
Nanzenji 5:330b
Fushimi Inari Shrine 伏見稲荷大社 2:357a; 3:283a; 7:126b
Fushin bugyō
Kobori Enshū 4:238b
Fūshinjō 風信帖 1:234a
Fusō ryakki 扶桑略記 1:76a; 3:153a
Fusō shūyō shū 扶桑拾葉集 8:105a
Fussa 福生 2:375a
Fusuma (kimono-like coverage) 1:148b
Fusuma (sliding door) 1:82b
Fusuma-e 7:42a
Fusumashōji 7:41b
Futabatei Shimei 二葉亭四迷 2:375a-376a; 7:81a, 103b
Futabatei Shimei ron 5:315a-315b
gembun itchi 3:16b
personal life 2:375a-375b
Russian literature translations 2:375a-375b
Futabu Industries, Ltd
Toyota Motor Co, Ltd 8:93b
Futagawa Buntarō 二川文太郎 2:268a
Futagawa Dam 二川ダム 1:83a
Futagawa ware 二川焼 2:295b
Fūtai 4:116a
Futaki Kenzō 二木謙三 2:376a
Futamigaura 二見浦 2:376a, *376b*
Futamunerō 7:111a
Futarasan. 二荒山 *See* **Nantaisan**
Futarayama Shrine 二荒山神社 2:376a
Futari (or *Ninin*) *daimyō* 二人大名 4:327a
Futasujimichi 二筋道 7:108a
Futatsu chōchō kuruwa no nikki 双蝶蝶曲輪日記 4:95b
Fūten rōjin nikki (Diary of a Mad Old Man) 瘋癲老人日記 6:230a; 7:343a
Futofude (thick brush) 1:*233a*, 233b
Futokoro nikki ふところ日記 4:180a
Futon. *See* **Bedding**
Futon (quilt) 蒲団 7:358b
Futsunomitama no Ōkami 布都御魂大神 3:348a
Futsū Senkyo Kisei Dōmeikai 普通選挙期成同盟会 2:376a-377b
Futsū Senkyo Undō. *See* **Universal Manhood Suffrage Movement**
Futtsu 富津 2:376b
Fuwa 不破 4:98b

Fuwa no Seki. 不破関 *See* **Sekisho**
Fuyu and funyū 不輸不入 **2**:376b
Fuyuhikoshū 冬彦集 **8**:11a
Fuyu kodachi 冬木立 **6**:297b
Fuyukusa ふゆくさ **8**:112a
Fuyu no yado 冬の宿 **1**:4b
Fuzambō **2**:376b-377a
Fūzokuga **2**:377a-378a
emergence **2**:377b
Kambun **2**:378a
Kan'ei **2**:377b-378a
Keichō **2**:377b
painting subjects **6**:158b
precursors **2**:377b
Fūzoku shōsetsu **2**:378a-378b; **5**:315a-315b; **6**:221b
literary status **2**:378a
postwar changes **2**:378b

G

Ga 蛾 **4**:138b
Gagaku 雅楽 **1**:157a, 159b; **3**:1a-2b, *2b*; **6**:298b
bugaku **3**:1b
history **3**:1a-1b
instruments **3**:1b-2a
repertoire **3**:1a
theory and formal structure **3**:2a-2b
tsuzumi **8**:119b
Gagaku court music **5**:15b
Gagen shūran 雅言集覧 **3**:3a
Gago onjō kō 雅語音声考 **7**:281a
Gaiban tsūsho 外蕃通書 **4**:269b
Gaijin **2**:314a
Gaikoku bugyō 外国奉行 **3**:3a
Gaikoku hōjin **3**:3a
Gaikokujin gakkō **3**:3a
Gaikokusen Uchiharai Rei 外国船打払令 **3**:3a-3b; **7**:125b
Gaimushō 外務省 **5**:188a-189b
Gaki-zōshi 餓鬼草紙 **1**:190b, *191a*
Gakkai. *See* **Learned societies**
Gakken Co, Ltd **3**:3b
Gakkiron 楽毅論 **1**:232a
Gakkō **1**:*187a*, 198a
Gakkō Kyōiku Hō 学校教育法 **7**:36a
Gakkōrei 学校令 **7**:36b
Gakubatsu (academic clique) 学閥 **1**:147a; **3**:3b-4a; **6**:205b
Gakudō 咢堂 **6**:140a
Gakukan'in **2**:77a
Gakumon no susume 学問ノスヽメ **1**:207b; **2**:183a, 368a; **3**:4a-4b
Gakuō Zōkyū 岳翁蔵丘 **3**:4b-5a
Gakureki shakai **3**:5a
Gakuren Incident 学連事件 **4**:339a
Gakusei 学制 **2**:182b-183a
Gakushūin University **1**:5a; **3**:5a
Konoe Atsumaro **4**:272b
Gakushū shidō yōryō **7**:34a
Gakusō 楽箏 **3**:2a; **4**:297a
Gakusoku 学則 **6**:72b
Galilean theory **5**:356a
Gamagōri 蒲郡 **3**:5a
Gambaru **3**:5a
Gambler (yakuza) **8**:286b
Gambling **3**:5b-6a
cockfighting **1**:333b-334a
hanafuda **3**:93a-93b
mah-jongg **3**:6a
pachinko **3**:6a
playing cards **6**:192a
professional **3**:5b
urban life **8**:177b
Western influence **3**:5b
Games **3**:6a
bean bag (otedama) **1**:148a
children's **4**:105a; **5**:359b
iroha karuta **3**:332a
dogfighting **2**:124a-124b
Edo period **4**:108a
fireworks **2**:281a
foreign influences **7**:195a
fukubiki **2**:361b
fuku warai **2**:367a
go **3**:37b-38a
hanafuda **3**:93a-93b
Heian period **4**:108a
indoor **4**:381a-381b
injiuchi **3**:305b
jūroku musashi **4**:86a
Kagome Kagome **4**:105a
Kai-awase **4**:108a
kemari (kickball) **1**:106b
mah-jongg **5**:84a
menko **5**:162b
outdoor **4**:381a-381b
pachinko **6**:143a
playing cards **3**:6a; **6**:192a
renju **6**:300a
shōgi **7**:158b-159b
sugoroku **7**:259a
sumō wrestling **7**:270b-271a
word **8**:269b-270a
Gamō Katahide 蒲生賢秀 **3**:6b
Gamō Kumpei 蒲生君平 **1**:76b; **3**:6a-6b
Gamō Masuhide 蒲生賦秀 **3**:6b
Gamō Ujisato 蒲生氏郷 **3**:6b
Gan **3**:13b
Gangōji 元興寺 **3**:6b-7a; **7**:16b
Kanroku **4**:151b
Gangster (yakuza) **8**:286b
Ganjin 鑑真 **3**:7a-7b; **5**:237a
Buddhist sculpture **3**:*7a*
China **1**:282b
Ritsu sect **6**:332a
statue of **3**:*7a*
Tōshōdaiji **8**:83b
Gankake **3**:7b
Ganku 岸駒 **3**:7b-8a
Gankutsuō 巌窟王 **4**:316b
Gannen-mono **4**:13b
Gan (The Mistress) 雁 **8**:90b
Garabō **3**:8a
Garakuta bunko 我楽多文庫 **4**:198b; **6**:139b; **8**:288b
Garan **1**:182a
Garashiya Hosokawa fujin がらしあ・細川夫人 **7**:339b
Gara Spinning **3**:8a
Garasu **3**:35b
Garbhadhātu **7**:310a
"Garden Guard" **6**:22b
Gardenia [(kuchinashi) *Gardenia jasminoides* f. *grandiflora*)] **3**:8a
Gardens **3**:8a-11b
Byōdōin **1**:227a-227b
designers
Kobori Enshū **3**:9b; **4**:238b
Musō Soseki **3**:10a; **5**:287b
Hama Detached Palace Garden **3**:90a
history **3**:8b-10a
Katsura Detached Palace **3**:*9b*; **4**:172b-173a
Kenrokuen **3**:*9a*; **4**:198b
Kinkakuji **4**:213a
Kōrakuen **4**:276a, *276b*
Ritsurin Park **6**:321b-322a, *322b*
Ryōanji **3**:*8b*; **6**:347b
scenic composition **3**:11a-11b
Shugakuin Detached Palace **7**:181b-182a
space **3**:10b-11a
styles **3**:10a-11b
funa asobi **3**:10b-11a
kaiyū **3**:10a-11a
kanshō **3**:10b-11a
rock and sand garden (kare sansui) **3**:9b
shūyū **3**:10b-11a
tea garden (roji niwa) **3**:9b
technique and composition **3**:10b
GARIOA **2**:155a, 158a-158b; **7**:253a
GARIOA-EROA **3**:11b-12a
Garment industry **3**:12a
Kashiyama & Co, Ltd **4**:163a
Renown, Inc **6**:300b
Wacoal Corporation **8**:197b
Gasan **4**:116a
Gas industries
Nippon Sanso **6**:12a
Ōsaka Gas Co, Ltd **6**:121a
Teisan **7**:376b
Tōkyō Gas Co, Ltd **8**:67a
Gassan 月山 **1**:136b; **3**:13a
Gasshō-zukuri **5**:*192b*
Gates **3**:12a-13a
chūmon (inner gate) **3**:*12b*
city **3**:12b
domestic **3**:13a
fortifications **3**:12a
karamon **3**:*12b*, 13a
nagayamon (rowhouses) **3**:13a
temple **3**:12a-12b
yakuimon **3**:13a
Gāthā **3**:58a
GATT. *See* General Agreement on Tariff and Trade
Gauffrage (blind printing) **8**:142a
Gaun nikkenroku 臥雲日件録 **3**:13b
Gaun Tatsumune 臥雲辰致 **3**:8a
Gauzes (ra and sha) **8**:17b
Gay life **8**:177b-178a
Gazoku setchū **4**:243a
Geba **7**:252b
Gebaruto **7**:252b
Gedatsu 解脱 **4**:98b
Geese [(gan; kari) family Anatidae] **3**:13b
Geiami 芸阿弥 **1**:52b; **3**:14a
works **1**:52b
Geibikei 猊鼻渓 **3**:14a
Geidō-mono **2**:271a
Geijutsu ha sengen
Shinkō Geijutsu Ha **7**:119b
Geijutsusai Taishō (National Art Festival Grand Prize) **8**:289a
Geisha **3**:14a-15b; **6**:257a
dance, traditional **2**:75b
fees **3**:15a
history **3**:15a-15b
Morgan, Yuki **5**:248b
organization **3**:14b-15a
profession **3**:14a-14b
ryūkōka **6**:354a
shimpa **7**:108a
Shindō Kaneto **7**:111a
tattoos **7**:350b
training **3**:14b

geisha houses ··· **3**:14b
traditional arts ··· **3**:14b
urban life ··· **8**:177b
Geiyo Islands ··· 芸予諸島 ··· **3**:15b
Innoshima ··· **3**:308b
Ōkunojima ··· **6**:97b-98a
Gejijō ··· 下知状 ··· **3**:15b
Gekika jiken ··· **1**:271b; **2**:335b; **4**:89a
Geki nikki ··· 外記日記 ··· **3**:219a
Gekken ··· **4**:195b
Gekokujō ··· 下剋上 ··· **3**:15b-16a
bushidō ··· **1**:222a
gōson system ··· **3**:50a-51a, 173a
Sengoku period ··· **7**:64b
Gembaku no ko
Shindō Kaneto ··· **7**:111a-111b
Gembakushō ··· 原爆症 ··· **1**:111b-114a
Gembikei ··· 厳美渓 ··· **3**:16a
Gembō ··· 玄昉 ··· **3**:16a
Gembudō ··· 玄武洞 ··· **3**:16b
Gembun itchi ··· 言文一致 ··· **3**:16b
Futabatei Shimei ··· **2**:375b
Japanese language reform ··· **4**:30a
Ken'yūsha ··· **4**:199a
Yamada Bimyō ··· **8**:288b
Gembun itchiron gairyaku
··· 言文一致論概略 ··· **8**:288b
Gemmei, Emperor 元明天皇 ··· **2**:350a
Gemmu monogatari 幻夢物語 ··· **6**:130a
Gempei jōsuiki. *See* **Gempei seisuiki**
Gempei no Sōran
··· 源平の争乱 ··· **7**:299b-300b
Gempei seisuiki
··· 源平盛衰記 · **1**:294a; **3**:16b;
5:44a, 246a
Gempei War. *See* **Taira- Minamoto War**
Gempuku ··· **3**:17a; **5**:325a-326a
Gendaigeki ··· **2**:267b, 269b, 271b
Gendai Haiyū Kyōkai ··· **8**:289a
Gendaijin no kenkyū
··· 現代人の研究 ··· **4**:125b
Gendai kanazukai ··· **4**:134b
Gendai Nihon bungaku
zenshū 現代日本文学全集 **1**:276b; **2**:212b
Genda Minoru ··· 源田実 ··· **3**:17a-17b
Gendarme force in Korea ··· **4**:282a
Gen'e ··· 玄恵 ··· **3**:17b
Genealogy ··· **3**:17b-18a
charting ··· **3**:17b-18a
compilations ··· **3**:17b-18a
imperial ··· **3**:152b
medieval tables ··· **7**:227a
noble families of Heian period ··· **7**:124b
Sompi bummyaku ··· **3**:*17a*
Gene marker ··· **4**:35b-36b
General accounts ··· **2**:281a-281b
General Agreement on Tariffs and Trade
(GATT) **1**:117b; **2**:320b; **3**:13a-13b; **8**:324a
tariffs ··· **7**:346b-347a
United Kingdom ··· **8**:153a
United States ··· **8**:161a
General clause ··· **3**:18a
General Corporation ··· **3**:18a
General Council of Trade Unions of
Japan · **4**:188b; **6**:212b; **7**:188b, 223b-224a
General Electric ··· **2**:317a
General Federation of Korean Residents
··· **4**:286b
General Headquarters (GHQ) ··· **3**:30a
Generally Accepted Accounting
Principles (GAAP) ··· **1**:8b
General Sekiyu ··· **3**:18a-18b
General Strike of 1947 ··· **3**:18b; **4**:351b
communist influence ··· **3**:18b
Occupation Purge ··· **6**:58b
Sambetsu Kaigi (Congress of Industrial
Labor Unions of Japan) ··· **7**:6a
General trading companies ··· **2**:324a;
3:18b-20a; **7**:268a
C. Itoh & Co, Ltd ··· **1**:316a
functions and characteristics ··· **3**:19a-19b
financial ··· **3**:19a
personnel ··· **3**:19a-19b
future ··· **3**:19b-20a
Japanese business in U.S. ··· **4**:22b
Kanematsu-Gōshō, Ltd ··· **4**:139a
keiretsu ··· **4**:189b
Marubeni Corporation ··· **5**:120b
Mitsubishi Corporation ··· **5**:207a
Mitsui & Co, Ltd ··· **5**:210b-211a
multinational enterprises ··· **5**:263a
Nisshō-Iwai Co, Ltd ··· **6**:21a-21b
origins ··· **3**:18b-19a
zaibatsu vs non-zaibatsu ··· **3**:19a
strategy and competition ··· **3**:19b
international ··· **3**:19a
Sumitomo Corporation ··· **7**:268a
Toyō Menka Kaisha, Ltd ··· **8**:92a
Geneticists
Kihara Hitoshi ··· **4**:204b
Kimura Motoo ··· **4**:211b
Toyama Kametarō ··· **8**:88a
Genetics ··· **1**:156a
Geneva Naval Conference of 1927 · **3**:20a
Geneva Whaling Control Convention
of 1931 ··· **8**:250b
Gengenshū ··· 元元集 ··· **4**:224b
Gengō. 元号 *See* **Nengō**
Gengo ··· 玄語 ··· **5**:214b
Gengyo shishu ron
··· 言語四種論 · **4**:31b; **7**:281a
Genin ··· 下人 ··· **3**:20a; **7**:62a
Genji 源氏
Murakami ··· **5**:177b-178a
Seiwa ··· **5**:178a-178b
See **Minamoto family**
Genji Keita ··· 源氏鶏太 ··· **2**:274a; **3**:20a
Genji monogatari. 源氏物語 *See* **Tale of Genji**
Genji monogatari emaki
··· 源氏物語絵巻 ··· **3**:20a-21a
Genji monogatari
shinshaku 源氏物語新釈 ··· **4**:129b
Genjitsu ··· 現実 ··· **4**:125a
Genka ··· 幻化 ··· **8**:147b
Genkai ··· 言海 ··· **2**:57a
Ōtsuki Fumihiko ··· **6**:134b
Genkainada ··· 玄海灘 ··· **4**:211a
Genkai Sea ··· 玄界灘 ··· **3**:21a
Genkan (entry hall) ··· **7**:162b
Genkan (musical instrument) ··· **7**:195a
Genkō Incident ··· 元弘の変 ··· **3**:21a
Ashikaga Takauji ··· **1**:100a
Kemmu restoration ··· **4**:192a
Kikuchi Taketoki ··· **4**:206b
Kōgon, Emperor ··· **4**:249a
Kojima Takanori ··· **4**:252a
Kusunoki Masashige ··· **4**:321a
Genkō shakusho 元亨釈書 ··· **1**:294b;
3:21a-21b; **4**:252b
Genkun ··· **3**:21b
Genre painting ·· **2**:377a-378a; **6**:153b, *155a*
Genrin, Yamaoka 山岡元隣 ··· **3**:77b
Genrō ··· 元老 ··· **3**:21b-22a
influence on government ··· **3**:197b-198a
members
Inoue Kaoru ··· **3**:310a-310b
Itō Hirobumi ··· **3**:352a-353b
Katsura Tarō ··· **4**:173b-174a
Kuroda Kiyotaka ··· **4**:314a-314b
Matsukata Masayoshi ··· **5**:134b-136a
Ōyama Iwao ··· **6**:138a-138b
Saigō Tsugumichi ··· **6**:367a
Saionji Kimmochi ··· **6**:371b-372b
Yamagata Aritomo ··· **8**:290b-292a
political system ··· **6**:214a, 216b
prime minister and cabinet ·· **6**:241b-242b
Genrōin ··· 元老院 ··· **3**:22a
early Meiji Dajōkan ··· **2**:70b
Meiji Constitution ··· **2**:1b
Ōsaka Conference of 1875 ··· **6**:121a
shigi kempō ··· **7**:92b
Genroku era ··· 元禄時代 ··· **1**:211b;
3:22a-23a, 191a
arts and crafts ··· **3**:23a
education ··· **3**:22b
Forty-Seven Rōnin Incident ··· **2**:328a
historical accounts ··· **4**:102a
kabuki ··· **4**:90b
literature ··· **3**:22b-23a; **4**:102a
periodization ··· **6**:175a
puppet theater ··· **3**:22b
scholars ··· **3**:23a
textiles ··· **8**:19a
Tokugawa Tsunayoshi ··· **8**:56a
Genroku literature
··· 元禄文学 ··· **5**:46b-47b
Bashō ··· **1**:144a-145b; **5**:46b-47a
Chikamatsu Monzaemon ··· **1**:275a-276b;
5:47a
Saikaku ··· **5**:47a; **6**:369b-370b
Gensen ··· 言泉 ··· **3**:23a-23b
Gense shugi ··· **8**:24b
Genshi, josei wa taiyō de atta ··· **7**:339b
Genshin ··· 源信 ··· **3**:23b
beliefs ··· **3**:23b
nembutsu ··· **4**:67a-67b
raigōzu ··· **6**:277a
Sanzen'in ··· **7**:19b
wasan ··· **8**:231a
works ··· **3**:23b
Gensuikin. *See* **Atomic weapons, movement to ban**
Gensuikyō. *See* **Atomic weapons, movement to ban**
Gentians [(rindō) family Gentianaceae)]
··· **3**:24a
Gentlemen's Agreement of 1907
··· **3**:24a-24b; **8**:156a
Japanese Americans ··· **4**:14a
Japanese Associations of America ··· **4**:22a
Okinawa ··· **6**:87b
Roosevelt, Theodore ··· **6**:339a
segregation of Japanese schoolchildren in
the United States ··· **7**:49a
United States Immigration Acts of 1924,
1952, and 1965 ··· **8**:164b
Gen'yōsha ··· 玄洋社 ··· **3**:24b-25a
Amur River Society ··· **1**:53b
nationalism ··· **5**:342b-343a
tactics ··· **3**:24b-25a
tairiku rōnin ··· **7**:302b
Tōyama Mitsuru ··· **8**:88a
Uchida Ryōhei ··· **8**:124a
ultranationalism ··· **8**:145b
Genzammi Yorimasa. 源三位頼政
See **Minamoto no Yorimasa**
Genzu mandara
Ryōbu Mandara ··· **6**:348a
Geographers
Iizuka Kōji ··· **3**:264a
Inō Tadataka ··· **3**:309a
Kiuchi Shinzō ··· **4**:231b
Nagakubo Sekisui ··· **5**:301b-302a
Nishikawa Joken ··· **6**:17a
Ogawa Takuji ··· **6**:70a
Shiga Shigetaka ··· **7**:91b
Tada Fumio ··· **7**:293b
Takahashi Kageyasu ··· **7**:312a
Yamamura Saisuke ··· **8**:300a
Yamazaki Naomasa ··· **8**:313a
Geographical names ··· **5**:326a-326b
Geographic Survey Institute ··· **3**:25a

maps 5:112a
National Atlas of Japan 5:336b
Geographies, regional 6:288a
Geography 3:25a-26a
organizations 3:25b-26a
regional 6:288a
school education 3:25b
studies 3:25a-25b
foreign influence 3:25a-25b
Nishikawa Joken 3:25b
Geography in Japan 3:26a
Geological Society of Japan 2:329b
Geological structure 4:8a-9b
crustal movement 4:8b-9a
history of Japanese Islands 4:9a-9b
Northeastern and Southwestern Japan 4:8b
topography 4:8b
Geological Survey of Japan 1:21b; 3:26a
Naumann, Edmund 5:358a
Geologische Arbeiten in Japan 5:358a
Geologists
Naumann, Edmund 5:358a
Ogawa Takuji 6:70a
Yabe Hisakatsu 8:283a
Geology 2:141a
Geomancy 4:163a
Geophysicists
Tanakadate Aikitsu 7:336a
German Academic Exchange Service
3:28a
Germany and Japan 3:26a-28a
Anti-Comintern Pact 1:65a-65b
Edo period 3:26a-26b
interwar period 3:27a-27b
economic 3:27a-27b
political 3:27b
Japanese studies 4:42b-43a
Jiaozhou concession 4:53a
late 1860s to World War I 3:26b-27a
medicine, influence on 5:147a-147b
Russia and Japan 6:342a
Tripartite Pact 8:107a
World War II to present 3:27b-28a
economic 3:27b-28a
Gero 下呂 3:28a
Gesaku 戯作 3:28a-29a; 5:48b; 7:103a
early 3:28b
gōkan 4:42a-42b
kibyōshi 4:201b
kokkeibon 4:256a
late 3:28b-29a
ninjōbon 6:5b-6a
rise 3:28b
sharebon 7:79b-80a
tradition and modern literature 3:29a
writers 3:29b
yomihon 8:336a
Geschichte des Wahlrechts zum englischen Parlament 6:312a
Gesshō 月照 3:29a
Gestures 3:29a-30a
significance 3:29b
types 3:29a-30a
Gesu 下司 4:63a
Geta 3:30a
footgear, traditional 2:308a
Gewalt 7:252b
Gezairoku 戯財録 5:16b
Ghost of Tomomori, The 8:184a
Ghosts 1:130b; 3:30a; 8:357a
Ghost Story of Tōkaidō Yotsuya
8:41b-42a
GHQ 3:30a
Gi 4:141b
Gidayū-bushi 義太夫節 2:301a; 3:30a-30b; 4:99a
jōruri 4:77a
Gidō Shūshin 義堂周信 3:30b
Gift giving 2:17b; 3:30b
chūgen 1:312a
condolence 3:30b
etiquette 2:232b-234a
kaeshi 1:102a
miyage 5:217a
occasions 3:30b
otoshidama 6:133a
seibo 7:49a
shūgi 7:183a
significance 3:30b
Gifu 岐阜 3:31a
Gifu Castle 岐阜城 3:31a
Gifu Prefecture 岐阜県 3:31a-31b
Gifu-Yōrō Prefectural Park
岐阜養老県立公園 8:338b
Gigaku 伎楽 2:297b; 3:31b-32a; 7:148b, 195a
dance, traditional 2:73b-74a
masks 5:125b-126a
Gigaku mask 5:*125a*
Gigen yōki shū 戯言養気集 6:282a
Giin Shōgen Hō 4:262a
Gijō (officials) 議定 7:16b
Gijutsu dōnyū 3:32a-32b
Gijutsu iten. *See* **Technology transfer**
Gijutsu kakushin. *See* **Technological innovation**
Gikai Deiri Kishadan (Diet Journalists Club) 6:236a
Gikeiki 義経記 3:32b; 7:152b
summary 3:32b
Giko monogatari (pseudoclassical tales)
擬古物語 3:32b-33a; 5:246a
Gila River Relocation Center 3:33a
Gimbura 7:250a
Ginkakuji 銀閣寺 3:33a-33b; 4:336a
paintings 4:147b
structure 3:33a
tea ceremony 7:361a
Ginkgo [(ichō) *Gingko biloba*] 3:33b
Gin no saji (The Silver Spoon) 銀の匙 5:314a
Ginowan 宜野湾 3:33b
Ginsekai 銀世界 8:143a
Ginseng 7:334b
Ginza 銀座 8:63a
Ginzan Hot Spring
銀山温泉 3:33b
Giōji 祇王寺 3:33b
Gion Festival 祇園祭 2:255b; 3:33b-34a; 4:336a, *336b*; 8:316b
dashi 2:78a
depiction in art 2:377b
floats 3:34a
fūryū 2:374a
Gion Nankai 祇園南海 1:211a; 3:34a
Gion no shimai (Sister of the Gion) 祇園の姉妹 8:289a
Gion Shrine 祇園社 4:59b
Girard case 3:34a-34b
United States-Japan security treaties
8:167b
Girard, P.S.B. 4:32a
Girard, William S. 3:34a-34b
Giri (obligation) 1:149b
Giri and ninjō (obligation and human feeling) 2:232a; 3:34b; 6:206a
Chikamatsu Monzaemon 1:276a
etiquette 2:233a
gakubatsu 3:4a
groups 3:63a
literary criticism, premodern 5:16b
on 6:105a
political culture 6:206a
Giri ninjō i ro ha ni ho he to hen 4:157b
Girl Scouts 3:34b
Girls' Festival. *See* **Doll Festival**
Girls' high schools 4:297a-297b
Gisaku. *See* **Gesaku**
Giseigo 6:110b
Gishi wajinden. 魏志倭人伝
See **Wei zhi (Wei chih)**
Gissha 3:35a; 6:301a
Kasuga gongen genki 3:*35a*
Gitaigo 6:110b
Giwadan no Ran
義和団の乱 1:166a-166b
Glass 3:35b-36b
Edo period (1600-1868) 3:36a-36b
Heian period (794-1185) 3:36a
Kamakura, Muromachi, and Azuchi-Momoyama periods (1185-1600)
3:36a
Kofun period (ca 300-710) 3:35b
Meiji period (1868-1912) to present 3:36b
Nara period (710-794) 3:35b-36a
Satsuma cut glass 3:*35a*
Yayoi period (ca 300 BC-ca AD 300) 3:35b
Glass industry 3:36b
Glazes 1:265a-265b
Globefishes [(fugu) family Tetraodontidae] 3:36b-37a
Glover, Thomas Blake 3:36b-37a
Glycine max 7:239a
Gneist, Rudolf von 2:2b; 3:37b, 194a
Go (game) 3:37b-38a; 6:300a
basic rules 3:37b-38a
equipment 3:38a
grandmaster, title of 3:222b
history 3:38a
schools 3:38a
Nihon Kiin 5:380b
professional and international rankings 3:38a
Gō (village) 郷 3:38b
Goban Tadanobu
Onoe Matsunosuke 6:109b
Go-betweens (Nakōdo) 5:4b, 320b-321a
Gobies [(haze) family Gobiidae] 3:38b
Goble, Jonathan 1:142a
Gobō 御坊 3:38b
Gobō no Keiji 五榜の掲示 3:38b
Gobuji chūshingura
御無事忠臣蔵 8:183b
Gobusho 五部書 3:38b-39a; 8:236b
Gochi Kokubunji
五智国分寺 4:69a
7:66a
Go-Daigo, Emperor
後醍醐天皇 1:99a; 3:39a; 7:66a, 84a
Ashikaga Takauji 1:100a-100b; 3:172b
Fujiwara no Fujifusa 2:350b
Gen'e 3:17b
Genkō Incident 3:21a; 4:206b
Kanenaga, Prince 4:139b
Kemmu nenchū gyōji 4:191b
Kemmu Restoration 4:191b
Kimbusenji 4:208a
Kitabatake Akiie 4:224a
Kojima Takanori's support 4:252a
Nakasendai Rebellion 5:317b
Northern and Southern Courts 6:39a
rule 2:204b
warrior government 8:229b
Godaiō ki. *See* Godai teiō monogatari
Godai teiō monogatari
五代帝王物語 3:39a
historiography 3:154a
Godai Tomoatsu 五代友厚 3:39a-39b; 7:52a

diplomat 3:39a-39b
economic development 3:39a-39b
Kaigun Denshūjo 4:110a
Gods. *See* **Kami**
Godzilla 2:273b
Gofu 3:39b
Gofuchinin tomura 4:112b
Go-Fukakusa, Emperor 後深草天皇 3:39b
Fushimi, Emperor 2:375a
Kameyama, Emperor 4:125b
Northern and Southern Courts 6:39a
succession 4:192a
Gōgai 3:40a
Gōgaku 3:40a
Gogaku shinsho (New Book on Linguistics) 語学新書 8:243a
Gōgawa. 江川 *See* **Gōnokawa**
Go Haifu 呉佩孚 8:279b
Go-Hanazono, Emperor 後花園天皇 3:40a; 7:9b
Gohei 3:40a; 4:195a; 7:249b, 272b
origami 6:116b
Gohonzon 7:225a
Go-Horikawa, Emperor 後堀河天皇 4:72a
Gohō shinan (A Guide to Grammar) 語法指南 6:134b
Goichigo Jiken 五・一五事件 5:142b-143a
Go-Ichijō, Emperor 後一条天皇 3:40a-40b
Fujiwara no Yorimichi 2:357b
regency 2:353a
Goikō 語意考 4:129b
Gōi shinjū 7:262a
Gojira (Godzilla) ゴジラ 8:111a
Gojō 五條 3:40b
Gojūon ('50-sound') chart 8:221b
Gojūon zu 3:40b-41a
siddham 7:192b
Gokaidō 五街道 3:41a-41b
centralized government 3:41b
ekisei 2:188b
history 3:41a-41b
Kōshū Kaidō 3:41b
Nakasendō 5:318a
Nikkō Kaidō 3:41b
Ōshū Kaidō 3:41b
sankin kōtai 7:14a
sekisho 7:57a
sukegō 7:265a
Tōkaidō 8:40b
Gokajō no Goseimon. *See* **Charter Oath**
Go-Kameyama, Emperor 後亀山天皇 3:41b-42a; 4:319b; 5:49a
Gōkan 合巻 3:42a-42b; 7:18a
Jippensha Ikku 4:61a
kabuki influence 3:42a-42b
Shikitei Samba 7:96b-97b
Tamenaga Shunsei 7:333b-334a
writers 3:42a-42b
Gokanoshō 五家荘 3:42b
Gokasegawa 3:42b
Gokasho shōnin 五箇所商人 3:42b
Gokasho Shōnin Kaisho 五箇所商人会所 5:304a
Gōkawa. *See* **Gōnokawa**
Gokayama 五箇山 3:42b
Gokenin 御家人 1:131b; 2:264a-264b; 3:42b; 4:122a, 196b; 7:183a
ienoko and rōtō 3:261a
kobushin 4:239a
protection 3:42b
Shōheikō 7:162a
yoriki and dōshin 8:338b
Goken Sampa Naikaku 護憲三派内閣 3:43a
Goken Undō. *See* **Movement to Protect Constitutional Government**
Gōke shidai 江家次第 3:43a
Goki Shichidō 五畿七道 3:43a
Gokō gomin 五公五民 3:43a
Gokokuji 護国寺 3:43a
Go-Komatsu, Emperor 後小松天皇 3:43b; 6:39a; 8:356a
Gokuchū jūhachinen (Eighteen Years in Jail) 獄中十八年 8:44b
Gokurakubō 極楽坊 3:6b-7a
Gokuraku Jōdo kubon ōjō gi 極楽浄土九品往生義 6:351b
Gokyō (Defending the Faith) 8:296a
Go-Kyōgoku Yoshitsune 後京極良経 2:358a
Gold beetle [(koganemushi) *Minela splendens*] 3:43b
Golden Pavilion 4:*212b*
Goldfish [(kingyo) *Carassius auratus*] 3:43b
Goldmines 3:365a; 6:363a
Goldmining 3:184b-185a
Gold standard, return to 7:173b
Golf 3:43b
Golovnin, Vasilii Mikhailovich 3:43b-44a
capture by Japanese 3:44a
memoirs 3:44a
Goma 3:127b
Goma ceremony 1:188a
Gomi Yasusuke 五味康祐 3:44b; 7:85a
Go-Mizunoo, Emperor 後水尾天皇 3:44b; 7:255a, 270a
Katsura Detached Palace 4:172b
Shie Incident 7:89b
Gomoku narabe. *See* **Renju**
Gonaisho 御内書 3:44b
Goncharov, Ivan Aleksandrovich 3:44b-45a
Gondō Nariaki. *See* **Gondō Seikyō**
Gondō Seikyō 権藤成卿 3:45a
Gongan 4:234a
Gonge 1:122b-123a
Gongen. *See* **Avatar**
Goningumi (five-family associations) 五人組 3:45a-45b; 6:198a
function 3:45a-45b
gōson system 3:50a-51a
model 3:45a
registers 3:45b
tonarigumi 8:74a
Gonjinshū 言塵集 3:272a
Gonki 権記 3:45b
Gōnō 豪農 2:335a; 3:45b-46a
Gōnokawa 江川 3:46a
Gonorrhea 8:189b
Gonrei 権令 4:197b
"Good-for-nothing" 8:286b
Good luck charms 3:91a
Goodman, Mary Ellen 4:39b
Go on 呉音 3:46a
on readings 6:112b
Gorer, Geoffrey 4:38a
Gorges
Chōmonkyō 1:5a, 300a
Dangyokei 2:76b
Dorokyō 2:131b
Enakyō 2:213a
Geibikei 3:14a
Gembikei 3:16a
Iyadani 3:364a
Kurobe Kyōkoku 4:314a
Nagatoro 5:307b
Nakatsu Keikoku 5:318b
Nakatsukyō 5:318b
Nakayama Shichiri 5:319a
Nezamenotoko 5:373b
Ōboke 6:49b
Omogokei 6:103a
Shōsenkyō 7:167b
Sōunkyō 7:234b
Taishakukyō 7:303b
Takachihokyō 7:310b
Tenninkyō 8:7b
Yabakei 8:283a, 297a
Gorintō 五輪塔 3:46a
Gōri system 郷里制 3:46a-46b
gō 3:38b
ritsuryō system 6:325b
Goroku 語録 3:46b
Goryō 3:46b-47a; 4:126a
festivals 3:147a
Goryōkaku 五稜郭 3:*85a*; 7:160a
Goryōkaku, Battle of 五稜郭の戦 1:165a; 3:47a
Go-Saga, Emperor 後嵯峨天皇 3:47a
Fujiwara no Tameie 2:356a
Kameyama, Emperor 4:125b
succession 4:192a
Go-Sanjō, Emperor 後三条天皇 3:47a
Fujiwara family 2:348b
Fujiwara no Yorimichi 2:357b
insei 3:314b
Kiroku Shōen Kenkeijo 4:222a
Gosanjū Jiken 五・三〇事件 5:143b
Gosanke 御三家 3:47b, 186b
shimpan 7:108a
Gosankyō 御三卿 3:47b
shimpan 7:108a
Gosannen kassen ekotoba 後三年合戦絵詞 4:369a
Gosannen no Eki 後三年の役 4:368b-369a
Gose 御所 3:47b
Gosechi no mai 五節舞 3:47b
Goseda Hōryū 五姓田芳柳 8:298a
Goseibai Shikimoku 御成敗式目 1:212a; 3:47b-48a; 4:377a; 7:96a
Daibon Sankajō 2:55b
Hōjō Yasutoki 3:212a
nenki 5:361b
Gō Seinosuke 郷誠之助 3:48a
Gosekke 五摂家 3:48a-48b
Fujiwara family 2:348b, 349a-349b
kampaku 4:130a
Konoe family 4:272b
Kujō family 4:303b
Sanjō Sanetomi 7:12b
Gosekku 五節句 2:299a
Gosen 五泉 3:48b; 7:62a
Gosenshū. *See* **Gosen wakashū**
waka 8:204a
Gosen wakashū 後撰和歌集 3:48b; 4:132b; 5:33a; 6:105a
poets 3:48b
Gosetsu
ink painting 3:306b
Gōshi 郷士 3:48a-49a
functions 3:49a
Gōshidai 江次第 3:43a
Goshikinuma 五色沼 1:137a; 3:49a
Goshintai 3:49a-49b
origin 3:49a
Go-Shirakawa, Emperor 後白河天皇 3:49b; 7:13a, 68a, 96b, 279b
Hōgen Disturbance 3:209a

insei · 3:315a
Ryōjin hishō · 6:352a
Taira-Minamoto war · 7:299b, 300b
Goshi Undō 五・四運動 · 5:143a-143b
Goshkevich, Iosif Antonovich · 3:49b-50a
Goshogawara 五所川原 · 3:50a
Gosho Heinosuke
五所平之助 · 2:269a, 270a, 272a; 3:50a; 7:102b
Gōshō hensō 迎接変相 · 6:276b-277b
Gōshō mandara 迎接曼荼羅 · 6:276b-277b
Gosho ningyō · 2:*128b*
Goshūishū 後拾遺集 2:353a; 8:210a
Goshun. 呉春 *See* **Matsumura Goshun**
Gōso 強訴 · 3:50a
Gōson system 郷村制 · 3:50a-51a
dissolution · 3:51a
responsibilities · 3:50b-51a
social stratification · 3:50b
Gossha ごっしゃ · 4:119b
Gosu · 4:179a
Gotemba 御殿場 · 3:51a
Gotō Art Museum · 3:51a; 5:276b; 8:341a
Go-Toba, Emperor
後鳥羽天皇 · 1:40a; 2:355b, 357b, 358a; 3:51a-52b; 5:14b; 6:297a; 7:13a, 96b
abdication and exile · 3:52b
Bureau of Poetry · 3:52a
calligraphy · 1:235a
imperial poetry anthologies · 2:354a
Jien · 4:53b-54a
Jōkyū Disturbance · 4:192a
Lady Daibu · 4:197b
patron of arts · 3:51a-52b
poet · 3:51b-52a
works · 3:52a-52b
portraits · 2:353b
Shin kokinshū · 7:119b
waka · 8:212a-212b
Go-Toba In-bon
後鳥羽院本 · 4:161b
Go-Toba In Kumano gyokō ki
後鳥羽院熊野御幸記 · 8:105b
Go-Toba no in gokuden
後鳥羽院御口伝 · 3:52b
Gotō Chūgai 後藤宙外 · 3:52b
Gotō Fumio 後藤文夫 · 3:52b
Gotō Islands 五島列島 · 2:363a; 3:52b-53a
Gotō Katsu 後藤濶 · 3:53a
Gotō Keita 五島慶太 · 3:53a
Gotō Konzan 後藤艮山 · 3:53a, 239a
Kagawa Shūtoku · 4:103b
Gotō Mitsutsugu 後藤光次 · 3:53a; 7:274b
Gotō Ryūnosuke
後藤隆之助 · 3:53b
Gotō Shimpei 後藤新平 · 3:53b-54a
foreign affairs · 3:53b-54a
Gotō Shōjirō 後藤象二郎 · 1:34b; 2:56a, 336a; 3:54a; 7:23b
Freedom and People's Rights Movement · 2:333b-334a
Fukuoka Takachika · 2:365b
Itagaki Taisuke · 3:349b
Jiyūtō · 4:65a-65b
Gotō Shōzaburō. *See* **Gotō Mitsutsugu**
Gotō Shuichi 後藤守一 · 1:77b; 3:54a-54b
Gotō Tokujō 後藤徳乗 · 3:53a
Gōtsu 江津 · 3:54b
Go-Uda, Emperor
後宇多天皇 · 3:54b
Emperor Fushimi · 2:375a
Kameyama, Emperor · 4:125b
Government: [Premodern (to 1868)]
insei ("cloister government") · 3:166b; 3:314b-315a
regency government · 3:166a-166b; 6:286a-288a
ritsuryō system · 3:162b-166a; 6:322a-332a
emperor · 2:203b-204a
warrior government · 8:228b-230b
Kamakura shogunate · 3:169a-171a, 172a; 4:121b-122b
Muromachi shogunate · 3:172a-175a; 5:271b-274a
Shokuhō seiken ("Oda-Toyotomi regime") · 3:177a-180b; 7:164b-165a
Tokugawa shogunate · 3:185b-189b, 192a-192b; 8:52b-56a
bakuhan system · 1:131a-133a
Yamato court · 3:160a-162b; 8:308b-309a
emperor · 2:203a-203b
Government: [Modern (1868-1945)]
early Meiji
Dajōkan system · 2:70a-70b
political system · 6:213b-214b
under Meiji Constitution
cabinet · 6:240b-242b
emperor · 2:205b-207a
genrō · 3:21b-22a
Great Court of Cassation · 3:60b
Imperial Diet · 3:275b-277a
Meiji Constitution · 2:1a-3b
Privy Council · 6:252b-253b
Government [Contemporary (1945-present)]
Constitution of 1947 · 2:3b-7a, 9b-13a
Diet
House of Councilors · 2:188a-188b
House of Representatives · 2:188a-188b
Executive · 3:55b-56a
Prime Minister and cabinet · 6:240b-244a
Judiciary · 4:80b-81b
constitutional rights · 2:337a-339a, 369a-369b
supreme court · 7:277a-277b
Government, executive branch 3:55b-56a
Government agricultural policy. *See* **Agriculture**
Government and Relief in Occupied Areas-Economic Rehabilitation in Occupied Areas (GARIOA-EROA) · 3:11b-12a
Government bonds · 3:54b
Government compensation · 3:54b-55b
Government educational policy. *See* **Education**
Government-General of Korea · 4:283a
Government grants-in-aid · 3:56a
taxes · 7:353b
Government-operated factories, Meiji period · 2:361a; 3:56a-56b
sale · 4:138a
Government school · 4:140a
Governors and mayors · 3:56b
election · 3:56b
· 3:38b
Gowland, William · 1:77a
Goyō eshi · 7:270b
Goyōkin · 3:56b-57a
Goyō shōnin 御用商人 · 3:57a; 5:209b; 7:267a
goyōkin · 3:56b-57a
Goza · 4:160b
Gozan 五山 · 2:358b; 3:57a-58a; 4:120b
decline · 3:57b-58a
descriptions · 4:302b
formation · 3:57a-57b
ink painting · 3:306a
Nanzenji · 5:330a-330b
political and economic background · 3:57b
religious and cultural factors · 3:57b
literature · 3:58a-59a
Gozan editions 五山版 · 1:152b
Gozan literature 五山文学 · 1:150b, 294b; 3:57b, 58a-59a
Betsugen Enshi · 1:150b
Chūgan Engetsu · 1:311b
development and change · 3:58b
Gidō Shūshin · 3:30b
Gozan monasteries · 3:58a
Issan Ichinei · 3:348b
Kokan Shiren · 4:252b
Kyōshi · 1:295b
outstanding figures · 3:58b
poetry and prose in Chinese · 6:194b-195a
quality · 3:58a-59a
scholarship · 3:58b-59a
Sesson Yūbai · 7:70b
Zekkai Chūshin · 8:369b
zen · 8:370b
Goze 瞽女 · 3:59a; 5:45a; 7:250a
Gozen gikeiki 御前義経記 · 6:20a
Gozen kaigi 御前会議 · 3:59a-59b
Graduate schools · 3:59b; 8:171a
Graffiti · 3:59b-60a
Daidairon · 3:*59a*
political · 3:59b-60a
Grain embargo controversy · 3:60a-60b; 4:281a
Grammar · 4:24b-27b
Grand chamberlain · 7:207b
Grand Council of State · 2:69a-70b; 4:187b
Grand Order of the Chrysanthemum · 8:297b
Grant, Ulysses Simpson · 3:60b, 359a
Grants-in-aid · 3:56a
Grapefruit · 6:112a
Grapes · 3:60b
Grape Society, The (Budō no Kai) 8:299b
Grave goods. *See* **Beads, ancient; Ear ornaments, ancient; Funerary sculptures**
Great Court of Cassation (Daishin'in) · 2:13b; 3:60b, 135a; 4:383a; 7:277a
"Great East Academy" · 2:67b-68a
Great East Asia Conference · 3:321b
Great elder · 7:302b-303a
Greater East Asia Conference · 8:20b
Greater East Asia Coprosperity Sphere · 2:320a, 325a; 3:60b-62a; 7:235a; 8:273b
Asia Development Board · 1:102b
background · 3:60b-61a
Japanese expansionism · 3:61a-61b
conference · 3:61b-62a
participants · 3:61b
international relations · 3:321b-324a
Konoe Fumimaro · 4:273a
ministry · 3:61b
"Greater East Asia War" · 3:61b
Greater Japan Production Party · 3:25a
Great Fish Panic of 1973 · 2:304b
Great Japan Agricultural Association · 7:109a
Great Japan Association (Dai Nihon Kyōkai) · 8:91a
Great Japan National Essence Society · 2:66a
Great Japan Production Party · 7:108a
Great Japan Women's Society · 2:65b
Great Learning for Women, The · 6:108a
Great Mirror, The · 6:79a
Great Mirror of the Erotic Way, The · 7:95b-96a
Green, Thomas Hill · 4:178a
Green Breeze Society · 6:352a
Green Tuff zone · 4:9b

Greeting cards 5:372b
Gregorian chant 5:283b
Grew, Joseph Clark 3:62a-62b; 7:246b
  World War II 3:62a
Grid-pattern city 1:245b
Grievance procedure 3:62b
  labor unions 4:348a
Griffis, William Elliot 2:311a; 3:62b
Grillo, Pompeo 3:350b
Groom, Arthur H. 3:43b
Gross domestic product 2:145b-146b
Gross national product (GNP) 2:145a-145b, 159a-159b, 161b-162a, 163a-165b
  capital formation 1:240a-242a
  defense industry 2:82a
  land problem 4:363b
  monetary policy 5:241a
  national income 5:339a-341b
Ground Self Defense Forces 7:60a-60b
Group consciousness 3:260a
Group hiring 3:62b-63a
Group responsibility 6:301b
Groups 3:63a-63b
  batsu-type 1:146b
  family 2:241b-245b
  motivation 3:63a
  murahachibu (ostracized household) 5:266a
  occupational
    hereditary (be) 1:147b
  paternalism 6:165a
  ranking system 3:63a
Group travel 3:63b; 8:104b
Growth industries 3:63b
Guadalcanal 3:63b; 8:275a
Guam 3:63b-64a
Guandong (Kwantung) Army 関東軍 3:64a-64b; 7:89a
  activists 3:64a-64b
  Doihara-Qin (Doihara-Ch'in) Agreement 2:126b
  Guandong (Kwantung) Territory 3:64b-65a
  Honjō Shigeru 3:223b
  Ishiwara Kanji 3:345b
  Manchukuo 5:96a-97b
  Manuchurian Incident 5:97b-99a
  Mutō Akira 5:288a
  post-World War I 3:200a
  Shanghai Incident 7:77b
  Soviet Union vs. 3:64a-64b
  Tanggu (Tangku) Truce 7:340b-341a
  Tatekawa Yoshitsugu 7:349a
Guandong (Kwantung) Territory 3:64b-65a
  administration 3:64b
  Twenty-One Demands 8:120b
Guanjing xuanyi 4:67b
Guanyin 4:144b-145a
Guan Yu (Kuan Yü). 4:154a
Guardian 4:253b-254a
Gubijinsō 虞美人草 5:350a
Guest room 6:124b
Guidebooks 8:41b
Guideline for Peoples' Action 4:260b
Gukanshō 愚管抄 2:101b, 102b; 3:65a-65b
  historiography 3:153b
  Jien 4:53b
  secular concerns 3:65a
  theological principles 3:65a-65b
Gullion, Allen 4:17b
Gulls [(kamome) family Laridae] 3:65b
Gumbatsu 軍閥 3:65b-67a
  Imperial Way vs Control factions 3:66b
  Satsuma 3:65b-67a
Gumbu 軍部 3:67a-67b
Gumbu daijin gen'eki bukan sei 軍部大臣現役武官制 3:67b
Gumma Incident 群馬事件 3:67b-68a
Gumma Prefecture 群馬県 3:68a
Gun. 郡 *See* **Kokugun system**
Gunchūjō 軍忠状 3:68a
Gundai 郡代 3:68a
  kanjō bugyō 4:144a
Gundan 軍談 3:68b
Gunji 郡司 3:68b
Gunjin Chokuyu 軍人勅諭 3:279b-280a
Gunji Shigetada 郡司成忠 3:68b
Gunka 3:69a
  Mikado, The 3:69a
  ryūkōka 6:354a
Gunki monogatari 軍記物語 1:294a; 2:101b; 3:69a-69b; 5:39b, 246a
  development 3:69a-69b
  Gikeiki 3:32b
  Heiji monogatari 3:123b
  Heike monogatari 3:124a-125a
  Hōgen monogatari 3:209b
  influence 3:69b
  kōdan tradition 4:241b
  Shōmonki 7:165b
  Soga monogatari 7:221a
  Taiheiki 7:295a
Gunnery 3:283b
Gunpowder 7:106b
Gunreibu 軍令部 5:358b
Guns 3:140a
Gunseki yōran 群籍要覧 1:154a
Gunsho ichiran 群書一覧 1:154a
Gunsho kaidai 群書解題 1:154b
Gunsho ruijū 群書類従 1:154b; 3:69b; 7:294b
  Hanawa Hokiichi 3:95a
  historiography 3:155b
  Kuroita Katsumi 4:316a
Guntai nikki 軍隊日記 4:318b
Gun'yaku 軍役 3:69b-70a
Gunze, Ltd 3:70a
Guomindang [(Kuomintang (KMT)] 1:270b; 2:59a; 3:128b
Guo Moruo (Kuo Mo-jo) 3:70a-70b
  works 3:70a
Guo Songling (Kuo Sung-ling) 3:70b
Gurin. 愚林 *See* **Chūyūki**
Gusai 救済 3:70b
  Shinkei 7:119a
Gushikawa 具志川 3:70b
Gūzō saikō (Resurrecting Idols) 偶像再興 8:237b
Gymnastics 3:70b-71a
Gyōda 行田 3:71a
Gyōdō mask 5:*126a*, 126b
Gyōgi 行基 1:159b; 3:71a
  education 2:172a
  monasticism 5:237a
Gyōji ryōri cuisine 行事料理法 2:22a
Gyojū gaigen (An Outline on the Subduing of Foreigners) 馭戎慨言 8:306a
Gyōki. 行基 *See* **Gyōgi**
Gyokudō. 玉堂 *See* **Uragami Gyokudō**
Gyokudō Art Museum 3:71a; 4:178b
Gyokudō Kinshi. *See* **Uragami Gyokudō**
Gyokuen Bompō 玉畹梵芳 3:70a-70b
Gyokugan 3:71b
Gyokukai 玉海 3:71b
Gyokusai ("total sacrifice") 1:116a
Gyokusen School 3:336a
Gyokuyō 玉葉 3:71b
  Kujō Kanezane's diary 4:303b
  8:213b, 214b
Gyokuyō wakashū 玉葉和歌集 3:71b-72b; 4:329b; 7:302a
  Eifuku Mon'in 2:186a
  poets 3:71b-72a
  structure 3:72a
  styles 3:71b-72a
Gyōkyō 行教 3:363a
Gyōmin Kyōsantō (Awakened People's Communist Party) 暁民共産党 6:210b
Gyomotsu sekki 御物石器 7:248a
Gyōnen 凝然 3:72b
Gyō no tetsugaku (Philosophy of Spiritual Discipline) 行の哲学 4:204b
Gyōsai. *See* **Kawanabe Gyōsai**
Gyōsai gadan 暁斎画談 4:182a
Gyōsai manga shinseki 暁斎漫画真蹟 4:182a
Gyōsei Kanri Chō 行政管理庁 1:14a
Gyōsei shidō 1:12a-13a
Gyōsho ("running-style" script) 1:233b; 7:*171a*
Gyōshōnin 7:250b
Gyōzui 3:72b
Gyūnabe 7:265b

H

Habachi (sawflies) 1:149a
Habaki 4:323b
Habatsu (cliques) 派閥 1:147a; 3:73a; 6:205b; 7:62b
Habeas Corpus Law 2:6b; 3:73a
Habikino 羽曳野 3:73a
Habōhō. *See* **Subversive Activities Prevention Law**
Haboku 破墨 3:73a-73b
  artists 3:73b
  ink painting technique 3:305b
Haboku landscape 7:*69a*
Habomai Islands 歯舞諸島 3:73b
  Soviet-Japanese relations 7:10b
Hachi 1:149a
Hachigyaku 八虐 3:73b
Hachihachi Kantai 八八艦隊 1:87b; 3:73b
  Nagato 5:307a
Hachiichi sengen 八一宣言 1:116b
Hachijōjima 八丈島 3:74a
Hachijō susuki 7:279a
Hachiku (*Phyllostachys nigra* var. *henonis*) 1:136a
Hachimaki 2:253b; 3:74a
  morning glory fair 3:*74b*
  tasuki 7:348a
Hachiman 八幡 3:74a-74b; 7:*134b*, 136a
  Iwashimizu Hachiman Shrine 3:363a
  religious symbolism 6:295b
  theories of origin 3:74a-74b
Hachimantai 八幡平 3:74b
Hachimonjiya-bon 八文字屋本 3:74b; 8:144b

Hachimonjiya Jishō ············ 八文字屋自笑 · **2**:188a; **5**:16b, 48b
Hachinohe ··········· 八戸 ········· **3**:74b
Hachiōji ··········· 八王子 ········· **3**:74b
silk weaving ···················· **2**:296a
Hachirōgata ··········· 八郎潟 ········· **3**:74b
Hachisu no tsuyu
Ryōkan ······················· **6**:352a
Hadairo no tsuki · 肌色の月 ······· **3**:151b
Ha Daiusu ······· 破提宇子 ········· **2**:241a
Hadaka no shima ·· 裸の島 ········· **3**:75a
Shindō Kaneto ··················· **7**:111b
Hadano ··········· 秦野 ········· **3**:75a
Haedong chegukki ··················· **8**:325a
"Haedong jegukki" ··················· **4**:278b
Haerbin ························· **3**:103b
Ha-erh-pin ························· **3**:103b
Hagakure ··········· 葉隠 · **1**:222b, 223b; **3**:75a-75b
Haga Yaichi ····· 芳賀矢一 ········· **3**:75b
Gensen ························· **3**:23a-23b
Hagerty Incident ··················· **3**:75b
Hagi (city) ··········· 萩 ········· **3**:75b
Hagi [(Japanese bush clover) *Lespedeza bicolor* var. *japonica*] ········ **3**:75b-76a
types ························· **3**:75b
Haginoya ··········· 萩の舎 ········· **3**:136a
Hagi Rebellion of 1876 ············ 萩の乱 · **3**:76a; **5**:79b; **7**:152a
chitsuroku shobun ··················· **1**:298a
Hagiwara Kyōjirō 萩原恭次郎 ······ **3**:76a
Hagiwara Sakutarō ············ 萩原朔太郎 ····· **3**:76a-76b
"voluptuous grave" ··················· **5**:57a
Western influence ··················· **3**:76a
works ························· **3**:75b-76a
Hagiwara Yūsuke 萩原雄祐 ········· **3**:76b
Hagi ware ··········· 萩焼 ····· **3**:76b-77a
:ollections ························· **3**:77a
glazes ························· **3**:76b
tea ceremony ······················· **7**:363b
Hagi-yaki Tōgei Kaikan ··············· **3**:77a
Hagnenauer, Charles ··················· **4**:42b
Hagoita ························· **3**:77a
Hagoita ichi ························· **3**:77a
Hagoromo ··········· 羽衣 · **2**:*73a*; **5**:295a
Hagoromo Falls ·· 羽衣ノ滝 ········· **8**:7b
Hagoromo legend ··················· **3**:77a
Nō ························· **6**:28b
prototypes ························· **2**:341a
Hagurosan ········· 羽黒山 · **1**:136b-137a; **3**:77a
Haha (*The Mother*) ····· 母 ········· **8**:117a
Haibun ························· **1**:295b; **3**:77a-78a; **6**:297b-298a
anthologies ······················· **3**:77b-78a
Bashō ························· **1**:144a; **3**:77b
categories ························· **3**:78a
characteristics ······················· **3**:77a-77b
decline ························· **3**:78a
early ························· **3**:77b
Issa ························· **3**:348a
Yokoi Yayū ························· **8**:331b
Haibutsu kishaku 廃仏毀釈 ········· **3**:78a
Haifū yanagidaru ············· 誹風柳多留 ········ **4**:157a
Haigon ························· **3**:78b
Haihan chiken ··· 廃藩置県 ··· **6**:233b-235a
Haikai ··········· 俳諧 **6**:296b-300a; **7**:208a
compared to renga ··················· **3**:78b
criticism ························· **5**:16a
haiku, hokku, haikai
distinction between ··················· **3**:78b
literary groups ······················· **5**:18a
Haikai gosan ····· 俳諧五山 ········· **7**:140a
Haikai jūron ······ 俳諧十論 ········· **4**:102b
Haikai jūsanjō · 俳諧十三条 ········ **6**:126a
Haikaishi ··········· 俳諧師 ········· **7**:311b
Haikai shichibushū ············· 俳諧七部集 · **3**:78a; **4**:102b
Haiku ··········· 俳句 ···· **3**:78a-82a
abroad ························· **3**:80b
cicadas as symbols ··················· **1**:315a
development (premodern) ······ **3**:78b-79b
decline ························· **3**:79a
Matsunaga Teitoku ··········· **3**:78b-79b
notable poets ························· **3**:79a
haibun ························· **3**:77b
hokku, and haikai ··················· **3**:78b
modern ························· **3**:79b-80b
factions ························· **3**:80a
magazines ························· **3**:80a
Masaoka Shiki's reform ··· **3**:79b; **5**:123b
moon viewing ························· **5**:248a
principles ························· **3**:80b-82a
seasons depicted ··················· **1**:325b-326b
travel diaries ························· **8**:105b
writing in English ··················· **3**:80b-82a
metrical pattern ······················· **3**:81a
seasonal theme principle ······ **3**:81b-82a
subjects ························· **3**:80b
technique of cutting ··········· **3**:81a-81b
Haiku contests ························· **5**:15a
Haiku literary groups (modern) ····· **5**:20a
Haiku paintings ······················· **4**:201a
Haiku poets
Arakida Moritake ··················· **1**:73b
Awano Seiho ························· **1**:124b
Bashō ············ **1**:144a-145b, 224b-225a
Buson ························· **1**:224b-225a
Hattori Ransetsu ····················· **3**:114a
Hattori Tohō ························· **3**:114a
Hōjō Dansui ························· **3**:210b
Iida Dakotsu ························· **3**:262a
Ikenishi Gonsui ······················· **3**:266b
Ishida Hakyō ························· **3**:340a
Ishida Mitoku ························· **3**:340a
Issa ························· **1**:224b; **3**:348b
Kagami Shikō ························· **4**:102b
Kaga no Chiyo ························· **4**:102b
Katō Kyōtai ··················· **4**:168b-169a
Katō Shūson ························· **4**:169b
Kawabata Bōsha ······················· **4**:175a
Kawahigashi Hekigotō ················ **4**:178a
Kawai Sora ························· **4**:179a
Kaya Shirao ························· **4**:185a
Kitamura Kigin ························· **4**:227a
Kitao Shigemasa ··················· **4**:228a-228b
Konishi Raizan ························· **4**:270a
Kubota Mantarō ··················· **4**:301a-301b
Masaoka Shiki ··················· **5**:123b-124a
Matsue Shigeyori ······················· **5**:133a
Matsumura Goshun ······················· **5**:138a
Matsunaga Teitoku ··············· **5**:138b-139a
Miura Chora ························· **5**:215a
Mizuhara Shūōshi ······················· **5**:225b
Morikawa Kyoroku ······················· **5**:250a
Mukai Kyorai ························· **5**:262a
Murakami Kijō ··················· **5**:266a-266b
Naitō Jōsō ························· **5**:311a
Nakamura Kusatao ······················· **5**:315a
Nakarai Bokuyō ························· **5**:317b
Nonoguchi Ryūho ··················· **6**:34b-35a
Nozawa Bonchō ························· **6**:42a
Ochi Etsujin ························· **6**:59b
Ogiwara Seisensui ······················· **6**:70b
Okanishi Ichū ························· **6**:80b
Ōshima Ryōta ························· **6**:126a
Ōsuga Otsuji ························· **6**:127b
Ozaki Hōsai ························· **6**:139a
Satō Nempuku ························· **7**:28a
Sugiyama Sampū ························· **7**:259a
Takahama Kyoshi ··················· **7**:311a-311b
Takai Kitō ························· **7**:313b-314a
Takano Sujū ························· **7**:317a-317b
Takarai Kikaku ························· **7**:318a
Takebe Ayatari ··················· **7**:321a-321b
Takii Kōsaku ························· **7**:326b
Taneda Santōka ························· **7**:340a
Tan Taigi ························· **7**:344b-345a
Uejima Onitsura ························· **8**:127a
Yamaguchi Seishi ··················· **8**:295a-295b
Yamaguchi Sodō ························· **8**:295b
Yamazaki Sōkan ························· **8**:331a
Yasuhara Teishitsu ······················· **8**:318b
Yokoi Yayū ························· **8**:331b
Hairstyles ········ **2**:38a; **3**:82a-83b; **4**:127b
aristocratic ························· **3**:82a
Chinese influence ······················· **3**:82b
clothing ························· **1**:332b
combs ························· **1**:337a
Heian period (794-1185) ················ **3**:82b
kanzashi ························· **4**:154b
samurai ························· **3**:82b-83b
Tokugawa shogunate (1603-1868) ··· **3**:83a
Western influence ······················· **3**:83a
Haishō hitosuji 廃娼ひとすじ ······ **4**:301b
Haitoku no mesu ············· 背徳のメス ········ **4**:316b
Haitōrei ··········· 廃刀令 ·· **1**:89a; **3**:83b
Dampatsurei ························· **2**:72a
Haiya-bushi ······ ハイヤ節 ········ **2**:301b
Haiyūza ························· **7**:113b
Haji (shame) ······················· **3**:83b-84a
Hajibe ··········· 土師部 ········· **1**:147b
Haji Seiji ········· 土師清二 ········· **3**:84a
Haji ware ··········· 土師器 **1**:258a; **2**:305b; **3**:84a-84b; **7**:30b, 256a
archaeological dating ··················· **3**:84b
characteristics ··················· **3**:84a-84b
functions ························· **3**:84a-84b
jar ························· **3**:*84b*
kofun deposits ························· **4**:245b
rokuro ························· **6**:335b
typological studies ······················· **1**:79a
Hakamada Satomi ············· 袴田里見 ········· **4**:11b
Hakamagoshi ········ 袴腰 ······· **1**:183a
Hakase ························· **3**:84b; **4**:140a
Hakata. 博多 *See* **Fukuoka**
Hakata Dontaku ············ 博多どんたく ········· **3**:85a
Hakata merchants ············ 博多商人 ········· **3**:85a
tally trade ······················· **7**:331b-332a
Hakata Station film decision ··· **3**:85a-85b
"Hakidame" ··········· 塵溜 ········ **4**:179b
Hakkōdasan ····· 八甲田山 ········· **3**:85b
Hakkō Hikka Incident ············ 白虹筆禍事件 ········ **6**:120a
Hakkō ichiu ······ 八紘一宇 ········· **3**:85b
Hakoda Rokusuke ············ 箱田六輔 ········· **8**:88a
Hakodate ··········· 函館 ········· **3**:85b
Goryōkaku ························· **3**:*85a*
Hakodate bugyō · 箱館奉行 ········· **3**:86a
Hakodate Dock Co, Ltd ··············· **3**:86a
Hakone ··········· 箱根 ········· **3**:86a
Hakone Canal ··· 箱根用水 ········· **3**:86a
Hakone Museum of Art ·· **3**:86a-86b; **7**:56a
Hakone no Seki ··· 箱根関 ·· **3**:86b; **7**:57a
Hakone Open-Air Museum **3**:87a; **5**:279b
Hakone Pass ······ 箱根峠 ········· **3**:87a
Hakoneyama ······ 箱根山 · **2**:347b; **3**:87a; **8**:194a
Hakoniwa ························· **3**:87a
Hako otoko ··········· 箱男 ········· **1**:3a
Hakozaki Shrine ··· 筥崎宮 ········· **3**:87a
Hakuba ··········· 白馬 ········· **3**:87a
Hakubakai (White Horse Society) ········· 白馬会 ······ **2**:345b; **3**:87a-87b; **8**:328a

Hakubakai exhibition **1**:69a
Hakubunkan **3**:87b
children's literature **1**:279b
Ōhashi Sahei **6**:73b
Ozaki Kōyō **4**:198b-199a
Hakubyōga 白描画 **3**:87b
precedents **3**:87b
Hakugō shugi (White Australia) **1**:119a
Hakuhō culture 白鳳文化 **3**:87b-88a
Hakuhōdō **1**:17a
Hakuhōdō, Inc **3**:88a
founder **7**:56b
Seki Hironao **7**:56b
Hakuhō period **6**:175b
Hakui 羽咋 **3**:88a
Hakuin 白隠 **1**:179b, *193a*, 194a; **3**:88a-88b; **7**:89b
calligraphy **3**:88b
paintings **3**:88b
Rinzai sect **6**:320a
teachings **3**:88a
writings **3**:88a
Hakurai **3**:88b
Hakusan 白山 **3**:88b
Hakusan National Park 白山国立公園 **2**:364a; **3**:88b-89a
Hakusan Volcanic Zone 白山火山帯 **3**:89a
Hakushaku fujin (The Countess) 伯爵夫人 **6**:221a
Hakusho **8**:251b
Hakusōrei 薄葬令 **7**:296b
Hakusukinoe, Battle of 白村江の戦 **1**:4a; **3**:89a; **7**:260a, 263a
Paekche **6**:146b
Taika Reform **7**:296b
Yamato's foreign relations **4**:277b
Hakuyōkyū 白羊宮 **7**:279b
Halberd heads **1**:175a
Hall, John W. **4**:41b; **5**:228b
Hamada 浜田 **3**:89a; **7**:101a
Hamada Hikozō 浜田彦蔵 **3**:89a-89b
Hamada Kōsaku 浜田耕作 **1**:77a; **3**:89b
Hamada Shōji 浜田庄司 **2**:294a; **3**:89b
Hamada Yahyōe 浜田弥兵衛 **3**:89b-90a; **7**:255b
Hama Detached Palace Garden 浜離宮庭園 **3**:90a
Hamaguchi Osachi 浜口雄幸 **3**:90a; **7**:88b
Hamaguchi Osachi cabinet
Dan Takuma **2**:77b
Nakano Seigō **5**:316a-316b
Hamaguchi Yūkō. 浜口雄幸 *See* **Hamaguchi Osachi**
Hamaguri Gomon Incident 蛤御門の変 **3**:90a; **5**:317b
Kido Takayoshi **4**:202b
Shimonoseki Bombardment **7**:106a
Shinsengumi **7**:124b
Hamakita 浜北 **3**:90b
Hamamatsu 浜松 **3**:90b
Nippon Gakki Company **3**:*90b*
Hamamatsu Chūnagon monogatari 浜松中納言物語 **3**:90b-91a; **7**:257b
theme **3**:90b
Hamana, Lake 浜名湖 **3**:91a
Hamao Arata 浜尾新 **3**:91a
Hamaya and Hamayumi **3**:91a
Hamayū (*Chrinum asiaticum* var. *japonicum*) **3**:91a
Hamayumi **3**:91a
Hamba seido **3**:91b
conditions **3**:91b
Hambatsu (domain clique) 藩閥 **1**:147b; **3**:91b-92a; **4**:340a
influence on government **3**:91b-92a
use **3**:92a
Hambun hiraita mado 半分開いた窓 **6**:112a
Hamlet **7**:112b
Hammotsu 判物 **2**:*100a-100b*
Hampon **2**:295b
Han (domain) 藩 **3**:92b
common features **3**:92b
productivity **3**:92b
size **3**:92b
"Hana" 鼻 **1**:45a
Hanabachi (bees) **1**:149a
Hanabatake Kyōjō 花畠教場 **3**:265b
Hanabusa Itchō 英一蝶 **3**:92b-93a
Hanabusazōshi (A Garland of Tales) 英草紙 **8**:336b
Hanada Kiyoteru 花田清輝 **3**:93a; **5**:13b
Hanafuda **3**:93a-93b; **6**:192a
origin **3**:93a-93b
Hanagatami 花筐 **2**:76b
Hanagoi (carp) **1**:244a
Hanagoyomi hasshōjin 花暦八笑人 **6**:359a
Hanaike **1**:136a
Hanai Takuzō 花井卓蔵 **3**:94a
Hanakago **1**:136a
Hana Karuta **3**:5b, 93a
Hanako, Princess 華子妃 **3**:*277a*
Hanamaki 花巻 **3**:94a
Hana Matsuri 花祭 **2**:260a; **3**:94a
yudate rites **4**:107b
Hanami **3**:94a-94b; **4**:381a
flower viewing (Ueno Park) **3**:*94b*
Hanamichi **4**:91a, 93a-94a, *95a*, 95b; **7**:272a
Hanamori 花守 **8**:334a
Hana no byakkotai 花の白虎隊 **4**:174b
Hana no sugao 花の素顔 **6**:78a
Hanaoka Seishū 華岡青洲 **3**:94b
Hanasaka jijii 花咲翁 **3**:94b
Hana saku minato 花咲く港 **4**:207a
Hanasanjin 鼻山人 **3**:94b-95a
Hanashi (stories) **6**:282a
Hanashōbu **4**:22b
Hanawa Hokiichi 塙保己一 **1**:154a; **3**:95a
Gunsho ruijū **3**:69b
historiography **3**:155b
Hanayagiryū 花柳流 **2**:*74b*
Hanayagi Shigeka 花柳茂香 **2**:*74b*
Hanayagi Shōtarō 花柳章太郎 **3**:95a
shimpa **7**:108a
Hanayagi Suzushi 花柳寿々紫 **2**:76a
Hanazono, Emperor 花園天皇 **5**:291a
Hanazono Tennō shinki 花園天皇宸記 **3**:95a
Handa 半田 **3**:95a
Handen shūju system 班田収授法 **2**:104a; **3**:95a-96a, 162b; **4**:76a; **7**:89a-89b, 296a
abandonment of land **1**:303b
breakdown **3**:95b-96a
Chinese model **3**:95a-95b
economy **2**:147a
keichō **4**:187b
ko (household) unit **4**:233b-234a
process **3**:95b
regulations **3**:95b
ritsuryō system **6**:326b
ryōshu **6**:353a
shōen **7**:155b
Handicapped
aid **7**:212a
discrimination **5**:195b
schools **7**:241b
Handicraft industry **2**:150a
taxes **7**:239b
Handscrolls (emakimono) **2**:198a-200a
format **2**:198a-199a
history **2**:199a-200a
painting **6**:150a
Han dynasty **4**:55b
Haneda Airport **5**:371a
Han'ei sembai 藩営専売 **3**:96a-96b
Kaiho Seiryō **4**:110a
Hanetsuki **3**:77a, 96b
Hanging scroll **4**:116a
"Hangman, The" (Maedakō Hiroichirō) **5**:80a
Han'gŭl **3**:96b; **4**:289b, 291a
Hani Gorō 羽仁五郎 **3**:96b
Hani Motoko 羽仁もと子 **2**:344a; **3**:96b-97a
publications **3**:96b
Shin Kyōiku Undō **7**:121b
Hani Susumu 羽仁進 **2**:274a; **3**:97a-97b
documentary techniques **3**:97a-97b
films **3**:97a-97b
Haniwa 埴輪 **1**:75b, 77a, 147b, 197a-197b, 257b; **3**:97b-98a, *98b, 99a*; **7**:*143a*
chokkomon **1**:299b
falconry **2**:241b
kofun **4**:244b
origins **3**:98a; **4**:84b
placement patterns **3**:97b-98a
ritual function **3**:98a
surface detail **3**:97b
Haniya Yutaka 埴谷雄高 **3**:98a-98b
Hankanfu 藩翰譜 **1**:72b; **3**:98b-99a
Hanko. *See* **Seals**
Hankyū Corporation **3**:99a-99b; **4**:188b
Hankyū Department Stores, Inc **3**:99b
Hankyū Electric Railway Co **4**:188b
Hannō 飯能 **3**:99b
Han pronunciation **4**:148a
Hanren **4**:123b
Hansatsu 藩札 **3**:99b; **5**:*242a-242b*
economy **2**:150a
Hanshan (Han-shan) and Shide (Shih-te). *See* **Kanzan and Jittoku**
Hansharo 反射炉 **3**:99b
Hanshi **4**:196a
Hanshichi torimonochō 半七捕物帳 **6**:80b
Hanshin Industrial Zone **3**:100a; **8**:326b
Ōsaka **6**:120a
Han shu (History of the Former Han Dynasty) **8**:197a
Hansŏng **6**:146a
Hansŏng sunbo **4**:280b
Hanwa Co, Ltd **3**:100a
Hanwen **4**:123b
Hanyū 羽生 **3**:100a
Hanzei 半済 **3**:100a
Ashikaga Yoshimitsu **1**:101b
Kaei sandai ki **4**:101b
Muromachi shogunate **5**:272a
shōen **7**:158a
Hara **3**:100a-100b
Harada Magoshichirō 原田孫七郎 **3**:100b; **4**:369a
Harada Naojirō 原田直次郎 **3**:100b

Harada Yoshito 原田淑人 3:100b
Harae 3:100b-101b
 atonement 3:100b
  offerings 3:100b
 purification rite 3:100b-101a
 variant forms 3:101a-101b
Haragei 3:100a
Hara Katsurō 原勝郎 3:156b
Hara Kei. 原敬 *See* **Hara Takashi**
Harakiri 3:101b-102a; 4:84b; 7:68b, 261a
 ritual 3:101b
 Seppuku 7:68b
Haramachi 原町 3:102a
Hara Martinho 原マルチノ 3:102a
Hara Setsuko 原節子 2:*271a*; 3:102a-102b
Hara Takashi 原敬 3:102b-103b, 198a
 historical significance 3:102b
 party leader 3:102b
 Rikken Seiyūkai 6:315a-315b
 Shandong (Shantung) Question 7:77b
 suffrage 3:103a
Hara Tamiki 原民喜 3:103b
Hara Yasusaburō 原安三郎 3:103b
Harbin 3:103b
Hare 2:253b-254a; 4:186a; 6:362a-362b
Hare of Inaba 5:293b
Hares. *See* **Rabbits**
Hari 1:10b
Haribako 3:103b
Hari kuyō 針供養 3:104a
Hari kuyō observance 2:*260b*
Harima industrial area 3:146b
Harima Plain 播磨平野 3:139a
Harima school 播磨節 4:77a
Harima Sea 播磨灘 3:104a
Haring, Douglas 4:38b
Harinoki Pass 針ノ木峠 3:104a
Harivarman 4:71a
Harquebus 3:140a
Harriman, E. H. 4:268a
Harris, Merriman Colbert 3:104a
Harris, Thomas Lake 1:73a; 3:104a-104b; 5:306b
Harris, Townsend 3:104b-105a; 7:104b
 Harris Treaty 3:105a
 Heusken, Henry C. J. 3:128b
 Opening of Japan 5:155b
Harris Treaty 2:319b; 3:105a
 fumie prohibition 2:368a
 Ii Naosuke 3:263b
 Inoue Kiyonao 3:310b
 Iwakura Tomomi and 3:360a
 Iwase Tadanari 3:363a
 Kanrin maru 4:151b
 Kawaji Toshiakira 4:179b
 Kōmei, Emperor 4:266a
 Muragaki Norimasa 5:265b
 Nakahama Manjirō 5:313a-313b
 national flag 5:339a
 provisions 3:105a
 shogunal succession 5:156a
 Tokugawa Nariaki 8:52a
 United States 8:154b
 Yokohama 8:329b
Hart, H.L.A. 4:85b
Hartmann, Carl Sadakichi 3:105a-105b
Haru ichiban 4:8a
Haru Koma 春駒 7:250a
Haruma Wage 波留麻和解 3:105b; 8:242b
 Inamura Sampaku 3:282b
Haruna, Lake 榛名湖 3:105b
Harunasan 榛名山 3:106a; 7:86a
Harunobu 春信 3:106a-106b; 5:18a; 7:84a
 pictorial calendars 3:106a-106b
 techniques 3:106a
 works 3:106a
Haru no shiro 春の城 1:21a
Harusame monogatari (Tales of the Spring Rain) 春雨物語 5:48b; 8:126b
"Haru wa basha ni notte" (Spring, Riding in a Carriage) 春は馬車に乗つて 8:332a
Harvard Journal of Asiatic Studies 2:196b
Harvard-Yenching Institute 2:196b
Harvest rites 1:23a
Hase 初瀬 3:106b
Hasebe Kotondo 長谷部言人 3:106b; 4:74a
 physical characteristics of Japanese people 4:35a
Hasedera 長谷寺 3:106b-107a
 Shingon sect 7:115a
Hasegawa Kazuo 長谷川一夫 3:107a
Hasegawa Kiyoshi 長谷川清 3:107a
Hasegawa Nyozekan 長谷川如是閑 1:155b; 3:107a
Hasegawa Roka 長谷川路可 3:107a-107b
Hasegawa school 長谷川派 3:107b; 4:146a
 founding 3:108b-109a
 Kanō school rivalry 4:147b
Hasegawa Shin 長谷川伸 3:107b-108a
 "Kutsukake Tokijirō" 7:121a
 literary genre 3:107b
 "Mabuta no haha" 7:121a
 "Seki no Yatappe" 7:121a
 shin kabuki 4:92a
 Shinkokugeki 7:121a
 themes used 3:108a
Hasegawa Shirō 長谷川四郎 3:108a
Hasegawa Tai 長谷川泰 3:108a
Hasegawa Tatsunosuke 長谷川辰之助 2:375b
Hasegawa Tenkei 長谷川天渓 3:108a-108b; 5:13a
Hasegawa Tōhaku 長谷川等伯 3:108b, 182a, *307a*; 7:*41a-41b*, 42b, 70a
 Hasegawa school 3:107b
 ink painting 3:108b
 Pine Trees 3:*108b*
 works 3:108b
Hasekura Tsunenaga 支倉常長 3:*109a*
 French-Japanese relations 2:330a
 Vatican expedition 4:369a
Hashiguchi Goyō 橋口五葉 3:109a-109b
Hashikuiiwa 橋杭岩 3:109b
Hashima (city) 羽島 3:109b
Hashima (island) 端島 3:109b
Hashimoto 橋本 3:109b
Hashimoto Gahō 橋本雅邦 3:109b
 Shimomura Kanzan 7:105a-105b
 works 3:109b
Hashimoto Kansetsu 橋本関雪 3:110a
Hashimoto Kingorō 橋本欣五郎 3:110a
 Sakurakai (Cherry Blossom Society) 7:5a
Hashimoto Sanai 橋本左内 3:110a-110b; 7:3b
 Ansei purge 1:63b
 fukoku kyōehi 2:360b
Hashimoto Shinkichi 橋本進吉 3:110b
 orthographic studies 4:134b
Hashimoto Shinobu 橋本忍 3:110b
Hashimoto Toshio 橋本敏雄 1:124b
Hashira-e (pillar prints) 柱絵 8:141a
Hassōan 八窓庵 5:333a
Hasu 5:73b-74a
Hasuda 蓮田 3:111a
Hata. *See* **Flags and banners**
Hata family 秦氏 3:111a
 Aya family 1:125b
 Inari 3:283a
 kikajin 4:205b
 Kōryūji built for 4:294a
 Nagaokakyō 5:303b
Hatakebiraki 7:109b
Hatakenaoshi shinkai 7:109b
Hatakeyama family 畠山氏 3:111a; 7:83b
 kanrei 4:151a
Hatakeyama Kinenkan 3:111a-111b
Hatakeyama Kizan 畠山箕山 7:95b-96a
Hatakeyama Masanaga 畠山政長 8:303b
Hatakeyama Museum 3:111a-111b; 5:276b
Hatakeyama Shigetada 畠山重忠 3:111b
Hatakeyama Yoshinari 畠山義就 8:303b
Hatakeyama Zekan 畠山是閑 2:144a
Hatamoto 旗本 1:131b; 2:340b; 3:111b-112a
 decline 3:111b-112a
 genealogies 4:138a
 heirs 3:111b
 kanjō gimmiyaku 4:144a
 kobushin 4:239a
 registers 1:206a
 ryōshu 6:353a
 Shōheikō 7:162a
 status 3:111b
Hatamoto ryō 8:10a
Hatamoto yakko 旗本奴 3:112a
 behavior 3:112a
Hatanagi Daiichi Dam 畑薙第1ダム 2:73b
Hatano Kanji 波多野完治 3:112a
Hata no Kimi Irogu 秦公伊呂具 3:283a
Hatano Seiichi 波多野精一 3:112b
Hata Sahachirō 秦佐八郎 3:112b
Hata Toyokichi 秦豊吉 3:112b
Hatogaya 鳩ケ谷 3:112b
Hatoyama Haruko 鳩山春子 3:112b
Hatoyama Hideo 鳩山秀夫 3:112b-113a
Hatoyama Ichirō 鳩山一郎 1:97b; 3:113a; 4:386a; 7:92a
 founding Liberal Party (Jiyūtō) 4:387b
 Liberal Democratic Party 4:386a
 Nihon Jiyūtō (Japan Liberal Party) 4:65b
 Nihon Minshutō (Japan Democratic Party) 5:381a
 Prime minister 3:113a
Hatoyama Kazuo 鳩山和夫 3:113a
Hatsuboku 溌墨 3:305b
Hatsukaichi 廿日市 3:113b
Hatsukari 初雁 1:237a
Hatsumōde 2:*259b*
Hatsuse. 初瀬 *See* **Hase**
Hatsushima 初島 3:113b
Hatsusugata 初姿 4:296a
Hatsuuma 初午 2:260a; 3:113b
Hatta, Mohammad 3:113b; 7:253b
Hattori Dohō 服部土芳 3:114a
Hattori Kintarō 服部金太郎 3:113b; 4:200b
Hattori Nankaku 服部南郭 3:113b-114a
Hattori Ransetsu 服部嵐雪 3:114a
Hattori Shirō 服部四郎 3:114a

Japanese language studies 4:31b
orthographic studies 4:134b
Hattori Shisō 服部之総 3:114a
Shinjinkai 7:115b
Hattori Tohō 服部土芳 3:114a; 5:16a
Hausknecht, Emile 3:114a-114b
Hauta 端唄 4:64b
Hawaii
Japanese immigration 2:200b; 4:13b
Japanese labor disputes 3:53a
Hawai-Marē oki Kaisen (The War at Sea from Hawaii to Malaya) ハワイ・マレー沖海戦 8:111a
Hawks and eagles 3:114b
Hayabusa 隼 3:114b
Hayachinesan 早池峰山 3:114b
Hayagawari 4:94a
Hayaishi Osamu 早石修 3:114b
Hayakawa Sesshū 早川雪洲 3:115a; 4:127b
Hayama 葉山 3:115a
Hayama Yoshiki 葉山嘉樹 3:115a-115b
Bungei sensen 1:209b
labor activities 3:115a-115b
proletarian literature movement 6:255a
work 3:115a-115b
Hayami Gyoshū 速水御舟 3:115b
Hayariuta はやり唄 4:296a
Hayashi 3:115b; 4:99a
Hayashi Akira. *See* **Hayashi Fukusai**
Hayashi Fubō 林不忘 3:116a
Hayashi Fukusai 林復斎 3:116a
Hayashi Fumiko 林芙美子 2:274a; 3:116a-116b; 7:25a
childhood 3:116a-116b
poetry 3:116a
works 3:116a-116b
Hayashi Fusao 林房雄 3:116b; 7:103b
Shinjinkai 7:115b
Hayashi Gahō 林鵞峰 1:154a; 3:116b; 8:295b
historiography 3:154b
Hayashi Hōkō 林鳳岡 3:116b
Hayashi Jussai 林述斎 3:116b-117a; 7:27a
Hayashikane Shōten. *See* **Taiyō Fishery Co, Ltd**
Hayashi Razan 林羅山 2:241a; 3:117a; 5:16b; 7:274b; 8:290a
Fujiwara Seika 2:358b
historiography 3:154b
Kan'ei shoka keizu den 4:138a
promotion of Zhu Xi Neo-Confucianism 3:117a
Tokugawa shogunate service 3:117a
works 3:117a
Hayashi Senjūrō 林銑十郎 3:117b-118a; 7:28a
Hayashi Senjūrō cabinet 8:337a
Hayashi Shihei 林子平 3:118a
naval defense 3:118a
Hayashi Tadasu 林董 3:118a
Hayashi Yūzō 林有造 3:118a-118b
Hayashizaki Jinsuke Shigenobu 林崎甚助重信 3:253a
Hayato 隼人 3:118b
dialects 2:91b
Kagoshima Prefecture 4:105b
Hayatozuka 隼人塚 3:118b
Hazama-Gumi, Ltd 3:118b
Hazama Shigetomi 間重富 3:309a
Haze (gobies) 3:38b
Headgear 3:118b-119b
categories 3:118b
ceremonial 3:118b
functional 3:119a
Western influence 3:119a-119b
Headquarters for Pacification and Defense 1:296a
Health and Welfare, Ministry of 7:206a
Health care system 3:119b-120b
health care activity 3:120a
medical education system 3:120a
medical facilities 3:120a-120b
medical services 3:120a
National Health Administration 3:119b-120a
personnel 3:120a
present conditions and priorities for future 3:120b
Western influence 3:119b
Health Insurance Law (Kenkō Hoken Hō) 5:144b; 8:270a
Health insurance system 4:47a
Hearken to the Ocean's Voice! 4:206a
Hearn, Lafcadio 2:41b; 3:120b-121a
works 3:120b-121a
Hearst, William Randolph 8:323a
"Heart Learning" 7:111b-112a
Heart Mountain Relocation Center 3:121a
Heaven 2:80b; 3:121a-121b
Heban shi shinrigaku 奚般氏心理学 6:260b
Hebei-Chahar (Hopeh-Chahar) Political Council. *See* **Ji-Cha (Chi-Ch'a) Autonomous Political Council**
Hebi 7:206b
Hebi Hime sama (Snake Princess) 蛇姫様 8:289a
Heco, Joseph 3:89a
Heda Museum of Shipbuilding and Folk Arts 6:270b
Hedonism in art 2:378a
Hegurajima 舳倉島 3:121b
Heianchō bumpō shi (History of Heian Period Grammar) 平安朝文法史 8:290a
Heian history. *See* **History of Japan**
Heian ibun (Documentary Remains of the Heian Period) 平安遺文 2:104b
Heiankyō 平安京 2:350a; 3:121b-122b; 4:128a-128b, 334b; 5:303b
administration 3:122a
crime 3:122a
design 3:121b-122b
inhabitants 3:122a
urban life 8:176a 177a
urban planning 8:179b
Heian literature. *See* **Literature**
Heian period 平安時代 3:122b
Heian Shrine 平安神宮 3:122b; 4:336a
Heibonsha, Ltd, Publishers 3:122b
founder 7:105b
Heichū monogatari 平仲物語 3:122b-123a; 5:246a
kakekotoba 4:115b
monogatari bungaku 5:246a
Heifuku Kumiuchi 4:82a
Heigenji 平間寺 4:183a
Heiji Disturbance 平治の乱 3:123a; 7:96b
Fujiwara no Michinori, death of 2:353a
Go-Shirakawa, Emperor 3:49a
Minamoto no Yorimasa 5:180b
Minamoto no Yoshitomo 5:182b
samurai 7:7b
Taira-Minamoto War 7:299b
Taira no Kiyomori 7:301a
Taira no Shigemori 7:302a
warrior government 8:229a
Heiji monogatari 平治物語 3:69a, 123a-123b; 5:43b, 246a
gunki monogatari 3:69a-69b
Heiji monogatari ekotoba (Tale of Heiji scrolls) 平治物語絵詞 6:152a
Heiji monogatari emaki 平治物語絵巻 1:137a; 3:123b
episodes illustrated 3:123b
styles 3:123b
Heiji no Ran. *See* **Heiji Disturbance**
Heijōkyō 平城京 2:350a; 3:124a; 5:303b
artifacts 3:124a
design 3:124a
Kizugawa and 4:233b
Nara National Research Institute of Cultural Properties 5:333a-333b
temples 3:124a
urban life 8:176a, 177a
urban planning 8:179b
Heijō Palace site 平城宮址 5:334a
Heike monogatari 平家物語 1:40a, 294a; 2:101b, 241a; 3:124a-125a; 5:43b, 246a; 7:270a, 299a
gunki monogatari 3:69a-69b
Buddhist doctrine 3:125a
chanting 3:125a
biwa hōshi 1:157b
heikyoku 3:125a
episodes 3:124b
Giōji 3:33b
gunki monogatari 3:69a-69b
historiography 3:154a
Jakkōin 4:1a
Jesuit mission press 4:52a
Nō 6:26a
ochiudo legends 6:60a
otogi-zōshi 6:130a
Taira no Kiyomori 7:301a
Tomoe Gozen 8:73a
travel diaries 8:105a
Heikyoku 平曲 2:301a; 3:125a
Nasu no Yoichi 5:336a
repertoire 3:125a
Heimin 平民 3:125b; 7:151a
shi-nō-kō-shō 7:122b
Heiminsha 平民社 1:72a; 3:125b
Fukuda Hideko 2:362a
Ishikawa Sanshirō 3:344a
Kōtoku Shūsui 3:125b; 4:279b
newspapers 3:125b
Russo-Japanese War 6:347a
Sakai Toshihiko 6:377a
Heimin shimbun 平民新聞 1:2a; 3:125b; 8:296b
pacifism 6:144a
Russo-Japanese War 6:346b
suspension 1:252b
Heimin shugi 8:60b
Heimon 3:126a
Heinō bunri 兵農分離 3:187b; 4:194a; 7:285a
Heirs, adopted 1:14b
Heishi. 平氏 *See* **Taira family**
Heiwa (Peace) 平和 4:174b
Heiwa Mondai Danwa Kai (Discussion Committee on the Problems of War) 6:144a, 145b
Heizei, Emperor. 平城天皇 *See* **Kusuko Incident**
Hekian 4:133b
Hekigotō kushū 碧梧桐句集 4:178a
Hekinan 碧南 3:126a
Hekisho 壁書 4:90a
Hekizan nichiroku 碧山日録 3:126a
Hell 2:80b; 3:126a
Emma 2:201b

Hemeden ·········· 変目伝 ········ **3**:151a
Hemp ································ **1**:91b
Henderson, Harold G ········ **3**:126a-126b
Henjō ·············· 遍昭 · **3**:126b; **7**:13a
Kokinshū ·························· **4**:245b
Rokkasen ························· **6**:334b
Hennen kiryaku · · 編年紀略 ········ **5**:381a
Hentai kambun · · 変体漢文 · · **3**:126b-127a; **7**:230a
characteristics ······················ **3**:127a
styles ······························ **3**:126b
used in *Kojiki* ······················ **4**:251a
Hepburn, James Curtis ····· **1**:150b, 171a, 308a; **3**:127a-127b
Hepburn system ···················· **6**:335b
Herbicides ·························· **6**:309a
Herbs and spices ·········· **2**:306b; **3**:127b
Hermit, The ························ **3**:328b
Heroic tales ················· **5**:296a-296b
Heroin abuse ························ **2**:134a
Herons [(sagi) family Ardeidae] ··················· **3**:127b-128a
Hero worship ········· **3**:128a; **8**:311a-311b
characteristics ······················ **3**:128a
ochiudo legends ····················· **6**:60a
Herring [(nishin) *Clupea pallasi*] · · **2**:285b; **3**:128a
Hetsumiya Shrine ················· 辺津宮 · · · **5**:264b-265a
Hettsui ····························· **4**:120b
He-Umezu (Ho-Umezu) Agreement ········ 梅津-何応欽協定 **2**:126b; **3**:128b
He Yingqin (Ho Ying-ch'in) ······· **3**:128b
Umezu Yoshijirō ···················· **8**:147b
Heusken, Henry C.J. ·············· **3**:128b
Harris, Townsend ··················· **3**:104a
Heya (sumō) ················ **7**:272b-273a
He Yingqin (Ho Ying-ch'in) ······· **3**:128b
Hiai no kōchō · 悲哀の高調 ·········· **8**:116a
Hibachi ······· **1**:267a; **2**:371b; **3**:128b-129a
Hibakusha ·········· 被爆者 · · **1**:111a, 114b
Hibakusha Special Welfare Law · · · **1**:110b
Hibara, Lake ······· 檜原湖 ········ **3**:129a
Hibari ······························ **4**:368b
Hibi Ōsuke ······ 日比翁助 ········ **3**:129a
Hibiya Incendiary Incident · · **3**:129a-129b; **4**:274a
Taishō democracy ·················· **7**:304b
Hibiya Park ···· 日比谷公園 ········ **3**:129b
Hibiya Yakiuchi Jiken. 日比谷焼打事件 *See* **Hibiya Incendiary Incident**
Hiburishima ········ 日振島 ········ **3**:129b
Hichiriki ·························· **3**:129b
gagaku ······························ **3**:1b
kagura uta ·························· **4**:108a
Hida Folklore Village ·············· **3**:129b
Hidaka Mountains ················ 日高山脈 · · **3**:130a; **4**:9b
Hida-Kisogawa Quasi-National Park ······ 飛驒木曽川国定公園 ········ **5**:319a
Hida Mountains · 飛驒山脈 ········ **3**:130a
Hidari Jingorō ··· 左甚五郎 ········ **3**:130a
Hidari Sachiko ····· 左幸子 ······· **2**:*274b*; **3**:130a-130b
director ···························· **3**:130b
films ······························· **3**:130a
Hiden'in ··········· 悲田院 · **3**:130b; **7**:74a
Kōfukuji building ·················· **4**:243b
Kōmyō, Empress ··················· **4**:268b
seyakuin ···························· **7**:74a
Hie
Shintō ······························ **7**:126b
Hieda no Are ···· 稗田阿礼 ······· **3**:130b; **6**:112a
kataribe ···························· **4**:166b
Kojiki ······························· **4**:251a
Hieizan ············· 比叡山 **2**:220a; **3**:130b; **7**:333a
Hie Shrine ······· 日吉大社, 日枝神社 · · **3**:130b-131a; **4**:137a; **6**:133b; **7**:91a, 180a
annual festival ······················ **3**:131b
jinnin ······························· **4**:59b
religious symbolism ················ **6**:295b
Sannō Festival ······················ **7**:15a
Shintō architecture ················· **7**:133b
Hifuryaku ·········· 秘府略 ········ **1**:151b
Higaki kaisen (lozenge-fenced cargo ship) ·········· 菱垣廻船 **4**:112b; **7**:*144b*
Higambana [(herb) *Lycoris radiata*] ······························· **3**:131a
Higambana (Equinox Flower) ·········· 彼岸花 ········ **6**:141b
Higamu ······························ **7**:275b
Higan ················ 彼岸 · · · **2**:22a, 260a; **3**:131a-131b; **7**:276b
Higashi Ajia bunkaken
Higashi Hiroshima · 東広島 ········ **3**:131b
Higashi Honganji 東本願寺 · · · **3**:131b-132a
architecture ················ **3**:131b-132a
Higashikuni Naruhiko ············· 東久邇稔彦 · · **2**:3b; **3**:132a; **7**:92a
Higashi Kurume · 東久留米 ········ **3**:132a
Higashi Matsuura Peninsula ···· 東松浦半島 ········ **3**:132a
Higashi Matsuyama 東松山 ········ **3**:132a
Higashi Murayama · 東村山 ········ **3**:132a
Higashine ··········· 東根 ········ **3**:132a
Higashi Nihon ······ 東日本 ········ **2**:142b
Higashi Ōsaka ····· 東大阪 ··· **3**:132a-132b
Higashi Shinakai · 東シナ海 ········ **2**:142a
Higashiyama culture 東山文化 **1**:101a; **3**:132b
Higashi Yamato ···· 東大和 ········ **3**:132b
Higashiyama Zoological Gardens · **8**:379b
Higeki kigeki ···· 悲劇喜劇 ········ **3**:132b
High courts ······· **3**:138a; **4**:80b-81a, 190a
High Energy Physics, National Laboratory for ····························· **3**:133a
Higher education ··········· **3**:133a-135a
and culture ················· **3**:134a-135a
development ················ **3**:133a-133b
government institutions ·········· **3**:133a
Imperial University ··············· **3**:133a
post-World War II ················ **3**:133b
private institutions ··············· **3**:133a
finance ····························· **3**:134a
multilayered multisector structure · **3**:133b
private vs public sector ···· **3**:133b-134a
types of schools ···················· **3**:133b
Higher Girls' School Order in 1899 **8**:260a
Higher schools ····················· **3**:135a
Highlands
Ebino Kōgen ······················· **2**:143b
Hachimantai ························ **3**:74b
Hiruzen Kōgen ····················· **3**:151b
Kirigamine ························· **4**:220b
Konsen ····························· **4**:275b
Kujū Kōgen ························ **4**:303b
Midagahara ························ **5**:166b
Nasu Kōgen ················ **5**:335b-336a
Sengokuhara ························ **7**:64a
Senjōgahara ························ **7**:65b
Shiga Kōgen ························ **7**:89b
Sugadaira ·························· **7**:256b
Tateshina Kōgen ···················· **7**:349a
High schools (Kōtō gakkō) ········ **2**:195b
High Treason Incident of 1910 ······ **1**:2a; **2**:241b; **3**:135a-136a; **4**:345a; **6**:127b; **7**:241b, 281a; **8**:296b
Futsū Senkyo Kisei Dōmeikai
dissolution ························· **2**:376b
impact on intelligentsia ······ **3**:133b-134a
Kanno Suga ························ **4**:145b
Kōtoku Shūsui ······················ **4**:297b
prosecution's case ·········· **3**:135a-135b
Red Flag Incident ·················· **6**:285b
sentences ·················· **3**:135a-135b
Uemura Masahisa ··················· **8**:128a
Universal Manhood Suffrage Movement ······························· **8**:169a
Highways ··························· **6**:332b
Higuchi Ichiyō ··· 樋口一葉 · · **3**:136a-136b; **5**:11b
early career ················ **3**:136a-136b
later career and death ············· **3**:136b
works ······················ **3**:136a-136b
youthful literary interests ·········· **3**:136a
Higuma *(Ursus arctos)* ············ **1**:148b
Higurashi suzuri ··· 日暮硯 ········ **6**:106a
Hihyō ················· 批評 ········ **8**:298b
Hiikawa ··········· 斐伊川 ········ **3**:136b
Hijikawa ··········· 肱川 ········ **3**:136b
Hijiki [(alga) *Hizikia fusiformis*] ···· **3**:136b
Hijiri ················ **3**:136b-137a; **4**:299a
nembutsu ··························· **4**:67a
oshi ································ **6**:124b
"Hikage no hana" ·············· ひかげの花 ········ **7**:176a
Hikaku Sangensoku ·········· **3**:137a-137b
national defense ············ **5**:336b-338b
Hikan ················· 被官 ········ **3**:137b
Hikari ················· 光 ········ **3**:137b
Hikari to sono kaichō (Light and Its Harmony) ··········· 光とその諧調 ········ **6**:186a
Hikawa Shrine ··· 氷川神社 ········ **3**:137b
Hikeshi ············· 火消 ········ **3**:*137a*, 137b-138a
fireman's uniforms, traditional ························· **2**:280b-281a
Hikiate ······························ **4**:117a
Hikidemono ························ **3**:138a
Hikiita. *See* **Naruko**
Hikimawashi ······· 引回し ········ **3**:138a
Hikime Kagibana 引目鉤鼻 ·········· **3**:20b
Hikitsuke ··········· 引付 **3**:138a; **4**:122a
Hikitsukeshū ······· 引付衆 ········ **4**:122a
Hiki Yoshikazu · 比企能員 · · · **3**:138a-138b
assassination ························ **1**:51a
Hikone ·············· 彦根 ········ **3**:138b
Hikone byōbu ···· 彦根屛風 · · **2**:*377a*, 378a
Hikone domain ····· 彦根藩 ········ **3**:263a
Hikosan ············ 英彦山 ········ **3**:138b
Hikoshima ··········· 彦島 ········ **3**:138b
Hikyaku ············· 飛脚 · · · **3**:138b-139a
postal service ······················ **6**:229a
Hill, James Jerome ················ **3**:139a
Hill-on-the-plain castle (hirayamajiro) ······························· **1**:247b
Hills
Iimoriyama ························ **3**:262b
Kasugayama ························ **4**:164a
Kiyosumiyama ·············· **4**:232b-233a
Kunōzan ··························· **4**:310b
Kuramayama ······················· **4**:311b
Miwayama ························· **5**:216b
Myōkensan ························· **5**:290b
Nokogiriyama ························ **6**:32b
Ogurayama ·························· **6**:71b
Ōsakayama ················ **6**:123a-123b
Senjōsan ···························· **7**:66a
Shigisan ····························· **7**:92b
Shiroyama ·························· **7**:148a
Tama ······························· **7**:332b
Tennōzan ···························· **8**:8b
Togakushi Kōgen ···················· **8**:35b
Tōnomine ··························· **8**:75a

Yamato Sanzan 8:310b
Himachi and tsukimachi 3:139a
Hi Matsuri (Kurama Fire Festival) 火祭 2:*259a*; 4:311b
Himebachi (*ichneumons*) 1:149a
Himeji 姫路 3:139a
Himeji Castle 姫路城 1:*247a*; 3:139a
Himeji Plain 姫路平野 3:139a
Himemasu 4:321b
Himeyuri Butai 姫百合部隊 3:139b
Himi 氷見 3:139b
Himiko 卑弥呼 3:139b-140a, 160b; 8:305a-305b
Wei China 3:139b-140a
Wei zhi (Wei chih) 8:240a
Himitsu mandara jūjūshin ron 秘密曼荼羅十住心論 4:83b
Himmin shinri no kenkyū 貧民心理の研究 4:104a
Hinagu Hot Spring 日奈久温泉 8:320a
Hina Matsuri 雛祭 2:127b-128a
Hinatsu Kōnosuke 日夏耿之介 3:140a
Hinawajū 火縄銃 3:140a
Hinin 非人 3:140a; 7:62a
shi-nō-kō-shō 7:122b
Hino 日野 3:140b
Hino Ashihei 火野葦平 3:140b; 7:103b
Hino family 日野氏 3:140b
Hi no hashira (Pillar of Fire) 火の柱 6:254b
Hinoki 2:53b-54b
Hinomaru. *See* **National flag**
Hino micro-mixing system 3:140b
Hinomisaki 日御碕 3:140b
Hino Motors, Ltd 3:140b-141a
automotive industry 1:121b
Hino Tomiko 日野富子 3:141a
Hinoyama Park 火の山公園 7:105b
Hinuma 涸沼 3:141a
Hirabayashi Hatsunosuke 平林初之輔 3:141a
Hirabayashi Taiko 平林たい子 3:141a-141b
proletarian literature movement 6:255a
Hirabayashi v *US* (320 US 81) 4:18a
Hirado 平戸 3:141b; 7:256b
Dutch East India Company 2:330b
Hiradoshima 平戸島 3:141b
Hirafuku Hyakusui 平福百穂 3:141b-142a
Kaburagi Kiyokata 4:100b
Hiraga Gennai 平賀源内 1:225a; 3:142a-142b
gesaku 3:28b
herbal medicine 3:142a
kokkeibon 4:256a
Nakagawa Jun'an 5:313a
pseudonyms 3:142a
Satake Shozan 7:25b
sharebon 7:80a
Shikitei Samba 7:97a
taketombo 7:325b
works 3:142a-142b
Hiraga Motoyoshi 平賀元義 3:142b
Hiragana 1:153b; 4:131b; 6:248b; 7:163a
Hiraga Renkichi 平賀練吉 3:142b
Hiraga Yuzuru 平賀譲 3:142b
Hiragushi Denchū 平櫛田中 3:142b-143a
Hiraide site 平出遺跡 3:143a
Hiraizumi 平泉 3:143a
Ōshū Fujiwara family 6:126a-127a
urbanization 8:176a
Hirakata 枚方 3:143a
Hira maki-e 平蒔絵 4:240b, *360b*
Hira Mountains 比良山地 3:143a
Hirano Ken 平野謙 3:143b; 5:13b, 316b-317a
Hirano Kuniomi 平野国臣 3:143b
Hirano Yoshitarō 平野義太郎 3:143b
Hiranuma Kiichirō 平沼騏一郎 3:143b-144a
Ministry of Justice 3:143b
National Spiritual Mobilization Movement 5:347a
prime minister 3:144a
right wing philosophy 3:143b
Hiranuma Kiichirō cabinet
Arita Hachirō 1:85a
Yonai Mitsumasa 8:337a
Hiranuma Ryōzō 平沼亮三 3:144b
Hirao 4:308a
Hiraodai 平尾台 3:144b
Hiraoka Kōtarō 平岡浩太郎 8:88a
Hirara 平良 3:144b
Hirasawa Tsunetomi. 平沢常富 *See* **Hōseidō Kisanji**
Hirase Sakugorō 平瀬作五郎 3:144b-145a
Koishikawa Botanic Garden 4:250a
Hirashimizu ware 平清水焼 3:145a
decoration 3:145a
Hirata 平田 3:145a
Hirata Atsutane 平田篤胤 1:211b; 3:145a-145b; 5:17b; 7:28b, 94b, 264a
Kokugaku 4:257b-258b
works 3:145a-145b
Hirata Gōyō 平田郷陽 2:*130b*; 3:145b
Hirata Tokuboku 平田禿木 3:145b
Hirata Tōsuke 平田東助 1:21b; 3:145b
Hiratsuka 平塚 3:146a; 4:135a; 7:*335a*
Hiratsuka Raichō 平塚雷鳥 1:155b; 3:146a; 7:54b
Fujin kōron publication 2:344a
Ichikawa Fusae 3:257a
photo 3:*146b*
Seitōsha 7:54b
Shin Fujin Kyōkai 7:111b
social concerns 3:146a
Hiratsuka Tsunejirō 平塚常次郎 3:146a
Hiratsuka Un'ichi 平塚運一 3:146b
modern prints 5:232b
Hirayama Teruo 平山輝雄 4:31b
Hirayu Hot Spring 平湯温泉 1:5a; 3:146b
Hiro, Prince 浩宮 3:147b, *277a*
Hiroba no kodoku (Alone in the Marketplace) 広場の孤独 3:240a; 6:231a
Hirohata 広畑 3:146b
Hirohito, Emperor 天皇,裕仁 2:207a-207b; 3:*147a*, 147b; 277a
February 26th Incident 2:249b
politics 3:147a
renunciation of divinity by emperor 2:209a
Sakuradamon Incident 7:4b
Hirohito, Prince Regent 8:76a
Hiroi Isamu 広井勇 3:147b
Hiroioya 7:279b
Hironaka Heisuke 広中平祐 3:147b
Hirosaki 弘前 3:147b
Hirose 7:126b
Hirose Saihei 広瀬宰平 3:147b; 7:267a
Hirose Shrine 広瀬神社 3:147b-148a
Tatsuta Shrine 7:350a
Hirose Takeo 広瀬武夫 3:148a
Hirose Tansō 広瀬淡窓 3:148a; 4:233a; 7:94b
Hiroshige 広重 1:211b, *300b*; 3:148a-149b; 8:*144b*
illustrations 3:148a-148b
kachōga prints 3:148b
landscapes 3:148a-148b
Shōno (Rain at Shōno) 3:*148b*
Tōkaidō gojūsantsugi (Fifty-three Stations of the Tōkaidō) 3:*148b*
Hiroshige II 広重(二代) 3:149a
Hiroshige III 広重(三代) 3:149a
Hiroshige IV 広重(四代) 3:149a-149b
Hiroshima 広島 1:*108b*; 3:149b; 8:276a
atomic bomb 3:149b
atomic bomb related diseases 1:111b-112a
Chūgoku region 1:312a
Peace Memorial Park cenotaph 3:*149a*
peace movement 6:166a-166b
Shindō Kaneto 7:111b
Hiroshima Bay 広島湾 3:149b
Hiroshima Maidens programs 1:111a
Hiroshima Peace Center 7:340b
Hiroshima Plain 広島平野 3:149b
Hiroshima Prefectural Women War Victims (1948) 1:111a
Hiroshima Prefecture 広島県 3:149b-150a
Hiroshima University 3:150a
Hirota 7:126b
Hirota-Karakhan fishing agreements 3:150a
Hirota Kōki 広田弘毅 3:150a-150b; 7:28a; 8:225a
February 26th Incident 2:250a
military policies 3:150b
Hirota Kōki cabinet
Arita Hachirō 1:85a
Nagano Osami 5:302b
Hirota Shrine 広田神社 3:150b
Hirotsu Kazuo 広津和郎 3:151a; 5:13a
Hirotsu Ryūrō 広津柳浪 3:151a
Ken'yūsha 4:199a
Shinshōsetsu 7:125b
"tragic novels" 3:151a
Hiru 4:374b
Hirugao [(bindweed) *Calystegia japonica*] 3:151a
Hiruzen Kōgen 蒜山高原 3:151b
Hisago 3:151b
Hisai 久居 3:151b
Hisaita Eijirō 久板栄二郎 3:151b
Hisamatsu Sen'ichi 久松潜一
Kokutai no hongi, prepared draft 4:264a
Hisamatsu Shin'ichi 久松真一 3:151b
Hisao Jūran 久生十蘭 3:151b
Hishi 1:153b
Hishida Shunsō 菱田春草 3:151b-152a; 6:*157a*
style 3:152a
Hishikawa Moronobu 菱川師宣 5:255b-256a; 6:*155b*; 8:*138b*
Hishizashi stitches 7:24b
Historians. *See* **Discipline of Japanese history: a guide to research**
Historical documents. *See* **Diplomatics**
Historical Materials of Great Japan 2:65b
Historical periods. *See* **Periodization**
Historical scholarship 2:101a-116b
diplomatics. *See* **Diplomatics**
history, views of 2:101a-102b
Confucian 2:102a
laws of history 2:101b-102a
loyalty, theory of 2:102a
modern period 2:102a-102b

myth and history 2:101a-101b
as story 2:101b
local 5:71a-71b
medieval and early modern 2:106-110a
Azuchi-Momoyama and Edo periods 2:108a-109b
Kamakura period 2:106b-107a
Muromachi period 2:107b-108a
modern and contemporary 2:110a-112b
modern Japan 2:110a-111a
research areas 2:111a-112b
prehistory and ancient history 2:102b-106b
arts 2:150a-150b
documentary sources 2:104b-105a
fifth century and earlier 2:103a-103b
ninth to eleventh centuries 2:104b
religion 2:105a
seventh and eighth centuries 2:104a-104b
sixth century 2:103b-104a
source materials 2:115a-116a
ancient period 2:115b
early modern period 2:116a
general 2:115a-115b
medieval period 2:116a
modern and contemporary periods 2:116a-116b
Historical tales (rekishi monogatari) 5:246a
Historik: ein Organo geschichtlichen Denkens und Forschens 6:312a
publications 3:156b
Historiographical Institute, Tokyo University 2:65a; 3:152a
Dajōkan (Grand Council of State) 2:70b
publications 3:156b
Historiography 3:152a-158a
aristocratic age 3:152a-153b
official histories 3:152a-153b
unofficial histories 3:152a-153b
Edo period 3:154b-156a
beginnings of modern 3:155a
critical historical scholarship 3:155b
Japanese classicists 3:155a
new national histories 3:154b
feudal age 3:153b-154b
contemporary affairs 3:154a
critical approach 3:153b-154b
Gukanshō 3:65a-65b
popular literature 3:153b-154a
traditional writing 3:154a
modern period 3:156a-157b
new academic tradition 3:156a
perspectives and interests 3:156b-157b
scholarship 3:156a
recent trends 3:157b
Marxist influence 3:157b-158a
Western influence 3:156a-157b
specialization 3:156b-157a
cultural 3:156b-157a
historical materialism 3:156a-156b
socioeconomic 3:156a-157b
History of Great Japan 2:65a-65b; 7:164a
History of Japan 2:101b; 3:158a-206a; 4:101b
Asuka 3:161b-163b
Buddhism and Soga family 3:162a-162b
Fujiwara capital 3:163a-163b
Korea 3:162a-162b
Taika Reforms 3:162b; 7:295a-297a
Temmu 3:162b-163a
Yamato court 3:161b-162a; 8:308b-309a
Azuchi-Momoyama 3:177b-185b
culture 3:180b-181a
institutional developments 3:178b-180b
international dimension 3:184b-185b
periodization 3:177b-178b
Shokuhō seiken 7:164b-165a
Edo 3:185b-192b
bakuhan state 3:188b-189b
bakuhan system, administration 3:187a-187b
bakuhan system, social structure 1:131a-133a; 3:187b-188b
bakumatsu 3:192a-192b
economy and culture 3:189b-191a
intellectual ferment 3:191a-192a
seclusion 3:188b; 5:346b-347a
Tokugawa power structure 3:186a-186b
Tokugawa regime 3:186b-187a
Tokugawa shogunate 8:52b-56a
Heian 3:165a-169b
art 3:169a-169b
cultural life 3:168a
institutions 3:165b-166a
landholding system 3:166b-168a
literature 3:168b-169a
Nara, Nagaoka, Kyōto 3:121b-122b, 165a-165b
politics and government 3:166a-166b
regency government 6:286a-290a
religion 3:168a-168b
Kamakura 3:169b-172a
arts 3:171b-172a
background 3:170a
Buddhism 3:171a-171b
constitution of military class 3:170a-170b
economy 3:171a
Hōjō Regency 3:170b-171a; 7:97
life of warrior 3:170b
Mongol invasions 3:171a; 5:243b-245a
shogunate 3:172a; 4:121b-122b
Meiji 3:192b-197b
abolition of feudalism 3:193a-194b
constitutional government 3:195b-196b
institution building 3:194b-195b
Meiji Constitution 2:1a-3b
Meiji Restoration 5:155a-160a
role of emperor 3:192b-193a
Russo-Japanese War 3:196b-197a; 6:345b-347a
Sino-Japanese War of 1894-1895 7:197b-198b
Muromachi 3:172a-177b
central government 3:173a-174b
economic and social developments 3:175a-176b
interpretations 3:173a
local rule 3:174b-175a
Muromachi shogunate 5:271b-274a
Northern and Southern Courts 6:39a-40a
religion and culture 3:176b-177b
Sengoku period 7:64a-64b
Nara 3:163b-165a
end of period 3:164b-165a
Heijōkyō 3:124a
ritsuryō system 3:163b-164a; 6:322a-332a
Tempyō culture 3:164a-164b
postwar 3:203a-206a
Constitution of 1947 2:3b-7a
economic development 3:205a
economic growth 3:203a-203b
educational system 3:204a
end of era 3:205b-206a
foreign affairs 3:205a
political system 3:204a-205a; 6:213b-217a
social changes 3:203b-204a
prehistory 3:158a-160a
Jōmon period 3:158b-159b; 4:72a-74a
Paleolithic period 3:158a-158b; 6:159b-160a
Yayoi period 3:159b-160a; 8:321a-322a
protohistory 3:160a-161b
early and middle Kofun period 3:160b-161b; 4:244a-246a
late Yayoi period 3:160b
Taishō and early Shōwa 3:197b-203a
bureaucratic government 3:200b
change in leadership 3:197b-199a
China War 3:201a-202a; 7:199a-202a
economic recovery 3:201a
Pacific War 3:202a-203a; 8:271b-278b
wartime boom and postwar depression 3:199b-200a; 8:270b-271b
wartime political structure 3:202a
World War I and postwar foreign policy 3:199a
years of crisis 3:200a-200b
History of Japanese Religion 1:56b
Hita (city) 日田 3:206a
Hita Basin 日田盆地 3:206a-206b
Hitachi, Prince 常陸宮 3:207b
Hitachi (city) 日立 3:206b
Hitachibō Kaison 常陸坊海尊 1:42a
Hitachi Cable, Ltd 3:206b
Hitachi Chemical Co, Ltd 3:206b
Hitachi Corporation
Tōshiba Corporation 8:82b
Hitachi Ltd 3:206b-207a
in *Pak Chong-sŏk* v. *Hitachi, Ltd* 4:291b
Hitachi Metals Ltd 3:207a
Hitachi Ōta 常陸太田 3:207a
Hitachi Plant Engineering & Construction Co, Ltd 3:207a
Hitachi Sales Corporation 3:207b
Hitachi Zōsen Corporation 3:207b
Hitler, Adolf 8:272b
Hitobashira 3:207b
Hitodama 3:207b
Hitoegusa (seaweed) 7:47a
Hitogaeshi 人返し 3:207b-208a
Hitogata 4:166b
Hitojichi 人質 3:208a
Hitomi Kinue 人見絹枝 3:208a
Hito no Michi Kyōdan ひとのみち教団 6:192b
Hitori musuko (The Only Son) 一人息子 6:141b
Hitorishizuka *(Chloranthus japonicus)* 3:208a
Hitō Shōgō Sakusen 比島捷号作戦 6:115a
Hitosuji no michi ひとすじの道 4:169b
Hitotsubashi University 3:133a, 208a-208b
Hitotsume kozō 3:208b
Hitoyogiri 3:208b; 7:75b
Hitoyoshi (city) 人吉 3:208b
Hitoyoshi Basin 人吉盆地 3:208b
Hitsuji no uta 羊の歌 4:169b
Hittōsha 3:240a
Hiuchigadake 燧ケ岳 2:366b; 3:208b
Hiyuka poems 5:105b
Hizakurige series 4:61a-61b
Hizōhōyaku 秘蔵宝鑰 4:83b
Hō 2:91b
Hoan Jōrei 保安条例 6:167b
Hoantai 5:346a
Hoashi Banri 帆足万里 3:208b-209a
Ho Chi Minh 2:333a
Hōchi shimbun 報知新聞 3:209a; 8:355a
Hoderi no Mikoto 火照命 5:294b-295a
Hodosan 宝登山 3:209a
Hoes 4:322a
Hoffman, Hermann 7:229a
Hoffman, Johann Joseph 3:209a
Hōfu 防府 3:209a
Hōgen 法眼 7:270a
Hōgen Disturbance of 1156 保元の乱 3:209a-209b

Fujiwara family ····· 2:348b
Go-Shirakawa, Emperor ····· 3:49b
insei ····· 3:315a
Minamoto no Yorimasa ····· 5:180b
samurai ····· 7:7b
Taiki ····· 7:297b
Taira family ····· 7:299a
Taira-Minamoto War ····· 7:299b
Taira no Kiyomori ····· 7:301a
Taira no Shigemori ····· 7:302a
Taira no Tadamori ····· 7:302a
Toba, Emperor ····· 8:31b
warrior government ····· 8:229a
Hōgen monogatari ····· 保元物語 ····· **3**:69a-69b, 209b; **5**:43b, 246a
Heiji monogatari ····· **3**:123b
texts ····· **3**:209b
Hōgen no Ran. *See* **Hōgen Disturbance**
Hōgen to kaishaku ····· 方言と解釈 ····· **7**:259a
Hōgo. *See* **Goroku**
Hōhei kōshō ····· 砲兵工廠 ····· **3**:210a
Hohnen Oil Co, Ltd ····· **3**:210a
Hōitsu. 抱一 *See* **Sakai Hōitsu**
Hōji Conflict ····· 宝治合戦 ····· **3**:210a-210b
Hōjin ····· **3**:210b
tax law ····· **7**:355a-358b
Hōjō ····· 北条 ····· **3**:210b
Hōjō Dansui ····· 北条団水 ····· **3**:210b-211a
Hōjō family ····· 北条氏 ····· **3**:211a; **7**:58a, 70a
Hōjō Masako ····· **4**:122a
Hōjō Sōun ····· **4**:118b
Kamakura shogunate ····· **4**:122a
Mongol invasions of Japan ····· **5**:244a
museums ····· **5**:277a
Nakasendai Rebellion ····· **5**:317b
rule ····· **2**:204b
Samurai-dokoro (Board of Retainers) **7**:8b
shikken ····· **7**:97b
Taira no Yoritsuna ····· **7**:302b
Uesugi Kenshin ····· **8**:129b-130a
warrior government ····· **8**:229b
Hōjō godai ki ····· 北条五代記 **2**:279a; **3**:211a; **4**:187b
Hōjō Hideji ····· 北条秀司 ····· **3**:211a-211b
"Ōshō" ····· **7**:121a
Hōjōki (An Account of My Hut) ····· 方丈記 ····· **4**:129a; **5**:43b
Hojokin ····· **3**:56a
Hōjō Masako ····· 北条政子 ····· **3**:211b
Eisai ····· **2**:187a
Jōkyū Disturbance ····· **4**:72a
Minamoto no Yoriie ····· **4**:122a
Minamoto no Yoritomo ····· **4**:181a
Hōjō no umi (The Sea of Fertility) ····· 豊饒の海 ····· **6**:231b
Hōjō Sanetoki. *See* **Kanazawa Bunko**
Hōjō Sōun ····· 北条早雲 ····· **3**:211a, 211b; **7**:64b
Sōunji Dono Nijūikkajō ····· **4**:118b
Hōjō Takatoki ····· 北条高時 ····· **3**:172a, 211b; **5**:317b
Hōjō Tamio ····· 北条民雄 ····· **3**:211b-212a
Hōjō Tokimasa ····· 北条時政 ····· **3**:211a, 212a; **4**:181a; **7**:97b
Hōjō Tokimune ····· 北条時宗 ····· **3**:171a, 212a
Hōjō Tokiyori ····· 北条時頼 ····· **1**:11a; **3**:212a; **7**:58a, 80b
Hōjō Tokiyuki ····· 北条時行 ····· **5**:317b
Hōjō Yasutoki ····· 北条泰時 ····· **3**:212a-212b; **7**:85b, 97b
Jōkyū Disturbance ····· **4**:72a
Hōjō Yoshitoki ····· 北条義時 ····· **3**:212a-212b
Hōjō Sanetoki ····· **4**:136a
Jōkyū Disturbance ····· **4**:72a
Hōka ····· 放下 ····· **3**:212b
Hōkaiji ····· 法界寺 ····· **3**:212b
Hōkan ····· 幇間 ····· **7**:342b
Hokekyō ····· 法華経 ····· **5**:74a
Hōken seido ····· 封建制度 ····· **2**:263a
Hōken taiki ····· 保建大記 ····· **4**:313b
Hokkaidō ····· 北海道 ····· **3**:212b-213a; **4**:7a
area ····· **4**:2b
capital ····· **7**:20a
population density ····· **4**:2b, 7a
Russia ····· **6**:340b
Hokkaidō Colonization Office (Kaitakushi) ····· 開拓使 **1**:243b; **4**:113a; **5**:299a
Hokkaidō Colonization Office Scandal of 1881 ····· **3**:213a-213b; **4**:113a
Hokkaidō Development Agency ····· **1**:219a; **3**:213a-214b
Hokkaidō Electric Power Co, Inc ····· **3**:214a
Hokkaidō Kaihatsu Hō ····· **3**:213b-214a
Hokkaidō shimbun ····· 北海道新聞 ····· **3**:214a
Hokkaidō Takushoku Bank, Ltd ····· **1**:139a; **3**:214a
Hokkaidō University ····· **3**:214a
Hokkatei ····· 北花亭 ····· **4**:189b
Hokke gengi shakusen ····· 法華玄義釈選 ····· **6**:248a
Hokke gisho (Commentary on the Lotus Sutra) ····· 法華義疏 ····· **1**:*234b*
Hokkeji ····· 法華寺 ····· **3**:214a-214b
Kōmyō, Empress ····· **4**:268b
Hokkekyō ····· 法華経 ····· **1**:180b
Hokke metsuzai no tera ····· 法華滅罪之寺 ····· **4**:257a
Hokku ····· **3**:78b
Hokkyō ····· 法橋 ····· **7**:270a
Kōrin's award ····· **4**:293a
Hōkō Fishing Co, Ltd ····· **2**:284a; **3**:214b
Hōkōji. 法興寺 *See* **Asukadera**
Hōkōnin ····· **2**:211b-212b
Hokubei yūzeiki (A Stumping Tour of North America) ····· 北米遊説記 ····· **8**:117a
Hokuetsu Paper Mills, Ltd ····· **3**:214b
Hokuetsu seppu (Annals of Snow in the Hokuetsu Region) ····· 北越雪譜 ····· **3**:214b
Hokuman Tetsudō ····· 北満鉄道 ····· **1**:292a-292b
Hokumen no bushi ····· 北面の武士 ····· **3**:214b-215a
Shirakawa, Emperor ····· **7**:146b
takiguchi no bushi ····· **7**:326b
Hokuriku ····· 北陸 ····· **7**:46a
Hokuriku Electric Power Co, Inc ····· **3**:215a
Hokuriku Industrial Zone ····· **8**:87b
Hokusai ····· 北斎 ····· **1**:170a, 211b; **3**:215a-216a; **5**:*101a*; **7**:17b, 79a; **8**:*143b*
Fugaku sanjūrokkei (Thirty-six Views of Mt Fuji) ····· **3**:*215a*
Mt Fuji Viewed Through Waves Off the Coast of Kanagawa ····· **3**:*215a*
Hokusai manga ····· 北斎漫画 ····· **8**:143b
Hokushin Jihen ····· 北清事変 ····· **1**:166a-166b
Hokutei ····· 北亭 ····· **4**:189b
Holding companies ····· **2**:31b; **3**:216a
Antimonopoly Law ····· **3**:216a
Holidays ····· **3**:216b
national. *See* **Festivals**
Holy Orthodox Church ····· **1**:308a; **3**:216b
Holy Spirit Association for the Unification of World Christianity ····· **3**:216b-217a
Hombyakushō ····· 本百姓 ····· **3**:217a
gōson system ····· **3**:50b-51a
shinden kaihatsu ····· **7**:110a
Home economics
school curriculum ····· **7**:35b
Home life
family. *See* Family life
lifestyles ····· **5**:7b
Home Ministry (Naimushō) ····· **3**:217a-217b; **6**:198a
fukoku kyōhei leadership ····· **2**:361a
Ōkubo Toshimichi ····· **6**:94b
urban planning ····· **8**:180a
Homma Art Museum ····· **5**:276b
Homma Kazuo ····· 本間一夫 ····· **4**:10b
Hommonji ····· 本門寺 ····· **3**:217b
Hommon sect ····· 本門宗
Taisekiji ····· **7**:303b
Homosexuality ····· **3**:217b-218a
legal history ····· **3**:218a
Hōmushō ····· 法務省 ····· **5**:191b
Homutawake no Mikoto ····· 誉田別尊 ····· **6**:76b
Hon'ami Kōetsu ····· 本阿弥光悦 ····· **1**:153a, 166b, 193b, *235a*, 236a; **3**:182a, *218b*, 218b-219a
Furuta Oribe ····· **2**:373b
rimpa ····· **6**:317b
Honchō gashi ····· 本朝画史 ····· **4**:148b, 150a
Honchō jinja kō ····· 本朝神社考 ····· **7**:128b
Honchō monzui ····· 本朝文粋 **1**:293a; **2**:350a; **3**:219a; **5**:37b
Honchō seiki ····· 本朝世紀 **2**:353a; **3**:219a
Honchō shojaku mokuroku ····· 本朝書籍目録 **1**:154a; **3**:219a
Honchō tsugan (Speculum of Japan) ····· 本朝通鑑 **3**:154b; **7**:191a; **8**:49a
Honda Kōtarō ····· 本多光太郎 ····· **3**:219a
Honda Motor Co, Ltd ····· **3**:219a-219b
Honda Sōichirō ····· **3**:219b
passenger car production ····· **1**:122a
Honda Sado no Kami Masanobu ····· 本多佐渡守正信 ····· **3**:226b
Honda Seiroku ····· 本多静六 ····· **3**:219b
Honda Shūgo ····· 本多秋五 ····· **3**:219b
Honda Sōichirō ····· 本田宗一郎 ····· **3**:219b
Honda Toshiaki ····· 本多利明 ····· **3**:219b-220a
Honda Yasuji ····· 本田安次 ····· **2**:297b, 374a
Honden (main hall) ····· **4**:*297a*
Hondo ····· 本渡 ····· **3**:220a
Hōnen ····· 法然 ····· **3**:220a-220b
Hōnen shōnin eden ····· **3**:*220b*
Jōdo sect ····· **4**:67a-68a
raigōzu ····· **6**:277a
Senchakushū (Senchaku hongan nembutsu shū) ····· **7**:63a, 123a
Shinran ····· **7**:122b
Hōnen shōnin eden ····· 法然上人絵伝 ····· **7**:42b
Honest John Incident ····· **3**:220b-221a
Honeysuckle, Japanese [(nindō) *Lonicera japonica*] ····· **3**:221a
Hongaku ····· 本覚 ····· **3**:221a; **7**:5a, 114a
Honganji ····· 本願寺 ····· **3**:221a-222b
division ····· **3**:221b-222b
history ····· **4**:68a
Oda Nobunaga vs ····· **3**:222a-222b; **6**:63a
Ōtani University ····· **6**:129a
political and military power ····· **3**:221b-222b
Rennyo ····· **3**:221b; **6**:300a
Shinran ····· **7**:123b
Hongawara-buki ····· **6**:337b
Hon'imbō ····· 本因坊 ····· **3**:222b
Honjibutsu ····· 本地仏 ····· **3**:222b-223a
Honjin (daimyō inns) 本陣 **3**:223a; **6**:229b

Honjin satsujin jiken 本陣殺人事件 8:333b
Honji suijaku 本地垂迹 3:223a; 7:80b
Honjō (northern Honshū) 本荘 3:223a
Honjō (central Honshū) 本庄 3:223a
Honjō Mutsuo 本庄陸男 3:223b
Honjō Shigeru 本庄繁 3:223b
Honkadori 本歌取 2:357a; 3:223b; 5:42b
Honke and bunke 3:223b-224a; 4:218a
Honke and ryōke 本家, 領家 3:224a; 7:156b
Honke-gaeri 4:151a
Honkyōgen 本狂言 4:326b
Honkyoku 7:75b
Honne 6:204b
Honnōji Incident of 1582 本能寺の変 3:224a
 Akechi Mitsuhide 1:41a
 Oda Nobunaga 6:64b
 Shinchō kō ki 7:109b
 Tsutsui Junkei 8:118b
Hōnoki *(Magnolia obovata)* 3:224a-224b
Honor 3:224b
Honorific language 3:224b-226a
 diplomatics 2:97b
 speech style 3:225a
 third person reference 3:226a
 types 3:225a-226a
 world perspective 3:226a
Honors system 2:187b
Hō no shihai to saiban 法の支配と裁判 7:337b
Honryō ando. 本領安堵
Honsaroku 本佐録 3:226b
Honshū 本州 3:226b
 area 4:2b
 dialects 2:91b-92a
 electric power 2:191b
 population density 4:2b, 7a
Honshū Paper Co, Ltd 3:226b
Honto mononari 本途物成 3:226b-227a; 4:267b; 5:360b
Honzen ryōri 本膳料理 2:21b, 305a, 306a
Honzōgaku 本草学 1:155b
 Abe Shōō 1:4b
 Iinuma Yokusai 3:263b
 Inō Jakusui 3:308b
 Itō Keisuke 3:354b
 Iwasaki Kan'en 3:361b
 Matsuoka Joan 5:139a
 Ono Ranzan 6:111b
 Tamura Ransui 7:334b
Honzō kōmoku keimō 本草綱目啓蒙 6:111b
Honzō wamyō 本草和名 4:50b, 374b; 7:179b
Hōō 法皇 3:227a
Hoori no Mikoto 火遠理命 5:294b-295a
Hoover-Stimson Doctrine 6:35b
Hōōzan 鳳凰山 3:227a
Hopeh-Chahar Political Council. *See* **Ji-Cha (Chi-Ch'a) Autonomous Political Council**
Hoppō Bunka Museum 5:276b
Horagai 3:227a
Hōraichiku *(Bambusa nana* var. *normalis)* 1:136a
Hōraijisan 鳳来寺山 3:227a
Hōreki Incident 宝暦事件 3:227a-227b
Horie Ken'ichi 堀江謙一 3:227b
Horie Shigeo 堀江薫雄 3:227b
Horiguchi Daigaku 堀口大学 3:227b
Horiguchi Sutemi 堀口捨巳 1:81a; 3:227b
Hori Hidemasa 堀秀政 3:227b-228a
Hori Hidenari 堀秀成 1:104a
Horikawa hyakushu 堀河百首 5:38a
Hori Keizan 堀景山 4:258a; 5:257b
Horikoshi Jirō 堀越二郎 3:228a
Horikoshi Kubō 堀越公方 3:228a; 7:64b
Hori Kyūsaku 堀久作 3:228a
Horimono. *See* **Tattoos**
Hori Ryūjo 堀柳女 3:228a
Horishi
 tattoos 7:350a
Hori Tatsuo 堀辰雄 3:228a
Hōritsu 3:228a-228b
Hōritsu shakaigaku no shomondai 法律社会学の諸問題 4:112a
Horiuchi Masakazu 堀内正和 3:228b
Horn, musical 3:227a
Hōroku 3:228b
Horsecars 3:228b
Horse chestnut, Japanese [(tochinoki) *Aesculus turbinata*] 2:326b; 3:228b-229a
Horsemanship 3:229a
 martial arts 1:206a
Horseracing at the Kamo Festival 4:320b
Horse-rider theory 1:78b; 2:103b; 3:229a-231a; 4:276b
 criticism and revisions 3:230b
 Egami Namio 3:229b-230a
 historical perspective 3:230a-230b
 1948 Symposium on Japanese origins 3:229b-230a
 Oka Masao 3:229b
 origin of Japanese people 4:34b
 physical characteristics of Japanese people 4:35a
Horses (uma) 3:231a
 breeding 7:116a
Horseshoe crab [(kabutogani) *Tachypleus tridentatus*] 3:231a; 5:352a-352b
Horse trappings, ancient 1:78a; 3:231a-231b
 of kofun 4:245a
Horticulture 1:30a; 3:231b
 bonsai 1:161b-163a
 modern and contemporary 3:231b
 mosses 5:256b
Hōryūji 法隆寺 1:178a, 182a, *185a*; 3:231b-233b; 4:145a; 7:13b, 42a, 85a, 264a
 founding 3:232a
 gates 3:12a
 graffiti 3:59b
 images 3:232a
 main hall (kondō) 3:*232b*
 pagoda 3:*232b*
 rebuilding controversy 1:79b
 textiles 8:17a
 treasures of 3:233b-234b
Hōryūji Great Treasure House 法隆寺大宝蔵殿 3:233b
 treasures of 3:*233a*, 233b-234b
  Kanchōban 3:*233a*
  Queen Māya figurines 3:*233a*
Hōsa Bunko 蓬左文庫 3:234b
Hōseidō Kisanji 朋誠堂喜三二 3:234b
Hōsei University 3:234b-235a
"Hōsenka" 鳳仙花 4:183a
Hōshakaigaku kōza 法社会学講座 4:184b
Hoshina Masayuki 保科正之 3:235a; 7:81a
Hoshino site 星野遺跡 3:235a
Hoshi Ryō. 星良 *See* **Sōma Kokkō**
Hoshi Shin'ichi 星新一 3:235a
 science fiction 7:38b-39a
Hoshi Tōru 星亨 2:56a; 3:235a-235b
 Sandai Jiken Kempaku Movement (Movement to Memorialize Three Important Items) 7:9b
Hōshō 5:144a-144b
Hōshō Fusao 宝生英雄 6:*24b*
Hōshō Kan 宝生閑 6:*26b*
Hōshō school 宝生流 3:235b
Hōshosen 奉書船 3:235b
 National Seclusion 5:347a
Hōsho Shūzai 宝所周財 3:33a
Hōshō Yaichi 宝生弥一 6:*26b*
Hōsō Bunka Shō (Broadcasting Prize) 8:299b
Hosoda Eishi 細田栄之 3:235b
Hōsō Daigaku 1:171a-171b
Hosoda Tokitomi. *See* **Hosoda Eishi**
Hosofude 1:*233a*, 233b
Hōsōhō. *See* **Broadcasting Law**
Hosoi Heishū 細井平洲 3:235b-236a; 7:71a
Hosoi Kōtaku 細井広沢 3:236a
Hosoi Wakizō 細井和喜蔵 4:71b
Hosokawa family 細川氏 3:236a; 7:83b
 kanrei 4:151a
Hosokawa Fujitaka. 細川藤孝 *See* **Hosokawa Yūsai**
Hosokawa Gracia 細川ガラシア 3:236a-236b
Hosokawa Karoku 細川嘉六 3:236b
Hosokawa Katsumoto 細川勝元 3:236b; 6:107a
Hosokawa Sansai. 細川三斎 *See* **Hosokawa Tadaoki**
Hosokawa Tadaoki 細川忠興 3:236a-237a
Hosokawa Tama 細川玉 3:236a-236b
Hosokawa Yūsai 細川幽斎 3:236a, 237a; 8:215b
 Kokin denju 4:254a
Hospitals 3:120a
Hosshinshū 発心集 4:129a
Hossō School 1:312b
Hossō sect 法相宗 1:106a, 178b; 3:237a-237b
 Dōshō 2:132a
 headquarters 5:332b
Hōssō shiyō shō 法曹至要抄 4:376b
Hostages 3:208a
Host-guest relationship 2:233b
Hotakadake 穂高岳 3:237b; 4:127a
Hotakayama 武尊山 3:237b
Hotaru 2:280a-280b
Hotarugari. *See* **Firefly viewing**
Hotarugusa (The Dayflower) 螢草 6:221a
Hotei 布袋 5:296a
Hoteichiku *(Phyllostachys bambusoides* var. *aurea)* 1:135b-136a
Hotels
 Hotel Ōkura 7:341b
 Imperial Hotel 3:277b
Hōten Kaisen 5:262b
Hōtetsugaku 4:85a-85b
Hotoke. *See* **Buddha**
Hō to shūkyō to shakai seikatsu 法と宗教と社会生活 7:337b
Hototogisu ホトトギス 3:237b; 4:178a; 5:20a; 8:295a
 haiku 3:79b-80a

Masaoka Shiki ······ 5:123b
Natsume Sōseki ······ 5:350a
Satō Nempuku ······ 7:28a
Takahama Kyoshi ······ 7:311a
Hototogisu [(little cuckoo) *Cuculus poliocephalus*] ······ 1:223a
Hototogisu (Namiko) ······ 不如帰(浪子) · 6:221a; 8:59b
Hototogisu [(toad lily) *Tricyrtis hirta*] ······ 3:237b
Hot Spring Law ······ 3:239b
Hot springs ······ 3:238a-239b; 7:191b
Akakura ······ 1:40a; 8:293b
Arima ······ 1:83b
Asama ······ 1:95b
Asamushi ······ 1:95b
Atagawa ······ 1:107b
Atami ······ 1:107b
Awara ······ 1:124b-125a
Azusagawa ······ 1:127b
balneotherapy in Japan ······ 3:239a-239b
history ······ 3:239a
present conditions ······ 3:239a-239b
Beppu ······ 1:150a
Dake ······ 2:70b-72a
definition ······ 3:238a
distribution ······ 3:238a
in Japan ······ 3:238a
world ······ 3:238a
Dōgo ······ 2:126a
geothermal electrical generation ······ 3:238b-239a
Ginzan ······ 3:33b; 8:293b
Higashine ······ 8:293b
Hirayu ······ 1:5a; 3:146b
Iizaka ······ 3:264a
Isobe ······ 1:62b
Japanese attitude ······ 3:238a-238b
Kaminoyama ······ 8:293b
Kami Suwa ······ 4:127b
Katsuura ······ 5:300a
Kawaji ······ 4:179b
Kinugawa ······ 4:219a
Kusatsu ······ 4:319b
Manza ······ 5:111a
Masutomi ······ 5:130a
Ōwakudani ······ 6:136b
Sakunami ······ 7:4a
Shima ······ 7:99a
Shirahone ······ 7:145a
Sukayu ······ 7:265a
Tamatsukuri ······ 7:332b-333a
Tawarayama ······ 7:351b
Tōgatta ······ 8:36a
Tsubaki ······ 8:109b
Uchinomaki ······ 1:102b
utilization ······ 3:238b
water volume and radiation ······ 3:238a
Yamanaka ······ 8:300b
Yuda ······ 8:294a
Yudanaka ······ 8:355a
Yugashima ······ 1:49b; 8:355a
Yukawa ······ 5:300a
Yumoto ······ 8:295a
Yunoyama ······ 8:357b
Zaō ······ 8:293b, 367b
Hotta Masatoshi ·堀田正俊 ······ 3:239b
Hotta Masayoshi ·堀田正睦 ······ 3:239b
Hotta Shōzō ····堀田庄三 ······ 3:239b
Hotta Yoshie ····堀田善衛 ··· 3:239b-240a
Hou Han shu (History of the Later Han Dynasty) ······ 6:258b; 7:264a; 8:232b
Ho-Umezu Agreement. *See* **He-Umezu (Ho-Umezo) Agreement**
House, Edward Howard ······ 3:240a
House arrest ······ 3:126a
House codes. *See* **Kakun**
"House elders" ······ 4:160a
House Food Industrial Co, Ltd ······ 3:240a
Household ······ 3:259a-260b; 7:213a
contemporary standard of living ······ 7:243b-245a
importance ······ 7:212a
paternalism ······ 6:165a
See also **Ie**
Household furnishings ······ 1:148b; 5:8a
Household-Precept Letter Writer ·· 7:376a
Household precepts ·· 4:118a-119a; 7:234b
Household registers ·· 3:240a-241a; 5:321a
history ······ 3:240b-241a
minority rights ······ 5:195b
ryōmin ······ 6:352b
social classes
heimin ······ 3:125b
Housemen ······ 3:42b; 4:196b
House name (yagō) ······ 8:284a
House of Councillors · 2:189a-189b; 6:214b
Diet member legislation ······ 2:96b
Ryokufūkai ······ 6:352a
Tanaka Kōtarō ······ 7:337b
House of Ono ······ 6:110a
House of Peers ····· 3:241a; 6:171a; 7:304a
factions ······ 3:276b
House of Representatives ··· 2:188b-189b, 190a; 3:276a; 6:214b
Diet member legislation ······ 2:96b
House of Representatives Members Election Law ······ 6:212a
House of the Sleeping Beauties ··· 4:176b
Housewives ······ 3:241a-242a
nature of job ······ 3:241b
preparation ······ 3:241b-242a
relations with husbands ······ 3:242a
Housewives Association (Shufuren) ······ 8:263b
Housing
apartments ······ 5:6a
construction ······ 5:6a
consumer expenditure ······ 2:17a
exterior ······ 3:*243a*
history ······ 3:242b-244b
ancient religious influence ·· 3:243a-243b
architecture ······ 3:244a
modern ······ 3:244a-245b
prehistoric dwellings ······ 3:243a
residential styles emergence of ······ 3:243b-244a
interior ······ 3:*242b*
lifestyles ······ 5:6a
minka ······ 5:192a-194a
modern ······ 3:244a-245b
changes in design ······ 3:244b-245a
danchi ······ 3:245a
multiunit dwellings ······ 3:245a-245b
problems ······ 3:245b-246b
quality ······ 7:245a
rents ······ 4:363b
Yayoi ······ 8:321b-322a
Housing and Urban Development Corporation ······ 3:321b-322a
Housing Construction Planning Law ······ 3:246a
Housing developers ······ 3:242b
Housing Loan Corporation ······ 3:244b
fiscal system ······ 2:281b
Howling at the Moon ······ 3:76a
Hōya ······ 保谷 2:305b; 3:246b
Ho Ying-ch'in. *See* **He Yingqin (Ho Ying-ch'in)**
Hōyō kazoku ····抱擁家族 ······ 4:252a
Hōza ······ 6:321b
Hōzan Tankai. 宝山湛海 *See* **Tankai**
Hozugawa ······保津川 ······ 3:246b
Hōzuki [(ground cherry) *Physalis alkekengi*] ······ 3:246b
noisemaking toy ······ 3:246b
plant ······ 3:246b
Hōzuki ichi ······ 3:247a
Hozumi Nobushige ······ 穂積陳重 2:319a; 3:247a
Hozumi Shigetō ·穂積重遠 ······ 3:247a
Nakagawa Zennosuke ······ 5:313a
Hozumi Yatsuka ·穂積八束 ······ 3:247a
Ernest Francisco Fenollosa ······ 2:251b
Hsien-jen ······ 7:67a
Hsin-min Hui. *See* **Xinmin Hui (Hsin-min Hui)**
Hsu, Francis L.K. ······ 4:38b
Huang Xing (Huang Hsing) ······ 3:247b
Huang Zunxian (Huang Tsun-hsien) ······ 3:247b; 4:141a
Huiguo ······ 6:348a
Huike (Hui-k'o) Severing His Arm · 8:*371a*
Hukbalahap ······ 3:247b
Hukbo ng Bayan Laban sa Hapon (People's Anti-Japanese Army) ·· 3:247b
"Huks, the" ······ 3:247b
Hull, Cordell ······ 3:247b-248a
Hull note ······ 3:321b
Human rights ······ 4:379b
government compensation ······ 3:54b-55a
protection of civil liberties ······ 1:317b
Hundred Days' Reform ······ 4:141a
Hundred-Poem Sequences ······ 3:52a
Hundred Regiment Offensive ······ 3:248a
Hungary ······ 2:142b
Hŭngsŏn'gun. *See* **Taewŏn'gun**
Hunting ······ 3:248a-248b
falconry ······ 2:241b
policy ······ 3:248a-248b
use of hawks ······ 3:114b
Hunting and gathering economy ··· 4:72a
Husband ······ 2:244a-244b; 3:242a
Husi san xiao ······ 4:253b
Hu-ssu san hsiao ······ 4:253b
Hyakudan Taisen 百団大戦 ······ 3:248a
Hyakuichi shinron (New Theory of the Hundred and One) ······百一新論 ······ 6:14a
Hyakumantō darani ("mantras of the million stupas") ···百万塔陀羅尼 1:152a; 6:247b
Hyakunin isshu ··百人一首 ·· 1:4a; 2:354b; 3:248b-249a; 4:161b; 7:61b; 8:184a
Hon'ami Kōetsu ······ 1:*235a*
Ōeyama ······ 6:67b
uta karuta ······ 3:*248b*
Hyakurenshō ······百練抄 ······ 3:249a
historiography ······ 3:154a
Hyakushō ····· 3:249a-249b; 4:194b; 5:360b
Hyakushōdai ······百姓代 ·· 4:55a; 5:270a
Hyakushō ikki ···百姓一揆 ······ 3:192a, 249b-250b, 269a; 7:5a, 345b; 8:293a, 337b
Marxist vs non-Marxist interpretations ······ 3:250a-250b
phases ······ 3:269a
Hyakushōuke ······百姓請 ······ 3:250b
Hydrangea, Japanese [(ajisai) *Hydrangea macrophylla* var. *otaksa*] ······ 3:251a
Hydroelectric power ······ 2:190b-192a; 5:353a-353b
dams ······ 2:72a-72b
Hyō, Lake ······ 瓢湖 ······ 3:252a
Hyōe ······ 兵衛 ······ 2:184a
Hyōgikai ······ 4:11a; 7:344a
Hyōgo Prefecture ··兵庫県 ······ 3:251b
Hyōgo Shipyards ······ 兵庫造船所 ······ 3:252a
Hyōjōsho (Judicial Council) 評定所 8:53a

Hyōjōshū 評定衆 3:252a; 4:122a; 7:97b
keishi 4:190a
Hyōjun system 6:335b
Hyŏn Chun-Gŭk 4:287a
Hyŏn Chun-hyŏk 4:208b
Hyōrōmai 兵糧米 3:252a-252b
Hyōsō 4:116a
Hyōtan 3:151b
Hypothec 3:252b
Hyūga 日向 3:252b

I

Iai 3:253a
Iaidō 居合道 3:253a
Ianfu 4:159b
Ibara 井原 3:253a
Ibaraki 茨城 3:253a
Ibaraki Prefecture 茨城県 3:253a
industrial development 3:253a
tourist attractions 3:253b
Ibaraki Satellite Communication station 7:311a
Iba site 伊場遺跡 3:253b
Ibigawa 揖斐川 3:253b; 5:303b
IBM Japan, Ltd 3:253b
computer industry 1:345a
United States economic relations (1945-1973) 8:162a
IBRD 3:253b-254a
Ibuka Masaru 井深大 3:254a
Ibuse Masuji 井伏鱒二 3:254a-255a; 5:55b-56a; 7:119b
awards 3:255a
works of 3:254b-255a
Ibusuki 指宿 3:255a
Ichi 市 5:114b-115a
Ichiba 市場 5:114b-115a
Ichiba machi 市場町 5:115a-115b
Ichibō 一房 4:62a
Ichibukin 一分金 5:*242a-242b*
Ichidai toshiyori 7:274a
Ichien chigyō 一円知行 1:274a; 3:255a
shōen 7:157a
Ichigo ichie 一期一会 1:52b
Ichigō Sakusen 6:115a
Ichihara 市原 3:255b
Ichii [(Japanese yew) *Taxus cuspidata*] 3:255b
Ichijitsu shintō ki 一実神道記 3:255b
Ichijō, Emperor 一条天皇 3:255b-256a; 7:52b
Fujiwara no Kaneie 2:351b
Fujiwara no Korechika 2:352b
Fujiwara no Teishi 2:356b
regency 2:352b
Sei Shōnagon 7:52b
Ichijō family. 一条家 *See* **Gosekke**
Ichijō Kaneyoshi 一条兼良 3:256a
handbook on statecraft 1:207b
poet and critic 3:256a
politician 3:256a
scholar 3:256a
works 3:256a
Ichijō Norifusa 一条教房 3:256b
Ichijō Sanetsune 一条実経 3:256b
Ichijō Tsunetsugu 一条経嗣 3:256b
Ichikawa 市川 3:256b
Ichikawa Beian 市河米庵 3:256b-257a
Chinese influence 3:256b
Ichikawa Danjūrō 市川団十郎 3:257a; 5:49b
debut 4:91a
jōruri 4:77a
kabuki jūhachiban 4:97b
style 3:257a
Ichikawa Danjūrō XI 4:*90b*
Ichikawa Fusae 市川房枝 3:257a
Fusen Kakutoku Dōmei 2:374b
politician 3:257a
Shin Fujin Kyōkai 7:111b
work for women's rights 3:257b
Ichikawa Gakusan 市川岳山 6:*116b*
Ichikawa Kon 市川崑 2:272a, 273a, 274a; 3:257b-258a
films 3:257b
Shindō Kaneto 7:111a
style 3:257b
Ichikawa Shōichi 市川正一 3:258a
Ichikawa Utaemon 市川右太衛門 2:269b; 3:258a
Ichikishima Hime no Mikoto 市杵島姫命 3:357a
Ichimon 7:108a, 273b
Ichimonji 4:116a
Ichimura Kiyoshi 市村清 3:258a
Ichimura Sanjirō 市村瓚次郎 3:258a
Ichinen yūhan (A Year and a Half) 一年有半 5:311b-312a
Ichinomiya 一宮 3:258a
Ichinoseki 一関 3:258b
Ichi no Shōnin 市の聖人 7:166b
Ichinotani, Battle of 一谷の戦
Taira no Munemori 7:301b
Taira no Shigehira 7:302a
Taira no Tadanori 7:302a
Taira no Tomomori 7:302b
"Ichioku sōhakuchika" 6:138b
Ichirinsō *(Anemone nikoensis)* 3:258b
Ichirizuka 一里塚 3:258b
Ichiyō joshi no haka 一葉女史の墓 4:100b
Ichizoku 7:108a
Ichizoku rōtō 一族郎党 3:260b
Ichō 3:33b
Icons 7:67b
Idealism vs pragmatism 6:232b
Ideals of the East, The 5:12a; 6:79b; 7:294b
Idemitsu Art Gallery 3:258b
Idemitsu Kōsan Co, Ltd 3:258b-259a
Idemitsu Sazō 出光佐三 3:259a
Idemitsu Art Gallery 3:258b
Idemitsu Kōsan Co, Ltd 3:258b
Ideographs 4:141b-143b
Ideological "conversion." *See* **Tenkō**
Idioms 3:303b-304a
Idiophones 5:282b
Idojiri Archaeological Hall 3:259a
Ie (household) 2:241b-242a; 3:259a-260b; 4:217b
composition 3:259a
concept 3:259a-260b
in group consciousness 3:260a
functional meaning and its decline 3:260a
economic factors 3:260a
samurai status 3:260a
industry 3:260b
principle of succession 3:259b-260a
adoption 3:259b
inheritance 3:259b
rice culture 6:309b
sibling relationships 3:259b
Iejima 伊江島 3:260b
Iemoto 2:291b; 3:260b
disciples 3:260b
ie pattern 3:260b
Ienaga Saburō 家永三郎 3:261a; 4:67b
Ienaga textbook review case 3:261a
Ie no hikari 家の光 3:261a
Ienoko and rōtō 家子,郎党 3:261a; 7:7a
Iesu no Mitama Kyōkai Kyōdan イエス之御霊教会教団 7:242b
Iesu no shōgai イエスの生涯 2:214a
Ietsukasa 家司 4:190a
Igai 意外 4:181a
Igakujo 医学所 3:261b
Koishikawa Yōjōsho 4:250b
Igarashi Chikara 五十嵐力 3:261b
Iga ware 伊賀焼 2:295b; 3:261b; 7:256a
characteristics 3:261b
production 3:261b
Igaya Chiharu 猪谷千春 3:262a
Igo. 囲碁 *See* **Go**
Igusa 7:266a
Iha Fuyū 伊波普猷 3:262a
Ihara Saikaku. 井原西鶴 *See* **Saikaku**
Iha shell mound 伊波貝塚 3:262a
Ii 6:288b
Iida 飯田 3:262a
Iida Dakotsu 飯田蛇笏 3:262a
Iida Incident 飯田事件 3:262b
Iimoriyama 飯盛山 1:38b; 3:262b
Ii Naomasa 井伊直政 3:262b; 7:56b
Ii Naosuke 井伊直弼 3:263a-263b; 4:179b; 5:156a; 7:4b, 102a-102b
Ansei Purge 1:63b; 3:263b
Harris Treaty 3:105a
Meiji Restoration 5:156a
Movement for Union of Court and shogunate 5:260a-260b
Sakurada mongai Incident 1:84a; 7:4b
Iinuma Yokusai 飯沼慾斎 3:263b
Iiyama 飯山 3:263b-264a
Ii Yōhō 伊井蓉峰 3:264a
Iizaka Hot Spring 飯坂温泉 3:264a
Iizawa Tadasu 飯沢匡 3:264a
radio drama 6:275b
Iizuka 飯塚 3:264a
Iizuka Kōji 飯塚浩二 3:264a
I-jan 3:357a-357b
Ijūin family 伊集院氏 3:264b
Ika 7:243a-243b
Ikaho 伊香保 3:264b
Ikai 位階 2:39b-41a
Ikaruga 斑鳩 3:264b
Ikarugadera 斑鳩寺 3:231b
Ikaruga no Miya 斑鳩宮 3:264b
Ikat 4:164a-165a
Ikawa Dam 井川ダム 2:73b
Ikazuchi Kai いかづち会 5:19b
Ikebana 2:288a-292a
Ikebana International 2:292a
Ikebe Sanzan 池辺三山 3:264b
Ikeda (city) 池田 3:264b-265a
Ikeda (town) 池田 3:265a
Ikeda, Lake 池田湖 3:265b
Ikeda Daisaku 池田大作 3:265a
Ikeda-Diefenbaker communique 1:238a
Ikeda Hayato 池田勇人 2:333a; 3:265a; 7:275b
Income-Doubling 3:287a
Japanese self-defense 3:265a
Kōno Ichirō 4:274a
normalization with Korea 4:285a
prime minister 3:265b

Sakurada Takeshi ········ 7:4b
Satō Eisaku ········ 7:26a
Ikeda-Kennedy Agreements ········ 3:265a; 8:160a
Ikeda Kikunae ··· 池田菊苗 ··· 1:39a, 268a; 3:265b
Ikeda Mitsumasa 池田光政 1:158a; 3:265b
Confucianism ········ 3:265b
Ikeda Museum of Twentieth-Century Art ········ 5:279b
Ikeda Nagaoki ··· 池田長発 ··· 3:265b-266a
Ikeda-Robertson Talks ········ 3:266a
Ikeda Shigeaki ·池田成彬 ········ 3:266a
Ikeda Terumasa ·池田輝政 · 3:266a; 7:56b
Ikeda Yaemon ········ 池田八右衛門 ········ 6:359a
Ikedaya Incident ········ 池田屋騒動 ··· 3:266a-266b
Kondō Isami ········ 4:269a
Shinsengumi ········ 7:124b
Ikeda Yoshinobu 池田義信 ········ 4:189b
Ikegai Shōtarō 池貝庄太郎 ········ 3:266b
Ikejima Shimpei ·池島信平 ········ 3:266b
Ikenishi Gonsui ·池西言水 ········ 3:266b
Ike no Gyokuran ···池玉瀾 1:211a; 3:266b
Ike no mokuzu ···池の藻屑 ········ 1:73b
Ikeno Seiichirō 池野成一郎 ········ 3:266b
Ike no Taiga ······ 池大雅 ·· 1:193b, *210b*, 211a, 225a; 3:267a-267b; 7:17b
as calligrapher ········ 3:267b
influences ········ 3:267a
Sanzui jimbutsu zu ········ 3:*267a*
techniques ········ 3:267a
Ike no Zenni ······ 池禅尼 ········ 3:267b
Iki (island) ········ 壱岐 ········ 3:267b
Iki and sui (ideals) ········ 3:267b-268a
iki ········ 3:268a
sui ········ 3:267b-268a
Ikigai ········ 3:268a
Ikigami ········ 3:268a
Iki no Hakatoko ··伊吉博徳 ········ 3:268b
Iki no Muraji Hakatoko no fumi ······ 伊吉連博徳書 ········ 3:268b
kokiroku ········ 4:255a
Ikiru ········ 生きる 2:272a; 3:268b
Shimura Takashi ········ 7:108b
Ikiteiru heitai ········ 生きてゐる兵隊 ········ 7:176b
Ikite iru Yuda (The Living Judas) ··· 生きているユダ ········ 6:139a
Ikkai Gyojin. *See* **Soganoya Gorō**
Ikka shinjū ········ 7:262a
Ikki ········ 一揆 ········ 3:268b
kokujin ········ 4:260a
types ········ 3:268b-269a
Ikkō ikki ········ 一向一揆 ········ 3:269b
Ikkoku Ichijō Rei ········ 一国一城令 ········ 3:269b
Ikkōshū. *See* **Jōdo Shin sect**
Ikko sono ta ···一個その他 ········ 5:301b
Ikkyū ········ 一休 ········ 1:294b; 3:269b-270b
portrait ········ 3:*270b*
works ········ 3:270a
Ikkyū Sōjun ······ 一休宗純 ········ 1:192a; 3:269b-270b
portrait painting ········ 6:227b
Ikoku nikki ······ 異国日記 3:270b; 7:255a
Ikokusen Uchiharai Rei. 異国船打払令 *See* **Gaikokusen Uchiharai Rei**
Ikoma ········ 生駒 ········ 3:270b
Ikomayama ········ 生駒山 ········ 3:270b
Ikudama manku ·生玉万句 ········ 2:77b
Ikukunitama Shrine ········ 生国魂神社 ··· 3:270b-271a
Ikumatsu ········ 幾松 ········ 4:202b
Ikuno Disturbance ········ 生野の変 ········ 3:271a
Tenchūgumi Rebellion ········ 8:4a
Ikuno Silver Mine 生野銀山 ········ 3:271a
Ikushima Shingorō ········ 生島新五郎 ········ 2:188a
Ikuta Chōkō ···· 生田長江 · 3:271a; 7:54b
Ikuta Kengyō ···· 生田検校 ········ 4:64b
Ikuta Shungetsu ·生田春月 ········ 3:271a
Iku Tatsufu ········ 郁達夫 ········ 8:355a
Ikuta Yorozu, Rebellion of ········ 生田万の乱 ········ 3:271a
IL ········ イル ········ 4:139a
Ilchin-hoe ········ 4:282a
Illegitimacy ········ 6:163a
Illumination painting ········ 6:150a
Illustrated Sutra of Cause and Effect (E inga kyō) ········ 6:*149a*
Illustration, book ········ 1:163b-164a
Imabari ········ 今治 ········ 3:271b
Imado shinjū ···· 今戸心中 3:151a; 4:199b
Imagawa family ···· 今川氏 · 3:271b; 7:84a, 274b
Imagawa Kana Mokuroku ········ 今川仮名目録 ········ 3:271b
Imagawa Yoshimoto ········ 3:272b
Shingen Kahō ········ 7:113b
Imagawa Sadayo ········ 今川貞世 3:272a; 4:140a; 8:215a
military career ········ 3:272a
poetic activities ········ 3:272a
poetic diction ········ 3:272a
Imagawa Ujichika 今川氏親 ········ 3:271b
Imagawa Yoshimoto ········ 今川義元 ········ 3:272b
Imaichi ········ 今市 ··· 3:272b-273a
Imai Sōkyū ······ 今井宗久 · 3:181a, 273a; 7:67a
Imai Tadashi ····· 今井正 ·· 2:272a-272b; 3:273a
film-making style ········ 3:273a
Shindō Kaneto ········ 7:111a
works ········ 3:273a
Imakagami ········ 今鏡 · 3:273b; 5:39b
Imaki no tehito 今来の才伎 ········ 4:205b
Ima monogatari ···· 今物語 ········ 3:69b
Imamukashi ayatsuri nendaiki ···今昔操年代記 ········ 6:20a
Imamura Arao ···今村荒男 ········ 3:273b
Imamura Shikō ··今村紫紅 3:273b; 6:*158b*
Imamura Shōhei ·今村昌平 · 2:273b-274a, 275b; 3:273b-274a
film protagonists ········ 3:273b
films ········ 3:274a
methods ········ 3:274a
Imanishi Kinji ···· 今西錦司 3:274a; 6:240a
monkeys ········ 1:156a
Imari ········ 伊万里 ········ 3:274a
Imari ware. *See* **Arita ware**
Imari ware jar ········ 1:*260b*
Imbanuma ········ 印旛沼 · 3:274b; 7:4a
Tanuma Okitsugu ········ 7:345a-346a
Imbe ········ 忌部, 斎部 ········ 1:147b
Imbe Family ·· 忌部氏, 斎部氏 ··· 3:274b
Imbe no Hironari 斎部広成 ········ 1:116a
IMF ········ 3:274b
Japan's membership ········ 3:274b
yen exchange system ········ 3:274b
IMF-JC (International Metalworkers Federation-Japan Council) 3:274b-275a; 4:360a
Jidōsha Sōren ········ 4:53b
Imiki ········ 忌寸 ········ 4:89a
Imikotoba ········ 7:291b
Immediate acquisition ········ 7:68a
Immigrants. *See* **Kikajin**
Immigration
Australia ········ 1:116b-117a, 119a
Brazil ········ 1:169a-169b
Hiraga Renkichi ········ 3:142b
Wako Shungorō ········ 8:221b
Canada ········ 1:238b
Hawaii
Irwin, Robert Walker ········ 3:336a
United States Immigration Acts of 1924, 1952, and 1965 ········ 8:164b-165a
Immigration control. *See* **Emigration and immigration control**
Immigration Control Law ········ 2:313b
Immigration Control Order ········ 1:47b
Immigration Exclusion Act (1924) ·· 4:13a
Immortality ········ 1:20a; 2:80b-81a
Imochibyō ········ 6:310a
Imohori chōja ··· 芋掘長者 ········ 7:269b
Imo Mutiny ········ 2:361a; 3:275a; 4:280a
draft notification slips ········ 7:167b
Kaehwap'a ········ 4:101b
Taewŏn'gun ········ 7:294a
Imori [newt *(Triturus pyrrhogaster)*] ········ 3:275a
Imoseyama onna teikin ········ 妹背山婦女庭訓 ········ 1:274b
Imo to sekagami ········ 妹と背かゞみ ········ 8:110b
Impāru Sakusen ········ 3:281b
Impeachment ········ 3:275a; 6:242b
grounds ········ 3:275b
Imperial Academy Prize ········ 7:315b
Imperial anthologies 2:354a; 3:275b; 7:94b
Chinese poetry
Bunka shūreishū ········ 1:211b-212a
Keikokushū ········ 4:189a
Ryōunshū ········ 4:109a, 189a; 5:29b
waka
Fūgashū ········ 3:275b
Go shūishū ········ 2:353a
Gyokuyō wakashū ········ 3:71b
Kin'yō wakashū ········ 4:219a-219b
Kokinshū ········ 4:254b-255a
Senzai wakashū ········ 7:68a
Shika wakashū ········ 7:95a
Shin chokusenshū ········ 2:354a
Shin kokinshū ········ 7:119b-120b
Shin shūishū ········ 8:73b
Shin zoku kokinshū ········ 7:170b; 8:204a
Shūi wakashū ········ 7:184b
Imperial Art Academy ········ 4:178b
Imperial authority ········ 3:152b
Imperial conferences ········ 3:59a-59b
Imperial Diet ········ 3:275b-277a; 6:214a
armed forces ········ 8:85a
Genrōin ········ 3:22a
history: Meiji period ········ 3:276b
political parties & factions ········ 3:276b
history: Shōwa period ········ 3:276b-277a
history: Taishō period ········ 3:276b
Itō Hirobumi ········ 3:353a
Meiji, Emperor ········ 5:153a
Meiji Constitution 2:2b, 8a, 8b, 9a; 3:195b
operation ········ 3:276a
sessions ········ 3:276a
organization ········ 3:276a
House of Peers ········ 3:241a, 267a
House of Representatives ········ 3:276a
powers ········ 3:276a
Taishō, Emperor ········ 2:207a
Taishō democracy ········ 7:304a
Universal Manhood Suffrage Movement ········ 8:169a
Imperial edict ········ 3:277a
rinji ········ 6:318a
semmyō ········ 7:62a-62b
senji ········ 7:65b
Imperial family ········ 3:*277a*
Fujiwara family ········ 2:348a, 350b
Shintō rituals surrounding ········ 7:126b

See also **Imperial household**
Imperial Fine Arts Academy (Teikoku Bijutsuin) ········ **8**:318b
Imperial Guard, Office of ········ **2**:184a
Imperial Headquarters ········ **2**:58b
independence ········ **1**:86b-87a
Imperial Hotel ········ **3**:277b; **8**:279a
Raymond, Antonin ········ **6**:284b
Imperial household ········ **3**:277b
Imperial Household Agency ········ **1**:218b; **3**:277b-278a; **6**:214a
Imperial Household Council ········ **2**:377b
Imperial Household Law ··· **2**:6b, 8a, 206a; **3**:278a; **7**:69b
commentary ········ **4**:192b
Daijōsai ········ **2**:59a-59b
Itō Hirobumi ········ **3**:353a
kōgō defined ········ **4**:249a
Imperialism ········ **4**:387a; **7**:198b
Imperial Japanese Army ········ **3**:278a
Nakano School ········ **5**:316a
Imperial Japanese Navy ········ **3**:278a
Naval Academy ········ **5**:358a-358b
Naval General Staff Office ········ **5**:358b
Imperial Law of the Houses ········ **2**:95a
Imperial legitimacy, historical debate ········ **5**:323b-324a
"Imperial loyalists" ········ **2**:205a
Imperial Military Reservists' Association ········ **3**:278a; **5**:174a
Imperial Rule Assistance Association ········ **3**:280b
Tanaka Giichi ········ **7**:336a-336b
Imperial Mirror ········ **4**:148b
Imperial National Defense Policy ··· **1**:87b
Imperial New Year's Poetry Reading ········ **3**:278b
Imperial ordinance ········ **3**:278b
Imperial Diet ········ **3**:276a
Imperial Palace ········ **8**:*61a*
Imperial Palace Music Department ·· **3**:1b
Imperial Party ········ **7**:376b
Imperial police ········ **4**:185b
Imperial Prize of the Japan Academy ········ **4**:9b
Ogura Shimpei (1935) ········ **6**:71b
Tawara Sunao (1914) ········ **7**:351b
Imperial regalia **1**:51b; **3**:278b-279a; **7**:278b
death of Tokiko ········ **1**:67b
Ise Shrine ········ **3**:338a
Kusanagi no Tsurugi ("grass-cutting" sword) ········ **1**:115b-116a
legend ········ **3**:278a
magatama ········ **1**:147b
mythology ········ **5**:293b
Shintō ········ **7**:126a
Shintō art ········ **7**:135a
Taira-Minamoto War ········ **7**:300b
Imperial Rescript on Education of 1890 · **1**:165b, 252b; **2**:175a; **3**:195b, 279a-279b; **6**:192b; **8**:28b, 291b
basis ········ **3**:279a
Confucianism ········ **1**:358a
historical background ········ **3**:279a
Inoue Kowashi ········ **3**:311a
kokutai ········ **4**:263a
modern philosophy ········ **5**:229b
Motoda Nagazane ········ **5**:257a
nationalism ········ **5**:342b
policy ········ **2**:182a
principles ········ **2**:183a-183b
religion ········ **6**:293b
Imperial rescripts ········ **1**:165b
Imperial Rescript to Soldiers and Sailors ········ **3**:279b-280a; **5**:173b; **7**:65b; **8**:291a
political circumstances ········ **3**:280a
precedents ········ **3**:279b-280a
principles of conduct ········ **3**:279b-280a

Takehashi Insurrection ········ **7**:324a
Imperial Rule Assistance Association (IRAA) ···· **1**:40a, 84a; **2**:94b; **3**:280a-281a; **6**:207a; **6**:211b; **8**:277b
China War ········ **3**:202a
cultural section ········ **7**:176b
Gotō Ryūnosuke ········ **3**:53b
Kawakami Jōtarō ········ **4**:181a
Konoe Fumimaro ········ **4**:273a
local level ········ **3**:280b
Nagai Ryūtarō ········ **5**:301b
Nakano Seigō ········ **5**:316a-316b
New Order Movement ········ **5**:366a
Occupation Purge ········ **6**:58a
"reformists" vs "Japanists" ········ **3**:280a
Rikken Seiyūkai ········ **6**:315b
Tōjō Hideki ········ **8**:39b
Imperial Shintō ········ **2**:300b
Imperial Theater ········ **2**:75b-76b
Imperial universities ········ **3**:281a
higher schools ········ **3**:135a
privileges ········ **3**:281b
research and development ··· **6**:303b-305b
systematizing higher education ···· **3**:133a
Imperial Universities Athletic Association ········ **7**:242b
Imperial University Order ········ **8**:170a
Imperial Veterans Association ········ **3**:278a
Imperial Way faction ········ **1**:74a; **4**:243a
Imphal Campaign ········ **3**:281b
United Kingdom ········ **8**:152b
Important Cultural Properties. *See* **National Treasures**
Important Intangible Cultural Assets. *See* **Living National Treasures**
Imports. *See* **Foreign trade;** *and specific country*
Imprisonment ········ **6**:172b
Imprisonment of the Companions of Barbarian Studies ········ **1**:141b
In. *See* **Seals**
Ina ········ 伊那 ········ **3**:281b
Ina Basin ········ 伊那盆地 ········ **3**:281b
Inada Ryōkichi ·· 稲田龍吉 ········ **3**:282a
Inagaki Hiroshi ···· 稲垣浩 ·· **2**:269b-270a, 271a; **3**:282a
Inagaki Taruho ·· 稲垣足穂 ········ **3**:282b
works ········ **3**:282a
Inagi ········ 稲城 ········ **3**:282b
Inago ········ **5**:72a
Inaka kyōshi ····· 田舎教師 ········ **7**:359a
Inamura Junzō ··· 稲村順三 ········ **4**:48b
Inamura-Morito dispute ········ **4**:48b
Inamura Sampaku ········ 稲村三伯 ········ **3**:282b
Haruma wage ········ **3**:105b
Inari ········ 稲荷 ·· **3**:282b-283a, 375a
Hatsuuma ········ **3**:113b
origins ········ **3**:283a
symbol ········ **3**:283a
Inariyama tomb ········ 稲荷山古墳 ··· **1**:79a; 233b; **3**:283a
Ina Tadatsugu ··· 伊奈忠次 ········ **3**:283b
Inatomi Naoie ··· 稲富直家 ········ **3**:283b
Inatomi school of gunnery ········ **3**:283b
Inawashiro, Lake 猪苗代湖 **1**:137a; **3**:283b
Inawashiro Kensai ········ 猪苗代兼載 ········ **3**:283b
Shinsen tsukubashū ········ **7**:124b
Inayama Yoshihiro ········ 稲山嘉寛 ········ **3**:284a
Inazawa ········ 稲沢 ········ **3**:284a
Incantations, prayer ········ **6**:233a
Incarceration ········ **2**:48b-49a
wartime ········ **4**:17a-17b

Incense ceremony ········ **3**:284a-285a
history ········ **3**:284b
various ceremonies ········ **3**:284b-285a
"Incident of the Bell Inscription" ·· **7**:165b
Income, national ········ **5**:339b-341b
complementary structure and economic growth ········ **5**:340a-340b
consumption behavior ········ **2**:18a-20b
disposable ········ **2**:18a-20b
public sector ········ **5**:340b-341a
savings behavior ········ **2**:18a-20b
size and structure ········ **5**:339b-340a
transfer payments ········ **5**:341a-341b
wealth ········ **5**:349a-349b
Income distribution ·· **3**:285b-287a; **7**:216b
factors of ········ **3**:286a
international comparisons ···· **3**:285b-287a
economic ········ **3**:286a
historical ········ **3**:286a
social ········ **3**:286b-287a
statistical ········ **3**:286a
life-cycle differences ········ **3**:286a-287a
modern ········ **2**:165a
prewar and postwar patterns ········ **3**:285b
urban/rural differentials ········ **3**:285b
taxes ········ **7**:353b-354a
Income-Doubling Plan ····· **3**:287a; **8**:180a
technological development ········ **7**:370a
Income per capita ········ **2**:16b-17a
Incomes policy ········ **3**:287b
industrial policy ········ **3**:296b
Income Tax Law ········ **2**:276b
tax accounting ········ **7**:352a
Increase Production and Promote Industry ········ **7**:165b
Indebtedness ········ **6**:105a
Indebtedness, certificate of ········ **2**:81a
Independence Club ········ **3**:287b; **6**:307b
anti-Russian activities ········ **4**:281b
Independence Party ········ **4**:101b
Independent act ········ **4**:86a
Independent movie productions ········ **3**:287b-288a
India
Bose, Rash Behari ········ **1**:164a-164b
military commanders ········ **7**:197a
nationalist leaders
Bose, Subhas Chandra ······ **1**:164b-165a
religion ········ **6**:290a-293b
Ryōbu Mandara ········ **6**:347b
India and Japan ········ **3**:288a-289b
British India ········ **3**:288a
early attitude ········ **3**:288a
early Buddhist influences ········ **3**:288a
postwar cultural relations ········ **3**:289a
postwar economic relations ········ **3**:289a
postwar political relations ···· **3**:288b-289a
Indian National Army (INA) ········ **1**:164b; **2**:348b; **3**:289b-290a; **6**:260a; **7**:197a
Indian Ocean Fisheries Commission ········ **2**:283a
Indian-Pacific Ocean Fisheries Commission ········ **2**:283a
Indigents' Party ········ **1**:272a; **4**:267a
Indigo ········ **2**:136a, 296a; **3**:290a; **7**:24a
vat-dye method ········ **3**:290a
Individual autonomy, principle of ··· **4**:86a
Indochina
French-Japanese relations ········ **2**:333a
Japanese occupation ········ **3**:290b
Indonesia and Japan ········ **3**:290b-291a
immigration ········ **3**:290b
World War II ········ **3**:290b-291a
Indonesian Pembela Tanah Air ···· **6**:179b
Industrial Bank of Japan, Ltd ····· **1**:139a; **3**:291a; **5**:319a-319b; **8**:357b
Industrial complexes ········ **3**:291b

Industrial design. *See* **Design**
Industrial funds 3:291b-292a
lending rates 3:291b
sources 3:291b
Industrial injuries 3:292a
Industrial insurance 3:317a
Industrial Investment Special Account 1:139b
Industrialization
class structure 1:323a
"closed" employment systems 4:344a-344b
company welfare system 1:342b
crime rate 7:209a
dekasegi 2:83b-84a
early modern economy 2:151a-153b
effect on today's society 7:213a-218b
labor 4:343a
modern employment system 2:210b
Shibusawa Eiichi 7:86a-86b
social welfare as outgrowth 7:211a
Industrial organization 3:292a-296b
capital concentration 3:293b-294a
contemporary 2:162b-163a; 3:296a
historical background 3:292a
modern vs traditional 3:292a
post-World War II 3:292b
history of economic concentration 3:292b-293b
cartels 3:293a
zaibatsu 3:292b
importance of groups 3:295a
intercorporate stockholding 3:295a
shihon keiretsu 3:295b
industrial policy 3:296b
market concentration 3:294a-295a
low vs high 3:294a
role of legal cartels 3:295b-296a
types 3:296a
Industrial Patriotic Association 4:345b
Industrial plants, production 1:27b
Industrial policy 3:296b-297a
categories 3:296b-297a
means of implementation 3:297a
Industrial property 3:297a
classes 3:297a
registration 3:297b
rights 3:297a
Industrial relocation policy 3:297b
goals 3:297b
Industrial Relocation Promotion Law of 1972 3:297b
Industrial reorganization 3:298a
Industrial revolution in Japan 3:298a; 7:198b
Industrial robots 3:298b-299b
economic and social role 3:299a
government programs to faster use 3:299b
growth of robot industry 3:298b-299a
development 3:298b
exports 3:298b-299a
types and primary uses of 3:299a
Industrial Standard, Japanese (JIS) 4:61b-62a
Industrial Standardization Law of 1949 4:61b-62a; 6:273b
Industrial structure 3:299b-302a
changes in manufacturing 3:300b-301b
conclusion 3:302a
economic sectors 3:299b
industrial policy 3:296b
Japan's historical experience 3:299b-300b
national income 5:339b-341b
relationship to foreign trade structure 3:301b-302a
Industrial Structure Council 1:12a; 3:302a
economic planning 2:167a
functions and council reports 3:302b
organization and membership 3:302a
Industrial waste 3:302b
contamination 3:302b
disposal 3:302b
Industrial zones 3:303a
Industries
chemical 1:267b
commodities 3:313a
computer 1:344a
Japanese market share 1:344a
construction 2:14a
construction machinery 2:14a
copper 2:372a
declining 2:81b
development
industrial robots 3:298b
electrical equipment 2:342a, 372b
energy 2:214a-214b
fish and shellfish farming 2:281b-282b
fishing 2:284a-287b
food processing 2:307a
garment 3:12a
glass 3:36b
government-operated factories 3:56a-56b
government promotion of 7:165b
growth 3:63b
input-output analysis 3:313a
internal organization 3:318a
iron 3:333b-336a
knowledge-intensive 3:63b
machine tool 5:78b
mining 5:184b-185a
modern vs traditional 3:19a
monopoly and oligopoly 5:247a-247b
nonferrous metals 6:34b
petrochemical 6:180a
pharmaceutical 6:182a
precision machinery 6:233b
primary industries 6:239b
public corporations 6:263a
public utilities 6:266b
public utility rates 6:266b
publishing 6:267a
secondary 7:47b
service 3:313a
sewing machines 4:2a
shipbuilding 7:141b-143a
silk production 7:194a
steel 3:333b-336a
subcontractors 2:14a
tertiary industries 8:14b-15a
textile 8:16a-16b
whaling 8:249b-250b
Infancy 5:4a
Infanticide 2:246b; 6:224a
Inflation
Dodge line 2:122b
land reform 4:365a
Political Crisis of 1881 6:202b
Inflation and price stability 3:303a
economic indicators 3:303a
input-output analysis 3:313a
types of inflation 3:303a
Inga 3:303b
Ingaōhō 4:93b
Ingen 隠元 1:179b; 3:303b
Itsunen 3:357a
Ingo 3:303b-304a
Inheritance 1:14b; 6:244b
adoption 1:15a-15b
land 7:232a
principle of succession 3:259b
Inheritance law 3:304a-305b; 4:379a
history of inheritance system 3:304a
Edo period (1600-1868) 3:304a
Meiji period (1868-1912) 3:304a
summary of present 3:304a-305b
acceptance and renunciation 3:304b
administration of estate 3:305a
disinheritance 3:304b
disqualification 3:304b
order of inheritance 3:304b
partition of estates 3:305a
principle 3:304a
secured portions 3:305a
shares 3:304b-305a
In Hōkichi 伊奉吉 8:357b-358a
Injiuchi 3:305b; 8:325b
Injū 陰獣 2:170b
"Ink-flow" 7:266b
"Inki na tanoshimi" 陰気な愉しみ 8:319b
Ink line painting (hakubyōga) 3:87b
Ink painters. *See* Painters, ink
Ink painting (suibokuga) 1:192a; 3:305b-307b; 6:150b
China 1:283a
Hasegawa Tōhaku 3:307a
Higashiyama culture 3:132b
history 3:306a-307a
rise 3:306a
Kanō school 4:149a, 150a
Kaō Ninga 3:*305a*
Rimpa 6:317b
Sesshū Tōyō 7:69b-70a
Ama no Hashidate 6:152a
Haboku Landscape 7:68a
Landscape of the Four Seasons 3:306b
Shūbun 3:180b-181a
subjects 3:306a
Inkyo 3:307b-308a
ideals 3:307b
kanreki 4:151a
social class 3:307b
Inland Sea 瀬戸内海 3:308a, *308b*; 7:97b
Awajishima 1:124a-124b
Inland Sea Industrial Region 3:308a
Inland Sea National Park 瀬戸内海国立公園 1:124b; 4:103b
Okayama Prefecture 6:83a
"Innate Buddhahood" 8:27a
Inner minister 5:310a-310b
Inner Mongolia, Russo-Japanese agreements of 1907-1916 6:344b
Innoshima (city) 因島 3:308b
Innoshima (island) 因島 3:308b
Inns 3:308b
"Inochi no Shoya" いのちの初夜 7:176a
Inō Jakusui 稲生若水 3:308b
Kaibara Ekiken 4:108b
Inokuchi Ariya 井口在屋 3:309a
Inō maps 伊能図 3:309a
Inomata Tsunao 猪俣津南雄 3:309a
Inoshishi 8:253a
Inō Tadataka 伊能忠敬 2:65a; 3:309a; 7:31b
Inoue Enryō 井上円了 3:309b
Fenollosa, Ernest Francisco 2:251b
Inoue Hisashi 井上ひさし 3:309b
Inoue Junnosuke 井上準之助 3:309b-310a
assassination 4:373a
Inoue Kaoru 井上馨 1:160a; 2:56a; 3:310a; 5:314a-314b; 7:9b, 29a, 86a
diplomat 3:310a
financial policies 3:310a
foreign minister 3:310b
Fujita Denzaburō 2:346a
genrō 3:310b
Hara Takashi 3:102b
Kanghwa, Treaty of 4:140b
naichi zakkyo 5:309b-310a
Treaty of Seoul 4:280b
Inoue Kiyonao 井上清直 3:310b-311a

Inoue Kowashi 井上毅 2:2b, 332a; 3:311a
Imperial Rescript on Education 3:279a
Meiji Constitution 2:2b
Minister of Education 2:176a
natural science 5:356b
Inoue Masao 井上正夫 2:268b
Inoue Mitsuharu 井上光晴 3:311a
Inoue Mitsusada 井上光貞 4:261b
Inoue Nisshō 井上日召 3:311a; 7:108a
Inoue Tetsujirō 井上哲次郎 1:223a; 3:311a; 7:270b
Fenollosa, Ernest Francisco 2:251b
Inoue Yasushi 井上靖 1:164a, 207a; 3:311b; 7:103b
awards 3:311b
works 3:311b
I-novel 3:312a; 7:175b-176a
bundan 1:208b
criticism 3:312a
evolution 3:312a
modern 5:54a-54b
postwar literature 6:230b-231a
Input-output analysis 3:312b-313a
commodities and services industries 3:313a
Japan vs West Germany 3:312b
relative price changes 3:312b-313a
"skyline" of Japanese industry 3:312b
Inrō 印籠 1:166b; 3:313a
construction 3:313b
functions 3:313b
netsuke 3:313a
Yamada Jōka 3:313a
Inryōken nichiroku 蔭凉軒日録 4:147b
Insai Hakusui 淫斎白水 4:189b
Insanity 5:162b
Insatsu Kōgyō Kai (Japan Printers' Associations) 6:246b
In school 3:313b
Inson 3:315a
Inscriptions 3:313b-314a
calligraphy 1:233b
historical sources 3:314a
methods 3:313b
studies 3:314a
Insect Book (Ehon mushi erami) 8:142a
Insecticides 6:309a
Insects 1:61a
ants 1:67b-68a
bees and wasps 1:149a
butterflies 1:225b-226a
cicadas 1:315a
crickets 2:43b-44a
dragonflies 2:133b
fireflies 2:280a
gold beetle 3:43b
Japanese beetle 4:22b
kirigirisu 4:220b
plant hopper 6:190a
spiders 7:242b
Insei 院政 3:314b-315a; 7:69b
factional strife 3:315a
interpretation 3:315a
Kōgon headed 4:249a
political structure 3:314b
reassertion of Imperial Rule 3:314b
after Shirakawa 3:315a
Shirakawa and the establishment 3:314b-315a
Inshō 7:45b-46a
Insignias 2:42a-43b
Inson 院尊 1:199b; 3:315a
Inspectors general *(ōmetsuke)* 6:101a
Installment Sales Law 3:315b
freedom of contract 2:337b
provisions 3:315b
Instant foods 3:315b
Institute for Infectious Diseases 4:229a; 6:305b
Institute for the Investigation of Barbarian Books 1:141b-142a
Institute of Asian Economic Affairs 3:319b
Institute of Japanese Culture and Classics 4:259b
Institute of Oriental Culture, Tōkyō University 3:315b
Institute of Pacific Relations 3:315b-316a
Institute of Physical and Chemical Research 1:268a; 3:316a, 372a; 4:207a; 6:303b, 305b, 311b
Ikeda Kikunae 3:265b
natural science 5:356b
Ōkōchi Masatoshi 6:93a
technology, modern 7:372b
Institute of Statistical Mathematics 4:116b; 6:261a
Institut Franco-Japonaise 2:332b
Insurance
casualty 3:316a-316b
life 5:5b
medical 3:120a
medical and health 5:144b-145b
miscellaneous 3:316a-316b
unemployment 8:148a
Insurance Business Law (Hokengyō Hō) 8:316a
Insurance companies
Dai-Ichi Mutual Life Ins Co 2:58b-59a
Meiji Mutual Life Insurance Co 5:154b
mutual company 5:289b
Nippon Life Insurance Co 2:58b; 6:10b
Sumitomo Mutual Life Insurance Co 7:269b
Taishō Marine & Fire Insurance Co, Ltd 7:305b
Tokio Marine & Fire Insurance Co., Ltd 8:43a
Yasuda Fire & Marine Insurance Co, Ltd 8:317b-318a
Insurance system 3:316b-317a
government 3:317a
history 3:316b
private insurance companies 3:316b-317a
Intangible property rights 3:317a-317b
Intendants 2:60a; 8:292b
Interdependent origination 2:217a-217b
Interest groups 6:236b
Interest Limitation Law 3:317b
Interest rate structure 3:317b-318a
corporate finance 2:29a
discount rate 3:317b
monetary policy 5:239b
prime lending rate 3:317b
"Interference by Demons"
Shimomura Kanzan 7:105b
Inter-Governmental Group on Indonesia (IGGI) 3:291a
Interim Measure Law concerning Fishing Zones 2:283a
Interim Treaty for the Preservation of Fur Seals in the North Pacific Ocean 2:283b
Intermediaries 2:233a
Internal organization of Japanese companies 3:318a-318b
decision-makeup 3:318a
impact of technological progress 3:318a
research and development 3:318a
International Accounting Standards Committee (1973) 1:8b
International Air Transport Association, (IATA) 4:10a
International Bank for Reconstruction and Development (BRD) 3:253b-254a
International Banking Consortium for China 7:297a-297b
International Christian University 3:318b
International Commerce 4:11a
International communications 3:318b-319a
business communications 3:319a
news agencies
foreign 3:319a
Japanese 3:318b
television relay 3:319a
International Confederation of Free Trade Unions (ICFTU) 4:347a; 7:223b
International Convention for the Regulation of Whaling of 1946 8:250b
International Court of Justice 7:337b
International crimes 3:319a
International Criminal Police Organization 3:319a
International cultural exchange 3:319a
government involvement 3:319b
organizations 3:319b
programs 3:319b
International Energy Agency 2:215b
International Federation for the Promotion of Sister Cities 7:202a
International Finance Bureau 5:188a
International friendship organizations 3:319b-320a
diplomacy 3:320a
economy 3:319b
International Geographical Union 7:293b
International Geophysical Year 7:240a
International Jūdō Federation 4:82b
International Kendō Federation 4:196a
International Labor Organization (ILO) 4:344b, 351a, 373a; 4:178b; 7:209a
occupational structure 6:55b
International Latitude Observation Project Center 1:104a
International law, private 6:250a-252b
choice-of-law rules 6:250a-251b
adoption 6:251a-251b
decree of legal death 6:250b
inheritance 6:251b
legal acts and contracts 6:250b
legal capacity 6:250b
legal incompetency 6:250b
legitimacy 6:251a
marriage and divorce 6:251a
national law determination 6:251b
obligations 6:251a
parent-child relationship, rights and duties 6:251b
paternity 6:251a
property rights 6:250b-251a
renvoi 6:251b
civil procedure 6:251b-252a
foreign judgments 6:252a
jurisdiction over foreigners 6:251b-252a
standing to sue 6:251b
International Metalworkers' Federation-Japan Council (IMF-JC) 3:274b; 4:348a; 7:189b
International Military Tribunal for the Far East 8:223b
International Monetary Fund (IMF) 2:310a; 3:13b, 274b; 8:324a
import liberalization 2:323b
United States 8:161a
International Origami Association 6:118b
International Planned Parenthood Federation (IPPF) 2:247b
International Polar Motion Observation Project Center 1:104a
International relations 3:320a-325b

economic issues 3:325a
evolving relations with the United States 3:325a
expansion on the Asian mainland 3:320b
future prospects 3:325b
incursions in Manchuria and China 3:321b
Japan as a major power 3:320b-321a
Japan in the cold war 3:324a-324b
occupation period 3:324a
opening of Japan 3:320a
selected indicators of Japan's foreign relations 3:322a-323b
territorial issues and treaty revision 3:320b
toward a more independent diplomacy 3:324b-325a
World War I and its aftermath 3:321a
World War II and the Greater East Asia Coprosperity Sphere 3:321b-324a
See also each country
International trade. *See* **Foreign trade**
International Travel Inns 3:308b
International Treaty concerning Fishing on the High Seas in the North Pacific Ocean 2:282b
International Treaty for the Preservation of Tuna in the Northwest Atlantic Ocean 2:282b
International Tribunal of the Far East 8:36b, 223b
International Whaling Commission 8:249b
International Whaling Control Treaty 2:282b; 8:250a
International Whaling Convention of 1937 8:250b
Internists. *See* **Medicine,** internists
Interrogation (jimmon) 2:49b
Into a Black Sun 4:111b
Intoku taiheiki 陰徳太平記 6:132b
Intoxication 2:48a
Inu 2:124b-126a
Inubōzaki 犬吠埼 3:325b
Inu hariko 3:325b; 8:*96b*
Inuiyama 乾山 4:199b
Inu jinin 犬神人 4:59b
Inukai Tsuyoshi 犬養毅 3:326a-326b; 4:384b; 5:316a-316b; 7:4b, 78a, 276b
assassination (May 15th Incident) 4:373a; 5:142b
cabinet 1:74a
goals 3:326a
Kakushin Kurabu 4:120a
support of Sun Yat-Sen 3:326a
Inuoumono 犬追物 3:326b; 4:160b
Inu tsukubashū 犬筑波集 7:140a
Inuyama 犬山 3:326b
Invasions of Korea in 1592 and 1597 3:326b-327b
Bunroku Campaign 3:326b-327a
causes 3:326b
Chinese involvement 3:326b-327a
difficulties 3:327b
Fujiwara Seika 2:358b
Fukushima Masanori 2:366b
Keichō Campaign 3:327a
Korean-Japanese relations 4:140b
Korean potters 6:320b
national flag 5:339a
National Seclusion 5:347a
peace negotiations 3:327a
supply base 4:127b
Tōdō Takatora 8:34b
Ukita Hideie 8:137b
waegwan 8:198a
Investments
character of Japanese 5:263b
foreign 2:29a-30b
monetary policy 5:240b
industrial funds 3:291b
monetary policy 5:239b-240a
savings 2:160b-161a
Investment trusts 3:327b-328a
In-yō (Chinese: yin-yang) 5:151a
Inzō 印相 3:328a
Iodochlorhydroxyquin 7:206a
Ioffe (Joffe), Adolf Abramovich 2:248b; 3:328a
Iō Islands 硫黄列島 3:328a
Iōjima 硫黄島 3:328b; 4:207a; 8:276a
4:207a; 8:276a
Iōjima (Iwojima), Battle of 3:328b
Ionushi いほぬし 3:328b
"Ippeisotsu" 一兵卒 7:358b
Ippen 一遍 3:328b-329b
Ippen shōnin eden 3:*329a*
Ji sect 4:62a
studies 3:328b-329a
travels 3:329a
Ippen shōnin eden (Pictorial Biography of the Monk Ippen) 一遍上人絵伝 3:329b; 8:29b
Ippitsuan Kakō 一筆庵可候 4:189b
Ippitsusai Bunchō 一筆斎文調 3:329b
Ippon-gatana dohyōiri 一本刀土俵入 3:108a; 4:166a
IPR 3:315b-316a
Iragomisaki 伊良湖岬 3:329b
Irako Seihaku 伊良子清白 3:329b
Iran Committee 4:188a
Irejichi 7:87a
Irezumi 入墨 8:73a
Iriai 入会 3:329b-331a
fertilizers 3:330b
legal battles over 3:330b
Meiji government 3:331b
tomeyama 8:70b
types 3:330a
Iriaiken no kaitai 入会権の解体 4:184b
Iriai no kenkyū 入会の研究 4:111b
Irie Takako 入江たか子 3:331a
Iriomotejima 西表島 3:331a
Iriomote National Park 西表国立公園 3:331a
Irises (family Iridaceae) 3:331b-332a
cultivation 3:331b
introduction to West 3:331b
Iris Screens 6:*154a-154b*
Irodorareru kuchibiru (Painted Lips)彩られる唇 8:90b
Irogoi (carp) 1:244a
Iroha jirui shō 色葉字類抄 2:93b; 3:332a
Iroha karuta 3:332a, *332b*; 6:192a
Iroha poem 3:332a-332b
Irohazaka いろは坂 3:332b
Iron age 鉄器時代 3:332b-333a
Iron and steel 3:333a-333b
Iron and steel industry 3:*333a*, 333a-336a
companies
Kawasaki Steel Corporation 4:184a
Kōbe Steel, Ltd 4:238a
Nippon Kōkan 6:10a-10b
Nippon Steel Corporation 6:12b-13a
Sumitomo Metal Industries, Ltd 7:269a
economic independence 2:165b
economic planning 2:165b
exports 3:335b-336a
facilities and technology 3:335b
finance 3:335b
labor and industrial relations 3:335a
Meiji period 2:153a
modern 3:333b
origins 3:333b-334a
English furnaces 3:333b
government involvement 3:333b-334a
postwar recovery and growth 3:334a-334b
competition 3:334b
rationalization programs 3:334b
problems and prospects 3:336a
raw material supply 3:335a
structure 3:334b-335a
swords 3:333a-333b
tatara-buki 3:333a; 7:348a-348b
wage bargaining 7:189b
Irori tan 囲炉裡譚 7:292a
Irōzaki 石廊崎 3:336a
Irozange (Confession) 色ざんげ 8:173a
Irregular Militia 4:204b
Irrigation
dams 2:72b
ritsuryō system 6:329a
techniques 1:29b
Iruma 入間 3:336a
Iruman 1:145b
Irwin, Robert Walker 3:336a
Japanese American 4:13b
Irwin, Sophia A. 3:336a
Irwin Convention 4:13b
Irwin School 3:336b
Isahaya 諫早 3:336b
Isamu Noguchi イサムノグチ 8:295b
Isanatori いさなとり 4:242b
Isa Tomomune 伊佐朝宗 2:78a
Isawa (city) 石和 3:336b
Ise (city) 伊勢 3:336b
Ise (poet) 伊勢 3:336b
Kokinshū 4:254b
Sanjūrokkasen 7:13a
Ise Bay 伊勢湾 3:336b-337a
Isehara 伊勢原 3:337a
Ise kagura 伊勢神楽 4:107b
Iseki 伊勢記 4:128b
Iseki & Co, Ltd 3:337a
Ise monogatari 伊勢物語 1:85b; 3:337a; 4:129b; 5:245b; 8:118b
commentaries 3:337a; 4:188a
influence 3:337b
manuscripts 3:337a
monogatari bungaku 5:245b
parody 4:136b
waka 8:208b, 212a
Isenoumi Prefecture Natural Park 伊勢海県立自然公園 1:45a
Ise Plain 伊勢平野 3:337b
Ise Province 伊勢国 3:337b
Ise Rebellion 伊勢暴動 3:337b-338a
Ise Sadamichi 伊勢貞陸 8:303b
Isesaki 伊勢崎 3:338a
Ise-Shima National Park 伊勢志摩国立公園 1:21b; 3:338a
Ise Shrine 伊勢神宮 2:248a, 300b; 3:338a-339a; 7:80b, 180a, 248a, 250a
Amaterasu Ōmikami 1:51a; 4:144a
architecture 3:338a
cult of 3:338b
"eejanaika" 2:184a
"emperor art"
Taut, Bruno 7:351a-351b
inner shrine 3:338a
Inner Shrine, main building 3:*338b*
kamikaze 4:126b
okage mairi 6:79a
outer shrine 3:338b
rites 3:338a
Ryōbu Shintō 6:351a
sacred fire 2:53b
Shintō 7:126a
Shintō architecture 7:132b

Shintō rites 7:137b
tama 7:332a
Usa Hachiman Shrine 8:181b
Isetan Co, Ltd 3:339a
I-shan I-ning 3:348b
Ishibashi Ningetsu .... 石橋忍月 · 3:339a; 5:13a; 7:125b
Ishibashi Shian · · 石橋思案 4:198b
Ishibashi Shōjirō .... 石橋正二郎 1:170b; 3:339a
Western-art museums 5:279a
Ishibashi Tanzan 石橋湛山 · 3:339b; 7:92a
Ishibashiyama, Battle of .... 石橋山の戦 2:342b
Kajiwara Kagetoki 4:114b
Minamoto no Yoritomo 5:181a
Sasaki Takatsuna 7:23a
Taira-Minamoto War 7:300a
Ishibatsuki 4:195a
Ishibutai tomb · 石舞台古墳 · · 3:*339a*, 339b
Ishida Baigan · · · · 石田梅岩 · · 3:339b-340a
doctrines 3:340a
Shingaku 7:111b
Teshima Toan 4:120a
works 3:340a
Ishida Eiichirō · 石田英一郎 2:312a; 3:340a
Ishida Hakyō · · · · 石田波郷 3:340a
Ishida Mitoku · · · · 石田未得 · · 3:340a; 5:48a
Ishida Mitsunari · 石田三成 · · 3:340a; 7:9a, 99a
Sekigahara, Battle of 7:56b
Ishida Taizō · · · · · 石田退三 3:340b
Ishi-dōrō lanterns 4:367b-368a
Ishigaki .... 石垣 3:340b
Ishigakijima .... 石垣島 3:340b
Ishiguro Munemaro .... 石黒宗麿 · · · 3:340b-341a
glazes 3:340b
Ishiguro Tadaatsu .... 石黒忠篤 3:341a
Ishihara Kanji · · · · 石原莞爾 · · · 3:345b-346a
Ishihara Shinobu .... 石原忍 3:341a
Ishihara Shintarō 1:209a; 2:273b; .... 石原慎太郎 3:341a
Ishii Baku .... 石井漠 2:75b
Ishii Hakutei · · · · · 石井柏亭 3:146b
Ishii Kikujirō · 石井菊次郎 3:341a; 4:366b; 7:88a
League of Nations 4:373a
Ishii-Lansing Kyōtei · · · · 石井–ランシング協定 · · 4:366b-367b
Ishii Mitsujirō · 石井光次郎 3:341b
Ishii Ryōsuke · · · · 石井良助 3:341b
Ishii Teabowl Art Museum 3:77a
Ishikari Coalfield 石狩炭田 · 1:39a; 3:341b
Ishikaridake .... 石狩岳 3:341b
Ishikarigawa .... 石狩川 3:342a
Ishikari Mountains .... 石狩山脈 3:342a
Ishikari Plain · · · · 石狩平野 · 3:342a; 7:20a
Ishikawa .... 石川 3:342a
Ishikawa Chiyomatsu .... 石川千代松 1:156a; 3:342a
Ishikawa Ichirō · · 石川一郎 3:342a
Ishikawajima-Harima Heavy Industries Co, Ltd 3:342b; 4:139a, 183b
defense industry 2:82b
Dokō Toshio 2:127b
history 3:342b
Mutsu 5:288a
Suzuki shōten subsidiary 4:238a
Ishikawa Jōzan · · 石川丈山 3:342b
Ishikawa Jun .... 石川淳 · · 3:342b-343b
critiques 3:343a
lifestyle 3:343a
novels 3:343a
translations 3:342b
Ishikawa Masamochi .... 石川雅望 2:303b; 3:343b; 7:95a
Gagen shūran 3:3a
Ishikawa Prefectural Art Museum · 4:198a
Ishikawa Prefecture .... 石川県 3:344a
industries 3:344a
tourist attractions 3:344a
Ishikawa Sanshirō .... 石川三四郎 · · 3:344a; 7:56a
Fukuda Hideko 2:362b
works 3:344a
Ishikawa Tairō · · · 石川大浪 3:344a
Ishikawa Takeyoshi .... 石川武美 3:344b
Ishikawa Takuboku .... 石川啄木 · · 3:344b-345a; 5:12b, 290b; 7:253b
influence 3:345a
works 3:344b
Ishikawa Tatsuzō 石川達三 3:345a; 7:103b
fūzoku shōsetsu 2:378b
Ishikawa Toyonobu .... 石川豊信 3:345a
Ishimoto Yasuhiro 石元泰博 6:*186b*
Ishin denshin 3:29b
Ishinomaki .... 石巻 3:345a
Ishioka .... 石岡 3:345a
Ishisaji 7:247b
Ishiwara Jun .... 石原純 3:345a
Ishiwara Kanji · · · 石原莞爾 · 3:345b-346a
China policy 3:345b-346a
in Manchuria 3:345b
political machinations 3:345b
theory of war 3:345b
Ishiwara Ken .... 石原謙 3:346a
Ishiyamadera .... 石山寺 · 3:346a; 7:91a
art treasures 3:346b
patrons 3:346b
Ishiyama Honganji .... 石山本願寺 · · 3:221a-222b, 346b-347a
Oda Nobunaga vs 3:179a
Ōsaka Castle 6:120a
screen paintings 4:148a
Ishizaka Kimishige .... 石坂君茂 3:347a
Ishizaka Taizō · · · 石坂泰三 3:347a
Ishizaka Yōjirō 石坂洋次郎 2:270b; 3:347a; 7:103b
fūzoku shōsetsu 2:378b
Ishizara 7:247b
Ishizuchi Quasi-National Park .... 石鎚国定公園 · · 2:185a-185b
Ishizuchisan .... 石鎚山 · 3:347a; 7:97b
Ishizuka Tatsumaro .... 石塚龍麿 3:347a
orthographic studies 4:134a
Ishō nihonden · 異称日本伝 3:347b
Ishō ningyō 2:*129a*
Islam 8:70b
Island, The 3:75a; 7:111b
Islands
Amakusa 1:50a
Amami 1:50a
Aoshima 1:70b
Awajishima 1:124a-124b
Bentenjima 1:150a; 4:2b
Birōjima 1:156b
Chichijima 1:272a-272b
Chikubushima 1:276b
Dejima 2:83a-83b
Dōgashima 2:123a
Enoshima 2:220a
Etorofu 2:234a
Fukuejima 2:363a
Geiyo 3:15b
geological structure 4:9a-9b
Gotō 3:52b-53a
Habomai 3:73b
Hachijōjima 3:74a
Hashima 3:109b
Hatsushima 3:113b
Hegurajima 3:121b
Hiburishima 3:129b
Hikoshima 3:138b
Hiradoshima 3:141b
Hokkaidō 3:212b-213a
Honshū 3:226b
Iejima 3:260b
Iki 3:267b
Innoshima 3:308b
Iō 3:328b
Iōjima 3:328b
Iriomotejima 3:331a
Ishigakijima 3:340b
Itsukushima 3:357a
Izu Islands 3:365a
Jōgashima 4:69a
Kakuijima 4:118a
Kashikojima 4:162a
Kerama 4:200a
Kikaishima 4:205a
Kinkazan 4:213a
Kōjima 4:251b
Koshikijima 4:295b
Kumejima 4:307b
Kunashiri 4:308b
Kurahashijima 4:311a
Kuril 4:313a
Kyūshū 4:341a
Matsushima 5:140a
Megijima 5:152a
Minami Daitōjima 5:176b
Minami Torishima 4:2b; 5:176b
Mishima 5:199a
Miyakejima 5:218a
Miyako 5:219b
Miyakojima 5:219b
Naoshima 5:331b
Nōmijima 6:33b-34a
Ogasawara 4:2b; 6:68b
Oki 6:84a-85b
Okinawa 4:2b
Okinoerabujima 6:92a
Okinoshima 6:92b
Okinotorishima 4:2b; 6:93a
Ōkunojima 6:97b-98a
Okushiri 6:98b
Ōmishima 6:102a
Ōshima (Izu Ōshima) 6:125a
Ōshima (Inland Sea) 6:125b
Rebun 6:284b
Rishiri 6:320b
Sado 6:362b-363b
Sakhalin 7:1b-2a
Sakishima 7:3a
Sakurajima 7:4b
Satsunan Islands 7:30b
Senkaku 7:66a
Sensuijima 7:67b
Shikanoshima 7:94b
Shikoku 7:97b
Shikotan 7:98a
Shisakajima 7:148a
Shōdoshima 7:155a
Taketomijima 7:325b
Tanegashima 7:340a
Tobishima 8:32b
Tokara 8:42b
Tokunoshima 8:58a
Torishima 8:80b
Toshima 8:83a
Tsushima 8:117b-118a, 325b

Yaeyama 8:283b
Yakushima 8:286b
Yonagunijima 4:2b; 8:337a
Yoronjima 8:339a
Isoda Kōichi 磯田光一 3:347b
Isoda Koryūsai 磯田湖龍斎 3:347b
Isoda Kyūjirō 磯田久次郎 4:171b
Isoho monogatari 伊曽保物語 3:347b; 4:52a, 136b; 5:46a
Isonokami no Yakatsugu 石上宅嗣 3:347b
Kaifūsō 4:109a
Untei 8:174a
Isonokami Shrine 石上神宮 3:348a; 7:126b
Isozaki Arata 磯崎新 3:348a
Israel 4:43b
Issa 一茶 1:182a; 3:79b, 348a; 5:16a; 7:5b
style 3:348b
works 3:348a
Issai-kyō 一切経 1:187b; 4:136a, 299b
Issan Ichinei 一山一寧 3:348b; 7:70b
Gozan literature 3:58a-59a
Issei 4:12b-13b, 14b-15a; 6:179a
Gentlemen's Agreement 4:22a
major organizations 4:22a
political involvement 4:15b
United States Immigration Acts of 1924, 1952, and 1965 8:165a
voting 4:15b
World War II incarceration 4:17a-17b
Issekikai (political group) 8:39b
Isshin Tasuke 一心太助 8:339a
Issuikai 一水会 8:318b
Issumbōshi 一寸法師 3:348b; 5:296a
folk tales 2:302b
Isuzu Motors, Ltd 3:348b
Diesel Kiki Co, Ltd 2:94a
Itabashi Ward 板橋区 3:349a
Itadori [(Japanese knotweed) *Polygonum cuspidatum*] 3:349a
Itagaki Seishirō 板垣征四郎 3:349a
Itagaki Taisuke 板垣退助 1:271b; 2:56a; 3:349a-350a
Aikoku Kōtō 1:34b
Aikokusha 2:366a
Freedom and People's Rights Movement 2:334a-334b, 373a
hambatsu 3:91b
Hayashi Yūzō 3:118a
Jiyūtō 4:65a-66a
Kenseitō 4:198b
Kōno Hironaka 4:273b
popular rights advocacy 3:349b
rise in power 3:349b
Sandai Jiken Kempaku Movement (Movement to Memorialize Three Important Items) 7:9b
Seikanron issue 7:50b
Itaguwa 4:322a
Itai itai disease イタイイタイ病 2:226b; 4:61a; 5:185b; 6:218b
Itako 潮来 3:350a
Itakura Katsukiyo 板倉勝静 3:350a
Itakura Katsushige 板倉勝重 1:301b; 3:350a; 4:338b
Italy and Japan 3:350b-351b
Anti-Comintern Pact 1:65a
Catholic missionaries 3:350b
cultural exchange after 1868 3:350b-351a
arts 3:350b
technology 3:350b
Japanese studies 4:43a
relations after World War II 3:351a
Itamae 2:25b
Itami 伊丹 3:351b
Itami Mansaku 伊丹万作 2:270a, 271a; 3:351b
Itaya Hazan 板谷波山 3:351b
Itchakushu-han 1:203a
Itō 伊東 3:351b
Itō, Mancio 伊東満所 3:355a
French-Japanese relations 2:330a
Ito Castle 怡土城 3:354b
Itō Chūta 伊東忠太 1:80b
Itō Daisuke 伊藤大輔 2:268b; 3:351b-352a
Itō Eiga Kenkyūjo 3:351b
Itō Einosuke 伊藤永之介 3:352a
Itō Gemboku 伊東玄朴 3:352a; 7:16a
Itō Ham Provisions Co, Ltd 3:352a
Itō Hirobumi 伊藤博文 1:11b, 86b, 120a; 2:334a; 3:352a, *352b*, 353a-353b; 4:198b 241a; 7:29a, 51a, 105a, 255b
Anglo-Japanese Alliance 1:56b
assassination 1:55a; 4:282b
diplomat 3:353a
early career 3:353b-354a
genrō 3:21b
Gneist, Rudolf von 3:37b
hambatsu 3:91b
Imperial Diet 3:276a
Inoue Kaoru 3:310a
Inoue Kowashi 3:311a
Itō Miyoji 3:355a
Jiyūtō 4:65b
Kaneko Kentarō 4:138b
Kojong abdicated throne 4:252b
Korea 4:280b, 282a
last years 3:353a
Li Hongzhang 5:9b
Meiji Constitution 2:1b
nationalism 5:342b
party politics 3:353a
prime minister 6:*243a*
Rikken Seiyūkai 6:315a
Treaty of Shimonoseki 7:106a
youth 3:353a
Itoigawa 糸魚川 3:352b
Itoigawa-Shizuoka tectonic line 糸魚川-静岡構造線 4:8b
Itō Jakuchū 伊藤若冲 3:353b-354a
religious scrolls 3:353b
Itō Jinsai 伊藤仁斎 1:357a; 3:354a; 4:58b, 247b; 7:94b
Confucian teachings 1:355b-357b
Kagawa Shūtoku 4:103b
Kogaku proponent 4:246b
Kogidō founded and directed by 4:248b
Kogigaku 3:354a
works 3:354a
Itojō 怡土城 3:354b
Itokawa Hideo 糸川英夫 3:354b
Itō Keiichi 伊藤圭一 3:354b
Itō Keisuke 伊藤圭介 1:76b; 3:354b
Itokoku 伊都国 3:354b
Itoman 糸満 3:354b
Itōman & Co, Ltd 3:355a
Itō Michio 伊藤道郎 2:75b
Itō Miyoji 伊東巳代治 2:2b; 3:355a
Kaneko Kentarō 4:138b
Meiji Constitution drafting 2:2b
Itō Noe 伊藤野枝 3:355a; 7:57a
Kamichika Ichiko 4:126a
murder 4:125a; 6:128a
Ōsugi Sakae 6:127b
Seitōsha 7:54b
Itō Sachio 伊藤左千夫 1:74b; 3:355a
Nagatsuka Takashi 5:307b
Itō Sei 伊藤整 3:355b-356a; 5:275b
awards 3:355b-356a
critical essays 3:355b
new psychological literature 3:355b
novels 3:355b-356a
Shinchō 7:109a
Itō Shinsui 伊東深水 3:356a
Kaburagi Kiyokata 4:100b
Itō Shizuo 伊東静雄 3:356a
Itō Sukechika 伊東祐親 3:356a
Itō Sukeyuki 伊東祐之 8:287a
Itō Tōgai 伊藤東涯 3:356a
Itowappu 糸割符 3:356b; 5:323a-323b
National Seclusion 5:346b-347a
Itō-Yōkadō Co, Ltd 3:356b
Itsukaichi 五日市 3:356b
Itsuki Hiroyuki 五木寛之 3:356b-357a
fūzoku shōsetsu 2:378b
Itsukushima 厳島 3:357a
Itsukushima Shrine 厳島神社 1:187b; 3:*357a*; 5:277b; 7:232b
Itsunen 逸然 3:357a
Itsu no Kotowaki 稜威言別 7:292b
Itsuō Art Museum 3:357b
Ittsui otoko hayari no Utagawa (Two Stars of the Utagawa School) 一対男時花歌川 8:184b
Iva Toguri D'Aquino 4:15a
Tōkyō Rose 8:68b
IVR 4:85b
Iwafune no ki 磐舟柵 3:357b
Iwafune no saku 磐舟柵 3:357b
Iwai 岩井 3:357b
Iwai, Rebellion of 磐井の乱 3:357b-358a
Iwai Akira 岩井章 3:357b
Iwajuku site 岩宿遺跡 1:38a, 76a; 3:358a
Iwaki 磐城 2:367a; 3:358a
Iwakigawa 岩木川 3:358a
Iwakisan 岩木山 3:358a
Iwakuni 岩国 3:358a
Iwakura 岩倉 3:358b; 7:248b
Iwakura mission of 1871 岩倉遣外使節 1:119b-120a; 2:311a; 3:358b-360a; 7:50b, 270b
Bacon, Alice Mabel 1:129b
Hayashi Tadasu 3:118a
influence on Japanese policies 3:359b
Itō Hirobumi 3:352b
Iwakura Tomomi 3:360a
Kido Takayoshi 4:203a
Kume Kunitake 4:307b
Nagayo Sensai 5:308a
Parkes, Sir Harry Smith 6:164a
purpose 3:358b-359a
reception 3:359a
route map 3:*358b*
Sasaki Takayuki 7:23b
Seikanron 7:50b
shogunate missions to the West 7:161b
Tanabe Taichi 7:335b
Tanaka Fujimaro 7:336a
tour 3:358b-359a
Tsuda Umeko 8:112b
Unequal Treaties revision 8:148b
Verbeck, Guido Herman Fridolin 8:190a
Iwakura Tomomi 岩倉具視 3:360a; 7:29a
Iwakura mission 3:358b-360a
Meiji Restoration 3:360a
Sanjō Sanetomi 7:12b
Iwakuro Hideo 岩畔豪雄 7:197a
Iwami Silver Mine 石見銀山 3:360a; 4:127b

Iwamizawa ········· 岩見沢 ········· **3**:360b
Iwamoto Yoshiharu
·················· 巌本善治 **1**:208b; **3**:360b
Iwanaga News Agency ············· **3**:360b
Iwanaga Yūkichi · 岩永裕吉 ········· **3**:360b
Furuno Inosuke ····················· **2**:373a
Iwanami Bunko ·· 岩波文庫 ··· **3**:360b-361a
Iwanami Shigeo · 岩波茂雄 ········· **3**:360b
Iwanami Shoten Publishers · **3**:360b-361a; **7**:55b
publications ·················· **3**:360b-361a
series ·························· **3**:361a
Iwanari Tomomichi
················· 岩成友通 ········· **5**:224a
Iwano Hōmei ···· 岩野泡鳴 · **3**:361a; **7**:54b
critiques ························ **3**:361a
novels ··························· **3**:361b
plays ···························· **3**:361a
poetry ··························· **3**:361a
Shinshichō ······················ **7**:124b
Shinshōsetsu ···················· **7**:125b
Iwanuma ············· 岩沼 ········· **3**:361b
Iwasaki Kan'en ·· 岩崎灌園 ········· **3**:361b
Iwasaki Koyata 岩崎小弥太 ·· **3**:361b-362a; **7**:50b
Iwasaki Yanosuke
················ 岩崎弥之助 ········· **7**:50b
Iwasaki Yatarō 岩崎弥太郎 ·· **3**:362a; **7**:52a
Kaiseikan of Tosa ················ **3**:362a
Mitsubishi ······················· **5**:205b
Shinagawa Yajirō ················· **7**:109a
shipping business ················ **3**:362a
tactics ·························· **3**:362a
Taiwan Expedition ················ **3**:362b
Iwasa Matabei · 岩佐又兵衛 ··· **3**:362b-363a
works ···························· **3**:363a
I was Born, But ············ **8**:146a-146b
Iwase Tadanari ·· 岩瀬忠震 ········· **3**:363a
Iwase "thousand-mound" tomb cluster
·········· 岩橋千塚古墳群 ········· **3**:363a
Iwashi ··························· **7**:21b
Iwashimizu Hachiman Shrine ····· 石清水八幡宮 ···· **3**:74a-74b, 363a; **4**:164a; **7**:126b
Shintō architecture ·············· **7**:133b
Iwashimizu monogatari (Tale of Iwashimizu)
·············· 石清水物語 ········· **5**:246a
Iwashimotsuke ···················· **7**:107a
Iwashita Shima ··· 岩下志麻 ········· **2**:*274b*
Iwashita Sōichi ·· 岩下壮一 ··· **3**:363a-363b
Iwata ················· 磐田 ········· **3**:363b
Iwatahara ·········· 磐田原 ········· **3**:363b
Iwata Sentarō · 岩田専太郎 ········· **1**:*163a*
Iwata Toyoo. *See* **Shishi Bunroku**
Iwate Prefecture ··· 岩手県 ········· **3**:363b
tourist attractions ·············· **3**:363b
Iwatesan ············ 岩手山 ········· **3**:363b
Iwatsuki ·············· 岩槻 ········· **3**:364a
Iwayagawachi kiln
·············· 岩谷川内窯 ········· **5**:299a
Iwaya Sazanami · 巌谷小波 **1**:164a; **3**:364a
children's literature ············· **1**:279b
Ken'yūsha ························ **4**:199a
Iwojima. 硫黄島 *See* **Iōjima**
Iyadani ············· 祖谷渓 · **3**:364a; **7**:97b
Iyo ······················ 伊予 ········· **3**:364a
Iyo Mishima ····· 伊予三島 ········· **3**:364b
Izanagi and Izanami
········· 伊弉諾, 伊弉冉 · **2**:302b, 376a; **3**:364b-365a; **4**:125b; **5**:292b-293a
leech baby ······················· **4**:374b
Izanagi no Mikoto
················ 伊弉諾尊 ··· **3**:364b-365a
Izanami no Mikoto
················ 伊弉冉尊 ··· **3**:364b-365a
Izawajō ············ 胆沢城 **3**:365a; **6**:379a; **7**:3a
Izawa Shūji ····· 伊沢修二 ········· **3**:365a
Izayoi nikki (Diary of the Waning Moon)
·············· 十六夜日記 ····· **1**:5b-6a; **6**:2b; **8**:105a-105b
Izu Dancer, The ··················· **4**:175b
Izu Gold Mine ···· 伊豆金山 ········· **3**:365a
Ōkubo Nagayasu ··················· **6**:93b
Izuhara port ········ 厳原港 ········· **8**:*117a*
Izui Hisanosuke
·············· 泉井久之助 ········· **4**:20a
Izu Islands ······· 伊豆諸島 **2**:342b; **3**:365a
Hachijōjima ······················ **3**:74a
Ōshima ··························· **6**:125a
Izumi (northern Honshū)
························ 泉 ········· **3**:365a
Izumi (central Honshū)
······················ 和泉 ········· **3**:365a
Izumi (Kyūshū) ······· 出水 ··· **3**:365a-365b
Izumidono ························ **7**:111a
Izumi Kyōka ······· 泉鏡花 **3**:365b; **7**:103b
Ken'yūsha ························ **4**:199a
shimpa ··························· **7**:108a
Shinshōsetsu ···················· **7**:125b
style ···························· **3**:365b
works ···························· **3**:365b
Yashagaike ······················ **7**:122b
Izumi Motohide ·· 和泉元秀 ········· **4**:*327a*
Izumi Mountains · 和泉山脈 ········· **3**:366a
Izumi Ōtsu ········· 泉大津 ········· **3**:366a
Izumi Sano ········· 泉佐野 ········· **3**:366a
Izumi school ······· 和泉流 **3**:366a; **4**:325b
Izumi Seiichi ······· 泉靖一 ········· **3**:366a
Izumi Shikibu ···· 和泉式部 · **3**:366a; **5**:34b; **7**:52b, 95a
poetry ··························· **3**:366a
Shin kokinshū ···················· **7**:120a
Izumo ···················· 出雲 **3**:367a; **7**:101a
Izumo cycle of mythology ···· **5**:293b-295a
Izumo kagura ···· 出雲神楽 ········· **4**:107b
Izumo no Okuni · 出雲阿国 · **3**:367a; **6**:97a
Izumo Plain ····· 出雲平野 · **3**:*366b*, 367a
Izumo Province ·· 出雲国 ········· **3**:367a
Izumo Shrine ···· 出雲大社 **3**:367a; **7**:100b
architecture ····················· **3**:367b
festivals ························ **3**:367b
Lake Shinji ······················ **7**:115a
main building ···················· **3**:*367a*
mythic origins ··················· **3**:367b
Ōkuninushi no Mikoto ············· **6**:97b
Shintō ··························· **7**:126a
Shintō architecture ·············· **7**:133a
Taisha ··························· **7**:303b
Izu Nagaoka ····· 伊豆長岡 ········· **3**:367b
Izu no odoriko · 伊豆の踊子 · **1**:49b; **4**:175b
Izu Ōshima ······· 伊豆大島 ········· **6**:125a
Izu Ōshima volcano 伊豆大島火山 **8**:194b
Izu Peninsula ···· 伊豆半島 **2**:342b; **3**:367b
Izura ················· 五浦 ········· **3**:367b
Izu Shrine ········ 伊豆神社 ········· **7**:206b

J

JACL ························· **4**:12b-13a
Jagatara-bumi
············ ジャガタラ文 ········· **4**:1a
Jaguaré Fertilizer Company ······· **5**:317b
Jahana Noboru ···· 謝花昇 ········· **4**:1a
Jaimini ··········· 闍威弥尼 ········· **1**:69a
Jakkōin ············ 寂光院 ········· **4**:1a
origins ·························· **4**:1a
Jakuchū. 若冲 *See* **Itō Jakuchū**
Jakugon ················ 寂厳 ······· **4**:1a-1b
Jakuren ················ 寂蓮 ···· **4**:1b; **5**:41a
Fujiwara no Ietaka ················ **2**:351a
Kenshō ··························· **4**:198b
Shin kokinshū ···················· **7**:119b
Jakushitsu Genkō
················ 寂室元光 ······· **4**:1b-2a
JAL (Japan Air Lines Co, Ltd) ······ **4**:10a
JALPAK ··························· **4**:10a
JALTOS ··························· **4**:10a
Janes, Leroy Lansing ············ **4**:2a
Jan Joosten, Lodenstijn ········ **4**:2a; **5**:3b
Janken. *See* **Ken**
Janome Sewing Machine Co, Ltd ··· **4**:2a
Jansen, Marius B. ················· **5**:228b
Japan ················ **4**:2b-9b; **6**:135a, 288a
geological structure ············· **4**:8a-9b
crustal movement ················ **4**:8b-9a
history of islands ·············· **4**:9a-9b
northeastern and southwestern ······ **4**:8b
topography ······················· **4**:8b
maps ···························· **4**:*3a-6b*
natural features ················ **4**:7b-8a
climate ············ **1**:325a-328b; **4**:7b-8a
life and nature ··················· **4**:8a
topography ························ **4**:7b
territory and administrative divisions
····························· **4**:2b-7b
changes in ························ **4**:7a
formation of country ··············· **4**:7a
modern administrative system ·· **4**:7a-7b
population ········ **4**:2b-7a; **6**:222a-225b
territory of Japan ······· **4**:2b; **8**:13b-14b
See also **Prefectures**
Japan, Past and Present ··········· **6**:289a
Japan: The Story of a Nation ······ **6**:289a
Japan Academy ········ **4**:9b; **7**:3b; **8**:289b
Japan Advertiser ··········· **4**:49b; **7**:229b
Japan Advertisers Association ······ **4**:9b
Japan Advertising Artists Club (JAAC)
································· **2**:89b
Japan Advertising Review Organization ·················· **4**:9b-10a
Japan Air Lines Co, Ltd (JAL) ····· **1**:48a; **4**:10a; **8**:102b
Japan Air Lines Development Co ··· **4**:10a
Japan Air Lines Law ··············· **4**:10a
Japan Alpine Club ········· **5**:259b; **8**:249a
Japan Amateur Sports Association **4**:10a, 82b; **7**:243a
founding ························· **4**:147a
Kishi Seiichi ····················· **4**:223b
National Sports Festival ·········· **5**:348a
Japan Amateur Wrestling Association
································· **8**:279a
Japan-American Institute of Management Science (JAIM) ··················· **2**:347b
Japan-American Student Conference
······························ **4**:10a-10b
Japan Art Academy ················ **4**:10b
Kitamura Rokurō ·················· **4**:227a
Kosugi Tengai elected to ·········· **4**:296a
Takii Kōsaku ······················ **7**:326b
Tanaka Chikao ····················· **7**:335b
Japan Art Academy (Nihon Geijutsuin)
································· **6**:158a
Japan Art Academy Literary Prize
Ikko sono ta (1965) ·············· **5**:301b
Japan Art Academy Prize
Yamamoto Kenkichi (1966) ·········· **8**:298b
Japan Art Association ············· **7**:359a
Japan Association for Legal Philosophy
································· **4**:85b
Japan Association of National Universities ······················· **4**:10b

Japan Association of Tax Accounting 7:351b
Japan Atomic Power Company 4:10b
Japan-Australia Business Cooperation Committee 1:118b-119a
Japan Book Publishers Association 4:10b
Japan Braille Library 4:10b-11a
Japan Broadcasting Association 1:11a
Japan Broadcasting Corporation. *See* **NHK**
Japan Buddhist Federation. *See* **Zen Nihon Bukkyō Kai**
Japan Center for Area Research and Development 4:11a
Japan Chamber of Commerce and Industry 1:11a; 4:11a, 188a; 6:237b
collective bargaining 4:348b
international friendship organizations 3:320a
Nagano Shigeo 5:303a
Japan Chemical Society 4:373b
Japan-China Cultural Association 7:323b
Japan Chronicle 4:49b
Japan Commercial Arbitration Association 2:118b
Japan Committee for Economic Development (Keizai Dōyū Kai) 4:11a, 188a, 348b; 5:319a-319b; 6:238a; 8:367a
Japan Communist Party 2:7a; 4:11a-12a; 6:210b; 7:25a, 215b, 251b, 264b; 8:296b
Akahata 1:39b
Akamatsu Katsumaro 1:40a
Arahata Kanson 1:72a
campaign to destroy 7:242a
Diet 2:95a
Fukumoto Kazuo 2:364a; 4:180b
history
postwar 4:11b-12a
through 1945 4:11a-11b
Ichikawa Shōichi 3:258a
Inoue Mitsuharu 3:311a
Japan Socialist Party 4:48b
labor reforms 4:358a
March 15th Incident 5:112b
Minsei 5:197a
Miyamoto Kenji 5:220a
Miyamoto Yuriko 5:220b
Mizuno Shigeo 5:226b
modern philosophy 5:231b
national defense 5:336b-338b
National Railway Workers' Union 7:107a
Nosaka Sanzō 8:315b
Occupation 6:54a
party strength 4:12a
peace movement 6:166b
Peace Preservation Law of 1925 6:168b
Planning Board Incident 6:189b
postwar activity 3:204b-205a
Red Purge 6:285b
Sakai Toshihiko 6:377a
Sambetsu Kaigi (Congress of Industrial Labor Unions of Japan) 7:7a
Shiga Yoshio and 7:91b
Shinjinkai 7:115b
Taira Incident 7:299b
Tanno Setsu 7:344a
Tokuda Kyūichi 8:44b
Watanabe Masanosuke 8:236a
Yamakawa Hitoshi 8:296b
Japan Confederation of A- and H-bomb Sufferers Organizations 1:111a
Japan Council against Atomic and Hydrogen Bombs 6:166a
Japan Creative Tours Co 4:10a
Japan Current. *See* **Kuroshio**
Japan Democratic Party (Nihon Minshutō) 4:384b; 5:381a
Japan Design Promotion Organization (JIDPO) 2:90a
Japan Development Bank 1:139b; 4:12b; 5:319a-319b; 6:263b
fiscal system 2:281b
Japan Development Bank Law 4:12b
Japan Electronic Industry Development Association 2:193b
Japan Emigration Promotion Company 2:201a
Japan Emigration Service (JEMIS) 2:201a
Japanese, The 6:289a
"Japanese Adam Smith, The" 7:294b
Japanese Agricultural Standard 4:50b
Japanese Alps 4:*12b*, 224a
Akaishi Mountain range 1:39b
Chūbu region 1:311a
mountaineering 5:259b
Japanese American Bar Association 4:14b
Japanese American Citizens League (JACL) 4:12b-13a, 15a
voter registration 4:15b
Japanese American Claims Act of 1948 4:13a, 17b
Japanese American Relations Committee 1:47a
Japanese Americans 4:13a-16a
cultural changes and adaptation 4:15b
current issues 4:15b-16a
evacuation during World War II 4:14a-14b
442nd Regimental Combat Team 2:329b
Gentlemen's Agreement 3:24b
Hawaii 4:16a-17a
cultural continuity and change 4:16b-17a
immigration history 4:16a
occupational trends and economic standing 4:16b
political participation 4:16b
immigration background 4:13b-14a
as inu 4:13a
Japanese American Citizens League 4:12b-13a
Japan's 4:15a-15b
military service 4:15a, 18a
organizations 4:14b-15a
political involvement 4:15b
Topaz Relocation Center 8:75b
War Relocation Authority (WRA) 8:228b
wartime relocation centers 1:48b
wartime relocation of 4:13a, 14a-14b, 17a-18a; 8:158b
aftermath 4:18a
evacuation and relocation 4:17b-18a
genesis of evacuation 4:17a-17b
Rohwer Relocation Center 6:334a
Japanese andromeda 1:97a
Japanese angelica tree 7:346a
Japanese Asian Solidarity Committee 1:19b
Japanese Association of International Law 8:289b
Japanese Association of Medical Sciences 4:374a
Japanese Associations of America 4:22a-22b
Japanese American Citizens League 4:22b
Japanese American Organizations 4:14b-15a
Japanese beauty-berry 5:269b
Japanese beetle [(manekogane) *Popillia japonica*] 4:22b
Japanese box 8:113a-113b
Japanese bush clover 3:75b-76a
Japanese business in America 4:22b-23a
basic resources 4:22b-23a
conclusions 4:23a
manufacturing 4:23a
sales and distribution 4:23a
service industries 4:22b
Japanese cedar 7:257b
Japanese Chronological Tables 1:231b
Japanese Cities, A Geographical Approach 4:23b
Japanese Confederation of Labor 2:130a; 7:189a
peace movement 6:166b
Japanese Culture Research Institute 1:2b
Japanese Culture Society of Brazil 5:317b (Sociedade Brasileira de Cultura) 8:298b
Japanese Exclusion Act of 1924 4:23b
United States 8:157b
Japanese Fair Trade Commission 6:268b
Japanese Folklore Studies 6:118b
Japanese Gospel Society of San Francisco 4:14b
Japanese hop 4:135b
Japanese Industrial Standard 4:61b-62a
Japanese Institute of Certified Public Accountants (JICPA) 1:8b
Japanese knotweed 3:349a
Japanese-Korean Treaty of Alliance 4:281a
Japanese labor movement 6:129a
Japanese language 4:23b-29b
accent in. *See* **Accent in Japanese language**
alleged difficulty 4:28a
Altaic languages 4:18b-20b
comparative method 4:19a-20b
conclusions 4:20a
classical. *See* **Classical Japanese**
classical standard 4:30a
colloquial standard 4:30a
dialects 2:91b-92a; 4:23b-24a
dialects and speech of Tōkyō 4:23b-24a
dictionaries 2:93a-94a
feminine. *See* **Feminine language**
as foreign language 4:21a-22a
pre-World War II 4:21a
World War II 4:21a
post-World War II 4:21a-22a
genetic relationships 4:23b
gojūon zu 3:40b-41a
grammar 4:24b-27a
adjectives 4:26a-26b
copula 4:26a-26b
levels of speech 4:26b
modern 4:24b-27a
nouns 4:24b-25a
sentence 4:26b-27a
verbs 4:24a-26a
vocabulary 4:27a
Hawaii 4:17a
history 4:28b-29b
honorific. *See* **Honorific language**
hyōjungo 4:23b
kana. *See* **Kana**
kanji. *See* **Kanji**
Korean language 4:289b-291a
Malayo-Polynesian languages 4:20a-21a
masculine. *See* **Masculine language**
medieval 7:165b-166a
morphology 4:19b
onomatopoeia. *See* **Onomatopoeia**
phonology 4:24a-24b
consonants 4:24a-24b
of the standard 4:24a-24b
stress accent 4:24b
syllable 4:24a-24b
vowels 4:24a-24b
process theory 8:42b
reforms 4:29b-30b
first period (1868-1900) 4:29b-30a
second period (1900-1960) 4:30a-30b
third period (1960-present) 4:30b

future ··· 4:30b
romanization of ··· 6:335b-336b
school curriculum ··· 7:34b
speech of Tōkyō ··· 4:23b-24a
studies, history of ··· 4:30b-32a
vernacular. *See* **Gembun itchi**
writing
jōyō kanji ··· 4:27b
kana ··· 4:27b-28a
kun readings ··· 4:27b-28a
on readings ··· 4:27b-28a
writing system ··· 4:27a-28a
Japanese language studies ··· 4:21a-22a
Japanese laurel ··· 1:68b
Japanese literature and Christianity ··· 4:32a-32b
Japanese Literature Patriotic Association ··· 7:316a
Japanese National Commission for UNESCO. *See* **UNESCO activities in Japan**
Japanese nationalism ··· 7:320a
Japanese nationality ··· 2:313b; 4:32b-33a
acquisition ··· 4:32b-33a
konketsuji ··· 4:271b
of Koreans in Japan ··· 4:291b
loss ··· 4:33a
naturalization ··· 5:351b
Japanese National Railways (JNR) ··· 4:33b; 6:278a; 7:14b; 8:99a-99b
background ··· 4:33b
fiscal system ··· 2:281b
Kōrōkyō membership ··· 4:294a
organization and scale of operation ··· 4:33b
problems and plans ··· 4:33b
Shinkansen ··· 7:116b-119a
Teito Rapid Transit Authority ··· 7:377a
Yamanote Line ··· 8:302a
Japanese National Railways Labor Union ··· 4:84a
Japanese Newspaper Association ··· 4:79a
Japanese Olympic committee ··· 7:310a
Japanese people
origins ··· 4:33b-35a
formation of the Yamato ··· 4:34b
Jōmon hunters and Yayoi cultivators ··· 4:34a-34b
modern man ··· 4:34a
time depth and early man ··· 4:33b-34a
physical characteristics ··· 4:35a-38a
abnormal hemoglobins ··· 4:36b
adaptation ··· 4:37a-37b
blood group antigens ··· 4:35b-36a
color blindness ··· 4:36b
descriptive traits ··· 4:35a
earwax ··· 4:35b
fingerprints ··· 4:35b
gamma globulins ··· 4:36a-36b
glandular secretions ··· 4:36b-37a
hair follicles ··· 4:35b
mate selection and inbreeding ··· 4:38a
morphological types ··· 4:35a-35b
red cell enzymes ··· 4:36a
regional variability ··· 4:35b
secular trend increases ··· 4:37b-38a
serological gene markers ··· 4:35b
serum proteins ··· 4:36a
virus studies ··· 4:36b
psychology of ··· 4:38a-40b
achievement orientation ··· 4:39b
compulsive personality theory ··· 4:38b
early national character studies ··· 4:38a-39a
modal personality-conceptual problems ··· 4:39a-40b
psychological reductionism ··· 4:39a
reaction formation ··· 4:38b
rituals ··· 4:38b
Japanese pittosporum ··· 8:32a-32b
Japanese Political League of Small and Medium Enterprises ··· 6:238a
Japanese privet ··· 5:374a
Japanese Psychological Association (Nihon Shinri Gakkai) ··· 6:260b
Japanese Red Cross Society ··· 4:40b
Sano Tsunetami ··· 7:16a
Japanese robin ··· 4:264b
Japanese Romantic School ··· 5:381b
Japanese sago palm ··· 7:233a
Japanese scabiosa ··· 5:138b
Japanese serow ··· 4:129b
Japanese snowbell ··· 2:184b
Japanese society, interpretations of ··· 7:217b-218a
Japanese Society for Science of Design (JSSD) ··· 2:90a
Japanese Society for the Study of Wooden Documents ··· 1:80a
Japanese spaniel (chin) ··· 4:40b-41a
Japanese spicebush ··· 4:316b
Japanese spirit, Chinese learning ··· 8:221a
Japanese spirit, Western learning ··· 8:221a-221b
Japanese studies abroad ··· 4:41a-45a
Japanese as foreign language ··· 4:45a
multidisciplinary approach ··· 4:41b-42a
Japanese Studies in the United States ··· 4:41b
Japanese Studies in the Universities and Colleges of the United States ··· 4:41b
Japanese-style painting ··· 5:379a-380a; 6:154a, 155a
Japanese-style Painting Society ··· 4:175b; 8:13a
Japanese Tax Law Review Commission ··· 7:355a-358b
Japanese terrier (Nippon teriya) ··· 4:45a
Japanese Utility-Model Law of 1905 ··· 8:187a
Japanese yew ··· 3:255b
Japan Esperanto Association ··· 2:231b
Japan Esperanto Institute ··· 2:231b
Japan Euthanasia Association ··· 2:236a
Japan External Trade Organization. *See* **JETRO**
Japan Fabian Society
founding ··· 1:2a
Kimura Ki ··· 4:211a
Japan Family Planning Association ··· 2:247b
Japan Family Planning Federation 2:247b
Japan Farmers' Union ··· 1:84a
Japan Federation of Bar Associations ··· 4:45b
civil liberties ··· 1:318a
Japan Federation of Employers' Associations. *See* **Nikkeiren**
Japan Federation of Engineering Societies ··· 4:374a
Japan Federation of Japanese Overseas Associations ··· 2:201a
Japan Federation of Labor ··· 1:2a; 7:219a-219b
Japan Federation of Labor Unions 6:212b
Japan Federation of Proletarian Literature ··· 7:175a
Japan Federation of Religions ··· 4:45b
Japan Federation of Tax Agents Associations ··· 1:9a
Japan Federation of Textile Industry Workers Unions ··· 8:376b
Japan Fine Arts Academy (Nihon Bijutsuin) ··· 1:154b; 4:45b-46a
modern painting ··· 6:156a
Okakura Kakuzō ··· 6:79b
Rimpa ··· 6:318a
Shimomura Kanzan ··· 7:105b
Yokoyama Taikan ··· 8:334b
Japan Fine Arts Association ··· 4:175b
Japan Fisheries Agency ··· 2:304b
Japan Folk-Craft Museum ··· 4:46a
Japan Folk Craft Society ··· 2:294b
Japan Folklore Institute ··· 2:296b
Japan Foundation ··· 3:341a; 4:46a
Malaysia ··· 5:88b
Japan Foundation Library ··· 4:46a
Japan Graphic Designers Association ··· 2:89b
Japan Greening Center ··· 4:11a
Japan Handicrafts Association ··· 3:341a
Japan Herald ··· 4:46a
Japan Highway Public Corporation ··· 4:46a-46b
expressways ··· 2:238a
roads ··· 6:332b
Japan Historical Geography Society (Nihon Rekishi Chiri Kenkyū kai) 4:228b
Japan Housewives Association. *See* **Shufuren**
Japan Housing Corporation. *See* **Housing and Urban Development Corporation**
Japan-Hungary Cultural Agreement ··· 2:142a
Japan Imperial Table Tennis Association ··· 7:291b
Japan Imperial Volleyball Association (Japan Volleyball Association) ··· 8:195b
Japan Incorporated ··· 4:46b-47a
Ministry of International Trade and Industry ··· 5:190a
Japan Industrial Council (Nihon Sangyō Kyōgikai) ··· 4:188a
Japan Industrial Designers Association ··· 2:89b
Japan Industrial Robots Association ··· 3:298b
Japan Information Center for Science and Technology ··· 7:38a
Japan International Cooperation Agency ··· 4:47a
foreign aid policy ··· 2:310a
international friendship organizations ··· 3:319b
Overseas Economic Cooperation Fund ··· 4:47a
Japanism. *See* **Nihon shugi**
Japan Labor Council ··· 7:189a
Japan Labor-Farmer Party. *See* **Nihon Rōnōtō**
Japan Liberal Party ··· 4:274a; 6:211b
Japan Line, Ltd ··· 4:47a
Japan Literati Painting Association ··· 7:344b
Japan Magazine Publishers Association ··· 4:47a
Japan Mail ··· 4:49b
Japan Mathematical Society ··· 4:373b
Japan Medical Association (Nihon Ishikai) ··· 4:47a-47b; 6:237a, 238a; 8:263a
Japan Metals & Chemicals Co, Ltd 4:47b
Japan Monopoly Corporation ··· 6:263b
Japan Mountaineering Association 5:259b
Japan National Oil Corporation (JNOC) ··· 6:182a
Japan Newspaper Publishers and Editors Association ··· 4:47b
Japan Opera Association ··· 8:289a
Japan Overseas Cooperation Volunteers ··· 1:19b; 4:47b
Japan Painting Association (Nihon Kaiga Kyōkai)
Uemura Shōen ··· 8:128a

Japan Peasant Union (Nihon Nōmin Kumiai) ··· 4:363a
Japan P. E. N. Club ··· 4:47b-48a
Japan Petroleum Exploration Co, Ltd ··· 6:181b
Japan Physics Society ··· 4:373b
Japan Productivity Center ··· 1:11a; 4:48a
  collective bargaining ··· 4:348b
Japan Proletarian Arts League (Nihon Puroretaria Geijutsu Remmei) ··· 6:255a
Japan Proletarian Literary Arts League (Nihon Puroretaria Bungei Remmei) ··· 6:254b-255a
Japan Proletarian Party ··· 5:381a
Japan Pulp & Paper Co, Ltd ··· 4:48a
Japan Punch ··· 8:254b
Japan Railway Company ··· 5:384b
Japan Reform Party ··· 1:40b
Japan Research Council on Economics Education ··· 4:11a
Japan Review ··· 5:380a
Japan Robot Leasing Corporation 3:299b
Japan Science Council ··· 4:256b
Japan Securities Finance Co, Ltd ··· 4:48a
Japan Shōgi Federation ··· 7:158b-159a
Japan-Singapore Association ··· 7:196b
Japan Socialist League. *See* **Nihon Shakai Shugi Dōmei**
Japan Socialist Party
  postwar ··· 1:2b; 2:7a; 4:48a-49a, 285b; 6:211b-212a; 7:215b
    Arahata Kanson ··· 1:72a-72b
    Asanuma Inejirō ··· 1:96a
    Asukata Ichio ··· 1:107b
    ban-the-bomb movement ··· 1:114b-115a
    Democratic Socialist Party ··· 2:85a-85b
    Den Hideo ··· 2:86b
    Diet ··· 2:96b
    Eda Saburō ··· 2:168b
    Katayama Tetsu ··· 4:167b
    labor unions ··· 4:347a
    Narita Tomomi ··· 5:334b
    national bureaucracy ··· 1:220b
    national defense ··· 5:336b-338b
    Occupation ··· 6:54a
    Ōuchi Hyōe ··· 6:135a
    peace movement ··· 6:166b
    Planning Board Incident ··· 6:189b
    postwar power ··· 3:204b
    pressure groups ··· 6:236b, 238a
    Sasaki Kōzō ··· 7:22b-23a
    United Social Democratic Party ··· 8:154b
    Sakisaka Itsurō ··· 7:3a
  pre-World War II ··· 4:48a; 6:210b
    Heimin shimbun ··· 3:125b
    Katayama Sen ··· 4:167a
    Kōtoku Shūsui ··· 4:298a
    Nishikawa Mitsujirō ··· 6:17a
    Sakai Toshihiko ··· 6:377a
    Tazoe Tetsuji ··· 7:359b
Japan Society for the Promotion of Science ··· 4:49a-49b; 6:303b
Japan Society for the Study of Education ··· 2:181a
Japan Society in London ··· 6:188a
Japan Sociological Society ··· 8:34b
Japan-Soviet Committee ··· 4:188a
Japan State Socialist Party ··· 1:40b
Japan Statutory Auditors Association ··· 1:9a
Japan Steel Works, Ltd ··· 4:49b
Japan Sumō Association ··· 7:271b
Japan Symphony Orchestra ··· 5:287a
Japan Synthetic Rubber Co, Ltd ··· 4:49b
Japan Teachers' Union. *See* **Nikkyōso**
Japan Times ··· 4:49b-50a
Japan Times and Mail ··· 6:343a
Japan Tobacco and Salt Public Corporation ··· 4:50a; 7:14b
  Kōrōkyō membership ··· 4:294a
Japan Travel Bureau, Inc ··· 4:50a
  railways ··· 6:280a
Japan-United States Educational Commission ··· 4:50a-50b
Japan-United States Extradition Treaty ··· 2:238a
Japan Upper Secondary School Teachers' Union ··· 7:366b
Japan-U.S.-Canada Fishery Agreement ··· 2:285b
Japan-U.S.S.R. Fishery Agreement ··· 2:285b
Japan Women's College ··· 8:267b
Japan Women's University ··· 4:50b; 7:54a
  founder ··· 5:335a
Japan Wool Textile Co, Ltd ··· 4:50b
Japan Wrestling Association ··· 8:279a
Japan Yearbook ··· 4:44a
Japan Youth Painting Society (after 1897 the Japanese-Style Painting Society, Nihonga Kai) ··· 8:13a
Japan Zoological Society ··· 4:373b
JAPEX. *See* Japan Petroleum Exploration Co, Ltd
JAS (Japanese Agricultural Standard) ··· 4:50b
Jashūmon (Heathen Gate) ··· 邪宗門 ··· 8:13a
Jayanagi ··· 蛇柳 ··· 4:99a
Jazz ··· 1:44b
Jellyfish (kurage) ··· 4:50b
JEMIS (Japan Emigration Service) 2:201a
Jerome Relocation Center ··· 4:50b-51a
Jesuit mission press ··· キリシタン版 ··· 4:51a, 119b; 5:322a-323a; 6:248a; 8:248b
  Doctrina Christan ··· 4:52a, *52b*
  Korean moveable type ··· 4:279a
Jesuits ··· 1:306b; 4:51a-51b; 6:334a
  mission to Europe of 1582 ··· 5:203a
  namban art ··· 5:322a-323a
  Ōmura Sumitada ··· 6:104b
  Ōtomo Sōrin ··· 6:132b
  romanization of Japanese ··· 6:336a
JETRO (Japan External Trade Organization) ··· 1:120a; 1:168b; 2:321a; 4:52a; 7:257b
  Ministry of International Trade and Industry ··· 5:191a
Jewelry
  bracelets, ancient ··· 1:167a
JGC Corporation ··· 4:52b
Jiaozhou (Kiaochow) concession ··· 4:53a
Ji-Cha (Chi-Ch'a) Autonomous Political Council ··· 4:53a; 6:260a
Jichikai (self-governing associations) ··· 自治会 ··· 7:252a-252b; 8:375a
Jichin ··· 慈鎮 ··· 4:53b-54a
Jichinsai ··· 4:195a
Jichirō (All Japan Prefectural and Municipal Workers' Union) ··· 自治労 ··· 4:53a; 4:348b; 6:238a
Jichishō. 自治省 *See* **Ministry of Home Affairs**
Jidai Festival ··· 時代祭 ··· 2:*258b*; 4:53a, 336a
  Heian Shrine ··· 3:122b
Jidai fudō uta-awase ··· 時代不同歌合 ··· 4:161b
Jidaigeki (period drama) ··· 2:267b-268a, 269b, 271b, 274a; 7:31a
Jidai-mono (historical plays) ··· 時代物 4:91a, 93a-94a; 5:234b
  acting style ··· 4:94a
  costume, wig and makeup ··· 4:95b
  dialogue ··· 4:94a
Jidan ··· 4:53b
Jidong Fanggong Zizhi Zhengfu ··· 2:142b
Jidōsha Sōren ··· 4:53b
Jieikan ··· 7:58b, 60b
Jieitai. *See* **Self Defense Forces**
Jien ··· 慈円 ··· 4:53b-54a
  Fujiwara no Tameie ··· 2:356a
  Fujiwara no Yoshitsune ··· 2:358a
  Gukanshō ··· 3:65a-65b
  historical principles ··· 3:153b
  Shin kokinshū ··· 7:120a
Jigabachi (sand wasps) ··· 1:149a
Jige (groundlings) ··· 地下 ··· 2:40a; 4:54a
Jigenin ··· 地下人 ··· 4:54a
Jigeuke ··· 地下請 ··· 3:250b
Jigoku. *See* **Hell**
Jigokumon ··· 地獄門 ··· 2:56b
  Daiei Co, Ltd ··· 2:56b
Jigoku-zōshi ··· 地獄草紙 ··· 1:190b; 4:54a-54b; 5:333a
Jihon ··· 3:255b
Jiji Press ··· 4:54b
  directorship ··· 2:373a
  international communications ··· 3:318b
Jiji shimpō ··· 時事新報 ··· 1:16b; 2:367b; 4:54b, 206b; 5:314a-314b
  Sankei shimbun ··· 7:13b
Jiji Tsūshinsha ··· 4:54b
Jikaku ni okeru chokkan to hansei (Intuition and Reflection in Self-consciousness) ·自覚に於ける直観と反省 ··· 6:15a
Jikan (vice-ministers) ··· 8:191a-191b
"Jikan" (Time) ··· 時間 ··· 8:332b
Jikata ··· 地方 ··· 4:54b-55a
Jikata hanrei roku ··· 地方凡例録 ··· 4:55a-55b
Jikata sanchō ··· 地方三帳 ··· 4:55a
Jikatasho ··· 地方書 ··· 4:55a
Jikatatori ··· 地方取 ··· 4:55a
Jikei University School of Medicine ··· 7:311a
Jikifu ··· 食封 ··· 4:55b
Jikiso ··· 直訴 ··· 4:55b
Jikkan ··· 十干 ··· 1:232a
Jikkan jūnishi 十干十二支 ··· 4:55b-57a
  calendar, dates, and time ··· 1:232a-232b
  kanreki ··· 4:151a
  kigen ··· 4:204a
  kōshin ··· 4:57a
  periodization ··· 6:174b-175a
Jikken shitsu (The Laboratory) ··· 実験室 ··· 8:289b
Jikkinshō ··· 十訓抄 ··· 4:57a; 7:72a
Jikkoku Pass ··· 十国峠 ··· 4:57a
Jikkunshō ··· 十訓抄 ··· 4:57a
Jimbō Kaku ··· 神保格 ··· 4:31b
Jimbutsuga (figure painting) 1:156a; 7:17b
Jimmeiyō kanji beppyō (A Supplementary Table of Chinese Characters for Use in Personal Names) ··· 8:91b
Jimmeiyō kanji tsuika hyō (Table of Additional Characters for Use in Personal Names) ··· 8:91b
Jimmin bunko ··· 人民文庫 ··· 7:176b
Jimmin Sensen Jiken. 人民戦線事件 *See* **Popular Front Incident**
Jimmu, Emperor ·神武天皇 ··· 4:57a-57b; 7:264b
  folktales ··· 2:302b
  hakkō ichiu ··· 3:85b

imperial era 4:203b
Kigensetsu controversy 4:204a
Kojiki 5:27b
Nihon shoki 5:384a
Jimoku 除目 4:57b-58a
Jimpūren Rebellion
神風連の乱 4:58a; 7:152a
chitsuroku shobun 1:298a
Jin 3:354a; 4:141b
Itō Jinsai's concept 4:247b
Jinaichō 寺内町 4:58a
Jinan (Tsinan) Incident 4:373b
Jindaiji 深大寺 4:58a
Jindai moji 神代文字 4:58a
Jing 7:263b; 8:119a-119b
Jingi 仁義 4:58a-58b
Jingikan. 神祇官 *See* **Dajōkan**
Jingō, Empress. 神功皇后 *See* **Jingū, Empress**
Jingoji 神護寺 2:355b; 4:58b
Shinshōji 7:125a
Jingo Jihen 壬午事変 3:275a
Jingōki. 塵劫記 *See* **Yoshida Mitsuyoshi**
Jingū, Empress 神功皇后 4:59a; 8:286b
Hirota Shrine 3:150b
Ōjin, Emperor 6:76b
Jingū Bunko 4:58b-59a
Jingūreki (Ise Shrine Calendar) 1:*231a*
Jinin. 神人 *See* **Jinnin**
Jinja. *See* **Shrines**
Jinja Honchō 神社本庁 7:139b
Jinja Shintō 神社神道 7:180b
Jinjiin. 人事院 *See* **National Personnel Authority**
Jinkaishū 塵芥集 4:59a
Date family 2:78a
Jinken shinsetsu 人権新説 4:168b
Jinken yōgo 1:317b-318a
Jinkōki 塵劫記 8:231b
Jinku 甚句 2:301b; 7:272b
Jinnin 神人 4:59b
Jinnō shōtō ki 神皇正統記 1:67b; 2:101b-102a; 4:59b-60a
historiography 3:153b
Nambokuchō seijun ron 5:323b
Jinrikisha. *See* **Rickshaw**
Jinsei gekijō 人生劇場 6:140a
Jinsei sampō setsu (Theory of the Three Human Treasures)
人生三宝説 6:14a
Jinshin Disturbance (672)
壬申の乱 2:103a; 4:60a-60b; 8:285b
handen shūju system 3:96a
poetry 4:117a
Taika Reform 7:296b
toneri 8:74b
Jinshin Koseki 壬申戸籍 4:60b-61a
Jinshin no Ran. 壬申の乱 *See* **Jinshin Disturbance**
Jinzūgawa 神通川 4:61a
Jion kanazukai 4:134a
Jippensha Ikku 十返舎一九 1:211b; 2:378a; 3:42a; 5:49a; 4:61a-61b; 7:97a
kokkeibon 4:256a
Ji Qiao Tian
Tanabata Festival 7:334b-335a
Jiraigen 地雷原 7:334b
Jiriki. *See* **Tariki**
JIS (Japanese Industrial Standard)
4:61b-62a
Ji sect 時宗 3:177a; 4:62a; 8:356a
Ippen 3:328b-329b
nembutsu 5:359b
temples 2:345b
Jisha bugyō 寺社奉行 4:62b; 7:6a
Jishi 地子 4:62b
Jishimban and tsujiban
自身番と辻番 4:62b
Jishoiron 8:28a, 335b
Jishōji. 慈照寺 *See* **Ginkakuji**
Jishū 時宗 4:62a
Jissatsu 十刹 3:57a
Jisshinshi (real parent-child relationships) 6:162b
Jitō, Empress 持統天皇 4:63b-64a; 8:285b
court 2:350a
Kakinomoto no Hitomaro 4:117a
Naniwakyō 5:328b
Jitō 地頭 4:62b-63b
appointment 4:121b
corvée labor 1:226b
dismissal 4:108b
economy 2:147b
governmental functions 2:264a-264b
kokujin 4:260a
shitaji chūbun 7:149b
shōen 7:157a
Jitsugakutō (Practical Party) 実学党 8:331a
Jitsugyō Dōshikai
実業同志会 4:64a
Jitsugyō no shisō
実業の思想 6:93a
Jitsugyō semmon gakkō 7:62a
Jitsuin 4:156a
Jitsuin ("true seals") 7:46a
Jitsuroku 6:316a
Jitsurokumono 実録物 4:64a
Jitte 4:64a
Jiun Onkō 慈雲飲光 4:64a-64b
Jiun Sonja. 慈雲尊者 *See* **Jiun Onkō**
Jiuta 地唄 4:64b-65a
Jiutamai 地唄舞 4:65a
7:148b
Jiyū gakkō (Freedom School) 自由学校 6:221b; 7:148b
Jiyū Gakuen 3:96b; 7:121b
Jiyū Gekijō (Free Theater)
Pan no Kai 6:161b
shingeki 7:112b
Jiyūkei 自由刑 7:140b
Jiyū Minken Undō. 自由民権運動 *See* **Freedom and People's Rights Movement**
Jiyū Minshutō. 自由民主党 *See* **Liberal Democratic Party**
Jiyū shimbun 自由新聞 4:65a
Jiyū Shisō (Free thought)
自由思想 4:145b
Jiyūtō (Liberal Party)
自由党 1:34b; 4:65a-65b; 6:207a; 7:66b, 255b
Baba Tatsui 1:129a
Chichibu Incident 1:271b
dissolution 2:336a
establishment 2:335a
Freedom and People's Rights Movement
2:333b-336a
Furusawa Shigeru and 2:373b
Imperial Diet 3:276b
Itagaki Taisuke 3:349a
Kishida Toshiko 4:223a
Korean contact 4:280b
local affiliates 2:366a
predecessor 4:372b
Rikken Teiseitō 6:315b
Shimpotō 7:108b
Takenouchi Tsuna 7:325a
Ueki Emori 8:127b
Jiyūtō (post-World War II). *See* **Liberal Party**
Jiyūtō shi 自由党史 4:65b-66a
Jizaikagi 2:371b; 4:66a
open hearth (irori) 4:*66b*
Jizamurai 地侍 2:265a; 4:66a
Jizō 1:159b, *201a*; 4:66a, *66b*, 144b; 5:43b
JMPA (Japan Magazine Publishers Association) 4:47a
Jōban Coalfield 常磐炭田 4:66a
Job placement 2:210a
Job tenure 4:356b-357b
Jōchi Daigaku 7:229a
Jōchō 定朝 1:199b, *201a*, 227b; 4:66a-66b
In school 3:313b
Jōdai 城代 4:66b
Jōdai kanazukai 4:134a
Jōdogahama 浄土ケ浜 4:67a
Jōdoji 浄土寺 6:108b
Jōdo mandara-zu
浄土曼荼羅図 5:333a
Jōdo sect 浄土宗 4:67a-68a; 7:63a
Azuchi Disputation 1:126b-127a
Byōdōin temple 1:227b
doctrinal basis 4:67a
Fujiwara culture 2:347b
Fukuda Gyōkai 2:361b-362a
Hōnen 3:220a
Japanese foundation 4:67b-68a
lineage 4:67a
painting 6:149b
pure land faith 4:67a-67b
tariki 7:347a
Jōdo Shin sect 浄土真宗 3:177a; 4:62a, 68a-69a; 6:300a; 7:84b
doctrines 4:68b
historical developments 4:68a
Ikkō ikki 3:269b
Kiyozawa Manshi 4:233a
mandalas 5:100b
naikan therapy 5:310b-311a
popularization of Buddhism 3:171a
Shimaji Mokurai 7:99b
Shimazu Yoshihiro
1597 prohibition 7:102b
shinjin 4:68b
Shinran 7:122b
Temmon Hokke Rebellion 7:381b
Toyotomi Hideyoshi 8:95a
vow
tariki 7:347a
Jōdo Shinshū 浄土真宗 4:68a-69a
Jōdo sugoroku 浄土双六 7:259a
Jōdo wasan 浄土和讃 8:231a
Jōei Shikimoku. 貞永式目 *See* **Goseibai Shikimoku**
Jōetsu 上越 4:69a
Joffe, Adolf Abramovich 3:328a
Jogaku shinshi 女学新誌 4:69a; 8:268a
Jogaku zasshi 女学雑誌 1:208b; 4:69a; 7:23b
Iwamoto Yoshiharu 3:360b
Jōganjigawa 常願寺川 4:69a
Jōgashima 城ケ島 4:69a
Jōgū Shōtoku Hōōtei setsu 上宮聖徳法王帝説 4:69a; 7:376a
Jōha 紹巴 6:299b
Jōhana-nuri 城端塗 8:181a
Jōhei and Tengyō Rebellions.
承平・天慶の乱 *See* **Fujiwara no Sumitomo; Taira no Masakado**
Jōheisō 常平倉 4:69b
Jōhikeshi 定火消 3:137a
John Gabriel Borkman
shingeki 7:112b

Johnston, Percy H. 4:69b
Johnston Report 4:69b
Jōin 4:69b
Joint acts 4:86a
Joint Council of Fellow Activists on the Peace Question 3:129a-129b
Joint Staff College 4:69b
Joint Staff Council 2:82a; 4:69b-70a; 7:59a
Joint-stock company 2:31b-32a, 37b; 4:70a-71a; 7:247a
  articles of association 2:37b
  vs. limited liability company 5:10a
Joint ventures 4:71a; 6:164b
  multinational enterprises 5:263b
Jōjitsuron (Satyasiddhi) 成実論 1:178b; 4:71a, 132b; 5:332b
Jōjitsu school 成実宗 1:178b; 4:71a-71b
Jojōshi 抒情詩 4:309a
Jōka machi. *See* **Castle towns**
Jōkō 上皇 4:71b
Jokō aishi (The Tragic History of Women Workers) 女工哀史 4:71b; 8:264a
Jō komononari 定小物成 4:267b
Jokotoba 4:71b-72a
  waka 8:203a
Jokō to kekkaku (Women Workers and Tuberculosis) 女工と結核 8:264a
Jōkyū Disturbance (1221) 承久の乱 2:107a; 4:72a
  Fujiwara no Tameie 2:355b
  Goseibai Shikimoku 3:47b-48a
  Go-Toba, Emperor 3:51a-52b
  jitō appointments 4:122a
  Kaidōki 4:108b
  Kamakura shogunate 4:122a
  Shin kokinshū 7:120a
  shōen 7:157b
  Takeda family 7:322a
  thought and culture 8:26b
  Tsuchimikado, Emperor 8:112a
Jomei, Emperor 舒明天皇 2:55a; 8:303b
Jōmen 定免 4:72a; 4:331b
  nengu 5:360b
Jōmō Kyōkai geppō 上毛教会月報 4:162b
Jōmon culture 縄文文化 3:158b-159b; 4:72a-74a; 7:178b-179a
  artifacts 4:153b
  economy 2:147a
  final 4:73b-74a
  housing 3:243a
  late 4:73a-73b
  middle 4:72b
  origin of 4:276b
Jōmon figurines 4:74a-74b, *74b*
  Kamegaoka site 4:125a
  Shintō 7:125b
Jōmon peoples, diet of 7:83a
Jōmon period 縄文時代 4:75a
  archaeological remains 4:34a-34b
  culture 4:72a-74a
  figurines 4:74a-74b
  pottery 4:75a-75b
  religion 7:125b
  stone tools 7:247b
Jōmon pottery 縄文式土器 1:76a, 256b; 4:75a-75b
  lacquer use 4:361a
Jonidan 7:272a, 273a
Jonokuchi 7:272a, 273a
Jon Shirubā 4:157b
Jōrei 5:71b; 7:56a
Jōri 条理 4:75b, 247a; 5:214b-215a
Jōri system 条里制 2:104a; 4:75b-76a; 7:296a
  handen shūju system 3:95b
  Haorigata method 4:75b
  Nagachigata method 4:75b
  ri 6:308a
  Temmu, Emperor 7:381b-382b
Jōruri 浄瑠璃 2:267b; 4:76a-77b; 5:45a; 7:249b
  bun'ya-bushi 4:77a
  criticism 5:16a
  dan-mono shū 4:77a
  development 4:76b-77a
  Gidayū-bushi 4:77a-77b
  Jippensha Ikku 4:61a
  kabuki adaptations 4:91a
  kiyomoto-bushi 4:77a
  ningyō 4:77a
  origin 4:76b
  sekkyō 4:77a
  Takemoto Gidayū I 7:324b
  tokiwazu-bushi 4:77a
  See also **Bunraku**
Jōruri hime monogatari (*Jōruri Hime*) 浄瑠璃姫物語 3:184a; 4:76b
Jōruriji 浄瑠璃寺 4:77b
Joseigo 2:250b
Josetsu 如拙 4:77b-78a; 7:70a
  Catching a Catfish With a Gourd (Hyōnenzu) 4:*78b*
  screen painting 7:42b
Jōshi 7:262a
Joshi Eigaku Juku (Tsuda College) 8:267b
Jōshin'etsu Kōgen National Park 上信越高原国立公園 1:95b; 4:78a
Joshi Rōdo Teishintai (Volunteer Labor Corp) 女子労働挺身隊 8:261a
Josūshi 2:39a
JOTF (Kyokutō Hōsō) 4:332b
Jōtō Mon'in 上東門院 4:78a
Jōun 浄雲 4:76b-77a
Journalists
  American
    House, Edward Howard 3:240a
    Vaughn, Miles W. 8:189a
  Anglo-Irish
    Brinkley, Frank 1:170b-171a
  British
    Black, John Reddie 1:158b
    Murdoch, James 5:270b
  Chinese
    Dai Jitao (Tai Chi-t'ao) 2:59a
    Wang Tao (Wang T'ao) 8:222b
    Zou Taofen (Tsou T'ao-fen) 8:380a
  Japanese
    Abe Shinnosuke 1:4b
    Akiyama Teisuke 1:44a
    Arahata Kanson 1:72a-72b
    Baba Tsunego 1:129a-129b
    Fukuchi Gen'ichirō 2:361b
    Furugaki Tetsurō 2:371b
    Furuno Inosuke 2:373a
    Hani Motoko 3:96b-97b
    Hasegawa Nyozekan 3:107a
    Hosokawa Karoku 3:236b
    Ikebe Sanzan 3:264b
    Ishibashi Tanzan 3:339b
    Iwanaga Yūkichi 3:360b
    Kanagaki Robun 4:135a
    Kaneko, Josephine Conger 4:138a
    Kikutake Sunao 4:207b
    Kiryū Yūyū 4:222a
    Kishida Ginkō 4:222b
    Kiyosawa Kiyoshi 4:232b
    Komatsubara Eitarō 4:265b
    Kuga Katsunan 4:302a
    Kurimoto Joun 4:313a-313b
    Maeda Yoshinori 5:81b
    Miura Saku 5:216a
    Miyatake Gaikotsu 5:221a
    Motoyama Hikoichi 5:259a
    Murayama Ryōhei 5:270a-270b
    Nakano Seigō 5:316a-316b
    Narushima Ryūhoku 5:335b
    Numa Morikazu 6:44b
    Ogata Taketora 6:69a-69b
    Oka Shigeki 6:81a
    Ozaki Hotsumi 6:139b
    Seki Hironao 7:56b
    Shimada Saburō 7:99a
    Suehiro Tetchō 7:255b
    Sugimura Sojinkan 7:258a
    Taoka Reiun 7:346a
    Torii Sosen 8:79b-80a
    Ueno Riichi 8:129a
    Yamaji Aizan 8:296a
    Yanagawa Shunsan 8:313b
  Mexican
    Tablada, Josē Juan 7:291a
Jōwa Conspiracy 承和の変 4:78a
  Fujiwara no Yoshifusa 2:358a
Jōyaku kaisei. *See* **Unequal Treaties, revision of**
Joya no kane 5:*371a*
Jōyō 城陽 4:78b
Jōyō kanji 4:30b, 78b-79a
  Japanese language reform 4:30b
  Japanese writing 4:27b
Jōyō kanji hyō 4:78b-79a
Jōyuishiki ron 成唯識論 6:247b
Jōzankei Hot Spring 定山渓温泉 4:79a; 7:98a
JSC (Science Council of Japan) 7:38a
JSP (Japan Socialist Party) 4:48a-49a
JTB (Japan Travel Bureau, Inc) 4:50a
J-turn phenomenon 8:176b
Jūbako 4:79a
Judaism, tolerance in Japanese religion 8:70b
Judges 4:79a-79b
  impeachment 3:275a
  responsibilities
    civil cases 1:320a-320b
Judicial Committee of the House of Councillors 4:81a
Judicial precedents 4:79b
Judicial review 2:13a; 4:79b-80a; 7:275a
  administrative law 1:13a
  fundamental liberties and 2:369b
  introduction 4:378a
Judicial scrivener 4:80a-80b
Judicial system 4:80b-81b
  Administrative Court 1:11b-12a, 13a
  administrative litigation 1:13b
  bail 1:130a
  judges 4:79a-79b
  Supreme Court 7:277b
Judiciary 6:215a
  constitutional litigation 2:13a-13b
  source of information on 7:181b
Jūdō 柔道 1:34a; 4:82a-83a, *83a*
  competition techniques 4:82b-83a
  expansion 4:82b
  history and development 4:82a-82b
  Ippon 4:82b-83a
  kangeiko 4:140b
  Kōdōkan 4:243a
  ranks 4:83a
  schools 4:147a

swordplay vs ····· 5:119a
Jūgatsu Jiken ···· 十月事件 ····· 6:60a
Jūgatsukai ····· 十月会 ····· 5:19b
Jūgoya ····· 十五夜 ····· 5:248a
Jūgoya festivities ····· 1:23a
Jūhachi Daitsū ·· 十八大通 ····· 4:83a
Jūichigatsu Jiken
····· 十一月事件 ····· 6:41b-42a
Jūichikai (Society of Eleven) ····· 十一会 ····· 8:327b
Jui ippon ····· 儒医一本 ····· 4:103b
Jūjiro ····· 十字路 ····· 2:269a
Kinugasa Teinosuke ····· 4:218b
Jūjō Paper Co, Ltd ····· 4:83a-83b
Jūjūshin ron ····· 十住心論 ····· 4:83b
Kūkai ····· 4:304a
Jūjutsu. *See* **Jūdō**
Juka bijin ····· 樹下美人 ····· 4:83b
Jukaie ····· 授戒会 ····· 7:234a
Jūkan kaishū shōkai shingo 重刊改修倢解新語 ····· 7:163a
Jūkei seifu ····· 重慶政府 ····· 1:300b
Juki sampō ····· 拾璣算法 ····· 8:231b
Juku ····· 4:83b-84a
cram schools ····· 2:41b
Jumbungaku ····· 3:312a
Toyoda Shirō ····· 8:90b
Jūmin soshō ····· 4:84a
Jumpō tōsō ····· 4:84a; 7:250b
Jūnidan ····· 十二段 ····· 4:76b
Jūnidan sōshi · 十二段草子 ····· 4:76b
Jūnikyū Undō ····· 2:81a-81b
Junior colleges ····· 4:84a-84b; 8:170b
Junior Pilot Training Corps (Yokaren) ····· 8:329a
Jūnishi ····· 十二支 ····· 1:232a
Junnin, Emperor · 淳仁天皇 ····· 4:253b
Junrei monogatari ····· 巡礼物語 ····· 4:187b
Junshi ····· 4:84b-85a
Nogi Maresuke ····· 6:31a
Junsō ····· 4:84b
Junsui haiku ····· 純粋俳句 ····· 8:298b
Jun tian ····· 3:95b
Juntoku, Emperor 順徳天皇 ····· 4:85a
Fujiwara no Sadaie ····· 2:354b
Fujiwara no Tameie ····· 2:355b
Jōkyū Disturbance ····· 4:72a
Juntoku In Mishō ····· 順徳院御抄 ····· 4:210b
Jūō-gyō ····· 十王経 ····· 1:20a
Juridical Foundation Hikari Association ····· 6:220a
Juridical Persons Tax Law ··· 7:355a-358b
Jurisprudence ····· 4:85a-85b
Juristic act ····· 2:20a; 4:86a
general clause ····· 3:18a
kōjo ryōzoku ····· 4:252b
Juristic person. *See* **Hōjin**
Jurōjin ····· 寿老人 ····· 5:296a
Jūroku musashi ····· 4:86a
Jurong Industrial Complex ····· 7:196b
Jūron ibenshō · 十論為辯抄 ····· 4:102b
Jūryō ····· 7:272a, 273a
Jury system ····· 4:81b
Jūsan, Lake ····· 十三湖 ····· 4:86a
Jusco Co, Ltd ····· 4:86a-86b
Jushi ····· 4:325a
Jūshichijō no Kempō. 十七条の憲法 *See* **Seventeen-Article Constitution**
Jūshin ····· 4:86b
Jus sanguinis ····· 4:32b
Jus soli ····· 4:32b
Juvenile crime ····· 4:86b-87a
Juvenile delinquency ····· 2:44b
penalties ····· 2:45b
Juvenile labor ····· 4:87a
Juvenile Law ···· 2:246a; 4:87a-87b; 6:172a
juvenile crime ····· 4:86b
Juvenile Law of 1948 ····· 2:51b
Juvenile reformatories and classification centers ····· 4:87b
Juvenile workers, protective legislation for ····· 4:87b-88a
Jūyokkakai ····· 十四日会 ····· 5:281a
Jūyō Sangyō Tōsei Hō. *See* **Law concerning the Control of Important Industries**
Juzu ····· 1:197a

K

Kabane ····· 姓 ····· 5:324b
ason ····· 1:103a
uji-kabane system ····· 8:131b
Yakusa no Kabane ····· 4:89a
Kabasan Incident ····· 加波山事件 ····· 4:89a-89b
Freedom and People's Rights Movement ····· 2:335b; 4:89a
Mishima Michitsune ····· 4:89a
Kabayama Sukenori ····· 樺山資紀 ····· 4:89b-90a
Kabegaki ····· 壁書 ····· 4:90a
domainal codes ····· 4:90a
Kemmu irai tsuika hō ····· 4:90a
Ōuchike Kabegaki ····· 6:135b
Ruijū fusen shō ····· 4:90a
sata mirensho definition ····· 4:90a
Tokusei edicts ····· 4:90a
Kabi (Mold) ····· 黴 ····· 8:45a
Kabo Reform ···· 甲申政変 ····· 4:90a
Kabu ····· 4:100a
Kabufuda ····· 株札 ····· 4:100a
Kabuki ····· 歌舞伎 ····· 2:74b; 4:90a-97b, 336b; 5:46a; 7:31a, 43a, 97a, 249b; 8:21b-23a
acting families ····· 4:94b-95a
acting roles ····· 4:94a
acting style ····· 4:94a
actor-centered theater ····· 4:94a-94b
Aoto-zōshi hana no nishiki-e ····· 4:95a
Bandō Tamasaburō ····· 4:91a
costume, wig, and makeup ··· 4:95b; 8:24a
Kumadori ····· 4:95b
dance, traditional ····· 2:73b
dialogue ····· 4:94a
Edo period ····· 4:92a
late ····· 5:49b-50a
fashion ····· 1:332b
folk versions ····· 2:296b
formalized behavior ····· 4:93b
furyū influence ····· 2:374a
future ····· 4:95b-96a
fūzokuga ····· 2:378a
Genroku era ····· 4:91a
hanamichi ····· 4:95a
Ichikawa Danjūrō ····· 3:257a
Ichikawa Danjūrō XI ····· 4:90b
jōruri ····· 4:77a
kakubei-jishi ····· 4:118a
Kanjinchō ····· 4:94b
Kanze Nobumitsu ····· 4:154b
Kataoka Takao ····· 4:91a
Kyōganoko musume Dōjōji ····· 4:93a
ma, use of ····· 5:77a
Matsumoto Kōshirō VIII ····· 4:94b
Meiboku sendai hagi ····· 4:94b
Mokuami and the Meiji period ····· 4:92a
Morita Kan'ya ····· 5:253b
music and dance. *See* **Kabuki music**
nagauta ····· 5:307b
Nakamura Kanzaburō XVII ····· 4:94b
Nakamura Utaemon ····· 5:315b
Nakamura Utaemon VI ····· 4:93a, 94b
Okuni ····· 6:97a
onnagata ····· 6:108a
Onnagoroshi abura no jigoku ····· 4:91a
Onoe Kikugorō ····· 6:109a
Onoe Matsunosuke ····· 6:109b
Onoe Shōroku ····· 4:92b
origin ····· 3:184a-184b; 4:90b
Ōsaka school ····· 6:123a
other traditional dramas ····· 4:92b
performances ····· 4:93b-94a
plays ····· 4:93a
post-Meiji ····· 4:92a
post-World War II ····· 4:92a-92b
puppet theater ····· 4:91b, 93a
Sakata Tōjūrō I ····· 6:379b
San'yūtei Enchō ····· 7:19b
Sawamura Sōjūrō ····· 7:31a
Shibaraku ····· 4:92b
shimpa ····· 7:107b
shingeki ····· 7:112a
Shinkokugeki ····· 7:121a
Shinoda Masahiro ····· 7:122b
after 1652 ····· 4:90b-91a
social position of actors ····· 4:95a-95b
stage ····· 4:95b
stage assistants ····· 4:94a
staging ····· 4:93b
Sukeroku yukari no edo-zakura ····· 4:90b
Takeda Izumo ····· 7:322b
tattoos ····· 7:350b
Tokugawa thought ····· 4:93b
Tōkyō ····· 8:63b
Torii school ····· 8:79a
tsuzumi ····· 8:119b
Kabuki Jūhachiban ····· 歌舞伎十八番 ····· 1:213b; 4:97b-99a
Ichikawa Danjūrō ····· 3:257a; 4:97b
Kabukimono ····· 歌舞伎者 ····· 4:332b
Kabuki music ····· 4:91b-92a, 99a-100a
early history ····· 4:99a
form ····· 4:99b-100a
functions ····· 4:99b
Nagauta school ····· 4:91b
performance practice ····· 4:99a
traditional ····· 5:285a
types ····· 4:99a
Kabuki theater
Okuni ····· 6:97a
puppet theater influence ····· 1:215a
Kabunakama ····· 株仲間 ·· 2:147b-148a; 4:100a
apprentice system ····· 1:71a
dissolution ····· 4:100a
fudasashi ····· 2:340b
increase ····· 4:100a
kokuso used against ····· 4:262b
membership ····· 4:100a
monopoly status ····· 1:132b
opposition ····· 4:100a
premodern economy ····· 2:149b
Tanuma Okitsugu ····· 7:345a-346a
Kaburagi Kiyokata ····· 鏑木清方 ··· 4:100a-100b
Kaburaya ····· 4:160b
Kabushiki kaisha. *See* **Joint-stock company**
Kabushiki kaisha keizai ron ····· 株式会社経済論 ····· 8:127a
Kabutogani ····· 3:231a

Kachikachi Mountain 4:100b
Kachikachi yama かちかち山 2:303a; 4:100b
Kachikoshi 7:273a
Kachō 1:14b
Kachōga 花鳥画 1:156a-156b; 7:17b
  subjects 6:158b
Kadankai 5:19b
Kada no Arimaro 荷田在満 4:100b
  Kada no Azumamaro 4:100b
Kada no Azumamaro 荷田春満 1:154a; 4:100b-101a
  Kada no Arimaro 4:100b
  Kamo no Mabuchi 4:100b, 129a
  Kokugaku 4:257b
  Man'yōshū scholarship 5:110b
Kada zenshū 荷田全集 4:101a
Kadena 嘉手納 4:101a
Kades, Charles Louis 4:101a
Kadokawa Gen'yoshi 角川源義 4:101a
Kadokawa Publishing Co, Ltd 4:101a; 6:268a
Kadoma 門真 4:101a
Kadomatsu 5:*371a*
Kadoya Shichirobei 角屋七郎兵衛 4:101a
Kadozuke 4:101a-101b
Kaede 4:64b; 5:111b-112a
Kaedegawa Shiin 楓川市隠 4:189b
Kaehwap'a (Enlightenment Faction) 4:101b, 280b
  Fukuzawa Yukichi 4:101b
  Kapsin Political Coup 4:156b
  Kim Ok-kyun 4:101b, 209a
  Pak Yŏng-Hyo 4:101b; 6:159b
  Sugup'a 4:101b
Kaei sandai ki 花営三代記 4:101b
Kaempfer, Engelbert 1:237a, 269b; 4:101b-102a
  German-Japanese relations 3:26a
  History of Japan 4:101b-102a
  sazanka 7:32a
  Shizuki Tadao 4:102a
Kaerazaru natsu 帰らざる夏 4:102b
Kaeriten 4:124a
Kaeriyama Norimasa 帰山教正 2:268a
Kaeru 2:339b-340a
Kaesen 替銭 4:102a
Kaeshi 4:102a
  gift giving 3:31a
Kaezeni 替銭 4:102a
Kaezeniya 替銭屋 4:102a
Kaga 加賀 4:102a-102b
Kaga Bunko Collection 8:67b
Kagaku Gijutsu Chō 科学技術庁 7:37b-38a
Kagaku Gijutsu Kaigi 7:38a
Kagakukai 歌学会 5:19b
Kagakuron (On Science) 科学論 8:81b
Kagaku teiyō 歌学提要 4:103a
Kagami Kenkichi 各務鎌吉 4:102b
Kagami Shikō 各務支考 4:102b; 5:16a; 6:299b
Kaga no Chiyo 加賀千代 4:102b
Kaga no Jō 加賀掾 4:77a
Kaga Otohiko 加賀乙彦 4:102b
Kagawa Gen'etsu 賀川玄悦 4:102b
Kagawa Kageki 香川景樹 4:102b-103a; 5:17a, 48a
  Kamo no Mabuchi 4:103a
  Ki no Tsurayuki 4:103a
  Masaoka Shiki 4:103a
  Ozawa Roan 4:103a
Kagawa Prefecture 香川県 4:103a-103b
  history 4:103b
  Sanuki Mountains 4:103a
  tourist attractions 4:103b
Kagawa Shūtoku 香川修徳 3:239a; 4:103b
  Gotō Konzan 4:103b
  Itō Jinsai 4:103b
Kagawa Toyohiko 賀川豊彦 1:84a; 4:103b-104a
  Kaizō 4:113b
  labor movement activities 4:104a
  pacifism 6:144a
  social gospel 4:103b
Kagayakeru yami 輝ける闇 4:111b
Kageki Shakai Undō Torishimari Hōan 2:133a-133b
Kagekiyo 景清 4:98b
Kagemusha 影武者 8:36b
Kagerō かげろう 7:111b
Kagerō nikki 蜻蛉日記 4:104a-104b; 6:2a; 7:257b
  Fujiwara no Michitsuna no Haha 4:104a
Kageyama Hideko 景山英子 2:362a
Kageyu 勘解由 4:104b
Kageyujō 勘解由状 4:104b
Kageyushi 勘解由使 4:104b
Kagi (The Key) 鍵 6:230a; 7:343a
Kago (baskets) 4:104b-105a
Kago (conveyance) 4:104b
Kagome Co, Ltd 4:105a
Kagome kagome かごめかごめ 4:105a
Kagoshima 鹿児島 4:105a, *105a*, 105b, 221b
Kagoshima Bay 鹿児島湾 4:105b
Kagoshima Bombardment 薩英戦争 1:86a; 4:105b; 8:253b
Kagoshima Juzō 鹿児島寿蔵 4:105b
Kagoshima Prefecture 鹿児島県 4:105b-106a; 7:30a
  economy 4:106a
  geography 4:105b
  history 4:105-106a
  tourist attractions 4:106a
Kagura 神楽 2:255b, *297a*, 297b; 4:106a-108a; 7:148b
  dance, traditional 2:73b
  forms 4:107a-108a
    ise 4:107b
    izumo 4:107b
    mikagura 4:107a
    miko 4:107b
    minkan 4:107b
    sato 4:107b
    shishi 4:107b
  gagaku 3:1a
  importance 2:137a-138a
  kannamesai 4:144b
  nature 4:106b-107a
  Shintō rites 7:139b
Kagurabue 4:108a
Kagura uta 神楽歌 4:108a
  accession ceremony performance 4:108a
  gagaku style 4:108a
  modern performances 4:108a
  parts 4:108a
Kahō 家法 4:119a
Kahokugata 河北潟 4:108a
Kai 花彙 6:111b
Kai-awase 貝合せ 4:108a; 7:82a
Kaibara Ekiken 貝原益軒 4:108a-108b
  Onna daigaku 4:108b; 6:108a
  Yōjōkun 8:328b
Kaibun (palindromes) 8:270a
Kaichōon 海潮音 8:127a
Kaidan jidaigeki 2:273a
Kaidō 4:108b
  Gokaidō 4:108b
  post-station towns 4:108b
Kaidōki 海道記 1:294a; 4:108b, 128b; 8:104b-105a
Kaieki 改易 4:108b-109a
Kaientai 海援隊 4:109a; 5:313b-314a
  Sakamoto Ryōma 4:109a
Kaifūsō 懐風藻 1:180b; 2:350b; 4:109a; 5:26a; 6:193a
  authorship 4:109a
  Chinese literary influence 1:293a; 4:109a
  Kōbun, Emperor 4:239a
  Ōmi no Mifune 6:102a
  poetic style 4:109a
Kaigai Ijū Shinkō Kabushiki Kaisha 2:201a
Kaigai Tokō Kinshi Rei 海外渡航禁止令 4:109b
Kaigata Hot Spring 海潟温泉 7:347b
Kaigenrei 5:120a
Kaigetsudō Ando 懐月堂安度 4:109b
Kaigetsudō school 懐月堂派 4:109b; 8:140a, *140b*
Kaigo Tokiomi 海後宗臣 4:109b
  Imperial Rescript on Education 4:109b
Kaigun 海軍 7:148b, 263a
Kaigun Denshūjo 海軍伝習所 4:110a
  Enomoto Takeaki 4:110a
  Godai Tomoatsu 4:110a
  Katsu Kaishū 4:110a
  Kimura Yoshitake 4:211b
  Sano Tsunetami 4:110a
Kaigun Heigakkō. *See* **Naval Academy**
Kaigun Kōshō 海軍工廠 8:334a
Kaigunshō 海軍省 5:358b
Kaihaku Goshi Shinrei. 海舶互市新例 *See* **Shōtoku Nagasaki Shinrei**
Kaihō school 海北派 4:110a, 146a
  Kaihō Yūshō 4:110a, 110b-111a
  Kanō school rivalry 4:150b
  style 4:110a
Kaiho Seiryō 海保青陵 4:110a-110b
  domainal monopoly advocacy 4:110a
Kaihō Yūshō 海北友松 4:110b-111a; 7:42b
  Clouds and Dragons 4:*110a-110b*
Kaijin nijūmensō 怪人二十面相 7:166b
Kaijō geijutsu 会場芸術 4:175b
Kaikaha 開化派 4:101b
Kaikei 快慶 1:199a, *201a*; 4:111a
Kaikei Kensa In 1:159a
Kaikō 歌意考 4:129b; 7:196a
Kaikō Ken 開高健 1:209a; 4:111a-111b; 7:85a
Kaikoku. 開国 *See* **Opening of Japan**
Kaikoku heidan (Military Discussion of a Maritime Country) 海国兵談 8:243a
Kaikoma 甲斐駒 4:265a
Kai Komagatake 甲斐駒ケ岳 4:265a
Kaikō Takeshi. 開高健 *See* **Kaikō Ken**
Kaikyū oyobi daisan shikan 階級及び第三史観 7:319b
Kaimondake 開聞岳 4:105b, 111b
Kainan 海南 4:111b
Kainan Gisha 海南義社 4:166a
Kainan Jiyūtō 海南自由党 6:321a

Kain no matsuei カインの末裔 **1**:84b
Kainō Michitaka 戒能通孝 **4**:111b-112a
civil rights **4**:112a
early research **4**:112a
war crimes trials **4**:112a
Kaionji Chōgorō 海音寺潮五郎 **4**:112a
Kairaishi ki (Account of Kairaishi) 傀儡子記 **6**:269b
Kairakuen 偕楽園 **4**:112a, 198a
Kairō ni te 廻廊にて **8**:113b
Kaisaku bugyō 改作奉行 **4**:112b
Kaisakuhō 改作法 **4**:112a-112b
administrators **4**:112b
effects **4**:112a
Maeda family **4**:112a
peasants' tax burden **4**:112b
tax rate **4**:112b
Kaiseijo 開成所 **1**:142a
Kaiseikan 開成館 **3**:362a
Kaiseki gairon 解析概論 **7**:311a
Kaiseki ryōri 会席料理 **2**:22a, 305a
Kaisen 廻船 **4**:112b-113a
higaki **4**:112b
kitamaebune **4**:112b
ports **4**:112b
sea routes **4**:112b-113a
sengokubune **4**:112b
steamboat replacements **4**:113a
taru **4**:113a
Kaisen shikimoku 廻船式目 **4**:112b
Kaishi **4**:113a; **6**:362b, 363a
Kaishiki **2**:25b; **6**:362b, 363a
Kaishin shimbun 改進新聞 **1**:155a
Kaishintō. 改進党 *See* **Rikken Kaishintō**
Kai Shirane. *See* **Shirane Sanzan**
Kaisho **4**:142a-142b; **7**:*171a*, 172b
Kaitai shinsho 解体新書 **4**:173a; **5**:82a; **6**:65a; **7**:258b; **8**:242a
Kaitakushi 開拓使 **4**:113a
budget **4**:113a
Hokkaidō Colonization Office **4**:113a
Kuroda Kiyotaka **4**:113a
militia system **4**:113a
Kaitakushi Kan'yūbutsu Haraisage Jiken 開拓使官有物払下げ事件 **3**:213a-213b
Kaitakushi Scandal of 1881. *See* **Hokkaidō Colonization Office Scandal of 1881**
Kaitei Ritsurei 改定律例 **4**:113b
Shinritsu Kōryō **7**:124a
Kaiten 回天 **4**:113b
Kaito **4**:308a
Kaitokudō 懐徳堂 **4**:113b
curriculum **4**:113b
Miyake Sekian **4**:113b
Nakai Riken **5**:313b
Kaitoku Shoin. 懐徳書院 *See* **Kaitokudō**
Kai tsūshō kō (Study of Commercial Intercourse with the Chinese and Other Foreigners) 華夷通商考 **8**:241b, 242a
Kaizei Yakusho 改税約書 **4**:113b
import tariff reduction **4**:113b
shogunate trade control **4**:113b
Kaizō (Reconstruction) 改造 **4**:113b-114a; **6**:267b; **7**:309a; **8**:297a
censorship **1**:253a
Chūō Kōron **4**:114a
Yamamoto Sanehiko **4**:113b
Yokohama Incident **8**:330a
Kaizōsha **8**:298b
Kaizuka (city) 貝塚 **4**:114a
Kaizuka. *See* **Shell mounds**
Kajii Motojirō 梶井基次郎 **4**:114a-114b
Kajikisen (facsimiles) 加治木銭 **4**:239a
Kajima Corporation **4**:114b
Taisei Corporation **7**:303a
Kajimaya 加島屋 **4**:114b
daimyō loans **4**:114b
Dōjima Rice Market activities **4**:114b
Kaji shōzoku **2**:280b-281a
Kajiwara Kagetoki 梶原景時 **4**:114b; **7**:80b
Minamoto no Yoriie **4**:114b
Minamoto no Yoritomo rescue **4**:114b
Minamoto no Yoshitsune **4**:114b
Taira-Minamoto War **4**:114b
Kajiwara Shōzen 梶原性全 **4**:114b-115a
Ban'ampō **4**:114b-115a
Ton'ishō **4**:114b
Kajiya **7**:206a
Kajiyama Toshiyuki 梶山季之 **4**:115a
Kakamigahara 各務原 **4**:115a
Kakari 懸 **4**:191a
Kakari-musubi **4**:115a
Kakashi **4**:115a
Kake **1**:273a
Kakebuton **1**:148b
Kakegawa 掛川 **4**:115a
Kakei Katsuhiko 筧克彦 **4**:115a-115b
Dai Nippon teikoku kempō no kompongi **4**:115b
Hirata Atsutane **4**:115b
Kami nagara no michi **4**:115b
Koshintō taigi **4**:115b
Minobe Tatsukichi **4**:115b
Motoori Norinaga **4**:115b
Kakeizu 家系図 **3**:17b
Kakekomidera **4**:115b
Kakekotoba (pivot words) 掛詞 **4**:115b
word games **8**:269b
Kakemono **4**:116a, *116b*
Kakemonokake **4**:116a
Kakeya 掛屋 **2**:340b; **4**:116a
daimyō loans **2**:64b; **4**:116a
Kōnoike family **4**:116a, 274a
Kakeya Sōichi 掛谷宗一 **4**:116b
Kakibe 部曲 **1**:147b
Kakiemon ware 柿右衛門手 **1**:85a-85b, 260a; **4**:116b
Edo period **1**:263b
foreign imitations **4**:116b
jar **1**:*261a*
Sakaida Kizaemon **4**:116b
typical forms **4**:116b
Kaki futatsu 柿二つ **7**:311b
Kakihan 書判 **4**:155b
Kakiire **7**:87a
main suit **4**:117a
money suit **4**:117a
Kaki no ki no aru ie 柿の木のある家 **8**:110a
Kakinomoto no Hitomaro 柿本人麻呂 **1**:299b; **4**:117a-117b; **5**:13a, 104b; **7**:13a; **8**:287b
chōka **4**:117a
Jinshin Disturbance of 672 **4**:117a
Man'yōshū **4**:117a; **5**:107b
Shin kokinshū **7**:120a
style **4**:117a
Kakitsubata. *See* **Irises**
Kakitsubata gunraku カキツバタ群落 **7**:339b
Kakitsu Incident 嘉吉の乱 **1**:40b
Kakiuchi 垣内 **4**:119b
Kakizaki family 蠣崎氏 **2**:238b
Kakizome **2**:*259b*
Kakogawa (city) 加古川 **4**:117b
Kakogawa (river) 加古川 **4**:117b
Kako genzai inga kyō emaki. 過去現在因果経絵巻 *See E inga kyō*
Kakoimai 囲米 **4**:117b
Kaku **4**:131a
Kakuban 覚鑁 **4**:117b-118a
Dai Dembōin **4**:118a
Kūkai **4**:304a
Pure Land worship **6**:270a
Shingon sect **7**:115a
Kakubei-jishi **4**:118a, *118b*
Kakubetsu chigyō 格別知行 **3**:255b
Kakuda 角田 **4**:118a
Kakudai **4**:308a
Kakuijima 鹿久居島 **4**:118a
Kakujō 覚盛 **2**:187b
Kaku Matsujaku 郭沫若 **3**:70a-70b
Kakun 家訓 **4**:118a-119a
Asakura Takakage Jōjō **4**:118b
Asakura Toshikage, 17-Article Code of **1**:94b-95a
Gokurakuji Dono Goshōsoku **4**:118b
kabegaki **4**:90a
Kibi no Makibi **4**:118a
Kōnoike constitution **4**:274b
Mōri Motonari **4**:118b
okibumi similarity **4**:118b
Rokuhara Dono Gokakun **4**:118b
Shingen Kahō **7**:113b
Sōunji Dono Nijūikkajō **4**:118b
Kakunodate 角館 **4**:119a
Kakure Kirishitan **4**:119a-120a
Francis Xavier **8**:281a
fumie **2**:368a
lay leadership **4**:119a-119b
orashio **4**:119b
persecution **6**:118a
sacraments **4**:119b
Taketa **7**:325b
Kakushiaji **2**:25b
Kakushin Kurabu 革新倶楽部 **4**:120a
dissolution **4**:120a
goals **4**:120a
Inukai Tsuyoshi **3**:326a; **4**:120a
Kenseikai **4**:120a, 198a
Kiyoura Keigo **4**:233a
movement to protect constitutional government **4**:120a
Ozaki Yukio **4**:120a
Rikken Kokumintō **4**:120a
support **4**:120a
Kakushin Ni 覚信尼 **4**:68a
Kakushi toride no san akunin
Shimura Takashi **7**:108b
Kaku Shōrei 郭松齢 **3**:70b
Kakushu gakkō **5**:198b
Kakuyū. *See* **Toba Sōjō**
Kakuzenshō 覚禅鈔 **4**:120a
Buddhist sculpture **1**:203b
Kakyō hyōshiki 歌経標式 **8**:209a
Kama **4**:120a
Kama and kamado (rice pot and hearth) **2**:25a
Kamada Ryūō 鎌田柳泓 **4**:120a
Kamado **4**:120a-120b; **5**:*193a*
cultural significance **4**:120a
history **4**:120b
types **4**:120b
Kamadogami **4**:120b
Kamagaya 鎌ケ谷 **4**:120b
Kamahige 鎌髭 **4**:99a
Kamaishi 釜石 **4**:120b
Kamaishi Iron Mine **3**:333b
Kamakura 鎌倉 **2**:*252b*; **4**:120b, 135a; **7**:161a

Daibutsu ········ 4:120b
Engakuji ········ 4:120b
Gozan ········ 4:120b
Kenchōji ········ 4:120b
Minamoto no Yoritomo ········ 4:120b
Tōkeiji ········ 4:120b
Tsurugaoka Hachiman Shrine ········ 4:*120b*
urbanization ········ 8:176a

Kamakura bakufu. *See* **Kamakura shogunate**

Kamakura-bori 鎌倉彫 2:295a; 4:121a

Kamakura Daibutsu 鎌倉大仏 ········ 2:*55a*

Kamakurafu ········ 鎌倉府 ········ 5:272b

Kamakura Gozan. 鎌倉五山 *See* **Gozan**

Kamakura history. *See* **History of Japan**

Kamakura Matsuri ········ 2:*252b*

Kamakura National Treasure House ········ 5:276b

Kamakura ōzōshi ········ 鎌倉大草紙 ········ 4:121a
Kantō Kanrei ········ 4:121a
Kūbo ········ 4:121a
Taiheiki ········ 4:121a

Kamakura period 鎌倉時代 ········ 4:121b

Kamakura shogunate ········ 鎌倉幕府 ·· 4:121b-122b
Azuma kagami ········ 1:127a
character ········ 4:122a
Jōkyū Disturbance of 1221 ········ 4:122a
lord-vassal relationship ········ 4:122a
shiki ········ 4:122a
Council of State ········ 3:252a
decrees (tokusei) ········ 8:58b
development ········ 4:122a-122b
exchange economy ········ 4:122b
Goseibai shikimoku ········ 3:47b; 5:101b
Hōjō family ········ 4:122a
mandokoro ········ 4:122a
Minamoto no Sanetomo ········ 4:122a
Minamoto no Yoriie ········ 4:122a
monchūjo ········ 4:122a
Mongol invasions ········ 4:122a
overthrow ········ 4:122b
political change ········ 4:122a
samurai-dokoro ········ 4:122a
toimaru ········ 4:122b
education ········ 2:172b
establishment ········ 4:122a
jitō appointments ········ 4:122a
Minamoto no Yoritomo ········ 4:122a
shugo appointments ········ 4:122a
Taira family defeat ········ 4:122a
Go-Daigo, Emperor ········ 3:39a
inheritance of land ········ 7:232a
Kameyama, Emperor ········ 4:125b
kokushi's status during ········ 4:262b
Korean court, relations between ········ 4:276a
military governors ········ 7:220a
Minamoto family ········ 5:178a
Minamoto no Yoriie ········ 5:180b
Minamoto no Yoritomo ········ 5:181a-182b
Mongol invasions of Japan ········ 5:243b
nenki ········ 5:361b
samurai ········ 7:8a
sekke shōgun ········ 7:57b-58a
shikken (shogunal regent) ········ 7:97b
trade ········ 2:148a
yoriai ········ 8:338a

Kamanashigawa 釜無川 2:341b, 343b; 4:122b

Kamasu ········ 4:123a

Kamba Falls ········ 神庭滝 ········ 4:123a

Kamban ········ 7:193b

Kambara Ariake 蒲原有明 ········ 4:123a
Shinshichō ········ 7:124b

Kambayashi Akatsuki ········ 上林暁 ········ 4:123a

Kambun ········ 1:293a-293b; 2:97b; 4:31a, 123a-124b; 7:34b, 62a

Kambun Master ········ 4:124b

Kame ········ 8:120a-120b

Kameda Bōsai 亀田鵬斎 ········ 2:347a; 4:124b-125a

Kamegaoka site ········ 亀ヶ岡遺跡 ········ 4:74a, 75b, 125a
beads ········ 4:125a
bone articles ········ 4:125a
fern frond designs ········ 4:125a
Jōmon figurines ········ 4:125a
stone tools ········ 4:125a

Kameido Incident ········ 亀戸事件 ········ 4:125a
Tanno Setsu ········ 7:344a
Tōkyō Earthquake of 1923 ········ 8:66b

Kamei Katsuichirō ········ 亀井勝一郎 ·· 4:125a-125b; 5:13a
Nihon Rōmanha ········ 4:125a; 5:381b
Proletarian literature movement involvement ········ 4:125a
Shinjinkai ········ 4:125a; 7:115b
Yasuda Yojūrō ········ 4:125a

Kamei Nammei 亀井南冥 ········ 1:76b

Kamen no kokuhaku (Confessions of a Mask) ········ 仮面の告白 ········ 6:231a

Kameoka ········ 亀岡 ········ 4:125b
Akechi Mitsuhide rule ········ 4:125b
post-station ········ 4:125b

Kameyama (city) ········ 亀山 ········ 4:125b

Kameyama, Emperor ········ 亀山天皇 ········ 4:125b
Emperor Fushimi ········ 4:125b
Emperor Go-Fukakusa ········ 4:125b
Emperor Go-Saga ········ 4:125b
Emperor Go-Uda ········ 4:125b
Northern and Southern Courts ········ 6:39a
succession ········ 4:192a

Kami ········ 1:62a, 122b-123a; 2:236b-237a; 4:125b-126a; 7:263a, 361b
earthly divinities ········ 4:125b
exorcism ········ 4:126a
heavenly divinities ········ 4:125b
High Celestial Plain ········ 4:126a
kagura ········ 4:106b
kites ········ 4:229b-231b
manifestation ········ 4:126a
mountains, worship of ········ 5:259b-260a
religion and society ········ 6:293b
in Shinto art ········ 7:134b
tatari ········ 7:257a
thought and culture ········ 8:25a-26a
vengeful spirits ········ 3:46b-47a
worship ········ 7:179b-180a
See also Deities

Kamichika case ········ 6:250a

Kamichika Ichiko 神近市子 4:126a; 6:250a
Hikage Teahouse Incident ········ 4:126a
Kamichika Ichiko jiden: Waga ai waga tatakai ········ 4:126a
Ōsugi Sakae ········ 4:126a
Seitōsha membership ········ 4:126a

Kamidana ("god shelf"). *See* **Shintō family altars**

Kami Fukuoka ········ 上福岡 ········ 4:126a

Kami fūsen. *See* **Paper balloons**

Kamigata ········ 上方 ········ 4:151b

Kamigumi Co, Ltd ········ 4:126b

Kamikakushi ········ 4:126b

Kamikawa Basin 上川盆地 ········ 4:*126b*

Kamikaze ········ 神風 ········ 1:123b; 4:126b; 7:262a-262b
literary usage ········ 4:126b
Mongol armada destruction ········ 4:126b

Kamikaze Special Attack Force ········ 神風特別攻撃隊 4:127a; 8:276a
effectiveness ········ 4:127a
suicide weapons ········ 4:127a

Kamikōchi ········ 上高地 ········ 4:*127a*
Yakedake volcano ········ 8:285a

Kami no Hakubutsukan ········ 6:162a

Kaminoyama ········ 上山 ········ 4:127a

Kamiokuri ········ 1:155a

Kami Shiiba Dam 上椎葉ダム ········ 2:73a

Kami Suwa Hot Spring ········ 上諏訪温泉 ········ 4:127b

Kami tobi (paper hawk kite) ········ 4:229b

Kami to hito no aida ········ 神と人の間 ········ 7:342b

Kamitsukasa Shōken ········ 上司小剣 ········ 4:127b

Kamiyama Sōjin 上山草人 ········ 4:127b
Ai yo jinrui to tomo ni are ········ 4:127b
Shingeki movement ········ 4:127b
Thief of Baghdad, The ········ 4:127b

Kamiya Sōtan ········ 神谷宗湛 ········ 4:127b; 7:99a
Kamiya Sōtan nikki ········ 4:127b
Kobayakawa Hideaki ········ 4:127b
Shimai Sōshitsu ········ 4:127b
Toyotomi Hideyoshi ········ 4:127b

Kamiya Ten'yū ········ 神谷天遊 ········ 8:297a

Kamiyui ········ 4:127b
Dampatsurei law ········ 4:127b
hairstyles ········ 4:127b
Ukiyodoko descriptions ········ 4:127b

Kammon Bridge ········ 関門橋 ········ 7:*106b*
Shimonoseki ········ 7:105b

Kammon gyoki 看聞御記 ········ 4:127b-128a

Kammon nikki 看聞日記 ········ 4:127b

Kammon Strait 関門海峡 ········ 4:128a
Shimonoseki ········ 7:105b

Kammon Tunnels ········ 7:105b

Kammu, Emperor 桓武天皇 ········ 4:128a; 7:62b
Heiankyō ········ 3:121a
Kūkai ········ 4:128a
monasticism ········ 5:237b
Saichō ········ 4:128a

Kammuri ········ 3:119a

Kammuriyama ········ 冠山 ········ 4:128a

Kamo (city) ········ 加茂 ········ 4:128a

Kamo. *See* **Wild ducks**

Kamochi Masazumi ········ 鹿持雅澄 ········ 4:128a
Man'yōshū scholarship ········ 5:110b

Kamogawa (city) ········ 鴨川 ········ 4:128a

Kamogawa (river) 賀茂川 ········ 4:128a-128b, 338a

Kamon ········ 家門 ········ 7:108a

Kamo no Chōmei 鴨長明 ········ 1:181b, 294a; 4:128b-129a; 5:14b, 43b; 7:72a
elderly recluse ········ 4:128b-129a
Hōjōki ········ 4:129a; 5:43b
poet and literary critic ········ 4:128b
mujō ········ 4:129a; 5:262a
yūgen advocacy ········ 4:128b; 8:355b
Tosa Mitsuhide ········ 4:*128b*

Kamo no Chōmei shū ········ 鴨長明集 ········ 4:128b

Kamo no kurabeuma ········ 賀茂競馬 ········ 4:129a
depiction in art ········ 2:377b

Kamo no Mabuchi ········ 賀茂真淵 ········ 1:154a; 4:129a-129b; 5:17a
chōka revival ········ 4:129a
Genji monogatari shinshaku ········ 4:129b
Ise monogatari commentaries ········ 4:129b
Kada no Arimaro ········ 4:100b
Kada no Azumamaro ········ 4:100b, 129b
Kagawa Kageki ········ 4:103a
Kanjikō ········ 4:129b
Katō Chikage ········ 4:129b

Katori Nahiko 4:129b
Keichū 4:129a
Kokugaku 4:257b
Man'yōshū commentaries 4:129a-129b
Man'yōshū scholarship 5:110b
Motoori Norinaga 4:129b
Murata Harumi 4:129b
Niimanabi 4:129b
poetic style 4:129b
Tale of Genji commentaries 4:129b
Tayasu Munetake 4:129b
Tokugawa Yoshimune 4:129b
Kamoshika [(Japanese serow) *Capricornis crispus*] 4:129b
Kamo Shrines 賀茂神社 4:128a, 130a, 336b; 7:180a
Aoi Festival 1:68a; 4:130a
horse race 4:129a
Kamo no Chōmei 4:128b
origins 4:130a
Kampaku 関白 2:204a-204b, 348a, 351b; 4:130a; 7:69b
Fujiwara no Yoshifusa 4:130a
Gosekke family 4:130a
Ichijō Norifusa 3:256b
Ichijō Sanetsune 3:256b
Ichijō Tsunetsugu 3:256b
Kujō family eligible for 4:303b
political power 4:130a
regency government 4:130a
Toyotomi Hidetsugu 4:130a
Toyotomi Hideyoshi 4:130a
Kampan Batabiya shimbun 官板バタビヤ新聞 4:130a
Kampan kaigai shimbun 官板海外新聞 4:130a
Kampō. *See* **Official Gazette**
Kampō (medicine) 5:150b-151b
characteristics 5:151a
examination methods 5:151b
schools 5:146a-146b, 150b-151a
Kampu 官符 4:130a-130b
dajōkam-pu 4:130a
Kampūzan 寒風山 4:130b
Kamu 4:106b
Kamuikotan 神居古潭 4:130b
Kamura Isota 嘉村礒多 4:130b
Shinkō Geijutsu Ha 7:119b
Kamurikiyama 冠着山
Obasuteyama 6:48a-48b
Kamu Yamato Iware Hiko no Mikoto 神日本磐余彦尊 4:57a-57b
Kan 4:130b-131a
aspects 4:130b
kaku 4:131a
kotsu 4:131a
Kuroda Ryō 4:130b
Kana 仮名 1:151b, 153b, 233a; 2:348a; 4:131a-135a; 6:248b; 7:34b
Gojūon zu 3:40b-41a
hiragana 4:132b
Kokin wakashū 4:132b
onnade 4:132b
Tosa nikki 4:*133b*
use by women 4:132b
ideographs 4:141b-143b
Japanese language 4:27a-28a
Japanese language reform 4:30a
kambun 4:124a
kaō 4:155b
katakana 4:132a-133a
earliest examples 4:132b-133a
Gosen wakashū 4:132b
Kanamajiri bun 4:132b
Konjaku monogatari 4:132b
mnemonic function 4:132a-132b
Tōdaiji fujumon kō 4:132b
variant symbols 4:133a
man'yōgana 4:131b-132b, *133a;* 5:109a-109b
characters 4:131b-132a
gisho reading 4:131b
kun reading 4:132a
Man'yōshū writing system 4:131b
on reading 4:132a
syllables 4:131b
orthography 4:132b-135a
Fujiwara no Teika (sadaie) 2:354a-355a
gendai 4:134b-135a
jion 4:134a
jōdai 4:134a-134b
Keichū 4:187b-188a
Monnō 4:134a; 5:245b
Motoori Norinaga 4:134a; 5:257a-258b
rekishiteki 4:133b-134a
Teika 4:133a-133b
Ryūkyū dialects 6:355b
sōgana 4:132a
studies 4:31a-31b
"Kanadehon chūshingura" 仮名手本忠臣蔵 1:*212b*; 4:61a, 93b
Shinkokugeki 7:121a
Kanagaki Robun 仮名垣魯文 4:135a; 7:103a
Agura nabe 4:135a
fūzoku shōsetsu 2:378b
Seiyō dōchū hizakurige 4:135a
Kanagawa Prefectural Museum of Modern Art 4:135a
Kanagawa Prefecture 神奈川県 4:135a; 8:355a
Fuji-Hakone-Izu National Park 4:135a
Kamakura 4:135a
Kawasaki 4:135a
Tōkyō Earthquake of 1923 4:135a
Yokohama 4:135a
Kanagawa shimbun 神奈川新聞 4:211a
Kanagawa Treaty 神奈川条約 1:3b; 2:331a; 4:135a-135b; 7:104b; 8:329b
Kawaji Toshiakira 4:179b
Kōmei, Emperor 4:266a
National Seclusion termination 4:135b
Perry, Matthew Calbraith 4:135a-135b; 6:177b
United States 8:154b
Kanai Akira 金井章 6:*24b*
Kanai Noburu 金井延 4:135b
Ernest Francisco Fenollosa 2:251b
Shakai keizaigaku 4:135b
Shakai mondai 4:135b
Shichihakase Jiken 4:135b
Kanamajiri bun 4:132b
Kan'ami 観阿弥 4:135b; 5:43a; 6:24a
Kanze school 4:135b, 155a
Zeami 4:135b; 8:369a
Kan'ami Kiyotsugu 観阿弥清次 4:135b
Kanamori Tokujirō 金森徳次郎 2:4a; 4:135b
constitution 4:135b
Minobe Tatsukichi 4:135b
National Diet Library 4:135b
Yoshida Shigeru cabinet 4:135b
Kanamugura [(Japanese hop) *Humulus japonicus*] 4:135b
Kanashiki chichi 哀しき父 4:160b
Kanashimi no daika (Prince in Sadness) 悲しみの代価 8:332a
Kanaya 金谷 4:136a
post-station 4:136a
tea cultivation 4:136a
Kanazawa 金沢 4:136a
Kanazawa Bunko 金沢文庫 1:151b; 4:136a
Hōjō Sanetoki 4:118b, 136a
Kanazawa Plain 金沢平野 4:136a
Kana-zōshi 仮名草紙 1:94a; 3:347b; 4:136b; 5:46a; 8:144a
Kanazukai 4:132b-133a
Kanazukai oyobi kana jitai enkaku shiryō 6:138b
Kanchiku (*Chimonobambusa marmorea)* 1:136a
Kanchōban 灌頂幡 3:*233a*
Kanchōrō Kakai 観潮楼歌会 5:19b
Kanchūki 勘仲記 4:136b-137a
Mongol invasions 4:137a
shōen disputes 4:137a
Kanda Akiko 2:76a
Kanda Aqueduct 神田上水 4:137a
Tamagawa Aqueduct 7:332b
Kandachime 上達部 4:302b
Kanda Festival 神田祭 4:137a; 7:15a
dashi 4:137a
Kanda Shrine 4:137a
mikoshi 4:137a
shogunal patronage 4:137a
Kandaka 貫高 4:137a
eidaka 4:137a
eirakusen 4:137a
Kammon 4:137a
replaced by kokudaka 4:257b
replacement 4:137a
Kanda Kōhei. *See* **Kanda Takahira**
Kanda Shrine 神田明神 4:137a
Kanda Festival 4:137a
Ōkuninushi no Mikoto 6:97b
Taira no Masakado 4:137a
Kanda Takahira 神田孝平 4:137a-137b
Kanden (official fields) 官田 2:104b
Kanebō, Ltd 4:137b
Kaneda Masaichi 金田正一 4:137b
Kanegafuchi Bōseki 4:64a
Kanegafuchi Chemical Industry Co, Ltd 4:137b
Kan'ei House Genealogies 4:138a
Kan'eiji 寛永寺 4:137b-138a, 163a
Tenkai 4:138a
Tokugawa Iemitsu 8:48a
Kan'ei jigyō haraisage 官営事業払下げ 4:138a
Furukawa 4:138a
government-operated factories 3:56a-56b; 4:138a
Mitsubishi 4:138a
Mitsui 4:138a
seishō 4:138a
zaibatsu 4:138a
Kan'ei kōjō 官営工場 3:56a-56b
"Kan'ei Sampitsu" 寛永三筆 1:236b; 4:273b
Kan'ei shoka keizu den 寛永諸家系図伝 4:138a
Fujiwara 4:138a
Hayashi Razan 4:138a
Minamoto 4:138a
miscellaneous 4:138a
Taira 4:138a
Kan'ei tsūhō 寛永通宝 5:*242a-242b*
Kaneko, Josephine Conger 4:138a-138b
Kaneko Fumiko 金子文子 6:159a
Kaneko Kentarō 金子堅太郎 2:2b; 4:138b
diplomatic career 4:138b
drafting of Meiji Constitution 4:138b

Inoue Kowashi 4:138b
Itō Hirobumi 4:138b
Itō Miyoji 4:138b
Kaneko Mitsuharu 金子光晴 4:138b-139a
antiwar poems 4:138b; 5:57b
Kaneko Naokichi 金子直吉 4:139a
Ishikawajima-Harima Heavy Industries Co, Ltd 4:139a
Kōbe Steel, Ltd 4:139a
Suzuki Shōten 4:139a
Teijin, Ltd 4:139a
Kanematsu-Gōshō, Ltd 4:139a-139b
Kanemi kyō ki 兼見卿記 4:139b
Oda Nobunaga 4:139b
Toyotomi Hideyoshi 4:139b
Kanemi Oil Poisoning Incident 2:304b; 4:139b
Kanegafuchi Chemical 4:139b
Kanemi Sōko Co 4:139b
legal aspects 4:139b
Kanenaga, Prince 懐良親王 4:139b-140a
Emperor Go-Daigo 4:139b-140a
Imagawa Sadayo 4:140a
Kanenaka ki 兼仲記 4:136b
Kanenaka Kyō ki 兼仲卿記 4:136b
Kanesawa Bunko 金沢文庫 *See* **Kanazawa Bunko**
Kanesawa Sanetoki. 金沢実時 *See* **Kanazawa Bunko**
Kaneshige Tōyō 金重陶陽 1:158a; 4:140a
bizen ware 4:140a
Living National Treasure 4:140a
Tea ceremony vessels 4:140a
Kanga 漢画 4:157a
Kangaku 4:140a
Daigaku 4:140a
Daigakuryō 4:140a
Fujiwara no Fuyutsugu 4:140a
Kangakuin 勧学院 4:140a; 2:350b; 4:140a
Kangeiko 4:140a-140b
Kanghwa, Treaty of 4:140b-141a, 279a; 7:7a, 197b; 8:325b
Inoue Kaoru 4:140b
Kanghwa Incident 4:140b
Kuroda Kiyotaka 4:140b
relations with China 1:286b
Sino-Japanese War of 1894-1895 4:140b
Taewŏn'gun rule 4:140b
terms 4:140b
waegwan 8:198a
Kanginshū 閑吟集 2:301b; 4:141a; 7:64b
musical structure 4:141a
themes 4:141a
Kango 敢語 5:214b
Kangō bōeki 勘合貿易 7:331b-332a
Kang Youwei (K'ang Yu-wei) 4:140a-140b, 384a
Huang Zunxian 4:141a
Hundred Days' Reform 4:141a
Miyazaki Tōten 4:141b
Ōkuma Shigenobu 4:141a
Prince Konoe Atsumaro 4:141a
Treaty of Shimonoseki rejection 4:141a
Wang Tao 4:141a
Kan Hasshū 関八州 4:141b
Kani 2:41a-41b
Kan'i jūnikai 官位十二階 2:39b; 4:141b; 7:264a
chi 4:141b
gi 4:141b
jin 4:141b
rei 4:141b
ritsuryō system 6:322a
shin 4:141b
toku 4:141b
Kani kōsen (The Cannery Boat) 蟹工船 7:175b
Kan'in, House of 閑院宮 4:141b
Arai Hakuseki 4:141b
commoner status 4:141b
Kani yamabushi 蟹山伏 4:327b
Kanji 4:141b-143b; 7:*170b*
Ashide style 1:97b
calligraphy 1:233a
character styles 4:142b-143a
clerical 4:143a
greater seal 4:143a
gyōsho 4:143a
kaisho 4:143a
kimbun 4:143a
lesser seal 4:143a
oracle bone 4:142b-143a
sekibun 4:143a
sōsho 4:143a
tadpole 4:143a
zokuji 4:143a
go on 3:46a
kan on 4:148a
kun readings 4:310b
on and kun readings
go on 4:143a
jukuji kun 4:143b
kan on 4:143a-143b
tō on 4:143a-143b
script style 7:170a
Shinsen jikyō 7:124b
styles 7:170a
tō on 8:75b
types of Chinese characters 4:142a-142b
borrowing 4:142b
combined meanings 4:142a
diagrammatic 4:142a
dictionary arrangement 4:142b
domestic 4:142b
extension 4:142b
numbers 4:142b
pictographs 4:142a
Kanjiki 4:143b
Kanjikō 冠辞考 4:129b
Kanjin 3:137a
Kanjinchō 勧進帳 4:*94b*, 98a
Kanjō 灌頂 1:179a; 4:117b
Kanjō bugyō 勘定奉行 4:143b-144a; 7:6a
daikan 4:144a
gundai 4:144a
kattegakari 4:144a
kattekata 4:144a
kujikata 4:144a
Rōjū 4:144a
tenryō 4:144a
Tokugawa Yoshimune 4:144a
Kanjō gimmiyaku 勘定吟味役 4:144a
Kanjō Jōyaku 漢城条約 7:68b
Kanjō rekimei 灌頂歴名 4:58b
Kankakei 寒霞渓 4:144a
Kanken 観賢 2:57b
Kanko 官戸 7:62a
Kankoku Tōkanfu 韓国統監府 6:306a
Kankō maru 観光丸 4:110a
Kanku kidōtai 6:320b
Kankyōchō 環境庁 2:224a
Kannamesai 神嘗祭 4:144a-144b
Daijōsai 2:59a-59b
Engi shiki description 4:144a
Shintō rites 7:138b-139b
Taihō Code description 4:144a
Kannen shōsetsu 4:179b, 199a
Kannō Disturbance 観応の擾乱 4:144b
Ashikaga Tadayoshi 1:100a; 4:144b
Ashikaga Takauji 1:100b; 4:144b
Kō no Moronao 4:144b
Kan no kenkyū 勘の研究 4:131a
Kannon 1:122b-123a, 159b; 2:376b; 4:144b-145a; 5:43b; 7:20a, 67b
Amida 4:144b
Byōdōin temple 1:227a
Daianji 2:55a-55b
Daigoji 2:57a
Daitokuji 2:68b
feminine representation 4:144b-145a
Hall of Dreams (Yumedono) 4:*145a*
Ishiyamadera 3:346a
Lotus Sutra depiction 4:144b
miracles 4:144b
Nanzenji 5:330b
Omizutori 6:102b
pilgrimages 4:144b
Pure Land Buddhism 4:144b
ritual implements 1:196a
Takasaki 7:318b
Kannon, Eleven-Headed 1:187b, 189a
Kannonji Castle 観音寺城 1:126b
Kannon Riding on a Dragon 8:328a
Kanno Suga 管野スガ 4:145a-145b
Arahata Kanson 1:72a; 4:145b
High Treason Incident of 1910 3:135a; 4:145b
Jiyū shisō 4:145b
Kōtoku Shūsui 4:145b
Kyōfūkai membership 4:145a
Red Flag Incident of 1908 4:145b
"Shide no michikusa" 4:145b
Kannoura 甲浦 4:145b
Kan no Wa no Na no kokuō no in 漢委奴国王印 1:76b; 4:*145a*, 145b; 5:321b
Kannushi 4:145b-146a; 6:238b-239a
Edo period 4:145b
gūji 4:146a
hafuri 7:138b
Heian period 4:145b
hereditary nature 4:145b
miyaza 5:221a
negi 6:239a
Kanō Einō 狩野永納 4:148b
Kanō Eitoku 狩野永徳 1:157b; 2:*377a*; 4:146a-146b; 7:42b
Azuchi Castle paintings 4:146a
Azuchi-Momoyama history 3:177b
Birds and Flowers 4:146a
Chao Fu 4:146b
Chinese Lions (Karajishi zu) 4:*146a-146b*
Chinese Mythical Lions 4:146b
Cypress Trees 4:146b
developed style 4:146b
early style 4:146a
Four Elegant Pastimes, The 4:146a
fūzokuga 2:377b
Kaihō Yūshō 4:110b
Kanō Motonobu 4:146a
Nanzenji 5:330b
Ōsaka Castle paintings 4:146a
Scenes in and around Kyōto 4:146a
Uesugi Kenshin 4:146a
yamato-e style 4:146a
Kanoe saru 庚申 4:295b
Kanogawa 狩野川 4:146b
Kanō Hōgai 狩野芳崖 4:146b-147a; 6:*378b*
Deva Seizing a Demon 4:147a
Ernest F. Fenollosa 4:147a
Hashimoto Gahō 4:147a
Kanō Tan'yū 4:146b-147a
Merciful Mother Kannon 4:147a
Okakura Kakuzō 4:147a

Sakuma Shōzan **4**:146b
Sesshū Tōyō **4**:146b
Sesson Shūkei **4**:146b
Shimazu family **4**:146b
Shimomura Kanzan **7**:105a-105b
Kanō Jigorō ... 嘉納治五郎 ... **4**:82a-83a, 147a; **7**:270b
Ernest Francisco Fenollosa **2**:251b
Japan Amateur Sports Association leadership **4**:147a
jūdō activities **4**:147a
Kōdōkan established by **4**:243a
Kanō Kōkichi .... 狩野亨吉 **4**:147a
Andō Shōeki **1**:155b
Shizuki Tadao **7**:152b
Kanō Masanobu · 狩野正信 · · **4**:147a-147b; **7**:42b
Admiring Lotus Blossoms **4**:147b
Ashikaga Yoshimasa **4**:147b
Bamboo and White Crane **4**:147b
Eight Views of Xiao and Xing, The ... **4**:147b
Fujiwara no Yoshitsune **4**:147b
Inryōken nichiroku **4**:147b
Kanō school **4**:147a
Oguri Sōtan **4**:147b
Shūbun **4**:147b
Kanō Mitsunobu · 狩野光信 **4**:147b
Azuchi Castle paintings **4**:147b
Hasegawa school rivalry **4**:147b
Kanō Eitoku **4**:147b
Nanzenji **5**:330b
Ōsaka Castle paintings **4**:147b
Toyotomi Hideyoshi **4**:147b
Kanō Motohide ... 狩野元秀 **6**:*62a*
Kanō Motonobu · 狩野元信 · **1**:156a, 192b; **4**:*147a*, 147b-148a; **7**:42b
bird-and-flower painting **4**:148a
Daitokuji temple paintings **4**:148a
fusuma-e **4**:148a
ink painting **4**:148a
Kaihō Yūshō **4**:110b
Kanō Eitoku **4**:148a
Kanō Masanobu **4**:147b
Myōshinji temple paintings **4**:148a
Nanzenji **5**:330b
sansuiga (landscape painting) **7**:17b
shogunal patronage **4**:148a
yamato-e painting style **4**:148a
Kan on **4**:148a
go on **3**:46a
on readings **6**:112b
Kanō Naganobu · 狩野長信 **6**:*155a*
Kan'onji .... 観音寺 **4**:148b
Kanō Sakujirō · 加能作次郎 **4**:148b
Kanō Sanraku ... 狩野山楽 · **2**:57b; **3**:181b; **4**:148b; **6**:*153a*; **7**:42b
Battle of the Carriages **4**:148b
Birds of Prey **4**:148b
Imperial Mirror **4**:148b
Kanō Eitoku **4**:148b
Kanō Mitsunobu **4**:148b
Kanō school of painting **4**:148b
Nanzenji **5**:330b
Kanō Sansetsu · · 狩野山雪 ... **4**:148b-149a
Honchō gashi **4**:148b
Kanō Sanraku **4**:148b
Kanō school **4**:148b
Winter Seascape with Birds **4**:148b
Kanō school .... 狩野派 · **4**:149a-150b; **7**:84a, 270a
art historical significance **4**:150b
Hashimoto Gahō **4**:150b
heterodox tradition **4**:150b
Kanō Hōgai **4**:150b
Printing Appreciation Society **4**:150b
bunjin artists **1**:210b
"Eight Views" themes **7**:167b
fūzokuga **2**:377b
Hashimoto Gahō **4**:178b
history **4**:149a
ink painting **4**:149a
Kanō Eitoku **4**:149a
Kanō Masanobu **4**:149a
Kanō Motonobu **4**:149a
Kanō Sanraku **4**:149a
Kanō Tan'yū **4**:149a
screen and wall painting **4**:149a
Shōkokuji **4**:149a
Shūbun **4**:149a
yamato-e style **4**:149a
impact on screen and wall painting · **7**:43a
ink painting **4**:150a
suiboku **4**:150a
Tan'yū copies **4**:150a
Kanō Eitoku **4**:146a
Kanō lineage **4**:149a
Kajibashi branch **4**:149b
Kanō Mitsunobu **4**:149b
Kanō Sansetsu **4**:149b
Kanō Tan'yū **4**:149b
Kobikichō branch **4**:149b
machieshi **4**:149b
okueshi **4**:149b
omoteeshi **4**:149b
studio system **4**:149a
Kanō Masanobu **4**:147a
kara-e-mekiki painters **5**:305b
namban screens **5**:322a-323a
painting **6**:151b, *153a*
screen painting **4**:150a-150b
Birds and Flowers of the Four Seasons **4**:150b
Cypress Trees **4**:150b
heroic style **4**:150b
Kanō Eitoku **4**:150b
Kanō Mitsunobu **4**:150b
Kanō Sanraku **4**:150b
military patronage **4**:150a
seals **6**:281b
Shimomura Kanzan **7**:105b
style **4**:110a
stylistic and thematic range · · **4**:149b-150a
Battle of the Carriages **4**:149b
Craftsmen of Various Trades **4**:150a
ema **4**:149b
emakimono **4**:149b
Festival of Hōkoku Shrine **4**:150a
Hanabusa Itchō **4**:150a
kakemono **4**:149b
kanga **4**:150a
Maple Viewing at Takao **4**:150a
Merrymaking under the Cherry Blossoms **4**:150a
Rakuchū rakugai zu **4**:149b
Seiryōji engi emaki **4**:149b
Tōshōgu engi emaki **4**:149b
yamato-e **4**:149b
Takahashi Yuichi **7**:313b
Tatebayashi Kagei **7**:349a
Terazaki Kōgyō **8**:13a
Western-style pictures **8**:248b
Kanō Shōsen'in .... 狩野勝川院 **4**:146b
Kanō Tan'yū ..... 狩野探幽 **1**:193b; **4**:150b-151a; **7**:43a; **8**:*49a*
art connoisseurship **4**:151a
Edo Castle paintings **4**:151a
hōgen title **4**:151a
Kanō Eitoku **4**:150b
Nagoya Castle paintings **4**:151a
Nanzenji **5**:330b
Nanzenji temple paintings **4**:151a
Nijō Castle paintings **4**:151a
Tokugawa official painter **4**:151a
Tōshōgū engi **4**:151a
Tōshōgū paintings **4**:151a
yamato-e painting style **4**:151a
Kanoya .... 鹿屋 · · **4**:106a, 151a
Kanrai .... 寒雷 **4**:169b
Kanrei .... 管領 · **4**:151a; **7**:64b, 83b
Hatakeyama family **4**:151a
Hosokawa family **4**:151a
proclamations **4**:90a
Shiba family **4**:151a
shitsuji **4**:151a
Kanrei kabegaki · 管領壁書 **4**:90a
Kanreki **4**:151a
inkyo status **4**:151a
jikkan jūnishi **4**:57a
Kanrin maru (warship) .... 咸臨丸 · · **1**:175a-175b; **2**:367b; **4**:151b; **8**:154b
Admiral Kimura Yoshitake **4**:151b
Captain Katsu Kaishū **4**:151b
Kimura Yoshitake **4**:211b
national flag **5**:339a
Kanroku .... 観勒 **4**:151b
calendrical science **4**:151b
Empress Suiko **4**:151b
Gangōji temple lectures **4**:151b
Kanryō .... 管領 **4**:151a
Kansai .... 関西 **2**:364a; **4**:151b
Chūgoku region **4**:151b
Kantō **4**:151b
Kinki region **4**:151b
Kansai Electric Power Co, Inc **1**:97a, 311a; **4**:151b-152a
Kurobe Dam No. 4 hydroelectric plant **4**:151b
nuclear power development **4**:151b
Tōkyō Electric Power Co, Inc **4**:151b
Kansai Fine Arts Academy (Kansai Bijutsuin) **7**:326a; **8**:328a
Kansai Paint Co, Ltd **4**:152a
Kansai region ... 関西地方 **4**:153b
Kansatsushi .... 監察使 **4**:104b
Kan Sazan .... 菅茶山 **1**:295a; **4**:152a; **7**:94b
Kansei Calendar
Takahashi Yoshitoki **7**:313b
Kansei chōshū shoka fu .... 寛政重修諸家譜 **4**:152a
Hayashi Jussai **4**:152a
Kan'ei shoka keizu den supplement ... **4**:152a
Yashiro Hirokata **4**:152a
Kansei Gakuin University **4**:152a
Kansei Reforms .... 寛政の改革 · **1**:157a, 211b; **3**:189b; **4**:152a-152b; **7**:87a, 95a
administrative efficiency **4**:152b
Ban on Heterodoxy **4**:152b
censorship **1**:252a
conservatism **4**:152b
Decree of the Cancellation of Debts **4**:152b
economic **4**:152b
fudasashi **2**:340b; **4**:152b
gesaku **3**:28b
hitogaeshi **2**:207b-208a
kabunakama dissolution **4**:100a
Kameda Bōsai **4**:124b
Koikawa Harumachi's satire **4**:250a
Matsudaira Sadanobu **4**:152a
Neo-Confucianism **1**:356a
Rōjū **4**:152b
rural reconstruction **4**:152b
sharebon **7**:80a
Shōheikō **7**:162a
sobayōnin **4**:152b
social atmosphere **4**:157a
Tokugawa Ienari **8**:48a
Tokugawa shogunate **8**:55b
Kansha **7**:96a

Kanshi. *See* **Poetry and prose in Chinese**
Kanshibun 6:193b
Kan Shinsui 菅晋帥 4:152a
Kan susuki 7:279a
Kantan 邯鄲 4:201b
Kantei style 勘亭流 4:153a
  kabuki 4:153a
  sumō wrestling 4:153a
Kantō 関東 2:*255a*; 4:153a
  Tanabata Festival 4:153a
Kantō Auto Works, Ltd 4:153a
  Toyota Motor Co, Ltd 4:153a; 8:93b
Kantō Daishinsai. 関東大震災 *See* **Tōkyō Earthquake of 1923**
Kantō Earthquake. *See* **Tōkyō Earthquake of 1923**
Kantō Electrical Construction Co, Ltd 4:153a
  Tōkyō Electric Power Co, Inc 4:153a
Kantōgun. 関東軍 *See* **Guandong (Kwantung) Army**
Kantō kanrei 関東管領 4:121a, 153a
  Muromachi shogunate 4:153a
  Uesugi family 4:153a
Kantō loam 1:38a; 4:153a-153b
  Iwajuku site 3:358a
  Jōmon culture artifacts 4:153b
  Kantō Plain 4:153a-153b
  paleolithic culture artifacts 4:153b
Kantō Mountains 関東山地 1:272a; 4:153b
  Kimpusan 4:153b
  Kobushigadake 4:153b
Kantō Oxygen 3:342a
Kantō Plain 関東平野 4:153b
Kantō region 関東地方 4:141b, 153b-154a
  agricultural production 4:153a
  border 4:154b
  frontier status 4:153b
  Keihin Industrial Zone 4:154a
  Tokugawa shogunate 4:153b
  Tōkyō 4:153b
  Tonegawa 4:153b
Kantōshū. 関東州 *See* **Guandong (Kwantung) Territory**
Kantsubaki (*Camellia hiemalis*) 1:237a
Kan U 関羽 4:98b, 154a
  deification 4:154a
  pictorial depiction 4:154a
Kanuchibe 鍛冶部 1:147b
Kanuma 鹿沼 4:154a
  post-station towns 4:154a
  Tokugawa Ieyasu mausoleum 4:154a
Kanwa jiten 漢和辞典 2:93b-94a
Kan'yagami 紙屋紙 8:233a
Kan'ya no shikishi 紙屋色紙 8:233a
Kanzaki Paper Mfg Co, Ltd 4:154a
  Occupation monopoly policy 4:154a
  Ōji Paper Co, Ltd affiliation 4:154a
Kanzan 寒山 3:*305a*
  See also **Kanzan and Jittoku**
Kanzan and Jittoku 寒山拾得 4:154a
  ink painting subjects 4:154a
  Zen spirit 4:154a
Kanzanchiku (*Pleioblastus hindsii*) 1:136a
Kanzanji 寒山寺 4:154b
Kanzanji temple 4:154b
Kanzashi 4:154b
  hairstyles 3:83a
Kanzei. *See* **Tariffs**
Kanze Motokiyo. 観世元清 *See* **Zeami**
Kanze Motomasa 観世元雅 4:154b
  Kanze school 4:155a
Kanze Nobumitsu 観世信光 4:154b
  Kanze school 4:155a
Kanze school 観世流 4:155a
  Nō 6:24a
  Yūzaki troupe 4:135b
Kanze-yori 4:299b
Kao (face) 4:155a
Kaō (monograms) 花押 4:*155a-155b*; 155a-156a; 7:45b
  diplomatics 2:98a; 4:156a
  Edo period 4:155b-156a
  Heian period 4:155b
  jitsuin 4:156a
  kakihan 4:155b
  Kamakura period 4:155b
  Meiji Restoration 4:156a
  Muromachi period 4:155b
  seals 6:281b
  Sengoku period 4:155b
  Zen Buddhist 4:155b
Kaō Corporation 4:156a
Ka Ōkin 何応欽 3:128b
Kaō Ninga 可翁仁賀 3:*305a*; 4:156a-156b
  Koga bikō 4:156a
  Takuma school 4:156a
Kappa 河童 4:156b; 7:263b
  Akutagawa Ryūnosuke 1:45b
  bakemono 1:130b
"Kappan'ya no hanashi" 活版屋の話 5:301b
  Ogawa Usen 6:70a
Kapsan Faction 4:208b
Kapsin Political Coup (1884) 4:156b-157a, 280b
  fukoku kyōhei 2:361a
  Kaehwap'a 4:101b, 156b
  Kim Ok-kyun 4:156b
  Pak Yŏng-hyo 4:156b
  Sugup'a 4:156b
  Tianjin Convention 4:157a; 8:29b
  Treaty of Seoul 4:157a; 7:68b
Kara-e (Chinese-style painting) 唐絵 4:157a; 7:42a
  Heian period 4:157a
  Kanga 4:157a
  Tang dynasty 4:157a
  yamato-e contrast 4:157a
Kara-e-mekiki painters 5:305b
Karafuto. 樺太 *See* **Sakhalin**
Karafuto-Chishima Kōkan Jōyaku. *See* **St. Petersburg, Treaty of**
Karagoromo Kisshū 唐衣橘洲 4:157a
  Kyōka poetry 4:157a, 332a
Karaguwa 4:322a
Karai Hachiemon 柄井八右衛門 4:157a
Karai Senryū 柄井川柳 4:157a-157b; 8:368a
Kara Jūrō 唐十郎 4:157b
Karakami (kagura uta) 4:108a
Karakhan, Lev Mikhailovich 4:157b
Karaki Junzō 唐木順三 5:13b
Karako site 唐古遺跡 4:157b; 7:265b
  bone articles 4:157b
  bronze bell molds 4:157b
  excavation 1:77b
  pit houses 4:157b
  rokuro 6:335b
  stone tools 4:157b
  Yayoi pottery 4:157b
Karamatsu. *See* **Larch, Japanese**
Karamete (castle entrance) 搦手 1:248a
Karamon (gate) 3:*12b*, 13a
Kara-ori 4:158a
Karasu 2:51b-52a
Karasumaru Mitsuhiro 烏丸光広 4:158a; 5:48a
Karate 空手 4:158a-159a
  modern development 4:158b
    clubs 4:158b
    federation of organizations 4:158b
    Funakoshi Gichin 4:158b
    schools 4:158b
    styles 4:158b
  origins 4:158a-158b
    legendary 4:158a
    Okinawa 4:158b
    quanfa 4:158a
    Ryūkyū Islands 4:158b
    Shōrinji kempō 4:158a
    tōde 4:158b
  technique and contests 4:159a
    form competitions 4:159a
    practice methods 4:159a
    sparring matches 4:159a
Karatedō 4:158b
Karatsu 唐津 4:159a
  Karatsu ware 4:159a
  Niji no Matsubara 4:159a
Karatsu ware 唐津焼 1:*260b*, 263b; 2:295b; 4:159a-159b
  Agano ware 1:20b
  first written record 4:159b
  Furuta Oribe 4:159b
  kilns 4:159b
  Korean pottery techniques 4:159b
  Korean style 4:159a
  museums 5:279b
  Nakazato Tarōemon XII 4:159b
  plain 4:159a
  Sen no Rikyū 4:159b
  Takatori ware 7:320a
  Tea ceremony 4:159a-159b; 7:363b
  underglazed 4:159a
Karayō 唐様 1:236a
Karayuki san 4:159b-160a
  film
    Imamura Shōhei 3:274a
  Indonesia and Japan 3:290b
  Manchurian Incident of 1931 4:159b
  military prostitution 4:159b
"Kareki no aru fūkei" 枯木のある風景 7:176a; 8:173b
Kare no kokyō 彼の故郷 6:69b
Kari 3:13b
Kariage 借上 4:161b
Karikachi Pass 狩勝峠 4:160a
Kariya 刈谷 4:160a
Karlgren, Bernhard 4:160a
  Chinese phonology studies 4:160a
  Museum of Far Eastern Antiquities Bulletin, The 4:160a
Karmic evil 4:68b
Karō 家老 4:160a
  administrative responsibilities 4:160a
  toshiyori 4:160a
Karuizawa 軽井沢 4:160b
  Onioshidashi 4:160b
  Shiraito Falls 4:160b
Karurusu Hot Spring 4:160b
Karuta. *See* **Playing cards**
Karyūkai 3:14a
Kasa 3:119a
Kasabuta Shikibu kō かさぶた式部考 1:42a
Kasagake 笠懸 4:160b
  Kaburaya 4:160b
  Kamakura period 4:160b
  Muromachi period 4:160b
Kasagi Mountains 笠置山地 5:332a
Kasai 加西 4:160b
Kasai Zenzō 葛西善蔵 4:160b

I-novel 3:312a; 4:160a
Kasa jizō 笠地蔵 4:160b
Kasama 笠間 4:161a
Kasaneori 6:118a
Kasa no Kanamura 笠金村 4:161a; 8:206b
Man'yōshū 4:161a
poems in *Man'yōshū* 5:107b
Kasaoka 笠岡 4:161a
Kasaya Yukio 笠谷幸生 4:161a
Sapporo Winter Olympic Games 7:20b
Kaseda 加世田 4:161a
Kasen-e 歌仙絵 4:161a-161b
Agedatami-bon 4:161b
Buson 4:161b
formats 4:161b
Fujiwara no Nobuzane 4:161b
Go-Toba In-bon 4:161b
hyakunin isshu 4:161b
Jidai fudō uta-awase 4:161b
Kakinomoto no Hitomaro 4:161b
Kōrin 4:161b
Narikane-bon 4:161b
Sanjūrokunin sen 4:161b
Satake-bon 4:161b
yamato-e theme 4:161a
Kasen koi no bu (Selected Poems on Love)
歌撰恋の部 8:186b
Kashi 6:47a
Kashiage 借上 4:122b, 161b
Kashihara 橿原 4:162a
Fujiwarakyō site 4:162a
Jimmu enthronement 4:162a
Kashihara Shrine 橿原神宮 4:162a
Kashihon'ya Library
Tamenaga Shunsei 7:333b-334a
Kashii Shrine 香椎宮 4:162a
imperial patronage 4:162a
Kashii-zukuri style 4:162a
Kashii-zukuri 香椎造 4:162a
Kashikojima 賢島 4:162a
Kashima (city) 鹿島 4:162a
Kashima (town) 鹿島 4:162a
Kashima Sea 鹿島灘 2:285b; 4:162a
Kashima Shrine 鹿島神宮 4:162b
festival 4:162a
Takemikazuchi no Mikoto 4:162a
Kashima Yarigatake
鹿島槍ケ岳 4:162b
Kashindan 家臣団 1:131b
Kashin (Good News) 嘉信 8:315b
Kashiwa 柏 4:162b
Kashiwabara Hyōzō
柏原兵三 4:162b
Kashiwadebe 膳部 1:147b
Kashiwagi Gien 柏木義円 4:162b
Kashiwagi Yoshimaru
柏木義円 4:162b
Ashio Copper Mine Incident involvement 4:162b
Jōmō kyōkai geppō 4:162b
Niijima Jō 4:162b
Kashiwara 柏原 4:162b-163a
Kashiwazaki 柏崎 4:163a
Kashiyama & Co, Ltd 4:163a
Kasho 過書 4:163a
firearms 4:163a
tegata 4:163a
women 4:163a
Kasho-bune 過書船 4:163a
Kashōki 可笑記 4:136b
Kasō 家相 4:163a
Kimon 4:163a
Ommyōryō 4:163a
Kasori shell mounds
加曽利貝塚 4:163b
bone articles 4:163b
Jōmon pottery 4:163b
pit houses 4:163b
stone tools 4:163b
Kasō Sōdon 華叟宗曇 3:269b
Kassen Togamegoto
合戦咎事 4:196b
Kasshi Reform 甲子の改革 7:296b
Kasuga 春日 4:163b; 7:136a
Occupation military base 4:163b
Shintō 7:126b
Suku site 4:163b
Kasuga gongen genki 春日権現験記 3:*35a*
Kasugai 春日井 4:163b
Kasuga Ikkō 春日一幸 4:163b; 7:23a
Kasuga mandara
春日曼荼羅 4:164a; 5:100a
Kasuga no Tsubone
春日局 4:163b
Akechi Mitsuhide 4:163b
Ōoku 4:163b
Tokugawa Iemitsu 4:163b; 8:48a
Kasuga Shrine 春日大社 4:163b-164b, 169a, 368a; 5:*331a*
architectural style 4:164a
branch shrines 4:164a
festival 4:164a
Kasuga mandara 5:100a
Kōfukuji 4:243b
sacred symbol 4:163b
Shintō architecture 7:132a
Kasugayama 春日山 4:164a
Kasukabe 春日部 4:164a
Kasumigaseki 霞が関 8:*62b*
Kasumigaura 霞ケ浦 4:164a, *164b*
Kasuri 2:295b; 4:164a-165a, 312a, 318b; 8:19b
cottage industry 4:164b
e-dai 4:164b
e-gasuri 4:*164b*
kosode 4:164a
local textile areas 4:164b
Nō costumes 4:164a
patterns 4:164b
weaving development 4:164a-164b
Kata 4:196a
Katagami Noburu 片上伸 4:165a
Katagami Tengen 片上天弦 4:165a
Katagi 4:165a
Katagimono 気質物 2:188a; 8:144b
Katagiri Katsumoto
片桐且元 4:165a
Battle of Shizugatake 4:165a
daimyō status 4:165a
Kimura Shigenari 4:165a
Ono Harunaga 4:165a
Shōmei Incident 4:165a
Tokugawa Ieyashu 4:165a
Toyotomi Hideyoshi 4:165a
Toyotomi Hidiyori 4:165a
Katakago 堅香子 4:165b
Katakana. *See* **Kana**
Katakiuchi 4:165a-165b
archetype of practice 4:165b
dramatic subject 4:165b
Edo period 4:165b
Forty-Seven Rōnin Incident 2:327a
justification 4:165a-165b
prohibition 4:165b
rules 4:165b
Soga brothers 4:165b
Katakuri [(trout lily) *Erythronium japonicum]* 4:165b
Katakuriko 片栗粉 4:165b
Katamewaza 4:82b
Katamino 7:249a
Katanagari. 刀狩 *See* **Sword hunt**
Katano 交野 4:166a
Kataoka Chiezō
片岡千恵蔵 4:166a
Kataoka Kenkichi
片岡健吉 4:166a
Aikokusha formation 4:166a
Freedom and People's Rights Movement 2:334b; 4:166a
Itagaki Taisuke 4:166a
Jiyūtō formation 4:166a
League for Establishing a National Assembly representation 4:166a
Risshisha formation 4:166a
Sandai Jiken Kempaku Movement (Movement to Memorialize Three Important Items) 7:9b
Kataoka Takao 片岡孝夫 4:*91a*
Kataoka Teppei 片岡鉄兵 4:166a-166b; 7:175a
Bungei jidai 4:166b
fūzoku shōsetsu 2:378b
Proletarian literature movement involvement 4:166b
Shinkankaku school 4:166b; 7:116a-116b
Kataribe 語部 4:166b
ceremonial role 4:166b
Engi shiki 4:166b
forerunner 4:166b
Hieda no Are 3:130b
Katari-mono 語り物 4:93a
Katashiro 4:166b
Doll Festival 2:128a
mamako nagare rite 4:166b
nagoshi 5:308b
Nagoshi observance 4:166b
origami 6:116b
Snake Day exorcism 4:166b
Katatagae 4:166b
"Kataude" 片腕 4:176b
Katauta
Takebe Ayatari 7:321a
waka 8:202b
Katayama Sen 片山潜 4:166b-167a, 382b; 7:74a-74b
antiwar activities 4:167a
Bolshevism 4:167a
expatriation 4:167a
Futsū Senkyo Kisei Dōmeikai 2:376b
Kōtoku Shūsui 4:167a
labor movement 4:345a
Rōdō sekai editorship 4:167a
trade union movement 4:167a
"Katayama's Formula" 1:268b
Katayama Tetsu 片山哲 4:167a-167b; 7:74b
Abe Isoo 4:167a
coalition cabinet 4:167b
Democratic Socialist Party formation 4:167b
Japan Socialist Party 4:48b, 167b
Shakai Minshūtō membership 4:167a
Shakai Taishūto membership 4:167a
Katayama Tōkuma
片山東熊 1:80b
Katazome 4:167b; 8:19b
bokashi 4:167b
kimono 4:167b
komon 4:167b
kōzo 4:167b
patterns 4:167b
technical development 4:167b
Katei shōsetsu 4:199b
Katō case 6:250a
Katō Chikage 加藤千蔭 4:167b
Kamo no Mabuchi 4:129b, 167b
Man'yōshū scholarship 5:110b
Katō Gen'ichi 加藤元一 4:167b
Katō Hajime 加藤土師萌 1:261a, *262b*; 4:168a
Living National Treasure 4:168a
Mino ware 4:168a

Seto ware ········· 4:168a
Katō Hiroharu ··· 加藤寛治 ········· 4:168a
London Naval Conference ········· 4:168a
militarism ········· 4:168a
Washington Conference of 1921-22 4:168a
Katō Hiroyuki ···· 加藤弘之 ··· 4:168a-168b
Freedom and People's Rights Movement
opposition ········· 4:168b
Kaiseijo position ········· 4:168a
Meirokusha membership ········· 4:168a
Sakuma Shōzan ········· 7:3b
Social Darwinism ········· 4:168a-168b
Western Learning ········· 4:168a
Katō Kanji. 加藤寛治 *See* **Katō Hiroharu**
Katō Kiyomasa ·· 加藤清正 ·· 4:168b, 305b
Battle of Sekigahara ········· 4:168b
Battle of Shizugatake ········· 4:168b
invasions of Korea ········· 3:327a; 4:168b
Konishi Yukinaga ········· 4:168b
Tokugawa Ieyasu ········· 4:168b
Toyotomi Hideyori ········· 4:168b
Toyotomi Hideyoshi ········· 4:168b
Katō Kōmei. 加藤高明 *See* **Katō Takaaki**
Katoku ········· 3:304a
Katō Kyōtai ······ 加藤暁台 ········· 1:225a; 4:168b-169a
Buson ········· 4:168b-169a
Katō Michio ····· 加藤道夫 ········· 4:169a
shingeki ········· 7:113a
Katorikku daijiten ········· 1:250b
Katori Nahiko ··· 楫取魚彦 ········· 4:169a
Kamo no Mabuchi ········· 4:129b, 169a
Katori Shrine ··· 香取神宮 ·4:162b, 169a; 7:31b
festival ········· 4:169a
Fujiwara family patronage ········· 4:169a
Katō Sawao ······ 加藤沢男 ········· 4:169a
Katō Shizue ··· 加藤シヅエ ··· 4:169a-169b
Facing Two Ways ········· 4:169b
family planning activities ········· 4:169a
Hitosuji no michi ········· 4:169b
Japan Socialist Party membership ·· 4:169a
Margaret Sanger ········· 4:169a
Katō Shūichi ····· 加藤周一 ········· 4:169b
Katō Shūson ····· 加藤楸邨 ········· 4:169b
Katō Takaaki ···· 加藤高明 ········· 3:198a; 4:169b-170b; 7:270b
Goken Sampa Naikaku ········· 3:43a
Inukai Tsuyoshi ········· 4:120a
Iwasaki Yatarō ········· 4:169b
Kenseikai ········· 4:198a
premiership ········· 4:170a-170b
movement to protect constitutional
government ········· 4:170a
Peace Preservation Law of 1925 ·· 4:170a
public life ········· 4:169b
Katsura Tarō cabinet ········· 4:170a
Rikken Dōshikai leadership ········· 4:170a
Saionji Kimmochi cabinet ········· 4:170a
Twenty-One Demands ········· 4:170a
Shidehara Kijūrō ········· 7:88b
Katō Takeo ······ 加藤武男 ········· 4:170b
Iwasaki Koyata ········· 4:170b
Mitsubishi directorship ········· 4:170b
Shinkō Geijutsu Ha ········· 7:119b
Katō Tōkurō ··· 加藤唐九郎 ········· 4:170b
Katō Tomosaburō
········· 加藤友三郎 ········· 4:170b
Battle of Tsushima ········· 4:170b
on Japanese-American relations ········· 1:57a
Washington Conference delegation 4:170b
Katō Works Co, Ltd ········· 4:170b-171a
Katsu Awa. 勝安芳 *See* **Katsu Kaishū**
Katsugo danzoku fu
········· 活語断続譜 ········· 7:281a
Katsugo shinan · 活語指南 ········· 8:39b
Katsu Kaishū ····· 勝海舟 ········· 1:165a; 4:171a-171b; 7:3b, 263b
Kaigun Denshūjo ········· 4:110a, 171a
Kanrin maru ········· 4:151b, 171a
Kimura Yoshitake ········· 4:211b
Saigō Takamori ········· 4:171a
Tokugawa shogunate negotiator ··· 4:171a
Tokugawa Yoshinobu ········· 4:171a
Katsukawa school · 勝川派 ········· 4:171b
Katsukawa Shunshō ········· 4:171b
nigao-e ········· 4:171b
yakusha-e ········· 4:171b
Katsukawa Shun'ei
········· 勝川春英 · 4:171b; 7:79a; 8:141b
kabuki actor portraits ········· 4:171b
Katsukawa Shunshō ········· 4:171b
Sharaku ········· 4:171b
sumō wrestler portraits ········· 4:171b
Utagawa Kunimasa ········· 4:171b
Utagawa Toyokuni ········· 4:171b
Katsukawa Shunshō
········· 勝川春章 ·· 4:171b-172a; 8:141a
kabuki actor portraits ········· 4:171b-172a
pupils ········· 4:172a
sumō wrestler portraits ········· 4:171b-172a
Katsuki Yasuji ··· 勝木保次 ········· 4:172a
Katsumoto Seiichirō
········· 勝本清一郎 ········· 4:172a
Katsunuma ········· 勝沼 ········· 4:172a
Katsunuma Seizō 勝沼精蔵 ········· 4:172a
Katsuo. *See* **Bonito**
Katsuo no eboshi ········· 4:50b
Katsurada Fujio
········· 桂田富士郎 ········· 4:172a
Katsura Detached Palace
········· 桂離宮 ········· 3:*9b*; 4:172b-173a, *172b*, 336a; 7:*265a*, 266a
"emperor art"
Taut, Bruno ········· 7:351a-351b
gardens ········· 3:10a
shoin-zukuri architecture ········· 4:172b
sukiya-zukuri architecture ········· 4:172b
tea gardens
Kobori Enshū ········· 4:238a
Toshitada, Prince ········· 4:172b
Katsuragawa ········· 桂川 ·· 4:128a-128b, 173a, 338a
Katsuragawa Hoshū
········· 桂川甫周 4:173a; 7:258b
Daikokuya Kōdayū ········· 2:60b
Hokusa bunryuaku ········· 4:173a
Izak Titsingh ········· 4:173a
Kaitai shinsho ········· 4:173a
Maeno Ryōtaku ········· 4:173a
Roshia shi ········· 4:173a
Sugita Gempaku ········· 4:173a
Thunberg, Peter ········· 4:173a
Katsuragi, Prince. 葛城王 *See* **Tachibana no Moroe**
Katsurahama ········· 桂浜 ········· 4:173a
Katsura Kogorō. 桂小五郎 *See* **Kido Takayoshi**
Katsura-Taft Agreement (1905) ··· 桂-タフト協定 ·· 4:173a-173b; 8:156a
Korea and Japan ········· 4:282a
Korea's annexation ········· 4:287b
Katsura Tarō ······ 桂太郎 ·· 1:86b, 165b; 2:241b; 3:198a; 4:173b-174a; 7:88a
Anglo-Japanese Alliance ···· 1:56b; 4:173b
Hara Takashi ········· 3:103a; 4:173b
Hibiya Incendiary Incident ········· 3:129a
High Treason Incident of 1910 ····· 4:174a
Kiyoura Keigo ········· 4:233a
Kodama Gentarō cabinet ········· 4:241a
Korea annexation ········· 4:173b
Movement to Protect Constitutional
Government ········· 4:174a
Ōyama Iwao ········· 4:173b
Rikken Dōshikai ········· 4:173b; 6:314b
Rikken Seiyūkai ········· 4:173b
Russo-Japanese War ········· 4:173b
Saionji Kimmochi ········· 4:173b
Sino-Japanese War of 1894-1895 ·· 4:173b
Taishō political crisis ······ 4:174a; 7:305b
Tokutomi Sohō ········· 4:174a
Treaty of Portsmouth ········· 4:174a
Yamagata Aritomo ········· 4:173b
Katsura tree [(katsura) *Cercidiphyllum japonicum*] ········· 4:174a-174b
Katsureki-mono ···· 活歴物 ········· 5:234b
Katsu Rintaro. 勝麟太郎 *See* **Katsu Kaishū**
Katsushika Hokusai. 葛飾北斎 *See* **Hokusai**
Katsushika Ward ·· 葛飾区 ········· 4:174b
Katsu Shintarō · 勝新太郎 2:274b; 4:174b
Katsuta ········· 勝田 ········· 4:174b
Katsuura ········· 勝浦 ········· 4:174b
Katsuyama ········· 勝山 ········· 4:175a
Kattegakari rōjū (councillors) · 勝手掛老中 ········· 4:331a
Katydid ········· 4:220b
Kauffman, James Lee ········· 4:175a
Kawabata Bōsha 川端茅舎 ········· 4:175a
Kawabata Gyokushō
········· 川端玉章 ··· 4:175a-175b
bunjinga ········· 4:175a
Charles Wirgman ········· 4:175a
Hirafuku Hyakusui ········· 4:175b
Mitsui family commissions ········· 4:175b
Kawabata Nobukazu
········· 川端信一 ········· 4:175a
Kawabata Ryūshi 川端龍子 ········· 4:175b
Kawabata Shōtarō
········· 川端昇太郎 ········· 4:175b
Kawabata Yasunari
········· 川端康成 2:274a; 4:*175a*, 175b-177a; 5:13a; 7:103b
Bungeijidai ········· 1:209a
death ········· 4:176b
early years ········· 4:175a
"Izu no odoriko" ········· 4:175a
last years ········· 4:176b-177a
Nemureru bijo ········· 4:176b
postwar years ········· 4:176a-176b
Nobel prize (1969) ········· 4:176b
Sembazuru ········· 4:176b
Yama no oto ········· 4:176b
Shinkankaku school · 4:175b; 7:116a-116b, 175a-175b
war years ········· 4:176a
Yukiguni ········· 4:176a
Kawabiraki ········· 4:177a
Kawachi Nagano 河内長野 ········· 4:177a
Kawagoe ········· 川越 ········· 4:177b
Kawaguchi ········· 川口 2:345a; 4:177b
Kawaguchi, Lake · 河口湖 ········· 4:177b
Kawaguchi Ekai · 河口慧海 ········· 4:177b
Chibetto ryokōki ········· 4:177a
Inoue Enryō ········· 4:177a
Kawaguchi Matsutarō
········· 川口松太郎 2:274a; 4:177b
fūzoku shōsetsu ········· 2:378b
Kawahara Keiga · 川原慶賀 ·· 4:177b-178a; 5:306a
Dejima ········· 4:177b-178a
Hendrick Doeff portrait ········· 4:178a
Ishizaki Yūshi ········· 4:177b-178a
Philipp von Siebold ········· 4:178a; 7:192b
yamato-e ········· 4:178a
Kawahigashi Hekigotō
········· 河東碧梧桐 ········· 4:178a

haiku 3:79b
Hototogisu 3:237b; 4:178a
Kawai Eijirō 河合栄治郎 4:178a-178b
fascism opposition 4:178b
idealist socialism 4:178b
labor reform advocacy 4:178b
Publication Law of 1893 violation 4:178b
Kawai Gyokudō 川合玉堂 4:178b
Gyokudō Art Museum 3:71a; 4:178b
Hashimoto Gahō 4:178b
Kōno Bairei 4:178b
Kawai Kanjirō 河井寛次郎 2:294a; 4:178b-179a
Kawai Matahei 河井又平 4:179a
Kawai Michi 河井道 4:179a
Nitobe Inazō 4:179a
Tsuda Umeko 4:179a
Uemura Masahisa 4:179a
Young Women's Christian Association 4:179a
Kawai Musical Instruments Mfg Co, Ltd 4:179a
Kawai Sora 河合曽良 1:*144b*; 4:179a
Kawai Suimei 河井酔茗 4:179a-179b
Kawai Tsugunosuke 河井継之助 4:179b
National Seclusion opposition 4:179b
Sakuma Shōzan 4:179b
Kawaji Hot Spring 川治温泉 4:179b
Kawaji Ryūkō 川路柳虹 4:179b
Kawaji Toshiakira 川路聖謨 4:179b
Egawa Tarōzaemon 4:179b
Evfimii Vasil'evich Putiatin 4:179b
Fujita Tōko 4:179b
Hotta Masayoshi 4:179b
Inoue Kiyonao 4:179b
Satō Issai 4:179b
Watanabe Kazan 4:179b
Kawakami Bizan 川上眉山 1:209b; 4:179b-180a
Futokoro nikki 4:180a
haibun 3:78a; 4:180a
Harin 4:180a
Kannen shōsetsu 4:179b-180a
Kannon iwa 4:180a
Ken'yūsha 4:180a, 199a
naturalism influence 4:180a
Ozaki Kōyō 4:180a
"Sodezukin" 4:180a
Yamada Bimyō 4:180a
Kawakami Gen'ichi 川上源一 4:180b
Yamaha Motor Co, Ltd 4:180b
Yamaha Music Foundation 4:180b
Kawakami Hajime 河上肇 1:155a; 4:180b-181a; 7:251a
Kawakami Jōtarō 河上丈太郎 4:181a
Kawakami Otojirō 川上音二郎 4:181a-181b
Freedom and People's Rights Movement's activities 4:181a
Igai 4:181a
Kawakami Sadayakko 4:181b
Oppekepē-bushi 4:181a
shimpa 7:107b
shimpa theatrical tradition 4:181a
Kawakami Sadayakko. 川上貞奴 *See* **Kawakami Otojirō**
Kawakami Sōroku 川上操六 4:181b
Kawakami Tetsutarō 河上徹太郎 4:181b; 5:13a
Kawakami Tōgai 川上冬崖 4:181b; 8:327a
Kawamoto Kōmin 川本幸民 4:181b
Bansho Shirabesho 4:181b
Kikai kanran kōgi 4:181b
Shimazu Nariakira 4:181b
Kawamura Zuiken 河村瑞賢 1:38b; 4:182a
rice tax transport 4:112b
Kawanabe Gyōsai 河鍋暁斎 4:182a
Josiah Conder 4:182a
Kanō school 4:182a
Toba Sōjō 4:182a
Utagawa Kuniyoshi 4:182a
Kawanabe Nobuyuki 河鍋陳之 4:182a
Kawanakajima, Battles of 川中島の合戦 4:182a
military chronicles 4:182a
site 5:302a
Takeda Shingen 4:182a; 7:323a
Uesugi Kenshin 4:182a; 8:129b
Kawanishi 川西 4:182a
Kawanoe 川之江 4:182a-182b
Kawaraban 瓦版 4:182b
newspapers 5:369a
Kawaradera remains 川原寺址 4:182b
Kawaramono 河原者 4:182b-183a; 7:12a
acting profession association 4:95b
discriminatory policy 4:182b-183a
entertainers 4:182b
Kawara nadeshiko 2:339b
Kawari-e origami 6:118a
Kawasaki 川崎 4:135a, 183, *183a*
Kawasaki Daishi 4:183a
Keihin Industrial Zone 4:183a
Kawasaki Aircraft Co, Ltd 4:183b
Kawasaki asthma 川崎喘息 4:183b
Kawasaki Car Manufacturing Co, Ltd 4:183b
Kawasaki Chōtarō 川崎長太郎 4:183a
Aka to kuro 4:183a
Kikuchi Kan 4:183a
Kawasaki Daishi 川崎大師 4:183a-183b
festivals 4:183b
Hirama Kanenori 4:183a
Kūkai 4:183a
Kawasaki disease 川崎病 4:183b
Kawasaki Heavy Industries, Ltd 4:183b-184a
aviation 1:124a
defense industry 2:82b
Kawasaki Kisen Kaisha, Ltd 4:183b
Kawasaki Steel Corporation 4:183b
original technologies 4:183b
overseas markets 4:183b
Kawasaki Hyōgo Shipyard 4:183b
Kawasaki Kisen Kaisha, Ltd 4:183b-184a
Kawasaki Heavy Industries, Ltd 4:183b
Kawasaki Steel Corporation 4:183b
Kawasaki Natsu 河崎なつ 4:184a
Fusen Kakutoku Dōmei 2:374b; 4:184a
Miyamoto Yuriko 4:184a
Tatewaki Sadayo 4:184a
Kawasaki Shipbuilding Co 4:184a
Kawasaki Shipyard Co 4:183b
Kawasaki Steel Corporation 4:184a
Chiba steel mill 4:184a
Kawasaki Heavy Industries, Ltd 4:184a
Kawasaki Tsukiji Shipyard 4:183b
Kawase kaisha 為替会社 1:138a; 4:184a-184b
Mitsui 4:184a
Ono-Gumi 4:184a
technological development 7:369a
Kawashi 為替 4:102a
Kawashima Takeyoshi 川島武宜 4:184b
Kawashima Yūzō 川島雄三 2:273a
Kawashō Corporation 4:184b
Kawasumi Hiroshi 河角広 2:139a
Kawatake Mokuami. 河竹黙阿弥 *See* **Mokuami**
Kawate Bunjirō 川手文治郎 4:271b
Kawauso [(otter) *Lutra lutra*] 4:184b
Kawazu, Seven Falls of 4:184b
Kaya (Korea) 伽倻 4:185a, 195a, 276a; 7:2a
Iwai, Rebellion of 3:357b
Keitai, Emperor 4:190b
Mimana 4:276a
Kaya (mosquito net) 1:148b
Kayaba Industry Co, Ltd 4:185a
Kayabuki 7:249b
Kayari 4:185a
Kaya Seiji 茅誠司 4:185a
Kaya Shirao 加舎白雄 4:185a
Kayōkyoku (popular music) 歌謡曲 4:248a
Kazami Akiko 風見章子 2:*269a*
Kazan, Emperor 花山天皇 4:185a
abdication 2:351b; 4:185a
Fujiwara no Kaneie 4:185a
Fujiwara no Korechika 2:352b
imperial poetry anthology 2:352a
Kazarinashi 加佐里那止 4:185a
Kaze ni soyogu ashi (Like a Reed Shaken in the Wind) 風にそよぐ葦 8:330a
"Kaze tachinu" 風立ちぬ 7:176a
Kazo 加須 4:185b
Kazoku. 華族 *See* **Peerage**
Kazoku (Where Spring Comes Late) 家族 8:290a
Kazoku kaigi (Family Conference) 家族会議 7:176a; 8:333a
Kazoku kokka 4:185b
Kazu, Princess 和宮 4:185b
Kazuken 4:193a
Kazuno 鹿角 4:185b
KDD (International Telegram and Telephone Public Corporation) 4:261b
Ke 2:253b-254a; 6:362a-362b
Kebiishi 検非違使 4:185b
police system 6:2a
ryōge no kan 6:351b
Kebukigusa 毛吹草 6:258b
Keenan, Joseph Berry 4:185b-186a
Kegare 4:186a-186b
categories 4:186a
taboo 7:291b
tsumi 8:115a-115b
Kegon 華厳 4:175a
Kegon Falls 華厳滝 4:*186b*
Kegonkyō 華厳経 4:186b
Kegon sect 華厳宗 1:178b; 4:186b
Dōsen 2:131b; 4:186b
Gangōji 3:6b
Gyōnen 3:72b; 4:186b
headquarters 5:332b
Kōzanji 4:300a
Rōben 6:333a
Kehi Shrine 気比神宮 4:186b
Shintō 7:126b
Keian Genju 桂庵玄樹 4:186b-187a
Gozan training 4:187a
Kenninji 4:187a
Keian Incident (1651) 慶安事件 4:187a
Abe Tadaaki 1:4b
literary portrayal 4:187a
Marubashi Chūya 4:187a; 5:120a
Matsudaira Nobutsuna 4:187a
Sumpu burning 4:187a

Tokugawa Iemitsu ················ 4:187a
Tokugawa Ietsuna ·········· 4:187a; 8:49a
Yui Shōsetsu ······················ 4:187a
Keian no Ofuregaki
············ 慶安の御触書 1:131b; 4:187a; 8:266a
Keian taiheiki ·· 慶安太平記 ········ 4:187a
Keibatsu ·············· 1:147a; 4:187a-187b
Keichō ··············· 計帳 ········ 4:187b
Keichō Campaign (1597-98) ······· 3:327a
Keichō kemmon shū
··············· 慶長見聞集 ········ 4:187b
Keichō koban 慶長小判 ···· 4:234b; 5:*242a*
Keichū ··············· 契沖 ········ 1:154a; 4:187b-188a; 5:17a; 7:105a
historiography ····················· 3:155a
Japanese language studies ··········· 4:31a
Kamo no Mabuchi ·········· 4:129a, 188a
kana research ······················ 4:187b
Kokugaku forerunner ·············· 4:257b
Man'yōshū scholarship ········ 5:110a-110b
orthographic studies ··············· 4:133b
Waji shōran shō ············ 4:188a; 8:201a
Keidanren ·········· 経団連 ··· 4:188a-188b
Dokō Toshio ······················ 2:127b
functions ···················· 4:188a-188b
Ishikawa Ichirō ··················· 3:342a
Ishizaka Taizō ···················· 3:347a
leadership effectiveness ············ 4:188a
oil crisis of 1973 ·················· 4:188b
political influence ················· 4:188b
Uemura Kōgorō ············ 4:188b; 8:127b
Keiei keizaigaku sōron
·········· 経営経済学総論 ········ 8:127a
Keien isshi ······ 桂園一枝 ········ 4:103a
Keien school ······· 桂園派 ········ 8:216a
Keifugaku. 系譜学 *See* **Genealogy**
Keigo. *See* **Honorific language**
Keihan Electric Railway Co, Ltd ·· 4:188b
Keihin Electric Express Railway Co, Ltd ·························· 4:188b
Keihin Industrial Zone
············ 京浜工業地帯 ·· 4:154a, 183a, 188b-189a; 8:329b
Ōta Ward ························ 6:129b
Shinagawa Ward ··················· 7:108b
Keiji soshōhō kōgi
············ 刑事訴訟法講義 ········ 6:111b
Keijō nippō ······ 京城日報 ········ 4:283b
Keijo Shūrin ····· 景徐周麟 ········ 4:147b
Keikō, Emperor · 景行天皇 ········ 4:189a
Yamatotakeru, Prince ·············· 8:311a
Keikō film ···················· 2:269b-270a
Keikokushū ········ 経国集 1:293a; 4:189a; 5:29b
Keiō University ·············· 3:133a; 4:189a
Keiō University Hiyoshi Dormitory · 7:341b
Keiran jūyō shū
·············· 渓嵐拾葉集 ········ 7:127b
Keiretsu ···· 4:47a, 189a-189b; 7:266b-267a
general trading companies ········· 4:189b
kigyō ···························· 4:189a
kin'yū ··························· 4:189a
modern economy ··················· 2:163a
ownership ties ···················· 4:189b
shihon ··························· 4:189a
zaibatsu subsidiaries ·············· 4:189a
Keirin Gakumei (Statecraft Study Association) ···················· 8:130b
Keisai ··················· 渓斎 ······· 4:189b
Keisai Eisen ····· 渓斎英泉 ··· 4:189b-190a
erotica ·························· 4:189b
Mumeiō zuihitsu ··················· 4:189b
surimono ························ 4:189b
Keisatsu Yobitai. *See* **National Police Reserve**
Kei school ························ 4:190a
Keisei ehon ······ 傾城絵本 ········· 8:78b
Keisei Electric Railway Co, Ltd ··· 4:190a
Keisei irojamisen (Courtesan Samisen of Love) ······ 傾城色三味線 ········ 8:144a
Keisen Jogakuen ··················· 4:179a
Keishi ··············· 家司 ········ 4:190a
Keishichō ········· 警視庁 ····· 8:67b-68a
Keishinshi (stepparent-child relationships) ···················· 6:162b
Keishū Bungaku Kai
·············· 閨秀文学会 ········· 7:54b
Keitai, Emperor · 継体天皇 ·· 4:190a-190b
Emperor Jimmu ···················· 4:57b
Emperor Ōjin ·················· 4:190a-190b
Nihon shoki ······················· 4:190a
Ōtomo no Kanamura ··············· 4:190a
Keiyaku ·························· 4:308a
Keiyakuhō ········· 契約法 ········ 7:255b
Keiyō Industrial Region
············ 京葉工業地帯 ········ 8:339a
Keizai Antei Hombu ················ 2:168a
Keizai Dōyū Kai. 経済同友会 *See* **Japan Committee for Economic Development**
Keizai hakusho ···················· 8:251b
Keizai hyōron ···· 経済評論 ········ 4:300a
Keizai Jissō Hōkokusho (Report on Actual Economic Conditions)
········· 経済実相報告書 ········ 8:251b
Keizai kanchō ··················· 4:190b
Economic Planning Agency ········ 4:190b
Ministry of Construction ··········· 4:190b
Ministry of Finance ··············· 4:190b
Ministry of Foreign Affairs ········ 4:190b
Ministry of International Trade and Industry ························ 4:190b
Ministry of Transport ············· 4:190b
Keizai Kikaku Chō. 経済企画庁 *See* **Economic Planning Agency**
Keizai rinri no kōzō
········· 経済倫理の構造 ········ 7:258a
Keizai sanron (Essays on Economics) ···· 経済纂論 ········ 6:126a
Keizai shinkaron
·············· 経済進化論 ········ 7:359a
Keizai shōgaku ·· 経済小学 ········ 4:137b
Keizai tetsugaku no kihon mondai
····· 経済哲学の基本問題 ········ 7:258a
Keizai zasshi ····· 経済雑誌 ········ 4:316a
Keizan Jōkin ···· 瑩山紹瑾 ········ 4:190b
Keizan oshō shingi
············ 瑩山和尚清規 ········ 4:190b
Keizu ··················· 系図 ········ 3:17b
Kellner, Oscar ·················· 4:190b-191a
Kellogg-Briand Pact (1928) 4:191a; 8:272b
Tanaka Giichi ················ 7:336a-336b
war crimes trials ·················· 8:224b
Kelsen, Hans ······················ 4:375a
Kelsenists ························ 4:375a
Keman ···························· 1:*196b*
Kemari ··············· 蹴鞠 ·· 4:191a, 381a
Asukai Masatsune ················· 1:106b
leisure-time activities ············· 4:381a
Kembun gunshō · 見聞軍抄 ········ 4:187b
Kembunshū ········ 見聞集 ········ 4:187b
Kemi ················ 検見 ·· 4:191a-191b
inspection methods ············ 4:191a-191b
Land Tax Reform of 1873-1881 ···· 4:191b
tax-adjustment methods ······· 4:191a-191b
Kemmi ·················· 検見 ·· 4:191a-191b
Kemminshi ·········· 遣明使 ········ 7:144a
Kemmu irai tsuika hō
········· 建武以来追加法 ········ 4:90a
Kemmu nenchū gyōji
············ 建武年中行事 ········ 4:191b
Kemmu nenkan ki
·············· 建武年間記 ········ 4:191b
Kemmu Restoration
················ 建武中興 ········ 3:172a; 4:191b-192b; 7:66a
Ashikaga Takauji ···· 1:100a; 4:191b-192b
court ceremonies ·················· 4:191b
failure ··················· 4:139b, 192b
Fujiwara no Fujifusa ·············· 2:350b
Go-Daigo, Emperor ··· 3:39a; 4:191b-192b
Go-Fukakusa, Emperor ············ 4:192a
historical assessment ············· 4:192b
Hōjō family ·············· 3:211a; 4:192b
imperial restoration concept ······· 4:191b
Jinnō shōtōki ···················· 4:59b-60a
Kamakura shogunate ·············· 4:192a
Kameyama, Emperor ·············· 4:192a
Kōgon's abdication ··············· 4:249a
Kusunoki Masashige ·············· 4:192b
Nawa Nagatoshi ·················· 5:353b
Nitta Yoshisada ·················· 4:192a
restoration ······················ 4:192a
rinji ···························· 6:318a
Sasaki Takauji ···················· 7:23b
shōen ··························· 7:158a
warrior government ··············· 8:229b
Kemmu Restoration government
Nakasendai Rebellion ············· 5:317b
Kemmu Shikimoku
················ 建武式目 · 4:192b, 377a; 7:73b, 96a
dosō ···························· 2:132a
Sasaki Takauji ···················· 7:23b
supplementary articles ············· 4:90a
Kempei. *See* Military police (pre-World War II)
Kempeitai in Korea ················ 4:282a
Kempō Chōsakai. *See* **Commission on the Constitution**
Kempō gige ····· 憲法義解 ··· 4:192b-193a
Kempō Mondai Kenkyūkai. *See* **Constitutional Problems Study Group**
Kempō satsuyō · 憲法撮要 ········ 4:193a
Hozumi Yatsuka ·················· 4:193a
Minobe Tatsukichi ················ 4:193a
Uesugi Shinkichi ················· 4:193a
Ken ···················· 拳 ········ 4:193a; 8:239b, 240a
standardization ···················· 1:82b
Kenchi ·············· 検地 ·· 4:193a-195a
Chōsokabe family ················ 4:193b
cultivator class ············· 4:194a-194b
Edo period ······················ 4:193a
heinō bunri ····················· 4:194a
Hōjō family ····················· 4:193b
Imagawa family ·················· 4:193b
Ishida Mitsunari ················· 4:193b
kokudaka ························ 4:194a
land registration ················· 4:194a
Land Tax Reform of 1873-1881 ···· 4:195a
Mōri family ····················· 4:193b
Muromachi period ················ 4:193a
national implementation ··········· 4:193b
Oda Nobunaga ···················· 4:193b
samurai ···················· 4:194a-194b
sashidashi ······················· 4:193a
sengoku daimyō ············· 4:193a-193b
Shimazu family ·················· 4:193b
social results ··············· 4:194b-195a
standard measures ·········· 4:193b-194a
Taikō ····················· 4:193b-195a
Takeda family ··················· 4:193b
Tokugawa family ················· 4:193b
Toyotomi Hideyoshi ·············· 4:193b
yield measurements ··············· 4:194a
Kenchichō (land register)
················· 検地帳 ········ 4:194b
Kenchiku girei ···················· 4:195a
chōna hajime ····················· 4:195a
ishibatsuki ······················· 4:195a

jichinsai 4:195a
koyairi 4:195a
muneage 4:195a
omoto 4:195a
shimenawa 4:195a
shinchiku iwai 4:195a
tatemae 4:195a
tōryō okuri 4:195a
yautsuri 4:195a
Kenchōji 建長寺 4:120b, 195a-195b
Kenchōji-bune 建長寺船 4:195b
Kenchū 検注 4:193a
Kenchūchō 検注帳
ōtabumi 6:128a
Kendan 検断 4:195b
jitō 4:195b
shugo 4:195b
Kendan sata 検断沙汰 4:195b
Kendō 剣道 4:195b-196a, *196b*
All Japan Kendō Federation 4:196a
grades 4:196a
International Kendō Federation 4:196a
kangeiko 4:140b
matches 4:196a
naginata 5:308a-308b
school curriculum 4:196a
schools 4:196a
training 4:196a
Ken'eki 6:274a
Ken'etsu Seido Kaisei Kisei Dōmei (Organization for the Revision of the Censorship System) 1:253a
Kengiroku 顕偽録 7:186a
Kenin 家人 4:196b; 7:7b, 62a
Kenjichi 7:87a
Kenjinkai (group of persons born in the same prefecture) 4:14b; 6:205b
Kenji sannen ki 建治三年記 4:255b
Kenjutsu 剣術 3:253a; 4:195b
Kenka ryōseibai
喧嘩両成敗 4:196b
Kujikata Osadamegaki 4:196b
Sengoku daimyō 4:196b
Kenkoku Kinembi
建国記念日 4:204a
Kenkyō ruiten 憲教類典 4:269b
Kennaiki 建内記 4:196b-197a
Kennedy, John F. 3:265a
Ikeda Hayato 4:285a
Kennedy Round talks 8:161b
tariffs 7:346b-347a
Kenninji 建仁寺 4:197a-197b
paintings 4:110b
Kennyo Kōsa 顕如光佐 3:346b
Kenrei 県令 4:197b
Kenrei Mon'in 建礼門院 4:1a
Kenrei Mon'in Ukyō no Daibu shū
建礼門院右京大夫集 4:197b-198a; 5:40a
Kenrikin. *See* **Key money**
Kenri ran'yō no kenkyū
権利濫用の研究 7:255b
Kenri shingai ron
権利侵害論 7:255b
Kenrokuen 兼六園 3:*9a*; 4:136a, 198a
Kenryaku gyoki 建暦御記 4:210b
Kensatsukan (public prosecutors) 6:266a
Kensei Hontō (True Constitutional Party)
憲政本党 4:198a; 6:210a
Kenseitō 4:198b
Ōkuma Shigenobu 4:198a; 6:96a
Rikken Kokumintō 6:314b
Rikken Seiyūkai alliance 4:198a
Kenseikai (Constitutional Association) 憲政会 4:198a; 5:316a-316b; 6:210a; 7:55a, 66b
Kakushin Kurabu 4:120a
Katō Takaaki 4:198a
Kiyoura Keigo 4:233a
Peace Preservation Law of 1925 4:198a
Rikken Minseitō 4:198a; 6:315a
Rikken Seiyūkai alliance 4:198a
Tanaka Giichi 4:198a
Universal Manhood Suffrage Movement 8:169b
Wakatsuki Reijirō 4:198a
Kenseitō (Constitutional Party) 憲政党 3:196b; 4:198a-198b 6:210a
hambatsu 3:92a
Itagaki Taisuke 3:350a; 4:198b
Itō Hirobumi 3:353a
Ozaki Yukio 4:198b
Rikken Seiyūkai 4:198b; 6:315a
Shimpotō 7:108b
Kensei Yōgo Undō. *See* **Movement to Protect Constitutional Government**
Kensetsushō. 建設省 *See* **Ministry of Construction**
Kenshō 顕昭 4:198b; 5:15a
Jakuren 4:1b, 198b
Kenshōin 見性院 8:302a
Kenshō In Naifu ki
建聖院内府記 4:196b
Kentōshi. 遣唐使 *See* **Sui and Tang (T'ang) China, embassies to**
Kenuki 毛抜 4:98a-98b
Ken'yakurei 倹約令 4:198b
Ken'yūsha 硯友社 1:163b, 208a; 4:198b-199b; 5:18b, 7:358b
evolution 4:198b-199a
Garakuta bunko 4:198b; 5:22a
Ozaki Kōyō 4:199b; 6:139b
significance 4:199b
Yamada Bimyō 4:198b; 8:288b
Kenzan 乾山 2:346a; 4:199b-200a, 337a
Hon'ami Kōetsu 4:199b
Kōrin's collaborations 4:293a
Nonomura Ninsei 4:199b; 6:35a
plate by 1:*262b*
Raku ware 4:199b
teabowl by 4:*199a*
Kenzō. *See* **Takada Kenzō**
Kenzuishi. 遣隋使 *See* **Sui and Tang (T'ang) China, embassies to**
Kenzuishi and kentōshi
遣隋使, 遣唐使 7:259b-261a
Keppan 血判 4:200a
Kerama Islands
慶良間列島 4:200a
Kesaku. *See* **Gesaku**
Kesatuan Melayu Muda (KMM) 2:348b
Kesennuma 気仙沼 4:200a
Keshin 1:122b-123a
Keshōjio 2:25b
Keshōmawashi 7:272a
Kessen no ōzora e (Toward a Decisive Battle in the Sky)
決戦の大空へ 8:319b
Ketsumeidan
Inoue Nisshō 3:311a
Ketsumeidan Jiken. 血盟団事件 *See* **League of Blood Incident**
Ketsuzei ikki 血税一揆 4:200a-200b
Keyaki 8:369b
Key money 4:200b
K. Hattori & Co, Ltd 3:113b; 4:200b
Khubilai Khan 忽必烈汗 3:171a; 5:243b-245a
Khvostov, Nikolai Aleksandrovich 6:341a
Ki 気 4:200b-201a; 7:190a-190b
Kiaochow concession. *See* **Jiaozhou (Kiaochow) concession**
Kibachi (horntails) 1:149a
Ki Baitei 紀梅亭 1:211a; 4:201a
Kiba minzoku setsu 3:229a-231a
Kibei 4:14b
Kibi Daijin nittō ekotoba
吉備大臣入唐絵詞 4:201b
Kibi Kōgen 吉備高原 4:128a, 201a
Kibi no Makibi 吉備真備 4:201a-201b
Abe no Nakamaro 4:201a
Fujiwara no Hirotsugu, Rebellion of 2:351a
Fujiwara no Nakamaro 4:201a
Gembō 3:16a; 4:201a
kakun 4:118a
ritsuryō system 6:331b
Sui and Tang (T'ang) China, embassies to 7:260a
Tachibana no Moroe 4:201a
Kibune Shrine 貴船神社 4:201b
Kibuneyama 貴船山 4:201b
Kibutsu poetry 5:106a
Kibyōshi 黄表紙 4:61a, 201b-202a; 5:49a; 7:18a, 96b; 8:141b
format 4:201b
Hōseidō Kisanji 3:234b; 4:202a
Koikawa Harumachi 4:250a
Shikatsube Magao 7:95a
Kichigai buraku shūyū kikō 気違い部落周遊紀行 4:202a
Kichijō Kekae ceremony 8:286a
Kichijōten 吉祥天 1:*185a*; 4:77b
Kichi mondai 8:167b-168b
Kidai 3:81b
Kida Minoru きだみのる 4:202a
Kido Jun'ichirō 木戸準一郎 4:203a
Kido Kanji 木戸貫治 4:203a
Kido Kōichi 木戸幸一 4:202a
Konoe Fumimaro cabinet 4:202a
lord keeper of the privy seal 5:310a-310b
war crimes conviction 4:202a
Kido Kōin. 木戸孝允 *See* **Kido Takayoshi**
Kido nikki 木戸日記 4:202a
Kido Shirō 城戸四郎 4:202a
Kidōtai 6:320a-320b
Kido Takayoshi 木戸孝允 4:202b-203a; 7:29b, 51a
cabinet critic 4:203a-203b
Assembly of Prefectural Governors 4:203a
Land Tax Reform of 1873-1881 4:203a
Chōshū samurai 4:202b
Egawa Tarōzaemon 4:202b
Western Learning 4:202b
Yoshida Shōin 4:202b
Meiji councillor 4:203a
Charter Oath 1:267a; 4:203a
Iwakura mission 4:203a
modernization policies 4:203a
Restoration activist 4:202b
Coup d'Etat of 30 September 1863 4:202b
Hamaguri Gomon Incident 4:202b
Sakamoto Ryōma 4:203a
Shinagawa Yajirō 7:109a
Kienrei 棄捐令 4:203b
Ki family 紀氏 4:203b
Kiga kaikyō (The Straits of Starvation) 飢餓海峡 8:89a
Uchida Tomu 8:124a
Kiganjo 4:195b

Kigen 紀元 1:232a; 4:203b-204a
Emperor Jimmu 4:57a, 203b
Kigensetsu 4:204a
periodization 6:175a
Tokugawa Nariaki 4:204a
Kigensetsu 紀元節 4:204a
Kigensetsu controversy 4:204a
Kiguchi Kohei 木口小平 4:204a
Kihara Hitoshi 木原均 1:156a; 4:204b
Kihara Institute for Biological Research 4:204b
Kiheitai 奇兵隊 1:86a; 4:204b
Boshin Civil War 4:204b
Ikuno Disturbance 3:271a
Shimonoseki Bombardment 4:204b
Takasugi Shinsaku 4:204b; 7:319a-319b
Yamagata Aritomo 4:204b
Kihira Masami 紀平正美 4:204b
Kihira Tadayoshi 紀平正美 4:204b
Kii Channel 紀伊水道 4:204b
Kii Mountains 紀伊山地 4:204b
Kii Ōshima 紀伊大島 6:125a
Kii Peninsula 紀伊半島 4:205a
Kiji. *See* **Pheasants**
Kijibiki 4:205a
Kijishi 4:205a
Kijiya 4:205a
rokuro 6:335b
Kikai kanran (Beholding the Waves in the Sea of Ether) 気海観瀾 8:242b
Kikai kanran kōgi 気海観瀾広義 4:181b
"Kikai" (Machine) 機械 8:332b
Kikaishima 喜界島 4:205a
Kikajin 帰化人 1:147b; 4:205a-205b, 338a; 7:256a
Aya family 4:205b
Buddhism introduction 4:205b
court rank 4:205b
Hata family 4:205b
periods of arrival 4:205b
Sakanoue family 4:205b
Shiba Tatto 4:205b
titles 4:89a
Wani 4:205b
Yamato court 4:277a
Yuzuki no Kimi 4:205a
Kikakuin Jiken 企画院事件 6:189b
Kikawada Kazutaka 木川田一隆 2:167b; 4:205b
Kike wadatsumi no koe きけわだつみのこえ 4:206a
Kikikata 聞方 4:119b
Kikkōchiku 1:135b
Kikkōman Corporation 4:206a
Kikkōman Foods, Inc 4:206a
Kikkōman International, Inc 4:206a
Kikkōman Trading Europe, GmbH 4:206a
Kikō 8:104b-106a
Kiku 1:310a-311a
Kikuchi 菊池 4:206a
Kikuchi Dairoku 菊池大麓 4:206a
Kikuchi family 菊池氏 4:206a-206b
Kikuchi Hiroshi 菊池寛 4:206b
Kikuchi Kan 菊池寛 4:206b-207a; 7:81a, 103b, 109a, 125a, 126b
Bungei Shunjū 1:209b-210a; 4:206b
fūzoku shōsetsu 2:378b
literary prizes 4:206b-207a; 5:24b
radio drama 6:275a
sponsorship of Furukawa Roppa 2:373a
Yamamoto Yūzō 4:206b
Kikuchi Seishi 菊池正士 4:207a
Kikuchi Taisuke 菊池太輔 7:96b-97b
Kiku gashira kōmori *(Rhinolophus ferrumequinum)* 1:146b
Kikumura Itaru 菊村到 4:207a
Kiku no Sekku. 菊の節句 *See* **Chrysanthemum Festival**
Kikuta Kazuo 菊田一夫 4:207a-207b
dramatic serials 4:207a
Furukawa Roppa 2:373a; 4:207a
plays 4:207a
radio drama 6:275b
Kikutake Kiyonori 菊竹清訓 4:207b
Kikutake Sunao 菊竹淳 4:207b
Kikuta Noboru 菊田登 1:15b
Kikyō [(balloonflower) *Platycodon grandiflorum*] 4:207b
Kikyō (Homecoming) 帰郷 6:221b
Kilns 1:256a-265b; 7:91a
Kimbusenji 金峰山寺 4:207b-208a
Kimbusen Shugen Honshū 金峰山修験本宗 4:207b
Kim Ch'angam 4:208a
Kim Ch'angsu 4:208a
Kim Dae-jung 4:211a
Kim Gu 4:208a
Kimi 君 4:89a, 310a
Kimigayo (His Majesty's Reign) 君が代 5:336a
Kimiidera 紀三井寺 4:208a
Kim Il-sŏng 4:208b
Japanese imperialism 4:284a
Kapsan faction 4:208b
Korean People's Liberation Army 4:208b
premiership 4:208b
Kimi no na wa (What's Your Name?) 君の名は 6:275b
Kimi Pass 紀見峠 4:208b
Kimitsu 君津 4:208b
Kim Jong-p'il 4:211a, 285a
Kimmeichiku *(Phyllostachys bambusoides var. castillonis)* 1:135b
Kimmei, Emperor 欽明天皇 4:208b; 7:264a
Kimmon Incident. 禁門の変 *See* **Hamaguri Gomon Incident**
Kim-Ōhira Memorandum 4:288a
Kimoiri. *See* **Shōya**
Kim Ok-kyun 4:209a
assassination of 4:281a
Fukuzawa Yukichi 4:209a
Independence Party 4:209a
Japanese visit 4:280b
Kaehwap'a 4:101b, 209a
Kapsin Political Coup 4:156b, 209a
Kimon 4:163a
Kimono 着物 1:329a; 4:*209a, 209b*, 210a-210b; 7:272b; 8:*358b*
atsuita 1:115b
caring 4:210b
dyes and dye colors 2:136b
how to wear 4:210a
kara-ori 4:158a
kosode predecessor 1:332b; 2:90b; 4:209a
men's 4:209b
ro and sha 6:333a
sarasa (calico; batik) silk 7:21a
style and tailoring 4:210a
tasuki 7:348a
textiles, care and preservation of 8:20a
women's 4:209b-210a
Kimpira 金平 4:77a
Kimpishō 禁秘抄 4:210b
Kimpokusan 金北山 4:210b
Kimpusan 金峰山 1:272a; 4:153b, 211a
Kim Sŏng-ju 4:208b
Kim Tae-jung 4:211a
Japanese-Korean relations 4:286a
Kim Tal-su 4:211a
Kimura Hisashi 木村栄 4:211a
Kimura Ihei 木村伊兵衛 6:*185a*
Kimura Kaishū. 木村芥舟 *See* **Kimura Yoshitake**
Kimura Ki 木村毅 4:211a-211b
Kimura Motoo 木村資生 4:211b
Kimura Shigenari 木村重成 4:211b
Tōdō Takatora 4:211b
Tokugawa Hidetada 4:211b
Tokugawa Ieyasu 4:211b
Toyotomi Hideyori 4:211b
Uesugi Kagekatsu 4:211b
Kimura Toshio 木村俊夫
visit to Africa 1:19b
Kimura Yoshitake 木村喜毅 4:211b
Kanrin maru 4:151b, 211b
Katsu Kaishū 4:211b
Kin 7:87b
Kinai 畿内 4:211b-212a
Kin Bay 金武湾 4:212a
Kinchū Narabi ni Kuge Shohatto 禁中並公家諸法度 3:186b; 4:212a
Tokugawa shogunate 8:53a-53b
Kindai bungaku 近代文学 4:212a; 6:230b
Kindai bungaku nōto 近代文学ノート 4:172a
Kindai Bungaku Kondan Kai 5:19b
Kindaichi Haruhiko 金田一春彦 4:31b
Kindaichi Kyōsuke 金田一京助 1:36b; 4:212a
Kin Daichū 金大中 4:211a
Kindai Eiga Kyōkai 2:275b
Kindai kaiga 近代絵画 5:13a
Kindai keizaigaku shi 近代経済学史 7:258a
Kindai ōshū keizaishi josetsu (Introduction to Modern European Economic History) 近代欧州経済史序説 6:134a
Kindai seikatsu 近代生活 7:175b
Kindai shisō (Modern Thought) 近代思想 1:72a
Ōsugi Sakae 6:127b
Kindergarten Order (Yōchien Rei) 6:235b
Kindergartens. *See* **Preschool education**
Kinema Jumpō Prize
Tanaka Kinuyo 7:337a
King of Chūzan 中山王 1:314b
Kingu キング 4:212b
Kingu Prize 4:242a
Kingyo 3:43b
Kin Gyokukin 金玉均 4:209a
Kingyotsubaki 1:237a
Kinkafu 琴歌譜 4:297a
early Japanese songs 2:138a
Kinkai wakashū 金槐和歌集 4:212b
Minamoto no Sanetomo 4:122a, 212b; 5:179a
Kinkakuji 金閣寺 4:213a, 336a-336b
Golden Pavilion 4:*212b*
Kinkazan 金華山 4:213a; 7:16a
Kinki Electrical Construction Co, Inc 4:213a
Kinki kakumei 錦旗革命
October Incident 6:60a
Kinkikan Incident 錦輝館事件 6:285a-285b
Kinki Nippon Railway Co, Ltd 4:213b
Nagoya Railroad Co, Ltd 5:309b

Kinkin sensei eiga no yume (Mr. Glitter n' Gold's Dream of Splendor) 金々先生栄花夢 4:201b, 250a
Kinki region 近畿地方 4:151b, 213b
parks 4:213b
urban planning 8:179b
Kinki Region Development Law 4:213b
Kinki shoga 琴棋書画 4:213b-214a
Kinko (cucumber) 7:45a
Kinkō Bay 錦江湾 4:105b
Kinkō bunseki no kihon mondai (Basic Problems of Equilibrium Analysis) 均衡分析の基本問題 8:319a
Kinkyōrei 禁教令 1:64b-65a
Kin Kyū 金九 4:208a
Kin Nissei 金日成 4:208a-208b
Kinnōka 勤皇家 2:205a
Ki no Kaion 紀海音 4:214a
jōruri plays 4:77a
Kyūemon and Matsuyama romance 4:93b
Kinokawa 紀ノ川 4:214a
Kinoko 5:282a-282b
Kinokuniya Bunzaemon 紀国屋文左衛門 4:214a
chōnin 1:302a
Kinosaki 城崎 4:214a; 7:11b
Kinoshita Chōshōshi 木下長嘯子 4:214b; 7:105a; 8:215b
Kinoshita Jun'an 木下順庵 4:214b
Amenomori Hōshū 4:214b
Arai Hakuseki 4:214b
Kaibara Ekiken 4:108b
Maeda Tsunanori 4:214b
Matsunaga Sekigo 4:214b
Miyake Kanran 4:214b
Muro Kyūsō 4:214b
Tokugawa Tsunayoshi 4:214b
Kinoshita Junji 木下順二 2:76b; 4:214b-215b; 5:59b
Shingeki 7:112a, 113a
Yamamoto Yasue 4:214b; 8:299b
Kinoshita Keisuke 木下恵介 2:272a-272b, 273b-274a; 4:215b
Shindō Kaneto 7:111a
Kinoshita Mokutarō 木下杢太郎 4:215b; 7:253b
Kinoshita Naoe 木下尚江 1:155a; 4:215b-216a; 7:74a-74b
Futsū Senkyo Kisei Dōmeikai 2:376a
pacifism 4:215b-216a; 6:143b
Kinoshita Rigen 木下利玄 4:216a
Kinoshita Takafumi 木下幸文 4:216a
Kinoshita Takeji 木下竹次 7:36a
Ki no Tomonori 紀友則 4:216a-216b; 7:13a
Kokinshū 4:254b
Ki no Tsurayuki 紀貫之 1:18a, 85b; 2:301b; 4:216b-217a; 5:14a; 6:113b, 299a; 7:13a, 42b; 8:287b
court poet 4:216b
imperial poetry anthology 4:216b
Kagawa Kageki 4:103a
Kokinshū 4:254b
poetic style 2:352a
Shin kokinshū 7:120a
Tosa nikki 4:216b
Kinō wa kyō no monogatari きのふはけふの物語 6:282a
Kinran and ginran 4:217a
Kinrō Kokumintō 勤労国民党 1:2b
Kinroku kōsai 金禄公債 4:217a
Kinsaku 1:144a
Kinsei kijin den 近世畸人伝 4:217a
Kinsei Nihon kokumin shi (A History of Early Modern Japan) 近世日本国民史 8:60a
Kinsekibun 金石文 3:313b-314a
Kinshi Kunshō 金鵄勲章 4:217a
Kinship 4:217a-218b
affines 4:217b
bilateral pattern 4:217a
cognates 4:217b
composition of shinrui 4:217b
head of household 4:217b
socioeconomic obligation 4:217b
Confucian influence 1:353b
consanguinity 1:358b-359a
dominant tendency of male side 4:217b-218a
dōzoku 4:218a
surnames 4:218a
virilocal marriage 4:217b
honke and bunke 3:223b-224a
ie 3:260a
importance of women in network 4:218a-218b
terminology 4:217a
Kinshō-Mataichi Corporation 4:218b
Kintarō 金太郎 4:218b
Kintōshū 公任集 8:188a
Kinu 7:194a
Kinugasa Teinosuke 衣笠貞之助 2:56b, 269a, 271a, 273b; 4:218b-219a
Jigokumon 4:219a
Jūjiro 4:218b
Kawabata Yasunari 4:218b
Kurutta ippeiji 4:218b
onnagata 4:218b
Kinugawa 鬼怒川 4:219a
Shimotsuma 7:107a
Kinugawa Hot Spring 鬼怒川温泉 4:219a
Kinunuibe 衣縫部 1:147b
Kinuta 砧 7:293a
Kin'yōshū 金葉集 4:219a-219b
Kin'yō wakashū 金葉和歌集 2:350a; 3:275b; 4:219a-219b; 5:38a, 179b; 7:95a
major poets 4:219a-219b
Minamoto no Toshiyori 4:219a-219b; 5:179b
Kin'yū keiretsu 4:189a
Kinza, ginza, and zeniza 金座, 銀座, 銭座 4:219b-220a
Gotō family 4:219b-220a
ōban 6:48a
Tokugawa Ieyasu 4:219b-220a
Kioku to genzai 記憶と現在 6:113b
Kira Yoshinaka 吉良義央 4:220a
Forty-Seven Rōnin Incident 2:327a
Kiri. *See* **Paulownia**
Kiribi 4:220a
Kirigamine 霧ケ峰 4:127b, 220b
Kirigirisu [(katydid) *Gampsocleis buergeri*] 4:220b
Kirikane 切金 4:220b-221a
Kirimai 切米 4:221a
Kirin 麒麟 7:342b
Kirin Brewery Co, Ltd 4:221a
Kiri no naka 霧の中 7:334a
Kirino Toshiaki 桐野利秋 7:51a
Kirishima Volcanic Zone 霧島火山帯 4:221a
Kirishima-Yaku National Park 霧島屋久国立公園 4:105a, 106a, 221a-221b; 5:304a
Kirishimayama 霧島山 4:105b, 221b
Kirishitan. *See* **Kakure Kirishitan**
Kirishitan-ban. 切支丹版 *See* **Jesuit mission press**
Kirishitan daimyō. *See* **Christian daimyo**
Kirishitan monogatari 切支丹物語 2:241a; 4:221b
Kirishitan Yashiki 切支丹屋敷 4:221b-222a
Kirisute gomen 切捨御免 4:222a
Kirisutoki 契利斯督記 7:186a
Kirisutokyō no gaidoku キリスト教の害毒 4:168b
Kiritake Monjūrō II 桐竹紋十郎(二代) 4:222a
Kiritsunagi origami 6:118a
Kiroku Shōen Kenkeijo 記録荘園券契所 4:222a
Kirokutai 3:126b-127a
Kiryoka (travel poems) 羇旅歌 8:104b
Kiryū 桐生 4:222a
silk weaving 2:296a
Kiryū Yūyū 桐生悠々 4:222a
Kisaku. *See* **Gesaku**
Kisarazu 木更津 4:222b
Kisatsu Seimu Iinkai 冀察政務委員会 4:53a
Kisegawa 黄瀬川 4:222b
Kisen
Kokinshū 4:254b
Kisen Shūshō 亀泉集証 4:147b
Kishibojin 鬼子母神 4:222b
Kishida Ginkō 岸田吟香 4:222b
Kishida Kunio 岸田国士 4:222b
fūzoku shōsetsu 2:378b
shingeki 7:113a
Kishida Ryūsei 岸田劉生 4:223a
Kishida Ginkō 4:223a
Kuroda Kiyoteru 4:223a
modern painting 6:156a
Mushanokōji Saneatsu 4:223a
Kishida Toshiko 岸田俊子 4:223a; 7:54a
Fukuda Hideko 2:362a
Kishi-Eisenhower joint declaration 8:160b
Kishi Nobusuke 岸信介 2:333a; 3:289a; 4:223a-223b; 7:275b
Fujiyama Aiichirō 2:359a
national defense 5:336b-338b
United States-Japan security treaties 8:166b
Kishi school 岸派 3:7b-8a
Kishi Seiichi 岸清一 4:223b
Kishiwada 岸和田 4:223b
Kishō-bori
tattoos 7:350a
Kishōchō 気象庁 5:165a
Kishōgaku 気象学 6:78b
Kishōgaku kōwa 気象学講話 6:78b
Kiska 4:223b
Kisodani 木曽谷 4:223b
Kiso Fukushima 木曽福島 4:223b-224a
Kisogawa 木曽川 4:224a; 5:303b
Kiso Kaidō rokujūkutsugi (69 Stations of the Kiso Kaidō Road) 木曽街道六十九次 4:190a
Kisokoma 木曽駒 4:265a
Kiso Komagatake 木曽駒ケ岳 4:265a
Kiso Mountains 木曽山脈 4:224a-224b
Kiso Ontake 木曽御岳 6:112b
Kiso Yoshinaka. 木曽義仲 *See* **Minamoto no Yoshinaka**
Kissaten 1:334a-334b
Kissa yōjō ki 喫茶養生記 2:187a
Kisuge 2:78b-79a

Kitabatake Akiie · 北畠顕家 **4**:224a
Kō no Moronao destroyed **4**:275a
Kitabatake Chikafusa 北畠親房 **4**:224a; **7**:164b
historiography **3**:153b
Kitabatake family · 北畠氏 **4**:224b
Kita Chishima ainugo 北千島アイヌ語 **1**:36b
Kita Daitōjima · 北大東島 **4**:224b
Kitadake 北岳 **4**:224b
Shirane Sanzan **7**:147a
Kitagata, Lake 北潟湖 **1**:125a
Kitagawa Fuyuhiko 北川冬彦 **4**:224b
Kajii Motojirō **4**:114a
Kitagawa Morisada. 喜田川守貞 *See* **Morisada mankō**
Kitagawa school · 喜多川派 **4**:224b-225a
Kitagawa Utamaro. 喜多川歌麿 *See* **Utamaro**
Kitahara Hakushū 北原白秋 **4**:225a; **7**:253b; **8**:341a
"Jōgashima no ame" **4**:69a
Kitahara Takeo · 北原武夫 **4**:225a-225b
Kitahara Tasaku · 北原多作 **4**:225b
Kita Ibaraki 北茨城 **3**:367b; **4**:225b
Kita Ikki 北一輝 **4**:225b-226a
February 26th Incident **2**:250a
Kitakami (city) 北上 **4**:226a
Kitakami Basin · 北上盆地 **4**:226a
Kitakamigawa 北上川 **4**:226a
Kitakami Mountains 北上山地 **4**:226a-226b
Kitakata 喜多方 **4**:226b
Kita Kyūshū 北九州 **2**:364b-365a; **4**:*226b*
Kita Kyūshū Municipal Art Museum **5**:279a
Kitamaebune 北前船 **4**:112b
Kitami 北見 **4**:226b
Kitami Mountains 北見山地 **4**:226b
Kitamori Kazō · 北森嘉蔵 **4**:227a
Kita Morio 北杜夫 **4**:227a
Kitamoto 北本 **4**:227a
Kitamura Kigin · 北村季吟 **4**:227a
Man'yōshū scholarship **5**:110b
Kitamura Kusuo 北村久寿雄 **4**:227a
Kitamura Rokurō 喜多村緑郎 **4**:227a
shimpa **7**:107b
Kitamura Sayo · 北村サヨ **4**:227b; **7**:76b
Kitamura Seibō · 北村西望 **5**:*304b*
Kitamura Tōkoku 北村透谷 **4**:227b-228a; **5**:11b
Bungakukai **1**:208b
pacifism **6**:143b-144a
Kitano 北野
Shintō **7**:126b
Kitano Shrine · 北野天満宮 **4**:228a; **7**:257a
Takayama Sōzei **7**:320a
temmangū **7**:381a
Kitano Tenjin engi 北野天神縁起 **4**:228a; **7**:*136b*
Kitaōji Rosanjin 北大路魯山人 **4**:228a-228b
Kitao Masanobu · 北尾政演 **7**:18a
Kitao Shigemasa 北尾重政 **4**:228b
Santō Kyōden **7**:18a
Kita Sadakichi · 喜田貞吉 **1**:77b; **4**:228b
Kita school 喜多流 **4**:228b-229a
Kitaura 北浦 **4**:229a
Kita Ward 北区 **4**:229a
Kitayama culture 北山文化 **4**:229a
Kitazato Institute **4**:229a
Kitazato Shibasaburō 北里柴三郎 **4**:229a; **7**:89b
Kitazono Katsue · 北園克衛 **4**:229a
Kite, black [(tobi) *Milvus migrans*] **4**:229b
Kite battles **4**:230a, 231a
Kite makers **4**:229b-232a
Kites · **2**:296a; **4**:229b-230a, *230b*, 231a-231b
for Children's Day **1**:279b
decoration **4**:230a-231a
as folk craft **4**:231a-231b
military history **4**:230a
modern **4**:230b-231a
premodern **4**:229b-230b
Kitō 几董 **6**:297b, 298b
Kitō Bōkyō Jichi Seifu 冀東防共自治政府 **2**:142b
Kitsuki 杵築 **4**:231b
Kitsune **2**:330a
Kitsuneken **4**:193a
Kitsutsuki **8**:269b
Kiuchi Sekitei 木内石亭 **1**:75b; **4**:231b
Kiuchi Shinzō 木内信蔵 **4**:231b
Geography in Japan **3**:26a
Kiuchi Sōgorō. 木内惣五郎 *See* **Sakura Sōgorō**
Kiwanis Club **4**:231b
Kiwanis Japan **4**:231b
"Kiyō bimbō" (Clever Poverty) 器用貧乏 **8**:173b
Kiyokawa Shōji · 清川正二 **4**:231b
Kiyomizudera 清水寺 **3**:*9a*; **4**:231b-232a, *334b*, 336a; **7**:256b
Kiyomizudera engi (Legends of Kiyomizudera) 清水寺縁起 **6**:*153b*
Kiyomizu monogatari 清水物語 **4**:136b
Kiyomizu ware. 清水焼 *See* **Kyōto ceramics**
Kiyomizuyaki 清水焼 **4**:337a
Kiyomoto-bushi 清元節 **4**:91b, 99a, 232a-232b
tokiwazu-bushi **8**:43b
Kiyonaga. 清長 *See* **Torii Kiyonaga**
Kiyono Kenji 清野謙次 **4**:232b
Kiyooka Takayuki 清岡卓行 **4**:232b
Kiyosato 清里 **4**:232b
Kiyosawa Kiyoshi · 清沢洌 **4**:232b
Kiyose 清瀬 **4**:232b
Kiyosumiyama 清澄山 **4**:232b-233a
Kiyoura Keigo 清浦奎吾 **3**:198a; **4**:233a; **7**:55a
cabinet **4**:120a, 198a
Kiyozawa Manshi 清沢満之 **4**:233a
Jōdo Shin sect **4**:68b
Kiyū shōran (Diversions for One's Amusement) 嬉遊笑覧 **4**:233b
Kizetsukyō gorge 奇絶峡
Tanabe **7**:335a
Kizewa-mono 生世話物 **4**:91b-92a
Kizokuin. 貴族院 *See* **House of Peers**
Kizugawa 木津川 **4**:233b
Knitting **7**:106b
Knives (hōchō) **2**:24b
Know-how **4**:233b
Ko (household) **4**:233b-234a
Kō (associations) 講 **4**:234a
Kōain 興亜院 **1**:102b
Kōan **4**:234a; **8**:373b
Hakuin **3**:88a
riddles **6**:311b
Kōan Chōsa Chō 公安調査庁 **6**:266b
Kōan jōrei 公安条例 **4**:234a-234b
Tōkyō ordinance decision (20 July 1960) **8**:68b
Kōa Oil Co, Ltd **4**:234b; **6**:181b
Kobachi *(chalcids)* **1**:149a
Koba Ichirō 木庭一郎 **5**:315a-315b
Koban (gold coins) · 小判 · **4**:234b; **7**:67b
ōban (coins) **6**:47b
Kōban (police box) **4**:234b-235a
Kobanashi **4**:235a-235b
Kobayakawa Hideaki 小早川秀秋 **4**:235b-236a; **7**:56b, 99a
Kamiya Sōtan **4**:127b
Kobayashi 小林 **4**:236a
Kobayashi Ataru 小林中 **4**:236a
Kobayashi Hideo 小林秀雄 **1**:209a; **4**:236a-236b
literary criticism **5**:13a
Kobayashi Ichizō 小林一三 **4**:236b
Furukawa Roppa **2**:373a
Hankyū Corporation **3**:99a
Itsuō Art Museum **3**:357b
Kobayashi Issa. 小林一茶 *See* **Issa**
Kobayashi Kiyochika 小林清親 **4**:236b-237a
modern prints **5**:232a
Kobayashi Kokei 小林古径 **4**:237a
Kobayashi Masaki 小林正樹 **2**:272a-272b, 274a; **4**:237a
Seppuku **7**:68b
Kobayashi Shigeru · 小林茂 **4**:237a
Kobayashi Takiji 小林多喜二 **4**:237a-238a; **7**:25a, 66b
proletarian literature movement **6**:255b-256a
Kobayashi Yukio · 小林行雄 **1**:77b
Kōbe 神戸 **4**:238a, *238b*
Kobē Bank Ltd **8**:96a
Kōbe Port Island **4**:*364b*
Kōbe Steel, Ltd **4**:139a, 238a
Kōbetsu **7**:124b
Kōbe University **4**:238a-238b
Kōbō Daishi. 弘法大師 *See* **Kūkai**
Kōbō Daishi gyōjō 弘法大師行状 **4**:295a
Kobori Enshū 小堀遠州 **4**:238b
Furuta Oribe **2**:373b
Iga ware **3**:261b
Kōrakuen **4**:276a
Kobori Jinji 小堀甚二 **3**:141a
Kobotoke Pass 小仏峠 **4**:238b
Kōbu Bijutsu Gakkō (Technical Fine Arts School) **7**:43b
Kōbu currency 洪武銭 **4**:239a
Kōbu gattai 公武合体 **5**:260a-260b
Kōbu Gattai Undō. 公武合体運動 *See* **Movement for Union of Court and Shogunate**
Kōbun, Emperor · 弘文天皇 **4**:238b-239a
Jinshin Disturbance **4**:60b
Kobunjigaku 古文辞学 **4**:239a
Kōbusen 洪武銭 **4**:239a
Kobushi *(Magnolia kobus)* **4**:239a
Kobushigadake 甲武信ヶ岳 **1**:272a; **4**:239a
Kobushin 小普請 **4**:239a-239b
Kobutori jiiji ("The Old Man Who Lost His Wen") 瘤取爺 **4**:239b
Kōbu tsūhō 洪武通宝 **4**:239a
Kobuuri 昆布売 **4**:328a
Kōchi (city) 高知 **4**:239b
Kōchi kōmin system 公地公民制 **5**:333b
Kōchi Plain 高知平野 **4**:239b
Kōchi Prefecture 高知県 **4**:239b
Kochō 蝴蝶 **8**:288b
Kōchō jūnisen · 皇朝十二銭 **4**:239b-240a; **7**:277a
Wadō kaihō **8**:198a
Kōda Aya 幸田文 **4**:240a

Kodai ··· 4:258a
Kōdaiji maki-e · 高台寺蒔絵 ·· 4:240a-240b; 4:360b
Kodai kenkyū (The Study of Ancient Times) ··· 古代研究 4:240b; 6:119a
Kodaira ··· 小平 ··· 4:241a
Kodaira Kunihiko 小平邦彦 ··· 4:241a
Kodakara ("child-treasure") ··· 1:277a
Kodama (train) ··· 6:279a
Kodama administration
  Taiwan ··· 7:307b
Kodama Gentarō ··· 児玉源太郎 ··· 4:241a
Kodama Yoshio ··· 児玉誉士夫 ··· 4:241a
Kōdan ··· 4:241a-241b; 6:263a-264a; 7:65a
  film influence ··· 2:267b
Kōdansha, Ltd · 4:241b-242a; 6:246a, 268a
  Noma Seiji ··· 4:212b
Kōda Rohan ··· 幸田露伴 ··· 2:291b; 4:242a-243a; 5:13a; 7:103a
  fūryū concept ··· 2:374b
  Ken'yūsha ··· 4:199a
  life ··· 4:242a-243a
  Shinshōsetsu ··· 7:125b
  works ··· 4:242a-243a
Kodemari
  shimotsuke ··· 7:107a
Kōden ··· 公田 ··· 4:243a
Kodera Kambyōe ··· 小寺宮兵衛 ··· 4:315a
Kōdō ··· 講堂 ··· 1:182b;
Kōdō ··· 香道 ·· 3:284a-285a
Kōdōha ··· 皇道派 ··· 4:243a
  Nagata Tetsuzan ··· 5:307a
  Tōseiha ··· 8:82b
  Watanabe Jōtarō ··· 8:235b
Kōdōkan ··· 講道館 ··· 4:243a
  kangeiko ··· 4:140b
Kōdōkan (school for Western Learning) ··· 弘道館 ··· 8:52a
Kōdōkan Jūdō school ··· 4:82b
Kōdōkan ki jutsugi ··· 弘道館記述義 ··· 4:243b
Kōdō Kyōkai ··· 公道協会 ··· 3:262b
Kodomo no Hi ··· 子供の日 ·· 1:279a-279b
Kodomo no shiki ··· 子供の四季 ··· 8:110a
Kōeki kokusan kō ··· 広益国産考 ··· 6:98a
Kōen ··· 皇円 ··· 3:153a
Kōenkai ··· 7:272b
Kōetsu. 光悦 *See* **Hon'ami Kōetsu**
Kōfu (city) ··· 甲府 ··· 4:243b
Kōfu Basin ··· 甲府盆地 ··· 4:243b
Kōfukuji ··· 興福寺 · 1:152b, 182a; 4:243b-244a; 5:270b-271a, *331a*, 332a; 7:74a
  edokoro
    Kose-school painters in ··· 4:295a
  hiden'in ··· 3:130b
  Taira-Minamoto War ··· 7:299b
  Tamon'in nikki ··· 7:334a-334b
Kōfukuji Treasure House ··· 4:244a
  Ashura ··· 4:*244b*
Kofun ··· 古墳 ·· 4:244a-245b; 7:30b, 256a
  early-period ··· 4:244a-245b
  Eta Funayama tomb ··· 2:231b
  first systematic investigation ··· 1:76b
  Horse-rider theory ··· 4:277a
  Ishibutai tomb ··· 3:339b
  Iwase "thousand-mound" tomb cluster ··· 3:363a
  Kakogawa ··· 4:117b
  late-period ··· 4:245b-246a
  middle-period ··· 4:245a-245b
  Nagoya ··· 5:308b-309a
  Nintoku Mausoleum ··· 4:*246b*
  Ōzuka tomb ··· 6:141a
  Shintō ··· 7:126a
  Takamatsuzuka tomb ··· 7:314b-315a
  Takehara tomb ··· 4:*247a*
  Yame tomb cluster ··· 8:313a-313b
Kofun period ··· 古墳時代 ··· 3:160b-161b; 4:246a
  archaeology of ··· 4:246a
  economy ··· 2:147a
  periodization ··· 6:175b
  religion during ··· 7:126a
Kofun studies
  new trends ··· 1:79a
  protohistoric ··· 1:77a, 78b
Kofun to jōdai bunka ··· 古墳と上代文化 ··· 7:312a
Koga ··· 古河 ··· 4:246a
Koga bikō ··· 古画備考 ··· 4:156a
Kōgai ··· 笄 ·· 4:246a, 295b
Kōgaibyō ··· 6:217b-220a
Koga Issaku ··· 古賀逸策 ··· 4:246a-246b
Kogaku (Ancient Learning) ··· 古学 ·· 4:246b-248a, 258b; 7:71a, 190b-191a
  Itō Jinsai ··· 3:354a; 4:247b
  Ogyū Sorai ··· 4:247b-248a; 6:72b-73a
  Yamaga Sokō ··· 4:247a-247b; 8:290b
Koga kubō ··· 古河公方 ··· 4:248a
Koga Masao ··· 古賀政男 ··· 4:248a
Koganei ··· 小金井 ··· 4:248a
Koganei Yoshikiyo ··· 小金井良精 ··· 4:248a-248b
Koganemaru (Golden Boy) ··· こがね丸 ··· 4:199a
Koganemushi ··· 3:43b
Koganemushi ··· こがね蟲 ··· 4:139a
Kōgei ··· 2:293b-294a; 4:179a
Kōgei (Decorative Arts) ··· 工芸 ··· 8:314a
Kogen eeben shōho ··· 古言衣延弁小補 ··· 6:138b
Kogentei ··· 古言梯 ·· 4:134a, 169a
Kōgi ··· 公儀 ··· 4:248b
Kogidō ··· 古義堂 3:354a; 4:248b; 7:94b
Kogidō Bunko · 古義堂文庫 ··· 8:8b
Kogigaku ··· 古義学 3:354a; 4:247b
Kogin ··· 2:*295a*; 7:24b
Kōgi seitai ron 公議政体論 ··· 4:248b-249a
  Taisei Hōkan ··· 7:303a
Kogito ··· コギト ··· 7:176a
Kōgō ··· 皇后 2:356b; 4:249a
Kōgoishi ··· 神籠石 ··· 4:249a
Kōgo Kaikaku ··· 甲午改革 ··· 4:90a
Kōgon, Emperor · 光厳天皇 ··· 4:249a
Kōgonen-jaku ··· 庚午年籍 ··· 4:249a-249b
Kogosho Kaigi 小御所会議 ··· 4:249b
Kogo shūi ··· 古語拾遺 · 4:249b; 5:26a
  mythology ··· 5:292a
  thought and culture ··· 8:25b
  Wani ··· 8:223a
Koguryŏ ··· 1:159b; 2:287b, 303b; 4:249b; 6:146a; 7:16b
  in Korean Three Kingdoms period · 4:292a
  language of ··· 4:291a
Kōgyō Gijutsu In ··· 工業技術院 ··· 1:21b
Kōgyō iken ··· 興業意見 4:249b; 6:232a
Kōgyō keiei sōron ··· 工業経営総論 ··· 6:93a
Kōgyoku, Empress. 皇極天皇 *See* **Saimei, Empress**
Kohan shuki ··· 湖畔手記 ··· 4:160b
Kohitsugire ··· 古筆切 ··· 1:233b
Kōhōdō ··· 1:16b
Koi ··· 1:244a
Koicha ··· 7:363a
Koicha-demae ··· 7:363a-363b
Koichijō In ··· 小一条院 ··· 4:249b-250a
Koide Narashige 小出楢重 ··· 4:250a
Koihō school ··· 古医方
  natural sciences ··· 5:356b
Koikawa Harumachi ··· 恋川春町 · 4:250a; 7:95a, 97a
Koikawa Sukimachi ··· 恋川好町 ··· 7:95a
Kōiki shichōsonken ··· 4:250a
Koinuma Kuhachirō 鯉沼九八郎 ··· 4:89a
Koishibara ware · 小石原焼 ··· 4:250b
Koishikawa Botanic Garden ··· 1:165b; 4:250a; 8:320a
Koishikawa Yōjōsho ··· 小石川養生所 ··· 4:250a-250b
Koishiwara ware · 小石原焼 2:295b; 4:250b
  Onta ware ··· 6:113a
Koiso Kuniaki ··· 小磯国昭 4:250b; 7:258b
Koizumi Chikashi ··· 古泉千樫 ··· 4:250b
Koizumi Shinzō ·· 小泉信三 ·· 4:250b-251a
Koizumi Yakumo. 小泉八雲 *See* **Hearn, Lafcadio**
Kojidan (Stories About the Past) ··· 古事談 ··· 4:251a
Kōjien ··· 広辞苑 ··· 4:31b
Kojiki (Record of Ancient Matters) ··· 古事記 ·· 1:20a, 151b, 293a; 2:101a; 4:251a-251b; 5:25b, 27a; 6:290b; 7:48a, 128a, 143b, 310b, 324b, 376a, 382b
  analysis ··· 5:27a-28a
  Chinkon ritual ··· 4:107a
  content ··· 5:27b
  dance, traditional ··· 2:73b
  early Japanese song ··· 2:137a-138a
  English translation ··· 1:266b
  falconry ··· 2:241b
  fishing references ··· 2:283b
  folktales ··· 2:302b
  frogs ··· 2:340a
  historiography ··· 3:152b
  Hieda no Are ··· 3:130b
  Japanese language, history ··· 4:28b
  jellyfish ··· 4:50b
  Jimmu, Emperor ··· 4:57a-57b
  Kada no Azumamaro lectures ··· 4:100b
  Kakei Katsuhiko ··· 4:115b
  literary analysis ··· 2:346b
  Motori Norinaga's study of ··· 4:258b
  mythology ··· 5:292a-295a
  nature in ··· 5:357b
  Ōkuninushi no Mikoto ··· 6:97b
  Ō no Yasumaro ··· 6:112a
  pheasants ··· 6:182b
  preface ··· 5:27a
  rabbits ··· 6:275a
  religious symbolism ··· 6:295b
  Shintō ··· 7:126a
  Tokoyo ··· 8:44a
  use of language ··· 5:104a
  waka ··· 8:204a
  Wani ··· 8:223a
  Watarai Shintō ··· 8:236b
  whales ··· 8:249a
  women in Japan ··· 8:258a
  women in Japanese religion ··· 8:256b
  women's education ··· 8:267a
  Yamatotakeru, Prince ··· 8:311a-311b
Kojiki den ··· 古事記伝 2:102b; 4:188a, 251b, 258b
Kōjima ··· 幸島 ··· 4:251b
Kojima Bay ··· 児島湾 ··· 4:251b
  reclamation ··· 4:364a

Kojima Gen'nosuke ··· 小島源之助 ··· 4:157a
Kojima Iken ··· 児島惟謙 ··· 4:251b-252a
Kōjima Island ··· 幸島 ··· 4:251b
Kojima Korekata ··· 児島惟謙 ··· 4:251b-252a
Kojima Moriyoshi 小島守善 ··· 4:308b
Kojima Nobuo ··· 小島信夫 1:209a; 4:252a
Kojima Takanori ··· 児島高徳 ··· 4:252a
Kōjin ··· 荒神 ··· 4:252a
Kōjinsama ··· 荒神様 ··· 4:120b
Koji ruien ··· 古事類苑 ··· 4:252a
  Ōtsuki Fumihiko ··· 6:134b
Kōjō Hō ··· 工場法 ··· 2:241a-241b
Kojong, King ·· 4:140b, 252a-252b; 7:259b; 8:293b
  Japanese gunboat diplomacy ··· 4:279b
  Kabo Reform ··· 4:90a
  pro-Russian, anti-Japanese activities ··· 4:281b
  Samil Independence Movement ··· 7:6b
  Taewŏn'gun ··· 7:293b-294a
  Tonghak Rebellion ··· 8:74b
"Kōjō no tsuki" (The Moon over the Ruined Castle) ··· 荒城の月 ··· 2:126a-126b
Kōjo ryōzoku ··· 4:252b
Kō Junken ··· 黄遵憲 ··· 3:247b
Kōjunsha ··· 交詢社 ·· 2:1b; 4:252b
Kōkaido Ō ryō hi. 広開土王陵碑 *See* **Kwanggaet'o monument**
Kōka no Miya ··· 甲賀宮 ··· 7:91a
Kokan Shiren ··· 虎関師錬 ·· 4:252b-253a; 7:70b; 8:341b
  calligraphy ··· 1:235b
  Genkō shakusho ··· 3:21a
Kōkatō Jōyaku 江華島条約 ··· 4:140b-141a
Kōkato Treaty. *See* **Kanghwa, Treaty of**
Kōke ··· 高家 4:253a; 5:256b
Kōkechi (tie-dyeing) ·纐纈 ··· 7:13b
Kōkei ··· 康慶 1:199a; 4:253a
  Fukū Kensaku Kannon ··· 4:253a
  Kaikei ··· 4:111a
  Kōfukuji commission ··· 4:244a
Kokei sanshō ("The Three Laughters of Tiger Ravine") 虎渓三笑 ··· 4:253b
Kokemi ··· 小検見 ··· 4:191a
Koken (bill of sale) ··· 沽券 ··· 4:253b
Kōken, Empress ·孝謙天皇 ··· 4:253b
  Fujiwara no Nakamaro ··· 2:353b
Kōkennin ··· 4:253b-254a
Kokeshi ··· 4:254a-254b
  Shiroishi ··· 7:148a
Kōki ··· 皇紀 ··· 1:232a
Kōkigyō ··· 6:263a-264a
Kokin chomonshū ··· 古今著聞集 ··· 4:256b
Kokin Denju ··· 古今伝授 ··· 4:254a-254b
Kokinshū ··· 古今集 ·1:293b; 2:57a; 4:133a, 254b-255a; 5:31b; 6:299a; 7:12b, 42b, 61b, 95a, 161b-162a; 8:114b, 287b, 328b
  commentaries ··· 4:188a, 198b
  compilation ··· 2:352b
  Fujiwara no Kanesuke ··· 2:351b
  Gosen wakashū ··· 3:48b
  imperial anthologies ··· 3:275b
  kagura uta ··· 4:108a
  Ki no Tomonori ··· 4:216a-216b
  Ki no Tsurayuki ··· 4:216b-217a
  Mibu no Tadamine ··· 5:166a-166b
  Ono no Takamura ··· 6:111b
  Ōshikōchi no Mitsune ··· 6:125a
  preface ··· 1:85b; 2:353a
  Rokkasen ··· 6:334b
  Senzai wakashū ··· 7:68a
  Tō no Tsuneyori ··· 8:75a
Kokinshū style ··· 5:31a
Kokin waka rokujō (Six Books of Japanese Poetry Ancient and Modern) ··· 古今和歌六帖 ·5:35a; 8:204b
Kokin wakashū.古今和歌集 *See* **Kokinshū**
Kokin wakashū seigi ··· 古今和歌集正義 ··· 4:103a
Kokiroku ··· 古記録 ··· 4:255a-255b
Kokka ··· 国華 ··· 1:154b; 4:255b; 6:204b
Kokka hachiron (Eight Matters of Concern in the National Poetry) ··· 国歌八論 4:100b; 8:215b
Kokkai. *See* **Diet**
Kokkai Kisei Dōmei. 国会期成同盟 *See* **League for Establishing a National Assembly**
Kokka Kōan Iinkai. *See* **National Public Safety Commission**
Kokkakuki ··· 骨角器 ··· 1:160a-160b
Kokka Shintō. *See* **State Shintō**
Kokka shugi ··· 5:342a-343b
Kokka Sōdōin Hō. 国家総動員法 *See* **National Mobilization Law**
Kokka taikan ··· 国歌大観 ··· 5:140b
Kokkeibon ··· 滑稽本 ··· 4:61b, 256a; 7:18a
  Hiraga Gennai ··· 3:142a
  late Edo ··· 5:49a
  sharebon ··· 7:80a
  Shikitei Samba ··· 7:96b-97b
Kokkeibon fiction ··· 5:49a
Kokkei wagōjin 滑稽和合人 ··· 6:359a
Kokken hanron ··国憲汎論 ··· 6:109a
Kokkuri ··· 4:256a
Kō Kō ··· 黄興 ··· 3:247b
Kōkō Emperor ··· 光孝天皇 ··· 1:45a
Kōkogaku Kenkyūkai ··· 1:77b
Kokon chomonjū ··· 古今著聞集 4:256b; 7:328a
Kokoro ··· 心 ··· 4:85a
Kokoromi no kishi ··· 試みの岸 ··· 6:69b
Kokoronashi ··· 心無し ··· 5:282a
Kokorozuke ··· 4:256b
Kōkotsu no hito ·恍惚の人 ··· 6:99a
Koku ··· 石 2:340a; 4:256b
Kokubō ··· 5:336b-338b
Kokubō Fujinkai. *See* **Dai Nippon Kokubō Fujinkai**
Kokubō Kaigi ··· 5:338b
Kokubu ··· 国分 ··· 4:256b
Kokubungaku Kenkyū Shiryōkan ··· 4:256b-257a
Kokubunji (city) ··· 国分寺 ··· 4:257a
Kokubunji (provincial temple) ··· 国分寺 ··· 4:257a
  Kōmyō, Empress ··· 4:268b
Kokubunniji ··· 国分尼寺 ··· 4:268b
Kokudainō ··· 石代納 ··· 4:257a
Kokudaka ··· 石高 ··· 3:188a; 4:257a-257b; 5:360b
  shimpan ··· 7:108a
  shinden kaihatsu ··· 7:109b
  Tanuma Okitsugu ··· 7:345a-346b
Kokudo Chiriin ··· 3:25a
Kokudochō. *See* **National Land Agency**
Kokufu ··· 国府 ··· 4:257b
  kokushi assigned to ··· 4:262a
Kokugaku (National Learning) ··· 国学 2:172b; 4:140a, 257b-259b; 6:306b; 7:28b, 190b, 256b
  Edo period ··· 4:257b-259b
    Ban Nobutomo ··· 1:141b
    Hirata Atsutane ··· 4:259a
    Kada no Azumamaro ··· 4:258a
    Kamo no Mabuchi ··· 4:129a-129b
    Keichū ··· 4:257b-258a
    Motoori Norinaga ··· 4:258a-258b
    Ōkuni Takamasa ··· 6:97b
    Tayasu Munetake ··· 7:359a
  historiography ··· 3:155a
  Japanese language studies ··· 4:31a
  Kojiki's status ··· 4:251b
  kokutai and ··· 4:263a
  later developments ··· 4:257b-259b
  nationalism ··· 5:342b
  objectivism ··· 4:188a
  Shintō and Buddhism, separation of ··· 7:132a
  Tanigawa Kotosuga ··· 7:341b
  Tarui Tōkichi ··· 7:347a
  thought and culture ··· 8:25a
Kokugakuin University ··· 4:259b
Kokugaku no hongi ··· 国学の本義 ··· 4:259a
Kokugaku scholars ··· 5:17a
Kokugaryō (public lands) ··· 国衙領 ··· 4:193a
Kokuga Sōsaku Kyōkai (National Creative Painting Association) ··· 8:111b
  modern painting ··· 6:156b
Kokugikan ··· 4:259b
Kokugo Chōsa Iinkai ··· 4:31b
Kokugogaku shi (History of Japanese Language Studies) ··· 国語学史 ··· 8:290a
Kokugo jiten ··· 国語辞典 ··· 2:93b-94a
Kokugo Shingikai. *See* **Council on the National Language**
Kokugun system 国郡制 2:104a; 4:259b
  agatanushi in ··· 1:21a
  ko (household) unit ··· 4:233b-234a
  provinces ··· 6:258b, 260a
  ritsuryō system ··· 6:329a
  Tōkyō ··· 8:61b
Kokuhō *See* **National Treasures**
Kokuhonsha ··· 国本社 ··· 4:259b-260a
  Hiranuma Kiichirō ··· 3:144a
  Toranomon Incident ··· 8:76b
Kokuikō ··· 国意考 ··· 4:129b
Kokujin ··· 国人 2:265a; 4:260a; 7:64b
  Akutō as ··· 1:46a
  kuni ikki ··· 4:309a
  shōen ··· 7:158a
Kokumin Bungei Kai ··· 5:19a
Kokumin Chōyō Rei. 国民徴用令 *See* **National Service Draft Ordinance**
Kokumin Dōmei ·国民同盟 ··· 4:260a
  Adachi Kenzō ··· 1:11a
  Russo-Japanese War ··· 6:346a
  Tairo Dōshikai ··· 7:303a
  Tōhōkai (Far East Society) ··· 8:36b
Kokumin Dōshikai ··· 国民同志会 ··· 4:64a
Kokumin gakkō ·· 4:260a-260b; 7:36a, 51a,
Kokumin Jissen Yōryō 国民実践要領 ··· 4:260b
Kokumin kenkō hoken. *See* **National health insurance**
Kokumin Kyōdōtō (National Cooperative Party) ··· 国民協同党 4:260b; 6:212a
Kokumin Kyōkai ·国民協会 ··· 1:40a; 4:260b-261a
  ritō ··· 6:321b
  Shinagawa Yajirō ··· 7:109a
  Teikokutō ··· 7:376b
Kokumin no tomo (Friend of the People) ·国民之友 ·4:261a; 8:60a; 296a
Kokumin seikatsu hakusho ··· 8:251b

Kokumin Seikatsu Shingikai · 2:168a-168b
Kokumin Seishin Bunka Kenkyūjo 4:204b
Kokumin Seishin Sōdōin Remmei
 ······ 国民精神総動員連盟 ········ 4:284a
Kokumin Seishin Sōdōin Undō. *See* **National Spiritual Mobilization Movement**
Kokumin shimbun
 ················ 国民新聞 ········ 4:261a
Kokumin shukusha ··············· 4:261a
Kokumin Taiiku Taikai ·············· 5:348a
Kokumintō (National People's Party)
 ················· 国民党 ··· 5:311b-312a
Kōkuri. 高句麗 *See* **Koguryŏ**
Kokuritsu Daigaku Kyōkai ·········· 4:10b
Kokuritsu ginkō. *See* **National banks**
Kokuritsu Kagaku Hakubutsukan
 ································ 5:346a
Kokuritsu Kōbunshokan. *See* **National Archives**
Kokuritsu Kokkai Toshokan
 ········· 国立国会図書館 ··· 5:338b-339a
Kokuritsu Kokugo Kenkyūjo ······· 5:343b
Kokuritsu Kyōiku Kenkyūjo ········ 2:181a
Kokuritsu Minzokugaku Hakubutsukan
 ········ 国立民族学博物館 ········ 5:344a
Kokuritsu Rekishi Minzoku Hakubutsukan
 ······ 国立歴史民俗博物館 ········ 4:261b
Kokuritsu Seiyō Bijutsukan ········ 5:344b
Kokurō (National Railway Workers' Union) ···· 国労 ········ 6:238a
Kokuryūkai ········ 黒龍会 ········ 1:53b
Kokusai Bunka Shinkōkai ··· 3:319b; 4:41a
Kokusai Denshin Denwa Co, Ltd (KDD)
 4:261b; 7:86b
 radio law ······················· 6:276a
 telephones ······················ 7:380a
Kokusai Kirisutokyō Daigaku · 国際基督教大学 ········ 3:318b
Kokusai Kōryū Kikin ··············· 4:46a
Kokusai shihō (Private International Law) ··········· 国際私法 ········ 8:289b
Kokusaku kaisha 国策会社 ··· 4:261b-262a
Kokusan kaisho · 国産会所 ········ 4:262a
Kokusei chōsaken ················ 4:262a
 Diet ···························· 4:262a
Kokusen (Black Fan) ·黒扇 ········ 2:*346b*
Kokusen'ya Kassen
 ·············· 国性爺合戦 ········ 1:275b
Kokushi ············ 国司 ··· 4:262a-262b
 kageyushi ······················· 4:104b
 Taika Reform ···················· 7:296a
 yōnin ··························· 8:338a
Kokushigatake 国師ケ岳 ··········· 4:153b
Kokushi musō (Peerless Patriot) ········· 国士無双 ········ 8:289a
Kokushi no kenkyū
 ·············· 国史の研究 ········ 6:176a
Kokushi taikei ··· 国史大系 ········ 4:262b
 Kuroita Katsumi and ·············· 4:316a
Kokusho kaidai ·· 国書解題 ··· 1:154a-154b
Kokusho sōmokuroku
 ·············· 国書総目録 ········ 1:154b
Kokushunrō ········ 国春楼 ········ 4:189b
Kokuso ····················· 国訴 ········ 4:262b
Kokutai (national polity)
 ··················· 国体 ·· 4:262b-263b; 5:348a; 6:204b, 236b; 7:190b
 academic freedom ················ 1:6b
 Imperial Rescript on Education ···· 3:279a
 Kanamori Tokujirō ··············· 4:135b
 Kokugaku as the elucidation of ···· 4:257b
 Kokutai no hongi ················ 4:264a
 nationalism ····················· 5:343a
 Occupation ······················ 6:51a
Kokutai debate ·············· 4:263b-264a
Kokutai meichō mondai. 国体明徴問題 *See* **Kokutai debate**
Kokutai no hongi
 ·············· 国体の本義 ········ 4:264a
 kokutai ························· 4:263b
 nationalism ····················· 5:342b
Kokutai shinron ·· 国体新論 ·· 4:168a, 263a
Kokutetsu. *See* **Japanese National Railways**
Kokutōkai ························ 6:159a
Kōkū Uchū Gijutsu Kenkyūjo ······ 5:336a
Kokuyaku ············ 国役 ········ 4:310a
Kokuyo Co, Ltd ·················· 4:264b
Kokuzei. *See* **Taxes, national and local**
Kokyakujō (deed) ·················· 4:253b
Kōkyō Kigyōtai Tō Rōdō Kumiai Kyōgikai ························ 4:294a
Kokyū ·························· 4:264b
 jiuta ···························· 4:64b
 ryūkōka ························· 6:354a
Kokyū wasureubeki
 ········· 故旧忘れ得べき ·· 7:176a, 315a
Kolchak, Aleksander Vasilievich ··· 7:192a
Koma. *See* **Tops**
Komachishū ········ 小町集 ········ 6:111a
Komadori [(Japanese robin) *Erithacus akahige*] ······················· 4:264b
Komae ············· 狛江 ········ 4:264b
Komagaku ·········· 高麗楽 ·········· 3:1a
Komagane ········· 駒ケ根 ········ 4:264b
Komagatake (mountain, Akaishi) ··········· 駒ケ岳 ········ 4:265a
Komagatake (mountain, Kiso) ··············· 駒ケ岳 ········ 4:265a
Komagatake (mountain, northern Honshū) 駒ケ岳 ········ 4:265a
Komagatake (volcano, Hokkaidō) ········ 駒ケ岳 ········ 4:264b
Komagatake (volcano, Honshū) ········· 駒ケ岳 ··· 4:264b-265a
Komainu ·········· 狛犬 ········ 4:265a
Komaki ············ 小牧 ········ 4:265a
Komaki Dam ····· 小牧ダム ········ 2:72b
Komaki Nagakute Campaign
 ······· 小牧・長久手の戦 ········ 4:265b
 Toyotomi Hideyoshi ··············· 8:95a
Komatsu ··········· 小松 ········ 4:265b
Komatsubara Eitarō
 ·········· 小松原英太郎 ········ 4:265b
Komatsu, Ltd ··············· 4:265b-266a
Komatsu Minoru ··· 小松実 ········ 4:266a
Komatsu Ryūnosuke
 ············ 小松竜之介 ········ 2:170b
Komatsu Sakyō ·· 小松左京 ········ 4:266a
 science fiction ·················· 7:38b
Komatsu Seisakusho ·············· 4:265b
Komatsushima ····· 小松島 ········ 4:266a
Komatsu Tatewaki
 ··············· 小松帯刀 ········ 4:266a
Koma-yaki ········· 高麗焼 ········ 7:226b
Komayubachi *(braconids)* ·········· 1:149a
Kombu (seaweed) ·················· 7:47a
Kome ························ 6:308b-310a
Kōmei bijin rokkasen ·············· 8:*142b*
Kōmei, Emperor · 孝明天皇 ··· 4:266a-266b
Kōmei Political Federation ·········· 4:266b
Kōmeitō (Clean Government Party)
 ················ 公明党 ·· 4:266b-267a; 6:205b, 212b, 213a
 future outlook ·············· 4:266b-267a
 Ikeda Daisaku ···················· 3:265a
 national defense ············ 5:336b-338b
 organization ····················· 4:266b
 policies ·························· 4:266b
 postwar status ···················· 3:205a
 Takeiri Yoshikatsu ··············· 7:324a
Kome kitte ········· 米切手 ········ 4:267a
Kome sōdō. 米騒動 *See* **Rice riots of 1918**
Kome Yokose Mēdē. 米よこせメーデー *See* **Shokuryō Mēdē**
Kōmin ················ 公民 ········ 6:352b
 koshiro and nashiro relabeled ····· 4:296a
Kōminkan ························· 1:341a
Komiya Toyotaka 小宮豊隆 1:155b; 4:267a
Kommintō ·········· 困民党 ········ 4:267a
Komon ·························· 4:267a
Komonjo. 古文書 *See* **Diplomatics**
Komonjo gaku ··· 古文書学 ···· 2:97a-100b
Komononari ········ 小物成 ·· 4:267a-267b; 5:360b
Kōmori ··························· 1:146b
Kōmorigasa ("bat umbrellas") ····· 1:146b
Komoro ············· 小諸 ········ 4:267b
Komparu Nobutaka
 ··············· 金春信高 ········ 4:267b
Komparuryū ········ 金春流 ········ 4:267b
Komparu school ··· 金春流 · 4:267b; 6:24a
Komparu Ujinobu 金春氏信 ········ 4:267b
Komparu Zempō · 金春禅鳳 ········ 4:267b
Komparu Zenchiku
 ··············· 金春禅竹 · 4:267b; 5:15b
Kompira. 金毘羅 *See* **Kotohira Shrine**
Kompon Chūdō ·· 根本中堂 ········ 2:*220b*
Kompon Daitō ··· 根本大塔 ········ 4:269b
Komugi ··························· 8:251a
Kŏmundo Incident
 ············· 巨文島事件 ··· 4:267b-268a
Komura Jutarō 小村寿太郎 ··· 4:268a-268b
Komura-Vaeber Memorandum
 ···· 小村-ウェーバー覚書 · 4:268a, 281b; 5:196b-197a; 8:293b
 Russo-Japanese War ··············· 6:346a
Komusō. *See* **Shakuhachi**
Komusubi ························· 7:272a
Kōmyō, Empress 光明皇后 ········ 4:268b
 calligraphic collections ··········· 1:234a
 Fujiwara no Nakamaro ············ 2:353b
 Hiden'in ························· 3:130b
Kōmyōshi ··········· 光明子 ········ 4:268b
Kōnan ·············· 江南 ········ 4:268b
Kondei ·············· 健児 ········ 4:268b
Konden ······················ 7:109b-110a
Konden Einen Shizai Hō. 墾田永年私財法 *See* **Konden Eisei Shizai Hō**
Konden Eisei Shizai Hō
 ········· 墾田永世私財法 ·· 4:268b-269a; 7:19b
Kondō (main hall) ··· 1:182b; 3:*232b*; 8:*83a, 285a, 376b*
Kondō butsu ···················· 4:269a
Kondō Heisaburō
 ············· 近藤平三郎 ········ 4:269a
Kondō Isami ······· 近藤勇 ········ 4:269a
 Shinsengumi ······················ 7:124a
Kondō Jūzō ····· 近藤重蔵 ········ 1:154a; 4:269a-269b
Kondō Keitarō · 近藤啓太郎 ········ 4:269b
Kondō Kenzō ···· 近藤賢三 ········ 4:69a
Kondō Morishige. *See* **Kondō Jūzō**
Kondō Yoshirō ··· 近藤義郎 ········ 1:79a
Kondō Yūzō ····· 近藤悠三 ········ 1:261a
Kongōbuji ······ 金剛峰寺 ········ 4:269b
 Takuma Tametō ··················· 7:328a
Kongōchō-gyō ··· 金剛頂経 ········ 4:270a
Kongōfukuji, temple of
 ················ 金剛福寺 ········ 1:102b
Kongō Iwao ········ 金剛巌 ········ 6:*26b*
Kongōkai ········· 金剛界 ··· 4:269b-270a
 Dainichi ························· 2:64b
 Shingon sect ····················· 7:115a
Kongōkai mandara
 ··········· 金剛界曼荼羅 4:270a; 6:347b, *348b*, 349a-351a

Kongōsan 金剛山 4:270a
Kongō school 金剛流 4:270a
Kongōsen 金剛山 4:270a
Kon Hidemi 今日出海 4:270a
Konica 4:270b
Kō Nihon bunten (Comprehensive Grammar of Japanese) 広日本文典 6:134b
Konishi Jin'ichi 小西甚一 6:297a
Konishi Raizan 小西来山 4:270a
Konishiroku Photo Industry Co, Ltd 4:270b
Konishiroku Shashin Kōgyō 4:270b
Konishi Yukinaga 小西行長 1:83b; 4:270b; 7:56b, 83b, 98b-99a
  Christian daimyō 1:306a
  invasions of Korea in 1592 and 1597 3:327a
  Luis Frois 2:340a
Konjaku monogatari 今昔物語 1:180b; 2:296a; 4:132b, 270b-271a; 5:44a; 7:61b, 72a
  Chinese literature 1:294a
  folktales 2:304a
  fox legends 2:330a
  Fujiwara no Kintō 2:352a
  obasute 6:48a
  Obasuteyama 6:48b
  Warashibe chōja ("The Straw Millionaire") 8:223b
Konjiki yasha (The Golden Demon) 金色夜叉 4:199a; 6:221a; 7:107b
Konjin 金神 4:271b
Konketsuji 4:271a-271b
Konkō Daijin 金光大神 4:271b
Konkō Daijin Oboe 金光大神覚え 4:272a
Konkō Daijin Rikai 金光大神理解 4:272a
Konkōkyō 金光教 2:300b; 4:271b-272a; 7:48a
Konkōmyō Shitennō gokoku no tera 金光明四天王護国寺 4:257a
Konnyaku 7:105b
Kōno Bairei 幸野楳嶺 4:272a
Konoe Atsumaro 近衛篤麿 4:272a-272b
Konoe family 近衛家 4:272b; 7:29b
  Gosekke 3:48a
Konoe Fumimaro 近衛文麿 2:3b; 4:272b-273b; 7:258b
  Gotō Ryūnosuke 3:53b
  Imperial Rule Assistance Association 3:280a
  New Order Movement 5:365b
  Sasaki Sōichi 7:23a
Konoe Fumimaro cabinet
  Araki Sadao 1:74a
  Arima Yoriyasu 1:84a
  Arita Hachirō 1:85a
  Nagai Ryūtarō 5:301a
  Yonai Mitsumasa 8:337a
Konoe Hidemaro 近衛秀麿 5:286b
Konoe Iehiro 近衛家熙 4:273b
Konoe Nobutada 近衛信尹 4:273b
Konohanasakuya Hime 木花開耶姫 5:294b
Kōno Hironaka 河野広中 4:273b-274a
  Freedom and People's Rights Movement 2:335a
  Fukushima Incident 2:366a
  Futsū Senkyo Kisei Dōmeikai 2:376b
  League for Establishing a National Assembly 4:372b
Kōno Hisashi 河野寿 2:250a
Kōno Ichirō 河野一郎 4:274a
Kōnoike family 鴻池家 4:274a-274b
Kōnoike shinden 鴻池新田 4:274b
Kōnoike Zen'emon. *See* **Kōnoike family**
Kōno Kenzō 河野謙三 4:274b
Kōno Michiari 河野通有 4:274b
Kō no Moronao 高師直 4:274b-275a
  Kannō Disturbance 4:144b
Kōnosu 鴻巣 4:275a
Kōno Togama 河野敏鎌 4:275a
Kōno Yōhei 河野洋平 4:275a
Konrad, Nikolai Iosifovich 4:275b
Konsei 金精 4:275b
Konsei Pass 金精峠 4:275b
Konsei sama 金精さま 4:275b
Konsen Highlands 根釧台地 4:275b
Kon Tōkō 今東光 4:275b
"Ko o kashiya" 子を貸し屋 8:173b
Kōrai 高麗 4:294a
Kōraimon (castle gate) 高麗門 1:248b
Kōrakuen 後楽園 4:198a, 276a, *276b*
Kōrakuen Garden (Tōkyō) 後楽園(東京) 4:276a
Korea
  annexation 4:287a-287b
  cultural sphere 2:142a
  historical works
    Samguk sagi (History of the Three Kingdoms) 7:6a
    Samguk yusa (Memorabilia of the Three Kingdoms) 7:6a
  language
    han'gŭl 3:96b
  religion 6:290a-293b
  Samil Independence Movement 7:6a-6b
  wakō 8:220b
  See also **Korea and Japan**
Korea, annexation of 4:287a-287b
  historical context 4:282a
  Korean-Japanese Convention of 1905 4:289b
Korea and Japan 4:276a-287a
  Democratic People's Republic of Korea (1953-) 4:286a-287a
  early modern relations
    Chemulp'o, Treaty of 1:268b
    Japanese control and annexation 4:281b-282a
    Kanghwa, Treaty of 4:140b-141a
    Kŏmundo Incident 4:268a
    Korea, annexation of 4:287a-287b
    Korean-Japanese Convention of 1905 4:289b
    opening of Korea 4:279b-280a
    reaction to Japanese control 4:282a-282b
    Russian influence 4:281b
    Sino-Japanese War of 1894-1895 4:281a-281b; 7:197b-198b
    Treaty of Shimonoseki 7:106a
  early postwar (1945-1952) 4:284a-284b
  independence 7:106a
  invasions of Korea in 1592 and 1597 3:326b-327b
  Japanese Colonial Control of Korea (1910-1945)
    Korea, annexation of 4:287b
  Japanese colonial control (1910-1945) 4:283a-284a
    administration 4:283a
    establishment 4:283a-283b
    Japanese militarization 4:284a
    reforms 4:283b-284a
  Koreans in Japan 4:292a
  patriotic groups of 7:196a
  premodern relations (to 1875) 4:276a-279b
    foreign influences and consolidation of Yamato State 4:277a-277b
    Jingū, Empress 4:59a
    Kaya 4:185a
    Koryŏ Period (935-1391) 4:278a-278b
    prehistoric and protohistoric 4:276b-277a
    Silla 4:277b-278a; 7:196a
    wakū 8:220b
    Yi Dynasty to 1875 4:278b-279a; 8:324b-325a
  Republic of Korea (1953-) 3:324a; 4:284b-286a
    deterioration in 1950s 4:284b-285a
    normalization 4:285a-285b
    postnormalization 4:285b-286a
    tensions 4:286a
  Silla kingdom 7:196a
  Sino-Japanese War of 1894-1895 7:197b
  YMCA 7:196a
Korea-Japan Treaty of 1965 4:287b-288a
  historical context 4:285b
  supplementary agreements 4:288a-288b
Korea-Japan Treaty of 1965, supplementary agreements 4:288a-288b
  historical context 4:285b
Korean Armistice 4:286b
Korean campaigns of 1592 and 1597. *See* **Invasions of Korea in 1592 and 1597**
Korean Central Intelligence Agency 4:286a
Korean Communist Party 4:283b
Korean Daily News 4:282b
Korean debate 2:334a
Korean Empire 7:293b
Korean "Independence Party." *See* **Kaehwap'a**
Korean-Japanese Convention of 1905 4:289a-289b; 26a
  historical context 4:282a
  Itō Hirobumi 3:353b
  Resident General 6:306a
  Russo-Japanese War 6:347a
  territory of Japan 8:14a
Korean language 4:289b-291a
  grammar 4:290b
  history 4:291a
  romanization 4:289b-290a
  sounds 4:290a-290b
  spelling 4:289b
  writing 4:289b
Korean National Art Museum 2:293b
Korean National Association 4:208b
Korean Patriotic League 8:357b
Korean People's Liberation Army 4:208b
Korean phonetic alphabet 7:163a
Korean Railway 6:346b
Koreans in Japan 4:291a-292a
  konketsuji 4:271b
  Korea-Japan Treaty of 1965, supplementary agreements 4:288a
  minorities 5:195a-195b
  resident foreigners 2:313a-313b
Korean Three Kingdoms period 4:292a; 7:6a
  Koguryo 4:249b
  Tachan Empire 7:293b
"Korean Tripitaka" 4:278b
Korean War 4:292a-292b
  Acheson statement 1:10a-10b
  foreign procurements (tokuju) 8:57b
  Japanese economy 2:158a
  Korean-Japanese relations 4:284a
  Occupation 6:54b
  Ōsu Incident 6:128a
  role in Self Defense Forces creation 7:58b
Korea Strait 朝鮮海峡 4:292b
Korematsu v US (323 US 214) 4:18a

Koretaka, Prince 惟喬親王 **4**:205a
Koretō Hyūga no Kami. 惟任日向守
  See **Akechi Mitsuhide**
Koreyuki 尹行 **1**:234b-235a
Kōrin 光琳 **1**:*166b, 262b;*
  2:346a; **4**:292b-293b; **6**:153a, *154a-154b;*
  7:43a
  Red and White Plum Trees (Kōhakubai zu) **4**:*293a-293b*
  Rimpa **6**:317b
Kōriyama 郡山 **2**:367a; **4**:293b
Kōriyama Basin 郡山盆地 **4**:293b
Kōrogi **2**:43b-44a
Kōrokan 鴻臚館 **4**:293b-294a
Kōrōkyō **4**:294a
Koryō **4**:294a; **7**:6a
  Japanese relations **4**:278a
  Mongol invasions of Korea and **5**:245a
Kōryūji 広隆寺 **4**:294a-294b, 334b
Kosai 湖西 **4**:294b
Kosaka Zentarō 小坂善太郎 **4**:285a
Kosaku sōgi. *See* **Tenant farmer disputes**
Kōsei shimpen 厚生新編 **4**:294b
Kōseishō. 厚生省 *See* **Ministry of Health and Welfare**
Koseki. *See* **Household registers**
Kose no Kanaoka 巨勢金岡 **4**:294b
  Kose school **4**:295a
Kose school 巨勢派 **4**:295a
  Kose no Kanaoka, founder **4**:294b
Kōsha **6**:263a-264a
Kōshaku **4**:241a
Kōshakushi **4**:241b
Koshi **4**:295a
Koshigaya 越谷 **4**:295b
Koshiki **2**:305a
Koshikijima Islands 甑島列島 **4**:295b
Koshimino **7**:249a
Kōshin 甲申 **4**:295b
Kōshin Jihen 甲申事変 **4**:156b-157a
Kōshin machi 庚申待 **4**:295b
Koshirae **4**:295b
Koshiro 子代 **1**:147b; **7**:296a
Koshiro and nashiro 子代, 名代 **4**:296a
Kōshitsu **3**:277b
Koshitsū (Survey of Ancient History) 古史通 **2**:102b; **8**:306a
Kōshitsu Tempan. 皇室典範 *See* **Imperial Household Law**
Koshō 小姓 **4**:296a, *304b, 322b*
Kōshōgaku school 考証学派 **3**:155b
Kōshoku 更埴 **4**:296a
Kōshokubon 好色本 **4**:296a; **8**:144a
Kōshoku ichidai otoko 好色一代男 **4**:136b; **8**:144a
Kōshoku-mono (armorous pieces) 好色物 **8**:144a
Kōshoku Tsuihō **6**:57b-58b
Koshoku zensho 古織全書 **4**:159b
Koshu 戸主 **4**:60b-61a
Kōshū Gakusei Jiken 光州学生事件 **4**:323b
Kōshū Kaidō 甲州街道 **3**:41a
Kōshūwan soshakuchi 膠州湾租借地 **4**:53a
Kōsō 高宗 **4**:252a-252b
Kosode 小袖 **8**:23b
  designs **2**:90b
Kōsō wasan 高僧和讃 **8**:231a
Kosugi Isamu 小杉勇 **2**:*269a, 270b*
Kosugi Tengai 小杉天外 **4**:296a-296b
  fūzoku shōsetsu **2**:378b
"Kosui to karera" 湖水と彼等 **8**:92b
Kōtai Ō hi 好太王碑 **4**:323a-323b
Kōtaishi Shōtoku hōsan 皇太子聖徳奉讃 **8**:231a
Kotani Kimi 小谷喜美 **4**:296b
Kotani Yasukichi 小谷安吉 **6**:289a
Kotatsu **1**:267a
Kōten Kōkyūjo 皇典講究所 **4**:259b
Koto **4**:296b-297a; **7**:75b, 87b, 225b-226a
  gagaku **3**:2a
Kotobagaki **4**:297a
Kotoba no tama no o 詞玉緒 **4**:31b
Kotoba no yachimata 詞八衢 **4**:31b
Koto hajime **4**:298a
Kotohira 琴平 **4**:297a
Kotohira Shrine 金刀比羅宮 **4**:103b, 297a
  main hall (honden) **4**:*297a*
Kōtō jogakkō **4**:297a-297b
Kōtoku, Emperor 孝徳天皇 **4**:297b
  Taika Reform **7**:296a
Kōtoku Incident 幸徳事件 **3**:135a
Kōtoku Shūsui 幸徳秋水 **4**:297b-298a; **7**:56a, 74a-74b; **8**:296b
  Fukuda Hideko **2**:362b
  Futsū Senkyo Kisei Dōmeikai **2**:376b
  Heiminsha **3**:125b
  High Treason Incident of 1910 **3**:135a
  Kamitsukasa Shōken **4**:127b
  Kanno Suga **4**:145b
  pacifism **6**:144a
Koto osame **4**:298a
Kōtō semmon gakkō. *See* **Technical colleges**
Kōtō Ward 江東区 **4**:298a
Kotowaza **6**:258b
Kotoyōka 事八日 **3**:208b; **4**:298a
Kotsu **4**:131a
Kōtsū Hakubutsukan **8**:104a
Kotsutsubo **2**:370a
Kottai-san 太夫さん
  shimpa **7**:108a
Kouta 小唄 **4**:298a-298b
Kouta (small song) **4**:328a
Kōwaka (ballad-drama) 幸若 **4**:298b; **5**:45a
Kōwaka-mai 幸若舞 **4**:298b
Kōwa Mondai Dōshi Rengōkai 講和問題同志連合会 **3**:129a-129b
  Tairo Dōshikai **7**:303a
Kōya 空也 **4**:322a-322b
Kōyagire 高野切 **4**:*133a*
Koyairi **4**:195a
Koyama Shōtarō 小山正太郎 **8**:341a
Koyama Yūshi 小山祐士 **4**:298b-299a
Kōyasan (monastic complex) 高野山 **4**:299a-299b, 304a; **6**:248a
Kōyasan (mountain) 高野山 **4**:299a
Kōyasan Treasure House **4**:299b
Kōyō gunkan 甲陽軍鑑 **4**:299b
Koyori **4**:299b
Kōyō Seikō Co, Ltd **4**:299b
Kōyō sekiyō sonsha shi 黄葉夕陽村舎詩 **4**:152a
Kōyōsha **8**:88a
Kōyō wakaskū 黄葉和歌集 **4**:158a
Kō Yūi 康有為 **4**:141a-141b
Kōyū Kurabu 公友倶楽部 **4**:198a
Kōzaha 講座派 **4**:299b-300a; **7**:3a; **8**:289a
  Rōnōha **6**:337b
Kozai Shikin 古在紫琴 **4**:300a
Kozaki Hiromichi 小崎弘道 **4**:300a
Kōzanji 高山寺 **4**:300a-300b
Kōzen gokoku ron 興禅護国論 **2**:187a; **4**:300b
Kōzo **4**:167b
Kozuka **4**:295b
Kōzuke monuments 上野三碑 **4**:300b
Kōzuki 上月 **8**:301a
Kū. 空 *See* **Emptiness**
Kuan-yin **4**:144b-145a
Kuan Yü. *See* **Kan U**
Kubō 公方 **4**:121a, 300b
Kubo Kakutarō 久保角太郎 **6**:289a
Kubokawa Tsurujirō 窪川鶴次郎 **4**:300b; **7**:25a
Kubo Ryōgo 久保亮五 **4**:300b-301a
Kubo Sakae 久保栄 **4**:301a
  shingeki **7**:113a
Kubo Shumman 窪俊満 **4**:301a
Kubota, Ltd **4**:301a
Kubota Mantarō 久保田万太郎 **4**:301a-301b
  shin kabuki **4**:92a
Kubota Michiharu 久保田通治 **4**:301b
Kubota Utsubo 窪田空穂 **4**:301b
Kubunden 口分田 **4**:301b
Kubushiro Ochimi 久布白落実 **4**:301b
  fusen Kakutoku Dōmei **2**:374b
Kuchiei and kuchimai 口永, 口米 **4**:301b; **5**:360b
Kuchigin 口銀 **4**:301b
Kuchimane muko 口真似聟 **4**:327b
Kuchinashi (gardenia) **3**:8a
Kuchizeni 口銭 **4**:301b
Kūchō **6**:357b
Kudamatsu 下松 **4**:302a
Kudara 百済 **6**:146a-146b
Kudara Daiji 百済大寺 **2**:55a
Kudaradera remains 百済寺址 **4**:302a
Kudashibumi 下文 **4**:302a
  chōsen **1**:303b
  gejijō **3**:15b
Kuden. 公田 *See* **Kōden**
Kudo **4**:120b
Kudō Heisuke 工藤平助 **1**:39a; **4**:302a
Kudō Suketsune 工藤祐経 **3**:356a
Kudzu vine **4**:323a
Kueiden (publicly managed fields) 公営田 **2**:104b
Kuga Katsunan 陸羯南 **4**:302a-302b
Kugatachi 盟神探湯 **4**:302b
Kuge (Court nobles) 公家 **4**:191a
Kuge (age of aristocratic houses) **6**:176b
Kuge bunko (private libraries) **8**:174a
Kūge nichiyō kufū ryakushū. 空華日用工夫略集 *See* **Kūge nikkushū**
Kūge nikkushū 空華日工集 **4**:302b
Kugo **7**:195a
Kugutsume 傀儡女 **8**:259a
Kugyō 公卿 **1**:96b; **2**:40a; **4**:302b
Kuhara Fusanosuke 久原房之助 **4**:302b-303a; **7**:276b
Kuiawase **4**:303a
Kuina **6**:277b
Kuji 旧辞 **4**:340b
Kuji (city) 久慈 **4**:303a
Kuji ("public matters") 公事 **4**:303a
Kujigawa 久慈川 **4**:303a
Kujikata Osadamegaki 公事方御定書 **4**:303a-303b
  Ofuregaki Shūsei **6**:68a

shioki ························· 7:140b
Kujikata Osadamegaki
code ······公事方御定書 ···8:53a, 113b
Kuji kongen ····公事根源 ········4:303b
Kujira ····················· 8:249a-249b
Kujō family ········九条家 ·4:303b; 7:58a
Fujiwara no Nobuzane ············ 2:353b
Kujō Kanezane ··九条兼実 ········4:303b
Fukuharakyō ···················· 2:363a
Gyokuyō ························ 3:71b
Jien ······························ 4:53b
Kujō family descended from ······ 4:303b
literature ························· 5:40a
Kujū Kōgen ······久住高原 ········4:303b
Kujūkurihama 九十九里浜 ·1:92a; 4:303b
Kujūsan ··········久住山 ········4:303b
Kukadachi ······盟神探湯 ········4:302b
Kūkai ················空海 1:178b; 4:183a, 304a; 5:30a, 295a
Buddhist sculpture ··········· 1:198a-198b
charcoal making ·················· 1:267a
Chinese poetry ··················· 1:293b
collection in Kōyasan Treasure House ························· 4:299b
education ························ 2:172b
esoteric ritual implements ········ 1:196a
Fushimi Inari Shrine ·············· 2:375a
iroha poem ························ 3:332a
Jingoji ···························· 4:58b
Kakuban ··························· 4:118a
Kammu, Emperor ··················· 4:128a
Kongōbuji ························ 4:269b
Kōshō ····························· 4:*304b*
monasticism ················· 5:237b-238a
Shingon sect ······················ 7:113b
Shinshōji ························· 7:125a
Shintō ···························· 7:127a
Kukatachi ······盟神探湯 ········4:302b
Kuki ················久喜 ········4:304a
Kuki Ryūichi ····九鬼隆一 ········4:255b
Kuki Shūzō ······九鬼周造 ········4:304b
Kuma (bears) ······················ 1:148b
Kumade ···························· 8:*80b*
Kumadori ··········隈取 ········4:95b
Kumagai Gumi Co, Ltd ············ 4:304b
Kumagai Hisatora熊谷久虎 ········2:270b
Kumagai Naoyoshi
···············熊谷直好 ········4:304b
Kumagai Naozane
···············熊谷直実 ········4:305a
Kumagaisō *(Cypripedium japonicum)* ························· 4:305a
Kumagai Taizō ··熊谷岱蔵 ········4:305a
Kumagawa ········球磨川 ···4:305a-305b
Kumagaya ·············熊谷 ········4:305b
Kumai Kei ·········熊井啓 ········4:305b
Kumamoto ···········熊本 ········4:305b
"Kumamoto Band" ········4:306b; 6:258a
Kumamoto Plain 熊本平野 ········4:305b
Kumamoto Prefectural Art Museum ························· 4:305b
Kumamoto Prefecture
···············熊本県 ········4:306a
Kumamoto Yōgakkō
···········熊本洋学校 ···4:306a-306b
Janes, Leroy Lansing ··············· 4:2a
Kumano ·············熊野 ········4:306b
Kumanogawa ······熊野川 ········4:306b
Kumano Sanzan Shrines
···············熊野三社 ··4:306b-307a; 5:300a
Shingū ···························· 7:115a
Kumano Sea ······熊野灘 ········4:307a
Kumano Shingū 熊野新宮··········6:124b
Kumano shrines 熊野神社 ··········7:160a
Kumārajīva ························· 4:71a
Kumashiro Hi ·····熊代斐 ········4:307a
Kumashiro Tatsumi
···············神代辰巳 2:275b; 4:307a
Kumashiro Yūhi ·熊代熊斐 4:307a; 5:306a; 7:83b
Kumaso ·············熊襲 ········4:307a
Kagoshima Prefecture ·············· 4:105b
suppression ······················· 4:189a
Yamatotakeru, Prince ·············· 8:311a
Kumaya Art Museum ················· 3:77a
Kumazasa *(Sasa albo-marginata)* ·1:136a
Kumazawa Banzan
···············熊沢蕃山 ··4:307a-307b; 5:16b; 8:335b
Kumejima ··········久米島 ········4:307b
Kume Kunitake ··久米邦武 3:359b; 4:307b; 7:92b
historiography ···················· 3:156a
Kume Masao ····久米正雄 ···4:307b-308a
fūzoku shōsetsu ··················· 2:378b
Shinshichō ······················· 7:125a
Kume no Sennin ·久米仙人 ···5:295b-296a
Kumi ·····················組 ········4:308a
Kumiai batsu (labor-union clique) ··········組合閥 ········6:205b
Kumiai Chemical Industry Co, Ltd 4:308a
Kumigashira ·········組頭 ··4:55a; 5:270a
Kumihimo ························ 4:308a
Kumo ······························ 7:242b
shingeki ·························· 7:113b
Kumoi Tatsuo ··雲井龍雄 ···4:308a-308b
Kumon ···············公文 ········4:308b
Kumonjo ··········公文所 ··4:308b; 7:8b
Taira-Minamoto War ················ 7:300b
Kumo no hate ·····雲の涯 ········7:335b
Kumonosujō ····蜘蛛巣城 ········7:108b
Kumootoko ·······蜘蛛男 ········2:170b
Kumosuke ···········雲助 4:308b; 7:265b
Kunaichō. 宮内庁
See **Imperial Household Agency**
Kunaichō Shoryōbu. *See* **Archives and Mausolea Department, Imperial Household Agency**
Kunaichō Zushoryō
···········宮内庁図書寮 ········1:82b
Kunashiri ···········国後 ··4:308b-309a
Kundoku kambun ···················· 4:124a
Kung-an ··························· 4:234a
Kuni ························ 6:258b-260a
Kuni ikki ··········国一揆 3:268b; 4:309a
kokujin leadership ················ 4:260a
Kunikida Doppo
···············国木田独歩 ···4:309a-309b
naturalism ························ 5:351a
Kunimidake ·······国見岳 ········4:309b
Kuninaka no Muraji Kimimaro ·国中連公麻呂 1:199b; 4:309b
Kuni no mikotomochi 国司 ········4:310a
Kuni no Miya ······恭仁京 ···4:309b-310a
Kuni no miyatsuko ··国造 ···1:21a, 147b; 4:310a
uji-kabane system ················· 8:134a
Kunisada. 国貞 *See* **Utagawa Kunisada**
Kunisada Chūji 国定忠治
Shimozawa Kan ····················· 7:107b
Shinkokugeki ······················ 7:121a
Kunisaki Peninsula
···············国東半島 ········4:310a
Kunishū (provincials) 国衆 ········4:260a
Kunitachi ···········国立 ········4:310a
Kunitsukami ·······国津神 ········4:125b
Kunitsu tsumi ······国津罪 ········3:101a
Kuniyaku ·············国役 ········4:310a
Kuniyakukin ·······国役金 ········4:310a
Kuniyoshi. 国芳 *See* **Utagawa Kuniyoshi**
Kuniyoshi, Yasuo国吉康雄 ········4:310b
Kunji ······························ 4:143b
Kunōji kyō ······久能寺経 ········8:183a
Ku no sekai (World of Woe) ········苦の世界 ········8:173b
Kuno Yasu ········久野寧 ········4:310b
Kuno Yasushi ······久野寧 ········4:310b
Kunōzan ···········久能山 ········4:310b
Kunōzan-Tōshōgū
···········久能山東照宮 ········7:153b
Kun readings ············ 4:310b; 5:324b
ideographs ················· 4:143a-143b
Shinsen jikyō ····················· 7:124b
Kunshō ····························· 2:81b
Kunugi ····························· 4:22b
Kunuhi ··········公奴婢 ········7:62a
Kuo Mo-jo. *See* **Guo Moruo (Kuo Mo-jo)**
Kuonji. 久遠寺 *See* **Minobusan**
Kuo Sung-ling. *See* **Guo Songling (Kuo Sung-ling)**
Kura ··························4:106b; 7:248b
Kurabō Industries, Ltd ············ 4:311a
Kurage ······················ 2:305b; 4:50b
Kurahara Korehito
···············蔵原惟人 ·4:311a; 7:66b, 122a
proletarian literature movement
························· 6:255-255b
Kurahashijima ····倉橋島 ········4:311a
Kurahashi Juhei ·倉橋寿平 ········4:201b
Kurahashi Kaku ···倉橋格 ········4:250a
Kurahashi Yumiko
···········倉橋由美子 ········1:209a; 4:311a-311b
Shinchō ·························· 7:109a
Kurai ·····················位 ········7:248b
Kurai e (Dark Pictures)
···············暗い絵 ········6:230b
Kurakata no Okite
···············倉方の掟 ········4:59a
Kuramai ·············蔵米 ········4:311b
kokudainō and ····················· 4:257a
Kuramayama ······鞍馬山 ········4:311b
Kuramoto ···············蔵元 ········4:312a
"Kura no naka" ····蔵の中 ········8:173b
Kuraray Co, Ltd ················· 4:311b
Kurashiki ·············倉敷 ········4:311b
Kurashiki Folkcraft Museum ······ 4:*311a*
Kurata Chikara ··倉田主税 ···4:311b-312a
Kurata Hyakuzō 倉田百三 ··4:312a; 7:81a
Kuratsukuribe ·······鞍作部 ········1:147b
Kuratsukuri no Tori
···············鞍作鳥 ·1:*197a*; 2:55b; 4:312a; 7:85a
sanzonzō ·························· 7:20a
Kurayashiki ·······蔵屋敷 ········4:312a
kome kitte ························ 4:267a
Kurayoshi ···········倉吉 ········4:312a
Kurayoshi Plain 倉吉平野 ···4:312a-312b
Kure ····················呉 ········4:312b
Kureha Chemical Industry Co, Ltd 4:312b
Kure Ken ·············呉健 ········4:312b
Kuri ······························ 1:270a
Kurihama ···········久里浜 ········4:312b
Kurihara, Thomas
···········栗原トーマス ········2:268a
Kurikaradani, Battle of
·········倶利伽羅谷の戦 ········4:312b
Kurikara Pass ·倶利伽羅峠 ···4:312b-313a
Kurikomayama ·····栗駒山 ········4:313a
Kuril Current. 千島海流 *See* **Oyashio**
Kuril Islands ·····千島列島 ········4:313a
Russia and Japan ············ 6:340b, 344a
Kurimoto Hōan ··栗本鋤庵 ········4:313a
Kurimoto Iron Works, Ltd ········· 4:313a
Kurimoto Joun ··栗本鋤雲 ···4:313a-313b
French-Japanese relations ·········· 2:331b
Kurimoto Kon ······栗本鯤 ········4:313a
Kurishima Sumiko
···············栗島すみ子 ········4:313b

Kuriyagawa Hakuson 厨川白村 4:313b
Kuriyama Sempō 栗山潜鋒 4:313b
Kurobe 黒部 4:313b
Kurobe Dam 2:73a; 4:151b; *313a*, 313b
Kurobegawa 黒部川 4:314a
Kurobe Kyōkoku 黒部峡谷 4:314a
Kurobon 黒本 4:201b
Kurochiku *(Phyllostachys nigra)* 1:136a
Kuroda family 黒田氏 7:320a
Kuroda Hisao 黒田寿男 4:314a
Kuroda Josui 黒田如水 4:315a
Kuroda Kiyotaka 黒田清隆 3:213a-213b; 4:314a-314b
 Kaitakushi 4:113a
 Kanghwa, Treaty of 4:140b
 Sakhalin 7:1b
Kuroda Kiyoteru. *See* **Kuroda Seiki**
Kuroda Nagamasa 黒田長政 4:314b; 7:56b, 99a
 Fukuoka 4:127b
Kurodani shōnin gotō roku 黒谷上人語燈録 6:248a
Kuroda Seiki 黒田清輝 4:314b-315a; 6:*156b*; 8:328a
 Maiko 4:*315a*
 modern painting 6:155b
Kuroda Yoshitaka 黒田孝高 4:315a-315b
Kurōdo-dokoro 蔵人所 2:350b; 4:315b; 7:65b
 rinji 6:318a
 takiguchi no bushi 7:326b
Kurofune 黒船 4:315b
 technology transfer 7:374a
Kurohimeyama 黒姫山 4:315b
Kurohon 黒本 4:319b
Kuroi ame 黒い雨 3:255a
Kuroi kiri 黒い霧 4:315b-316a
Kuroi Senji 黒井千次 4:316a
Kuroishi 黒石 4:316a
Kuroiso 黒磯 4:316a
Kuroita Katsumi 黒板勝美 1:154a; 4:316a
 historiography 3:156b
 Shintei zōho kokushi taikei editor 4:262b
Kuroiwa Jūgo 黒岩重吾 4:316b
Kuroiwa Ruikō 黒岩涙香 4:316b; 8:339a
 Futsū Senkyo Kisei Dōmeikai 2:376b
Kuroiwa Shūroku 黒岩周六 4:316b
Kurokamiyama. 黒髪山 *See* **Nantaisan**
Kurokawa Kishō 黒川紀章 4:316b
Kurokawa Toshio 黒川利雄 4:316b
Kurokawa v *Chiba Prefectural Election Administration Commission* 4:80a
Kuromaru odori (dance) 黒丸踊 2:*299a*
Kuromoji [(Japanese spicebush) *Lindera umbellatum; Benzoin umbellatum*] 4:316b
Kuro no shisōsha 黒の試走車 4:115a
Kuropatkin, Aleksei Nikolaevich 4:317a
Kurosawa Akira 黒沢明 2:56b, 272a, 273a, 274a; 4:*317a*, 317b-318a
 Hashimoto Shinobu 3:110b
 Ikiru 3:268b
 Rashōmon 6:283b
 Seven Samurai 7:73a
 Shimura Takashi 7:108b
Kuroshima Denji 黒島伝治 4:318a-318b
Kuroshio 黒潮 2:284a; 4:318b
Kuroshio current 8:118a
Kuroshoin 黒書院 7:*162b*
Kurotokage 黒蜥蜴 3:151a; 4:199a
Kurozumikyō 黒住教 4:318b; 7:48a
Kuruidako 狂ひ凧 8:147b
Kurume 久留米 1:276b; 2:365b; 4:318b
Kurume Civic Center 4:207b
Kurume-gasuri 久留米絣 1:276b
Kurusu Saburō 来栖三郎 4:318b
Kurutta ippeiji (A Page Out of Place) 狂った一頁 2:*268b*; 4:176a
Kuruwa kotoba 2:92b
Kuruwa zōdan (Tales of the Pleasure District) 廓雑談 3:95a
Kusaboke 6:274b
Kusaka Genzui 久坂玄瑞 3:90a; 4:319a
Kusakezuri kuwa 4:322a
Kusama Isuke 草間伊助 4:319a
Kusamakura 草枕 5:350a
Kusama Naokata 草間直方 4:319a
Kusanagi 草薙 5:293b
Kusanagi no Tsurugi ("grass-cutting" sword) 草薙剣 1:115b-116a
Kusano Shimpei 草野心平 4:319a
Kusarigama 4:319a
Kusarigamajutsu 4:319a
Kusatsu (city) 草津 4:319a-319b
Kusatsu (town) 草津 4:319b
Kusatsu Shirane. *See* **Shiranesan**
Kusawakaba 草わかば 4:123a
Kusazōshi 草双紙 1:163b; 4:201b, 319b-320a; 5:49a; 7:103a
 akahon 4:319b
 Bakin 1:130b
 Izumi Kyōka 3:365b
 kibyōshi 4:201b-202a, 319b
 kurohon 4:319b
Kusemai 曲舞 4:135b
Kusharon 倶舎論 1:178b; 4:320a; 5:332b
Kusha school 倶舎派 1:178b; 4:320a
Kushida Tamizō 櫛田民蔵 4:320a
Kushida Tamizō zenshū 櫛田民蔵全集 4:320a
Kushikino 串木野 4:320a
Kushima 串間 4:320a
Kushimoto 串本 4:320a-320b
Kushiro 釧路 4:320b
Kushirogawa 釧路川 4:320b
Kussharo, Lake 屈斜路湖 4:321b
Kusu (camphor tree) 1:237a
Kusuko Incident 薬子の変 4:320b
 Fujiwara no Fuyutsugu 2:350b
 Kurōdo-dokoro 4:315a
Kusumi Morikage 久隅守景 4:320b-321a
Kusunoki. *See* **Camphor tree**
Kusunoki Masashige 楠木正成 4:321a
 Chihaya Castle 4:270a
Kusunoki Masatsura 楠木正行 4:275a
Kusunokiryū hanami no makubari 樟紀流花見幕張 4:187a
Kutaiji 九体寺 4:77b
Kutani ware 九谷焼 4:136a, 321b, 337a
 Kaga 4:102b
 Komatsu 4:265b
 medieval 1:263b
 museums 5:279b
 plate 1:*261a*
Kutcharo, Lake 屈斜路湖 4:321b
Kutōten. *See* **Punctuation marks**
Kutsukake Tokijirō 沓掛時次郎 3:107b
Kutsuki Masatsuna 朽木昌綱 4:321b
Kuttara, Lake 倶多楽湖 4:321b; 7:98a
Kuwa 4:322a; 7:265b
Kuwabara Takeo 桑原武夫 4:322a
 haiku 3:80b
Kuwada Yoshinari 桑田義備 4:322a
Kuwaki Gen'yoku 桑木厳翼 4:322a
 modern philosophy 5:230b
Kuwana 桑名 4:322a
Kuwayama kofun shikō 桑山古墳私考 1:76b
Kuwayoboro 钁丁 8:327a
Kūya 空也 4:322a-322b; 6:335a
 Kōshō 4:*322b*
 nembutsu 4:67a
Kuze Hirochika 久世広周 1:55a; 4:322b-323a
Kuzu [(kudzu vine) *Pueraria thunbergiana*] 4:323a
Kuzu no matsubara 葛の松原 4:102b
Kuzuryūgawa 九頭竜川 2:364a; 4:323a
Kwanggaet'o monument 4:*323a*, 323a-323b; 8:220a
 Japanese battles in Korea 4:277a
Kwangju Student Resistance Movement 7:6b
 historical context 4:284a, 323b
Kwantung Army. *See* **Guandong (Kwantung) Army**
Kwantung Territory. *See* **Guandong (Kwantung) Territory**
Kyahan 4:323b
Kyaku and shiki. 格, 式 *See* **Engi Shiki**
Kyakushiki compilations 格式編纂 4:376a
Kyan taiheiki mukō hachimaki 侠太平記向鉢巻 7:97a
Kyaramakura (Aloewood Pillow) 伽羅枕 4:199a
Kyobuntō jiken 巨文島事件 4:267b-268a
Kyōbushō 教部省 4:323b
 Taikyō Sempu 7:297b
Kyōdai Jiken. 京大事件 *See* **Kyōto University Incident**
Kyōdō Bokin 1:341a-341b
Kyōdo geinō 2:296b
Kyōdō Insatsu sōgi. 共同印刷争議 *See* **Kyōdō Printing Company strike**
Kyōdo kenkyū 郷土研究 4:323b-324a
Kyōdō News Service 4:324a; 5:369a
 international communications 3:318b
Kyōdō Oil Co, Ltd 4:324a
Kyōdō Printing Company strike 4:324a
Kyōdō Shimbun Kisha Kurabu (Associated Newspapers Journalist Club) 6:236a
Kyōdo shinsho 郷土新書 6:288a
Kyōdō Shiryō Co, Ltd 4:324a
Kyōdō Tsūshinsha 4:324a
Kyōdō Un'yu Kaisha 7:109a
Kyōfūkai 矯風会 4:324b; 7:23b, 54a; 8:257b
 Kanno Suga 4:145a
 prostitution 6:257a
 Yajima Kajiko 8:284b
Kyōga 4:201a
Kyōgaku Taishi 教学大旨 2:175b-176a
Kyōganoko musume Dōjōji 京鹿子娘道成寺 4:*93a*
Kyōgen 狂言 2:74b-75a; 4:324b-329a, 336b; 5:15b; 7:80b; 8:21b-22a
 Bōshibari 4:*326b*
 classification and content 4:326b-328a
  daimyō (feudal lord) 4:327a
  first-group plays 4:327a
  Mai (dance) 4:327b

Muko (bridegroom, son-in-law) ············ 4:327a-327b
Oni (Devil) ············ 4:327b
Shukke (Buddhist priest) ············ 4:327b
Tarō Kaja or Shōmyō ············ 4:327a
Yamabushi (mountain ascetic) ············ 4:327b
Zatō (blind men) ············ 4:327b
costume ············ 4:328b; 8:23b
Fuku no kami ············ *4:325a*
Fuse nai kyō ············ *4:328b*
general characteristics ············ 4:388b-329a
history ············ 4:324b-325b
Iizawa Tadasu ············ 3:264a
independent plays ············ 4:326b
Izumi Motohide ············ *4:327a*
Jippensha Ikku ············ 4:61b
kabuki ············ 4:90b-91a
kabuki adaptations ············ 4:92a
masks ············ 4:328b
Nakajima Noboru ············ *4:325a*
name and variants ············ 4:324b
Nomura Mansaku ············ *4:326b*
Nomura Matasaburō ············ *4:327a*
Nō plays ············ 4:326a-326b
sarugaku and ············ 7:22a
schools
Izumi ············ 3:366a
Ōkura ············ 6:98a
schools and players ············ 4:325b-326a
Setsubun ············ *4:327a*
Shigeyama Sengorō ············ *4:328b*
Shigeyama Sensaku ············ *4:329a*
song, music and dance ············ 4:328a
stage properties ············ 4:328a-328b
Takai Noriyasu ············ *4:325a*
Tsukimi zatō ············ *4:329a*
Yamamoto Tōjirō ············ *4:325a*
Kyōgen ki ······ 狂言記 ······ 4:328a
Kyōgen mask ············ 5:*127b*
Kyōgen nō ······ 狂言能 ······ 4:324b
Kyōgen plays, masks for ······ 5:127a-127b
Kyōgoku ······ 京極 ······ 2:186a
Kyōgoku family ······ 京極氏 ·· 4:329a-329b; 7:8b
Fujiwara no Sadaie ············ 2:355a
Kyōgoku Tamekane
············ 京極為兼 ·· 4:329b-330a; 5:14b
Kyōgyōshinshō ·· 教行信証 ······ 4:68a, 330a-330b; 8:28a
Shinran ············ 7:123a
Kyōha Shintō. 教派神道 *See* **Sect Shintō**
Kyōha Shintō Rengōkai
······ 教派神道連合会 ····· 7:48a-48b
Kyōhō Famine · 享保の飢饉 ······ 4:330b
rice storage ············ 4:117b
Kyōhō Reforms 享保の改革 ······ 3:189a; 4:330b-331b
meyasubako ············ 5:165b
tashidaka ············ 7:347b
Tokugawa shogunate ············ 8:55b
Tokugawa Yoshimune ············ 8:56b
Kyōiku ······ 教育 ······ 7:335b
Kyōiku Chokugo. 教育勅語 *See* **Imperial Rescript on Education**
Kyōiku chokugo seiritsushi no kenkyū
···· 教育勅語成立史の研究 ······ 4:109b
Kyōiku kaikaku ron
············ 教育改革論 ······ 1:4b
Kyōiku kanji ············ 4:331b; 7:34b
Kyōiku Kihon Hō
············ 教育基本法 ··· 2:182a-182b
Kyōiku kihonhō no riron
······ 教育基本法の理論 ······ 7:337b
Kyōiku mama ············ 2:181b
Kyōikurei ······ 教育令 ······ 2:183a
Kyōiku Sasshin Iinkai ············ 2:183a
Kyōiku shinron ·· 教育新論 ······ 7:315b
Kyōja no kenri no kyōsō/ Der kampf ums Recht des Stärkeren und seine Entwicklung
······ 強者の権利の競争 ······ 4:168b
Kyo-jitsu (emptiness-fullness) ····· 5:151a
Kyōka ············ 狂歌 ·· 4:331b-332a; 7:18a
Karagoromo Kisshū ············ 4:157a
later Edo period ············ 5:48a
Ōta Nampo ············ 6:129a
Shikatsube Magao ············ 7:95a
travel diaries ············ 8:105b
Kyōka iezuto ··· 狂歌家づと ······ 4:332a
Kyōkai jigen ······ 教界時言 ······ 4:233a
Kyōkaku ············ 4:332b
Kyōka poets
Ishida Mitoku ············ 3:340a
Ishikawa Masamochi ············ 3:343b
Karagoromo Kisshū ············ 4:157a
Kubo Shumman ············ 4:301a
Nagata Teiryū ············ 5:307a
Nakarai Bokuyō ············ 5:317b
Ōta Nampo ············ 6:129a
Shikatsube Magao ············ 7:95a
Kyōka sakehyakushu
············ 狂歌酒百首 ······ 4:331b
Kyōkasho Gigoku 教科書疑獄 ······ 8:16a
Kyōka wakabashū
············ 狂歌若葉集 ······ 4:157a
Kyōkechi (block-resist technique) ······ 夾纈 ······ 7:13b
Kyokutei Bakin. 曲亭馬琴 *See* **Bakin**
Kyokutō Hōsō (JOTF) ············ 4:332b
Kyokutō Iinkai ············ 2:248a
Kyokutō Kyōwakoku ············ 2:248b
Kyokuyō Co, Ltd ······ 2:284a; 4:332b
Kyō Machiko ······ 京マチ子 ······ 4:332b
Kyōnyo Kōju ···· 教如光寿 ······ 3:346b
Kyōō Gokokuji 教王護国寺 ······ 8:38a
Kyorai ············ 去来 ······ 6:299b
Kyoraishō ······ 去来抄 ······ 4:169a
Kyorin ············ 4:140b
Kyoryūchi ············ 4:333a
Kyōsai. 狂斎 *See* **Kawanabe Gyōsai**
Kyōsai gafu ······ 狂斎画譜 ······ 4:182a
Kyōsei shikkō ············ 4:333a
Kyōshi and kyōbun ············ 4:333a-334a
poets ············ 4:333b
themes and techniques ······ 4:334b-335a
Kyōtai kushū ····· 暁台句集 ······ 4:169a
Kyōtaku ············ 4:334a
Kyōto ············ 京都 ··· 4:334a-335b
Arashiyama ············ 1:74b
chōnin class ············ 1:301a-301b
gardens ············ 3:8b-9a
Gion Festival ············ *4:336b*
growth ············ 2:149a-150b
Heiankyō ············ 3:121b-122b
Kiyomizudera ············ *4:334b*
Kyōto Imperial Palace ············ *4:336b*
language ············ 4:24a
map ············ *4:335a-335b*
Nijō Castle ············ *4:334b*
Kyōto Art Association ············ 4:272a
Kyōto Basin ····· 京都盆地 ·· 4:336b-337b
Kyōto ceramics ······ 京焼 ·· 1:*262b*, 263b; 2:295b; 4:336a, 337a-338a; 6:35a
Kyōto Ceramics Testing Institute ·· 4:178b
Kyōto Daigaku Jimbun Kagaku Kenkyūjo. *See* **Kyōto University Research Institute for Humanistic Studies**
Kyōto Fu Tojaku Shihō of 1868 ···· 4:60b
Kyōto Gozan. 京都五山 *See* **Gozan**
Kyōto Imperial Palace 京都御所 ···· 4:*336b*
Kyōto Institute for the Blind and Deaf ············ 7:241b
Kyōto National Museum ····· 4:336a, 337b
Kyōto Prefectural Painting School 4:272a
Tanomura Chokunyū ············ 7:344b
Kyōto Prefecture ··· 京都府 ·· 4:337b-338b
geography and climate ······ 4:337b-338a
history ············ 4:338a
industries ············ 4:338a
tourism and culture ······ 4:338a-338b
Kyōto printing ············ 6:248a
Kyōto shoshidai
············ 京都所司代 ······ 4:338b
Itakura Katsushige ············ 3:350a
Kyōto shugoshoku
············ 京都守護職 ··· 4:338b-339a
Shinsengumi ············ 7:124b
Kyōto University ············ 4:339a
Tanimoto Tomeri ············ 7:342a
Kyōto University Incident
············ 京大事件 ·· 4:339a-339b; 7:251b, 255b; 8:116a
Gakuren Incident ············ 4:339a
Takikawa Incident ··· 4:339b; 7:326b-327a
Kyōto University Research Institute for Humanistic Studies ············ 4:339b
Kyōto ware ······ 京焼 ······ 6:*35a*
plate ············ 1:*262b*
Kyōwa Bank, Ltd ············ 4:339b-340a
Kyōwa Hakkō Kōgyō Co, Ltd ····· 4:340a
Kyōwakai. 協和会 *See* **Concordia Society**
Kyō-yaki. 京焼 *See* **Kyōto ceramics**
Kyōyujo ············ 教諭所 ······ 4:340a
Kyōzon Dōshū ············ 6:109a
Kyōzuka ············ 経塚 ······ 7:280a
Kyū. *See* **Moxa treatment**
Kyūchū Bō Jūdai Jiken
······ 宮中某重大事件 ······ 4:340a
Kyūdō ············ 弓道 ·· 4:340a-340b
Kyūha ············ 2:267b
Kyūji ············ 旧辞 1:151a; 4:340b
historiography ············ 3:152a
Kojiki based on ············ 4:251a
Kyūjutsu ············ 4:340a
Kyūkakoku Jōyaku
············ 九か国条約 ······ 6:4b
Kyūketsu hime ····· 吸血姫 ······ 4:157b
Kyūkokukai ············ 5:346a
Kyū nihonhei mondai ······ 8:278b-279a
Kyūritsū (Physics) ·· 窮理通 ······ 6:187a
Kyūrō gafu ······ 九老画譜 ······ 4:201a
Kyūsei Atami Art Museum. *See* **MOA Museum of Art**
Kyūseigun ······ 救世軍 ······ 7:5b-6a
Kyūsei Hakone Art Museum. *See* **Hakone Museum of Art**
Kyūsei kōtō gakkō ············ 3:135a
Kyūsekki bunka
············ 旧石器文化 ·· 6:159b-160a
Kyūsekki jidai ·· 旧石器時代 ······ 6:160a
Kyūshū 九州
area ············ 4:2b
dialects ············ 2:91b
population density ············ 4:2b, 7a
Kyūshū Electric Power Co, Inc ··· 4:340b
Kyūshū Matsushita Electric Co, Ltd ············ 4:340b-341a
Kyūshū Mountains
············ 九州山地 ······ 4:341a
Kunimidake ············ 4:309b
Kyūshū region ··· 九州地方 ······ 4:341a
Kyūshū theory ····· 九州説 ······ 8:306a
Kyūshū University ············ 4:341b
Kyūtei Edokoro (Imperial Court Office of Painting) ······ 宮廷絵所 ······ 2:171a

L

LaBarre, Weston 4:38b
Labor 4:343a-349b
Allied Occupation labor reforms 4:345b-346a
arubaito (part-time student) 2:209b
"closed" employment systems 4:344a-344b
collective bargaining 4:348a-348b
company welfare system 2:209b
compensation 4:346a
bonus 4:348a
nenkō and benefits 4:348a
shuntō wage pattern 4:348a
corvée 1:226a-226b
corvée (yōeki) 8:327a
distribution 2:162a-162b
dualistic labor markets 4:343b
early patron-client system 4:343b-344a
economic growth 2:160a-161b
General Strike of 1947 3:18b
government role 4:348b
growth of unionism (1945-1950) 4:346a-346b
indentured servants 2:211b
industrial labor force, emergence of 4:343a-343b
industrial structure 3:301a
inflation and price stability 3:303a
Japanese emigrants 2:200b, 201b
labor-management relations outlook 4:348b-349b
managerial ideology 5:91b-92b
Meiji period 2:152a-152b
minors 2:209b
modern employment system 2:210a-211a
nenkō wages and benefits 4:344b-345a
premodern system 2:211b-212b
pressure groups 6:237a
pre-World War II labor movement 4:345a
Proletarian literature movement 6:254b
reemergence of rival labor federations 4:346b
restraints on unionism after 1947 4:346b-347a
salaried 8:251b
Sampō: wartime labor front 4:345b
shagaikō (noncompany workers) 2:209b
shortage 2:211a
industrial robots 3:298b-299a
shuntō wage pattern 4:348a
Sōhyō and Dōmei 4:347a-347b
structure and function of Japanese unionism 4:347b-348a
white-collar workers 8:251a-251b
women's rights
Tanino Setsu 7:342a
worker's compensation 8:270a
work hours 8:270a-270b
work regulations 8:270b
Yūaikai and Sōdōmei 4:345a-345b
yui 8:356a
Labor boss system 3:91b
Labor centers 4:359b
Labor Dispute Mediation Law (Rōdō Sōgi Chōtei Hō) 4:351a
Labor disputes 4:349b-351a
Ashio Copper Mine 1:102a
at Besshi Copper mine 1:150a
in Hawaii
Gotō Katsu 3:53a
pre-World War II 4:345a
resolution procedures 4:349b-350a
strikes 7:250b-251a
Takita Minoru 7:327a
work slowdowns 7:250b-251a
Laborers
dekasegi (work away from home) 2:83b-84a
hereditary occupations 1:147b
Labor-Farmer Party. *See* **Rōdō Nōmintō**
Labor federations 4:360a
IMF-JC 3:274b-275a
Labor force
contemporary 2:161a
employee dismissal 2:117a
industrial 4:343a
participation 4:354b-355b
women 8:264a-266a
protective legislation 8:269a
Labor laws 4:351a-353b
Allied Occupation reforms 4:351a-351b
Labor Relations Adjustment Law of 1946 4:351b
Labor Standards Law of 1947 4:351b
Labor Union Law of 1945 4:351b
company welfare system 1:342b
labor protection 4:352b
Labor Standards Law of 1947 4:352b
Minimum Wage Law of 1959 4:352b
Vocational Training Law of 1958 4:352b
prewar legislation 4:351a
Factory Law of 1911 4:351a
Labor Dispute Mediation Law of 1926 4:351a
Public Order and Police Law of 1900 4:351a
revisions 4:351b-352a
Public Corporations and Government Enterprises Labor Relations Law of 1948 4:352a
rights under collective bargaining 1:334b
social security 4:352b-354a
Employment Security Law of 1947 4:352b
Unemployment Insurance Law of 1947 4:352a-353a
unfair labor practices 8:149b
Labor management relations
government role 4:348b
outlook 4:348b
Labor market 4:353b-357b
changing nature 4:353b
dualistic 4:343b
industrial 4:343a-343b
job tenure 4:356b-357b
labor force participation 4:354b-355b
retired workers 4:355b-356a
unemployment workers 4:356a-356b
women 4:355b
Labor organizations 7:164a
Labor protection laws 4:352b
Labor reforms of 1945-1947 4:357b-358b
Employment Security Law (1947) 4:358a
Labor Relations Adjustment Law (1946) 4:357b
Labor Standards Law (1947) 4:357b-358a
Labor Union Law (1945) 4:357b
National Personnel Law (1948) 4:358b
Public Corporation Labor Relations Law (1948) 4:358b
Unemployment Compensation Law (1947) 4:358a
Workers' Accident Compensation Law (1947) 4:358a
Labor relations
collective labor agreements 1:334b
conditions of factory workers, study of 7:164a
iron and steel industry 3:335a
Labor Relations Adjustment Law of 1946 (Rōdō Kankei Chōsei Hō) 4:351b, 358a
amendments 4:346b
labor dispute resolution 4:349b
1952 amendment 4:352a
Labor relations commissions 4:346a, 358b
collective bargaining 1:334b
conciliation 4:349b
labor reform 4:358a
unfair labor practices 8:149b
Labor relations laws 4:351a-352b
Labor rights
establishment 4:359a
fundamental 4:345b
Labor Safety and Sanitation Law 3:292a
Labor Safety Law 4:358b
Labor Standards Act of 1947
women 8:265b
workers' compensation 8:270a
Labor standards inspection offices 2:117a; 4:358b
work regulations 8:270b
Labor Standards Law (1947) 2:6b; 2:209b, 241b; 4:87a, 346a, 351b, 352b, 358a
enforcement 4:358b
industrial injuries 3:292a
women in 8:261b, 8:269a
work regulations 8:270b
See also **Labor laws**
Labor Standards Law (1949)
work hours 8:270a
Labor Thanksgiving Day 2:262a
Labor Union Law. *See* **Labor laws**
Labor Union Law (1946) 4:345b-346a, 351b, 357b; 6:313a
since 1948 4:352a
1948 revision 4:358a
1949 revisions 4:352a
unfair labor practices 8:149b
See also **Labor laws**
Labor Union Law (1949) 6:264b
Labor unions 2:32b, 36b-37a; 4:358b-360a; 6:206b; 7:219a; 8:376b
chartering 4:360a
collective bargaining 4:360a
Dōmei 2:130a
enterprise 2:211a
internal involvement 4:360a
national labor federations 4:359b
organization 4:358b
post-World War II 2:156a-156b
public corporations 6:263b
rights 4:360a
right to organize 6:312a-312b
secondary 4:359a
Shinsambetsu 7:124a
Takano Minoru 7:317a
wage level 8:198b
Lacquer
making 4:361a
production 4:361a
uses 4:361a
See also **Lacquer ware**
Lacquer pictures 8:181a
Lacquer sap 4:360a
Lacquer tree [(urushi) *Rhus verniciflua*] 4:360a
Lacquer ware 4:360b-362a
boxes 1:166b-167a

decorative techniques ······ **5**:85a-85b
general ······ **4**:360b-361a
gold- or silver-leaf ······ **4**:220b
hira maki-e ······ **4**:*360b*
history ······ **4**:361a-362a
Azuchi-Momoyama period (1568-1600) ······ **4**:361b
early ······ **4**:361a
Edo period (1600-1868) ······ **4**:361b
Heian period (794-1185) ······ **4**:361a-361b
Kamakura and Muromachi (1133-1568) ······ **4**:361b
Kamakura period (1185-1333) ······ **4**:361b
Meiji period ······ **4**:361b
Nara period (710-794) ······ **4**:361a
kamakura-bori ······ **4**:121a
kijiya ······ **4**:205a
maki-e ······ **5**:85a-85b
museums ······ **5**:280a
negoro-nuri ······ **5**:359a-359b
Ladybird Incident ······ **4**:362a
Lady Chatterley's Lover case ······ **4**:362a
Itō Sei ······ **3**:355b-356a
obscenity ······ **6**:50b
Lady Ōtomo of Sakanoue ······ 大伴坂上郎女 ······ **6**:131a
Lafcadio Hearn Bunko ······ **8**:9a
Lagoons
Hachirōgata ······ **3**:74b
Hinuma ······ **3**:141a
Jūsan ······ **4**:86a
Kahokugata ······ **4**:108a
Saroma ······ **7**:22a
Laity ······ **4**:362a
lay Buddhist movement ······ **4**:372a
ubasoku ······ **8**:123a
zaike ······ **8**:367b
Lakes
Hokkaidō
Abashiri ······ **1**:1b-2a
Akan ······ **1**:40b
Fūren ······ **2**:370b
Kutcharo ······ **4**:321b
Kuttara ······ **4**:321b
Mashū ······ **5**:125b
Notoro ······ **6**:41b
Ōnuma ······ **6**:113a
Saroma ······ **7**:22a
Shikotsu ······ **7**:98a
Tōfutsu ······ **8**:35b
Tōya ······ **8**:87b
Uryū ······ **8**:181a
Honshū
Biwa ······ **1**:157b-158a
Chūzenji ······ **1**:315a
Fuji Five ······ **2**:342b
Hachirōgata ······ **3**:74b
Hamana ······ **3**:91a
Haruna ······ **3**:105b
Hibara ······ **3**:129a
Hyō ······ **3**:252a
Imbanuma ······ **3**:274b
Inawashiro ······ **3**:283b
Kasumigaura ······ **4**:164a
Kawaguchi ······ **4**:177b
Kitagata ······ **1**:125a
Kitaura ······ **4**:229a
Mikata Five ······ **5**:170b
Nojiri ······ **6**:32b
Shinji ······ **7**:115a
Shirakaba ······ **7**:145b
Tama ······ **7**:332b
Tazawa ······ **7**:359a
Towada ······ **8**:87a
Yamanaka ······ **8**:300b
Kyūshū
Ikeda ······ **3**:265b
"Lamenting the Deviations." *See* **Tannishō**
"Lampoons." *See* **"Nijōgawara no rakusho"**
Lamps ······ **5**:9a
Land
distribution systems
handen shūju system ······ **2**:104b; **3**:95a-96a
private estates
shitaji chūban ······ **7**:149b
Land allotment system ······ **3**:95a-96a
Land conservation ······ **2**:326b
Landed estates ······ **7**:155a-158a
managers ······ **7**:163a
Landholders, local (myōshu) ······ **5**:291b
Land laws
Sanze Isshin no Hō (Law of Three Generations or a Lifetime) ······ **7**:19b
Landlordism ······ **4**:362b-363a; **6**:353a
cooperatives ······ **1**:22a
decline ······ **4**:363a
development ······ **4**:362b-363a
land reforms of 1946 ······ **4**:365a
Land Tax Reform of 1873-1881 ······ **4**:365b
origins ······ **4**:362b
Landlord-tenant relationships ······ **2**:107b
Land of the Wa ······ **8**:305a
Landowners ······ **6**:137b
collective
iriai ······ **3**:329b-331a
ichien chigyō ······ **3**:255a
rights and obligations ······ **3**:255b
shiryō ······ **7**:148a
Land problem ······ **4**:363b-364a
housing developers ······ **3**:242b
Land Purchase and Mortgage Regulation of 1873 ······ **2**:151a
Land reclamation ······ **4**:364a
Edo period ······ **4**:364a
Kōbe Port Island ······ **4**:*364b*
Meiji period ······ **4**:364a
post-World War II ······ **4**:364a
Land reform
Kansei Reforms ······ **4**:152b
religion and ······ **6**:292b
Land reforms of 1946 · **1**:31a; **4**:364a-365b; **6**:52b, 212a
agriculture ······ **1**:24b
income distribution ······ **3**:285b
Okinawa ······ **6**:87b
women, rural ······ **8**:266b
Land registers ······ **6**:128a-128b
Land rent ······ **4**:62b
Land Requisition Orders ······ **1**:21a
Land rights ······ **1**:274a
Landscape ······ **4**:110b
Landscape of the Four Seasons ······ **3**:*306b*
Landscape painting, traditional. *See* **Sansuiga**
Landscapes in miniature ······ **1**:161a
Land System History Association ······ **8**:289a
Land Tax Reform Agency ······ **4**:366a
Land Tax Reform of 1873-1881 ······ **2**:151b, 361a; **4**:365b-366b
bureaucratic development ······ **1**:217b
chitsuroku shobun ······ **1**:297b
general description ······ **4**:365b-366a
Ise Rebellion ······ **3**:337b
Kanda Takahira ······ **4**:137b
kemi discontinuation ······ **4**:191b
kenchi ······ **4**:195a
ketsuzei ikki ······ **4**:200a
komononari abolished ······ **4**:267b
Mutsu Munemitsu ······ **5**:288b
nengu ······ **5**:360b
reforms ······ **4**:366a
results ······ **4**:366b
shizoku ······ **7**:151b
women, rural ······ **8**:266b
Land tenancy ······ **2**:186b
Land tenure system ······ **4**:362b
Language. *See* **Japanese language**
Language of the court ladies ······ **6**:45a-45b
Lan-chi tao-lung ······ **6**:283b
Lansing-Ishii Agreement ······ **3**:341b; **4**:366b-367b; **8**:271a
Terauchi Masatake ······ **8**:12b
Washington Conference ······ **8**:234a-235a
Lansing, Robert ······ **4**:367b
Ishii Kikujirō ······ **3**:341b
Lantern plants, Chinese ······ **3**:246b-247a
Lanterns ······ **2**:371b; **4**:367b-368a; **5**:9a
andon ······ **4**:368a
bombori ······ **4**:368a
chōchin ······ **4**:368a
ishi-dōrō ······ **4**:368a
tōrō ······ **4**:368a
Langi Daolong ······ **6**:283b
Laos refugees ······ **6**:286a
LARA (Licensed Agencies for Relief in Asia) ······ **4**:368a
Larch, Japanese [(karamatsu) *Larix leptolepis*] ······ **4**:368b
Large Japanese-Russian Dictionary ······ **4**:275b
Larks [(hibari) family Alaudidae] ······ **4**:368b
Later Collection of Japanese Poetry ······ **3**:48b
Later Three Years' War · **1**:4a; **4**:368b-369a
samurai in ······ **7**:7b
Lathes ······ **6**:335b
Latin America and Japan ······ **4**:369a-370a
diplomatic relations ······ **3**:*323a–323b*
economic relations ······ **4**:369b-370a
premodern relations ······ **4**:369a-369b
since 1868 ······ **4**:369b
trade ······ **3**:*323a–323b*
Latitude Observatory of Mizusawa **7**:336a
Latter Age of the Law (mappō) ······ **5**:43b
Lattimore, Owen ······ **3**:316a
Laurel, José Paciano ······ **4**:370a
Laures, Johannes ······ **4**:370a
Laurilignosa culture. *See* **Shōyō jurin bunka**
Laver ······ **6**:37a-37b
Law ······ **4**:375b-380b
Absolute Government under Military Law (ca 1500-1868) ······ **4**:377b-378a
Chinese
ritsuryō system ······ **6**:324b
consumer protection ······ **2**:15b-16b
Installment Sales Law ······ **3**:315b
contemporary ······ **4**:379a-381b
criminal justice ······ **4**:380a
custom ······ **4**:379a-379b
disputes and their settlement ······ **4**:379b
legal profession and public ······ **4**:380a
legal tensions ······ **4**:380a-380b
perceptions and uses ······ **4**:379b-380a
sources ······ **4**:379a
copyright ······ **2**:25b-26a
Corporate Reorganization Law of 1952 ······ **2**:33b-34a
criminal ······ **2**:47b-49b
Keihō ······ **7**:123b-124a
Criminal Compensation Law of 1950 **2**:47a
Cultural Properties Law of 1950 **2**:52b-53a
customary (kanshūhō) ······ **2**:53b
early state (600-800) ······ **4**:376a-376b
equality ······ **2**:230a-230b
equality of sexes ······ **2**:229b-230a
Institutionalization of Absolutist Monarchy (1868-1945) ······ **4**:378a
land
bunchi seigen rei ······ **1**:208a

legal liability of a third party (suretyship) ······ **7**:278a
military houses ······ **1**:206b-207a
morality ······ **5**:248b
to preserve Buddhist temples ······ **1**:203b
rule of law (1945 to present) · **4**:378a-379a
Shōen period: decentralized jurisdiction (800-1500) ······ **4**:376b-377b
warrior class ······ **1**:206b
See also **Legal system**
Law, attitudes toward ······ **4**:370a-370b
Law, constitutional litigation under · **2**:13a
Law concerning Compensation for Nuclear Energy Damages of 1961 ······ **1**:114b
Law concerning Prevention of Radiation Sickness Due to Radioactive Isotopes of 1957 ······ **1**:114b
Law concerning Regulation of Nuclear Raw Materials, Nuclear Fuel Materials, and Nuclear Reactors of 1957 ··· **1**:114b
Law concerning Technical Standards for the Prevention of Radiation of 1957 ······ **1**:114b
Law concerning the Control of Important Industries ······ **4**:370b
Law Concerning the Counting of Age (1902) ······ **1**:21a
Law concerning the Settlement of Environmental Pollution Disputes **2**:225a
Law concerning the Special Measures for Atomic Bomb Sufferers of 1968 ······ **1**:110b
Law concerning the Treatment and Clearing of Discharge ······ **3**:302b
Law examination ······ **4**:370b-371a
Law Examination Control Committee ······ **4**:370b
Law for Examination and Control of Chemical Materials ······ **6**:220a
Law for Health Protection and Medical Care for the Atomic Bomb Explosion Sufferers ······ **1**:110b
Law for the Acceleration of Electric Power Development ······ **2**:191b
Law for the Payment of Compensation to Crime Victims (Hanzai Higaisha Tō Kyūfukin Shikyū Hō) ······ **2**:46b
Law for the Prevention of Capital Flight ······ **2**:320a
Law for the Punishment of Crimes Relating to the Environmental Pollution that Adversely Affects the Health of Persons ······ **2**:224b
Law Governing Monks and Nuns ·· **4**:372a
Law of evidence ······ **2**:50b; **4**:371a-371b
Law of Fire Defense Organization · **2**:279b
Law of Summary Procedures for Police Offenses ······ **5**:196a
Law on Provisional Measures relating to the Fisheries Zone ······ **2**:283b
Law on Territorial Waters (No. 30 of 2 May 1977) ······ **8**:13b
Laws for the Military Houses · **1**:206a-207a
Laws Governing the Imperial Court and Nobility ······ **4**:212a
Laws restricting the partitioning of farm lands ······ **1**:208a
Law to Prevent Excessive Premiums and Unreasonable Representations ··· **1**:67b
Lawyers ······ **4**:371b-372a
court-appointed ······ **2**:39b
law examination ······ **4**:370b-371a
limited role ······ **4**:371b
Laxman, Adam Erikovich ··· **2**:60b; **4**:372a
Golovnin, Vasilii Mikhailovich ······ **3**:44a
Russia ······ **6**:341a
Laxman, Kiril ······ **2**:60b
Lay, Horatio Nelson ······ **4**:372b
Lay Buddhist movement ······ **4**:372a
LDP (Liberal Democratic Party) ······ **4**:384b-386b
Le ······ **3**:304a
Leach, Bernard Howell ···· **2**:294a; **4**:372b
Leach Pottery, The ······ **4**:372b
Lead-glazed wares. *See* **Ceramics**
League for Establishing a National Assembly (Kokkai Kisei Dōmei) ·· **1**:34b; **2**:334b; **4**:372b-373a; **6**:207a
League for the Establishment of Universal Suffrage ······ **8**:169a
League of Blood Incident (1932) ·· **4**:373a
Dan Takuma ······ **2**:77b
League of Nations ······ **3**:199a
Thailand and Japan ······ **8**:20b
Tripartite Pact ······ **8**:107a
Washington Naval Treaty of 1922 · **8**:235a
League of Nations and Japan ······ **4**:373a-373b
League of the Divine Wind. *See* **Jimpūren Rebellion**
League to Petition for Universal Suffrage ······ **2**:376a-376b
Lealand, George A. ······ **7**:242b
Learned societies ······ **4**:373b-374a
legal ······ **4**:375b
Learning of the Southern Barbarians ······ **8**:241a
Leased House Law ······ **4**:374a
freedom of contract ······ **2**:337b
Leased house rights ······ **4**:374a
Leased Land Law
freedom of contract ······ **2**:337b
land lease rights ······ **4**:374a
Leased land rights ······ **4**:374a-374b
Leasing
deposit money ······ **2**:87b
Orient Leasing Co, Ltd ······ **6**:116a-116b
Leaves of Jade ······ **3**:71b
"Lectures" faction ······ **4**:299b
Lectures on the Development of Japanese Capitalism ······ **8**:289a
Leeches [(hiru) class Hirudinea] ·· **4**:374b
Lee Hwe-song ······ **4**:374b
Left-wing Socialist Party ······ **8**:296b
Legal Affairs Bureaus ······ **4**:80b
Legal cases
After the Banquet case ······ **1**:20a-20b
Naganuma case ······ **5**:303a
Legal education ······ **4**:374b-375a
Legal Reform in Occupied Japan: A Participant Looks Back ······ **6**:115b
Legal rights ······ **3**:252b
Legal scholarship ······ **4**:375a-375b
associations ······ **4**:375a
civil law ······ **4**:375a
constitutional law ······ **4**:375a
criminal law ······ **4**:375a
"Japanese philosophy of law" ······ **4**:375a
Legal specialists ······ **6**:323a
Legal system ······ **4**:375a-380b
administrative law ······ **1**:13a-13b
administrative litigation ······ **1**:13b-14a
administrative procedures ······ **1**:14a
administrative scrivener ······ **1**:14a-14b
attitudes toward ······ **4**:370a-370b
cabinet orders (seirei) ······ **1**:229a
confessions ······ **1**:350b
contracts ······ **2**:20a-20b
criminal procedures ······ **2**:49b-51b
domainal ······ **1**:212a
education ······ **2**:182b
history ······ **4**:375b-376a
absolutist government under military law (CA 1500-1868) ······ **4**:377b-378a
absolutist monarchy (1868-1945) · **4**:378a
contemporary ······ **4**:379a-380b
early state (600-800) ······ **4**:376a-376b
rule of law (1945 to the present) ······ **4**:378a-379a
Shōen period: decentralized jurisdictions (800-1500) ······ **4**:376b-377b
Legal Training and Research Institute ······ **2**:246a; **4**:380a-381a
Chūō University ······ **1**:313b
law examinations ······ **4**:371a
structure ······ **4**:380b
Le Gendre, Charles William ······ **4**:381a
Legends
fireflies ······ **2**:280a-280b
ochiudo ······ **6**:60a
Legends of Mt. Shigi, The ····· **7**:92b-93a
Legends of Tōno, The ······ **8**:75a
Legislation
delegation of power ······ **2**:84a
modernization of business ······ **2**:30a
small- and medium-sized businesses ······ **7**:205b
Legislative reapportionment ······ **4**:80a
Legislative supremacy ······ **4**:81a
Legislature. *See* **Diet**
Leisure dress ······ **5**:7b-8a
Leisure-time activities ······ **4**:381a-382b; **5**:7a-7b
early historical period: courtly pastimes ······ **4**:381a
early modern period: leisurely pursuits of the townspeople ······ **4**:381b
industry growth ······ **4**:382a
introduction of Western ······ **4**:381b-382a
mass ······ **4**:382a-382b
participation sports ······ **4**:382a
television ······ **4**:382a
medieval period: warrior pastimes · **4**:381a
post-World War II ······ **4**:382a
western influence ······ **5**:7b-8a
Lelang (Lolang) ······ **4**:382b
commerce of, in prehistory ······ **4**:276b
Japanese and Korean ties ······ **4**:276a
Lenin, Vladmir Il'ich. *See* **Lenin and Japan**
Lenin and Japan ······ **4**:382b-383a
conversations with Japanese journalists ······ **4**:383a
publication of works in Japan ······ **4**:383a
Russia and Japan ······ **6**:342b
view of Japan ······ **4**:383a
Lennon, John ······ **6**:112a
Léonard, Foujita ······ **2**:347a
Leontief, Wassily ······ **2**:144b
Lerch, Theodore von ······ **1**:120a; **4**:383a; **7**:242b
Les Aïnou des Iles Kouriles ······ **1**:36a
Lese majesty ······ **4**:383a-383b
food demonstrations ······ **7**:165a
Les Grimmaces ······ **4**:178a
Letters, Japanese ······ **7**:231b
Leyte Gulf, Battle of ······ レイテ沖海戦 ······ **4**:383b; **5**:307b; **8**:276a
Li ······ **6**:288b
Liability ······ **4**:383b-384a
Automobile Liability Security Law of 1955 ······ **1**:120b
compensation for damages ······ **7**:226a
employers' ······ **2**:209a
government ······ **3**:55a
for negligence ······ **4**:383b
without fault ······ **4**:383b-384a
Liancourt Rocks ······ **7**:325a-325b
Liang Kai ······ **4**:78a
Liang Qichao (Liang Ch'i-ch'ao) · **1**:229b; **4**:384a-384b
influence of seiji shōsetsu ······ **7**:50a

Liao Chengzhi (Liao Ch'eng-chih) 4:384b
Libel Law of 1875 1:252a; 4:384b; 6:262b
Press Ordinance of 1875 6:236a
Liberal Democratic Party (LDP) 1:220a; 2:85a; 4:384b-386b; 6:212b, 215a, 216b; 7:26a, 28b, 215b
committees 4:384b
Diet 2:95a
as government 4:386a-386b
factions 4:385b
funding 4:384b
Hatoyama Ichirō 3:113a
ideology and policies 4:385a
Ishii Mitsujirō 3:341b
Japan Socialist Party 4:48a
Kishi Nobusuke 4:223a-223b
Kōno Kenzō 4:274b
"money politics" 4:385b
national defense 5:336b-338b
New Liberal Club 5:365a
Ōno Bamboku 6:109a
organization of leadership 4:385a-385b
pacifism 6:145a
peace movement 6:166b
postwar dominance 3:204b
pressure groups 6:236b
prime minister and cabinet 6:242b
reform 4:385b-386a
support 4:384b
Tanaka Kakuei 7:337a
Liberalism 4:386b-387a
Liberal Party (post-World War II) 4:66a, 223a-223b, 387b; 6:211b; 7:26a
Liberal Party (prewar). *See* **Jiyūtō**
Librarians (shisho) 5:1b; 7:36a-36b
assistant *(shishoho)* 5:2b
Libraries 5:1a-3a
Asakusa Bunko 1:95a-95b
Ashikaga Gakkō Iseki Toshokan 1:100a
Cabinet Library 1:229a
cataloging 5:2b
classification system 5:2b
film 2:276a
history 5:1a
Hōsa Bunko 3:234b
Japan Foundation Library 4:46a
Jingū Bunko 4:58b-59a
Kanazawa Bunko 4:136a
Matsugaoka Bunko 5:133a
Mitsui Research Institute for Social and Economic History 5:212b
Nanki Bunko 5:329a
National Diet Library 5:338b-339a
problems 5:3a
profession 5:2a
professional journals for 5:2b
roles and functions of modern 5:1b
school 7:36a-36b
Seikadō Bunko 7:50b
Sonkeikaku Library 1:151b; 7:228a
subject heading assignments 5:2b
technical processing 5:2b
Tenri Central Library 8:8b-9a
Tōkyō Metropolitan Archives and Records Institute 8:67b
Tōkyō Metropolitan Hibiya Library 8:67b
Tōyō Bunko 8:89b-90a
types 5:1b, 5:3a
academic 5:2a, 5:3a
children's 5:2a
national 5:1b
prefectural 5:2a
public 5:2a, 5:3a
school 5:3a; 7:36a
special 5:2a
Untei 8:174a
Yōmei 8:335a
Zushoryō 8:381a-381b
Library Law of 1950 5:1b
Licensed Agencies for Relief in Asia (LARA) 4:368a
Licensing System 6:276a
Liefde 1:11a; 2:135b; 5:3a
Life Composition Movement (Seikatsu Tsuzurikata Undō) 6:233a
Life cycle 5:3b-5b
age reckoning and 5:3b
change and conflict 5:5a
childhood 5:4a
infancy 5:4a
maturity 5:4b-5a
old age 5:5a
postmortem 5:5a
religious rituals 6:292a
youth 5:4a; 8:352a-353b
Life expectancy 6:222a
economic implications 6:232a
Life insurance 5:5b
Lifelong learning 5:5b
Life of Jesus, A 2:214a
Life stages 5:3b
Lifestyles 5:5b-8b
education 5:6b
elderly 5:7a
home life 5:7b
housing 5:6a
modern and traditional elements 5:7b-8b
education 5:8b
food and diet 5:8a
household furnishings 5:8a
leisure time activities 5:8a
occupations 5:8a
social status 5:8b
women 5:8b
schoolchildren 5:6b
standard of living and leisure time 5:7a
time and space 5:6a
women 5:6b-7a
Lighting equipment 2:370b; 5:8b-9b
Li Hongzhang (Li Hung-chang) 5:9b
Treaty of Shimonoseki 7:106a
Li ji 4:165b
Lilies [(yuri) *Lilium* spp.] 5:9b-10a
Limestone 7:278b
Limited liability company 2:31b, 37b; 5:10a
Limited Liability Company Law (Yūgen Kaisha Hō) of 1938 5:10a
Limited partnership company 2:31b, 37b; 5:10b; 6:164a
Lin Biao 7:200a
Lindera 4:316b
Linguistics 4:30b-32a
Linji Yixuan (Lin-chi I-hsüan; Rinzai Gigen) 6:318b-319a
Lion Corporation 5:10b
Lion dance 2:74a
Lions Club 5:10b
Li-po y otros Poemas 7:291a
Li-qi dualism 7:191a
Li-qi monism 7:191a
Liquefied natural gas (LNG) 2:216a, 217a
Tōkyō Electric Power Co, Inc 8:67a
Tōkyō Gas Co, Ltd 8:67a
Liquor Tax Law 2:276b
Literacy 2:174b-175a
Literacy rate 5:10b-11a
Literary Age 1:209a-209b
Literary Arts 1:209a
Literary Club 1:209b
Literary criticism 5:11a-17b
modern 5:11a-13b
first modernists 5:11a
practical critics 5:13a
professional critics 5:13a
traditionalists 5:11b-12a
Western influence 5:11a
Westernization, second wave 5:12a
premodern 5:13b-17b
conclusions 5:17b
didactic theories 5:16b-17a
early thoughts 5:13b-14a
fiction 5:14a
haikai and haiku 5:16a
Heian Court poetry 5:14a
jōruri and kabuki 5:16a
Kokugaku scholars 5:17a-17b
medieval waka aesthetics 5:14b
Nō drama 5:15b-16a
renga and structural principles 5:15a
valuational criticism in poetry contests 5:14b-15a
Literary critics
Ara Masahito 1:74a
Etō Jun 2:234a
Fukuda Tsuneari 2:362b
Hanada Kiyoteru 3:93a
Haniya Yutaka 3:98a-98b
Hirabayashi Hatsunosuke 3:141a
Hirano Ken 3:143b
Hirotsu Kazuo 3:151a
Honda Shūgo 3:219b
Ikuta Chōkō 3:271a
Ishibashi Ningetsu 3:339a
Ishikawa Jun 3:342b-343b
Itō Sei 3:355b-356a
Iwano Hōmei 3:361a
Kamei Katsuichirō 1:209a; 4:125a
Katō Shūichi 4:169b
Katsumoto Seiichirō 4:172a
Kawakami Tetsutarō 4:181b
Kimura Ki 4:211a
Kitamura Tōkoku 4:227b
Kobayashi Hideo 4:236a-236b
Komiya Toyotaka 4:267a
Kubokawa Tsurujirō 1:209a; 4:300b
Kurahara Korehito 4:311a
Kuriyagawa Hakuson 4:313b
Masaoka Shiki 5:123b-124a
Nakamura Mitsuo 5:315a-315b
Nakamura Shin'ichirō 5:315b
Nakano Shigeharu 5:316b-317a
Nakano Yoshio 5:317a-317b
Narushima Ryūhoku 5:335b
Odagiri Hideo 6:61a
Oda Makoto 6:61b
Ozaki Hotsuki 6:139a
Shimamura Hōgetsu 7:99b-100a
Takayama Chogyū 7:320a
Taoka Reiun 7:346a
Terada Tōru 8:11a
Uno Kōji 1:209a
Usui Yoshimi 8:182a
Yamamoto Kenkichi 8:298b
Yamazaki Masakazu 8:312b-313a
Yasuda Yojūrō 8:318a
Yoshimoto Takaaki 8:348a
Literary Front 1:209b
Literary groups 5:17b-21b
bundan 1:208a-208b
modern 5:18b-21b
fiction 5:18b-19b
haiku 5:20a
other special-purpose 5:21a
poetry 5:20a
politically oriented 5:20b-21a
tanka 5:19b-20a
women's 5:20b
premodern 5:17b-18b
Chinese learning 5:18b
haikai 5:17b
publishers and printers 5:18a
renga 5:17b
writers and artists 5:18a

Literary magazines · · · 5:21b-24b
early development (1868-1885) · · · 5:22a
large literary and comprehensive magazines (1895-1900) · · · 5:22a
Leftist literary movement (1925-1935) · · · 5:23a
mid- and late Taishō period (1915-1925) · · · 5:23a
modern developments (1955-1975) · · · 5:24a
modern literature (1885-1895) · · · 5:22a
naturalist literature (1905-1910) · · · 5:22b
journals opposing (1910-1915) 5:22b-23a
non-leftist · · · 5:23b
postwar (1945-1955) · · · 5:24a
types · · · 5:21b-22b
dōjin zasshi · · · 5:22a
kikanshi · · · 5:22a
War (1935-1945) · · · 5:23b-24a
Literary names · · · 5:325a-326a
Literary prizes · · · 5:24b-25a
Akutagawa Ryūnosuke · · · 1:46a
Akutagawa Ryūnoske Shō (Akutagawa Prize) · · · 5:24b
Dazai Osamu Shō (Dazai Prize) · · · 5:24b
Edogawa Rampo Prize · · · 2:171a
H-Shi Prize · · · 5:25a
Mainichi Geijutsu Shō (Mainichi Art Award) · · · 5:24b
Naoki Sanjūgo Shō (Naoki Prize) · · · 5:24b
Nihon Geijutsuin Shō (Japan Art Academy Award) · · · 5:24b
Noma Bungei Shō (Noma Literary Prize) · · · 5:24b
Shinchō Bungaku Shō (Shinchō Literary Prize) · · · 5:24b
Tanizaki Jun'ichiro Shō (Tanizaki Prize) · · · 5:24b
Yomiuri Bungaku Shō (Yomiuri Literary Prize) · · · 5:25a
Literary societies · · · 1:208a
Literary vocational organizations · · · 5:21a-21b
Literary World, The · · · 1:208a-208b
Literati painters · · · 6:154a
Literati painting. *See* **Bunjinga**
Literature · · · 5:25a-60a
authors (premodern). *See* Authors, premodern
criticism
modern · · · 5:11a-13b
premodern · · · 5:13b-17b
critics. *See* Literary critics
essayists. *See* Essayists
foreign influence
Chinese · · · 1:292b-296a
Western · · · 8:243a-247b
genre (modern)
biography and biographical · 1:155a-155b
book illustration · · · 1:163b-164a
children's · · · 1:279b-280a
chūkan shōsetsu · · · 1:312b-313a
drama · · · 5:57b-60a
fūzoku shōsetsu · · · 2:378a-378b
I-novel · · · 3:312a
mystery stories · · · 5:291b-292a
naturalism · · · 5:351a-351b
poetry · · · 5:56a-57b
popular fiction · · · 6:220b-221a
proletarian literature · · · 6:254b-256a
science fiction · · · 7:38a-39a
seiji shōsetsu · · · 7:50a-50b
shimbun shōsetsu · · · 7:103a-104a
tanka · · · 7:343b
war literature · · · 8:225b-228a
genre (premodern)
chōka · · · 1:299a-299b
enkyoku · · · 2:218b
fūryū · · · 2:374a-374b
gesaku · · · 3:28a-29a
giko monogatari · · · 3:32b
gōkan · · · 3:42a
Gozan literature · · · 3:58a-59b
gundan · · · 3:68b
gunki monogatari · · · 3:69a-69b
hachimonjiya-bon · · · 3:74b
haibun · · · 3:77a-78a
haiku · · · 3:78b-82a
honkadori · · · 3:223b
imperial anthologies · · · 3:275b
jitsurokumono · · · 4:64a
jokotoba · · · 4:71a-72a
kakekotoba · · · 4:115b
kana-zōshi · · · 4:136b
kawaraban · · · 4:182b
kibyōshi · · · 4:201b-202a
kobanashi · · · 4:235a-235b
Kokin denju · · · 4:254a
kokkeibon · · · 4:256a
kotobagaki · · · 4:297a
kusazōshi · · · 4:319b-320a
kyōka · · · 4:331b-332a
kyōshi and kyōbun · · · 4:333a-334a
makura kotoba · · · 5:87b-88a
monogatari bungaku · · · 5:245b-246a
nikki bungaku · · · 6:2a-2b
ninjōbon · · · 6:5b-6b
otogi-zōshi · · · 6:129b-130b
poetry and prose in Chinese · · · 6:193b-197b
renga and haikai · · · 6:296b-300a
Rokkasen · · · 6:344b
saijiki · · · 6:369a
sakimori uta · · · 7:2a-2b
senryū · · · 8:368a-368b
setsuwa bungaku · · · 7:72a-72b
sharebon · · · 7:79b-80a
shikashū · · · 7:94b-95a
travel diaries · · · 8:104b-106a
ukiyo-zōshi · · · 8:144a-144b
uta-awase · · · 8:182a-182b
utagaki · · · 8:183a
uta makura · · · 8:185b
uta monogatari · · · 5:245b-246a
waka · · · 8:201b-217a
yomihon · · · 8:336a-336b
zappai and senryū · · · 8:368a-368b
zuihitsu · · · 8:380a-380b
groups (modern) · · · 5:17b-21b
bundan · · · 1:208a-208b
Ken' yūsha · · · 4:198b-199b
Nihon Bungaku Hōkokukai · · · 5:379a
Nihon Rōman Ha · · · 5:381b
Pan no Kai · · · 6:161b
Shinkankaku school · · · 7:116a-116b
Shinkō Geijutsu Ha · · · 7:119b
Shirakaba school · · · 7:145b-146b
Zen Nihon Musansha Geijutsu Remmei (NAPF) · · · 6:255b
history
early · · · 5:25b-28b
Edo · · · 5:46a-50b
Heian · · · 5:28b-41b
medieval · · · 5:41b-46a
modern · · · 5:50b-60a
postwar · · · 6:230a-231b
Shōwa · · · 7:174b-176b
institutions
Kokubungaku Kenkyū Shiryōkan · · · 4:256b-257a
Museum of Modern Japanese Literature · · · 5:275b
novelists. *See* Novelists (modern)
playwrights. *See* Playwrights
poets
free verse. *See* Poets
haiku. *See* Haiku poets
renga. *See* Renga poets
tanka. *See* Tanka poets
waka. *See* Waka poets
religion and literature
Buddhism · · · 1:180a-182a
Christianity · · · 4:32a
works (modern)
"Abe ichizoku" · · · 5:252b
An'ya kōro · · · 7:90a
Bokutō kidan · · · 5:300b
Gan · · · 5:252b
"Haguruma" · · · 1:45b
Hakai · · · 7:101a
Hototogisu · · · 8:59b
"Jigokuhen" · · · 1:45b
Kamen no kokuhaku · · · 5:200b
"Kani kōsen" · · · 4:237b
Kuroi ame · · · 3:255b
"Maihime" · · · 5:252a
Miyamoto Musashi · · · 8:347a
Mon · · · 5:350b
Sanshirō · · · 5:350a
Sasameyuki · · · 7:343a
Sembazuru · · · 4:176b
Shōsetsu shinzui · · · 8:110b
Sorekara · · · 5:350a
Suna no onna · · · 1:3a
"Takekurabe" · · · 3:136b
Tsuchi · · · 5:307b
Ukigumo · · · 2:375b
Yama no oto · · · 4:176b
Yoakemae · · · 7:101b
Yukiguni · · · 4:176a
works (premodern)
Azuma kagami · · · 1:127a-127b
fudoki · · · 1:341a-341b
Hamamatsu Chūnagon monogatari · · · 3:90b-91a
Heichū monogatari · · · 3:122b-123a
Heiji monogatari · · · 3:123a-123b
Heike monogatari · · · 3:124a-125a
Hōgen monogatari · · · 3:209b
Hōjōki · · · 3:129a
Ise monogatari · · · 3:337a-337b
Izumi Shikibu nikki · · · 3:366b
Kagerō nikki · · · 4:104a-104b
Kaifūsō · · · 4:109a
Kinkai wakashū · · · 4:212b
Kojiki · · · 4:251a-251b
Kokinshū · · · 4:254b-255a
Konjaku monogatari · · · 4:270b-271a
Makura no sōshi · · · 7:52a-53a
Man'yōshū · · · 5:102b-110b
Nansō Satomi hakkenden · · · 5:329a-329b
Ochikubo monogatari · · · 6:59b-60a
Ōkagami · · · 6:79a
Sarashina nikki · · · 7:21a-21b
Shasekishū · · · 7:80b-81a
Shin kokinshū · · · 7:119b-120b
Taiheiki · · · 7:295a
Taketori monogatari · · · 7:325a-326b
Tale of Genji · · · 7:328b-331b
Tōkaidōchū hizakurige · · · 4:61a
Tosa nikki · · · 4:216b-217a
Towazugatari · · · 8:87a-87b
Tsurezuregusa · · · 8:341b-342b
Tsutsumi Chūnagon monogatari · · · 8:118b-119a
Uji shūi monogatari · · · 8:137b
Utsubo monogatari · · · 8:187a-188a
Lithography · · · 5:233a-233b
Litigation · · · 4:81b
Liutiaogou (Liu-t'iao-kou) Incident · 5:60a
Vaughn, Miles W. · · · 8:189a

Liu Yongfu (Liu Yung-fu) · 5:60a
Livelihood Protection Law (Seikatsu Hogo Hō) · 4:353a; 5:60a-60b; 7:55b, 209b
Livestock. *See* **Agriculture**
Livestock Communicable Disease Control Law · 6:274a
Livestock production · 1:27b-28a
  climate · 1:28a
  historical perspective · 1:28a
  native breeds · 1:28b
Living National Treasures · 5:60b-61a
  Arakawa Toyozō (1955) · 1:73b
  Cultural Properties Law of 1950 · 2:52b
  Hamada Shōji · 3:89b
  Hanayagi Shōtarō · 3:95a
  Hirata Gōyō · 3:145b
  Hori Ryūjo · 3:228a
  Ishiguro Munemaro · 3:340a-341b
  kabuki actors · 4:95b
  Kaneshige Tōyō · 4:140a
  Katō Hajime · 4:168a
  Kiritake Monjūrō II · 4:222a
  Miwa Kyūwa · 5:216a
  Nakamura Utaemon VI · 5:315b
  Nakazato Tarōemon XII · 4:159b
  potters · 1:260b
  puppeteers · 1:215b
  Serizawa Keisuke · 7:69a
  Shōno Shōunsai (1967) · 1:136a
  Tomimoto Kenkichi · 8:71a-71b
  Toyotake Yamashiro no Shōjō · 8:93b
Lizards · 8:40a
Loans · 3:56b-57a
  education · 6:174a
  goods (suiko) · 7:264a
  interest rate structure · 3:317b-318a
  priority system · 3:291b
  seed rice (suiko) · 7:264a
  small and medium-sized businesses · 6:174a; 7:205b-206a
Loanwords · 5:61a-62a
  Chinese · 5:61b
  differences in meaning · 5:62a
  Dutch · 5:61b
  English · 5:61b
  French · 5:61b
  general description · 5:61a-61b
  introductory form · 5:61b
  Japanese language · 4:23b-24a, 27a-27b
  Portuguese · 5:61b
  Russian · 5:61b
  Spanish · 5:61b
  transformation into Japanese · 5:62a
Local autonomy · 5:62a-62b
Local Autonomy Law of 1947 3:56a; 4:84a
  direct demand · 2:101a
Local Civil Service Law (Chihō Kōmuin Hō), Law No. 261 (1950) · 4:351b; 6:264b
Local government · 5:62b-71a
  Allied Occupation · 5:65b-67a
    decentralization · 5:65b-66a
    new system · 5:66a-66b
    problems · 5:66b
  Assembly of Prefectural Governors 1:103b
  early Meiji period (1868-1878) · 5:63a
  grants-in-aid · 3:56a
  Meiji local autonomy system · 5:63b-64b
    administrative justice · 5:64b
    district code · 5:64b
    municipal code · 5:64a
    prefectural code · 5:64a-64b
    reform · 5:64b-65b
    town code · 5:64a
    village code · 5:64a
  politics · 5:69a-71a
    prewar · 5:69a-69b
  post-Occupation evolution · 5:67a-69a
    administrative recentralization 5:67a-68a
    finance · 5:68b-69a
    local control · 5:68a-68b
    stable growth adjustment · 5:68b
  postwar · 5:69b-71a
  prewar · 5:65b, 69a-69b
  Three New Laws System (1878-1888) · 5:63a-63b
    districts · 5:63b
    local taxes · 5:63b
    prefectural assemblies · 5:63b
    towns · 5:63b
    villages · 5:63b
    wards · 5:63b
  time of Restoration · 5:62b-63a
  wartime · 5:65b
Local history · 5:71a
  birthplace history · 5:71b
  forerunners · 5:71a
  "Study of the Lore of Rural Localities" · 5:71b
Local ordinances · 5:71b
Lo Chen-yü. *See* **Luo Zhenyu (Lo Chen-yü)**
Lockheed Scandal · 2:45a; 4:386a; 5:72a; 8:160b
  Kodama Yoshio · 4:241a
  Tanaka Kakuei · 7:337a
Locusts (inago) · 5:72a
Loew, Oscar · 5:72a
London, Jack · 5:72a
London Naval Armaments Limitation Treaty
  Uchida Ryōhei · 8:124a
London Naval Conferences · 5:72b-73a; 7:88b
  Hamaguchi Osachi · 3:90a
  militarism · 5:173a, 174b
  Nagano Osami · 5:302b
  United States · 8:158b
  Wakatsuki Reijirō · 8:219a
London Naval Limitations Treaty
  power of supreme command · 8:85a
London Naval Treaty · 8:308a
  Takarabe Takeshi · 7:317b
London Telegram · 7:193b
Long-Term Credit Bank of Japan, Ltd · 1:139b; 5:73a
Long-term credit banks · 1:139b
  establishment · 1:139b
  floating debentures · 1:139b
Looms · 5:73a-73b
Lord keeper of the privy seal. *See* **Naidaijin**
"Lord of a sixth" · 7:184a
"Lord Tamesuke's Thousand-Poem Sequence" · 6:290a
Loti, Pierre · 5:73b
Lotte Co, Ltd · 5:73b
Lotteries, public · 5:73b
  Dai-Ichi Kangyō Bank, Ltd · 2:58b
Lotus [(hasu) *Nelumbo nucifera*] · 5:73b-74a
Lotus Confederation · 1:267b
Lotus Sutra 1:177b, 178b-179a, 180b, 186a, 187b, 193b, 282b, 292b; 5:74a, *74b*; 7:172a
  Eisai · 2:187a
  exorcism · 2:236b-237a
  Fuju Fuse sect · 2:359b
  Genshin · 3:23b
  Kannon · 4:144b
  Lotus Sutra scroll · 5:*74b*
  Namu Myōhō renge kyō · 5:327b
  new religions · 5:366b
  Nichiren · 5:375b
  Nichiren sect · 5:376b
  Rinzai sect · 6:319b
  Sangyō gisho · 7:11b
  Tendai sect · 8:4b
  thought and culture · 8:26b
  uta-e · 8:183a
Love marriage (ren'ai kekkon) · 5:320b
Love Suicides at Sonezaki, The · 4:77a
Lowborn (semmin) · 7:62a
Lowell, Percival · 5:74a
Low-income family slums · 7:202b
Low-pollution engines · 5:74a-75a
  catalytic converter · 5:75a
  CVCC (combined vortex controlled combustion) · 5:75a
  electric automobile · 5:75a
  ERG (exhaust gas recirculation) · 5:75a
  general description · 5:74a-74b
  hydrogen · 5:75a
  TGP (turbulence-generating pot) · 5:75a
Loyalty · 5:75a; 6:163a; 7:213b
  filial piety · 2:267a
  Seiken igen · 7:51b
Loyalty to the emperor · 5:75b
Luck of the Mountains · 5:294b-295a
Luck of The Sea · 5:294b-295a
Lucky Dragon Incident · 1:113b, 114b; 5:75b-76a; 6:166a
  peace movement · 1:111a
Luedorf, August · 3:26b
Lu Hsün. *See* **Lu Xun (Lu Hsün)**
Lunch box (warigo) · 8:225b
Luncheonettes · 7:164b
Luo Zhenyu (Lo Chen-yü) · 5:76a
Lüshun · 6:226a-226b
Lute priest · 1:157b
Lutheran Church · 5:76a
Lu Xun (Lu Hsün) · 5:76b
Luzon · 8:276a
Lyman, Benjamin Smith · 5:76b
Lytton Commission · リットン調査団 · 1:253a; 5:76b; 7:246b

M

Ma · 間 · 1:82a-82b; 5:77a
Mabechigawa · 馬淵川 · 5:77a
Mabe Manabu · 間部学 · 5:77a
Mabuchi Kazuo · 馬淵和夫 · 4:31b
Mabuta no haha (Mother in My Dreams) · 瞼の母 3:107b; 4:166a
Macaque · 5:245a-245b
MacArthur, Douglas · 2:4b, 185b, 248a; 5:77a, *77b*, 78a; 6:302b; 7:32b, 47a, 89a, 278a, 245b
  Aguinaldo, Emilio · 1:32b
  Akahata · 1:39b
  Diet · 2:94b
  Dulles, John Foster · 2:135a
  General Strike of 1947 · 3:18b; 4:11b
  Korean War · 4:292b
  Nine Principles for Economic Stabilization · 6:5a
  Occupation · 6:51b
  Red Purge · 6:285b
  renunciation of war · 6:301b
  role in constitutional revision · 2:3b
  San Francisco Peace Treaty and 7:10a-10b
  Self Defense Forces · 7:58b
  United States-Japan security treaties · 8:165b

World War II 8:273a
MacArthur, His Rendezvous with History 8:252b
MacArthur Line 6:307b
MacArthur, 1941-1951 ..... 8:253b
McCarran-Walter Act 8:164b
McCarthy, Joseph 3:316a
McDonald, Davidson 1:237b
MacDonald, Ranald 5:78a
Machi bugyō 町奉行 5:78b; 8:338b
Edo 2:171a
Machibure 町触 5:78b
Machida 町田 5:78b
Machieshi (town painters) 4:149b; 7:43a
Machi hikyaku 町飛脚 3:138a
Machine industries
Ebara Corporation 2:142b-143a
Katō Works Co, Ltd 4:170b-171a
Komatsu, Ltd 4:265b-266a
Kubota, Ltd 4:301a
Nachi-Fujikoshi Corporation 5:299b
NHK Spring Co, Ltd 5:374b
Niigata Engineering Co, Ltd 5:385a-385b
Nippon Seikō 6:12a
Sumitomo Heavy Industries, Ltd 7:268b
Tōshiba Machine Co, Ltd 8:82b
Toyoda Automatic Loom Works, Ltd 8:90a
Yanmar Diesel Engine Co, Ltd 8:316a
Machine Poetiku (Matinée Poetique) 5:19a
Machine tool industry 5:78b
"Machi no odoriba" 町の踊り場 7:176a
Machishū 町衆 5:78b-79a; 7:64b
Machi yakko 町奴 4:332b; 5:79a; 6:221a
Machi yakunin 町役人 5:79a
Mackerel [(saba) *Scomber japonicus*] 2:284b; 5:79a
Macroeconomics 2:144a-144b
Madai (sea bream) 7:45a
Madake 1:135b
Madenokōji Tokifusa 万里小路時房 4:196b
Madre de Deus Incident 1:83b; 5:79a-79b, 323a-323b
Mad verse 4:331b-332a
Maebara Issei 前原一誠 5:79b
Maebashi 前橋 5:79b
Maeda Construction Co, Ltd 5:79b
Maeda family 前田氏 5:79b-80a
Ishikawa Prefecture 3:344a
Kaisakuhō 4:112a
Kanazawa 4:136a
Maeda Ikutoku Kai Sonkeikaku Bunko 7:228a
Maedakō Hiroichirō 前田河広一郎 5:80a
Maeda Magoemon 前田孫右衛門 5:80a-80b
Maeda Seison 前田青邨 5:80b
Maeda Tamon 前田多門 5:80b
Maeda Toshiie 前田利家 5:80b-81a
Maeda Tsunanori 前田綱紀 5:81a-81b
Kaisakuhō 4:112a
Kanazawa Bunko 4:136a
Sonkeikaku Library 7:228a
Maeda Yoshinori 前田吉徳 5:81b
Maeda Yūgure 前田夕暮 5:81b
Maegashira 7:272a
Maehata Hideko 前畑秀子 5:81b
Maejima Hisoka 前島密 5:81b-82a
Maekawa Kunio 前川国男 1:81a; 5:82a
Kumamoto Prefectural Art Museum 4:305b
Tange Kenzō 7:340b
Maeku zuke 4:157a
Maeno Ryōtaku 前野良沢 5:82a-82b, 313a; 7:258b
Maezumō 7:273a
Mafune Yutaka 真船豊 5:82b
Mafutsusan 麻沸散 3:94b
Magariya 5:*193a*
Magatama. *See* **Beads, ancient**
Magazine of Women's Learning 4:69a
Magazines 5:82b-83a
advertising 1:17a
censorship 1:253a, 254b
current trends 5:83a
literary 5:21b-24b
Meiji period 5:82b
personal advice columns (minoue sōdan) 5:196a
post-World War II 5:83a
publishing 6:267b
Taishō and Early Shōwa periods 5:82b-83a
weekly 8:239a-239b
women's 6:221a; 8:268a-268b
Magemono 2:*294b*, 295a; 5:83a
Magic 8:273b
dog, Japanese 2:125b-126a
dolls 2:128a, 129b
Magnolia Kobus 4:239a
Magnolias 3:224a-224b; 4:239a
Mago 5:83a-83b
Magome Pass 馬籠峠 5:83b
Magoshi Kyōhei 馬越恭平 5:83b
Maguro 8:120a
Magusaba 秣場 5:83b
Mahāvairocana 2:64b
Mahāvairocana-sūtra 7:113b
Mahāyāna Buddhism マハーヤーナ教 1:177b-179b; 4:67a, 68b; 6:270a
architecture 1:185b
art 1:184b-187b
calligraphy 1:187a-187b
early texts 1:177b
Lotus Sutra 5:74a
Mādhyamika school 1:177b
printing 1:187a-187b
Yogācāra school 1:177b
Mahiru no ankoku (Darkness at Noon) 真昼の暗黒 5:83b-84a; 8:284b
Mahito 真人 1:103a
Mah-Jongg 4:382a; 5:7b, 84a
"Maiden Sano no Chigami, The" 7:15b-16a
Maigoto 舞事 2:74b
Maihara 米原 5:84a-84b
Maiko (apprentice geisha) 3:14b
Maiko 舞子 5:84b
Maikov, Nikolai Apollonovich 3:44b
Mai-mai 舞舞 4:298b
Mainichi Book Award
Kita Morio (1964) 4:227a
Mainichi Broadcasting System, Inc (MBS) 1:311a; 5:84b
Mainichi shimbun 毎日新聞 1:4b; 5:84b; 8:330b
Mai no hon 舞の本 4:298b
Mai (dance) plays 4:327b
Maisaka 舞阪 5:84b-85a
Maison Franco-Japonaise 2:332b
Maitreya. *See* **Miroku**
Maitreya, age of 8:337b
Maizuru 舞鶴 4:337b; 5:85a
Mājan 5:84a
Majima Toshiyuki 真島利行 1:268b; 5:85a
Majime ningen (A Serious Person) マジメ人間 8:294b
Major Industries Control Law 3:293a
Makekoshi 7:273a
Maki 牧 5:85a
Maki Asami Ballet Company 2:76a
Maki-e 4:136a, 361a; 5:85a-85b
inrō 3:313b
mother-of-pearl inlay 5:256b
wooden ware 8:269b
Maki Fumihiko 牧文彦 5:85b
Makiguchi Tsunesaburō 牧口常三郎 5:85b
Makihanashi 4:240b
Maki Itsuma 牧逸馬 3:116a
Maki Izumi 真木和泉 5:86a
Hamaguri Gomon Incident 3:90a
Makimono 4:116a
Makino Eiichi 牧野英一 5:86a
Makinohara 牧ノ原 4:136a; 5:86b
Makino Masahiro マキノ雅弘 2:268b; 5:86b
Fuji Junko 2:343a
Makino Nobuaki 牧野伸顕 5:86b
February 26th Incident 2:249b
Makino Shin'ichi 牧野信一 5:86b
Makino Shinken. *See* **Makino Nobuaki**
Makino Shōzō 牧野省三 2:267b; 5:87a
Makino Tomitarō 牧野富太郎 1:156a; 5:*87a*
Makioka Sisters, The 1:102a
Maki Ryōko 巻菱湖 5:87a-87b
Makisu 2:25a
Maki Yasuomi. 真木保臣 *See* **Maki Izumi**
Maki Yūkō 槇有恒 5:87b
"Makkō Chō" 抹香町 4:183a
Makoto 5:87b
Kogaku concept 4:247a
in Konishi Raizan's verse 4:270a
Maksimovich, Kark Ivanovich 5:87b
Maku ga orite kara 幕が下りてから 8:319b
Makura-e 7:187a
Makura kotoba 4:115b; 5:87b-88a
jokotoba 4:72a
waka 8:203a
Makura no sōshi 枕草子 4:166b; 7:52a, 241a
cats 1:251a
cattle 1:251a-251b
Makurazaki 枕崎 5:88a
Makushita 7:272a, 273a
Makuuchi 7:272a, 273a
Malayan Campaign 5:88a
Malayo-Polynesian languages, Japanese and 4:20a-21b
Malay Peninsula 5:88a
Malaysia and Japan 5:88a-88b
Japanese occupation of 5:88a
Japanese settlement in 5:88a-88b
postwar Japanese relations 5:88b
World War II campaign 2:348b
Mamako nagare 継子流れ 4:166b
Mameita gin 豆板銀 5:*242a-242b*
Mamiya Rinzō 間宮林蔵 5:88b-89a
Sakhalin 7:1b
Mamizukurage 4:50b
Mammals 1:59a-59b, 61b
bats 1:146b
bears 1:148b
cats 1:251a
cattle 1:251a-251b
deer, Japanese 2:82a
dog, Japanese 2:124b-126b
dormouse, Japanese 2:131a-131b
flying squirrels 2:293b
foxes 2:330a
horses 3:231a
Japanese spaniel 4:40b-41a

Japanese terrier ········· 4:45a
Kamoshika ········· 4:129b
Kawauso ········· 4:184b
marine mammals ········· 5:114a
moles ········· 5:235b
monkeys ········· 5:245a-245b
rabbits ········· 6:275a
rats and mice ········· 6:284a
tanuki ········· 7:345a
Tosa dog ········· 8:81a-81b
weasels ········· 8:238a
whales ········· 8:249a-249b
wild boar ········· 8:253a
wildcats ········· 8:253a
wolf, Japanese ········· 8:255b-256a

Mammō Dokuritsu Undō ········· 満蒙独立運動 ········· 5:99a-99b

Mampukuji ········· 万福寺 ········· 5:89a
Ingen ········· 3:303b

Manabe Akifusa 間部詮房 ········· 5:89a-89b

Manabe Akikatsu 間部詮勝 ········· 5:89b

Management ········· 5:89b-91a
conflict resolution ········· 1:351b
foreign executives ········· 2:318a-318b
multinational enterprises ········· 5:263b
organizational structure and decision making ········· 5:90a-91a
personnel practices ········· 5:89b-90a
seniority system ········· 5:92b

Management familism ········· 4:356b

Management of affairs ········· 5:91a

Managerial careers ········· 5:91a-91b

Managerial ideology ········· 5:91b-92b
antibusiness activities ········· 5:92a
contracts ········· 5:92a
definition ········· 5:91b
postwar ········· 5:92a-92b
prewar ········· 5:91b-92a
vs government regulation ········· 5:92a

Managers
career development ········· 5:91b
industrial
managerial ideology ········· 5:91b-92b
promotion ········· 5:91b
recruitment ········· 5:91a-91b
retirement ········· 5:91b

Ma namako (sea cucumber) ········· 7:45a

Man and vegetation in prehistoric Japan ········· 5:92b-96a
anthropogenic period ········· 5:95b-96a
late-glacial period ········· 5:93b
paleolithic period ········· 5:92b-94a
postglacial period ········· 5:93b-95b

Manase Dōsan 曲直瀬道三 ········· 5:96a

Manazuru ········· 真鶴 ········· 5:96a

Manchukuo ········· 満州国 ········· 5:96a-97b; 6:302a; 7:78a, 264b
Anti-Comintern Pact ········· 1:65b
"bandits" and border skirmishes ········· 5:97a
formation ········· 5:96b-97a
immigration ········· 5:97a
industries ········· 5:97a
land and people ········· 5:96b
Provisional Government of the Republic of China ········· 6:260a
Russia and Japan ········· 6:343a
South Manchuria Railway ········· 7:237a
war in the Pacific ········· 5:97a-97b
World War II role ········· 5:97a-97b

Manchuria
Bohai (Po-hai) ········· 1:159b
Concordia Society ········· 1:349a
Guandong Army ········· 3:64a-64b
Japanese conquest
Manchukuo ········· 5:96a-97b
U.S. reaction ········· 5:96b
Japanese immigration ········· 2:200b
Japanese takeover ········· 5:98a-98b
Manchurian Incident ········· 5:97b-99a
Toi ········· 8:38a
U.S.-Japanese confrontation ········· 3:321b

Manchurian Incident 満州事変 1:11a, 88a, 237b; 5:97b-99a; 7:74b, 92a, 199a, 228a, 251b; 8:271b
background ········· 5:97b-98a
colonial rule in Korea ········· 4:283b
Dai Jitao (Tai Chi-t'ao) ········· 2:59a
foreign trade ········· 2:320a
freedom of speech restrictions ········· 2:339a
Grew, Joseph Clark ········· 3:62a
Inukai Tsuyoshi ········· 3:326a
Itagaki Seishirō ········· 3:349a
Kellogg-Briand Pact ········· 4:191a
League of Nations ········· 4:373b
Lytton Commission ········· 5:76b
military operations ········· 5:98a-98b
Puyi (P'u-i) ········· 6:271a
Russia and Japan ········· 6:343a
Shanghai Incident ········· 7:77b-78a
Shidehara Kijūrō ········· 7:89a
significance ········· 5:99a
socio-political context ········· 2:250a
takeover ········· 5:98a-98b
Tatekawa Yoshitsugu ········· 7:349a
Tripartite Pact ········· 8:107a
Uchida Kōsai ········· 8:123b
United Kingdom ········· 8:152a
Wakatsuki Reijirō ········· 8:219a
women's suffrage ········· 8:268b

Manchurian Industrial Development Company ········· 7:237b

Manchurian-Mongolian Independence Movement ········· 5:99a-99b
Koiso Kuniaki ········· 4:250b

Mandala ········· 曼荼羅 ·· 1:188a, 196a; 5:99b-100b
Dainichi ("Great Sun") ········· 2:64b
Japanese ········· 5:100a-100b
meanings ········· 5:99b
Ryōbu mandara ········· 6:347b-351b
Shingon sect ········· 7:113b-115a
types ········· 5:99b-100a
general ········· 5:99a
Kongōkai mandara · 5:100a; 6:349a-351a
Taizō mandara ········· 5:100a; 6:348a-349a

Mandara. *See* **Mandala**

Mandarin duck [(oshidori) *Aix galericulata*] ········· 5:100b-101b

Mandokoro ········· 政所 · 5:101b; 7:97b
keishi ········· 4:190a
Minamoto no Yoritomo ········· 4:122a
Ōe no Hiromoto ········· 6:67a
proclamations ········· 4:90a

Manekineko ········· 5:*101a*, 101b

Manekogane ········· 4:22b

Man'en Kembei Shisetsu ········· 万延遣米使節 ········· 8:168b

Manga ········· 5:101b-102a
Ancient period ········· 5:101b-102a
Edo period ········· 5:102a
Hokusai ········· 5:*101a*
Middle Ages ········· 5:102a
modern times ········· 5:102a

Mange jigoku ········· 万花地獄 ········· 4:166a

Manginshū ········· 漫吟集 ········· 4:188a

Manila Declaration ········· 7:236a

Manji ········· 卍 ········· 7:342b

Manjirō, John ········· 5:313a

Manjushage ········· 3:131a

Mannensha ········· 1:17a

Manners. *See* **Etiquette**

Mannō Pond ········· 満濃池 ········· 5:102a

Manor Regulation Edit of 902 ········· 4:364a

Mansai ········· 満済 ········· 2:57b; 5:102a-102b

Mansaku ········· 8:255a

Manshū Jihen. 満州事変 *See* **Manchurian Incident**

Manshūkoku. 満州国 *See* **Manchukuo**

Mantetsu. *See* **South Manchuria Railway**

Mantra ········· 5:102b
Shingon sect ········· 7:113b

Manufacturing ········· 7:47b
distribution system ········· 2:119b
industrial robots ········· 3:298b-299a
industrial structure ········· 3:300b-301b
iron
Tetsuzan hitsuyō kiji ········· 7:348a
light vs heavy ········· 3:300b-301b

Manuscripts ········· 1:152a
binding ········· 1:153a-153b
paper ········· 1:153b
script styles ········· 1:153b

Man'yō Botanical Gardens ········· 4:257a

Man'yō daishō ki 万葉代匠記 4:188a, 258a

Man'yōgana ········· 万葉仮名 · 4:131b, *133a*; 5:109a-109b

Man'yōkō ········· 万葉考 ········· 4:129b

Man'yōshū ········· 万葉集 1:151b, 165b, 180b; 5:26a, 28a-28b, 102b-111a; 7:96a-96b, 131a; 8:286b
anonymous poems and problem of social range ········· 5:108b-109a
chōka ········· 1:299b
commentaries ········· 4:188a, 198b
compilation ········· 2:352b
content and structure ········· 5:105a-107a
Book 1 ········· 5:105a
Book 2 ········· 5:105a-105b
Book 3 ········· 5:105b
Book 4 ········· 5:105b
Book 5 ········· 5:105b
Book 6 ········· 5:105b
Book 7 ········· 5:105b-106a
Book 8 ········· 5:106a
Book 9 ········· 5:106a
Book 10 ········· 5:106a
Books 11 and 12 ········· 5:106a
Book 13 ········· 5:106a-106b
Book 14 ········· 5:106b
Book 15 ········· 5:106b
Book 16 ········· 5:106b-107a
Book 17 ········· 5:107a
Book 18 ········· 5:107a
Book 19 ········· 5:107a
Book 20 ········· 5:107a
decipherment and exegesis ········· 5:109b-111a
early Japanese song ········· 2:137a, 138a-138b
firefly viewing ········· 2:280b
folk songs ········· 2:301b
Fujiwarakyō references ········· 2:350a
Fujiwara no Toshinari ········· 2:357b
historical context ········· 5:103a-105a
Japanese language, history ········· 4:28b
Japanese language studies ········· 4:31a
Kada no Azumamaro lectures ········· 4:100b
kakekotoba ········· 4:115b
Kakinomoto no Hitomaro ········· 4:117a
Kamo no Mabuchi ········· 4:129a
Keichū's study ········· 4:258a
Kodai kenyū ········· 4:240b
Kojiki quotations ········· 4:251b
literary analysis ········· 2:346b
literary criticism ········· 5:13b
major poets ········· 5:107a-108b
Kakinomoto no Hitomaro 4:117a; 5:107b
Kasa no Kanamura ········· 4:161a; 5:107b
Nukata no Ōkimi ········· 5:107a-107b; 6:44a
Ōtomo no Sakanoue no Iratsume ········· 5:108a-108b; 6:131a
Ōtomo no Tabito ········· 5:108a; 6:131b
Ōtomo no Yakamochi ········· 5:108b; 6:131b
Takahashi no Mushimaro ·· 5:107b-108a; 7:313a

Tanabe no Fubito Sakimaro ······ **5**:108a
Yamabe no Akahito ····· **5**:107b; **8**:287b
Yamanoue no Okura ············ **5**:108a; **8**:302a-303a
Man'yō writing system ······· **5**:109a-109b
Motoori Norinaga ·············· **5**:257b
matsuri ························ **2**:253b
mythology ··················· **5**:292a-292b
nature in ······················ **5**:357b
Ōnakatomi no Yoshinobu ·········· **6**:105b
orthography ····················· **4**:134b
pheasants ······················· **6**:182b
poetry of sakimori ··················· **7**:2a
poets ··························· **5**:28a
prosodic features ············ **5**:104a-104b
sakimori uta ··················· **7**:2a-2b
Sano no Chigami no Otome ········ **7**:15b
Sasaki Nobutsuna ················· **7**:23a
scholarship ····················· **5**:109a
Senkaku's study of ················ **7**:66a
Shimokōbe Chōryū's research ····· **7**:105a
Tachibana Akemi ············ **7**:291b-292a
Tayasu Munetake ················· **7**:359a
thought and culture ··············· **8**:25b
title and compilation ············· **5**:103a
Tokoyo ························· **8**:44b
travel diaries ···················· **8**:104b
waka ··························· **8**:204a
women in Japan ·················· **8**:258a
writing system ··················· **4**:131b
Man'yōshū kogi
··············· 万葉集古義 ········ **4**:128a
Man'yōshū ryakuge
··············· 万葉集略解 ········ **4**:167b
Manza Hot Spring
··············· 万座温泉 ········ **5**:111a
Manzai ··················· **5**:111a; **7**:250a
Manzai kyōkashū
··············· 万載狂歌集 ········ **4**:157a
Manzanar Relocation Center **5**:111a-111b
Mao Zedong (Mao Tse-tung) ····· **1**:289a; **5**:111b
Maples [(kaede; momiji) *Acer* spp.]
··························· **5**:111b-112a
Maple Viewing at Takao ·········· **4**:150a
Mappō. *See* **Eschatology**
Maps ··················· **2**:65a; **5**:112a-112b
cartographers
Inō Tadataka ················· **3**:309a
Nagakubo Sekisui ·········· **5**:301b-302a
Dai Nihon enkai jissoku zenzu ········ **5**:*112b*
Marathons ···················· **5**:112b
March 15th Incident ·· **5**:112a-113b; **7**:99b, 251b
Shinjinkai ······················ **7**:115b
Tanaka Giichi ·············· **7**:336a-336b
Tanno Setsu ···················· **7**:344a
"Thought Criminal" Probation Law · **8**:29a
Watanabe Masanosuke ············ **8**:236a
March Incident ·· 三月事件 ··· **5**:112b-113a
Koiso Kuniaki's role ·············· **4**:250b
Tatekawa Yoshitsugu ·············· **7**:349a
Ugaki Kazushige ················· **8**:130b
Marco Polo Bridge Incident ······ 蘆溝橋事件 ······· **3**:201b; **5**:113b; **7**:199a, 228a; **8**:272a, 344a
Tanggu (Tangku) Truce ······ **7**:340b-341a
Marebito ·············· 客人 · **5**:113b; **8**:44b
Marē Oki Kaisen
··············· マレー沖海戦 ········ **7**:234b
Marē Ran'in kikō
········· マレー蘭印紀行 ········ **4**:139a
Mari ··············· 毬(鞠) ········ **4**:191a
Maria Luz Incident ··· **5**:113b-114a; **6**:178b
DeLong, Charles E. ················ **2**:84a
Terashima Munenori ··············· **8**:12a
Maria no kubi · マリアの首 ········ **7**:335b
shingeki ························ **7**:113a
Marijuana ······················ **2**:134a-134b
Marine accidents inquiry ·········· **5**:114a
Marine insurance ··················· **3**:316b
Marine mammals ················ **5**:114a
Marine parks ···················· **5**:114b
Ocean resource development ······· **6**:59a
Marine products, processing of ··· **7**:105b
Marine resources
Ocean resource development ··· **6**:58b-59a
Marine Science and Technology Center
Ocean resource development ······· **6**:59a
Marine transportation ·············· **8**:102a
Maritime Guard ···················· **7**:59a
Maritime policies ··················· **3**:3b
Maritime Self Defense Forces ·· **7**:60a-60b
Marketing interdependency ········ **2**:318a
Markets ······················ **5**:114b-115a
consumer ························ **2**:17b
Market towns ··· **2**:148a-148b; **5**:115a-115b
premodern ······················ **2**:148a
urban planning ··················· **8**:179b
Marquat, William Frederic ········· **5**:115b
Marriage ······················ **5**:115b-118a
adoptive ···················· **2**:242a-242b
age for ···························· **5**:4b
"arranged" (miai) ················ **5**:320b
changes ···················· **5**:116a-116b
common-law ················ **1**:340a-340b
consanguineous ··················· **4**:38a
dissolving ······················· **5**:118b
Edo period ······················ **5**:117a
family decisions ············· **2**:243b-244a
go-betweens, role of ···· **5**:116a, 117a-118a
housewives ················· **3**:241a-242a
husbands ························ **3**:242a
ie ······························· **5**:116a
industrialization ············ **5**:117a-118a
investigations ···················· **1**:217a
legal requirements ··········· **5**:118a-118b
love ···························· **2**:244a
"love" (ren'ai kekkon) ············· **5**:320b
matrilocal ······················· **5**:262b
matrilocal (mukoirikon) ············ **5**:262b
miai ···························· **5**:166a
minors ··························· **1**:16a
modern trends ·············· **5**:117a-118a
permanent ·················· **5**:116b-117a
polygamous ················· **5**:116a-116b
regulation ······················· **5**:117a
social factors ·············· **5**:115a-116b
traditionally arranged ············· **2**:244a
Marriage alliances ············ **5**:116b-117a
Marriage customs
abalones ························· **1**:1b
yomeirikon ······················ **8**:336a
Marriage interview ··················· **5**:4b
Marriage law ················ **5**:118a-118b
Marriage negotiations ········ **5**:320b-321a
Marshal ························ **5**:118b
Martha Graham Dance Company ··· **2**:76a
Martial arts ·················· **5**:118b-120a
aikidō ···························· **1**:34a
bugei jūhappan ··················· **1**:206a
characteristics ···················· **5**:119a
essence ·························· **5**:119b
iai ······························ **3**:253a
implements for training of samurai **1**:206a
jūdō ·························· **4**:82a-83a
karate ······················ **4**:158a-159a
kendō ······················ **4**:195b-196b
kusarigamajutsu ················· **4**:319a
kyūdō ······················ **4**:340a-340b
methods of practice ·········· **5**:119b-120a
philosophy ················· **5**:119a-119b
skills ···························· **5**:119b
sōjutsu ·························· **7**:224a
spiritual training ············ **5**:119a-119b
Martial law ······················ **5**:120a
Marubashi Chūya
················· 丸橋忠弥 ··· **5**:120a-120b
Maruba shimotsuke ················ **7**:107a
Marubeni Corporation ·············· **5**:120b
Marudai ························ **4**:308a
Marudai Food Co, Ltd ············· **5**:120b
Marugame ············ 丸亀 **4**:103b; **5**:120b
Maruhon-mono ···· 丸本物 ···· **4**:91b, 93b
dialogue ·························· **4**:94a
Maruichi Steel Tube, Ltd ····· **5**:120b-121a
Marui Co, Ltd ···················· **5**:121a
Marumino ························ **7**:249b
Maruoka Hideko · 丸岡秀子 ··· **5**:121a-121b
Maruoka Kyūka ·· 丸岡九華 ········ **4**:198b
Maruyama Hiroshi · 丸山博 ········ **5**:251a
Maruyama Kaoru ·· 丸山薫 ········ **5**:121b
Maruyama Kenji · 丸山健二 **1**:209a; **5**:121b
Maruyama Masao
················ 丸山真男 · **5**:121b; **6**:73b
gekokujō ·························· **3**:16a
Maruyama Ōkyo · 円山応挙 **1**:156b; **5**:*121a*, 121b-122a; **7**:17b
Maruyama-Shijō school
·············· 円山四条派 ·· **5**:122a-122b
Atomi Kakei ····················· **1**:115a
Hiroshige ······················· **3**:148a
Kanō Tan'yū ····················· **4**:150a
Kōno Bairei ················ **4**:178b, 272a
Maruyama Ōkyo ············ **5**:121b-122a
Matsumura Goshun ················ **5**:138a
modern painting ················· **6**:155b
painting ························ **6**:153b
Takeuchi Seihō ·················· **7**:326a
Tani Bunchō ····················· **7**:341a
Terazaki Kōgyō ··················· **8**:13a
Uemura Shōen ···················· **8**:128a
ukiyo-e ························· **8**:144a
Maruzen Co, Ltd ················· **5**:122b
Maruzen Oil Co, Ltd ······· **5**:122b; **6**:182a
Daikyō Oil Co, Ltd ··········· **2**:60b-61a
Marxism ····· **2**:102b-103a, 142b; **4**:11b, 85b
historiography ·············· **3**:157b-158a
philosophical aspects ········ **5**:231a-232a
postwar adoption ················· **3**:203b
pragmatism ······················ **6**:232b
Masakadoki. 将門記 *See* ***Shōmonki***
Masamune Hakuchō
················ 正宗白鳥 ········ **5**:13a, 122b-123a
middle years and turn to drama ··· **5**:123a
move to Tōkyō ··················· **5**:123a
Shinshichō ······················· **7**:124b
Masanobu. 正信 *See* **Kanō Masanobu**
Masaoka Shiki ··· 正岡子規 · **4**:103a; **5**:11b, 123b-124a, 315a; **7**:27b, 99b, 311b; **8**:216b
Araragi ················· **1**:74b; **5**:19b
haiku ······················ **3**:78b-79a
haiku reform ······················ **3**:79b
Hototogisu ················ **3**:237b; **5**:20a
Itō Sachio ······················· **3**:355b
Nagatsuka Takashi ················ **5**:307b
Shin kokinshū ··················· **7**:120b
Masculine language ·········· **5**:124a-125a
Mashi ··························· **1**:153b
Mashiko (town) ······ 益子 ········ **5**:125a
Mashiko ware ······ 益子焼 ········ **5**:125a
teapot ·························· **2**:*294b*
Mashū, Lake ······· 摩周湖 ·· **5**:*124b*, 125b
Masks ················ **1**:197a; **5**:125b-127b
festivals ···················· **5**:126b-127a
Karura, gigaku mask ·············· **5**:*125a*
Katen, gyōdō mask ················ **5**:*126a*
Kobuaku, kyōgen mask ············ **5**:*127b*
Koomote, Nō mask ················ **5**:*126b*
museums ························ **5**:280a
Okame and Hyottoko ··············· **6**:80a
Okina, Nō mask ·················· **5**:*127a*
ryōō bugaku mask ················· **5**:*125b*

Mason, Luther Whiting · **5**:127b-128a, 286a
Massage
amma method · **1**:53a
shiatsu vs · **7**:83b
Mass Communication Ethics Group · **1**:255a
Mass communications · **5**:128a-129b
broadcasting · **1**:171b-173a
education, culture and society **5**:129a-129b
historical development · **5**:128a
international communications **3**:318b-319a
journalists and their audience · **5**:128-129a
news, opinion and politics · **5**:129a
newspapers · **5**:369a-370a
structures and functions · **5**:128a-128b
treatment of law · **4**:380a
Massey, Elizabeth and Joseph · **4**:41b
Master of Go, The · **4**:176a
Masu · **7**:5b
Masuchi Yōjirō 増地庸治郎 · **5**:129b
Masuda 益田 **5**:129b; **7**:101a
Masuda Takashi · 益田孝 · **5**:129b-130a
Masugata (castle entrance) · 枡形 · **1**:248b
Masugatamon · **3**:13a
Masukagami · 増鏡 · **5**:130a
Masumoto Hakaru · 増本量 · **5**:130a
Masumura Yasuzō · 増村保造 · **2**:272b, 273b
Masutomi Hot Spring · 増富温泉 · **5**:130a
Masuzawa Dam · 桝沢ダム · **7**:116a
Matabei. 又兵衛 *See* **Iwasa Matabei**
Matagi · **5**:130a
Matamono · 又者 · **1**:130a
Matatabi-mono · 股旅物 · **3**:108a
Matchlocks. *See* **Hinawajū**
Materialism Study Society · **5**:231b
Material on the History of Northern Japan and Her Relations with the Asiatic Continent and Russia · **6**:232b
Mathematicians
Hironaka Heisuke · **3**:147b
Kakeya Sōichi · **4**:116b
Kikuchi Dairoku · **4**:206a
Kodaira Kunihiko · **4**:241a
Ogura Kinnosuke · **6**:71a
Oka Kiyoshi · **6**:79b
Seki Takakazu · **7**:57b
Shōda Kenjirō · **7**:154b
Takagi Teiji · **7**:311a
Takebe Katahiro · **7**:321b
Yoshida Mitsuyoshi · **8**:342b
Mathematics
abacus · **1**:1a
modern · **5**:130a-131a
premodern. *See* **Wasan**
school curriculum · **7**:35a
Taisei sankyō · **7**:321b
Takagi class-field theory · **7**:311a
yōsan · **8**:231a
Matrix Realm · **7**:310a
Matsu. *See* **Pines**
Matsubame-mono (adaptations of Nō drama) · 松羽目物 · **5**:235a
Matsubara · 松原 · **5**:131a
Matsuda Eiko · 松田英子 · **2**:*275a*
Matsudaira family. *See* **Tokugawa family**
Matsudaira Hirotada · 松平広忠 · **8**:49a
Matsudaira Ietada · 松平家忠 · **5**:131a
Matsudaira Katamori · 松平容保 · **5**:131a-131b
Matsudaira Keiei. *See* **Matsudaira Yoshinaga**
Matsudaira Nobutsuna · 松平信綱 · **5**:131b
Matsudaira Sadanobu · 松平定信 · **5**:49a, 131b-132a; **7**:84a, 87a
bakuhan state · **3**:189b
Bunka and Bunsei eras · **1**:211b
education · **2**:174a
Hayashi Jussai · **3**:116b-117a
hitogaeshi · **3**:208a
Kansei Reforms · **4**:152a
Matsudaira Tadanao · 松平忠直 · **5**:132a
Matsudaira Tadayoshi · 松平忠吉 · **5**:132b; **7**:56b
Matsudaira Yoshinaga · 松平慶永 **5**:132b; **8**:302b
Matsuda Masaki · 松田正恭 · **5**:135a
"Matsuda reorganization" · **6**:158a
Matsudo · 松戸 · **5**:132b
Matsue · 松江 **5**:132b; **7**:100b
Matsue Hot Spring 松江温泉 · **7**:115a
Matsue Plain · 松江平野 · **5**:133a
Matsue Shigeyori 松江重頼 · **5**:133a
Matsugaoka Bunko · 松ケ岡文庫 · **5**:133a
Matsui Sumako · 松井須磨子 **4**:181b; **5**:133a; **7**:31a
Matsukata fiscal policy · **2**:361a; **5**:133a-134b
financial crisis of 1878-1880 · **5**:133b
impact · **5**:134a-134b
industrial revolution in Japan · **3**:298a
kan'ei jigyō haraisage · **4**:138a
Matsukata Reform · **5**:133b-134a
national banks · **5**:336b
Matsukata Masayoshi · 松方正義 **1**:140b; **3**:194a; **5**:134a-136a; **7**:66b, 263b
Aoki Shūzō · **1**:69a
Chichibu Incident · **1**:271b
Kabasan Incident · **4**:89a
Kabayama Sukenori · **4**:89b
Kiyoura Keigo · **4**:233a
military career · **5**:135a
political career · **5**:135b-136a
Shimpotō · **7**:108b
Shinagawa Yajirō · **7**:109a
Matsukawa Incident · 松川事件 · **5**:136a-136b; **7**:25a, 147b
Hirotsu Kazuo · **3**:151a
Shimoyama Incident · **7**:107b
Tanaka Kōtarō · **7**:337b
Matsukaze · 松風 · **4**:135b
Matsukura Shigemasa · 松倉重政 · **5**:136b-137a
Matsumae (town) · 松前 · **5**:137a
Matsumae family · 松前氏 · **5**:137a
Russia · **6**:340b
Matsumoto (city) · 松本 · **5**:137b
Matsumoto Basin 松本盆地 · **5**:137b
Matsumoto Castle · 松本城 · **5**:137b
Matsumoto Folk Arts Museum · **5**:137b
Matsumoto Hikoshichirō · 松本彦七郎 · **1**:76a
Matsumoto Jōji · 松本烝治 · **2**:3b, 319a; **5**:137b
Matsumoto Kōshirō VIII 松本幸四郎(八代) · **4**:*94b*
Matsumoto Nobuhiro · 松本信広 · **4**:20a
Matsumoto Seichō · 松本清張 **5**:138a; **6**:268b; **7**:103b
Shimoyama Incident · **7**:107a-107b
Matsumura Akira · 松村瞭 · **4**:35a
Matsumura Goshun · 松村呉春 · **1**:211a, 224b; **5**:138a
Kōno Bairei influenced by · **4**:272a
Matsumura Jinzō 松村任三 · **5**:138a
Matsumura Keibun · 松村景文 · **5**:138a-138b
Matsumura Kenzō · 松村謙三 · **5**:138b
Matsumushisō [(Japanese scabiosa) *Scabiosa japonica*] · **5**:138b
Matsunaga Memorial Gallery · **5**:138b
Matsunaga Sekigo · 松永尺五 · **5**:138b; **7**:94b
Fujiwara Seika · **2**:358b
Kaibara Ekiken · **4**:108b
Matsunaga Teitoku · 松永貞徳 · **2**:77a-77b; **5**:18a, 138b-139a, 317b; **6**:298b; **7**:96a
haikai · **3**:79a
Matsunaga Yasuzaemon · 松永安左衛門 **4**:205b; **5**:139a
Matsu no koe · 松の声 · **4**:102b
Matsu no uchi · 松の内 · **8**:110b
Matsuo Bashō. 松尾芭蕉 *See* **Bashō**
Matsuoka Eikyū · 松岡映丘 · **5**:139a
Kaburagi Kiyokata · **4**:100b
Matsuoka Gentatsu · 松岡玄達 · **1**:75b
Matsuoka Joan · 松岡恕庵 · **5**:139a
Matsuoka Komakichi · 松岡駒吉 · **5**:139a
Matsuoka Yōsuke · 松岡洋右 · **5**:139a-139b
League of Nations · **4**:373b
Matsuo Munefusa · 松尾宗房 · **1**:144a
Matsuratō · 松浦党 · **5**:139b-140a
Matsuri · **1**:22b-23a; **2**:252b-258a; **7**:139a-139b
dancing · **2**:255b
essentials · **2**:254a-255b
communion · **5**:331a-331b
offerings · **2**:254b
purificatory asceticism · **7**:139a
hare and ke · **7**:362a
modern society · **2**:258a
seasons · **2**:254a
ujigami · **8**:131a-131b
ujiko · **2**:255b
village and city festivals · **2**:255b
See also **Festivals**
Matsusaka · 松阪 · **5**:140a
Matsushima · 松島 · **5**:140a, *140b*
Matsushima Bay · 松島湾 · **5**:140a
Matsushiro · 松代 · **5**:140a
Matsushita Communication Industrial Co, Ltd · **5**:140a
Matsushita Daizaburō · 松下大三郎 · **5**:140a-140b
Matsushita Electric Industrial Co, Ltd · **4**:340b-341a; **5**:140b; **7**:19a
Matsushita Electric Trading Co, Ltd · **5**:140b
Matsushita Electric Works, Ltd · **5**:140b-141a
Matsushita Kenrin · 松下見林 · **3**:347b
Matsushita Kōnosuke · 松下幸之助 · **5**:141a
Matsushita-Kotobuki Electronics Industries, Ltd · **5**:141a-141b
Matsushita Reiki Co, Ltd · **5**:141b
Matsuura · 松浦 · **5**:141b
Matsuura Historical Museum · **5**:276b

Matsuura Takeshirō ··· 松浦武四郎 ··· 5:141b
Matsuyama ··· 松山 ··· 5:141b
Dōgo Hot Spring ··· 5:*141a*
Matsuyama Plain 松山平野 ··· 5:141b
Matsuyama Zenzō ··· 松山善三 ··· 5:141b-142a
Matsuzaka. 松阪 *See* **Matsusaka**
Matsuzakaya Co, Ltd ··· 5:142a
Matsuzaki tenjin engi ··· 松崎天神縁起 ··· 7:42b
"Matters to be announced" ··· 6:67b
Mattō ··· 松任 ··· 5:142a
Mawaributai ··· 4:91b, 95b
Mawari-dōrō ··· 5:142a
Mawashi ··· 7:271b
Mayama Seika ··· 真山青果 ··· 5:142a
shin kabuki ··· 4:92a
Shinseisakuza ··· 7:124a
May Day Incident ··· 5:142a-142b; 7:252a
Mayet, Paul ··· 3:27a; 5:142b
May 15th Incident ··· 五・一五事件 ··· 5:142b-143a
Aikyōjuku ··· 1:34b
Inukai Tsuyoshi ··· 3:326b
Shimpeitai Incident ··· 7:108b
Tachibana Kōzaburō ··· 7:292a
May Fourth Movement 五・四運動 ··· 1:288a; 5:143a-143b
Kita Ikki ··· 4:226a
Nishihara loans ··· 6:16a
Shandong (Shantung) Question ··· 7:77b
Mayoke ··· 5:143b
Mayors ··· 3:56b
May 30th Incident ··· 五・三〇事件 ··· 5:143b; 7:78a
Mayuzumi Toshirō · 黛敏郎 ··· 5:144a
Mazaki Jinzaburō ··· 真崎甚三郎 ··· 5:144a
February 26th Incident ··· 2:250a
Hayashi Senjūrō ··· 3:117b
Kōdōha leader ··· 4:243a
Mazda ··· 6:339b
Mazushiki shinto ··· 貧しき信徒 ··· 8:284a
Mead, George H. ··· 2:184b
Meakandake ··· 雌阿寒岳 ··· 5:144a
Meakashi ··· 目明 5:144a; 8:338b
Meanings of Sound, Word, and Reality, The ··· 7:114b
Measure
architectural units ··· 1:82b
weights and measures ··· 8:239b-240a
Meat packing industries
Itō Ham Provisions Co, Ltd ··· 3:352a
Marudai Food Co, Ltd ··· 5:120b
Nippon Meat Packers, Inc ··· 6:11a
Prima Meat Packers, Ltd ··· 6:239b
Meckel, Klemens Wilhelm Jakob ·· 1:86b; 4:241a; 5:144a
Medake *(Arundinaria simonii)* ··· 1:136a
Medals of honor ··· 5:144a-144b
Mēdē Jiken ·· メーデー事件 ·· 5:142a-142b
Median Tectonic line ··· 4:8b
Mediation
contemporary law ··· 4:379b
labor
Tripartite commissions ··· 4:351b
litigation vs ··· 4:370b
Medical and health insurance ··· 4:353a; 5:144b-145b
financing ··· 5:145a
health insurance society ··· 5:145a
national ··· 5:339a-339b
structure ··· 5:144b
Medical care
health care system ··· 3:119b-120b
Medical research. *See* **Medicine**
Medicine ··· 5:145b-152a
acupuncture ··· 1:10b
diseases ··· 5:147b-149a
characteristics ··· 5:147b-149a
common ··· 5:147b
drugs ··· 5:150a-150b
approval and reevaluation ··· 5:150a
consumption and related problems ··· 5:150a-150b
manufacture and supply ··· 5:150a
euthanasia ··· 2:235b-236a
general ··· 5:145b
history ··· 5:145b-147a
Chinese medicine and Western medicine (16th-19th centuries) ··· 5:146b-147a
classicist school (17th-19th centuries) ··· 5:146a-146b
from 8th century ··· 7:170a
introduction of Chinese ··· 5:146a
latter-day school (16th-19th centuries) ··· 5:146a
modernization ··· 5:147a-147b
industrial
occupational diseases ··· 6:55b
Kampō ··· 5:150b-151b
Old-Age Welfare Law ··· 6:100a
physicians
Adachi Buntarō ··· 1:11a
Aoyama Tanemichi ··· 1:71a
Asada Gōryū ··· 8:292a
Asada Sōhaku ··· 1:92a
Bälz, Erwin von ··· 1:135b
Dohi Keizō ··· 2:126a
Furuhata Tanemoto ··· 2:371b-372a
Gotō Konzan ··· 3:53a
Hanaoka Seishū ··· 3:94b
Iinuma Yokusai ··· 3:263b
Imamura Arao ··· 3:273b
Inada Ryōkichi ··· 3:282a
Itō Gemboku ··· 3:352a
Kaempfer, Engelbert ··· 4:101b-102a
Kagawa Gen'etsu ··· 4:102b
Kagawa Shūtoku ··· 4:103b
Katsunuma Seizō ··· 4:172a
Katsuragawa Hoshū ··· 4:173a
Kumagai Taizō ··· 4:305a
Kure Ken ··· 4:312b
Kurokawa Toshio ··· 4:316b
Maeno Ryōtaku ··· 5:82a-82b
Manase Dōsan ··· 5:96a
Mitsuda Kensuke ··· 5:209b
Mitsukuri Gempo ··· 5:213b
Miura Kinnosuke ··· 5:215b
Nagoya Gen'i ··· 5:309b
Nakagawa Jun'an ··· 5:313a
Ogata Kōan ··· 6:69a
Ogata Koreyoshi ··· 6:69a
Ogino Ginko ··· 6:70a-70b
Ogino Kyūsaku ··· 6:70b
Okinaka Shigeo ··· 6:84b
Shimazono Junjirō ··· 7:101b
Shioda Hiroshige ··· 7:140a
Sugita Gempaku ··· 7:258b
Taki Mototaka ··· 7:327a
Tamba Yasuyori ··· 7:333b
Tashiro Sanki ··· 7:347b
Udagawa Yōan ··· 8:125b
Yamawaki Tōyō ··· 8:311b-312a
Yoshimasu Tōdō ··· 8:347b
Yoshioka Yayoi ··· 8:349b
public health ··· 5:149a-150a
aging ··· 5:149a
death trends ··· 5:149a-149b
future problems ··· 5:149b-150a
Health Service System ··· 5:149a
prevention of infectious diseases · 5:149b
Public Health Service ··· 5:149b
research ··· 5:151b-152a
smallpox vaccine ··· 3:352a
traditional ··· 5:150b-151b
characteristics ··· 5:151a
examination methods ··· 5:151b
febrile disease ··· 5:151b
shiatsu ··· 7:83b
Shō ··· 5:151a-151b
two major schools ··· 5:150b-151a
venereal disease ··· 8:189b
Medieval ceramics. *See* **Ceramics**
Medieval literature. *See* **Literature**
Meditation (zazen) ··· 8:*372b*
music ··· 7:75b
Medium (shamanism) ··· 7:76b
Megijima ··· 女木島 ··· 5:152a
Meguro Ward ··· 目黒区 ··· 5:152a
Meian ··· 明暗 ··· 5:350b
Meiboku sendai hagi ··· 伽羅先代萩 ··· 4:94a, *94b*
Meibutsugire ··· 5:152b
Meidensha Electric Mfg Co, Ltd ·· 5:152b
Meigen ··· 鳴弦 ··· 5:152b
Meigetsuki ··· 明月記 2:354b; 5:152b
Meigō ōrai ··· 明衡往来 ··· 2:350a; 5:152b-153a
ōraimono ··· 6:115b
Meigō shōsoku. *See* **Meigō ōrai**
Meiji, Emperor ··· 明治天皇 ··· 5:*153a*, 153b-154a; 7:27a
Iwakura mission ··· 3:358b-360a
plot to assassinate ··· 3:135a
Meiji Bijutsukai (Meiji Fine Arts Society) ··· 6:155b
Meiji Bunka Kenkyūkai ··· 4:211a
Meiji bunka zenshū ··· 明治文化全集 ··· 8:349a
Meiji Canal ··· 明治用水 ··· 5:153a
Meiji Colonization Company ··· 6:178b
Meiji Constitution. *See* **Constitution; Constitution of the Empire of Japan**
Meiji Enlightenment ··· 5:154a; 7:54b
Mori Arinori ··· 5:249a
shogunate missions to the West ··· 7:161b
technological innovation ··· 7:371b
Meiji era ··· 明治時代 ··· 6:176a
Meiji Fine Arts Society (Meiji Bijutsukai) ··· 8:328a
Meiji Gakuin University ··· 5:154a; 6:258a
Hepburn, James Curtis ··· 3:127a-127b
Meiji government. *See* Government, modern
Meiji history. *See* **History of Japan**
Meiji ichidai onna 明治一代女 ··· 7:108a
Meiji Ishin. *See* **Meiji Restoration**
Meiji Jogakkō ··· 3:360b
Meiji Jūyonen no Seihen. *See* **Political Crisis of 1881**
Meiji Kempō ··· 明治憲法 ··· 2:1a-3b
Meiji Milk Products Co, Ltd ··· 5:154b
Meiji-mono ··· 2:271a
Meiji Mura ··· 明治村 ··· 5:*154b*
Meiji Mutual Life Insurance Co ··· 5:154b
Meijin ··· 名人 ··· 4:176a
Meiji no Mori Takao Quasi-National Park 明治の森高尾国定公園 ··· 7:317b
Meiji period ··· 明治時代 ··· 5:155a
Meiji Restoration (1868) ··· 明治維新 · 1:159b, 223a; 2:1a; 5:155a-160b; 7:30a, 7:31b, 102a
background ··· 5:155a-155b
chōnin ··· 1:301a
educational policies ··· 3:279a
emperor ··· 2:205b-206b
fudasashi ··· 2:340b
fukoku kyōhei ··· 2:360b
genrō ··· 3:21b
gesaku ··· 3:29a

Gobō no Keiji ··· **3**:38b
hambatsu ··· **3**:91b
impact of Ii Naosuke ··· **5**:156a-157a
industrialization ··· **4**:14a
interpretations ··· **5**:160a-160b
Iwakura Tomomi ··· **3**:360a
Japanese emigration ··· **4**:14a
Japanese language ··· **4**:24a
kōgi seitai ron used on the eve of ··· **4**:248b
Meiji, Emperor ··· **5**:153a
nationalism ··· **5**:342b
natural science ··· **5**:356b
Occupation ··· **6**:51a
Okinawa ··· **6**:87a
Ōkubo Toshimichi ··· **6**:93b
Opening of Japan ··· **6**:115a
painting ··· **6**:154a
peerage ··· **6**:170b
periodization ··· **6**:177a
provinces ··· **6**:260a
regional reform ··· **5**:158a-159a
religion ··· **6**:290b
restoration ··· **5**:159a-160a
rōnin ··· **6**:337a
Russo-Japanese War ··· **6**:347a
samurai ··· **7**:8b
Shinritsu Kōryō ··· **7**:124a
tattoos ··· **7**:350a-350b
technological development ··· **7**:368a
textiles ··· **8**:16a
Tōkyō ··· **8**:61b
"Union of Court and Shogunate" ··· **5**:157a-158a
World War II ··· **8**:271b
United Kingdom ··· **8**:151a
Meiji Seika Kaisha, Ltd ··· **5**:160b
Meiji Shrine ··· 明治神宮 ··· **5**:160b
Meiji Shrine games ··· **7**:243a
Meiji 6 Society ··· **5**:161a-161b
Meiji Sugar Mfg Co, Ltd ··· **5**:160b
Meiji University ··· **5**:160b-161a
Meiji Village Museum ··· **5**:278b
Meireki Fire ··· 明暦の大火 **4**:182a; **5**:161a; **8**:350a
Meirokusha ··· 明六社 ··· **5**:161a-161b
Meiroku zasshi (Journal of Meiji) ··· 明六雑誌 ··· **6**:246a
Meiryō kōhan ··· 明良洪範 · **4**:85a; **5**:161b
Meisaku gekijō (Masterpiece Theater) ··· 名作劇場 ··· **6**:275b
Meishi. *See* **Name cards**
Meishin Expressway ··· **4**:46b
Meisho-e (famous places) paintings ··· 名所絵 ··· **8**:309b
Meisho zue ··· 名所図絵 ··· **5**:161b-162a
Meitokuki ··· 明徳記 ··· **4**:84b
Meitoku Rebellion ··· 明徳の乱 ··· **5**:162a
Meitō Tax Evasion Case ··· **6**:201b
Meiwa Incident ·· 明和事件 **5**:162a; **8**:292b
Mekiki ··· **4**:177b
Membranophones ··· **5**:282b
Memorial services ··· **8**:319b
Memorial tablet (ihai) ··· **5**:5a
Memushiri kouchi 芽むしり仔撃ち · **6**:66a
Men ··· 面 ··· **8**:73a
Mencius ··· **4**:58a
Itō Jinsai's study ··· **4**:247b
Mendenhall, Thomas Corwin ··· **5**:162a
Mengjiang ··· **7**:201a
Menko ··· **5**:162b
Men's names ··· **5**:325a-326a
artistic and literary ··· **5**:325a-326a
Buddhist ··· **5**:325a-326a
until 8th century ··· **5**:325a-326a
premodern ··· **5**:325a-326a
scholars ··· **5**:325a-326a
Mental illness ··· **5**:162b-163b; **6**:261a
attitudes toward ··· **5**:163b
changes in symptoms over time ··· **5**:163a-163b
introduction ··· **5**:162b
social causes ··· **5**:162b-163a
Mental impairment ··· **2**:48a
Mentally Disabled Welfare Law ··· **7**:209b
Menuki ··· **4**:295b
Meoto-jawan ··· **5**:163b
Meoto zenzai (Marital Relations) ··· 夫婦善哉 ··· **8**:319b
Meranoshō ··· 米良荘 ··· **5**:164a
Merchant class ··· **1**:300b
Merchant guilds. *See* **Kabunakama**
Merchant houses ··· **2**:29b-30a; **6**:110a
Merciful Mother Kannon (Hibo kannon) ··· **4**:147a; **5**:*378b*
Mercury pollution ··· **6**:218a-218b
Merger, corporate ··· **5**:164a
regulation of ··· **1**:66a-66b
Meriyasu ··· **4**:99b
Merodorama ··· **2**:269b
Merrimac ··· **1**:175b
Merrymaking under the Cherry Blossoms ··· **4**:150a; **6**:*155a*
Meshi ··· めし **5**:164a; **5**:335a
Metabolist group ··· **4**:207b
Metal industries
Mitsubishi Metal Corporation ··· **5**:208a
Mitsui Mining & Smelting Co, Ltd · **5**:211b
Nippon Mining Co, Ltd ··· **6**:11a
Sumitomo Metal Mining Co, Ltd ·· **7**:269b
Tōhō Zinc Co, Ltd ··· **8**:37b-38a
Metallurgists
Masumoto Hakaru ··· **5**:130a
Mishima Tokushichi ··· **5**:199a
Murakami Takejirō ··· **5**:266b
Noro Kageyoshi ··· **6**:39a
Ōshima Takatō ··· **6**:126a
Metallurgy ··· **7**:266b
Metals and minerals ··· **5**:353b-354a
iron and steel ··· **3**:333a-333b
nonferrous ··· **6**:34b
manufacturers ··· **7**:268b-269a
Metalwork ··· **5**:164a, *164b*, 165a
folk craft ··· **2**:295b
"Metamorphosis" ··· **7**:109a
Metempsychosis ··· **1**:20a
Meteorological Agency ··· **5**:165a
typhoons ··· **8**:122b
Metric system ··· **8**:239b
Metropolitan Expressway Public Corporation ··· **5**:165a
expressways ··· **2**:238a
Metropolitan Police Department (MPD) ··· **8**:68a
Metsuke ··· 目付 ··· **5**:165a
Mexico and Japan ··· **5**:165b
diplomatic ties ··· **4**:369b
Meyasubako ··· 目安箱 ··· **5**:165b
Mi ··· **5**:165b
Miai ··· 見合 **2**:244a; **5**:166a
Mibuchi Tadahiko ··· 三淵忠彦 ··· **5**:166a
Mibudera ··· 壬生寺 ··· **5**:166a
Mibunkei ··· 身分刑 ··· **7**:140b
Mibu no Tadamine ··· 壬生忠岑 ·· **5**:166a-166b; **7**:13a
Kokinshū ··· **4**:254b
Mice. *See* **Rats and mice**
Michi ··· **5**:166b
ancient Japanese literature ··· **4**:258b
kogaku ··· **4**:247b
Michiko, Princess ··· 美智子妃 **3**:*277a*; **5**:166b
Michikusa ··· 道草 **4**:183a; **5**:350b
Michinoku no Kuni · 陸奥国 ··· **5**:289a-289b
Michiyukiburi ·· 道ゆきぶり ··· **3**:272b
Microeconomics ··· **2**:144b
Midagahara ··· 弥陀ヶ原 ··· **5**:166b
Midaregami ··· みだれ髪 ··· **8**:340a
Middle East and Japan ··· **5**:167a-167b
diplomatic relations ··· **3**:*322a-322b*
trade ··· **3**:*322a-322b*
Middle Kingdom, The ··· **8**:253b
Middle schools. *See* **Elementary and secondary education**
Midō Kampaku. 御堂関白 *See* **Fujiwara no Michinaga**
Midō Kampaku ki ··· 御堂関白記 **2**:353a; **4**:255b; **5**:167b
Midorikawa ··· 緑川 ··· **5**:167b
Midway, Battle of ··· ミッドウェー海戦 ·· **5**:167b, 307b
Mie ··· **4**:94a
Mieidō ··· **1**:182b
Mie Prefecture ··· 三重県 ··· **5**:167b-168a
Mifune Kyūzō ··· 三船久蔵 ··· **5**:168a
Mifune Toshirō 三船敏郎 ··· **2**:*270b*, *271a*; **5**:168a-168b
Migration ··· **4**:15a
Migration routes ··· **4**:33b
Migyōsho ··· **2**:*98a-98b*
Mihara ··· 三原 ··· **5**:168b-169a
Miharayama ··· 三原山 **2**:347b; **5**:169a
Mihashi Michiya 三橋美智也 ··· **6**:355a
Miho no Matsubara ··· 三保ノ松原 **5**:169a; **7**:*103a*, 104a
Mihonoseki ··· 美保関 ··· **5**:169a
Mihoro Dam ··· 御母衣ダム ·· **2**:73b; **5**:169a
Miidera ··· 三井寺 ·· **5**:169a; **7**:91a
ōtsu-e ··· **6**:133b
Miike Coal Mines 三池炭鉱 ·· **1**:74b; **2**:31b; **5**:169b
Dan Takuma ··· **2**:77b
Miike strike 三池争議 · **4**:349b; **5**:169b-170a
Sakisaka Itsurō ··· **7**:3a
Miira no kuchibeni ··· 木乃伊の口紅 ··· **7**:334b
Mikage ··· 御影 ··· **5**:170a
Mikagura ··· 御神楽 ··· **4**:107a
Mikami Akira ··· 三上章 ··· **5**:170a
Mikami Sanji ··· 三上参次 ··· **5**:170a
Mikan [(citrus) family Rutaceae] ··· **5**:170a-170b
Mikasa, Prince ··· 三笠宮 ··· **5**:170b
Mikasa (city) ··· 三笠 ··· **5**:170b
Mikata Five Lakes ··· 三方五湖 ··· **5**:170b
Mikatagahara ··· 三方ヶ原 ··· **6**:63a
Mikatahara ··· 三方原 ··· **5**:170b
Mikawa Bay ··· 三河湾 ··· **5**:170b
Mikawa monogatari ··· 三河物語 ··· **5**:170b-171a
Ōkubo Hikozaemon ··· **6**:93b
Mikazuki (Crescent Moon) ··· 三日月 ··· **6**:221a
Miki ··· **5**:171a
Miki Bukichi ··· 三木武吉 ··· **5**:171a
Miki Kiyoshi ··· 三木清 ··· **5**:171a
Miki Kiyoshi ni okeru ningen no kenkyū 三木清に於ける人間の研究 ··· **4**:270a
Mikimoto Kōkichi ··· 御木本幸吉 ··· **1**:21b; **5**:171a-171b
Miki Rofū ··· 三木露風 ··· **5**:171b
Miki Takeo ··· 三木武夫 **2**:333a; **5**:171b
Miki Tokuchika ·· 御木徳近 ··· **5**:171b
Mikkabi ··· 三ケ日 ··· **5**:171b-172a
Mikkyō. *See* **Esoteric Buddhism**
Miko ··· **5**:172a
shamanism ··· **7**:76b

Miko kagura ········ 4:106b, 107b
Miko mai ········ 4:107b
Mikoshi 御輿 ··· 4:137a; 5:172a-172b; 7:74a
festivals ········ 2:253b
Sanja Festival ········ 5:*172b*
Mikoto ········ 1:62a
Mikotonori. 詔 *See* **Imperial edict**
Mikudarihan ······ 三行半 ······ 5:172b
Mikuni Mountains
········ 三国山脈 ······ 5:172b
Mikuni Pass ······ 三国峠 ······ 5:172b
Mikuni Rentarō 三国連太郎 ·· 5:172b-173a; 7:68b
Milestones ········ 3:258b
Militarism ········ 5:173a-175a
growth ········ 5:173a
international relations ········ 3:321a
Military Armory Bribery case ······ 6:201b
Military brigade ········ 6:317a
Military chronicles. *See* **Gunki monogatari**
Military cliques. *See* **Gumbatsu**
Military commissioner for Kyōto
········ 4:338b-339a
Military education in the schools · 5:175a
Military factions. *See* **Gumbatsu**
Military forces. *See* **Armed forces, imperial Japanese; National defense; Self Defense Forces**
Combined Fleet, Imperial Japanese Navy
········ 1:336b
Imperial Japanese Army ········ 3:278a
Imperial Japanese Navy ········ 3:278a
Indian National Army ········ 3:289b-290a
self-defense ········ 3:266a
training ········ 3:279b-280a
Military governors ········ 7:183a-184a
Military kites ········ 4:230a
Military leaders, modern
Army
Abe Nobuyuki ········ 1:3b-4a
Anami Korechika ········ 1:53b
Araki Sadao ········ 1:74a
Doihara Kenji ········ 2:126b
Fukushima Yasumasa ········ 2:367a
Hashimoto Kingorō ········ 3:110a
Hayashi Senjūrō ········ 3:117b
Higashikuni Naruhiko ········ 3:132a
Ishiwara Kanji ········ 3:345b-346a
Itagaki Seishirō ········ 3:349a
Katsura Tarō ········ 4:173b-174a
Kawakami Sōroku ········ 4:181b
Kodama Gentarō ········ 4:241a
Koiso Kuniaki ········ 4:250b
Mazaki Jinzaburō ········ 5:144a
Minami Jirō ········ 5:176b
Miura Gorō ········ 5:215a-215b
Mutō Akira ········ 5:288a
Nagata Tetsuzan ········ 5:307a
Nogi Maresuke ········ 6:31a-31b
Ōmura Masujirō ········ 6:104b
Ōyama Iwao ········ 6:138a-138b
Saigō Takamori ········ 6:366a-367a
Sugiyama Hajime ········ 7:258b
Tachibana Shūta ········ 7:293a
Tanaka Giichi ········ 7:336a-336b
Tani Kanjō ········ 7:341b-342a
Tatekawa Yoshitsugu ········ 7:349a
Terauchi Hisaichi ········ 8:12a
Terauchi Masatake ········ 8:12b
Tōjō Hideki ········ 8:39b-40a
Tsuji Masanobu ········ 8:113b-114a
Uehara Yūsaku ········ 8:127a
Ugaki Kazushige ········ 8:130b-131a
Umezu Yoshijirō ········ 8:147b
Watanabe Jōtarō ········ 8:235b
Yamagata Aritomo ········ 8:290a-292a
Yamashita Tomoyuki ········ 8:305a
Navy
Genda Minoru ········ 3:17a-17b
Hiraga Yuzuru ········ 3:142b
Hirose Takeo ········ 3:148a
Kabayama Sukenori ········ 4:89b
Katō Hiroharu ········ 4:168a
Katō Tomosaburō ········ 4:170b
Nagano Osami ········ 5:302b
Nomura Kichisaburō ········ 6:34a
Okada Keisuke ········ 6:78a-78b
Saigō Tsugumichi ········ 6:367a
Saitō Makoto ········ 6:374a
Suzuki Kantarō ········ 7:282a
Takarabe Takeshi ········ 7:317b-318a
Tōgō Heihachirō ········ 8:36a-36b
Yamamoto Gonnohyōe ········ 8:297b
Yamamoto Isoroku ········ 8:298a
Yonai Mitsumasa ········ 8:337a
Military police (pre-World War II) ·· 6:198b
Tōkyō Earthquake of 1923 ········ 8:66b
Military Procurement Ministry (Gunjushō)
········ 8:40a
Military tales (gunki monogatari) ·· 5:246a
Military uniforms ········ 1:332b
Military Vehicle Subsidy Law (1918)
········ 1:121a
Milne, John ········ 5:175a
seismology ········ 2:140b
Mimai ········ 5:175a-175b
Mimana ········ 任那 ·· 4:185a, 276a
Mimasaka ········ 美作 ······ 5:175b
Mimashi ········ 味摩之 ······ 3:32a
Mimikawa ········ 耳川 ······ 5:175b
Miminashiyama ···· 耳成山 ······ 8:310b
Mimizu ········ 2:141a-141b
Mimpō no hone ·· 民法之骨 ······ 6:109a
Mimpon shugi ··· 民本主義 ······ 5:175b
Mimpōten. 民法典 *See* **Civil Code**
Mimpōten ronsō
········ 民法典論争 ·· 1:316b-317b
Mimpō yōgi ····· 民法要義 ······ 8:147a
Min, Queen ········ 5:196b-197a
Min. *See* **Min, Queen; Sōmin** (Buddhist priest)
Minabuchi no Shōan
········ 南淵請安 5:175b; 7:260a
Minakami ········ 水上 ······ 5:176a
Minakami Takitarō
········ 水上滝太郎 ······ 5:176a
Minakami Tsutomu 水上勉 5:176a; 7:103b
Minakata Kumakusu
········ 南方熊楠 ······ 5:176a
Minakuchi ········ 水口 ······ 5:176a
Minamata (city) ····· 水俣 ······ 5:176a
Minamata disease ·· 水俣病 ······ 2:224a, 226a-226b, 304a; 6:218b
Minami Arupusu Kokuritsu Kōen 南アルプス国立公園 ······ 7:236a
Minami Ashigara ··· 南足柄 ······ 5:176b
Minami Bōsō
Quasi-National Park
········ 南房総国定公園 ······ 1:277a
Minami Chita ····· 南知多 ······ 5:176b
Minami Daitōjima 南大東島 ······ 5:176b
Minami Jirō ······ 南次郎 ······ 5:176b
Minami Kikan ····· 南機関 1:221a; 5:176b
Minami Manshū Tetsudō
········ 南満州鉄道 ·· 7:237a-238a
Minami Torishima · 南鳥島 ·· 4:2b; 5:176b
Minamoto family ···· 源氏 ·· 5:176b-178b, *177a-177b*
alliances ········ 2:264a
flags and banners ········ 2:288a
Fujiwara no Michinaga ········ 2:353a
Heike monogatari ········ 3:124a-124b
Kitabatake Chikafusa ········ 4:224a-224b
Murakami Genji ········ 5:177b-178a
Musashi Shichitō ········ 5:275b
Ogasawara family ········ 6:68b
origins ········ 5:176b-177a
samurai ········ 7:7b
Seiwa Genji ········ 5:178a-178b
structure ········ 5:177a-177b
Taira-Minamoto War ········ 7:299b
Wada Yoshimori ········ 8:197b
warrior government ········ 8:229a
Minamoto no Akikane
········ 源顕兼 ······ 4:251a
Minamoto no Michichika
········ 源通親 ······ 3:52a
Minamoto no Raikō. 源頼光
See **Minamoto no Yorimitsu**
Minamoto no Sanetomo
········ 源実朝 ······ 1:11a; 5:178b-179a; 7:58a, 97b
character and cultural interests ···· 5:178b
Fujiwara no Sadaie ········ 2:354a
Kamo no Chōmei ········ 4:128b
Kinkai wakashū ········ 4:212b
Minamoto no Yoritomo ········ 4:122a
poetry ········ 5:178b-179a
Minamoto no Shitagau
········ 源順 ·· 5:179a; 7:13a
Minamoto no Takakuni
········ 源隆国 ······ 4:270b
Minamoto no Tametomo
········ 源為朝 ··· 5:179a-179b
harakiri ········ 3:101b
Minamoto no Tameyoshi. 源為義
See **Hōgen Disturbance**
Minamoto no Toshiyori
········ 源俊頼 ···· 5:14a, 38a, 179b-180a; 7:68a, 95a
Fujiwara no Akisuke ········ 2:350a
Fujiwara no Mototoshi ········ 2:353b
Fujiwara no Toshinari ········ 2:357b
Kamo no Chōmei ········ 4:128b
poetic style ········ 5:179b-180a
works ········ 5:180a
Minamoto no Tsunenobu
········ 源経信 ······ 5:38a, 180a-180b; 8:210a
Shin kokinshū ········ 7:120a
Minamoto no Yoriie 源頼家 · 5:180b; 7:58a
Kajiwara Kagetoki ········ 4:114b
Minamoto no Yoritomo ········ 4:122a
Minamoto no Yorimasa
········ 源頼政 2:280b; 5:180b
rebellion ········ 2:363a
Minamoto no Yorimitsu
········ 源頼光 ··· 5:180b-181a
Minamoto no Yoritomo
········ 源頼朝 ·· 5:181a-182b; 7:7b-8a, 25b, 57b, 85b, 97b, 101b
assessment ········ 5:182a-182b
Battle of Fujigawa ········ 2:342b
bugyō ········ 1:206a
collection in Kōyasan Treasure House
········ 4:299b
consolidation of power ········ 5:182a
feudalistic government ········ 2:264a
Fujiwara no Takanobu ····· 2:355b; 5:*181a*
Gikeiki ········ 3:32b
gokenin ········ 3:42b
Ike no Zenni ········ 3:267b
Itō Sukechika ········ 3:356a
jitō ········ 4:63a
Kajiwara Kagetoki ········ 4:114b
Kamakura ········ 4:120b
Kamakura shogunate ········ 4:121b-122b
Kōfukuji rebuilt ········ 4:244a
portrait painting ········ 6:227a
post-station system ········ 2:188b
revolt against Taira family ········ 2:363a
rule ········ 2:204a-204b
Samurai-dokoro ········ 7:8b

Sasaki Takatsuna · · · 7:23a
shugo · · · 7:183a
Taira-Minamoto War · · · 5:181a-182a
warrior ethic · · · 1:221b
warrior government · · · 8:229a
Minamoto no Yoshiie
· · · 源義家 · · 5:182b; 7:7b
Earlier Nine Years' War · · · 2:137a
Later Three Years' War · · · 4:369a
Minamoto no Yoshinaka
· · · 源義仲 · · · 5:182b
Minamoto no Yoshitomo
· · · 源義朝 · · · 5:182b
Fujiwara no Michinori · · · 2:353a
Heiji Disturbance · · · 3:123a
Minamoto no Yoshitsune
· · · 源義経 · · · 5:44b, 182b-183a;
Benkei · · · 4:98a
biography · · · 3:32b
collection in Kōyasan Treasure House · · · 4:299b
Dannoura, Battle of · · · 2:77a
Kajiwara Kagetoki · · · 4:114b
Sasaki Takatsuna · · · 7:23a
Minamoto-Taira War. 源平の争乱 *See* **Taira-Minamoto War**
Minase sangin hyakuin
· · · 水無瀬三吟百韻 · · · 6:297a
Minashiguri · · · 虚栗 · · · 8:295b
Minasu · · · 5:183a-183b
Minatogawa, Battle of
· · · 湊川の戦 · · · 5:183b
Minato machi. *See* **Port towns**
Minato Ward · · · 港区 · · · 5:183b
Minatsuki-barae · · · 5:308b
Minazuki no tsugomori no ōharae 水無月の晦の大祓 · · · 2:232a
Minchō · · · 明兆 · · 1:192a, *192b*; 5:183b-184a
Nanzenji · · · 5:330b
works · · · 5:183b-184a
Mine · · · 美祢 · · · 5:184a
Mineral rights · · · 5:184a
Minerals · · · 5:353a-354b
Mines Law (Kōgyō Hō) · · · 6:181b
Ming dynasty
invasions of Korea in 1592 and 1597 · · · 3:327a
Ryūkyū trade · · · 6:358a
script style · · · 7:170a
Mingei. *See* **Folk crafts**
Mingu · · · 2:295b; 5:184a
Miniature gardens. *See* **Hakoniwa**
Minidoka Relocation Center · · · 5:184b
Minimum Wage Law (1959) · · · 4:352b; 5:184b
enforcement · · · 4:358b
Mining · · · 5:184b-185a
coal · · · 1:333a-333b
history · · · 5:184b
Meiji period · · · 2:151b
modernization · · · 2:31a-31b
Mining industry · · · 5:185a
Mining industry companies · · · 5:185a
Dōwa Mining Co, Ltd · · · 2:132b-133a
Mitsubishi Mining & Cement Co, Ltd · · · 5:208a-208b
Mitsui Mining & Smelting Co, Ltd · 5:211b
Mitsui Mining Co, Ltd · · · 5:211b-212a
Nittetsu Mining Co, Ltd · · · 6:22b
Takashima Coal Mine · · · 7:318b-319a
Mining Law (Kōgyō Hō) · · · 5:184a
Mining Memorandum of 1872 · · · 2:151b
Mining pollution · · · 5:185a-186a
Ashio Copper Mine Incident · 1:101b-102a
classification · · · 5:185a
countermeasures and problems in future · · · 5:186a
history · · · 5:185b
recent problems · · · 5:185b
Tanaka Shōzō · · · 7:338b-339b
Ministerial deliberative council · · · 1:12b; 5:186a
Ministers of State · · · 2:7b
Ministries, governmental · · · 1:218b-219a
Ministry of Agriculture and Commerce · · · 6:41a-41b
Ministry of Agriculture and Commerce Ordinance · · · 8:250b
Ministry of Agriculture, Forestry, and Fisheries · · · 2:284a; 5:186a; 6:238a
Ministry of Central Imperial Affairs · 7:62b
Ministry of Construction · · · 4:190b; 5:186a-186b
roads · · · 6:332b
transportaton · · · 8:99a
urban planning · · · 8:180b
Ministry of Education · · · 5:186b; 7:34a
educational research · · · 2:180b
educational technology · · · 2:181b
education law · · · 2:182b
function · · · 2:177b-178a
higher education system · · · 3:133a
Historical Documents Division in Kokubungaku Kenkyū Shiryōkan · · · 4:257a
Imperial Rescript on Education · · · 3:279a
influence · · · 2:175b
teachers · · · 7:365a-367a
universities and colleges · · · 8:170b
university autonomy · · · 8:171a
Ministry of Education Fine Arts Exhibition · · · 1:215b
Ministry of Finance · · 4:190b; 5:186b-188a; 7:48b
advisory council · · · 2:316b
auditing practices · · · 1:9a
budgeting · · · 5:187b-188a
Business Accounting Council · · · 2:278a
foreign exchange control · · · 2:315b
foreign trade policy · · · 2:325b
history · · · 5:187a
monetary policy · · · 5:239b
monopolies · · · 4:50a
other functions · · · 5:188a
regulatory agent
insurance · · · 3:316b-317a
role in economic growth · · · 5:187a-187b
Securities Bureau · · · 1:8b; 2:278a
status · · · 5:187b
technological development · · · 7:369a
transportation · · · 8:99a
Ministry of Foreign Affairs · · 5:188a-189b; 6:244b
functions · · · 5:189a
future prospects · · · 5:189b
organization and personnel · · · 5:189a-189b
origin and development · · · 5:188a-189a
Ministry of Health and Welfare · · · 3:119b; 5:189b; 7:211a
establishment · · · 4:351b
Maternal and Child Health Division of the Children and Families Bureau · · · 2:247b
public health · · · 5:149a
Ministry of Home Affairs · · · 5:189b
kōiki shichōsonken · · · 4:250a
Ministry of International Trade and Industry (MITI) · · · 1:12a; 2:315b; 4:190b; 4:62a; 5:189b-191b; 6:304a; 7:253b
automotive industry · · · 1:122a
computer technology · · · 1:346b
electronics industry · · · 2:193b-194a
foreign trade · · · 2:320b
foreign trade regulation · · · 2:325a
function · · · 2:165b-168a
industrial policy · · · 3:296b
Industrial Structure Council · · · 3:302a
legal cartels · · · 3:295b-296a
Ministry of Foreign Affairs · · · 5:189a
origins and development · · · 5:190a-191a
pollution standards · · · 2:226a
powers and influence · · · 5:191a-191b
public utilities · · · 6:266b
technological development · · · 7:370a
technology, modern · · · 7:373a
transportation · · · 8:99a
United States economic relations (1945-1973) · · · 8:162a
Ministry of Justice · · 4:80b; 5:191b; 6:198a; 7:93b
civil liberties · · · 1:317b
Public Security Investigation Agency · · · 6:266b
Ministry of Labor · · · 4:190b; 5:191b
Central Labor Relations Commission (Chūō Rōdō Iinkai) · · · 1:256a
establishment · · · 4:351b
group hiring · · · 3:62b
Labor Relations Commission · · · 4:358b
retirement · · · 6:306b
shuntō negotiations · · · 7:189b
Ministry of Posts and Telecommunications · · · 5:191b; 6:276a
Ministry of Public Works · · · 7:165b
Ministry of Punishments · · · 4:185b
Ministry of Religion · · · 4:323b
Ministry of Transport 4:190b; 5:191b-192a; 8:99a-103b
marine accidents inquiry · · · 5:114a
Minjihō Hanrei Kenkyūkai (Civil Case Study Group) · · · 4:375a
Minjuŭiwŏn · · · 4:208a
Minka · · · 5:192a-194a
design characteristics · · · 5:192a-192b
differences in · · · 5:193b-194a
farmhouses · · · 5:192b-193b
gasshō-zukuri · · · 7:158b
preservation · · · 5:194a
roof forms · · · 5:192b
townhouses · · · 5:193b
types and construction materials · · · 5:192a
Minkan denshō · · 民間伝承 2:302a; 5:194a
Minkan geinō · · · 2:296b
Minkan Jōhō Kyōiku Kyoku · · · 1:317b
Minkan kagura · · · 4:107b
Minkan shinkō · · · 2:298a
Minkan Shintō · · · 民間神道 · · · 2:300b
Minken jiyūron 民権自由論 · · · 8:127b
Mino (city) · · · 美濃 · · · 5:194a
Mino. *See* **Straw raincoats**
Minobe Ryōkichi
· · · 美濃部亮吉 · · · 5:194a
Minobe Tatsukichi
· · · 美濃部達吉 · · · 5:194b
emperor-as-organ of state theory · · 4:375a; 8:8a
Kanamori Tokujirō · · · 4:135b
kokutai debate · · · 4:263b
kokutai interpretation · · · 4:263b
Minobōshi · · · 7:249b
Minobu · · · 身延 · · · 5:194b
Minobusan · · · 身延山 · · · 5:194b
Mino Kamo · · · 美濃加茂 · · · 5:194b
Minolta Camera Co, Ltd · · · 5:194b-195a
Minomura Rizaemon
· · · 三野村利左衛門 · · · 5:195a
Minoo · · · 箕面 · · · 5:195a
Mino Province · · · 美濃国 · · · 5:195a
Minorities · · · 5:195a-195b; 7:217a
Minority rights · · · 5:195b-196a
among konketsuji · · · 4:271b

Minority shareholders 4:71a
Minor Offenses Law 5:196a
Minors 1:16a
Minoue sōdan 5:196a
Mino ware 美濃焼 1:259a; 2:295b; 5:196a-196b
Arakawa Toyozō 1:73b
museums 5:279b
Tajimi 7:310a
tea ceremony 7:364b
Minsei 民青 5:197a; 7:252b
Minsei Dōmei 4:12a
Minshatō. 民社党 *See* **Democratic Socialist Party**
Minshingaku 明清楽 5:197a-197b
Minshu Chōsen 民主朝鮮 4:211a
Minshu Jiyūto (Democratic Liberal Party) 民主自由党 6:212a
Minshuka Dōmei (Democratization League) 民主化同盟 6:212b
Minshuku 5:197b
Minshū no teki (Enemy of the People) 民衆の敵 8:319b
Minshu Shakaitō 民主社会党 2:85a-85b
Minshutō (Democratic Party) 民主党 5:197b; 6:212a
Japan Socialist Party 4:48b
Mintō 民党 2:335a; 5:197b-198a
ritō 6:321b
Minumadai Canal 見沼代用水 5:198a
Min'yō 2:300b-301b
Min'yūsha (Society of the People's Friends) 民友社 4:261a
Minzokugaku 2:296a-296b
Minzoku geinō 2:296b-298a
Minzoku shugi 5:342a-343b
Minzoku to rekishi (Race and History) 民族と歴史 4:228b
Mio. 三尾 *See* **Amerika Mura**
"Miraculous Teakettle, The" 1:207a-207b
Miroku 1:159b; 2:83a; 5:198a; 8:337b
image in Kōryūji 4:294a
Shinran 7:123b
statues 1:197b; 4:111a
Mirror of Eastern Japan 1:127a-127b
Mirror of Gesture, The 8:21b
Miruna no zashiki 見るなの座敷 5:198a
Misasa 三朝 5:198a
Misato 三郷 5:198a
Misawa 三沢 5:198b
Misawa Homes Co, Ltd 5:198b
Miscellaneous schools 5:198b
gaikokujin gakkō 3:3a
Miserables, Les 4:316b
Mishihase 粛慎 5:198b
Mishima (city) 三島 5:199a
Mishima (island) 見島 5:199a
Mishima Michitsune 三島通庸 5:199a
Fukushima Incident 2:366a
Kabasan Incident 4:89a
Mishima Tokushichi 三島徳七 5:199a
Mishima Tsūyō. 三島通庸 *See* **Mishima Michitsune**
Mishima Yukio 三島由紀夫 1:3a, 20b, 85a, 223b; 2:274a; 5:199a-202a, 315b; 7:261a
February 26th Incident 2:250b
first writings 5:199b-200b
harakiri 3:102a
1950s 5:200b-201a
1960s 5:201a-202a
obscenity case 1:255a
Shinchō 7:109a
Shingeki 7:112a, 113b
Mishina Shōei 三品彰英 8:307a
Mishōtai 5:202a
Shintō art 7:135a
Miso 2:305a, 306b; 5:202a; 6:283a; 7:239a, 265b
brewing 1:170a
Shimo Suwa 7:106b
Misogi 3:100b; 5:202a-202b
Misogikyō 禊教 5:202b
Misora Hibari 美空ひばり 5:202b
ryūkōka 6:355a
Missan roku 密参録 7:234a
Missionaries, Christian 1:306a
Catholic 1:249b-251a
English 8:249a
friars 1:307a
Jesuit 1:306b
Mission schools 5:202b-203a; 8:257b
Mission to Europe of 1582 5:203a-203b
achievements 5:203a-203b
aims 5:203a
Arima Harunobu 1:83a
Chijiwa Miguel 1:274b
Hara Martinho 3:102a
Itō, Mancio 3:355a
journey 5:203a
members 5:203a
Nakaura Julião 5:318b
Ōmura Sumitada 6:104b
Ōtomo Sōrin 6:132b
Misumi 三角 5:203b
Mita bungaku 三田文学 2:214a; 4:301a; 5:203b, 300b
Mitaka 三鷹 5:203b-204a
Mitaka Incident 三鷹事件 5:204a; 7:147b
Shimoyama Incident 7:107b
Mitake Shrine 御岳神社 1:272a
Ontake 6:112b
Mitama. *See* **Tama**
Mitamura Engyo 三田村鳶魚 5:204a
Mitasareta seikatsu 充たされた生活 1:83b
Mitate-e (parodies of classics) 見立絵 8:140b
Mitaue Matsuri 御田植祭 1:103b
Mitegura. *See* **Gohei**
Mitford, Algernon 5:204a-204b
MITI. *See* **Ministry of International Trade and Industry**
Mito 水戸 5:204b
Mito Civil War 天狗党の乱 5:204b-205a
Takeda Kōunsai 7:322b
Mito Kōmon. *See* **Tokugawa Mitsukuni**
"Mito Kōmon" (television series) 水戸黄門 2:219b
Mito school 水戸学 5:205a-205b
Gamō Kumpei 3:6a-6b
kokutai 4:263a
National Seclusion 5:347b
scholars
Aizawa Seishisai 1:38a
Asaka Tampaku 1:94b
Kuriyama Sempō 4:313b
Shinron 7:124a
sonnō jōi 7:228b
Mitoshiro 7:109b
Mitoshiroda 7:109b
Mitsuba 3:127b
Mitsubachi (honey bees) 1:149a
Mitsubishi 三菱 5:205b-206b; 7:30b, 50b, 88a, 266b
government enterprise sales 4:138a
Ikuno Silver Mine 3:271a
interaffiliate stockholding 3:295a
Iwasaki Koyata 3:361b-362a
Iwasaki Yatarō 3:362b
seishō 7:52a
Takashima Coal Mine 7:319a
Tōyama Mitsuru 8:88b
Mitsubishi Bank, Ltd 5:206b-207a
Mitsubishi Chemical Industries, Ltd 5:207a
Mitsubishi Corporation 3:18b-20a; 5:207a; 7:258a
Mitsubishi Electric Corporation 2:82b; 5:207a-207b
Mitsubishi Estate Co, Ltd 5:207b
Mitsubishi Gas Chemical Co, Inc 5:207b-308a
Mitsubishi Gōshi 3:361b-362a
Mitsubishi group 1:92b
Mitsubishi Heavy Industries, Ltd 4:183b; 5:208a
automotive 1:121b
defense industry 2:82b
Nagasaki Shipyards 5:306a
Mitsubishi Metal Corporation 5:208a
Mitsubishi Mining & Cement Co, Ltd 5:208a-208b; 7:267b
Mitsubishi Motors Corporation 5:208b
Mitsubishi Oil Co, Ltd 5:208b; 6:181b
Mitsubishi Paper Mills, Ltd 5:208b
Mitsubishi Petrochemical Co, Ltd 5:208b-209a; 6:180a
Mitsubishi Rayon Co, Ltd 5:209a
Mitsubishi Steel Mfg Co, Ltd 5:209a
Mitsubishi Trust & Banking Corporation 5:209a
Kagami Kenkichi 4:102b
Mitsubishi Warehouse & Transportation Co, Ltd 5:209b
Mitsuchi Chūzō 三土忠造 5:209b
Mitsuda-e 5:209b
Mitsuda Kensuke 光田健輔 5:209b
Mitsui 三井 1:138a, 165a; 2:30a, 359a; 5:209b-210b; 7:86a, 266b
Chōnin kōkenroku 1:303a
government enterprise sales 4:138a
Ikeda Shigeaki 3:266a
Inoue Kaoru 3:310a
interaffiliate stockholding 3:295a
seishō 7:52a
Mitsui & Co, Ltd 3:18b-20a; 5:210b-211a
international communications 3:319a
Mukai Tadaharu 5:262a
Tashiro Shigeki 7:347b
Mitsui Bank, Ltd 5:211a
Dai-Ichi Kangyō Bank, Ltd 2:58b
Mitsui Bunko 三井文庫 5:212b
Mitsui Bussan Company 7:193b
Mitsui Construction Co, Ltd 5:211a-211b
Mitsui Engineering & Shipbuilding Co, Ltd 5:211b
Mitsui group 7:305b
Mitsui Mining & Smelting Co, Ltd 4:61a; 5:211b; 6:219a
Mitsui Mining Co, Ltd 5:211b-212a
Miike Coal Mines 5:169b
Mitsui O.S.K. Lines, Ltd 5:212a
Daiichi Chūō Kisen Kaisha 2:58b
Mitsui Petrochemical Industries, Ltd 5:212a; 6:180a
Mitsui Real Estate Development Co, Ltd 4:190a; 5:212a-212b
Mitsui Research Institute for Social and Economic History 5:212b
Mitsui Sugar Co, Ltd 5:212b
Mitsui Takatoshi 三井高利 5:212b
Mitsui Tōatsu Chemicals, Inc 5:212b
Mitsui Trust & Banking Co, Ltd 5:212b-213a
Mitsui Warehouse Co, Ltd 5:213a
Mitsukaidō 水海道 5:213a

Mitsuke 見附 5:213a
Mitsukoshi, Ltd 5:213a-213b
Mitsukuri Gempachi 箕作元八 5:213b
Mitsukuri Gempo 箕作阮甫 5:213b
Mitsukuri Kakichi 箕作佳吉 5:213b
Mitsukuri Rinshō 箕作麟祥 5:213b
  Civil Code 2:319a
Mitsukuri Shūhei 箕作秋坪 5:213b
Mitsuminesan 三峰山 5:214a
Mitsumine Shrine 三峰神社 1:272a; 5:214a
Mitsunaga Hoshio 光永星郎 5:214a
Mitsu no hamamatsu (The Pine on the Beach at the Royal Port) 御津の浜松 5:36a
Mitsutani Kunishirō 満谷国四郎 5:214a
Mitsuya plan 5:214a
Mitsuzōin 密蔵院 4:163b
Miura 三浦 5:214a-214b
Miura Anjin. 三浦按針 *See* **Adams, William**
Miura Baien 三浦梅園 5:214b-215a
  jōri 4:247a; 5:214b
  main works 5:214b-215a
    Gengo 5:214b
    Kango 5:215a
    Zeigo 5:214b-215a
  social and educational activity 5:215a
Miura Chora 三浦樗良 5:215a
Miura family 三浦氏 5:215a
Miura Gorō 三浦梧楼 4:281b; 5:215a-215b
Miura Hiroyuki 三浦周行 5:215b
  historiography 3:156b
Miura Jōshin 三浦浄心 4:187b
Miura Ken'ya 三浦乾也 5:215b
Miura Kinnosuke 三浦謹之助 5:215b
Miura Peninsula 三浦半島 5:215b-216a
Miura Saku 三浦鑿 5:216a
Miura Shumon 三浦朱門 5:216a
Miura Tetsuo 三浦哲郎 5:216a
Miwa Kyūwa 三輪休和 5:216a
Miwa Shissai 三輪執斎 5:216a; 8:335b
Miwata Masako 三輪田真佐子 5:216a-216b
Miwayama 三輪山 5:216b
Mixed-blood children 4:271a-271b
Miyabe Kingo 宮部金吾 5:216b
Miyagawa 宮川 5:216b
Miyagawa Chōshun 宮川長春 5:216b
Miyagawa Kazuo 宮川一夫 5:216b-217a
Miyage 5:217a
Miyagi Michio 宮城道雄 5:217a-217b
Miyagi Prefecture 宮城県 5:217b-218a
  attractions 5:218a
  history 5:217b
  Tagajō 7:294a
Miyagi Tamayo 宮城タマヨ 5:218a
Miyagi Yotoku 宮城与徳 5:218a; 7:229b
Miyajima. 宮島 *See* **Itsukushima**
Miyajima Seijirō 宮嶋清次郎 5:218a
Miyake Issei 三宅一生 5:218a
Miyakejima 三宅島 5:218a
Miyake Kaho 三宅花圃 5:218b
Miyake Kanran 三宅観瀾 5:218b
Miyake Sekian 三宅石庵 5:218b
  Kaitokudō 4:113b
Miyake Setsurei 三宅雪嶺 5:218b-219a, 311a; 7:51b, 91b, 258b
  Ernest Francisco Fenollosa 2:251b
Miyake Shōsai 三宅尚斎 5:219a
Miyake Yonekichi 三宅米吉 1:77a; 5:219a
Miyake Yoshinobu 三宅義信 5:219a
Miyako 宮古 5:219a
  Ryūkyū Islands 6:357a
Miyakogusa (*Lotus corniculatus* var. *Japonicus*) 5:219a
Miyako Islands 宮古諸島 5:219b; 7:3a
Miyakoji Bungonojō 宮古路豊後掾 8:43b
Miyakojima 宮古島 5:219b
Miyako no hana 都の花 4:199a
Miyakonojō 都城 5:219b
Miyakonojō Basin 都城盆地 5:219b
Miyako no Nishiki 都の錦 5:219b
Miyako no Yoshika 都良香 5:219b
Miyako shimbun 都新聞 5:219b-220a
  Kokumin shimbun merged with 4:261a
Miyamairi 宮参り 5:220a
Miyamoto Kenji 宮本顕治 5:220a; 7:25a
Miyamoto Musashi 宮本武蔵 1:193b, 222a; 5:220a; 8:295a-295b
Miyamoto Musashi series 6:221b
Miyamoto Yuriko 宮本百合子 1:155b; 5:220a-221a; 7:25a
  Shin Nihon bungaku 7:122a
  works 5:220b-221a
Miyanouradake 宮之浦岳 4:105b; 5:221a
Miyashita Takichi 宮下太吉 3:135a-136a
Miyatake Gaikotsu 宮武外骨 5:221a
Miyatsuko 造 4:89a
Miyaza 宮座 4:145b; 5:221a
Miyazaki 宮崎 5:221a-221b
Miyazaki Ichisada 宮崎市定 5:221b, 311b
Miyazaki Plain 宮崎平野 5:221b
Miyazaki Prefecture 宮崎県 5:221b
Miyazaki Shrine 宮崎神宮 5:222a
Miyazaki Tōten 宮崎滔天 5:222a-222b; 7:276b
  tairiku rōnin 7:302b
Miyazaki Yasuji 宮崎康二 5:222b
Miyazaki Yasusada 宮崎安貞 1:24a; 5:222b
Miyazawa Kenji 宮沢賢治 5:222b-223b
  works 5:223a
Miyazawa Toshiyoshi 宮沢俊義 2:13b; 5:223b
Miyazu 宮津 5:223b
Miyoshi 三次 5:223b
Miyoshi Basin 三次盆地 5:223b
Miyoshi Jūrō 三好十郎 5:223b-224a
Miyoshi Kiyoyuki 三善清行 5:224a
Miyoshi Manabu 三好学 5:224a
Miyoshi Masayasu 三好政康 5:224a
Miyoshi Nagayoshi 三好長慶 5:224a
Miyoshi Nagayuki 三好長逸 5:224a
Miyoshi Sanninshū 三好三人衆 5:224a
Miyoshi Tatsuji 三好達治 5:224a-224b
  Kajii Motojirō 4:114a
Miyoshi Yasunobu 三善康信 5:57b, 224b-225a
  works 5:224b
Mizoguchi Kenji 溝口健二 2:268b-269a, 270b-271a, 272a; 5:225a-225b
  Shindō Kaneto 7:111a
  Shinoda Masahiro 7:122a
Mizuhara Shūōshi 水原秋桜子 5:20a, 225b; 8:295a
  haiku 3:80b
Mizuhiki 5:225b-226a
  kokorozuke placed in 4:256b
Mizuho Station 瑞穂基地 1:64b
Mizukata 水方 4:119b
Mizuki 水城 5:226a
Mizuki Yōko 水木洋子 5:226a
Mizukurage 4:50b
Mizunami 瑞浪 5:226a
Mizuno Corporation 5:226a
Mizunomi-byakushō 水呑百姓 5:226a-226b
Mizuno Rentarō 水野錬太郎 5:226b
Mizuno Seiichi 水野清一 1:78b
Mizuno Shigeo 水野成夫 5:226b
  Sankei shimbun 7:13b-14a
Mizuno Tadakuni 水野忠邦 1:21a; 5:226b-227b; 7:28b
  as rōjū 5:227a-227b
  hitogaeshi 3:208a
  Tempō Reforms 3:189b; 5:226b, 227b; 8:2a
Mizusawa 水沢 5:227b
Mizusawa Ken'ichi 水沢謙一 2:302b
Mizusawa, Latitude Observatory of 5:227b
  discoveries 1:104b
Mizushima 水島 5:*227a*, 227b
Mizushima Coastal Industrial Region 水島臨海工業地域 6:83a; 7:312a
Mizushima San'ichirō 水島三一郎 1:268b; 5:227b-228a
Mizutani Yaeko 水谷八重子 5:228a
  shimpa 7:108a
MOA Museum of Art 5:228a; 7:56a
Mobara 茂原 5:228a
Mobil Sekiyu 5:228a
  Tōa Nenryō Kōgyō 8:30b
Mochi 2:253b, 262a
Mochizuki Yūko 望月優子 5:228b
Modern age 6:176b
Modern Art Association 8:294b
Modern art museums 5:279a
Modernization 5:228b-229b
Modern philosophy 5:229b-232a
  formation of academic philosophy 3:112b; 4:322a
  Hiratsuka Un'ichi 5:232b
  introduction of Western philosophy 5:161a-161b, 311b-312a; 6:14a-14b
  Marxist philosophy 4:180b; 5:171a; 6:367a-367b
  Nishida and Tanabe 6:14b-15b; 7:335a-335b
  post-World War II 5:232a
  Taishō democracy and philosophy 1:2b; 4:304b; 8:237b
  traditional thought 5:229b-230a
Modern poetry literary groups 5:20a-20b
Modern prints 5:232a-233b
  Munakata Shikō 5:*233a*
  1960s and 1970s 5:233a-233b
  Nyonin Kanzeon 5:*233a*
  Onchi Kōshirō 5:*232b*
  sōsaku hanga 5:232b-233a
Mo Di 4:58b
Modorikago 戻駕 8:43b
Modoshi 4:119b
Moetsukita chizu (1968, The Burned-up Map) 燃えつきた地図 1:3a; 8:15a
Mogamigawa 最上川 5:233b
Mogami Tokunai 最上徳内 5:233b
Mogi Keizaburō 茂木啓三郎 5:233b
Mogura 5:235b

Mohan Singh 7:197a
Mō hitori no Keitarō .... もう一人の啓太郎 6:275b
Mōka .... 真岡 5:234a
Mokkan .... 木簡 .. 1:80a; 5:234a
inscriptions 3:314a
Mokkei .... 牧谿 .. 1:192a-192b; 5:234a
Mōko Shūrai ..... 蒙古襲来 ... 5:243b-245a
Mōko shūrai ekotoba .... 蒙古襲来絵詞 · 1:89b; 4:274b; 5:*243a-243b*
Mokuami .... 黙阿弥 5:50a, 234b-235a
kabuki plays 4:91b
Sakura Sōgorō tale 7:5a
Mokuami, Kawatake .... 河竹黙阿弥 7:4a
Mokuan Reien ... 黙庵霊淵 ... 5:235a-235b
ink painting 3:306b
works 5:235b
Mokubei. 木米 *See* **Aoki Mokubei**
Mokugyo. 木魚 *See* **Asai Chū**
Mokujiki .... 木食 1:199b; 5:235b
Mokujiki Gogyō .. 木食五行 1:194a; 5:235b
Mokujiki Ōgo .... 木食応其 5:235b
Mokuyōkai (Thursday Club) .... 木曜会 5:18b
Moles [(mogura) family Talpidae] · 5:235b
Mollusks. *See* **Shellfish**
Molony, James Clark 4:38b
Mombatsu 1:147a
Mombetsu .... 紋別 5:236a
Mombi 7:58a
Mombushō. *See* **Ministry of Education**
Momiji 5:111b-112a
Momijigari .... 紅葉狩 4:154b; 5:236a
Momijioroshi 2:25b
Momi no ki wa nokotta (The Fir Tree Still Stands) .. 樅の木は残った 6:221b
Mommu, Emperor .... 文武天皇 · 5:236a; 7:62b
court 2:350a
Fujiwara family 2:348a, 350b
Kakinomoto no Hitomaro 4:117a
Momo 6:169b
"Mōmoku" .... 盲目 7:176a
Mōmoku monogatari .... 盲目物語 7:342b
Momonga 2:293b
Momo sumomo .... 桃李 6:298b
Momotarō .... 桃太郎 2:302a; 5:236a; 7:149b
Momoyama period. 桃山時代 *See* **Azuchi-Momoyama period**
Mon .... 門 5:350b
Monasticism 5:236a-239a
administrative framework 5:236b-237a
discipline problems 5:236b-237a
Ganjin 3:7a-7b
reform movement 5:238a-238b
secular control 5:237a
Tokugawa Reform 5:238b-239a
warrior control 5:238b
wealth and power 5:237b
Monchūjo .... 問注所 .. 5:239a; 7:8b
keishi 4:190a
Minamoto no Yoritomo 4:122a
Taira-Minamoto War 7:300b
Monetary expansion 2:148a
Monetary policy 5:239b-242a
banking system 5:240a
before the late 1960s 5:240b-241a
industrial policy 3:296b
mechanics 5:239b-240b
1970s and beyond 5:241a-242a
reserve money 5:239b-240a
Monetary system
Meiji period 2:151b
Muromachi history 3:175a-176b
premodern 2:147b-148a
Wadō kaihō 8:198a
Money. *See* **Money, premodern; Yen**
Money changers (ryōgaeshō) 6:351b
Money offerings 5:242a
Money, premodern 5:242a-243a
eirakusen 2:186b
hansatsu 5:*242a-242b*
ichibukin 5:*242a-242b*
Kan'ei tsūhō 5:*242a-242b*
Keichō koban 5:*242a-242b*
kōchō jūnisen 4:239b
mameita gin 5:*242a-242b*
Tenshō naga ōban 5:*242a-242b*
Wadō kaihō 5:*242a-242b*
See also Coins
Mongaku .... 文覚 .. 5:243a-243b; 7:85b
Jingoji 4:58b
Mongolia 4:18b
Manchurian-Mongolian Independence Movement 5:99a-99b
Mongol invasions of Japan .. 5:243a-245a; 7:70b, 94b, 97b, 183b, 263a
Akutō 1:46a
challenge and response 5:243b-244a
effects 5:244a
Eizon 2:188a
fortifications 2:364b
Hōjō Tokimune 3:212a
Japanese defense 5:244a
kamikaze 4:126b
Kikuchi Takefusa 4:206b
Kōno Michiari 4:274b
Koryŏ-Japan relations 4:278a
location 2:365a
Mōko shūrai ekotoba 5:*243a-243b*
national flag 5:339a
regency politics 4:122a
Takezaki Suenaga 7:326b
warrior government 8:229b
Mongol invasions of Korea 5:245a
Mongoloid features 4:35a-35b
Monkeys [(saru) *Macaca fuscata*] 5:245a-245b
Mori Sosen 5:253a
Monnō .... 文雄 5:245b
phonological works 4:134a
Mono-awase 4:381a
Monobi 7:58a
Monochrome ink painting 6:150b
Monogatari bungaku 5:245b-246b
Chinese literature 1:293b
gunki monogatari (military tales) 3:69a-69b; 5:246a
rekishi monogatari (historical tales) 5:246a
rise 5:14a
setsuwa bungaku 5:246b; 7:72a-72b
Tale of Genji 7:330a
tsukuri monogatari (courtly romances or prose fiction) 5:246a
uta monogatari (stories about poems or poem tales) 5:245b-246a
Monograms 4:155a-156a
Monographs 4:23b
Mono no aware .... 物のあはれ · 2:273b; 5:17a, 246b-247a
Motoori Norinaga 4:258b
Mononobe family .. 物部氏 5:247a; 7:264a
Buddhism 4:277a
Keitai, Emperor 4:190a
Nakatomi family alliance 2:351a
Yamato court 8:308b
Mononobe no Moriya .... 物部守屋 5:247a
Mononoke 5:247a
Monopolization, private 1:65b-66b
Monopoly and oligopoly 5:247a-247b
coin mints 4:219b
domainal 3:96a-96b
industrial organization 3:292b-293b
private
control 1:66a
definition 1:65b
exclusion 1:65b
public interest and particular field of trade 1:66a
regulation of stock acquisitions and mergers 1:66a-66b
silk trade 3:356b
Monopoly Bureau 4:50a
Monosodium glutamate (MSG) 3:265b
Monshō 2:42a-43b
Monshō (Family Crest) .... 紋章 8:333a
Montages 2:378a
Montblanc, Charles, Comte des Cantons de 5:247b
Months 1:232a-232b
Monumenta Nipponica 1:250a
Monuments, natural 5:352a-352b
Monzen machi ..... 門前町 ... 5:247b-248a
Moon and agricultural rites 1:23a
Moon viewing 5:248a
cooking 2:22a
Moraes, Wenceslau de 5:248a
Moral Adoption program 1:111a
Moral education 2:181a; 5:248a-248b; 7:34a-34b
Moral excellence (toku) 4:141b
Morality 5:248b
vs etiquette 2:232b
"Moral" training 7:191b
Morgan, George Dennison 5:248b
Morgan, Yuki .. モルガン雪 5:248b
Mori Arimasa ...... 森有正 5:248b
Mori Arinori .... 森有礼 .. 5:248b-249b
education 2:176a
educational policies 3:279a
Japanese language reform 4:29b
Meirokusha 5:161a
school orders 7:36b
Moribana 2:290b-291a
Moribana-style 2:*291a*
Mōri family .... 毛利氏 5:249b; 7:104a
Moriguchi .... 守口 5:249b
Mori Hanae .... 森英恵 5:249b
Mori Kaku .... 森恪 5:249b; 7:276b
Mori Kansai .... 森寛斎 ... 5:249b-250a
style 5:250a
Morikawa Kyoroku .... 森川許六 · 1:295b; 5:16a, 250a
Morikawa Yoshinobu .... 森川義信 1:82b
Mori Masayuki ..... 森雅之 2:*272b*; 5:250a
Morimoto Kaoru ... 森本薫 ... 5:250a-250b
shingeki 7:113a
Mōri Motonari ... 毛利元就 5:250b; 7:277a
kakun 4:118b
Morimoto Rokuji · 森本六爾 · 1:77b; 5:250b
Mōri Museum 5:276b
Morinaga, Prince 護良親王 5:251b
Morinaga & Co, Ltd 5:250b
Morinaga Milk Industry Co, Ltd ... 5:251a; 6:220a
Morinaga Powdered Milk Incident 2:304b; 5:251a-251b; 6:253b
Mori Nobuteru ..... 森矗昶 5:251b
Mori Ōgai .... 森鷗外 · 1:155b; 5:11b, 52b-54a, *251a*, 251b-252b; 7:103b, 253b

education 5:251b
Nakamura Fusetsu 5:314b
works 5:252a-252b
Morioka 盛岡 5:252b
Morioka Emigration Company 6:178b
Mori Rammaru 森蘭丸 5:252b
Mori Rintarō 森林太郎 5:251b-252b
Morisada mankō 守貞漫稿 2:296a; 5:252b-253a
Morishige Hisaya 森繁久弥 5:253a
Morishima Michio 森嶋通夫 5:253a
Morishita Yōko 森下洋子 2:76a
Mori Shushō 森守象 5:253a
Mori Sosen 森狙仙 5:253a
Morita Akio 盛田昭夫 5:253a
Morita Kan'ya 守田勘弥 5:253b
kabuki leadership 4:92b
Moritake senku 守武千句 1:73b
Morita Masatake 森田正馬 5:253b-254a
Morita Sōhei 森田草平 5:253b
Morita therapy 5:253b-254a; 6:261b
central tenet 5:254a
Moritaza 守田座 5:253b
Morito Incident 森戸事件 5:254a-254b
Morito Tatsuo 森戸辰男 5:254b
dispute 4:48b
Mori Tsutomu 森恪 5:249b
Moriyama 守山 5:254b
Moriyama Shigeru 森山茂 4:279a
Moriyama Takichirō 森山多吉郎 5:254b-255a
Moriyoshi, Prince 護良親王 *See* **Morinaga, Prince**
Morning glories [(asagao) *Pharbitis nil; Ipomoea nil*] 5:255a
Morning glory fair 5:255a
Morning Toilette 8:328a
Morohashi Tetsuji 諸橋轍次 2:60a; 5:255a-255b
Moromoriki 師守記 5:255b
Moronobu 師宣 1:163b; 2:373b; 5:255b-256a; 6:155b; 7:*258a*; 8:*138b*
Kaigetsudō school 4:109b
Kambun Master 4:124b
style 5:255b
Morrison Bunko 8:90a
Morrison expedition 6:258a
Morrison Incident モリソン号事件 5:256a
Gaikokusen Uchiharai Rei 3:3b
Shinkiron 7:119a
Morse, Edward Sylvester 1:75b, 155b; 2:311a; 5:256a
Faulds, Henry 2:249b
Fenollosa, Ernest Francisco 2:251b
Ōmori shell mounds 6:103a
shell mounds 7:81b
Mortality rates 5:149a-149b
Mortars. *See* **Usu**
Moscow 4:44a
Mōsōchiku *(Phyllostachys pubescens)* 1:135b
Mosse, Albert 2:2b; 5:256a-256b
Meiji Constitution 3:195a
Mosses [(koke) division *Bryophyta*] 5:256b
Mō Takutō 毛沢東 5:111b
Moteru kuni Nihon 持てる国日本 6:93a
Motherhood Protection League [Boshi Hogo Remmei (Bosei Hogo Dōmei)] 8:289b, 307b
Mother-of-pearl inlay 2:371b; 5:256b
Motion Picture Code Committee 2:273a; 5:256b
Motion Picture Code of Ethics 1:254b
Motion Picture Film Censorship Regulations 2:339a
Motion Picture Law 2:339a
Motion pictures. *See* **Film, Japanese**
Motivation
employment
internal organization of Japanese companies 3:318a-318b
group 3:63a
Moto 4:108a
Motobu 本部 5:256b
Motoda Nagazane 元田永孚 5:257a
Imperial Rescript on Education 3:279a
nationalism 5:342b
Moto Gangōji. *See* **Asukadera**
Motoki Shōzō 元木昌造 6:245b
Motomezuka 求塚 4:135b
Motonobu. *See* **Kanō Motonobu**
Motoori Haruniwa 本居春庭 5:257a; 7:281a
Fujitani Nariakira 2:346b
Motoori Norinaga 本居宣長 1:20a, 154a; 2:346b; 3:155a; 5:13a, 17a, 257a-258b; 7:94b, 263b-264a, 281a; 8:216a
childhood and youth 5:257b
early works in literary criticism 5:257b-258a
Genji monogatari tama no ogushi 5:258a; 7:331a
Hirata Atsutane 3:145a
impact 5:258b
influenced by Ogyū Sorai 4:248a
Japanese language studies 4:31a
Kamo no Mabuchi 4:129b
Kojikiden 4:251b
Kokugaku 4:257b, 258a
later years 5:258a-258b
literary scholar to classicist 5:258a
mono no aware 5:246b-247a
orthographic studies 4:134a
self-portrait 5:*257a*
writings 5:258a-258b
Motoori Ōhira 本居大平 5:259a
Motorcycle gangs 4:86b
Motorcycle theft 4:86b
Motor vehicles 8:102a
Motoyakushiji remains 本薬師寺跡 5:259a
Motoyama Hikoichi 本山彦一 5:259a
Mōtsuji 毛越寺 3:*8b*; 5:259a
Mōtsuji remains 毛越寺跡 5:259a-259b
Mt. Asama 浅間山 8:194b
Mt. Bandai 磐梯山 8:194a
Mt. Fuji 富士山 2:344b-345b; 8:194a
Mt. Fuji Pilgrimage Mandala 7:136a
Mountain ash 5:327b
Mountain climbing 8:287b
Mountaineering 5:259b
Mountaineering and Exploration in the Japanese Alps 4:12b; 8:249a
Mountain fort 1:246b
Mountain fortress (yamajiro) 1:246a
Mountain passes
Abō 1:5a
Amagi 1:49a
Daibosatsu 2:55b
Hakone 3:87a
Harinoki 3:104a
Jikkoku 4:57a
Karikachi 4:160a
Kimi 4:208b
Kobotoke 4:238b
Konsei 4:275b
Kurikara 4:312b-313a
Magome 5:83b
Mikuni 5:172b
Ningyō 6:5b
Nomugi 6:34a
Sayo no Nakayama 7:31b
Torii 8:79a
Usui 8:182a
Wada 8:197b
"Mountain people" 7:13b
"Mountain preserves" regulations (tomeyama) 8:70b-71a
Mountain ranges
Akaishi 1:39b
Abukuma 1:5b
Asahi 1:92b-93a
Chūgoku 1:312a
Dewa 2:91a
Echigo 2:143b
Ezo 2:239a-239b
Hidaka 3:130a
Hida 3:130a
Hira 3:143a
Ishikari 3:342a
Izumi 3:366a
Japanese Alps 4:12b
Kantō 4:153b
Kii 4:204b
Kiso 4:224a
Kitakami 4:226a
Kitami 4:226b
Kyūshū 4:341a
Mikuni 5:172b
Oku Chichibu 6:95a
Oku Tama 6:98b
Ōu 6:135b-136a
Sanuki 7:18b
Sefuri 7:48b
Shikoku 7:97b
Suzuka 7:280b
Tamba 7:333a
Tango 7:341a
Teshio 8:15b
Tsukushi 8:115a
Yamizo 8:313b
Yūbari 8:354b
Mountains
Hokkaidō
Ashibetsudake 1:97a
Daisetsuzan 2:67b
Ishikaridake 3:341b
Yūbaridake 8:354b
Honshū
Adatarasan 1:11b
Akaishidake 1:39b
Amagisan 1:49b
Bukōsan 1:207a
Daisen 2:67a
Dōgoyama 2:126a
Enasan 2:213a
Fujisan 2:344b-345b
Hagurosan 3:77a
Hakusan 3:88b
Hayachinesan 3:114b
Hieizan 3:130b
Hodosan 3:209a
Hōōzan 3:227a
Hōraijisan 3:227a
Hotakadake 3:237b
Ikomayama 3:270b
Kammuriyama 4:128a
Kashima Yarigatake 4:162b
Kimpokusan 4:210b
Kimpusan 4:211a
Kitadake 4:224b
Kobushigadake 4:239a
Komagatake (central Honshū/Akaishi) 4:265a
Komagatake (central Honshū/Kiso) 4:265a

Komagatake (northern Honshū) · · **4**:265a
Kongōsan · · · **4**:270a
Kōyasan · · · **4**:299a
Mitsuminesan · · · **5**:214a
Myōgisan · · · **5**:290b
Nachisan · · · **5**:300a
Obasuteyama · · · **6**:48a-48b
Ōdaigaharasan · · · **6**:61a
Ōeyama · · · **6**:67b
Ōminesan · · · **6**:102a
Ōtakineyama · · · **6**:129a
Ōyama · · · **6**:137b
Rokkōsan · · · **6**:334b-335a
Rokkōzan · · · **1**:83b
Ryōzen · · · **6**:353a
Senjōgatake · · · **7**:66a
Sentsūzan · · · **7**:67b
Shiomidake · · · **7**:141a
Shirane Sanzan · · · **7**:147a
Shiroumadake · · · **7**:148a
Taishakusan · · · **7**:303b
Takaosan · · · **7**:317b
Tanigawadake · · · **7**:341a-341b
Tanzawasan · · · **7**:346a
Tateyama · · · **7**:349b
Togakushiyama · · · **8**:35b
Tsubakurodake · · · **8**:109b
Tsukubasan · · · **8**:114b
Tsurugidake · · · **8**:116b
Yahikoyama · · · **8**:284b
Yakushidake · · · **8**:285b
Yarigatake · · · **8**:316b
Kyūshū
Hikosan · · · **3**:138b
Kujūsan · · · **4**:303b
Kunimidake · · · **4**:309b
Miyanouradake · · · **5**:221a
Sobosan · · · **7**:207b
Shikoku
Ishizuchisan · · · **3**:347a
Tsurugisan · · · **8**:116b
worship · · · **5**:259b-260a
Mountains, worship of · · · **5**:259b-260a
Mourning · · · **2**:370a; **5**:260a
Movement for Union of Court and Shogunate · · · **1**:55a-55b; **4**:308b; **5**:260a-260b, 317b; **7**:102a
Iwakura Tomomi · · · **3**:360a
Kōmei, Emperor · · · **4**:266a
Nabeshima Kansō · · · **5**:299a
Sakuma Shōzan · · · **7**:4a
Tokugawa Iemochi · · · **8**:48a
Movement to Memorialize Three Important Items · · · **7**:9b
Movement to Protect Constitutional Government · **3**:198a; **5**:260b-261a; **6**:211a
Imperial Diet · · · **3**:276b
Kakushin Kuarabu · · · **4**:120a
Kenseikai · · · **4**:198a
Kiyoura Keigo · · · **4**:233a
Kōjunsha · · · **4**:252b
Rikken Seiyūkai · · · **6**:315a
Taishō political crisis · · · **7**:305b
Takahashi Korekiyo · · · **7**:312b
Moxa treatment · · · **1**:10b; **5**:261a-261b
Moxibustion · · · **5**:146a, 261a-261b
Moyoro shell mound · · · モヨロ貝塚 · · **1**:1b; **5**:261b
Okhotsk culture · · · **6**:84a
Mozaemon IV · · · 茂左衛門(四代) · · · **5**:334b
Mozu · · · **7**:179b
Mozume Takami · 物集高見 · · · **5**:261b
M. R. Seni Pramot · · · **7**:65b
Mu · · · **6**:41b
Mube (*Stautonia hexaphylla*) · · · **5**:261b
Muchaku · · · 無著 · · · **1**:*186b*
Mu-ch'i. *See* **Mokkei**
Muchigoma ("whip top") · · · **1**:149b
Muchō (pen name). *See* **Ueda Akinari**
Muchū mondōshū (Collections of Questions and Answers [Exchanged] in a Dream) · · · 夢中問答集 · · · **8**:28a
Mudaiki · · · 無益委記 · · · **4**:250a
Mudrā · · · **3**:328a
Mugaen · · · 無我苑 · · · **4**:180b
Mugenkyū · · · 無弦弓 · · · **4**:179b
Mugen no michi · 無限の道 · · · **4**:165a
Mugi · · · **8**:251a
Mugi to heitai · · · 麦と兵隊 · · · **7**:176b
Mugiwara-bōshi · · · **3**:119a
Muharras Oil Co, Ltd · · · **2**:61a
Muika · · · 六日 · · · **5**:261b
Mujin · · · 無尽 · · · **5**:261b-262a
insurance system · · · **3**:316b-317a
Mujina. *See* **Tanuki**
Mujō · · · 無常 · **1**:180b, 181b; **4**:129a; **5**:262a; **6**:299a
kabuki interpretations · · · **4**:93b
Mujū Ichien. 無住一円 *See* ***Shasekishū***
Mukai Kyorai · · · 向井去来 · · · **5**:16a, 262a; **6**:299b
Mukai Tadaharu · 向井忠晴 · · · **5**:262a
Mukashi-banashi kenkyū · · · 昔話研究 · · · **2**:302a
Mukashi-banashi saishu techō · · · 昔話採取手帖 · · · **2**:302a
Mukawa · · · 鵡川 · · · **5**:262a-262b
Mukden, Battle of · · · 奉天会戦 **3**:197a; **5**:262b
Russo-Japanese War · · · **6**:347a
Mukō (city) · · · 向日 · · · **5**:262b
Mukōgaoka shell mound · · · 向ケ岡貝塚 · **1**:76b; **5**:262b
Mukogawa · · · 武庫川 · · · **5**:262b
Mukoirikon · · · **5**:262b
Muko (bridegroom, son-in-law) plays · · · **4**:327a
Muko yōshi · · · **2**:242a-242b
Mukyōkai (non-church movement) · · · 無教会 · · **5**:262b-263a, 323b
Uchimura Kanzō · · · **8**:124b-125a
Multinational enterprises · · · **5**:263a-264a
investment character · · · **5**:263b
Japanese · · · **5**:263a-263b
problems in 1980s · · · **5**:263b-264a
Mumeiō · · · 無名翁 · · · **4**:189b
Mumyōshō · · · 無名抄 · · · **4**:128b
Mumyō-zōshi · · · 無名草子 · · · **5**:39b, 264a
Munabetsusen · · · 棟別銭 · · · **5**:264a
Munakata Shikō · 棟方志功 **2**:294a; **5**:*233a*, 264a-264b
Aomori Prefectural Museum · · · **1**:69b
modern prints · · · **5**:232b
style · · · **5**:264b
Munakata Shrines · · · 宗像神社 · · · **5**:264b-265a
Okinoshima · · · **6**:92b
Munakata Taisha Treasure House **5**:277b
Muneage · · · **4**:195a
Munebetsusen. *See* **Munabetsusen**
Munenaga, Prince · · · 宗良親王 · · · **5**:265a
Munetaka, Prince 宗尊親王 · · · **5**:265a
Mung, John · · · **5**:313a-313b
Municipal museums · · · **5**:279a
Muqi (Mu-ch'i). *See* **Mokkei**
Mura · · · **5**:265a-265b
Muragaki Norimasa · · · 村垣範正 · · · **5**:265b
Murahachibu · · · 村八分 · · · **5**:265b-266a
Muraji. 連 *See* **Kabane**
Murakami · · · 村上 · · · **5**:266a
Murakami Genzō 村上元三 **2**:274a; **5**:266a; **7**:103b
Murakami Kagaku · · · 村上華岳 · · · **5**:266a
Murakami Kijō · · · 村上鬼城 · · · **5**:266a-266b
Murakami Makoto · · 村上信 · · · **5**:266b
Murakami Namiroku · · · 村上浪六 · · · **5**:266b
Murakami Naojirō · · · 村上直次郎 · · · **5**:266b
Murakami Shōtarō · · · 村上荘太郎 · · · **5**:266a-266b
Murakami Takejirō · · · 村上武次郎 · · · **5**:266b
Murakami Yoshiteru · · · 村上義光 · · · **3**:101b-102a
Mural painting. *See* **Screen and wall painting**
Muramatsu Aizō · 村松愛蔵 · · · **3**:262b
Muramatsu Giichi 村松義一 · · · **5**:266b
Muramatsu Shōfū · · · 村松梢風 · · · **5**:266b
"Mura no ie" · · · 村の家 · · · **7**:176a
Murano Shirō · · · 村野四郎 · · · **5**:266b-267a
style · · · **5**:267a
Murano Tōgo · · · 村野藤吾 · · · **5**:267a
Muraoka Hanako 村岡花子 · · · **5**:267a
Muraoka Iheiji · 村岡伊平治 · · · **5**:267a-267b
Muraoka Tsunetsugu · · · 村岡典嗣 · · · **4**:259a
Murasaki (*Lithospermum erythrorhizon*) · **5**:267b
Murasaki no hitomoto · · · 紫の一本 · · · **8**:34b
Murasaki Shikibu · · 紫式部 · · · **1**:18a, 266a; **2**:280a; **5**:14a-14b, 267b-269a, 325a; **7**:52b
Chinese literature · · · **1**:293b
at court · · · **5**:268a-269a
Fujiwara no Kintō · · · **2**:352a
Fujiwara no Teishi · · · **2**:356b
Kagerō nikki · · · **4**:104a
late years and achievement · · · **5**:268b-269a
middle years · · · **5**:268a-268b
name, family and early life · · **5**:267b-269a
Sei Shōnagon · · · **7**:52b
Tale of Genji · · · **7**:328b-331a
Murasaki shikibu [(Japanese beautyberry) *Callicarpa japonica*] · · · **5**:269b
Murasaki Shikibu nikki · · · 紫式部日記 · · · **2**:186a; **5**:267b-268a
Murasaki Shikibu shū · · · 紫式部集 · · · **5**:269a
Murasaki susuki · · · **7**:279a
Murasakizome (purple dye) · · · **1**:237a
Murata Harumi · · 村田春海 · · · **5**:269b
Kamo no Mabuchi · · · **4**:129b
Murata Kiyokaze · 村田清風 · · · **5**:269b-270a
Murata Minoru · · · 村田実 **2**:268a; **5**:269b; **7**:102b
Murata Seifū · · · 村田清風 · · · **5**:269b-270a
Murata Shōzō · · · 村田省蔵 · · · **5**:270a
Mura (village) · · · **5**:265b
Mura yakunin · · · 村役人 · · · **5**:270a
Murayama · · · 村山 · · · **5**:270a
Murayama Reservoir. *See* **Tama, Lake**
Murayama Ryōhei · · · 村山龍平 · · · **5**:270a-270b
Murayama Shichirō · · · 村山七郎 · · **1**:36b; **4**:18b, 20b
Murayama Tomoyoshi · · · 村山知義 · · · **5**:270b
Murdoch, James · · · **5**:270b
Muri shinjū · · · **7**:262a

Murō-Akame-Aoyama Quasi-National Park 室生赤目青山国定公園 …… **5**:299a
Murōji 室生寺 …… **5**:270b-271a
Muro Kyūsō 室鳩巣 …… **5**:271a-271b
  Forty-Seven Rōnin Incident …… **2**:327b
Muromachi bakufu. 室町幕府 *See* **Muromachi shogunate**
Muromachi history. *See* **History of Japan**
Muromachi ki 室町記 …… **4**:101b
Muromachi period 室町時代 …… **5**:271b
Muromachi shogunate 室町幕府 …… **1**:212a; **5**:271b-274a; **7**:8a, 12a, 64b, 161a
  Council of State …… **3**:252a
  decline and demise …… **5**:274a
  distribution of power …… **5**:272b-273a
  feudalism …… **2**:265a
  founding …… **1**:99a
  Kamakura shogunate military governors under …… **7**:184a
  machinery of government …… **5**:273a-274a
  patronage of arts …… **5**:273a
  powers of the shogunate …… **5**:273a
  shōgun and shugo …… **5**:272a-272b
  warrior government …… **8**:229b
Muroo Saisei 室生犀星 …… **5**:274a-274b
  Hagiwara Sakutarō …… **3**:76a
Muroran 室蘭 …… **5**:274b
Muroto 室戸 …… **5**:274b
Muroto-Anan Coast Quasi-National Park 室戸阿南海岸国定公園 …… **1**:53b
Murotozaki 室戸岬 …… **5**:274b
Murray, David …… **2**:311a; **5**:275a; **7**:35b
Musan Fujin Geijutsu Remmei …… **7**:316b
Musansha undō to fujin no mondai (The Proletarian Movement and Problems of Women) 無産者運動と婦人の問題 …… **8**:297a
Musasabi …… **2**:293b
Musashi 武蔵 …… **5**:275a
  loss …… **4**:383b
Musashi Murayama 武蔵村山 …… **5**:275a
Musashino 武蔵野 …… **5**:275a
Musashino Department Store …… **7**:49a
Musashino Plateau 武蔵野台地 …… **5**:275a
Musashino Tetsudō …… **7**:49b
Musashi Province 武蔵国 …… **5**:275a-275b
Musashi Shichitō 武蔵七党 …… **5**:275b
Muscular dystrophy …… **2**:143a
Museki isshi 夢跡一紙 …… **4**:154b
Museum of Modern Japanese Literature …… **5**:275b
  Takami Jun …… **7**:315a
Museums …… **5**:275b-280b
  archaeological …… **5**:277b-278a
  ceramics …… **5**:279b
  educational activities …… **5**:280a-280b
  ethnographical …… **5**:278a-278b
  exhibition principles …… **5**:280b
  foreign …… **5**:280b
  funding …… **5**:280a-280b
  individual artists …… **5**:279b-280a
  modern art …… **5**:279a
  municipal …… **5**:279a
  national …… **5**:276a-276b
  prefectural …… **5**:278b
  private …… **5**:276b-277b
  religious foundation …… **5**:280a
  special …… **5**:280a
  treasure houses …… **5**:277b
  Western-art …… **5**:279a-279b
Musha Incident 霧社事件 …… **5**:280b
Mushanokōji Saneatsu 武者小路実篤 **2**:344a; **4**:114a; **5**:281a-281b
  Christianity …… **4**:32a
  Shirakaba school …… **7**:145b-146b
Mushi …… **5**:281b-282a
Mushifūji …… **5**:282a
Mushi mo ki mo 虫も樹も …… **6**:139b
Mushin 無心 **5**:282a; **6**:297a
Mushi no iroiro 虫のいろいろ …… **6**:139b
Mushin (poetry term) 無心 …… **8**:181b
Mushi okuri 虫送り …… **6**:309b
Mushiro …… **7**:249b
Mushrooms (kinoko) …… **5**:282a-282b
  production …… **1**:27b
Music
  accompaniment …… **3**:115b
  Ainu …… **1**:36a
  from Bohai …… **1**:159b
  children's songs …… **1**:280a
  composers
    Akiyoshi Toshiko …… **1**:44b
    Dan Ikuma …… **2**:76b
    Fukushima Kazuo …… **2**:366b
    Koga Masao …… **4**:248a
    Mayuzumi Toshirō …… **5**:144a
    Miyagi Michio …… **5**:217a-217b
    Nakanoshima Kin'ichi …… **5**:317a
    Nakayama Shimpei …… **5**:319a
    Takemitsu Tōru …… **7**:324b
    Taki Rentarō …… **7**:327a
    Yamada Kōsaku …… **8**:289a
  conductors
    Ozawa Seiji …… **6**:140b
  dengaku …… **2**:86a-86b
  folk song …… **2**:300b-301a
  gagaku …… **3**:1a-2a
  gidayū-bushi …… **3**:30a-30b
  gigaku …… **3**:31b-32a
  hayashi …… **3**:115b
  heikyoku …… **1**:157a
  Italian influence …… **3**:351a
  of Japanese imperial court …… **3**:1a-2b
  jiuta …… **4**:64b-65a
  jōruri …… **4**:76a-77b
  kabuki music …… **4**:99a-100a
  kiyomoto-bushi …… **4**:232a-232b
  kouta …… **4**:298a-298b
  meter in Ryūkyū …… **6**:357b-358a
  military songs (gunka) …… **3**:69a
  minshingaku …… **5**:197a-197b
  modal systems …… **3**:2a-2b
  nagauta …… **5**:307b
  naniwa-bushi …… **5**:328a
  national anthem …… **5**:336a
  notation …… **6**:86b
  puppet theater …… **1**:214a
  religious …… **5**:283a-284a
    Buddhist …… **5**:283a-283b
    Christian …… **5**:283b-284a
    Shintō …… **5**:283a
  ryūkōka …… **6**:353b-355a
  Ryūkyū music …… **6**:357a-358a
  saibara …… **6**:365a
  sōkyoku …… **7**:225b-226a
  song, early …… **2**:137a-138b
    Heian sources …… **2**:137b
    singers and song use …… **2**:138a
    sources …… **2**:137a
  tokiwazu-bushi …… **8**:43b
  traditional …… **5**:284a-285b
    early history (400-1200) …… **5**:284a-284b
    modern period …… **5**:285a-285b
    1200-1500 …… **5**:284b
    1500-1868 …… **5**:284b-285a
  Western …… **5**:285b-287b
    Meiji period (1868-1912) …… **5**:285b-286a
    ryūkōka …… **6**:354a
    Taishō and prewar Shōwa periods (1912-1940) …… **5**:286a-287a
    World War II and after (1940-) …… **5**:287a-287b
Musical instruments …… **5**:282b
  aerophones …… **5**:282b
  Ainu …… **1**:37b
  biwa …… **1**:157a-157b
  chordophones …… **5**:282b
  companies
    Kawai Musical Instruments Mfg Co, Ltd …… **4**:179a
    Nippon Gakki Co, Ltd …… **6**:9b-10a
  denden taiko …… **2**:85b-86a
  Esoteric Buddhist rites …… **1**:195b-196a
  gagaku …… **3**:1b-2a
  hichiriki …… **3**:129b
  hitoyogiri …… **3**:208b
  idiophones …… **5**:282b
  kokyū …… **4**:264b
  koto …… **4**:296b-297a
  lute …… **1**:157a-157b
  membranophones …… **5**:282b
  percussion …… **3**:2a
  Pure Land Buddhist rites …… **1**:196a-196b
  sasara …… **7**:24a
  shakuhachi …… **7**:75a-76a
  shamisen …… **1**:157a, 212b-214a
  shichigenkin …… **7**:87b
  shō …… **7**:154a
  stringed …… **3**:2a
  taiko …… **7**:297b
  tsuzumi …… **8**:119b-120a
  Western …… **5**:285b-287b
  wind …… **3**:1b-2a
  Zen rites …… **1**:196b
Musket, matchblock …… **3**:140a
Musō Soseki 夢窓疎石 …… **3**:33a; **5**:287b; **6**:*152b*
  gardens …… **3**:9a-9b
  Josetsu …… **4**:77b
  kakun …… **4**:118b
  portrait painting …… **6**:227b
Musubinokami (god) 産霊神 …… **4**:259a
Musume Dōjōji 娘道成寺 …… **6**:108a
Musume-gumi 娘組 …… **8**:353b
Musume to watashi 娘と私 …… **7**:148b
Mutai Risaku 務台理作 …… **5**:287b-288a
Mutō Akira 武藤章 …… **5**:288a
Mutobe Yoshika 六人部是香 …… **4**:259a
Mutō Nobuko 武藤能婦子 …… **2**:66a
Mutō Sanji 武藤山治 …… **2**:32b; **5**:288a
Mutō Shūji …… **6**:*152b*
Mutsu (city) むつ …… **5**:288a
Mutsu (battleship) 陸奥 …… **5**:288a, 307b
Mutsu (nuclear-powered ship) むつ …… **5**:288a-288b
Mutsu Bay 陸奥湾 …… **5**:288b
  …… **5**:288a
Mutsu family 陸奥氏 …… **6**:126b-127a
Mutsu Munemitsu 陸奥宗光 …… **5**:288b-289a; **7**:99a
  Hara Takashi …… **3**:102b
Mutsu Province 陸奥国 …… **3**:363b; **5**:289a-289b
Mutsu waki 陸奥話記
  Earlier Nine Years' War …… **2**:137a
Mutual company …… **5**:289b
Mutual Cooperation and Security, Treaty of …… **6**:167a

United States-Japan Administrative Agreement. *See* **United States-Japan security treaties**
Mutual Security Agreement **5**:289b; **8**:345a
  Occupation **6**:55a
Mutual Security Agreement of 1952 **7**:252a
My Fair Lady (Japanese) **4**:207b
"My heart is Buddha" **8**:27a-27b
My Lantern **4**:179a
Myōe 明恵 **5**:289b-290a; **7**:85b
  Hōnen **4**:67b
  portrait **5**:*289a*
  writings **5**:290a
Myōen 明円 **5**:290a
Myōga **3**:127b
Myōgakin 冥加金 **4**:100a; **5**:290a, 360b
  unjō **8**:172a
Myōgisan 妙義山 **5**:290b
Myōjinshō 明神礁 **5**:290b
Myōji taitō 苗字帯刀 **5**:290b
Myōjō 明星 **2**:346a; **5**:290b; **8**:340b
  founding **5**:19b
Myōkensan 妙見山 **5**:290b
Myōkō, Naganuma 妙佼長沼 **6**:321a
Myōkōnin 妙好人 **5**:290b-291a
Myōkōsan 妙高山 **2**:347b; **5**:291a
Myōō **5**:291a
  Tankai **7**:343b
Myōren 妙蓮 **2**:199b; **7**:92b, 93a
Myōshinji 妙心寺 **5**:291a; **7**:76a
  paintings **4**:148a
Myōshu 名主 **5**:291b
  bushidan **1**:221b
  gōson system **3**:50a-51a
  nago **5**:308b
  shōen **7**:157a
Myōtei mondō 妙貞問答 **2**:241a
Mystery stories **2**:170a-171a; **5**:291b-292a; **6**:221b
  orthodox vs innovative authors **5**:292a
Mythology **5**:292a-297b
  Amaterasu and Susanoo **5**:293a-294b
    birth **5**:293a
    disappearance of Sun **5**:293b
    feuding **5**:293a-293b
  badgers **5**:296b
  cats **5**:296b
  cycles
    Izumo **5**:293b-295a
    Yamato **5**:292b-293b
  Dragon Palace **5**:295b
  fairies and celestial beings **5**:295a-295b
  fountains **5**:295a
  foxes **5**:296b
  heaven **3**:121a-121b
  heroic tales **5**:296a-296b
  Hoderi no Mikoto **5**:294b
  Hoori no Mikoto **5**:294b
  Izanagi and Izanami **3**:364b-365a; **5**:292b-293a
    land of Yomi **5**:293a
  nefarious spirits **5**:296a
  Ninigi no Mikoto **5**:294b; **6**:5b
  Ōkuninushi no Mikoto **5**:293b-294a
    Amaterasu's messengers **5**:294a-294b
    hare of Inaba **5**:293b
    Sukunahikona no Mikoto **5**:294a
    trials **5**:293b-294a
  sennin **5**:295b-296a
  Seven Gods of Good Fortune **5**:296a
  Shintō **7**:130b
  sources
    Kogo shūi (Gleanings from Ancient Stories) **5**:292a
    Kojiki ("Records of Ancient Matters") **5**:292a-295a
    Izumo fudoki **2**:341a
    Nihon shoki ("Chronicles of Japan") **5**:383b-384a
    Shoku nihongi (Chronicles of Japan, Continued) **5**:292
  sparrow **5**:296b
  Takamagahara **7**:314a
  Tanabata **5**:105a
Myths
  Chinese **7**:163b
  discipline of Japanese history **2**:101a-101b
  monkeys **5**:245a-245b
Myths, agricultural **7**:177b

N

Nabari 名張 **5**:299a
Nabe (saucepans or pots) **2**:24b
Nabeshima family 鍋島氏 **5**:299a
Nabeshima Kansō 鍋島閑叟 **5**:299a
Nabeshima Naomasa. 鍋島直正 *See* **Nabeshima Kansō**
Nabeshima Naoshige 鍋島直茂 **5**:299a
Nabeshima ware 鍋島焼 **1**:85b; **5**:299a-299b
  Edo period **1**:263b
  museums **5**:279b
Nachi Falls 那智滝 **5**:*299b*, 300a; **8**:348b
Nachi-Fujikoshi Corporation **5**:299b
Nachi-Katsuura 那智勝浦 **5**:300a
Nachisan 那智山 **5**:300a
Nada 灘 **5**:300a
Nademono **4**:166b
Naeba International Skiing Ground **5**:300a
Naebasan 苗場山 **5**:300a
Nagahama 長浜 **5**:300a
Nagai 長井 **5**:300a
Nagai Kafū 永井荷風 **1**:164a; **2**:274a; **5**:55b, 300a-301a; **7**:26b, 103b, 125b, 253b; **8**:328b
  education and early career **5**:300a
  Ken'yūsha **4**:199a
  western influence **5**:300b
  works **5**:300b-301a
Nagai Nagayoshi 長井長義 **1**:268a; **5**:301a
Nagai Ryūtarō 永井柳太郎 **5**:301a-301b
  education **5**:301a
  political career **5**:301a
Nagai Tatsuo 永井龍男 **5**:301b
Nagai Uta 長井雅楽 **5**:301b
Nagajuban **4**:210b
Nagako, Empress 皇后, 良子 **3**:*277a*; **5**:301b
Nagakubo Sekisui 長久保赤水 **5**:301b-302a
Nagamaki **1**:89a
Nagamochi **5**:302a
Nagano 長野 **5**:302a
Nagano Basin 長野盆地 **5**:302b
Nagano Osami 永野修身 **5**:302b
Nagano Prefecture 長野県 **5**:302b-303a; **8**:355a
Nagano Shigeo 永野重雄 **5**:303a
Naganuma case **5**:303a; **7**:275b
Nagaoka 長岡 **5**:303b
Nagaoka Hantarō 長岡半太郎 **5**:303b
Nagaokakyō (city) 長岡京 **5**:303b
Nagaokakyō (Imperial capital) 長岡京 **4**:128a; **5**:303b
Nagaragawa 長良川 **5**:303b
Nagareru 流れる **4**:240a
Nagareyama 流山 **5**:303b
Nagasaki 長崎 **5**:303b-304a; **8**:276a
  atomic bomb related diseases **1**:111a-112b
  food riot **8**:124a
Nagasakibana 長崎鼻 **5**:304a
Nagasaki boat races **6**:171b
Nagasaki Flag Incident **5**:304a
  Korean (Democratic People's Republic)-Japanese trade suspended **4**:286b
Nagasaki Haruma 長崎波留麻 **2**:123a
Nagasaki Kaisho 長崎会所 **5**:304a-304b, 306a
Nagasaki miyage **5**:305a
Nagasaki Naval Training Academy. *See* **Kaigun Denshūjo**
Nagasaki Prefecture 長崎県 **5**:304b-305a
  capital **5**:303b
  port **5**:304b
  principal products **5**:304b
  tourist attractions **5**:304b
Nagasaki school 長崎派 **5**:305a-306a; **7**:83b
  individualists **5**:306a
  official painters **5**:305b
  screen and wall painting **7**:43a
  Shen Nanpin school **5**:305b-306a
  woodblock prints **5**:305a-305b
Nagasaki Shipyards **2**:31a; **5**:306a, *306b*
Nagasaki trade 長崎貿易 **1**:211b; **5**:306a;
  Dutch trade **2**:135b
  strict regulation **7**:171a
Nagasawa, Kanaye **5**:306a-306b
Nagasawa Rosetsu. 長沢蘆雪 *See* **Rosetsu**
Nagase & Co, Ltd **5**:306b
Nagashikan **2**:25a
Nagashino 長篠 **6**:63b
Nagashino, Battle of 長篠の戦 **5**:306b
  ashigaru **1**:98a
  firearms usage **2**:279a
  Takeda Katsuyori **7**:322b
Nagashizuki (method of molding paper) **8**:234a
Nagata Masaichi 永田雅一 **5**:306b-307a
Nagata Teiryū 永田貞柳 **5**:307a
Nagata Tetsuzan 永田鉄山 **5**:307a
  February 26th Incident **2**:250a
Nagata Tokuhon 永田徳本 **5**:307a
Nagata Zenkichi. *See* **Aōdō Denzen**
Nagato (battleship) 長門 **5**:307a-307b
Nagato (city) 長門 **5**:307a
Nagatoro 長瀞 **1**:73b; **5**:307b
Nagatsuka Takashi 長塚節 **5**:307b; **7**:103b
Nagauta 長唄 **2**:301a; **4**:77a, 99a; **5**:307b; **7**:149a
  Tōkyō **8**:63b
Nagauta school **4**:91b
Nagaya **3**:245a
Nagayamon (gate) **3**:13a

Nagaya no Ō, Rebellion of 長屋王の変 5:307b-308a
Nagayo Sensai 長与専斎 5:308a
Nagayo Yoshirō 長与善郎 1:155b; 5:308a
Nagegane 投銀 5:308a
Nageire (modern, free-style) 2:289b, *291a*
Nageshi 7:265b
Nagewaza 4:82b
Nagai michi 長い道 4:162b
Naginata 1:89a-89b; 5:308a-308b
Nago (city) 名護 5:308b
Nago (peasant status) 名子 5:308b
Nago Bay 名護湾 5:308b
Nagoshi 夏越 5:308b
Nagoya 名古屋 5:308b, *309a*
  Chūbu region 1:311a
  history 5:308b-309a
  products 5:309a-309b
  tourist attractions 5:309a-309b
Nagoya Castle 名古屋城 5:309a-309b
  paintings 4:151a
Nagoya Gen'i 名古屋玄医 5:309b
Nagoya Railroad Co, Ltd 5:309b
Nagoya Tansuishi 名古屋丹水子 5:309b
Nagoya University 5:309b
Nagusazan Gokokuin 名草山護国院 4:208a
Naha 那覇 5:309b
Nahiko kashū 魚彦歌集 4:169a
Naichi zakkyo 内地雑居 4:333a; 5:309b-310a
Naidaijin 内大臣 5:310a-310b
  inner minister 5:310a-310b
  lord keeper of the privy seal 5:310a-310b; 6:242a
Naikaku Bunko. 内閣文庫 *See* **Cabinet Library**
Naikan therapy 5:310b-311a; 6:261b
Naikasho 内科書 4:312b
Naiken 内検 4:191a
Naikoku Kangyō Hakurankai 内国勧業博覧会 5:341b
Naimushō. 内務省 *See* **Home Ministry**
Naitō Jōsō 内藤丈草 5:311a
Naitō Konan 内藤湖南 5:311a; 7:51b
Naitō Torajirō. 内藤虎次郎 *See* **Naitō Konan**
Naizai hihyō ijō no mono 内在批評以上のもの 4:165a
Nakabashira 7:266a
Nakabayashi Chikutō 中林竹洞 1:211a; 5:311a-311b
Nakadai Motohisa 仲代元久 5:311b
Nakadai Tatsuya 仲代達矢 2:*273a*; 5:311b; 7:68b
Nakada Kaoru 中田薫 5:311b
Nakae Chōmin 中江兆民 1:19a; 2:2a, 332a; 5:311b-312a
  education 5:311b-312a
  Freedom and People's Rights Movement 2:335b
  fukoku kyōhei 2:361a
  Genrōin 5:311b-312a
  political activities 5:311b-312a
  Tōyō jiyū shimbun (Oriental Free Press) 5:311b-312a
  works 5:311b-312a
Nakae Tōju 中江藤樹 5:312a-312b; 7:94b; 8:335a
  Shingaku 7:111b
Nakagawa (Honshū) 那珂川 5:312b
Nakagawa (Shikoku) 那賀川 5:312b
Nakagawa Gorōji 中川五郎治 5:312b-313a
Nakagawa Jun'an 中川淳庵 5:313a; 7:258b
Nakagawa Yoichi 中河与一 5:313a
Nakagawa Zennosuke 中川善之助 5:313a
Nakahama Manjirō 中浜万次郎 5:313a-313b
Nakahara Chūya 中原中也 5:313b
Nakahara Moromori 中原師守 5:255b
Nakai Riken 中井履軒 5:313b
Nakajima Atsushi 中島敦 5:313b
Nakajima Chikuhei 中島知久平 2:343a; 5:313b
Nakajima Mitsuzō. *See* **Takamura Kōun**
Nakajima Nobuyuki 中島信行 5:313b-314a
Nakajima Shōen. *See* **Kishida Toshiko**
Nakajima Toshiko. *See* **Kishida Toshiko**
Nakajō 中条 5:314a
Naka Kansuke 中勘助 5:314a
Nakama 仲間 4:100a; 5:314a
Naka Michiyo 那珂通世 5:314a
Nakamigawa Hikojirō 中上川彦次郎 5:314a-314b
  Fujiyama Raita 2:359a
Nakaminato 那珂湊 5:314b
Nakamura 中村 5:314b
Nakamura Chōhachi 中村長八 5:314b
Nakamura Fusetsu 中村不折 5:314b
Nakamura Gakuryō 中村岳陵 5:314b
Nakamura Hajime 中村元 5:314b-315a
Nakamura Kanzaburō XVII 中村勘三郎(十七代) 4:*94b*
Nakamura Keiu 中村敬宇 5:315a
Nakamura Kenkichi 中村憲吉 5:315a
Nakamura Kichiemon 中村吉右衛門 2:*274b*
Nakamura kiln 中村窯 7:226b
Nakamura Kinnosuke 中村錦之助 8:339a
Nakamura Kusatao 中村草田男 5:315a
  haiku 3:80a
Nakamura Masanao 中村正直 1:237b; 5:315a
  liberalism 4:387a
Nakamura Mitsuo 中村光夫 5:13b, 315a-315b
Nakamura Sakutarō 中村鈼太郎 5:314b
Nakamura Seiichirō 中村清一郎 5:315a
Nakamura Shin'ichirō 中村真一郎 5:315b
Nakamura Tekisai 中村惕斎 5:315b
Nakamura Tsuruzō 中村鶴蔵 6:109b
Nakamura Utaemon 中村歌右衛門 5:315b
  kabuki leadership 4:92b
Nakamura Utaemon VI 4:*93a, 94b*
Nakamura v *Japan (1962)* 2:13a
Nakane Chie 中根千枝 7:218a
  vertical society 8:191a
Nakanishi Seiko. *See* **Arima Ineko**
Nakano 中野 5:315b-316a
Nakano kennel 7:167a
Nakanomikado, Lord 中御門殿 2:358a
Naka no Ōe, Prince. 中大兄皇子 *See* **Tenji, Emperor**
Nakano School 5:316a
Nakano Seigō 中野正剛 5:316a-316b
  ideas 5:316a-316b
  Kokumin Dōmei 4:260a
  political activities 5:316a-316b
Nakano Shigeharu 中野重治 5:13a, 316b-317a; 7:66b
  Kurahara Korehito 5:316b-317a
  novels 5:316b-317a
  proletarian literature movement 6:255a
  Sata Ineko 7:25a
  Shinjinkai 7:115b
  Shin Nihon bungaku 7:122a
Naka no Shima 中之島 6:*119a*
Nakanoshima Kin'ichi 中能島欣一 5:317a
Nakano Tomonori 中野友礼 5:317a
Nakanoumi 中海 5:318b
Nakano Ward 中野区 5:317a
Nakano Yoshio 中野好夫 1:155b; 5:317a-317b
Nakaoka Shintarō 中岡慎太郎 5:317b; 7:3b
Nakaoku koshō 中奥小姓 4:296a
Nakao Kumaki 中尾熊喜 5:317b
Nakarai Bokuyō 半井卜養 5:317b
Nakarai Tōsui 半井桃水 3:136a
Nakasendai Rebellion 中先代の乱 5:317b
Nakasendō 中山道 3:40b-41a; 5:303a, 318a; 6:229b; 8:41a
  railways 6:278a
Nakasone Yasuhiro 中曽根康弘 2:82b; 5:318a
Nakatsu 中津 5:318a
Nakatsukasa Naishi no nikki 中務内侍日記 5:318a-318b
Nakatsu Keikoku 中津渓谷 5:318b
Nakatsukyō 中津峡 5:318b
Nakatsumiya Shrine 中津宮 5:265a
Nakauchi Isao 中内功 2:56b
Nakaumi 中海 5:318b
Nakaura Julião 中浦ジュリアン 5:318b
Nakayama Gishū 中山義秀 5:318b
Nakayama Heijirō 中山平次郎 1:77a
Nakayama Ichirō 中山伊知郎 5:318b
Nakayama Miki 中山みき 5:319a; 7:76b
  Tenrikyō 8:9a
Nakayama Shichiri 中山七里 5:319a
Nakayama Shimpei 中山晋平 5:319a
Nakayama Sohei 中山素平 5:319a-319b
Nakayama Steel Works, Ltd 5:319b
Nakayama Tadamitsu 中山忠光 5:319b
Nakayama Yoshihide 中山義秀 5:318b
Nakaya Ukichirō 中谷宇吉郎 5:319b
Nakazato Kaizan 中里介山 1:164a; 2:268a; 5:319b-320a
  Daibosatsu Tōge 5:320a; 6:221a; 7:121a
  early career 5:319b
  later period 5:320a
Nakazawa Dōni 中沢道二 5:320a
  Shingaku 7:112a
Nakijin castle remains 今帰仁城跡 5:320b
Nakōdo 5:320b-321a
  love marriage and arranged marriage 5:320b
  marriage negotiations 5:320b-321a
  social context 5:320b
Nakoku 奴国 5:321a-321b; 7:266a

Nakoso no Seki 勿来関 5:321b
Namahage 5:*321a*, 321b
Namako. *See* **Sea cucumbers**
Namamugi Jiken. 生麦事件 *See* **Richardson Affair**
Namazu 1:249b; 6:44b
Namba Daisuke. 難波大助 *See* **Toranomon Incident**
Namban 5:321b-322a; 7:104b
Namban art 5:322a-323a, *322a-322b*, 6:153b
Kanō school 4:150a
museums 5:280a
Nambanji 南蛮寺 5:323a
Namban maki-e (lacquer ware) 南蛮蒔絵 4:240b, 361b
Namban screens 5:322a-323a
Nambantetsu 3:333a
Namban trade 5:323a-323b
ships 7:144a
Nambara Shigeru 南原繁 5:323b
Shimoyama Incident 7:107b
Nambokuchō period. *See* **Northern and Southern Courts**
Nambokuchō seijun ron 南北朝正閏論 5:323b-324a
Namboku sōhō 南北相法 6:160b
Nambu Chūhei 南部忠平 5:324a
Nambu Yoshikazu 南部義籌 4:30a
Nambyō 難病 2:116b
Name cards 5:324a
Namerikawa 滑川 5:324a
Names 5:324a-326b
group (clan and family) 5:324b-325a
men's 5:325a-326a
people's 5:324b
personal 5:325a
place 5:326a-326b
women's 5:326a
Nametoko 滑床 5:326b
Nami 波 4:179b
Namida o shishi no tategami ni
Shinoda Masahiro 7:122a
Namiki Gohei 並木五瓶 4:91b; 5:50a, 326b-327a
Namiki Shōzō 並木正三 4:91b; 5:50a, 327a
Namiki Shōzō II 5:16b
Namiki Sōsuke 並木宗輔 5:327a
Namiko 浪子 8:59b
Nam II 4:286b
Nampo Jōmyō 南浦紹明 5:327a
Namu Amida Butsu 南無阿弥陀仏 5:327a-327b
Namu Myōhō renge kyō 南無妙法蓮華経 5:327b
Namura Shipbuilding Co, Ltd 5:327b
Nanakamado [(mountain ash) *Sorbus commixta*] 5:327b
Nanao 七尾 5:327b
Nanatsugama 七ツ釜 5:327b
Nanatsumen 七つ面 4:98b
Nandin 5:329b-330a
Nando 7:248b
Nanga 南画 5:327b-328a
See also **Bunjinga**
Nangakuha 南学派 5:328a
Tani Jichū 7:341b
Nangawara kiln 南川原窯 5:299a
Nangnang 4:382b
Nangoku 南国 5:329a
Naniwa (now Ōsaka) 難波 8:176a
Naniwa-bushi 浪花節 5:328a
kōdan 4:241a-241b
Naniwa erejii (Ōsaka Elegy) 浪花エレジー 8:289a
Naniwakyō 難波京 5:328b; 7:91a
Naniwa miyage 難波土産 5:328b
Naniwa Palace 難波京 2:58a
Nanjing (Nanking) Incident 5:328b-329a
1927 1:288b; 5:328b
1937–1938 5:329a
Shidehara Kijūrō 7:88b
Nanjō Bun'yū 南条文雄 5:329a
Nanki Bunko 南葵文庫 5:329a
Nankoku 南国 5:329a
Nankyō shinshō 南京新唱 1:38b
Nansei Islands. 南西諸島 *See* **Ryūkyū Islands**
Nansenshō Somabito. 南仙笑楚満人 *See* **Tamenaga Shunsui**
Nanshinron. 南進論 *See* **Southern expansion doctrine**
Nansō Satomi hakkenden 南総里見八犬伝 1:130b, 295b; 5:16b, 329a-329b; 8:336b
Nan taiheiki. 難太平記 *See* **Imagawa Sadayo**
Nantaisan 男体山 5:329b; 6:*3a*
Nanten [(nandin) *Nandina domestica*] 5:329b-330a
Nanushi. 名主 *See* **Shōya**
Nan'yō 南陽 5:330a
Nan'yō Eiga Kyōkai 4:202a
Nan'yō no daiharan 南洋の大波瀾 6:332b
Nanzan University 5:330a
Nanzenji 南禅寺 4:125b, 336a; 5:330a-330b; 7:255a
paintings 4:151a
tea gardens
Kobori Enshū 4:238b
Nanzonghua 5:328a
Naobi no Kami 直毘の神 5:330b
Naohi no Kami. *See* **Naobi no Kami**
Naoki Prize 7:293a
Dan Kazuo 2:76b
Genji Keita 3:20a
Hisao Jūran 3:151b
Ibuse Masuji 3:254a-255b
Kaionji Chōgorō 4:112a
Kikuchi Kan 4:206b
Kon Hidemi 4:270a
Kon Tōkō 4:275b
Kuroiwa Jūgo 4:316b
Minakami Tsutomu 5:176a
Nosaka Akiyuki 6:40b
Shiba Ryōtarō 7:84b
Shiroyama Saburō 7:148a
Tachihara Masaaki 7:293a
Umezaki Haruo 8:147b
Yamaguchi Hitomi 8:294b
Naoki Sanjūgo 直木三十五 5:330b-331a
Bungei Shunjū, Ltd 1:210a
Naorai 直会 2:254b-255b; 5:331a-331b; 7:139b
Daijōsai 2:59a-59b
Naoshima Islands 直島諸島 5:331b
NAPF (All Japan Proletarian Arts League) 7:175b
Nara. *See* **Oaks**
Nara (city) 奈良 5:331b-332a; 6:47a
contemporary 5:331b
excavations 5:331b
Heijōkyō 3:124a
history 5:331b
Kasuga Shrine 5:*331a*
natural features 5:331b
pagoda 5:*331a*
Sarusawa Pond 5:*331a*
tourism and culture 5:332a
Nara Basin 奈良盆地 5:332a-332b
Nara Buddhism 2:178a-178b; 5:332b
Narachō bumpō shi (History of Nara Period Grammar) 奈良朝文法史 8:290a
Narahara Shigeru 奈良原繁 4:1a
Nara history. *See* **History of Japan**
Narai 奈良井 5:332b-333a
Nara Kashiwara Archeology Research Institute
Takamatsuzuka tomb 7:314b-315a
Nara Kokuritsu Bunkazai Kenkyūjo. *See* **Nara National Research Institute of Cultural Properties**
Nara Kokuritsu Hakubutsukan. *See* **Nara National Museum**
Nara National Museum 5:276b, 333a; 7:170a
Nara National Research Institute of Cultural Properties 5:333a-333b
Nara Park 5:332a
Nara period 奈良時代 5:333b
Nara Prefecture 奈良県 5:333b-334a
geography and climate 5:334a
history 5:334a
industries 5:334a
tourism and culture 5:334a
Narashino 習志野 5:334a
Nara Women's University 5:334a
Narayama-bushi kō 6:99a
Naraya Mozaemon 奈良屋茂左衛門 5:334a-334b
Narcotics. *See* **Drug abuse**
Narcotics Control Law 2:134a-134b; 5:334b
Narihiradake (*Semiarundinaria fastuosa)* 1:136a
Narikane-bon 業兼本 4:161b
Narita 成田 5:334b
Narita Airport. *See* **New Tōkyō International Airport**
Narita Shinkansen 6:279b
Narita Tomomi 成田知巳 5:334b
Japan Socialist Party 4:49a
Narōdo 7:115b
Narrative literature 5:245b-246b
Narrative of the Expedition of an American Squadron to the China Seas and Japan 6:177b, 185b
Narrow Road through the Provinces 6:297b
Narrow Road to The Deep North, The 8:185b
Narukami 鳴神 4:97b, 98b
Narukami Fudō kitayama-zakura 鳴神不動北山桜 4:98a
Naruko (town) 鳴子 5:334b
Naruko ("bird rattles") 鳴子 5:334b
Naruse Jinzō 成瀬仁蔵 5:335a
Naruse Mikio 成瀬巳喜男 2:270a, 271a, 272a; 5:335a-335b
Narushima Ryūhoku 成島柳北 5:335b
Narutaki Gumi 鳴滝組 2:270a
Naruto 鳴門 5:335b
Naruto Strait 鳴門海峡 5:*335a*, 335b
Nashi 6:170a
Nashiji 梨地 4:240b
Nashimotoshū 梨本集 8:34b
Nashiro 名代 1:147b
Nasu 那須 2:184b; 5:335b
Nasudake 那須岳 5:335b
Nasu Kōgen 那須高原 5:335b-336a
Nasu no Yoichi 那須与一 4:326b; 5:336a
Nasu Volcanic Zone 那須火山帯 1:11b; 5:335b-336a; 8:352a, 368a
Nation, The 4:261a

National Administrative Organization Law 1:13a
National Aerospace Laboratory ... 5:336a; 7:38a
National Alliance. *See* **Kokumin Dōmei**
National anthem 5:336a
National Archives 1:218b; 5:336a-336b
Cabinet Library 1:229a
National assemblies 3:275b
National Association of Chairmen of Town and Village Assemblies 6:238a
National Association of Commercial Broadcasting in Japan 5:366b
National Association of Progressive Mayors 1:107b
National Association of Towns and Villages 6:238a
National Atlas of Japan 5:336b
National Bank Act 4:184b
National Bank Ordinance of 1872 . 1:138a
national banks 5:336b
shizoku 7:151b
National Banks 5:336b
founding 2:30b
National Capital Region Development Law (Shutoken Seibi Hō) 8:67b
National Center for University Entrance Examinations 2:222b
National character 4:38a-39b
opinion surveys 4:40a
National Chemical Laboratory for Industry 1:21b
National Civil Service Law (1948) . 4:351b; 6:264b
National Personnel Authority 5:344b
National Council for Peace and against Nuclear Weapons 6:166b
National Council of State Garden Clubs 2:292a
National Council of Women's Organizations of Agricultural Cooperatives 8:263b
National defense 5:336b-338b
evolving attitudes 5:337b
Japanese-American relations 5:338a
policy of major political parties 5:337b-338a
public attitudes 5:338a-338b
Self Defense Forces 7:58b-60b
National Defense Academy . 5:338b; 7:60a
National Defense College 5:338b
National Defense Council .. 1:218b; 2:82a; 5:338b; 6:244a; 7:60a
National Defense Program 7:60a
National Defense Women's Association. *See* **Dai Nippon Kokubō Fujinkai**
National Diet Library .. 2:95a; 5:338b-339a; 7:50b; 8:90a
Cabinet Library 1:229a
Kanamori Tokujirō 4:135b
National Education Association ... 2:180b
National Enterprise and Public Corporation Labor Relations Commission (Kōkyō Kigyōtai Tō Rōdō Iinkai) 6:265a
National Environmental Policy Act 2:224a, 225a
"National era" 1:232a
periodization 6:175a
National Eugenic Law 2:234b; 6:224a
National Federation of Industrial Labor Organizations 7:124a
National Federation of Regional Women's Organization 1:273b
National Federation of Research Institutes for School Curricula ... 2:180b
National flag 5:339a
National Foundations Society 4:259b-260a
National health insurance ... 5:339a-339b
National Health Resort Hot Spring 7:351b
National Herbarium (Leyden) 7:193a
National holidays 2:262a
National income 5:339b-341b
complementary structure and economic growth 5:340a-340b
flow of funds 2:292a
public sector 5:340b-341a
size and structure 5:339b-340a
transfer payments 5:341a-341b
National Income Taxation 7:355a-358b
National Industrial Exhibition 5:341b
National Institute for Research Advancement (NIRA) 3:127b; 5:341b-342a
National Institute of Genetics 4:204b
National Institute of Japanese Literature 4:256b-257a
Nationalism ... 5:342a-343b; 6:214a; 7:214a
education 2:172a, 183b
historiography 3:157b
managerial ideology 5:91b-92a
patriots and nationalists 1850-1890 5:342b
popular 5:342b-343a
popular 1890-1945 .... 5:342b-343a
postwar 5:343a-343b
premodern patriotism 5:342a-342b
statist 1890-1945 .... 5:342b
ultranationalism 8:145a
Nationalist Association 4:260b-261a
Nationalist Labor Party 1:2b
Nationality, legal
loss of 4:32b-33a
Nationality Law. *See* **Japanese nationality**
National Japanese Language Research Institute 5:343b
National Laboratory for High Energy Physics 6:306a
National Land Agency 1:219a; 5:343b
National Learning School (Kokugaku) 1:75b
National Mobilization Law 1:229a; 5:343b-344a
China War 3:201b
Konoe Fumimaro 4:273b
National Service Draft Ordinance . 5:347b
National Museum of Ethnology ... 5:344a; 6:306a; 7:193a
National Museum of Japanese History 4:261b
National Museum of Modern Art, Tōkyō 5:344a-344b
National Museum of Natural History (Leyden) 7:193a
National Museum of Western Art . 5:344b
National museums 5:276a-276b
National parks and quasi-national parks 5:344b
Abashiri 1:1b
Akan 1:40b
Akiyoshidai 8:295a
Ashizuri-Uwakai 1:102b
Aso 1:103a; 6:76a
Bandai-Asahi 1:11b, 127b, 136b-137a
Chichibu-Tama 1:272a; 6:239a
Chōkai 8:293b
Chūbu Sangaku 1:5a, 127b
Daisen-Oki 2:67a-67b; 6:84b
Daisetsuzan 1:92b; 2:67b
Fuji-Hakone-Izu 1:49b, 107b; 2:342b-343a; 6:125a
Hakusan 3:88b-89a; 7:375a
Inland Sea 1:124b; 6:76a, 335a
Iriomote 3:331a; 6:92a
Ise-Shima 1:21b; 3:338a
Jōshin'etsu Kōgen 1:95b; 4:78a
Kirishima-Yaku 7:310b
Kita Nagato Coast 6:102a
Kongō-Ikoma 6:122b
Kurikoma 8:293b
Meiji no Mori Minoo 6:122b
Myōgi-Arafune-Saku Kōgen 7:105b
Nikkō 6:3a
Oga 6:68a
Ogasawara 6:68b-69a
Okinawa Coast 5:308b
Rikuchū Coast 6:67b
Rishiri-Rebun-Sarobetsu 6:320b
Saikai 6:369b
San'in Coast 4:338b
Shikotsu-Tōya 7:347a
Shiretoko 7:147b
Sobo-Katamuki 7:310b
Southern Alps 1:39b; 7:236a
Southern Bōsō 7:349b
Suigō-Tsukuba 8:313b
Tanzawa-Ōyama 7:346a
Towada-Hachimantai 1:43a
Unzen-Amakusa 1:50a
Yōrō-Sekigahara-Ibi 6:68a
Yoshino-Kumano 6:125a; 7:115a
Zaō 8:293b
National Pearl Research Institute ... 1:21b
National Pension Insurance 7:211b
National Pension Law (Kokumin Nenkin Hō) 6:173a; 7:55b
pensions 4:353a
National People's School Order ... 4:260b
National Personnel Authority 1:218b; 4:351b; 5:344b; 6:264b
impeachment 3:275b
Occupation 6:53b
public employees 6:264b
recommendations 5:344b-345a
Satō Tatsuo 7:29a
shuntō 4:352a
National Personnel Law (Kokka Kōmuin Hō) of 1948 .... 4:358a
National Police Agency 6:198a-198b
National Police Reserve .. 5:345b; 6:198b; 7:58b-59a; 8:344b
defense industry 2:82b
national defense 5:336b-338b
National Safety Forces 5:346a
Occupation 6:54b
United States-Japan security treaties 8:166a
United States military bases, disputes 8:168a
"National polity." *See* **Kokutai**
National Public Safety Commission 1:219a; 5:345b-346a
Tōkyō Metropolitan Police Department 8:67b
National Railway Workers' Union .. 7:107a
National Research Institute of Police Science 2:47a
National Research Laboratory of Metrology 1:21b
National Rural Police (Kokka Chihō Keisatsu) 6:198b
National Safety Forces 5:346a; 7:59a; 8:344b
national defense 5:336b-338b
National Police Reserve 5:345b
United States military bases, disputes 8:168a
National Salvation Association ... 5:346a; 7:78b; 8:380a
December Ninth Movement 2:81b

National Science Museum 5:346a
National Seclusion 1:161b; 5:346a-347b; 7:8a, 256b, 263a, 266b
abandonment 3:192a
Austro-Hungarian relations 1:119b
China 1:284b
Chōsen tsūshinshi 1:304a
criticism 1:39a, 141b
Daikokuya Kōdayū 2:60b
Dutch Factory 2:135b
eating habits 2:305a
Edo period 3:185b
foreign trade policy 2:324b
Gaikokusen Uchiharai Rei 3:3b
Indonesia and Japan 3:290b
Kaempfer, Engelbert 4:102a
Kaigai Tokō Kinshi Rei 4:109b
Kakure Kirishitan 4:119a
Kanagawa Treaty 4:135b
Kawai Tsugunosuke 4:179b
Kawaji Toshiakira 4:179b
missionary work 2:330b
Morrison Incident 5:256a
Nagasaki trade 5:306a
naichi zakkyo 5:309b-310a
Nakahama Manjirō 5:313a-313b
Opening of Japan 6:114b
Perry, Matthew Calbraith 6:177b
Phaeton Incident 6:182a
plants 6:191a
port towns 6:228b
Russia 6:340b
Sakuma Shōzan's violation 7:3b
Shinkiron 7:119a
Shinron 7:124a
Shinsui Kyōyo Rei 7:125b
Spanish relations 4:369b
technological development 7:368b
temples 8:1b
Thailand and Japan 8:20b
Tokugawa Iemitsu 8:48a
Tokugawa shogunate 8:56a
trade regulations 7:171a
transportation 8:98a
United Kingdom 8:150b
United States 8:154b
Vietnam 8:191b
warriors 1:222b
Watanabe Kazan 8:235b
Western learning 8:241b
whaling 8:249b
National Service Draft Ordinance 5:347b; 8:277b
Koreans in Japan 4:291a
National Socialist Party 8:296a
National Space Development Agency of Japan 1:172b; 5:347b; 7:38a, 240a
National Spiritual Mobilization Movement 5:348a; 8:277a
National Sports Festival 5:348a; 7:243a
National Sports Stadium 7:116a
National Tax Administration Agency 5:188a
tax office 7:358b
National Tax Agency 7:355a-358b
National Tax Tribunal 5:348a-348b
National Trade Union of Metal and Engineering Workers 1:72a
National Union of Agricultural Cooperative Women's Guild 8:267a
National University of Singapore 7:196b
National Vacation Village 7:303b
National Veterans' Association (Gōyūren) 6:238b
National wealth 5:349a-349b
Natori 名取 5:349b
Natorigawa 名取川 4:328a
Natsuigawa 夏井川 5:349b
Natsukodachi 夏木立 8:288b
Natsume Sōseki 夏目漱石 1:5a, 74a, 155b; 2:274a, 291b; 5:12b, 314a, 349b-350a, *350b*, 351a; 7:103b, 125b
biography 5:349b-350a
fūryū concept 2:374b
Komiya Toyotaka's teacher 4:267a
works 5:350a-351a
Natsu no heitai (Summer Soldiers) 夏の兵隊 8:15a
Natsu no yami 夏の闇 4:111b
Nattō 2:306a; 5:351a
Natural disasters 5:351a
Natural features. *See* **Japan**
Natural gas 2:216a; 3:344b; 5:353a
Naturalism 5:351a-351b
Iwano Hōmei 3:361b
literary criticism 5:12a
literary expression 2:378b
modern 5:54a-54b
Shimazaki Tōson 7:101a
Tayama Katai 7:358b-359a
Tokuda Shūsei 8:44b
Uno Kōji 8:173b
Naturalist literary movement
Iida Dakotsu 3:262b
I-novel 3:312a
Naturalization 4:32b-33a; 5:351b
grand 4:33a
of Koreans in Japan 4:291b
ordinary 4:32b-33a
special 4:33a
Natural monuments and protected species 5:352a-352b
animals 5:352a
plants 5:352a-352b
protected areas 5:352a
Natural resources 5:352b-355a
coal 5:352b-353a
economic efficiency 2:146a
hydroelectric power 5:353a-353b
metals and minerals 5:353b-354a
natural gas 5:353a
nuclear power and alternative sources 5:353b
petroleum 5:353a
prospects 5:354b-355a
wood and pulp 5:354a-354b
Natural sciences 5:355a-357a
Chinese influences 5:355a
early Edo period 5:355a-355b
after Meiji period 5:356b-357a
modern science and Western Learning 5:355b-356b
postwar era 5:357a
western (Namban) culture 5:355a
Nature, concept of 5:357a-357b
religious symbolism 6:295b
Nature Conservation Law 2:228a
Nature in Japanese religion 5:357b-358a
Nature Protection District 5:352a-352b
Nature religion 6:291a
Naumann, Edmund 5:358a-358b
geology 2:141a
Naval Academy 5:358a-358b
National Defense Academy 5:338b
Naval bases 1:296a
Naval General Staff Office 5:358b
independence 1:87a
power 8:85a
Naval Institute. *See* **Kaigun Denshūjo**
Navy, Imperial Japanese 3:278a
militarism 5:173b-174b
shipbuilding industry 7:141b-142a
World War II 8:271b
Navy Day 6:347a
Navy Ministry 5:358b
Nawabari 5:358b
Nawa Nagatoshi 名和長年 5:358b
Naya Sukezaemon 納屋助佐衛門 6:340b
Nayoro 名寄 5:358b
Nayosechō 名寄帳 5:359a
Nayotake なよたけ 4:169a
Naze 名瀬 4:106a; 5:359a
Nazo nazo 6:311b
NCR Japan, Ltd (Nippon NCR) 5:359a
NDL (National Diet Library) 5:338b-339a
Nebuta Festival ねぶた祭 1:69b, 160b; 2:*255a*; 5:359a
Neesima, Joseph Hardy. *See* **Niijima Jō**
Negi. *See* **Welsh onion**
Negishi Tanka Kai (Negishi Tanka Society) 根岸短歌会 5:19b; 8:216b
Negoro-nuri 根来塗 2:295a; 5:359a-359b
Nehru, Jawaharlal 3:289a
Neighborhood associations 1:300a; 5:359b; 8:277b
Imperial Rule Assistance Association 3:281a
Neighborhood groups 5:359b
Nekki 5:359b
Nekkoku no maki (The Tropics) 6:*158b*
Neko 1:251a
Neko to Shōzō to futari no onna (A Cat, Shōzō, and Two Women) 猫と庄造と二人のをんな 8:319b
Nema 7:248b
Nembutsu 念仏 1:194b; 4:67a; 5:359b; 6:270a; 7:63a, 347a
Ippen 3:328b-329b; 4:62a
kakun 4:118b
religious symbolism 6:295b
Shinran 7:123a
Yūzū Nembutsu sect 8:359b
Nembutsu odori 念仏踊 2:374a; 4:62a; 5:360a; 7:149a
Nemure Pari 眠れパリ 4:139a
Nemureru bijo 眠れる美女 4:176b
Nemuro 根室 5:360a
Nemuro harbor 5:*360b*
Nemuro Peninsula 根室半島 5:360a
Nemuro Strait 根室海峡 5:360a
Nenashigusa 根なし草 4:256a
Nenchū gyōji 年中行事 2:252b-253a, 258a-262a, 299a
Heian period 2:259b-261b
post-Heian period 2:260b-262a
pre-Heian antecedents 2:258b-259b
sources 2:258a-258b
See also **Festivals**
Nenchū gyōji emaki 年中行事絵巻 7:42b
shinden-zukuri 7:110b
Sumiyoshi school 7:270a
Nengajō 5:372b
Nengō 年号 1:231b-232a; 5:360a
Nengu 年貢 5:360a-361b
kokudainō 4:257a
tansen and tammai 7:344b
Nenjū gyōji emaki. 年中行事絵巻 *See Nenchū gyōji emaki*
Nenki 年紀 5:361b
Nenkō joretsu 7:189a
Nenkō system. *See* **Seniority system**
Nenkō wages and benefits 4:344b
"Nennen saisai" 年年歳歳 1:21a
Neo-Confucianism. *See* **Confucianism; Shushigaku; Yōmeigaku**
Neo-Kantian school 7:335a-335b
Neolithic period 5:361b

Neo-Thomism 4:85b
Nerima Ward 練馬区 5:361b
Nerimiso (miso paste) 2:25b
Netherlands and Japan 5:361b-363a
  influence on medicine 5:146b-147a
  Japanese studies 4:43a-43b
  modern period 5:362b-363a
  premodern period 5:362a
Netherlands Trading Company 5:362b; 7:193a
Netsuke 3:*313a*; 5:*363a*, 363b-365a
  inrō 3:313b
Neuer Tanz (new dance) 2:76a
Nevskii, Nikolai Aleksandrovich 5:365a
New Asian order 8:159a
New Collection of Ancient and Modern Times 7:119b-121a
New Drama 7:112a
New Education Movement 7:367a-367b
New Fourth Army Incident 7:48a
New industrial cities 5:365a
New Japan Philharmonic Orchestra 6:140b
New Left Movement 6:284b; 7:252a
New Liberal Club 5:365a; 6:213a
  Kōno Yōhei, founder and chairman 4:275a
"New Order in East Asia." *See* **Tōa Shinchitsujo**
New Order in Europe and Greater East Asia 8:107b
New Order Movement 5:365a-366a; 8:277b
  Asō Hisashi 1:103a
  Imperial Rule Assistance Association 3:280a
  Konoe Fumimaro 4:273a
  National Mobilization Law 5:343b-344a
New People's Society 8:281b
New Photography Movement 6:186a
New religions 2:300a; 5:366a-368b; 6:292a
  early development 5:367a-367b
  lay Buddhist movement 4:372a
  priesthood 6:238b
  Shintō 7:129b
  significance 5:368b
  social and religious background 5:366b-367a
  twentieth century 5:367b-368b
  Union of New Religious Organizations of Japan 8:150a
  women in 8:257b
News agencies 5:368b-369a
  mass communications 5:128b
Newspaper Law 2:339a
Newspapers 5:369a-370a
  advertising 1:16b
  censorship 1:252a-252b, 253b
  history 5:369a-369b
  journalists 5:370a
  local 5:370a-370b
  mass communications 5:128a-128b
  mass media 5:369b-370a
  Meiji period (1868-1912) 4:46a
  monopoly dealerships 5:370a
  nationwide 5:370b
  publishing 6:267b
  sociocultural contributions 5:129a
News services 3:318b
New Theater movement 8:300a
New Tōkyō International Airport 1:37b; 5:*370b*, 371a-371b
Newtonianism 5:356a
New Trunk Line. *See* **Shinkansen**
Newt. *See* **Imori**
New Tsukiji Theater Company (Shin Tsukiji Gekidan) 8:299b
New Woman's Association. *See* **Shin Fujin Kyōkai**
New Year 1:160b; 2:258a-260a, 262a; 5:371b-372a
  cooking 2:22a
  enkai (banquet) 2:218a
  folk religion 2:299a
  games 2:367a
  joya no kane 5:*371a*
  kadomatsu 5:*371a*
  New Year's Day 5:371b
  New Year's Eve 5:371b
  Ōshōgatsu and Koshōgatsu 5:372a
  religion 6:291b
  rice growing rites 1:23a
New Year's cards 5:372b
New Year's Scene at Nihombashi 8:78b
New York City Ballet 2:76a
New York Herald Tribune 3:151b
New Zealand and Japan 5:372b-373a
  Japanese studies 4:44b
Neyagawa 寝屋川 5:373a
Nezame monogatari emaki 寝覚物語絵巻 5:373a-373b
Nezamenotoko 寝覚ノ床 5:373b
Nezu Art Museum 5:276b, 373b
Nezu Bijutsukan 5:373b
Nezu Kaichirō 根津嘉一郎 5:373b-374a
Nezumi 6:284a
Nezumimochi [(Japanese privet) *Ligustrum japonicum*] 5:374a
Nezu no seki 念珠関 7:146b
NGK Insulators, Ltd 5:374a
NHK (Japan Broadcasting Corporation) 1:4b, 93a, 171b-173b; 5:374a-374b; 6:275a
  folk song collection 2:301b
  international communications 3:318b
  wire-relayed broadcasting 8:254b
NHK Spring Co, Ltd 5:374b
Nichibei Gakusei Kaigi 4:10a-10b
Nichibei Gyōsei Kyōtei 8:165a-165b
Nichibei Kyōiku Iinkai 4:50a-50b
Nichibei Shinshi Kyōyaku 日米紳士協約 3:24a-24b
Nichibei Shūkō Tsūshō Jōyaku. *See* **Harris Treaty**
Nichibei Sōgo Bōei Enjo Kyōtei 8:165b
Nichibei Washin Jōyaku. 日米和親条約 *See* **Kanagawa Treaty**
Nichidokui Sangoku Dōmei 日独伊三国同盟 8:107a-107b
Nichiei Dōmei. 日英同盟 *See* **Anglo-Japanese Alliance**
Nichietsu Bōeki Kai (Japan-Vietnam Trade) 8:192a
Nichiei Tsūshō Kōkai Jōyaku. 日英通商航海条約 *See* **Anglo-Japanese Commercial Treaty of 1894**
Nichifutsu Kyōyaku 日仏協約 2:333b
Nichifutsu tsūshin 日仏通信 7:310b
Nichii Co, Ltd 5:374b
Nichimen Co Ltd 5:374b
Nichinan 日南 5:375a
Nichinan Coast, Quasi-National Park 日南海岸国定公園 1:70b
Nichinichi shimbun 日日新聞 4:100a
Nichiō 日奥 5:375a
  Fuju Fuse sect 2:359b
Nichiren 日蓮 5:375a-376b
  daimoku 5:327b
  Fuju Fuse sect 2:359b
  Hōnen 4:67b
  Lotus Sutra 5:74a
  portrait 5:*375a*
  Risshō ankoku ron 6:321a
  Tainoura 7:298b
Nichiren sect 日蓮宗 1:178b-179a; 5:376b-377b
  Azuchi Disputation 1:126b-127a
  basic doctrines and controversies 5:376b-377a
  climax and decline 5:377a-377b
  Fuju Fuse branch 2:359b
  mandalas 5:100b, 376a
  modern period (1868-); "Nichirenism" 5:377b
  Nichiren 5:375a-376b
  Namu Myōhō renge kyō 5:327b
  Nichiō 5:375a
  Temmon Hokke Rebellion 7:381b
Nichiren Shōshū 7:303b
Nichirenshū Fujiha 7:303b
Nichiren: the Buddhist Prophet 1:56b
Nichirin (The Sun) 日輪 8:332a
Nichiro Gyogyō Kaisha, Ltd 2:284a; 5:378a
  Hiratsuka Tsunejirō 3:146a
Nichiro kyōyaku. *See* **Russo-Japanese agreements of 1907-1916**
Nichiro Sensō. 日露戦争 *See* **Russo-Japanese War**
Nichirōto. 日労党 *See* **Nihon Rōnōtō**
Nichiyō gorakuban 日曜娯楽版 6:275b
Nicknames 5:325a-326a
Nifon no cotoba to historia uo narai xiran to fossvrv fito no tameni xeva ni yava ragvetarv Feige no monogatari 2:241a
Night Drum 8:339b
Night schools 5:378a
"Nights of Fitful Waking" 8:339a-339b
Night View of Kanazawa in Musashi Province 8:143b-144a, *144b*
Nigite. *See* **Gohei**
Nihommachi 日本町 5:378a-378b
Nihommatsu 二本松 5:378b
Nihon 日本 5:378b
Nihon Aeroplane Manufacturing Co, Ltd 8:353b
Nihon Apatchi zoku 日本アパッチ族 4:266a
Nihon Arupusu 4:12b
Nihon Baputesuto Dōmei 1:142a
Nihon Baputesuto Remmei 1:142a
Nihon Beikoku Kabushiki Kaisha (Japan Rice Company, Ltd) 日本米穀株式会社 2:127a
Nihon-Betonamu Yūkō Kyōkai (Japan-Vietnam Friendship Association) 8:192a
Nihon Bijutsuin. 日本美術院 *See* **Japan Fine Arts Academy**
Nihon bukkyō shi: Jōseihen (History of Buddhism in Japan, Ancient Period) 日本仏教史:上世編 2:105a
Nihon bukkyō shi no kenkyū (Studies on the History of Buddhism in Japan) 日本仏教史の研究 8:114a
Nihon bumpōgaku gairon (Outline of Japanese Grammar) 日本文法学概論 8:290a
Nihon bumpōron (Japanese Grammar) 日本文法論 8:290a
Nihon bumpō yōron (Essentials of Japanese Grammar) 日本文法要論 8:290a

Nihon Bungaku Hōkokukai ··· **5**:379a

Nihon Bunka Kenkyūjo ··· 日本文化研究所 ··· **1**:2b

Nihon buppō chūkō gammon ··· 日本仏法中興願文 ··· **2**:187a

Nihon Cement Co, Ltd. ··· **1**:96a; **5**:379a

Nihon chimbotsu 日本沈没 ··· **4**:266a

Nihon Chiri Gakkai ··· **1**:103b

Nihon chishi ··· 日本地誌 ··· **6**:288a

Nihon Chōkoku Kai ··· **3**:143a

Nihon dai bunten ··· 日本大文典 ··· **6**:59b

Nihon daijisho 日本大辞書 ··· **5**:379a

Nihondaira ··· 日本平 **5**:379a; **7**:104a

Nihon Dempō Tsūshinsha (Dentsū) **1**:16b

Nihon eitaigura 日本永代蔵 ··· **8**:144a

Nihonga ··· **5**:379a-380a

  Japan Fine Arts Academy ··· **4**:45b

Nihon gaikō shi ··· 日本外交史 ··· **4**:232b

Nihon Gakujutsu Kaigi. *See* **Science Council of Japan**

Nihon Gakujutsu Shinkōkai. *See* **Japan Society for the Promotion of Science**

Nihon Gakushiin. *See* **Japan Academy**

Nihon Geijutsuin. *See* **Japan Art Academy**

Nihon Genshiryoku Kenkyūjo ··· **1**:114b

Nihongi. 日本紀 *See* **Nihon shoki**

Nihon Ginkō. *See* **Bank of Japan**

Nihon Harisuto Seikyōkai ··· 日本ハリスト聖教会 ··· **3**:216b

Nihon Heimintō (Japan Commoners' Party) ··· 日本平民党 ··· **6**:210b

Nihon Heiwa Gakkai (Peace Studies Association of Japan) ··· **6**:145b

Nihon Heiwa Kenkyū Kondan Kai (Japan Peace Research Group) ··· **6**:145b

Nihon hyōron (Japan Review) ··· 日本評論 **5**:380a; **8**:127b

Nihon infureishon no kenkyū (Study of Japanese Inflation) ··· **6**:135b

Nihon Ishikai ··· **4**:47a-47b

Nihon Jidō Bungakusha Kyōkai ··· **5**:19a

Nihon Jidō Bungeika Kyōkai ··· **5**:19a

Nihonjin ··· 日本人 ··· **5**:11b, 380b; **7**:51b, 258b

Nihonjin no hōishiki ··· 日本人の法意識 ··· **4**:184b

Nihonjin no seishin shi kenkyū ··· 日本人の精神史研究 ··· **4**:125b

Nihonjin reika · 日本人霊歌 ··· **8**:114a

Nihon Jiyūtō ··· 日本自由党 **4**:274a; **6**:211b

  Ashida Hitoshi ··· **1**:97b

Nihon Joshi Daigaku ··· **4**:50b

Nihonkai ··· 日本海 ··· **7**:46a

Nihon Kaigai Kyōkai Rengōkai ··· **2**:201a

Nihonkai Kaisen ··· 日本海海戦 ··· **8**:118a

Nihon kaika shōshi ··· 日本開化小史 ··· **7**:294b

Nihon kaizō hōan taikō ··· 日本改造法案大綱 **4**:225b; **8**:359a

Nihon Kajin Kyōkai ··· **5**:19b

Nihon Kakushintō (Japan Reform Party) 日本革新党 ··· **1**:40a; **4**:261a

Nihon keizai shimbun ··· 日本経済新聞 ··· **5**:380b

  Television Tōkyō Channel 12, Ltd · **7**:380b

Nihon keizai shinshi ··· 日本経済新誌 ··· **4**:180b

Nihon Kiin ··· **5**:380b

Nihon Kindai Bungakukan ··· 日本近代文学館 ··· **5**:275b

Nihon Kirisuto Kyōdan ··· **8**:150a

Nihon Kirisutokyō Fujin Kyōfūkai ··· 日本基督教婦人矯風会 ··· **4**:324b

Nihon Kirisutokyō Rengōkai ··· **1**:305a

Nihon kirui. 日本紀類 *See* **Nihon kiryaku**

Nihon kiryaku ··· 日本紀略 ··· **5**:381a

Nihon Kōfuku Bunsho ··· **7**:278a-278b

Nihon kōki ··· 日本後紀 ··· **6**:315b

Nihon Kokka Shakaitō ··· 日本国家社会党 ··· **1**:40a

Nihon Kōkokunushi Kyōkai ··· **4**:9b

Nihon Kōkoku Shinsa Kikō ··· **4**:9b-10a

Nihon Koku ··· 日本国 ··· **4**:7a

Nihonkoku genzaisho mokuroku ··· 日本国見在書目録 ··· **1**:154a

Nihon kokugo daijiten ··· 日本国語大辞典 ··· **2**:93b

Nihonkoku kokken an ··· 日本国国憲按 ··· **8**:127b

Nihon kokusei chizu 日本国勢地図 · **5**:336b

Nihon koten bungaku taikei (Compendium of Japanese Classical Literature) ··· 日本古典文学大系 ··· **2**:104b

Nihon Kyōdōtō (Japan Cooperative Party) ··· 日本協同党 ··· **6**:211b

Nihon kyōiku shōshi ··· 日本教育小史 ··· **4**:109b

Nihon Kyōsantō. 日本共産党 *See* **Japan Communist Party**

Nihon Kyōshokuin Kumiai Rengō ··· 日本教職員組合連合 ··· **7**:366b

Nihon Kyōshokuin Remmei · 日本教職員連盟 ··· **7**:366b

Nihon meizan zue ··· 日本名山図絵 ··· **7**:341a

Nihon Mingeikan ··· **4**:46a

Nihon Mingei Kyōkai ··· **4**:179a

Nihon Minkan Hōsō Remmei ··· **5**:336b

Nihon Minshutō (Japan Democratic Party) ··· 日本民主党 ··· **5**:381a

  Hatoyama Ichirō ··· **3**:113a

  Rikken Minseitō ··· **6**:315a

  Tanaka Kakuei ··· **7**:337a

Nihon Montoku Tennō jitsuroku. 日本文徳天皇実録 *See* **Rikkokushi**

Nihon Musantō (Japan Proletarian Party) ··· 日本無産党 **5**:381a; **6**:211b

Nihon no autosaidā ··· 日本のアウトサイダー ··· **4**:181b

Nihon no fujin: Fujin undō no hatten o megutte ··· **7**:349b

Nihon nōgyō no tenkai katei (The Development of Japanese Agriculture) ··· 日本農業の展開過程 ··· **8**:36b

Nihon nōgyō seisanryoku kōzō 日本農業生産力構造 ··· **8**:289a

Nihon no kasō shakai (Japan's Lower Classes) ··· 日本の下層社会 **7**:164a; **8**:264a, 334b

Nihon no kōkogaku ··· 日本の考古学 ··· **1**:76a

Nihon no kuroi kiri ··· 日本の黒い霧 ··· **4**:315b

Nihon Nōmin Kumiai ··· 日本農民組合 ··· **1**:84a

Nihon no rōdō mondai ··· 日本の労働問題 ··· **7**:281a

Nihon Nōsan Kōgyō ··· **5**:381a

Nihon nōson fujin mondai (The Problems of Rural Women in Japan) ··· 日本農村婦人問題 ··· **8**:266b

Nihon oyobi nihonjin (Japan and the Japanese) · 日本及日本人 ··· **5**:316a

Nihon oyobi nihonjin no michi 日本及び日本人の道 ··· **6**:82a

Nihon Pen Kurabu ··· **4**:47b-48a

Nihon Radiator Co, Ltd ··· **5**:381b

Nihon reiiki. *See* **Nihon ryōiki**

Nihon Rekishi Chiri Gakkai ··· **3**:156b

Nihon rekishi dai jitten ··· 日本歴史大辞典 ··· **8**:240a

Nihon rettō kaizō ron ··· 日本列島改造論 ··· **5**:381b

Nihon Rōdō Kumiai Zenkoku Hyōgikai (All-Japan Council of Labor Unions) · 日本労働組合全国評議会 ··· **6**:222a

Nihon Rōmanha ··· 日本浪曼派 ··· **5**:19a, 381b; **7**:176a

  Kamei Katsuichirō ··· **4**:125a

Nihon Rōnōtō (Japan Labor-Farmer Party) ··· 日本労農党 ··· **5**:382a

  Asō Hisashi ··· **1**:102b

Nihon ryōiki ··· 日本霊異記 · **1**:180b; **5**:26a, 29b, 382a; **7**:67a, 72a

  folktales ··· **2**:304a

  Shintō ··· **7**:126b

Nihon sammon opera ··· 日本三文オペラ ··· **4**:111b

Nihon sandai jitsuroku. 日本三代実録 *See* **Rikkokushi**

Nihon Sankei ··· 日本三景 ··· **5**:382a

Nihon seiji shisōshi kenkyū ··· 日本政治思想史研究 **4**:259a; **5**:121b

Nihon seiki ··· 日本政記 ··· **6**:281a

Nihon Seikōkai 日本聖公会 ··· **7**:51b

Nihon Seinen Kaigai Kyōryoku Tai · **4**:47b

Nihon seishin (The Spirit of Japan) ··· 日本精神 ··· **4**:204b

Nihon Sekijūjisha ··· **4**:40b

Nihon shakai no kazokuteki kōsei ··· 日本社会の家族的構成 ··· **4**:184b

Nihon Shakai Shugi Dōmei (Japan Socialist League) ··· 日本社会主義同盟 ··· **5**:382a-382b; **6**:210b

  Sekirankai auxiliary ··· **7**:57a

Nihon Shakaitō. 日本社会党 *See* **Japan Socialist Party**

Nihon shihon shugi hattatsu shi kōza · 日本資本主義発達史講座 **3**:361a; **5**:382b

Nihon shihon shugi ronsō ··· 日本資本主義論争 · **4**:362b; **5**:382

  central issues ··· **5**:382b-383a

  historical context ··· **5**:383a-383b

  postwar significance ··· **5**:383b

Nihonshi jiten ··· 日本史辞典 ··· **8**:240a

Nihon Shimbun Kyōkai ··· **4**:47b

Nihon Shimpotō (Japan Progressive Party) ··· 日本進歩党 ··· **6**:211b

Nihon shoki ··· 日本書紀 · **1**:106a, 141b, 151b, 353b; **2**:259b; **4**:259b; **5**:25b, 383b-384a; **6**:290b; **7**:69a, 85a, 143b, 296a-297a, 310b, 324b, 376a, 382b; **8**:285b

  analysis ··· **5**:27a

  Chinese literature ··· **1**:293a

  commentaries ··· **5**:384a

compilation 5:383b-384a
early Japanese song 2:137a, 138b
Five Kings of Wa 2:287b
folktales 2:303b
fudoki 2:341a
Fujiwarakyō references 2:350a
historiography 3:152b-153a
horse-rider theory 3:230a
Japanese language, history 4:28b
Jimmu, Emperor 4:57a-57b
Kada no Azumamaro lectures 4:100b
Keitai, Emperor 4:190a
kikajin 4:205a
Kojiki compared 4:251a
mythology 5:292a-295a
nature, concept of 5:357a-357b
nature in 5:357a
Ōjin, Emperor 6:76b
orthography 4:134b
periodization 6:176a
pheasants 6:182b
religious symbolism 6:295b
Rikkokushi 6:315b
roof tiles 6:337b
Shaku nihongi 7:76a
Shintō 7:126a
tattoos 7:350a
tokoyo 8:44a
use of language 5:104a
wagtails 8:201a
waka 8:204a
Wani 8:223a
wild ducks 8:253a
women in Japan 8:258a
Yamato court 8:308b
Yamatotakeru, Prince 8:311a-311b
Nihon shoki tsūshō 日本書紀通証 7:341b
Nihon Shōkō Kaigisho 日本商工会議所 4:11a
Nihon shomin kyōikushi 日本庶民教育史 6:133b
Nihon Shoseki Shuppan Kyōkai 4:10b
Nihonshu (Japanese sake) 7:1a
Nihon shugi 日本主義 5:384a-384b
Daitōjuku 2:68a
ultranationalism 8:144b
Nihon Shūkyō Remmei. *See* **Japan Federation of Religions**
Nihon suidokō 日本水土考 3:25b
Nihon Tenji Toshokan 4:10b-11a
Nihon Tetsudō Kaisha 5:384b; 6:278b-279a
Nihon Tokushukō, Ltd 2:56b
Nihon University 5:384b
university upheavals of 1968-1969 8:171b
Nihon yakkyokuhō 6:182b
Nihon yūyō shokubutsu zusetsu 日本有用植物図説 7:339b
Nihon Zasshi Kyōkai 4:47a
Niichi Suto. *See* **General Strike of 1947**
Niigata 新潟 5:385a
Niigata Engineering Co, Ltd 5:385a-385b
Niigata hanjō ki 新潟繁昌記 8:11b
Niigata Plain 新潟平野 5:385b
Niigata Prefecture 新潟県 5:385b-386a
Niihama 新居浜 5:386a
Niijima Jō 新島襄 5:386a-386b
Niimanabi にひまなび(新学) 4:129b
Niimanabi iken 新学異見 4:103a
Niimi 新見 5:386b
Niinamesai (harvest rites) 新嘗祭 5:386b; 8:311a
Niitsu 新津 5:386b
Niiza 新座 5:386b
Niji 虹 7:311b
Niji no Matsubara 4:159a; 5:386b-387a
Nijō, Lady 二条后 8:87a
Nijō Castle 二条城 2:375a; 4:*334b*; 5:387a; 7:*162b*
Kobori Enshū 4:238b
paintings 4:151a
Nijōgawara no rakusho 二条河原落書 5:387a
transcriptions 4:191b
Nijō poetic school 二条流 7:170b
Nijō school 二条派 8:213b
Nijō Tameyo 二条為世 5:387a-387b
Kokin denju 4:254a
Nijō Yoshimoto 二条良基 1:181b; 5:15a, 43a, 387b; 6:297a, 298b
Nijūhasshuku 二十八宿 8:334a
Nijūichinichi Kai 二十一日会 6:221a
Nijūsannen miraiki 二十三年未来記 7:255b
Nijūshikumi-doiya 二十四組問屋 6:1a
kaisen management 4:113a
monopolistic trade rights 4:100a
Nijūshi no hitomi 二十四の瞳 2:*272b*, 272b; 6:1a; 8:110a
Nikaidō family 二階堂氏 6:1a
Nikakai 二科会 6:156a, 157b
Nika Society. *See* Nikakai
Nikkan gendai 日刊現代 6:268a
Nikkan Kihon Jōyaku 日韓基本条約 4:287b-288a
Nikkan Kyōyaku, Dai Niji 日韓協約(第二次) 4:289a-289b
Nikkatsu 2:275a
Imamura Shōhei 3:274a
Nikkatsu Corporation 2:267b-268a, 270b; 3:102a; 6:1a-1b
Daiei Co, Ltd 2:56b
Tasaka Tomotaka 7:347b
Uchida Tomu 8:124a
Nikka Whisky Distilling Co, Ltd 6:1b
Nikkeiren (Japan Federation of Employers' Associations) 日経連 4:188a, 348a; 6:1b, 237b; 8:199a, 367a
Sakurada Takeshi 7:4b
Nikki bungaku 日記文学 6:2a-2b
Nikkō 日光 1:*187a*; 6:2b-3a; 7:15b
Nikkō Kaidō 日光街道 3:41a
Nikkō National Park 日光国立公園 6:3a
Irohazaka 3:332b
Lake Chūzenji 6:*3a*
Nantaisan 6:*3a*
Tōshōgū 8:84b
Nikkō Onari Kaidō 日光御成街道 8:220a
Nikkō Securities Co, Ltd 6:3a
Nikkō Shirane. *See* **Shiranesan**
Nikkyōso (Japan Teachers' Union) 日教組 6:3a-3b, 237a, 238a
atom bomb film 7:111b
teachers 7:366a
Nikō Jiken. *See* **Nikolaevsk Incident**
Nikolaevsk Incident 6:3b; 7:238a
Nikolai, Archbishop 6:3b-4a
Holy Orthodox Church 3:216b
spread of Christianity 1:308a
Nikutai no mon (The Gate of Flesh) 肉体の門 6:221b; 7:334b
Nimbetsu aratame 人別改 6:4a
Nimbetsuchō 人別帳 6:4a
Nimono 2:306a
Ninagawa Torazō 蜷川虎三 6:4a-4b
Nin'ami Dōhachi 仁阿弥道八 6:4b
Nindō 3:221a
Nine-Power Treaty (1922) 6:4b; 8:272b
China 1:288a
Lansing-Ishii Agreement 4:367a
United States 8:157a
Nine Principles for Economic Stabilization 6:4b-5b
evaluation 6:5a
implementation 6:5a
inflation 6:5a
prior attempts 6:5a
provisions 6:4b-5b
Ningen Kokuhō 5:60b-61a
Ningen no higeki 人間の悲劇 4:139a
Ningen no jōken (The Human Condition) 人間の条件 2:*273a*
"Ningen ōrai" (Human Comings and Goings) 人間往来 8:173b
Ningen shikkaku 人間失格 2:80a
Ningyō jōruri 人形浄瑠璃 1:275a
Ningyō mawashi 7:250a
Ningyō Pass 人形峠 6:5b
Ningyō Sashichi torimonochō 人形佐七捕物帳 8:333b
Ningyō shibai 2:267b
Ninigi no Mikoto 瓊瓊杵尊 5:294b; 6:5b
imperial regalia 3:278b
story in *Kojiki* 4:251a
Niniroku Jiken. 二・二六事件 *See* **February 26th Incident**
Ninja. *See* **Ninjutsu**
Ninjin kōsakuki 人参耕作記 7:334b
Ninjō 2:269b
Ninjōbon 人情本 5:49b; 6:5b-6b; 7:97a
Hanasanjin 3:94b
Santō Kyōden 7:18a
sharebon 7:80a
Tamenaga Shunsui 7:333b-334a
Ninjō kamifūsen (Humanity and Paper Balloons) 人情紙風船 8:300b
Ninjutsu 忍術 6:6b-7a
Ninkyō gaiden: Genkainada 任侠外伝:玄海灘 4:157b
Ninkyō Tōkaidō 任侠東海道 4:166a
Ninnaji 仁和寺 4:336b; 6:7a
Kakuban 4:117b
Shingon sect 7:115a
Ninnaji shojaku mokuroku 仁和寺書籍目録 3:219a
Ninohe 二戸 6:7a
Ninomiya Sontoku 二宮尊徳 6:7a-8a; 7:338b
Ninsei. 仁清 *See* **Nonomura Ninsei**
Ninshikiron 認識論 4:204b
Ninshō 忍性 2:187b-188a; 5:238b
Ninsoku yoseba 人足寄場 6:8a
Nintoku, Emperor 仁徳天皇 2:287b; 6:8a
tomb 2:303b
Nintoku Mausoleum 仁徳陵 4:*246b*; 6:8a-8b
Niō 1:*186b*
Nippara Shōnyūdō 日原鍾乳洞 6:8b
Nippo jisho 日葡辞書 6:8b, 228b
Nippon 日本 1:76b, 123a
Nippon, Archiv zur Beschreibung von Japan 7:192b
Nippon Beet Sugar Mfg Co, Ltd 6:8b

Nippon Broadcasting System, Inc 1:173b; 2:347a; 6:8b; 7:14a
Nippon Chisso Fertilizer Co 7:57b
Nippon Columbia Co, Ltd 6:8b
Nippon Credit Bank, Ltd 1:139b; 6:9a
Nippon Cultural Broadcasting, Inc 1:173b; 2:347b; 6:9a; 7:14a, 86b
Nippon Dempō Tsūshinsha (Japan Telegraphic News Agency) 5:369a
Nippondensō Co, Ltd 6:9a
  Toyota Motor Co, Ltd 8:93b
Nippon Educational Television (NET) 1:93a
Nippon Electric Co, Ltd (NEC) 6:9a-9b
Nippon Electric Industries 7:173a
Nippon Express Co, Ltd 6:9b
Nippon Flour Mills Co, Ltd 6:9b
Nippon Formula Feed Mfg Co, Ltd 6:9b
Nippon Gakki Co, Ltd 3:90b; 4:179a; 6:9b-10a
  Kawakami Gen'ichi 4:180b
Nippon Hodō Co, Ltd 6:10a
Nippon Hōsō Kyōkai 日本放送協会 2:179a, 182a; 5:374a-374b
  establishment 2:192a
Nippon Iodine Co 7:173a
Nipponjin no higeki 日本人の悲劇 4:139a
Nippon Kangyō Bank 1:139a
Nippon Kangyō Bank, Ltd 2:58b
Nippon Kayaku Co, Ltd. 6:10a
  Hara Yasusaburō 3:103b
Nippon Kōgaku 6:10a
Nippon Kōkan 6:10a-10b; 7:269a
  Tōshin Steel Co, Ltd 8:83b
Nippon Koku 日本国 4:7a
Nippon konchūki (The Insect Woman) にっぽん昆虫記 2:*274b*
Nippon Life Insurance Co 6:10b
Nippon Light Metal Co, Ltd 2:372b; 6:10b-11a
Nippon Meat Packers, Inc 6:11a
Nippon Menka Kaisha (Japan Cotton Trading Company) 5:374b
Nippon Metal Industry Co, Ltd 6:11a
Nippon Mining Co, Ltd 6:11b
Nippon mukashi-banashi meii 日本昔話名彙 2:302b
Nippon mukashi-banashi shūsei 日本昔話集成 2:302b
Nippon News Network (NNN) 8:337a
Nippon no mukashi-banashi 日本の昔話 2:302a
Nippon Oil & Fats Co, Ltd 6:11b
Nippon Oil Co, Ltd 6:11b, 182a
Nippon Paint Co, Ltd 6:11b
Nippon Petrochemical 6:180a
Nippon Reizō 6:11b-12a
Nippon Sanso 6:12a
Nippon Seikō 6:12a
Nippon Sharyō Seizō Kaisha, Ltd 6:12a
Nippon Sheet Glass Co, Ltd 6:12a
Nippon shimbun 日本新聞 7:258b
Nippon Shimbun Rengōsha (Japan Associated Press) 3:360b; 5:369a
Nippon Shinpan Co, Ltd 6:12a
Nippon Shokubai Kagaku Kōgyō Co, Ltd 6:12a-12b
Nippon Soda Co, Ltd 5:317a; 6:12b
Nippon Stainless Steel Co, Ltd 6:12b
Nippon Steel Corporation 2:343a; 3:*333a*, 333b; 6:12b-13a; 7:269a
  Inayama Yoshihiro 3:284a
  Nagano Shigeo 5:303a
  Pacific Metals Co, Ltd 6:143b
  Sankyū, Inc 7:15a
  Shinwa Kaiun Kaisha, Ltd 7:139b
  Topy Industries, Ltd 8:76a
Nippon Suisan Kaisha, Ltd 2:284a; 6:13a
Nippon Telegraph and Telephone Public Corporation 6:13a, 263b; 7:14b
  administrative committee 2:373a
  fiscal system 2:281b
  Kokusai Denshin Denwa Co, Ltd separated from 4:261b
  Kōrōkyō membership 4:294a
  radio law 6:276a
  telecommunications systems 7:377a
  telephones 7:380a
Nippon Television Network Corporation (NTV) 1:172a; 6:13a-13b
Nippon teriya 4:45a
Nippon Times 4:50a
Nippon Univac Kaisha, Ltd 6:13b
Nippon Yakin Kōgyō Co, Ltd 6:13b
Nippon Yūsen 2:31a; 6:13b
  history 2:151b, 153a
  Kagami Kenkichi 4:102b
Nippon Zeon Co, Ltd 6:13b
NIRA. *See* **National Institute for Research Advancement**
Nirasaki 韮崎 6:13b-14a
Nireke no hitobito 楡家の人びと 4:227a
Niroku shimpō 二六新報 1:44a
Nirvāna 1:177a
Nisai tōki 二彩陶器 1:262a
Nisei 4:12b-13a, 13a-15a; 6:179a
  dual citizenship 4:16b
  Hawaiian politics 4:16b
  Japan 4:15a
  United States Immigration Acts of 1924, 1952, and 1965 8:165a
  wartime relocation 4:18a
Nisei hibakusha 4:15a
Niseko ニセコ 6:14a
Nise monogatari 仁勢物語 4:136b
Nise Murasaki inaka Genji (Rustic Genji, Imitation Murasaki) 偐紫田舎源氏 3:42a; 5:49a; 6:359a
"Nisen dōka" 二銭銅貨 2:170b
Nisengohyakunen shi 二千五百年史 7:324a
Nishi Amane 西周 6:14a-14b, 260b
  Freedom and People's Rights Movement 2:335b
  Imperial Rescript to Soldiers and Sailors 3:280a
  shigi kempō 7:92b
Nishida Kitarō 西田幾多郎 6:*14b*, 15a-15b
  philosophies 5:230a-230b
Nishida Mitsugi 西田税 6:15b-16a
  February 26th Incident 2:250a
Nishigoribe 錦織部 1:147b
Nishihara loans 西原借款 3:199a; 6:16a
  Duan Qirui (Tuan Ch'i-jui) 2:134b
  Terauchi Masatake 8:12b
Nishi higashi 西東 4:139a
Nishi Honganji 西本願寺 6:16a-17a
Nishijin-ori 西陣織 4:338a; 6:17a
Nishikawa Joken 西川如見 4:1a; 6:17a
  geography studies 3:25b
Nishikawa Kōjirō. *See* **Nishikawa Mitsujirō**
Nishikawa Mitsujirō 西川光二郎 6:17a
Nishikawa Shōji 西川正治 6:17a
Nishikawa Sukenobu 西川祐信 6:17a-17b; 7:187b
Nishiki 4:158a; 6:17b
  Atsuita 1:115b
Nishiki-e origami 6:118a
Nishikigoi (carp) 1:244a
Nishimatsu Construction Co, Ltd 6:17b
Nishimura Isaburō 西村伊三郎 2:66a
Nishimura Shigeki 西村茂樹 6:17b-18b; 7:3b
  Koji ruien 4:252a
Nishimura Shigenaga 西村重長 8:*141a*
Nishin 3:128a
Nishina Yoshio 仁科芳雄 6:18b
Nishi-Nippon Railroad Co, Ltd 6:18b
Nishi Nippon shimbun 西日本新聞 6:18b
Nishinomiya 西宮 6:19a
Nishinoomote 西之表 6:19a
Nishio 西尾 6:19a
Nishio Suehiro 西尾末広 6:19a
  Democratic Socialist Party 2:85b
  Japan Socialist Party 4:48b
Nishi-Rosen Agreement 6:19a; 8:293b
  Korea 4:281b
  Russo-Japanese War 6:346a
Nishi Sonogi Peninsula 西彼杵半島 6:19a-19b
Nishi Takeichi 西竹一 6:19b
Nishiwaki 西脇 6:19b
Nishiwaki Junzaburō 西脇順三郎 6:19b-20a
Nishiyama Sōin 西山宗因 2:77a-77b; 6:20a, 297a
  haikai 3:79a
Nishiyama Suishō 西山翠嶂 6:20a
Nishiyama Usaburō. 西山卯三郎 *See* **Nishiyama Suishō**
Nishizawa Ippū 西沢一風 5:48b; 6:20a
Nissan Chemical Industries, Ltd 6:20a
  Ishikawa Ichirō 3:342a
Nissan Diesel Motor Co, Ltd 6:20b
Nissan Motor Co, Ltd 1:33b; 2:343a; 6:20b
  Atsugi Motor Parts Co, Ltd and 1:115b
  Daidō Steel Co, Ltd 2:56b
  early automotive industry 1:121b
  unions 4:53b
Nissan Shatai Co, Ltd 6:20b
Nisshin Flour Milling Co, Ltd 6:20b-21a
Nisshin Oil Mills, Ltd 6:21a
Nisshin Sensō. *See* **Sino-Japanese War of 1894-1895**
Nisshin Shūkō Jōki 日清修好条規 7:197b
Nisshin Spinning Co, Ltd 6:21a
  Sakurada Takeshi 7:4b
  Takita Minoru 7:327a
Nisshin Steel Co, Ltd 6:21a
Nisshō 4:11a
Nisshō-Iwai Co, Ltd 6:21a-21b
  Takahata Seiichi 7:313b
Nissin Food Products Co, Ltd 6:21b
Nissin Sugar Mfg Co, Ltd 6:21b
Nisso Kihon Jōyaku 日ソ基本条約 7:238a
Nisso Kyōdō Sengen 7:238b-239a
Nitaika fūga 二大家風雅 4:333b
Nitchū Heiwa Yūkō Jōyaku 日中平和友好条約 1:291b-292a
Nitchū Sensō. *See* **Sino-Japanese War of 1937-1945**
Nitobe Inazō 新渡戸稲造 1:223a; 6:21b-22a
  League of Nations 4:373a
Nito monogatari 二都物語 4:157b
Nitta family 新田氏 6:22a
Nittai Dōmei 日・タイ同盟 8:20a
Nitta Isamu 仁田勇 1:268b; 6:22a
Nitta Yoshisada 新田義貞 6:22a-22b

betrayal 4:192a
defeat 1:94b
Nitten (Nihon Bijutsu Tenrankai; Japan Art Exhibition) 1:215b; 6:158a
Nittetsu Mining Co, Ltd 6:22b
Nittō Bōseki Co, Ltd 6:22b
Nittō Chemical Industry Co, Ltd 6:22b
Nittō guhō junrei kōki 入唐求法巡礼行記 8:105b
Nittsū. *See* **Nippon Express Co, Ltd**
Niwaban 庭番 6:22b
Niwabi 4:108a
Niwa Fumio 丹羽文雄 2:274a; 6:22b-23a
fūzoku shōsetsu 2:378b
Niwaka 俄 7:221b
Niwano Nikkyō 庭野日敬 6:23a; 6:321a
Niwatori 1:272b-273b
Niwa Yasujirō 丹羽保次郎 6:23a
Nixon shocks 6:23a-23b
foreign trade policy 2:326a
Satō Eisaku 7:26b
Niyodogawa 仁淀川 6:23b
NLC 5:365a
Nō 能 2:*73a*; 4:336b; 6:23b-29b, 298b; 7:64b, 79a; 8:21b-22a
audience 6:27b-28a
costume 4:158a; 6:26a; 8:23b
criticism 5:15b
dance, traditional 2:75b
evolution 6:24a-24b
fans 2:248a
folk versions 2:296b
Hōshō school 3:235b
kabuki adaptations 4:92b
Kanze school 4:155a
Kita school 4:228b-229a
Komparu school 4:267b
kyōgen 5:43a
ma, use of 5:77a
masks 5:*127a-127b*; 6:26a
musical influence 2:366b
Ōkura school 6:98a
origins 6:23b-24a
performance 6:26a-27b
performers 6:25b-26a
plays 6:26a-27a; 7:61b
properties 6:26a
sarugaku 5:43a; 7:22b
shingeki 7:112a
stage 6:24b-25b
tsuzumi 8:119b
Zen influence 5:43a
Nōami 能阿弥 1:52b; 6:29b-30a
Nobel Prize
Esaki Reona 2:231b
Fukui Ken'ichi 2:363b
Kawabata Yasunari 4:176b
Satō Eisaku 7:26a
Tomonaga Shin'ichirō 8:73a
Yukawa Hideki 8:356b
Nobeoka 延岡 6:30a
Nobeyama 野辺山 6:30a
Nobi (Fires on the Plain) 野火 2:*273a*; 6:113b
Nōbi Earthquake of 1891 8:194b
Nōbi Plain 濃尾平野 6:30a
Nagoya 5:308b-309a
Nobori 2:288a
Noboribetsu 登別 6:30a
Noborigama (climbing kiln) 1:263b, 264b; 4:159b
Nobunaga Kō ki 信長公記 7:109a-109b
Nobushi (armed peasants) 1:97b; 6:30a
Nobuzumi 信澄 3:117a
Noda 野田 6:30a-30b
Noda Kōgo 野田高梧 2:272a; 6:30b
Noda Shōyu Co 4:206a
Noda Soy Sauce Co, case of 1957 1:66a
Nogami Yaeko 野上弥生子 6:30b-31a
Nōgata 直方 2:365a; 6:31a
Nogawa site 野川遺跡 6:31a
Nogi Maresuke 乃木希典 1:87b, 223a; 3:102a; 6:31a-31b
Noguchi, Isamu 6:31b
Noguchi Hideyo 野口英世 6:31b
Noguchi Shitagau 野口遵 6:32a
Noguchi Yonejirō 野口米次郎 6:32a
Nōgyōkai (Agricultural Association) 1:22a
Nōgyō kyōdō kumiai 1:21b-22b
Nōgyō zensho 農業全書 1:24a; 6:32a
Nōhon shugi 農本主義 6:32a-32b; 8:144b
Noibara. *See* **Roses**
Nōin 能因 6:32b; 8:210b
Nōin uta makura 能因歌枕 8:185b
Noise pollution 2:228a
Noise Regulation Law 2:228a
Nojima Kōzō 野島康三 6:*185a*
Nojiri, Lake 野尻湖 6:32b
Nojiri Kiyohiko 野尻清彦 6:123b
Nōkō girei 1:22b-23a
Nokogiriyama 鋸山 6:32b
Nōkyō 1:21b-22b
Noli me Tangere 6:332b
Noma Hiroshi 野間宏 6:32b-33a
Shin Nihon bungaku 7:122a
Noma Institute of Educational Research 6:33a-33b
Noma Kyōiku Kenkyūjo. *See* **Noma Institute of Educational Research**
Nomaoi Matsuri 野馬追祭 2:*254b*
Noma Prize
Endō Shūsaku 2:214a
Nagai Tatsuo 5:301b
Nakayama Gishū 5:318b
Shōno Junzō 7:167a
Takami Jun 7:315a
Yasuoka Shōtarō 8:319b
Noma Seiji 野間清治 6:33b
Dai Nippon Yūben Kai Kōdansha 4:241b
Noma Shōichi 野間省一 6:33b
Kōdansha's president 4:242a
Nō mask 5:*126b-127a*
Nōmijima 能美島 6:33b-34a
Nōmin Bungaku Konwa Kai 農民文学懇話会 5:19a
Nōmin Bungei Kondankai 7:176b
Nomonhan Incident (1939) ノモンハン事件 1:88b; 6:34a, 343b
Tsuji Masanobu 8:113b
Nomori no kagami 野守の鏡 4:329b
Nomugi Pass 野麦峠 6:34a
Nomura Hōtei 野村芳亭 2:268a
Nomura Kichisaburō 野村吉三郎 6:34a
Nomura Kodō 野村胡堂 6:34a
Nomura Mansaku 野村万作 4:*326b*
Nomura Matasaburō 野村又三郎 4:*327a*
Nomura Motoni 野村望東尼 6:34a-34b
Nomura Securities Co, Ltd 6:34b
Tōyō Trust & Banking Co, Ltd 8:96a
Nonaka Kenzan 野中兼山 6:34b
Nonaka Shirō 野中四郎 2:250a
Nonchurch Christianity. *See* **Mukyōkai**
Nonchurch Movement. *See* **Mukyōkai**
Nonferrous metals industry 6:34b
Nonki-megane 暢気眼鏡 6:139b; 7:176a
Nonki na kanja のんきな患者 4:114a
Non-nuclear principles 8:168b
Nonoguchi Ryūho 野々口立圃 6:34b-35a
Nonomura Ninsei 野々村仁清 2:346a; 6:35a
Kyōto ware 6:*35a*
Nonpenal fines 6:35a-35b
Nonprint media 6:268a
Nonrecognition policy 6:35b; 7:246b
Shandong (Shantung) Question 7:77b
Nonverbal communication 6:36a-37a
historical factors 6:36a
social factors
artifacts 6:36b-37a
body motion (kinesics) 6:36b
group importance 6:36a
long-range goal perseverance 6:36a-36b
mother-child closeness 6:36a
paralanguage 6:36b
social obligations 6:36a
space (proxemics) 6:36b
Noodles (menrui) 6:283a
Japanese cooking methods 2:24a-24b
Norainu 野良犬 7:108b
Noren 2:295b; 6:*37a*
Nori, Princess 3:*277a*
Nori (laver) 2:281b-282a; 6:37a-37b
Norikuradake 乗鞍岳 6:37b
Norikura Volcanic Zone 乗鞍火山帯 6:37b
Norimono 4:104b
Nōrin Chūkin Bank 1:22a; 6:37b
Nōrin Suisan Shō. 農林水産省 *See* **Ministry of Agriculture, Forestry, and Fisheries**
Noritake Co, Ltd 6:37b-38a
Tōtō, Ltd 8:85b
Norito 祝詞 6:38a
Shintō rites 7:138b
Normal schools 6:38a
teachers 7:365b
Norman, Egerton Herbert 1:238a; 6:38b
Normanton Incident ノルマントン号事件 6:38b; 8:151b
Noro Eitarō 野呂栄太郎 6:38b
Noro Genjō 野呂元丈 6:39a
Noro Kageyoshi 野呂景義 6:39a
North China Area Army 6:260a
North China Incident 7:199a
North China Political Council 6:260b
Northern and Southern Courts 6:39a-40a
estate stewards 4:63b
feudalism 2:265a
Go-Kameyama, Emperior 3:41b-42a
Jinnō shōtōki 4:59b-60a
Kaei sandai ki 4:101b
Kōgon, Emperor 4:249a
periodization 6:175b
reunification 3:41b-42a
Taiheiki 7:295a
Northern sea operations 2:285b
Northern Territory issue. *See* **Territory of Japan**
North Korea, Japanese relations with. *See* **Korea and Japan**
North Kyūshū Industrial Zone 6:40b
North Pacific Paper Corporation 4:83b
Norway 4:43b
Noryang, Battle of 3:327b
Nosaka Akiyuki 野坂昭如 6:40b; 8:328b
Nosaka Sanzō 野坂参三 6:40b
Japan Communist Party 4:11a-11b
Shinjinkai 7:115b
Nosappumisaki 野寒布岬 6:40b
"Nose, The" 1:45a
Noshappumisaki 納沙布岬 6:41a
Noshi 1:1b; 6:41a
kokorozuke placed in 4:256b
Noshi awabi 6:118a

Noshiro ·············· 能代 ········· 6:41a
Noshiro Plain ···· 能代平野 ·········· 6:41a
Nōshōmushō ···· 農商務省 ····· 6:41a-41b
Nōshū ················ 能衆 ········ 2:297b
"Nosongdang Ilbon haengnok" ·· 4:278b; 7:227b
Notary public ················· 1:16a; 6:41b
Notes on the Rectification of the Japanese Writing ················ 8:201a
Nothingness ··········· 2:212b-213a; 6:41b
Notkome ························· 6:340b
Noto Peninsula ·· 能登半島 ········· 6:41b
Notoro, Lake ······· 能取湖 ········· 6:41b
Notsukezaki ········ 野付崎 ········· 6:41b
Novelists
Abe Kōbō ························ 1:2b-3b
Abe Tomoji ························· 1:4b
Aeba Kōson ························ 1:18a
Agawa Hiroyuki ···················· 1:21a
Akutagawa Ryūnosuke ········· 1:45a-46a
Amino Kiku ················· 1:52a-52b
Aono Suekichi ·············· 1:70a-70b
Arishima Takeo ···················· 1:84b
Ariyoshi Sawako ···················· 1:86a
Chikamatsu Shūkō ··········· 1:276a-276b
Dan Kazuo ························· 2:76b
Dazai Osamu ·················· 2:79b-80a
Edogawa Rampo ············ 2:170b-171a
Enchi Fumiko ······················ 2:213b
Endō Shūsaku ······················ 2:214a
Fujieda Shizuo ···················· 2:342a
Fujimori Seikichi ·················· 2:343b
Fujioka Sakutarō ············ 2:344a-344b
Fujisawa Takeo ····················· 2:345b
Fukazawa Shichirō ················· 2:360a
Fukunaga Takehiko ················ 2:364a
Funahashi Seiichi ·················· 2:368b
Furui Yoshikichi ···················· 2:372a
Furuyama Komao ··················· 2:373b
Futabatei Shimei ············ 2:375a-376a
Genji Keita ························ 3:20a
Gomi Yasusuke ······················ 3:44b
Haji Seiji ·························· 3:84a
Haniya Yutaka ················ 3:98a-98b
Hara Tamiki ························ 3:103b
Hasegawa Shirō ···················· 3:108a
Hayama Yoshiki ·············· 3:115a-115b
Hayashi Fubō ······················ 3:116a
Hayashi Fumiko ············· 3:116a-116b
Hayashi Fusao ······················ 3:116b
Hino Ashihei ························ 3:140b
Hirabayashi Taiko ·················· 3:141b
Hirotsu Kazuo ······················ 3:151a
Hirotsu Ryūrō ······················ 3:151a
Hisao Jūran ························ 3:151b
Hōjō Tamio ·················· 3:211b-212a
Honjō Mutsuo ······················ 3:223b
Hori Tatsuo ························ 3:228a
Hoshi Shin'ichi ····················· 3:235a
Hotta Yoshie ················ 3:239b-240a
Ibuse Masuji ························ 3:255a
Inagaki Taruho ·············· 3:282a-282b
Inoue Hisashi ······················ 3:309b
Inoue Mitsuharu ···················· 3:311a
Inoue Yasushi ······················ 3:311b
Ishihara Shintarō ···················· 3:341a
Ishikawa Jun ················ 3:342b-343b
Ishikawa Tatsuzō ··················· 3:345a
Ishizaka Yōjirō ······················ 3:347a
Itō Einosuke ························ 3:352a
Itō Sei ····················· 3:355b-356a
Itsuki Hiroyuki ·············· 3:356b-357a
Iwano Hōmei ················ 3:361a-361b
Izumi Kyōka ························ 3:365b
Kaga Otohiko ······················· 4:102b
Kaikō Ken ··················· 4:111a-111b
Kaionji Chōgorō ···················· 4:112a
Kajii Motojirō ··············· 4:114a-114b
Kajiyama Toshiyuki ················ 4:115a
Kambayashi Akatsuki ·············· 4:123a
Kamitsukasa Shōken ··············· 4:127b
Kamura Isota ······················ 4:120b
Kanō Sakujirō ······················ 4:148b
Kasai Zenzō ························ 4:160b
Kashiwabara Hyōzō ················ 4:162b
Kataoka Teppei ···················· 4:166a
Kawabata Yasunari ·········· 4:175b-177a
Kawaguchi Matsutarō ·············· 4:177b
Kawakami Bizan ············· 4:179b-180a
Kawasaki Chōtarō ·················· 4:183a
Kida Minoru ························ 4:202a
Kikuchi Kan ················· 4:206a-207a
Kikumura Itaru ····················· 4:207a
Kikuta Kazuo ······················ 4:207a
Kim Tal-su ························· 4:211a
Kinoshita Naoe ·············· 4:215b-216a
Kitahara Takeo ·············· 4:255a-255b
Kita Morio ·························· 4:227a
Kobayashi Takiji ············ 4:237a-237b
Kōda Rohan ················ 4:242a-243a
Kojima Nobuo ······················ 4:252a
Komatsu Sakyō ···················· 4:266a
Kondō Keitarō ····················· 4:269b
Kon Tōkō ·························· 4:275b
Kosugi Tengai ······················ 4:296a
Kubota Mantarō ···················· 4:301a
Kunikida Doppo ············· 4:309a-309b
Kurahashi Yumiko ··········· 4:311a-311b
Kuroi Senji ························· 4:316a
Kuroiwa Jūgo ······················ 4:316b
Kuroshima Denji ············ 4:318a-318b
Lee Hwe-song ······················ 4:374b
Maedakō Hiroichirō ················· 5:80a
Makino Shin'ichi ···················· 5:86b
Maruyama Kenji ···················· 5:121b
Masamune Hakuchō ········· 5:122b-123a
Matsumoto Seichō ·················· 5:138a
Minakami Takitarō ·················· 5:176a
Minakami Tsutomu ················· 5:176a
Mishima Yukio ·············· 5:199a-202a
Miura Shumon ······················ 5:216a
Miura Tetsuo ······················· 5:216a
Miyamoto Yuriko ··········· 5:220a-221a
Mori Ōgai ·················· 5:251b-252b
Morita Sōhei ························ 5:253b
Murakami Genzō ···················· 5:266a
Muramatsu Shōfū ·················· 5:266b
Muroo Saisei ··············· 5:274a-274b
Mushanokōji Saneatsu ······ 5:281a-281b
Nagai Kafū ················· 5:300a-300b
Nagai Tatsuo ······················· 5:301b
Nagatsuka Takashi ················· 5:307b
Nagayo Yoshirō ···················· 5:308a
Nakagawa Yoichi ··················· 5:313a
Nakajima Atsushi ··················· 5:313b
Naka Kansuke ······················ 5:314a
Nakamura Shin'ichirō ·············· 5:315b
Nakano Shigeharu ··········· 5:316b-317a
Nakayama Gishū ··················· 5:318b
Nakazato Kaizan ············ 5:319b-320a
Naoki Sanjūgo ·············· 5:330b-331a
Narushima Ryūhoku ················ 5:335b
Natsume Sōseki ············· 5:349b-351a
Niwa Fumio ·················· 6:22b-23a
Nogami Yaeko ················ 6:30b-31a
Noma Hiroshi ················ 6:32b-33a
Nomura Kodō ························ 6:34a
Nosaka Akiyuki ······················ 6:40b
Oda Makoto ·························· 6:61b
Oda Sakunosuke ····················· 6:65a
Ōe Kenzaburō ················ 6:66a-66b
Ogawa Kunio ························ 6:69b
Ogawa Mimei ························ 6:70a
Oguri Fūyō ··························· 6:71b
Okamoto Kanoko ····················· 6:80a
Okamoto Kidō ························ 6:80b
Ōoka Shōhei ························ 6:113b
Osaragi Jirō ················· 6:123b-124a
Ozaki Kōyō ················· 6:139b-140a
Ozaki Shirō ························ 6:140a
Saitō Ryokuu ······················ 6:374b
Sakagami Hiroshi ·················· 6:375a
Sakaguchi Ango ············ 6:375a-375b
Sata Ineko ···················· 7:25a-25b
Satō Haruo ···················· 7:26b-27a
Satomi Ton ·························· 7:27b
Serizawa Kōjirō ······················ 7:69a
Setouchi Harumi ····················· 7:71a
Shiba Ryōtarō ························ 7:84b
Shibata Renzaburō ··················· 7:85a
Shibata Shō ·························· 7:85a
Shiga Naoya ·················· 7:89b-90b
Shiina Rinzō ·················· 7:93b-94a
Shimaki Kensaku ····················· 7:99b
Shimao Toshio ······················ 7:101a
Shimazaki Tōson ············ 7:101a-101b
Shimozawa Kan ····················· 7:107b
Shiroyama Saburō ·················· 7:148a
Shishi Bunroku ····················· 7:148b
Shōji Kaoru ························ 7:163a
Shōno Junzō ························ 7:167a
Sono Ayako ························· 7:228b
Suzuki Miekichi ····················· 7:282b
Tachihara Masaaki ·················· 7:293a
Takahashi Kazumi ··················· 7:312a
Takami Jun ·························· 7:315a
Takayama Chogyū ·················· 7:320a
Takeda Rintarō ·············· 7:322b-323a
Takeda Taijun ······················ 7:323b
Takii Kōsaku ························ 7:326b
Tamura Taijirō ······················ 7:334b
Tamura Toshiko ····················· 7:334b
Tanabe Seiko ························ 7:335b
Tanaka Hidemitsu ··················· 7:336b
Tanizaki Jun'ichirō ·········· 7:342a-343b
Tayama Katai ················ 7:358b-359a
Tōkai Sanshi ························· 8:42a
Tokuda Shūsei ················· 8:44b-45a
Tokunaga Sunao ······················ 8:58a
Tokutomi Roka ················· 8:59b-60a
Tomita Tsuneo ························ 8:73a
Tonomura Shigeru ···················· 8:75a
Tsuboi Sakae ························ 8:110a
Tsubota Jōji ························· 8:110a
Tsubouchi Shōyō ············ 8:110a-111a
Tsuji Kunio ························· 8:113b
Uchida Hyakken ····················· 8:123b
Umezaki Haruo ··············· 8:147a-147b
Uno Chiyo ·························· 8:173a
Yamada Bimyō ······················ 8:288b
Yamada Tomohiko ·················· 8:289b
Yamamoto Shūgorō ·········· 8:299a-299b
Yamamoto Yūzō ···················· 8:300a
Yamate Kiichirō ····················· 8:307b
Yoshikawa Eiji ······················ 8:347a
Yasuoka Shōtarō ···················· 8:312b
Yokomitsu Riichi ············· 8:331b-333b
Yoshiya Nobuko ············· 8:351a-351b
Yoshiyuki Junnosuke ········ 8:351b-352a
Novelists (premodern). *See* Authors (premodern)
Novels
home (katei shōsetsu) ················ 4:199b
opinion (kannen shōsetsu) ··········· 4:199a
November Incident ············ 十一月事件 ····· 6:41b-42a
Nozarashi kikō ············ 野ざらし紀行 ········ 1:144a
Nozawa Bonchō · 野沢凡兆 ·········· 6:42a
Nozoe Tetsuo ··· 野副鉄男 · 1:268b; 6:42a
Nozomi naki ni arazu (Not without Hope) ·········· 望みなきに非ず ········ 6:221b

NSK (Japanese Newspaper Publishers and Editors Association) ········ **4**:47b
NTN Tōyō Bearing Co, Ltd ········ **6**:42a
Nuchi ········ **6**:324b
Nuclear energy ······ **1**:114a-114b; **2**:216b; **5**:353b
laws ········ **1**:114a-114b
peaceful use ········ **1**:114a-114b
Nuclear energy policy ········ **6**:42a-43b
history ········ **6**:42b
need ········ **2**:191b
unresolved problems ········ **6**:43a
Nuclear family ········ **7**:208b
Nuclear Non-Proliferation Treaty · **4**:386b; **8**:154a
Nuclear policy ········ **3**:137b; **6**:43b-44a
military ········ **6**:43b-44a
peaceful ········ **6**:44a
Nuclear reactors ········ **2**:216b
Nuclear Test Ban Treaty (1963) ········ **6**:166b; **8**:154a
Nuclear weapons ········ **1**:114-115a
Nue ········ **6**:44a
Nuhi ········ 奴婢 · **1**:147b; **6**:44a; **7**:62a
Nukata no Ōkimi ··· 額田王 ········ **6**:44a
poems in *Man'yōshū* ········ **5**:107a-107b
Nukina Kaioku ·· 貫名海屋 ········ **6**:44b
Numa Morikazu · 沼間守一 ········ **6**:44b
Numata ········ 沼田 ········ **6**:44b
Numazu ········ 沼津 ········ **6**:44b
Numeral classifiers ········ **2**:39a
Nunobiki maru ····· 布引丸 ········ **1**:32a
Nunohiki Dam ···· 布引ダム ········ **2**:72b
Nurigome ········ **7**:111a
Nursery songs. *See* **Children's songs**
Nurses ········ **3**:119b-120a
Nusa. *See* **Gohei**
Nutari no ki ········ 渟足柵 ····· **6**:44b-45a
Nu, U ········ **6**:45a
Nyōbō hōsho ···· 女房奉書 ········ **6**:45a
Nyōbō kotoba ······ 女房詞 ····· **6**:45a-45b
Nyohōzan ········ 女峰山 ········ **6**:45b
Nyoirin Kannon ········ **1**:*188b*
Nyokōba ········ **6**:45b
Nyonin Kanzeon ········ **5**:*233a*
Nyonin kinzei ········ **6**:45b
Nyorai ········ **2**:64b; **6**:45b
Shinran ········ **7**:123b
Nyoraidō ········ 如来堂 ········ **1**:182b
Nyūan zakki (Miscellaneous Record of a Sexton) ········ 入庵雑記 ········ **6**:139a
Nyūtōzan ········ 乳頭山 ········ **6**:45b

O

Oakandake ······ 雄阿寒岳 ········ **6**:47a
Oaks [(kashi; nara) *Quercus* spp.] · **6**:47a
Ōama, Prince ·· 大海人皇子 ········ **4**:60a
Ōarai ········ 大洗 ········ **6**:47a
Ōashi. *See* **Tageta**
Ōatari kyōgen (Successful Plays) · **8**:183a
Oats ········ **8**:251a
Ōaza ········ **5**:265b
Ōba Hideo ······· 大庭秀雄 ········ **2**:272b
Ōbaiin ········ **8**:*172b*
Obake ········ **1**:130b
Ōbaku Sampitsu · 黄檗三筆 ········ **1**:236a
Ōbaku sect ········ 黄檗宗 ········ **1**:179b; **6**:47a-47b; **8**:371b
Ingen ········ **3**:303b
Itsunen ········ **3**:357a
Tetsugen ········ **8**:16a
Ōbakushū ········ 黄檗宗 ···· **6**:47a-47b
Obama (city) ········ 小浜 ········ **6**:47b
Obama (town) ········ 小浜 ········ **6**:47b
Ōban ········ 大判 ···· **6**:47b-48a
Obanazawa ········ 尾花沢 ········ **6**:48a
Obara Kuniyoshi 小原国芳 ········ **6**:48a
Shin Kyōiku Undō ········ **7**:121b
Obasute ········ 姨捨 ········ **6**:48a
Fukazawa Shichirō ········ **2**:360a
old age and retirement ········ **6**:99a
Obasuteyama ······ 姨捨山 ···· **6**:48a-48b
obasute ········ **6**:48a
Ōbe Masuo ········ 大邊男 ········ **6**:93a
Obi ········ 帯 ········ **4**:308a; **6**:48b-49a; **7**:87b
Obidome ········ **4**:308a
Obihiro ········ 帯広 ········ **6**:49a
Obi iwai ········ 帯祝 ········ **6**:49a
Obito ········ 首 ········ **4**:89a
Obligation, default of ········ **6**:49a-49b
Obligations ········ **6**:301a
human feelings (ninjō) ········ **3**:34b
social (giri) ········ **3**:34b
Oblomov ········ **3**:44b
Oboe ········ **3**:129b
Ōboke ········ 大歩危 ·· **6**:49a; **7**:97b
Ōbora shell mounds 大洞貝塚 ······ **4**:75b
Obscenity ········ **6**:49b-50b
censorship ········ **1**:254b
freedom of speech ········ **2**:338a, 339a
Japanese Supreme Court ········ **6**:50b
law today ········ **6**:49b-50a
pictures ········ **6**:50a
writings ········ **6**:50a-50b
Ōbu ········ 大府 ········ **6**:50b
Ōbunsha Publishing Co, Ltd ··· **6**:50b-51a
Occupation ·· **2**:13b; **6**:51a-55b; **7**:29a, 58b, 93b; **8**:278a
bureaucracy ········ **1**:218a-218b
business reforms ········ **2**:34b
censorship ········ **1**:254a-255b
censorship repeal ········ **2**:339a
Commercial Code ········ **1**:338a
conclusion ········ **6**:55a-55b
Constitution, enactment of ········ **2**:3b
Crisis of 1947 ········ **6**:53a-54a
Crisis of 1950 ········ **6**:54b-55a
Daitōjuku ········ **2**:68a
Diet ········ **2**:94b
economic reforms ········ **6**:52b-53a
economy ········ **2**:154a-158b
educational reforms ··· **2**:180a-180b; **6**:53a
Eichelberger, Robert Lawrence ····· **2**:185b
Far Eastern Commission (FEC) ····· **2**:248a
film censorship policy ········ **2**:271b
foreign trade regulation ········ **2**:314b
foreign trade restoration ········ **2**:320a
General Strike of 1947 ········ **3**:18b
general trading companies ········ **3**:19a
imperial ordinance ········ **3**:278b
international relations ········ **3**:324a
iron and steel industry ········ **3**:334a
Japanese language reform ········ **4**:30a
labor rights, fundamental ········ **4**:359a
land reforms ········ **4**:345b, 364a
life under ········ **6**:55a
local government ········ **5**:65b-71a
MacArthur, Douglas. *See* **MacArthur, Douglas**
Ministry of Finance ········ **5**:187a
Occupation Purge ········ **6**:57b
Okinawa ········ **6**:88b
Oppler, Alfred C. ········ **6**:115a
Ōsu Incident ········ **6**:128a
policy and structure ········ **6**:51b
political parties ········ **6**:207a, 211b
political reforms ········ **6**:51b-52b
political trends ········ **6**:54a-54b
prostitution ········ **6**:257a
public assistance during ········ **7**:210a
Red Purge ········ **6**:285b
renunciation of war ········ **6**:301b
Russia and Japan ········ **6**:343b
San Francisco Peace Treaty ····· **7**:10a-11a
SCAP during ········ **7**:32b
science ········ **5**:357a
Shimoyama Incident ········ **7**:107a-107b
social prejudice ········ **4**:271a
social reforms ········ **7**:211a
student movements ········ **7**:251b-252a
surrender terms ········ **6**:51a
technological development ··· **7**:369b-370a
technology transfer ········ **7**:374b
United States economic relations ··· **8**:161a
war criminals ········ **4**:273a
Warner, Langdon ········ **8**:228a
Willoughby, Charles Augustus ···· **8**:253b
women in ········ **8**:261b
women's suffrage ········ **8**:268b
World War II, Japanese society during ········ **8**:278b
Occupational diseases ········ **6**:55b
Occupational structure ········ **6**:55b-57b
individual behavior ········ **6**:57b
1920-1940 ········ **6**:56b
postwar recovery ········ **6**:56b-57b
pre-1920 ········ **6**:56a-56b
Occupation-period economy. *See* **Economic history**
Occupation Press Code ········ **1**:254a
Occupation Purge ······ **6**:57b-58b; **7**:86b; **8**:344b
Occupations
lifestyle ········ **5**:8a
self-employment ········ **7**:60b
Ocean resource development ·· **6**:58b-59a
Ochanomizu University ········ **6**:59a
Ochanomizu Women's University ·· **6**:59a
Ochiai Eiji ······· 落合英二 ········ **6**:59a
Ochiai Naobumi · 落合直文 ····· **6**:59a-59b
Ochi Etsujin ····· 越智越人 ········ **6**:59b
Ochikubo monogatari ········ 落窪物語 ··· **5**:34a, 246a; **6**:59b-60a
Ochitaru tennyo ········ 堕ちたる天女 ······· **8**:289a
Ochiudo legends ········ **6**:60a
Ō Chōmei ········ 汪兆銘 ······· **8**:222a
Ochūdō ········ **2**:345b
October Incident ········ **6**:60a
Octopuses [(tako) order Octopoda] ········ **2**:287a; **6**:60a-60b; **7**:81b
Ōda ········ 大田 ········ **6**:60b
Oda family ········ 織田氏 ····· **6**:60b-61a
Odagiri Hideo · 小田切秀雄 ········ **6**:61a
Shin Nihon bungaku ········ **7**:122a
Oda Gōichi. 小田剛一 *See* **Takakura Ken**
Ōdaigaharasan 大台ケ原山 ········ **6**:61a
Odaira Namihei ·· 小平浪平 ········ **6**:61a
Odaishi Sama ···· 御大師様 ········ **4**:269b
Odaka Tomoo ··· 尾高朝雄 ····· **6**:61a-61b
Oda Makoto ········ 小田実 · **6**:61b; **7**:85a
Oda Mikio ······· 織田幹雄 ········ **6**:61b
Odani no Kata ··· 小谷の方 ········ **6**:61b
Oda Nobukatsu ·· 織田信雄 ········ **4**:265b
Oda Nobunaga ·· 織田信長 ········ **1**:193a; **6**:61b-65a; **7**:8a, 14a, 64a, 67a, 84a, 90b-91a, 104a
abolition of barrier stations ········ **7**:57a
Anegawa, Battle of ········ **1**:56a

assassination 1:41a; 3:224a
Azuchi Castle 1:126b; 4:146a
Azuchi Disputation 1:126b-127a
campaigns 3:178b
chōnin 1:301a
Christianity 5:323a
climax and end of career 6:63b-65a
corvée labor 1:226b
Enryakuji temple 2:220b-221a
feudalism 2:266a
free markets 6:283a
Furuta Oribe 2:373b
Gamō Ujisato 3:6b
government 3:178b
Honganji vs. 3:221a-222b
Honnōji Incident 3:224a
Imai Sōkyū 3:273a
Kaihō Yūshō 4:110b
Kanemi kyō ki 4:139b
Kanō Motohide 6:*62b*
Komaki developed 4:265a
Luis Frois 2:340a
military practices 2:279a
monasticism 5:238b
Nagashino, Battle of 5:306b
Nagoya Castle 5:309a-309b
provenance and early career 6:62a-62b
rise to hegemony 6:62b-63b
seal of 7:45b
Shibata Katsuie 7:84b
Shinchō kō ki 7:109a-109b
Shokuhō seiken 7:164b
Odano Naotake 小田野直武 6:65a; 7:25b
Oda Sakunosuke 織田作之助 6:65a
fūzoku shōsetsu 2:378b
Ōdate 大館 6:65a
Ōdate Basin 大館盆地 6:65a
Oda-Toyotomi regime 織田豊臣政権 3:178b
accomplishments 3:180b
Oda Uraku 織田有楽 6:65a-65b
Odawara 小田原 6:65b
Odawara Campaign 小田原征伐 6:65b
firearms usage 2:279a
Fukushima Masanori's role 2:366b
Keichō kemmon shū 4:187b
Sanada Yukimura 7:9a
Toyotomi Hideyoshi 8:95b
Uesugi Kagekatsu 8:129b
Ukita Hideie 8:137b
OECD (Organization for Economic Cooperation and Development) 1:238a; 6:65b
Ōei Invasion 応永の外寇 6:65b-66a
Ōei Rebellion 応永の乱 6:66a
Ōe Kenzaburō 大江健三郎 1:209a; 2:274a; 6:66a-66b; 7:109a
Ōendan 6:66b
Ōe no Hiromoto 大江広元 6:66b-67a
Ōe no Masafusa 大江匡房 1:151b; 6:67a; 7:72a, 95a
Fujiwara no Michitoshi 2:353a
Gōke shidai 3:43a
Ōe Taku 大江卓 6:67a-67b
Ōeyama 大江山 6:67b
Tango Mountains 7:341a
Ōeyama emaki 大江山絵巻 6:*106b*
Offenders Rehabilitation Law 2:49a
Offerings, Shintō rites 7:138b
Office of Municipal Affairs 4:185b
Officers, imperial court 1:206a-206b
Official Development Assistance (ODA) 2:308b
Africa 1:19b
Official documents 4:308b
Official Gazette (Kampō) 6:67b; 8:106a
Offset printing 6:246a
Ofuda 3:39b
Ofudesaki 2:82b
Ofukuro おふくろ 7:335b
Ōfunato 大船渡 6:67b
Ofuregaki 御触書 6:67b-68a
Ofuregaki Shūsei 御触書集成 6:68a
Oga 男鹿 6:68a
Ōgaki 大垣 6:68a
Oga Peninsula 男鹿半島 6:68a-68b
Ogasawara family 小笠原氏 6:68b
Ogasawara Islands 小笠原諸島 4:2b, 7a; 6:68b
Ogasawara National Park 小笠原国立公園 1:272b; 6:68b-69a
Ogasawara school of etiquette 2:258b; 6:69a
Ogasawara family 6:68b
Ogata Kenzan 尾形乾山 1:*262b*; 4:199b, 337a
Ogata Kōan 緒方洪庵 6:69a
Nagayo Sensai 5:308a
school for Dutch studies 2:367b
Ogata Koretomi 尾形惟富 4:292b-293b
Ogata Koreyoshi 緒方惟準 6:69a
Ogata Kōrin 尾形光琳 4:292b-293b; 6:153a
Ogata Shinsei 尾形深省 4:199b
Ogata Taketora 緒方竹虎 6:69a-69b
Ogata Tomosaburō 緒方知三郎 6:69a; 7:101b
Ogawa Heikichi 小川平吉 6:69b
Ogawa Isshin 小川一真 6:*184b*
Ogawa Kunio 小川国夫 6:69b
Ogawa Mimei 小川未明 1:279b; 6:70a
Ogawa Mokichi 小川茂吉 6:70a
Ogawa Shinsuke 小川紳介 2:275b
Ogawa Takuji 小川琢治 6:70a
Ogawa Usen 小川芋銭 4:*156b*; 6:70a
Ōgi. *See* **Fans**
Ogidō 荻堂 6:85a
Ogidō shell mound 荻堂貝塚 6:70a
Ogino Ginko 荻野吟子 6:70a-70b
Ogino Kyūsaku 荻野久作 2:247a; 6:70b
Ogin sama お吟さま 4:275b
Ogiwara Morie 荻原守衛 6:70b; 7:*44b*
Ogiwara Seisensui 荻原井泉水 6:70b
haiku 3:79b
Ogiwara Shigehide 荻原重秀 6:70b
Ogōchi Dam 小河内ダム 6:71a
Ōgon kamen 黄金仮面 2:170b
Ogōri (city) 小郡 6:71a
Ogōri (town) 小郡 6:71a
Ōgosho 大御所 6:71a
Oguma Hideo 小熊秀雄 6:71a
Ogura hyakunin isshu 小倉百人一首 3:248b
Ogura Kinnosuke 小倉金之助 6:71a
Ogura Masatsune 小倉正恒 6:71a
Ogura Shimpei 小倉進平 6:71b
Ogurayama 小倉山 6:71b
Oguri Eijirō 小栗栄次郎 6:71b
Oguri Fūyō 小栗風葉 6:71b; 7:124b
fūzoku shōsetsu 2:378b
Oguri Mushitarō 小栗虫太郎 6:71b; 7:38b
Oguri Ryōun 小栗了雲 3:339b
Oguri Sōtan 小栗宗湛 6:72a
Oguri Tadamasa 小栗忠順 6:72a-72b
Ogyū Sorai 荻生徂徠 4:247b-248a; 6:72b-73a; 7:281a
education 2:173b
Forty-Seven Rōnin Incident 2:327b
Kobunjigaku exponent 4:239a
Kogaku proponent 4:246b
Motoori Norinaga's study of 4:258a
Seidan 7:49b
Ohachimeguri 2:345b
Ohajiki 6:73a
Ōhara 大原 6:73a
Ōhara Art Museum 5:279a
Ōharae 大祓 3:101a
Ohara Hōun 小原豊雲 2:291b
Ōhara Institute for Social Research 5:254b; 6:73b, 305b
Miyagi Tamayo 5:218a
Ōhara Magosaburō 6:73b
Takano Iwasaburō 7:317a
Ōhara Magosaburō 大原孫三郎 2:294a; 6:73b
Western-art museums 5:279a
Oharame 大原女 6:73b
Ōhara Shakai Mondai Kenkyūjo. *See* **Ōhara Institute for Social Research**
Ōhara shakai mondai kenkyūjo zasshi 大原社会問題研究所雑誌 6:337b
Ōhara Sōichirō 大原総一郎 6:73b
Ohara Unshin 小原雲心 2:290a
Ōhara Yūgaku 大原幽学 6:73b
Ōhashi Sahei 大橋佐平 6:73b-74a
Hakubunkan 3:87b
Ohayō おはよう 8:146b
Ohbayashi-Gumi, Ltd 6:74a
Ōhira Masayoshi 大平正芳 2:309b; 6:74a
election 4:386a
Ōhiroma 大広間 6:74a
Oichi no Kata お市の方 6:61b
Ōichōmage 7:272a-272b
Ōi Dam 大井ダム 2:72b
Oie sōdō 御家騒動 6:74a-74b
Ōigawa 大井川 6:74b
Oikawa Heiji 及川平治 6:74b-75a
Shin Kyōiku Undō 7:121b
Ōi Kentarō 大井憲太郎 6:75a
Freedom and People's Rights Movement 2:335a
Fukuda Hideko 2:362a
Ōsaki Incident 6:121b
Oil, dependence on Middle East 5:167a-168b
Oil crisis of 1973 2:214b-215b; 6:75a-75b; 7:24a, 204a-204b, 253b
balance-of-trade effects 2:326a
coal 1:333b
consumer movements 2:15a
declining industries 2:81b
economic effects 2:164a-164b, 292b
employment system, effect on 2:34b
IMF and 3:274b
iron and steel industry 3:336a
Japanese economy 1:133b
nuclear energy policy 6:42a-44a
personal consumption 7:244a
quality control 6:273b
Sankō Steamship Co, Ltd (Sankō Kisen) 7:14b
transportation 8:99a
wage level 8:199a
Oil refiners 7:176b
"Oil shock" 6:75a
Oirasegawa 奥入瀬川 6:75b; 8:*87a*
Ōishi Hisatake 大石久敬 4:55a
Ōishi Kuranosuke. 大石内蔵助 *See* **Ōishi Yoshio**
Ōishi Yoshio 大石良雄 2:327b; 6:75b
Ōiso 大磯 6:75b
Ōita 大分 6:75b

Ōita Plain 大分平野 6:75b
Ōita Prefecture 大分県 6:75b-76a; 8:355a
Oiwake 追分 2:301b
Ojigi 6:76a
Ōjin, Emperor 応神天皇 2:287b; 6:76a-76b
 horse-rider theory 3:230a
 Iwashimizu Hachiman Shrine 3:363a
 Keitai, Emperor 4:190a
Ōjin Mausoleum 応神天皇陵 6:76b
 Ōsaka Prefecture 6:122a
Ōji Paper Co, Ltd 2:348b, 359a; 4:83a; 6:77a; 7:86a
Ojiya 小千谷 6:77a
Ōjōya 大庄屋 5:270a
Ōjōyōshū 往生要集 1:20a; 3:23b; 6:77a
 nembutsu 5:359b
Oka Asajirō 丘浅次郎 6:77b
 Esperanto promotion 2:231b
Okabe Kinjirō 岡部金次郎 6:77b
 electronics 2:192a
Okada Beisanjin 岡田米山人 1:211a; 6:77b
Okada Eiji 岡田英次 6:78a
Okada Hankō 岡田半江 1:211a; 6:78a
Okada Keisuke 岡田啓介 3:202a; 6:78a-78b; 7:92a
 February 26th Incident 2:249b
Okada Mokichi 岡田茂吉 6:78b
 Sekai Kyūsei Kyō 7:56a
Okada Saburōsuke 岡田三郎助 6:78b
Okada Takematsu 岡田武松 6:78b
Okada Yasui 岡田野水 6:299b
Okadera 岡寺 6:78b
Ōkagami 大鏡 2:102b; 5:37a, 246a; 6:79a
 Fujiwara no Kintō 2:352a
 narrative histories 3:153a
Okage mairi 御蔭参り 6:79a-79b
Oka Kiyoshi 岡潔 6:79b
Okakura Kakuzō 岡倉覚三 1:154b; 5:12a; 6:79b; 7:270b
 Fenollosa, Ernest Francisco 2:251b
 Hishida Shunsō 3:151b
 Japan Fine Arts Academy 4:45b
 Kokka founder 4:255b
 Rimpa 6:318a
 Shimomura Kanzan 7:105b
 Tagore, Rabindranath 7:294b
Oka Masao 岡正雄 1:120a
 horse-rider theory 3:229b
Okame and Hyottoko 6:80a, *80b*
Okamezasa *(Shibataea kamasaca)* 1:136a
Okami 7:108a
Ōkami [(wolf) *Canis lupus hodophilax*] 8:255b-256a
Okamisan 7:273a
Okamoto Kanoko 岡本かの子 6:80a; 7:71a
Okamoto Kansuke 岡本監輔 6:80a
Okamoto Keiji 岡本敬二 6:80b
Okamoto Kidō 岡本綺堂 6:80b
 kabuki 4:92a
 radio drama 6:275a
 Tamura Toshiko 7:334b
Okamoto Kihachi 岡本喜八 2:274a
Okamoto Toyohiko 岡本豊彦 6:80b
Okanishi Ichū 岡西惟中 6:80b
Okano Keijirō 岡野敬次郎 2:319a; 6:80b-81a
Okashi をかし 6:81a
Oka Shigeki 岡繁樹 6:81a-81b
Okauchi Hideo 岡内英夫 6:81a-81b
Ōkawa 大川 6:81b
Ōkawabata 大川端 6:123b
Ōkawa Heizaburō 大川平三郎 6:81b
Ōkawa Shūmei 大川周明 6:81b-82b
Okaya 岡谷 6:82b
Okayama 岡山 6:82b
Okayama Astrophysical Observatory 1:104b
Okayama Plain 岡山平野 6:82b-83a
Okayama Prefecture 岡山県 6:83a
Okazaki 岡崎 6:83a
Okazaki Katsuo 岡崎勝男 6:83a
Okazaki Kunisuke 岡崎邦輔 6:83a
Oke 6:83b
Okegawa 桶川 6:83b
Okehazama, Battle of 桶狭間の戦 6:83b
 Imagawa Yoshimoto 3:272b
 Oda Nobunaga 6:62a
 Takeda Shingen 7:323a
Ōkemi 大検見 4:191a
Okera *(Atractylis ovata)* 6:83b
Okhotsk culture 1:160a; 6:83b-84a; 7:30b
Okhotsk Current 6:138b
Okhotsk Sea オホーツク海 6:84a
Okibumi 置文 6:84a
 kakun 4:118b
Okibutai 4:93b
Oki Electric Industry Co, Ltd 6:84a
Okigome 4:117b
Oki Islands 隠岐諸島 6:84a-84b
Okina 翁 4:326a
Okina ebisugai 7:81b
Okinaka Shigeo 沖中重雄 6:84b
Okina mondō (Dialogues with an Old Man) 翁問答 5:312a-312b
Okina no fumi (Writings of an Old Man) 翁の文 8:71b
Okinawa (Ryūkyū) 沖縄 6:84b-91a
 agricultural rites 1:23a
 agricultural productivity 6:86b-87a
 cultural characteristics 6:85a
 dialects 6:385a
 earliest times to 1945 6:84b-85a
 early dynasties 6:85b-86a
 economic grievances and protests 6:87b-88b
 financial problems 6:87a
 Japanese militarism and Pacific War 6:88b
 liberalizing American control 6:90a
 military bases and land issue 6:89a-89b
 military government 6:88b-89a
 postwar 6:88b
 prehistory 6:85a-85b
 reversion issue 6:90a-91a
 San Francisco Peace Treaty 7:10b
 Satō-Nixon Communiqué 7:28b
 Second Golden Age 6:86a-86b
 sovereignty issue 6:87a-87b
 taxation 6:87a
 under dual sovereignty 6:86a
 Western pressures 6:87a
 World War II 8:276a
Okinawa (city) 沖縄 6:84b
Okinawa Coast Quasi-National Park 沖縄海岸国定公園 5:308b
Okinawa culture 3:262a
Okinawa Day 6:284b
Okinawa Day demonstration of April 28
 university upheavals of 1968-1969 8:171b
Okinawa Development Agency 沖縄開発庁 1:219a; 6:91a
Okinawa Islands 沖縄諸島 4:2b; 6:91a
 population density 4:2b
Okinawa issennen shi 沖縄一千年史 6:88a
Okinawans 4:35a
Okinawan textiles 2:294a; 6:91a-91b
Okinawa People's Party 沖縄人民党 7:63a
Okinawa Prefecture 沖縄県 6:91b-92a
 capital 5:309b
 Ryūkyū Islands 6:357a
Okinoerabujima 沖永良部島 6:92a
Okinoshima 沖ノ島 6:92b
Okinoshima site 沖ノ島遺跡 6:92b
Okinotorishima 沖ノ鳥島 4:2b; 6:93a
Ōki Takatō 大木喬任 6:93a
Ōkita Saburō 大来佐武郎 2:154b
 economic planning 2:168a
Okitsumiya Shrine 沖津宮 5:265a
Okitsu Yagoemon no isho 興津弥五右衛門の遺書 4:85a
Okiya 3:14b
Ōkōchi Denjirō 大河内伝次郎 2:*268b*; 6:93a
Ōkōchi Masatoshi 大河内正敏 6:93a-93b
Ō Kokubin 王克敏 8:222b
Ōkōmori [(flying fox) *Pteropus* spp.] 1:146b
Ōkubi-e, (close-up bust portrait) 大首絵 8:142b
Ōkubo Hikozaemon 大久保彦左衛門 6:93b
 Mikawa monogatari 5:170b-171a
Ōkubo Nagayasu 大久保長安 6:93b
Ōkubo Toshimichi 大久保利通 1:86b, 150a; 2:30a, 332a; 6:93b-94b; 7:29b, 102a
 Freedom and People's Rights Movement 2:334a-334b
 Political Crisis of 1881 6:202b
 sangi (councillor) 7:11b
 Seikanron issue 7:50b
Ōkuchi 大口 6:95a
Oku Chichibu 奥秩父 1:272a; 6:95a
Okuda Eisen 奥田穎川 6:95a
Okueshi 4:149b
Oku Koshō 奥小姓 4:296a
Ōkuma cabinet 6:95a
Ōkuma Kotomichi 大隈言道 6:95a-95b
Ōkuma Shigenobu 大隈重信 2:30a; 5:314a-314b; 6:95b-96b; 7:29a, 66b, 86a, 88a, 99a, 276b
 Freedom and People's Rights Movement 2:334a
 Gen'yōsha 3:24b
 Itagaki Taisuke 3:349b
 Itō Hirobumi 3:353a
 Kenseitō 4:198b
 naichi zakkyo 5:309b-310a
 Political Crisis of 1881 6:202a
 Rikken Kaishintō 6:314b
 Shimpotō 7:108b
 Waseda University 8:232a
Okumiya Kenshi. *See* **Okumiya Takeyuki**
Okumiya Takeyuki 奥宮健之 6:96b
Oku Mumeo 奥むめお 6:96b
 Shin Fujin Kyōkai 7:111b
Okumura Corporation 6:96b
Okumura Ioko 奥村五百子 6:96b-97a
Okumura Masanobu 奥村政信 6:97a

Okunchi ・・・・・・・・・・ おくんち ・・・・・・・・ 2:*258b*
Okuni ・・・・・・・・・・・・・・・・・ 阿国 ・ 3:184a; 4:90b; 6:97a
Ōkunimi ・・・・・・・・・・・・ 大国見 ・・・・・・・・ 4:309b
Ōkuninushi no Kami. *See* **Ōkuninushi no Mikoto**
Ōkuninushi no Mikoto
・・・・・・・・・・・・・・・・ 大国主命 ・ 6:97a; 1:149a; 4:125b; 5:293b-294a; 6:97b; 7:73a, 280a
Izumo Shrine ・・・・・・・・・・・・・・・・・・・・ 3:367b
Kanda Shrine ・・・・・・・・・・・・・・・・・・・・ 4:137a
Ōkuni Takamasa 大国隆正 ・・・・・・・・・ 6:97b
Fukuba Bisei ・・・・・・・・・・・・・・・・・・・・ 2:361b
Hirata Atsutane's influence ・・・・・・・・ 4:259a
Oku no hosomichi (The Narrow Road to the Deep North) ・・・・ 奥の細道 1:145a; 4:179a; 6:297b; 8:104a-104b; 185b
Ōkunojima ・・・・・・・ 大久野島 ・・・・・ 6:97b-98a
Ōkura & Co, Ltd ・・・・・・・・・・・・・・・・・・ 6:98a
Ōkura Commercial School ・・・・・・・・・・ 6:98a
Ōkura Kihachirō
・・・・・・・・・・・・・・・ 大倉喜八郎 ・・・・・・・・・ 6:98a
collections ・・・・・・・・・・・・・・・・・・・・・・・ 5:277a
Hakodate Dock Co, Ltd ・・・・・・・・・・・・ 3:86a
Ōkura Museum ・・・・・・・・・・・・・・・・・・ 5:277a
Ōkura Nagatsune 大蔵永常 ・・・・・・・・・ 6:98a
Ōkura school ・・・・・・ 大蔵流 ・ 4:325b; 6:98a
Ōkurashō ・・・・・・・・・・ 大蔵省 ・・ 5:186b-188a
Ōkura Toraakira ・ 大蔵虎明 ・・・・ 5:15b-16a
Okushiri ・・・・・・・・・・・・・・ 奥尻 ・・・・・・・・ 6:98b
Oku Tadami Dam
・・・・・・・・・・・・・・ 奥只見ダム ・・ 2:73a; 6:98b
Oku Tama ・・・・・・・・・・ 奥多摩 ・ 1:272a; 6:98b
Oku Tama, Lake ・ 奥多摩湖 ・・ 1:272a; 8:*62b*
Ōkyo. 応挙 *See* **Maruyama Ōkyo**
Old age ・・・・・・・・・・・・・・・・・・・・・・・・・・・・ 5:5a
Old age and retirement 4:356a; 6:98b-100a
family solidarity ・・・・・・・・・・・・・・・・・・ 6:99b
obasute ・・・・・・・・・・・・・・・・・・・・・・・・・・ 6:48a
population change ・・・・・・・・・・・・・・・・ 6:98b
prospects ・・・・・・・・・・・・・・・・・・・・・ 6:99b-100a
social services ・・・・・・・・・・・・・・・・・ 6:99a-99b
traditional themes ・・・・・・・・・・・・・・・・ 6:98b
work ・・・・・・・・・・・・・・・・・・・・・・・・・・・・ 6:99a
Old-Age Welfare Law ・・・・・・ 6:100a; 7:209b
Old Ash Spreader, The ・・・・・・・・・・・・・ 3:94b
Old Goose Hunter, The ・・・・・・・・・・・・・ 3:94b
"Old Man Who Lost His Wen, The" ・・・・・・・・・・・・・・・・・・・・ 4:239b
Old Pine Tree in Snow (Setchū rōshō zu or Sesshōzu) ・・・・・・・・・・・ 5:*121a*
Oligopoly ・・・・・・・・・・・・・・・・・・・・・・ 2:162b-163a
Oliphant, Laurence ・・・・・・・・ 5:306b; 6:100a
Harris, Thomas Lake ・・・・・・・・・・・・・・ 3:104b
Olivetti ・・・・・・・・・・・・・・・・・・・・・・・・・・ 7:196a
Olympic games ・・・・・・・・・・・・・・・・・・・・ 7:243a
Sapporo Winter Olympic Games ・・・ 7:20b
Tōkyō ・・・・・・・・・・・・・・・・・・・・・・ 8:61b, 353b
Olympus Optical Co, Ltd ・・・・・・・・・ 6:100a
Ōmachi ・・・・・・・・・・・・・・・ 大町 ・・・ 6:100a-100b
Omaezaki ・・・・・・・・・・ 御前崎 ・・・・・・・・ 6:100b
Ōmagari ・・・・・・・・・・・・・・・ 大曲 ・・・・・・・・ 6:100b
Omamori ・・・・・・・・・・・・・・・・・・・・・・・・・・・ 3:39b
Ōmazaki ・・・・・・・・・・ 大間崎 6:100b; 7:105a
Ombashira ・・・・・・・・・・・ 御柱 ・・・・・・・・ 7:280b
Ombin ・・・・・・・・・・・・・・・・・・・・・・・ 6:100b-101a
Ombu ・・・・・・・・・・・・・・・・・・・・・・・・・・・・ 6:101a
Ōme ・・・・・・・・・・・・・・・・・・ 青梅 ・・・・・・・・ 6:101a
Ōme Marathon
・・・・・・・・・・・・・ 青梅マラソン ・・・・・・・・ 7:243a
Ōmetsuke ・・・・・・・・・・ 大目付 ・・・・・・・・ 6:101a
Omi ・・・・・・・・・・・・・・・・・・・・ 臣 ・・・ 4:89a, 310a
uji-kabane system ・・・・・・・・・・・・・・・・ 8:131b
Ōmi Basin ・・・・・・・ 近江盆地 ・・・・・・・・ 6:101a
Ōmi Code ・・・・・・・・・・・ 近江令 ・・・・・・・・ 1:151a; 6:101a-101b
Kōgonen-Jaku
Taika Reform ・・・・・・・・・・・・・・・・・・・・ 7:296b
ritsuryō system ・・・・・・・・・・・・・・・・・・・ 6:331a
Ōmi Hachiman ・・ 近江八幡 ・・・・・・・・ 6:101b
Ōmi Hakkei *(Eight Views of Ōmi)* ・・・・・・・・・ 近江八景 6:101b; 8:184b
Ōmikenshi Co, Ltd ・・・・・・・・・・・・・・・・ 6:101b
Omikuji ・・・・・・・・・・・・・・・・・・・・・・・・・・ 6:101b
Ōmi Mission ・・・・・・・・・・・・・・・・・・・・・・ 8:195b
Ominaeshi *(Patrinia scabiosaefolia)* ・・・・・・・・・・・・・・・・・・・・・・・・・・・・・・・・ 6:101b
Ōminesan ・・・・・・・・・・ 大峰山 6:102a; 8:349b
Ōmi no Mifune ・・ 淡海三船 ・・・・・・・・ 6:102a
Kaifūsō ・・・・・・・・・・・・・・・・・・・・・・・・・・・ 4:109a
Ōmiryō. 近江令 *See* **Ōmi Code**
Ōmi sales ・・・・・・・・・・・・・・・・・・・・・・・・ 8:195b
Ōmishima (Island, central Inland Sea) ・・・・・・・ 大三島 ・・・・・・・・ 6:102a
Ōmishima (Island, Sea of Japan) ・・・・・・・・・・・ 青海島 ・・・・・・・・ 6:102a
Ōmi Shrine ・・・・・・ 近江神宮 ・・・・・・・・ 6:102a
Ōmiwa Shrine ・ 大三輪神社 ・・ 6:102a-102b, 259b-260a
tama ・・・・・・・・・・・・・・・・・・・・・・・・・・・・・ 7:332a
Ōmiya ・・・・・・・・・・・・・・・ 大宮 ・・・・・・・・ 6:102b
Omizutori ・・・・・・・・・・ 御水取 ・・・・・・・・ 6:102b
Tōdaiji ・・・・・・・・・・・・・・・・・・・・・・・・・・・ 6:*102b*
Ommitsu ・・・・・・・・・・・・・ 隠密 ・・・ 6:102b-103a
Ommyōdō ・・・・ 2:259a; 6:103a, 187a; 8:285a
kaō ・・・・・・・・・・・・・・・・・・・・・・・・・・・・・・・ 4:156a
Konjin's origins ・・・・・・・・・・・・・・・・・・ 4:271b
Ommyōji ・・・・・・・・・・・ 陰陽師 ・・・・・・・・ 4:166b
Omogashi, tea ceremony ・・・・ 7:362b-363a
Omogokei ・・・・・・・・・・ 面河渓 ・・・・・・・・ 6:103a
Omoide no ki ・・・・ 思出の記 ・ 1:155a; 8:59b
Omoide o uru otoko
・・・・・・・・・・ 思ひ出を売る男 ・・・・・・・・ 4:169a
Omoigawa (*Love Stream*)
・・・・・・・・・・・・・・・・・・・・ 思ひ川 ・・・・・・・・ 8:173b
Omonogawa ・・・・・・・ 雄物川 ・・・・・・・・ 6:103a
Ōmori Fusakichi ・ 大森房吉 ・・・・・・・・ 6:103a
earth sciences ・・・・・・・・・・・・・・・・・・・・ 2:141a
Ōmori shell mounds
・・・・・・・・・・・・・・・・ 大森貝塚 ・・・・・・・・ 1:75b; 6:103a-103b
Omoro sōshi おもろさうし
Ryūkyū dialects ・・・・・・・・・・・・・・・・・・ 6:355b
Ryūkyū music ・・・・・・・・・・・・・・・・・・・・ 6:357b
Omoshiro hambun
・・・・・・・・・・・・・・・・ 面白半分 ・・・・・・・・ 8:328b
Omotedaka ・・・・・・・・・・・ 表高 ・・・・・・・・ 6:103b
Omoteeshi ・・・・・・・・・・・・・・・・・・・・・・・・ 4:149b
Omote Nihon ・・・・・・ 表日本 ・・・・・・・・ 6:103b
Omoto *(Rohdea japonica)* ・ 4:195a; 6:103b
Ōmoto (new religion) 大本教 6:103b-104a; 7:48b, 56a, 76b
Deguchi Nao ・・・・・・・・・・・・・・・・・・ 2:82b-83a
Deguchi Onisaburō ・・・・・・・・・・・・・・・・ 2:83a
Taniguchi Masaharu ・・・・・・・・・・・・・・ 7:341b
Omron Tateisi Electronics Co, Ltd 6:104a
Ōmugaeshi bumbu no futamichi ・・ 4:250a
Ōmugi ・・・・・・・・・・・・・・・・・・・・・・・・・・・・ 8:251a
Ōmura ・・・・・・・・・・・・・・・ 大村 ・・・・・・・・ 6:104a
Ōmura Bay ・・・・・・・・・ 大村湾 ・・・・・・・・ 6:104b
Ōmura Masujirō
・・・・・・・・・・・・・・ 大村益次郎 ・・・ 1:86a, 165a; 6:104b
Ōmura Sumitada 大村純忠 3:184b; 5:306a; 6:104b
Christian daimyō ・・・・・・・・・・・・ 1:305b, 306b
Omuro shojaku mokuroku
・・・・・・・・・・・・ 御室書籍目録 ・・・・・・・・ 3:219a
Ōmuta ・・・・・・・・・・・・・・・ 大牟田 ・・・・・・・・ 2:365b; 6:104b-105a
On ・・・・・・・・・・・・・・・・・・・・・・・・・・ 1:149b; 6:105a
Onagawa ・・・・・・・・・・・・・・ 女川 ・・・ 6:105a-105b
Ōnakatomi no Yoshinobu
・・・・・・・・・・・・・・・ 大中臣能宣 ・・ 6:105a-105b; 7:13a
Ōnanjiyama ・・・・・・・・ 大汝山 ・・・・・・・・ 7:349b
Onarimon ・・・・・・・・・・・・・・・・・・・・・・・・・ 1:183a
"On a Winter Garden" ・・・・・・・・・・・・・・ 8:214a
Onchi Kōshirō ・ 恩地孝四郎 5:*232b*; 6:105b
modern prints ・・・・・・・・・・・・・・・・・・・・ 5:232b
Onda Moku ・・・・・・ 恩田木工 ・・・ 6:105b-106a
Onda Takumi ・・・・ 恩田木工 ・・・・・・・・ 6:105b
Onda ware ・・・・・・・・ 小鹿田焼 ・・・・・・・・ 6:113a
Ondo Strait ・・・・・・ 音戸瀬戸 ・・・・・・・・ 6:106a
"One Arm" ・・・・・・・・・・・・・・・・・・・・・・・・ 4:176b
One-set principle ・・・・・・・・・・・・・・・・ 6:106a
Ongagawa ・・・・・・・・・ 遠賀川 ・・・・・・・・ 6:106a
Oni ・・・・・・・・・・・・・・・・・・・・・・・・・・ 6:106a, *133a*
Ōeyama emaki ・・・・・・・・・・・・・・・・・・・・・ 6:*106b*
On'i ・・・・・・・・・・・・・・・・・・・・・・・・・・・・・・・ 2:40b
Onibaba ・・・・・・・・・・・・・・ 鬼婆 ・・・・・・・・ 7:111b
Onibi ・・・・・・・・・・・・・・・・・・ 鬼火 ・・・・・・・・ 8:333b
Oni (devil) plays ・・・・・・・・・・・・・・・・・・ 4:327b
Ōnie ceremony ・・・・ 大嘗祭 ・・・・・・・・ 2:128b
Oni no ko no uta
・・・・・・・・・・・・・・ 鬼の児の唄 ・・・・・・・・ 4:138b
Ōnin War ・・・・・・・・ 応仁の乱 ・・ 6:106b-107b; 7:19b, 45b, 64a, 84a
Ashikaga hegemony ・・・・・・・・・ 6:106b-107a
economic effects ・・・・・・・・・・・・・・・・・ 2:260b
events ・・・・・・・・・・・・・・・・・・・・・・・ 6:107a-107b
Gozan monasteries ・・・・・・・・・・・・・・・・・ 3:58a
Hatakeyama family ・・・・・・・・・・・・・・・・ 3:111a
historiography ・・・・・・・・・・・・・・・・・・・ 3:154b
role of Hino Tomiko ・・・・・・・・・・・・・・・ 3:141a
samurai ・・・・・・・・・・・・・・・・・・・・・・・・・・・ 7:8a
Shiba family ・・・・・・・・・・・・・・・・・・・・・・ 7:84a
Shinkei ・・・・・・・・・・・・・・・・・・・・・・・・・・ 7:119a
shōen ・・・・・・・・・・・・・・・・・・・・・・・・・・・・ 7:158a
shōgun ・・・・・・・・・・・・・・・・・・・・・・・・・・・ 7:160b
sociopolitical consequences ・・・・・・・・ 2:265a
succession disputes ・・・・・・・・・・・・・・・ 6:107a
textiles ・・・・・・・・・・・・・・・・・・・・・・・・・・・ 8:18b
Toki family ・・・・・・・・・・・・・・・・・・・・・・・ 8:43a
Uragami family ・・・・・・・・・・・・・・・・・・・ 8:174b
warrior government ・・・・・・・・・・・・・・・ 8:229b
Yamana family ・・・・・・・・・・・・・・・・・・・・ 8:300b
Onioshidashi ・・・・・・・ 鬼押出 ・ 1:95b; 4:160b; 6:107b
Ōnishi Hajime ・・・・・・ 大西祝 ・・・・・・・・ 6:107b
Ōnishi hakase zenshū
・・・・・・・・・・・・ 大西博士全集 ・・・・・・・・ 6:107b
Onjōji. 園城寺 *See* **Miidera**
Onjō shugi ・・・・・・・・・・・・・・・・・・・ 6:165a-165b
Onjuku ・・・・・・・・・・・・・・・・ 御宿 ・・・・・・・・ 6:107b
Onkō, Jiun Sonja
・・・・・・・・・・・・・ 飲光慈雲尊者 ・・・・・・・・ 1:179b
Onna (Woman) ・・・・・・・・・・ 女 ・・・・・・・・・・ 7:*44b*
Onna daigaku ・・・・・・ 女大学 ・ 6:108a; 7:81a; 8:259a, 267a
Onnade ・・・・・・・・・・・・・・・・・・・・・・・・・・・ 4:133a
Onna-e painting ・・・・・・・・・・・・・・・・・・・ 6:150a
Onnagata (female impersonator) ・・ 2:268a; 4:218b; 6:108a-109b; 7:48b
development ・・・・・・・・・・・・・・・・・・・・・・ 4:91a
Hanayagi Shōtarō ・・・・・・・・・・・・・・・・・ 3:95a
makeup ・・・・・・・・・・・・・・・・・・・・・・・・・・・ 4:95b
Nakamura Utaemon ・・・・・・・・・・・・・・・ 5:315b
Onoe Kikugorō ・・・・・・・・・・・・・・・ 6:109a-109b
roles ・・・・・・・・・・・・・・・・・・・・・・・・・・・・・ 4:94a
Sawamura Sōjūrō ・・・・・・・・・・・・・・・・・ 7:31a
shimpa ・・・・・・・・・・・・・・・・・・・・・・・・・・・ 7:108a
Onnagoroshi abura no jigoku
・・・・・・・・・・・・・・・・・・ 女殺油地獄 ・・・・・・・・ 4:*91a*
Onnakeizu (Lineage of Women) ・・・・・・・・・・ 婦系図 ・・・・・・・・ 8:289a
Onnakotoba ・・・・・・・・・・・・・・・・・・・・・・・ 2:250b
Onna nidai no ki (A Story of Mother and Daughter)
・・・・・・・・・・・・・・・ 女二代の記 ・・・・・・・・ 8:297a

Onna sakusha ····· 女作者 ········ 7:334b
Onnazaka (The Waiting Years) ·············· 女坂 ········ 6:231a
Ono (city, Hyōgo Prefecture) ········· 小野 ········ 6:108b
Ōno (city, Fukui Prefecture) ········· 大野 ········ 6:108b
Ono Azusa ········· 小野梓 ··· 6:108b-109a
 Fuzambō ································ 2:377a
Ōno Bamboku ··· 大野伴睦 ········ 6:109a
Onoda ·············· 小野田 ········ 6:109a
Onoda Cement Co, Ltd ············ 6:109a
Onoda Hiroo ·· 小野田寛郎 ········ 8:279a
Ōno Dam ········ 大野ダム ········ 8:358a
Onoe Hachirō ··· 尾上八郎 ········ 6:110a
Onoe Kikugorō 尾上菊五郎 ········ 4:92a; 6:109a-109b
Onoe Matsunosuke ··············· 尾上松之助 ······· 2:267b; 6:109b-110a
Onoe Saishū ····· 尾上柴舟 ········ 6:110a
Onoe Shōroku ·· 尾上松緑 ········ 4:*92b*
Ono ga tsumi ······ 己が罪 ········ 7:107b
Ōnogawa ··········· 大野川 ········ 6:110a
Ono-Gumi ··········· 小野組 ········ 6:110a
Ōno Harunaga ··· 大野治長 ········ 6:110a
Ōnojō ············ 大野城 ········ 6:110a
Ōnojō Castle ······· 大野城 ········ 6:110a
Onomatopoeia ······················ 6:110b
Onomichi ············· 尾道 ········ 6:110b
Ono no Imoko ·· 小野妹子 2:288a; 6:110b; 7:253a, 260a
Ono no Komachi 小野小町 ·· 6:110b-111a; 7:13a, 53b, 96b; 8:208b
 Ise ····································· 3:336b
 Kenuki ································· 4:98a
 Kokinshū ······························· 4:254b
 Rokkasen ······························· 6:334b
Ono no Michikaze. *See* **Ono no Tōfū**
Ononomiya Sanesuke ··············· 小野宮実資 ········ 7:179a
Ono no Takamura · 小野篁 ··· 6:111a-111b
Ono no Tōfū ····· 小野道風 1:234a; 6:111b
 Fujiwara no Sukemasa ··············· 2:355a
Ono Ranzan ····· 小野蘭山 1:155b; 6:111b
Ono Seiichirō · 小野清一郎 ··· 6:111b-112a
Ōno Susumu ······· 大野晋 ········ 4:31b
Ono Tōzaburō · 小野十三郎 ········ 6:112a
Ō no Yasumaro · 太安万侶 ········ 6:112a
 Chinese literature ················· 1:293a
 Kojiki ································· 4:251a
Ono Yōko ······· 小野洋子 ········ 6:112a
"On Parting from His Wife as He Set Out from Iwami for the Capital" ······ 8:206a
On readings ··· 4:57a; 5:324b; 6:112a-112b
 go on ·································· 3:46a
 ideographs ······················ 4:143a-143b
 kan on ································· 4:148a
 nengō ·································· 1:231b
 Shinsen jikyō ·························· 7:124b
 tō on ·································· 8:75b
Onryō. *See* **Goryō**
Onryōken nichiroku ·············· 蔭涼軒日録 ········· 1:52b
Onsen. *See* **Hot springs**
Ontake ··············· 御岳 ······ 6:112b, 259b-260a; 7:48a
Ontakesan ········· 御岳山 ··· 6:112b-113a
Ontake Shrine ·· 御岳神社 ········ 6:112b
Onta ware ······ 小鹿田焼 2:295b; 6:113a
On the Unity of Learning and Culture ······································· 1:207b
Ontleedkundige Tafelen ··········· 7:258b
Ōnuma ··············· 大沼 ········ 6:113a
Ōnuma Chinzan · 大沼枕山 ········ 6:113a
On'yōryō ·········· 陰陽寮 ··· 6:113a-113b
Ōoka Echizen no Kami Tadasuke nikki ······ 大岡越前守忠相日記 ········ 6:113b
Ōoka Makoto ······ 大岡信 ········ 6:113b
Ōoka seidan ····· 大岡政談 ········ 6:113b
Ōoka Shōhei ···· 大岡昇平 2:274a; 6:113b
Ōoka Tadamitsu · 大岡忠光 3:189a; 8:292b
Ōoka Tadasuke ·· 大岡忠相 ········ 6:113b
Ōoku ················ 大奥 ·· 6:113b-114a
OPEC, nuclear energy policy ··· 6:42a-44a
Open Door policy ········· 4:366b; 6:114a
 Franco-Japanese Agreement of 1907 ······································· 2:233b
 Roosevelt, Theodore ··············· 6:339a
 Russo-Japanese agreements of 1907-1916 ··································· 6:344b
 Shandong (Shantung) Question ····· 7:77b
Open guilds ························· 6:282b
Opening of Japan ··········· 6:114a-115a
 consequences ················ 5:155b-156a
 Dutch trade ························ 2:135b
 international relations ············ 3:320a
 Netherlands ························ 5:362a
 periodization ······················ 6:176b
 Perry, Matthew Calbraith ·········· 6:177b
 technological development ········ 7:368b
Opera. *See* **Music**
Operation Number One ············ 6:115a
Operation Victory ················· 6:115a
Opium ································ 2:134a
Opium War ··························· 6:114b
Oppekepei bushi ········· オッペケペー節 ········ 4:181a
Oppler, Alfred C. ··········· 6:115a-115b
Oraga haru ······ おらが春 ········ 6:298a
Ōraimono ·········· 往来物 ········ 6:115b
 school textbooks ··················· 7:37b
Oral Folklore ························ 5:194a
Oranda bōeki. *See* **Dutch trade**
Oranda chikyū zusetsu ······· オランダ地球図説 ········ 5:355b
Oranda fūsetsugaki ········· オランダ風説書 ··· 6:115b-116a
Oranda honzō wage (Dutch Botanicon Translated) 和蘭本草和解 ········ 8:242b
Oranda kotohajime 和蘭事始 ······ 6:283b
Oranda Shōgatsu ··········· オランダ正月 ········ 6:116a
 Ichikawa Gakusan ················ 6:*116b*
Oranda Shōkan ··········· オランダ商館 ········ 2:135b
Oranda tsūji · オランダ通辞 ········ 6:116a
Orange War ························ 6:116a
 Rainbow plan ······················ 6:280a
Orashio ·········· オラショ ········ 4:119b
Orashū ······························· 4:119b
Order for the Repelling of Foreign Ships ························· 3:3a-3b
Order of Culture ······················ 2:81b
 Andō Hirotarō (1956) ··············· 1:55a
 Asakura Fumio (1948) ·············· 1:94b
 Nagai Tatsuo (1981) ················ 5:301b
 Nagaoka Hantarō (1937) ··········· 5:303b
 Nitta Isamu (1966) ················· 6:22a
 Nozoe Tetsuo (1958) ················ 6:42a
 Okada Saburōsuke (1937) ············ 6:78b
 Okada Takematsu (1949) ············ 6:78b
 Takagi Teiji (1940) ················ 7:311a
 Takahama Kyoshi (1954) ··········· 7:311b
 Tamiya Hiroshi (1977) ·············· 7:334a
 Tanakadate Aikitsu (1944) ·········· 7:336a
 Tawara Kuniichi (1946) ············· 7:351b
 Yabe Hisakatsu (1953) ············· 8:283a
 Yabuta Teijirō (1964) ·············· 8:283b
 Yagi Hidetsugu (1956) ·············· 8:283b
 Yamagata Masao (1967) ············ 8:293b
 Yamamoto Yūzō (1965) ············· 8:300a
 Yasuda Yukihiko (1948) ············ 8:318a
 Yasui Sōtarō (1952) ················ 8:318b
 Yasui Takuma (1971) ··············· 8:318b
 Yokoyama Taikan (1937) ··········· 8:334b
Order of the Golden Kite ···· 2:81b; 4:217a
Order of the Precious Crown ········ 2:81b
Order of the Rising Sun ···· 2:81b; 4:381a
Order of the Sacred Treasure ······ 2:81b
Ordnance Manufacturing Law (1953) ······································· 1:90b
"Organic Act" ························ 7:54a
Organization for Economic Cooperation and Development (OECD) · 2:159b, 175b; 3:13b, 265a; 4:386b; 6:65b
 Development Assistance Committee ······································· 2:308b
 Foreign Investment Council ········ 2:316b
 foreign trade ······················ 2:322b
 income distribution ·········· 3:285b-286a
 technological assistance codes ······ 2:316a
 United States ······················ 8:162a
Organization for Pacific Trade and Development ················ 1:117b-118b
Organized crime ······················ 2:45a
Oribe ware ······· 織部焼 ········ 1:*258b*
 See also **Mino ware**
Oriental Development Company ···· 8:93b
Oriental Economic Review, The ··· 1:129a
Oriental Liberal Party ················ 8:91a
Oriental Socialist Party ······· 1:53b; 8:92b
Orient Emigration Company ········ 6:178b
Orient Leasing Co, Ltd ······· 6:116a-116b
Orient Steamship Company ········ 6:179a
Origami ······················ 6:116b-118b
 background ················· 6:116b-118a
 education and art ·················· 6:118b
 making ······················ 6:118a-118b
 outside Japan ······················ 6:118b
 types ······························· 6:118a
 Yoshizawa Akira ················· 6:*116b*
Origami Center of America ········ 6:118b
Orihon ················ 折本 ········ 1:153a
Orikuchi Shinobu 折口信夫 · 2:296b, 297b; 5:13b; 6:118b-119a
 Kodai kenkyū ························ 4:240b
Orimposu no kajitsu ········ オリンポスの果実 ········ 7:336b
Oritaku shiba no ki ········ 折たく柴の記 ·· 1:73a; 3:155a
Ornamental and ritual objects
 beads, ancient ····················· 1:147b
Ornamented tombs ··· 4:*247a*; 6:119a-119b
 chokkomon ························· 1:299b
 fern frond design ················· 2:252a
Oroshigane (grater) ················· 2:25a
Orthodox Church. *See* **Holy Orthodox Church**
Ōryōshi ············ 押領使 ········ 6:119b
Osabyakushō ······ 長百姓 ········ 6:119b
Ō Sadaharu ········ 王貞治 ········ 6:119b
Osadamegaki ······ 御定書 ········ 4:318b
Ōsaka ················ 大阪 ·· 4:58a; 6:120a
 chōnin class ······················· 1:301b
 Dōtombori ························· 6:*119a*
 growth ······················ 2:149a-150b
 language ··························· 4:24a
 Nakanoshima ····················· 6:*119a*
Ōsaka Asahi Hikka Incident ······· 大阪朝日筆禍事件 2:338b; 6:120a
 Hasegawa Nyozekan ··············· 3:107a
Ōsaka asahi shimbun ············ 大阪朝日新聞 ·· 4:180b, 320a
Ōsaka Bay ········ 大阪湾 ········ 6:120a
Ōsaka Castle ······ 大阪城 ········ 2:375a; 6:120a-120b; 7:274b
 jōdai ································ 4:66b
 Kanō Mitsunobu ···················· 4:147b

Kimura Shigenari **4**:211b
Ōsaka Prefecture **6**:122b
paintings **4**:151a
sieges of **6**:120b
Toyotomi Hideyoshi **4**:146a
Ōsaka Cement Co, Ltd **6**:120b-121a
Ōsaka Conference of 1875 **1**:34b; **2**:334b; **6**:121a
Assembly of Prefectural Governors **1**:103b
Itagaki Taisuke **3**:349b
Kido Takayoshi **4**:203a
Ōsaka Dōjima Beikoku Torihikisho 大阪堂島米穀取引所 **2**:127a
Ōsaka Dōjima Komeshō Kaisho
Dōjima Rice Market **2**:127a
Ōsaka Expo '70. *See* **Expo '70**
Ōsaka Gas Co, Ltd **6**:121a
Ōsaka Incident 大阪事件 **2**:336a; **6**:121a-121b
Ōsaka International Airport **1**:37b
Ōsaka mainichi shimbun 大阪毎日新聞 **4**:265b; **7**:279b
Ōsaka Municipal Museum of Fine Arts **6**:121b
Ōsaka no Jin. 大坂の陣
See **Ōsaka Castle, Sieges of**
Ōsaka Plain 大阪平野 **6**:121b
Ōsaka Prefecture 大阪府 **6**:122a-122b
Ōsaka school 大坂派 **6**:123a
Ōsaka School of Foreign Languages **6**:123a
Ōsaka Shōsen Kaisha Co **5**:270a
Ōsaka Spinning Mill **6**:123a
industrial revolution in Japan **3**:298a
Ōsaka tube **2**:192a
Ōsaka University **6**:123a
Ōsaka University of Foreign Studies **6**:123a
Ōsakayama 逢坂山 **6**:123a-123b
Ōsakazuki 大盃 **4**:180a
Osanai Kaoru 小山内薫 **2**:268a; **6**:123b
shingeki **7**:112b-113a
Shinshichō **7**:124b
Osaragi Jirō 大仏次郎 **1**:164a; **6**:123b-124a; **7**:103b
contemporary novels **6**:123b-124a
historical novels **6**:123b
other works **6**:124a
Ōseidasaresho 被仰出書 **6**:124a
education theory **2**:182b-183a
Ō Seiei 汪精衛 **8**:222a
Ōsei Fukko 王政復古 **6**:124a
Kogosho Kaigi **4**:249b
Ō Seitei 王正廷 **8**:222b-223a
Ōse Jintarō 大瀬甚太郎 **6**:124a-124b
Osenkorogashi おせんころがし **4**:174b; **6**:124b
Ōsetsuma **2**:253b; **6**:124b
Oshi 御師 **6**:124b
Oshidashibutsu **6**:125a
Amida triad **6**:*124b*
Oshidori **5**:100b-101b
Oshiekata 教方 **4**:119b
Oshika Peninsula 牡鹿半島 **6**:125a
Ōshikōchi no Mitsune 凡河内躬恒 **6**:125a; **7**:13a
Kokinshū **4**:254b
Oshikōji ware 押小路焼 **4**:337a
Oshima Fuji 渡島富士 **4**:264b
Ōshima Hiroshi 大島浩 **6**:125b
Ōshima (island, Wakayama Prefecture) 大島 **6**:125a
Ōshima (island, western Inland Sea) 大島 **6**:125b
Ōshima (volcanic island) 大島 **6**:125a
Ōshima Nagisa 大島渚 **2**:273b, 275b; **6**:125b-126a; **7**:122a
obscenity case **1**:255a
Oshima Peninsula 渡島半島 **6**:126a
Ōshima Ryōta 大島蓼太 **6**:126a
Ōshima Sadamasu 大島貞益 **6**:126a
Ōshima Takatō 大島高任 **6**:126a
blast furnace construction **4**:120b
iron and steel industry **3**:333b
Oshimodoshi 押戻 **4**:98b
Ōshio Chūsai 大塩中斎 **6**:126a
Ōshio Heihachirō 大塩平八郎 **1**:141b; **6**:126a-126b; **8**:335b
Ōshū Fujiwara family 奥州藤原氏 **1**:189b-190a; **6**:126b-127a
Fujiwara no Hidesato **2**:350b
seat
Hiraizumi **3**:143a
Taira-Minamoto War **7**:300b
Ōshū kikō (European Travel Diary) 欧州紀行 **8**:333a
Osoreyama 恐山 **6**:127a
Osorezan 恐山 **6**:127a; **7**:76b, 105a
Osso 越訴 **4**:55b; **6**:127a-127b
Osso bugyō (commissioner of appeals) 越訴奉行 **6**:127a
Ostasien 1860–62 **2**:235a
Osteoporosis **6**:219a
Ostracism. *See* **Murahachibu**
Ōsuga Isao 大須賀績 **6**:127b
Ōsuga Otsuji 大須賀乙字 **6**:127b
Ōsugi Sakae 大杉栄 **1**:54a, 155a; **6**:127b-128a; **7**:54b, 93b
Itō Noe **3**:355a
Kaizō **4**:113b
Kamichika Ichiko **4**:126a
murder **4**:125a
Red Flag Incident **6**:285a
Ōsu Incident 大須事件 **6**:128a
Ōsumi Peninsula 大隅半島 **6**:128a
Ōsuzumebachi (*Vespa mandarinia latilineata*) **1**:149a
Ōta 太田 **6**:128a
Ōtabumi 太田文 **4**:193a; **6**:128a-128b
Ōta Dōkan 太田道灌 **6**:128b
Ōtagaki Rengetsu 太田垣蓮月 **6**:128b
Ōtagawa 太田川 **6**:128b
Ōtaguro Tomoo 大田黒伴雄 **4**:58a
Ōtaka Hiroshi 大鷹弘 **8**:295b
Ōta Kaoru 太田薫 **6**:129a
Ōtake 大竹 **6**:129a
Otake Kōkichi 尾竹紅吉 **7**:54b
Ōtakineyama 大滝根山 **6**:129a
Ōta Nampo 大田南畝 **6**:129a; **7**:79a-79b
kyōka **4**:332a
kyōshi **4**:333b
Ōtani University **6**:129a
Otaru 小樽 **6**:129a-129b
Ōta Shokusanjin. 大田蜀山人
See **Ōta Nampo**
Ōta Sukenaga 太田資長 **6**:128b
Ōtaue (rice transplanting festival) **2**:*254b*
Ōtawara 大田原 **6**:129b
Ōta Ward 大田区 **6**:129b
Ōta Zensai 太田全斎 **4**:31b
Ōte 大手 **1**:248a
Otedama **1**:148a
Ōtemmon Conspiracy 応天門の変 **6**:129b
Fujiwara no Yoshifusa **2**:358a
Ōte Takuji 大手拓次 **6**:129b
Ō Tō 王韜 **8**:222b
Otogi bunko (The Companion Library) 御伽文庫 **6**:130a
Otogishū 御伽衆 **6**:129b, 282a
Otogi-zōshi 御伽草子 **2**:303a; **5**:45a; **6**:129b-130b; **7**:64b
Ochikubo monogatari **6**:59b
painting **6**:150b
Otoko-e painting **6**:150a
Otoko wa tsurai yo; Torajirō wasurenagusa (Hard to Be a Man; Tora's Forget-me-not) 男はつらいよ **1**:115b; **2**:*275a*
Otometsubaki **1**:237a
Ōtomo 大友氏 **7**:102b
Ōtomo family (fl 8th century) 大伴氏 **6**:130b
Ōtomo family (fl 12th-16th centuries) 大友氏 **6**:130b
Ōtomo no Kanamura 大伴金村 **6**:130b-131a
Keitai, Emperor **4**:190a
Ōtomo no Kuronushi 大伴黒主 **4**:254b
Ōtomo no Miyuki 大伴御行 **1**:107a
Ōtomo no Sakanoue no Iratsume 大伴坂上郎女 **6**:131a
poems in *Man'yōshū* **5**:108a-108b
Ōtomo no Tabito 大伴旅人 **5**:104b-105a; **6**:131a-131b; **8**:206b, 303a
poems in *Man'yōshū* **5**:108a
Ōtomo no Yakamochi 大伴家持 **6**:131b-132a; **7**:13a; **8**:207a
Man'yōshū compilation **5**:103a
poems in *Man'yōshū* **5**:108b
sakimori uta **7**:2b
Ōtomo, Prince 大友皇子 **4**:60a
Ōtomo Sōrin 大友宗麟 **6**:132a-132b; **7**:99a-99b
Christian daimyō **1**:305a
Luis Frois **2**:340a
Ōtomo Yoriyasu 大友頼泰 **3**:329a
Ōtomo Yoshishige 大友義鎮 **6**:132a
Otona 乙名 **6**:132b
Ōtori Keisuke 大鳥圭介 **6**:133a
Kabo Reforms **4**:281a
Otoshiana (Pitfall) おとし穴 **8**:15a
Otoshidama **6**:133a
Ōtoshi no kyaku 大歳の客 **6**:133b
Ototake Iwazō 乙竹岩造 **6**:133b
Otowa Nobuko 乙羽信子 **6**:133b
Ōtsu 大津 **6**:133b; **7**:90b
urbanization **8**:176a
Ōtsubo Noboru 大坪昇 **7**:93b-94a
Ōtsu-e 大津絵 **2**:296a; **6**:133b-134a
Ki Baitei **4**:201a
oni **6**:*133a*
Ōtsu Incident 大津事件 **6**:134a
Kojima Iken's sentencing **4**:251b
Otsuji haironshū 乙字俳論集 **6**:127b
Otsuji kushū 乙字句集 **6**:127b
Otsuji shokanshū 乙字書簡集 **6**:127b
Ōtsuka Hisao 大塚久雄 **6**:134a
Ōtsuki 大月 **6**:134a
Ōtsuki Fumihiko 大槻文彦 **2**:57a, 377a; **6**:134a-134b
Ōtsuki Gentaku 大槻玄沢 **6**:134b; **7**:258b
Kōsei shimpen translator **4**:294b
Rangaku kaitei **6**:283b
Ōtsuki Joden 大槻如電 **6**:134b

Ōtsuki Nyoden 大槻如電 6:134b
Ōtsukyahan 4:323b
Otsuni, Iwama 岩間乙二 3:79b
Ōtsu no Miya 大津宮 6:134b-135a
Ōtsu pictures 6:133b-134a
Ottama, U 6:135a
Ottawa Conference (1932) 8:152b
Ott, Eugen 6:135a
Otter 4:184b
Ottō to yobareru nihonjin 7:113a
Ōuchi family 大内氏 6:135a
  Ōuchike Kabegaki 6:135b
  Sesshū Tōyō 7:69b
  tally trade 7:332a
Ōuchi Hyōe 大内兵衛 2:13b; 6:135a-135b
  Sakisaka Itsurō 7:3a
Ōuchike Kabegaki 大内家壁書 6:135b
  Ōuchi family 6:135a
Ōuchi Yoshitaka 大内義隆 6:135b; 7:277a
Ōuetsu Reppan Dōmei 奥羽越列藩同盟 6:135b
Ōu Mountains 奥羽山脈 2:366b; 6:135b-136a
Ōura Kanetake 大浦兼武 6:136a
  senkyo kanshō 7:66b
Our Jungle Road to Tokyo 2:185b
Outcasts (semmin) 7:62a
Outer Gardens of the Meiji Shrine
  Shinjuku Ward 7:116a
Outline of a Theory of Civilization, An 1:207b
Overseas colonization theory 7:236b
Overseas Development Company 6:178b
Overseas Economic Cooperation Fund 6:136a; 8:324a
  foreign aid policy 2:310a
  international friendship organizations 3:319b
Overseer 6:136a; 7:254a
Ōwakudani 大涌谷 6:136b
Ōwani 大鰐 6:136b
Owari Asahi 尾張旭 6:136b
Owari no Kuni 尾張国 6:136b
Owari Province 尾張国 6:136b
Owarishi michi no shirube ni (Marking the Road I Have Come) 終りし道の標べに 6:230b
Owase 尾鷲 6:136b
Ownership rights 6:136b-137a, 288a
  abuse 1:5b
Ōya 大家 6:137a
Oyabe 小矢部 6:137a
Oyabun-kobun 2:243a; 4:344a; 6:137a-137b
  "parent-child" relationship 1:207b
Oyakata 1:71a-71b; 7:273a
Oyakata and hikan 親方, 被官 6:137b
Oyakata-kokata. *See* **Oyabun-kobun**
Oya-ko 6:204b
Oyakodaka 父子鷹 7:107b
Oyama (city) 小山 6:137b
Ōyama (mountain) 大山 6:137b
Ōyama Ikuo 大山郁夫 1:313b; 6:137b-138a
Ōyama Iwao 大山巌 1:86b, 87b; 6:138a-138b
Oyama Shrine 雄山神社 7:349b
Oyashio 親潮 2:284a; 6:138b
Oyashirazu 親不知 6:138b
Ōyashirokyō 大社教 3:367b
Ōya Sōichi 大宅壮一 6:138b
  literary prize 1:209b-210a
Oyatoi gaikokujin 2:310b-311b
Ōya Tōru 大矢透 6:138b
Ōyodogawa 大淀川 6:138b
Ō Yōmei 王陽明 8:335a
Oysters [(magaki) *Crassostrea gigas*] 2:282a
  cultivation 2:231b; 7:266a
Oyudono no Ue no nikki 御湯殿上日記 4:255b
Ōyu stone circles 大湯環状列石 6:139a, *139a*, 235a
Ozaki Hōsai 尾崎放哉 6:139a
Ozaki Hotsuki 尾崎秀樹 6:139a
Ozaki Hotsumi 尾崎秀実 6:139b; 7:229b
Ozaki Kazuo 尾崎一雄 6:139b
Ozaki Kōyō 尾崎紅葉 1:164a; 5:11b; 6:139b-140a
  fūzoku shōsetsu 2:378b
  "Golden Demon, The" 7:121a
  Izumi Kyōka 3:365b
  Ken'yūsha 4:198b
Ozaki Memorial Hall 6:140b
Ozaki Shirō 尾崎士郎 6:140a
Ozaki Yukio 尾崎行雄 6:140a-140b
  Kakushin Kurabu 4:120a
  Kenseitō 4:198b
Ozawa Roan 小沢蘆庵 5:17a-17b; 6:140b
  Kagawa Kageki 4:103a
Ozawa Seiji 小沢征爾 6:140b
Ozawa Shigeo 小沢重男 4:18b
Oze 尾瀬 6:*140b*
Ōzeki 7:272a
Ozeki San'ei 小関三英 6:140b-141a
Ōzu 大洲 6:141a
Ōzu Castle 大洲城 6:141a
Ōzuka tomb 王塚古墳 6:141a
Ozu Yasujirō 小津安二郎 2:269b-270a; 3:102b; 6:*141a*, 141b-142b
  Shinoda Masahiro 7:122a
  Umarete wa mita keredo, (I Was Born, But . . .) 8:146a

P

Pabst, Jean Charles 6:143a
Pachinko 4:382a; 5:7b; 6:*143a*
Pacific Affairs 3:316a
Pacific Basin Economic Council 6:143a-143b
  founding 1:118b-119a
Pacific Economic Committee 4:188a
Pacific Islands
  Japanese occupation 7:235a
  relations with Japan 7:234b-236a
    diplomatic relations 3:322a-322b
    trade 3:322a-322b
  Southern expansion doctrine 7:236a-237a
Pacific Islands Agency 7:235a
Pacific Metals Co, Ltd 6:143b
Pacific Ocean
  earthquakes 2:139b
  natural features of Japan 4:7b
Pacific Painting Society (Taiheiyō Gakai) 4:175b; 8:328a, 341a
Pacific plate
  volcanoes 8:193b
Pacific War 太平洋戦争 3:202a-202b
  See also **World War II**
Pacifism 6:143b-146a
  partisan politics 6:145a-145b
  peace research 6:145b-146a
  postwar era 6:144b-145a
  post-World War I 1:88a
  prewar development 6:143b-144b
  United States-Japan security treaties 8:165b
Packhorsemen 5:83a-83b
Packhorse service (chūma) 1:313a
Pact of Paris 4:191a
Paddy field remains
  historical 1:80a
Paekche 2:287b; 6:146a-146b
  Chinese relations 6:146b
  Hakusukinoe, Battle of 3:89a
  in Korean Three Kingdoms period 4:292a
  Japanese relations 6:146b
  Kanroku 4:151b
  language of 4:291a
  origins and society 6:146a
  relations among Korean Kingdoms 6:146a-146b
  religion and culture 6:146b
Page 4:296a
Page of Madness, A 4:176a
Pagès, Léon 6:146b-147a
  works 6:146a
Pagoda 3:*232b*; 5:*331a*; 6:147a-147b; 8:*285a*, 285b
  architecture 1:182a-182b
Painters
  Akita
    Odano Naotake 6:65a
    Satake Shozan 7:25b
  bunjinga
    Aoki Mokubei 1:68b
    Buson 1:224b-225a
    Gion Nankai 3:34a
    Ike no Gyokuran 3:266b
    Ike no Taiga 3:267a
    Ki Baitei 4:201a
    Nakabayashi Chikutō 5:311a-311b; 8:297a
    Okada Beisanjin 6:77b
    Okada Hankō 6:78a
    Rai San'yō 6:28b
    Tani Bunchō 7:341a
    Tanomura Chikuden 7:344b
    Tazaki Sōun 7:359a
    Tomioka Tessai 8:72a-73a
    Totoki Baigai 8:85b
    Tsubaki Chinzan 8:109b
    Uragami Gyokudō 8:175a
    Uragami Shunkin 8:175b
    Watanabe Kazan 8:235b
    Yamamoto Baiitsu 8:297a-297b
    Yokoi Kinkoku 8:330b-331a
  Chinese
    Itsunen 3:357a
    Mokkei 5:234a
    Shen Nanpin (Shen Nan-p'in) 7:83b
  emakimono
    Toba Sōjō 8:31b-32a
  English
    Wirgman, Charles 8:254b-255a
  French
    Bigot, Georges 1:154b-155a
  Hasegawa
    Hasegawa Tōhaku 3:108b
  illustrators
    Andō Hiroshige 1:163b
    Hanabusa Itchō 3:92b-93a
    Ishikawa Tairō 3:344a
    Kaburagi Kiyokata 1:164a
    Katsushika Hokusai 1:163b
    Kitagawa Utamaro 1:163b
    Suzuki Harunobu 1:163b
    Takehisa Yumeji 1:164a; 7:324a
    Torii Kiyonaga 1:163b

ink
Gakuō Zōkyū 3:4b
Geiami 3:14a
Gyokuen Bompō 3:71a-71b
Hasegawa Tōhaku 3:108b-109a, *307a*
Josetsu 4:77b-78a
Kaihō Yūshō 4:110b
Kameda Bōsai 4:124b-125a
Kanō Masanobu 4:147b
Kaō Ninga 4:156a
Mokkei 5:234a
Minchō 5:183b
Mokuan Reien 5:235a-235b
Nōami 6:29b-30a
Oguri Sōtan 6:72a
Sesshū Tōyō 7:69b
Sesson Shūkei 7:70a
Shōkei 7:163b
Shūbun 7:180b-181a
Shūgetsu Tōkan 7:182b-183a
Sōami 7:207b
Sōen 7:219b-220a
Tesshū Tokusai 8:15b-16a
Italian
Chiossone, Edoardo 1:296b
Fontanesi, Antonio 2:304a
Japanese-style, modern
Dōmoto Inshō 2:130b
Fukuda Heihachirō 2:362a
Hashiguchi Goyō 3:109b
Hashimoto Kansetsu 3:110a
Hayami Gyoshū 3:115b
Hirafuku Hyakusui 3:141b-142a
Hishida Shunsō 3:151b-152a
Imamura Shikō 3:273b
Itō Shinsui 3:356a
Kaburagi Kiyokata 4:100a
Kawabata Ryūshi 4:175b
Kawai Gyokudō 4:178b
Kobayashi Kokei 4:237a
Maeda Seison 5:80b
Murakami Kagaku 5:266a
Nakamura Gakuryō 5:314b
Nishiyama Suishō 6:20a
Ogawa Usen 6:70a
Shimomura Kanzan 7:105a-105b
Takeuchi Seihō 7:326a
Terazaki Kōgyō 8:13a
Tomita Keisen 8:73a
Tsuchida Bakusen 8:111b
Uemura Shōen 8:128a
Yasuda Yukihiko 8:318a
Kaihō
Kaihō Yūshō 4:110b-111b
Kanō
Hashimoto Gahō 3:109b
Kanō Eitoku 4:146a
Kanō Hōgai 4:146b-147a
Kanō Masanobu 4:147a
Kanō Mitsunobu 4:147b
Kanō Motonobu 4:147b-148a
Kanō Sanraku 4:148b
Kanō Sansetsu 4:148b-149a
Kanō Tan'yū 4:150b
Kusumi Morikage 4:320b
Mori Sosen 5:253a
Kishi
Ganku 3:7b-8a
Kose
Kose no Kanaoka 4:294b
Maruyama-Shijō
Kawabata Gyokushō 4:175a
Kōno Bairei 4:272a
Maruyama Ōkyo 5:121b-122a
Matsumura Goshun 5:318a
Matsumura Keibun 5:138a-138b
Mori Kansai 5:249b-250a
Mori Sosen 5:253a
Okamoto Toyohiko 6:80b
Rosetsu 6:339a
Watanabe Nangaku 8:236a
nanga
See Painters, bunjinga
nihonga
See Painters, Japanese-style, modern
portraiture
Fujiwara no Nobuzane 2:353b-354a
Fujiwara no Takanobu 2:355b
Rimpa
Kenzan 4:199b
Kōrin 4:292b-293b
Sakai Hōitsu 6:376b
Sōtatsu 7:232b
Watanabe Shikō 8:236a
Soga
Soga Shōhaku 7:222a
Takuma
Takuma Eiga 7:327b
Takuma Shōga 7:328a
Takuma Tamenari 1:190a; 7:328a
Takuma Tametō 7:328a
ukiyo-e
Chōkyōsai Eiri 1:300a
Furuyama Moromasa 2:373b
Harunobu 3:106a-106b
Hiroshige 3:148a
Hokusai 3:215a-216a
Hosoda Eishi 3:235b
Ishikawa Toyonobu 3:345a
Isoda Koryūsai 3:347b
Katsukawa Shunchō 4:171b-172a
Kawanabe Gyōsai 4:182a
Kobayashi Kiyochika 4:236b-237a
Miyagawa Chōshun 5:216b
Nishikawa Sukenobu 6:17a-17b
Sharaku 7:78b-79a
Taiso Yoshitoshi 7:306a
Torii Kiyonobu I 8:78b-79a
Totoya Hokkei 8:85b
Utagawa Kunimasa 8:183a
Utagawa Kunisada 8:183a
Utagawa Kuniyoshi 8:183b-184a
Utagawa Toyoharu 8:184b
Utagawa Toyohiro 8:184b
Utagawa Toyokuni 8:184b
Utamaro 8:185b-187a
Unkoku
Unkoku Tōgan 8:172b-173a
Western-style
Aōdō Denzen 1:68a
Aoki Shigeru 1:69a
Asai Chū 1:93b
Fujishima Takeji 2:345b-346a
Fujita Tsuguharu 2:347a
Harada Naojirō 3:100b
Hasegawa Roka 3:107a-107b
Kawahara Keiga 4:177b-178a
Kawakami Tōgai 4:181b; 8:327a
Kishida Ryūsei 4:223a
Koide Narashige 4:250a
Kuniyoshi, Yasuo 4:310b
Kuroda Seiki 4:314b
Mitsutani Kunishirō 5:214a
Nakamura Fusetsu 5:314b
Okada Saburōsuke 6:78b
Sakamoto Hanjirō 6:378a
Takahashi Yuichi 7:313b
Umehara Ryūzaburō 8:146b
Wada Eisaku 8:197b
Yamaguchi Kaoru 8:294b
Yamamoto Hōsui 8:298a
Yasui Sōtarō 8:318b
yamato-e
Iwasa Matabei 3:362b-363a
Matsuoka Eikyū 5:139a
Reizei Tamechika 6:289b
Zen
Fūgai Ekun 2:341b
Hakuin 3:88a
Sengai Gibon 7:63b
Takuan Sōhō 7:327b
Painting 6:147b-158b
Amanohashidate 6:*152b*
Ban Dainagon ekotoba (Picture Story of the Courtier Ban Dainagon) 6:*152a*
Beauties beneath Trees (juka bijin) 6:*149a*
bird-and-flower 1:156a-156b
Black Cat 6:*157a*
bunjinga school 1:210a-211a
Chinese influence 7:167b
Diamond realm mandala 6:*150b*
dōshakuga 1:192a
Engeki zukan 6:*155b*
esoteric Buddhist 1:188b-189a
Fudō Myōō 6:*151a*
haboku 1:193a
handscrolls (emakimono) 2:198a-200a
Heiji monogatari ekotoba (Tale of Heiji scrolls) 6:*152a*
Hishida Shunsō 6:*157a*
Hishikawa Moronobu 6:*155b*
Illustrated Sutra of Cause and Effect (E inga kyō) 6:*149a*
Imamura Shikō 6:*158b*
ink painting 1:192a; 3:305b-307b
Iris Screens (Kakitsubatazu) 6:*154a-154b*
Italian influence 3:350b
Kanō Naganobu 6:*155a*
Kanō Sanraku 6:*153a*
Kiyomizudera engi (Legends of Kiyomizudera) 6:*153b*
Kōrin 6:*154a-154b*
Kuroda Seiki 6:*156b*
latter-day Buddhist 1:193a-194b
Mahāyāna Buddhist 1:185b-187a
emakimono 1:186b-187a
Merrymaking under the Cherry Blossoms 6:*155a*
modern 6:155a-158b
Shōwa period 6:157b-158b
Taishō period 6:156a-157b
Musō Soseki 6:*152b*
Mutō Shūi 6:*152b*
nanga. *See* **Bunjinga**
Nekkoku no maki (The Tropics) 6:*158b*
premodern 6:147b-148a
Azuchi-Momoyama and Edo period 6:151b-155a
Buddhist 6:148a-149b
ink 6:150b-151b
scroll 6:149b-150b
Pure Land Buddhist 1:189b-191a
raigōzu 1:190a; 6:*151b*
schools
Ami school 1:52b-53a
Kanō school 4:149a-151a
Maruyama-Shijō school 5:122a-122b
Rimpa 6:317b-318a
Takuma school 7:328a
Sesshū Tōyō 6:*152b*
screen and wall 7:41a-43b
subjects 6:158b-159a
suibokuga 1:192a
Tamamushi Shrine 6:*148b*
Tanomura Chikuden 6:*155b*
Tosa Mitsunobu 6:*153b*
Umehara Ryūzaburō 6:*156b*
wall painting 6:*148b*
Western-style (yōga) 8:327a-328b
yamato-e 8:309b
early 8:248b-249a
Yokoyama Taikan 6:*157a*
Yoshiwara 6:*155b*

Yunazu · · · 6:*155a*
Zen · · · 1:192a-194a; 8:374b-375b
Painting Appreciation Society · · · 4:150b
Painting subjects · · · 6:158b-159a
bird-and-flower painting (kachōga) · · · 6:158b-159a
figure painting (jimbutsuga) · · · 6:158b
landscape painting (sansuiga) · · · 6:158b
Pak Chŏng-hŭi · · · 6:159a
Pak Chong-sŏk v. Hitachi, Ltd · · · 4:291b
Pakutari no saiban · · · 朴達の裁判 · · · 4:211a
Pak Yŏl · · · 6:159a-159b
plot · · · 6:159a
Pak Yŏng-hyo · · · 6:159b
Japanese visit · · · 4:280b
Kaehwap'a · · · 4:101b
Kapsin Political Coup · · · 4:156b
Palace Guards. *See* **Efu**
Paleolithic culture · · · 6:159b-160a
artifacts · · · 4:153b
Iwajuku site · · · 3:358a
Paleolithic period · · · 6:160a
Paleontological Society of Japan · 2:329b
Paleontology · · · 2:328a
cenozoic · · · 2:329a
development · · · 2:328a
mesozoic · · · 2:328b
paleozoic · · · 2:328b
Palisades (ki) · · · 1:246b
Pallada · · · 6:270b
Palmistry · · · 6:160b
Palms
Cycas revoluta · · · 7:233a
Pan American Treaty on Tropical Tuna · · · 2:282b-283a
Pan-Asianism · · · 1:164b; 6:160b-161a; 7:51b; 8:144b
Amur River Society · · · 1:53b
nationalism · · · 5:343b
United States · · · 8:156a
World War II · · · 8:272a
Panay Incident · · · パネー号事件 · · · 6:161a-161b
Panē gō Jiken. *See* **Panay Incident**
Pan no Kai (Pan Society) · · · パンの会 · 5:18b; 6:161b; 8:346b
Paper · · · 8:232b-234a
book · · · 1:153b
marbled design techniques · · · 7:266b
pattern technique · · · 7:280b
traditional furniture material · · · 2:371b
Paper, hand-made. *See* **Washi**
Paper and pulp industry
Daishōwa Paper Mfg Co, Ltd · · · 2:67b
Honshū Paper Co, Ltd · · · 3:240a
Jūjō Paper Co, Ltd · · · 4:83a-83b
Ōji Paper Co, Ltd · · · 6:77a
Paperback books · · · 6:162a
major series · · · 6:162a
Paper balloons · · · 6:162a
Paper-folding
origami · · · 6:116b-118b
"Paper Lining of the Sliding Doors of a Four-and-a-Half-Mat Room" · · · 8:328b
Paper mill · · · 8:233a
Paper Museum · · · 6:162a
Papier-mâché · · · 2:371b
Pardon · · · 2:49a; 6:162a-162b
Pardon Law of 1947 · · · 6:162b
Parental power · · · 6:162b
Parent and child, legal definition of · · · 6:162b-163a
adoptive · · · 6:163a
illegitimacy · · · 6:163a
legitimate · · · 6:162b-163a
recorded and nonexistent · · · 6:163a
rights and obligations · · · 6:163a
Parenticide · · · 6:163a-163b
Parhae · · · 1:159b-160a
Paris Exposition of 1878 · · · 4:182a
Paris Peace Conference · · · 4:367b
United States · · · 8:157a
Versailles, Treaty of · · · 8:190b
Parkes, Sir Harry Smith · · · 1:175b; 4:372b; 6:163b-164a
French-Japanese relations · · · 2:331b
Satow, Ernest Mason · · · 7:29a
Shimonoseki Bombardment · · · 7:106a
Parlor · · · 6:124b
Parole · · · 6:172b
Parties himachi and tsukimachi · · · 3:139a
Partnership · · · 6:164a-164b
Pasture lands, regulation · · · 5:85a
Patent agent · · · 1:16a
Patent Law of 1959 · · · 6:164b-165a
Patent Office · · · 3:297a
Patents, Design Law · · · 2:91a
Paternalism · · · 6:165a-165b; 7:213b
"closed" employment systems · · · 4:344b
job tenure · · · 4:357a
managerial ideology · · · 5:91b-92a
Paternity suit · · · 6:163a
Pathologists
Katsurada Fujio · · · 4:172a
Kiyono Kenji · · · 4:232b
Ogata Tomosaburō · · · 6:69b
Tawara Sunao · · · 7:351b
Yamagiwa Katsusaburō · · · 8:294a
Yoshida Tomizō · · · 8:346a-346b
Patrimonial rule
ritsuryō system · · · 6:322a
Patriotic Association for Japanese Literature · · · 5:379a
Patriotic Labor Party · · · 7:108a
Patriotic Women's Association · · · 1:34a; 6:165b
Patriotism · · · 6:165b
Patron-client system · · · 4:343b-344a
Patterns of Culture · · · 4:39a
Pauley, Edwin Wendell 6:165b-166a, 302b; 7:250b
Paulownia [(kiri) *Paulownia tomentosa*] · 2:371b; 6:166a
Pavlova, Anna · · · 2:75b
Pawnbrokers · · · 2:148a-148b
Pawning · · · 7:87a
Peabody Museum · · · 5:256a
Peace for Vietnam Committee · · · 6:166a
Oda Makoto · · · 6:61b
peace movement · · · 6:167a
Peace Memorial Park · · · 3:*149a*, 149b
Peace movement · · · 1:111a; 6:166a-167b
Anti-Nuclear-Bomb Movement · · · 6:166a-166b
Anti-Security-Treaty Movement · · · 6:166b-167a
Vietnam and Okinawa Movement · · · 6:167a-167b
women in · · · 8:263b
"Peace police" · · · 7:241b
Peace Preservation Law of 1887 · 1:252b; 6:167b
Daidō Danketsu Movement · · · 2:56a
Freedom and People's Rights Movement · · · 2:336a
Kishida Toshiko · · · 4:223a
Kiyoura Keigo · · · 4:233a
Nakae Chōmin · · · 5:311b-312a
Nakajima Nobuyuki · · · 5:313b-314a
Sandai Jiken Kempaku Movement (Movement to Memorialize Three Important Items) · · · 7:9b
Peace Preservation Law of 1925 · · 1:253a; 2:337b-338a; 3:198b; 4:339a, 345b, 378a; 6:168a-169b; 6:266a; 7:229a, 242a, 251b, 254a
democracy · · · 2:84b
fundamental liberties limitation · · · 2:369b
Kakushin Kurabu · · · 4:120a
Kawakami Hajime · · · 4:181a
Kenseikai · · · 4:198a
kokutai discussed · · · 4:263b
March 15th Incident · · · 5:113a
Planning Board Incident · · · 6:189b
Taishō democracy · · · 7:305a
Tanaka Giichi · · · 7:336a-336b
"Thought Criminal" Probation Law · 8:29a
Tosaka Jun · · · 8:81b
United States · · · 8:157b
Wakatsuki Reijirō · · · 8:218b
Yokohama Incident · · · 8:330a
"Peach Boy" · · · 5:296a-296b
Peaches *(Prunus persica)* · · · 6:169b
Pearl Harbor, attack on · · · 6:169b; 8:273a
Genda Minoru · · · 3:17a-17b
Grew, Joseph Clark · · · 3:62a
Roosevelt, Franklin Delano · · · 6:339a
United States · · · 8:159a
Pearl industry · · · 1:21b
Pearls · · · 2:287a; 6:*169a*, 169b-170a
classification · · · 6:170a
commercial production · · · 6:170a
composition · · · 6:170a
cultivation · · · 7:266a
cultured · · · 6:169b
formation · · · 6:169b-170a
freshwater · · · 6:170a
shellfish · · · 6:169b
Pears [(nashi) *Pyrus serotina*] · · · 6:170a
Peasant Family beneath a Hanging Gourd Trellis · · · 4:320b
Peasant landholders (hombyakushō) · · · 4:362b
Peasant leagues. *See* **Tsuchi ikki**
Peasant protest · · · 8:337a
Peasants · · · 3:217a
hyakushō · · · 3:249a-249b
rebellions
ikki · · · 3:268b
rōnin · · · 6:336b
Peasant uprisings · · · 2:107b-108a
Pecuniary sanctions · · · 2:49a
Peel Island · · · 1:272a-272b
Peerage · · · 6:170a-172b; 7:151a
abolition · · · 6:171b
adoption · · · 6:170a-170b
court ranks · · · 2:39b-41a
historical evolution · · · 6:170b
House of Peers · · · 6:171a-171b
Meiji Restoration · · · 6:170b-171a
Occupation · · · 6:52a
Peerage Act of 1884 · · · 6:171a
shi-nō-kō-shō · · · 7:122b
Peerage Act · · · 6:171a
Peerage rights · · · 4:362b
Peers' School (Gakushūin) · · · 1:5a; 4:82b; 6:171a
Peiron boat race · · · 5:304a; 6:171b
Peiron Festival · · · 1:37b
Penal Code · · · 2:339a
Penal sentences
death · · · 2:48b
incarceration · · · 2:48b-49a
pecuniary sanctions · · · 2:48b-49a
Penal system · · · 2:45b; 6:171b-172b
contemporary · · · 6:172a-172b
capital punishment · · · 6:172b
juvenile offenders · · · 6:172a
number of offenses · · · 6:172a
parole · · · 6:172b
prison terms · · · 6:172b
prosecution · · · 6:172b

exile (entō) ········ 2:222a
history ········ 6:171b-172a
premodern
banishment ········ 1:137b
Peninsulas
Atsumi ········ 1:115b
Bōsō ········ 1:165b
Chita ········ 1:297b
Higashi Matsuura ········ 3:132a
Izu ········ 3:367b
Kii ········ 4:205a
Kunisaki ········ 4:310a
Miura ········ 5:215b-216a
Nemuro ········ 5:360a
Nishi Sonogi ········ 6:19a-19b
Noto ········ 6:41b
Oga ········ 6:68a-68b
Oshika ········ 6:125a
Oshima ········ 6:126a
Ōsumi ········ 6:128a
Satsuma ········ 7:29b
Shakotan ········ 7:75a
Shima ········ 7:101a
Shimabara ········ 7:98b
Shimane ········ 7:100b
Shimokita ········ 7:105a
Shiretoko ········ 7:147b
Tsugaru ········ 8:113a
Pensions ········ 6:172b-173b
development ········ 7:210b
national ········ 6:173a
Onkyū system ········ 6:172b
private ········ 6:172b
public ········ 6:172b
railroad workers ········ 6:172b
retirement plans ········ 6:99a, 307a
social security ········ 6:173a
Penta-Ocean Construction Co, Ltd ········ 6:173b
Peonies [(botan; shakuyaku) family Ranunculaceae] ········ 6:173b-174a
People's Cooperative Party ········ 4:260b
People's Council to Prevent the Security Treaty Revision ········ 6:167a
People's Finance Corporation ········ 6:174a; 7:204b
People's Party (Kokumintō) ········ 4:260b
People's Republic of China
postwar relations ········ 1:290a
Pēpābakku ········ 6:162a
Perfect Liberty, The Church of. *See* **PL Kyōdan**
Periodicals, censorship of ········ 1:253a
Periodization ········ 6:174a-177b
dating system ········ 6:174b-175a
"national era" ········ 6:175a
nengō (imperial name era) ········ 6:174b
60-year cycles ········ 6:174b-175a
sovereign reign ········ 6:175a
historiographical ········ 6:175a-177a
conceptual systems ········ 6:176a-176b
era names ········ 6:175a-175b
European models ········ 6:176b
jidai (epoch, age, period) ········ 6:175b-176a
scholarly debates over ········ 6:176b-177a
Permanent Court of International Justice ········ 4:373a
Perry, Matthew Calbraith ········ 2:64a; 6:*177a*, 177b-178a; 7:3b, 8b, 86a
bureaucratic development ········ 1:217b
end of Tokugawa regime ········ 3:192a-192b
imperial rule ········ 2:205b
Kanagawa Treaty ········ 2:331a; 4:135a, 140b
Nakahama Manjirō ········ 5:313a-313b
National Seclusion ········ 5:346b-347b
Opening of Japan
daimyō response ········ 5:155b-156a
Persecution, religious ········ 6:294b
Persecutions at Urakami (Urakami kuzure) ········ 6:178a
Persimmons *(Diospyros kaki)* ········ 6:178a
"Personal collections" (shikashū) ········ 8:204a
Personal field allotment ········ 4:301b
Personal names ········ 5:324b-325a
kana ········ 5:325a
Personal suretyship ········ 6:178a-178b
Personification, waka ········ 8:203b
Personnel
foreign firms ········ 2:318a
training ········ 2:318a
Person without capacity ········ 6:178b
Peru, diplomatic ties ········ 4:369b
Peru and Japan ········ 6:178b-179b
Japanese immigrants ········ 6:178b-179a
Maria Luz Incident ········ 6:178b
World War II ········ 6:178b
PETA Army ········ 6:179b
Petrochemical industry ········ 1:267b; 6:180a-180b
companies
Kanegafuchi Chemical Industry Co, Ltd ········ 4:137b
Mitsubishi Petrochemical Co, Ltd ········ 5:208b-209a
Mitsui Petrochemical Industries, Ltd ········ 5:212a
Sekisui Chemical Co, Ltd ········ 7:57b
energy revolution ········ 2:214b
Petrochemicals, manufacturers ········ 7:173a
Petroleum ········ 5:353a; 6:180b-182a
alternatives ········ 6:181a
conservation ········ 6:181a
consumption ········ 6:181a
imports ········ 6:180b-181a
production ········ 6:181b-182a
products ········ 6:181a
Petroleum industries
Arabian Oil Co, Ltd ········ 1:71b-72a
Daikyō Oil Co, Ltd ········ 2:60b-61a
Esso Standard Oil Co, Ltd ········ 2:231b
Fuji Kōsan Co, Ltd ········ 2:343b
General Sekiyu ········ 3:18a-18b
Idemitsu Kōsan Co, Ltd ········ 3:258b-259a
Kōa Oil Co, Ltd ········ 4:234b
Kyōdō Oil Co, Ltd ········ 4:324a
Maruzen Oil Co, Ltd ········ 5:122b
Mitsubishi Oil Co, Ltd ········ 5:208b
Mobil Sekiyu ········ 5:228a
Nippon Mining Co, Ltd ········ 6:11a
Nippon Oil Co, Ltd ········ 6:11b
Shell Oil Co, Ltd ········ 7:83a-83b
Shōwa Oil Co, Ltd ········ 7:176b
Teikoku Oil Co, Ltd ········ 7:376a-376b
Tōa Nenryō Kōgyō ········ 8:30b
Phaeton Incident ········ フェートン号事件 1:211b; 6:182a
Doeff, Hendrik ········ 2:123a
National Seclusion ········ 5:347b
Phan Boi Chau ········ 2:53a; 6:182a
Pharmaceutical industry ········ 5:150a; 6:182a-182b
companies
Eisai Co, Ltd ········ 2:187b
Fujisawa Pharmaceutical Co, Ltd ········ 2:345b
Kanebō, Ltd ········ 4:137b
Sankyō Co, Ltd ········ 7:15a
Shionogi & Co, Ltd ········ 7:141a
Takeda Chemical Industries, Ltd ········ 7:321b-322a
Tanabe Seiyaku Co, Ltd ········ 7:335b
Pharmacists in health care system 3:120a
Pharmacognosists. *See* Honzōgaku
Pharmacognosy ········ 1:155b
Pharmacologists
Asahina Yasuhiko ········ 1:93a
Nagai Nagayoshi ········ 5:301a
Tawara Yoshizumi ········ 7:351b
Pharmacopoeia of Japan ········ 6:182b
Pheasants [(kiji; yamadori) family Phasianidae] ········ 6:182b
Phenylthiocarbamide ········ 4:36b-37a
Phibul Songkhram ········ 6:183a; 7:65b
Philip Jaisohn
Independence Club ········ 4:281b
Philippine Executive Commission ········ 6:184a
Philippines and Japan ········ 6:183a-184b
before 1898 ········ 6:183a-183b
Japanese-Philippine Trade (1899-1941) ········ 6:183b-184a
postwar relations ········ 6:184b
wartime relations ········ 6:184a-184b
Philippine Sea, Battle of ········ 5:307b; 6:184b-185a
Philosophers
Aizawa Seishisai ········ 1:38a
Andō Shōeki ········ 1:55b-56a
Ban Nobutomo ········ 1:141b
Dazai Shundai ········ 2:80b
Fujita Tōko ········ 2:347a
Fujiwara Seika ········ 2:358b-359a
Hasegawa Nyozekan ········ 3:107a
Hashimoto Sanai ········ 3:110a-110b
Hatano Seiichi ········ 3:112b
Hayashi Razan ········ 3:117a-117b
Hisamatsu Shin'ichi ········ 3:151b
Inoue Tetsujirō ········ 3:311a
Ishida Baigan ········ 3:339a-340a
Itō Jinsai ········ 3:354a
Itō Tōgai ········ 3:356a
Iwashita Sōichi ········ 3:363a-363b
Jien ········ 4:53b-54a
Kaibara Ekiken ········ 4:108a-108b
Kameda Bōsai ········ 4:124b-125a
Kanō Kōkichi ········ 4:147a
Kawakami Hajime ········ 4:107b-181a
Kihira Tadayoshi ········ 4:204b
Kuki Shūzō ········ 4:304b
Kumazawa Banzan ········ 8:335b
Kuwaki Gen'yoku ········ 4:322a
Maruyama Masao ········ 5:121b
Miki Kiyoshi ········ 5:171a
Miura Baien ········ 5:214b-215a
Mori Arimasa ········ 5:248b
Muro Kyūsō ········ 5:271a-271b
Mutai Risaku ········ 5:287b-288a
Nakae Tōju ········ 8:335b
Nakamura Hajime ········ 5:314b-315a
Ninomiya Sontoku ········ 6:7a-8a
Nishi Amane ········ 6:14a-14b
Nishida Kitarō ········ 6:14b-15b
Nishimura Shigeki ········ 6:17b-18b
Ogyū Sorai ········ 6:72b-73a
Oka Asajirō ········ 6:77b
Okakura Kakuzō ········ 6:79b
Ōkuni Takamasa ········ 6:97b
Ōnishi Hajime ········ 6:107b
Ōshio Heihachirō ········ 6:126a-126b
Rai San'yō ········ 6:280b-281a
Saigusa Hiroto ········ 6:366a-366b
Sakuma Shōzan ········ 7:3b-4a
Shibukawa Shunkai ········ 7:86a
Sugiura Shigetake ········ 7:258b
Suzuki Shōsan ········ 7:283a-283b
Tachibana Shiraki ········ 7:293a
Takahashi Satomi ········ 7:313a
Tanabe Hajime ········ 7:335a-335b
Tanaka Ōdō ········ 7:338a-338b
Teshima Toan ········ 8:15a-15b
Tosaka Jun ········ 8:81b
Tsuda Sōkichi ········ 8:112b
Watsuji Tetsurō ········ 8:237b
Yamaga Sokō ········ 8:290a-290b
Yamagata Bantō ········ 8:292a-292b

Yamakawa Hitoshi 8:296a-297b
Yamazaki Ansai 8:312a-312b
Yanagi Muneyoshi 8:314a
Yokoi Shōnan 8:331a-331b
Yoshida Shōin 8:345b-346a
Yoshino Sakuzō 8:348b-349a
Philosophy
comprehensive dialectical whole 7:313a
Confucianism 1:352b-358b
emptiness 2:212b-213a
ethics 2:232a-232b
existentialism 2:236b
Marxist 5:231a-232a
modern 5:229b-232a
wakon yōsai (Japanese spirit, Western knowledge) 8:221a
Philosophy of law 4:85b
Phoenix Hall (Hōōdō) 1:*226b*
Phonetics. *See* **Japanese language**
Phonics, Ryūkyū dialects 6:355a-357a
Phonorecord 6:354b
Photographers
Ishimoto Yashuiro 6:*186b*
Kimura Ihei 6:*185a*
Nojima Kōzō 6:*185a*
Ogawa Isshin 6:*184b*
Photography 6:185a-186a
industry companies
Asahi Optical Co, Ltd. 1:93a
Canon, Inc. 1:239b
Nippon Kōgaku 6:10a
Olympus Optical Co, Ltd 6:100a
Ricoh Co, Ltd 6:311b
19th century 6:185a-185b
professional photographers 6:185b
Shimazu Nariakira 6:185a
studios 6:185b
techniques 6:185b
20th century 6:185b-186a
artistic or salon photography 6:185b-186a
eizō or personal vision 6:186a
wartime 6:186a
Physical education 4:10a; 7:35b
Physically Handicapped Welfare Law of 1949 6:186a-186b; 7:209b
investigation 6:186a-186b
rehabilitation 6:186a
technical guidance 6:296a
Physicists
Esaki Reona 2:231a
Honda Kōtarō 3:219a
Ishiwara Jun 3:345a
Kaya Seiji 4:185a
Kikuchi Seishi 4:207a
Kubo Ryōgo 4:300b
Nagaoka Hantarō 5:303b
Nakaya Ukichirō 5:319b
Nishikawa Shōji 6:17a
Nishina Yoshio 6:18b
Sakata Shōichi 6:379b
Terada Torahiko 8:11a
Tomonaga Shin'ichirō 8:73a
Yukawa Hideki 8:356b
Physics 3:133a; 6:186b-187a
Physiognomy 6:187a-187b
Physiologists
Katō Gen'ichi 4:167b
Katsuki Yasuji 4:172a
Kuno Yasu 4:310b
Shibata Keita 7:84b
Tamiya Hiroshi 7:334a
Physiology 1:156a
Physiology of Human Perspiration, The 4:310b
Physique 4:37a
Piccadilly 6:100a
Pickles 2:52b; 6:187b
Picture brides 6:187b-188a
Hawaii 4:16a
Japanese American 4:14a
Japanese Associations of America 4:22a
Picture scrolls. *See* **Emakimono**
Piggott, Francis Stewart 6:188a
Pilgrimages 1:194b; 6:188a-188b, 291a
gankake 3:7b
Ise Shrine 3:338a-339a
prayer 6:233a
Pillow Book. *See* **Sei Shōnagon**
Pillow words 5:87b-88a
Pimiko 3:139b
Pine and Hawk 4:150a
Pines [(matsu) *Pinus* spp.] 2:326b; 6:188b-189a
Pines on a Beach 4:111a
Pine Trees 3:*108b*
Ping-Pong. *See* **Table tennis**
Pinku 2:275a
Pioneer Electronic Corporation 6:189a
Pipe organs 6:9b-10a
Pirates 8:220a-221a
Pit houses 1:78a; 4:72b; 6:189a-189b; 7:30b
Hiraide site 3:143a
Iba site 3:253b
Karako site 4:157b
shell mounds 7:82b-83a
Toro site 6:*189a*
Pittosporum. *See* **Tobera**
Place names 5:326a-326b
administrative 5:326a-326b
Chinese 5:326a-326b
geographical 5:326a-326b
historical 5:326a-326b
Plain castle (hirajiro) 1:247b
Plains
Hokkaidō
Ishikari 3:342a
Sarobetsu 7:22a
Teshio 8:15b
Tokachi 8:40a
Honshū
Akita 1:42b
Fukui 2:363b
Himeji 3:139a
Hiroshima 3:149b
Ise 3:337b
Izumo 3:367a
Kanazawa 4:136a
Kantō 4:153b
Kurayoshi 4:312a-312b
Matsue 5:133a
Niigata 5:385b
Nōbi 6:30a
Noshiro 6:41a
Okayama 6:82b-83a
Ōsaka 6:121b
Sendai 7:63b
Shizuoka 7:153b
Shōnai 7:166a
Tonami 8:73b
Tottori 8:86a
Toyama 8:88b
Tsugaru 8:113a
Wakayama 8:219b
Kyūshū
Fukuoka 2:364b
Kumamoto 4:305b
Miyazaki 5:221b
Ōita 6:75b
Tsukushi 8:115a
Shikoku
Kōchi 4:239b
Matsuyama 5:141b
Sanuki 7:18b
Tokushima 8:58b-59a
Planning Board Incident 6:189b
Planning Board (Kikakuin) 1:8a-8b
Plant breeding 1:30a
Plant Communicable Disease Control Law 6:274a
Plant conservation 6:192a
Plant crops. *See* **Agriculture**
Plant diseases 1:30b
rice 6:310a
Plant export 6:190a
Plant hopper (unka) 6:190a
Plants 6:190a-192a
folklore 6:191b
garden flowers 6:192a
in literature 6:191a
in visual arts 6:191a-191b
modern Japan 6:192a
protected 5:352a-352b
religion 6:191b-192a
trees and shrubs 6:192a
types 6:190a-191a
endemic species 6:190a-191a
floricultural 6:191a
naturalized 6:191a
plant distribution zones 6:190a
uses 6:191a
wild flowers 6:192a
Playing cards 6:192a-192b
Play therapy 6:261b
Playwrights
Abe Kōbō 1:3b
Akimoto Matsuyo 1:42a
comic
Shibuya Tengai 7:86b
Soganoya Gorō 7:221b
French
Claudel, Paul Louis Charles 1:325a
Fujimori Seikichi 2:343b
Inoue Hisashi 3:309b
kabuki
Chikamatsu Monzaemon 1:276a
Mokuami 5:234b-235a
Okamoto Kidō 6:80b
Sakurada Jisuke 7:4a
Segawa Jokō 7:48b
Tsuruya Namboku 8:117b
Kawaguchi Matsutarō 4:177b
Kikuchi Kan 4:206b
Kinoshita Mokutarō 4:215b
Kishida Kunio 4:222b
Koyama Yūshi 4:298b
Kume Masao 4:307b
Mafune Yutaka 5:82b
Mayama Seika 5:142a
Morimoto Kaoru 5:250a-250b
Murayama Tomoyoshi 5:270b
Nō
Kan'ami 4:135b
Kanze Motomasa 4:154b
Kanze Nobumitsu 4:154b
Komparu Zenchiku 4:267b
Zeami 8:369a-369b
puppet theater (bunraku) 1:214a
Chikamatsu Hanji 1:274b
Chikamatsu Monzaemon 1:214a, 275a-276a
Namiki Sōsuke 5:327a
radio
Kikuta Kazuo 4:207a
Kinoshita Junji 4:214b-215b
Kubota Mantarō 4:301a-301b
Tanaka Sumie 7:339b
Uchimura Naoya 8:125a
Tanaka Chikao 7:335b
theater
Hōjō Hideji 3:211a-211b
Iizawa Tadasu 3:264a
Kara Jūrō 4:157b
Katō Michio 4:169a

Kikuta Kazuo ········ 4:207a
Kinoshita Junji ········ 4:214b-215b
Kubo Sakae ········ 4:301a
Kubota Mantarō ········ 4:301a-301b
Osanai Kaoru ········ 6:123b
Shimamura Hōgetsu ········ 7:99b-100a
Terayama Shūji ········ 8:12b-13a
Tsubouchi Shōyō ········ 8:110a-111a
Yamamoto Yūzō ········ 8:300a
Yamazaki Masakazu ········ 8:312b-313a
Yashiro Seiichi ········ 8:317a
Plea bargaining ········ 6:172b
Pleasure quarters, popular fiction ········ 7:79b-80a
PL Kyōdan ········ 5:171b; 6:192b
Plovers [(chidori) family Charadriidae] ········ 6:192b
Plum, Japanese [(ume) *Prunus mume*] ········ 6:192b-193b
Plum and Pine Discourse, The ········ 1:130a-130b
Plural suicide ········ 7:262a
Poetic Memoirs of Lady Daibu, The ········ 4:197b-198a
Poetry ········ 5:13b-14a
chōka ········ 1:299a-299b
early Japanese song ········ 2:137a-138b
haiku ········ 3:78a-82a
imperial anthologies ········ 3:275b
kanshi ········ 6:193b-197b
kyōka ········ 4:331b-332a
kyōshi ········ 4:333a-333b
modern ········ 5:56a-57b
renga ········ 6:296b-300a
senryū ········ 8:368b
tanka ········ 7:343b
waka ········ 8:201b-217a
zappai ········ 8:368a
Poetry, Bureau of ········ 3:52a
Ōnakatomi no Yoshinobu ········ 6:105a
Poetry and prose in Chinese ········ 4:109a; 6:193b-197b
general ········ 6:193b
history ········ 6:193b-195b
Ishikawa Jōzan ········ 3:342b
method and forms ········ 6:195b-197b
"Poetry Contest at the Residence of the Minister of Public Affairs" ········ 8:209b
Poetry Contest in Six Hundred Rounds ········ 4:1b, 198b; 5:40b
Poetry contests ········ 8:209b
Poetry match ········ 8:182a-182b
Poetry, modern. *See* **Literature**
Poets
haiku. *See* Haiku poets
modern
Anzai Fuyue ········ 1:68a
Doi Bansui ········ 2:126a-126b
Hagiwara Sakutarō ········ 3:76a-76b
Horiguchi Daigaku ········ 3:227b
Hori Tatsuo ········ 3:228a
Itō Shizuo ········ 3:356a
Kambara Ariake ········ 4:123a
Kaneko Mitsuharu ········ 4:138b-139a
Kawaji Ryūkō ········ 4:179b
Kinoshita Mokutarō ········ 4:215b
Kitagawa Fuyuhiko ········ 4:224b
Kitahara Hakushū ········ 4:225a
Kusano Shimpei ········ 4:319a
Miki Rofū ········ 5:171b
Miyazawa Kenji ········ 5:222b-223b
Miyoshi Tatsuji ········ 5:224a-224b
Murano Shirō ········ 5:266b-267a
Nishiwaki Junzaburō ········ 6:19b-20a
Ōoka Makoto ········ 6:113b
Saijō Yaso ········ 6:369b
Satō Hachirō ········ 7:26b
Senke Motomaro ········ 7:66b
Susukida Kyūkin ········ 7:279b
Tachihara Michizō ········ 7:293a
Takahashi Mutsuo ········ 7:312b
Takahashi Shinkichi ········ 7:313a
Takamura Kōtarō ········ 7:315b-316b
Ueda Bin ········ 8:126b-127a
Yagi Jūkichi ········ 8:284a
Yamamura Bochō ········ 8:300a
Yosano Akiko ········ 8:340a
renga. *See* Renga poets
tanka. *See* Tanka poets
waka. *See* Waka poets
Po-hai. *See* **Bohai (Po-hai)**
Poisoning ········ 5:148b-149a
Poland, Japanese studies ········ 4:43b
Police, criminal investigation ········ 2:49b
Police box (kōban) ········ 6:*200b*
Police Duties Law of 1938 ········ 2:49b
Police Offenses Penal Regulations 5:196a
Police system ········ 6:198a-201a
administration (keimu) ········ 6:200a
brutality ········ 6:200b
community relations ········ 6:200a-201a
counselors ········ 6:200b
crime prevention (bōhan) ········ 6:200a
criminal investigation (keiji) ········ 6:200a
historical development ········ 6:198a-198b
neighborhood association (chōnaikai) ········ 6:200b
police officers ········ 6:200a
present structure ········ 6:198b-199b
riot police (kidōtai) ········ 6:200a
security (kōan) ········ 6:200a
specializations ········ 6:199b-200a
traffic (kōtsū) ········ 6:200a
traffic safety ········ 6:200b
Political asylum ········ 6:201a
Political cliques ········ 6:165a
Political commentary ········ 7:119a
Political concepts ········ 3:15b-16a
Political corruption ········ 6:201a-202a
history ········ 6:201b
postwar ········ 6:201b-202a
prospects for reducing ········ 6:202a
Political Crisis of 1881 ········ 4:113a; 6:202a-203a; 7:92b, 99a
Political culture ········ 6:203a-207a
continuities and changes ········ 6:206a-207a
emperor ········ 6:203b-204a
hara, kan, newaza ········ 6:205b-206a
kenryoku (political power) ········ 6:206a
political parties, cliques, and factions ········ 6:205b
power ········ 6:203a-203b
pragmatism ········ 6:206a
public ········ 6:205a-205b
state ········ 6:204b-205a
yokubō shizen shugi (Doctrine of Natural Desire) ········ 6:204a-204b
Political Ethicization Movement (Seiji Rinrika Undō) ········ 8:117a
Political Fund Control Law ········ 4:386a
Political Fund Regulations Law ········ 2:337b
Political groups, right-wing extremists ········ 7:176b-177a
Political memorandum ········ 7:337b
Political movements, Marxist student ········ 7:251a-253a
"Political novel" ········ 7:50a-50b
Political parties ········ 6:207a-213a
Diet (1890–1898) ········ 6:207b-210a
Jiyūtō ········ 6:207b, 210a
Shimpotō ········ 6:207b, 210a
Meiji constitutional government ········ 3:195a-195b
Military Takeover (1932-1945) ········ 6:211a
Occupation (1945-1952) ········ 6:211b-212b
communists ········ 6:212b
conservative parties ········ 6:211b-212a
multiparty competition ········ 6:212a
reorganization ········ 6:211b
Socialists ········ 6:211a-211b
"One-and-a-Half-Party System" (1952-1977) ········ 6:212b-213a
origins (1874-1889) ········ 6:207a-207b
Itagaki Taisuke ········ 6:207a-207b
Ōkuma Shigenobu ········ 6:207a
politics of compromise (1898-1924) ········ 6:210a-211a
civil bureaucracy ········ 6:210b-211a
Kenseikai vs. Seiyūkai ········ 6:210a-210b
party cabinet of 1898 ········ 6:210a
proletarian groups ········ 6:210b
Yamagata cabinet of 1900 ········ 6:210a
"reformist" ········ 3:280a-281a
rise of ········ 3:276b
temporary command (1924-1932) ········ 6:211a-211b
noncommunist proletarian groups 6:211a
repression of proletarian groups ·· 6:211a
Taishō democracy ········ 6:211a
Political scandals ··· 5:72a; 6:202a; 7:143a, 173a, 375b
Political Study Association ········ 1:2a
Political suppression of writers in Shōwa period ········ 7:175b-176a
Political system ········ 6:213b-217a
conclusion ········ 6:216b-217a
democracy ········ 2:84a-85a
origins ········ 6:213b
postwar ········ 6:214b-216b
centralization ········ 6:215a-215b
participation ········ 6:215b-216b
structure ········ 6:214b-215a
postwar changes ········ 3:204a-205a
power structure under the Meiji Constitution ········ 6:213b-214b
Political thought, Confucianism ········ 1:352b-358b
Politics, student movements ········ 7:115b
Polivanov, Evgenij Dmitrievich ········ 4:20b; 6:217a
writings ········ 6:217a
Polluter Pays Principle (PPP) ········ 2:225a, 226a, 229a
Pollution
automobile emissions ········ 2:236a-236b
control ········ 2:224a, 225b
industrial complexes ········ 3:291b
industrial waste ········ 3:302b
laws against ········ 2:224a-225b
mining ········ 5:185a-186a
modern economy ········ 2:165a
plants ········ 6:192a
victim compensation ········ 2:225a
See also **Environmental quality**
Pollution Control Public Works Cost Allocation Law ········ 2:224b
Pollution Countermeasures Basic Law ········ 6:217a
Pollution litigation ········ 6:217b
Ashio Copper Mine Incident ········ 1:102a
Pollution-related diseases ········ 2:224a, 226a-226b, 304a; 6:217b-220a
air pollution ········ 6:217b-218a
photochemical smog ········ 6:218a
respiratory disorders ········ 6:217b-218a
food poisoning ········ 6:219b-220a
dried milk poisoning (arsenic) ········ 6:220a
milk contamination (BHC) ········ 6:220a
rice oil poisoning (PCB) ········ 6:219b-220a
land pollution ········ 6:218b-219a
arsenic poisoning, chronic ········ 6:219a
itai itai disease ········ 6:218b-219a
Pollution-Related Health Damage Compensation Law ········ 6:219a-219b

pressure groups ········ **6**:237b
water pollution ········ **6**:218a-218b
Minamata disease ········ **6**:218a-218b
Niigata mercury poisoning ········ **6**:218b
Pollution-Related Health Damage Compensation Law ········ **2**:225a
Polyandry. *See* Polygamy
Polychlorinated biphenyl poisoning ········ **2**:304b
Polychrome Corporation ········ **4**:23a
Polychrome screen and wall painting ········ **6**:151b
Polygamy ········ **5**:116a-117a
Polygyny. *See* Polygamy
Polytheism ········ **6**:290a
Po mo ········ **3**:73a-73b
Pompe van Meerdervoort, Johannes Lydius Catherinus ········ **6**:220a-220b
Poporo Players case (1963) ········ **6**:220b
university autonomy ········ **8**:171a
Poppe, N. N. ········ **4**:18b
Popper, Karl ········ **4**:85b
Popular fiction ········ **6**:220b-221b
Daibosatsu Tōge ········ **5**:320a
Popular Front Incident ········ **6**:221b-222a; **7**:74b; **8**:296b
Sakisaka Itsurō ········ **7**:3a
Popular parties ········ **5**:197b-198a
Popular Rights Movement. *See* **Freedom and People's Rights Movement**
Popular sovereignty ········ **6**:222a
Population ········ **4**:7a; **6**:222a-225b
historical patterns ········ **6**:222b-224a
Edo-period (1600-1868) ········ **6**:222b-223b
1868 to 1940 ········ **6**:223b-224a
postwar ········ **6**:224a-225b
changing patterns ········ **6**:224b-225a
decline of growth rate ········ **6**:224a-224b
increase ········ **6**:224a
regional differences and redistribution ········ **6**:225a
special features ········ **6**:225a-225b
urban densities ········ **7**:214a
Population censuses ········ **6**:4a
Population density, land rents ········ **4**:363b
Population Problems Council ········ **6**:224a
Population Problems Research Council ········ **2**:247b
Population redistribution ········ **6**:225b-226a
Porcelain ········ **1**:260a
Porcelain industry ········ **1**:85a
Pork production ········ **1**:28b
Pornography ········ **6**:49b-50b
Poroshiridake ········ 幌尻岳 ········ **6**:226a
Port Arthur ········ **6**:226a-226b; **7**:277b
Hirose Takeo ········ **3**:148a
Port Hamilton Incident ········ **4**:267b-268a
Portman, Anton L. C. ········ **6**:226b
"Portrait of Tenshin" ········ **7**:105b
Portrait painting ········ **6**:226b-228a
Ashikaga Takauji ········ **1**:*100b*
China ········ **1**:283a
early ········ **6**:226b
Edo ········ **6**:227b-228a
Fujiwara no Takanobu ········ **5**:*181a*; **6**:*227a*
Ikkyū ········ **3**:*270b*
Kamakura ········ **6**:227a-227b
Muromachi and Momoyama ········ **6**:227b
Myōe ········ **5**:*289a*
Nichiren ········ **5**:*375a*
Shōtoku, Prince ········ **7**:*172b*
subjects ········ **6**:158b
Taira no Shigemori ········ **6**:*227a*
Tokugawa Ieyasu ········ **8**:*49a*
Toyotomi Hideyoshi ········ **8**:*94b*
Watanabe Kazan ········ **8**:236a
Portraits of Eminent Tendai Monks **6**:227a
Portraiture
kabuki actors ········ **7**:79a
Sharaku ········ **7**:79a
Portsmouth, Treaty of ········ ポーツマス条約 ········ **3**:197a; **6**:228a-228b; **7**:88a, 237a, 238a
China ········ **1**:288b
Guandong Territory ········ **3**:64b-65a
Hibiya Incendiary Incident ········ **3**:129a-129b
Japan's interest in Korea ········ **4**:282a
Komura Jutarō ········ **4**:268a
Korea's annexation ········ **4**:287b
mandates ········ **6**:228a
Russo-Japanese fisheries ········ **6**:345a
Russo-Japanese War ········ **6**:347a
Tairo Dōshikai ········ **7**:303a
Takahira Kogorō ········ **7**:313b
Port towns ········ **6**:228b
urban life ········ **8**:177b
urban planning ········ **8**:179b
Portugal and Japan ········ **6**:228b
Namban trade ········ **5**:323a-323b
Possession ········ **7**:67b-68a
Postal savings system ········ **1**:139b
Postal service ········ **6**:229a-229b
founder of ········ **5**:81b-82a
history ········ **6**:229a
present state ········ **6**:229a-229b
Postal system, early ········ **3**:138a
Postindustrialism ········ **3**:302a
Poston Relocation Center ········ **6**:229b
Post-station system ········ **2**:188b
Post-station towns ········ **6**:229b-230a; **7**:4b
bashaku ········ **1**:144a
urban planning ········ **8**:179b
Postwar history. *See* **History of Japan**
Postwar literature ········ **6**:230a-231b
chūkan shōsetsu ········ **1**:312b-313a
decadence (buraiha) phenomenon ········ **6**:230a
democratic literature ········ **6**:230a
mass communications ········ **6**:231a
renewed activity of major writers ········ **6**:230a-230b
sengo bungaku school ········ **6**:230b
"first wave" ········ **6**:230b
"second wave" ········ **6**:230b-231a
"third new generation" ········ **6**:231a
United States-Japan Security Treaty **6**:231a
Postwar reforms. *See* **Occupation**
Post-World War II reparations ········ **7**:235b
Potatoes and yams ········ **6**:231b
Potsdam Declaration ········ **1**:108a, 290a; **6**:231b-232a; **7**:28a, 246b, 278a; **8**:276b
Anami Korechika ········ **1**:53b
Far Eastern Commission ········ **2**:248a
Government-General of Korea ········ **4**:283a
Hirohito, Emperor ········ **3**:147a
Kido Kōichi ········ **4**:202a
Occupation ········ **6**:51b
Occupation Purge ········ **6**:57b
religious freedom ········ **6**:294b
Taiwan ········ **7**:309a
women's suffrage ········ **8**:268b
Potter's Book, A ········ **4**:372b
Potter's wheels. *See* **Rokuro**
Pottery
Agano ware ········ **1**:20b
Arakawa Toyozō ········ **1**:73b
Asahi ware ········ **1**:93b
Banko ware ········ **1**:141a
Haji ········ **1**:79b
high-fired ········ **1**:258a
Jōmon ········ **1**:76a
Ōmori shell mounds ········ **6**:103a
Onta ware ········ **6**:113a
paleolithic culture ········ **6**:159b
Sue ········ **1**:79b
Tamba ware ········ **7**:333a
yayoi ········ **1**:76b-77a
Poverty ········ **6**:232a-232b
Power of supreme command ········ **8**:85a
Pozdneev, Dmitrii Matveevich ········ **6**:232b
Pragmatism ········ **6**:232b-233a; **7**:149a-149b
Prajñapāramitā sutras ········ **2**:213a
Pratītya-samutpāda ········ **2**:217a-217b
Prawns. *See* **Shrimps, prawns, and lobsters**
Prayer ········ **6**:233a
Precepts for Health ········ **8**:328b
Preceramic period ········ **6**:233a-233b
Precision machinery industry ········ **6**:233b
companies ········ **1**:239b, 316a; **4**:200b; **6**:10a; **7**:99a
Prefectural governor ········ **4**:197b
Prefectural museums ········ **5**:278b
Prefectural public safety ordinance ········ **4**:234a-234b
Prefectural system, establishment of ········ **2**:1a; **6**:233b-235a; **7**:30a
abolition of domains ········ **6**:234a-235a
bureaucratic development ········ **1**:217b
compromise settlement ········ **6**:234a
establishment ········ **4**:7a
hambatsu ········ **3**:91b
hanseki hōkan ········ **6**:233b-234a
provinces ········ **6**:260a
Verbeck, Guido Herman Fridolin ········ **8**:190a
Prefectures
Hokkaidō ········ **3**:212b-213a
Honshū
Aichi ········ **1**:33a
Akita ········ **1**:42b-43a
Aomori ········ **1**:69b-70a
Chiba ········ **1**:271a
Fukui ········ **2**:364a
Fukushima ········ **2**:366b-367a
Gifu ········ **3**:31a-31b
Gumma ········ **3**:68a
Hiroshima ········ **3**:149b-150a
Hyōgo ········ **3**:251b
Ibaraki ········ **3**:253a-253b
Ishikawa ········ **3**:344a
Iwate ········ **3**:363b
Kanagawa ········ **4**:135a
Kyōto ········ **4**:337b-338b
Mie ········ **5**:167b-168a
Miyagi ········ **5**:217b-218a
Nagano ········ **5**:302b-303a
Nara ········ **5**:333b-334a
Niigata ········ **5**:385b-386a
Okayama ········ **6**:83a
Ōsaka ········ **6**:122a-122b
Saitama ········ **6**:372b-373a
Shiga ········ **7**:90b-91a
Shimane ········ **7**:100b
Shizuoka ········ **7**:153b-154a
Tōkyō ········ **8**:60b-66a
Tochigi ········ **8**:33a
Tottori ········ **8**:86a-86b
Toyama ········ **8**:88b-89a
Wakayama ········ **8**:219b
Yamagata ········ **8**:293b
Yamaguchi ········ **8**:295a
Yamanashi ········ **8**:301a-301b
Kyūshū
Fukuoka ········ **2**:364b-365b
Kagoshima ········ **4**:105b-106a
Kumamoto ········ **4**:306a
Miyazaki ········ **5**:221b
Nagasaki ········ **5**:304b-305a
Ōita ········ **6**:75b-76a
Saga ········ **6**:363b-364a
Okinawa ········ **6**:91b-92a
Shikoku
Ehime ········ **2**:185a-185b
Kagawa ········ **4**:103a

Kōchi ··· 4:239b
Tokushima ··· 8:59a
See also maps ··· 4:4a-4b
Pregnancy ··· 6:49a
Prehistoric burials ··· 6:235a-235b
hōkei shūkōbo ··· 4:244a
Prehistoric relics ··· 7:82b-83a
Prehistory. *See* **History of Japan**
Preparatory Commission for Establishing a New Political Order ··· 3:280b
Preparatory school (Juku) ··· 5:6b
Preschool education ··· 2:195b; 6:235b
Prescriptive period ··· 6:235b-236a
Press
influence ··· 5:129a
regulation ··· 5:129a
Press clubs ··· 5:128b-129a; 6:236a
Press Code and Radio Code for Japan ··· 2:339a
Press Law of 1909 ··· 1:72a; 1:252b; 2:338a-338b; 6:236a
Morito Incident ··· 5:254b
Torii Sosen ··· 8:80a
Press Ordinance of 1875 ·· 1:252a; 6:236a, 262b
Pressure groups ··· 6:236a-238b
agriculture ··· 6:238a
business ··· 6:237b-238a
Federation of Economic Organizations (Keidanren) ··· 6:237b
Japan Chamber of Commerce and Industry (Nisshō) ··· 6:237b-238a
Japan Committee for Economic Development (Keizai Dōyū Kai) · 6:238a
Japan Federation of Employers' Associations (Nikkeiren) ··· 6:237b
history ··· 6:236b
interaction with government · 6:236b-237a
labor ··· 6:238a
General Council of Trade Unions of Japan (Sōhyō) ··· 6:238a
Japanese Confederation of Labor (Dōmei) ··· 6:238a
major ··· 6:237b-238b
medical ··· 6:238a-238b
methods ··· 6:237a-237b
courts ··· 6:237b
election to Diet ··· 6:237a-237b
information ··· 6:237a
meetings ··· 6:237a
money ··· 6:237a
retired bureaucrats ··· 6:237b
Preternatural beings ··· 1:130b
Price changes ··· 3:312b-313a
Price Control Order of 1946 ··· 6:238b
Price controls ··· 6:310a
Price stability ··· 3:303a
Pridi Phanomyong ··· 2:339b; 6:238b
Priest and His Disciples, The ··· 4:312a
Priesthood ··· 6:238b-239b
Buddhism ··· 6:239a-239b
new religions ··· 6:239b
Shintō ··· 4:145b-146a
Priest of Hitachi, The ··· 1:42a
Primal Vow ··· 4:68b-69a
Prima Meat Packers, Ltd ··· 6:239b
Primary industries ··· 6:239b-240a
secondary industries ··· 7:47b
"Primary union" ··· 4:359b
Primate Research Institute ··· 6:240a
Primate studies ··· 6:240a-240b
infrahuman culture ··· 6:240a
Macaca Fuscata society ··· 6:240b
Prime minister and cabinet ·· 6:240a-244a
cabinet system
origins ··· 6:241a-241b
party to military ··· 6:242a-242b
postwar changes ··· 6:242b
powers and organizations ·· 6:244a-244b
decentralization ··· 6:241b-242a
government, executive branch ·· 3:55b-56a
prime minister
powers and functions ··· 6:242a
selection process ··· 6:242b-244a
"transcendental" cabinets ··· 8:97b
Prime ministers
Abe Nobuyuki ··· 1:3b-4a
Ashida Hitoshi ··· 1:97b
Fukuda Takeo ··· 2:362b
Hamaguchi Osachi ··· 3:90a
Hara Takashi ··· 3:102b-103b
Hatoyama Ichirō ··· 3:113a
Hayashi Senjūrō ··· 3:117b
Higashikuni Naruhiko ··· 3:132a
Hiranuma Kiichirō ··· 3:143b-144a
Hirota Kōki ··· 3:150a
Ikeda Hayato ··· 3:265a
Inukai Tsuyoshi ··· 3:326a; 4:373a
Ishibashi Tanzan ··· 3:339b
Itō Hirobumi ··· 3:353a
Katayama Tetsu ··· 4:167a
Katō Takaaki ··· 4:169b-170b
Katō Tomosaburō ··· 4:170b
Katsura Tarō ··· 8:291b
Kishi Nobusuke ··· 4:223a-223b
Kiyoura Keigo ··· 4:233a
Koiso Kuniaki ··· 4:250b
Konoe Fumimaro ··· 4:272b; 6:189b
Kuroda Kiyotaka ··· 4:314a-314b
Matsukata Masayoshi ··· 5:134b-136a
Miki Takeo ··· 5:171b
Nakasone Yasuhiro ··· 5:318a
Ōhira Masayoshi ··· 6:74a
Okada Keisuke ··· 6:78a-78b
Ōkuma Shigenobu ··· 6:95b-96a
Saionji Kimmochi ··· 6:371b-372b
Saitō Makoto ··· 6:374a
Satō Eisaku ··· 7:26a-26b
Shidehara Kijūrō ··· 7:88a-89a
Suzuki Kantarō ··· 7:282a
Suzuki Zenkō ··· 7:284a
Takahashi Korekiyo ··· 7:312a-312b
Tanaka Giichi ··· 7:336a-336b
Tanaka Kakuei ··· 7:337a
Terauchi Masatake ··· 8:12b
Tōjō Hideki ··· 1:32a
Wakatsuki Reijirō ··· 8:218b-219a
Yamagata Aritomo ··· 8:290b-292a
Yamamoto Gonnohyōe ··· 8:297b
Yonai Mitsumasa ··· 8:337a
Yoshida Shigeru ··· 8:343a-345a
Prime Minister's Office ··· 1:218b; 6:244b
Council for Science and Technology (Kagaku Gijutsu Kaigi) ··· 7:38a
external organs ··· 6:244b
National Land Agency ··· 5:343b
Primeval forest ··· 5:352a-352b
Primogeniture ··· 2:242a; 6:244b
Primroses [(sakurasō) *Primula* spp.] ··· 6:245a
Principle of changed circumstances ··· 6:245a-245b
Principle of fidelity and good faith 6:245b
Principles of Newspaper Ethics, The ··· 1:254b
Principles of Publishing Ethics, The ··· 1:254b
Printing ··· 1:152a-153a, 187a-187b, 233b; 6:245b-249a
modern ··· 6:245b-246b
history ··· 6:245b-246a
industry today ··· 6:246a-246b
movable-type ··· 8:325a
premodern ··· 6:246b-249a
book illustration ··· 6:247a
Kyōto ··· 6:247b-248a
legacy from China ··· 6:246b-247a
luxury printing ··· 6:248b
movable type ··· 6:248a-248b
Nara ··· 6:247b
origins ··· 6:247a-247b
woodblock printing ··· 6:247a
17th to 19th centuries ··· 6:248b-249a
Printing Bureau ··· 6:246a
Print media ··· 6:268a
Prints. *See* **Ukiyo-e; Modern prints**
Priority production program ··· 6:249a
business cycles ··· 1:224a
Reconstruction Finance Bank ··· 6:284b
Priority Production System ··· 1:84b
Prisoners' rights ··· 6:249b
Prison Law (Kangoku Hō) of 1908 6:249b
Prisons ··· 2:51b; 6:172a, 249a-249b
Kirishitan yashiki ··· 4:221b-222a
premodern ··· 6:8a
Privacy, invasion of ··· 1:255a
Privacy, right of ··· 6:249b-250a
After the Banquet case (1964) ··· 1:20b
judicial decisions ··· 6:250a
privacy law ··· 6:249b-2450a
society ··· 6:249b
Private international law ··· 1:316b, 337b-339a; 6:250a-252a
Private Investment Company for Asia (PICA) ··· 6:143b
Private museums ··· 5:276b-277b
Private schools ··· 2:179a; 6:252a-252b; 7:94a-94b
Private universities ··· 6:252b
Privy Council ··· 2:2b, 4a; 6:214a, 242a, 252b-253b; 7:304a
Hiranuma Kiichirō ··· 3:143b-144b
Imperial Diet ··· 3:276a
Itō Hirobumi ··· 3:353a
Konoe Fumimaro ··· 4:273a
Kōno Togama ··· 4:275a
Meiji Constitution ··· 3:195a
power of supreme command ··· 8:85a
Probation ··· 4:87a-87b
Probation officers ··· 2:246a
Proceedings of the Japan Academy or *Gakushiin kiyō* ··· 4:9b
Proclamation concerning the Encouragement of Education ··· 6:124a
Proclamation of Neutrality (Proclamation No. 546 of 1870) ··· 8:13b
Proclamation of the Great Doctrine. *See* **Taikyō Sempu**
Product distribution ··· 2:162a
Production Research Council ··· 7:372b
Product liability ··· 6:253b-254b
burden of proof ··· 6:254a
government liability for negligence ··· 6:253b-254a
legal theories ··· 6:253b
proximate causation ··· 6:254a
scope ··· 6:254a-254b
standard of care ··· 6:254a
strict ··· 6:254a
Professional School Order (Semmon Gakkō Rei) ··· 7:62a; 8:170a
Professional Writers' Guild of Japan ··· 4:207a
Profitability, Japanese corporate view ··· 2:35b
Progovernment parties ··· 6:321b
Progressive Education Movement ··· 7:367a-367b
Progressive Party ··· 7:108b
The Progressive Woman ··· 4:138b
Prohibitions of Foreign Voyages ·· 4:109b
Proletarian literary groups ··· 5:20b
Proletarian literature movement · 1:209a-209b; 6:254b-256a; 7:25a, 66b, 69a

Aono Suekichi ········ 1:70a
areas of dispute ········ 6:255b
Bungei sensen period (1924-1932) ········ 6:254b-255b
children's literature ········ 1:279b
film ········ 2:269b
fūzoku shōsetsu ········ 2:378b
Hayama Yoshiki ········ 3:115a
Hayashi Fusao ········ 3:116b
Hirabayashi Hatsunosuke ········ 3:141a
Hirabayashi Taiko ········ 3:141b
Hirotsu Kazuo ········ 3:151a
Hisaita Eijirō ········ 3:151b
Itō Einosuke ········ 3:352a
Kamei Katsuichirō ········ 4:125a
Kataoka Teppei ········ 4:166b
Kikuchi Kan ········ 4:206b
Kindai bungaku ········ 4:212a
Kobayashi Takiji ········ 4:237a
Kurahara Korehito ········ 4:311a
Maedakō Hiroichirō ········ 5:80a
Miyoshi Jūrō ········ 5:223b
Nakano Shigeharu ········ 5:316b-317a
NAPF-KOPF period (1928-1934) ········ 6:255b-256a
postwar literature ········ 6:230a
schisms ········ 6:255a
Senki ········ 7:66b
Shinkō Geijutsu Ha ········ 7:119b
Shin Nihon bungaku ········ 7:122a
Takeda Rintarō ········ 7:323a
Tane maku hito ········ 7:340a-340b
Tane maku hito period (1920-1922) ·· 6:254b
Tokunaga Sunao ········ 8:58a
Tsuboi Sakae ········ 8:110a
Tsuboi Shigeji ········ 8:110a
Tsubota Jōji ········ 8:110a
Western literature in Japanese translation ········ 8:248a
Proletarian theater movement (puroretaria engeki) ········ 6:255a
Promotion of Zen in Defense of the Country ········ 6:319a
Promotive establishment ········ 2:37b
Propagation of Zen for the Protection of the Country, The ········ 8:370b
Property, ownership ········ 7:155a-158a
right to control ········ 6:312a
Property, registration of ········ 6:288a-288b
Property deed ········ 8:359b
Property law ········ 8:238a
Property rights ········ 6:256a-256b
abuse ········ 1:5b
ando ········ 1:55a
managerial ideology ········ 5:92b
ownership rights ········ 6:136b
principle rights ········ 6:256a
shitaji chūbun ········ 1:101b
Proprietary lords ········ 6:353a
Proprietary province ········ 1:274a-274b
Proprietorship (chigyō) ········ 1:274a-274b; 3:255a
Prose, Buddhist ········ 1:180b, 181b
Prosecution review commissions (Kensatsu shinsakai) ········ 6:256b, 266a
Prostitution ········ 6:256b-257b; 7:234b-235a
karayuki san ········ 4:159b
Meiji to World War II ········ 6:257a
postwar ········ 6:257a-257b
premodern ········ 6:256b-257a
Shikidō ōkagami ········ 7:95b-96a
tsutome hōkō ········ 2:211b-212a
Prostitution Prevention Law ········ 6:257b; 8:349b
Miyagi Tamayo ···· 2:49a; 5:218a; 6:257b; 8:189b
Protected species ········ 5:352a-352b
Protectionism ········ 2:325a
Protectorate Treaty ········ 4:289a
Protestant missionaries ········ 6:257b-258b
Proto history. *See* **History of Japan**
Proverbs ········ 6:258b
Provinces ········ 6:258b-260a
Provincial capitals ········ 4:257b
Provincial governors · 3:174b; 4:262a-262b
"Provincial levies" ········ 4:310a
Provisional disposition ········ 6:260a
Provisional Government of Free India ········ 6:260a
Provisional Government of Korea 6:260a, 307b
Provisional Government of the Republic of China ········ 6:260a-260b, 285b, 302a
Wang Kemin (Wang K'o-min) ········ 8:222b
Wu Peifu (Wu P'ei-fu) ········ 8:279b
Xinmin Hui (Hsin-min Hui), (New People's Society) ········ 8:281b
Provisional Joint Agreement ········ 4:281a
"Prussia of the Far East" ········ 1:86b
PS-1 seaplane ········ 6:260b
Psychodrama ········ 6:261b
"Psychologism" ········ 7:175b
Psychologists. *See* **Psychology in Japan**
Psychology, concepts in
akirame ········ 1:42a
amae ········ 1:48b
educational counseling ········ 2:179a-179b
ego ········ 2:184b
hara ········ 3:100a
Psychology in Japan ········ 6:260b-261a
Psychotherapy ········ 6:261a-262a
Buddhist-based ········ 6:261b-262a
morita ········ 6:261b
naikan ········ 6:261b
shadan ········ 6:261b-262a
mental hospitals ········ 6:262a
mental process ········ 6:261b
naikan ········ 5:310b
physical process ········ 6:261a-261b
Ptarmigan [(raichō) *Lagopus mutus*] ········ 6:262b
PTAs ········ 6:262b
Public Accounts law ········ 2:276b
Public assembly, restriction ········ 7:185a
Public Assembly Ordinance ········ 7:185a
Public assistance. *See* **Social Welfare**
Publication Law of 1893 ········ 1:252b; 2:338a-338b; 4:339a; 6:236a, 262b
fundamental liberties limitation ········ 2:369b
Kawai Eijirō ········ 4:178b
Publication Ordinance of 1869 ··· 1:252a; 6:262b
Publications, distributors ········ 1:163b
Publications Law ········ 2:339a
Public auction ········ 6:262b-263a
Public bathhouses. *See* **Bath**
Public Corporation Labor Relations Law of 1948 ········ 4:358a
Public corporations ········ 6:263a-264a
bonds ········ 3:54b
finance ········ 1:139b
kokusaku kaisha ········ 4:262a
public investment ········ 6:265a
role ········ 6:264a
types ········ 6:263a-264a
union members ········ 4:348b
Public Corporations and Government Enterprises Labor Relations Law ·· 4:352a, 358a, 360a; 6:264b; 7:189b, 279b
Kōrōkyō restricted ········ 4:294a
Public Corporations and National Enterprise Labor Relations Commission (Kōkyō Kigyōtai Tō Rōdō Iinkai) ········ 4:358b
Public deposit ········ 4:334a
Public Employee Law ········ 2:339a
Public employees ········ 6:264b-265a
legal restrictions ········ 4:360a
Public employment security offices ········ 2:210a; 6:265a
Public fields (kōden) ········ 4:243a
Public Finance Law ········ 3:54b
Public health ········ 5:149a-150a
environmental law ········ 2:224a-225b
Ministry of Health and Welfare ··· 5:189b
pollution ········ 2:226a-226b
Public Housing Law ········ 3:245b
Public Information and Cultural Affairs Bureau ········ 3:319b
Public investment ········ 6:265a-265b
Public law ········ 6:265b
"Public matters" ········ 4:303a
Public Office Election Law ········ 2:189a
Public Opinion Survey Department 6:265b
Public opinion surveys ········ 6:265b-266a
Public Order and Police Law of 1900 ·· 2:337a-337b; 4:345a, 351a; 6:210b, 266a; 7:241b, 317a; 8:291b
sex discrimination ········ 2:362a
women's suffrage ········ 8:268b
Public Order and Police Law (1922) ········ 8:268b
Public Party of Patriots ········ 1:34b
Public Peace Police Law ········ 2:337a
Public prosecutor ····· 2:45b; 6:256b, 266a
criminal investigation ········ 2:47a-47b
Public Safety ········ 5:345b-346a
Public Safety Examination Commission ········ 2:337b
Public schools, construction ········ 7:33b
Public Security Investigation Agency ········ 6:266b
Public Telecommunications Law ·· 6:276a
Public utilities ········ 6:266b
Public utility rates ········ 6:266b-267a
Public welfare ········ 6:267a
establishment of principal ········ 1:5b
Public works
national budget ········ 1:205a-205b
Public Works Research Institute ·· 6:267a
Publishers' Weekly ········ 6:268a
Publishing ········ 6:267a-269a
freedom of the press ········ 2:339a
industry structure ········ 6:268a-268b
buying and selling ········ 6:268b
distribution system ········ 6:268a
size ········ 6:268a
after Meiji Restoration ········ 6:267b-268a
contemporary book ········ 6:267b
magazine ········ 5:82b-83a; 6:267b-268a
translations ········ 6:268a
postwar reforms ········ 6:268b-269a
printing ········ 6:267a-267b
reference ········ 7:105b
Publishing companies
Bungei Shunjū, Ltd ········ 1:209a
Chikuma Shobō Publishing Co, Ltd ········ 1:276b; 7:309b
Chūō Kōron Sha, Inc ········ 1:313b
Fuzambō ········ 2:376b-377a
Gakken Co, Ltd ········ 3:3b
Hakubunkan ········ 1:209b; 7:309b
Heibonsha, Ltd, Publishers 3:122b; 7:309b
Iwanami Shoten Publishers ·· 3:360b-361a; 7:149a
Kadokawa Publishing Co, Ltd ········ 4:101a
Kaizōsha
Bungei ········ 1:209a
Kōdansha, Ltd ········ 4:241b
Ōbunsha Publishing Co, Ltd ···· 6:506-51a
Shinchōsha Company ········ 7:109b
Shōgakukan Publishing Co, Ltd ···· 7:158a
Shūeisha Publishing Co, Ltd ········ 7:181a

Publishing Ordinance of 1869 ····· **2**:338b
Pueraria thunbergiana ············· **4**:323a
Pu Fa zhan ji (P'u-Fa chan chi; The Franco-Prussian War) ············ **8**:222b
P'u-i. *See* **Puyi (P'u-i)**
"Pulling boards." *See* **Naruko**
Pulp ························· **5**:354a-354b
Punctuation marks ··········· **6**:269a-269b
Punishments
criminal ························ **3**:138a
heimon ························· **3**:126a
hell ···························· **3**:126a
tojime ·························· **3**:126a
Puns ··························· **8**:269b
Puppeteers
dress ······················ **1**:213a-213b
Kiritake Monjūrō II ·············· **4**:222a
Puppet heads ······················ **1**:*214b*
Puppets ··················· **2**:128a-129a
Puppet theater ······· **1**:212a-215b; **2**:267b; **6**:269b-270a
Azuchi-Momoyama ··············· **3**:184a
dolls ···························· **2**:128a
kabuki adaptations ········ **4**:91b, 93a, 99a
music, traditional ················ **5**:284b
Pure Land Buddhism ·· **1**:178b-179a, 185a; **6**:270a-270b
Amida ··························· **1**:189a
architecture ····················· **1**:189b
art ······················· **1**:189a-191a
Genshin ·························· **3**:23b
Hōnen ··························· **1**:190b
Ippen ····················· **3**:328b-329b
Kakuban ························· **1**:191a
Kannon ·························· **4**:144b
modern philosophy ··············· **5**:230b
monasticism ····················· **5**:238a
musical instruments ········· **1**:196a-196b
Myōe ···························· **5**:289b
Ōbaku sect ·················· **6**:47a-47b
painting ··················· **1**:189b-191a
poems and songs ················ **8**:231a
Pure Land ······················· **4**:307b
Rinzai sect ······················ **6**:319b
Risshō ankoku ron ················ **6**:321a
ritual implements ··········· **1**:196a-196b
rosaries ························· **1**:197a
schools ·························· **1**:179a
sculpture ·················· **1**:189b-191a
Senchakushū (Senchaku hongan nembutsu shū) ····················· **7**:63a
Shinran ························· **1**:190b
Tannishō ························ **7**:344a
thought and culture ············ **8**:27a-28a
Purification. *See* **Misogi**
Puroretaria geijutsu (Proletarian Arts) ········ プロレタリア芸術 ········ **6**:255a
Putiatin, Evfimii Vasil'evich · **6**:270b, 278a
Goncharov, Ivan Aleksandrovich ···· **3**:44b
Puyi (P'u-i) ················· **6**:270b-271b

Q

Qin (Ch'in) dynasty
calligraphic styles ················ **7**:170a
Qincuxū (Kinkushū) ················ **2**:241a
Qing (ch'ing) dynasty ················ **4**:18b
Qingdao (Tsingtao) ················ **6**:273a
concession ························· **4**:53a
Qing period ················ **7**:307a-307b
Qinqi shuhua ··············· **4**:213b-214a
Q. P. Corporation ················ **6**:273a
Quality control ············ **6**:273a-274a
automation ················· **6**:273b-274a
Deming, Edward ················ **6**:273b
history ···················· **6**:273a-273b
principles ······················ **6**:273b
Quanfa ··························· **4**:158a
Quarantine ······················ **6**:274a
Quasi-legal professions ············ **4**:371b
Quezon, Manuel Luis ········ **6**:274a-274b
Quilting ····················· **7**:24a-24b
Quince, dwarf Japanese [(kusaboke) *Chaenomeles japonica*] ·········· **6**:274b
Quinoform ························ **7**:206a

R

Rabbits [(usagi) family Leporidae] ······························· **6**:275a
Rabies Prevention Law ············ **6**:274a
Raccoon dog. *See* **Tanuki**
Racial discrimination ············· **7**:209a
Radar ···························· **2**:192a
Raden. *See* **Mother-of-pearl inlay**
Radiation Effects Research Foundation (RERF) ······················· **1**:112a
Radio
broadcasting ·········· **1**:171b-172a, 173a
educational ····················· **2**:179a
censorship ······················ **2**:339a
late-night ······················· **1**:173b
mass communications ············· **5**:128b
technology ··············· **2**:192a, 193b
Radioactive isotopes laws ········· **1**:114b
Radio Code for Japan ·············· **2**:339a
Radio drama ················ **6**:275a-276a
Radio Law ·········· **1**:171b-172a; **6**:276a
Radio Press (RP) ················· **5**:369a
Radio serials ····················· **4**:207a
Radishes [(daikon) *Raphanus sativus* var. *acanthiformis*] · **6**:276a-276b
production ······················· **1**:27a
Ragusa, Vincenzo ········ **2**:304a; **6**:276b
"Rai" ·················· 癩 ········ **7**:176a
Raichō ··························· **6**:262b
Raigō triptych ···················· **4**:299b
Raigōzu ············ 来迎図 ·· **1**:*190a-190b*; **6**:*151b*, 276b, *277a*, 277b
Rails [(kuina) family Rallidae] ····· **6**:277b
Railway industries
Kinki Nippon Railway Co, Ltd ···· **4**:213b
Hankyū Corporation ·············· **3**:99a
Nagoya Railroad Co, Ltd ·········· **5**:309b
Nishi-Nippon Railroad Co, Ltd ····· **6**:18b
Seibu Railway Co, Ltd ············· **7**:49b
Tōbu Railway Co, Ltd ·········· **8**:32b-33a
Tōkyū Corporation ················ **8**:70a
Railway Nationalization Law ········ **4**:33b
Railways ·········· **6**:277b-280a; **8**:99a-99b
boxed meals (ekiben) ········ **2**:188a-188b
electric ··················· **7**:116a-119a
high-speed ················· **7**:116a-119a
history ···················· **6**:278a-279a
importance ······················ **6**:277b
Meiji period ····················· **2**:153a
nationalization ············ **2**:31a; **6**:279a
other service ·············· **6**:279b-280a
passenger ················· **7**:116a-119a
Shinkansen ················ **6**:279a-279b
size and complexity ·············· **6**:278a
urban life ························ **8**:178b
Railway Technical Research Institute ······························· **7**:117b
Rain, rituals for ················· **6**:280b
Rainbow plan ···················· **6**:280a
Raingear, traditional ········ **6**:280a-280b
Rain supplication (amagoi) rites ···· **1**:23a
Rainy season ························ **4**:8a
Rai San'yō ········ 頼山陽 ········ **1**:211a; **5**:311a-311b; **6**:280b-281a
Kan Sazan ······················· **4**:152a
Rai San'yō to sono jidai ············ **5**:315b
Uragami Shunkin ················· **8**:175b
Rajio monogatari (radio story) ···· **6**:275b
Rakan ·············· 羅漢 ········ **2**:346a; **6**:281a-281b
Takuma Eiga ····················· **7**:327b
Rakkan ············· 落款 ········ **6**:281b
Rakkasan ·········· 落下傘 ········ **4**:138b
Rakuchū rakugai 洛中洛外 ········ **7**:270a
Rakuchū rakugai zu ················ **2**:*377a*
Rakugaki (graffiti) ············· **3**:59b-60a
Rakugo ············· 落語 ······ **2**:267b; **6**:281b-282b
influence on Shikitei Samba ········ **7**:97a
Jippensha Ikku ···················· **4**:61b
kōdan ··························· **4**:241a
kokkeibon influenced ·············· **4**:256a
San'yūtei Enchō ··················· **7**:19b
Yanagiya Kosan V ················· **6**:*282b*
Rakuichi and rakuza ··············· 楽市楽座 ··· **6**:282b-283a
Rakujitsu moyu ·· 落日燃ゆ ········ **7**:148a
Rakujō ··············· 落城 ········ **7**:334a
Rakurō ················ 楽浪 ········ **4**:382b
Rakusho ··························· **3**:59b
Rakusho roken ·· 落書露顕 ·········· **3**:272b
Raku ware ··········· 楽焼 · **1**:20b; **4**:337a; **6**:283a; **7**:67a
originator ······················· **1**:298b
teabowl ························· **1**:*258b*
tea ceremony ····················· **7**:363b
Rakuzenkai Institute for the Blind · **7**:241b
Rāmen ·························· **6**:283a
Ramies ···························· **8**:17b
Rangaku. 蘭学 *See* **Western Learning**
Rangaku kaitei ·· 蘭学階梯 ········ **6**:283b
Ōtsuki Gentaku ··················· **6**:134b
Rangaku kotohajime ·············· 蘭学事始 **6**:283b; **7**:258b
Rangakusha (Scholars of Dutch studies) ························ **8**:235b
Ranke, Leopold von ··············· **3**:156a
Rankei Dōryū ···· 蘭渓道隆 **5**:327a; **6**:283b
Rantō kotohajime 蘭東事始 ········ **6**:283b
Ranwa tsūben (Dutch-Japanese Conversations) · 蘭和通弁 ········ **6**:245b
Ranzan ··············· 嵐山 ········· **1**:74b
Rape of Nanjing ·········· **5**:329a; **7**:199b
Ra Shingyoku ······ 羅振玉 ·········· **5**:76a
Rashōmon ·········· 羅生門 ··· **2**:56b, 272a; **4**:154b, 317b; **5**:217a, 307a; **6**:283b-284a
Daiei Co, Ltd ······················ **2**:56b
Hashimoto Shinobu ················ **3**:110b
Rastvorov, Yuri ··················· **6**:284a
Rastvorov Incident ··············· **6**:284a
Ratification ····················· **6**:284a

Rationing, rice ··· 6:310a
Rats and mice [(nezumi) suborder Myomorpha] ··· 6:284a
Rausudake 羅臼岳 ··· 6:284b
Raymond, Antonin ··· 6:284b
Reading in the Bamboo Study (Chikusai dokusho zu) ··· 7:181a, *181a*
Real estate
  religious ownership ··· 7:109b
"Realizing Buddhahood" ··· 8:27a
Realm ··· 4:269b-270a
Real property registration ··· 6:288a
Realtors ··· 6:137a
Rebirth ··· 6:318b
Rebun 礼文 ··· 6:284b
  Rishiri-Rebun-Sarobetsu National Park ··· 6:320b
Recession ··· 2:146b, 157b-158a, 163b-164a
Reconstruction Finance Bank ··· 6:249a, 284b
  Dodge line ··· 2:122b
Reconstruction Finance Board
  economic reform ··· 2:155b-156a, 157a
Record of three generations of flowery rule ··· 4:101b
Records, historiography ··· 3:152a-158a
Records of Ancient Matters ··· 4:251a-251b
Records of a Tibetan Journey ··· 4:177b
"Records of the Eastern Barbarians" ··· 7:264a
Red algae ··· 7:46b
Red and White Plum Trees (Kōhakubai zu) ··· 4:*293a-293b*
Red Army faction ··· 6:284b-285a; 7:252b
  pacifism ··· 6:145b
Red Bird ··· 1:39b
Red Cross ··· 4:40b
  Sano Tsunetami, founder ··· 7:16a
Red Cross Service Organization (Nisseki Hōshidan) ··· 6:238b
Red Flag ··· 1:39b
Red Flag Incident of 1908 ··· 6:285a-285b; 8:296b
  High Treason Incident of 1910 ··· 3:135a
  Kanno Suga ··· 4:145b
Red Purge ··· 6:285b; 7:91b, 252a; 8:344b
  Japan Communist Party ··· 4:11b
  Occupation ··· 6:54b
  Sambetsu Kaigi (Congress of Industrial Labor Unions of Japan) ··· 7:6a
Red Wave Society (Sekirankai) ··· 7:57a
"Reed script painting" ··· 1:97b
Reed warblers [(yoshikiri) family Muscipapidae] ··· 6:285b
Reform Club ··· 4:120a
Reformed Government of the Republic of China
  Wu Peifu (Wu P'ei-fu) ··· 8:279b
Reform Government of the Republic of China ··· 6:285b-286a, 302a; 8:279b
  New Order in East Asia ··· 3:61a
Refractories
  Shinagawa Refractories Co, Ltd ··· 7:108b
Refugees ··· 6:286a
Refuge temples ··· 4:115b
Regency government 摂関政治 ··· 2:104b, 106b, 348b; 6:286a-288a
  culmination ··· 6:286b
  decline ··· 6:286b-287b
  establishment ··· 4:130a
  Fujiwara no Yoshifusa ··· 2:358a
  Fujiwara Regency ··· 6:286a-286b
  post of Regent ··· 6:286b
  ritsuryō state ··· 6:287b-288a, 322a
  Shirakawa, Emperor ··· 7:146b
  traditional and modern views ··· 6:287b
Regent (sesshō) ··· 7:69b
Regional development
  Comprehensive National Land Development Plan ··· 1:343b
Regional geographies ··· 6:288a
Register of Foreign Affairs ··· 3:270b
Register of the Kōgo Year ··· 4:249a
Registration ··· 6:306a
Registration of property ··· 6:288a-288b
Regulations for the Control of Factory-Ship Whaling ··· 8:250b
Rei ··· 4:141b; 6:288b
Reichōrui Kenkyūjo ··· 6:240a
Reign years ··· 1:232a
Reiheishi Kaidō 例幣使街道 ··· 8:220a
Reikai monogatari 霊界物語
  Deguchi Onisaburō ··· 2:83a
Reimeikai 黎明会 2:362b; 6:288b
Reincarnation ··· 2:80b
Reischauer, August Karl ··· 6:288b-289a
Reischauer, Edwin Oldfather ··· 2:196b; 6:289a
  modernization ··· 5:228b
Reisho (clerical script) ··· 1:233b, 1:*170b*
Reiss, Ludwig ··· 3:156a
Reiyūkai 霊友会 ··· 6:289a-289b
Reizei family 冷泉家 ··· 4:329b
Reizei Tamechika 冷泉為恭 ··· 6:289b
  Fukko Yamato-e school ··· 2:360b
Reizei Tamehide 冷泉為秀 ··· 3:272a
Reizei Tamesuke 冷泉為相 ··· 1:5b; 6:289b-290a
Rekishi chiri 歴史地理 ··· 4:228b
Rekishi kagaku 歴史科学 ··· 4:300a
Rekishi monogatari ··· 2:186a; 5:246a; 6:79a; 7:153a; 8:242b
Rekishiteki kanazukai ··· 4:133b, 134b
Rekishō shinsho (New Book of Astronomical Calculations) 暦象新書 7:153a; 8:242a
Relic hall (shariden) ··· 1:*191a*
Religion ··· 6:290a-293a
  afterlife ··· 1:20a
  animism ··· 1:62a
  asceticism ··· 1:96b
  cosmogony ··· 2:38b
  eschatology ··· 2:231a
  freedom of religious faith ··· 2:337a-338a
  historical formation ··· 6:290a-291b
  heaven and hell ··· 3:121a-121b, 126a
  monasticism ··· 5:236a-239a
  nature ··· 5:357b-358a
  prayer ··· 6:233a
  priesthood ··· 6:238b-239b
  sacred, the ··· 6:361b-362b
  sacrifice ··· 6:362b
  society and ··· 6:293b-294b
  state and ··· 6:294b-295a
  sin ··· 8:115a-115b
  syncretism ··· 7:288b-290b
  this-worldliness ··· 8:24b
  tolerance ··· 8:70b
  See also **Buddhism, Christianity, New religions, Shintō**
Religion and modernization ··· 6:293a-293b
Religion and society ··· 6:293b-294b
Religion and the state in modern Japan ··· 6:294b-295a
Religious associations (kō) ··· 4:234a
Religious education ··· 6:295a-295b
Religious foundation museums ··· 5:280a
Religious freedom ··· 6:292b
Religious inquiry census registers 7:186b
Religious inquisition ··· 7:185b-186b
Religious Organizations Law ··· 8:150a
Religious symbolism ··· 6:295b-296a
Reliquary (sharitō) ··· 1:*195a*
Reluctant Admiral, The: Yamamoto and the Imperial Navy ··· 1:21a
Remon 檸檬 ··· 4:114a
Ren ··· 4:295a
"Ren'ai kassen" 恋愛合戦 ··· 8:173b
Ren'ai kekkon ··· 2:244a
Rendai ··· 6:296a
  Utagawa Toyokuni ··· 6:*296b*
Rendaku 連濁 ··· 6:296a-296b
  constraints ··· 6:296a
  origins ··· 6:296a-296b
Renga and haikai 連歌俳諧 ··· 1:181b; 6:296b-300a; 7:64b, 222b-223b
  canons ··· 6:298a-298b
  criticism and examples 5:15a; 6:298b-300a
  general description ··· 6:296b-297a
  history ··· 6:297a-298a
  kakekotoba ··· 4:115b
  Kanemi kyō ki ··· 4:139b
  Shinsen tsukubashū ··· 7:124b
  Tsukubashū ··· 8:144b
Renga poets
  Arakida Moritake ··· 1:73b
  Asayama Bontō ··· 1:96a
  Gusai ··· 3:70b
  Imagawa Sadayo ··· 3:272a
  Inawashiro Kensai ··· 3:283b
  Nishiyama Sōin ··· 6:20a
  Satomura Jōha ··· 7:27b
  Shōhaku ··· 7:161b-162a
  Takayama Sōzei ··· 7:320b-321a
  Yamazaki Sōkan ··· 8:313a
Renge Kokūzō 蓮華虚空像 ··· 1:*187a*
Rengeōin 蓮華王院 ··· 7:13a
Rengetsu. 蓮月
  See **Ōtagaki Rengetsu**
Rengō Co, Ltd ··· 6:300a
Rengō Sekigun (United Red Army) 6:285a
Renju ··· 6:300a
Rennyo 蓮如 ··· 4:68a; 6:300a-300b
  Honganji ··· 3:221b
  Ikkō ikki ··· 3:296b
  Ishiyama Honganji ··· 3:346b
Rennyo Kenju. 蓮如兼寿 *See* **Rennyo**
Renown, Inc ··· 6:300b
Rensageki ··· 2:267b
Rensha ··· 6:301a
Rensho 連署 ··· 6:301a
Rentai saimu ··· 6:301a
Rents, land ··· 4:363b
Renunciation of war 2:82a; 4:378a; 6:166a, 301a-301b; 7:274b
  Occupation ··· 6:52a
Renza 連坐 ··· 6:301a
Reorganization Loan ··· 1:287b; 6:302a; 7:277b
Reorganized National Government of the Republic of China ··· 6:260b, 286a, 302a-302b
  Wu Peifu (Wu P'ei-fu) ··· 8:279b
Reparations for Southeast Asia ··· 6:302b
Report cards ··· 6:302b-303a
Report on the Ezo Lands ··· 1:39a
Repoussé. See **Oshidashibutsu**
Reprieve (kei no shikkō menjo) ··· 2:49a
Reptiles ··· 1:60a-60b, 62a
Republic of Korea, Japanese relations with. *See* **Korea and Japan**
Republic of the Philippines ··· 6:184a
Research and development ··· 6:303a-305b
  current efforts ··· 6:304a
  economic growth ··· 2:161b
  electric power ··· 2:192a
  electronics ··· 2:195a, 325a
  government ··· 6:304a-304b
  historical background ··· 6:303a-304a

private sector ··· 6:305a-305b
summary ··· 6:305b
universities ··· 6:304b-305a
Research Institute for Iron, Steel and Other Metals ··· 6:305b
Research institutes ··· 6:305b-306a
Educational Research, National Institute for ··· 2:181a
Electric Power Industry, Central Research Institute of ··· 2:192a
Institute of Pacific Relations ··· 3:315b-316a
Institute of Physical and Chemical Research ··· 3:316a
Nara National Research Institute of Cultural Properties ··· 5:333b
National Institute of Japanese Literature ··· 4:256b
National Japanese Language Research Institute ··· 5:343b
National Laboratory for High Energy Physics ··· 3:133a
Ōhara Institute for Social Research ··· 6:73b
Science Council of Japan ··· 7:38a
Tōkyō National Research Institute of Cultural Properties ··· 8:68a-68b
Reservoirs ··· 2:72b
Resident General in Korea, Office of ··· 6:306a
opening of ··· 4:282a
Resident registration ··· 6:306a
Resignation ··· 1:42a
Resist-dyed textiles. *See* **Sankechi**
Respect for the Aged Day ··· 2:254a; 5:5a
Responsibility
ethical concept ··· 2:232a
Restorationism ··· 8:144b
Restoration of Imperial Rule
Ōsei Fukko ··· 6:124a
Restoration of rights (fukken) ··· 2:49a
Restoration Shintō ··· 6:306a-306b; 7:129a-129b
Restoration War of 1868. *See* **Boshin Civil War**
Restraint of trade, unreasonable
cartels ··· 1:66b
definition ··· 1:66b
exemptions ··· 1:66b
international cartels ··· 1:66b-67a
trade associations ··· 1:66b
"Restructuring Theory" ··· 2:168b
Retailers
distribution system ··· 2:119b
Itō Yōkadō Co, Ltd ··· 3:356b
Retired shōgun ··· 6:71a
Retirement ··· 2:245b; 4:348b, 356a; 5:5a; 6:306b-307a; 7:65a, 216b
head of household
inkyo ··· 3:307b-308a
lifestyles ··· 5:7a
payments and benefits ··· 8:200a
pensions ··· 4:353a-353b
Return of Political Rule to the Emperor. *See* **Taisei Hōkan**
Reverberatory furnace ··· 3:99b
"Revere the Emperor, Expel the Barbarians." *See* **Sonnō jōi**
Revised Kansei Genealogies ··· 4:152a
Rezanov, Nikolai Petrovich ··· 4:372a; 6:307a-307b
Gaikokusen Uchiharai Rei ··· 3:3b
Golovnin, Vasilii Mikhailovich ··· 3:44a
Russia ··· 6:341a
Rhee, Syngman ··· 6:307b-308a
Korean independence activist ··· 4:284a
Rhee line established ··· 4:288a
Rhee line ··· 6:307b
fishing restrictions ··· 4:285a
Korea-Japan Treaty of 1965, supplementary agreements ··· 4:288b
Rhodesia ··· 1:19b
Rhododendrons [(shakunage) *Rhododendron* spp.] ··· 6:308a
Ri (village) ··· 里 ··· 6:308a
Ri (law, principle) ··· 6:308a
Riccar Art Museum ··· 6:308a-308b; 7:190a-190b
Rice ··· 6:308b-310a
botanical characteristics ··· 6:308b
cooking methods ··· 2:305a
cultivation history ··· 6:309a
religious aspects ··· 2:254a
folk beliefs ··· 6:309b-310a
food staple ··· 2:306a
Japanese cooking methods ··· 2:24a
patterns in consumption ··· 6:309a-309b
plant damage ··· 6:309a
price stabilization ··· 2:307b
production ··· 2:149b 308a
seed rice loans ··· 7:264a
storage ··· 4:117b; 7:248a-249a
straw sacks ··· 7:351b
taxes ··· 7:239b
ritsuryō system ··· 6:326b
technique ··· 6:309a
varieties and improvements ··· 6:308b-309a
See also **Agriculture**
Rice blight ··· 6:309a, 310a
Rice Control Law ··· 6:310a
religious aspects ··· 2:254a
Rice farming
development ··· 7:178a
influence on village design ··· 7:179a
Iseki & Co, Ltd ··· 3:337a
Rice growing rites
rain supplication ··· 1:22b
seedling-transplanting ··· 1:22b
sowing ··· 1:22b
Rice Law ··· 6:310a
Rice planting techniques ··· 1:28b-29a
Rice price controls ··· 6:310a-310b
land reform programs ··· 1:24b
Rice riots of 1918 ··· 6:310b-311a; 7:242a; 8:124b
China ··· 1:388a
cooperatives, role of ··· 1:22a
employment ··· 4:344b
Korea ··· 4:283b
Taishō democracy ··· 7:304b
Terauchi Masatake ··· 8:12b
World War I ··· 8:271a
Rice stipend (kirimai) 切米 ··· 4:221a
Rice-transplanting dances ··· 2:86a
Rice wine. *See* **Sake**
Richardson, Charles ··· 6:311a
Richardson Affair ··· 6:311a
Kagoshima Bombardment ··· 4:105b
United Kingdom ··· 8:150b
Willis, William ··· 8:253b
"Rich Nation and a Strong Army" 2:311b
Richō ··· 李朝 ··· 8:324b-325b
Rickshaw ··· 6:311a-311b; 8:350b
Ricoh Co, Ltd ··· 6:311b
Riddles ··· 6:311b
Ridgway, Matthew Bunker ··· 2:248a; 6:311b-312a; 7:32b
Riess, Ludwig ··· 6:312a
Rigaku kōgen (An Exploration of the Principles of Philosophy) ··· 理学鉤玄 ··· 5:311b-312a
Rigen shūran ··· 俚言集覧 ··· 6:312a
Japanese dialects ··· 4:31b
Righteous Army Movement ··· 4:282a
resistance of Japanese control through ··· 4:282b
Righteousness (gi) ··· 4:141b
Rights
abuse ··· 1:5b
control property ··· 6:312a
in things ··· 6:312a
of possession ··· 7:67b-68a
proprietary ··· 1:55a
to organize labor unions ··· 6:312a-312b
collective bargaining ··· 1:334b
to remain silent ··· 6:312b
to strike ··· 6:312b-313a; 7:250b
to sunshine ··· 6:313a
Rights in things ··· 6:312a
Right to organize labor unions ··· 6:312a-312b
collective bargaining ··· 1:334b
Right to remain silent ··· 6:312b
Right to strike ··· 6:312b-313a; 7:250b
collective bargaining ··· 1:334b
Right to sunshine ··· 6:313a
Right wing ··· 6:313a-314b
Amur River Society ··· 1:53b
Gen'yōsha ··· 3:24b-25a
Kita Ikki ··· 4:225a
Kodama Yoshio ··· 4:241a
Ōkawa Shūmei ··· 6:81b
Tōyama Mitsuru ··· 8:88a
Uchida Ryōhei ··· 8:124a
ultranationalism ··· 8:144b-146a
Rijichō ··· 7:274a
Rikagaku Kenkyūjo. *See* **Institute of Physical and Chemical Research**
Ri Kaisei. 李恢成 *See* **Lee Hwe-song**
Ri Kan'yō ··· 李完用 ··· 8:326a
Rikka ··· 2:288b-289b, *293a*
Rikka-style ··· 2:*288b*
Rikken Dōshikai (Constitutional Association of Friends) ··· 立憲同志会 ··· 6:210a, 314b; 7:66b
Adachi Kenzō ··· 1:11a
Katsura Tarō ··· 4:173b
Kenseikai ··· 4:198a
Taishō Political Crisis ··· 7:305b
Wakatsuki Reijirō ··· 8:218b
Rikken Kaishintō (Constitutional Reform Party) ··· 立憲改進党 ··· 6:207b, 314b; 7:99a, 255b
democracy ··· 2:84b
Freedom and People's Rights Movement ··· 2:335a
Imperial Diet ··· 3:276b
Inukai Tsuyoshi ··· 3:326a
Jiyūtō ··· 4:65a-65b
Kōno Togama founded ··· 4:275a
Ōkuma Shigenobu ··· 6:96a
Rikken Teiseitō ··· 6:315b
senkyo kanshō ··· 7:66b
Shimpotō ··· 7:108b
Takada Sanae ··· 7:310b
Rikken Kokumintō (Constitutional Nationalist Party) ··· 立憲国民党 ··· 6:210a, 314b-315a
Inukai Tsuyoshi ··· 3:326a
Kakushin Kurabu ··· 4:120a
Universal Manhood Suffrage Movement ··· 8:169b
Rikken Minseitō (Constitutional Democractic Party) ··· 立憲民政党 ··· 5:316a-316b; 6:211a, 315a; 7:52a, 55a, 66b, 74b
Kenseikai ··· 4:198a
Tokonami Takejirō ··· 8:44a

Rikken seitai ryaku ········立憲政体略 ········4:168a
Rikken Seiyūkai (Friends of Constitutional Government Party) ········立憲政友会 ·1:97b; 3:198a; 6:210a, 315a-315b; 7:52a, 55a, 66b
Arima Yoriyasu ········1:84a
Hara Takashi ········3:103a
Imperial Diet ········3:227b
Itō Hirobumi ········3:353a
Jiyūtō ········4:65b
Kakushin Kurabu ········4:120a
Kaneko Kentarō ········4:138b
Kenseikai ········4:198a
Kenseitō ········4:198b
Kiyoura Keigo ········4:233a
Kōno Ichirō ········4:274a
Mori Kaku ········5:249b
Nakajima Chikuhei ········5:313b
Ozaki Yukio ········6:140a
Pak Yŏl ········6:159a
power of supreme command ········8:85a
Rikken Minseitō ········6:315a
Taishō democracy ········7:304a-304b
Takahashi Korekiyo ········7:312a-312b
Takegoshi Yosaburō ········7:324a
Tanaka Giichi ········7:336a-336b
Teikokutō ········7:376b
Tokonami Takejirō ········8:44a
Universal Manhood Suffrage Movement ········8:169b
Rikken Teiseitō立憲帝政党 2:366a; 6:315b
Rikkokushi (Six National Histories) ········六国史 ········1:354a; 6:315b-317a; 7:62b, 257a
Dai Nihon shiryō ········2:65b
general description ········6:315b-316a
historiography ········3:152b-153a
Miyako no Yoshika ········5:219b
Nihon kōki (Later Chronicle of Japan) ········6:316b
Nihon Montoku Tennō jitsuroku (Veritable Record of Emperor Montoku of Japan) ········6:316b
Nihon sandai jitsuroku (Veritable Record of Three Generations [of Emperors] of Japan) ········6:316b; 7:257a
Nihon shoki (Chronicle of Japan) ····6:316a
Shinkokushi ········7:121b
Shoku nihongi (Chronicle of Japan, Continued) ········6:316a-316b
Shoku Nihon kōki (Later Chronicle of Japan, Continued) ········6:316b
Rikkyō University ········6:317a
Ri Kō ········李滉 ········8:325b
Rikord, Petr Ivanovich ········3:44a
Ri Kōshō ········李鴻章 ········5:9b
Rikuchū Coast National Park ···陸中海岸国立公園 ··6:*317a*; 7:16a
Rikuentai ········陸援隊 ········5:317b; 6:317a-317b
Rikugien Garden ···六義園 ········6:317b
Rikugō zasshi ····六合雑誌 4:300a; 8:127b, 138a
Ōnishi Hajime ········6:107b
Rikugun Nakano Gakkō ········5:316a
Rikugun Shikan Gakkō. *See* **Army Academy**
Rikugunshō. 陸軍省 *See* **Army Ministry**
Rikuzen Takata ·陸前高田 ········6:317b
Rikyū ········利休 ········6:299b
Rimpa ········琳派 1:210a; 4:361b; 6:317b-318a
Fukuda Heihachirō ········2:362a
Kōrin ········4:292b
painting ········6:153a, *154a-154b*
screen and wall painting ········7:43a
seals ········6:281b
Rimpohan ········4:308a
Rin ········8:323b
Rindō. *See* **Gentians**
Ringi system. *See* **Management**
Ringo ········1:71a
Rinji ········綸旨 ········6:318a
Rinji Kyōiku Kaigi ········2:176a; 6:318b
Rinne ········6:318b
Rinrigaku ········倫理学 ········8:237b
Rinzai sect ········臨済宗 ·1:179b, 294a; 6:318b-320a; 7:80b
China ········1:253a
Chinese émigré masters ········6:319b
Daitokuji ········2:68a
founder ········2:187a; 6:319a-319b
Gozan network ········6:319b-320a
monks
Bankei Yōtaku ········1:137b
Eisai ········6:319a-319b
Hakuin ········6:320a
Jakushitsu Genkō ········4:1b-2a
Shidō Bunan ········7:89b
Yinyuan Longji (Yin-yüan Lung-chi; Ingen Ryūki) ········6:320a
Ryōanji temple ········6:347b
Tenryūji ········8:10b
Riot Police ········6:320a-320b
Riron keizaigaku no kihon mondai ····理論経済学の基本問題 ········7:258a
Riryō ········李陵 ········5:313b
Ri Sampei ········李参平 ·1:85b; 6:320b
Rise and Fall of the Genji and Heike, The ········3:16b
Ri Seikei ········李成桂 ········8:326a
Rishi keizairon (Economics of Ricardo) ········李氏経済論 ········6:126a
Rishiri ········利尻 ········6:320b
Rishiri-Rebun-Sarobetsu National Park 利尻礼文サロベツ国立公園 ········6:320b
Ri Shōban ········李承晩 ········6:307b
Ri Shōban rain ········李承晩ライン ········6:307b
Ri Shunshin ········李舜臣 ········8:326a
Risshakuji ········立石寺 ···6:320b-321a
Risshisha ········立志社 ·1:34b; 2:334a, 373b; 6:207a, 321a
Hayashi Yūzō ········3:118a
Itagaki Taisuke ········3:349b
Taoka Reiun ········7:346a
Risshō ankoku ron ········立正安国論 5:375b; 6:321a; 8:28a
Risshō Gokoku Dō ········立正護国堂 ········3:311a
Risshō Kōseikai ········立正佼成会 ···6:321a-321b
Niwano Nikkyō ········6:23a
Reiyūkai ········6:289b
Risshū ········6:332a
Ri Taiō ········李太王 ···4:252a-252b
Rites and ceremonies
agricultural ········1:22b-23a
Buddhist ········1:194b-195a
for laity ········1:194b
for monks ········1:194b-195a
Confucianism ········4:247b
religion ········6:290b
Shintō ········7:139a
Rites of passage ········2:299b
Ritō ········吏党 ········6:321b
Ritsu ········律 ··6:327b-328b
ritsuryō system ········6:322b
Ritsuko, sono shi ········リツ子・その死 ········2:76b
Ritsumeikan University ········6:321b
Ritsurin Park ····栗林公園 ········4:103b; 6:321b-322a, *322b*
Sanuki Folk Arts Museum ········7:18b
Takamatsu ········7:314a-314b
Ritsuryō system · 律令制 ······2:106b; 6:322a-332a; 7:11a, 57a, 89a-89b, 274b
agatanushi in ········1:21a
barter ········6:326b
classes defined ········7:62a
Confucian influence ········1:353b
Confucianism ········6:322b
corvée labor ········1:226a-226b; 8:327a
court hierarchy ········4:141b
court rank ········2:40a
criminal law ········6:327a
currency minting ········6:328a
Dajōkan ········2:69a-70a
decline ········8:338a
diplomatics ········2:97b
economy ········2:147a
filial piety ········6:325b
general principles of Ritsuryō Law ········6:322a-323a
Goki Shichidō ········3:43a
gōri system ········3:46a-46b
hakase ········3:84b
history ········6:330b-332a
Asuka Kiyomihara Code ········6:331a
compendium of regulations ······6:331b
Ōmi Code ········6:331a
"revised ritsuryō" and "revised ryōkyaku" ········6:331b-332a
Ryō no gige ········6:332a
Taihō Code ········6:331a-331b
Taika Reform ········6:331a
Yōrō Code ········6:331b
impeachment and legal process ········6:327a-328b
imperial edict ········3:277a
imperial rule ········2:203b-204b
inheritance ········6:326a
inheritance law ········3:304a
kinship rules ········6:325a
kōden under ········4:243a
kōgō status ········4:249a
ko (household) unit ········4:233b-234a
Koken under ········4:253b
kokufu under ········4:257b
kokugun system under ········4:259b
law
education in ········6:323a
philosophies of ········6:322b
legal specialists ········6:323a-327a
mura (village) ········5:265a
nengu ········5:360a
official salaries ········2:360b
premodern employment ········2:211b
real property ········6:326a
renza ········6:301b
ri ········6:308a
ritsu ········6:327b-333b
"ritsuryō state" ········6:329a-332a
ru ········6:339b
ryō ········6:347a
ryōge no kan ········6:351b
ryō, rules of ········6:324a-327a
sakimori ········7:2a
Sanze Isshin no Hō (Law of Three Generations or a Lifetime) ········7:19b
shichi ········7:87a
shinden ········7:109b
Shintō ········7:126b
shōen ········7:155b
uniforms ········8:149b

warrior government 8:228b
yakko (slaves) 8:285a
Ritsu school 5:238b
Ritsu sect ..... 律宗 .. 1:178a-178b; 6:332a
headquarters 5:332b
Rittō ..... 栗東 6:332a
Ritual impurity 4:186a-186b
Ritualism 4:38b
Rivers
Hokkaidō
Ishikarigawa 3:342a
Kushirogawa 4:320b
Mukawa 5:262a-262b
Sarugawa 7:22b
Shiribetsugawa 7:147b
Teshiogawa 8:15b
Tokachigawa 8:40a
Tokorogawa 8:44a
Honshū
Abekawa 1:2b
Abugawa 1:5a
Abukumagawa 1:5a
Adogawa 1:14b
Aganogawa 1:20b
Agatsumagawa 1:21a
Ajikawa 1:38b
Arakawa 1:73a-73b
Aridagawa 1:83a
Asahigawa 1:92b
Asukagawa 1:106b
Azusagawa 1:127b
Chikumagawa 1:276b
Edogawa 2:170b
Fuefukigawa 2:341b
Fujikawa 2:343b
Gōnokawa 3:46a
Hiikawa 3:136b
Hozugawa 3:246b
Ibigawa 3:253b
Iwakigawa 3:358a
Jinzūgawa 4:61a
Jōganjigawa 4:69a
Kakogawa 4:117b
Kamanashigawa 4:122b
Kamogawa 4:128a-128b
Kanogawa 4:146b
Kinokawa 4:214a
Kinugawa 4:219a
Kisegawa 4:222b
Kisogawa 4:224a
Kitakamigawa 4:226a
Kizugawa 4:233b
Kujigawa 4:303a
Kumanogawa 4:306b
Kurobegawa 4:314a
Kuzuryūgawa 4:323a
Mabechigawa 5:77a
Miyagawa 5:216b
Mogamigawa 5:233b
Mukogawa 5:262b
Nagaragawa 5:303b
Nakagawa 5:312b
Natsuigawa 5:349b
Ōigawa 6:74b
Oirasegawa 6:75b
Omonogawa 6:103a
Ōtagawa 6:128b
Setagawa 7:70b
Shinanogawa 7:109a
Shōgawa 7:158b
Sumidagawa 7:266a
Tadamigawa 7:293b
Takahashigawa 7:312a
Tamagawa 7:332b
Tatsutagawa 7:349b
Tedorigawa 7:375a
Tenryūgawa 8:10b
Tonegawa 8:74a
Totsukawa 8:85b
Ujigawa 8:131b
Watarasegawa 8:236b
Yahagigawa 8:284a-284b
Yamatogawa 8:309b-310a
Yasugawa 8:318b
Yodogawa 8:326b
Yoneshirogawa 8:337b-338a
Yōrōgawa 8:339a
Yoshiigawa 8:346b
Yuragawa 8:358a
Kyūshū
Chikugogawa 1:83a, 276b
Gokasegawa 3:42b
Kumagawa 4:305a
Midorikawa 5:167b
Mimikawa 5:175b
Ongagawa 6:106a
Ōnogawa 6:110a
Ōyodogawa 6:138b
Sendaigawa 7:63b
Shirakawa 7:146b
Yabegawa 1:83a
Yamakunigawa 8:297a
Shikoku
Hijikawa 3:136b
Nakagawa 5:312b
Niyodogawa 6:23b
Shimantogawa 7:101a
Rizal, José 6:332b
Roads 6:332b
Road Traffic Law 2:48a; 6:332b-333a
drivers' licenses 2:133b-134a
Ro and sha 6:333a
Rōben ..... 良弁 6:333a
Ishiyamadera 3:346a
Roberts Commission
Warner, Langdon 8:228a
Robertson, Walter S. 3:266a
Robins 4:264b
Robinson no matsuei
..... ロビンソンの末裔 4:111b
Robō no hana ... 路傍の花 4:179b
Robō no ishi 路傍の石
Shindō Kaneto 7:111a
Robots, industrial 3:298b-299b
Rochdale Society of Equitable Pioneers 1:22a
Roches, Léon ... 1:229b, 267a; 6:333a-333b
French-Japanese relations 2:331a
Rockets 7:239b-241a
Rock formations 3:109b
Rōdō Kumiai Kiseikai (Society for Formation of Labor Unions)
..... 労働組合期成会 4:345a
Takano Fusatarō 7:317a
Rōdō Nōmintō (Labor-Farmer Party)
..... 労働農民党 · 1:96a; 6:333b; 7:74b
Japan Communist Party 4:11a
Yamamoto Senji 8:299a
Rōdō sekai ..... 労働世界 4:167a; 7:164a
Rōdōsha Nōmintō
..... 労働者農民党 6:333b
Rōdōshō. 労働省 *See* **Ministry of Labor**
Rōdō undō nijūnen
..... 労働運動二十年 7:281a
Rōdō wa shinsei nari
..... 労働は神聖なり 7:281a
Rodrigues, João 4:51a; 6:334a
Jesuit mission press .....
Rōei ..... 朗詠 3:1a
Rōen (The Aging Monkey) 老猿 7:*43a*
Roesler, Karl Friedrich Hermann ... 1:8a; 2:2b, 311a; 6:334a
Commercial Code 1:338a
legal reform activities 2:319a
Rohen ..... 炉辺 4:301b
Rohen sōsho ..... 炉辺叢書 2:302a
Rohwer Relocation Center 6:334a
Roji 7:361b
Rojin ..... 魯迅 5:76b
Rojō no reikon 路上の霊魂 5:269b
Rōjū ..... 老中 · 4:109b, 160a; 6:334a-334b
Roka Tokutomi Kenjirō
..... 蘆花徳富健次郎 · 1:155b; 8:60a
Rōkechi ..... 臈纈 7:13b; 8:237b-238a
Rōketsu 8:237b-238a
Rokkaku family ..... 六角氏 6:334b
free markets 6:283a
Rokkakushi Shikimoku
..... 六角氏式目 8:346b
Rokkasen ..... 六歌仙 6:334b
Ariwara no Narihira 1:85b
Fujiwara no Kintō 2:352a
Fujiwara no Sadaie 2:354b
Henjō 3:126b
Ono no Komachi 6:110b-111a
Rokkō ..... 六甲 4:207b
Rokkōsan ..... 六甲山 1:83b; 6:334b-335a
Rokōkyō Jiken 蘆溝橋事件 5:113b
"Rōko shiiki" ..... 聾瞽指帰 4:269b
Rokudai shōjiki 六代勝事記 3:154a
Rokuhara deputies 六波羅探題 ... 6:335a
Rokuharamitsuji
..... 六波羅蜜寺 6:335a
Rokuhara tandai
..... 六波羅探題 6:335a; 7:340a
Rokujō Madenokōji bussho 六条万里小路仏所 3:313b
Rokujō no Akisuke
..... 六条顕輔 2:350a
Rokujō poets ..... 六条派 4:1b
Rokumeikan ..... 鹿鳴館 ... 6:335a-335b
Yōshū Chikanobu 6:*335a*
Rokuon'indono Itsukushima mōde no ki
..... 鹿苑院殿厳島詣記 3:272b
Rokuonji ..... 鹿苑寺 4:213a
Rokuon nichiroku
..... 鹿苑日録 ·· 1:264a-264b; 6:335b; 6:335b
Rokuro 6:*335b*
Karako site 5:157b
Rokuroshi 4:205a
Rōkyoku 2:267b; 5:328b
Romances 5:246a
Romanization of Japanese ·· 6:335b-336b
difficulties 6:336a
early systems 6:336a
general description 6:335b-336a
Hepburn system 6:336a
Hyōjun system 6:336a
International Organization for Standardization (ISO) 6:336a
Kokutei system 6:336a
Kunrei system 6:336a-336b
Rōmajikwai 6:336
Roman poruno 2:275a
Rōnin ..... 浪人 · 6:336b-337a; 7:75b
Forty-Seven Rōnin Incident 2:327a
movie theme 2:268a
Shinsengumi 7:124a
Rōninkai ..... 浪人会 ·· 6:337a-337b
Rōnō ..... 労農 6:337b; 8:297a
Rōnōha 6:337b
Rōnōha ..... 労農派 · 1:72a; 6:337b; 8:289a, 296b
Sakisaka Itsurō 7:3a

Rōnōtō. 労農党
See **Rōdō Nōmintō; Rōdōsha Nōmintō**
Roofs ········· 5:192b
Roof tiles ········· 6:337b-339a
general description ········· 6:337b
hongawara-buki ········· 6:337b-338a
karakusa-gawara ········· 6:338b
onigawara ········· 6:338a-338b
sangawara-buki ········· 6:338a
Roosevelt, Franklin Delano 6:339a; 7:246b
atomic bomb ········· 1:108a
wartime relocation of Japanese Americans ········· 4:17b
World War II ········· 8:272b
Yalta Conference ········· 8:286b
Roosevelt, Theodore ········· 6:339a; 7:49a
Gentlemen's Agreement ········· 3:24a-24b
Korean appeal to ········· 4:282b
Root, Elihu ········· 3:24a-24b
Rosanjin. 魯山人 *See* **Kitaōji Rosanjin**
Rosaries, Buddhist ········· 1:197a
Rosario kiroku ········· ロザリオ記録 ········· 7:241a
Rosario no kyō ········· ロザリオの経 ········· 7:241a
Roses (*Rosa* spp.) ········· 6:339a
Rosetsu ········· 蘆雪 ········· 6:339a-339b
Roshia Gunkan Tsushima Senryō Jiken ロシア軍艦対馬占領事件 ········· 8:118a
Roshia shi ········· ロシア史 ········· 4:173a
Rōshigumi
Shinsengumi ········· 7:124a
Rosny, Léon Louis Lucien Prunol de ········· 6:339b
Rōsōkai (Society of the Old and the Young) ········· 老壮会 ········· 8:359a
Rossi, Giovanni V. ········· 2:75b
Rossi, Vittorio ········· 3:351a
Rotary Club ········· 6:339b
Rotary engine ········· 6:339b
Rotary press ········· 6:246a
Rotenshō ········· 7:250a
Rōtō ········· 郎党 ········· 3:261a
Rouge (beni) ········· 2:38a
Royal Co ········· 7:196a
Royalty rights ········· 6:164b
Rōyama Masamichi 蠟山政道 ········· 7:115b
Ru ········· 流 ········· 6:339b-340a
Rubber industry
Bridgestone Tire Co, Ltd ········· 1:170b
Yokohama Rubber Co, Ltd ········· 8:330b
Ruijū fusen shō ········· 類聚符宣抄 ········· 4:90a
Ruijū jingi hongen ········· 類聚神祇本源 ········· 7:128a
Ruiju karin (Classified Forest of Verse) 類聚歌林 ········· 8:303a
Ruijū kokushi ········· 類聚国史 1:151b; 6:340a
Ruiju myōgi shō ········· 類聚名義抄 ········· 1:7b; 6:340a
Ruijū uta-awase (Classified Texts of Poetry Contests) ········· 類聚歌合 ········· 8:204b
Ruined Map, The ········· 1:3a
Rules of court ········· 6:340a-340b
Rumoi ········· 留萌 ········· 6:340b
Rumpen-mono
Shindō Kaneto ········· 7:111a
Runners. *See* Couriers
Rural Samurai ········· 3:48b-49a
Rural women ········· 8:266a-267a
Rushana ········· 盧遮那 ········· 1:*199a*
Rusk, Dean ········· 4:285b
Ruson Sukezaemon ········· 呂宋助左衛門 ········· 6:340b
Russia and Japan ········· 6:340b-344b
early relations ········· 6:340b-341b
Entente ········· 6:341b-342a
espionage ········· 7:229a-230a
Ezo ········· 2:238b
Ioffe (Joffe), Adolf Abramovich ········· 3:328a
Japanese studies ········· 4:44a
Korean Question ········· 6:341b
Laxman, Adam Erikovich ········· 4:372a
neutrality ········· 6:343a-343b
Nishi-Rosen Agreement ········· 6:19a
normalization of relations ········· 6:344a-344b
Northern Territories Issue ········· 6:344a
occupation ········· 6:343b-344a
Pacific War ········· 6:343b
postwar relations ········· 3:205b
recognition of the USSR ········· 6:343a
refugees ········· 6:286a
Shichihakase Jiken ········· 7:87b-88a
Siberian Intervention ········· 6:342b-343a
Tairo Dōshikai (anti-Russian group) 8:88b
Treaty of Portsmouth ········· 6:342a-342b
Tripartite Intervention ········· 6:341b
Russia Japan Expedition of 1852-1855
Putiatin, Evfimii Vasil'evich ········· 6:270b
Russian Orthodox Church ········· 6:258a
Archbishop Nikolai ········· 6:3b
Russian Soviet Federated Socialist Republic ········· 2:248b
Russo-Japanese agreements of 1907–1916 ········· 6:344b
Russo-Japanese Alliance ········· 6:342b
Russo-Japanese fisheries ········· 6:344b-345b
Cooperative Fishery Agreement of 1978 ········· 6:345b
Fishery Convention of 1907 ········· 6:345a
Fishery Convention of 1928 ········· 6:345a-345b
Fishery Convention of 1956 ········· 6:345b
Fishery Agreement of 1975 ········· 6:345b
Russo-Japanese Treaty of Amity ········· 6:270b
Russo-Japanese War ········· 1:166a; 6:342a, 345b-347a; 8:287a
Akiyama Saneyuki's battle plan ········· 1:144a
annexation of Korea and ········· 4:281b
background ········· 6:345b-346b
Denison, Henry Willard ········· 2:86b
Eastern European nations and Japan ········· 2:142a
events ········· 6:346b-347a
French-Japanese relations ········· 2:332b
Fukushima Yasumasa ········· 2:367a
Gen'yōsha ········· 3:25a
growth of business ········· 2:30b
Hibiya Incendiary Incident ········· 3:129a
Hirose Takeo ········· 3:148a
Kaneko Kentarō ········· 4:138b
Komura Jutarō ········· 4:268a
Korean-Japanese relations ········· 4:279b
Korea's annexation ········· 4:287b
Mukden, Battle of ········· 5:262b
nationalism ········· 5:343a
periodization ········· 6:177a
photography ········· 6:185b
Portsmouth, Treaty of ········· 6:228a, 347a
Roosevelt, Theodore ········· 6:339a
Russian influence in Korea ········· 4:90a
Russo-Japanese agreements of 1907–1916 ········· 6:344b
Sakhalin ········· 7:2a
Shichihakase Jiken ········· 7:87b-88a
Shimose Masachika ········· 7:106b
Tachibana Shūta ········· 7:293a
Tairo Dōshikai ········· 7:303a
Takahira-Root Agreement ········· 7:313b
Tatekawa Yoshitsugu ········· 7:349a
Tōgō Heihachirō ········· 8:36a
territory of Japan ········· 8:14a
Tripartite Intervention ········· 8:107a
United Kingdom and Japan ········· 8:152a
victory ········· 1:87b
war literature ········· 8:226a
World War I ········· 8:271a
Wu Peifu (Wu P'ei-fu) ········· 8:279b
Rusui ········· 留守居 ········· 6:347a
Rye and oats ········· 8:251a
Ryō ········· 令 ········· 6:324a-327b, 347a-347b
ritsuryō system ········· 6:322b
Ryōanji ········· 龍安寺 ········· 3:*8b*; 6:347b
Ryōben ········· 良弁 ········· 6:333a
Ryōbu
Shintō ········· 7:127b-128a
Ryōbu Mandara ········· 両部曼荼羅 ········· 6:347b-351a
general description ········· 6:347a-348a
Kongōkai ········· 4:270a
Kongōkai mandara ········· 6:349a-351a
Gōzanze katsuma e ········· 6:350b
Gōzanze sammaya e ········· 6:351a
Ichiin e ········· 6:350b
Kompon jōshin e ········· 6:349b-350b
Kuyō e ········· 6:350b
Misai e ········· 6:350b
Rishu e ········· 6:350b
Sammaya e ········· 6:350b
Shiin e ········· 6:350b
Kongōkai mandara (Diamond Realm Mandala) ········· 6:*348b*
Taizō mandara ········· 6:348a-349a
Chūtai hachiyō in ········· 6:348b
Henchi in ········· 6:348b-349a
Jimyō in ········· 6:348b
Jizō in ········· 6:349a
Jogaishō in ········· 6:349b
Kannon in ········· 6:349a
Kokūzō in ········· 6:349a
Kongōshu in ········· 6:349a
Monju in ········· 6:349a
Saige in ········· 6:349a
Shaka in ········· 6:349b
Soshitsuji in ········· 6:349a
Taizō mandara (Womb Mandala) ········· 6:*348a*
Ryōbun ········· 3:92b
Ryōbu Shintō ········· 両部神道 ········· 1:187b-188a; 6:351a-351b; 7:289b
Sannō Ichijitsu Shintō ········· 7:15a
Shingon sect ········· 7:115a
Shintō and Buddhism, separation ········· 7:132a
Ryōgae nendaiki ········· 両替年代記 ········· 6:351b
Ryōgaeshō ········· 両替商 ········· 1:137b; 6:351b; 7:268b
Kōnoike family ········· 4:274a
Ryōgae nendaiki ········· 6:351b
Ryōgen ········· 良源 ········· 6:351b
Ryōge no kan ········· 令外官 ········· 6:351b
kageyushi ········· 4:104b
kebiishi ········· 4:185b
naidaijin ········· 5:310a-310b
Sangi ········· 7:11a
Ryōjin hishō ········· 梁塵秘抄 ········· 3:49b; 5:40a; 6:351b-352a
Ryojun ········· 旅順 ········· 6:226a-226b
Ryōkai Mandara. 両界曼荼羅
See **Ryōbu Mandara**
Ryokan. *See* **Inns**
Ryōkan ········· 良寛 ········· 5:48a; 6:352a
Ryō Keichō ········· 梁啓超 ········· 4:384a-384b
Ryōken ········· 亮賢 ········· 3:43a
Ryōko ········· 良戸 ········· 7:62a
Ryokufūkai ········· 緑風会 ········· 6:352a-352b
Ryokuyū tōki ········· 緑釉陶器 ········· 1:263a
Ryōmin ········· 良民 ········· 6:352b
ritsuryō system ········· 6:324a
Ryōmō Railway Company
Taguchi Ukichi ········· 7:294b

Ryōnin 良忍 6:352b; 8:359b
nembutsu 4:67a
Sanzen'in 7:20a
Ryō no gige 令義解 6:352b; 7:54a; 8:339a
commentary 6:352b
ritsuryō system 6:332a
Ryō no shūge 令集解 6:352b-353a; 7:295b; 8:339a
Ryōō bugaku mask 5:*125b*
Ryō Shōshi 廖承志 4:384b
Ryōshu 6:353a
shitaji chūbun 7:149b
shōen 7:156a
yorioya-yoriko relationship 8:338b
Ryoshū (A Traveler's Sadness) 旅愁 8:333a-333b
Ryōshun. 了俊 *See* **Imagawa Sadayo**
Ryōshun isshi den 了俊一子伝 3:272b
Ryōtsu 両津 6:353a
Ryōunshū ("Cloud-borne Collection") 凌雲集 4:109a, 189a; 5:29b
Ryōzen 霊山 6:353a-353b
Ryūchikai (Dragon Pond Society) 龍池会 6:155a; 8:327b
Ryū Chishū 笠智衆 2:*271a*; 6:353b
Ryū Eifuku 劉永福 5:60a
Ryūgadō 竜河洞 6:353b
Ryūgaiji 龍蓋寺 6:78b
Ryūgasaki 竜ケ崎 6:353b
Ryūgū Soga monogatari 竜宮曽我物語 4:319b
Ryūjōkō Jiken 柳条溝事件 5:60a
Ryūkōgo 6:353b
Ryūkōka 6:353b-355a
early history 6:353b-354a
Edo-period 6:354a
late 1920s and 1930s 6:354b-355a
after 1941 6:355a
Meiji-period 6:354a-354b
Taishō-period 6:354b
Ryūkyū dialects 6:355a-357a
external history 6:355a-355b
Okinawan 6:355b-356b
morphology and syntax 6:356a
phonology 6:355b-356a
written language 6:355b
Outer Islands 6:356b-357a
Hirara 6:356b-357a
Sakishima 6:356b
Ryūkyū Islands 琉球諸島 6:84b-91a, 356b, 357a; 7:30b; 8:13b
San Francisco Peace Treaty 7:10b
Taiwan Expedition of 1874 7:309a
Ryūkyū Kingdom. *See* **Okinawa**
Ryūkyū kizoku mondai 6:357a
Ryūkyū music 6:357a-358a
Ryūkyū Rettō 琉球列島 6:357a
Ryūkyū territorial question 6:357a
Ryūkyū trade 6:358a-358b
Ryūkyū University 6:358b-359a
Ryūnōgiku (Chrysanthemum makinoi) 6:359a
Ryū Seiryū 柳成龍 8:358b
Ryūsendō 竜泉洞 6:359a
Ryūshi shinron 柳子新論 8:292b-293a
Ryūtanji Yū 竜胆寺雄
Hōrō jidai 7:119b
Machi no nansensu 7:119b
Ryūtei Rijō 滝亭鯉丈 6:359a
Ryūtei Tanehiko 柳亭種彦 1:119b, 211b; 3:42a-42b; 5:49a; 6:359a-359b
fūzoku shōsetsu 2:378a
Ryūzōji 龍造寺 7:102b
Ryūzōji family 龍造寺氏 6:359b

S

Saba 5:79a
Sabae 鯖江 2:364a; 6:361a
Sabi 寂び 1:145a; 5:42a; 6:146a, 297b, 361a-361b; 7:85b
ferns 2:252a
Jakuren 4:1b
Saburō Masaaki 三郎正明 4:270a
Sacks, straw 7:351b
Sacred, the 6:361b-362b
hare 2:253b-254a
kami 4:125b-126a
kami-hotoke 6:361b-362a
ke 2:253b-254a
kegare 4:186a-186b
Sacred fire 4:220a
Sacred Nachi Waterfall, The 7:136a
Sacrifice 6:362b
Sacrifice, human 3:207b
Sadae Party. *See* **Sugup'a**
Sada Keiji 佐田啓二 6:362b
Sadamisaki Peninsula 佐田岬半島 6:362b
Sadanobu 定信 1:234b
Saddlery 1:90a
Sadō. *See* **Tea ceremony**
Sado 佐渡 6:363a-363b; 7:360a-365a
Sado bugyō 佐渡奉行 6:363a
Sado mines 佐渡金山 6:363a
Ōkubo Nagayasu 6:93b
Saekibe 佐伯部 1:147b
Safety Agency 7:59a
Safety ordinances 4:234a-234b
Saga-bon 嵯峨本 3:182a; 6:248b
Saga, Emperor 嵯峨天皇 6:363b
Fujiwana no Yoshifusa 2:358a
Fujiwara family 2:350b
rule 2:204a
Saga (city) 佐賀 6:363a
Sagae (city) 寒河江 6:363a
Sagami Bay 相模湾 6:363b
Sagamigawa (river) 相模川 4:135a; 6:363b
Sagamihara (city) 相模原 6:363b
Sagamihara (upland) 相模原 6:363b
Sagami, Lake 相模湖 6:363b
Saga ningyō 2:*129a*
Saga Prefecture 佐賀県 6:363b-364a
Sagara Sōzō 相楽総三 6:364a
Saga Rebellion 佐賀の乱 1:34b; 6:364b-365a; 7:152a
Sagi 3:127b-128a
Sagi school 鷺流 4:325b
Sagisō (*Habenaria radiata; Pecteilis radiata*) 6:365a
Sagoromo monogatari 狭衣物語 5:36b; 6:365a
Sahara Makoto 佐原真 1:78b
Sahogawa 佐保川 6:365a
Saiban shiyō shō 裁判至要抄 4:376b
Saibara 催馬楽 4:108a; 6:365a
folk song 2:138b
gagaku 3:1a
Saichō 最澄 1:178b; 2:60b; 5:30a; 6:365a-366a
autonomous ordination system 6:365b-366a
Buddhist sculpture 1:198a-198b
early life 6:365a-365b
education 2:172a
Eisai 2:187a
Enryakuji temple 2:220b
esoteric ritual implements 1:196a
founding of Tendai sect 6:365b
Kammu, Emperor 4:128a
monasticism 5:237b-238a
portrait painting 6:227a
relationship with Kūkai 6:365b
Sanzen'in temple 7:19b
Shintō 7:127a
voyage to China 6:365b
Saidaiji 西大寺 6:366a
Saifu 割符 4:102a; 6:366a
Saifuya 割符屋 4:102a
Sai Gaku 蔡鍔 1:229b
Saiga no tsugunoi (What Cai Wo [Tsai Wo] Wrote instead of Napping) 宰我の償 8:292a
Saigawa 犀川 6:366a
Saigoku risshi hen 西国立志編 6:366a
Saigō Takamori 西郷隆盛 1:87a, 165a; 6:366a-367a; 7:29b, 102a
Chiossone, Edoardo 6:*366b*
Freedom and People's Rights Movement 2:334a
Itagaki Taisuke 3:349a
Iwakura Tomomi 3:360a
Satsuma Rebellion 7:30a
Seikanron issue 7:50b
Saigō Tsugumichi 西郷従道 6:367a
Kokumin Kyōkai founder 4:260b
Shinagawa Yajirō 7:109a
Saigusa Hiroto 三枝博音 6:366a-366b
Saigyō 西行 1:181a-181b; 2:303b; 5:39a; 6:299b, 367b-368b; 7:72a
Fujiwara no Ietaka 2:351a
Fujiwara no Toshinari 2:357b
Ihon Sankashū (variant Sankashū) 6:368b
Kamo no Chōmei 4:128b
Kikigakishū and *Kikigaki zanshū* 6:368b
life 6:367a-368a
poetry 6:368b
Sankashū 6:368a
Shin kokinshū 7:120a
Saihōji 西芳寺 6:368b-369a
gardens 3:9a-9b
Saiiki monogatari 西域物語 6:369a
Saijiki 歳時記 2:258b; 6:369a
Saijō 西条 6:369b
Saijō Yaso 西条八十 6:369b
Saika 7:129a, 139a
Saikai National Park 西海国立公園 6:369b
Saikaku 西鶴 2:77b; 5:11b, 47a; 6:369b-371a
fiction
Kōshoku gonin onna (Five Women Who Loved Love) 5:47a; 6:370b
Kōshoku ichidai onna (The Life of an Amorous Woman) 5:47a; 6:370b
Kōshoku ichidai otoko (The Life of an Amorous Man) 5:47a; 6:370a
Kōshoku nidai otoko 6:370a
Koyomi 6:370b
Nanshoku ōkagami 6:370b
Nippon eitaigura (The Japanese Family Storehouse) 5:47a; 6:370b
Saikaku shokokubanashi 6:370b
Seken munesan'yō (Worldly Mental Calculations) 6:370b

- *Shoen ōkagami* 6:370a-370b
- fūzoku shōsetsu 2:378a
- haikai 3:79a; 6:369b-370a
  - "arrow counting" (yakazu) 6:370a
  - "Dutch style" 6:370a
- influence of *Shikidō ōkagami* 7:95b
- life 6:369b
- posthumously published works 6:370b

Saikaku ichidai onna (The Life of Oharu) 西鶴一代女 2:*270b*
Saikaku shokokubanashi 西鶴諸国噺 6:370b; 8:144a
Saiken 再建 7:176b
Saiki 佐伯 6:371a
Saikontan 菜根譚 6:371a
Saikun 細君 8:110b
Saimei, Empress 斉明天皇 5:328b; 6:371a
Saimoppo Jōyaku 済物浦条約 1:268b
"Saint of Kasuya" 8:60a
St. Petersburg, Treaty of 4:7a; 6:371a
- Russia and Japan 6:344a
- Terashima Munenori 8:12a

Saionji, Prince 西園寺公 3:200b
Saionji family 西園寺家 6:371b
Saionji Kimmochi 西園寺公望 1:165b; 2:332b; 5:310a-310b; 6:371b-372b
- genrō 3:21b
- Hiranuma Kiichirō 3:144a
- Hirohito, Emperor 3:147a
- Nakae Chōmin 5:311b-312a
- Ritsumeikan University 6:321b

Saionji Kintsune 西園寺公経 6:372b
Sairan igen 采覧異言 4:369b; 8:241b
Saisei itchi 祭政一致 7:245b
Saisen 5:242a
Saishōkōin wall paintings 6:227a
Saitama Bank, Ltd 6:372b
Saitama Prefecture 埼玉県 6:372b-373a
Saito 西都 6:373a
Saitobaru Burial Mounds Museum 5:277b
Saitobaru tomb cluster 西都原古墳群 6:373a
- excavation 1:77b
- ships 7:144a

Saitō Dōsan 斎藤道三 6:373a-373b
Saitō Gesshin 斎藤月岑 6:373b
Saitō Hiroshi 斎藤博 6:373b-374a
Saitō Makoto 斎藤実 3:117b; 6:374a; 7:92a
- February 26th Incident 2:249b
- Samil Independence Movement 7:6b

Saitō Mokichi 斎藤茂吉 1:74b; 5:13a; 6:374a-374b
- Kaminoyama museum 4:127a

Saitō Mokichi nōto 斎藤茂吉ノオト 5:316b-317a
Saitō Rinjirō. 斎藤林次郎 *See* **Takayama Chogyū**
Saitō Ryokuu 斎藤緑雨 5:13a; 6:374b
Saitō Sanemori 斎藤実盛 6:374b
Saitō Setsudō 斎藤拙堂 6:374b
Saitō Tatsuo 斎藤達雄 2:*269a*
Saiyūki 西遊記 8:106a
Saji Keizō 佐治敬三 6:375a; 7:276a
Sakado 坂戸 6:375a
Sakadoza 坂戸座
- Kongō school 4:270a

Sakagami Hiroshi 坂上博 6:375a
Sakaguchi Ango 坂口安吾 6:375a-375b
Sakaguchi Kin'ichirō 坂口謹一郎 6:375b
Sakai 堺 2:295a; 4:112b; 6:375a-376b; 7:99a
- Oda Nobunaga 6:63a
- machishū 5:78b

Sakai, Frankie フランキー堺 6:376a-376b
Sakaida Kakiemon 酒井田柿右衛門 1:*261a*; 4:116b
Sakaide 坂出 4:103b; 6:376a
Sakai Hōitsu 酒井抱一 6:376b
- Kameda Bōsai 4:125a

Sakai merchants 6:376b
- gokasho shōnin 3:42b
- shipping 4:113a
- tally trade 7:331b-332a

Sakaiminato 境港 6:376b-377a
Sakai Spinning Mill 堺紡績所 6:377a
Sakai Tadakiyo 酒井忠清 6:377a
Sakai Toshihiko 堺利彦 6:377a; 7:56a
- Baibunsha 1:129b-130a
- Fukuda Hideko 2:362b
- Heiminsha 3:125b
- *Kaizō* 4:113b

Sakaki (*Cleyera ochnacea*) 6:377a-377b
Sakakibara Yasumasa 榊原康政 6:377b
Sakaki Hyakusen 彭城百川 1:211a; 6:377b-378a
Sakakura Junzō 坂倉準三 6:378a
Sakamoto Hanjirō 坂本繁二郎 6:378a
Sakamoto Ryōma 坂本龍馬 5:317b; 6:378a-378b; 7:3b, 23b, 29b
- Kaientai 4:109a

Sakana 2:25b
Sakanishi Shiho 坂西志保 6:378b-379a
Sakanoue family 坂上氏 6:379a
- Aya family 1:125b

Sakanoue no Tamuramaro 坂上田村麻呂 6:379a
- pardon of Fun'ya no Watamaro 2:370b
- shōgun 7:160a

Sakasafuji 逆富士 4:177b
Sakashitamon Incident 坂下門外の変 6:379a
Sakata 酒田 6:379b
Sakata Shōichi 坂田昌一 6:379b
Sakata Tōjūrō 坂田藤十郎 5:16b, 47a
- acting style 4:91a

Sakata Tōjūrō I 坂田藤十郎(初代) 6:379b
Sakawagawa 酒匂川 6:379b
Sakaya 6:379a-380b
Sakaya Kaigi 酒屋会議 6:380a-380b
Sake (dog salmon) 7:5b
Sake 1:46b; 2:306a; 4:336a, 338a; 7:1a-1b, 5b, 207a, 257b
- brewing 1:170a; 7:1a-1b
- ceremonial use 1:46b
- current drinking patterns 7:1b
- economy 2:148b
- origin 1:46b
- present day
  - social 1:47a
  - wedding ceremony 1:47a
- present day use 1:47a
- production 1:46b
- refined 7:1a
- rice consumption 6:309b
- shōchū 7:1a-1b
- songs
  - *Taue-zōshi* 7:351a
- Takara Shuzō Co, Ltd 7:318a
- tōji (brewer) 8:38a
- transport 4:113a

Sake brewers 6:379b-380a
Sake brewing 4:226b
Sake Production Bureau 1:46b
Sakhalin 7:1b-2a
- acquisition 4:7a
- international relations 3:320b
- Mamiya Rinzō 5:88b-89a

Sakhalin-Kuril Islands Exchange Treaty. *See* **St. Petersburg, Treaty of**
Sakimori 防人 7:2a
Sakimori uta 防人歌 7:2a-2b
- defined 5:106b

Sakisaka Itsurō 向坂逸郎 7:2b-3a
Sakishima Islands 先島諸島 7:3a
- Ryūkyū dialects 6:355a

Sakka shiron 作家私論 8:11a
Sakoku 鎖国 5:346b-347b
Saku (city) 佐久 7:3a
Saku Basin 佐久盆地 7:3a
Saku (stockades) 柵 7:3a
Sakugami. *See* **Ta no kami**
Sakuma Dam 佐久間ダム 2:73a; 7:3a-3b
Sakuma Kanae 佐久間鼎 7:3b
Sakuma Kōho 佐久間珖甫 2:*129a*
Sakuma Shōzan 佐久間象山 7:3b-4a, 27a; 8:221a-221b, 313b
- fukoku kyōhei 2:360b

Sakunami Hot Spring 作並温泉 7:4a
Sakura (city) 佐倉 7:4a
Sakura (flowering cherry tree) 1:269a-270a
Sakurada Ichirō 桜田一郎 1:268b; 7:4a
Sakurada Jisuke 桜田治助 4:91b; 7:4a-4b
- kabuki plays 4:91b

Sakuradamongai Incident 桜田門外の変 1:55a, 84a, 263b; 7:4b
Sakuradamon Incident 桜田門事件 7:4b
Sakurada Takeshi 桜田武 7:4b
Sakurai 桜井 7:4b
Sakurai Prize 1:268a
Sakurajima 桜島 4:105a-105b; 7:4b; 8:147b, 194a
Sakurakai 桜会 7:5a
Sakurama Michio 桜間道雄 4:267b; 6:*26b*
Sakurama Sajin 桜間左陣 4:267b
Sakurasō. *See* **Primroses**
Sakura Sōgorō 佐倉惣五郎 7:5a
Sakushiki 作職 7:5a
Salamanders [(sanshōuo) family Salamandridae] 7:5a-5b
Sales contract 2:20a-20b
Salmon and trout 2:284a
Salmons [(sake; masu) family Salmonidae] 7:5b
Salt fields 2:213b
Salvation Army 7:5b-6a
- prostitution 6:257a
- Yamamuro Gumpei 8:300a
- Yamamuro Kieko 8:300a

Samādhi 4:304a
Sambesan 三瓶山 7:6a, 101a
Sambetsu Kaigi 産別会議 4:346b, 358a; 6:212b; 7:6a
- Shinsambetsu 7:124a

Sambō Hombu 参謀本部 1:90b-91a
Sambōin 三宝院 2:57b
Sambugyō 三奉行 7:6a
Same 鮫 4:138a
Samgha
- monasticism 5:236b

Samguk sagi 6:146a; 7:6a
- Korean Three Kingdoms period 4:292a

Samguk sidae 4:292a
Samguk yusa 7:6a
- Korean Three Kingdoms period 4:292a

Samil Independence Movement 6:159a; 7:6a-6b, 242a
- historical context 4:283b

Sammaioroshi 2:25b
Samma [(saury) *Cololabis saira*] 7:6b-7a

Sammon **1**:183a
Sampitsu 三筆 **1**:234a
Sampō (Industrial Patriotic Association) **4**:345b
Samp'o Incident **7**:7a
Sampō kōjin (god) 三宝荒神 **4**:252a
Sampo no Ran. *See* **Samp'o Incident**
"Sampō" (Sangyō Hōkoku Kai) **4**:351a
Sampū kushū 杉風句集 **7**:259a
Samsara **1**:181a
Samurai 侍 **7**:7a-8b, 247a, 251a, 258b, 261a
- abolition of class **3**:192a
- administrative units (yakukata) **1**:137b
- arms bearing **1**:88b-89a
- bakuhan system **1**:131a-131b
- bushidō **1**:221b-223b
- Christian conversion **1**:308b
- Dampatsurei **2**:72a
- declassment **4**:108b-109a
- descendants **1**:324b
- dissolution **7**:8b
- Edo **2**:168b-169b
- Edo period **3**:186a
- education **2**:172b, 174b
- employees **2**:212a-212b
- ethics **1**:221b-223b, 276b
- feudalism **2**:263b-264a
- fighting units (bankata) **1**:137b
- geisha **3**:15b
- Genroku era **3**:22b
- gōshi (rural) **3**:48b-49a
- hatamoto yakko **3**:112a
- ie system **3**:260a
- Japanese immigration to U.S. **4**:13b
- kana-zōshi **4**:136b
- kenka ryōseibai **4**:196b
- kirisute gomen (privilege to kill) **4**:222a
- leaders **7**:7b
- martial arts **1**:206a
- Medieval Age **7**:7b-8a
- Meiji Restoration **5**:156b
- myōji taitō **5**:290b
- militarism **5**:173a
- organization **7**:7a-7b
- origins **7**:7a
- pension **2**:151b
- physical characteristics **4**:35a
- salaries **2**:340a
- Satsuma Rebellion **4**:105b
- shimpan **7**:108a
- shi-nō-kō-shō **7**:122b
- sword fights (chambara) **1**:266a
- Taira and Minamoto struggle **7**:7b
- technological development **7**:368b
- Tokugawa shogunate **7**:8a-8b
- urban life **2**:150b-151a; **8**:177b

Samurai declassment
- Edo period **4**:108b
- Muromachi period **4**:108b

Samurai descent **7**:151a-152a
Samurai-dokoro 侍所 **4**:122a; **5**:273b; **7**:8b, 97b
- Kajiwara Kagetoki **4**:114b
- Minamoto no Yoritomo **4**:122a

Samurai society
- lineage **7**:108a
- related houses **7**:108a

Sanada Nobushige 真田信繁 **7**:9a
Sanada Yukimura 真田幸村 **7**:9a
- Sekigahara, Battle of **7**:56b

Sanage 猿投 **1**:258a, 261b-262a; **7**:9a-9b, 71a
- green-glazed wares **1**:263a
- Tokoname ware **8**:44a

Sancho Kurabu **5**:19a
Sanchū hōrō 山中放浪 **4**:270a
Sanda 三田 **7**:9b
Sandai Jiken Kempaku Movement 三大事件建白運動 **7**:9b
Sandaikō 三大考
- Hirata Atsutane influenced **4**:259a

Sandaishū ("The Collections of Three Eras") 三代集 **8**:204a
Sandakan hachiban shōkan サンダカン八番娼館 **4**:159b-160a
Sandakan hachiban shōkan: Bōkyō サンダカン八番娼館:望郷 **7**:337a
Sandamme **7**:272a, 273a
San'en **8**:29a-29b
Sanetaka Kō ki 実隆公記 **7**:9b, 12b
San Felipe Incident **7**:9b-10a
San Francisco Board of Education **7**:49a
San Francisco Peace Treaty **6**:178b, 302b; **7**:10a-11a, 28a, 275a; **8**:160a-160b, 165b, 344b
- Article 14 **7**:235b
- atomic bomb **1**:110b
- Cambodia **1**:236b
- Canada **1**:238a
- Communist purge termination **2**:339a
- Dulles, John Foster **2**:135a
- Far Eastern Commission **2**:248a
- French-Japanese relations **2**:333b
- Hiratsuka Raichō **3**:146a
- Indonesia and Japan and **3**:291a
- Latin American emigration **4**:369b
- Netherlands **5**:362b
- New Zealand **5**:372b
- Occupation **6**:51a
- Okinawa **6**:88b
- Ōsu Incident **6**:128a
- peace movement **6**:166b
- Philippines **6**:184b
- postwar relations with China **1**:290a
- Russia and Japan **6**:344a
- territory of Japan **8**:14b
- United Kingdom **8**:153a
- United States military bases, disputes **8**:168a

San Francisco Symphony Orchestra
- Ozawa Seiji **6**:140b

San Francisco World's Fair of 1939 **8**:228a
Sangaku 散楽 **7**:22a
Sangaku shinkō 山岳信仰 **5**:259b-260a
Sangatsu Jiken 三月事件 **5**:112b-113a
Sangawara-buki **6**:338a
Sanger, Margaret **2**:246b; **7**:11a
Sangha **1**:177a
Sangi 参議 **2**:70a-70b; **7**:11a-11b
Sangoku jidai 三国時代 **4**:292a; **7**:6a
Sangoku Kanshō. 三国干渉 *See* **Tripartite Intervention**
Sangoku shiki 三国史記 **7**:6a
Sangō shiki 三教指帰 **4**:304a
Sanguo zhi **7**:264a
Sangyō gisho 三経義疏 **7**:11b, 172a
Sangyō kumiai (production unions) **1**:21b
San'ichi Dokuritsu Undō 三・一独立運動 **7**:6a-6b
San'ichigo Jiken. *See* **March 15th Incident** 三・一五事件
San'in Coast National Park 山陰海岸国立公園 **4**:338b
Sanja Festival 三社祭 **2**:*253a*; **5**:*172b*; **7**:11b
Sanjiin **8**:291a
Sanjo (people) 散所 **7**:11b-12a
Sanjō, Emperor 三条天皇 **7**:12a
Sanjō (city) 三条 **7**:12a
Sanjōgatake 山上ケ岳 **6**:102a
Sanjōnishi Sanetaka 三条西実隆 **7**:12a-12b
- diary **7**:9b
- incense ceremony **3**:285a
- Kokin denju **4**:254a

Sanjō Sanetomi 三条実美 **7**:12b, 88a
- lord keeper of the privy seal **5**:310a-310b
- Seikanron issue **7**:50b

Sanjō wasan 三帖和讃 **8**:231a
Sanjūrokkasen 三十六歌仙 **2**:354a; **4**:161b; **7**:12b-13a
- Ariwara no Narihira **1**:85b
- Ōnakatomi no Yoshinobu **6**:105a-105b

Sanjūrokunin sen 三十六人撰 **4**:161b
Sanjūrokunin Kashū (Collection of Thirty-six Master Poets) 三十六人歌集 **7**:266b; **8**:233a
Sanjūsangendō 三十三間堂 **1**:*189a*; **4**:145a; **7**:*13a*, 13b, 67b
Sanjūyonka no kotogaki (The Thirty-Four Articles) 三十四箇事書 **8**:27a
Sanka **7**:13b
Sankan. 三関 *See* **Sekisho**
Sanka zui 三貨図彙 **4**:319a
Sankechi **7**:13b; **8**:17b
Sankeien 三渓園 **7**:13b
Sankei shimbun サンケイ新聞 **2**:347b; **7**:13b-14a
Sanki Engineering Co, Ltd **7**:14a
Sankin kōtai 参勤交代 **1**:131b, 132a; **7**:14a-14b, 265a; **8**:98a
- Edo **2**:168b, 170a
- Edo-period **2**:171b
- feudalism **2**:266b
- Gokaidō **3**:41a-41b
- Hakone no Seki **3**:86b
- urban life **8**:177b

Sankōsha gogengyō **7**:14b
Sankō Steamship Co, Ltd **7**:14b
Sankyō Aluminium Industry Co, Ltd **7**:14b
Sankyō Co, Ltd **7**:15a
Sankyō Seikō Co, Ltd **7**:15a
Sankyū, Inc **7**:15a
Sanlüe **4**:82a
Sannō 山王 **7**:136a
Sannō Festival 山王祭 **4**:137a; **7**:15a
Sannō Ichijitsu Shintō 山王一実神道 **7**:15a-15b
- *Ichijitsu shintō ki* **3**:255b
- Shintō **7**:127b

Sannō Nijūissha 山王二十一社 **3**:130b
Sano 佐野 **7**:15b
Sano Manabu 佐野学 **7**:15b
Sano no Chigami no Otome 狭野茅上娘子 **7**:15b-16a
Sano Tsunetami 佐野常民 **1**:119b-120a; **7**:16a
- Kaigun Denshūjo **4**:110a

Sanoyasu Dockyard Co, Ltd **7**:16a
Sanraku. 山楽 *See* **Kanō Sanraku**
Sanriku Coast 三陸海岸 **2**:285b; **7**:16a
Sanrizuka 三里塚 **7**:16a
Sanron 産論 **4**:102b
Sanron school 三論宗 **1**:178b; **4**:71b; **5**:332b; **7**:16a-16b
Sansai tōki 三彩陶器 **1**:263a
Sansei **4**:13a-13b, 14b-15a
- Hawaiian politics **4**:16b
- Japan **4**:15a-15b

marriage ······ **4**:17a
Sanseki (Three [Brush] Traces) ······ 三蹟 ··· **1**:234a-234b
Sanshimpō (Three New Laws) ······ 三新法 · **1**:103b; **7**:16b
Sanshin
Ryūkyū music ······ **6**:357a
Sanshirō ······ 三四郎 ······ **5**:350a
Sanshō ······ **2**:305a; **3**:127b
Sanshoku ······ 三職 ······ **7**:16b-17a
Sanshōuo ······ **7**:5a-5b
Sanshu no jingi
······ 三種の神器 ··· **3**:278b-279a
Sanskrit drama ······ **8**:22a
Sanskrit language ······ **7**:192b
Sanskrit treatises ······ **8**:21b
Sansom, George Bailey ······ **7**:17a-17b
works ······ **7**:17a-17b
Sansui Electric Co, Ltd ······ **7**:17b
Sansuiga ······ 山水画 · **6**:151a, 158b; **7**:17b
Autumn and Winter Landscapes ······ **7**:*17a*
Sesshū Tōyō ······ **7**:*17a*
subjects ······ **6**:158b
Santai (Three Truths) 三諦 ······ **8**:29a
Santō Kyōden ··· 山東京伝 · **1**:130b; **5**:48b; **7**:18a-18b, 96b
fūzoku shōsetsu ······ **2**:378a
gesaku ······ **3**:28b
sharebon ······ **7**:79b
Santō Mondai. 山東問題
See **Shandong (Shantung) Question**
"Santō senkyaku" (The Steerage Passengers)
······ 三等船客 ······ **5**:80a
Sanuki Folk Arts Museum ······ **7**:18b
Sanuki Mountains
······ 讃岐山脈 · **4**:103a; **7**:18b
Sanuki no Suke no nikki
······ 讃岐典侍日記 ··· **5**:38b; **6**:2b; **7**:18b
Sanuki Plain ······ 讃岐平野 ······ **7**:18b
Sanwa Bank, Ltd ······ **7**:18b-19a
Tōyō Trust & Banking Co, Ltd ······ **8**:96a
San'yaku ······ **7**:272a
San'yō Electric Co, Ltd ······ **7**:19a
San'yo-Kokusaku Pulp Co, Ltd ······ **7**:19a
San'yūtei Enchō
······ 三遊亭円朝 ······ **7**:19b
Sanze Isshin no Hō
······ 三世一身の法 ······ **7**:19b
Sanzen ······ **7**:234a
Sanzen'in ······ 三千院 ······ **7**:19b-20a
Sanzenri ······ 三千里 ······ **4**:178a
Sanzonzō ······ 三尊像 ······ **7**:20a
Saotome ······ **7**:20a
Sapporo ······ 札幌 **7**:20a, *20b*, 98a
Sapporo band ······ **6**:258a
Sapporo Breweries, Ltd **4**:221a; **7**:20a-20b
Sapporo Winter Olympic Games ··· **7**:20b
Sararīman ······ **7**:20b-21a; **8**:251b
urban life ······ **8**:178b
Sarasa ······ **7**:21a
Sarashina nikki ·· 更級日記 · **1**:154a; **5**:35b; **6**:2a; **7**:21a-21b, 257b; **8**:104b
Sarcoli, Adolfo ······ **3**:351a
Sardines [(iwashi) family Clupeiformes]
······ **2**:284b; **7**:21b
Saris, John ······ **7**:21b-22a
Sarobetsu Plain
······ サロベツ原野 ·· **7**:22a; **8**:15b
Rishiri-Rebun-Sarobetsu National Park
······ **6**:320b
Saroma, Lake ···· サロマ湖 ······ **7**:22a
Saru ······ **5**:245a-245b
Sarugaku ······ 猿楽 **1**:216a; **2**:297b; **5**:43a; **7**:22a-22b
dance, traditional ······ **2**:74a-74b
Sarugaku nō ······ 猿楽能 ······ **4**:324b
Sarugawa ······ 沙流川 ······ **7**:22b
Sarukani kassen · 猿蟹合戦 ······ **7**:22b
Saru mawashi ······ **7**:250a
Sarumino ······ 猿蓑 ······ **6**:298b
Sarusawa Pond ··· 猿沢池 · **5**:*331a*; **7**:22b
Sasa ······ **1**:135b-136a
Sasagawanagare 笹川流れ ······ **7**:22b
Sasago Pass ······ 笹子峠 ······ **7**:22b
Sasaki Dōyo ··· 佐々木道誉 ······ **7**:23b
Sasaki Eigyōbu Co, Ltd ······ **6**:300b
Sasaki Kojirō 佐々木小次郎 ······ **6**:221b
Sasaki Kōzō ··· 佐々木更三 ····· **7**:22b-23a
Sasaki Nobutsuna
······ 佐佐木信綱 ······ **7**:23a
Sasaki Ryōsaku
······ 佐々木良作 ······ **7**:23a
Sasaki Sōichi · 佐々木惣一 ···· **2**:3b; **7**:23a
Sasaki Takaoki 佐々木隆興 ······ **7**:23a
Sasaki Takasada
······ 佐々木高貞 ······ **4**:275a
Sasaki Takatsuna
······ 佐々木高綱 ····· **7**:23a-23b
Sasaki Takauji 佐々木高氏 ······ **7**:23b
Sasaki Takayuki
······ 佐々木高行 ······ **7**:23b
Sasaki Toyoju · 佐々城豊寿 ······ **7**:23b
Sasamegoto ··· ささめごと **7**:23b-24a, 80b
Sasameyuki (The Makioka Sisters) ······ 細雪 **1**:102a; **6**:230a; **7**:176b, 343a
Sasanqua ······ **7**:31b-32b
Sasara ······ **7**:24a
Sasayama ······ 篠山 ······ **7**:24a
Sasebo ······ 佐世保 ······ **7**:24a
Sasebo Heavy Industries Co, Ltd ·· **7**:24a
Sase Yojiemon
······ 佐瀬与次右衛門 ······ **1**:38b
Sashidashi ······ 指出 ······ **4**:193a
Sashi-e ······ **1**:163b-164a
Sashi hijiki ······ **1**:183b
Sashiko ······ **2**:294a; **7**:24a-24b
techniques ······ **7**:24a-24b
Sashimi ······ **2**:305b-306a; **7**:24b; **8**:323b
Sāstra ······ **1**:177a
Sata ······ 沙汰 ······ **7**:25a
Sata Ineko ······ 佐多稲子 ······ **6**:255a; **7**:25a-25b, 66b
works ······ **7**:25a
Satake-bon ······ 佐竹本 ······ **4**:161b
Satake family ······ 佐竹氏 ······ **7**:25b
Satake Shozan ·· 佐竹曙山 ······ **7**:25b
Sata mirensho · 沙汰未練書 ······ **7**:25b
kabegaki definition ······ **4**:90a
Satamisaki ······ 佐多岬 ······ **7**:25b
Satchō Dōmei. 薩長同盟
See **Satsuma-Chōshū Alliance**
Satellites, artificial. *See* **Space technology**
Sato ······ **6**:308a
Satodairi ······ 里内裏 ······ **7**:26a
Satō Eisaku ······ 佐藤栄作 ······ **1**:159a; **7**:26a-26b, 28a, 252b
Fujiyama Aiichirō defeat ······ **2**:359a
hikaku sangensoku ······ **3**:137a
Satō Genchō ···· 佐藤元萇 ·· **5**:251b, 252b
Satogo ······ **7**:26b
Satō Hachirō
······ サトウハチロー ···· **7**:26b, 27b
Satō Haruo ······ 佐藤春夫 ······ **5**:13a; **7**:26b-27a, 253b
fiction ······ **7**:27a
poetry ······ **7**:27a
samma (saury) in poetry ······ **7**:7a
Satō Issai ······ 佐藤一斎 ·· **5**:315a; **7**:3b, 27a; **8**:335b
Satokagami (Mirror of Flower Town) ······ 里鏡 ······ **3**:95a
Sato kagura ······ 里神楽 **4**:107b; **5**:283a
Satō Kōgyō Co, Ltd ······ **7**:27a-27b
Satō Kōroku ···· 佐藤紅緑 ···· **7**:27b, 121a
Satō Hachirō ······ **7**:26b
Satomi and the Eight "Dogs" **5**:329a-329b
Satomi Ton ······ 里見弴 ······ **7**:27b
radio drama ······ **6**:275a
Satomura Jōha ·· 里村紹巴 · **6**:297a; **7**:27b
Satō Naokata (Neo-Confucian scholar) ······ 佐藤直方 ····· **7**:27b-28a
Satō Naotake (diplomat)
······ 佐藤尚武 ······ **7**:28a
Satō Nempuku ·· 佐藤念腹 ······ **7**:28a
Satō-Nixon Communiqué ······ **7**:28a-28b; **8**:160a
Japanese-Korean cooperation ······ **4**:286a
trade with China ······ **1**:291a
United States-Japan Security Treaties ······ **8**:167b
Satō Nobuhiro ··· 佐藤信淵 ······ **7**:28b
Satori ······ **7**:28b; **8**:373b-374a
Satō Satarō ···· 佐藤佐太郎 ······ **7**:28b
Satō Takeo ······ 佐藤武夫 ······ **7**:28b
Satō Tatsuo ······ 佐藤達夫 ····· **7**:28b-29a
Satō Toshi. *See* **Tamura Toshiko**
Satow, Ernest Mason ······ **1**:77a; **7**:22a, 29a-29b, 270b
Satsuban ······ **2**:*260b*
Satsuei Sensō ·· 薩英戦争 ······ **4**:105b
Satsuki *(Rhododendron indicum)*
······ **1**:126a-126b
Satsuma and Chōshū oligarchs. *See* **Hambatsu**
Satsuma-Chōshū Alliance
······ 薩長同盟 **4**:109a; **5**:317b; **7**:29b
Inoue Kaoru ······ **3**:310a
Komatsu Tatewaki ······ **4**:266a
Shinagawa Yajirō ······ **7**:109a
Satsuma Peninsula
······ 薩摩半島 ······ **7**:29b
Satsuma Province · 薩摩国 ···· **7**:29b-30a; **8**:323b
Satsuma Rebellion
······ 西南戦争 ·· **1**:85a; **7**:16a, 30a, 152a; **8**:291a
chitsuroku shobun ······ **1**:298a
Fujita Denzaburō ······ **2**:346a
Hayashi Yūzō ······ **3**:118a
Kabayama Sukenori ······ **4**:89b
Kawakami Sōroku ······ **4**:181b
Kido Takayoshi ······ **4**:203b
Kōno Togama ······ **4**:275a
location ······ **4**:105b
Red Cross Society ······ **4**:40b
Saigō Takamori ······ **6**:367a
samurai ······ **7**:8b
Sasaki Takayuki ······ **7**:23b
Seikanron issue ······ **7**:51a
Shiroyama ······ **7**:148a
Takehashi Insurrection ······ **7**:324a
Takenouchi Tsuna ······ **7**:325a
Tani Kanjō ······ **7**:341b-342a
Terauchi Masatake ······ **8**:12b
Willis, William ······ **8**:253b
Satsuma Tayū ·· 薩摩太夫 ····· **4**:76b-77a
Satsuma ware ····· 薩摩焼 ····· **7**:30a-30b
Satsumon culture
······ 擦文文化 ······ **7**:30b
Satsunan Islands 薩南諸島 · **6**:357a; **7**:30b
Saury ······ **7**:6b-7a
Savings, consumer ······ **2**:17b
Savings and loan banks (sōgo ginkō)
······ **1**:139b
Savings Bank Ordinance of 1890 · **1**:138b
Sawada Miki ····· 沢田美喜 ······ **7**:30b
Elizabeth Saunders Home ······ **2**:196b

Sawada Shōjirō 沢田正二郎 2:268a; 7:30b-31a
Shinkokugeki 7:121a
Sawamura Sōjūrō 沢村宗十郎 7:31a
Sawa Nobuyoshi 沢宣嘉 7:31a-31b
Sawara 佐原 7:31b
Sawayanagi Masatarō 沢柳政太郎 7:31b
school curriculum 7:36a
Shin Kyōiku Undō 7:121b
Saya 4:295b
Sayama 狭山 7:31b
Sayama Kengyō 佐山検校 4:65a
Sayama, Lake 狭山湖 7:31a
Sayo no Nakayama 小夜ノ中山 7:31b
Sazae san サザエさん 6:275b
Sazanka [(sasanqua) *Camellia sasanqua*] 7:31b-32b
Scandinavia
Japanese studies 4:43b
SCAP 7:32b-33a, 47a
civil information and education section 1:317b
deputy chief 4:101a
normalization negotiations 4:284b
Sorge Affair 7:229b
Scapegoats
dolls 2:128a
Scarecrows 4:115a
Scenes in and around Kyōto 4:146a
Schnell, John Henry 4:13b
Scholars' names 5:325a-326a
Scholastic Shintō 2:300b
School Administration 7:33a
School administration and finance. *See* **Education**
School architecture 7:33a-33b
Schoolchildren, life of 5:6b
School course guidelines 7:34a
textbooks 7:37b
School curriculum 7:34a-36a
history of 7:35b-236a
revision 2:180b
structure 7:34b-35b
extracurricular activities 7:35b
foreign language 7:35b
health and physical education 7:35b
home economics 7:35b
language 7:34b
mathematics 7:35a
music and art 7:35b
science 7:35a
social studies 7:34b-35a
School Education Law of 1947 2:179b; 6:235b; 7:34a, 36a-36b, 241b
higher education 3:133a
outline 2:180a
private schools 6:252a
structure 2:182b
School entrance examinations 2:222a-224b
School libraries 7:36a-36b
School lunch program 7:36b
School orders 7:36a-36b
teachers 7:365b
Schools for Japanese children abroad 7:36a-37b
School system. *See* **Education**
School system administration and finance 2:177a-178b
School textbooks 7:37b
Science and International Affairs Bureau 3:319b
Science and Technology, Council for 7:38a
Science and Technology Agency 1:219a; 6:304a; 7:37b-38a
1977 White Paper on Science and Technology 7:372b
Ocean resource development 6:59a
technology, modern 7:373a
Science Council of Japan 1:218b; 7:38a
natural science 5:357a
Science fiction 6:221b; 7:38a-39a
Edo-period 7:38a-38b
Meiji period to World War II 7:38b
mystery stories 5:292a
post-World War II 7:38b-39a
Scientific research
natural science 5:356b-357a
Scientific thought, premodern 7:39a-41a
astronomy 7:39a, 40a
Confucianism 7:40a-40b
emperor's mandate 7:39a-39b
mathematics 7:39b-40a; 8:231a-232a
medicine 5:145b-147a
Shibukawa Shunkai 7:40a, 86a
Western influences 7:39b-40a
Scott, Marion McCarrell 7:35b, 41a
Screen 2:371a
Screen and wall painting 3:181a-183a; 6:151b; 7:41a-43b
byōbu-e 7:41b-42a
Chinese Lions 4:146a-146b
Cherries and Maples panels 7:*41a-41b*
early shōbyōga 7:42a-42b
Edo-period shōbyōga 7:43a-43b
Hikone byōbu 2:377a
Iris Screens 6:154a-154b
Kanō school 4:149a, 150a
medieval shōbyōga 7:42b-43a
shōhekiga 7:41b
rakuchū rakugai zu 2:*377a*
Script style 7:170a
"Scriptures of the Konkōkyō" 4:272a
Scroll of Hungry Ghosts 1:*191a*
Scrolls of Frolicking Animals and Humans. *See* **Chōjū giga**
Scrolls of Hells 4:54a-54b
Sculptors
Buddhist
Chōsei 1:303b
Enkū 2:218a-218b
Inson 3:315a
Jōchō 4:66a-66b
Kaikei 4:111a
Kōkei 4:253a
Kuninaka no Muraji Kimimaro 4:309b
Kuratsukuri no Tori 4:312a
Myōen 5:290a
Tankai 7:343b
Unkei 8:172a
Yamaguchi no Atai Ōguchi 8:294b
modern
Asakura Fumio 1:94b
Hiragushi Denchū 3:142b-143a
Horiuchi Masakazu 3:228b
Noguchi, Isamu 6:31b
Ogiwara Morie 6:70b
Takada Hiroatsu 7:310b
Takamura Kōun 7:316b
Takeuchi Kyūichi 7:326a
modern
Sculpture. *See* **Buddhist sculpture; Masks; Sculpture, modern**
Sculpture, modern 7:43b-44b
international participation 7:44b
Meiji and Taishō (1912-1926) 7:43b-44a
neoclassicism 7:44a
object in space 7:44b
Ogiwara Morie 7:*44b*
Onna (Woman) 7:*44b*
outdoor 7:44b
Rōen (The Aging Monkey) 7:*43a*
romanticism 7:44a-44b
Shōwa period 7:44a-44b
Takamura Kōun 7:*43a*
Western-style 7:43b-44a
See also Sculptors
Sculpture, premodern. *See* **Buddhist sculpture**
Sculptures
haniwa 3:97b-98a
SDF 7:58b-60b
Sea bream [(tai) family Sparidae] 2:284a; 5:352a-352b; 7:45a
Sea cucumbers [(namako) class Holothuroidea] 2:287a; 7:45a
Seafood 7:179b
Seagulls. *See* **Gulls**
Seals 4:*145a*; 7:45b-46a
artist's 6:281b
diplomatic 2:99b-100a
tensho 1:233b
Seamen's Insurance Law 6:172b
Sea of Japan 7:46a
Sea of Japan, Battle of. 日本海海戦 *See* **Tsushima, Battle of**
Search and seizure (sōsaku, sashiosae) 2:49b
Seas, marginal 4:8b
Seasonal festival 7:58a-58b
Seasonal workers
dekasegi 2:83b
Seasonings 2:21a-21b
Seasons 4:8a
festivals 2:254a
folk beliefs 2:297a-297b
folk religion 2:298b
haiku 3:81b-82a
Sea urchins [(uni) class Echinoidea] 7:46a-46b
Seaweed 7:46b
Seaweed cultivation 2:284a; 7:46b, *47a*
Sebald, William Joseph 7:47a
Sebiki Kemi 畝引検見 4:191a
Seburi Mountains 背振山地 7:48b
Sechie-zumō 節会相撲 4:82a
SECOM Co, Ltd 7:47a-47b
Secondary education. *See* **Education, secondary**
Secondary industries 6:239b; 7:47b
"Secondary unions" 4:359b
Second National Bank 4:184b
Second United Front 7:47b-48a
Secret agents
ommitsu 6:102b-103a
Secret History of the Mongols 4:18b
Secret language 3:303b-304a
"Secret Selection of Dust and Motes" 6:351b-352a
Sect Shintō 教派神道 2:300b; 7:48a, 137a
Sect Shintō, Association of 教派神道連合会 7:48a-48b
Secularism 6:204a, 292b
Securities
American Depositary Receipts (ADR) 1:51b
bonds, government 1:160a
fixed-interest 1:160a
Securities Bureau of the Ministry of Finance 7:48b
Securities Exchange Law 1:8b-9a; 7:48b, 247a-247b, 254a
auditing practices 1:9a
financial reporting requirements 2:277b-278a
tax accounting 7:352a
Securities Investment Trust Law 3:327b

Security Consultative Committee
United States-Japan security treaties ······ **8**:167a
Sedōka 旋頭歌
waka ······ **8**:202b
Seedlings Law ······ **1**:30a
Sefuri Mountains 背振山地 ······ **7**:48b
Segawa Jokō ······ 瀬川如皐 ······ **7**:48b
Segregation of Japanese schoolchildren in the United States ······ **4**:14a; **7**:48b-49a
Sei ······ 生 ······ **7**:359a
Seian Jiken ······ 西安事件 ······ **8**:281a-281b
Seibo ······ **7**:49a
kaeshi ······ **4**:102a
Seibu Department Stores, Ltd · **7**:49a, 55a
Seibu Railway Co, Ltd ······ **7**:49b
Tsutsumi Yasujirō ······ **8**:119a
Seibutsu ······ 静物 ······ **7**:167a
Seichōkai ······ **5**:18b
Seichō no Ie ······ 生長の家 ······ **7**:49b
Taniguchi Masaharu ······ **7**:341b
Seidan ······ 政談 ······ **7**:49b
Seidō ······ 西堂 ······ **7**:49b
Seidōki jidai ······ 青銅器時代 ······ **1**:173b-174a
Seidōkyō ······ **1**:174a
Seifukugumi ······ 制服組 ······ **7**:58b
Seifū sagen ······ 清風瑣言 ······ **8**:126b
Seiiki monogatari (Account of the West) ······ 西域物語 ······ **8**:242a
Seii tai shōgun ······ 征夷大将軍 **3**:172b; **4**:122a, 192b
Seiji Kenkyūkai ······ **1**:2a
Seiji Kōgaku Kenkyūjo ······ **4**:275a
Seiji Shōsetsu ······ **7**:50a-50b, 255b
new literature ······ **7**:50a
rehabilitation of novel ······ **7**:50a
significance ······ **7**:50a
Seikadō Bunko 静嘉堂文庫 · **5**:277a; **7**:50b
Seikanron ······ 征韓論 ······ **7**:50b-51a
Seikan Tunnel 青函トンネル
Tappizaki ······ **7**:346a
Seikatsu Tsuzurikata Undō ······ 生活綴り方運動 ······ **7**:51a
Seiken igen ······ 靖献遺言 ······ **1**:95b; **7**:51b
Seiki ······ 清輝 ······ **8**:334a
Seikōkai ······ 聖公会 ······ **7**:51b
Seikōsha Co, Ltd ······ **4**:200b
Seikyōsha (Society for Political Education) ······ 政教社 ······ **7**:51b
Miyake Setsurei ······ **5**:218b
Shiga Shigetaka ······ **7**:91b
Seikyō yōroku ······ 聖教要録 · **4**:247a; **7**:51b; **8**:290a
Seimeikei ······ 生命刑 ······ **7**:140b
Seimi kaisō ······ 舎密開宗 ······ **8**:125b
Seimikyoku ······ 舎密局 ······ **7**:51b-52a
Seimino ······ **7**:249b
Seinan no Eki ······ 西南の役 ······ **7**:30a
Seinan Sensō. *See* **Satsuma Rebellion**
Seinen Bungaku Kai ······ **5**:18b
Seinen gakkō ······ 青年学校 ······ **7**:52a
training ······ **2**:183b
Seinen Geijutsu Ha ······ **5**:19a
Sei no yōkyū to bungaku ······ 生の要求と文学 ······ **4**:165a
Seiōbo ······ 西王母 ······ **5**:295b
Seirigaku ······ 生理学 ······ **4**:167b
Seiryōji engi emaki ······ 清凉寺縁起絵巻 ······ **4**:149b
Seiryōki ······ 清良記 ······ **7**:52a
Seiryūsha (Blue Dragon Society)
modern painting ······ **6**:157b
Seiryūtō-gata sekki ······ 青竜刀型石器 ······ **7**:248a
Seisetsu igen sūyō ······ 西説医原枢要 ······ **7**:316b
Seishin shugi (spiritualism) ······ **4**:233a
Seishin shūyō ······ **3**:63a
Seishō ······ 政商 ······ **7**:52a
kan'ei jigyō haraisage ······ **4**:138a
Sei Shōnagon ······ 清少納言 · **1**:18a; **2**:280a; **5**:325a; **7**:52a-54a
butterflies ······ **1**:226a
classical Japanese language ······ **1**:322a
feminine language ······ **2**:250b
Fujiwara no Kintō ······ **2**:352a
Fujiwara no Teishi ······ **2**:356b
literary significance ······ **7**:53b-54a
Makura no sōshi ······ **5**:34a-34b; **7**:52b-53a
personality ······ **7**:53a-53b
private life and career ······ **7**:53b
Seisho no kenkyū (Bible studies) ······ 聖書の研究 ······ **6**:144a
Russo-Japanese War ······ **6**:346b
Uchimura Kanzō ······ **8**:124b
Seishū ······ 勢州 ······ **3**:337b
Seismologists
Milne, John ······ **5**:175a
Ōmori Fusakichi ······ **6**:103a
Seismology ······ **2**:140b
Seisonkaku ······ 成巽閣 ······ **5**:276b
Seisuishō ······ 醒睡笑 ······ **1**:62a-63a; **6**:282a
Seitai ······ **4**:263a
Seitai no Eki ······ 征台の役 ······ **7**:309a-309b
Seitaisho ······ 政体書 **7**:16b, 54a, 55a
Fukuoka Takachika ······ **2**:365b
Seitō ······ 青鞜 · **7**:54b; **8**:297a
Seitōsha ······ 青鞜社**7**:54a-54b; **8**:289b
Hiratsuka Raichō ······ **3**:146a
Itō Noe ······ **3**:355a
Kamichika Ichiko ······ **4**:126a
Seiwa Genji. 清和源氏 *See* **Minamoto family**
Seiyō dōchū hizakurige ······ 西洋道中膝栗毛 ······ **4**:135a
Seiyō jijō ······ 西洋事情 **1**:207b; **2**:368a; **4**:387a; **7**:54b-55a
Seiyō kibun ······ 西洋紀聞 · **1**:72b; **7**:192b; **8**:241b
Seiyō zasshi (Journal of Western Affairs) 西洋雑誌 ······ **6**:245b
Seiyū Hontō (True Seiyū Party) ······ 政友本党 · **6**:211a; **7**:55a, 66b
Kenseikai ······ **4**:198a
Rikken Minseitō ······ **6**:315a
Tokonami Takejirō ······ **8**:44a
Seiyūkai. 政友会 *See* **Rikken Seiyūkai**
Seiyū Stores, Ltd ······ **7**:55a
Seiza ("quiet sitting") ······ **6**:261b
Seizonken ······ **7**:55a-55b
Seizure ······ **7**:55b
Seji kembunroku ······ 世事見聞録 ······ **7**:55b
Sekai ······ 世界 ······ **7**:55b-56a
Iwanami Shoten Publishers ······ **3**:361a
Sekai fujin ······ 世界婦人 · **2**:362a; **7**:56a
Sekai Heiwa Apīru Shichinin Iinkai **1**:340a
Sekaihō no riron ······ 世界法の理論 ······ **7**:337b
Sekai Keizai Hihan Kai ······ **1**:84a-84b
Sekai Kirisutokyō Tōitsu Shinrei Kyōkai ······ **3**:216b-217a
Sekai Kyūsei Kyō ······ 世界救世教 ······ **7**:56a
Okada Mokichi ······ **6**:78b
Sekai Meshiya Kyō ······ 世界メシア教 ······ **7**:56a
Sekai no meisaku (World Masterpieces) 世界の名作 ······ **6**:275b
Seken musuko katagi ······ 世間子息気質 ······ **8**:144b
Seken tekake katagi ······ 世間妾形気 ······ **8**:126a
Sekibō ······ **7**:247b
Seki (city) ······ 関 ······ **7**:56a
Seki (town) ······ 関 ······ **7**:56a-56b
Sekigahara ······ 関ケ原 ······ **7**:56b, 274b
Gifu Prefecture ······ **3**:31a-31b
Ōgaki ······ **6**:68a
Sekigahara, Battle of ······ 関ケ原の戦 · **1**:83b; **5**:299a; **7**:9a, 25b, 56b, 98b, 101b
Date Masamune ······ **2**:78a
fudai ······ **2**:340b
Fukushima Masanori's role ······ **2**:366b
Ishida Mitsunari ······ **3**:340a
Konishi Yukinaga ······ **4**:270b
Tōdō Takatora ······ **8**:34b-35a
Tokugawa Ieyasu ······ **3**:186a; **8**:50b
tozama (outside vassals) ······ **8**:97a
Uesugi family ······ **8**:129a
warrior government ······ **8**:230a
Sekigunha. *See* **Red Army faction**
Seki Hironao ······ 瀬木博尚 ······ **7**:56b
Hakuhōdō, Inc ······ **3**:88a
Sekihōji ······ 石峰寺 ······ **3**:353b
Sekimon Shingaku. *See* **Shingaku**
Sekine Shōroku · 関根祥六 ······ **6**:27a
Sekino Tadasu ······ 関野貞 ······ **1**:79b
Seki no to 関の扉
tokiwazu-bushi ······ **8**:43b
Sekirankai ······ 赤瀾会 · **7**:57a; **8**:260b
Itō Noe ······ **3**:355a
Tanno Setsu ······ **7**:344a
Yamakawa Kikue ······ **8**:297a
Sekirei ······ **8**:200b-201a
Sekisen ······ 関銭 ······ **7**:57a
Sekisho ······ 関所 · **4**:153b; **7**:57a
Sekisui Chemical Co, Ltd ······ **7**:57b
Sekisui House, Ltd ······ **7**:57b
Seki Takakazu ······ 関孝和 ······ **7**:57b
natural sciences ······ **5**:355b
Takebe Katahiro ······ **7**:321b
Sekitori ······ **7**:272a, 273a
Sekiwake ······ **7**:272a
Sekiya Kiyokage 関谷清景
earth sciences ······ **2**:140a
Sekkan ······ **7**:248a
Sekkan seiji ······ 摂関政治 ······ **6**:286a-288a
Sekke shōgun ······ 摂家将軍 ······ **7**:57b-58a
Sekki ······ 節気 · **1**:231a, 259b
Sekku ······ 節句 **2**:260a; **7**:58a-58b
"Selections of Poetry in the New Style" (Shintaishi shō) ······ **8**:216a
Self-defense, national right of ······ **7**:60b
Self Defense Forces (SDF) · **1**:219a; **2**:52a; **6**:198b; **7**:58b-60b; **8**:344b
arms and equipment ······ **7**:60a-60b
budget ······ **7**:59b-60a
constitutionality ······ **2**:218a
constitution and SDF ······ **7**:60b
defense buildup ······ **7**:60a
duties and operations ······ **7**:59a-59b
education and training ······ **7**:60a
history ······ **7**:58b-59a
judicial review ······ **4**:79b
maritime ······ **2**:231b
Naganuma case ······ **5**:303a
national defense ······ **5**:336b-338b
National Defense Academy ······ **5**:338b
National Police Reserve ······ **5**:345b
national right of self-defense ······ **7**:60b
Occupation ······ **6**:54b
organization and command ······ **7**:59a
pacifism ······ **6**:145a
personnel ······ **7**:59b
United States ······ **8**:160a

United States-Japan security treaties ········ 8:166b
United States military bases disputes ········ 8:168a
units ········ 7:60a
Self Defense Forces Law ········ 7:59a
Self-employment ···· 2:210b; 4:353b; 7:60b
Self-governing bodies ········ 7:207a
Self-help ········ 7:60b-61a
Self Help (Saigoku risshi hen) ····· 5:315a
Self Help Society ········ 6:321a
Sembakoki ········ 千歯扱 ········ 7:61a
Sembazuru (Thousand Cranes) ········ 千羽鶴 4:176b; 6:230a
Sembetsu ········ 2:249a
Sembon Matsubara ········ 千本松原 ········ 7:61a
Semburi *(Swertia japonica)* ···· 7:61a-61b
Sembutsu ········ 1:176a-176b
Semenov, Grigorii Mikhailovich ···· 7:61b
Semi ········ 1:315a
Semiconductor industry
Ibuka Masaru ········ 3:254a
silicon production ········ 7:111b
Semimaru ········ 蟬丸 ····· 7:61b-62a
Semmen koshakyō ········ 扇面古写経 ········ 7:266b
Semmin ········ 賤民 · 2:104a; 7:62a
ritsuryō system ········ 6:324a
Semmon gakkō ········ 7:62a; 8:170a
development ········ 2:175b-176a
training ········ 2:183b
Semmyō ········ 宣命 ····· 7:62a-62b
Rikkokushi ········ 6:316a
Sempai-kōhai ········ 7:62b
gakubatsu ········ 3:4b
Sempūyō ········ 1:153a-153b
Sen ········ 8:323b
Senaga Kamejirō ········ 瀬長亀次郎 ········ 7:63a
Senate ········ 3:22a
Sencha ········ 7:365a
Senchaku hongan nembutsushū ········ 選択本願念仏集 ·· 4:67b; 7:63a
Senchakushū ······ 選択集 ·· 3:220a-220b; 5:359b; 7:63a
Senchimentaru jānī ········ 感傷旅行 ········ 7:335b
Sendai (Honshū) ····· 仙台 ···· 7:*63a*, 63b
Sendai (Kyūshū) ····· 川内 ········ 7:63b
Sendai Bay ········ 仙台湾 ········ 7:63b
Sendaigawa ········ 川内川 ········ 7:63b
Sendai Plain ····· 仙台平野 ········ 7:63b
Sendan ········ 1:291b
Sendoki jidai ·· 先土器時代 ··· 6:233a-233b
Sengai Gibon ···· 仙厓義梵 · 1:194a; 7:63b; 8:*374b*
Idemitsu Art Gallery ········ 3:258b
"Sengen hitotsu" 宣言一つ ········ 1:84b
Sengen Shrine ··· 浅間神社 · 2:359b; 7:64a, 153b
Sengokubune ······ 千石船 ········ 4:112b
Sengoku daimyō 戦国大名 1:212a; 3:175a; 7:64a
Sengokuhara ······ 仙石原 ········ 7:64a
Sengoku period · 戦国時代 ····· 7:64a-64b
kabegaki ········ 4:90a
Ōnin War ········ 6:106b
samurai ········ 7:8a
Sen Hime ········ 千姫 ····· 7:64b-65a
Senior councillors ········ 6:334a-334b
Seniority system ········ 2:34a, 36a, 211a; 7:65a-65b, 214a
managerial ideology ········ 5:92a-92b
job tenure ········ 4:356b-357b
occupational structure ········ 6:56a
retirement ········ 6:306b
women in ········ 8:265b
Seni Pramot ········ 2:339b; 7:65b
Senji ········ 宣旨 ········ 7:65b
rinji ········ 6:318a
Senjinkun ········ 戦陣訓 ········ 7:65b
Senjōgahara ····· 戦場ケ原 ········ 7:65b
Senjōgatake ····· 仙丈ケ岳 ········ 7:66a
Senjōsan ········ 船上山 ········ 7:66a
Senjuji ········ 専修寺 ········ 7:66a
Senju Seijūsho 千住製絨所 ········ 7:66a
Senju Woolen Mill ········ 7:66a
Senkaku ········ 仙覚 ········ 7:66a
Man'yōshū exegesis ········ 5:110a
Senkaku Islands · 尖閣諸島 ········ 7:66a
Senkaku Islands, disputes over. *See* **Territory of Japan**
Senkan ········ 8:231a
Senkan Yamato (Battleship Yamato) ········ 戦艦大和 ········ 8:319b
Senkawa Aqueduct ········ 7:332b
Senke Motomaro 千家元麿 ········ 7:66b
Senki ········ 戦旗 ········ 7:66b
Senkō sanzenri (Three Thousand Miles Underground) ········ 潜行三千里 ········ 8:114a
Senku
Rōnōha ········ 6:337b
Shinjinkai ········ 7:115b
Senkyo kanshō ·· 選挙干渉 ········ 7:66b
Shinagawa Yajirō ········ 7:109a
"Senkyūhyaku nijūhachinen sangatsu jūgonichi" ········ 4:237b; 7:242a
Sennan ········ 泉南 ········ 7:66b
Sennimbari ········ 千人針 ········ 7:67a
Sennin ········ 仙人 · 5:295b-296a; 7:67a
Sen no Rikyū ······ 千利休 ·· 1:136a, 158a; 2:21b, 289b; 3:197a; 4:337a; 7:67a-67b
Furuta Oribe ········ 2:373b
tea ceremony ········ 7:361a
tea ceremony fans ········ 2:248a
tea gardens ········ 3:9b
Sen'oku Hakkokan ········ 泉屋博古館 ········ 7:67b
Senryōbako ········ 7:67b
Senryū. 川柳 *See* **Zappai and senryū**
Senryūhyō mankuawase ········ 川柳評万句合 ········ 4:157a
Senshi bankō ···· 千紫万紅 ········ 4:199b
Senshindō satsuki
Ōshio Heihachirō ········ 6:126b
Sensō to heiwa (War and Peace) ········ 戦争と平和 ········ 8:319b
Sensuijima ········ 仙酔島 ········ 7:67b
Sentai butsu ········ 7:67b
Senten sōhō ····· 先天相法 ········ 6:187a
Sentō ········ 1:146a
Sentsūzan ········ 船通山 ········ 7:67b
Sen'yū ········ 7:67b-68a
Sen'yū to shoyū ········ 専有と所有 ········ 7:255b
Senzaishū ········ 千載集 ····· 7:68a-68b
Senzai wakashū ········ 千載和歌集 · 4:198b; 5:39a; 7:68a-68b, 96b, 302a
compilation ········ 7:68a
composition and structure ········ 7:68a
Fujiwara no Ietaka ········ 2:351a
Fujiwara no Toshinari ········ 2:356b
Jakuren ········ 4:1b
major poets ········ 7:68a
poetic styles ········ 7:68a-68b
Senzui byōbu ···· 山水屛風 ····· 7:42a-42b
Senzui Kawaramono ········ 山水河原者 ········ 3:9b
Seoul, Treaty of ········ 4:280b; 7:68b
Kapsin Political Coup ········ 4:156b
Seoul-Inch'ōn Railroad ········ 4:281b
Seoul-Pusan Railroad ········ 4:281b
Seppuku ········ 切腹 ········ 2:274b; 7:68b
See also **Harakiri**
Sequential voicing ········ 6:296a-296b
Sericulture ········ 7:68b-69a
Serizawa Chōsuke ········ 3:358a
Serizawa Keisuke ········ 芹沢銈介 ·· 2:294a; 7:69a
Serizawa Kōjirō ········ 芹沢光治良 ····· 7:69a-69b
Serow. *See* **Kamoshika**
Servants, hereditary ········ 2:340b
Service population ········ 7:12a
Sessai. 折柴 *See* **Takii Kōsaku**
Sesshō ········ 摂政 · 2:204a; 7:69b
Sesshū Tōyō ···· 雪舟等楊 · 1:156a, 192b, 193a; 3:*306b*; 6:*152b*; 7:*17a*, 42b, 69b-70a; 8:*371a*
Gakuō Zōkyū ········ 3:4b
Haboku Landscape ········ 7:*69a*
ink painting ········ 3:306b
sansuiga (landscape painting) ········ 7:17b
Sesson Shūkei ··· 雪村周継 7:42b, 70a, *70b*
Sesson Yūbai ··· 雪村友梅 · 1:150b; 7:70b
Setagawa ········ 瀬田川 ········ 7:70b
Setagaya Ward ·· 世田谷区 ····· 7:70b-71a
Seta no Karahashi ········ 瀬田唐橋 ········ 4:333b
Setchōshū ········ 節用集 ········ 7:72b
Setchūbai ········ 雪中梅 ········ 7:255b
Setchūgakuha ··· 折衷学派 ········ 7:71a
Seto ········ 瀬戸 ········ 7:71a
Seto Naikai. 瀬戸内海 *See* **Inland Sea**
Setō Shōji ······· 瀬藤象二 ········ 7:71a
Setouchi ········ 瀬戸内 ········ 7:71a
Setouchi Harumi ········ 瀬戸内晴美 ········ 7:71a
Seto ware ········ 瀬戸焼 ········ 1:258b; 2:295b; 4:337a; 7:71a-71b
jar ········ 1:*257b*
museums ········ 5:279b
tea ceremony ········ 7:360b, 364b
Setsu ········ 節 ········ 1:231a
Setsubun ········ 節分 ·· 2:259a-259b; 4:*327a*, 327b; 7:71b
cooking ········ 2:22a
religious symbolism ········ 6:296a
Setsuhei
Tominaga Nakamoto ········ 8:71b
Setsuwa ········ 1:180b; 3:154a
Setsuwa bungaku (tale literature) ······ 説話文学 ··· 5:26a, 246b; 7:72a-72b, 131b
Kodai kenkyū ········ 4:240b
Setsuwa-mono (tales of the strange) ······ 説話物 ········ 8:144a
Setsuyōshū ········ 節用集 7:64b, 72b-73a
Setting Sun, The ········ 2:80a
Settlement regions (teijūken)
urban planning ········ 8:180b
Settsu ········ 摂津 ········ 7:73a
Seven Deities of Good Fortune ··· 5:296a; 7:73a, 250a
Daikokuten ········ 2:60b
dolls ········ 2:129b
Ebisu ········ 2:60b, 143b
Ōkuninushi no Mikoto ········ 6:97b
Shintō family altars ········ 7:137b
Seven Sages ········ 8:173a
Seven Sages in a Bamboo Grove · 4:110b
"Seven Sages of Renga" ········ 7:320a
Seven Samurai ·· 七人の侍 2:272a; 4:317b; 7:73a
Seven Shingon Patriarchs ········ 6:227a
Seventeen-Article Constitution ··· 6:205a; 7:73a-73b, 190b, 264a

China ········· 1:281b
codes of conduct ········· 1:207a
Shōtoku ········· 7:171b
Taika Reform ········· 7:295b-296a
Seventh-Day Adventists ········· 6:144b
Seven-Volume Haikai Collection ········· 3:78a
Sewa-mono (domestic plays) ········· 世話物 ········· 4:91a, 92a, 93a-94a; 5:234b
acting style ········· 4:94a
dialogue ········· 4:94a
costume, wig and makeup ········· 4:95b
Sewing box ········· 3:103b
Sewing ceremonies ········· 3:104a
Sexagenary cycle. *See* **Jikkan jūnishi**
Sex education ········· 7:73b
Sex in Japanese folk culture ········· 7:73b-74a
folk song ········· 7:73b-74a
religious observances ········· 7:74a
Sexual discrimination ········· 2:229b-230a
Seyakuin ········· 施薬院 ········· 7:74a
Kōfukuji building ········· 4:243b
Kōmyō, Empress ········· 4:268b
Shadan therapy ········· 6:261b
Shaga ········· 3:331b
Shain (permanent members of a company) ········· 4:344b
Shaka ········· 1:176a
Shakaigaku gairon ········· 社会学概論 ········· 7:319b
Shakai keizaigaku ········· 社会経済学 ········· 4:135b
Shakai Minshu Rengō ········· 社会民主連合 ········· 8:154b
Shakai Minshutō (Social Democratic Party) ········· 社会民主党 ········· 1:2b, 40b; 6:210b; 7:74a-74b; 8:349a
Shakai mondai ··· 社会問題 ········· 4:135b
Shakai Minshūtō ········· 社会民衆党 ········· 7:74b
Shakai mondai kenkyū ········· 社会問題研究 ········· 4:180b
Shakai Shimin Rengō. *See* **United Social Democratic Party**
Shakai shōsetsu ········· 4:180a
"Shakaishugi hyōron" ········· 社会主義評論 ········· 4:180b
Shakai Shugi Kenkyūkai (Socialist Study Party) ········· 社会主義研究会 ········· 1:2a, 72a; 6:210b; 7:74b
Shakai Shugi Kyōkai (Socialist Association) ········· 社会主義協会 ········· 6:210b
Tazoe Tetsuji ········· 7:359a-359b
Shakai shugi shinzui ········· 社会主義神髄 ········· 4:297b
Shakai Taishūtō (Socialist Masses Party) 社会大衆党 ········· 1:96a; 3:198b; 6:211a; 7:74b
Asō Hisashi ········· 1:102b-103a
founding ········· 1:2b
tenkō ········· 8:7a
Shakaitō ········· 社会党 ········· 7:74b-75a
Shakai to kokka ········· 社会と国家 ········· 7:319b
Shaka Triad ········· 1:*197a*
Shaken ········· 7:251b
Shakkintō ········· 借金党 ········· 4:267a
Shakotan Peninsula ········· 積丹半島 ········· 7:75a
Shakubyōshi ········· 4:108a
Shaku Chōkū ········· 釈迢空 ········· 6:118b
Shakuhachi ········· 7:75a-76a
history ········· 7:75a-75b
jiuta ········· 4:64b
music ········· 7:75b
musical instruments ········· 5:282b
Shakunage ········· 6:308a
Shaku nihongi ··· 釈日本紀 ········· 7:76a
Shaku Sōen ········· 釈宗演 ········· 7:76a, 281b
Shaku Unshō ········· 釈雲照 ········· 5:239a
Shakuyaken. *See* Leased house rights
Shakuyaku. *See* **Peonies**
Shamanism ········· 7:76a-76b
kagura ········· 4:107b
miko ········· 5:172a
Takamagahara ········· 7:314a
women in ········· 8:256b, 258a
yamabushi ········· 8:288a
Shame ········· 3:83b-84a
Shamisen ········· 1:161b; 7:75b, 76b-77a
film accompaniment ········· 2:267b
folk music accompaniment ········· 2:301a
kabuki music ········· 4:99a
musical instruments ········· 5:282b
nagauta ········· 5:307b
Okinawa ········· 6:86b
ryūkōka ········· 6:354a
Shamoji (spatula) ········· 2:25a
Shand, Alexander Allan ········· 1:8a
Shandao ········· 4:67a-67b
Shandong (Shantung) Question ········· 4:367a-367b; 7:77a-77b
Washington Conference ········· 8:234b
Shanghai Conspiracy: The Sorge Spy Ring ········· 8:253b
Shanghai Incident ········· 7:77b-78a, 92a
League of Nations ········· 4:373b
nationalist government ········· 1:289a
Sino-Japanese War 1937-1945 ········· 7:199b
Shanghai International Settlement ········· 7:78a-78b; 8:252b
Shanhai (Shanghai) ·· 上海 ········· 7:116b, 175b; 8:332b
Shanhai Jiken ··· 上海事件 ········· 7:77b-78a
Shanhai jing (Shan-hai ching; Classic of Mountains and Waterways) ········· 8:197a
Shan-hou Chieh-k'uan ········· 6:302a
Shanhou Jiekuan ········· 6:302a
Sharaku ········· 写楽 ········· 7:78b-79b; 8:*143a*
drawings ········· 7:79a
identity ········· 7:79a-79b
influence ········· 7:79b
prints ········· 7:78b-79a
Sanogawa Ichimatsu III ········· 7:*78b*
Sharebon ········· 洒落本 ········· 5:49a; 7:18a, 79b-80a; 8:141b
gesaku ········· 3:28b
Santō Kyōden ········· 7:18a
Shikitei Samba ········· 7:97a
Tamenaga Shunsui ········· 7:333b-334a
Shareholders, general meetings of 7:247a
Shares ········· 4:70a-70b
Sharp Corporation ········· 7:80a-80b
Shasei ········· 3:79b
Shaseiga (painting subjects) ········· 6:159a
Shasekishū ········· 沙石集 ········· 7:80b-81a
author ········· 7:80b-81a
Shasō ········· 社倉 ········· 7:81a
Shaw, Glenn William ········· 7:81a
Shayō (The Setting Sun) ········· 斜陽 ········· 6:230b
Shazensōsha ········· 車前草社 ········· 5:19b
Shellfish [(kai) phylum Mollusca] ········· 7:81a-82b
important species ········· 7:81b-82b
Shell mounds ········· 貝塚 ········· 1:75a, 160a; 4:163b; 6:235a; 7:82b-83a
Shell Sekiyu Co, Ltd ········· 7:83a-83b
Shenghuo zhoukan ········· 8:380a
Shen Nanpin (Shen Nan-p'in) ········· 1:211a; 5:305a; 7:83b
Shen Nanpin school ········· 5:305b-306a
Shen Weijing (Shen Wei-ching) ········· 7:83b
Shenxiang quanbian ········· 6:160b
Shiatsu ········· 7:83b
Shiawase no kiiroi hankachi (Yellow Handkerchief of Happiness) ········· 8:290a
Shiba family ········· 斯波氏 ········· 7:83b-84a
kanrei ········· 4:151a
Shiba Kōkan ········· 司馬江漢 ········· 7:84a
Shibano Ritsuzan 柴野栗山 ········· 7:84a-84b
Shibaraku ········· 暫 ········· 4:*92b*, 98a
Shiba Ryōtarō 司馬遼太郎 ········· 7:84b, 103b
Shibata ········· 新発田 ········· 7:84b
Shibata Katsuie 柴田勝家 ········· 7:84b
castle town ········· 2:363a
free markets ········· 6:283a
Shibata Keita ········· 柴田桂太 ········· 1:156a, 268b; 7:84b
Shibata Kyūō ········· 柴田鳩翁 ········· 7:84b-85a
Shingaku ········· 7:112a
Shibata Renzaburō ········· 柴田錬三郎 ········· 7:85a
Shibata Shō ········· 柴田翔 ········· 7:85a
Shiba Tatto ········· 司馬達等 ········· 7:85a
Shibata Zeshin ········· 柴田是真 ········· 7:85a-85b
Shiba Teikichi ··· 斯波貞吉 ········· 8:296a
Shiba Yoshimasa 斯波義将 ········· 3:173b
Shiberia Shuppei ········· 7:192a-192b
Shiberiya monogatari ········· シベリヤ物語 ········· 3:108a
Shibetsu ········· 士別 ········· 7:85b
Shibori ········· 8:29b-30a
Shiborizome ········· 8:29b-30a
Shibue Chūsai ··· 渋江抽斎 ········· 1:155b; 7:85b
Shibugaki ········· 渋柿 ········· 7:85b
Shibui ········· 6:361a; 7:85b-86a; 8:197a
Shibukan ········· 四部官 ········· 7:150b-151a
Shibukawa ········· 渋川 ········· 7:86a
Shibukawa Shunkai ········· 渋川春海 ········· 7:86a
Shibusawa Eiichi 渋沢栄一 ········· 2:58b, 332b; 7:52a, 86a-86b, 87b
Furukawa Ichibei ········· 2:372b
Hakodate Dock Co, Ltd ········· 3:86a
Ōji Paper Co, Ltd ········· 6:77a
Shibusawa Keizō 渋沢敬三 ········· 2:295b; 7:86b
Shibushi Bay ········· 志布志湾 ········· 1:83a; 7:86b
Shibuya Tengai · 渋谷天外 ········· 7:86b
Shibuya Ward ········· 渋谷区 ········· 7:87a
Shichi ········· 質 ········· 7:87a
Shichibukin tsumitate ········· 七分金積立 ········· 7:87a-87b
Shichidaiji junrei shiki ········· 七大寺巡礼私記 ········· 1:79a
Shichifukujin ········· 7:73a
Shichigenkin ········· 7:87b
Shichigosan ········· 2:*261b*, 262a; 7:87b
Shichihakase Jiken ········· 七博士事件 ········· 7:87b-88a
Kanai Noburu ········· 4:135b
Shichiire ········· 4:117a
Shichijō Ōmiya bussho ········· 七条大宮仏所 ········· 3:313b
Shichikyō Ochi ·· 七卿落ち ········· 7:88a
Shichimi tōgarashi ········· 3:127b
Shichinin no samurai (Seven Samurai) ········· 七人の侍 ········· 2:*277a*; 7:73a
Shichirigahama ·· 七里ケ浜 ········· 7:88a
Shichiseisha (Seven Lives Society)
Uesugi Shinkichi ········· 8:130b
Shichiya ········· 7:88a
Shichō ········· 1:149a
Shida ········· 2:252a
Shide. *See* **Gohei**
Shidehara Kijūrō ········· 幣原喜重郎 7:86b, 88a-89a
emperor's renunciation of divinity ········· 2:209a

Shiden 私田 7:89a-89b
Shidō Bunan 至道無難 7:89b
Shidō yōroku 2:53a
Shie Incident 紫衣事件 7:89b, 255a
Shields 1:89b
Shien (old paper owl kite) 4:229b
Shier zhi 4:57a
"Shifun no Kao" 脂粉の顔 8:173a
Shigajiku ("painting and poetry scrolls") 4:116a; 6:151a
Shiga Kiyoshi 志賀潔 7:89b
Shiga Kōgen 志賀高原 7:89b
Shigaku 2:172b
Shigakukai 6:312a
Shigaku kenkyū hō (Methods of Historical Research) 7:109b-110a
Shigaku zasshi 2:115a; 6:312a
Shiga Naoya 志賀直哉 1:313b; 2:274a; 4:114a; 7:89b-90b, 103b
I-novel 3:312a
Shiga Prefecture 滋賀県 7:90b-91a
Shigaraki 信楽 7:91a
Shigaraki no Miya 紫香楽宮 7:91a
Shigaraki Palace 紫香楽宮 7:91a
Shigaraki ware 信楽焼 4:337a; 7:91a-91b, 256a
similarity to Iga ware 3:261b
Shiga Shigetaka 志賀重昻 5:11b; 7:51b, 91b
Shiga Yoshio 志賀義雄 4:12a; 7:91b
Shinjinkai 7:115b
Shigemasa 重政 3:149a
Shigemitsu Mamoru 重光葵 6:302a; 7:91b-92a, 278a
Shigenobu 重宣 3:149a
Shigeno Yasutsugu 重野安繹 7:50b, 92b
historiography 3:156a
Shigeta Sadakazu 重田貞一 4:61a-61b
Shigeyama Sengorō 茂山千五郎 4:*328b*
Shigeyama Sensaku 茂山千作 4:*328b-329a*
Shigi kempō 私擬憲法 7:92b
Shigisan 信貴山 7:92b
Shigisan engi emaki 信貴山縁起絵巻 1:137a; 2:199b; 7:92b-93a; 8:32a
The Flying Granary 7:*93a*
Shigisanji 信貴山寺 7:93a-93b
Shihō Kenshūjo. *See* **Legal Training and Research Institute**
Shihon keiretsu 3:295b; 4:189b
Shihōshō 司法省 7:93b
Shiiba 椎葉 7:93b
Shiin 1:183a
Shiina Etsusaburō 椎名悦三郎 4:285b-286a
Shiina Rinzō 椎名麟三 7:93b-94a
Christianity 4:32a
Shijin 詩人 4:139a
Shijing
Kokinshū 4:255a
Shi jing (Shih ching or Book of Odes) 8:209a
Shi ji (Records of the Historian)
Tokugawa Mitsukuni 8:51b
Shijōnawate 四条畷 7:94a
Shijō school. *See* **Maruyama-Shijō school**
Shijūhattai Butsu 7:94a, *94b*
Shijuku 7:94a-94b
Shika 2:82a
Shikakudake *(Chimonobambusa quadrangularis)* 1:136a
Shikan Gakkō Jiken 士官学校事件 6:41b-42a
Shikanki 史官記 3:219a
Shikano Buzaemon 鹿野武左衛門 6:282a
Shikanoshima 志賀島 7:94b
Shikashū 私家集 4:117a; 7:94b-95b
Shikatsube Magao 鹿都部真顔 7:95a
Shika wakashū 詞花和歌集 2:350a; 5:38a; 7:95a-95b
Fujiwara no Toshinari 2:357a
Shiki 志木 7:95b
Shiki 職 1:274a; 2:263b
shogunal bestowal 4:122a
Shikibō, Ltd 7:95b
Shikibuton 1:148b
Shikidō ōkagami 色道大鏡 7:95b-96a
Shiki-e (four seasons) paintings 8:309b
Shikikin. *See* **Deposit money**
Shikimi (*Illicium religiosum; Illicium anisatum*) 7:96a
Shikimoku 式目 7:96a
Shikinaisha 式内社 7:96a
Shikinai shrines 式内社 7:96a
Shiki no Miko 志貴皇子 7:96a-96b
Shikirisen 7:271a
Shikisha 7:96a
Shikishi
Shin kokinshū 7:120a
Shikishiban 7:278a
Shikishi, Princess 式子内親王 2:357b; 7:96b
Shiki sōka
subjects 6:159a
Shikitei Samba 式亭三馬 1:146a; 5:16b; 7:79a, 96b-97b
fūzoku shōsetsu 2:378a
kamiyui descriptions 4:127b
kokkeibon 4:256a
works 7:96a-97a
Shikken 執権 4:122a; 7:97b
hereditary nature 4:151a
rensho 6:301a
Shikkongōshin, statue of 1:*198b*
Shiko 7:272b
Shikoku
area 4:2b
population density 4:2b, 7a
Shikoku Electric Power Co, Ltd 7:97b
Shikoku Kantai Shimonoseki Hōgeki Jiken 四国艦隊下関砲撃事件 7:105b-106a
Shikoku karst 四国カルスト 7:97b
Shikoku Mountains 四国山脈 7:97b
Shikoku region 四国地方 7:97b-98a
Shikotan 色丹 7:98a
Shikotsu, Lake 支笏湖 7:98a
Shikotsu-Tōya National Park 支笏洞爺国立公園 4:79a; 7:98a
Shikunshi 四君子 5:311a-311b; 7:98a-98b
Shikyō ruijū 私教類聚 4:201b
Shima, George 4:22a
Shima 島 2:302a
Shimabara 島原 7:98b
Shimabara Peninsula 島原半島 7:98b
Shimabara Uprising 5:323a-323b; 7:98b
anti-Christian policy 3:188b
Dejima 2:83b
Dutch trade 2:135b
National Seclusion 5:347b
Tokugawa Iemitsu 8:48a
Shimada 島田 7:99a
Shimada Saburō 島田三郎 7:99a
Kakushin Kurabu 4:120a
Shimadzu Corporation 7:99a
Shima Hot Spring 四万温泉 7:99a
Shimai Sōshitsu 島井宗室 4:127b; 7:99a-99b
Shimai toshi 7:202a
Shimaji Mokurai 島地黙雷 7:99b
Fukuda Gyōkai 2:362a
Shimaki Akahiko 島木赤彦 1:74b; 7:99b
Shimaki Kensaku 島木健作 7:99b
Shimamura Hōgetsu 島村抱月 5:12b; 7:31a, 99b-100a
Shimanaka Incident 嶋中事件 2:360a; 7:100a
Shimanaka Yūsaku 嶋中雄作 7:100a-100b
Shimane Peninsula 島根半島 7:100b
Shimane Prefecture 島根県 7:100b-101a
Shimantogawa 四万十川 5:326b; 7:101a
Shimanto geosyncline 四万十地向斜 4:9b
Shimao Toshio 島尾敏雄 7:101a
Shima Peninsula 志摩半島 2:234b; 7:101a
Shimazaki Shōji
Shimura Takashi 7:108b
Shimazaki Tōson 島崎藤村 5:52a-52b; 7:101a-101b, 103b
Japan P.E.N. club 4:47b
naturalism 5:351a-351b
Shinshōsetsu 7:125b
Shimazono Junjirō 島薗順次郎 7:101b
Shimazu 島津 7:56b
Shimazu family 島津氏 7:101b-102b
Kagoshima 4:105a
Satsuma Province 7:29b
Shimazu Genzō 島津源蔵 7:102a
Shimazu Hisamitsu 島津久光 7:102a
Richardson Affair 6:311a
Shimazu Nariakira 島津斉彬 7:102a-102b
Shimazu Yasujirō 島津保次郎 2:269a; 7:102a
Kamiyama Sōjin 4:127b
Shimazu Yoshihiro 島津義弘 7:101b, 102b
invasions of Korea in 1592 and 1597 3:327b
Shimbunshi Hō 新聞紙法 6:236a
Shimbunshi Jōrei. *See* **Press Ordinance of 1875**
Shimbun shōsetsu 7:103a-104a
golden age 7:103b
growth and development 7:103a-103b
popularization 7:103b
postwar period 7:103b
Shimbutsu bunri 神仏分離 7:132a
Shimbutsu Shūgō. *See* **Syncretism**
Shimenawa 7:249b
Shintō 7:*128b*
shrines 7:180a
Shīmensu Jiken シーメンス事件 7:193a-193b
Shimizu 清水 7:*103a*, 104a
Shimizu Construction Co, Ltd 7:104a
Shimizu Hamaomi 清水浜臣 7:104a
Shimizu Hiroshi 清水宏 2:270a
Shimizu Muneharu 清水宗治 7:104a
Shimmei Masamichi 新明正道 7:104b
Shimmei-zukuri 7:271a

Shimmi Masaoki 新見正興 ······ **7**:104a
Shimminato 新湊 ······ **7**:104a
Shimminkai ······ **8**:281b
Shimmura Izuru 新村出 ······ **7**:104b
Shimobe 下部 ······ **7**:104b
Shimoda 下田 **2**:342b; **7**:104b
Shimodate 下館 ······ **7**:104b
Shimoda Utako 下田歌子 ······ **7**:105a
Shimofuri ······ **2**:25b
Shimo-Gamo Shrine
  Takehara ······ **7**:324a
Shimokita Peninsula
  下北半島 ······ **7**:105a
Shimokōbe Chōryū
  下河辺長流 ······ **7**:105a
  Man'yōshū study ······ **5**:110a
Shimokōbe Nagaru
  下河辺長流 ······ **7**:105a
Shimomoto Kenkichi
  下元建吉 ······ **7**:105a
Shimomura Kanzan
  下村観山 ··· **7**:105a-105b
Shimonaka Yasaburō
  下中弥三郎 ······ **7**:105b
  Committee of Seven to Appeal for World Peace ······ **1**:340a
  Heibonsha, Ltd, Publishers ······ **3**:122b
Shimonita 下仁田 ······ **7**:105b
Shimonoseki 下関 ······ **7**:105b
  Chōfu ······ **1**:298b
Shimonoseki, Treaty of
  下関条約 ·· **3**:196a; **5**:9b; **7**:106a-106b, 197b, 198b
  Komura Jutarō and ······ **4**:268a
  Mutsu Munemitsu ······ **5**:289a
  rejection ······ **4**:141a
  relations with China ······ **1**:286b
  Shanghai International Settlement ··· **7**:78a
  Sino-Japanese War of 1894-1895 ·· **7**:198b
  Tripartite Intervention ······ **8**:106b
Shimonoseki Aquarium ······ **7**:105b
Shimonoseki Bombardment 馬関戦争 · **1**:86a; **5**:319b; **7**:105b-106a
  Itō Hirobumi ······ **3**:352b
  Kiheitai ······ **4**:204b
  Takasugi Shinsaku ······ **7**:319b
Shimose gunpowder
  developer ······ **7**:106b
Shimose Masachika
  下瀬雅允 ······ **7**:106b
Shimo Suwa 下諏訪 ······ **7**:106b
Shimotsuke (*Spiraea japonica*) ······ **7**:106b-107a
Shimotsuke Incident
  Taira no Yoritsuna ······ **7**:302b
Shimotsuki kagura
  霜月神楽 ······ **4**:107b
Shimotsuma 下妻 ······ **7**:107a
Shimoyama Incident
  下山事件 ·· **7**:107a-107b, 147b
  Furuhata Tanemoto ······ **2**:371b
Shimoyama Sadanori 下山定則 ··· **7**:107a
Shimozawa Kan 子母沢寛 **2**:274a; **7**:107b
Shimpa 新派 ······ **2**:267b; **4**:218b; **7**:31a, 107b-108a
  Hanayagi Shōtarō ······ **3**:95a
  Kawakami Otojirō ······ **4**:181a
  Shinkokugeki ······ **7**:121a
Shimpa higeki ······ **2**:268b
Shimpai 信牌 ······ **7**:171a
Shimpan 親藩 ······ **1**:131b; **2**:340b; **3**:186a; **7**:108a
Shimpeitai Incident
  神兵隊事件 ··· **7**:108a-108b
  Daitōjuku ······ **2**:67b
Shimpotō 進歩党 **4**:141a; **7**:108b
  Tanaka Kakuei ······ **7**:337a
Shimpukuji-bon 真福寺本 ······ **4**:251b
Shimura Takashi 志村喬 ······ **7**:108b
Shin ······ **4**:141b, 295b
Shinabe (workers) 品部 ······ **1**:147b
Shinagawa Refractories Co, Ltd ·· **7**:108b
Shinagawa Ward 品川区 ······ **7**:108b
Shinagawa Yajirō
  品川弥二郎 · **1**:21b; **7**:109a
  Kokumin Kyōkai founder ······ **4**:260b
Shinanogawa 信濃川 ······ **7**:109a
Shinano mainichi shimbun
  信濃毎日新聞 ······ **8**:296a
Shinano Province 信濃国 ······ **5**:303a
Shina shisō kenkyū
  支那思想研究 ······ **7**:293a
Shin Buddhism ······ **4**:68a-69a
Shinchiku iwai ······ **4**:195a
Shinchō 新潮 ······ **7**:109a
  Shinkō Geijutsu Ha ······ **7**:119b
Shincho hyakushu (A Hundred New Volumes) 新著百種 ······ **4**:199a
Shinchō Kō ki 信長公記 ··· **7**:109a-109b
Shin chokusenshū (New Imperial Collection)
  新勅撰集 ······ **8**:212b
Shinchō Literary Prize ······ **6**:66b
Shinchōsha Company ······ **7**:109b
Shinden 神田 ······ **7**:109b
Shinden kaihatsu 新田開発 ··· **7**:109b-110a
Shinden-zukuri 寝殿造 ······ **3**:243b; **7**:110a-111a
  design ······ **7**:110b-111a
  Fujiwara culture ······ **2**:348a
  gardens ······ **3**:9a
  history ······ **7**:110b
  main hall ······ **7**:111a
Shindō Kaneto 新藤兼人 ······ **2**:275b; **7**:111a-111b
  Hadaka no shima ······ **3**:75a
Shin'ei. *See* **Shinyei Kaisha**
Shi nengō 私年号 ······ **1**:232a
Shin'en (The Imperial Mausoleum) 寝園 ······ **8**:332b
Shin-Etsu Chemical Co, Ltd ······ **7**:111b
Shin Fujin Kyōkai (New Woman's Association)
  新婦人協会 ······ **7**:111b; **8**:260b, 268b
  Hiratsuka Raichō ······ **3**:146a
  Oku Mumeo ······ **6**:96b
Shingaku 心学 ······ **6**:260b; **7**:111b-112a
  Ishida Baigan ······ **3**:339b-340a
  Nakazawa Dōni ······ **5**:320a
  Shibata Kyūō ······ **7**:84b-85a
  Teshima Toan ······ **8**:15a
Shingaku tokeigusa
  心学時計草 ······ **4**:61a
Shingei. *See* **Geiami**
Shingeki (magazine) 新劇
  film influence ······ **2**:268a
  shimpa ······ **7**:107b
  Shinshichō ······ **7**:124b
  ······ **7**:112a
Shingeki (theater) ······ **7**:112a-113b, 368a
Shingen Kahō 信玄家法 ······ **7**:113b
Shin Gesaku Ha 新戯作派 ······ **5**:19b
Shingon (mantra) 真言 **5**:102b; **6**:233a
Shingon sect ··· **1**:178b-179a; **7**:113b-115a
  Akishinodera ······ **1**:42a
  Amida ······ **4**:67a
  doctrines ······ **7**:225a
  Hasedera ······ **3**:106b-107a
  Jingoji ······ **4**:58b
  Jiun Onkō ······ **4**:64a-64b
  Kakuban ······ **4**:117b
  Kōfukuji ······ **4**:244a
  Kongōbuji ······ **4**:299a-299b
  Kūkai ······ **4**:304a
  mandalas ······ **5**:100a
  mantra ······ **6**:233a
  Mokujiki Ōgo ······ **5**:235b
  monasticism ······ **5**:237b-238a
  Mongaku ······ **5**:243a-243b
  Okadera ······ **6**:78b
  Ryōbu Mandara ······ **6**:347b
  Ryōbu Shintō ······ **6**:351a
  Shinshōji ······ **7**:125a
  Shigisanji ······ **7**:93a-93b
  Tōji ······ **8**:38b
Shingū 新宮 ······ **7**:115a
Shin Heike monogatari (New Tales of Heike)
  新平家物語 ······ **6**:221b
Shin Ikei 沈惟敬 ······ **7**:83b
Shinji, Lake 宍道湖 ······ **7**:115a
Shinjin ······ **4**:68b
Shinjin (The New Person)
  新人 ······ **2**:143a
"Shinjin Celluloid Workers Union"
  Shinjinkai ·· **1**:40a; **7**:91b, 115b-116a, 251b
  Kamei Katsuichirō ······ **4**:125a
  Sano Manabu ······ **7**:15b
Shinjinkai (New Man Society) 新人会 ··· **5**:316b-317a
Shinjitsushō-gyō
  Ryōbu Mandara ······ **6**:348a
Shin Jiyū Kurabu
  新自由クラブ ······ **5**:365a
Shinjō 新庄 ······ **7**:116a
Shinjō Basin 新庄盆地 ······ **7**:116a
Shinjō Hot Spring 新庄温泉 ······ **7**:116a
Shinjū ······ **4**:93b; **7**:95b, 262a
Shinju fujin (Lady Pearl)
  真珠夫人 ······ **6**:221a
Shinjuku Gyoen National Garden **7**:116a
Shinjuku Ward 新宿区 ······ **7**:116a
Shinjū Ten no Amijima (Love Suicide at Amijima; Double Suicide)
  心中天網島 ······ **2**:274b
Shinkai 神誠 ······ **4**:272a
  shinden kaihatsu ······ **7**:109b-110a
Shinka Jōrei 新貨条例 ······ **8**:323b
Shin kanazukai ······ **4**:134b
Shinkankai 新幹会 ······ **7**:196a
Shinkankaku school
  新感覚派 ······ **2**:378b; **7**:116a-116b, 175a
  Literary Age ······ **1**:209a
  Shinchō ······ **7**:109a
  Nakagawa Yoichi ······ **5**:313a
  Western literature in Japanese translation ······ **8**:248a
  Yokomitsu Riichi ······ **8**:331b-333b
Shinkansen ······ **2**:345a; **4**:336a; **6**:278a; **7**:116b-119a
  development ······ **7**:117a-117b
  extension ······ **4**:33b
  operation and maintenance ··· **7**:118a-119a
  power source ······ **7**:118a
  Shinkansen central control room ··· **7**:*117a*
  technical aspects ······ **7**:117b-118a
Shinkei 心敬 · **1**:181b; **5**:15a, 42b; **6**:298b-299a; **7**:80b, 119a
  Sasamegoto (Murmured Conversations) ······ **7**:23b
  Shinsen tsukubashū ······ **7**:124b
Shinkeishitsu ······ **5**:253b-254a
Shin kigen 新紀元 ······ **1**:2a
Shinkiron 慎機論 ······ **7**:119a
Shinkō Geijutsu Ha
  新興芸術派 · **2**:378b; **5**:19a; **7**:119b
  Shinchō ······ **7**:109a

Shinkō Geijutsu Ha Kurabu 新興芸術派倶楽部 7:175b
Shin kokinshū (New Collection of Ancient and Modern Times) 新古今集 3:52a-52b; 5:15a, 41a, 42b; 7:96b, 119b-121a; 8:211a
Buddhist influence 5:43a
compilation 7:120a
compilers 2:351a; 5:41a
Fujiwara no Sadaie 2:354a
Fujiwara no Toshinari 2:357a
Fujiwara no Toshinari no Musume 2:357b
Fujiwara no Yoshitsune 2:358b
influence on later literature 7:120b
Jakuren 4:1b
Jien 4:54a
Kamo no Mabuchi 4:129b
Kinkai wakashū 4:212b
Kokinshū compared 4:255a
Kujō Kanezane in 4:303b
literary status 7:120a
poets 7:120a
qualities 5:42b-43a
structure 7:120a-120b
styles 7:120b
techniques 5:42b
Shin kokin wakashū. 新古今和歌集 *See* **Shin kokinshū**
Shinkoku 神国 4:59b
Shinkokugeki 新国劇 2:268a; 7:121a
Sawada Shōjirō 7:30b-31a
Shinkokushi 新国史 7:121a-121b
historiography 3:153a
Shinkoku shōsetsu 4:199a
Shin Kokuzō 新国造 4:310a
Shinkō shūkyō 5:366a-368b
Shinku (closely related verses) 親句 8:214b
Shinkun 神訓 4:272a
Shin Kyōiku Undō 新教育運動 7:121b
Tanimoto Tomeri 7:342a
Shinkyoku Urashima 新曲浦島 2:75b; 8:111a
Shinkyō Kyōdōtai 心境共同体 7:121b
Shinkyō Taamidabutsu 真教他阿弥陀仏 4:62a
Shin Nampin 沈南蘋 7:83b
Shin Nan'yō 新南陽 7:121b
Shin Nihon bungaku 新日本文学 7:122a
Shin Nihon Bungakukai (Society for a New Japanese Literature) 新日本文学会 5:316b-317a; 6:230b
Shin Nihon bungaku 7:122a
Tsuboi Shigeji 8:110a
Shin Nihon Bungaku Kyōkai 5:19a
Shin Nihon Kajin Shūdan 新日本歌人集団 5:20a
Shin Nihon Shūkyō Dantai Rengōkai 8:150a
Shin Nippon (New Japan) 新日本 5:301a
Shinobunoya. *See* **Tachibana Akemi**
Shinobunoya kashū 志濃夫廼舎歌集 7:292a
Shinoda Masahiro 篠田正浩 2:273b; 7:122a-122b
Shi no genri 詩の原理 3:76b
Shi-nō-kō-shō 士農工商 7:122b
Shin onna daigaku
Onna daigaku 6:108a
Shino ware. 志野焼 *See* **Mino ware**
Shinran 親鸞 3:171b; 4:67b-68b, 125a; 7:66a, 122b-123b
Jinen hōn'i shō 7:123a
Jōdo Shin sect 4:68a
Kagami no miei 7:*122b*
Kyōgyōshinshō 4:330a-330b
monasticism 5:238a
raigōzu 6:277a
Sen Amidabutsu 7:*122b*
Tannishō 7:344a
wasan 8:231a
Shinran's Kyōgyōshinshō
Kiyozawa Manshi 4:233a
Shinrigaku kenkyū (Psychological Research) 心理学研究 6:260b
Shinri ippan 真理一般 8:127b
Shinritsu Kōryō (New Legal Principles) 新律綱領 6:172a
Kaitei Ritsurei 4:113b
Shinroku Ujimasa 新六氏正 4:270a
Shinron 新論 1:38a; 7:124a
Shinrui (shinseki) 4:217b, 218a
Shinsai Yobō Chōsakai 2:140b
Shinsambetsu (National Federation of Industrial Organizations) 新産別 4:347b, 360a; 6:238a; 7:124a
Shin sarugaku ki 新猿楽記 4:325a
Shinsei 新声
Shinchō 7:109a
Shinchōsha Company 7:109b
Shinseisakuza 7:124a
Shinsei taii 真政大意 4:168a
Shinsekki jidai 新石器時代 5:361b
Shinsengumi 新撰組 7:124a-124b
Ikedaya Incident 3:266b
Kondō Isami, leader 4:269a
Serizawa Kamo 7:124a
Shinsengumi shimatsuki
Shimozawa Kan 7:107b
Shinsen jikyō 新撰字鏡 2:93a; 7:124b
Shinsen jisho
Ōtsuki Joden 6:134b
Shinsen rōeishū (Newly Selected Collection for Recitation) 新撰朗詠集 5:38b; 8:208a
Shinsen shōjiroku 新撰姓氏録 1:151b; 7:124b; 8:137a
Kōgonen-Jaku cited 4:249a
Shinsen tsukubashū 新撰菟玖波集 7:12b, 124b, 162a
Shinsetsu Ishikawa Goemon 真説石川五右衛門 2:76b
Shinsha 4:179a
Shin shakai 新社会 7:310a
Shinshibari 4:210b
Shinshichō 新思潮 7:124b-125a; 8:300a
"neorealist" school 5:19a
Osanai Kaoru 7:124b
Shinshiro 新城 7:125a
Shinsho 6:162a
Shinshō hōshi nikki 信生法師日記 8:105a
Shinshōji 新勝寺 5:334b; 7:125a
Shinshōji temple 1:271a
Shinshō maru (ship)
Daikokuya Kōdayū 2:60b
Shinshōsetsu 新小説 7:125a
Shin shūishū (New Collection of Gleanings) 新拾遺集 8:73b
Shinshūren 8:150a
Shinshū temma kyō 神州天馬俠 7:166b
Shinsō zempen 神相全編 6:187a
Shinsui Kyōyo Rei 薪水供与令 7:125a-125b
Shintaikei 身体刑 7:140b
Shin Taisei Undō 新体制運動 5:365a-366a
Shintaishi (new form poetry) style 4:225a
Shintaishi shō 新体詩抄 8:88a
Shin Tanka Kyōkai (New Tanka Society) 新短歌協会 5:19b
Shintei zōho kokushi taikei (Newly Revised and Supplemented Compendium of National History) 新訂増補国史大系 2:104b-105a; 4:262b; 7:262b
Shintō 神道 1:162b; 6:290a; 7:48a-48b, 64a, 99b, 125b-132a
afterlife 1:20a
dance, traditional 2:73b
doctrine
changeableness 8:25a-25b
community-ism 8:25b-26a
functionalism 8:25b
family altars 7:137b
festivals 2:252b-258a
folk religion 2:298a
Gobusho 3:38b-39a
government promotion 3:78a
historical developments
origins and formative period 7:125b-127a
medieval period 7:127a-128b
Edo period 7:128b-129b
Meiji period and after 7:129b
Inari 3:283a
kami 4:125b-126a
lay believers (ujiko) 4:362a-362b
miko 5:172a
music 5:283a
mythology 5:295a
nature in 5:357b
new religions 5:368a-368b
prayer 6:233a
priesthood 6:238b-239a
restructuring 2:206a-206b
ritual codification 7:126b
ritual dimensions and thought 7:129b-132a
ritual music and dance 3:1a, 2a
Sect Shintō
Confucian 7:48a
Faith-healing 7:48a
Mountain 7:48a
Pure 7:48a
Purification 7:48a
Restoration 7:48a, 129a-129b
Ryōbu 7:127b
Sannō Ichijitsu 7:127b
Suika 7:129a
Watarai 7:127b-128a
Yuiitsu 7:128a-128b
shimenawa 7:*128b*
Shingaku 7:112a
taboo expressions 7:291b
Taikyō Sempu 7:297b
tama 7:332a
thought and culture 8:25a-29a
tolerance in Japanese religion 8:70b
types 2:300b
Folk 2:300b
Imperial 2:300b
Scholastic 2:300b
Sect 7:48a
Shrine 7:180b
shūgyō 4:271b
weddings 8:239a
women in 8:256b, 258a

Shintō and Buddhism, separation of · · · 7:132a
Shintō architecture · · · 7:132a-134a
origin · · · 7:132a-132b
reconstruction · · · 7:134a
shrine complex buildings · · · 7:134a
shrine complexes · · · 7:132b-134a
Shintō art · · · 7:134b-137b
anthropomorphism · · · 7:126a
applied arts · · · 7:136b
architecture · · · 7:132a-134a, 135b
definition · · · 7:134b-135a
Hachiman · · · 7:*134b*
history · · · 7:136b-137a
imperial regalia · 3:278b-279a; 7:135a-135b
Kitano tenjin engi · · · 7:*136b*
painting · · · 7:136a-136b
sculpture · · · 7:136a
shūgō bijutsu · · · 7:*134b*
Shintō-Buddhist relationships 1:179b-180a
Honji Suijaku theory
religious literature concerning 7:127a-128b
Shintō charms · · · 3:91a
Shintō denju · · · 神道伝授 · · · 7:128b
Shintō family altars 2:307a; 6:291a; 7:137b
harvest rites · · · 1:22b
Shintō gobusho · · · 神道五部書 · · · 3:38b-39a; 7:128a; 8:236b
Shin Tōhō Co, Ltd · · · 2:271b, 273b; 7:137b
Shintō Jūsampa · · · 神道十三派 · · · 7:48a
Shin Tōkyō Kokusai Kūkō · · · 5:370b-371a
Shintō rites · · · 7:137b-139b
accessories and offerings · · · 7:138b
body of worshipers · · · 7:138a-138b
buildings and facilities · · · 7:138a
divisions · · · 7:137b-138a
Engi Shiki · · · 2:217b
festivals · · · 7:139a
Norito · · · 7:138b
religious banquets · · · 7:139b
saikai · · · 7:139a-139b
shrine · · · 7:138a
Shintō shrines · · · 7:179b-180b
Akama · · · 1:40a
Akiba · · · 1:41b
Aso · · · 1:103b
Atago · · · 1:107b
Atsuta · · · 1:115b-116a
Awa · · · 1:125a
Dazaifu · · · 2:79b
Fushimi Inari · · · 2:375a
Futarayama · · · 2:376a
Hakozaki · · · 3:87a
Heian · · · 3:122b
Hie · · · 3:130b
Hikawa · · · 3:137b
Hirose · · · 3:147b
Hirota · · · 3:150b
Ikukunitama · · · 3:270b-271a
Ise · · · 3:338a-339a
Isonokami · · · 3:348a
Itsukushima · · · 3:357a
Iwashimizu Hachiman · · · 3:363a
Izumo · · · 2:67a
Kamo · · · 4:130a
Kashihara · · · 4:162a
Kashii · · · 4:162a
Kashima · · · 4:162b
Kasuga · · · 4:163b-164a
Katori · · · 4:169a
Kehi · · · 4:186b
Kitano · · · 4:228a
Kotohira · · · 4:297a
Kumano Sanzan · · · 4:306b
land owned by · · · 7:109b
Meiji · · · 5:160b
Mitsumine · · · 5:214a
Miyazaki · · · 5:222a
money offerings · · · 5:242a
Munakata · · · 5:264b-265a
Ōmi · · · 6:102a
Ōmiwa · · · 6:102a-102b
pictorial votive offerings · · · 2:196b-198a
public · · · 7:180b
Sengen · · · 7:64a
Shiogama · · · 7:140a
Shōkonsha · · · 8:319a
Sumiyoshi · · · 7:270b
Tatsuta · · · 7:350a
Tōshōgū · · · 8:84b
Tsurugaoka Hachiman · · · 8:116b
Udo · · · 8:125b
Usa Hachiman · · · 8:181b
Yasukuni · · · 8:319a-319b
Shintō Shrines, Association of · · · 7:139b
Shintō symbols · · · 3:49a-49b
Shinuhi · · · 私奴婢 · · · 7:62a
Shinwa Kaiun Kaisha, Ltd · · · 7:139b
Shin Yakushiji · · · 新薬師寺 · · · 7:139a-140b
Shinyei Kaisha · · · 7:140a
Shin'yōkai · · · 5:19a
Shinza · · · 神座 · · · 4:107a
Shinzei · · · 信西 · · · 2:353a
Shinzei kogakuzu · · · 信西古楽図 · · · 3:32a
Shinzō inu tsukubashū · · · 新増犬筑波集 · · · 7:140a
Shinzoku Hō (family law)
Tomii Masaaki · · · 8:71a
Shin zoku kokinshū (New Collection of Ancient and Modern Times, Continued, 1439) · · · 新続古今集 7:170b; 8:204a
Shiobara · · · 塩原 · · · 7:140a
Shioda Hiroshige 塩田広重 · · · 7:140a
Shiogama · · · 塩竈 · · · 7:140a
Shiogama Jinja. *See* **Shiogama Shrine**
Shiogama Shrine 塩竈神社 · · · 7:140a
Shiohigari · · · 7:140b
Shioiri Matsusaburō · · · 塩入松三郎 · · · 7:140b
Shiojiri · · · 塩尻 · · · 7:140b
Shiokara · · · 2:305a
Shioki · · · 7:140b
Shiomidake · · · 塩見岳 · · · 7:141a
Shionogi & Co, Ltd · · · 7:141a
Shionomisaki · · · 潮岬 7:141a; 8:348b
Shiotsuki Yaeko · · · 塩月弥栄子 · · · 2:233b
Shiozawa · · · 塩沢 · · · 7:141a-141b
Shiozawa Masasada · · · 塩沢昌貞 · · · 7:141b
Shipbuilding companies
Hakodate Dock Co, Ltd · · · 3:86a
Hitachi Zōsen Corporation · · · 3:207b
Ishikawajima-Harima Heavy Industries Co, Ltd · · · 3:342b
Kawasaki Heavy Industries, Ltd · · · 4:183b
Mitsubishi Heavy Industries, Ltd · · · 5:208a
Mitsui Engineering & Shipbuilding Co, Ltd · · · 5:211b
Namura Shipbuilding Co, Ltd · · · 5:327b
Sanoyasu Dockyard Co, Ltd · · · 7:16a
Sasebo Heavy Industries Co, Ltd (Sasebo Jūkōgyō) · · · 7:24a
Shipbuilding industry 7:141b-143b; 8:102b
Edo · · · 2:149b
electronics · · · 2:192a
industrial organization and technology · · · 7:142a-143a
Meiji · · · 2:151b, 153a
postwar · · · 7:142a
pre-1945 · · · 7:141b-142a
Shimonoseki · · · 7:108b
Shipbuilding Scandal of 1954 · · · 7:143a-143b; 8:345a
Shipping industry companies · · · 7:142a
Daiichi Chūō Kisen Kaisha · · · 2:58b
Japan Line, Ltd · · · 4:47a
Kawasaki Kisen Kaisha, Ltd · · · 4:183b-184a
Mitsui O.S.K. Lines, Ltd · · · 5:212a
Nippon Yūsen · · · 6:13b
Sankō Steamship Co, Ltd · · · 7:14b
Shinwa Kaiun Kaisha, Ltd · · · 7:139b
Shōwa Line, Ltd · · · 7:174b
Yamashita-Shinnihon Steamship Co, Ltd · · · 8:304b
Shippō · · · 1:328b-329a
Ships · · · 7:143b-145a
haniwa · · · 7:*143a*
higaki kaisen (lozenge-fenced cargo ship) · · · 7:*144b*
types · · · 7:143b-144a
vermilion seal ship (shuinsen) · · · 7:*144b*
votive picture (ema) · · · 7:*144b*
Shirabe · · · 4:103a
Shirabyōshi · · · 白拍子 7:145a; 8:259a
geisha · · · 3:15a
Shiragi · · · 新羅 · · · 7:196a
Shiragikukai · · · 白菊会 · · · 5:19b
Shirahama (Chiba Prefecture) · · · 白浜 · · · 7:145a
Shirahama (Wakayama Prefecture) · · · 白浜 · · · 7:145a
Shirahone Hot Spring · · · 白骨温泉 · · · 7:145a
Shirahone Onsen. *See* **Shirahone Hot Spring**
Shirai Kyōji · · · 白井喬二 · · · 7:103b, 145b
Shirai Rittoku. *See* **Tatebayashi Kagei**
Shirai Seiichi · · · 白井晟一 · · · 7:145b
Shiraito Falls · · · 白糸の滝 4:160b; 7:145b
Shiraitowappu · · · 白糸割符 · · · 3:356b
Shirakaba, Lake · · · 白樺湖 · · · 7:145b-146b
Shirakaba · · · 白樺 · · · 5:19a, 281a, 308a
Shirakabaha, "White Birch school." *See* **Shirakaba school**
Shirakaba school · · · 白樺派 · 1:84b; 4:237b; 7:27b, 90b, 145b-146b
Christianity · · · 4:32a
founding · · · 5:19a
Leach, Bernard Howell · · · 4:372b
literary criticism · · · 5:12a
Shirakawa, Emperor · · · 白河天皇 · · · 7:26a, 146b, 279b
insei · · · 3:314b
Shirakawa (Fukushima Prefecture) · · · 白河 · · · 7:146b
Shirakawa (Gifu Prefecture) · · · 白川 · · · 7:146b
Shirakawa (river) · · · 白川 · · · 7:146b
Shirakawa no Seki · 白河関 · · · 7:146b-147a
Shiran (*Bletilla striata*) · · · 7:147a
Shiranami-mono (plays depicting activities of thieves) · · · 白浪物 · · · 5:234b
Shiranesan. *See* **Shirane Sanzan**
Shiranesan (Kusatsu) · · · 白根山 · · · 7:147a
Shiranesan (Nikkō) 白根山 · · · 7:147a
Shirane Sanzan · · · 白根三山 · · · 7:147a
"Shirano Benjūrō"
Shinkokugeki · · · 7:121a
Shirase Nobu · · · 白瀬矗 · · · 7:147a
Shirashi (ash-glazed wares) · · · 1:261b-262a
Shirasu · · · 白州 · · · 7:147a
Shirataki · · · 7:265b
Shiratori Incident 白鳥事件 · · · 7:147b

Shiratori Kurakichi 白鳥庫吉 7:147b
Shirauo 8:251a
Shiretoko Hantō. *See* **Shiretoko Peninsula**
Shiretoko National Park 知床国立公園 7:147b
Shiretoko Peninsula 知床半島 7:147b
Shiribetsugawa 尻別川 7:147b
Shiritori (capping) 8:269b
Shiroi keshi 白い罌粟 7:293a
Shiroi kyotō (The Ivory Tower) 白い巨塔 8:299a
Shiroishi 白石 7:148a
Shirō Katsuyasu 四郎勝康 4:270a
Shiron (Essays on Poetry) 詩論 6:112a
Shirone 白根 7:148a
Shiroumadake 白馬岳 7:148a
Shiroyama 城山 7:148a
Shiroyama Saburō 城山三郎 7:148a
Shiryō 私領 7:148a
Shiryō Hensanjo. *See* **Historiographical Institute, Tōkyō University**
Shisakajima 四阪島 7:148a
Shisei 刺青 7:342b
Shiseidō Co, Ltd 7:148b
Shisei System. *See* **Uji-kabane system**
Shisendō 詩仙堂 3:342b
Shisen o koete 死線を越えて 4:103b
Shisetsu jikenshū 師説自見集 3:272b
Shishi Bunroku 獅子文六 1:164a; 7:148b
  fūzoku shōsetsu 2:378b
Shishigatani Conspiracy 鹿ヶ谷の変 7:188b
  Taira no Shigemori 7:302a
Shishi kagura 獅子神楽 4:106b, 107b
Shishi-mai 獅子舞 7:*148b*, 148b-149a, 250a
  kadozuke 4:101b
Shishi odori 鹿踊 7:149a, *149a*
Shishi yuebao 7:337b
Shishōsetsu 3:312a-312b
Shisō 思想 3:127b; 7:149a
Shiso doll 4:105b
Shisōhan Hogo Kansatsu Hō. *See* **"Thought Criminal" Probation Law**
Shisōhan Hogo Kansatsu Hō 8:29a
Shisō kenji ("thought prosecutors") 6:168b
Shisō no kagaku 思想の科学 6:233a; 7:149a-149b
  members 7:149a
  pragmatism 6:232b-233a
  publications 7:149b
Shitaji chigyō 下地知行 1:274a
Shitaji chūbun 下地中分 7:149a
  Ashikaga Yoshimitsu 1:101b
  jitō 4:63b
  shōen 7:157b
Shitakiri suzume 舌切雀 2:302b; 7:149b
Shitamachi 7:149b-150b, 266a
  chōnaikai 1:300a
  urban life 8:178a
Shitaobi 2:369b
Shite kata 4:267b, 270a
Shitennōji 四天王寺 1:182a; 7:74a, 150b
Shitōkan 四等官 7:150b-151a
Shitomido 7:111a
Shiwaku Islands 塩飽諸島 1:125a
Shiwaza no kotoba 為業の言葉 7:281a
Shizen kankyō no hembō 自然環境の変貌 7:293b
Shizen shin'eidō 自然真営道 1:55b; 4:147a; 7:151a
Shizen shugi 5:351a-351b
Shizen shugi no shukanteki yōso 自然主義の主観的要素 4:165a
Shizoku 士族 7:151a-152a
  dissidence 7:151b-152a
  government policy 7:151a-151b
  shi-nō-kō-shō 7:122b
Shizoku jusan 士族授産 7:152a-152b
  shizoku 7:151b
Shizugatake, Battle of 賤ケ岳の戦 7:152b
  Fukushima Masanori's role 2:366b
  Shibata Katsuie 7:84b
Shizugatake no Tatakai. *See* **Shizugatake, Battle of**
Shizuka Gozen 静御前 7:152b
Shizukawa Hydroelectric Dam 2:72b
Shizuki Tadao 志筑忠雄 7:152b-153a
  Kaempfer, Engelbert 4:102a
  natural sciences 5:356a
Shizuoka 静岡 7:*153a*, 153a-153b
  shrines 7:153b
Shizuoka Bunko 静岡文庫 1:68a
Shizuoka Heiya. *See* **Shizuoka Plain**
Shizuoka Ken. *See* **Shizuoka Prefecture**
Shizuoka Municipal Toro Site Museum 7:153b
Shizuoka Plain 静岡平野 7:153b
Shizuoka Prefecture 静岡県 7:153b-154a; 8:355a
  cities 7:154a
  parks 7:154a
  rivers 7:153b
Shizuoka Shiritsu Toro Hakubutsukan. *See* **Shizuoka Municipal Toro Site Museum**
Shō 5:151a-151b; 7:154a
  determination 5:151a-151b
  use in gagaku 3:1b-2a
Shōan 咲庵 5:318b
Shōbara 庄原 7:154a
Shōbō genzō 正法眼蔵 2:123b; 7:154a; 8:28a
Shōbu [(sweet flag) *Acorus calamus* var. *asiaticus*] 7:154a-154b
Shōbungaku 4:199a
Shōbyōga 障屏画 7:41a-43b
Shōchi. 勝知 *See* **Takuma Tametō**
Shōchiku 2:268a, 269b
Shōchiku Co, Ltd 7:102b, 154b
Shōchiku Kinema 3:351b
Shōchiku Motion Picture Company
  Imamura Shōhei 3:274a
Shōchiku New Wave 7:122a
Shōchū (alcoholic beverages) 4:161a; 7:1a-1b
Shōchū Conspiracy 正中の変 7:154b
Shock therapy 6:261a
Shōda Heigorō 荘田平五郎 7:154b
Shōda Hidesaburō 正田英三郎 7:154b
Shōda Kenjirō 正田建次郎 7:154b
Shōdan chiyō 樵談治要 7:155a
Shōden Jiken. *See* **Shōwa Denkō Scandal**
Shodō 1:232b-236b
Shodō kikimimi sekenzaru 諸道聴耳世間猿 8:126a
Shōdoshima 小豆島 7:*155a*
Shoemaker, The 8:328a
Shōen 荘園 7:155a-158a, 277a
  corvée labor 1:226b
  early 7:155b-156a
  economy 2:147b-148a
  feudalism 2:263b
  honke and ryōke 3:224a
  hyakushō 3:249a
  iriai 3:330a
  kaezeni 4:102a
  Kamakura shogunate 7:157a-158a
  kenchi 4:193a
  kokugun system 4:259b
  mature 7:156a-157a
  rice tax 4:112b
  ryōshu 6:353a
  samurai 7:7a
  sanjo 7:12a
  shitaji chūbun 7:149b
  tax exemption rights 2:376b
  warriors 4:121b
Shōen-kōryō system (private estate-public land system) 荘園公領制 2:106b-107a
Shōen landholding system 1:80a
Shōen nikki 湘烟日記 4:223a
Shōga 2:305a; 3:127b
Shōgakukan Publishing Co, Ltd 7:158a-158b
Shōgatsu 正月 1:20a; 5:371b-372a
Shōgawa 庄川 7:158b
Shōgi 将棋 5:7b; 7:12b, 158b-159b
  game 7:159a-159b
  history 7:158b
  Japan Shōgi Federation 7:158b-159a
Shōgi Magajin 将棋マガジン 7:159a
Shōgi sekai 将棋世界 7:158b
Shōgitai 彰義隊 1:165a; 7:159b-160a
Shōgoin 聖護院 7:160a, 182a-182b
Shōgun 将軍 7:160a-160b
  Kamakura shogunate 4:121a-142b
    Kamakura shōguns 4:*122b*
  Muromachi shogunate 5:271b-274a
    Ashikaga shōguns 5:*272b*
  Tokugawa shogunate 8:52b-56a
    Tokugawa shogunal line 8:*45a*
  seii tai shōgun 2:204a-204b
Shogunal deputy 4:151a
Shogunal regent 7:97b
"Shōgun art"
  Taut, Bruno 7:351a-351b
Shogunate 7:160b-161a
Shogunate missions to the West 7:161a-161b
Shōhaku 肖柏 6:298b-299a; 7:161b-162a
  Kokin denju 4:254a
Shōheikō 昌平黌 1:157a; 4:140a; 7:84b, 162a
  Ban on Heterodoxy 4:152b
  Confucian academy 7:335b
  Nakamura Masanao and 5:315a
  religious education 6:295a-295b
  Satō Issai 7:27a
Shōhei no shiki
  Kojiki described 4:251b
Shōheizaka Gakumonjo. *See* **Shōheikō**
Shōhekiga 障壁画 7:41a-43b
Shōhisha undō 2:14a-15b
Shōhō Kōshūjo 商法講習所 5:249a
Shōhō Kōshū Jo (School for Commercial Law) 2:208a
Shōhon 正本 4:76b

Shoikō 書意考 4:129b
Shoin 7:266a
Shoin-zukuri 書院造り 2:295a; 7:162a-163a, 265b
Kuroshoin 7:*162b*
Nijō Castle 7:*162a*
shinden-zukuri 7:110a
shoin style 7:*162b*
Shōji 1:82b
Shōji Kaoru 庄司薫 7:163a
Shōji ninen nido hyakushu 正治二年二度百首 4:128b
Shōjin ryōri 2:*21a*, 22a
Shōji Tarō 東海林太郎 6:355a
Shōka 2:289b-290a, *293a*
Shōkadō Shōjō 松花堂昭乗 7:163a
Shō Kaiseki 蔣介石 1:270a-270b
Shōkai shingo 捷解新語 7:163a
Shōkai shingo bunshaku 捷解新語文釈 7:163a
Shōkaku 勝覚 2:57b
Shōkan 荘官 7:163a-163b
Shōka-style 2:*290b*
Shōkei 祥啓 7:163b
Geiami 3:14a
Shō Ki 鍾馗 7:163b
Shokikan 書記官 4:180a
Shokkiri 7:272b
Shokkō Giyūkai 職工義友会 7:164a
Takano Fusatarō 7:317a
Shokkō jijō 職工事情 7:164a; 8:264b
Shōko 3:2a
Shōkō Chūkin Bank 7:164a
Shōkōkan 彰考館 1:94b; 2:347a; 7:164a
Shōkō keiei 商工経営 8:127a
Shōkōki. 照光記 *See* **Meigetsuki**
Shokoku Fūzoku Toijō Kotae. *See* **Yashiro Hirokata**
Shōkokuji 相国寺 3:57a; 7:69b, 164b
Ginkakuji 3:33a
Itō Jakuchū 3:353b
Josetsu 4:77b-78a
Rokuon nichiroku 6:335b
Shokudō 7:165
Shokugaku keigen 植学啓原 8:125b
Shokugenshō 職原抄 4:224b; 7:164b
Shokugyō fujin
Oku Mumeo 6:96b
Shokuhō seiken 織豊政権 3:178b; 7:164b-165a
warrior government 8:230a
Shoku nihongi 続日本紀 4:249a; 7:248b
Kojidan, resource 4:251a
Rikkokushi 6:315b
Shoku Nihon kōki 続日本後紀 6:315b
Shokunin 7:165a
Shokuryō Mēdē 4:358a; 7:165a
Shoku sandai jitsuroku 7:121b
Shokusan Jūtaku Sōgo Co, Ltd 7:164a-164b
Shokusan kōgyō 殖産工業 7:165a-165b
National Industrial Exhibition 5:341b
technological development 7:369a
Shoku senzaishū (Collection of a Thousand Years Continued) 続千載集 8:73b
Shokushi, Princess. 式子内親王 *See* **Shikishi, Princess**
Shōman, Queen 勝鬘王妃 2:55b
Shōmei Incident 鐘銘事件 5:32b; 7:165b
Shōmonki 将門記 2:101b; 7:165b
Taira no Masakado 7:301b
Shōmono 7:165b-166a
Shōmu, Emperor 聖武天皇 1:184b; 5:308a; 7:91a, 166a; 8:287b
education 2:172a
Fujiwara family 2:348a, 350b
Fujiwara no Nakamaro 2:353b
Ishiyamadera 3:346a-346b
kokubunji decree 4:257a
Kōmyō, Empress, consort of 4:268b
monasticism 5:237b
Naniwakyō 5:328b
Shigaraki no Miya 7:91a
Shōmyō 声明 4:327a; 5:283a-283b
tonal system 5:283b
Shōmyō Falls 称名の滝 4:69a
Shōnai Plain 庄内平野 7:166a, *166b*
Shōnandō 小楠堂 8:331a
Shōnen 少年 7:166a, 342b
Shōnen kurabu 少年倶楽部 4:241b; 7:166b
Shōnen sekai 少年世界 7:309b
Shōni family 少弐氏 7:166b
Shōnin 7:166b-167a
Shōnindō 7:112a
Shōno Junzō 庄野潤三 7:167a
Shōnō ni kansuru kenkyū 小農に関する研究 8:331b
Shōno Shōunsai 生野祥雲斎 1:136a
Shōnyo Kōkyō 証如光教 3:346b
Sho o suteyo machi e deyō (Throw Away the Books, Take to the Streets) 書を捨てよ街へ出よう 8:13a
Shoplifting 4:86b
Shōriki Matsutarō 正力松太郎 7:167a
Short stories 5:42b
Shōrui Awaremi no Rei 生類憐みの令 7:167a-167b
Shōryoē Festival
dance, traditional 2:74a
Shosagoto 所作事 2:75b; 4:91a, 93a-93b, 95b
onnagata 6:108a
Shosai yori gaitō ni 書斎より街頭に 7:338b
Shosaizu 3:306a
Shōseikon (matrilocal marriage) 招婿婚 5:262b
Shōseikon no kenkyū 招婿婚の研究 7:316b
Shōsendō 象先堂 3:352a
Shōsenkyō 昇仙峡 7:167b
Shōsetsu Nihon ginkō 小説日本銀行 7:148a
Shōsetsu shinzui 小説神髄 5:11a
Shoshi Hatto (Regulations for the Vassals)
Tokugawa shogunate 8:53a
Shōshikai 尚歯会 1:141b; 7:167b
Takano Chōei 7:316b
Shōshimin geki 2:270a
Shōshin dokugo 称心独語 4:169b
"Shōshitsu" 消失 7:163a
Shōsho 詔書 3:277a-277b; 7:62a
Shōshō Hakkei 瀟湘八景 7:167b
Shōshō Shigemoto no haha 少将滋幹の母 7:343a
Shōshū reijō 召集令状 7:167b-168a
Shōsōin 正倉院 2:295a; 5:277b; 7:42a, 168a-170a
biwa 7:*168b*
bodhisattva (bosatsu) 7:*169a*
categories 7:169a-170a
ceramic bowl 7:*168b*
folding-screen panel 7:*169b*
furniture collection 2:371a
Kōmyō and Shōmu collection 4:268b
lead-glazed wares 1:262b
musical instruments 1:157a
preservation of treasures 7:170a
sankechi examples 7:13b
textiles 8:17a
treasures 7:169a
Shōsōin documents 正倉院文書 1:234a
Shōsōin textiles 正倉院染織 8:17b
Shotai 4:203a; 7:170a
calligraphy 1:233b
gyōsho 7:*171a*
kaisho 7:*171a*
kanji 7:*170b*
reisho 7:*170b*
sōsho 7:*171a*
tensho 7:*170b*
Shōta no uma 正太の馬 8:110a
Shōtatsu 聖達 3:328b-329a
Shōtetsu 正徹 5:14b; 7:170b; 8:215a
Shōtetsu monogatari 正徹物語 7:170b
Shotō chigyō 所当知行 1:274a
Shōtō Kokushi 正燈国師 4:1b-2a
Shōtoku, Empress 称徳天皇 4:253b
Shōtoku Nagasaki Shinrei 正徳長崎新令 7:171a
Dutch trade 2:136a
Shōtoku no Chi 正徳の治 7:171a
Shōtoku, Prince 聖徳太子 1:*234b*, 151a, 197b; 7:11b, 69b, 74a, 93a, 171b-172a, 260a, 264a
codes of conduct 1:207a
founding of Buddhism 1:178a
historiography 3:152a
Ikaruga no Miya 3:264b
imperial era 4:203b
Jōgū Shōtoku Hōōtei Setsu 4:69a
portrait 7:*172b*
Seventeen-Article Constitution 7:73a
Shinran 7:123a
treasure houses 5:277b
Shōtoku Taishi. *See* **Shōtoku, Prince**
Shōtoku Taishi 聖徳太子 4:125a; 1:197b
Shoup mission 7:172a-173a
taxes, national and local 7:354a-354b
Shōwa 昭和 3:147a
Shōwa Aluminum Corporation 7:173a
Shōwa bungaku shi 昭和文学史 7:175a
Shōwa Denkō 7:173a
pollution 2:226b
Shōwa Denkō Scandal 昭和電工事件 1:97b; 7:173a; 8:344b
Fukuda Takeo's involvement 2:362b
Shōwa Depression 昭和恐慌 7:173b-174a
cooperatives 1:22a
economy 2:153b
Financial Crisis of 1927 2:277a
landlordism 4:363a
Shōwa Electric Wire & Cable Co, Ltd 7:174a
Shōwa Fertilizer Co 7:173a
Shōwa Ishin. *See* **"Shōwa Restoration"**
Shōwa Kenkyūkai 昭和研究会 7:174a-174b
Shōwa Line, Ltd 7:174b
Shōwa literature 7:174b-176b
postwar literature 6:230a-231b
Shōwa Oil Co, Ltd 6:181b; 7:176b
Shōwa period 昭和時代 7:176b
Shōwa Research Association 3:53b; 7:174a
Shōwa Research Society 7:229b

Shōwa Restoration
昭和維新 7:176b-177a
Shōwa Sangyō Co, Ltd 7:177a
Shōwa Shinzan 昭和新山 7:98a, 177a
Shōwa Station 1:64a-64b
Shōya 庄屋 7:177a-177b
Shōyō jurin bunka
照葉樹林文化 7:177a-179a
Laurilignosa culture 7:177b-178a
development of agriculture 7:178a-178b
Jōmon cultures 7:178b-179a
material elements 7:177b
nonmaterial elements 7:177b-178a
Shōyu 2:305a, 306a; 7:239b
Shoyūken hō no riron
所有権法の理論 4:184b
Shōyūki 小右記 7:179a
Shozan 3:57a
Shōzei 正税 7:179a
Shōzōmatsu wasan
正像末和讃 8:231a
Shrikes [(mozu) *Lanius* spp.] 7:179b
Shrimps, prawns, and lobsters [(ebi) suborders Natantia and Palinura]
7:179b
Shrine Forest 5:352a-352b
Shrine Library 4:58b-59a
Shrine of Lady Tachibana
橘夫人厨子 1:21a
Shrines 7:138a, 179b-180b
kagura 4:106a-107b
Shintō 7:129b-131a
Shintō architecture 7:132a-134b
Shintō art 7:135b-136b
Shintō rites 7:137b-139b
ujigami 8:131a-131b
Shrine Shintō 神社神道 2:300b; 7:138a, 180b
goshintai 3:49a-49b
See also **Shintō**
Shūbun 周文 7:42b, 69b, 180b-181a
Gakuō Zōkyū 3:4b-5a
ink painting 3:306b
Reading in the Bamboo Study (Chikusai dokusho zu) 7:*181a*
sansuiga (landscape painting) 7:17b
Shuchiteki bungakuron
主知的文学論 1:4b
Shūdan shūshoku 3:62b-63a
Shūeisha Publishing Co, Ltd 7:181a
Shufu no tomo 主婦の友 7:181b; 8:289b
Shufuren 主婦連 6:238b; 7:181b
Oku Mumeo 6:96b
Shufu Rengōkai. *See* **Shufuren**
Shūgaishō 拾芥抄 7:181b
Shugakuin Detached Palace 修学院離宮 4:336a, 337a; 7:181b-182a
Shugakuin Rikyū. *See* **Shugakuin Detached Palace**
Shugei Shuchiin
綜芸種智院 7:182a
founding 2:172b
Kūkai founded 4:304a
Shugendō 修験道 2:57b, 88b; 7:67a, 182a-182b; 8:288a
En no Gyōja 2:219b
Shingon sect 7:115a
Shōgoin 7:160a
Shūgetsu Tōkan 秋月等観 7:70a, 182b-183a
Shūgi 7:183a
kokorozuke as 4:256b
Shūgigaisho 集義外書 4:307b
Shūgiwasho 集義和書 4:307b
Shugo 守護 7:64b, 183a-184a
appointment 4:121b
corvée labor 1:226b
governmental functions 2:264a-264b
kokujin 4:260a
mediation with shogunate 4:151a
Muromachi history 3:173a
provincial decrees 4:90a
shōen 7:157a
shogunate, shugodai and, relationships between 7:183b-184a
Shugo daimyō 守護大名 1:274a; 7:184a
Ōnin War and 6:106b
Shugō Incident 殊号事件 7:184a
Shūgō Shintō 4:271b
Shūgyō 1:96b
Shūgyokushū 拾玉集 4:54a
Shūhōdō. *See* **Akiyoshidō**
Shūhō Myōchō. *See* **Sōhō Myōchō**
Shuihuzhuan [Shui-hu-chan (All Men Are Brothers)] 8:336b
Shuinjō 朱印状 7:184a-184b, 256b, 266b
vermilion seal ship trade 8:190a
Shuinsen 朱印船 7:255a
Shuinsen bōeki 朱印船貿易 8:190a-190b
Shuinsen voyages 8:190a
7:184b-185a; 8:204a
Shūi wakashū 拾遺和歌集 1:41a; 5:35a; 7:42b, 184b-185a; 8:204a
Fujiwara no Kintō 2:352a
kagura uta 4:108a
Shūji. *See* **Calligraphy**
Shūkai Jōrei 集会条例 7:185a
Shūkai Oyobi Seisha Hō 6:266a
Shūkan shinchō 週刊新潮 6:267b
Shinchōsha Company 7:109b
Shūkan tōyō keizai (Weekly Eastern Economic Review) 週刊東洋経済 8:91b
Shūkiku 蹴鞠 4:191a
Shukke (Buddhist priest) plays 4:327b
Shukke taikō 出家大綱 2:187a
Shukke to sono deshi
出家とその弟子 4:312a
Shukkō 7:185a
Shū Kōkei Jiken
周鴻慶事件 8:379a
Shukuba machi. *See* **Post-station towns**
Shukushi (recycled paper)
宿紙 8:233a
Shukuzu 縮図 7:176b
Shindō Kaneto 7:111a
Shukuzu (Miniature)
Tokuda Shūsei 8:45a
Shukyūha 守旧派 7:259b
Shūmei 4:95a
Shūmeigiku 1:56a
Shummusō 春夢草 7:162a
Shūmon aratame 宗門改 7:185b-186b
Jinshin Koseki 4:60b
Shumpuden 春婦伝 7:334b
Shun 7:68a
Shunchōshū 春鳥集 4:123a
Shundō Junko 俊藤純子 2:343a
Shun'e 俊恵 7:186b-187a
Shunga 7:187a-188a, 258a; 8:*138b*
Shungiku 7:265b
Shunkan 俊寛 7:188a-188b
Shunran (*Cymbidium virescens*) 7:188b
Shunshoku tatsumi no sono 春色辰巳園 7:334a
Shunshoku umegoyomi
春色梅児誉美 7:333b-334a
Shuntō (spring labor offensive)
7:188b-190a, 250b
"Base-up" 7:189
collective bargaining 4:360a
enterprise-level unions 7:189a
Iwai Akira 3:357b
labor disputes 4:349b
negotiations 7:189b
origins 7:188b
Ōta Kaoru 6:129a
people's 7:189b-190a
spread 7:189a-189b
wage campaigns 1945-1955 7:188b-189a
wage level 8:198b
Shuntō wage pattern 4:348a
Shun'yōdō 春陽堂 4:199a
Shun'yōshū 春葉集 4:101a
Shū Onrai 周恩来 8:378b-379a
Shuppan Hō 出版法 6:262b
Shuppan Jōrei 出版条例 6:262b
Shuppan nenkan (Publisher's Yearbook)
出版年鑑 8:268a
Shuppan Rei 出版令 1:252a
Shurei no Mon 守礼の門 6:*84b*
Shuri castle 首里城 6:*84b*
Shuri castle remains
首里城遺構 7:190a
Shuriken 7:190a
Shū Sakujin 周作人 8:379a-379b
Shushi 4:325a
Shushigaku (Neo-Confucianism)
朱子学 1:354b-355a; 4:140a; 7:71a, 190a-191b
basic teachings 7:190a
education 2:173b-174a
new religions 5:366b
Shingaku 7:112a
shogunate patronage 1:355a
Shōheikō 7:162a
Tokugawa shogunate 8:53a
view of history 3:154b
view of literature 5:16b
warrior government 8:230b
Zhu Xi School 7:190b-191b
Shūshin 修身 7:35b, 191b
Shūshin koyō seido
technological development 7:369b
Shu Shunsui 朱舜水 7:191b
Shūsō Dōjin. 秋艸道人 *See* **Aizu Yaichi**
Shusse Kagekiyo 出世景清 1:275b; 4:77a
Shutaisei ("sense of self") debates
6:232b-233a
Shūto 8:230b-231a
Shūtō fukko 宗統復古 7:234a
Shutoken 8:67b
Shutsujin'ei
portrait painting 6:227b
Shutsujō kōgo (Buddha's Comments After His Meditation) 出定後語 8:71b
Shuzenji 修善寺 7:191b
Sian Incident. *See* **Xi'an (Sian) Incident**
Siberia
expedition of Japanese troops 7:192a
geological exploration 7:238b
natural resources 7:238b
Soviet-Japanese development 7:238a
Siberia, Japanese prisoners of war in
7:191b-192a
Siberian Intervention 1:74a; 7:192a-192b
China 1:288a
failure 1:88a
Kenseikai 4:198a
Tanaka Giichi 7:336a-336b
Terauchi Masatake 8:12b
Ugaki Kazushige 8:130b
United States 8:156b
Sickles. *See* **Kama**
Siddham 1:179a; 7:192b
Jakugon 4:1b
Sidotti, Giovanni Battista 7:192b

Siebold, Heinrich von ··· 1:120a
Siebold Philip Franz von ··· 1:76b; 7:192b-193a
German-Japanese relations ··· 3:26a
Inō Tadataka ··· 3:309b
Itō Gemboku ··· 3:352a
Sakhalin ··· 7:1b
Siemens Incident 7:99a, 193a-193b; 8:298b
Takarabe Takeshi ··· 7:317b
Signboards ··· 7:193b-194a
Silence ··· 2:214a
Silent Temple in Autumn Mountains ··· 6:77b
Silk ··· 7:21a, 194a-194b
fibers and yarns ··· 7:194a
history ··· 7:194a-194b
plain weave ··· 8:17b
production, sericulture ··· 7:68b
Silk crepe ··· 1:297a
Silk fabric ··· 7:194a
Silk industries
Shinyei Kaisha ··· 7:140a
Tomioka Silk-Reeling Mill ··· 8:72a
Silk Road ··· 1:26b; 7:194b-196a
in Japan ··· 7:195a-196a
motifs ··· 7:195b
musical instruments and game objects ··· 7:195a-195b
theater and acrobatics ··· 7:195a
West Asian design composition ··· 7:195b-196a
West Asian materials ··· 7:195b
West Asian objects and shapes ··· 7:195b
Silkscreen ··· 5:233a
Silk trade ··· 5:323a-323b
itowappu system ··· 3:356b
Taiwan ··· 7:306b-307a
Silkworms [(kaiko) *Bombyx mori*] ··· 7:196a
raising ··· 7:68b
Silla ··· 2:347b; 7:196a
in Korean Three Kingdoms period ··· 4:292a
language during ··· 4:291a
Silver mining ··· 5:184b-185a
Iwami Silver Mine ··· 3:360a
Silver Seikō, Ltd ··· 7:196a
Silver World ··· 8:143a
Simeão ··· 4:315a
Sin. *See* **Tsumi**
Sin'ganhoe ··· 7:196a
formation ··· 4:283b
Singapore and Japan ··· 7:196b
Malayan Campaign ··· 5:88a
postwar relations ··· 7:196b
Singapore-Malaya merger controversy
"Blood Debt" Incident ··· 1:158b-159a
Singer Sewing Machine Co ··· 7:196a
Singh, Mohan ··· 1:164b; 2:348b; 7:197a
Indian National Army ··· 3:289b
Single Poems by 100 Poets ··· 3:248b-249a
Sino-French War ··· 7:197a-197b
Sino-Japanese Amity Treaty of 1871 ··· 7:197b
Taiwan ··· 7:307a
Sino-Japanese Joint Defensive Military Agreement ··· 6:336a-336b
Sino-Japanese relations. *See* **China and Japan**
Sino-Japanese War of 1894-1895 ··· 1:286a; 7:29a, 197b-198b; 8:287a
Denison, Henry Willard ··· 2:86b
Ding Ruchang ··· 2:96b-97a
drama during ··· 7:107b
French-Japanese relations ··· 2:332b
Fukushima Yasumasa ··· 2:367a
Gen'yōsha ··· 3:25a
growth of business ··· 2:30b
Imo Mutiny ··· 3:275a
Imperial Japanese armed forces ··· 1:87a
Kabayama Sukenori ··· 4:89b
Kanghwa, Treaty of ··· 4:140b
Kawakami Sōroku ··· 4:181b
Kiguchi Kohei ··· 4:204a
Korean-Japanese relations ··· 4:279b
Mutsu Munemitsu ··· 5:288b
nationalism ··· 5:343a
Okinawa ··· 6:87b
Russo-Japanese War ··· 6:346a
Shimonoseki, Treaty of ··· 4:141a
Taewŏn'gun ··· 7:294a
Taiwan ··· 7:306b
Tanaka Giichi ··· 7:336a-336b
territory of Japan ··· 8:14a
Tianjin (Tientsin) Convention ··· 8:29b
Tōgō Heihachirō ··· 8:36a
Tonghak Rebellion ··· 8:74b
treaty concluding ··· 7:106a-106b
Tripartite Intervention ··· 8:106b
war literature ··· 8:225b
Sino-Japanese War of 1937-1945 ··· 1:286b-287a, 289b; 7:48a, 65b, 199a-202a
anticommunism ··· 7:201b-202a
background ··· 7:199a-199b
China ··· 6:302a
critics ··· 7:200a-200b
December Ninth Movement ··· 2:81b
Eastern European nations and Japan ··· 2:142a
French-Japanese relations ··· 2:333b
Guomindang (Kuomintang) government during ··· 1:300b
hostilities ··· 7:199a
Hundred Regiment Offensive ··· 3:248a
Imperial Japanese armed forces ··· 1:88b
Ishiwara Kanji ··· 3:346a
Konoe Fumimaro policy ··· 4:272b
Ladybird Incident ··· 4:362a
Marco Polo Bridge Incident ··· 5:113b
militarism as cause ··· 2:250a
military operations ··· 7:200a-200b
Nanjing Incident ··· 5:328b-329a
"New Policy for China" ··· 7:201b
peace initiatives and collaborationist governments ··· 7:200b-201b
photography ··· 6:185b
Puyi (P'u-i) ··· 6:271b
Reorganized National Government of the Republic of China ··· 1:289b
Russia and Japan ··· 6:344a
Shōwa Research Association ··· 7:174b
stalemate ··· 7:200a
Tanggu (Tangku) Truce ··· 7:340b-341a
Tripartite Pact ··· 8:107a
United Kingdom ··· 8:152b
Wang Jingwei (Wang Ching-wei) ··· 8:222a
war literature ··· 8:226b
Sister cities ··· 7:202a
Six National Histories ··· 6:315b-317a
"Six Poetic Geniuses" (Rokkasen) 8:207b
Six Poetic Sages, The ··· 6:334b
Six Scripts ··· 4:142a-142b
Sjahrir, Sutan. *See* **Syahrir, Sutan**
Skiing ··· 4:69a
introduction to Japan ··· 1:119b-120b; 4:383a
Sky House ··· 4:207b
Slang ··· 3:303b-304a
Slaves (yakko) ··· 6:44a; 8:285a
Slawik, Alexander ··· 4:43a
Slogans, political ··· 6:206a
Slums ··· 7:202a-203a
Small and Medium Business Cooperative Association ··· 7:164a
Small and Medium Enterprise Credit Insurance Finance Corporation Law ··· 7:205b
Small and Medium Enterprise Credit Insurance Law ··· 7:205b
Small and Medium Enterprise Group Organization Law ··· 3:295b
Small and Medium Enterprise Modernization Law ··· 7:205b
Small and medium enterprises ··· 7:203a-205b, 253b
bank for ··· 7:164a
developments ··· 7:204b
diversity of industries ··· 7:203b
foreign trade ··· 2:324a
government assistance ··· 7:204b-205a
growth ··· 7:203b-204a
international comparisons ··· 7:203a-203b
large companies ··· 7:203b
medium firms ··· 7:205a
national economy ··· 7:204a-204b
prospects ··· 7:205b
Small and medium enterprises, laws concerning ··· 7:205b
Small business. *See* **Small and medium enterprises**
Small Business Finance Corporation ··· 7:204b, 205b-206a
Smallpox vaccination ··· 5:312b-313a
Small-Scale Whaling Control Regulations ··· 8:250b
Smiths ··· 7:206a
Smiths, Bureau of ··· 7:206a
Smithsonian Agreements
United States economic relations (1945-1973) ··· 1:135a; 8:164a
Smog ··· 2:227b
SMON disease ··· 6:254a; 7:206a-206b
Tanabe Seiyaku Co, Ltd ··· 7:335b
Snails ··· 7:81b
Snakes [(hebi) suborder Serpentes] ··· 7:206b
"Snow" ··· 8:212b
Snowbell (tree), Japanese ··· 2:184b
Snow Brand Food Co, Ltd ··· 7:206b
Snow Brand Milk Products Co, Ltd ··· 7:206b
Snow Country ··· 4:176a
Snow Festival (Yuki Matsuri) ··· 2:252b; 7:206b-207a
Snow viewing ··· 7:207a
Snyder, Gary ··· 7:207a
Sō ··· 惣 ··· 7:207a-207b
Sōami ··· 相阿弥 ··· 1:52b; 7:42b, 70a, 207b
works ··· 1:52b
Sobayōnin ··· 側用人 ··· 7:207b
Sōbin. 僧旻 *See* **Sōmin**
Sobosan ··· 祖母山 ··· 7:207b
Sōbō Suisan Co ··· 7:173a
Sō Chae-p'il ··· 3:287b
Independence Club ··· 4:281b
Sōchō ··· 宗長 6:298b; 7:208a
Sōchū ··· 惣中 ··· 7:207a
Social Affairs Bureau of the Home Ministry ··· 7:211a
Japanese conception of ··· 1:324a
Social Democratic Party ··· 7:74a-74b
modern philosophy ··· 5:231a
Social hierarchy, class distinction ··· 7:122b
Social Insurance. *See* **Social security programs**
Social insurance ··· 3:317a
Social Insurance Payment Fund ··· 5:145a
Socialism
Arahata Kanson ··· 1:72a-72b
Asanuma Inejirō ··· 1:96a
censorship ··· 1:252a
High Treason Incident of 1910 ··· 3:135b-136a
labor federations ··· 4:346b
leaders
Abe Isoo ··· 1:2a

Harris, Thomas Lake ······ 3:104a-104b
Ishikawa Sanshirō ······ 3:344a
Kagawa Toyohiko ······ 1:2a
Kita Ikki ······ 4:225b-226a
Nishikawa Mitsujirō ······ 6:17a
Ōyama Ikuo ······ 1:2a
modern philosophy ······ 5:231a
national leadership ······ 3:198b
organizations
Baibunsha ······ 1:129b-130a
Heiminsha ······ 3:125b
pacifism ······ 6:144a
Shakai Shugi Kenkyūkai ······ 7:74b
Socialist Democratic Party ······ 1:2a
Socialism Study Society ······ 5:231a
Socialist Citizens League
Eda Satsuki ······ 2:168b
Socialist Democratic Party ······ 1:2a
Socialist Masses Party ··· 1:2b, 96a; 7:74b
"Socialist" novel
Proletarian literature movement ··· 6:254b
Socialist Party of Japan ······ 4:48a-48b
Socialist People's Party ······ 1:2b; 7:74b
Socialist Woman, The ······ 4:138b
Socialization ······ 4:39a
Social organization ······ 2:233a
ie ······ 3:259a-260b
Social problems ······ 7:208a-209a, 217b
Social relationships ······ 2:232b-234a
Social security, national budget
······ 1:204b-205a
Social security legislation ··· 4:352b-354a; 7:209a-209b
Employment Security Law of 1947 · 4:352b
Livelihood Protection Law of 1950 · 4:353a
National Pension Law of 1959 ····· 4:353a
Unemployment Insurance Law of 1947
······ 4:352b
Social security programs ···· 7:209b-210b
Ministry of Health and Welfare ··· 5:189b
Occupation reforms ······ 4:346a
Social Security System structure ·· 7:210a
Social Service Law (Shakai Jigyō Hō)
······ 6:235b
Social status, lifestyle ······ 5:8b
Social welfare ······ 7:210b-213a, 217b
aged ······ 7:211b-212a
early development ······ 3:71a; 7:210b
income maintenance ······ 7:211a-211b
industrialization ······ 7:211a
Ministry of Health and Welfare ··· 5:189b
other services ······ 7:212a-212b
postwar period ······ 7:211a
prospects ······ 7:212b-213a
social administration ······ 7:212b
Social Welfare Activities Law · 7:55b, 209b
Société Franco-Japonaise ······ 2:332b
Society ······ 7:213a-218b
class structure ······ 1:322b-324b
education ······ 7:215a-215b
employment ······ 7:216a-216b
government and business ···· 7:215b-216a
history, 1868-1945 ······ 7:213b-214a
income distribution ······ 7:216b
interpretations ······ 7:217b-218a
legacies ······ 7:213a-213b
marriage and family ······ 7:214b-215a
minorities ······ 7:217a-217b
occupation and postwar changes ··· 7:214a
problems ······ 7:217b
religion ······ 7:217a
stratification ······ 7:216a
unions ······ 7:216b-217a
urbanization and rural ······ 7:214a-214b
Society for Study of Meiji Civilization (Meiji Bunka Kenkyūkai) ······ 8:313b
Society for the Preservation of the Japanese Dog ······ 2:125b
Society for the Study of Marxist Arts (Marukusu Shugi Geijutsu Kenkyūkai)
······ 6:255a
Society for the Study of Socialism ·· 1:2a; 7:74b
Society of Commoners ······ 3:125b
Society of Masterless Samurai ···· 6:337a
Society of Patriots ······ 1:34b
Society of the Chemical Industry ·· 1:268a
Society to Protect Children ······ 1:255a
Sociologists
See **Sociology in Japan**
Sociology in Japan ······ 7:218b-219a
empirical ······ 7:218b-219a
formal ······ 7:218b
historical ······ 7:218b-219a
Marxist ······ 7:218b-219a
Meiji period ······ 7:218b
psychological ······ 7:218b
today ······ 7:219a
Sōda Kiichirō
······ 左右田喜一郎 ·· 7:219a, 258a
"Sodezukin" ······ 袖頭巾 ······ 4:180a
Sōdōmei (Federation of Labor) ······ 総同盟 ···· 1:2a, 150b; 4:345a, 346b; 6:212b; 7:74b, 219a-219b
democracy ······ 2:84b
Takano Minoru ······ 7:317a
Watanabe Masanosuke ······ 8:236a
Soejima Taneomi 副島種臣 · 3:349b; 7:54a, 219b
Seikanron issue ······ 7:50b
Sōen ······ 宗淵 ··· 7:219b-220a
Sō family ······ 宋氏 ······ 7:220a
trade policy ······ 4:278b
waegwan ······ 8:198a
Soft drinks ······ 7:220a-220b
Soga brothers. *See* **Soga monogatari**
Soga family ······ 蘇我氏 ·· 7:220b-221a, 264a
Aya family ······ 1:125b
Buddhism as power ploy ······ 4:277a
Fujiwara family rivalry ······ 2:348a
monasticism ······ 5:236b
Nakatomi family rivalry ······ 2:351a
Soga monogatari 曽我物語 · 1:294a; 5:44b, 47a; 7:221a-221b
kabuki depiction ······ 4:98a
otogi-zōshi ······ 6:130a
Sōgana ······ 4:131b
Soga no Emishi ·· 蘇我蝦夷 ······ 8:303b
Soga no Iruka ··· 蘇我入鹿 2:351b; 7:221b
Soga no Umako · 蘇我馬子 ··· 7:85a, 221b, 264a
Gangōji ······ 3:6b
monasticism ······ 5:236b
Soganoya Gorō
······ 曽我廼家五郎 ··· 7:221b-222a
Soga school ······ 曽我派 ······ 7:222a
Soga Shōhaku ··· 曽我蕭白 ··· 7:222a-222b
Sōgetsu Kaikan ······ 8:15a
Sōgi ······ 宗祇 · 5:15a; 6:297a, 298a, 299b; 7:24a, 222b-223b
Sanjōnishi Sanetaka ······ 7:12b
Shinkei ······ 7:119a
Shinsen tsukubashū ······ 7:124b
Sōgi dokugin nanibito hyakuin
······ 宗祇独吟何人百韻 ······ 6:298b
Sōgi shūenki ·· 宗祇終焉記 ······ 7:208a
Sogō Co, Ltd ······ 7:223b
Sōgō shōsha ······ 3:18b-20a
Sōhei ······ 僧兵 ··· 8:230b-231a
Sōhō Myōchō ···· 宗峰妙超 · 1:*235a*; 2:68a; 7:223b
calligraphy ······ 1:235b
Sōhyō (General Council of Trade Unions of Japan)
······ 総評 ·· 2:7a; 4:347a, 359b; 6:212b; 7:223b-224a, 366b
Iwai Akira ······ 3:357b
Japan Socialist Party ······ 4:48b-49a
Kōrōkyō affiliation ······ 4:294a
labor unions ······ 1:313b
national bureaucracy ······ 1:220b
Ōta Kaoru ······ 6:129a
Shinsambetsu ······ 7:124a
Takano Minoru ······ 7:317a
Takita Minoru ······ 7:327a
Sōja ······ 総社 ······ 7:224a
Sōjiji ······ 総持寺 ······ 7:224a
Sojinkan zenshū
······ 楚人冠全集 ······ 7:258a
Sō Jorin ······ 曹汝霖 ······ 1:239b
Sōjutsu ······ 7:224a-224b
Sōka ······ 草加 ······ 7:224b
Sōka Gakkai ····· 創価学会 ······ 6:212b; 7:224b-225a
Ikeda Daisaku ······ 3:265a
Makiguchi Tsunesaburō ······ 5:85b
Toda Jōsei ······ 8:34b
Sōkaiya ······ 7:225a
Sōkaiya kinjō ·· 総会屋錦城 ······ 7:148a
Sō Kikei ······ 宋稀璟 ······ 7:227b
Sōkonshū ······ 草根集 ······ 7:170b
Soku (distantly related verses) ······ 疎句 ······ 8:214b
Sokushin jōbutsu 即身成仏 ······ 7:114a, 225a-225b
Sokushin jōbutsu gi
······ 即身成仏義 ······ 4:304a
Sō Kyōjin ······ 宋教仁 ······ 7:227b
Sōkyoku ······ 7:225b-226a
Sōkyoku koto music ······ 5:317a
Solar energy ······ 2:216a-216b
Solatium ······ 7:226a-226b
Solf, Wilhelm ······ 3:27a
Sōma ······ 相馬 ······ 7:226b
Sōma family ······ 相馬氏 ······ 7:226b
Sōmagahara Incident
······ 相馬原事件 ····· 3:34a-34b
Sōma Kokkō ····· 相馬黒光 1:164b; 7:226b
Sōma Nomaoi Festival
······ 相馬野馬追い ······ 7:226b
Sōma ware ······ 相馬焼 ··· 7:226b-227a
Sōmin ······ 僧旻 · 7:227a, 260a
assassination ······ 4:90a
Sōmoku chūgyo · 艸木虫魚 ······ 7:279b
Sōmon ······ 1:183a
Sōmon poetry, defined ······ 5:105a
Sompi bummyaku
······ 尊卑分脈 ·· 3:*17a*; 7:227a
Sōmura ······ 惣村 ······ 7:207a
Sone no Yoshitada
······ 曽禰好忠 · 5:34b; 7:95a, 227a-227b
Fujiwara no Akisuke ······ 2:350b
Shin kokinshū ······ 7:120a
Sonezaki shinjū
······ 曽根崎心中 ·· 1:*212b*; 4:77a
Songai hoken ······ 3:316a
Songbirds ······ 7:179b
Song contests, early ······ 2:138a
Song Hŭi-gyŏng ······ 7:227b
envoy to Japan ······ 4:278b
Song Jiaoren (Sung Chiao-jen) ··· 7:227b
Sŏng, King ······ 6:146b
Songs. *See* **Music**
Song shu ······ 7:264a
"Song [Sung] coins" ······ 7:232a-232b
Song Zheyuan (Sung Che-yüan) ·· 7:228a
Sonkeikaku Library ······ 5:1a; 7:228a
Sonnō jōi ······ 尊王攘夷 · 1:86a; 2:102a, 347a; 7:228a-228b; 8:291a

Inoue Kaoru 3:310a
Meiji Restoration 5:156a
Mito school 5:205b
nationalism 5:342b
Ōkubo Toshimichi 6:94a
Sakuradamongai Incident 7:4b
Sanjō Sanetomi 7:12b
Shimonoseki Bombardment 7:106a
Shinagawa Yajirō 7:109a
Shinron 7:124a
Tachibana Akemi 7:292b
Takechi Zuizan 7:321b
Takeda Kōunsai 7:322b
Tenchūgumi Rebellion 8:4a
Tokugawa Nariaki 8:52a
Umeda Umpin 8:146b
Yoshida Shōin 8:346a
Sonnō jōi movement 5:317b, 319b
Sono Ayako 曽野綾子 7:228b
Sony Corporation 7:228b-229a
Ibuka Masaru 3:254a
Sōōji byōbu 相応寺屏風 2:378a
Sophia University 7:229a
Sora utsu nami 天うつ浪 4:242b
Sorekara それから 5:350a
Sorge Incident 7:229a-230a
Sorge, Richard. *See* **Sorge Incident**
Sōrifu 総理府 6:244b
Soroban 1:1a
Sōrōbun 7:230a-231b
epistolary form 7:231b
grammar 7:230b-231b
history 7:230a
ōraimono 6:115b
writing system 7:230a-230b
Sōrui 7:46b
Sōryō system 惣領制 7:232a
warrior government 8:229b
Sōsaku hanga 3:146b; 4:236b; 5:232b-233a
Onchi Kōshirō 6:105b
Sosei 素性 7:13a, 232a
Kokinshū 4:254b
Sōseki no geijutsu 漱石の芸術 4:267a
Sōsen 宋銭 7:232a-232b
"Sōshin" 喪神 3:44b
Sōsho ("grass writing") 1:233b; 7:*171a*, 207a
Sōshoku gakku 装飾楽句 8:114a
Sōshoku kofun 装飾古墳 6:119a-119b
Sōshū Masamune 相州正宗 7:*285a-285b*
Sosogi Coast 曽々木海岸 7:232b
Sōtan. 宗湛 *See* **Oguri Sōtan**
Sōtatsu 宗達 7:43a, 232b-233a
Hon'ami Kōetsu 3:182a-182b
rimpa 6:317b
Wind and Thunder Gods 7:*232a-232b*
Sotetsu [(Japanese sago palm) *Cycas revoluta*] 7:233a
Sō Tetsugen 宋哲元 7:228a
Sōtō, China 1:283a
Sotomo 蘇洞門 7:233a
Sōtō sect 曹洞宗 1:179b; 7:233a-234b
Dōgen 2:123b
Edo period and revitalization 7:234a-234b
Eiheiji temple 2:186a-186b
history 7:233b
popularization 4:190b; 7:224a
teachings 7:233b
Sound of a Waterfall 6:77b
Sōunji Dono Nijūikkajō 早雲寺殿廿一箇条 7:234b
Sōunkyō 層雲峡 7:234b
Soups 2:22b
South Africa 1:19b
South America, Japanese studies 4:45a
South China Sea, Battle of 7:234b
Southeast Asia, Pacific Islands, and Japan 7:234b-236a
anti-Japanese sentiment 7:236a
expansion 7:235a
Japanese influence 7:235b-236a
Meiji period 7:234b-235a
post-World War II relations 7:235b
World War II 7:235a
Southern Alps. *See* **Akaishi Mountains**
Southern Alps National Park 南アルプス国立公園 1:39b; 7:236a
Southern Baptist Mission 1:142a
"Southern barbarian" 5:321b-322a
Southern expansion doctrine 1:87b; 7:235a, 236a-237a
elements 7:236b
history 7:236b-237a
United Kingdom 8:152b
"Southern Learning" school 5:328a
"Southern painting" 5:327b-328a
Southern Song 7:167b
South Islands 6:35a
South Korea, Japanese relations with. *See* **Korea and Japan**
South Manchuria Railway 南満州鉄道 6:278b; 7:237a-238a
administration, 1906-1937 7:237a
conflict with China 7:237b
empire, 1906-1931 7:237a-237b
founding 7:237a
Japanese interest 1:288b
Komura Jutarō 4:268a
Manchukuo 5:96b-97a
Matsuoka Yōsuke 5:139b
after 1937 7:237b-238a
Shiratori Kurakichi 7:147b
Twenty-One Demands 8:120b
Uchida Kōsai 8:123b
South Manchuria Railway Research Institute 7:293a
Souvenirs, commemorative 3:138a
Sovereign, priestly retired 3:227a
Sovereigns
Emperor Shōmu 7:166a
residences 1:105a
Soviet-Japanese Basic Convention 7:238a
Russia and Japan 6:343a
Russo-Japanese fisheries 6:345a
Soviet-Japanese development of Siberia 7:238a-238b
Soviet-Japanese Joint Declaration 7:238b-239a
Cold War 3:324a
United Nations 8:153b
Soviet-Japanese Joint Economic Committee 7:238b
Soviet-Japanese Neutrality Pact 6:343b
Sōya Kaikyō 宗谷海峡 7:239a
Sōyamisaki 宗谷岬 7:239a
Sōya Strait 宗谷海峡 7:239a
Soybeans [(daizu) *Glycine max*] 7:239a
production 1:27a
So, yō, and chō 祖, 庸, 調 7:239a-239b, 296a
Soy sauce 2:305a, 306b; 7:239b
brewing 1:170a
production 5:233b
Sōzei 宗砌 6:297a
Sozō 7:239b
Sōzoku Hō (inheritance law) 8:71a
Sozoro monogatari そぞろ物語 4:187b
Space program. *See* **Aerospace**
Space technology 7:239b-241a
applications satellites 7:240b
plans 7:240b-241a
rockets 7:240a
scientific satellites 7:240a-240b
Spain and Japan 7:241a
San Felipe Incident 7:9b-10a
Spaniel, Japanese 4:40b-41a
Sparrows [(suzume) Passer spp.] 7:241a-241b
mythology 5:296b
Spearheads, bronze 1:175a
Spears 1:89b; 7:224a
Special accounts 2:281a-281b, 307b
Special education 7:241b
Special Higher Police (Tokubetsu Kōtō Keisatsu or Tokkō) 1:253a; 6:198b; 7:241b-242a
Yokohama Incident 8:330a
Special Measures Law 2:182b
Special procurements 8:57b-58a
Special tax measures 7:242a-242b
Spell master 4:325a
Spencer, Herbert 7:218b
Spices 2:306a; 3:127b
Japanese cooking 2:21a-21b
Spiders [(kumo) order Araneae] 7:242b
Spinning industries
Kanebō, Ltd 4:137b
Nisshin Spinning Co, Ltd 6:21a
Nittō Bōseki Co, Ltd 6:22b
Tōyōbō Co, Ltd 8:89b
Unitika, Ltd 8:168b
Spinning mills 2:31a
Spirit of Jesus Church 7:242b
Spirits
ancestral 5:260a
nefarious 5:296a-296b
Spiritual exercises 1:96b
Spitzer, H. M. 4:38b
Sponge bath 3:72b
Sporting goods manufacturers 7:269b
Sports 7:242b-243a
Sports and recreation regulation 4:10a
"Spring pictures" 7:187a-188a
Spring wage offensive 7:188b-190a
Spy ring 7:229a
Squid and cuttlefish [(ika) order Decapoda] 2:284b; 7:243a-243b
Squid fishing 2:286a
Stalactite grottos 7:312a
Stalin, Joseph 8:286b
Standard Classification of Occupations
occupational structure 6:55b
Standard-form contract 7:243b
Standard of living 2:165a; 6:225b; 7:243b-245a
changes in consumption patterns 7:244a-245a
leisure time 5:7a
living conditions 7:243b-244a
personal consumption 7:244a
Standing to sue doctrine 4:80a
State Ceremonials, Board of 7:180b
Statement on the Expulsion of the Bateren 1:65a
State policy company 4:261b-262a
State Shintō 国家神道 2:300b; 6:204b; 7:138a, 245b-246a
Deguchi Nao 2:82b
Fukko Shintō 6:306b
ikigami 3:268a-268b
Statistical Mathematics, Institute of 7:246a
Stature 4:37b
Status, concept of 1:207b

Status of Forces Agreement (SOFA)
United States-Japan Administrative Agreement · · · 8:165a-165b
United States military bases, disputes · · · 8:168a
United States-Japan security treaties · · · 8:167a
Statutory Law · · · 1:13a
Steaming, Japanese cooking method · · · 2:23b
Steel Industries
Aichi Steel Works, Ltd · · · 1:33a-33b
Daidō Steel Co, Ltd · · · 2:56b
Hitachi Metals, Ltd · · · 3:207a
Japan Steel Works, Ltd · · · 4:49b
Kamaishi · · · 4:120b
Kawasaki Steel Corporation · · · 4:184a
Kōbe Steel, Ltd · · · 4:238a
Maruichi Steel Tube, Ltd · · · 5:120b-121a
Mitsubishi Steel Mfg Co, Ltd · · · 5:209a
Nakayama Steel Works, Ltd · · · 5:319b
Nippon Kōkan · · · 6:10a-10b
Nippon Steel Corporation · · · 6:12b-13a
Nippon Yakin Kōgyō Co, Ltd · · · 6:13b
Nisshin Steel Co, Ltd · · · 6:21a
Pacific Metals Co, Ltd · · · 6:143b
Sankyū, Inc · · · 7:15a
Shin Nan'yō · · · 7:121b
Sumitomo Metal Industries, Ltd · · · 7:269a
Tōkyō Steel Mfg Co, Ltd · · · 8:69a
Tōshin Steel Co, Ltd · · · 8:83b
Yawata Iron and Steel Works 8:320b-321a
Yodogawa Steel Works, Ltd · · · 8:326b
See also **Iron and steel industry**
Stein, Lorenz von · · · 1:120a; 2:2b; 7:246a
Stencil dyeing · · · 4:167b
Stevens, Durham W. · · · 4:282b
Stews, Japanese cooking methods · 2:23a
Stick dance · · · 棒踊り · · · 7:246a
Ryūkyū music · · · 6:357b
Stilts · · · 7:246a
Stilwell, Joseph W. · · · 7:200b
Stimson, Henry Lewis · · · 7:246b
Stimson Doctrine. *See* **Nonrecognition policy**
Stipend · · · 7:347b
Stock acquisitions, regulation of · · · 1:66a-66b
Stock exchanges · · · 4:48a; 7:246b-247a
Stockholder, professional · · · 7:225a
Stockholders' general meeting · · · 1:159a; 7:247a-247b
overseer · · · 6:136a
Stockholm Appeal (1950) · · · 1:111a
Stock market · · · 2:35a
Stock ownership dividends · · 2:120b-121a
Stocks, corporate · · · 2:34a
Stoddard, George D. · · · 2:180a
Stone tools · · · 1:75b; 6:159b; 7:247b-248a
Fukui Cave · · · 2:363b
Iwajuku site · · · 3:358a
Kamegaoka site · · · 4:125a
Karako site · · · 4:157b
Okhotsk culture · · · 6:84a
paleolithic culture · · · 6:159a
Stoneware · · · 1:259b-260a
Stop Venereal Disease Week · · · 8:189b
Storehouses, traditional 7:248a-249a, *248b*
modernization · · · 7:249a
premodern · · · 7:248b-249a
Stories about the past · · · 4:251a
Storyteller · · · 6:281b
medieval · · · 5:44b-45a
Storytelling · · · 2:172a
kōdan (oral) · · · 4:241a-241b
Straight, Willard Dickerman · · · 7:249a
Straits
Kammon · · · 4:128a
Korea · · · 4:292b
Naruto · · · 5:335b
Nemuro · · · 5:360a
Ondo · · · 6:106a
Sōya · · · 7:239a
Tsugaru · · · 8:113a
Tsushima · · · 8:118a-118b
Strange, Fredric W. · · · 7:242b
Stranger, The · · · 7:109a
Strategic Bombing Survey, United States · · · 7:249a
Stratification, social · · · 7:216a
Stratovolcanoes · · · 8:194a
Straw boots. *See* **Waragutsu**
Straw raincoats · · · 6:280a; 7:249a-249b
Straw sandals. *See* **Waraji**
Straw ware · · · 7:249b
Stray Thoughts · · · 4:138b
Street dances · · · 2:74a
Street entertainment · · · 7:249b-250a
monkeys · · · 5:245b
Street stalls · · · 7:250a
Street vendors · · · 7:250b
Strike, Clifford Stewart · · · 7:250b
Strike, right to · · · 6:312b-313a
Strike for the Right to Strike · · · 7:279b
Strikes and other forms of labor dispute · 2:369a; 4:349b-350a; 7:250b-251a
Allied Occupation · · · 7:189a
injunctions · · · 4:352a
political implications · · · 4:350b-351a
public employees · · · 4:351a; 6:265a
Takita Minoru · · · 7:327a
Student associations. *See* **Zengakuren**
Student Federation of Social Science (Gakuren) · · · 6:168b
Student movement · · · 7:251a-253a; 8:375a-375b
armed confrontation · · · 7:252b
crisis of 1968-1969 · · · 7:252b-253a
Japan Communist Party (JCP) · · · 4:12a; 7:252a-252b
origins · · · 7:251a-251b
postwar reconstruction · · · 7:251b-252a
prewar Gakuren · · · 7:251b
revenue for higher education · · · 3:134a
Shinjinkai · · · 7:115b
suppression and decline · · · 7:251b
university autonomy · · · 8:171a
Zengakuren · · · 7:252a
Student protests of 1968-1969. *See* **University upheavals of 1968-1969**
Students, foreign · · · 2:319a-319b
Studies in Japanese Buddhism · · · 6:288b
Studies in the Intellectual History of Tokugawa Japan · · · 4:259a
Studio potter · · · 1:260a
Study abroad · · · 7:36b, 253a
Study of Ancient Times, The · · · 4:240b
Study of Good, A · · · 8:376a-376b
"Study of Local Rural Localities" · · 5:71b
Su, Prince · · · 粛親王 · · · 7:277b
Subarjo, Raden Akhmad · · · 7:253b
Subaru · · · スバル(昴) 2:343a; 7:253b
Subcontracting firms · · · 2:35b
Subcontractors · · · 7:253b
Subscriptive establishment · · · 2:37b
Subsidiaries, prevalence · · · 2:35b
Subsidiary companies · · · 7:253b-254a
stock · · · 4:189b
Subversive Activities Prevention Law of 1952 · · · 1:254b; 2:337b, 339a; 6:266b; 7:254a-254b
Japan Communist Party · · · 4:11b
Subways · · · 7:254b-255a; 8:103a
Succession
imperial household · · · 3:277b
principle of · · · 3:259b-260a
Sūden · · · 崇伝 · · · 7:255a
codes of conduct · · · 1:206b
Ikoku nikki · · · 3:270b
Sudō Sadanori · · · 角藤定憲 · · · 4:181a
Sue · · · 須恵 · · · 7:255a
Embree, John Fee · · · 2:200a
Sue Harukata · · · 陶晴賢 · · · 5:250b
Suehiro Izutarō 末弘厳太郎 · · · 7:255a-255b
case study approach · · · 4:375a
Suehiro Tetchō 末弘鉄腸 · · · 7:255b
fūzoku shōsetsu · · · 2:378b
hambatsu · · · 3:92a
seiji shōsetsu · · · 7:50a
Suekawa Hiroshi · · · 末川博 · · · 7:255b
Sue kilns · · · 7:256a
Suematsu Kenchō · · · 末松謙澄 1:159b; 7:255b
Suemitsu · · · 季光 · · · 5:249b
Suetsugu Heizō · 末次平蔵 · · · 7:255b-256a
Sue vessels · · · 7:256a
Sue ware · · · 須恵器 · · · 1:78a, 158a, 258a; 2:305b; 7:256a
ash glazing · · · 1:261b
jar · · · 1:*257a*
of kofun · · · 4:245a
Okinawa · · · 6:85b
rokuro · · · 6:335b
Sanage · · · 7:9a-9b
Sueyoshi Magozaemon · · · 末吉孫左衛門 · · · 7:256a-256b
Suffrage. *See* **Universal Manhood Suffrage Movement; Women's suffrage**
Suffrage movements · · · 8:169a-169b
Sugadaira · · · 菅平 · · · 7:256b
Sugae Masumi · · 菅江真澄 2:296a; 7:256b
Sugae Masumi yūranki · · · 菅江真澄遊覧記 · · · 7:256b
Sūgaku kyōiku no kompon mondai · · · 数学教育の根本問題 · · · 6:71a
Suganuma Teifū · 菅沼貞風 · · · 7:256b
Sugap'a · · · 7:259b
Sugar cane production · · · 1:50a
Sugar industries
Dai-Nippon Sugar Manufacturing Co, Ltd · · · 2:66b
Ensuikō Sugar Refining Co, Ltd · · · 2:221a-221b
Meiji Sugar Mfg Co, Ltd · · · 5:160b
Mitsui Sugar Co, Ltd · · · 5:212b
Nippon Beet Sugar Mfg Co, Ltd · · · 6:8b
Nissin Sugar Mfg Co, Ltd · · · 6:21b
Taitō Co, Ltd · · · 7:306a
Sugar industry · · · 2:152-153a
Sugata Sanshirō · 姿三四郎 · · · 8:36b, 73a
Sugawara Minoru. 菅原実 *See* **Uchimura Naoya**
Sugawara no Michizane 菅原道真 1:151b; 2:79a; 5:31a-31b; 7:21a, 256b-257b, 260a
China · · · 1:283a
Chinese poem · · · 1:293b
Fujiwara family · · · 2:348b
hero worship · · · 3:128a
Ruijū kokushi · · · 6:340a
Shin kokinshū · · · 7:120a
Shintō · · · 7:127a
vengeful spirit · · · 4:126a
works · · · 5:31b
Sugawara no Takasue no Musume · · · 菅原孝標女 · · · 7:257b
diary · · · 7:21a
Sarashina nikki · · · 5:35b; 7:21a-21b
Suggestion boxes · · · 5:165b
Sugi [(Japanese cedar) *Cryptomeria japonica*] · · · 7:257b
Sugihara Sōsuke 杉原荘介 · · · 3:358a

Sugihara Yoshie
  Ai no aru mura: Shinkyō Kyōdōtai no Kiroku 7:121b
  Sensei and His People: The Building of a Japanese Commune 7:121b
Sugi Michisuke 杉道助 7:257b
Sugimoto Eiichi 杉本栄一 7:258a
Sugimoto Ryōkichi 杉本良吉 3:261a
Sugimura Jihei 杉村治兵衛 7:258a
  Kaigetsudō school 4:109b
  Kambun Master 4:124b
Sugimura Kōzō 杉村広蔵 7:258a
Sugimura Sojinkan 杉村楚人冠 7:258a
Sugimura Yōtarō 杉村陽太郎 4:373a
Suginami Ward 杉並区 7:153a
Sugita Gempaku 杉田玄白 5:313a; 7:258b
  natural science 5:356b
  Rangaku kotohajime 6:283b
Sugiura Eiichi. 杉浦英一 *See* **Shiroyama Saburō**
Sugiura Shigetake 杉浦重剛 4:340a; 7:51b, 258b
Sugiyama Gen. *See* **Sugiyama Hajime**
Sugiyama Hajime 杉山元 7:258b
Sugiyama Naojirō 杉山直治郎 2:319a; 7:258a-259a
Sugiyama Sampū 杉山杉風 7:259a
Sugoroku 7:259a-259b
Sugup'a 7:259b
  Kaehwap'a clash 4:101b
  Kaehwap'a thwarted 4:280b
  Kapsin Political Coup 4:156b
Sui 粋 3:267b-268a
Sui and Tang (T'ang) China, embassies to 7:259b-261a
  abandonment 7:260a-261a
  Sui 7:260a
  Tang 7:260a
  Suibokuga. 水墨画 *See* **Ink painting**
Suichikushū 酔竹集 4:157a
Suicide 4:38b, 84b-85a; 7:261a-263a
  characteristics 7:261b-262a
    age 7:261b
    marital status 7:261b-262a
    occupation 7:262a
    plural suicide 7:262a
    region 7:261b
    sex differential 7:261b
  ethics 2:232a
  harakiri 3:101b-102a
  historical trends 7:261a-263a
  juvenile 4:87a
  psychological theories 7:262a-263a
  sociological approach 7:262a-263a
  statistics 7:261b
  theories 7:262a-263b
  types 7:261b-262a
Suiga Shintō 垂加神道 8:312a
Suigun 水軍 7:263a
Suijakuga 垂迹画 7:263a-263b
Suijin 水神 7:263b
Suijinroku 吹塵録 7:263b
Suijin yoroku 吹塵余録 7:263b
Suika Shintō 垂加神道 2:300b; 7:263b-264a; 8:312a-312b
Suiko 出挙 7:264a
  kōden 4:243a
Suiko, Empress 推古天皇 7:69b, 264a
  Kanroku 4:151b
Suinin, Emperor 垂仁天皇 4:84b
Suiren 8:237a
Suisei 水勢 4:139a
Suisha 8:237a-237b
Suishō gensō 水晶幻想 4:176a
Sui shu 7:264a-264b; 8:308b
Suita 吹田 7:264b
Suita Incident 吹田事件 7:264b
Suiteki 1:*233a*
Suiteki (small water-dropper) 1:233b
Suiyuan Incident 7:264b
Sujime 2:25b
Sujin, Emperor 崇神天皇 2:376a; 4:576; 7:264b
Sukagawa 須賀川 2:367a; 7:265a
Sukarno 3:290b-291a; 7:265a
  Hatta, Mohammad 3:113b
Sukayu Hot Spring 酸ケ湯温泉 7:265a
Sukegō 助郷 7:265a-265b
Sukeroku 助六 4:98a-98b
Sukeroku yukari no edo-zakura 助六由縁江戸桜 4:*90b*, 93a, 94a
Sukhāvatī 6:270a
Sukhāvatī-vyūha 4:330a
Suki 7:265b
Sukiwatadono
  shinden-zukuri 7:111a
Sukiya 7:265b
Sukiyaki 7:265b
Sukiya-zukuri 数寄屋造 7:265b-266a
  Katsura Detached Palace 7:*265a*
Sukumo 宿毛 7:266a
Sukumo Bay 宿毛湾 7:266a
Sukunahikona no Mikoto 少彦名命 5:294a
  Ōkuninushi no Mikoto 6:97b
Suku site 須玖遺跡 4:163b; 7:266a
Suma 須磨 7:266a
Sumi (Chinese ink) 1:232b, *233a*, 233b; 5:331b
Sumidagawa 隅田川 4:154b; 7:266a-266b
  firefly viewing 2:280b
Sumida Ward 墨田区 7:266b
Sumi-demae, tea ceremony 7:362b
Sumi-e 墨絵 3:305b-307b
Suminagashi (marbled paper) 墨流し 7:266b; 8:233a
Suminokura Ryōi 角倉了以 7:266b
Sumire 8:192a-192b
Sumitomo 住友 2:30a; 7:266b-267a, 268a-268b
  Hirose Saihei 3:147b
  interaffiliate stockholding 3:295a
Sumitomo Bakelite Co, Ltd 7:267a-267b
Sumitomo Bank, Ltd 7:267a-267b
Sumitomo Cement Co, Ltd 7:267b
Sumitomo Chemical Co, Ltd 6:180a; 7:267b-268a
Sumitomo Construction Co, Ltd 7:268a
Sumitomo Corporation 3:18b-20a; 7:268a
Sumitomo Electric Industries, Ltd 7:268a-268b
Sumitomo family 7:52a, 268b
Sumitomo Forestry Co, Ltd 7:268b
Sumitomo Heavy Industries, Ltd 7:268b
  Sanoyasu Dockyard Co, Ltd 7:16a
Sumitomo Kichizaemon 住友吉左衛門 7:267b, 268b
  museums 5:277a
  Sen'oku Hakkokan 7:67b
Sumitomo Light Metal Industries, Ltd 7:267b, 268b-269a
Sumitomo Metal Industries, Ltd 7:269a
Sumitomo Metal Mining Co, Ltd 7:269a
  pollution 2:226b
Sumitomo Mutual Life Insurance Co 7:267a, 269b
Sumitomo Rubber Industries, Ltd 7:269b
Sumitomo Trust & Banking Co, Ltd 7:267a, 269b
Sumitomo Warehouse Co, Ltd 7:269b
Sūmitsuin 枢密院 6:252b-253b
Sumiyaki chōja 炭焼長者 7:269b-270a
Sumiyoshi
  Shintō 7:126b
Sumiyoshi monogatari 住吉物語 5:246a; 7:270a
Sumiyoshi school 住吉派 2:360b; 7:270a-270b
Sumiyoshi Shrine 住吉神社 7:270b
Sumiyoshi-zukuri 住吉造 7:270b
Summary courts 4:80b, 81b
Summers, James 7:270b
Sumō 7:270b, *271a*, 271b-274a
  belt 7:271b
  ceremonies 7:272a-273a
  divisions and ranks 7:271b-272a
  dohyō 7:271a
  Japan Sumō Association 7:274a
  kappa 4:156b
  Kokugikan 7:274a
  object of match 7:271a-271b
  practice 7:273b-274a
  stable system 7:273a-273b
  techniques 7:271b
  tournaments 7:273a
  wrestlers 7:271b
Sumoto 洲本 7:274b
Sumō wrestlers
  fundoshi 2:369b
  physical adaptation 4:37a
Sumptuary edicts 4:198b
Sumpu 駿府 7:274b
Sumpuki 駿府記 7:274b
Sunagawa 砂川 7:274b
Sunagawa case 砂川事件 7:274b-275b
  judicial review 4:80a
  Tanaka Kōtarō 7:337a
Suna no onna (Woman in the Dunes) 砂の女 1:3a; 8:15a
Sunao 7:275b-276a
Sundry goods industry 7:276a
Suneru 7:275b
Sung Che-yüan. *See* **Song Zheyuan (Sung Che-yüan)**
Sung Chiao-jen. *See* **Song Jiaoren (Sung Chiao-jen)**
Sun goddess. *See* **Amaterasu Ōmikami**
Sun I-hsien 7:276b
Sunlight, access to 6:313a
Sun, The. *See* **Taiyō**
Suntory, Ltd 7:276a
  Torii Shinjirō 8:79b
Sun Wen. *See* **Sun Yat-sen**
Sun worship 7:276a-276b
Sūnyatā 1:177b-178a; 2:212b-213a
Sun Yat-sen 6:302a; 7:48a, 199b, 227b, 276b, 277b
  Chiang Kai-shek 1:270b
  Dai Jitao (Tai Chi-t'ao) 2:59a
  Inukai Tsuyoshi 3:326a
  Ioffe (Joffe), Adolf Abramovich 3:328a
  Kita Ikki 4:226a
  Provisional Government of the Republic of China 6:260b
Sun Yixian 7:276b
Suō no Kuni 周防国 7:276b-277a
Suō Ōshima 周防大島 6:125a-125b
Suō Province 周防国 7:276a-276b
Supermarkets distribution system 2:120b
Superstitions 5:245b
Support 7:277a
Supreme Commander for the Allied Powers (SCAP) 7:32b-33a
  Ball, William MacMahon 1:135a-135b
  dissension 2:154b
  economic planning 2:167b-168a

economic reforms 2:155a-155b
educational reform 2:180a-180b
Japanese economy 2:154b-155a, 156b-158a
labor unions 2:156b
LARA 4:368a
trade 2:157a
United States education missions to Japan 8:164b
United States-Japan security treaties 8:166a
Supreme Court .. 4:79a-81a; 6:214a; 7:93b, 277a-277b
customs 4:380a
delegation of power 2:84a
obscenity rulings 1:254b-255a
prime minister and cabinet 6:244a
religion 6:295a
rules of 6:340a
Supreme Order of the Chrysanthemum 2:81b
Suretyship 7:278a
Suretyship, personal 6:178a-178b
Suribachi and surikogi (mortar and pestle) 2:24b-25a
Surimono 7:278a; 8:183b-184a
Ōsaka school 6:123a
Surrender, Instrument of 7:278a-278b
Suruga Bay .... 駿河湾 7:278b
Susaki .... 須崎 7:278b
Susanoo no Mikoto .... 素戔嗚尊 7:278b; 8:307b
birth 5:293a
feuding with Amaterasu 5:293a-293b
Suseri Hime ... 須勢理毘売 5:294a
Sushi 2:24a, 306a; 7:278b-279a
chirashizushi 7:278b-279a
hakozushi 7:278b
makizushi 7:278b
nigirizushi 7:278b
Susono .... 裾野 7:279a
Sustenance allotments 4:55b
Susuki [(eulalia) *Miscanthus sinensis*] 7:279a
Susukida Kyūkin 薄田泣菫 7:279b
Kambara Ariake 4:123a
Susukita Rokuhei .... 寿々喜多呂九平 2:268a
Susumubeki haiku no michi .. 進むべき俳句の道 7:311b
Sutego 7:279b
Sū Tōfun .... 鄒韜奮 8:380a
Suto Ken Suto 7:279b
Sutoku, Emperor 崇徳天皇 7:68a, 279b-280a
Fujiwara no Toshinari 2:356b
Sūtra 1:177a
Sutra mounds 7:280a
gorintō 3:46a
inscriptions 3:313b
shellfish 7:82a
Suwa (city) .... 諏訪 7:280a
Suwa, Lake .... 諏訪湖 7:280a
Suwa Basin ...... 諏訪盆地 7:280a
Suwariwaza 4:82a
Suwa Seikōsha Co 4:200b
Suwa Shrine ..... 諏訪神社 ... 7:280a-280b
Suye Mura: A Japanese Village ... 2:200a; 7:255a
Suzaka .... 須坂 7:280b
Suzaku, Shinkokushi 7:121b
Suzu (city) .... 珠洲 .... 7:280b 7:280b
Suzu (bell) 7:280b
Suzuka .... 鈴鹿 7:280b
"Suzuka magouta" .... 鈴鹿馬子唄 7:281a
Suzuka Mountains .... 鈴鹿山脈 7:280b
Suzuka Pass .... 鈴鹿峠 ... 7:280b-281a
Suzuka Quasi-National Park .... 鈴鹿国定公園 8:357b
Suzuki Akira .... 鈴木朖 7:281a
Fujitani Nariakira 2:346b
Suzuki Bokushi .. 鈴木牧之 3:214b
Suzuki Bunji ..... 鈴木文治 7:281a
Yūaikai 4:345a
Suzuki Daisetsu . 鈴木大拙 7:281b
Suzuki, Daisetz Teitarō .... 鈴木大拙(貞太郎) ... 7:28b, 281b
Suzuki decision 4:79b; 7:281b-282a
Suzuki Eitarō .. 鈴木栄太郎 7:282a
Suzuki Harunobu. 鈴木春信 *See* **Harunobu**
Suzuki Kantarō 鈴木貫太郎 7:282a
February 26th Incident 2:249b
World War II 8:276a
Suzuki Kiitsu .... 鈴木基一 7:282a
Suzuki Kisaburō .... 鈴木喜三郎 ... 7:282a-282b
senkyo kanshō 7:66b
Suzuki Masatsugu鈴木雅次 7:282b
Suzuki Masaya 鈴木馬左也 .. 7:267a, 282b
Suzuki Masayuki · 鈴木雅之 4:259a
Suzuki Miekichi .... 鈴木三重吉 · 1:39b; 7:282b
Seikatsu Tsuzurikata Undō development 7:51a
Shinshōsetsu 7:125b
Suzuki Mosaburō .... 鈴木茂三郎 ... 7:282b-283a
Japan Socialist Party 4:48b
Suzuki Motor Co, Ltd 7:283a
Suzuki Ryōichi ... 鈴木良一 3:16a
Suzuki Shigetane 鈴木重胤 7:283a
Suzuki Shin'ichi · 鈴木鎮一 7:283a
Suzuki Shōsan .. 鈴木正三 1:179b; 7:283a-283b
Suzuki Shōten ... 鈴木商店 ... 2:31a, 277b; 4:139a; 7:283b
Takahata Seiichi 7:313b
Teijin Incident 7:375b
Suzuki Umetarō .... 鈴木梅太郎 1:268b; 7:283b
Suzuki violin method · 5:287a; 7:283b-284a
Suzuki Zenkō .... 鈴木善幸 7:284a
Suzume 7:241a-241b
Suzumebachi (hornets) 1:149a
Suzuri 1:*233a*, 233b
Suzuribako (writing-equipment box) 1:233b
Suzutake (*Sasa purpurascens*) 1:136a
Swallows [(tsubame) family Hirundinidae] 7:284a
Swami Vivekananda 3:288a-288b
Swearwords 7:284a
Sweden 4:43b
Sweetfish (ayu) 1:125b
Sweet flag 7:154a-154b
Swimming 7:284a-284b
Swiss Civil code 4:75b
Switzerland, Japanese studies 4:43a
Sword Ban Order of 1876 .... 7:151b
Sword-guards. *See* **Tsuba**
Sword hunt 1:89a; 7:84b, 284b-285a
Edo social structure and class policy 3:188a
Oda Nobunaga 6:63b
Sword Hunt of 1588 .... 7:122b
Sword-making
process 3:333a-333b
tatara furnace 3:333a-333b
Swordmanship
iai 3:253a
kendō 4:195b
training 5:119b-120a
Sword mountings 4:295b
Swordplay
jūjutsu vs. 5:119a
training 5:119b-120a
Swords 7:285a-288a
bronze 1:175a
early 1:87a
forging 7:285b-286a
Jōkotō (ancient sword) period 7:287a
Kotō (old sword) period 7:287a-287b
manufacture
Tawara Kuniichi 7:351b
modern period 7:288a
museums 5:280a
Shintō (new sword) period ... 7:287b-288a
Sōshū Masamune 7:*285a-285b*
swordsmiths 7:285b
tempering and polishing 7:286a-287a
Syahrir, Sutan 7:288b
Syllabic Dictionary of the Chinese Language, A 8:253b
"Symbol emperor system" (shōchō tennō sei) 2:208a
Symbolist movement 6:161b
Sympneumata 6:100a
Syncretism 7:288b-290b
evolution 7:288b-289a
examples 6:62a-62b; 8:221a, 347b
religious 3:223a; 6:351a-351b; 7:182a-182b, 190a-190b
terms 7:288b
Synthetic resins
manufacture 7:111b
Syphilis 6:257a; 8:189b

T

Taasobi 2:86a
Tabaruzaka .... 田原坂 7:291a
Tabei Junko ... 田部井淳子 7:291a
Tabi 4:210a; 7:291a
Tabi to densetsu · 旅と伝説 2:302a
Tablada, José Juan 7:291a
Table tennis 7:291b
Tableware 2:25a
bowls 2:25a
chawan 2:25a
hachi 2:25a
chopsticks (hashi) 2:25a
plate (sara) 2:25a
sake bottle and cup 2:25a
teapots (kyūsu and dobin) 2:25a
zen (table for one) 2:25a
Taboo 7:291b
Taboo expressions 7:291b
diplomatics 2:98a
Taboos 6:204a
harae 3:100b-101a
Tanabata Festival 7:334b-335a
Tachiai 7:271a
Tachibana Akemi .. 橘曙覧 5:48a; 7:291b-292a
Tachibana Chikage 橘千蔭 4:167b
Tachibana family ..... 橘氏 7:292a
Tachibana Kōsai · 橘耕斎 3:49b
Tachibana Kōzaburō .... 橘孝三郎 1:34b; 7:292a-292b
Tachibana Moribe · 橘守部 7:292b
travel diaries 8:106a

Tachibana no Hayanari 橘逸勢 7:292b
Jōwa conspiracy 4:78a
Sampitsu 1:234a
Tachibana no Moroe 橘諸兄 7:292b
Fujiwara no Hirotsugu, Rebellion of 2:351a
Tachibana no Narisue 橘成季 4:256b
Tachibana no Norimitsu 橘則光 7:53a
Tachibana no Tadakane 橘忠兼 3:332a
Tachibana no Ujikimi 橘氏公 2:77a
Tachibana Shiraki 橘樸 7:293a
Tachibana Shiraki chosakushū 橘樸著作集 7:293a
Tachibana Shūta 橘周太 7:293a
Tachihara Masaaki 立原正秋 7:293a
fūzoku shōsetsu 2:378b
Tachihara Michizō 立原道造 7:293a
Tachikawa 立川 7:293a
Tachikawa Bunko 立川文庫 7:293a-293b
Tachimochi 7:272b
Tachimono 7:293b
Tachioyama 4:95a
Tachiyaku 4:94a
Tada Fumio 多田文男 7:293b
Tadagoto uta (poetry employing the diction of ordinary speech) 6:140b
Tadamigawa 只見川 2:366b; 7:293b
Tadare (Festering) 爛 8:45a
Tadataka 忠教 6:93b
Tadayoshi 直義 8:341b
Tade 2:305a
Tade kuu mushi 蓼喰ふ虫 7:342b
Tadokoro 田荘 7:293b, 296a
Taehan Cheguk 7:293b
Taehan Empire 7:293b
Independence Club 3:287b
Korean-Japanese relations 4:281b
Taewŏn'gun 7:259b, 293b-294a
Japanese diplomacy 4:279b
Korean-Japanese relations 4:140b
Taft, William Howard 4:173a
Taga Castle 多賀城 7:294a
Tagajō (castle) 多賀城 7:3a, 294a
excavation 1:79b
Tagajō (city) 多賀城 7:294a
Taga no Ki. 多賀の柵 *See* **Tagajō**
Tagawa 田川 7:294a
Tageta 4:143b; 7:294b
Tagokura Dam 田子倉ダム 7:294b
Tagonoura 田子ノ浦 2:345a; 7:294b
Tagore, Rabindranath 1:164a; 3:288a; 7:294b
Taguchi Ukichi 田口卯吉 7:294b
historiography 3:156a
Kokushi taikei editor 4:262b
Tahata Eitai Baibai Kinshi Rei (of 1643) 田畑永代売買禁止令 1:131b; 7:294b-295a
Prohibition Against Permanent Alienation of Farm Lands 1:208a
Tokugawa Iemitsu 8:48a
Tai 1:244a; 7:45a
Taibei 7:307b
Tai Chi-t'ao. *See* **Dai Jitao (Tai Chi-t'ao)**
Taiga. 大雅 *See* **Ike no Taiga**
Taigyaku Jiken 大逆事件 3:135a-136a
Taiheiki 太平記 1:130b, 294a; 4:121a, 252a, 275a; 5:44a, 246a; 7:23b, 295a; 8:105a
gunki monogatari 3:69a
historiography 3:154a
kōdan tradition 4:241b
Taihei kōki 太平広記 4:121a
Taiheiyō Coal Mining Co. 7:295a-295b
Taiheiyō Kouhatsu, Inc 7:295a-295b
Taiheiyō Kyōkai (Institute of the Pacific)
Tsurumi Yūsuke 8:117a
Taiheiyō Mondai Chōsakai 3:315b-316a
Taiheiyō no washi (Eagles of the Pacific) 太平洋の鷲 8:111b
Taihō Code 大宝律令 1:151a; 7:11a, 62b, 295b
clothing styles 1:329b
compilation 1:20b
corvée labor 8:327a
court rank 2:40a
Daijōsai 2:59a-59b
Dazaifu 2:79a
education 2:171b, 172b
Fujiwara no Fuhito 2:350b
inheritance 6:244b
Kannamesai 4:144a
kokugun system 4:259b
ritsuryō system 6:329b, 331a
seals and 7:45b
Temmu, Emperor 7:382b
toneri 8:74b
uniforms 8:149b
Taihō Ritsuryō. 大宝律令 *See* **Taihō Code**
Taiinkun 大院君 7:293b-294a
Taika (Great Change) era 6:174b
Taika Nijūikkajō Yōkyū 対華二十一か条要求 8:120b-121b
Taika no Kaishin. *See* **Taika Reform**
Taika Reform 大化改新 1:293a; 2:102b; 7:2a, 90b, 100b, 172a, 260a, 295b-297a
China 1:282a
Chinese influence 4:277a
court rank 2:39b
corvée labor 8:327a
edict 7:296a
Fujiwara family 2:348a, 351a
immediate efforts 7:296a
iriai 3:330a
Jinshin Disturbance 4:60b
kokugun system 4:259b
Occupation 6:51a
opposition 7:296b
other reforms 7:296b
ritsuryō state 7:296b-297a
ritsuryō system 6:331a
sekisho establishment 7:57a
shōen 7:155b
645 Coup 7:296a
tadokoro 7:293b
technology transfer 7:374a
textiles 8:17b
uji-kabane system 8:131b
Uneme 8:147b
women in 8:258b
Yamato court 7:295b-296a
Taika Shakkandan 対華借款団 7:297a-297b
Taiki 台記 7:297b
Tai Kitō 戴季陶 2:59a
Taiko (drum) 2:301a; 4:193b; 7:297b
gagaku 3:2a
Ryūkyū music 6:357b
Taikō (title) 太閤 7:297b
Taikō kenchi 太閤検地 1:131b
Taikū (Big Sky) 大空 6:139a
Taikyō Sempu 大教宣布 7:297b
Taimadera 当麻寺 7:298a
Taima mandara engi 当麻曼荼羅縁起 7:42b
Taimitsu 2:231b
Tainichi Rijikai 1:47b-48a
Tai no kotoba 体の言葉 7:281a
Tainoura 鯛ノ浦 7:298a-298b
Tainoya 7:111a
Taipei Asian Problems Study Group 4:385a
Taiping Rebellion 2:319b
Taira 平氏 7:7b
Taira family 平氏 1:187b; 7:*298a-298b*, 298b-299a
alliances 2:264a
defeat 4:121b-122a
flags and banners 2:288a
Fujiwara family rivalry 2:348b
Hatakeyama family 3:111a
Heiji monogatari 3:123a
Heike monogatari 3:124a-124b
Ise Province 3:337b
ochiudo legends 6:60a
Sasaki Takatsuna 7:23a
warrior government 8:229a
Taira Incident 平事件 7:299b
Taira-Minamoto War 源平の争乱 1:51a, 67b; 2:264a, 363a; 7:93b, 183a, 299b-300b
aftermath 7:300b
battlefield 7:266a
Battle of Fujigawa 2:342b
crests 2:42b
Dannoura, Battle of 2:77a
defeat of Taira 7:300b
Heike monogatari 3:124b
jitō 4:63a
Koryŏ-Japan relations 4:278a
Minamoto family 5:178a
Mochihito, Prince 5:181a-181b
outbreak 7:299b
shōgun 7:160a
Taira family 7:299a
Tōdaiji 8:34a
warrior government 8:229a
Yoritomo's revolt 7:299b-300a
Yoshinaka and fighting 7:300a-300b
Taira no Atsumori 平敦盛 7:300b-301a
Taira no Kiyomori 平清盛 1:187b; 4:1a; 5:39b, 43b; 7:301a-301b
China 1:283a
court politics involvement 2:264a
Heiji Disturbance 3:123a
Heiji monogatari 3:123a
jitō 4:63a
Kōfukuji razed 4:244a
Ondo Strait 6:106a
residential estate 2:363a
Sanjūsangendō 7:13a
Taira no Sukemori 4:197b
Taira no Masakado 平将門 4:112a; 7:301b
Fujiwara no Hidesato 2:350b
Fujiwara no Takanobu 2:355b
Kanda Festival 4:137a
Shinshōji 7:125a
vengeful spirit 4:137a
Taira no Munemori 平宗盛 7:301b
Taira no Shigehira 平重衡 7:301b-302a
Taira no Shigemori 平重盛 6:*227a*; 7:302a
Fujiwara no Takanobu 2:355b
portrait painting 6:227a
Taira no Tadamori 平忠盛 7:302a
Taira no Tadanori 平忠度 5:39b; 7:302a
Taira no Tadatsune, Rebellion of 平忠常の乱 7:302a-302b
Taira no Tomomori 平知盛 7:302b
Taira no Yoritsuna 平頼綱 7:302b
Tairiku nippō 大陸日報 7:334b
Tairiku rōnin 7:302b
rōnin 6:337a
Tairō 大老 7:302b-303a

Tairo Dōshikai 対露同志会 4:272b; 7:303a
Tōyama Mitsuru 8:88b
Uchida Ryōhei 8:124a
Taisei Corporation 7:303a
firms of 7:303a
Taisei Hōkan 大政奉還 7:303a-303b
Taisei Kensetsu. *See* **Taisei Corporation**
Taisei kokuhō ron (On Western Law) 泰西国法論 8:112a
Taisei santen kō (Study of Three Changes in the World) 大勢三転考 2:102a; 3:155b
Taisei yochi zusetsu 泰西輿地図説 4:321b
Taisei Yokusankai 大政翼賛会 3:280a-281a
Taisekiji 大石寺 7:303b
Taisha 7:303b
Taishakukyō 帝釈峡 7:303b
Taishakusan 帝釈山 7:303b
Taishin'in. *See* **Great Court of Cassation**
Taishō, Emperor 大正天皇 7:69b, 305a-305b
Taishō and early Shōwa history. *See* **History of Japan**
Taishō Democracy 1:87a; 2:84b; 6:211a; 7:303b-305a
folk craft influence 2:295a
Gen'yōsha 3:25b
Imperial Diet 3:276b
limits 7:305a
mimpon shugi 5:175b
modern philosophy 5:230b-231a
Nagai Ryūtarō 5:301a-301b
popular involvement 7:304b
private interests vs. state interests 7:304b-305a
strengthening elected bodies 7:304a-304b
tennō kikan setsu 8:7b
theorists 2:362b
Ukita Kazutami 8:138a
Washington Conference 8:235a
women's suffrage 8:268b
Taishō Kaijō Kasai Hoken. *See* **Taishō Marine & Fire Insurance Co, Ltd**
Taishō Marine & Fire Insurance Co, Ltd 7:305b
Taishō period 大正時代 7:305b
Taishō Political Crisis 3:198a; 7:305b
Imperial Diet 3:276b
Taishō Seihen. 大正政変 *See* **Taishō Political Crisis**
Taishū bungaku. *See* **Popular fiction**
Taishū bungaku ron (Theory of Popular Literature) 大衆文学論 6:139a
Taishū tennōsei 大衆天皇制 6:204a
Taiso Hōnen. *See* **Taiso Yoshitoshi**
Taiso Yoshitoshi 大蘇芳年 7:306a
Kaburagi Kiyokata 4:100a
Taitō Co, Ltd 7:306a
Taitō Ku. *See* **Taitō Ward**
Taitō Ward 台東区 7:306a
Taiwan 台湾 1:286a; 7:306a-309a
acquisition of 4:7a; 7:198b
Chiang Kai-shek 1:270b
colonial politics 7:308b
colonial rule 7:307b
colonial society 7:308a-308b
Dutch and Zheng (Cheng) family periods 7:306b-307a
early reforms 7:307b
economic policy and development 7:307b-308a
Japanese contact 7:306b
modernization 7:308a
Musha Incident 5:280b
postwar era 7:309a
Qing period 7:307a-307b
Ryūkyū dialects 6:355a
Ryūkyū Islands 6:357a
wartime period 7:308b-309a
Taiwan Expedition of 1874 1:87a, 160a; 2:332a; 4:381a; 7:309a-309b
Iwasaki Yatarō 3:362b
Kido Takayoshi 4:203a
Ryūkyū kizoku mondai 6:357a
Taiwan Ginkō 2:277a-277b; 7:309b
Taiwan Seitō Co. 7:306a
Taiwan Shuppei 台湾出兵 7:309a-309b
Taiya Teiryū 鯛屋貞柳 5:307a
Taiyō 太陽 7:309b
Taiyō Fishery Co, Ltd 2:284a; 7:309b-310a
Taiyō Gyogyō. *See* **Taiyō Fishery Co, Ltd**
Taiyō Kōbe Bank, Ltd 1:140a; 7:310a
Taiyō no kisetsu (Season of Violence) 太陽の季節 6:231a
Taiyō no nai machi (Street without Sunshine) 太陽のない街 4:324a; 6:255b; 7:175b
Tokunaga Sunao 8:58a
Taiyōzoku 2:273b
Taizōkai 胎蔵界 7:310a
Kongōkai 4:269b-270a
Shingon sect 7:115a
Taizōkai mandara 胎蔵界曼荼羅 7:310a
Ryōbu Mandara 6:347b, 351a
Taizō mandara 胎蔵曼荼羅 7:310a
Taizō mandara (Womb Mandala) 胎蔵曼荼羅 6:*348a*
Tajima Naoto 田島直人 7:310a
Tajimi 多治見 7:276a, 310a
Tajō takon (Much Love Much Regret) 多情多恨 4:199a
Taka. *See* **Hawks and eagles**
Takabatake Motoyuki 高畠素之 7:310a
Takachiho 高千穂 7:310b
Takachihokyō 高千穂峡 7:310b
Takachihonomine 高千穂峰 4:221a; 7:310b
Takadachi 高館 4:76b
Takadai 4:308a
Takada Hiroatsu 高田博厚 7:310b
Takada Kenzō 高田賢三 7:310b
Takada Sanae 高田早苗 7:310b
Fenollosa, Ernest Francisco 2:251b
Taka-Diastase 7:315b
Takagari (falconry) 鷹狩 2:241b; 4:381a
Takagi Kanehiro. *See* **Takagi Kenkan**
Takagi Kenkan 高木兼寛 7:311a
Takagi Teiji 高木貞治 7:311a
Takahagi 高萩 7:311a
Takahama 高浜 7:311a
Takahama Kyoshi 高浜虚子 5:123b; 7:311a-311b; 8:295a
haiku 3:80a
Hototogisu 3:237b
Takahashi 高梁 7:311b
Takahashi Deishū 高橋泥舟 8:303a
Takahashi Dōhachi. 高橋道八 *See* **Nin'ami Dōhachi**
Takahashigawa 高梁川 7:312a
Takahashi Kageyasu 高橋景保 7:1b, 312a
Takahashi Kazumi 高橋和巳 7:85a, 312a
Takahashi Kenji 高橋健自 1:77b; 7:312a
Takahashi Kenzō 高橋建三
Kokka founder 4:255b
Takahashi Korekiyo 高橋是清 3:201a; 7:55a, 312a-312b
February 26th Incident 2:249b
Takahashi Mitsutoki. 高橋光時 *See* **Nin'ami Dōhachi**
Takahashi Mutsuo 高橋睦郎 7:312b
Takahashi no Mushimaro 高橋虫麻呂 7:313a; 8:207a
poems in *Man'yōshū* 5:107b-108a
sakimori uta 7:2b
"Takahashi no Mushimaro Collection" 8:207a
Takahashi Oden 高橋お伝 7:313a
Takahashi Satomi 高橋里美 5:230b; 7:313a
Takahashi Shinkichi 高橋新吉 7:313a
Nakahara Chūya 5:313b
Takahashi Yoshitoki 高橋至時 7:313b
Inō Tadataka 3:309a
Takahashi Yuichi 高橋由一 7:313b
Takahata Seiichi 高畑誠一 7:313b
Takahira Kogorō 高平小五郎 7:313b
Takahira-Root Agreement 高平-ルート協定 3:197a; 7:313b; 8:136a
Komura Jutarō 4:268b
Takaichi Kuroto. 高市黒人 *See* **Takechi no Kurohito**
Takai Kitō 高井几董 6:297b; 7:313b-314a
Takai Noriyasu 高井則安 4:*325a*
Takaishi 高石 7:314a
Takakura 1:*50b*
Takakura, Emperor 高倉天皇 1:67b
Takakura Ken 高倉健 7:314
Fuji Junko 2:343a
Takamagahara 高天原 4:126a; 7:278b, 314a
Takamanohara. *See* **Takamagahara**
Takamatsu 高松 4:103a; 7:314a-314b
Takamatsu, Prince 高松宮 7:314a
Takamatsu Castle 高松城 7:314a-314b
Takamatsu no Miya Nobuhito. 高松宮宣仁 *See* **Takamatsu, Prince**
Takamatsuzuka tomb 高松塚古墳 7:*314b*, 314b-315a
art objects 7:314b-315a
wall murals 1:79a
Takama Yoshio. 高間芳雄 *See* **Takami Jun**
Takami Jun 高見順 7:315a
February 26th Incident 2:250b
Takamine Hideko 高峰秀子 2:*272b*; 7:315a
Takamine Hideo 高嶺秀夫 7:315a-315b
Takamine Jōkichi 高峰譲吉 1:268a; 7:315b
Institute of Physical and Chemical Research 3:316a
Takami Senseki 鷹見泉石 7:315b
Takamuko no Kuromaro 高向玄理 7:260a, 315b
Takamura Kōtarō 高村光太郎 7:253b, 315b-316b
Takamura Kōun 高村光雲 7:*43a*, 316b
Takamure Itsue 高群逸枝 7:316b
Fujin kōron publication 2:344a
Takano Chōei 高野長英 1:141b; 7:28b, 316b-317a
Takano Fusatarō 高野房太郎 7:317a
labor movement 4:345a

Workers' Fraternal Society 7:164a
Takano Iwasaburō 高野岩三郎 7:317a
Takano Minoru 高野実 7:317a
Takano Sujū 高野素十 7:317a-317b
haiku 3:80a
Takaoka 高岡 7:317b
Takaosan 高尾山 7:317b
Takaosanji 高尾山寺 4:58b
Takarabe Takeshi 財部彪 7:317b-318a
Takarai Kikaku 宝井其角 1:225a; 7:318a
Ōshima Ryōta 6:126a
Takara kuji. *See* **Lotteries, public**
Takara Shuzō Co, Ltd 7:318a
Takarazuka 宝塚 7:318a
Takarazuka Girls Opera Company. *See* **Takarazuka Kagekidan**
Takarazuka Kagekidan 1:83b; 7:318a-318b
Otowa Nobuko 6:133b
repertoire 7:318b
Shōchiku Co, Ltd 7:318b
Takarazuka 7:318a
Takasago 高砂 7:318b
Takasago Netsugaku Kōgyō. *See* **Takasago Thermal Engineering Co, Ltd**
Takasago Thermal Engineering Co, Ltd 7:318b
Takasaki 高崎 7:318b
Takasakiyama 高崎山 7:318b
Takase Dam 高瀬ダム 2:73b
Takasegawa 高瀬川 7:318b-391a
Takashima Coal Mine 高島炭坑 2:31b; 7:318b-319a
Takenouchi Tsuna 7:325a
Takashimaryū teachings 7:319a
Takashima Shūhan 高島秋帆 7:319a
Takashima Tankō. 高島炭坑 *See* **Takashima Coal Mine**
Takashimaya Co, Ltd 7:319a
Takasugi Shinsaku 高杉晋作 1:86a; 7:319a-319b
Chōshū Expeditions 1:304a
Fujita Denzaburō 2:346a
Takataya Kahei 高田屋嘉兵衛 7:319b
Takata Yasuma 高田保馬 7:319b
Takatō 高遠 7:319b
Ejima Incident 2:188a
Takatō Castle 高遠城 7:319b
Takatori ware 高取焼 1:20b; 2:295b; 7:319b-320a
Kobori Enshū 4:238b
Takatori-yaki. 高取焼 *See* **Takatori ware**
Takatsuki 高槻 7:320a
Takatsu Tamaki 高津環 3:261a
Takaya Hikoshirō 高屋彦四郎 6:359a
Takayama 高山 7:320a
Takayama Basin 高山盆地 7:320a
Takayama Bonchi. *See* **Takayama Basin**
Takayama Chogyū 高山樗牛 5:12a; 7:320a
Takayama Festival 高山祭 7:320a, *320b*
Takayama Hikokurō 高山彦九郎 7:320b
Takayama Sōzei 高山宗砌 7:320b-321a
Takayama Ukon 高山右近 7:321a
Takayanagi Kenjirō 高柳建次郎 7:321a
electronics 2:192a
Takayanagi Kenzō 高柳賢三 2:319a; 7:321a
Commission on the 1947 Constitution 1:339b
Take 1:135b-136a
Takebe Ayatari 建部綾足 7:321a-321b
Takebe Katahiro 建部賢弘 7:57b, 321b
Takebu. 武生 *See* **Takefu**
Takechi no Kurohito 高市黒人 7:321b
Takechi Tetsuji 武智鉄二 2:274b-275a
Takechi Zuizan 武市瑞山 5:317b; 7:321b
Kōno Togama 4:275a
Takeda Chemical Industries, Ltd 7:321b-322a
Takeda family 武田氏 7:322a-322b
Kōfu, based in 4:243b
Shingen Kahō 7:113b
Uesugi Kenshin 8:130a
Takeda Izumo 竹田出雲 5:49b; 7:322a-322b
Forty-Seven Rōnin Incident 2:328a
productions 7:322b
Takeda Katsuyori 武田勝頼 7:322b
Nagashino, Battle of 5:306b
Takeda Kōunsai 武田耕雲斎 7:322b
Takeda Rintarō 武田麟太郎 7:322b-323a
Takeda Shingen 武田信玄 7:274b, 323a-323b
military practices 2:279a
Shingen Kahō 7:113b
Takeda Shirō. 武田四郎 *See* **Takeda Katsuyori**
Takeda Taijun 武田泰淳 7:323b
February 26th Incident 2:250b
Takefu 武生 2:364a; 7:323b
Takegoshi Yosaburō 竹越与三郎 7:323b-324a
Takehara 竹原 7:324a
Takehara tomb 竹原古墳 4:*247a*
Takehashi Insurrection 竹橋騒動 7:324a
Takehashi Sōdō. *See* **Takehashi Insurrection**
Takehisa Shigejirō. 竹久茂次郎 *See* **Takehisa Yumeji**
Takehisa Yumeji 竹久夢二 7:324a
Takeiri Yoshikatsu 竹入義勝 7:324a-324b
Takekoshi Yosaburō. 竹越与三郎 *See* **Takegoshi Yosaburō**
Takemi Tarō 武見太郎 4:47b
Takemitsu Tōru 武満徹 7:324b
Shinoda Masahiro 7:122a
Takemoto Gidayū 竹本義太夫 4:77a
Takemoto Gidayū I 竹本義太夫(初代) 3:30a; 7:324b
Takemotoza
Takeda Izumo 7:322a
Takemoto Gidayū I 3:30a; 7:324b
Takenaka Kōmuten Co, Ltd 7:324b
Takenouchi no Sukune 武内宿禰 7:324b-325a
Takenouchi Shikibu 竹内式部 7:325a
Takenouchi Tsuna 竹内綱 7:325a
Takenouchi Yasunori 竹内保徳 7:325a
Takeo 武雄 7:325a
Takeshima 竹島 7:325a-325b
Korea-Japan Treaty of 1965, supplementary agreements 4:288a
territorial claims 4:285b
Taketa 竹田 7:325b
Taketombo 竹蜻蛉 7:325b
Taketomijima 竹富島 7:325b
Taketori monogatari 竹取物語 5:32b-33a, 246a, 295a-295b; 7:325b-326a
Chinese literature 1:293b
monogatari bungaku 5:246a
Taketori no okina no monogatari. See **Taketori monogatari**
Takeuchi Kyūichi 竹内久一 7:326a
Takeuchi Seihō 竹内栖鳳 7:20a, 326a
Takeuchi Tsunekichi. 竹内恒吉 *See* **Takeuchi Seihō**
Takeuma 7:246a
Takezaki Suenaga 竹崎季長 7:326b
Mōko shūrai ekotoba commissioned 4:274b
Takiguchi no bushi 滝口の武士 7:326b
Takii Kōsaku 滝井孝作 7:326b
Takikawa 滝川 7:326b
Takikawa Incident 滝川事件 4:339b
Takikawa Yukitoki 滝川幸辰 7:251b, 326b-327a
Sasaki Sōichi 7:23a
Taki Mototaka 多紀元孝 7:327a
Taki Rentarō 滝廉太郎 7:327a
Takita Choin 滝田樗陰 7:100a, 327a
Chūō kōron 1:313a
Takita Minoru 滝田実 7:327a
Takizawa Bakin 滝沢馬琴 1:130b
Takizawa Eisuke 滝沢英輔 2:271a
Takizawa Okikuni 滝沢興邦 1:130b
Taki Zenzaburō 滝善三郎 3:101b-102a
Tako. *See* **Kites**
Tako (kite) 4:229b-231b
Tako (octopus) 6:60a-60b
Taku 多久 7:327b
Takuan Sōhō 沢庵宗彭 1:193b; 7:89b, 327b
Takuma Eiga 宅磨栄賀 2:346a; 7:327b
Takuma school 宅磨派 1:190a; 7:328a
Takuma Shōga 宅磨勝賀 7:328a
Takuma Tamenari 宅磨為成 1:227b; 7:328a
Takuma Tametō 宅磨為遠 7:328a
Tale of Flowering Fortunes 1:41a
Tale of Genji 1:293b; 4:188a; 5:35a-35b; 6:299b; 7:12b, 52a, 87b, 328b-331b
Buddhism 7:330b-331a
criticism 7:331a
divisions 7:328b-330b
early Japanese songs 2:138b
early stages 7:328b-330a
eschatology 7:331a
Fujiwara no Toshinari 2:357a
gagaku 3:1a
Genji monogatari emaki 3:87b; 7:*329a-329b*
Ichikawa Danjūrō 3:257a
influence 7:330b-331b
Kamo no Mabuchi commentary 4:129b
later stages 7:330a-330b
model for hero 2:352b
Motoori Norinaga's study of 4:258b
Murasaki Shikibu 5:267b-269a
Murasaki Shikibu nikki 7:328b
nature in Japanese religion 5:357b
Ochikubo monogatari 6:59b
paintings 4:148b
regency government 6:286b
Sarashina nikki 5:35b; 7:21b
Sengenshō 1:299b
studies of
Kodai kenkyū 4:240b
textual history 7:330b-331b
themes 7:330b-331b
translation 7:343a
waka 8:212b
women in Japan 8:258a
Tale of Lady Ochikubo, The 6:59b
Tale of Sagoromo 6:365a
Tale of the Bamboo Cutter, The (Taketori monogatari) 7:325b-326a

Tale of the Hamamatsu Middle Counselor ···· **3**:90b-91a
Tale of the Heike. See ***Heike monogatari***
Tale of the Hollow Tree ···· **8**:187b-188a
Tale of the Soga Brothers ···· **7**:221a-221b
Tale of the Tsutsumi Middle Counselor ···· **8**:118b-119a
Tales of Aesop ···· **2**:241a
Tales of Christians ···· **4**:221b
Tales of Glory ···· **2**:186a
Tales of Ise, The ···· **3**:337a-337b
Tales of Moonlight and Rain ···· **8**:126a
Tales of the Major Counselor from Uji ···· **8**:137b
Tales of the Spring Rain ···· **8**:126b
Tales of the West ···· **6**:369a
Tales of Times Now Past ···· **4**:270b-271a
Tales of Yamato ···· **8**:310a
Talisman
- inu hariko ···· **3**:325b

Talisman, protective ···· **8**:285a
Tally trade ···· **3**:174a; **7**:331b-332a; **8**:220b
- Ashikaga Yoshimitsu ···· **1**:101b
- kinds ···· **7**:332a
- Kōbe prospered in ···· **4**:238a
- Muromachi shogunate ···· **5**:273a
- National Seclusion ···· **5**:347a
- Ōuchi family ···· **6**:135a

Tama (city) ···· 多摩 ···· **7**:332a
Tama ···· **1**:62a, 147b-148a; **4**:126a; **7**:332a
- rites of pacification ···· **7**:332a
- types ···· **7**:332a

Tama, Lake ···· 多摩湖 ···· **7**:332b
Tamabachi (gall wasps) ···· **1**:149a
Tamagawa ···· 多摩川 **1**:272a; **4**:135a; **7**:332b
Tamagawa Aqueduct ···· **7**:332b
Tamagawa Daigaku. *See* **Tamagawa University**
Tamagawa Gakuen. *See* **Tamagawa University**
Tamagawa Jōsui. 玉川上水 *See* **Tamagawa Aqueduct**
Tamagawa University ···· **7**:332b
Tama Hills ···· 多摩丘陵 ···· **7**:332b
Tamai (field dance) ···· **2**:86a
Tamai Katsunori · 玉井勝則 ···· **3**:140b
Tamako. 多摩湖 *See* **Tama, Lake**
Tama Kyūryō. 多摩丘陵 *See* **Tama Hills**
Tamamushi Shrine 玉虫厨子 ···· **6**:*148b*
- urushi-e ···· **8**:181a

Tamana ···· 玉名 ···· **7**:332b
Tamana Hot Spring 玉名温泉 ···· **7**:332b
Tamano ···· 玉野 ···· **7**:332b
Tamari ···· **7**:265b
Tamatsukuri Hot Spring ···· 玉造温泉 ···· **7**:332b-333a
- Lake Shinji ···· **7**:115a

Tamatsukuri Onsen. *See* **Tamatsukuri Hot Spring**
Tama Zoological Park ···· **8**:379b
Tamba Mountains ···· 丹波高地 ···· **7**:333a
Tamba ware ···· 丹波焼 **2**:295b; **7**:333a
- glaze ···· **7**:333a
- kilns ···· **7**:333a
- museums ···· **5**:279b
- uses ···· **7**:333a

Tamba-yaki. *See* **Tamba ware**
Tamba Yasuyori · 丹波康頼 ···· **7**:333a-333b
Tameie ···· 為家 ···· **4**:54a
Tamenaga Shunsui ···· 為永春水 ···· **5**:49b; **7**:333b-334a
- fūzoku shōsetsu ···· **2**:378a

Tamerau nakare wakōdoyo ···· ためらうなかれ若人よ ···· **3**:102a
Tamezuki (method of molding paper) ···· **8**:234a
Tamiya Hiroshi ···· 田宮博 ···· **7**:334a
Tamiya Torahiko 田宮虎彦 ···· **7**:334a
Tamjing ···· **2**:130b
Tamon'in Diary. See ***Tamon'in nikki***
Tamon'in nikki 多聞院日記 ···· **7**:334a-334b
Tamura, Prince ·· 田村皇子 ···· **8**:303b
Tamura Denkichi 田村伝吉 ···· **1**:137a
Tamura Ransui ·· 田村藍水 **1**:225a; **7**:334b
Tamura Ryūichi ·· 田村隆一 ···· **1**:82b
Tamura Taijirō 田村泰次郎 ···· **7**:334b
- fūzoku shōsetsu ···· **2**:378b

Tamura Toshiko · 田村俊子 ···· **7**:54b, 71a, 334b
Tan ···· **4**:193b
Tana ···· **7**:266a
Tanabata Festival ·· 七夕 ···· **1**:160b; **2**:260b; **7**:334b-335a
- Hiratsuka ···· **7**:*335a*
- Kantō ···· **4**:153a
- religious symbolism ···· **6**:296a

Tanabe ···· 田辺 ···· **7**:335a
Tanabe Hajime ···· 田辺元 ···· **7**:335a-335b
- philosophies ···· **5**:230b

Tanabe Hajime zenshū ···· 田辺元全集 ···· **7**:335b
Tanabe no Sakimaro 田辺福麻呂 ·· **5**:108a
Tanabe Seiko ···· 田辺聖子 · **7**:103b, 335b
Tanabe Seiyaku Co, Ltd ···· **7**:335b
Tanabe Taichi ···· 田辺太一 ···· **7**:335b
Tanagokoro no shōsetsu ···· 掌の小説 ···· **4**:176a
Tanaka biwa ···· **7**:339b
Tanaka Chikao 田中千禾夫 ···· **7**:335b
- *Shingeki* ···· **7**:112a, 113a
- shingeki ···· **7**:113a

Tanaka Chōbei 田中長兵衛 ···· **3**:333b
Tanakadate Aikitsu 田中館愛橘 ···· **7**:336a
Tanaka Eizō ···· 田中栄三 ···· **2**:268a
Tanaka Fujimaro ···· 田中不二麿 **2**:175b; **7**:336a
Tanaka Fuyuji ···· 田中冬二 ···· **7**:336a
Tanaka Giemon. 田中儀右衛門 *See* **Tanaka Hisashige**
Tanaka Giichi ···· 田中義一 · **3**:200a; **7**:55a, 66b, 77b, 88b, 336a-336b
- cabinet ···· **2**:277b
- Jitsugyō Dōshikai ···· **4**:64a
- Kenseikai ···· **4**:198a
- resignation ···· **2**:207a-207b

Tanaka Giichi cabinet
- investigation ···· **5**:316a-316b
- Mizuno Rentarō ···· **5**:226b

Tanaka Hidemitsu ···· 田中英光 ···· **7**:336b
Tanaka Hisashige ···· 田中久重 ···· **7**:336b-337a
Tanaka Kakuei ···· 田中角栄 · **2**:309b, 333a; **7**:337a
- Lockheed Scandal ···· **5**:72a

Tanaka Kan'ichi · 田中寛一 ···· **2**:179a
Tanaka Kichinosuke. 田中吉之助 *See* **Tanaka Fuyuji**
Tanaka Kiichi. 田中喜一 *See* **Tanaka Ōdō**
Tanaka Kinuyo ·· 田中絹代 **2**:*270b*; **7**:337a
Tanaka Kōtarō 田中耕太郎 ·· **7**:275b, 337b
Tanaka Kyūgu ·· 田中丘隅 ···· **7**:337b
Tanaka Manufacturing Works **7**:336b-337a
Tanaka Memorandum ···· 田中覚え書 · **7**:337b; **8**:37a
Tanaka Mitsuaki · 田中光顕 ···· **7**:337b-338a
Tanaka Ōdō ···· 田中王堂 ···· **7**:338a-338b
Tanaka Shōsuke 田中勝助 ···· **7**:338b
Tanaka Shōzō ·· 田中正造 ···· **1**:73a; **7**:338b-339b
- ecologist ···· **7**:339a-339b
- fight for a village ···· **7**:339a
- Fukuda Hideko ···· **2**:362b
- pollution ···· **7**:338b-339a
- resistance to provincial misgovernment ···· **7**:338b

Tanaka Sumie ···· 田中澄江 ···· **7**:339b
Tanaka-Trudeau communique ···· **1**:238a
Tanaka Yoshio ·· 田中芳男 ···· **7**:339b
Tanaka Yutaka ···· 田中豊 ···· **7**:339b
Tanashi ···· 田無 ···· **7**:339b
Tanasue no mitsugi 手末調 ···· **7**:264b
Tandai ···· 探題 ···· **7**:340a
- Rokuhara ···· **6**:335a

Taneda Santōka ···· 種田山頭火 ···· **7**:340a
Tanegashima ···· 種子島 **3**:140a; **7**:340a
Tanegashima Space Center ···· **7**:240b
Tanegashima Tokitaka ···· 種子島時堯 **2**:279a; **7**:340a
Tanegashima Yukiko ···· 種子島有紀子 ···· **2**:76a
Tane maku hito ·· 種蒔く人 · **1**:70b; **7**:175a, 340a-340b
- proletarian literature movement ···· **6**:254b

Tang dynasty
- Dajōkan ···· **2**:69b
- kara-e painting ···· **4**:157a
- Taihō Code ···· **7**:295b

Tange Kenzō ···· 丹下健三 ···· **7**:340b
- buildings ···· **7**:340b

Tanggu (Tangku) Truce ···· **7**:340b-341a
Tango ···· 丹後 ···· **7**:341a
Tango fudoki · 丹後風土記 ···· **8**:44b
Tango Mountains 丹後山地 **4**:337b; **7**:341a
Tang style painting ···· **6**:148a
Tani Bunchō ···· 谷文晁 · **1**:211a; **7**:17b, 341a
- Kameda Bōsai ···· **4**:125a

Tanigawadake ···· 谷川岳 ···· **7**:341a-341b
Tanigawa Kotosuga ···· 谷川士清 ···· **7**:341b
Taniguchi Masaharu ···· 谷口雅春 ···· **7**:341b
- Seichō no Ie ···· **7**:49b

Taniguchi Yoshirō ···· 谷口吉郎 · **1**:81b; **7**:341b
- buildings ···· **7**:341b

Tani Jichū ···· 谷時中 ···· **7**:341b
Tani Jōji ···· 谷譲次 ···· **3**:116a
Tani Kanjō ···· 谷干城 ···· **7**:341b-342a
- Satsuma Rebellion ···· **7**:30a

Tanikawa Shuntarō ···· 谷川俊太郎 ···· **7**:342a
Tanimoto Tomeri ·· 谷本富 ···· **7**:342a
- Shin Kyōiku Undō ···· **7**:121b

Tanin no kao (The Face of Another) ···· 他人の顔 ···· **1**:3a; **8**:15a
Tanino Setsu ···· 谷野セツ ···· **7**:342a
Tani Tateki. 谷干城 *See* **Tani Kanjō**
Tanizaki Jun'ichirō ···· 谷崎潤一郎 ···· **1**:3a, 313b; **2**:268a, 274a; **5**:13a, 54b-55a; **7**:26b, 100b, 102b, 103b, 253b, 342a-343b
- shimpa ···· **7**:108a
- *Shinshichō* ···· **7**:125a

Tanizaki Jun'ichirō Prize
- Endō Shūsaku ···· **2**:214a
- Ōe Kenzaburō ···· **6**:66b

Tanka ···· **6**:296b; **7**:343b
- Hyakunin isshu (Single Poems by 100 Poets) ···· **3**:248b-249a
- kagura uta ···· **4**:108a
- *Man'yōshū* ···· **7**:343b
- predominance ···· **4**:115b
- sakimori uta style ···· **7**:2b
- Takechi no Kurohito ···· **7**:321b
- waka ···· **8**:201b

Tankai ···· 湛海 ···· **7**:343b
- statues ···· **7**:343b

Tanka literary groups ··········· 5:19a-20a
Tanka poets, modern
  Aizu Yaichi ··························· 1:38b
  Ishikawa Takuboku ·········· 3:344b-345a
  Itō Sachio ······························ 1:38b
  Kinoshita Rigen ···················· 4:216a
  Kitahara Hakushū ·················· 4:225a
  Kubota Utsubo ······················ 4:301b
  Maeda Yūgure ························ 5:81b
  Masaoka Shiki ··············· 5:123b-124a
  Miyazawa Kenji ·············· 5:222b-223b
  Ochiai Naobumi ······················ 6:59a
  Orikuchi Shinobu ············ 6:118b-119a
  Saitō Mokichi ················ 6:374a-374b
  Sasaki Nobutsuna ···················· 7:23a
  Shimaki Akahiko ····················· 7:99b
  Toki Zemmaro ························ 8:43b
  Tsuchiya Bummei ··················· 8:112a
  Wakayama Bokusui ················ 8:219a
  Yosano Akiko ························ 8:340a
  Yosano Tekkan ················ 8:340a-340b
  Yoshii Isamu ·················· 8:346b-347a
  Yoshino Hideo ······················ 8:348b
Tankei ················ 湛慶 · 1:200a; 7:13a, 343b-344a
  works ························ 7:343b-344a
Tankū Teisen Kyōtei. 塘沽停戦協定 *See* **Tanggu (Tangku) Truce**
Tanluan ··································· 4:67a
Tannishō ············ 歎異抄 ········ 7:344a
  Kiyozawa Manshi ··················· 4:233a
Tanno Setsu ····· 丹野セツ ········ 7:344a
Ta no kami ····· 4:125b-126a; 7:263b, 344a
  Daikokuten ···························· 2:60b
  scarecrows ··························· 4:115a
Tanomoshi ········· 頼母子 ········ 5:262a
Tanomura Chikuden
  ··············· 田能村竹田 1:211a; 6:*155b*; 7:344b
Tanomura Chokunyū
  ··············· 田能村直入 ········ 7:344b
Tansen and tammai
  ··············· 段銭, 段米 ········ 7:344b
  Kaei sandai ki ······················ 4:101b
Tansu ····································· 4:161a
Tan Taigi ··········· 炭太祇········ 1:225a; 7:344b-345a
Tantei sōshu ····· 端艇漕手 ········ 7:336b
Tanuki [(raccoon dog) *Nyctereutes procyonoides*] ······· 4:100b; 7:83a, 345a
Tanuma Okitsugu
  ················ 田沼意次 ··· 7:345a-346a
  Kansei Reforms ····················· 4:152b
Tanuma period
  kabunakama ·························· 4:100a
  merchant culture ··················· 2:340b
  Tanuma Okitsugu ············ 7:345a-346a
Tan'yū. 探幽 *See* **Kanō Tan'yū**
Tanzawasan ······· 丹沢山 ········ 7:346a
Tao-hsüan ······························· 2:131b
Taoism ················ 6:290a-292a; 8:372b
  holy men ································ 7:67a
  new religions ························ 5:366b
  thought and culture ················ 8:26b
  tolerance in Japanese religion ······· 8:70b
Taoka Reiun ····· 田岡嶺雲 ··· 7:51b, 346a
Taoka Reiun zenshū 田岡嶺雲全集 7:346a
Taoka Sayoji. 田岡佐代次 *See* **Taoka Reiun**
Taoshuo ·································· 1:68b
Tapestry ································ 1:189b
Tappizaki ·········· 竜飛崎 ········ 7:346a
Taradake ············ 多良岳 4:162a; 7:346a
Taranoki [(Japanese angelica tree) *Aralia elata*] ······················ 7:346a
Tarashikomi ···························· 7:233a
Tariff Convention of 1866 ·········· 4:113b
  Unequal Treaties revision ········· 8:148b
Tariffs ···························· 7:346b-347a
  government policy ················· 2:325a
  after World War II ·········· 7:346b-347a
  before World War II ·············· 7:346b
Tariki ······················ 2:293b; 7:347a
  Kiyozawa Manshi ··················· 4:233a
Taru ···································· 7:347a
Taruhito, Prince. 熾仁親王 *See* **Arisugawa no Miya Taruhito**
Tarui Tōkichi ···· 樽井藤吉 ········ 7:347a
  Futsū Senkyo Kisei Dōmeikai ······ 2:376a
Taru kaisen ········ 樽廻船 ········ 4:112b
Tarumaesan. *See* **Tarumaezan**
Tarumaezan ······· 樽前山 ··· 7:98a, 347b
Tarumizu ············· 垂水 ········ 7:347b
Tasaka Tomotaka
  ················ 田坂具隆 · 2:270b, 271b; 7:347b
Tashidaka ············ 足高 ········ 7:347b
Tashiro Gengoemon
  ·········· 田代源五右衛門 ········ 7:226b
Tashiro Sanki ···· 田代三喜 ········ 7:347b
Tashiro Shigeki ·· 田代茂樹 ········ 7:347b
Tashiro Shōi ····· 田代松意 ········ 2:77b
Task in Japan, The: A Study in Modern Missionary Imperatives ··········· 6:289a
Tass ····································· 7:192a
Tasuki ························ 2:253b; 7:348a
Tatami ········ 1:82b, 276b; 2:371a; 4:160b; 7:67a-67b, 249b, 273a, 348a, *348b*
  reed ······································ 4:231b
  rush production ······················ 1:27b
  standard size ························· 1:82b
Tatami rooms ···························· 5:8a
Tatara-buki ················· 7:348a-348b
Tatara furnace ························· 3:333a
Tatari ····································· 4:126a
Tatchū ···································· 1:183a
Tateana jūkyo ················ 6:189a-189b
Tateana sekishitsu (stone chamber)
  ·· 4:244b
Tatebayashi ·········· 館林 ········ 7:348b
Tatebayashi Kagei
  ················ 立林何帠 ········ 7:349a
Tatekawa Yoshitsugu
  ················ 建川美次 ········ 7:349a
Tatemae. *See* **Tatemae and honne**
Tatemae and honne ·· 4:39a, 195a; 6:204b; 7:349a
  etiquette ································ 2:233a
Tateshakai ······························· 8:191a
Tateshina Kōgen 蓼科高原 4:127b; 7:349a
Tatewaki Sadayo 帯刀貞代 ········ 7:349b
Tateyama (city) ······· 館山 ········ 7:349b
Tateyama (mountains)
  ····················· 立山 ········ 7:349b
Tateyama-Kurobe Alpine Route ··· 7:349b
Tatō ······································· 6:118a
Tatōgami ································ 4:113a
Tatsuno ················ 竜野 ········ 7:349b
Tatsuno Kingo ··· 辰野金吾 ········ 7:349b
Tatsuta ·································· 7:126b
Tatsutagawa ·········· 竜田川 ········ 7:349b
Tatsuta Shrine ··· 瀧田神社 ········ 7:350a
Tatsuta Taisha. *See* **Tatsuta Shrine**
Tattoos ······················ 7:350a-351a
  chronicles ······························ 7:350a
  Edo explosion ················ 7:350a-350b
  form of punishment ················ 7:350a
  full body ································ 7:350b
  lover's pledge ························ 7:350a
  meaning ································· 7:350a
  Meiji suppression ··················· 7:350b
  origins ··································· 7:350a
  Shimpen suiko gaden ·············· 7:350b
  today ·························· 7:350b-351a
  tools ····································· 7:351a
  Tsūzoku suikoden gōketsu hyakuhachinin ·· 7:350b
Taue-zōshi ······· 田植草紙 ········ 7:351a
Taut, Bruno ············ 4:173a; 7:351a-351b
Tawara ································ 7:351b
Tawara Kuniichi ··· 俵国一 ········ 7:351b
Tawara Sunao ····· 田原淳 ········ 7:351b
Tawarayama Hot Spring
  ················ 俵山温泉 ··· 7:351a-351b
Tawarayama Onsen. *See* **Tawarayama Hot Spring**
Tawaraya Sōtatsu. 俵屋宗達 *See* **Sōtatsu**
Tawara Yoshizumi
  ················ 田原良純 ········ 7:351b
Tax accountants ····················· 7:351b
Tax accounting ············· 7:351b-352a
Tax Account Law ······················ 7:351b
Tax Administration Agency ·········· 7:55b
Tax Advisory Commission ·········· 7:353a
Taxation
  demetaka ································ 2:84a
  Edo-period ···························· 4:267a
  recommendations by American specialists ··················· 7:172a-173a
  revisions in system ·········· 7:172a-173a
  tax rice ································· 7:179a
  tolls ······································ 7:57a
Tax Bureau ···················· 5:188a; 7:353a
Taxes ·························· 7:352a-354a
  administrative practices ············ 7:353b
  annual reductions ··················· 7:353a
  corporate income ···················· 7:352b
  early modern economy ·············· 2:151b
  economic incentives ·················· 2:29a
  eidaka ························ 2:185b-186a
  employee compensation ············ 7:353a
  estate ···································· 7:352b
  excise ···································· 7:352b
  expense accounts ···················· 7:353a
  gift ······································· 7:352b
  hanzei ··································· 3:100a
  income ·································· 7:352b
  income distribution ················· 3:285b
  industrial policy ············· 3:296b-297a
  inheritance ···························· 7:352b
  kuchiei and kuchimai ··············· 4:301b
  land
    annual (honto mononari) ··· 3:226b-227a
    handen shūju system ·········· 3:95a-96a
  Land Tax Reform of 1873-1881
    ···························· 4:365a-366b
  local revenue system ················ 7:353b
  military ························ 3:69b-70a
  national and local ·········· 7:354a-354b
  Occupation period ···················· 2:157a
  outline of system ············ 7:352b-353a
  premodern economy ·········· 2:148b-149a
  property ································ 7:353a
  real estate ····························· 7:353a
  records ·································· 5:234a
  retirement plans ······················ 7:353a
  ritsuryō system ··············· 6:322a, 329a
  shōen ···························· 7:155b-156a
  special features ·············· 7:353a-353b
    administrative practices ·········· 7:353b
    annual reductions ················· 7:353a
    employee compensation, expense accounts, and retirement plans
      ························ 7:353a-353b
    special measures ·················· 7:353a
  stipends ································· 1:297b
  tansen and tammai ··················· 7:344b
  types ····························· 7:352a-352b
  ukiyaku ("floating tax") ············ 8:138a
  unjō ····························· 8:171b-172a
  Urayaku ·································· 8:176a
Tax law ··············· 2:276b; 7:355a-358b
  individual income ··········· 7:356a-356b

juridical persons' income ····· 7:356b-358a
legislation and administration ······ 7:358a
national income taxation ····· 7:355a-356a
Tax office ························ 7:358b
Tax returns ··························· 1:9a
Tax revenues ························ 6:265a
Tax Special Measures Law ······· 7:353a, 355a-358b
Tax system
hanzei ······························ 1:101b
taxes, **national and local** ····· 7:354a-354b
tax law ························ 7:355a-358b
Tayama Katai ···· 田山花袋 ······· 1:155b; 7:358b-359a
I-novel ····························· 3:312a
Ken'yūsha ·························· 4:199a
naturalism ························ 5:351a-351b
Shinshōsetsu ······················ 7:125b
Tayasu Munetake
················ 田安宗武 ········ 7:359a
Kada no Arimaro ··················· 4:100b
Kamo no Mabuchi ··················· 4:129b
Toki Zemmaro ······················ 8:43b
Tayū ································ 4:298b
Tazaki Sōun ····· 田崎草雲 ········ 7:359a
Tazawa, Lake ······ 田沢湖 ········ 7:359a
Tazawako. *See* **Tazawa, Lake**
Tazawa volcano ····················· 7:359a
Tazoe Tetsuji ···· 田添鉄二 ··· 7:359a-359b
Tchaikovsky Memorial Tōkyō Ballet Co
······································ 2:76a
Tçuzzu, Rodrigues ·················· 3:183b
TDK Corporation ················· 7:359b
Tea ····························· 7:359b-360a
brewing ···························· 7:360a
history ···························· 7:360a
types ························ 7:359b-360a
bancha ······················ 7:359b-360a
gyokuro ··························· 7:359b
kamairicha ························ 7:359b
matcha ···························· 7:359b
sencha ···························· 7:359b
Tea ceremony ··· 4:337a, 381b; 7:64b, 71b, 360a-365a
Azuchi-Momoyama ·············· 3:180b-181a
Bizen ware ························· 1:158a
bokuseki ··························· 1:235b
chakaiseki ryōri ·················· 2:21b-22a
charcoal ceremony ·················· 7:362b
China ······························ 1:283a
confections ························ 1:350a
drinking ··························· 7:364a
dry sweets ························· 7:364b
Echizen ware ······················· 2:144a
examining utensils ··········· 7:364a-364b
flower arrangement ················· 2:289b
Furuta Oribe ······················· 2:373b
fūryū ······························ 2:374b
gardens ····························· 3:9b
Hagi ware ·························· 3:76b
Higashiyama culture ················ 3:132b
historical development ············· 2:295a
Iga ware ··························· 3:261b
Karatsu ware ······················· 4:159a
kogikushi paper ···················· 4:113a
Kutani ware ························ 4:321b
Murata Shukō, Takeno Jōō, and Sen no Rikyū ············ 7:360b-361a
nature in ·························· 5:358a
Nin'ami Dōhachi ······················ 6:4b
Oda Uraku ························ 6:65a-65b
origins in China ············· 7:360a-360b
presentation of thick tea ····· 7:363a-363b
presentation of thin tea ······ 7:364b-365a
principal sweet ·············· 7:362b-363a
Raku ware ·························· 6:283a
religion ··························· 6:292a
rimpa ······························ 6:317b
Satsuma ware ················· 7:30a-30b
schools ····················· 7:361a-361b
sencha ···························· 7:365a
Sen no Rikyū ························ 7:67a
service of tea and meal ············ 7:361b
Shigaraki ware ················ 7:91a-91b
Takatori ware ····················· 7:320a
tatami ···························· 7:348a
tatemae and honne ················· 7:349a
teabowl ····················· 7:363b-364a
tea garden ·················· 7:361b-362a
teahouse ···················· 7:361b-362a
tea in Japan ······················ 7:360b
tea meal ···················· 7:362a-362b
tearoom ·························· 7:*361a*
textiles ··························· 8:18b
thick tea ceremony ················ 7:363a
usucha temae ····················· 7:*364b*
vessels ··························· 4:140a
wabi ····························· 8:197a
Teachers ················· 7:365a-367a
appointment ················· 7:366a-366b
certification ····················· 7:366a
composition of personnel ···· 7:366b-367a
dismissal ··················· 7:366a-366b
in-service training ················ 7:366a
problems affecting profession ······ 7:367a
qualification ····················· 7:366a
remuneration ················ 7:366a-366b
responsibility ···················· 7:366b
training ···················· 7:365a-366a
unions ··························· 7:366b
Teacher's Association ·············· 6:90b
Teaching methods ·········· 7:367a-367b
Tea drinking ······················ 7:360b
Teahouse of the August Moon ···· 4:332b
Teahouses ························ 7:164b
Tea-leaf Picking at Uji ··········· 4:320b
Tearoom ·························· 7:*361a*
Teatoro ·················· 7:367b-368a
Teburi ························· 3:29a-30a
Technical colleges ········ 7:368a; 8:192b
Technological Art School (Kōbu Bijutsu Gakkō) ···· 2:304a; 8:327b
Technological assistance ···· 2:315b-316a
foreign investment ················ 2:316b
Technological development · 7:368a-371b
"A Model of Economic Growth" ··· 7:368a
compared with U.S. ·········· 7:370a-371b
contemporary ····················· 2:161b
history ····················· 7:368a-368b
17th century to 1930s ······· 7:368b-369b
World War II to 1970s ······· 7:369b-370a
Technological innovation ···· 7:371b-372b
environment ················· 7:371b-372a
fruits of ························· 7:372a
future ······················ 7:372a-372b
Technology
development of · 6:303a-305b; 7:368a-371b
economic growth ······ 2:159b-160a, 161b
economic planning ··········· 2:167a-167b
electronics ················· 2:193b-195a
electrotechnical ·················· 2:195a
labor unions' response ············· 2:36b
modern ··················· 7:372b-373b
characteristics ··················· 7:373a
developments ····················· 7:372b
history ····················· 7:372b-373a
recent trends ··············· 7:373a-373b
steel production ············ 3:333b, 336a
transportation ·············· 8:103a-104a
Technology transfer ·· 6:305a; 7:373b-375a
after Meiji Restoration ······· 7:374a-374b
cultural borrowing ················ 7:374a
modes ······················ 7:373b-374a
postwar experience ·········· 7:374b-375a
Tedorigawa ········ 手取川 ········ 7:375a
Teganuma ········ 手賀沼 ··· 7:375a-375b
Teganuma marshland
··················· 手賀沼 ·········· 1:5a
Tegata ···························· 4:163a
Tegoto-mono ······ 手事物 ········· 4:64b
Teigin Incident ·· 帝銀事件 ········ 7:375b
Furuhata Tanemoto ················· 2:372a
Tanaka Kōtarō ····················· 7:337b
Teigin Jiken. *See* **Teigin Incident**
Teihon kaeru ···· 定本蛙 ········ 4:319a
Teijin, Ltd ············· 4:139a; 7:375b-376a
Teijiin Incident ··················· 7:375b
Teijin Incident ··· 帝人事件 ········ 7:375b
Teijin Jiken. *See* **Teijin Incident**
Teijiin no Uta-awase
·············· 廷人の歌合 ········ 8:182a
Tei Joshō ·········· 鄭汝昌 ····· 2:96b-97a
Teijō zakki ······· 貞丈雑記 ········ 8:358b
Teika kanazukai
·············· 定家仮名遣 ········ 4:133b
Teiki ················· 帝紀 1:151a; 2:101a; 4:340b; 7:376a
historiography ···················· 3:152a
Kojiki based on ·················· 4:251a
Teikin ōrai ······· 庭訓往来 ········ 7:376a
Teikoku Bijutsuin (Imperial Fine Arts Academy) ······················ 6:158a
Teikoku bunko ··· 帝国文庫 ·········· 4:64a
Teikoku daigaku ············ 3:281a-281b
Teikoku Gikai ···· 帝国議会 ··· 3:275b-277a
Teikoku Ginkō ····················· 7:375b
Teikoku Jinzō Kenshi Co ···· 7:375b-376a
Teikoku Kaigun Rengō Kantai ····· 1:336b
Teikoku Nōkai ··· 帝国農会 ········ 7:376a
Teikoku Oil Co, Ltd ·· 6:182a; 7:376a-376b
Teikoku Sekiyu. *See* **Teikoku Oil Co, Ltd**
Teikokutō ·········· 帝国党 ········ 7:376b
Kokumin Kyōkai reorganized as ··· 4:261a
Teikoku Tsūshinsha ················· 1:16b
Teikoku Zaigō Gunjinkai. *See* **Imperial Military Reservists' Association**
Tei Kōsho ·········· 鄭孝胥 ········ 8:378b
Teimon school ····· 貞門派 ·········· 5:18a
Teinensei ························ 7:376b
Teisan ··························· 7:376b
Tei Seikō ·········· 鄭成功 ··· 8:378a-378b
Teisei zōyaku sairan igen
········ 訂正増訳采覧異言 ········ 4:369b
Teito Kōsokudo Kōtsū Eidan. *See* **Teito Rapid Transit Authority**
Teitoku kyōka hyakushu
············ 貞徳狂歌百首 ········ 4:332a
Teito nichinichi shimbun
············ 帝都日日新聞 ········ 8:330b
Teito Rapid Transit Authority ····· 6:264a; 7:376b-377a
Teiyū Ethics Society ··············· 6:107b
Teizambori ········ 貞山堀 ········ 7:377a
Tejima Seiichi ··· 手島精一 ········ 7:377a
Tekibo shoshi (legal wife-illegitimate child relationships) ············ 6:162b
Tekichū ōdan sambyakuri
········· 敵中横断三百里 ········ 7:349a
Tekijuku. *See* **Ogata Kōan**
Tekiya ···························· 7:250a
Tekki jidai ······· 鉄器時代 ··· 3:332b-333a
Tekkō ··························· 7:377a
Tekkō Rōren ······················· 3:335a
Telecommunications systems ···· 6:266b; 7:377a-379b
computer industry ················· 1:347b
future ····················· 7:378b-379b
history ····················· 7:377b-378a
Kokusai Denshin Denwa Co, Ltd ·· 4:261b
services ···················· 7:378a-378b
Telegraph ························· 3:319a
Telephones ················ 7:379b-380b
networks ···················· 7:380a-380b

international calls · · · 7:380b
modern services · · · 7:380b
other uses of circuitry · · · 7:380b
switchboards · · · 7:380a-380b
transmissions routes · · · 7:380b
Television · · · 6:268b
children's use · · · 1:278b-279a
educational broadcasting · · · 2:179a
growth · · · 2:192a, 193b
international communications · · · 3:319a
leisure-time activity · · · 4:382a
"Mito Kōmon" · · · 2:219b
sociocultural contribution · · · 5:129a-129b
Takayanagi Kenjirō · · · 7:321a
urban life · · · 8:179a
Yomiuri Telecasting Corporation · · · 8:337a
Television broadcasting · · · 1:172a-173b
late-night · · · 1:173b
mass communications · · · 5:128b
Television Tōkyō Channel 12, Ltd 7:380b
Television viewing · · · 1:173a
Temane · · · 3:29a-30a
Temari · · · 7:381a
Tembimbō · · · 7:381a
Tembu · · · 7:381a
Jōruriji · · · 4:77b
Temiya cave · · · 手宮洞窟 · · · 7:381a
Temiyage · · · 5:217a
Temmangū · · · 天満宮 · · · 7:381a
Temmei Famine
· · · 天明の飢饉 · · 7:28b, 345b, 381b
Temmei no Kikin. *See* **Temmei Famine**
Temmon Hokke no Ran. *See* **Temmon Hokke Rebellion**
Temmon Hokke Rebellion
· · · 天文法華の乱 · · · 7:381b
Temmu, Emperor 天武天皇 · 2:55a; 5:307b; 7:96a, 381b-382b; 8:285b
Hieda no Are · · · 3:130b
historiography · · · 3:152b
Jinshin Disturbance · · · 4:60b
Kōbun, Emperor · · · 4:239a
Naniwakyō · · · 5:328b
Silla relations · · · 4:277b
Temple attendants (chigo) · · · 1:274a
Temple gates · · · 3:12a-12b
Temple guarantee · · · 8:12b
"Temple guarantee system" · · · 7:186a
Temple of the Golden Pavilion, The
· · · 4:213a
Temple of the Silver Pavilion · · · 3:33a-33b
Temple refuge · · · 3:130b; 4:115b
Temples · · · 8:1a-2a
Akishinodera · · · 1:42a
Asukadera · · · 1:105b-106b
Buddhist sculpture · · · 1:197b-198a
Byōdōin · · · 1:227a-227b
construction of by Emperor Shōmu 7:166a
Honzan Shugenshū
Shōgoin · · · 7:160a
Hossō
Hōryūji · · · 3:231b-233b
Kōfukuji · · · 4:243b-244a
Yakushiji · · · 8:285b-286b
Ji
Yugyōji · · · 8:356a
Jōdo
Chion'in · · · 1:296b
Senjuji · · · 7:66a
Zōjōji · · · 8:379b
Jōdo Shin
Honganji · · · 3:221a-222b
Ishiyama Honganji · · · 3:346b
Nishi Honganji · · · 6:16a-17a
Senjuji · · · 7:66a
Kegon
Gangōji · · · 3:6b-7a
Shin Yakushiji · · · 7:139b-140a
Tōdaiji · · · 8:33b-34b
Nichiren
Hommonji · · · 3:217b
Minobusan · · · 5:194b
Tanjōji · · · 1:51b
Ōbaku
Mampukuji · · · 5:89a
Rinzai
Daitokuji · · · 2:68a-68b
Engakuji · · · 2:217a
Ginkakuji · · · 3:33a-33b
Kenchōji · · · 4:195a
Kenninji · · · 4:197a-197b
Kinkakuji · · · 4:213a
Myōshinji · · · 5:291a
Ryōanji · · · 6:347b
Shōkokuji · · · 7:164b
Tenryūji · · · 8:10b
Tōfukuji · · · 8:35a-35b
Zuisenji · · · 8:380b
Ritsu
Mibudera · · · 5:166a
Shingon
Chishakuin · · · 1:297a
Daianji · · · 2:55a
Daigoji · · · 2:57a-58a
Daikakuji · · · 2:59b
Gokokuji · · · 3:43a
Hasedera · · · 3:106b-107a
Hōkaiji · · · 3:212b
Hokkeji · · · 3:214a-214b
Ishiyamadera · · · 3:346a
Jingoji · · · 4:58a
Jōruriji · · · 4:77b
Kawasaki Daishi · · · 4:183a
Kimiidera · · · 4:208a
Kongōbuji · · · 4:269b
Kongōfukuji · · · 1:102b
Kōryūji · · · 4:294a-294b
Kōzanji · · · 4:300a-300b
Murōji · · · 5:270b-271a
Ninnaji · · · 6:7a
Okadera · · · 6:78b
Rokuharamitsuji · · · 6:335a
Shigisanji · · · 7:93a-93b
Shinshōji · · · 6:125a
Taimadera · · · 7:298a
Tōji · · · 8:38a-39a
Yakuōin · · · 7:317b
Zentsūji · · · 8:377b
Shingon Ritsu
Saidaiji · · · 6:366a
Shugendō
Kimbusenji · · · 4:207b-208a
Sōtō
Eiheiji · · · 2:186a-186b
Sōjiji · · · 7:224a
Tendai
Chūsonji · · · 1:314a
Daisenji · · · 2:67a
Enryakuji · · · 2:220a-221a
Fukidera · · · 2:360a
Jindaiji · · · 4:58a
Kan'eiji · · · 4:137b-138a
Miidera · · · 5:169a
Mōtsuji · · · 5:259a
Risshakuji · · · 6:320b-321a
Sanzen'in · · · 7:19b-20a
Shitennōji · · · 7:150b
Taimadera · · · 7:298a
Yamadadera · · · 8:288b-289a
Temple slaves · · · 2:132a
Temple supporters · · · 4:362b
Temple towns (monzen machi)
· · · 5:247b-248a
urban planning · · · 8:179b
Tempō Famine 天保の飢饉 · · · 7:87b; 8:2a
Tempō Reforms
· · · 天保の改革 · 1:21a; 3:189b; 7:102a; 8:2a-3a
Domainal reforms · · · 8:2b
fudasashi · · · 2:340b
kabunakama dissolution · · · 4:100a
kienrei · · · 4:203a
Mizuno Tadakuni · · · 5:226b, 227b
Ryūtei Tanehiko · · · 6:359b
shinden kaihatsu · · · 7:109b
Shogunate reforms · · · 8:2a
Tamenaga Shunsei · · · 7:333b-334a
Tokugawa shogunate · · · 8:55b-56a
Torii Yōzō · · · 8:80a
Tōyama Kinshirō · · · 8:88a
Tempura · · · 2:23a, 306a; 8:3a-3b
Tempyō culture · · 天平文化 · · · 8:3b
Ten. *See* **Heaven**
Tenant farmer disputes · · · 4:363a; 8:3b-4a
cooperatives · · · 1:22a
Tenant farmers (mizunomi-byakushō)
nago · · · 4:362b; 5:308b
Tenant farming · · · 1:31a
elimination · · · 4:364b
Tenant Rent Control Ordinance (Kosakuryō Tōsei Rei) · · · 4:363a
Tenant rights · · · 4:374a
Tenchi, Emperor. 天智天皇
See **Tenji, Emperor**
Tenchi kakitsuke 天地書附 · · · 4:272a
Tenchi nikyū yōhō
· · · 天地二球用法 · · · 5:355b
Tenchūgumi Rebellion
· · · 天誅組の乱 · · 5:319b; 8:4a
Tendai sect · · · 天台宗 · 1:178b; 7:13a, 80b; 8:4a-5b
Byōdōin temple · · · 1:227b
Chinese Tiantai · · · 8:4a
education · · · 2:172a
Eiheiji · · · 2:186a
Enryakuji · · · 2:220a-221a
founding of Japanese Tendai · · · 8:4b
bodhisattva precepts · · · 8:4b
Kūkai's esoteric Buddhism · · · 8:4b
Fujiwara culture · · · 2:347b
Fujiwara no Toshinari · · · 2:357a
Hōnen · · · 4:67b
Jindaiji · · · 4:58a
Kan'eiji · · · 4:137b
Kon Tōkō · · · 4:275b
meditation · · · 4:67a
monasticism · · · 5:237b
musical instruments · · · 1:157a
painting · · · 6:149b
poems and songs · · · 8:231a
priests
Annen · · · 8:5a
Enchin · · · 2:213b
Enkū · · · 2:218a-218b
Ennin · · · 2:219a
Genshin · · · 3:23b
Ryōgen · · · 6:351b
Senkaku · · · 7:66a
raigōzu · · · 6:277a
Saichō · · · 8:4a
Saichō's successors · · · 8:4b
Sannō Ichijitsu Shintō · · · 7:15a
Tendaishū · · · 天台宗 · · · 8:4a-5b
Tendō · · · 天童 · · · 8:5b
Tendō school · · · 天道流 · · 5:308a-308b
Tenement quarters · · · 7:202a
Tengu · · · 天狗 · 2:293b, 303a; 8:*5a*, 5b
kamikakushi · · · 4:126b
Tengutō no Ran
· · · 天狗党の乱 · · · 5:204b-205a
Tenioha · · · てにをは · · · 7:281a
Tenji, Emperor · · 天智天皇 · 7:96a; 8:5b-6a

descendants ····· 5:308a
Fujiwara family ····· 2:348a, 351b
Jinshin Disturbance ····· 4:60a
Ōmi Code ····· 6:101a
ritsuryō system ····· 4:277b
Tenjikuyō ····· 天竺様 ····· 3:12b
Tenjōbito ····· 殿上人 ····· 2:40a; 8:6a
Tenjōgawa ····· 天井川 ····· 8:6a
Tenjō Sajiki (Upper Balcony) ····· 天井桟敷 ····· 8:13a
Tenjukoku mandara shūchō. 天寿国曼荼羅繡帳 *See Tenjukoku shūchō*
Tenjukoku shūchō ····· 天寿国繡帳 ··· 2:200a; 4:69a
Tenkan nōryoku ····· 8:6a-6b
Tenka Ryūmon (Dragon Gate of the World) ····· 天下龍門 ····· 5:330a
Tenka taihei ki · 天下太平記 ····· 4:166a
Tenkō ····· 転向 · 8:6b-7b, 149b
forms of coercion ····· 8:6b
significance ····· 8:7b
"Thought Criminal" Probation Law · 8:29a
types of ····· 8:6b-7a
Tenkō bungaku ·· 転向文学 ····· 7:176a
Tennen kinembutsu ····· 5:352a-352b
Tenninkyō ····· 天人峡 ····· 8:7b
Tennis ····· 8:7b
Tennō ····· 天皇 ··· 2:203a-209a
Tennōki and Kokki ····· 天皇記, 国記 1:151a; 7:264a; 8:7b
Tennō kikan setsu ····· 天皇機関説 ····· 8:7b-8b
Kakei Katsuhiko ····· 4:115b
kokutai debate ····· 4:263b
"Tennō no bōshi" ····· 天皇の帽子 ····· 4:270a
Tennō no ningen sengen. *See* **Emperor, renunciation of divinity by**
Tennōzan ····· 天王山 ····· 8:8b
Tenrei banshō meigi ····· 篆隷万象名義 ····· 1:151b
Tenri ····· 天理 ····· 8:8b
Tenri Central Library ····· 8:8b-9a
Tenri Gaikokugo Gakkō (Tenri School of Foreign Languages) ····· 8:9b
Tenrikyō ····· 天理教 ····· 2:300b; 7:48a-48b; 8:9a-9b
doctrine ····· 8:9a
historical development ····· 8:9a
kokyū ····· 4:264b
museums ····· 5:280a
Nakayama Miki ····· 5:319a
scripture ····· 8:9b
Shinkyō kyōdōtai ····· 7:121b
Tenri University ····· 8:9b
Tenrō ····· 天狼 ····· 3:80b
Tenryō ····· 天領 ····· 8:9b-10a
kanjō bugyō ····· 4:144a
rural administration ····· 4:55a
Tenryū ····· 天竜 ····· 8:10a
Tenryūgawa ····· 天竜川 ····· 8:10b
Sakuma Dam ····· 7:3a
Tenryūji ····· 天龍寺 · 4:336a; 8:10b
Tenryūji-bune · 天龍寺船 ····· 8:10b-11a
Tenryūkyō ····· 天竜峡 ····· 8:11a
Tensho (archaic script) ····· 1:233b; 7:*170b*
Tenshō Ken'ō Shisetsu ····· 天正遣欧使節 ··· 5:203a-203b
Tenshō Kōtai Jingū Kyō ····· 天照皇大神宮教 ····· 4:227b
Tenshō Kōtai Jingū Kyō (Dancing Religion) ····· 8:257b
Tenshō kyōgen-bon ····· 天正狂言本 ····· 4:328a
Tenshō mission to Europe ····· 3:350b
Tenshō naga ōban 天正長大判 5:*242a-242b*
Tenshō onna gassen ····· 天正女合戦 ····· 4:112a
Tenson kōrin ····· 天孫降臨 ····· 2:101b
Ten to chi to ····· 天と地と ····· 4:112a
Ten to sen (Points and Lines) ····· 点と線 ····· 6:221b
Tenugui ····· 手拭 ····· 8:11a
headgear ····· 3:119a
Terada Torahiko · 寺田寅彦 ····· 8:11a
works ····· 8:11a
Terada Tōru ····· 寺田透 ····· 8:11a
works ····· 8:11a
Teradaya Incident ····· 寺田屋騒動 ·· 1:84a; 8:11b
Terakado Seiken 寺門静軒 ····· 8:11b
Terakoya ····· 寺子屋 · 1:152b; 7:37b, 94b; 8:11b-12a, 178a
education ····· 2:172b, 174b
literacy rate ····· 5:10b
ōraimono ····· 6:115b
religious education ····· 6:295a-295b
Shingaku ····· 7:112a
teaching methods ····· 7:367a-367b
Terashima Munenori ····· 寺島宗則 ····· 8:12a
Terauchi Hisaichi 寺内寿一 ····· 8:12a
Terauchi Masatake ····· 寺内正毅 ····· 8:12b
annexation of Korea ····· 4:282a
Kenseikai ····· 4:198a
Korea's annexation treaty ····· 4:287b
rice riots ····· 6:310b
Terauke ····· 寺請 ····· 4:119a; 7:185a-186b; 8:12b
Terayama Shūji ·· 寺山修司 ····· 8:12b-13a
Shinoda Masahiro ····· 7:122a
Terazaki Kōgyō ·· 寺崎広業 ····· 8:13a
Terebi Asahi. *See* **Asahi National Broadcasting Co, Ltd**
Terebijon ····· テレビジョン ····· 7:321a
Terebijon kōgaku ····· テレビジョン工学 ····· 7:321a
Terebi Tōkyō. *See* **Television Tōkyō Channel 12, Ltd**
Teriyaki ····· 8:13a, 323b
Terrace farming ····· 1:*25a*
Terrier, Japanese ····· 4:45a
Territorial waters ····· 4:2b; 8:13b
Territory and administrative divisions. *See* **Japan**
Territory of Japan ····· 8:13b-14b
Terrorism, political ····· 2:45a
government restriction ····· 7:254a
Tertiary industries ····· 6:239b; 8:14b-15a
Teshigahara Hiroshi ····· 勅使河原宏 · 2:274a, *292b*; 8:15a
Echizen ware ····· 2:144a
Teshigahara Sōfū ····· 勅使河原蒼風 ····· 2:291b
Teshikaga ····· 弟子屈 ····· 8:15a
Teshima Toan ··· 手島堵庵 ····· 8:15a-15b
disciples ····· 5:320a
Ishida Baigan ····· 4:120a
Shingaku ····· 7:112a
writings ····· 8:15a-15b
Teshiogawa ····· 天塩川 ····· 8:15b
Teshio Mountains ····· 天塩山地 ····· 8:15b
Teshio Plain ····· 天塩平野 ····· 8:15b
Tessai. 鉄斎 *See* **Tomioka Tessai**
Tessai Art Museum ····· 8:15b
Tesshū Tokusai · 鉄舟徳済 ····· 8:15b-16a
Tetsudō basha. *See* **Horsecars**
Tetsugakukan ····· 哲学館 3:309b; 4:177b
Tetsugen ····· 鉄眼 ····· 8:16a
Tetsujutsu sankei 綴術算経 ····· 8:231b
Tettei kojin-shugi ····· 徹底個人主義 ····· 7:338b
Teuchi ····· 8:16a
Textbook authorization system ····· 7:37b
Textbooks ····· 7:37b
Textbook Scandal of 1902-1903 ····· 8:16a
Textile industry ····· 8:16a-16b
companies
Fuji Spinning Co, Ltd ····· 2:346a
Gunze, Ltd ····· 3:70a
Itōman & Co, Ltd ····· 3:355a
Japan Wool Textile Co, Ltd ····· 4:50b
Kanebō, Ltd ····· 4:137b
Kurabō Industries Ltd ····· 4:311a
Kuraray Co, Ltd ····· 4:311b
Ōsaka Spinning Mill ····· 6:123a
Senju Woolen Mill ····· 7:66a
Shikibō, Ltd ····· 7:95b
Teijin, Ltd ····· 7:375b-376a
Tōhō Rayon Co, Ltd ····· 8:37b
Toyoda Automatic Loom Works, Ltd ····· 8:90a
Unitika, Ltd ····· 8:168b
cotton, worker exploitation ····· 4:343b
cotton spinning ····· 2:31a
female labor participation ····· 2:210b
industrial structure ····· 3:301a
Meiji period ····· 2:151b-152a
occupational structure ····· 6:56a
technological development ····· 7:369a
women in ····· 8:260a
working conditions ····· 2:241b; 4:71b
Textiles ····· 8:16b-20a
Asuka and Nara textiles ····· 8:17a
care and preservation of ····· 8:20a
Chinese influences ····· 7:195b
crepe ····· 1:274b
design ····· 2:90a-91a; 4:267a
Edo period ····· 8:19a
export ····· 7:203b
folk craft ····· 2:295b
Heian period and Kamakura period · 8:18a
Jōmon period ····· 8:16b
kara-ori ····· 4:158a
kasuri ····· 4:164a
Kurume-gasuri ····· 1:276b
Meiji period to present ····· 8:19b
Muromachi period and Azuchi-Momoyama period ····· 8:18b
Okinawan textiles ····· 6:91a-91b
Persian influence ····· 7:195b
Shōsōin ····· 8:17b
aya (figured twills) ····· 8:17b
nishiki (brocades) ····· 8:17b
plain weave silks and ramies ····· 8:17b
ra and sha ····· 8:17b
sankechi ····· 8:17b
shishū ····· 8:17b
silk ····· 7:194a
tsumugi ····· 8:116a
tsuzure-ori ····· 8:120a
wax-resist dyeing ····· 8:237b-238a
Yamato period ····· 8:17a
Yayoi period ····· 8:16b
Tezuka Ryokubin 手塚緑敏 ··· 3:116a-116b
Thai-Japanese Alliance ····· 8:20a
Thailand and Japan ····· 2:200a; 8:20a-21a
early relations ····· 8:20a
Free Thai Movement ····· 2:339b
postwar period ····· 8:20b
relations during World War II ····· 8:20b
1970s ····· 8:21a
Thalidomide children ··· 6:253b; 8:21a-21b
Thanksgiving pilgrimage ····· 6:79a-79b
Theater
female impersonators ····· 7:108a
leisure-time activity ····· 4:381b
onnagata ····· 6:108a-108b

periodicals 7:112a
political drama 7:112b-113a
puppet 1:212a-215b
shimpa 7:107b-108a
shingeki 7:112a-113b
Shinkokugeki 7:121a
Shinseisakuza 7:124a
traditional 8:21b-23a
bugaku 3:1b; 8:21b
bunraku 1:212a-215b; 8:22a
kabuki 4:90a-97b; 8:23a
kyōgen 4:324b-329a; 8:22a
Nō 6:23b-29b; 8:22a
urban life 8:178b
yose 8:340b
Theater critics
Aeba Kōson 1:18a
Tsubouchi Shōyō 8:110a-111a
Theatrical costumes 8:23a-24a
bugaku 8:23a
bunraku 8:23b
kabuki 8:24a
nō and kyōgen 8:23b
Theocracy 8:24a
Therapy 7:83b
Theravāda Buddhism · 1:177a-177b; 6:281a
Thermal pollution 2:227b
Thermal power 2:190b-191b
Third Comprehensive National Development Plan 6:228a
Third Domestic Industrial Exposition 1:71b
Third United Nations Conference on the Law of the Sea (UNCLOS III) 8:13b
Thirty-Six Poetic Geniuses (Sanjūrokkasen) 3:336b; 5:166a; 7:12b-13b
Thirty-Six Views of Mount Fuji (Fugaku sanjūrokkei) 8:143a, *143b*
Thistles [(azami) family Compositae] 8:24b
This-worldliness 8:24b
Thompson, Stith 2:302b
Thought and culture 8:24b-29a
development 8:26a
community-ism versus universalism 8:27b
functionalism and classicism 8:28a
life-centeredness versus transcendence 8:26b
stages of Chinese cultural influence 8:26a
traditional 8:25a
community-ism 8:25b
functionalism 8:25b
life centeredness 8:25b
Shintō changeableness 8:25a
"Thought Criminal" Probation Law · 8:7a, 29a
"Thought police" 6:168b
Thousand Cranes 4:176b
"Thousand-stitch" cloths 7:67a
"Three Arrows Studies" 5:214a
"Three Eccentrics" 7:320b
Threefold Pureland sutras 4:67a-67b
Three Hills of Yamato .... 大和三山 8:310b
"Three Labor Laws" (Rōdō Sampō) 4:357b
"Three Lords" 3:47b
Three Magistrates, The 7:6a
Three Monkeys 8:29a-29b
Three New Laws System 5:63a-63b
Three Nonnuclear Principles · 3:137a-137b
Three Offices 7:16b-17a
"Three press-dyes" 7:13b
Three Principles of Foreign Policy 8:153b
Three Regulations for Great Crimes 2:55b
Three Successor Houses, The 3:47b
Three Views of Japan 5:382a
Thrushes [(tsugumi) subfamily Turdidae] 8:29b
Thunberg, Carl Peter 5:313a; 8:29b
Thunderbolt realm 4:269b-270a
Tianjin (Tientsin) Convention 4:157a, 280b; 7:68b; 8:29b
Tianjin (Tientsin) Incident 8:152b
Tiatong Rujing 2:186a
Tidal waves 2:141a
Tie-dyeing 8:17b, 29b-30a
Tilapia 2:282b
Time of day 1:232b
Ting Ju-ch'ang. *See* **Ding Ruchang (Ting Ju-ch'ang)**
Tips or gratuities 7:183a
Title Incident 7:184a
Titsingh, Izaak 5:313a; 8:30a
works 8:30a
Toad lily 3:237b
Tōa Dōbunkai 東亜同文会 8:30a
Konoe Atsumaro 4:272b
Tōa Domestic Airlines Co, Ltd · 8:30a-30b
Tōagōsei Chemical Industry Co, Ltd 8:30b
Tōa Nenryō Kōgyō 6:181b; 8:30b
Tōa Remmei .... 東亜連盟 8:30b
Tōa Shinchitsujo .... 東亜新秩序 8:30b-31a
international relations 3:321b
Tōa Washinkai 東亜和親会 8:31a
Toba, Emperor ·· 鳥羽天皇 8:31b
Sanuki no Suke no nikki 7:18b
Toba .... 鳥羽 ·· 7:13a; 8:31a
Kakuban 4:118a
Sanzen'in 7:20a
Tobacco 8:31a
Tobacco production 1:27b
Toba-Fushimi, Battle of .... 鳥羽伏見の戦 · 1:165a; 8:31b
Tōbaku no mitchoku .... 討幕の密勅 8:31b
Toba Sōjō .... 鳥羽僧正 ·· 2:*199a-199b*; 8:31b-32a
Chōjū giga 1:299a
Tobe .... 砥部 8:32a
Tobera [(tobira) *Pittosporum tobira*] 8:32a-32b
Tobi 4:229b
Tobiganna ("jumping trimming tool") 1:264b
Tobira 8:32a-32b
Tobishima .... 飛島 8:32b
Tobishima Corporation 8:32b
Tobiume senku ·· 飛梅千句 1:73b
Tōbōsaku .... 東方朔 5:295b
Tōbu Railway Co, Ltd 8:32b-33a
Tochigi .... 栃木 8:33a
Tochigi Prefecture · 栃木県 8:33a
Tōchigyō (de facto rights) .... 当知行 1:274a
Tochinoki 3:228b-229a
Tochio .... 栃尾 8:33a-33b
Toda .... 戸田 8:33b
Toda Construction Co, Ltd 8:33b
Tōdaiji .... 東大寺 1:182a; 4:368a; 5:332a; 6:*106b*; 7:16b, 277a; 8:33b-34b
construction 2:327a
daibutsuden (great Buddha hall) 8:*33a*
Taira no Shigehira 7:302a
education 2:172a
Ganjin 3:7b
gates 3:12b
Kaikei 4:111a
Kegon sect 4:186b
Rōben 6:333a
Shintō 7:127a
Shōsōin location 2:371a
Taira-Minamoto War 7:299b
Takaoka 7:317b
tea ceremony 7:360a-365a
Tōdaiji fujumon kō .... 東大寺諷誦文稿 4:132b
Toda Jōsei .... 戸田城聖 8:34b
Toda Mosui .... 戸田茂睡 8:34b
"Toda of the Rice Bale" 5:296b
Toda Teizō .... 戸田貞三 8:34b
works 8:34b
Tōdatsu kikō (Record of Travels among the Eastern Tartars)東韃紀行 8:242b
Tōde 4:158b
Todoroki Falls · 等々力の滝 8:34b
Tōdō Takatora ·· 藤堂高虎 7:56b; 8:34b-35a
Tōei .... 塔影 4:179b
Tōei Co, Ltd 2:272a, 273a-273b, 274b, 359b; 8:35a
Mahiru no ankoku 5:83b
Takakura Ken 7:314a
Uchida Tomu 8:124a
Tōfu .... 豆腐 ·· 2:21b, 305a, 306a; 7:239a; 8:35a
Tōfukuji .... 東福寺 · 1:183a; 7:80b; 8:35a-35b
Tōfutsu, Lake .... 濤沸湖 8:35b
Tōgaku .... 唐楽 3:1a
composition categories 3:2b
Tōgaku no Ran ·· 東学の乱 8:74b
Togakushi Kōgen .... 戸隠高原 8:35b
Togakushiyama ·· 戸隠山 8:35b
Tōgane .... 東金 8:35b
Tōgarashi 3:127b
Togariishi site ·· 尖石遺跡 8:35b-36a
Togashi family ·· 富樫氏 8:36a
Tōgatta Hot Spring .... 遠刈田温泉 8:36a
Togawa Yūjirō · 戸川雄二郎 4:207a
Tōgō Bakuryō Gakkō 4:69b
Tōgō Bakuryō Kaigi 4:69b-70a
Tōgō Heihachirō .... 東郷平八郎 1:87b; 8:36a-36b
Tōgō Shigenori · 東郷茂徳 ·· 7:28a; 8:36b
Tōgyū. *See* **Bullfighting**
Tōhachiken 4:193a
Tōhaku. 等伯 *See* **Hasegawa Tōhaku**
Tōhata Seiichi ·· 東畑精一 8:36b
Tōhō Co, Ltd 2:270b; 3:102b; 8:36b
Tōhō Gakuen School of Music 8:36b
Tōhōkai .... 東方会 ·· 5:316a-316b; 8:37a
Tōhō Kaigi .... 東方会議 8:37a
Yamamoto Jōtarō 8:298b
Tōhoku Electric Power Co, Inc 8:37a
Tōhoku region ·· 東北地方 4:153b; 8:37a-37b
Tōhoku University 8:37b
Tōhō Rayon Co, Ltd 8:37b
Tōhō Strike 2:271b; 8:37b
Watanabe Tetsuzō 8:236b
Tōhō Symphony 5:287a
Tōhō Zinc Co, Ltd 8:37b-38a
Toi .... 刀伊 8:38a
Toilet training 4:38a-38b
Toimaru .... 問丸 · 4:122b; 8:38a
Toimisaki .... 都井岬 8:38a
Toiya .... 問屋 8:38a
monopoly status 1:132b
Tōji (sake) .... 杜氏 8:38a
Tōji (monastery-temple) .... 東寺 2:375a; 8:38b-39a;

construction 2:327a
Kūkai's headquarters 4:304a
sanjo 7:12a
wooden sculpture 1:198b-199a
Tōjimbō 東尋坊 8:*39a*
Tōjin Okichi 唐人お吉 8:39a
Harris, Townsend 3:104b
Tōji patriarch paintings 6:227a
Tōji Treasure House 東寺宝物館 8:39a-39b
Tōjō Gimon 東条義門 4:31b; 7:281a; 8:39b
Fujitani Nariakira 2:346b
Tōjō Hideki 東条英機 1:164b; 4:*273a;* 5:316a-316b; 7:92a; 8:39b-40a
Senjinkun 7:65b
Tōjō Misao 東条操 1:7a; 8:40a
works 8:40a
Tokachidake 十勝岳 8:40a
Tokachigawa 十勝川 8:40a
Tokachi Plain 十勝平野 8:40a
Tokage [(lizard) *Eumeces latiscutatus*] 8:40a
Tōkai (city) 東海 8:40b
Tōkai (village) 東海 8:40b
Tōkai Bank, Ltd. 8:40b
Tōkaidō 東海道 3:40b-41a, 86b; 6:229b; 8:40b-41b
development 8:40b
dialects 2:92a
history 8:40b
railways 6:278a
Shinkansen 7:116b
stages 8:41a
today 8:41b
travel 8:41a
travel diary 4:108b
travelers 8:41b
urban life 8:177b
Tōkaidō bunken ezu 東海道分間絵図 8:41b
Tōkaidōchū hizakurige (Shank's Mare) 東海道中膝栗毛 4:61a-61b, 256a; 8:104a
Tōkaidō gojūsantsugi (Fifty-three Stations of the Tōkaidō) 東海道五十三次 3:*148b*
Tōkaidō megalopolis 8:41b
Gokaidō 3:40b-41a
Tōkaidō Yotsuya kaidan 東海道四谷怪談 8:41b-42a
Tōkai Sanshi 東海散士 8:42a
seiji shōsetsu 7:50a
works 8:42a
Tōkai Shizen Hodō 東海自然歩道 8:42a
Tōkai University 8:42a
Tōkamachi 十日町 8:42a-42b
Tōkan kikō 東関紀行 4:108b, 128b; 8:42b, 104b
Tokara Islands 吐噶喇列島 7:30b; 8:42b
Tōka zuiyō 桃華蘂葉 8:42b
Tōkei 1:333b-334a
Tōkeiji 東慶寺 4:115b, 120b; 5:133a; 8:42b
Tōkei Sūri Kenkyūjo 7:246a
Toki 土岐 8:42b
Tokieda Motoki 時枝誠記 7:281a; 8:42b-43a
Toki family 土岐氏 8:43a
Tokio Marine & Fire Insurance Co, Ltd 8:43a
Kagami Kenkichi 4:102b
Tokitsugu Kyō ki 時継卿記 8:43a-43b
Tokiwa Mitsunaga 常盤光長 1:137a
Tokiwasusuki 7:279a
Tokiwazu-bushi 常磐津節 2:301a; 4:99a; 8:43b
repertoire 8:43b
Tokiwazu school 4:91b
Toki Zemmaro 土岐善麿 8:43b
Tōki zenshū 陶器全集 4:168a
Tokkō 特高 7:241b-242a
Tokkōtai 4:127a
Toko 7:266a
Toko jepang 7:235a
Tōkō kibun 東航紀聞 4:369b
Tokoname 常滑 8:43b
Tokoname ware 常滑焼 8:43b-44a
Tokonami Takejirō 床次竹二郎 7:55a; 8:44a
Tokonoma 2:289a
decoration 4:116a
Tokorogawa 常呂川 8:44a
Tokorozawa 所沢 8:44a
Tokoyo 8:44a-44b
Tokto. *See* **Takeshima**
Toku 4:141b
Tokubetsu Kōtō Keisatsu 特別高等警察 7:241b-242a
Tokuda Kyūichi 徳田球一 7:91b; 8:44b
Tokuda Shūsei 徳田秋声 1:155b; 7:103b; 8:44b-45b
Ken'yūsha 4:199a
works 8:45a
Tokugawa 徳川 7:161a
shōgun 7:160b
Tokugawa Akitake 徳川昭武 7:86a; 8:45b
French-Japanese relations 2:331b
Tokugawa Art Museum 5:276b
Tokugawa bakufu. 徳川幕府 *See* **Tokugawa shogunate**
Tokugawa family 徳川氏 8:45b-47b
Matsudaira and Tokugawa names 8:46a
origins 8:45b
shimpan 7:108a
shogunal line 8:47a
Tokugawa kinship group 8:46b
Tokugawa Hidetada 徳川秀忠 7:9a, 64b; 8:47b
codes of conduct 1:206b
daughter 8:51b
Furuta Oribe 2:373b
Saris, John 7:22a
Sekigahara, Battle of 7:56b
Tokugawa family 8:47a
Tokugawa Ieyasu 8:50b-51a
Tokugawa Ieharu 徳川家治 3:189a; 8:47b
Tokugawa Iemitsu 徳川家光 3:189a; 7:13b; 8:47b-48a
castle residences 2:375a
codes of conduct 1:207a
Hayashi Razan 3:117b
Kan'eiji 4:138a
local administration 4:55a
sankin kōtai (alternate attendance) system 7:14a
Tokugawa Iemochi 徳川家茂 8:48a
Chōshū Expeditions 1:304a
Tokugawa Ienari 徳川家斉 1:211a; 8:48a-48b
bakuhan state 3:189b
Tokugawa Ienobu 徳川家宣 8:48b
Tokugawa Iesada 徳川家定 8:47b
Tokugawa Iesato 徳川家達 8:48b
Tokugawa Ieshige 徳川家重 8:48b-49a
Tokugawa Ietsugu 徳川家継 8:47a
Tokugawa Ietsuna 徳川家綱 2:*100a-100b;* 8:49a
Tokugawa Ieyasu 徳川家康 1:11a, 83b, 151b, 156b, 193a; 7:8a, 14a, 25b, 64a, 65a, 84b, 98b, 101b, 102b, 255a, 256a, 270a, 274b; 8:49a-51a, 303a
background 8:49a
China 1:284b
codes of conduct 1:206b
early career 8:49b
Edo 2:168b
Edo Castle 2:170a
feudalism 2:266a
Fuju Fuse sect 2:359b
Fukushima Masanori 2:366b
Furuta Oribe 2:373b
Fushimi Castle residence 2:375a
goningumi 3:45a-45b
Hayashi Razan 3:117a
Ii Naomasa 3:262b
imperial institution 2:204b
Kanazawa Bunko 4:136a
Kanō Tan'yū 8:*49a*
Kōfukuji revived 4:244a
Komaki Nagakute Campaign 4:265b
Korean relations 4:276b, 279a
mausoleum 4:154a
military practices 2:279a
move to Edo 8:50a
Nagashino, Battle of 5:306b
Nagoya Castle 5:309a-309b
paintings 4:151a
portrait 8:*49a*
post-station system 2:188b
Sanada Yukimura 7:9a
Saris, John 7:22a
seal of 7:45b
Sekigahara, Battle of 7:56b
shimpan 7:108a
shōgun 8:50b
Spain 4:369a
vermilion seal ship trade 8:190a
warrior government 8:230a
Tokugawa Ieyoshi 徳川家慶 8:47b
Tokugawa jikki 徳川実紀 8:51a
Tokugawa Kazuko 徳川和子 8:51b
Tokugawa Keiki. 徳川慶喜 *See* **Tokugawa Yoshinobu**
Tokugawa kinrei kō 徳川禁令考 8:51b
Tokugawa mission 7:335b
Tokugawa Mitsukuni 徳川光圀 1:76b; 2:65a; 8:51b-52a
Dai Nihon Shi 2:347a
historiography 3:154b
inscriptions 3:314a
Kōrakuen Garden 4:276a
Tokugawa Musei 徳川夢声 8:52a
Furukawa Roppa 2:373a
Tokugawa Nariaki 徳川斉昭 8:52a
Fujita Tōko 2:347a
Kairakuen 4:112a
Tokugawa period 徳川時代 3:185b-192b
Tokugawa political system. *See* **Bakuhan system**
Tokugawa shogunate 徳川幕府 7:8a-8b, 91a-91b; 8:52b-56a
achievement 8:55b-56a
administrative system 8:55a
Bakuhan system 4:7a
Buddhism under 7:234a
Chōsen tsūshinshi 1:303b
codes of conduct 1:206b-207a
collapse 4:122a
copper coins 2:186b
copper mining 7:267a

decree concerning foreign ships ··· 7:125b
diplomacy ··· 7:220a
Edo ··· 2:168b
Edo city commissioners ··· 2:171a
emigration ··· 2:200b
erotic art ··· 7:187b-188a
feudalism ··· 2:266a-267a
financial position ··· 8:54b-55a
financial records ··· 7:263b
Gosanke ··· 3:47b
Gosankyō ··· 3:47b
government system ··· 7:164b-165a
highways ··· 4:108b
Ikeda Nagaoki ··· 3:265b-266a
imperial loyalism ··· 2:205a-205b
incident of bell inscription ··· 7:165b
Iwase Tadanari ··· 3:363a
Kira Yoshinaka ··· 4:220a
labor service under ··· 7:265a
military position ··· 8:54a-54b
missions from Korea ··· 4:279a
Mito Civil War ··· 5:204b-205a
National Seclusion ··· 5:346b-347b
Naval forces during ··· 7:263a
officials
ōmetsuke ··· 6:101a
rōjū ··· 6:334a
Sambugyō ··· 7:6a
wakadoshiyori ··· 8:217a
Ōoku ··· 6:113b-114a
Opening of Japan ··· 6:114a
post-station towns ··· 7:185a
powers ··· 8:53a-54a
prevention of cruelty to animals ··· 7:167a
religious inquisition ··· 7:185b
responsibilities ··· 8:52b-53a
rice tax transport ··· 4:112b
samurai retainers ··· 3:111b-112a
sankin kōtai (alternate attendance) system ··· 7:14a
Shie Incident ··· 7:89b
shimpan ··· 7:108a
shinden kaihatsu ··· 7:109b
social discrimination under ··· 7:209a
swordsmen ··· 7:124a
taxation ··· 7:109b
trade limitation regulations ··· 7:171a
trade with Southeast Asia ··· 7:234b
yoriai ··· 8:338a
Tokugawa Tsunayoshi ··· 徳川綱吉 ··· 7:270a; 8:56a-56b
Forty-Seven Rōnin Incident ··· 2:328a
Tokugawa family ··· 8:47a
Tokugawa Yoshimune ··· 徳川吉宗 ··· 7:49b; 8:56b-57a
Kaitokudō patronage ··· 4:113b
Kamo no Mabuchi ··· 4:129b
Kyōhō Reforms ··· 3:189a
Tokugawa family ··· 8:47a
Tokugawa Yoshinobu ··· 徳川慶喜 1:165a; 5:317b; 7:12b, 102a-102b; 8:57a-57b
Itakura Katsukiyo ··· 3:350a
Tokugawa family ··· 8:47a
Tokuju ··· 8:57b-58a
Japanese economy ··· 2:158a
Tokumi-doiya ··· 十組問屋 ··· 8:58a
kaisen management ··· 4:113a
monopolistic trade rights ··· 4:100a
Tokumitsukyō ··· 徳光教 ··· 6:192b
Tokunaga Sunao ·· 徳永直 ··· 7:66b; 8:58a
proletarian literature movement ··· 6:255b
Shin Nihon bungaku ··· 7:122a
works ··· 8:58a
Tokunō ··· 篤農 ··· 8:58a
Tokunoshima ··· 徳之島 ··· 8:58a
Tokura. *See* **Dosō**
Tokusei ··· 徳政 ··· 8:58b
Tokusei edict ··· 8:111b
Tokushima ··· 徳島 ··· 8:58b
Tokushima Plain 徳島平野 ··· 8:58b-59a
Tokushima Prefecture ··· 徳島県 ··· 8:59a
Tokushi yoron (Views of History) ··· 読史余論 2:102a; 3:155a
Tokushu kyōiku ··· 7:241b
Tokushu Seikō Co ··· 2:56b
Tokusō ··· 得宗 7:97b; 8:59a-59b
Tokutomi Iichirō. 徳富猪一郎 *See* **Tokutomi Sohō**
Tokutomi Roka ·· 徳富蘆花 1:155a; 7:103b; 8:59b-60a
Tokutomi Sohō ·· 徳富蘇峰 ··· 8:60a-60b
books ··· 8:60a
Kokumin no tomo founder ··· 4:261a
Kokumin shimbun founder ··· 4:261a
Tokuyama ··· 徳山 ··· 8:60b
Tokuyama Soda Co, Ltd ··· 8:60b
Tōkyō ··· 東京 ··· 8:60b-66a
Asakusa Kannon (Sensōji) ··· 8:*63a*
Azuma Ryūtarō (mayor) ··· 1:127b
business and entertainment center ··· 7:116a
cultural and recreational facilities ··· 8:63b
media ··· 8:63b
parks and sports facilities ··· 8:63b
daily life ··· 8:63b
entertainment areas ··· 2:237a-237b
fauna and flora ··· 8:61a
finance ··· 8:62a
Ginza ··· 8:*63a*
history ··· 8:61b
Imperial Palace ··· 8:*61a*
Kasumigaseki ··· 8:*62b*
Lake Oku Tama ··· 8:*62b*
local and traditional industry ··· 8:61b-62a
metropolitan area ··· 4:7a
modern industry ··· 8:62a
natural features ··· 8:61a
points of interest ··· 8:63b-66a
public institutions and services ··· 8:63a-63b
educational services ··· 8:63b
health services ··· 8:63a
police and fire departments ··· 8:63a
utilities ··· 8:63a
transportation ··· 8:62b-63a
urban planning ··· 8:180a
wards
Adachi ··· 1:11a
Arakawa ··· 1:73b
Bunkyō ··· 1:212a
Chiyoda ··· 1:298a
Chūō ··· 1:313b
Edogawa ··· 2:171a
Itabashi ··· 3:349a
Katsushika ··· 4:174b
Kita ··· 4:229a
Kōtō ··· 4:298a
Meguro ··· 5:152a
Minato ··· 5:183b
Nakano ··· 5:317a
Nerima ··· 5:361b
Ōta ··· 6:129b
Setagaya ··· 7:70b-71a
Shibuya ··· 7:87a
Shinagawa ··· 7:108b
Shinjuku ··· 7:116a
Suginami ··· 7:258a
Sumida ··· 7:266b
Taitō ··· 7:306a
Toshima ··· 8:83a-83b
See also **Edo**
Tōkyō Archaeological Society ··· 1:77b; 5:250b
Tōkyō Astronomical Observatory ··· 1:104b; 6:305b
discoveries ··· 1:104b
movement to Mitaka ··· 1:104b
photographs ··· 1:104b
Tōkyō Bay ··· 東京湾 ··· 8:66a
Tōkyō Bijutsu Gakkō ··· 8:327b
Tōkyō Biological Society ··· 8:320a
Tōkyō Botanical Society ··· 8:320a
Tōkyō Broadcasting System, Inc (TBS) ··· 1:173b, 311a; 8:66a
Tōkyō Chemical Society ··· 1:268a
Tōkyō Cuban Boys ··· 6:355a
Tōkyō Daigaku Shiryō Hensanjo ··· 3:152a
Tōkyō Daigaku Tōyō Bunka Kenkyūjo ··· 3:315b
Tōkyō Denki Kagaku Kōgyō. *See* **TDK Corporation**
Tōkyō Earthquake of 1923 ·2:*139a*; 7:80a; 8:61b, 66a-66b
dams ··· 2:72b
economic impact ··· 3:199b-200a
Financial Crisis of 1927 ··· 2:277a
Kameido Incident ··· 4:125a
magnitude ··· 2:138b-139a
political oppression following ··· 4:183a
prediction ··· 2:141a
transportation ··· 8:98b
Tōkyō Education Museum ··· 8:320a
Tōkyō Electric Power Co, Inc ··· 1:311a; 4:151b, 153a, 205b; 8:66b-67a
Tōkyō Gas Co, Ltd ··· 8:67a
Tōkyō Geographical Society ··· 8:67a
Kiuchi Shinzō ··· 4:231b
Tōkyō Higher Normal School (Tōkyō Kōtō Shihan Gakkō) ··· 8:327b
Tōkyō Hōsō. *See* **Tōkyō Broadcasting System, Inc. (TBS)**
Tōkyō Imperial Household Museum ··· 7:312a
Tōkyō Imperial University ··· 3:281a
Tōkyō Institute of Hygienic Sciences of the Home Ministry ··· 7:351b
Tōkyō Institute of Technology ··· 8:67a
Taniguchi Yoshirō ··· 7:341b
Tōkyō International Airport (Haneda) ··· 1:37b; 5:370a-371b
Tōkyō Joigakkō (Tōkyō Women's Medical School) ··· 8:267b, 349b
Tōkyō Kawa Kai ··· 東京歌話会 ··· 5:19b
Tōkyō keizai zasshi ··· 東京経済雑誌 ··· 7:294b
Tōkyō Kokuritsu Bunkazai Kenkyūjo. *See* **Tōkyō National Research Institute of Cultural Properties**
Tōkyō Kokuritsu Hakubutsukan. *See* **Tōkyō National Museum**
Tōkyō Kokuritsu Kindai Bijutsukan ··· 5:344a-344b
Tōkyō Laboratory of Hygienic Sciences ··· 6:305b
Tōkyō mainichi shimbun ··· 東京毎日新聞 ··· 8:330b
Tōkyō Mathematical Society (Tōkyō Sūgakusha) ··· 5:130b
Tōkyō Meteorological Observatory 6:305b
Tōkyō Metropolitan Archives and Records Institute ··· 8:67b
publications ··· 8:67b
Tōkyō Metropolitan Area ··· 8:67b
Tōkyō Metropolitan Art Museum ··· 5:279a
Tōkyō Metropolitan Hibiya Library · 8:67b
Tōkyō Metropolitan Police Department ··· 6:198a; 8:67b-68a
Tōkyō Metropolitan Police Ordinance of 1953 ··· 8:171a

Tōkyō monogatari 東京物語 2:*277a*; 3:102b; 6:141b
Tōkyō Municipal Ordinance in 1888 8:180a
Tōkyō Music School 5:286a
Tōkyō National Museum 5:276a; 8:68a
Takami Senseki 7:315b
Tōkyō National Museum of Modern Art 5:279a; 7:341b
Tōkyō National Research Institute of Cultural Properties 8:68a-68b
Tōkyō Naval Hospital 7:311a
Tōkyō nichinichi shimbun 東京日日新聞 4:170a
Tōkyō Olympic Games 8:68b
Tōkyō ordinance decision 8:68b
judicial review 4:80a
Tōkyō Philharmonic Society 5:286b
Tōkyō Police Department, Riot Police 6:320a
Tōkyō Rose 東京ローズ 8:68b-69a
D'Aquino, Iva Ikuko Toguri 4:15a
Tōkyō San'yō Electric Co, Ltd 8:69a
Tōkyō Semmon Gakkō 7:311b
Tōkyō Shibaura Electric 3:347a
Tōkyō shimbun 東京新聞 8:69a
Kokumin shimbun and *Miyako shimbun* merger formed 4:261a
Tōkyō Shiryō Collection 8:67b
Tōkyō station 7:349b
Tōkyō Steel Mfg Co, Ltd 8:69a
Tōkyō Stock Exchange 7:294b
Tōkyō Symphony Orchestra 5:286b-287a
Tōkyō Tower 8:69a
Tōkyō Trial 8:224a
Tōkyō University 8:69a-69b, 170a
entrance examinations 2:222a
Hiraga Yuzuru 3:142b
Historiographical Institute 3:152a
modern philosophy 5:229b
research and development 6:303a-305b
Tatsuno Kingo 7:349b
university upheavals of 1968-1969 8:171b
Tōkyō University of Education 8:69b
Tōkyō University of Fine Arts and Music 7:43b; 8:69b, 294b, 327b
Tōkyō University of Foreign Studies 8:69b
Tōkyō University of Science and Literature 2:179b
Tōkyō War Crimes Trial. *See* **War crimes trials**
Tōkyō Women's Christian University 8:69b
Tōkyō Women's Higher Normal School 7:315a-315b
Tōkyō Women's Medical School 8:267b, 349b
Tōkyō-Yokohama mainichi shimbun 東京横浜毎日新聞 8:330a
Tōkyū Car Corporation 8:69b
Tōkyū Construction Co, Ltd 8:70a
Tōkyū Corporation 4:188b; 8:70a
Gotō Keita 3:53a
major companies 8:70a
Tōkyū Land Corporation 8:70a-70b
Tōkyū Department Store Co, Ltd 8:70a
Tōkyū group
Tōkyū Car Corporation 8:69b
Tōkyū Construction Co, Ltd 8:70a
Tōkyū Corporation 8:70a
Tōkyū Department Store Co, Ltd 8:70a
Tōkyū Land Corporation 8:70a-70b
Tōkyū Land Corporation 8:70a-70b
Tolerance in Japanese religion 7:288b-290b; 8:70b
Tolls 7:57a
Tomabechi case 4:79b
Tomakomai 苫小牧 8:70b
Tomari Incident 泊事件 8:330a
Tomaso de Santo Domingo 2:330b
Tomato Kechappu Kōtei (Emperor Tomato Ketchup) トマトケチャップ皇帝 8:13a
Tomb mounds 4:244a-246a
decorations 3:97b-98a
Hayatozuka 3:118b
ornamented 1:77b
protohistoric
excavations 1:78b
dating 1:77b-78a
Tombo 2:133b
Tomb period. *See* **Kofun period**
Tombs
ornamented 6:119a-119b
tunnel 8:329b
Tomeyama 留山 8:70b-71a
Tomii Masaaki 富井政章 7:88a; 8:71a
Tōmi Kemi 遠見検見 4:191b
Tomikuji 富籤 8:71a
Tomimoto Kenkichi 富本憲吉 2:294a; 8:71a-71b
Tominaga Nakamoto 富永仲基 8:71b
Tomioka 富岡 8:71b-72a
Tomioka Kenzō 富岡謙蔵 1:77a
Tomioka Silk-Reeling Mill 富岡製糸所 7:86a; 8:72a
Ichiyōsai Kuniteru 8:*71a*
Tomioka Tessai 富岡鉄斎 1:211a; 8:72a-73a, *72b*
earliest paintings 8:72a
works 8:72a
Tomita Keisen 富田渓仙 8:73a
Tomita Tsuneo 富田常雄 8:73a
works 8:73a
Tōmitsu 東密 2:231b
Tomo 伴 1:147b; 8:131b
Tomobe 伴部 1:147b
Tomodachi 友達 1:3b
Tomoe 巴 8:73a
Tomoe Gozen 巴御前 8:73a
Tomoko Dōmei (Friend's League) 友子同盟 8:270a
Tomonaga Shin'ichirō 朝永振一郎 8:73a
publications 8:73a
Tōmon jissaku 答問十策 4:101b
Tomo no Dainagon ekotoba 伴大納言絵詞 1:137a
Tomo no Kowamine. 伴健岑 *See* **Jōwa Conspiracy**
Tomo no miyatsuko 伴造 1:147b; 8:73b
uji-kabane system 8:134a
Tomo no o 伴の男 1:147b
Tomo no Yoshio. 伴善男 *See* **Ōtemmon Conspiracy**
Tomura daikan 十村代官 4:112b
Tomuragumi 十村組 4:112b
Ton'a 頓阿 8:73b
Kokin denju 4:254a
writings 8:73b
Tonami 砺波 8:73b
Tonami Plain 砺波平野 8:73b
Tonarigumi 3:202a; 4:308a; 5:359b; 8:74a
National Spiritual Mobilization Movement 5:348a
women in 8:261a
Tonarigusa 鄰艸 4:168a
Tondabayashi 富田林 8:74a
Tondenhei 屯田兵 4:113a; 8:74a
Tondenhei settlement 屯田兵村 1:92b
Tonegawa 利根川 4:153b; 8:74a
Tonegawa zushi 利根川図志 8:74a-74b
Toneri, Prince 舎人親王 8:74b
Toneri 舎人 1:147b; 8:74b
ritsuryō system 6:326a
Toneribe 舎人部 1:147b
Tong'a ilbo 4:283b; 6:159b
Tonghak Rebellion 8:74b
Tongue twisters 8:269b
Ton'ishō 頓医抄 4:114b
Tōno 遠野 8:75a
Tōnomine 多武峰 8:75a
Tōno monogatari 遠野物語 4:275b; 8:75a, 315a
Tonomura Shigeru 外村繁 8:75a
trilogy 8:75a
works 8:75a
Tonoshō 土庄 8:75a
Tō no Tsuneyori 東常縁 8:75a-75b
Kokin denju 4:254a
Ton'ya. *See* **Toiya**
Tō on 8:75b
on readings 6:112b
Tooth blackening (ohaguro; kane) 2:38a
Topaz Relocation Center 8:75b-76a
Top Food (brand name) 8:85a
Toppan Printing Co, Ltd 8:76a
Tops 1:149b; 8:76a
Topy Industries, Ltd 8:76a
Toraijin. *See* **Kikajin**
Tōrai Sanna 唐来参和 4:201b
Torampu 6:192a
Toranomon Incident 虎ノ門事件 8:76a-76b, 297b
Tora San 寅さん 8:290a
Tōray Industries, Inc 8:76b-77a
Torch Festival 4:311b
Toride 取手 8:77a
Torii 鳥居 8:77a-77b
Itsukushima Shrine 3:357a
Torii ga keifu 鳥居画系譜 8:79b
Torii Kiyohiro 鳥居清広 8:77b
Torii Kiyomasu I 鳥居清倍(初代) 8:77b-78a, *140a*
Torii Kiyomasu II 鳥居清倍(二代) 8:78a
Torii Kiyomitsu I 鳥居清満(初代) 8:78a
Torii Kiyonaga 鳥居清長 8:78a-78b, *142a*
Torii Kiyonobu I 鳥居清信(初代) 8:78b-79a
Torii Kiyonobu II 鳥居清信(二代) 8:79a
Torii Pass 鳥居峠 8:79a
Torii Ryūzō 鳥居龍蔵 1:36a, 76a; 8:79a
research expeditions 8:79a
treatises 8:79a
Torii school 鳥居派 8:79a-79b, 139b, *140a*
Torii Shinjirō 鳥井信次郎 7:276a; 8:79b
Torii Sosen 鳥居素川 8:79b-80a
Torii Yōzō 鳥居耀蔵 1:141b; 8:80a
Torikaebaya monogatari とりかへばや物語 8:80a
Torimono 4:108a; 7:79b
Torimonochō 2:271b
Tori no ichi 酉の市 8:80a-80b
kumade 8:*80b*
Torinomi Palisade, Battle of 鳥海柵の戦 1:4a
Torishima 鳥島 8:80b
Tōrō (lanterns) 4:367b-368a
Tōrō nagashi 2:*261a*

Toro site 登呂遺跡 4:76a; 6:*189a*; 8:80b
excavation 1:78a
rice cultivation 6:309a
Shizuoka Municipal Toro Site Museum 7:153b
tageta 7:294b
Tortoises. *See* **Turtles**
Tortoiseshell ware 8:80b-81a
Torts 8:81a
government compensation 3:54b-55b
Torture, ritsuryō system 6:327a
Tōryō okuri 4:195a
Tosa 土佐 8:81a
Tosa Bay 土佐湾 8:81a
Tosa Diary, The 6:2a
Tosa dog 8:81a-81b
Tosa Hirokane 土佐広周 4:*128b*
Tosaka Jun 戸坂潤 5:231b; 8:81b
Tosa Kinnōtō 土佐勤王党 7:321b
Tosa Memorial of January 1874 2:234b
Tosa Mitsunobu 土佐光信 2:200a; 6:*153b*
Tosa Mitsuoki 土佐光起 5:*268b*
Tosa mizuki [(flowering hazel) *Corylopsis spicata*] 8:81b
Tosa nikki 土佐日記 1:154a; 4:*133b*; 5:32a-32b; 6:2a; 8:104b
Kino Tsurayuki 4:216b-217a
Tōsanjō Palace 7:110b
Tosa school 土佐派 1:210b; 2:360b; 6:150b, *153b*, 227b; 7:43a, 270a; 8:81b-82a
Tosa Shimizu 土佐清水 8:82a-82b
Tōsei 桃青 1:144a
Tōseiha 統制派 8:82b
Kōdōha's rivalry with 4:243a
Nagata Tetsuzan 5:307a
Tōsei shōnin katagi 当世商人気質 1:18a
Tōsei shosei katagi 当世書生気質 8:110b
Tōshiba Corporation 2:317a; 8:82b
Dokō Toshio 2:127b
Tōshin Steel Co, Ltd 8:83b
Tōshiba Machine Co, Ltd 8:82b
Toshigami 2:299a; 8:83a
Tōshi kaden 藤氏家伝 8:83a
Toshima 利島 8:83a
Toshima Ward 豊島区 8:83a-83b
Tōshin Denki Co 7:173a
Toshi no ichi (year-end fair) 歳の市 2:*262a*; 8:322b-323a
Tōshin Steel Co, Ltd 8:83b
Tōshin Tetsudō 東清鉄道 1:292a-292b
Tōshiya 7:13a-13b
Toshiyori 年寄 4:160a; 8:83b
rōjū 6:334a
Tōshōdaiji 唐招提寺 1:182a; 8:83b-84b
establishment 5:332a
Ganjin 3:7a
kondō (main hall) 8:*83a*
Ritsu sect 6:332a
Tankai 7:343b
Tōshōgū 東照宮 2:376a; 8:84b
paintings 4:151a
"shogun art" 7:351a-351b
Yōmeimon gate 8:*84b*
Tōshōgū engi 東照宮縁起 4:151a; 7:270a
Tōshōgū engi emaki 東照宮縁起絵巻 4:149b
Toshokan zasshi 図書館雑誌 5:1b
Tōshoku, Ltd 8:85a
Tōshūsai Sharaku. 東洲斎写楽 *See* **Sharaku**
Tōson Memorial Hall 藤村記念堂 7:341b
Tosu 鳥栖 8:85a
Tōsuiken 統帥権 8:85a
Tō Teikan 藤貞幹 1:75b, 79a
Totei seido 1:71a-71b
Totoki Baigai 十時梅厓 1:211a; 8:85b
Tōtō, Ltd 8:85b
Tōto shōkei ichiran (Fine Views of the Eastern Capital at a Glance) 東都勝景一覧 8:143b
Totoya Hokkei 魚屋北渓 8:85b
Tōtsubaki (*Camellia reticulata*) 1:237a
Totsukawa (village) 十津川 8:85b
Totsukawa (river) 十津川 8:85b
Tottori (city) 鳥取 8:85b-86a
Tottori Plain 鳥取平野 8:86a
Tottori Prefecture 鳥取県 8:86a-86b
Tottori Sand Dunes 鳥取砂丘 8:86b, *87a*
Towada (city) 十和田 8:86b
Towada, Lake 十和田湖 8:87a
Towada-Hachimantai National Park 十和田八幡平国立公園 1:43a; 8:86b
Towazugatari 問はず語り 7:21b; 8:87a-87b
Townhouses 5:193b
Town meetings (yoriari) 8:338a
Towns and villages, consolidation of 8:87b
Towns and Villages Annexation Promotion Law of 1953 4:7b
Towns and Villages Consolidation Promotion Law (Chōson Gappei Sokushin Hō) of 1953 8:87b
Townsmen 1:300b-302b
Toxicology, medical research 5:152b
Tōya 5:221a
Tōya, Lake 洞爺湖 8:87b
Toyama 富山 8:87b
Toyama Bay 富山湾 8:88a
Toyama Kametarō 外山亀太郎 1:156a; 8:88a
Tōyama Kinshirō 遠山金四郎 8:88a
Toyama Masakazu 外山正一 8:88a
Tōyama Mitsuru 頭山満 1:164a; 3:24b; 4:340a; 7:276b; 8:88a-88b
Toyama Plain 富山平野 8:88b
Toyama Prefecture 富山県 8:88b-89a
Tōya maru Disaster 洞爺丸事件 8:89a, 122a
Tōyashū kikigaki 東野州聞書 8:75b
Tōyo 東予 8:89a
Toyoake 豊明 8:89a
Tōyō Aluminium 8:89a-89b
Tōyōbō, Brazil 8:89b
Tōyōbō Co, Ltd 8:89b
Tōyō Rubber Industry Co, Ltd 8:94a
Tōyō Bunko 7:50b; 8:89b-90a
Toyoda Automatic Loom Works, Ltd 1:33a-33b; 8:90a
Ishida Taizō 3:340b
Toyoda Tsūshō Kaisha, Ltd 8:90b
Toyota Motor Co, Ltd 8:93b
Toyoda Sakichi 豊田佐吉 8:90a
Toyoda Shirō 豊田四郎 2:270b; 7:102b; 8:90a-90b
films 8:90b
Toyoda Tsūshō Kaisha, Ltd 8:90b
Toyogawa Canal 8:90b
Toyohashi 豊橋 8:90b
Tōyō Ink Mfg Co, Ltd 8:90b-91a
Tōyōjin no shii hōhō (Ways of Thinking of Eastern Peoples: India, China, Tibet, Japan) 東洋人の思惟方法 5:314b-315a
Tōyō Jiyūtō 東洋自由党 8:91a
Futsū Senkyo Kisei Dōmeikai 2:376a
Tōyō kanji 5:325a; 8:91a-91b
ideographs 4:143b
Tōyō kanji hyō (Table of Chinese Characters for Daily Use) 8:91a
Toyokawa 豊川 8:91b
Tōyō keizai shimpō 東洋経済新報 1:50b; 8:91b-92a
Tōyō Kōgyō Co, Ltd 8:92a
passenger car production 1:122a
rotary engine 6:339b
Tōyō Kōhan Co, Ltd 8:92a
Tōyō Seikan Kaisha, Ltd 8:92b
Toyokuni. 豊国 *See* **Utagawa Toyokuni**
Toyokuni Toyohiro ryōga jūni kō (Illustrations of the Twelve Months) 豊国豊広両畫十二考 8:184b
Tōyō Menka Kaisha, Ltd 8:92a
Toyonaka 豊中 8:92a-92b
Toyooka 豊岡 8:92b
Tōyō Rayon 7:347b
Toyosaka 豊栄 8:92b
Tōyō Seikan Kaisha, Ltd 8:92b
Tōyō Kōhan Co, Ltd 8:92a
Tōyō Shakaitō 東洋社会党 1:53b; 6:210b; 8:92b
Toyoshima Yoshio 豊島与志雄 8:92b
translations 8:92b
Tōyō Soda Mfg Co, Ltd 8:93a
Tōyō Suisan Kaisha, Ltd 8:93a
Toyota 豊田 8:*93a*
Toyota Auto Body Co, Ltd 8:93a
Toyota Motor Co, Ltd 8:93b
Toyotake Wakatayū 豊竹若太夫 4:77a
Toyotake Yamashiro no Shōjō 豊竹山城少掾 8:93b
Tōyō Takushoku Kaisha 8:93b
historical context 4:282a
Toyota Motor Co, Ltd
Aishin Seiki Co, Ltd 1:38a
Daihatsu Motor Co, Ltd 2:58b
early automotive industry 1:121b
Ishida Taizō 3:340b
Kantō Auto Works, Ltd affiliation 4:153a
Toyoda Automatic Loom Works, Ltd 8:90a
Toyoda Sakichi 8:90a
Toyoda Tsūshō Kaisha, Ltd 8:90b
Toyota Auto Body Co, Ltd 8:93a
unions 4:53b
Toyota Motor Corporation 8:93b
Tōyō Tire and Rubber Industry Co., Ltd 8:93b-94a
Toyotomi Hidetsugu 豊臣秀次 3:180b; 7:27b; 8:94a
Frois, Luis 2:340a
kampaku 4:130a
Toyotomi Hideyori 豊臣秀頼 7:9a, 64b, 93b, 274b; 8:94a
Tokugawa Ieyasu 8:50b-51a
Toyotomi Hideyoshi 豊臣秀吉 1:83b, 126b, 158a, 193a; 7:8a, 14a, 27b, 29b, 56b, 64a-64b, 74a, 83b, 84b, 101b, 104a, 255a, 266b, 274b; 8:94a-96a
abolition of barrier stations 7:57a
administration official 1:206a

anti-Christian edicts ······ **5**:306a
China ······ **1**:284a
chōnin ······ **1**:301a
Christianity ······ **5**:323a
corvée labor ······ **1**:226b
Dai Dembōin destruction ······ **4**:118a
Daigoji ······ **2**:57a-58a
depiction in art ······ **2**:377b
early years ······ **8**:94b
Fabian ······ **2**:241a
feudalism ······ **2**:266a
final years ······ **8**:95b
free markets ······ **6**:283a
Fuju Fuse sect ······ **2**:359b
Furuta Oribe ······ **2**:373b
Fushimi Castle residence ······ **2**:375a
general under Nobunaga ······ **8**:95a
Imai Sōkyū ······ **3**:273a
invasions of Korea in 1592 and 1597 ······ **3**:326b-327b; **8**:95b
Ishida Mitsunari ······ **3**:340a
Ishiyama Honganji ······ **3**:347a
Kaihō Yūshō ······ **4**:110b
Kamiya Sōtan ······ **4**:127b
kampaku ······ **4**:130a
Kanemi kyō ki ······ **4**:139b
kenchi ······ **4**:137a
kokudaka established ······ **4**:257b
koku standardized ······ **4**:256b
Komaki Nagakute Campaign ······ **4**:265b
Korean invasions ······ **4**:276a
Kyūshū campaign ······ **8**:95a
Latin America ······ **4**:369a
Luis Frois ······ **2**:340a
military practices ······ **2**:279a
Nanzenji ······ **5**:330a
nengu ······ **5**:360b
Ōno Harunaga ······ **6**:110a
Ōsaka Castle ······ **6**:120a-120b
Ōsakajō kabegaki ······ **4**:90a
portrait ······ **8**:*94b*
Sanada Yukimura ······ **7**:9a
San Felipe Incident (San Feripe go Jiken) ······ **7**:9b
Satake family ······ **7**:25b
Sen no Rikyū ······ **7**:67a
Seven Spears ······ **2**:366b
Shimai Sōshitsu ······ **7**:99a-99b
Shimazu Yoshihiro ······ **7**:102b
Shinchō kō ki ······ **7**:109b
shi-nō-kō-shō ······ **7**:122b
sword hunt ······ **7**:284b
taking reins of power ······ **8**:95a
Toyotomi Hidetsugu ······ **8**:94a
vermilion seal ship trade ······ **8**:190a
warrior government ······ **8**:230a
Tōyō Trust & Banking Co, Ltd ······ **8**:96a
Toyouke Daijin ··· 豊受大神 ······ **3**:338b
Toyouke no Ōkami 豊受大神 ······ **8**:236b
Ryōbu Shintō ······ **6**:351a
Tōyō University ······ **3**:133a
Toys, traditional ······ **8**:96a-96b
inu hariko ······ **8**:*96b*
materials used ······ **8**:96b
ohajiki ······ **6**:73a
regional variations ······ **8**:96b
tops (koma) ······ **1**:149b
Tōyūki ······ 東遊記 ······ **8**:106a
Tozama ······ 外様 ······ **1**:131b; **2**:340b; **7**:102a; **8**:97a
Tōzumō ······ 唐相撲 ······ **4**:326b
Track and field events ······ **8**:97a-97b
Trade. *See* **Foreign trade**
Trade associations (dōgyō kumiai) ······ **1**:66b; **2**:32a
Trade controls ······ **2**:314b
Trade diversion episode ······ **1**:116b-117a
Trademark Law ······ **6**:164b; **8**:97b
Trade name ······ **8**:97b
Trade secrets
"know-how" ······ **4**:233b
protection ······ **4**:233b
Trade Union Law ······ **4**:346b
Trading companies
Itōman & Co, Ltd ······ **3**:355a
Toyoda Tsūshō Kaisha, Ltd ······ **8**:90b
Tōyō Menka Kaisha, Ltd ······ **8**:92a
See also **General trading company**
Traditional Handcraft Products ······ **1**:261a
Traditional medicine ······ **5**:150b-151b
Training personnel ······ **2**:318a
"Transcendental" cabinets · **6**:241b; **8**:97b
Transistors ······ **2**:193b
Translation rights ······ **8**:98a
Translations
modern ······ **6**:246a
publishing ······ **6**:268a
Transliterating, romanization of Japanese ······ **6**:335b
Transmission of Dharma ······ **7**:114a
Transportation ······ **4**:336a; **8**:98a-104a
and society ······ **8**:103a
coordination and control ······ **8**:103a
new technology ······ **8**:103b
safety ······ **8**:103b
urban ······ **8**:103a
history ······ **8**:98a
Edo period ······ **4**:108b
Heian period ······ **4**:108b
Kamakura period ······ **4**:108b
Meiji period to World War II ······ **8**:98b
postwar ······ **8**:98b
postwar network ······ **8**:99a
administration ······ **8**:99a
air ······ **8**:102b
marine ······ **8**:102a
motor vehicles ······ **8**:102a
railroads ······ **8**:99a
railroad, high-speed ······ **7**:116b-119a
roads ······ **6**:332b
Road Traffic Law ······ **6**:332b
ships ······ **7**:143b-145a
urban life ······ **8**:179a
Transportation administration ······ **8**:99a
Transportation Museum ······ **8**:104a
Transportation safety ······ **8**:103b
Transportation services, land utilization ······ **4**:363b
Trans-Siberian Railway ······ **8**:255b
Travel ······ **8**:104a-104b
Travel diaries ······ **1**:294a; **8**:104b-106a
distinction between kikō and similar genres and ······ **8**:105a
language ······ **8**:105a
types of kikō ······ **8**:105b
Travel sections (michiyuki) ······ **8**:105a
Treasure houses ······ **5**:277b
Treaties ······ **8**:106a
Anglo-Japanese Commercial Treaty of 1894 ······ **1**:57b
Ansei commercial ······ **1**:63a
Anti-Comintern Pact ······ **1**:65a-65b
Chemulp'o ······ **1**:268b
China-Japan Peace and Friendship Treaty ······ **1**:291b-292a
Doihara-Qin (Doihara-Ch'in) Agreement ······ **2**:126b
Four-Power Treaty ······ **2**:330a
Franco-Japanese Agreement of 1907 ······ **2**:333b
Harris Treaty ······ **3**:105a
Kanagawa Treaty ······ **4**:135a
Kanghwa, Treaty of ·· **4**:140b-141a; **7**:197b
Korea-Japan Treaty of 1965 ······ **4**:287b
Nine-Power Treaty ······ **6**:4b
Portsmouth, Treaty of ······ **6**:228a
Potsdam Declaration ······ **6**:231b
Russo-Japanese agreements of 1907-1916 ······ **6**:344b
San Francisco Peace Treaty ······ **7**:10a-11a
Seoul, Treaty of ······ **7**:68b
Shimonoseki, Treaty of **7**:106a-106b, 197b
Sino-Japanese Amity Treaty of 1871 ······ **7**:197b
Soviet-Japanese Basic Convention ·· **7**:238a
Soviet-Japanese Joint Declaration ······ **7**:238b-239a
St. Petersburg ······ **6**:371a
Tianjin (Tientsin) Convention ······ **8**:29b
Tripartite Pact ······ **8**:107a-107b
Unequal Treaties ······ **8**:148a-149a
United States-Japan Administrative Agreement ······ **8**:165b
United States-Japan Mutual Defense Assistance Agreement, (MSA or Mutual Security Agreement) of 8 March 1954 ······ **8**:165b-167b
United States-Japan securities treaties ······ **8**:165b-167b
Versailles, Treaty of ······ **8**:190b-191a
Washington Naval Treaty of 1922 ·· **1**:88a; **8**:235a-235b
Treaty Concerning Fishing in the Northwest Atlantic Ocean ······ **2**:282b
Treaty for the Preservation of the Biological Resources of the Southeast Atlantic Ocean ······ **2**:282b
Treaty of Beijing ······ **4**:268a
Treaty of Edo (Tōkyō) of 26 August 1858 ······ **8**:150b
Treaty of Peace with Japan. *See* **San Francisco Peace Treaty**
Treaty of Territorial Waters and Contiguous Seas ······ **2**:282b
Treaty of the High Seas ······ **2**:282b
Treaty port system ······ **7**:78a
Trees. *See* **Plants**
Trench ······ **4**:8b-9a
Trial ······ **2**:50b
procedures ······ **2**:50b
public ······ **2**:50a
communists ······ **1**:340b-341a
speedy ······ **2**:50a
Tribal chieftains ······ **1**:21a; **7**:171b
Trio-Kenwood Corporation ······ **8**:106b
Tripartite Intervention ······ **1**:286b; **2**:332a; **8**:106b-107a
international relations ······ **3**:320b
Korean-Japanese relations ······ **4**:281b
Mutsu Munemitsu ······ **5**:289a
Russia and Japan ······ **6**:341b
Russo-Japanese War ······ **6**:346a
Sino-Japanese War of 1894-1895 ··· **7**:198a
Treaty of Shimonoseki ······ **7**:106b
ultranationalism ······ **8**:145a
Witte, Sergei Iul'evich ······ **8**:255b
Tripartite Pact ······ **1**:57b; **1**:65a-65b, 88a; **3**:202a; **8**:107a-107b, 272a, 344a
Konoe Fumimaro ······ **4**:273a
Matsuoka Yōsuke ······ **5**:139b
Tōjō Hideki ······ **8**:39b
United Kingdom ······ **8**:152b
United States ······ **8**:158b
Triple Alliance ······ **8**:270b
Triple Entente ······ **8**:270b
Trout lily ······ **4**:165b
Truck manufacturing ······ **3**:348b
True Constitutional Party ······ **4**:198a
True Pure Land school ······ 浄土真宗 ······ **4**:68a-69; **5**:238a
True Seiyū Party ······ **7**:55a
Truman, Harry S. ······ **2**:157a, 158a; **3**:62a; **6**:302b; **8**:107b

atomic bomb 1:108a
World War II 8:276b
Trust 8:107b-108a
Trust banks (shintaku ginkō) 1:139b; 3:327b
Trust Funds Bureau 1:140a
Trust Law (Shintaku Hō) of 1922 8:108a
Ts'ai O. *See* **Cai E (Ts'ai O)**
Ts'ao Ju-lin. *See* **Cao Rulin (Ts'ao Ju-lin)**
Tsingtao. *See* **Qingdao (Tsingtao)**
Tsou T'ao-fen. *See* **Zou Taofen (Tsou T'ao-fen)**
Tsu 津 8:108a
Tsuba 8:108a-109b, *108b*
Tsubaki 1:236b-237a
Tsubaki Chinzan 椿椿山 8:109b
Tsubaki Hot Spring 椿温泉 8:109b
Tsubaki Sanjūrō 椿三十郎 7:108b
Tsubakurodake 燕岳 8:109b
Tsubame 燕 7:276a; 8:109b
Tsubo 4:308a
Tsuboi Kumezō 坪井九馬三 8:109b-110a
Tsuboi Sakae 壺井栄 8:110a
Tsuboi Shigeji 壺井繁治 8:110a
Senki 7:66b
Shin Nihon bungaku 7:122a
works 8:110a
Tsuboi Shōgorō 坪井正五郎 1:75b; 8:110a
kōgoishi named by 4:249a
Tsubota Jōji 坪田譲治 8:110a
Tsubouchi Shōyō 坪内逍遙 5:315b; 7:31a, 99a; 8:110a, *110b*, 111a
Fenollosa, Ernest Francisco 2:251b
Futabatei Shimei 2:375b
fūzoku shōsetsu 2:378b
Shōsetsu shinzui 5:50b-51a
seiji shōsetsu 7:50a
shingeki 7:112b
Shinkokugeki 7:121a
Tsubouchi Memorial Theater Museum 8:232a
Tsuboya ware 壺屋焼 2:295b; 8:111a
Tsuburaya Eiji 円谷英二 8:111a-111b
Tsuburaya Special Productions 8:111b
Tsuchi 土 2:*269a*; 5:307b; 8:124a
Tsuchida Bakusen 土田麦僊 8:111b
Tsuchii Bansui. 土井晩翠 *See* **Doi Bansui**
Tsuchi ikki (peasant revolts) 土一揆 2:107b-108a; 3:268b-269a; 8:111b-112a
Tsuchimikado, Emperor 土御門天皇 8:112a
poetry 2:354b
Tsuchimoto Noriaki 土本典昭 2:275b
Tsuchi to heitai (Mud and Soldiers) 土と兵隊 2:*270b*
Tsuchiura 土浦 8:112a
Tsuchiya Bummei 土屋文明 8:112a
works 8:112a
Tsuchiya Yasuchika 土屋安親 8:*108b*
Tsuda College 8:112a
Tsuda Mamichi 津田真道 8:112a-112b
Tsuda Sen 津田仙 8:112b
Tsuda Sōgyū 津田宗及 7:67a; 8:112b
Tsuda Sōkichi 津田左右吉 8:112b
historiography 3:157a
on *Kojiki's* compilation 4:251b
works 8:112b
Tsuda Umeko 津田梅子 8:112b-113a
Bacon, Alice Mabel 1:129b
Tsūen 通円 4:327b
Tsugamonai hanashi no oyadama 無束話親玉 8:185a
Tsugaru Peninsula 津軽半島 1:69b; 8:113a
Tsugaru Plain 津軽平野 8:113a
Tsugaru Strait 津軽海峡 8:113a
Tsuga Teishō 都賀庭鐘 8:113a
works 8:113a
Tsuge [(Japanese box) *Buxus microphylla* var. *japonica*] 8:113a-113b
Tsugumi. *See* **Thrushes**
Tsuihō. *See* **Banishment**
Tsuina 7:71b
Tsuishu 4:116a
Tsu Islanders 4:35a
Tsuitate (free-standing screens) 7:41b
Tsuitate (single-panel screen) 7:42b
Tsujigahana 8:113b
Tsujigiri 8:113b
Tsuji Kunio 辻邦生 8:113b
Tsuji Masanobu 辻正信 8:113b-114a
Tsujimura Jusaburō 辻村ジュサブロウ 8:114a
Tsujimura Sumie. *See* **Tanaka Sumie**
Tsujiura 8:114a
Tsuji Zennosuke 辻善之助 8:114a
Tsuka 4:295b
Tsukamoto Kunio 塚本邦雄 8:114a
works 8:114a
Tsukasameshi no Jimoku 官召の除目 4:57b
Tsukebito 7:273a
Tsukemono 2:305a
Tsuki 4:196a
Tsukigase 月ヶ瀬 8:114a
"Tsukigata Hampeita" 月形半平太 7:121a
Tsukiji Little Theater (Tsukiji Shōgekijō) 7:112b; 8:299b
Tsukimi (moon viewing) 2:*261b*; 5:248a
Tsukimi zatō 月見座頭 4:327b, *329a*
Tsukimono 8:114a-114b
Tsukinami-e (activities of 12 months) paintings 8:309b
Tsuki ni hoeru 月に吠える 3:76a
Tsukinowaguma (*Selenarctos thibetanus*) 1:148b
Tsuki no yukue 月の行方 1:73b
Tsukioka Yoshitoshi 月岡芳年 7:306a
Tsuki wa higashi ni 月は東に 8:319b
Tsuki yori no shisha 月よりの使者 4:308a
Tsukuba Academic New Town 8:114b
Ibaraki Prefecture 3:253b
Tsukubasan 筑波山 8:114b
Tsukubashū 菟玖波集 5:18a; 8:114b
Shinsen tsukubashū 7:124b
Tsukuba University 2:179a-179b; 8:115a
Tsukuda 佃 8:115a
Tsukue Ryūnosuke 机龍之助 5:320a
Tsukumi 津久見 8:115a
Tsukumo shell mound 津雲貝塚 6:235a
Tsukuri 7:24b
Tsukuri monogatari (courtly romances or prose fiction) 作物語 5:246a
Tsukushi dōki 筑紫道記 6:299a
Tsukushi Mountains 筑紫山地 8:115a
Tsukushi Plain 筑紫平野 8:115a
Tsukuyomi no Mikoto 月読尊 5:293a
Tsuma 妻 2:25b; 7:359a
Tsumago 妻籠 8:115a
Tsuma yo bara no yō ni (Wife! Be like a Rose!) 妻よ薔薇のように 5:335a
Tsumegome 4:117b
Tsumi 2:232a-232b; 3:100b-101b; 4:186a-186b; 7:139a; 8:115a-115b
Tsumi-kegare 4:186a
Tsumugi 4:105a; 8:116a
Tsuna 7:272b
Tsunashima Ryōsen 綱島梁川 8:116a
Tsunetō Kyō 恒藤恭 8:116a
writings 8:116a
Tsunoda Ryūsaku 角田柳作 8:116a
Tsunokakushi 3:119a
Tsurane 4:94a
Tsure 4:298b
Tsurezuregusa 徒然草 4:136a; 5:44a; 8:341a-342b
Tsuridono 7:111a
Tsurigane ninjin (*Adenophora triphylla* var. *Japonica)* 8:116a-116b
Tsūron kōkogaku 通論考古学 1:77a, 79b
Tsuru. *See* **Ceramics**
Tsuruga 敦賀 2:364a; 8:116b
Tsuruga Bay 敦賀湾 8:116b
Tsurugaoka Hachiman Shrine 鶴岡八幡宮 4:*120b*; 8:116b
Shizuka Gozen 7:152b
Tsurugidake 剱岳 8:116b
Tsurugigasaki 剣ケ崎 7:293a
Tsurugisan 剣山 8:116b
Tsuruhachi Tsurujirō 鶴八鶴次郎 7:108a; 8:289a
Tsurukame 鶴亀 8:289a
Tsurumeso 弦召 4:59b
Tsurumi Shunsuke 6:233a; 7:149a-149b
Tsurumi Yūsuke 鶴見祐輔 8:116b-117a
Tsuru nyōbō 鶴女房 8:117a
Tsuruoka 鶴岡 8:117a
Tsuruta Yoshiyuki 鶴田義行 8:117a-117b
Tsuru wa yamiki 鶴は病みき 6:80a
Tsuruya Namboku 鶴屋南北 1:211b; 5:50a; 8:117b
kabuki plays 4:91a-92a
plays 8:117b
Tsuryō 津料 7:57a
Tsūsanshō 通産省 5:189b-191b
Tsushima (city) 津島 8:117b
Tsushima (island) 対馬 8:*117a*, 117b, 8:117b-118a
Izuhara port 8:*117a*
role in Korean-Japanese relations 4:278b
Silla pirates' attacks 4:277b
Sō family 7:220a
Sō Yoshitatsu 4:140b
Tsushima Current 対馬海流 3:21a; 8:118a
Tsushima, Battle of 3:197a; 8:118a
Russo-Japanese War 6:347a
Tōgō Heihachirō 8:36a
Tsushima Incident 対馬事件 8:118a
Tsushima Senryō Jiken 8:118a
Tsushima Shūji. 津島修治 *See* **Dazai Osamu**
Tsushima Strait 対馬海峡 8:118a-118b
Tsūshin seido. *See* **Telecommunications systems**
Tsūshō kaisha 4:184a; 8:118b
Tsūshō Sangyō Shō 通商産業省 5:189b-191b

Tsutaya Jūzaburō 蔦屋重三郎 **8**:186b
Tsutsui Junkei 筒井順慶 **8**:118b
Tsutsuji (azaleas) **1**:126a
Tsutsukyahan **4**:323b
Tsutsumi Chūnagon monogatari 堤中納言物語 **5**:36b, 42b; **8**:118b-119a
butterflies **1**:226a
Tsutsumi ware 堤焼 **8**:119a
Tsutsumi Yasujirō 堤康次郎 **8**:119a
Tsutsushimi **8**:119a-119b, 347b
Tsuwabuki *(Ligularia tussilaginea; Farfugium japonicum)* **8**:119b
Tsuwano 津和野 **8**:119b
Tsuyama 津山 **8**:119b
Tsuyama Basin 津山盆地 **8**:119b
Tsuyuharai **7**:272b
Tsuyu no atosaki つゆのあとさき **7**:176a
Tsuyu no Gorobei 露五郎兵衛 **6**:282a
Tsuzumi **8**:119b-120a
gigaku **3**:32a
Tsuzumi no onna 鼓の女 **7**:339b
Tsuzura **4**:105a; **8**:120a
Tsuzure-ori **8**:120a
Tsuzurikata **7**:51a
Tuan Ch'i-jui. *See* **Duan Qirui (Tuan Ch'i-jui)**
Tuberculosis **5**:147b
Tule Lake Relocation Center **8**:120a
Tuna [(maguro) *Thunnus* spp.] **2**:285b; **8**:120a
Tungusic **4**:18b
Tung-ya Ho-ch'in Hui **8**:31a
Turkic **4**:18b
Turtles [(kame) order Chelonia] **8**:120a-120b
Tutoring schools **2**:223a
Twenty-four Eyes **6**:1a; **8**:110a
Twenty-One Articles of Lord Sōunji, The **7**:234b
Twenty-One Demands **1**:239b, 287a-287b; **4**:367a; **8**:120b-121b, 270b, 354a
content **8**:121a
Japanese aspirations in China **8**:120b
Japanese ultimatum **8**:121b
response to **8**:121a
Shandong (Shantung) Question **7**:77b
Washington Conference **8**:235a
Twenty-Six Martyrs **5**:304a; **8**:121b
Toyotomi Hideyoshi **8**:96a
Two Mandalas, The **6**:347b-351a
Type and Motif Index of Japanese Folk Literature, A **2**:302b
Typhoons **8**:121b-122b
development and course **8**:122a
observation and forecasting **8**:122b
structure **8**:122a
Typhoon season **4**:8a
Typography **2**:296a

U

Ubasoku 優婆塞 **8**:123a
Ube 宇部 **8**:123a
Ube Industries, Ltd **8**:123a
U-BIX **4**:270b
Ubusunagami 産土神 **6**:205a; **8**:123a-123b
Uchida Ginzō 内田銀蔵 **8**:123b
historiography **3**:156b
works **8**:123b
Uchida Hyakken 内田百閒 **8**:123b
Uchida Kōsai 内田康哉 **8**:123b
Uchida Roan 内田魯庵 **5**:13a; **8**:123b-124a
Uchida Ryōhei 内田良平 **1**:164a; **8**:124a
Uchida Tomu 内田吐夢 **2**:270a; **8**:124a
Uchigeba **7**:252b
Uchikake (A Robe) 打掛 **8**:110a
Uchikowashi 打毀 **1**:132b; **7**:345b; **8**:124a-124b, 337b
Uchimura Kanzō 内村鑑三 **1**:84b, 155a, 223a; **5**:262b-263a; **7**:90b; **8**:124b-125a
geography **3**:25b
pacifism **6**:144a-144b
works **8**:124b
Uchimura Naoya 内村直也 **8**:125a
Uchinada 内灘 **8**:125a
Uchinada Incident **8**:125a
Uchinomaki Hot Spring 内牧温泉 **1**:103a
Uchinoura 内之浦 **8**:125a
Uchiura Bay 内浦湾 **8**:125a
Uchiwa (fans) **2**:247b-248a; **5**:331b
Uchū Kaihatsu Jigyōdan **5**:347b
Uda, Emperor 宇多天皇 **1**:45a; **7**:257a; **8**:125b
Fujiwara family **2**:348a-348b
Shinkokushi **7**:121b
Udagawa Yōan 宇田川榕庵 **8**:125b
Uda Tennō gyoki 宇多天皇御記 **8**:125b
Udon **7**:265b
Udonsuki **7**:265b
Udo Shrine 鵜戸神宮 **8**:125b
Ueda 上田 **8**:125b
Ueda Akinari 上田秋成 **5**:11b, 48b; **8**:126a-126b
early life **8**:126a
Fujitani Nariakira **2**:346b
Hachimonjiya-bon **3**:74b; **8**:126a
Harusame monogatari **8**:126b
poetry and scholarship **8**:126b
Ugetsu monogatari **8**:126a-126b
yomihon **8**:336a-336b
Ueda Bin 上田敏 **2**:296a; **5**:12b; **7**:253b; **8**:126b-127a
Kaichōon **8**:247b
Ueda Kazutoshi 上田万年 **2**:65a, 377a; **7**:104b; **8**:127a
Ueda Mannen. 上田万年 *See* **Ueda Kazutoshi**
Ueda Teijirō 上田貞次郎 **8**:127a
Uehara Yūsaku 上原勇作 **8**:127a
Uejima Onitsura 上島鬼貫 **3**:79a; **5**:16a; **8**:127a
Ueki Emori 植木枝盛 **8**:127a-127b
Freedom and People's Rights Movement **2**:334b-335a
political groups formed by **8**:127a
shigi kempō **7**:92b
Ueki Masayoshi 植木正義 **4**:166a
Uemura Kōgorō 植村甲午郎 **8**:127b
Uemura Masahisa 植村正久 **8**:127b-128a
Uemura Naomi 植村直己 **8**:128a
Uemura Ryūichi 上村隆一 **1**:125b-126a
Uemura Shōen 上村松園 **8**:128a-128b
Uemura Sōichi. 植村宗一 *See* **Naoki Sanjūgo**
Uemura Tamaki 植村環 **8**:128b
Ueno 上野 **7**:160a; **8**:128b
Ueno Basin 上野盆地 **8**:128b
Ueno Park 上野公園 **3**:*94b*; **8**:128b
modern architecture in **8**:128b-129a
Ueno Riichi 上野理一 **8**:129a
Ueno Zoological Garden **1**:71b; **8**:129a
Ueshiba Morihei 植芝盛平 **1**:34a
Uesugi family 上杉氏 **8**:129a
daimyō family **8**:129a
territorial warlords **8**:129a
Uesugi Harunori 上杉治憲 **8**:129a-129b
Uesugi Kagekatsu 上杉景勝 **3**:179b; **8**:129b
Sanada Yukimura **7**:9a
Uesugi Kenshin 上杉謙信 **8**:129b-130a
Kawanakajima, Battle of **4**:182a
Uesugi Norizane 上杉憲実 **8**:130a
Eiryō Rebellion **4**:248a
Uesugi Shinkichi 上杉慎吉 **8**:130a-130b
quasi-absolute power of emperor theory **4**:375a
Uesugi Yōzan. 上杉鷹山 *See* **Uesugi Harunori**
Uesugi Zenshū, Rebellion of 上杉禅秀の乱 **8**:130b
Uetsuka Shūhei 上塚周平 **8**:130b
Ugaki Kazushige 宇垣一成 **1**:88a; **8**:130b-131a
Uge no hitokoto. 宇下人言 *See* **Matsudaira Sadanobu**
Ugetsu monogatari (Tales of Moonlight and Rain) 雨月物語 **5**:48b; **8**:126a, 336b
Ugōkai 烏合会 **4**:100b
Uguisu (bush warbler) **1**:223b-224a
Uirōuri 外郎売 **4**:98b
Uji (city) 宇治 **4**:166b; **5**:324b; **8**:131a
chieftains **4**:89a
firefly viewing **2**:280b
Uji (political groups) 氏 **6**:176b; **8**:131a
uji-kabane system **8**:131b
Uji-bito 氏人 **4**:89a
Uji dainagon monogatari 宇治大納言物語 **8**:137b
Ujigami 氏神 **7**:179b; **8**:131a-131b
Shintō **4**:362b; **7**:126a
Ujigawa 宇治川 **4**:338a; **8**:131b
Uji-kabane system 氏姓制度 **8**:131b-137a
ason **1**:103a
history **8**:135b-137a
kabane **8**:134a-135b
Taika Reform **7**:295b
Uji structure **8**:132a-134a
Uji Kadayū 宇治嘉太夫 **4**:77a
Ujina 宇品 **8**:137a-137b
Uji no kami 氏上 **4**:89a
Uji shūi monogatari 宇治拾遺物語 **1**:137a; **2**:296a, 302b; **5**:43b-44a; **7**:72b, 93a, 149b; **8**:137b, 223b
Kobutori jijii in **4**:239b
Uji-Yamada 宇治山田 **8**:176a
Ukai **2**:26a
Ukaiki. 宇槐記 *See Taiki*
Ukanomitama no Kami 宇迦之御魂神 **2**:375a
Ukebumi 請文 **8**:137b
Ukemen'i 請免居 **4**:191b
Ukeragahana うけらが花 **4**:167b
Ukesho 請所 **4**:63b
Uki-e 浮絵 **8**:140b, *141a*
Ukigumo (Floating Clouds) 浮雲 **2**:*272b*; 375b
Uki komononari 浮小物成 **4**:267b
Ukita Hideie 宇喜多秀家 **8**:137b-138a
Ukita Kazutami 浮田和民 **8**:138a

Ukitōdai 浮き燈台 7:167a
Ukiyaku 浮役 5:360b; 8:138a
komononari 4:267b
Ukiyoburo 浮世風呂 4:256a; 7:97a
Ukiyodoko 浮世床 7:97a
Ukiyo-e 浮世絵 1:163b; 2:296a, 6:153b; 7:43a, 79b, 270a; 8:138a-144a
bijin-e 8:*140b*
Chōkyōsai Eiri 1:300a
design 2:88b
early 8:138a-139a
Edo 8:139b-140b
full-color printing 8:141a-141b
fūzokuga 2:377a
Gaifū kaisei or *Red Fuji* 8:*143b*
Genroku era 3:23a
Golden Age 8:142a-143a
Hiroshige 3:148a; 8:*144b*
Hishikawa Moronobu 8:*138b*
Hokusai 8:*143b*
Ishikawa Toyonobu 3:345a
Iwasa Matabei 3:363a
kabuki actor 8:*143a*
Kaigetsudō Ando 8:*140b*
Kaigetsudō school 4:109b; 8:*140b*
Kambun Master 4:124b
Katsukawa Shunshō 4:171b-172a
Kawanabe Gyōsai 4:182a
kibyōshi 8:141b-142a
Kitagawa school 4:225a
kyōka 8:141b-142a
landscape 8:143a-144a
mitate-e 8:141b-142a
modern prints 5:232a
Night View of Kanazawa in Musashi Province 8:*144b*
Nishimura Shigenaga 8:*141a*
Okumura Masanobu 6:97a
Ōsaka school 6:123a
Riccar Art Museum 6:308a
Sharaku 8:*143a*
shunga 8:*138b*
surimono 8:141b-142a
Suzuki Haruobu 8:*141b*
Takehisa Yumeji 7:324a
Thirty-Six Views of Mount Fuji (Fugaku sanjūrokkei) 8:*143b*
Torii Kiyomasu 8:*140a*
Torii Kiyonaga 8:*142a*
Torii school 8:*140a*
uki-e 8:*141a*
Utagawa Kunisada 8:*139a*
Utagawa Kuniyoshi 8:*145a-145b*
Utagawa school 8:184a-184b
Utagawa Toyokuni 8:184b-185b
Utamaro 8:*142b*
Western-style pictures 8:249a
woodblock printing 8:139a-139b
yokohama-e 8:330a
Ukiyogata rokumai byōbu 浮世方六枚屏風 1:119b
Ukiyo monogatari 浮世物語 4:136b
Ukiyo-zōshi 浮世草子 2:374b; 3:22b-23a; 4:136b; 5:48b; 7:333b-334a; 8:144a-144b
hachimonjiya-bon 3:74b
Saikaku 6:370a-370b
later Edo-period 5:48b-49b
Ukiyo-zōshi novels 浮世草子 6:247a
Ukon Ujinari 右近氏成 4:270a
Ŭlsa Treaty (1905) 4:289a
Ultranationalism 8:144b
contradictions in interpretations 8:145b-146a
genesis 8:145a-145b
modernization 5:229a
nationalism 5:342a-343b; 8:146a
Uma 3:231a
Umakaibe 馬飼部 1:147b
Uma no Kura 7:248b
Umarete wa mita keredo 生れてはみたけれど 6:141b; 8:146a-146b
Umarete wa mita keredo (I was Born But . . .) 2:*269a*
Umbrellas, traditional 6:280b; 8:146b
Ume 6:192b-193a
Umeboshi 8:146b
Umeda Umpin 梅田雲浜 8:146b
Umehara Ryūzaburō 梅原龍三郎 6:*156b*; 8:146b-147a
Umehara Sueji 梅原末治 1:77b; 8:147a
publications 8:147a
Ume Kenjirō 梅謙次郎 2:319a; 8:147a
Umemodoki (*Ilex serrata* var. *sieboldii*) 8:147a
Umetani Matsutarō 梅谷松太郎 7:107b
Umeyo fuyaseyo 生めよふやせよ 2:246b
Umezaki Haruo 梅崎春生 8:147a-147b
Umezawa Hamao 梅沢浜夫 8:147b
Umezu-Ka Ōkin Kyōtei 梅津-何応欽協定 3:128b
Umezu Masakage nikki 梅津政景日記 8:147b
Umezu Yoshijirō 梅津美治郎 7:278a; 8:147b
Umibe no kōkei 海辺の光景 8:319b
Umi ni ikuru hitobito (People Who Live on the Sea) 海に生くる人々 6:255a
Umi no Sachi (Gifts of the Sea) 1:*69a-69b*
Ummei 運命 4:114a
Unagi 2:184a
Unazuki 宇奈月 8:147b
Under the Persimmon Tree 8:110a
Un Dia 7:291a
Unebiyama 8:310b
Uneme 采女 1:147b; 8:147b-148a
Unemployment 4:356a; 7:216a; 8:148a
hidden 8:148a
public employment security offices 6:265a
Unemployment Compensation Law (1947) 4:358a
Unemployment insurance. *See* **Social security programs**
Unemployment Insurance Law (Shitsugyō Hoken Hō; Koyō Hoken Hō) of 1947 4:352b; 7:209b
Unequal Treaties 1:160a; 7:9b, 51a-51b
Austria 1:119b-120a
Denison, Henry Willard 2:86b
foreign trade development 2:320a
Mexico 5:165b
Ministry of Foreign Affairs 5:188b
naichi zakkyo 5:309b-310a
Unequal Treaties, revision of 8:148a
Aoki Shūzō 1:69a-69b
initiatives and negotiations 8:148b-149a
1868-1874 8:148b
1875-1879 8:148b
1880-1887 8:148b-149a
1888-1889 8:149a
1890-1894 8:149a
Tani Kanjō 7:341b-342a
treaties and problems 8:148a-148b
United Kingdom 8:151b
UNESCO (United Nations Educational, Scientific, and Cultural Organization) **activities in Japan** 2:175b, 181a; 8:149b
Unfair Competition Prevention Law (Fusei Kyōsō Bōshi Hō) 3:297b; 8:97b
Unfair labor practices 4:351b; 6:312b; 8:149b
collective bargaining 1:334b
Ungjin 6:146a
Uni 7:46a-46b
Unification, political before 1600 2:149a
Unification Church. *See* **Holy Spirit Association for the Unification of World Christianity**
Unification of the spoken and written word 3:16b
Uniforms 8:*149a*, 149b-150a
Unionism
labor reforms of 1945-1947 4:357b
labor relations 4:348b
national labor federations 4:345a-345b
pre-World War II 4:345a
reorganization and splits 4:347a
restraints 4:346b
rival federations 4:346b
structure and function 4:347b-348a
collective bargaining 4:347b
employment security 4:347b
grievance procedures 4:347b
membership 4:347b, 348b
wartime 4:345b
1945-1950 4:346a
Unionization 4:344b
Union of New Religious Organizations of Japan 8:150a
Union of Soviet Socialist Republics and Japan. *See* **Russia and Japan**
Unions 7:216b-217a
bureaucracy 1:220b
Federation of Independent Unions 1:313a-314a
labor unions 4:358b-360a
teachers 7:366b
Union Theological Seminary 6:288b
Unitarian Church 5:231a
United Church of Christ in Japan 8:150a
United Kingdom
Anglo-Japanese Alliance 1:56b-57b
Japanese studies 4:42a
United Kingdom and Japan 8:150a-153b
Alliance period 8:152a
early contacts 8:150b-151a
interwar period 8:152a-152b
Japan's modernization 8:151a-151b
Meiji period 8:151b-152a
post-World War II relations 8:152b-153b
United Nations and Japan 8:153b-154b
centrality of United Nations 8:153b
Japan's activities 8:154a-154b
UN agencies and UN nongovernmental organizations 8:153b-154a
United Nations Conference on the Law of the Sea (UNCLOS I) 8:13b
United Nations Conference on the Law of the Sea (UNCLOS II) 8:13b
United Nations Conference on Trade and Development (UNCTAD I) 2:309b
United Nations' Economic Commission for Asia and the Far East 7:235b
United Nations Law of the Sea Conference 6:345b
United Nations University 2:177a
United Social Democratic Party 8:154b
United States
influence on education 2:175a-176a
Japanese Americans 4:13a-16a
in Hawaii 4:16a-17a
Japanese immigrants 2:200b-201a
Japanese language studies 4:21a
Japanese studies in 4:41b
United States and Japan 6:289a; 8:154b-160b

armed forces in Japan ······ **8**:160b-161a
economic relations (1945-1973)
······ **2**:154a-165b; **8**:161a-164b
American foreign investment
······ **8**:162a-162b
American protectionism ···· **8**:163a-163b
dollar primacy ······ **8**:161b-162a
early postwar order ······ **8**:161a-161b
international economic system
······ **8**:162b-163a
international monetary crisis and yen revaluation ······ **8**:163b-164a
yen in new era of international financial relations ······ **8**:164a-164b
interwar period (1920-1930) ·· **8**:157a-158a
opening of relations (1853-1980)
······ **8**:154b-155b
postwar relations (1945-1980) **8**:159b-160b
power relations in Asia (1890-1920)
······ **8**:155b-157a
war period (1930-1945) ······ **8**:158a-159b
United States education missions to Japan ······ **8**:164b
romanization of Japanese ······ **6**:336a
school curriculum ······ **7**:36a
teachers ······ **7**:365b
United States Immigration Acts of 1924, 1952 and 1965 ··· **1**:136b; **4**:13a; **8**:164b-165a
United States-Japan Administrative Agreement ······ **8**:165a-165b
United States-Japan security treaties
······ **8**:166a
United States-Japan Commercial Treaty of 1858. *See* **Harris Treaty**
United States-Japanese Joint Committee of Trade and Economic Affairs
Ikeda-Kennedy Agreements ······ **3**:265a
United States-Japan Mutual Defense Assistance Agreement ······ **8**:165b
Ikeda-Robertson Talks ······ **3**:266a
United States-Japan Mutual Security Treaty
Tōkyō ordinance decision (20 July 1960)
······ **8**:68b
United States-Japan security treaties
······ **7**:235b; **8**:160a, 165b-167b, 344b
atomic bomb ······ **1**:110b
ban-the-bomb movement ······ **1**:115a
defense industry ······ **2**:82a-82b
Democratic Socialist Party ······ **2**:85b
Dulles, John Foster ······ **2**:135a
Japan Communist Party ······ **4**:12a
Japan Socialist Party ······ **4**:48b
judicial review ······ **4**:80a
Kishi Nobusuke ······ **4**:223a-223b
movement against. *See* **Peace movement**
national defense ······ **5**:336b-338b
Ōsu Incident ······ **6**:128a
reappraisal ······ **4**:386a
renunciation of war ······ **6**:301b
San Francisco Peace Treaty ····· **7**:10a-11a
Treaty of 1952 ······ **8**:165b-166b
Treaty of 1960 ······ **8**:166b-167b
United States armed forces in Japan
······ **8**:160b
United States military bases disputes
······ **8**:168a
university upheavals of 1968-1969 · **8**:171b
United States-Japan Treaty of Amity and Commerce of 1858 ······ **8**:168b
United States-Japan Treaty of Amity, 1854. *See* **Kanagawa Treaty**
United States military bases, disputes over ······ **8**:167b-168b
United States, mission of 1860 to · **8**:168b
United States National Security Council
······ **6**:54b
Unitika, Ltd ······ **8**:168b
Universal Copyright Convention
translation rights ······ **8**:98a
Wakatsuki Reijirō ······ **8**:218b
Universal Manhood Suffrage Law **2**:188b; **6**:168b, 211a
democracy ······ **2**:84b
Hara Takashi ······ **3**:103a
Ōyama Ikuo ······ **6**:138a
Universal Manhood Suffrage Movement
······ **3**:198b; **6**:210b; **8**:169a-169b
apathy and success ······ **8**:169b
arguments for ······ **8**:169b
beginnings (1897-1911) ······ **8**:169a
democracy ······ **2**:84b
early Diet activity ······ **8**:169a
eclipse and revival (1911-1919)
······ **8**:169a-169b
Inukai Tsuyoshi ······ **3**:326a
Taishō democracy ······ **7**:304b
Universities and colleges ···· **8**:170a-171a
academic freedom ······ **1**:6b
Aoyama Gakuin University ······ **1**:71a
associations ······ **4**:10b
Atomi Gakuen Women's University
······ **1**:115a
autonomy ······ **6**:220b, **8**:171a-171b
Chiba University ······ **1**:271a
Chūō University ······ **1**:313b
Dōshisha University ······ **2**:131b-132a
entrance examinations ······ **2**:222a-224a
finance ······ **3**:134a
Gakushūin University ······ **1**:5a; **3**:5a
Hiroshima University ······ **3**:150a
history ······ **3**:133a-133b; **8**:170a-170b
Hitotsubashi University ······ **3**:208a-208b
Hokkaidō University ······ **3**:214a
Hōsei University ······ **3**:234b-235a
imperial ······ **3**:281a
International Christian University ·· **3**:318a
Japan Women's University ······ **4**:50b
Kansei Gakuin University ······ **4**:152a
Keiō University ······ **4**:189a
Kōbe University ······ **4**:238a
Kokugakuin University ······ **4**:259b
Kyōto University ······ **4**:339a
Kyūshū University ······ **4**:341b
Meiji Gakuin University ······ **5**:154a
Meiji University ······ **5**:160b-161a
Nagoya University ······ **5**:309b
Nanzan University ······ **5**:330a
Nara Women's University ······ **5**:334a
National Defense College ······ **5**:338b
Nihon University ······ **5**:384b
Ochanomizu Women's University ·· **6**:59a
Ōsaka University ······ **6**:123a
Ōsaka University of Foreign Studies
······ **6**:123a
Ōtani University ······ **6**:129a
present status and problems ·· **8**:170b-171a
Rikkyō University ······ **6**:317a
Ritsumeikan University ······ **6**:321b
Ryūkyū University ······ **6**:358b
Sophia University ······ **7**:229a
Tamagawa University ······ **7**:332b
technical ······ **8**:192b
technical colleges ······ **7**:368a
Tenri University ······ **8**:9b
Tōhō Gakuen School of Music ····· **8**:36b
Tōhoku University ······ **8**:37b
Tōkai University ······ **8**:42a
Tōkyō Institute of Technology ······ **8**:67a
Tōkyō University ······ **8**:69a-69b
Tōkyō University of Education ····· **8**:69b
Tōkyō University of Fine Arts and Music
······ **8**:69b
Tōkyō University of Foreign Studies **8**:69b
Tōkyō Women's Christian University
······ **8**:69b
Tsuda College ······ **8**:112a
Tsukuba University ······ **8**:115a
Waseda University ······ **8**:232a
"University, The" ······ **2**:56a-57a
University Chartering Council (Daigaku Setchi Shingikai) ······ **8**:170b
University Law
university upheavals of 1968-1969 · **8**:171b
University Order (Daigaku Rei) ···· **8**:170a
University Upheavals of 1968-1969
······ **8**:171b
Riot Police ······ **6**:320b
Unjō ······ 運上 ······ **5**:360b; **8**:171b-172a
Unjō taxes ······ **1**:132a
Unjust enrichment ······ **8**:172a
Unka ······ **6**:190a
Unkei ······ 運慶 **1**:*186b*, 199a; **8**:172a
Kaikei ······ **4**:111a
Kōfukuji commission ······ **4**:244a
works ······ **8**:172a
Unknown War, The ······ **7**:200b
Unkoku school ···· 雲谷派 ··· **8**:172a-172b
Sesshū Tōyō ······ **7**:70a
Unkoku Tōgan ······ **8**:172b
Unkoku Tōeki ·· 雲谷等益 ······ **8**:172b
Unkoku Tōgan ··· 雲谷等顔 · **3**:182a; **7**:42b, 70a; **8**:172b-173a
Ōbaiin ······ **8**:*172b*
Unkoku school ······ **8**:172a
West Lake ······ **8**:*172b*
works ······ **8**:173a
Unlimited partnership company ··· **2**:31b, 37b; **6**:164a; **8**:173a
articles of association ······ **2**:37b
Uno Chiyo ······ 宇野千代 ······ **8**:173a
Kitahara Takeo ······ **4**:225b
works ······ **8**:173a
Unohana (*Deutzia crenata*) ······ **8**:173b
Uno Kōji ······ 宇野浩二 · **5**:13a; **8**:173b
Uno Kōzō ······ 宇野弘蔵 ·· **8**:173b-174a
Uno Kōzō chosakushū
······ 宇野弘蔵著作集 ······ **8**:174a
Unshū ······ 雲州 ······ **3**:367a
Unshū shōsoku. 雲州消息 *See* **Meigō ōrai**
Untei ······ 芸亭 ······ **8**:174a
Untei Library ······ **5**:1a
Isonokami no Yakatsugu ······ **3**:347b
U Nu. *See* **Nu, U**
Uny Co, Ltd ······ **8**:174a
Un'yō ······ 雲揚 ······ **4**:140b
Un'yushō. 運輸省
See **Ministry of Transport**
Unzen-Amakusa National Park ···
····· 雲仙天草国立公園 **1**:50a; **8**:174a-174b
Unzendake ······ 雲仙岳 ······ **8**:174b
Unzen Hot Spring
······ 雲仙温泉 ······ **8**:174a
Unzen volcano ······ **8**:195b
Uosuki ······ **7**:265b
U Ottama. *See* **Ottama, U**
Uozu ······ 魚津 ······ **8**:174b
Uplands
Iwatahara ······ **3**:363b
Makinohara ······ **5**:86b
Mikatahara ······ **5**:170b
Nihondaira ······ **5**:379a
Upright Party ······ **1**:314a
Urabon'e ······ 盂蘭盆会 ······ **1**:160b
Uraga ······ 浦賀 **4**:135a; **8**:174b
Uraga bugyō ····· 浦賀奉行 ······ **8**:174b
Uraga Channel ·· 浦賀水道 ······ **8**:174b
Uragami family ····· 浦上氏 ······ **8**:174b
Uragami Gyokudō
······ 浦上玉堂 **1**:211a; **8**:175a
Enkajō (Misty Landscapes Album) ·· **8**:*175a*

shichigenkin 7:87b
Uragami Shunkin 浦上春琴 1:211a; 8:175b
Urakami kuzure 6:178a
Uraminosuke うらみのすけ 4:136b
Ura Nihon 裏日本 8:175b
Uranouchi Bay 浦ノ内湾 8:175b
Uraomote うらおもて 4:180a
Uraomote (Inside Outside) 4:199a
Urashima Tarō 浦島太郎 2:302b; 5:295b; 8:175a-175b
  prototypes 2:341a
Urasoe 浦添 8:175b
Urawa 浦和 8:175b-176a
Urayaku 浦役 8:176a
  port or fishing official 8:176a
  tax 8:176a
Urayasu 浦安 8:176a
Urban administration 1:301b
Urban Construction Law 8:180a
Urbanization 2:108b-109a; 4:7a; 6:223b, 225a; 8:176a-177a
  before 1600 2:148b
  crime rate 7:209a
  Edo history 3:190a
  Edo period 2:149a-150a
  housing problems 3:245b
  land utilization 4:363b
  Meiji period 7:202a-203a
  Muromachi history 3:176a
  postwar 3:203b
  premodern 2:148b-150a
  rural society 7:214a
  studies 4:231b
  urban planning 8:180a
  Urban Planning Law 8:180b-181a
Urbanization Control Areas 8:180b
Urbanization Promotion Areas 8:180b
Urban life 8:177a-179b
  commerce and culture 8:177b-178a
  Edo (Tōkyō) 8:178a-178b
  functions and development 8:177a-177b
  leisure and entertainment 8:179a-179b
  modern city 8:178b-179a
Urban planning 8:179b-180b
Urban Planning Law 8:180b-181a
  Architectural Standards Law and 1:80b
  ownership rights 6:136b
Urban Planning Law of 1919 8:180a
Urban Planning Law of 1969 8:180b
Urban Redevelopment Act 8:180b
Urban residents 1:300b
Urban riots 8:124a-124b
Urban slums 7:202b-203a
Urban subcenters 8:181a
  Shinjuku Ward 7:116a
Urban transportation 8:103a
Ureshino 嬉野 8:181a
Urikohime 瓜子姫 8:181a
Urushi. *See* **Lacquer tree**
Urushi-e 漆絵 8:140b, 181a
Uryū, Lake 雨竜湖 8:181a
Usa 宇佐 8:181a
Usagi 6:275a
Usagi kōmori *(Plecotus auritus)* 1:146b
Usa Hachiman Shrine 宇佐八幡宮 3:74a; 8:181b
  Shintō 7:126b
Ushi 1:251a-251b
Ushibuka 牛深 8:181b
Ushin 有心 8:181b
  mushin vs. 5:282a
Ushinotoki mairi 2:128a
Ushin renga 有心連歌 6:297a
Usterling, Anders 4:177a
Usu 8:181b
Usucha Temae 7:*364b*
  tea ceremony 7:364b-365a
Usui Pass 碓氷峠 8:182a
Usuita 1:115b
Usui Yoshimi 臼井吉見 8:182a
Usuki 臼杵 8:182a, *182b*
Usury 2:132a
Usuyuki shō うすゆき抄 3:151b
Usuzan 有珠山 7:98a; 8:182a
Uta-awase (poetry contest) 歌合 5:14b-15a, 39a; 8:182a-182b
  advent 5:31a
  judgment 8:182b
  preparation 8:182a
  procedure 8:182a
Uta-e 歌絵 8:182b-183a
Utagaki 歌垣 2:138a; 4:108a; 8:183a
Utagaruta 歌骨牌 4:108a
Utagawa Hiroshige 歌川広重 3:148a-149b
Utagawa Kunimasa 歌川国政 7:79b; 8:183a
Utagawa Kunisada 歌川国貞 5:49a; 7:79b; 8:*139a*, 183a-183b
  daughters 8:183b
  Kunisada II 8:183b
  Kunisada III 8:183b
  secondary names 8:183b
Utagawa Kuniyoshi 歌川国芳 1:*251a*; 8:*145a-145b*, 183b-184a
Utagawa school 歌川派 8:184a-184b
  Western-style pictures 8:249a
Utagawa Toyoharu 歌川豊春 8:184b
  Utagawa school 8:184a
Utagawa Toyohiro 歌川豊広 8:184b
  Hiroshige 3:148a
  Utagawa school 8:184b
Utagawa Toyokuni 歌川豊国 6:*296b*; 7:79b, 96b; 8:184b-185b
  others with Toyokuni name 8:185a-185b
  Utagawa school 8:184b
Utage no ato (After the Banquet) 宴のあと 6:250a
Utakai Hajime. *See* **Imperial New Year's Poetry Reading**
Utakai Hajime 3:278b
Uta karuta 歌骨牌 3:*248b*
Uta makura 8:185b
  waka 8:203a
Utamaro 歌麿 7:79a; 8:*142b*, 185b-187a
  Fujin sōgaku juttai (Ten Studies of Women's Physiognomies) 8:*186b*
  illustrated books 8:185b
Uta monogatari (Tales about Poems) 歌物語 5:245b-246b
  Ise monogatari 3:337a
Utashinai 歌志内 8:187a
Utilities, public 6:266b
Utility companies
  Chūbu Electric Power Co, Inc 1:311a
  Chūgoku Electric Power Co, Inc 1:312a
  Kansai Electric Power Co, Inc 4:151a-151b
  Kyūshū Electric Power Co, Inc 4:340b
  Nippon Telegraph and Telephone Public Corporation 6:13a
  Ōsaka Gas Co, Ltd 6:121a
  Tōhoku Electric Power Co, Inc 8:37a
  Tōkyō Electric Power Co, Inc 8:66b-67a
  Tōkyō Gas Co, Ltd 8:67a
  Water Resources Development Public Corporation 8:237a
Utility-Model Patent Law 6:164b; 8:187a-187b
Uto 宇土 8:187b
Utokusen 有徳銭 8:187b
Utsubo monogatari 宇津保物語 1:73b; 5:34a, 246a; 8:187b-188a
  story 8:187b
Utsukushigahara 美ケ原 8:188a
Utsunomiya 宇都宮 8:188a-188b
Utsunomiya Daimyōjin 宇都宮大明神 2:376a
U-turn phenomenon 8:176b
Uwai Kakuken nikki 上井覚兼日記 8:188b
Uwajima 宇和島 8:188b
Uwanari 嫐 4:98b
Uwa Sea 宇和海 8:188b
Uyoku. *See* **Right wing**
Uzuragoromo 鶉衣 6:297b; 8:331b

V

Vaccination 6:164a
Vajra 1:*196b*
  esoteric ritual implements 1:196a
Vajradhātu 4:269b-270a
Vajraśekhara-sūtra 7:113b
Valignano, Alessandro 1:229b; 2:306b-307a; 8:189a
  Jesuit mission press 4:51a
  mission to Europe of 1582 5:203a
Valleys: Four Themes 8:13a
Valor of Ignorance, The 8:323a
Value-Creating Society 7:224b
Vanguard Artists League (Zen'ei Geijutsuka Dōmei) 6:255a
Van Reed, Eugene 4:13b
Vassalage system 1:131b
Vaughn, Miles W. 8:189a
Vegetables
  cucumber (kyūri) 2:52a-52b
  cucurbits 2:52a-52b
  eggplants 2:184b
  green 8:189a
  production 1:27a
  radishes 6:276a
  Welsh onions 8:241a
  Western 8:189a-189b
Vegetarian cooking 2:22a
Vegetation
  anthropogenic period 5:95b-96a
  late-glacial period 5:93a-93b
  paleolithic period 5:92b-93a
  postglacial period 5:93b-95b
Vehicles, diesel
  Hino Motors, Ltd 3:140b
  Nissan Diesel Motor Co, Ltd 6:20b
Vendetta. *See* **Katakiuchi**
Venereal disease 2:126a; 8:189b
  missionary 1:308a
Venereal Disease Prevention Law in 1948 8:189b
Verbeck, Guido Herman Fridolin 1:308a; 2:311a; 8:189b-190a
Vermilion-seal certificate 7:184a-184b
Vermilion seal ship (shuisen) 7:*144b*
Vermilion seal ship trade 1:74a, 83b; 5:306a; 7:255b, 256b; 8:190a-190b

Hamada Yahyōe ············· 3:89b-90a
licensed vessels ············· 3:235b
National Seclusion ············· 5:346b
Taiwan ············· 7:306b
Vernacular tracts ············· 7:80b-81a
Verny, François Léonce ····· 1:80b, 175b; 2:331b; 8:190b
Versailles, Treaty of ······· 3:199a; 7:235a; 8:190b-191a
China ············· 1:288a
territory of Japan ············· 8:14a
"White Australia" ············· 1:119a
Versailles Peace Conference ······ 6:307b
Vertical society ············ 2:245a; 8:191a
paternalism ············· 6:165a
Vice-ministers ············· 8:191a-191b
Victor Co of Japan, Ltd ············· 8:191b
Takayanagi Kenjirō ············· 7:321a
Vidyārāja ············· 5:291a
Vienna Exposition of 1873 ············· 4:182a
Viet Minh ············· 2:333a
Vietnam
activities ············· 2:53a
cultural sphere ············· 2:141b-142a
refugees ············· 6:286a
Vietnam and Japan ············· 8:191b-192a
Vietnam Duy Tan Hoi (Reformation Society) ············· 6:182a
Vietnam War ············· 6:166a; 8:192a
Okinawa ············· 6:90b
Viewing a Waterfall ············· 7:163b
Views of Sumiyoshi Handscroll ····· 6:78a
Vijf jaren in Japan (Five Years in Japan) ············· 6:220b
Village headman ············· 7:177a-177b
Village Japan ············· 4:41b
Villages
agricultural ············· 7:213a
museums ············· 5:278a-278b
Vinaya ············· 1:177a
Vining, Elizabeth Gray ············· 8:192a
Violets [(sumire) *Viola* spp.] · 8:192a-192b
Virilocal postmarital residence ···· 4:217b
Virus studies ············· 4:36b
Viscaino, Sebastian ············· 8:192b
Vivero de Velasco, Rodrigo ······· 8:192b
shipwreck ············· 4:369a
VLSI Research Center ············· 2:194b
Vocabulario ············· 4:51a
Vocabulario da Lingoa de Japam com a declaração em Portugues ·· 6:8b
Vocabulary development ············· 4:30a
Vocational education ········ 8:192b-193a
Vocational Training Law ····· 8:193a-193b
of 1958 ············· 4:352b; 8:193b
of 1969 ············· 8:193b
Volcanic front ············· 8:193b
Volcanic zones
Chishima ············· 1:297a
Chōkai ············· 1:299b
Fuji ············· 2:347b
Hakusan ············· 3:89a
Kirishima ············· 4:221a
Nasu ············· 5:336a
Norikura ············· 6:37b
Volcanoes ············· 4:7b; 8:193b-195b
caldera ············· 8:194b
distribution and makeup ············· 8:193b
eruption disasters and prevention ············· 8:195a-195b
Eurasia plate ············· 8:195a
history and present situation of volcanology ············· 8:194b-195a
Hokkaidō
Daisetsuzan ············· 2:67b
Komagatake ············· 4:264b
Meakandake ············· 5:144a
Oakandake ············· 6:47a
Rausudake ············· 6:284b
Shōwa Shinzan ············· 7:177a
Tarumaezan ············· 7:347b
Tokachidake ············· 8:40a
Usuzan ············· 8:182a
Yōteizan ············· 8:352a
Honshū
Adatarasan ············· 1:11b
Akagisan ············· 1:39a
Asamayama ············· 1:95b
Azumasan ············· 1:127b
Bandaisan ············· 1:137a
Chōkaisan ············· 1:299b
Daisen ············· 2:67a
Fujisan ············· 2:344b-345b
Gassan ············· 3:12a
Hakkōdasan ············· 3:85b
Hakoneyama ············· 3:87a
Hakusan ············· 3:88b
Harunasan ············· 3:106a
Hiuchigadake ············· 3:208b
Hotakayama ············· 3:237b
Iwakisan ············· 3:358a
Iwatesan ············· 3:363b
Kampūzan ············· 4:130b
Komagatake ············· 4:264b-265a
Kurikomayama ············· 4:313a
Kurohimeyama ············· 4:315b
Myōjinshō ············· 5:290b
Myōkōsan ············· 5:291a
Naebasan ············· 5:300a
Nantaisan ············· 5:329b
Nasudake ············· 5:335b
Norikuradake ············· 6:37b
Nyohōzan ············· 6:45b
Nyūtōzan ············· 6:45b
Ontakesan ············· 6:112b-113a
Osorezan ············· 6:127a
Sambesan ············· 7:6a
Shiranesan (Nikkō Shraine) ······ 7:147a
Shiranesan (Kusatsu Shirane) ···· 7:147a
Yakedake ············· 8:284b-285a
Yatsugatake ············· 8:320a
Zaōzan ············· 8:368a
Japanese people ············· 8:194b
Kyūshū
Asosan ············· 1:103a
Kaimondake ············· 4:111b
Kirishimayama ············· 4:221b
Takachihonomine ············· 7:310b
Takasakiyama ············· 7:318b
Taradake ············· 7:346a
Unzendake ············· 8:174b
large steam explosion ············· 8:194a
lava dome ············· 8:194a
monogentic ············· 8:194a
pyroclastic cone ············· 8:194a
pyroclastic eruption ············· 8:194b
pyroclastic flow ············· 8:194b
single eruption ············· 8:194a
structure and activity ········ 8:193b-194b
Volkskunde ············· 4:324b
Volleyball ············· 8:195b
Volta Redonda ············· 1:168a
Vories, William Merrel ············· 8:195b
Voting ············· 2:188b-190a
Votive offerings, pictorial ····· 2:196b-198a
VOU ············· 4:229a
Vukelic, Branco ············· 7:229b

W

Wa ············· 倭 7:259b; 8:197a
Five Kings ············· 2:287b
Wabi ············· 侘び ·· 3:267b-268a; 6:361a; 7:85b; 8:197a
ferns ············· 2:252a
Wabisuke ············· 1:237a
Wacoal Corporation ············· 8:197b
Wada ············· 和田 ······· 8:197b
Wada Eisaku ···· 和田英作 ······· 8:197b
Wada Hiroo ······ 和田博雄 ······· 2:168a
Wada Pass ········ 和田峠 ······· 8:197b
Wadatsumikai · わだつみ会 ······· 4:206a
Wada Yoshimori · 和田義盛 ··· 8:197b-198a
Samurai-dokoro (Board of Retainers) 7:8b
Wadō kaichin. 和同開珎 *See* **Wadō kaihō**
Wadō kaihō ······ 和同開珎 ·· 5:*242a-242b*; 8:198a
kōchō jūnisen ············· 4:240a
Waegwan ············· 8:198a
Japanese envoys ············· 4:279b
Wagahai wa neko de aru ········· 吾輩は猫である ······· 5:350a
Wagaku Kōdansho ············· 和学講談所 1:229a; 3:155b
"Wagakuni no shigeki" ············ わが邦の史劇 ······· 8:110b
Waga seishin no henreki ········· 我が精神の遍歴 ······· 4:125a
Waga seishun ni kui nashi ········ わが青春に悔なし ······· 7:108b
Waga tō wa soko ni tatsu ······ わが塔はそこに立つ ······· 4:339b
Wagatsuma Sakae · 我妻栄 ··· 8:198a-198b
works ············· 8:198b
Wage and lifetime employment systems ············· 8:199b
Wage bargaining ············· 7:188b
Wage determination ············· 8:199b
Wage differentials ········ 4:343b; 8:198b
factors ············· 8:198b
Wage level ············· 8:198b-199a
Wagener, Gottfried · 1:260a; 5:276a; 7:51b; 8:199a
Wages
base ············· 8:200a
bonus ············· 1:163a-163b
components ············· 7:189a
real ············· 8:199b
regulation ············· 4:352b
Wage system ············· 8:199b-200b
government guidelines ············· 3:287b
income distribution ············· 3:285b
nenkō ············· 4:345b
problems ············· 8:200b
salaries ············· 8:199b
seniority system ············· 2:211a
Wagon ············· 4:108a
Wagtails [(sekirei) family Motacillidae] ············· 8:200b-201a
Wainai Sadayuki ············· 和井内貞行 ······· 8:201a
Waisetsu ············· 6:49b-50b
Wajima ············· 輪島 ······· 8:201a
"Wajinden" ········ 倭人伝 ······· 8:240a

Waji shōran shō 和字正濫鈔 4:134a, 188a, 258a; 8:201a
Japanese language studies 4:31a
Wajū 輪中 8:*201a*, 201b
Ibigawa 3:253b
Wajū type embankments 8:338b
Waka 和歌 6:296b, 297b; 7:52b, 94b, 105a; 8:201b-217a
criticism 5:14b
early classical period (794-1100) 1:292b-293a; 8:207b-210b
Bo Juyi (Po Chii-i) and Tang poetry 8:210a
descriptive poetry 8:210a-210b
Kokinshū periods 4:254b-255a; 8:208b-209a
poetics 8:209a
poetry contests 8:209b
Six Dynasties poetry 8:208a-208b
early literary period (ca 610-784)
anonymous poems 8:207b
first *Man'yō* period 8:205a-205b
second *Man'yō* period and Hitomaro 8:205b-206a
third *Man'yō* period 8:206a-207a
fourth *Man'yō* period and Yakamochi 8:207a-207b
Edo period (1600-1868) 8:215b-216a
independents 8:216a
national scholars 8:215b-216a
general characteristics 8:201b-202a
honkadori 3:223b
imagery and metaphor 8:203b
imperial anthologies 3:275b
Kokin Denju 4:254a
late classical period (1250-1350) 8:213b-214b
abstractions 8:214b
new styles 8:214a-214b
other stylistic features 8:214b
Man'yōshū 5:102b-110b
mid-classical period (1100-1250) 8:210b-213b
aesthetic ideals 8:212a
conservatives and innovators 8:211a-211b
descriptive symbolism 8:211a
harmony and balance 8:211b
"old words, new treatment" 8:211b-212a
modern period (1867-present) 8:216a-217a
contemporary 8:217a
early twentieth century 8:216b-217a
Masaoka Shiki and shasei 5:123a; 8:216b
Myōjō school 5:290b; 8:216b
moon viewing 5:248a
post-classical period (1350-1600) 8:214b-215b
anti-Nijō forces 8:215a
decline of court poetry 8:215a-215b
primitive song and poetry (ca 550-686) 2:137a-138b; 8:204b-205a
prosody 8:202a-203a
revival (794-905) 5:29a-32a
rhetorical devices 8:203a-203b
engo 8:203b
jokotoba 4:71b; 8:203a
kakekotoba 4:115b; 8:203a-203b
makura kotoba 5:87a; 8:203a
uta makura 4:185b; 8:203a
Rokkasen 6:334b
Shin kokinshū 7:119a-120b; 8:212a-213b
association and progression principles 8:213a
attenuation and decline 8:213b
other poets 8:213a
Teika's styles 2:354a; 8:212b-213a
Shintō 7:131b
sources 8:204a-204b
subjects 8:203b
subjects, themes, and modes 8:203b-204a
themes 8:204a
travel diaries 8:105b
uta-awase 8:182a-182b
wabi 8:197a
writing style 4:132b
Wakaba no uta 若葉のうた 4:139a
Wakadokoro e fushin jōjō 和歌所へ不審条々 3:272a
Wakadoshiyori 若年寄 8:217a-217b
Wakai 8:217b
Wakai hito (Young People) 若い人 8:90b
Wakaki shijin no tegami 若き詩人の手紙 4:114a
Wakakusayama 若草山 8:*217a*, 217b
Wakamatsu colony 4:13b
Wakamatsusama 8:83a
Wakamatsu Shizuko 若松賤子 8:217b
Wakame (seaweed) 7:47a
Wakamono-gumi 若者組 8:217b-218a, 353b
Wakan 倭館 8:198a
Wakanoura 和歌浦 8:218a
Wakan rōeishū 和漢朗詠集 2:353b; 5:35a; 8:208a, 218a
compilers 8:218a
Fujiwara no Kintō 2:352a
Wakan sansai zue 和漢三才図絵 8:218a
Wakao Ayako 若尾文子 8:218b
films 8:218b
Waka poetry techniques 3:223b
Waka poets (modern). *See* Tanka poets
Waka poets (premodern)
Abutsu Ni 1:5b-6a
Akazome Emon 1:41a
Ariwara no Narihira 1:85b
Asukai Masaari 1:106b
Asukai Masatsune 1:106b
Eifuku Mon'in 2:186a
Fujitani Mitsue 2:346b
Fujiwara no Akisuke 2:350a
Fujiwara no Ietaka 2:351a
Fujiwara no Kanesuke 2:351b
Fujiwara no Kintō 2:352a
Fujiwara no Kiyosuke 2:352b
Fujiwara no Michitoshi 2:353a
Fujiwara no Mototoshi 2:353b
Fujiwara no Nobuzane 2:353b-354a
Fujiwara no Sadaie 2:354a-355a
Fujiwara no Takanobu 2:355b
Fujiwara no Tameie 2:355b-356b
Fujiwara no Toshinari 2:356b-357b
Fujiwara no Toshinari no Musume 2:357b
Fujiwara no Yoshitsune 2:358a
Go-Toba, Emperor 3:51a-52b
Henjō 3:126b
Hiraga Motoyoshi 3:142b
Hosokawa Yūsai 3:237a-237b
Ichijō Kaneyoshi 3:256a
Ike no Gyokuran 3:266b
Imagawa Sadayo 3:272a
Ise 3:336b
Izumi Shikibu 3:367a
Jakuren 4:1b
Jien 4:53b-54a
Kada no Arimaro 4:100b
Kada no Azumamaro 4:100b
Kagawa Kageki 4:102b-103a
Kakinmoto no Hitomaro 4:17a
Kamo no Chōmei 4:128b
Kamo no Mabuchi 4:129a
Karasumaru Mitsuhiro 4:158a
Kasa no Kanamura 4:161a
Katō Chikage 4:167b
Katori Nahiko 4:169a
Kenshō 4:198b
Kinoshita Chōshōshi 4:214b
Kinoshita Takafumi 4:216a
Ki no Tomonori 4:216a
Ki no Tsurayuki 4:216b-217a
Kitamura Kigin 4:227a
Kumagai Naoyoshi 4:304b
Kyōgoku Tamekane 4:329a-329b
Mibu no Tadamine 5:166a-166b
Minamoto no Sanetomo 5:178b
Minamoto no Shitagau 5:179a
Minamoto no Toshiyori 5:179b-180a
Minamoto no Tsunenobu 5:180a-180b
Munetaka, Prince 5:265a
Murata Harumi 5:269b
Nijō Tameyo 5:387a
Nijō Yoshimoto 5:387b
Nōin 6:32b
Nomura Motoni 6:34a-34b
Nukata no Ōkimi 6:44a
Ōkuma Kotomichi 6:95a-95b
Ōnakatomi no Yoshinobu 6:105a-105b
Ono no Komachi 6:110b-111a
Ono no Takamura 6:111a-111b
Ōshikōchi no Mitsune 6:125a
Ōtagaki Rengetsu 6:128b
Ōtomo no Sakanoue no Iratsume 6:131a
Ōtomo no Tabito 6:131a-131b
Ōtomo no Yakamochi 6:131b
Ozawa Roan 6:140b
Reizei Tamesuke 6:289b
Shimizu Hamaomi 7:104a
Shimokōbe Chōryū 7:105a
Shōhaku 7:161b-162a
Shōtetsu 7:170b
Sone no Yoshitada 7:227a-227b
Sosei 7:232a
Tachibana Akemi 7:291b-292a
Tachibana Moribe 7:292b
Takahashi no Mushimaro 7:313a
Takebe Ayatari 7:321a-321b
Takechi no Kurohito 7:321a
Tayasu Munetake 7:359a
Toda Mosui 8:34b
Ton'a 8:73b
Tō no Tsuneyori 8:75a-75b
Ueda Akinari 8:126b
Yamabe no Akahito 8:287a
Yamanoue no Okura 8:302b-303a
Wakasa Bay 若狭湾 2:364a; 4:338a; 8:*218b*
Wakatei jisshu ("Ten Styles of Waka") 和歌体十種 8:209a
Wakatoshisama 8:83a
Wakatsuki Reijirō 若槻礼次郎 7:78a, 88b; 8:218b-219a
cabinet 1:11a; 2:277a
Kenseikai 4:198a
Wakayama 和歌山 8:219a
Wakayama Bokusui 若山牧水 7:61a; 8:219a
works 8:219a
Wakayama Plain 和歌山平野 8:219b
Wakayama Prefecture 和歌山県 8:219b
Wake no Kiyomaro 和気清麻呂 8:220a
Heiankyō 3:121b
Jingoji 4:58b
Waki 4:298b
Wakiōkan 脇往還 8:220a

Wakkanai · · · 稚内 · · · **8**:220a
Wakō (city) · · · 和光 · · · **8**:220a
Wakō (pirates) · · · 倭寇 · · · **2**:148a; **8**:220a-221a
Japanese, in Koryŏ · · · **4**:278a
Korea · · · **8**:220b
Korean raids · · · **4**:276a
phases · · · **8**:220b
Ryūkyū trade · · · **6**:358a
Southeast Asia · · · **8**:221a
tally trade · · · **7**:331b-332a
Wakon kansai · · · 和魂漢才 · · · **8**:221a
Wakon yōsai · · · 和魂洋才 · · · **2**:34a; **8**:221a-221b, 290b
technological innovation · · · **7**:371b
Wako Shungorō
· · · 輪湖俊午郎 · · · **8**:221b
Wakun no shiori · · · 和訓栞 · · · **8**:221b
Waley, Arthur David · · · **8**:221b-222a
Chinese translations · · · **8**:221b
Japanese translations · · · **8**:221b
Wall painting · · · **6**:*148b*
Wamyō ruiju shō
· · · 倭名類聚鈔 · · · **4**:50b, 188a; **8**:222a
kites · · · **4**:229b
Wamyōshō. *See* **Wamyō ruiju shō**
Wands (gohei) · · · **3**:40a
Wang Chao-ming · · · **8**:222a
Wang Jingwei (Wang Ching-wei) · **3**:201b; **6**:302a-302b; **8**:222a
Wang Kemin (Wang K'o-min) · · · **8**:222b
Wang Kōn · · · **4**:278a
Wāngsōngguk · · · **4**:277b
Wang Tao (Wang T'ao) · · · **4**:141a; **8**:222b
"Wang Xizhi Writing on Fans" · · · **4**:77b
Wang Yangming philosophy. *See* **Yōmeigaku**
Wang Yangming school. *See* **Yōmeigaku**
Wang Zhaoming · · · **8**:222a
Wang Zhengting (Wang Cheng-t'ing) · · · **8**:222b-223a
Wani · · · 王仁 · · · **8**:223a
Yamato court visitor · · · **4**:277a
Wan Jingwei (Wang Ching-wei) · · · **7**:92a
Wankel engine
rotary · · · **6**:339b
Wa no Goō · · · 倭の五王 · · · **2**:287b-288a
Warabe uta. *See* **Children's songs**
Warabi · · · 蕨 · · · **8**:223a
Warabidemon · · · 蕨手文 · · · **2**:252a
Waragutsu · · · **7**:249b; **8**:223a
Warai no Ōkoku 笑いの王国 · · · **8**:52a
Waraji · · · **7**:249b; **8**:223a
Warambegusa · · · 童子草 · · · **4**:328a
Warashibe chōja
· · · わらしべ長者 · · · **8**:223a-223b
War chronicles · · · **7**:165b
medieval · · · **5**:43b
War crimes trials · · · **8**:223b-225b
defendant's list · · · **8**:224a-224b
Kainō Michitaka · · · **4**:112a
Ladybird Incident · · · **4**:362a
"minor" trials · · · **8**:223b-224a
Nanjing Incident · · · **5**:328b-329a
Tōkyō trial · · · **8**:224a-224b
Webb, Sir William Flood · · · **8**:238a
Ward, J · · · **3**:309b
Warigo · · · **4**:105a; **8**:225b
Warizansho (Writings on Division) · · · 割算書 · · · **8**:231b
War literature · · · **8**:225b-228a
Russo-Japanese War · · · **8**:226a
Sino-Japanese War · · · **8**:225b-226a
World War I · · · **8**:226b
World War II · · · **8**:226b
Warlords
Uesugi family · · · **8**:129a
Warner, Langdon · · · **8**:228a
Warplanes · · · **1**:123b
command reconnaissance · · · **1**:123b
Hayabusa · · · **1**:123b
Hayate · · · **1**:123b
Model 97 · · · **1**:123b
Shiden-modified · · · **1**:123b
Zero fighter · · · **1**:123b
War Relocation Authority (WRA)
Japanese Americans · · · **4**:17b
centers · · · **8**:228b
"Warring States" · · · **1**:99b
Warring States period · · · **7**:64a
Warrior class
eating habits · · · **2**:305b
feudalism · · · **2**:266b
Warrior ethic · · · **1**:221b-223b
kakun · · · **1**:222a
Warrior families
Hatekeyama family · · · **3**:111a
Hosokawa family · · · **3**:236a
Imagawa family · · · **3**:271b
Kyōgoku family · · · **4**:329a-329b
Matsumae family · · · **5**:137a
Minamoto family · · · **5**:176b-178b
Miura family · · · **5**:215a
Mōri family · · · **5**:249b
Nabeshima family · · · **5**:299a
Nitta family · · · **6**:22a
Ogasawara family · · · **6**:68b
Ōshū Fujiwara family · · · **6**:126b-127a
Ōtomo family · · · **6**:130b
Satake family · · · **7**:25b
Shiba family · · · **7**:83b-84a
Togashi family · · · **8**:36a
Tokugawa family · · · **8**:45b-47b
Uragami family · · · **8**:174b
vassals
ienoko and rōtō · · · **3**:261a
women · · · **8**:259a
Yamana family · · · **8**:300b
Warrior-farmer-artisan-merchant · · **7**:122b
Warrior government · · · **7**:8a; **8**:228b-230b
Ashikaga Takauji · · · **1**:100a
Hōgen and Heiji disturbances · · · **8**:229a
Kamakura shogunate · · · **8**:229a-229b
keishi · · · **4**:190a
laws · · · **1**:206b
Minamoto no Yoritomo · · · **5**:182a
Muromachi shogunate · · · **8**:229b-230a
Nobunaga and Hideyoshi · · · **8**:230a
overview · · · **8**:230b
peerage · · · **6**:170b
periodization · · · **6**:*174a-174b*
provinces · · · **6**:260a
Taira-Minamoto War · · · **7**:300b
Tokugawa Ieyasu · · · **8**:49a
Tokugawa shogunate · · · **8**:230a-230b
warrior class · · · **8**:228b-229a
Warrior leagues
kinship · · · **1**:221b
Tōryō · · · **1**:221b
Warrior library · · · **5**:1a
Warrior-monks · · · **8**:230b-231a
at Kōfukuji · · · **4**:244a
naginata · · · **5**:308a-308b
Taira no Tadamori · · · **7**:302a
Temmon Hokke Rebellion · · · **7**:381b-382b
Warriors
Abe no Munetō · · · **1**:4a
Ankokuji Ekei · · · **1**:62a
Aoto Fujitsuna · · · **1**:70b
Benkei · · · **1**:149b
Date Masamune · · · **2**:78a-79b
Forty-Seven Rōnin Incident · · **2**:327a-328a
Fujiwara no Hidesato · · · **2**:350b
Furuta Oribe · · · **2**:373b
Hatakeyama Shigetada · · · **3**:111b
Hori Hidemasa · · · **3**:227b
Ii Naomasa · · · **3**:262b
Imagawa Sadayo · · · **3**:272a
Ishida Mitsunari · · · **3**:340a
Itō Sukechika · · · **3**:356a
Kajiwara Kagetoki · · · **4**:114b
Katagiri Katsumoto · · · **4**:165a
Kimura Shigenari · · · **4**:211b
Kojima Takanori · · · **4**:252a
Kōno Michiari · · · **4**:274b
Kusunoki Masashige · · · **4**:321a
Matsudaira Ietada · · · **5**:131a
Minamoto no Yoshinaka · · · **5**:182b
Minamoto no Yoshitomo · · · **5**:182b
Minamoto no Yoshitsune · · · **5**:182b-183a
Musashi Shichitō · · · **5**:275b
Nasu no Yoichi · · · **5**:336a
Nitta Yoshisada · · · **6**:22a-22b
Ōishi Yoshio · · · **6**:75b
Ōkubo Hikozaemon · · · **6**:93b
Ōta Dōkan · · · **6**:128b
regulations for · · · **8**:50b
Sanada Yukimura · · · **7**:9a
Sasaki Takatsuna · · · **7**:23a
Shibata Katsuie · · · **7**:84b
Taira no Masakado · · · **7**:301b
Taira no Munemori · · · **7**:301b
Taira no Shigehira · · · **7**:301b-302a
Taira no Tadamori · · · **7**:302a
Taira no Tadanori · · · **7**:302a
Taira no Tomomori · · · **7**:302b
Takezaki Suenaga · · · **7**:326b
Yamanaka Shikanosuke · · · **8**:300b-301a
yoriki and dōshin · · · **8**:338b
yorioya-yoriko relationship · · · **8**:338b
See also **Daimyō**
Warriors' vassals · · · **3**:261a-261b
War songs. *See* **Gunka**
War stories · · · **3**:68b
Wartime relocation centers
Jerome Relocation Center · · · **4**:50b-51a
"Warui nakama" · 悪い仲間 · · · **8**:319b
War Victim Relief Law of 1942 · · · **1**:110b
Wasabi · · · **3**:127b
Wasan (mathematics) 和算 · · · **8**:231a-232a
Wasan · · · 和讃 · · · **8**:231a
religious symbolism · · · **6**:295b
Shinran · · · **7**:123a
Waseda bungaku
· · · 早稲田文学 **7**:309b; **8**:232a
Waseda University · · · **8**:232a
correspondence education · · · **2**:181b
Ōkuma Shigenobu · · · **6**:95b
Washi · · · **1**:125a; **2**:294a, 296a; **8**:232b-234a, *234b*
Azuchi-Momoyama period · · · **8**:233a-233b
Edo period (1600-1868) · · · **8**:233b
Heian period (794-1185) · · · **8**:232b-233a
invention and transmission · · · **8**:232b
Kamakura period · · · **8**:233a-233b
Meiji period (1868-1912) to present **8**:233b
molding · · · **8**:234a
Muromachi period · · · **8**:233a-233b
Nara period (710-794) · · · **8**:232b
raingear · · · **6**:280a
techniques · · · **8**:233b-234a
Washington Conference · · · **3**:199a; **7**:77a-77b; **8**:157a, 234a-235a, 343b
Anglo-Japanese Alliance · · · **1**:57a
China · · · **1**:288a
consequences · · · **8**:235a
Four-Power Treaty · · · **2**:330a
French-Japanese relations · · · **2**:332b
international relations · · · **3**:321a
Japan's response · · · **8**:234b
negotiations · · · **8**:234b-235a

Nine-Power Treaty ··· **6**:4b
origins ··· **8**:234a-234b
Shidehara Kijūrō ··· **7**:88a-88b
United Kingdom and Japan ··· **8**:152a
Wang Zhengting (Wang Cheng-t'ing) ··· **8**:222b
Washington Naval Treaty of 1922 · **8**:235a
Washington Naval Treaty of 1922 ··· **1**:88a; **8**:157a, 235a-235b
Japan's position ··· **8**:235a
negotiations ··· **8**:235a
origins ··· **8**:235a
power of supreme command ··· **8**:85a
significance ··· **8**:235b
terms ··· **8**:235b
"Washington System" ··· **3**:321a
Washiuzan ··· 鷲羽山 ··· **8**:235b
Wasps. *See* **Bees and wasps**
Waste, industrial ··· **3**:302b
Waste Land ··· **1**:82b-83a; **6**:19b
Wasuregusa ni yosu ··· 萱草に寄す ··· **7**:293a
Watakushi no aruita michi ··· 私の歩いた道 ··· **1**:155b
Watakushi shōsetsu ·· **3**:312a-312b; **8**:235b
Watanabe Gen ··· 渡辺元 ··· **2**:76a
Watanabe Jōtarō ··· 渡辺錠太郎 ··· **8**:235b
February 26th Incident ··· **2**:249b
Watanabe Kazan 渡辺崋山 · **1**:211a; **7**:27a, 28b; **8**:235b-236a
portrait painting ··· **6**:227b
Watanabe Kunio · 渡辺邦男 ··· **2**:272b
Watanabe Masanosuke ··· 渡辺政之輔 ··· **8**:236a
Watanabe Nangaku ··· 渡辺南岳 ··· **8**:236a
Watanabe Sadao 渡辺貞夫 ··· **8**:236a
Watanabe Shikō · 渡辺始興 ··· **8**:236a
Watanabe Tetsuzō ··· 渡辺銕蔵 ··· **8**:236b
Watarai Shintō ··· 度会神道 **2**:300b; **7**:128a, 263b; **8**:236b
Watarasegawa ··· 渡良瀬川 ··· **8**:236b
Watari yagura (tower) 渡櫓 ··· **1**:248b
Watatsumi ··· 海神 ··· **5**:294b
Wataya Bunko ··· 綿屋文庫 ··· **8**:8b
Watches ··· **6**:233b
Water deities ··· **7**:263b
Waterfalls
Akame, 48 Falls of ··· **1**:40b
Fukuroda Falls ··· **2**:365b
Kamba Falls ··· **4**:123a
Kegon Falls ··· **4**:186b
Nachi Falls ··· **5**:299b
Shiraito Falls ··· **7**:145b
Water lily [(suiren) *Nymphae tetragona* var. *angusta*] ··· **8**:237a
Water pollution
diseases ··· **2**:226a-226b
factors ··· **2**:227a
Water Quality Conservation Law ·· **2**:227a
Water Resources Development Public Corporation ··· **8**:237a
Waters, Thomas James ··· **1**:80b; **8**:237a
Waterwheels ··· **8**:237a-237b
Watsuji Tetsurō ·· 和辻哲郎 **5**:231a; **8**:237b
emperor theory ··· **2**:208a-208b
Shinshichō ··· **7**:125a
Wax-resist dyeing ··· **8**:17b, 237b-238a
Wayaku Tarō. 和訳太郎 *See* **Ueda Akinari**
Wayland, Francis ··· **3**:4b
Wayo ··· 和与 **1**:183a, 234b; **8**:238a
Way of Reason ··· **8**:26b
"Way of Yin and Yang, The" ··· **6**:103a
Ways of Thinking of Eastern Peoples: India, China, Tibet, Japan ··· **5**:315b
Waza ··· **4**:196a
Wazauta ··· **3**:59b
Wazoku dōjikun ··· 和俗童子訓 ··· **4**:108b
WCTU ··· **4**:324b
Wealth, national ··· **5**:349a-349b
Weaponry, bronze ··· **1**:174a-175a
Weapons
defense industry ··· **2**:82a-82b
See also **Arms and armor**
Weasels [(itachi) *Mustela sibirica*] · **8**:238a
Weaving. *See* **Textiles**
Webb, Sir William Flood ··· **8**:238a
Weddings ··· **5**:4b; **8**:238b-239a
courting procedures ··· **8**:238b
modern ··· **8**:239a
rituals ··· **8**:238b
traditional ··· **8**:238b-239a
Weekly magazines ··· **8**:239a-239b
Wei China
Himiko relations ··· **3**:139b-140a
Weight ··· **4**:37b
Weights and measures ··· **8**:239b-240a
koku ··· **4**:256b
monetary units ··· **8**:240a
premodern units ··· **8**:239b-240a
Wei lüe ··· **7**:264a
Wei zhi (Wei chih) ··· 魏志 · **1**:78b; **2**:365a; **7**:69a, 264a; **8**:240a-241a, 305a
history ··· **4**:28a-28b
Shintō ··· **7**:126a
Wa ··· **8**:197a
women in ··· **8**:256b
Welfare Acts for Working Women (1972) ··· **8**:265b
Welsh onion (*Allium fistulosum*) ··· **8**:241a
Shimonita ··· **7**:105b
Wen ··· **4**:123b
Wen-jen-hua ··· **1**:210a-211a
Wenrenhua ··· **1**:210a-211a
Wen xuan (*Monzen* or *Literary Selections*) ··· **4**:109a; **8**:208a
West
attitude toward ··· **2**:311b-312a
cultural sphere ··· **2**:142a
interest in Japan ··· **4**:41a-42b
West Asian design composition ··· **7**:195b-196a
West Asian materials ··· **7**:195b
West Asian objects and shapes ··· **7**:195b
Western-art museums ··· **5**:279a-279b
Western Electric Co, quality control ··· **6**:273a
Westernization
language reforms ··· **4**:29b
literary portrayal ··· **2**:378b
Western Japan ··· **8**:241a
Western Learning · **7**:16a, 94b; **8**:241a-243a
arts ··· **8**:242b
astronomy ··· **8**:242a-242b
botany ··· **8**:242b
campaigns against
Bansha no Goku ··· **1**:141b
chemistry ··· **8**:242b
Dejima ··· **2**:83b
Dutch ··· **8**:241b-242a
Dutch Factory ··· **2**:135b
education ··· **2**:174b
shogunate missions to the West ·· **7**:161b
educational institutions
Seimikyoku ··· **7**:51b
Fuseya Soteki ··· **2**:374b
geography ··· **8**:242a-242b
Iwakura mission ··· **3**:359a
Kawamoto Kōmin ··· **4**:181b
Kōsei shimpen stimulated ··· **4**:294b
language studies ··· **8**:242b-243a
mathematics ··· **8**:242b
medicine ··· **8**:242a
Meiji Restoration ··· **5**:155a-155b
military science ··· **8**:242b
National Seclusion ··· **5**:346b-347b
Ogata Kōan ··· **6**:69a
physics ··· **8**:242b
Rangaku kaitei ··· **6**:283b
Rangaku schools ··· **8**:243a
studies
Bansho Shirabesho ··· **1**:141b-142a
Titsingh, Izaak ··· **8**:30a
Western literature and Japanese literature ··· **8**:243a-247a
American influences ··· **8**:244a-244b
characteristics ··· **5**:25a
English and Irish influences ·· **8**:243b-244a
French influences ··· **8**:244b-246a
German influences ··· **8**:246b
Italian influences ··· **8**:246b-247a
Norwegian influence ··· **8**:247a
Russian influences ··· **8**:246a-246b
Spanish influences ··· **8**:247a
Western literature in Japanese translation ··· **8**:247a-248b
19th century ··· **8**:247b
20th century ··· **8**:247b-248b
Western music ··· **5**:285b-287b
Western-style dance. *See* **Dance, Western-style**
Western-style painting **6**:155b; **8**:327a-328b
Western-style pictures, early ··· **1**:43b; **8**:248b-249a
West Lake ··· **8**:172b
West Lake scene ··· **8**:173a
Weston, Walter ··· **4**:127a; **8**:249a
Japanese Alps ··· **4**:12b
mountaineering ··· **5**:259b
Weyerhaeuser Co of the United States ··· **4**:83b
Whales [(kujira) order Cetacea]
Whaling ··· **2**:284b; **8**:249b-250b
history ··· **8**:249b-250a
operations and whalers ··· **8**:250a
products ··· **8**:250a-250b
regulations ··· **8**:250b
supply and demand of products ··· **8**:250b
types ··· **8**:249b
Wheat and barley ··· **8**:251a
Wheel of Life ··· **8**:335a
"White Australia" ··· **1**:117b, 119a
Whitebait [(shirauo) *Salangichthys microdon*] ··· **8**:251a
White Clouds and Autumn Leaves **3**:109b
White-collar crime ··· **2**:45a
White-collar workers ··· **8**:251a-251b
"White Fox, The," ··· **7**:105b
White Horse Society ··· **3**:87a-87b; **8**:328a
White Mountain ··· **3**:88b
White Paper on Crime ··· **6**:172a
White Paper on Labor (1950) ··· **8**:251b
White Paper on Monopolies (1948) ··· **8**:251b
White Paper on the Economy ··· **2**:167b-168a; **8**:251b
Economic Planning Agency ··· **4**:190b
White Paper on the National Standard of Living ··· **2**:167b; **8**:251b
White Paper on Trade (1949) ··· **8**:251b
White papers ··· **8**:251b
White Russians ··· **8**:252a-252b
Whites, attitudes towards ··· **2**:312a-313a
White Tiger Brigade ··· **1**:226b
Whitman, Charles Otis ··· **8**:252b
Whitney, Courtney ··· **8**:252b-253a
Wholesale price index ··· **3**:303a
Wholesalers, distribution system ·· **2**:119b
"Why not, it's okay!" ··· **2**:184a

Wild boar [(inoshishi) *Sus scrofa leucomystax*] ········ **8**:253a
Wildcats [(yamaneko) family Felidae] ········ **8**:253a
Wild ducks [(kamo) family Anatidae] ········ **8**:253a-253b
Wild geese. *See* **Geese**
Williams, Samuel Wells ········ **8**:253b
Willis, William ········ **8**:253b
Willoughby, Charles Augustus ········ **8**:253b
Willows [(yanagi) *Salix* spp.] · **8**:253b-254a
Wills ········ **8**:254a
Wilson, Horace ········ **7**:242b
Wilson, Woodrow ········ **7**:192a
Wind and Thunder Gods ········ **7**:*232a-232b*
Wind-bells ········ **8**:254a
Winding Water Banquet ········ **2**:128a
Windows for the Crown Prince ········ **8**:192a
Winter hazel ········ **8**:81b
Winter Seascape with Birds ········ **4**:148b
Winter sports ········ **8**:254b
Wire-relayed broadcasting ········ **8**:254b
Wirgman, Charles ········ **8**:254b-255a
Wisdom (chi) ········ **4**:141b
Wisteria, Japanese [(fuji) *Wisteria floribunda*] ········ **8**:255a
Witch hazel [(mansaku) *Hamamelis japonica*] ········ **8**:255a
Witnesses ········ **8**:255a-255b
Witte, Sergei Iul'evich ········ **8**:255b
Wo. *See* **Wa**
Wolf, Japanese [(ōkami) *Canis lupus hodophilax*] ········ **8**:255b-256a
Woman ········ **6**:70b
Woman in the Dunes ········ **1**:3a
Womb Realm ········ **7**:310a
Women
  changing position ········ **4**:40a
  criminality ········ **2**:45a
  discrimination ········ **5**:196a
  housewives ········ **3**:241a-242a
  labor force ········ **4**:343b
  legal equality ········ **2**:229b-230a
  lifestyles ········ **5**:6b-7a, 8b
  poetry by ········ **6**:297b
  ritsuryō system ········ **6**:324b
  See also **Women in Japan, history of**
Women, rural ········ **8**:266a-267a
Women Bedecked with Feathers ········ **7**:196a
Women in Japan, history of · **8**:257b-263b
  contemporary ········ **8**:261b
    education ········ **8**:262b-263a
    family ········ **8**:262a-262b
    legal changes ········ **8**:261b-262a
    life expectancy and birthrates ········ **8**:263a
    political participation and volunteer work ········ **8**:263a-263b
  early high status ········ **8**:257b-258a
  Edo period ········ **8**:259a-260a
  impact of warfare ········ **8**:258b-259a
  lifestyle and attitude changes · **8**:260a-261a
  modernization ········ **8**:260a
  Taika Reform through Heian period ········ **8**:258b
  wartime ········ **8**:261a-261b
Women in Japanese religion **8**:256a-257b
  Buddhism ········ **8**:257a-257b
  Christianity ········ **8**:257b
  new religions ········ **8**:257b
  shamanism and Shintō ········ **8**:256b-257a
Women in labor force ········ **8**:264a-266a
  contemporary ········ **8**:264b
    distribution ········ **8**:265a-265b
    future problems and prospects ········ **8**:266a
    increasing number ········ **8**:264b
    other changes ········ **8**:264b-265a
    protective legislation ········ **8**:265b-266a
    wages ········ **8**:265b
    working time ········ **8**:265b-266a
  Meiji period through World War II ········ **8**:264a-264b
  modern ········ **2**:210a-210b
  protective legislation ········ **8**:269a
Women Lawyers' Association ········ **8**:263b
Women's and Minors' Bureau of the Labor Ministry ········ **4**:87a
  Tanino Setsu ········ **7**:342a
Women's and Young Workers' Bureau of the Ministry of Labor ········ **8**:263b
Women's Christian Temperance Union (Kyōfūkai) ········ **4**:324b; **8**:300a
Women's Democratic Club ········ **8**:263b
Women's education ········ **8**:267a-267b
  early history ········ **8**:267a
  feudal times ········ **8**:267a
  Japan Women's University ········ **4**:50b
  junior colleges ········ **4**:84a
  modernizing ········ **8**:267a-267b
  post-World War II ········ **8**:267b
Women's liberation ········ **8**:263b
Women's literary groups ········ **5**:20b
Women's magazines ········ **8**:268a-268b
Women's names ········ **5**:326a
Women's rights
  national organization ········ **7**:111b
Women's Social Reform League, (Chifuren) ········ **8**:307b
Women's suffrage ········ **8**:268b-269a
  Fusen Kakutoku Dōmei ········ **2**:373b
Women's Suffrage League ········ **2**:374b
Women's Suffrage Movement ········ **8**:169a
  Ichikawa Fusae ········ **3**:257a
Women workers ········ **8**:269a
  employment pattern ········ **4**:354a-354b
  Meiji period ········ **8**:260a
  professional and technical occupations ········ **4**:354a-354b
Women workers, protective legislation for ········ **8**:269a
Wood and pulp ········ **5**:354a-354b
Woodblock painting ········ **7**:187b
Woodblock printing ········ **6**:246b
  Ippitsusai Bunchō ········ **3**:329b
  modern ········ **5**:232a; **6**:245b
  ukiyo-e-style ········ **8**:330a
Woodblock prints. *See* **Ukiyo-e, modern prints**
Wood craftwork ········ **2**:295b
Wooden clogs. *See* **Geta**
Wooden tablets. *See* **Mokkan**
Woodenware ········ **8**:269a-269b
  kijiya ········ **4**:205a
Woodpeckers [(kitsutsuki) family Picidae] ········ **8**:269b
Word games ········ **8**:269b-270a
  hayakuchi or tongue twisters ········ **8**:269b
  kaibun or palindromes ········ **8**:270a
  shiritori or capping ········ **8**:269b
Word play ········ **8**:269b
Worker Farmer Artists League (Rōnō Geijutsuka Remmei)
  Proletarian literature movement ········ **6**:255a-255b
Worker-Farmer Party ········ **6**:333b
Workers Accident Compensation Law ········ **4**:358a; **7**:209b
  enforcement ········ **4**:358b
Workers' compensation ········ **7**:209b; **8**:270a
  industrial injuries ········ **3**:292a
  Occupation reforms ········ **4**:346a
Workers' Fraternal Society ········ **7**:164a
Work hours ········ **8**:270a-270b
Working Women's Welfare Law ········ **8**:262a
Workmen's Accident Compensation Insurance ········ **2**:241b
Work regulations ········ **4**:352b; **8**:270b
Work transfer, temporary ········ **7**:185a
World Bank ········ **3**:253b
World Design Conference ········ **2**:89a
World Economy Research Society ········ **1**:84a-84b
World Federation of Trade Unions (WFTU) ········ **4**:347a, 360a
World Health Organization ········ **6**:274a
World Intellectual Property Organization ········ **3**:317b
World Trade Mart ········ **4**:51b
World War I ········ **8**:270b-271b
  China ········ **1**:287b
  declaration of war ········ **8**:270b
  economic impact ········ **3**:199b
  international relations ········ **3**:321a
  military expansion and economic growth ········ **8**:271a-271b
  military operations ········ **8**:270b
  political relations with allies ········ **8**:270b-271a
  Taiwan ········ **7**:308b
  Twenty-one Demands ········ **8**:270b
  ultranationalism ········ **8**:145a
  war literature ········ **8**:226b
  Washington Conference ········ **8**:234a-234b
World War II ········ **8**:271b-277a
  Allied offensives ········ **8**:275a-275b
  Attu, battle of ········ **1**:116a
  and Australia ········ **1**:116b-117a
  bombings, study of effectiveness ········ **7**:249a
  Cairo Conference ········ **1**:229b
  casualties ········ **6**:224a
  China Incident ········ **7**:199b
  dissolution of Imperial Army ········ **1**:88b
  economic reconstruction ········ **2**:163a
  economy ········ **2**:153b-154a, 158b
  electronics industry ········ **2**:192a
  European War ········ **8**:272a
  Fujian, occupation of
    Taiwan ········ **7**:308b-309a
  Greater East Asia Coprosperity Sphere ········ **8**:273b
  Guangdong, occupation of
    Taiwan ········ **7**:308b-309a
  international relations ········ **3**:321b-324a
  invasion of China ········ **1**:289b-290a
  Iōjima (Iwojima), Battle of ········ **3**:328b
  Japan after ········ **2**:154a-155a
  Japan attacks ········ **8**:273a-273b
  Japanese-American confrontation ········ **8**:272a-273a
  Japanese expansionism ········ **8**:271b-272a
  Japanese society during ········ **8**:277a-278b
    full-scale participation ········ **8**:277b-278a
    Konoe's "New Order" ········ **8**:277b
    ravages ········ **8**:278a
    war and society ········ **8**:278a-278b
    war preparations ········ **8**:277a-277b
  Japan's surrender ········ **8**:276a-277a
  last assaults ········ **8**:275b-276a
  Luzon, invasion of
    Taiwan ········ **7**:308b-309a
  Malayan Campaign ········ **5**:88a
  Manchukuo role ········ **5**:97a-97b
  Marianas ········ **8**:275b
  nonrepatriated Japanese soldiers ········ **8**:278b-279a
  Operation Number One ········ **6**:115a
  Operation Victory ········ **6**:115a
  Pacific deadlock ········ **8**:273b-275a
  Potsdam Declaration ········ **6**:231b
  relocation centers ········ **4**:13a, 14a-14b
  reparations ········ **2**:155a
  Senjinkan ········ **7**:65b
  Tōkyō ········ **8**:61b
  United States ········ **8**:158a
  war crimes trials ········ **8**:223a-225b
  war literature ········ **8**:226b

Wrestling 8:279a
Wright, Frank Lloyd 8:279a
  Imperial Hotel 3:277b
"Writing for Sale Association" 1:129b-130a
Writings, inscriptions 3:313b-314a
Written vernacular Japanese, development of. *See* **Gembun itchi**
Wu 3:46a; 6:41b
Wu Peifu (Wu P'ei-fu) 8:279b

X

Xavier, Francis 1:150b; 2:306b; 7:30a, 64b; 8:281a
  Kakure Kirishitan 4:119a
Xerox Corporation 2:359a
Xianren 7:67a
Xi'an (Sian) Incident 1:116b; 2:342a; 8:281a-281b
  Second United Front 7:47b-48a
Xiliang ji 7:195a
Xinmin Hui (Hsin-min Hui) 6:260b; 8:281b
Xu'an Huaichang 2:187a
Xu You 4:146b

Y

Yabakei 耶馬渓 8:283a
Yabakei Gorge 1:70a
Yabegawa 矢部川 1:83a
Yabe Hisakatsu 矢部長克 8:283a
Yabukōji (*Ardisia japonica*) 8:283a
Yabukōjishū 藪柑子集 8:11a
Yabusame 流鏑馬 2:261a; 4:160b; 7:64a; 8:283a-283b
Yabusame ceremony parts 8:283a
Yabuta Teijirō 藪田貞治郎 8:283b
Yabutsubaki (*Camellia japonica*) 1:236b
Yachiyo 八千代 8:283b
Yadake *(Pseudosasa japonica)* 1:136a
Yaeyama Islands 八重山諸島 7:3a, 66a; 8:283b
  Iriomotejima 3:331a
  Ishigakijima 3:340b
  Ryūkyū Islands 6:357a
  Taketomijima 7:325b
  Yonagunijima 8:337a
Yafuki 野府記 7:179a
Yagi Hidetsugu 八木秀次 8:283b-284a
Yagi Jūkichi 八木重吉 8:284a
Yagisawa Dam 矢木沢ダム 8:237a
Yagi-Uda antenna 2:192a
Yagō 8:284a
Yaguramon (castle gate) 櫓門 1:248b
Yagyū 柳生 8:284a
Yagyū Munenori 柳生宗矩 8:284a
Yahagigawa 矢作川 8:284a-284b
Yahata. 八幡 *See* **Yawata**
Yahikoyama 弥彦山 8:284b
Yaita 矢板 8:284b
Yaizu 焼津 8:284b
Yajima Kajiko 矢島楫子 8:284b
  Sasaki Toyoju 7:23b
Yakai Incident 八海事件 8:284b
Yakaku teikinshō 夜鶴庭訓抄 1:235a
Yakata 7:271a
Yakazu haikai 矢数俳諧 3:79a
Yakedake 焼岳 4:127a; 8:284b-285a
Yakedake peak 焼岳 1:5a
Yakimono 2:306a
Yakishime 1:259b
Yakke 4:194b
Yakko 奴 1:147b; 8:285a
  Hatamoto 8:285a
  Machi 8:285a
  Sekisho (barriers) 8:285a
Yaku 4:95a
Yakubyōgami 1:155a; 8:285a
Yakudoshi 8:285a-285b
Yakukata 役方 1:137b
Yakumo mishō 八雲御抄 8:285b
Yakuō Tokken 約翁徳倹 4:2a
Yakusa no kabane 八色の姓 8:285b
Yakusha-e 役者絵 4:171b; 8:183a
Yakusha rongo 役者論語 6:108b; 8:21b
Yakushi 1:*188b*
Yakushidake 薬師岳 5:352b; 8:285b
Yakushiji 薬師寺 1:182a; 8:285b-286b
  kondō (main hall) 8:*285a*
  Pagoda 8:*285a*
  West Pagoda 5:332a
Yakushima 屋久島 4:105b; 8:286b
Yakushi Triad 1:*199a*
"Yakusoku" 約束 8:303a
Yakuza 2:343a; 8:286b
  gambling 3:5b
  oyabun-kobun 6:137a-137b
Yakuza, The ザ・ヤクザ 7:314a
  urban life 8:177b
Yakuza eiga 2:274b
Yakuza groups 7:209a
Yalta Conference 8:159b, 286b-287a
  Occupation 6:51a
  Roosevelt, Franklin Delano 6:339a
  Russia and Japan 6:344a
Yalu River, Naval Battle of 8:287a
Yama 2:201b; 3:329b
Yamabe 山部 1:147b
Yamabe no Akahito 山部赤人 7:13a; 8:206b, 287b
  poems in *Man'yōshū* 5:107b
Yamabe no Akahito shū 山部赤人集 8:287b
Yamabiraki 8:287b
Yamabito ("mountain people") 7:13b
Yama-boko 2:255b
Yamabōshi *(Cornus kousa)* 8:287b
Yamabuki (*Kerria japonica*) 8:287b-288a
Yamabukisō (*Hylomecon japonicum*) 8:288a
Yamabushi 山伏 4:327b; 7:182a; 8:288a
  conch-shell trumpet *(horagai)* 8:*288b*
  kagura 4:107b
  shamanism 7:76b
  Shōgoin 7:160a
Yamabushi kagura 山伏神楽 4:107b
Yamachawan 山茶碗 1:258b, 262a; 7:256a; 8:288a-288b
Yamada 山田 8:288b
Yamada Bimyō 山田美妙 5:379a; 8:288b
  Ken'yūsha 4:198b
Yamadadera remains 山田寺跡 8:288b-289a
Yamada Isuzu 山田五十鈴 8:289a
Yamada Jōka 山田常嘉 3:*313a*
Yamada Kengyō 山田検校 7:226a
Yamada Kōsaku 山田耕筰 8:289a
Yamada Moritarō 山田盛太郎 8:289a
Yamada Nagamasa 山田長政 8:289a-289b
Yamada Saburō 山田三良 8:289b
Yamada Tomohiko 山田智彦 8:289b
Yamada Waka 山田わか 8:289b
Yamada Yōji 山田洋次 2:275b; 8:289b-290a
Yamada Yoshihiko 山田芳彦 4:202a
Yamada Yoshio 山田孝雄 6:297a; 8:290a
  Kokugaku no hongi 4:259a
Yamaga 山鹿 8:290a
Yamagami Itarō 山上伊太郎 2:268b
Yamaga Sokō 山鹿素行 4:247a-247b; 8:290a-290b
  Chūchō jijitsu 1:311b
  Kogaku proponent 4:246b-247b
  nature, concept of 5:357b
  Seikyō yōroku 7:51b
Yamagata 山形 8:290b
Yamagata Aritomo 山県有朋 1:86a, 91a, 135b; 3:194b; 7:51a; 8:290b-292a
  Anglo-Japanese Alliance 1:56b
  Aoki Shūzō 1:69a
  Conscription Ordinance of 1873 4:204b
  Freedom and People's Rights Movement 2:334a
  genrō 3:21b
  gumbatsu 3:66a
  Kabasan Incident 4:89a
  Kabayama Sukenori 4:89b
  Kenseitō 4:198b
  Kiyoura Keigo 4:233a
  Kokumin shimbun influenced by 4:261a
  Rikken Seiyūkai 6:315a
  rules of military conduct 3:279b-280a
  Shandong (Shantung) Question 7:77a
  Uesugi Shinkichi 8:130a
Yamagata Bantō 山片蟠桃 8:292a-292b
Yamagata Basin 山形盆地 8:292b
Yamagata Daini 山県大弐 8:292b-293a
Yamagata Isoo 山県五十雄 5:270b
Yamagata-Lobanov Agreement 山県-ロバノフ協定 8:293a-293b
  Korea 4:281b
  Korea's independence 4:287b
  Russia and Japan 6:341b
  Russo-Japanese War 6:346a
Yamagata Masao 山県昌夫 8:293b
Yamagata Prefecture 山形県 8:293b, 355a
Yamagishikai 山岸会 8:293b-294a
Yamagiwa Katsusaburō 山極勝三郎 8:294a
Yamaguchi 山口 8:294a
Yamaguchi Basin 山口盆地 8:294a
Yamaguchi Hitomi 山口瞳 8:294b
Yamaguchi Kaoru 山口薫 8:294b
Yamaguchi no Atai Ōguchi 山口費大口 8:294b
Yamaguchi Prefecture 山口県 7:277a; 8:295a
Yamaguchi Reservoir 7:31b
Yamaguchi Saburō 山口三郎 7:108a
Yamaguchi Seishi 山口誓子 8:295a-295b

Yamaguchi Sodō 山口素堂 8:295b
Yamaguchi Yoshiko 山口淑子 8:295b
Yamaha Motor Co, Ltd 8:296a
  Kawakami Gen'ichi 4:180b
Yamaha Music Foundation 4:180b
Yamaichi Securities Co, Ltd 8:296a
Yamaji Aizan 山路愛山 5:13a; 8:296a
Yamajiro 山城 1:246b, 247b
Yamakawa Hitoshi 山川均 7:3a; 8:296a-297b
  Fukumoto Kazuo 2:364a
  Japan Communist Party 4:11a-11b
  Kaizō 4:113b
Yamakawa Kikue 山川菊栄 7:57a; 8:297a
  Fujin kōron publication 2:344a
Yama kōmori *(Nyctalus lasiopterus)* 1:146b
Yamakunigawa 山国川 8:297a
Yamamba 山姥 8:297a
Yamamichi 山道 7:334b
Yamamoto Baiitsu 山本梅逸 1:211a; 5:311a-311b; 8:297a-297b
Yamamoto Fujiko 山本富士子 8:297b
Yamamoto Gombei. *See* **Yamamoto Gonnohyōe**
Yamamoto Gonnohyōe 山本権兵衛 8:297b
Yamamoto Hokuzan 山本北山 8:297b-298a
Yamamoto Hōsui 山本芳翠 8:298a
  Fontanesi, Antonio 2:304a
  pupils 2:345b
Yamamoto Isoroku 山本五十六 1:21a; 8:298a
  World War II 8:273a
Yamamoto Jōtarō 山本条太郎 8:298a-298b
Yamamoto Kaichi 山本嘉一 2:*269a*
Yamamoto Kajirō 山本嘉次郎 2:270b, 271b; 8:298b
Yamamoto Kanae 山本鼎 5:232b
Yamamoto Kansai やまもと寛斎 8:298b
Yamamoto Kenkichi 山本健吉 5:13b; 8:298b
Yamamoto Kiyoshi 山本貴誉司 8:298b
Yamamoto Sanehiko 山本実彦 8:298b-299a
  Kaizō 4:113b
Yamamoto Satsuo 山本薩夫 2:272a, 274a; 8:299a
Yamamoto Senji 山本宣治 8:299a
  birth control movement 7:11a
Yamamoto Shūgorō 山本周五郎 7:103b; 8:299a-299b
Yamamoto Tamesaburō 山本為三郎 8:299b
Yamamoto Tōjirō 山本東次郎 4:*325a*
Yamamoto Yasue 山本安英 8:299b
Yamamoto Yūzō 山本有三 7:125a; 8:300a
Yamamura Bochō 山村暮鳥 8:300a
Yamamura Saisuke 山村才助 8:300a
Yamamuro Gumpei 山室軍平 8:300a
  Salvation Army (Kyūseigun) 7:5b
Yamamuro Kieko 山室機恵子 8:300a
Yamana family 山名氏 7:8b; 8:300b
Yamanaka (town) 山中 2:345a; 8:300b
Yamanaka, Lake 山中湖 8:300b
Yamanaka Sadao 山中貞雄 2:270a, 271a; 8:300b
Yamanaka Shikanosuke 山中鹿之介 8:300b-301a
Yamanashi (city) 山梨 8:301a
Yamanashi Prefecture 山梨県 8:301a-301b
Yamana Sōzen 山名宗全 8:301b
Yamane 2:131a-131b
Yamaneko 8:253a
Yamanobe no Michi 山辺の道 5:334a
Yama no kami 1:20a; 8:302a
  keshin forms 1:122b-123a
Yama no oto (The Sound of the Mountain) 山の音 6:230a
Yamanote 山手 4:176b; 8:178b, 302a
  shitamachi 7:149b-150a
Yamanouchi Hot Springs 山ノ内温泉 8:355a
Yamanouchi Kazutoyo 山内一豊 7:56b; 8:302a
  Kōchi 4:239b
Yamanouchi Pharmaceutical Co, Ltd 8:302b
Yamanouchi Sugao 山内清男 1:76a; 8:302b
  Jōmon pottery 4:75a
Yamanouchi Toyoshige 山内豊信 8:302b
Yamanoue no Okura 山上憶良 5:105a; 8:206b, 302b-303a
  poems in *Man'yōshū* 5:108a
  poetry 8:303a
Yamaoka Sōhachi 山岡荘八 7:103b; 8:303a
Yamaoka Tesshū 山岡鉄舟 8:303a-303b
Yamasa Shōyu Co, Ltd 8:303b
Yamashina Tokitsugu 山科言継
  Tokitsugu Kyō ki 8:43a
Yamashiro no Kuni fudoki 山城国風土記 7:139a
Yamashiro no Kuni Ikki 山城国一揆 8:303b
Yamashiro no Ōe, Prince 山背大兄王 8:303b
Yamashiro Province 山城国 8:303b-304a
Yamashiro Tomoe 山代巴 8:304a-304b
Yamashiroya Incident 山城屋事件 8:304b
Yamashiroya Wasuke 山城屋和助 8:304b
"Yamashita caveman" 6:85a
Yamashita-Shinnihon Steamship Co, Ltd 8:304b
Yamashita Tarō 山下太郎 1:71b; 8:304b
Yamashita Tomoyuki 山下奉文 8:305a
Yamatai 邪馬台 2:103b, 365a; 8:305a-307a
  Chen Shou and the *Wei zhi* 8:305a
  Itokoku 3:354b
  Kinai-Kyūshū standoff 8:306b-307a
  Kyūshū theory 8:306a-306b
  rulers
    Himiko 3:139b-140a
  Wa and Queen Himiko 8:305a-305b
  Yamatai debate 8:307a
  Yamato theory reborn 8:306b
Yamatai wa nakatta (There Was No Yamatai) 耶馬台はなかった 8:306b
Yamataka Shigeri 山高しげり 8:307b
Yamatake-Honeywell Co, Ltd 8:307b
Yamatane Museum of Art 8:307b
Yamata no Orochi 八岐大蛇 2:302b; 7:278b; 8:307b
Yamate Kiichirō 山手樹一郎 8:307b
Yamato (city) 大和 8:308a
Yamato ("Japanese") 大和 8:308a
  formation 4:34b
  gardens 3:8b
  Kinai 4:211b
Yamato (battleship) 大和 8:308a
Yamato Basin. *See* **Nara Basin**
Yamato Bunkakan 8:308a-308b
  iconographic drawings 7:328a
  museums 5:277b
Yamato court 大和朝廷 2:288a; 7:248a, 256a; 8:308b-309a
  cooking style 2:305b
  court titles 4:89a
  economy 2:147a
  formation of Japan 4:7a
  Fujwara no Kamatari 2:351a
  Hayato resistance 3:118b
  Imbe family 3:274b
  Inariyama tomb 3:283b
  Iwafune no ki 3:357b
  Iwai, Rebellion of 3:357b
  kikajin 4:205a-205b
  kokugun system to strengthen 4:259b
  Mononobe family 5:247a
  Ōjin Mausoleum 6:76b
  Ōtomo family 6:130b
  rise of 4:246a
  Taika Reform 7:295b-296a
  Takamuko no Kuromaro 7:315b
  Takenouchi no Sukune 4:203b; 7:325a
  Wani 8:223a
  women in 8:258b
Yamato cycle of mythology 5:292b
Yamato-damashii 大和魂 8:309a-309b
Yamato-e 大和絵 7:270a; 8:309b
  development 2:355b
  Fujiwara culture 2:348a
  Fukko school 2:360b
  fūzokuga 2:377a
  Genji monogatari emaki 3:20a
  Kaihō Yūshō 4:110b
  Kanō school 4:149b
  kara-e 4:157a
  Kose no Kanaoka, as founder 4:294b
  Kose school initiated 4:294b
  modern painting 6:156b
  Nakamura Gakuryō 5:314b
  painting 6:149b
  rimpa 6:317b
  subjects 6:158b
  Tazaki Sōun 7:359a
Yamatogawa 大和川 5:332b; 8:309b-310a
Yamatohime, Princess 倭姫命 8:310a
  Ise Shrine 3:338a
Yamato-hime no Mikoto seiki 倭姫命世記 7:263b
Yamato honzō 大和本草 4:108b
Yamato koji fūbutsushi 大和古寺風物誌 4:125a
Yamato Kōriyama 大和郡山 8:310a
Yamato leaders, technology transfer 7:374a
Yamato monogatari 大和物語 5:246a; 8:310a
  Obasuteyama 6:48b
Yamato period 大和時代 8:310b
  periodization 6:175b

Yama torikabuto (*Aconitum japonicum*) ········ **8**:310b
Yamato Sanzan 大和三山 ········ **8**:*310b*
Yamato Takada 大和高田 ········ **8**:310b
Yamatotakeru, Prince 日本武尊 ·· **8**:311a–311b
hero worship ········ **3**:128a
imperial regalia ········ **3**:278b
kofun ········ **5**:309a
Kumaso suppression ········ **4**:189a
Yamatotakeru no Mikoto. *See* **Yamatotakeru, Prince**
Yamato theory ········ **8**:306b
Yamawaki Izumi no Kami Motoyoshi 山脇和泉守元宜 ········ **3**:366a
Yamawaki Tōyō 山脇東洋 ·· **8**:311b–312a
Yamazaki 山崎 ········ **8**:312a
Yamazaki, Battle of 山崎の戦 · **1**:41b; **7**:104a; **8**:312b
Takayama Ukon ········ **7**:321a
Toyotomi Hideyoshi ········ **8**:95a
Yamazaki Ansai 山崎闇斎 ·· **7**:27b, 263b; **8**:119a–119b, 312a–312b
shasō ········ **7**:81a
Yamazaki Baking Co, Ltd ········ **8**:312b
Yamazaki Masakazu 山崎正和 ··· **8**:312b–313a
shingeki ········ **7**:113b
Yamazaki Naomasa 山崎直方 **1**:103b; **8**:313a
Yamazaki Sōkan 山崎宗鑑 ········ **8**:313a
Yambōshi (*Cornus kousa*) ········ **8**:287b
Yame 八女 ········ **8**:313a
Yame tomb cluster 八女古墳群 ··· **8**:313a–313b
Yamishio 闇潮 ········ **4**:180a
Yamizo Mountains 八溝山地 ········ **8**:313b
Yanagawa 柳川 ·· **8**:*313a*, 313b
Yanagawa Seigan 梁川星巌 ········ **8**:313b
Yanagawa Shunsan 柳川春三 ········ **8**:313b
Yanagi ········ **8**:253b–254a
Yanagida Izumi 柳田泉 ··· **8**:313b–314a
Yanagihara Byakuren 柳原白蓮 ········ **8**:314a
Yanagi Muneyoshi 柳宗悦 **2**:293a; **8**:314a
folklore studies ········ **2**:296b
Japan Folk-Craft Museum ········ **4**:46a
Koishiwara ware ········ **4**:250b
sashiko stitching ········ **7**:24a
Yanagisawa Kien 柳沢淇園 ········ **1**:211a; **8**:314a–314b
Ike no Taiga ········ **3**:267a
Yanagisawa Yoshiyasu 柳沢吉保 ········ **8**:314b
Yanagita Kunio 柳田国男 · **2**:296b, 297b, 302a; **5**:13b; **7**:256b; **8**:*315a*, 315b
festivals ········ **2**:253a–253b
folk religion ········ **2**:298a
historiography ········ **3**:157a
Yanagiya Kosan V 柳家小さん(五代) **6**:*282b*
Yanai 柳井 ········ **8**:315b
Yanaihara Tadao 矢内原忠雄 **5**:263a; **8**:315b
pacifism ········ **6**:144b
Yan'an (Yenan) Government · **8**:315b–316a
Yanmar Diesel Engine Co, Ltd ···· **8**:316a
Yano Fumio. 矢野文雄 *See* **Yano Ryūkei**
Ya no ne 矢の根 ········ **4**:98a
Yano Ryūkei 矢野龍渓 ········ **8**:316a
seiji shōsetsu ········ **7**:50a
Yano Tsuneta 矢野恒太 ········ **8**:316a
Yao 八尾 ········ **8**:316a
Yao Keijirō 八尾敬次郎 ········ **3**:18a
Yao Shōten Co, Ltd ········ **3**:18a
Yaoyorozu no kami ("The Eight Hundred Myriads") ········ **4**:126a
Yarigatake 槍ケ岳 ········ **8**:316b
Yarō kabuki 野郎歌舞伎 ········ **2**:75a
Yasaka 八坂 ········ **7**:126b
Yasaka Shrine 八坂神社 **4**:336a; **7**:278b; **8**:316b
Gion Festival ········ **3**:33b, 34a
Yasakayahama 八坂八浜 ········ **8**:316b
Yasan 野山 ········ **4**:299a
Yasato 八郷 ········ **8**:316b
Yashajin Pass 夜叉神峠 ········ **8**:316b
Yashi ········ **7**:250a
Yashica Co, Ltd ········ **8**:316b
Yashikigami ········ **2**:300b
Yashima 屋島 ··· **8**:316b–317a
Takamatsu ········ **7**:314a–314b
Yashio 八塩 ········ **8**:317a
Yashiro Hirokata 屋代弘賢 **2**:258b; **8**:317a
Yashiro Seiichi 矢代静一 ········ **8**:317a
shingeki ········ **7**:113b
Yaskawa Electric Mfg Co, Ltd ····· **8**:317a
Yasukawa Daigorō ········ **8**:319a
Yasoshima Matsuri 八十島祭 ········ **3**:271a
Yasotakeru 八十梟師 ········ **4**:57b
Yasuda 安田 ··· **8**:317a–317b
Yasuda Zenjirō ········ **8**:318a
Yasuda Fire & Marine Insurance Co, Ltd ········ **8**:317b–318a
Yasuda monogatari 安田物語 ········ **4**:76b
Yasuda plan ········ **8**:364a
Yasuda Trust & Banking Co, Ltd ········ **8**:318a
Yasuda Yojūrō 保田与重郎 · **5**:13b; **8**:318a
Kamei Katsuichirō ········ **4**:125a
Yasuda Yukihiko 安田靫彦 ········ **8**:318a
Yasuda zaibatsu (financial combine) 安田財閥 ········ **8**:357b
Yasuda Zenjirō 安田善次郎 ·· **7**:52a; **8**:318a
Yasuda Bank ········ **2**:342a
Yasugawa 野洲川 ········ **8**:318b
Yasugi 安来 ········ **8**:318b
Yasuhara Teishitsu 安原貞室 ········ **8**:318b
Yasui Sokken 安井息軒 ········ **8**:318b
Yasui Sōtarō 安井曾太郎 ········ **8**:318b
Yasui Takuma 安井琢磨 ··· **8**:318b–319a
Yasui Takuma chosakushū (Collected Works of Yasui Takuma) 安井琢磨著作集 ········ **8**:319a
Yasui Tetsu 安井てつ ········ **8**:319a
"Yasui-Umehara era" ········ **6**:157b
Yasukawa Daigorō 安川第五郎 ········ **8**:319a
Yasukuni Shrine 靖国神社 ········ **2**:300a; **8**:319a–319b
Yasumi Toshio 八住利雄 ········ **8**:319b
Yasunaka Hana 安中はな ········ **5**:267a
Yasuoka Shōtarō 安岡章太郎 ····· **8**:319b
Shinchō ········ **7**:109a
Yatabe Ryōkichi 矢田部良吉 ········ **1**:156a; **8**:319b–320a
Yatoi ········ **2**:311a
Yatomi 弥富 ········ **8**:320a
Yatsude (*Fatsia japonica*) ········ **8**:320a
Yatsugatake 八ケ岳 **2**:347b; **8**:320a
Yatsushiro 八代 ········ **8**:320a
Yatsushiro Kai 八代海 ········ **8**:320a
Yatsushiro Sea 八代海 ········ **8**:320a
Yautsuri ········ **4**:195a
Yawarasugi ········ **7**:257b
Yawata 八幡 ··· **8**:320a–320b
Yawatahama 八幡浜 ········ **8**:320b
Yawata Iron and Steel Company Political Donation Case ········ **6**:202a
Yawata Iron and Steel Works ····· **3**:284a, 333a; **4**:344a; **5**:303a; **8**:320b–321a
Yayoi culture 弥生文化 ··· **8**:321a–322a
affinity with Korea, Manchuria, and northern China ········ **4**:276b
archaeological study ········ **1**:77a–77b
belief systems ········ **8**:322a
clothing ········ **8**:321b–322a
economy ········ **2**:147a
folktales ········ **2**:303b
food ········ **8**:321b–322a
housing ········ **3**:243a; **8**:321b–322a
Jimmu, Emperor ········ **4**:57b
late ········ **8**:322a
magatama ········ **8**:*320b*
pottery jars ········ **8**:*320b*
technological advances ········ **8**:321a–321b
Toro site ········ **8**:80b
Yayoi period 弥生時代 ···· **4**:34a–34b; **8**:322a
archaeological sites ········ **7**:266a
burial mounds ········ **4**:244a
postwar research ········ **1**:78a–79a
religion ········ **7**:126a
rice cultivation ········ **7**:247b
Shintō ········ **7**:126a
stone tools ········ **7**:247b
Yayoi pottery 弥生式土器 ···· **1**:76b–77a; **8**:322a–322b, *323a*
fern frond design ········ **2**:252a
jars ········ **8**:*320b*
Karako site ········ **4**:157b
Year-end fair ········ **8**:322b–323a
Year of My Life, The ········ **6**:298a
"Yellow peril" ········ **1**:238b; **8**:323a–323b
Yellow Sea, Battle of. *See* **Yalu River, Naval Battle of**
Yellowtail [(buri) *Seriola quinqueradiata*] ········ **8**:323b
Yen 円 ········ **8**:240a, 323b–324a
exchange rate, monetary policy ···· **5**:241b
IMF ········ **3**:274b
premodern ········ **5**:243a
redenomination ········ **8**:324b
Yenan government. *See* **Yan'an (Yenan) Government**
Yen credit ········ **8**:324a–324b
Yen revaluation ········ **7**:223b
Yi Dong-wŏn ········ **4**:285b
Yi dynasty 李朝 ········ **4**:140b; **8**:324b–325b
founding ········ **8**:326a
Kojong, King ········ **4**:252a
Yi Sŏng-gye established ········ **4**:276a
Yi Ha-ŭng. *See* **Taewŏn'gun**
Yi Hoe-sŏng ········ **4**:374b
Yi Hwang ········ **8**:325b
Yin and Yang, Bureau of ····· **6**:113a–113b
Yin-dynasty, calendrical symbols ··· **4**:55b
Yin Rugeng (Yin Ju-keng) ········ **8**:325b
Yin-yang ····· **4**:55b; **5**:151a; **6**:103a; **7**:191a
Yiran ········ **3**:357a–357b
Yi Sam-p'yong. *See* **Ri Sampei**
Yishan Yining ········ **3**:348b
Yi Sŏng-gye ········ **8**:326a
wakō campaigns ········ **4**:276a, 278b
Yi Sŭng-man ········ **6**:307b–308a
Yi Sun-sin ········ **8**:326a
Yi Wan-Yong ········ **8**:326a
annexation treaty ········ **4**:282a, 287b
YMCA ········ **8**:326a
Yobai ········ **8**:326a–326b
Yobigoe 呼声 ········ **4**:328a
Yobikō ········ **2**:41b
Yoda Yoshikata 依田義賢 ········ **8**:326b

Yodogawa ············ 淀川 7:140a; 8:326b
Yodogawa Steel Works, Ltd ······· 8:326b
Yodogimi ············ 淀君 ········· 4:1a; 8:326b-327a
Yodo no koi shusse no taki nobori (The Carp of Yodo Climbs the Ladder of Success) 淀鯉出世滝徳 ······· 8:327a
Yodoya Tatsugorō
·············· 淀屋辰五郎 ······· 8:327a
Yōeki ················ 徭役 ······· 8:327a
corvée labor ···················· 1:226b
Yōga ················ 用賀 ··· 8:327a-328b
Yo ga kenshin no jikken
········ 予が見神の実験 ······· 8:116a
Yōgaku ·············· 洋学 ··· 8:241a-243a
Yōgakusho (Institute of Western Learning)
················· 洋学所 1:141b; 8:243a
Yoidore tenshi · 酔いどれ天使 ····· 7:108b
Yōjimbō ··········· 用心棒 ······· 7:108b
Yojō ··············· 余情 · 5:42a; 8:328b
origin ························· 8:328b
outside waka ··················· 8:328b
Yojōhan fusuma no shitabari trial
四畳半襖の下張り裁判 ······· 8:328b
Yōjōkun ·········· 養生訓 ······ 4:108b; 8:328a-329b
Yōju ················ 遙授 ······· 8:338a
Yōkai ·························· 1:130b
Yōkaichi ·········· 八日市 ······· 8:329a
Yōkaichiba ······ 八日市場 ······· 8:329a
Yokaren ··········· 予科練 ······· 8:329a
Yokkaichi ········ 四日市 ·· 8:*329a*, 329b
pollution of ··················· 2:226b
Yokoana ············· 横穴 ······· 8:329b
Yokoana sekishitsu (tomb chamber) ······ 横穴石室 ··· 4:245a-245b
Yokohama ·········· 横浜 4:135a; 8:*329a*, 329b
Yokohama Archives of History
······················· 8:329b-330a
Yokohama band ················· 6:258a
Yokohama-e ······ 横浜絵 ······· 8:330a
Yokohama Incident
················ 横浜事件 ······· 8:330a
Yokohama Kawase Kaisha ······· 4:184b
Yokohama mainichi shimbum ·· 横浜毎日新聞 ······ 6:245b; 8:330a-330b
Yokohama Rubber Co, Ltd 2:372b; 8:330b
Yokohama Specie Bank ···· 1:140b, 167b; 8:330b
establishment ············ 1:138b-139a
Takahashi Korekiyo ············ 7:312b
Yokoi Kinkoku ··· 横井金谷 ······· 1:211a; 8:330b-331a
Yokoi Myōdō ···· 横井妙幢 ······· 8:330b
Yokoi Shōichi ···· 横井庄一 ······· 8:279a
Yokoi Shōnan ··· 横井小楠 ··· 8:331a-331b
fukoku kyōhei ·················· 2:360b
Jitsugakutō (Practical Party) ······· 8:331a
schooling ······················ 8:331a
Shōnandō ······················ 8:331a
Yokoi Tokitsura ·· 横井時般 ······· 8:331b
Yokoi Tokiyoshi · 横井時敬 ······· 8:331b
Yokoi Yayū ····· 横井也有 6:297b; 8:331b
haibun ························· 3:78a
Yokomitsu Riichi 横光利一 2:274a; 7:103b; 8:331b-333b
early works ···················· 8:332a
fūzoku shōsetsu ················ 2:378b
Monshō ························ 8:333a
psychological monologues ······· 8:332b
Ryoshū ················ 8:333a-333b
Shanhai ······················· 8:332b
Shin'en ······················· 8:332b
Shinkankaku school ········ 7:116a-116b
Yokomizo Seishi 横溝正史 ······· 8:333b
Yokoo Tadanori · 横尾忠則 ······· 8:333b
Yokose Torahisa 横瀬虎寿 ······· 8:333b
Yokose Yau ····· 横瀬夜雨 ··· 8:333b-334a
Yokosuka ·········· 横須賀 4:135a; 8:334a
Yokosuka Naval Arsenal ·········· 8:334a
Yokosuka Shipyards
··········· 横須賀造船所 ·· 2:31a; 8:334a
foreign investment ·············· 2:316b
Oguri Tadamasa ·················· 6:72a
Yokota Kisaburō
·············· 横田喜三郎 ······· 8:334a
Yokote ················ 横手 ······· 8:334a
Yokote Basin ···· 横手盆地 ······· 8:334b
Yokoyama Gennosuke
·············· 横山源之助 ······· 8:334b
Yokoyama Taikan
················ 横山大観 ······· 6:*157a*; 8:334b-335a
Qu Yuan (Kutsugen) ·············· 8:*334b*
Yokozuna ················· 7:272a-272b
Yokozuna dohyōiri ··············· 7:272a
Yokubō shizen shugi
············· 欲望自然主義 ······· 6:204a
Yokusan Seijikai
·············· 翼賛政治会 ······· 3:281a
Yōmei Bunko ···· 陽明文庫 ······· 8:335a
Konoe collection ················ 4:273b
Konoe family collection ·········· 4:272b
Yōmeigaku ········ 陽明学 ·· 1:355a-357a; 7:71a; 8:335a-335b
Kaitokudō curriculum ············ 4:113b
Kumazawa Banzan ···· 4:307a-307b; 8:28a
Miwa Shissai ···················· 5:216a
Nakae Tōju ·············· 5:312a-312b
Ōshio Heihachirō ········ 6:126a-126b
Satō Issai ······················ 7:27a
Shingaku ······················· 7:111b
Yōmeigaku philosophy ··········· 5:315a
Yōmeimon gate ···· 陽明門 ········ 8:*84b*
Yomeirikon ··················· 8:336a
Yomena (*Aster yomena; Kalimeris yomena*) ··················· 8:336a
Yomi, land of ·················· 5:293a
Yomihon ·············· 読本 ······ 1:295a; 5:48b-49a; 7:18a; 8:336a-336b
Bakin ·························· 1:130b
composition ···················· 8:336a
history ························ 8:336a
Jippensha Ikku ·················· 4:61a
later Edo period ·········· 5:48b-49a
origin ························· 8:336a
purpose ························ 8:336a
Tamenaga Shunsei ········· 7:333b-334a
Yomi no kuni ····· 黄泉の国 ········ 1:20a
Yomise ························· 7:250a
Yomitan ·············· 読谷 ······· 8:336b
Yomiuri ·············· 読売 ······· 4:182b
Yomiuri Kinrei (Prohibition of Broadsides) · 読売禁令 ······· 1:252a
Yomiuri Literary Prize
Agawa Hiroyuki (1952) ············ 1:21a
Aizu Yaichi (1951) ··············· 1:38b
Amino Kiku (1967) ··············· 1:52b
Nakamura Mitsuo (1958) ····· 5:315a-315b
Shōno Junzō (1965) ·············· 7:167a
Tanaka Chikao (1953) ············ 7:335b
Yashiro Seiichi (1972) ··········· 8:317a
Yomiuri shimbun 読売新聞 · 1:18a; 4:127b, 184a, 199b, 207a; 7:310b; 8:336b-337a
Baba Tsunego ··················· 1:129b
Occupation ······················ 6:53b
Yomiuri Telecasting Corporation ·· 8:337a
Yōmonkai ··········· 陽門会 ······· 3:145b
Yomotsu Hirasaka
················ 黄泉平坂 ········ 1:69a
Yonago ··············· 米子 ······· 8:337a
Yonagunijima ···· 与那国島 ·· 4:2b; 8:337a
Yonai Mitsumasa 米内光政 ······· 8:337a
Arita Hachirō ···················· 1:85a
Yonaoshi rebellions
············ 世直し騒動 ··· 8:337a-337b
ikki ··························· 2:269a
Yoneda, Karl ···················· 4:15b
Yonemoto Masaaki. 米本正秋 *See* **Tachihara Masaaki**
Yoneshirogawa ···· 米代川 ··· 8:337b-338a
Yonezawa (city) ····· 米沢 ······· 8:338a
Yonezawa Basin · 米沢盆地 ······· 8:338a
Yonezawa Hikohachi
·············· 米沢彦八 ······· 6:282a
Yon'ichiroku Jiken. 四・一六事件 *See* **April 16th Incident**
Yōnin ················ 遙任 ······· 8:338a
Yōnin kokushi ··· 遙任国司 ······· 4:262a
Yonkakoku Jōyaku
·············· 四か国条約 ······· 2:330a
Yono ················ 与野 ······· 8:338a
Yo no naka e ···· 世の中へ ······· 4:148b
Yonsei ·························· 4:13b
Yoresugi ······················· 7:257b
Yoriai ··············· 寄合 ······· 4:122a; 8:338a-338b
group meetings ················· 8:338a
linked-verse ··················· 8:338b
secret council ·················· 8:338a
shogunal vassals ········ 8:338a-338b
Yoribito ··············· 寄人 ··· 8:339b-340a
Yoriki and dōshin
··············· 与力, 同心 ······· 8:338b
Yorimasa ············ 頼政 ······· 4:327b
Yorioya and yoriko
·············· 寄親, 寄子 ······· 8:338b
Yōrō ················ 養老 ······· 8:338b
Yoroboshi ·········· 弱法師 ······· 4:154b
Yōrō Code ······· 養老律令 ······· 7:11a; 8:338b-339a
clothing styles ················· 1:329b
court rank ······················ 2:40a
Dajōkan (Grand Council of State) ··· 2:70a
Fujiwara no Fuhito ·············· 2:350b
inheritance law ················· 3:304a
Rikkokushi ····················· 6:315b
ritsuryō system ················· 6:329b
Taihō Code ····················· 7:295b
Yōrōgawa ········· 養老川 ······· 8:339a
Yoroi kumiuchi ····· 鎧組打 ········ 4:82a
Yoronjima ········ 与論島 ······· 8:339a
Yōrō Ritsuryō. 養老律令 *See* **Yōrō Code**
Yorozu chōhō ······ 万朝報 1:129a; 6:144a; 8:339a
Ishikawa Sanshirō ··············· 3:344a
Kuroiwa Ruikō ·················· 4:316b
Naitō Konan ···················· 5:311a
Russo-Japanese War ············· 6:346b
Yorozuya Kinnosuke
·············· 萬屋錦之介 ······· 8:339a
Yorozuyo Bunko · 万代文庫 ·········· 8:9a
Yoru no kutsu (Shoes in the Night) ······· 夜の靴 ······· 8:333b
Yoru no nezame
·············· 夜の寝覚 ······ 7:257b; 8:339a-339b
Yoru no tsuzumi ··· 夜の鼓 ······· 8:339b
Shindō Kaneto ··················· 7:111a
Yoru to kiri no sumide
··········· 夜と霧の隅で ······· 4:227a
Yoryūdo ············ 寄人 ··· 8:339b-340a
farmers and laborers ······· 8:339b-340a
scribes ························ 8:339b
Yosa Buson ······ 与謝蕪村 ·· 1:*210b*, 224b; 6:297a
Yōsai. 栄西 *See* **Eisai**
Yōsan (mathematics) ············ 8:231a
Yosano Akiko · 与謝野晶子 · 2:344a; 7:54b, 253b; 8:340a

Myōjō 5:290b
Yosano Tekkan .... 与謝野鉄幹 8:216b, 340a-340b
Ishikawa Takuboku 3:344b
Myōjō 5:290b
Yose .... 寄席 8:340b
naniwa-bushi 5:328a
Yoseba kumiai mura .... 寄場組合村 1:211b
Yōshi. *See* **Adoption**
Yoshida-Acheson exchange of notes 8:340b-341a
Yoshida-Evarts Convention 8:12a
Yoshida Hideo 吉田秀雄 .. 1:17a; 8:341a
Yoshida Hiroshi .... 吉田博 8:341a
Yoshida Isoya 吉田五十八 .. 1:81a; 8:341a
Yoshida Issui .... 吉田一穂 8:341a
Yoshida Kanetomo .... 吉田兼倶 ... 8:341a-341b
Yoshida Kasaburō .... 吉田嘉三郎 8:341a
Yoshida Kenkō .. 吉田兼好 5:44a; 8:341a-342b, 380b
Tsurezuregusa 4:136a
writings 8:342b-343a
Yoshida Kōgyō 8:342b, 346a
Yoshida Mitsuyoshi .... 吉田光由 8:342b
Yoshida Seiichi .. 吉田精一 8:343a
Yoshida Shigeru ... 吉田茂 2:4a, 333a; 7:26a, 92a, 235b; 8:341a, *343a*, 343b-345a
Dulles, John Foster 2:135a
economic planning 2:168a
economy 2:157a-157b
Jiyūtō 4:65b
Kanamori Tokujirō 4:135b
Kigensetsu controversy 4:204a
Korean War 4:284b
labor unions 4:347a
land reforms of 1946 .... 4:365a
San Francisco Peace Treaty 7:11a
Shimoyama Incident 7:107a
Yoshida Shigeru cabinet 1:51a
Yoshida Shintō .. 吉田神道 .. 7:128a-128b; 8:345a-345b
Takamagahara 7:314a
Yoshida Shōin ... 吉田松陰 .. 5:156b; 7:3b, 94b; 8:345b-346a
Yoshida Tadao .. 吉田忠雄 8:346a
Yoshida Tōgo .. 吉田東伍 8:346a
Yoshida Tomizō 吉田富三 ... 8:346a-346b
Yoshida Tōyō .. 吉田東洋 8:346b
Yoshida Yoshishige .... 吉田喜重 2:273b
Yoshihara Oil Mill, Ltd 8:346b
Yoshiharu Shikimoku .... 義治式目 .. 7:96a; 8:346b
Yoshiigawa .... 吉井川 8:346b
Yoshii Isamu .... 吉井勇 7:253b; 8:346b-347a
Yoshikawa Eiji ... 吉川英治 1:164a; 2:274a; 7:65b, 103b; 8:347a
Yoshikawa Kōjirō .... 吉川幸次郎 ... 8:347a-347b
Yoshikawa Koretari .... 吉川惟足 8:347b
Yoshikiri 6:285b
Yoshimasu Tōdō 吉益東洞 8:347b
Yoshimi "hundred-cave" tunnel tombs .... 吉見百穴 ... 8:347b-348a
Yoshimitsu .... 義満 3:173b
Yoshimoto .... 良基 6:298b
Yoshimoto Ryūmei. 吉本隆明 *See* **Yoshimoto Takaaki**
Yoshimoto Takaaki .... 吉本隆明 .. 1:83a; 8:348a
Yoshimura Junzō 吉村順三 8:348a
Yoshimura Kōzaburō .... 吉村公三郎 .. 2:271b, 275b; 7:102b; 8:348a
Shindō Kaneto 7:111a
Yoshinogawa .... 吉野川 8:348a
Yoshino Hideo ... 吉野秀雄 8:348b
Yoshino-Kumano National Park ... 吉野熊野国立公園 5:299b; 8:348b, 349b
Yoshinokuzu .... 吉野葛 7:342b
Yoshino no tōzoku (Yoshino Bandits) .... 吉野の盗賊 8:319b
Yoshino Sakuzō .. 吉野作造 1:313b; 7:251a, 281a; 8:348b-349a
Fukuda Tokuzō 2:362b
mimpon shugi 5:175b
Reimeikai 6:288b
Yoshinoyama .... 吉野山 .. 8:*349a*, 349b
Yōshinshi (adoptive parent-child relationships) 6:162b
Yoshioka Kinzaburō. 吉岡金三郎 *See* **Taiso Yoshitoshi**
Yoshioka Yayoi .. 吉岡弥生 8:349b
Hani Motoko 3:96a
Yoshishige no Yasutane .... 慶滋保胤 .. 1:181a; 5:37b; 8:349b
Chiteiki 4:129a
Yoshiwara .... 吉原 .. 6:*155b*, 285b; 8:349b-351a
daily routine 8:350b-351a
end 8:351a
setting 8:350a
women 8:350a-350b
Yoshiwara keisei shin bijin awase jihitsu kagami 吉原傾城新美人合自筆鑑 8:142b
Yoshiya Nobuko .. 吉屋信子 7:103b; 8:351a-351b
fūzoku shōsetsu 2:378b
Yoshiyuki Eisuke 吉行エイスケ ... 7:119b
Yoshiyuki Junnosuke .... 吉行淳之介 1:209a; 8:351b-352a
Yoshizawa Akira ... 吉沢章 6:*116b*
Yoshizawa Kenkichi .... 芳沢謙吉 6:343a; 8:352a
Yōsho Shirabesho .... 洋書調所 1:142a
Yōteizan .... 羊蹄山 .. 7:98a; 8:352a
Yotsugi Soga .... 世継曽我 1:275a
Young, Ralph .... 2:157a-157b 8:354b
Young Men's Christian Association (YMCA) 8:326a
Young Officers' Movement 2:250a
Youth 5:4a-4b; 8:352a-353b
deviance 8:353a
education 5:4b
marriage 5:4b
modern period 8:352b
post-World War II 8:352b-353a
psychology 8:353a-353b
social roles 5:4a
traditional groups 8:352a-352b
Youth clubs 8:353b
Youth groups 8:217b-218a
Youth Labor Homes 4:87a
Yowa no nezame (Waking at Midnight) .. 夜半の寝覚 .. 5:35b; 7:21a
Yoyogi National Gymnasia 8:353b
YS-11 .... 8:353b-354a
Yūaikai .... 友愛会 1:2a, 72a; 4:345a-345b; 7:219a, 281a; 8:354a
Asō Hisashi 1:102b
Tanno Setsu 7:344a
Yuan shi 6:358a
Yuan Shikai (Yüan Shih-k'ai) 4:280b; 7:276b, 277b; 8:354a-354b
Kapsin Political Coup 4:280b
Reorganization Loan 6:302a
Yuasa Hachirō .. 湯浅八郎 3:318b; 8:354b
Yuasa Jōzan .... 湯浅常山 8:354b
Yuasa Yoshiko .. 湯浅芳子 5:220b
Yūbari .... 夕張 8:354b
Yūbaridake .... 夕張岳 8:354b
Yūbari Mountains .... 夕張山地 8:354b
Yūbe no kumo ... 夕べの雲 7:167a
Yūbin hōchi shimbun .... 郵便報知新聞 1:155a; 8:355a
Kurimoto Joun, editor 4:313b
Yūbin Jōkisen Kaisha 3:362b
Yu Dafu (Yü Ta-fu) 8:355a
Yudanaka Hot Spring .... 湯田中温泉 8:355a
Yūdansha (rank holders) 4:196a
Yudate kagura .. 湯立神楽 4:107b
Yudonosan .... 湯殿山 1:136b; 8:355a
Yuensai .... 油煙斎 5:307a
Yufuin .... 由布院 8:355
Yuga .... 瑜伽 .. 7:113b-115a
Yugake 4:340b
Yugashima Hot Spring .... 湯ケ島温泉 .. 1:49b; 2:342b; 8:355a
Yugawara .... 湯河原 8:355a
Yugei .... 靫負 1:147b
Yūgen .... 幽玄 1:181a; 2:355a; 5:39a, 42a, 43a; 8:355b-356a
Jakuren 4:1b
Yugishō .... 湯起請 4:302b
Yugyōji .... 遊行寺 8:356a
Ji sect 4:62a
Yuhazu no mitsugi 弓弭調 7:264b
Yūhitsu .... 右筆 8:356a
Yui .... 結い 8:356a
Yuiitsu shintō. *See* **Yoshida Shintō**
Yuiitsu shintō myōbō yōshū 唯一神道名法要集 7:128b
Yui Shōsetsu .... 由井正雪 ... 8:356a-356b
Yui Shōsetsu Disturbance .... 由井正雪の乱 4:187a
Yūkaku 3:15a
Yukar. *See* **Ainu language**
Yukar epics 1:37a
Yukawa Hideki .. 湯川秀樹 8:*356b*
Yuki (town) .... 油木 8:356b
Yūki (city) .... 結城 8:356b
Yūki family .... 結城氏 ... 8:356b-357a
Yuki fujin ezu (Portrait of Madame Yuki) .... 雪夫人絵図 6:221b
Yukiguni (Snow Country) .... 雪国 4:176a; 7:176a; 8:90b
"Yukihiko-Kokei era" 6:157b
Yukijirushi Shokuhin 7:206b
Yūkike Hatto .. 結城家法度 8:357a
Yūki Magosaburō .... 結城孫三郎 4:77a
puppet theater 6:270a
Yuki Matsuri .... 雪祭 ... 7:206b-207a
Yukimi (snow viewing) 4:381a; 7:207a
Yukinari Kyō ki .. 行成卿記 3:45b
Yuki onna .... 雪女 8:357a
Yūki Shōji .... 結城昌治 ... 8:357a-357b
Yūki Somei ...... 結城素明 4:175b
Yūki Toyotarō 結城豊太郎 8:357b
Yukitsubaki (*C. rusticana; C. japonica var. decumbens*) 1:236b
Yukiwarisō (*Anemone hepatica* var. *japonica; Hepatica acuta*) 8:357b
Yuku haru .... ゆく春 7:279b

Yukuhashi 行橋 8:357b
Yume no shiro (Instead of Dreams) 夢の代 8:292a
Yume no ukihashi 夢の浮橋 7:343a
Yumigahama 弓ケ浜 8:357b
Yūmoa gekijō (Humor Theater) ユーモア劇場 6:275b
Yuna 6:*155a*
Yun Ch'i-ho 4:281b
Yunoyama Hot Spring 湯の山温泉 8:357b
Yunoyama sangin hyakuin 湯山三吟百韻 6:298b
Yun Pong-gil 8:357b-358a
Yuragawa 由良川 4:338a; 8:358a
Yūrei (ghosts) 3:30a
Yuri 5:9b-10a
Yuri Kimimasa 由利公正 8:358a
Yuriwaka legend 百合若大臣 8:358a
Yūseishō. 郵政省 *See* **Ministry of Posts and Telecommunications**
Yūshi Kyōritsu Tōkyō Hospital 7:311a
Yushima Seidō. 湯島聖堂 *See* **Shōheikō**
Yūshi sensei 3:91b
Yūsoku kojitsu 有職故実 1:79a; 8:358a-358b
Yu Sŏng-nyong 8:358b
Yü Ta-fu. *See* **Yu Dafu (Yü Ta-fu)**
Yutai xinyong (Gyokudai shin'ei; New Songs from the Jade Terrace) 8:207a
Yuzawa (city) 湯沢 8:358b
Yuzawa (town) 湯沢 8:358b
Yūzen 友禅 4:336a, 338a; 8:238a; 8:359a
  kimono 8:*358b*
Yūzen-zome. 友禅染 *See* **Yūzen**
Yūzonsha 猶存社 8:359a
Yuzu 3:127b
Yūzuki 夕月 8:334a
Yuzuki no Kimi 弓月君 4:205b; 8:359a-359b
  Hata family 3:111a
Yūzū nembutsu engi (Buddhist hand scroll) 融通念仏縁起 8:82a
Yūzū Nembutsu sect 融通念仏宗 7:20a; 8:359b
  nembutsu 4:67a
  Ryōnin 6:352b
Yūzū Nembutsu Shū 融通念仏宗 8:359b
Yuzurijō 譲状 8:359b
Yūzuru (The Twilight Crane) 夕鶴 2:76b
  shingeki 7:113a
YWCA (Young Women's Christian Association) 8:257b, 359b
  Kawai Michi 4:179a
YX project 1:124a; 8:359b

Z

Za 座 4:100a; 8:361a-361b
Zabuton 2:371a
Zagashira 4:95a
Zaibatsu 財閥 1:147a; 7:214a, 267a-267b, 268b; 8:361b-363b
  centralized buying and selling 8:362b
  control through credit 8:362b
  "cordial oligopoly" 8:362b
  defined 8:361b-362a
  development 4:138a
  dissolution 1:8b; 2:35b; 4:364b, 378b; 8:363b-366a
  economic recovery 3:201a
  Financial Crisis of 1927 2:277b
  founders 2:30a, 31b-32a
  Furukawa 2:372b
  general trading companies 3:19a
  growth 2:153b
  holding companies 3:216a
  income distribution 3:285b
  industrial organization 3:292b-293b
  landlords 4:363a
  Mitsubishi 3:361b
  Mitsui 5:209b
  officer appointments and interlocks 8:362a-362b
  older and newer 8:363a
  ownership 8:362a
  political parties 3:198b
  public distrust 8:362b-363a
  reasons for growth 2:31b
  revival 8:363a-363b
  subsidiaries 4:189a
  Sumitomo 7:266b
  Taiwan 7:308a
  technological development 7:369b
  Yasuda 8:317a
Zaibatsu (film) 財閥 8:319b
Zaibatsu dissolution 2:372b; 7:267a, 268a, 269a; 8:363b-366a
  antitrust statute 8:364b-365a
  capital levy tax 8:365b
  Deconcentration Law 8:365a
  dissolution program 8:363b-364a
  economical purge 8:365b-366a
  Enterprise Reconstruction and Reorganization Law 8:365b
  Financial Institutions Reconstruction and Reorganization Law 8:365b
  Fuji Bank Ltd 2:342a
  Law for the Termination of Zaibutsu Family Control 8:365a-365b
  Mitsubishi Trading 8:365a
  Mitsui Trading 8:365a
  Occupation 6:52b-53a
  sale of securities 8:364b
  Sanwa Bank, Ltd 7:19a
  summary and assessment 8:366a
  Taisei Corporation 7:303a
  technological development 7:370a
  Yasuda plan 8:364a-364b
Zaigō shōnin 在郷商人 8:366a-366b
Zaikai 8:366b-367b
Zaikata kabu 在方株 4:100a
Zaike 在家 8:367b
  Buddhist laymen 8:367b
  laity 4:362a-362b
  lay Buddhist movement 4:372a
  peasants 8:367b
Zai Mimbukyō no Ie no Uta-awase 在民部卿家歌合 8:182a
Zaisankei 財産刑 7:140b
Zaiseigaku taikō (Principles of Public Finance) 財政学大綱 6:135b
Zaisei tōyūshi 8:367b
Zama 座間 8:367b
Zambōritsu. *See* **Libel Law of 1875**
Zangedō to shite no tetsugaku 懺悔道としての哲学 7:335b
Zangiri-mono ("cropped-hair" plays) 散切物 5:234b-235a
Zansetsu 残雪 7:359a
Zaō Gongen 蔵王権現 4:208a; 6:*24b*
Zaō Hot Spring 蔵王温泉 8:367b
Zaō Quasi-National Park 蔵王国定公園 8:368a
Zaōzan 蔵王山 8:*367a*, 368a
Zappai and senryū 8:368a-368b
  literary characteristics of senryū 8:368b
  senryū 8:368b
  types of zappai 8:368a-368b
Zaru (basket) 2:25a
Zashiki warashi 座敷童 8:368b
Zasshu bunka 雑種文化 4:169b
Zasso Ketsudansho 雑訴決断所 8:368b-369a
Zatō 5:45a; 8:369a
Zatō (blind men) plays 4:327b
Zatsumu sata 雑務沙汰 8:369a
Zazen (sitting meditation) 座禅 6:261b
  monasticism 5:238a
  See also **Zen**
Zeami 世阿弥 5:15b, 43a; 7:61b, 120b; 8:312b, 369a-369b
  artistic ideals 8:369b
  Kan'ami 4:135b
  Kanze Nobumitsu 4:154b
  Kanze school 4:155a
  life 8:369a
  works 8:369a-369b
  yūgen 8:355b
Zeigo 贅語 5:214b-215a
Zeimu kaikei. *See* **Tax accounting**
Zeimusho. *See* **Tax office**
Zeirishi. *See* **Tax accountants**
Zekkai Chūshin 絶海中津 8:369b
Zelkova [(keyaki) *Zelkova serrata*] 1:264b; 2:327a; 8:369b
Zempa 禅派 8:369b-370a
Zen 禅 1:178b-179b, 185b; 7:80b, 84a; 8:370a-374b
  architecture 1:191b-192a
  contemporary 8:374a-374b
  cultural and artistic dimension 8:374a
  Eiheiji temple 2:186a-186b
  existentialism 2:236b
  food and eating habits 2:305b
  Fujiwara no Nobuzane 2:354b
  Gozan 3:57a-58a
  Gozan literature 3:58a-59a
  history 8:370a-372a
    Chan in China 8:370a
    Zen in Japan 8:370b-372a
  Huike (Hui-k'o) Severing His Arm 8:*371a*
  influence on gardens 3:8b-9a
  ink painting 3:306a
  intellectual background 8:372a-373a
    cosmotheism (avatamsaka) 8:372a-372b
    idealism and consciousness (yogācāra) 8:372a
    Taoist contribution 8:372b
    wisdom and emptiness (prajñā and sūnyatā) 8:372a
    Zen masters 8:372b-373a
  Ishida Baigan 3:340a
  meditation (zazen) 8:*372b*
  monasticism 5:238a-238b
  monks
    Betsugen Enshi 1:150b
    Chūgan Engetsu 1:311b
    Dōgen 1:191b
    Eisai 1:191a; 2:187a
    Enni 1:191a, 192a; 2:219a
    Gidō Shūshin 3:30b
    Hakuin 3:88a

Ikkyū ··· 3:269b
Ingen ··· 3:303b
Issan Ichinei ··· 3:348b
Jakushitsu Genkō ··· 4:1b-2a
Keian Genju ··· 4:186b-187a
Kokan Shiren ··· 4:252b
Minchō ··· 5:183b-184a
Mokkei ··· 5:234a
Mokuan Reien ··· 5:235a-235b
Musō Soseki ··· 5:287b
Ryōkan ··· 6:352a
Sesshū Tōyō ··· 8:*371a*
Takuan Sōhō ··· 7:327b
musical instruments ··· 1:196b
Ōbaku sect ··· 6:47a-47b
painting ··· 1:210a-210b, 192a-193a; 6:158b
practice and enlightenment ··· 8:373a-374a
enlightenment (satori) ··· 7:28b; 8:373b-374a
kōan ··· 4:234a; 8:373b
lotus posture meditation (zazen) ··· 8:373a
psychotherapy ··· 6:261b
Rinzai sect ··· 6:318b
Rokuon nichiroku ··· 6:335b
Sasamegoto (Murmured Conversations) ··· 7:24a
sculpture ··· 1:192a-193a
Sōjiji ··· 7:224a
Sōtō sect ··· 7:233a-234b
Tang (T'ang) dynasty
tea ceremony ··· 7:360a
teachings ··· 3:46b
Waley, Arthur David ··· 8:221b
Zen calligraphy ··· 1:235b-236a
Zen'ei no bungaku ··· 前衛の文学 ··· 4:172a
Zen'ei (Vanguard) ··· 前衛 ··· 1:72a
Zenga ··· 禅画 ··· 6:153b; 8:374b-375a
Circle Triangle, and Square ··· 8:*374b*
Hakuin ··· 1:*193a*
Sengai Gibon ··· 8:*374b*
Zengakuren ··· 全学連 ··· 7:252a; 8:375a-375b
opposition to ··· 4:285b
United States-Japan security treaties ··· 8:167a
peace movement ··· 6:167a
Zengo Shakkan ··· 6:302a
Zenigata ("coin-shaped") ··· 7:41b
Zenitaka Corporation ··· 8:375b
Zeniya Gohei ··· 銭屋五兵衛 ··· 8:375b
Zeniza. *See* **Kinza, ginza, and zeniza**
Zenkōji ··· 善光寺 ··· 8:375b-376a
main hall (kondō) ··· 8:*376b*
urbanization ··· 8:176a
Zenkoku Chiiki Fujin Dantai Renraku Kyōgi Kai ··· 1:273b
Zenkoku Fujin Dōmei
Tatewaki Sadayo ··· 7:349b
Zenkoku hōgen jiten ··· 全国方言辞典 ··· 4:31b
Zenkoku mukashi-banashi kiroku ··· 全国昔話記録 ··· 2:302a
Zenkunen kassen emaki 前九年合戦絵巻
Earlier Nine Years' War ··· 2:137a
Zenkunen no Eki. 前九年の役 *See* **Earlier Nine Years' War**
Zen Nihon Bukkyō Kai ··· 8:376a
Zen Nihon Denki Kiki Rōdō Kumiai Rengōkai ··· 2:87a
Zen Nihon Gakusei Jichikai Sōrengō ··· 8:375a-375b
Zen Nihon Kendō Remmei ··· 4:196a
Zen Nihon Minshu Iryō Kikan Rengōkai ··· 4:12a
Zen Nihon Rōdō Sōdōmei ··· 全日本労働総同盟 2:130a; 7:219a
Zen no kenkyū ··· 善の研究 ··· 6:232b; 8:376a-376b
Zen painting. *See* **Zenga**
Zen printing, premodern ··· 6:248a
Zenrinkoku hōki ··· 善隣国宝記 ··· 8:376b
Zenrō ··· 7:327a
Zenrō Kaigi ··· 全労会議 ··· 7:189a
Zen school ··· 8:369b-370a
Zensen ··· 8:376b
Takita Minoru ··· 7:327a
Zenshinza ··· 前進座 ··· 8:377a
Zenshō ··· 7:273a
Zentsūji (city) ··· 善通寺 ··· 8:377a-377b
Zentsūji ··· 善通寺 ··· 8:377b
Shingon sect ··· 7:115a
ZERO ··· 4:10a
Zero Fighter ··· 5:313b; 8:377a, 377b
Zerosen ··· 零戦 ··· 8:377b
Zetsubō no seishin shi ··· 絶望の精神史 ··· 4:139a
Zeze Castle ··· 膳所城 ··· 6:133b
Zhang Jizhi (Chang Chi-chih) ··· 1:235b
Zhang Xueliang (Chang Hsüeh-liang) ··· 3:201b; 7:77b; 8:377b
Zhang Ziping (Chang Tzu-p'ing) ··· 8:377b-378a
Zhang Zuolin Incident 2:207b; 7:336a-336b
Zhang Zuolin (Chang Tso-lin) ··· 7:237b; 8:378a
Zheng Chenggong (Cheng Ch'eng Kung) ··· 8:378a-378b
Zheng-family rule ··· 7:307a
Zheng Xiaoxu (Cheng Hsiao-hsü) 8:378b
Zhong Gui ··· 7:163b
Zhonghua Minguo Linshi Zhengfu ··· 6:260a-260b
Zhonghua Minguo Weixin Zhengfu ··· 6:285b-286a
Zhou Enlai (Chou En-lai) ··· 8:378b-379a
Zhou Hongqing (Chou Hung-ch'ing) Incident ··· 8:379a
Zhou Maoshu Admiring Lotus Blossoms ··· 4:147b
Zhou Zuoren (Chou Tso-jen) 8:379a-379b
Zhu Shunshui ··· 7:191b
Zhu Xi (Chu Hsi) Neo-Confucianism ··· 3:117b; 7:190a-191b
Zhu Xi (Chu Hsi) school. *See* **Shushigaku**
Zōbiki ··· 象引 ··· 4:98b
Zōho gorin wakun no shiori ··· 増補語林和訓栞 ··· 8:221b
Zōho kai tsūshō kō ··· 増補華夷通商考 ··· 4:369b
Zōho rigen shūran ··· 増補俚諺集覧 ··· 6:312a
Zōjōji ··· 増上寺 ··· 8:379a
Zōka poetry ··· 5:105a
Zokkyoku no yurai (music) ··· 俗曲の由来 ··· 6:134b
Zoku hizakurige 続膝栗毛 ··· 4:61b
Zoku ichinen yūhan (A Year and a Half, continued) ··· 続一年有半 ··· 5:312a
Zoku sarumino ··· 続猿蓑 ··· 4:102b
Zoku Tokugawa jikki ··· 続徳川実紀 ··· 8:51a
Zoological gardens ··· 8:379b
Ueno Zoological Garden ··· 8:129a, 379b
Zoologists
Imanishi Kinji ··· 3:274a
Ishikawa Chiyomatsu ··· 3:342a
Mitsukuri Kakichi ··· 5:213b
Morse, Edward Sylvester ··· 5:256a
Toyama Kametarō ··· 8:88a
Whitman, Charles Otis ··· 8:252b
Zōri ··· 7:249b; 8:379b
Zoruge Jiken ··· ゾルゲ事件 ··· 7:229a-230a
Zōsen Gigoku. *See* **Shipbuilding Scandal of 1954**
Zōsen Oshoku. *See* **Shipbuilding Scandal of 1954**
Zōshi ··· 蔵志 ··· 8:311b
Zōshiki ··· 雑色 ··· 8:379b-380a
ritsuryō system ··· 6:324b
Zou Taofen (Tsou T'ao-fen) ··· 8:380a
Z Revolution ··· 8:293b
Zuihitsu ··· 8:380a-380b
Makura no sōshi ··· 7:52a
Shinkyō shōsetsu ··· 3:312a
Tsurezuregusa ··· 8:341b
Zuisenji ··· 瑞泉寺 ··· 8:380b
Zuisho ··· 隋書 ··· 7:264a-264b
Zukin ··· 3:119a
Zuryō ··· 受領 ··· 8:380b
Zushi ··· 逗子 ··· 8:381a
Zushoryō ··· 図書寮 ··· 1:151b; 5:1a; 8:381a-381b

APPENDIX

Nengō——Japanese Era Names and Dates

A

An'ei	安永	1772–1781
Angen	安元	1175–1177
Anna	安和	968–970
Ansei	安政	1854–1860 (1855–1860)
Antei	安貞	1227–1229 (1228–1229)

B

Bummei	文明	1469–1487
Bumpō	文保	1317–1319
Bun'an	文安	1444–1449
Bunchū	文中	1372–1375
Bun'ei	文永	1264–1275
Bunji	文治	1185–1190
Bunka	文化	1804–1818
Bunki	文亀	1501–1504
Bunkyū	文久	1861–1864
Bunna (N)	文和	1352–1356
Bun'ō	文応	1260–1261
Bunroku	文禄	1592–1596 (1593–1596)
Bunryaku	文暦	1234–1235
Bunsei	文政	1818–1830 (1818–1831)
Bunshō	文正	1466–1467

C

Chōgen	長元	1028–1037
Chōhō	長保	999–1004
Chōji	長治	1104–1106
Chōkan	長寛	1163–1165
Chōkyō	長享	1487–1489
Chōkyū	長久	1040–1044
Chōroku	長禄	1457–1460 (1457–1461)
Chōryaku	長暦	1037–1040
Chōshō	長承	1132–1135
Chōtoku	長徳	995–999
Chōwa	長和	1012–1017 (1013–1017)

D

Daidō	大同	806–810
Daiji	大治	1126–1131

E

Eichō	永長	1096–1097 (1097–1098)
Eien	永延	987–989
Eiho	永保	1081–1084
Eiji	永治	1141–1142
Eijō	永承	1046–1053
Eikan	永観	983–985
Eikyō	永享	1429–1441
Eikyū	永久	1113–1118
Eiman	永万	1165–1166
Einin	永仁	1293–1299
Eiroku	永禄	1558–1570
Eiryaku	永暦	1160–1161
Eishō	永正	1504–1521
Eiso	永祚	989–990
Eitoku (N)	永徳	1381–1384
Eiwa (N)	永和	1375–1379
Embun (N)	延文	1356–1361
Empō	延宝	1673–1681
Enchō	延長	923–931
Engen	延元	1336–1340
Engi	延喜	901–923
Enkyō	延慶	1308–1311
Enkyō	延享	1744–1748
Enkyū	延久	1069–1074
En'ō	延応	1239–1240
Enryaku	延暦	782–806
Entoku	延徳	1489–1492

G

Gangyō	元慶	877–885
Gembun	元文	1736–1741
Genchū	元中	1384–1392
Gen'ei	元永	1118–1120
Genji	元治	1864–1865
Genki	元亀	1570–1573
Genkō	元亨	1321–1324 (1321–1325)
Genkō	元弘	1331–1334
Genkyū	元久	1204–1206
Genna	元和	1615–1624
Gennin	元仁	1224–1225 (1225)
Gen'ō	元応	1319–1321
Genroku	元禄	1688–1704
Genryaku	元暦	1184–1185
Gentoku	元徳	1329–1332

H

Hakuchi	白雉	650–654
Heiji	平治	1159–1160
Hōan	保安	1120–1124
Hōei	宝永	1704–1711
Hōen	保延	1135–1141
Hōgen	保元	1156–1159
Hōji	宝治	1247–1249
Hōki	宝亀	770–781
Hōreki	宝暦	1751–1764
Hōtoku	宝徳	1449–1452

J

Jian	治安	1021–1024
Jingo Keiun	神護景雲	767–770
Jinki	神亀	724–729
Jiryaku	治暦	1065–1069
Jishō	治承	1177–1181
Jōan	承安	1171–1175
Jōei	貞永	1232–1233
Jōgan	貞観	859–877
Jōgen	貞元	976–978 (976–979)
Jōgen	承元	1207–1211
Jōhei	承平	931–938
Jōhō	承保	1074–1077 (1074–1078)
Jōji (N)	貞治	1362–1368
Jōkyō	貞享	1684–1688
Jōkyū	承久	1219–1222
Jōō	貞応	1222–1224 (1222–1225)
Jōō	承応	1652–1655
Jōryaku	承暦	1077–1081 (1078–1081)
Jōtoku	承徳	1097–1099 (1098–1099)
Jōwa	承和	834–848
Jōwa (N)	貞和	1345–1350
Juei	寿永	1182–1185

K

Kaei	嘉永	1848–1854 (1848–1855)
Kagen	嘉元	1303–1306 (1303–1307)
Kahō	嘉保	1094–1096 (1095–1097)
Kajō	嘉承	1106–1108
Kakitsu	嘉吉	1441–1444
Kakyō (N)	嘉慶	1387–1389
Kambun	寛文	1661–1673
Kampō	寛保	1741–1744
Kampyō	寛平	889–898
Kan'ei	寛永	1624–1644 (1624–1645)
Kan'en	寛延	1748–1751
Kangen	寛元	1243–1247
Kangi	寛喜	1229–1232
Kanji	寛治	1087–1094 (1087–1095)
Kankō	寛弘	1004–1012 (1004–1013)
Kanna	寛和	985–987
Kannin	寛仁	1017–1021
Kannō (N)	観応	1350–1352
Kansei	寛政	1789–1801
Kanshō	寛正	1460–1466 (1461–1466)
Kantoku	寛徳	1044–1046
Kaō	嘉応	1169–1171
Karoku	嘉禄	1225–1227 (1225–1228)
Karyaku	嘉暦	1326–1329
Kashō	嘉祥	848–851
Katei	嘉禎	1235–1238 (1235–1239)
Keian	慶安	1648–1652
Keichō	慶長	1596–1615
Keiō	慶応	1865–1868
Keiun	慶雲	704–708
Kemmu	建武	1334–1338
Kempō	建保	1213–1219 (1214–1219)
Kenchō	建長	1249–1256
Ken'ei	建永	1206–1207
Kengen	乾元	1302–1303
Kenji	建治	1275–1278
Kenkyū	建久	1190–1199
Kennin	建仁	1201–1204
Kenryaku	建暦	1211–1213 (1211–1214)
Kentoku	建徳	1370–1372
Kōan	弘安	1278–1288
Kōan (N)	康安	1361–1362
Kōchō	弘長	1261–1264
Kōei (N)	康永	1342–1345
Kōgen	康元	1256–1257
Kōhei	康平	1058–1065
Kōhō	康保	964–968
Kōji	康治	1142–1144
Kōji	弘治	1555–1558
Kōka	弘化	1844–1848 (1845–1848)
Kōkoku	興国	1340–1346 (1340–1347)
Kōnin	弘仁	810–824
Kōō (N)	康応	1389–1390
Kōryaku (N)	康暦	1379–1381
Kōshō	康正	1455–1457
Kōwa	康和	1099–1104
Kōwa	弘和	1381–1384
Kyōhō	享保	1716–1736
Kyōroku	享禄	1528–1532
Kyōtoku	享徳	1452–1455
Kyōwa	享和	1801–1804
Kyūan	久安	1145–1151
Kyūju	久寿	1154–1156

M

Man'en	万延	1860–1861
Manji	万治	1658–1661
Manju	万寿	1024–1028
Meiji	明治	1868–1912
Meiō	明応	1492–1501
Meireki	明暦	1655–1658
Meitoku (N)	明徳	1390–1394
Meiwa	明和	1764–1772

N

Nimbyō	仁平	1151–1154
Nin'an	仁安	1166–1169
Ninji	仁治	1240–1243
Ninju	仁寿	851–854
Ninna	仁和	885–889

Nengō——Japanese Era Names and Dates

O

Ōan (N)	応安	1368–1375
Ōchō	応長	1311–1312
Ōei	応永	1394–1428
Ōho	応保	1161–1163
Ōnin	応仁	1467–1469
Ōtoku	応徳	1084–1087
Ōwa	応和	961–964

R

Reiki	霊亀	715–717
Ryakunin	暦仁	1238–1239 (1239)
Ryakuō (N)	暦応	1338–1342

S

Saikō	斉衡	854–857
Shitoku (N)	至徳	1384–1387
Shōan	正安	1299–1302
Shōchō	正長	1428–1429
Shōchū	正中	1324–1326 (1325–1326)
Shōgen	正元	1259–1260
Shōhei	正平	1346–1370 (1347–1370)
Shōhō	正保	1644–1648 (1645–1648)
Shōji	正治	1199–1201
Shōka	正嘉	1257–1259
Shōkyō (N)	正慶	1332–1334
Shōō	正応	1288–1293
Shōryaku	正暦	990–995
Shōtai	昌泰	898–901
Shōtoku	正徳	1711–1716
Shōwa	正和	1312–1317
Shōwa	昭和	1926–
Shuchō	朱鳥	686

T

Taiei	大永	1521–1528
Taihō	大宝	701–704
Taika	大化	645–650
Taishō	大正	1912–1926
Tembun	天文	1532–1555
Temmei	天明	1781–1789
Tempō	天保	1830–1844 (1831–1845)
Tempuku	天福	1233–1234
Tempyō	天平	729–749
Tempyō Hōji	天平宝字	757–765
Tempyō Jingo	天平神護	765–767
Tempyō Kampō	天平感宝	749
Tempyō Shōhō	天平勝宝	749–757
Ten'an	天安	857–859
Tenchō	天長	824–834
Ten'ei	天永	1110–1113
Ten'en	天延	973–976 (974–976)
Tengen	天元	978–983 (979–983)
Tengi	天喜	1053–1058
Tengyō	天慶	938–947
Tenji	天治	1124–1126
Tenju	天授	1375–1381
Tenna	天和	1681–1684
Tennin	天仁	1108–1110
Ten'ō	天応	781–782
Tenroku	天禄	970–973 (970–974)
Tenryaku	天暦	947–957
Tenshō	天承	1131–1132
Tenshō	天正	1573–1592
Tentoku	天徳	957–961
Ten'yō	天養	1144–1145
Tokuji	徳治	1306–1308 (1307–1308)

W

Wadō	和同	708–715

Y

Yōrō	養老	717–724
Yōwa	養和	1181–1182

N indicates era names used by the Northern Court during the period of division into NORTHERN AND SOUTHERN COURTS; the Southern Court era names are widely regarded as more legitimate.

NOTE: The dates given here for era names are those to be found in standard Japanese historical reference works. For some eras prior to the adoption of the Western calendar on 1 January 1873 two sets of dates are given. In these cases the first set are the standard dates, which have not been corrected precisely for discrepancies between the Japanese lunar and Western solar New Year, and the second set (in parentheses) are the correctly converted dates. Since the discrepancies between the beginnings and ends of Japanese and Western years are often slight, the standard Japanese practice is to assign the first or last year of an era to the Western year within which most of the Japanese year falls. The standard *nengō* tables are widely used, and to avoid confusion it is the standard dates that are given throughout this encyclopedia whenever era names are identified. The dates of specific events have been precisely converted to the Western calendar whenever possible.